ALBERT

Other books by Stanley Weintraub

Private Shaw and Public Shaw

Journey to Heartbreak

Aubrey Beardsley: Imp of the Perverse

Whistler: A Biography

Four Rossettis: A Victorian Biography

The London Yankees

*A Stillness Heard Around the World:
The End of the Great War*

Victoria

Disraeli: A Biography

Shaw's People: Victoria to Churchill

'The Prince is become so identified with the Queen,
that they are one person, and as he likes and she dislikes
business, it is obvious that while she has the title he is
really discharging the functions of the Sovereign.
He is King to all intents and purposes.'

Charles Greville,
Clerk to the Privy Council

'He was part of my dream, of course –
but then I was part of his dream, too!'

Lewis Carroll,
Through the Looking Glass

Prince Albert in his last years, an engraving by William Holl from a photograph by O.G. Reylander

ALBERT
Uncrowned King

Stanley Weintraub

JOHN MURRAY
Albemarle Street, London

© Stanley Weintraub 1997

First published in 1997
by John Murray (Publishers) Ltd,
50 Albemarle Street, London W1X 4BD

A catalogue record for this book is available from the British Library

ISBN 0-7195-5756 9

Typeset in 11.75/13.5 Adobe Garamond by Pure Tech India Limited, Pondicherry, India
Printed and bound in Great Britain by The University Press, Cambridge

To my children
Mark and Judith
David and Carie Lee
Erica and Bruce

Contents

Illustrations

The author and publishers gratefully acknowledge the following for permission to reproduce illustrations: Plates 1, 6, 8, 9, 26, 27, The Royal Collection © Her Majesty Queen Elizabeth II; 2, Verwaltung de staatl. Schlosser, Garten u. Seen, Museumabteilung, München; 3 and 4, Herbert Appeltshauser, Coburg; 21, 24, The Royal Archives © Her Majesty Queen Elizabeth II; 17, Collection of Charles W. Mann; 28, *Illustrated London News*; 30, © English Heritage. Plates 5, 7, 22, 23 and 25 are from the collection of the author. The original of Plate 27 is untraced; photographic reproductions are held by the Wellcome Institute for the History of Medicine, and the Royal Collections.

The illustration reproduced on p.iv. is gratefully reproduced with the permission of The Royal Collection © Her Majesty Queen Elizabeth II.

Preface

HIS ROYAL DIADEM was a crown of thorns. Having come to an alien country to sire the succession, he remained always the alien. His ways were not English ways, and although he arrived at twenty with much to learn – and learned it, and more – he never adapted successfully to English society and culture, and his adopted people never fully accepted him. Yet the mark he left upon England as merely the Queen's husband was far greater than that of most monarchs, and his marriage, arranged as it was and as stormy as at times it could be, remains one of the most memorable of love stories.

Although his achievements were political and constitutional, scientific and economic, social and cultural, his life was also a romance. His biography opens almost as musical comedy in a feudal backwater that might have anticipated Ruritania, and closes as grand opera on an imperial stage. Nevertheless it is authentic history, not far removed in time from the memories of our great-grandparents, and taking place in the era of steamship, railway, telegraph and photograph.

Despite that sense of the near-present, his life possesses the makings not only of myth but of a complete mythology. At the beginning, one finds the boy from the bucolic village destined for transplantation to the great, sophisticated – and even wicked – city. The minor princeling in a place bypassed by time and destined to inherit nothing would become uncrowned king of the greatest empire on earth. Before that, however, he will be a child devastated when his beautiful mother is driven away by a villainous and dissolute father, for whom the son must thereafter feign affection. To fill the void he will become a Homeric Telemachus, finding, in a physician turned sage, his Mentor.

Here, too, as in many myths of East and West, is the pilgrimage of suitors from foreign lands for the hand of a young queen who rejects them all. Or, conversely, the sovereign summoning, and choosing, a spouse – only the throne is occupied by a woman and the supplicant is a man. Like others celebrated in song and story, the hero is a foreigner in a strange land who must struggle for acceptance by powerful figures whom he despises and whose values he rejects. Beset by enemies, he will best them all.

Also echoing myth, he has a principal heir who brings him little but grief, and a radiant and devoted daughter who is his greatest joy – but whom he must sacrifice. And, although a paragon of all the known virtues, and a seeker after a Utopia he has helped to formulate and which he can see in the near distance, he finds that fate will deny him entrance. Inevitably, a fatal flaw strikes him down at the pinnacle of his hard-won power and prestige.

Born, like Queen Victoria, in 1819, Prince Albert of Saxe-Coburg and Gotha was, from his marriage in 1840 until his death in 1861, the uncrowned king of England. The English had tolerated, uneasily, their fill of German occupants of Windsor Castle, both sovereigns and their spouses, before Albert became the last of them. The first George could not even speak English; even the fourth George, like his brother, William IV, was simultaneously king of a German state – Hanover, from which the first had been imported. Only the accident of Victoria's sex kept her, too, from being a German monarch. No one then alive could recall a regal personage of English descent on the British throne. That was handicap enough for Albert as royal immigrant, but the disability would be emphasized by each of his many public addresses. He could never abandon his heavy German accent, however eloquent or wise or persuasive was the English he spoke.

Albert also had to labour, from the beginning, under the handicap of being required to exercise virtues that were completely negative and went against the grain of his character. As the Queen's husband, he was not to act, but was instead to abstain from action and perform his role as royal cipher with exemplary tact and gravity. Passive excellence and regal inoffensiveness were expected to characterize him – yet whatever his intended public posture, a life of dignified unemployment could not be sustained in the man. He was no drone in a royal hive.

One of the myths that reflected his role as if in a distorting mirror materialized for Albert with a shock of recognition he almost certainly did not explain to anyone, let alone Victoria. In the legend of Omphale, Queen of Lydia, the queen bought the enslaved Hercules as a lover, and to father her sons. Reports would reach Greece that he was to be entirely ornamental while she ruled. Allegedly, he discarded the warrior's lion pelt that was his badge as well as his aspen wreath, and wore, in their place, jewelled necklaces and golden bracelets – even a woman's turban, rather than a crown. While Omphale issued commands, he sat with her Ionian maids and spun thread, outwardly displaying no shame. Hercules would in time, after siring three sons, reject his servitude and go on to perform the feats for which he was destined.

Early in his marriage, Albert encountered – and purchased – a large painting, by a German artist now otherwise forgotten, of Hercules in submission to Omphale (see chapter VIII). By the time of the acquisition Albert had already begun breaking out of his confines as mere consort. The queenly pregnancies which he had been imported to ensure were creating the conditions which enabled him to transform his role. Style would give way to substance. The picture, duly hung where the Prince could see it, remains, still, where he placed it.

With the sundered bondage to a queen, the mythic parallels strikingly intersect Albert's experience. Well aware of the situation awaiting him in England, he realized nevertheless that his alternatives made the risk worth taking. Rather than being mere succession insurance or ceremonial appendage, *Macmillan's Magazine* would later concede, he was 'a man of acute and strong intelligence, as capable as any within the whole circle of British aristocracy of acting a well-reasoned part, and as likely, if there were occasion, to act it resolutely. One even fancied that, at the [a]rouse of some not impossible juncture of affairs, that brain and head [of his] might turn out, in some less reversed manner than hitherto [expected], to be of some importance to the nation.'

Whether or not that reflected largely unspoken speculation as he arrived on the scene during an abyss in esteem for the Crown, it mirrored his own confidence. And so it would work out, although not without hazards and anxieties sufficient for a five-act drama. Barred from holding office or sitting in Parliament or signing an official paper, the Queen's husband created a role for himself above rank or office, and used himself up in its performance. The painting of Omphale and Hercules remained a picture rather than a prophecy.

Because Albert was much more than the Queen's husband – a reality that would cause him considerable misery as well as gratification – there has been no shortage of biographies. Since Theodore Martin's massive five-volume authorized life of 1875–1880, produced with Victoria's co-operation but also with Sir Theodore's sense of his sovereign looking over his shoulder, nearly every decade has seen the publication of another biography of the Prince Consort. Yet even now he emerges as a much more complex figure than we knew. As we look back at the decades since his premature death, we can perceive the potential for a far different history for his sceptred isle had the uncrowned king, as he had certainly become, lived out a biblical span of years.

That this volume parallels the first half of my *Victoria* is inevitable. The Queen and Prince shared lives as well as families, and lines from the distaff life will be echoed here. Events will also, inevitably, parallel and overlap, but from an Albertine perspective. Further, new sources have been exploited, and earlier documentation rediscovered. Clues have turned up in archives previously untapped, even in the sale catalogues of dealers and auction houses. Memoirs, letters and news-papers have been mined, even the scandalmongering press. Gossip and innuendo have value as an index to perception or reputation.

Further, aspects of Albert have been found in sources to which biographers of the Prince have never turned. No previous limner of his life has explored, for example, the American dimension. Although he travelled abroad very little after his marriage – only to France, Belgium, and Germany – an unceasing queue of people with royal business sought out the Prince. (Also, he was a public figure who endured the reality of the adage that a cat may look at a king.) Americans who encountered him included diplomats like Edward Everett and George Dallas, writers like Herman Melville and Washington Irving, artists like G.P.A. Healy, businessmen like George Peabody. Their pens preserved the moment.

Access to sources is not always by design. Some doors were opened by the publication of my *Victoria* and *Disraeli*. A biographer's mail may include happy and opportune leads and tips – even several of the illustrations reproduced here – as well as cranky observations and corrections of past inaccuracies for the next printing, 'if there is one'.

Someone, certainly, will deplore the loss of material from earlier lives of Albert. To create the illusion of a life, the biographer cannot replicate all the seemingly major events in it, let alone the everyday minutiae. In the course of reducing the Prince to a single volume of readable size, I have omitted particulars for which readers may wish to return to earlier biographies. Much must be left out to evoke the essentials of the man.

With changing times, there is also much that illustrates a life that seemed beyond the biographer in a more reticent day. One's subject may evidence vindictiveness as well as valour, obtuseness as well as foresight. One's subject is permitted a sex life, and may experience the unpleasantness of disease. His parents, both an allegedly revered father and a beautiful and beloved mother, may prove to be less than paragons. It diminishes none of his admirable qualities if he is also human enough to be spiteful at times, petty at others; or if he squabbles with his wife or, on occasion, arrogates to himself authority or perquisites not actually his, for power is a potent addiction, even to those who feel that they are eschewing it. That Albert spoke English in public and German in private in the edifice that, more than any other, symbolized monarchical England – Windsor Castle – would have caused royal embarrassment if revealed in the contemporary press, but that reflected a division of soul that was part of his personality. There were other such paradoxes in what was a distinguished and productive life which, however abbreviated, marks him still as the greatest of royal spouses. Tennyson got close to Albert's achievement, yet saddled him with a benign malediction in the form of a compliment when he wrote, in broad Laureate generosity, of a Prince

> Beyond all titles, and a household name,
> Hereafter, thro' all times, Albert the Good.

However well intended, the accolade did the Prince's posthumous reputation some harm. It suggested only gentility and passivity. On his record, Albert required an active, forceful adjective. The pages which follow illustrate why.

Stanley Weintraub

I
Leaving for Good
1839–1840

T HE DEPARTING PRINCE, if his circumstances were more believable, could have been the hero of a romantic play of 1898, *Alt Heidelberg*, later a long-running operetta with music by Sigmund Romberg. Much like the Karl Franz of venerable but mythic Sachsen-Karlsberg in *The Student Prince* (1924), the authentic prince, tall and handsome, with a light moustache and flashing eyes, had to forgo the remainder of his university days, including boon companions, singing clubs and *gemütlich* inns, to join his betrothed in an arranged marriage. The Saxon duchy was as minuscule as the fictional one, and the university was Bonn, but the bride was too august for credible operetta. Theatre requires some suspension of disbelief.

Prior to doing his marital duty, Prince Albrecht of Saxe-Coburg and Gotha,* like his stage counterpart, would even return to the scene of his student days for a nostalgic farewell. Yet for him, *Abschiednehmen* – leavetaking – was a month-long rite of passage from Coburg to Gotha and from youth-beneath-notice to person-of-consequence. The inner town of Gotha – the Frankish settlement of Gotaha founded in 775 – was already old when the imposing palace of Friedenstein was begun in 1643 by Duke Ernest the Pious on the site of the razed castle of Grimmenstein. Franz Albrecht August Karl

---

* In the bygone world of German dukedoms, baronies and petty principalities, the sons and daughters of Serene – rather than Royal – Highnesses were styled princes and princesses.

Emanuel, the twenty-year-old second son of Ernest I, the far-from-pious reigning duke, was departing from Gotha to become husband of Victoria of Great Britain and Ireland, the queen of the mightiest empire on the globe.

Home for the Prince had been a day's carriage journey to the south, in Coburg, known to history only since the tenth century. From 1353 it was the seat of the margraves of Meissen, descendants of the ambitious Wettin family, who elevated their titles to dukes as they accumulated castles and estates through marriages and inheritances. Franz Albrecht had been born a princeling of Saxe-Coburg-Saalfeld, but in a redivision of family lands after a death without male issue in 1826, Duke Ernest relinquished Saalfeld, to the north-east, for the larger province of Gotha, on the northern edge of the Thüringer Wald. More familiar to the Duke's sons was his Coburg country seat, once the round-towered residence of Adam Alexander von Rosenau, where Albert was born in 1819; and the Ehrenburg Palace, just off the market square, in the town, converted in 1543, early in the Reformation, from a dilapidated Franciscan monastery. In 1540 Martin Luther himself had resided in Coburg, in the Veste, a once-fortified hilltop castle that withstood sieges in the Thirty Years' War.

For all its venerable history and its happy commercial situation on the toll-road between Leipzig and Frankfurt, the Duchy of Coburg was only 201 square miles, half the size of the Isle of Wight, and had only 41,000 inhabitants, nine thousand of them in the town itself. Gotha and its detached principality to the east, Altenburg, added 596 square miles and sixty thousand subjects to Ernest I's domains, ranking him twelfth in the German Diet and requiring him to furnish a contingent of eight hundred soldiers – half his standing army – for the service of the German confederation.

Gotha boasted a population of 13,874 in the capital, by far the largest of twelve towns in the principality. Fifty miles north of Coburg, it was the last family destination on Albert's farewell journey toward England, and matrimony. Although he had not yet left the hourglass frontiers of Coburg and Gotha, he had already relinquished his German name, and understood that on his arrival on English soil he would be naturalized an English subject of the Queen. Nonetheless he vowed solemnly to his former University of Bonn companion, Prince William von Löwenstein-Wertheim-Freudenberg, 'Whilst striving and working

Die Ernestine Länder, 1741

The Ernestine principalities, dukedoms and dependencies in Saxony in pre-Napoleonic times. Coburg is to the south, Gotha to the north-west. By accretion they gradually expanded towards each other. Saalfeld, once a Coburg dependency, is to its north-east.

indefatigably for the country to which I shall belong in future and in which I shall be called to occupy a high position, I shall not cease to be a loyal German, Coburger, Gothaner.'

On the instructions of Victoria and with his father as her proxy in Gotha, on 23 January, 1840 her husband-to-be had been invested with the Order of the Garter in his new English guise. The Queen had been unable to invest him as well with an English peerage – a confirmation of the low esteem into which the monarchy had fallen – and he would be leaving Germany with only a bejewelled blue ribbon and an anglicized name.

In his last letter to Victoria from Coburg – each took seven or eight days by courier across Germany, Flanders and the Channel – Albert had written, having it both ways, 'I strongly approve of your method of writing to me in English when you feel you must express yourself very clearly, and I beg you to continue your habit of writing partly in German and partly in English, a method I shall likewise follow, and by which we shall not only be enabled to understand each other fully, but by which also my dearest Victoria will become the most amiable and useful language master I can possibly have.' It was dated three days before Christmas, his last at home among the German table-top evergreen trees bright with candles.

The formal declaration of Albert's betrothal had been made in Coburg two weeks earlier, in ceremonies on a scale that would have amused the English. The Court, he had explained the day before to Victoria, would gather 'in full dress to hear the Word of God; then it assembles in the Throne Room along with members of the Chamber, Delegates from the towns, chiefs of Colleges, the Army, the Clergy, etc., and, before Papa and myself, Minister von Carlowitz (after Saxon custom, the Ruler never speaking in Person) will read the Declaration, which will then be printed and sent throughout the country in a special newspaper issue. Then a Court [levée] for congratulations ... and then a state Banquet.' But solemnity was limited to the Saxon élite. Public reaction in Coburg was less restrained than in London, and dramatized the gulf between the two cultures. 'The joy of the people was so great', Albert wrote to Victoria on 10 December, two days after the official ceremonies in the duchy, 'that they went on firing in the streets with guns and pistols during the whole night, so that one might have imagined that a battle was taking place.'

Events affecting Coburg, a backwater even in fragmented Germany, created few ripples in relatively somnolent, post-Napoleonic Europe. A very young husband for a reigning queen seemed likely to have no impact other than to promise continuity for the royal line. In Britain, where the Whig grip on government had been slackening, strengthening the succession was a triumph for a party electorally imperilled since the coronation.

In London, Victoria had done no more, formally, than to read a paper – composed by Melbourne – to the Privy Council. Once the sovereign's private consultative body, it had lost most of its political powers to the Prime Minister's Cabinet as the Crown's powers declined, but membership remained a sought-after distinction although the Council met largely to formalize decisions already taken.* Victoria's assured presence before it, however, allayed concerns about the young queen's mishandling of her role, which had disquieted both government and opposition almost since her succession. Whatever common folk thought about the importation of a young and inexperienced foreigner to be her consort, the party in power saw in him a check on her more deplorable tendencies. As for the Tories, Sir James Graham wrote to the Conservative leader, Sir Robert Peel, 'no change can well be for the worse; and in such circumstances almost any change becomes desirable.'

On Christmas Day in London, after dining with the dowager queen, Adelaide, at Marlborough House, Lady Wharncliffe returned to her town residence in Curzon Street, Mayfair, and penned a gossipy letter to her daughter, Caroline Talbot. The former queen – she was only forty-seven, a quarter-century younger than the late William IV – was a favourite of Victoria, who liked her aunt far better than her own mother, the ambitious Duchess of Kent. The fondness had long been mutual. Unable to carry a child beyond stillbirth or early infancy, Adelaide had loved the young Victoria, destined by biology to be William's successor, as if she were their child. A Christmas parcel from Victoria had arrived, and Adelaide opened it in Lady Wharncliffe's presence. It contained a bracelet enclosing, in the custom of the day, a cutting of the giver's hair.

'She was much pleased with it', Lady Wharncliffe wrote of the dowager queen. Before her arranged marriage, Adelaide had been a

---

* The cabinet office of Lord President of the Council linked the two bodies.

princess of Saxe-Coburg-Meiningen – as Victoria's own mother had been a princess of neighbouring Saxe-Coburg-Saalfeld (and Albert's aunt). Protestant princesses of childbearing age had been much sought after by George III's sons after the death in childbirth of Princess Charlotte, the only child of the unadmirable Prince of Wales – who soon after became George IV.

Adelaide was charmed by the letter which accompanied Victoria's Christmas gift, 'which was in German & in German characters, & then told me that when she was at Windsor she had said to the Queen she should like much to get a German letter from her *some day*. She said it was very well written' – although Victoria afterward deplored her own early attempts at German as 'shocking bad' – '& that she now writes in German to Prince *Albert*. Of *him*, she' – Adelaide – 'gives a very favourable report, from all she has heard, & told us that he not only loved music – how lucky! – but *composed* very well indeed.' The young queen had even asked Adelaide to visit at five on an afternoon and listen to some of the Prince's songs. 'Accordingly she went, & I think it was in the Duchess of Kent's apartment – and there she remained singing her Albert's compositions till seven.' Lady Wharncliffe was weak on pronoun references but it was evident that Victoria's pride in her future husband was already substantial.

Reactions were very different elsewhere in London. The gutter press had quickly dampened the euphoria about the Queen's betrothal to a handsome and talented young prince. One broadside sold and sung in the streets, Charles Dickens alleged to the young MP Richard Monckton Milnes, not only emphasized Albert's foreign origins, but suggested a local pronunciation for his name that emphasized the Queen's own Saxon, and Hanoverian, origins:

> So let 'em say, whate'er thay may
> Or do whate'er they can;
> Prince Hallbert he will always be
> My own dear Fancy man.

Before the old year was out, even the Prime Minister was suggesting to the Queen that Albert was, in character and upbringing, alien to English ways, repeating to her a concern voiced by a lady in Melbourne's worldly circle that the Prince's German university traits would be made fun of by English university men, whose experience was less of learning than of license, and who emerged as gentlemen rather than as professors. 'Any attention to morality in universities [here] was ridiculed, which I said was too shocking', Victoria confessed in her diary on 31 December. 'I said funnily I thought Lord M. didn't like Albert so much as he would if he wasn't so strict. "Oh! no, I highly respect it," said Lord M. I then talked of A.'s saying I ought to be severe about people. "Then you'll be liable to make every sort of mistake. In this country all should go by law and precedent," said Lord M., "and not by what you hear." '

Two weeks later, Melbourne seemed concerned, in talking with the Queen, about 'Albert's indifference about Ladies'. He appeared innocent of female entanglements, too inexperienced to be a husband. 'A little dangerous, that's all it is', Melbourne explained. 'It's very well if that holds, but it doesn't always.'

Victoria was shocked. 'I said [to Lord M.] this was very wrong of him, and scolded him for it.'

The Saxon mini-states had furnished more than their share of spouses for English royalty, including Victoria's – and Albert's – uncle Leopold, who was Princess Charlotte of Wales's widower, but Gotha had not identified itself with the English royal house until its linkage with Coburg. The duchy's population of 96,000 – about five per cent of metropolitan London's two million in 1839 – was ecstatic about the rise of their own princeling to as high an estate as there was in the world. A new traffic count in London had tabulated seven thousand vehicles passing the intersection of Oxford Street and Newman Street in Soho daily. There were not that many carriages in all of Gotha. Now someone who otherwise at best would have been only a *Herzog zu Sachsen*, would, through marriage to a Wettin cousin for whom German was a foreign language, sit next to, if not upon, the throne of England.

Albert was under no illusions about his likely powerlessness. Still, the brilliant role in life arranged for him was better than life as a younger son in a third-class German statelet. Gotha had principally been known for the publishing house of Justus Perthes, which since 1753 had issued the *Gothaische Hofkalender*, better known as the *Almanach de Gotha*, the genealogical, diplomatic and statistical annual to which one referred for such information as the heads of ruling houses. This marriage would assure Albert a prominent place in it.

The high dignitaries converging upon Gotha for their farewells – a *Landgrave*, a *Landesherr*, a *Herzog* – were as nothing compared to those soon to crowd Albert's appointment book. For the visiting *Grossherzog* – Grand Duke – of nearby Weimar, a shooting party was arranged in the gross fashion of *Mitteleuropa*, a *battue* in which masses of game were driven into firing range. 'I took part,' Albert boasted to Victoria – he would be somewhat more cautious in England – 'and was so lucky as to kill 105 hares with my own gun.'

A few days before the colourful Garter ceremony, festive Gotha was plunged into mourning when Herr von Carlowitz, Duke Ernest's minister of state for eighteen years and his only intimate friend (three privy councillors completed the Lilliputian government), died suddenly of a stroke. Mourning had to be brief. The wedding at Windsor could not be postponed, and travel by the ducal entourage would not be easy.

No one told Albert, amid the festivities, that London rumour had it that the marriage might have to be postponed because of fears of revolution. Parliament had scorned a Chartist bill of rights for redress of grievances. (Much of it would be legislated piecemeal over the years.) A violent reaction was feared – even the Thames, it was rumoured, would be set on fire, and churches torched. The worst incident turned out to be a meeting in Bethnal Green which was broken up by the police.

While the outlook for order was improving, for Albert nothing good was happening in London. Despite Albert's origins in the duchy that had sheltered Luther, the Duke of Wellington, conservative even by Tory standards, moved in the Lords that a reference to Prince Albert be prefaced by the word 'Protestant', to protect England from Papist contamination. After all, members of his family, to rise in the world, had married Catholics, and Albert himself might have 'papistical leanings'. The amendment, Charles Greville, clerk to the Privy Council, observed in his diary, was 'a sop to the silly'. He was 'grieved' to see the elderly, doddering Wellington 'descend to such miserable humbug'. It was party posturing, with Albert as pawn.

Albert himself would have been grieved had he read in *Hansard* the debates in Parliament about granting him anything, from rank or title to an allowance befitting his station. 'Did the noble Lord', the Radical MP Joseph Hume taunted Viscount Melbourne's Chancellor of the Exchequer, Lord John Russell, 'know the dangers of setting a young man down in London with so much money in his pocket?' Laughter drowned out the difference between an annuity for the consort of the Queen and a pocketful of golden sovereigns carried down to Soho by a well-born blade from the country. As a further indignity, the bill as passed on 27 January would commence payment to Albert only on the day of the wedding, with the first instalment not due before Easter. Albert would have staff appointed for him and no means of paying them, a prospect which compelled him to plead, vainly, that he should have foisted upon him 'only enough gentlemen for appearance's sake'.

Through January the issue of his purse had been debated in print as well as in Parliament. 'Little Vic is in a dreadful stew', the irreverent weekly *The Satirist* reported, 'for ever since the prepayment system had been adopted she has got no letter of advice from Albert, as the Grand Duke of Saxe-Coburg refuses to sell his Duchy in order to enable the poor young man to prepay his letters.' (The Penny Post had just gone into effect in England.)

The Queen had been fearful of such stipulations when she formally opened Parliament on 16 January, but she went through her address with grace and dignity, breaking down only after Melbourne informed her, after eleven in the evening on the twenty-seventh, that the resolution on the Prince's status as proposed by Sir Robert Peel and his Tories had beaten the divided Whigs by 104 votes. The opposition had made every matter concerning Albert's perquisites a party question and Peel had sternly commanded Tory loyalty. 'We smashed the Government', the Tory MP from Maidstone, Benjamin Disraeli, gleefully reported to his sister, Sarah.

The royal earful which the Prime Minister received must have been much like the grievance which Victoria registered in her diary. The 'vile, confounded, infernal Tories' had aimed at embarrassing the shaky Whig government, and the Queen's marriage happened to be in the way, but Victoria took personally what Disraeli called 'a war to the knife'. 'As long as I live, I'll never forgive those infernal scoundrels, with Peel at their head ... for this act of personal spite!!'

Since the Duke of Wellington had insisted upon diminishing Prince Albert's allowance, Victoria declared to Melbourne that she would not extend the expected invitation to her wedding to the venerable hero of Waterloo. 'I really couldn't ask the Duke.' Only days before Albert's entourage clattered on toward Calais, Wellington remained intractable in the Lords, also objecting to a clause in the marriage act assigning

Albert precedence over all members of the royal family after the Queen. The royal dukes, Victoria's uncles, had objected and the Queen had even tried bribery, offering to give the Duke of Sussex's illegal wife (under the Royal Marriage Act) the title of Duchess of Inverness, and to have him give the bride away at the wedding. The Duke of Cambridge offered consent so qualified that Wellington interpreted it as an implicit rejection despite the Queen's public thanks. The Duke of Cumberland, now King Ernest Augustus of Hanover, would not hear of a mere princeling preceding him. On the twenty-sixth, a Sunday, Lord Clarendon intervened with Wellington, explaining in vain that Albert was marrying a queen, and that the precedents of Leopold and Charlotte, and – a century earlier – of Prince George of Denmark and the future Queen Anne, then a princess, did not apply. Wellington would not be budged, and Melbourne patiently counselled Victoria to give up the losing battle.

'I was perfectly frantic', the Queen confessed in her diary, '– this wicked old foolish Duke, these confounded Tories, oh! may they be well punished for this outrageous insult! I cried with rage... Poor dear Albert, how cruelly they are ill-using that dearest Angel! Monsters! You Tories shall be punished. Revenge! Revenge!'

Since anything less would have scandalized a still-adoring country, the avuncular Melbourne succeeded in obtaining for Wellington an invitation to the wedding. The Queen remained adamant about the wedding breakfast. The Duke intended no disrespect, Melbourne cajoled vainly: 'It's his conscience.' Still, Victoria had to inform Albert of his eroded position before his packet docked at Dover. Albert had lost on every issue, material and symbolic. Even before his round of farewells in Germany had begun, he had relinquished any hope of appointing his own Household other than for inferior servants. For private secretary and controller of his purse he had already accepted George Anson, the Prime Minister's secretary. It seemed almost as if Melbourne had arranged for a spy at Court. Albert's protest that he should remain outside 'party politics', earned him a wry history lesson from the Prime Minister. 'To compose your Household of persons who are neither themselves nor by their relations connected with political parties is impossible. So many neutral persons fit for the purpose do not exist and would form a strange assemblage if they could be found.' Rather, Melbourne saw the necessity for the appointment of 'persons of rank and character... with a decided leaning to the opinions of the present government.' Otherwise, he warned, the appearance would be created 'that Your Serene Highness is adverse to Her Majesty's ministers, and you will find yourself, in spite of yourself, taken up by the party in opposition . . .'

Unwilling to surrender easily, Albert had appealed from Gotha on 12 January 1840 that 'a mixed household of Whigs and Tories' would establish 'that I will belong to no party'. It was high-minded, but the Prime Minister was interested in perquisites rather than in principle, and although Albert sent copies of his exchanges to Victoria with the vow, 'I declare calmly that I will not take Mr Anson nor anybody now', he would have to back down. Melbourne left it to the Queen to appoint Anson. Too embarrassed to insult Albert directly by telling him what she had been required to do, having reaped the whirlwind of past political blunders, Victoria insulted him even further by leaving it to her confidante, Baroness Lehzen. Yet the Prince was trapped. 'I am leaving my home,' he had already objected to Victoria, 'with all its old associations, all my bosom friends, and going to a country in which everything is new and strange to me – men, language, customs, modes of life, position. Except yourself I have no one to confide in.'

The narrow streets of Gotha were dense with well-wishers as the Prince's carriages passed for the last time. In one was Colonel Charles Grey, who, to take a place in the Royal Household, had relinquished the parliamentary seat at High Wycombe he had first won in a contest with an ambitious upstart named Benjamin Disraeli. Grey had travelled to Gotha with Lord Torrington bearing the Queen's patent for emptily honouring Albert with the Garter. Torrington, the 7th Viscount and a young gentleman still in his twenties, was a favourite of the Queen but, unknown to her, a compulsive gossip who would soon feed hurtful stories about Albert to the press, particularly to *The Times*, as 'your Windsor special'. Yet at Court he would outlast the Prince. Another favourite whom Albert would shortly encounter, since he had been instructed to escort him across the Channel, was Lord Clarence Paget, one of the six sons of the Marquess of Anglesey, several of whom held Household posts. His brother, Lord Alfred Paget, was once rumoured as a possible mate for Victoria. Gossip referred to them as the 'Paget House Club' – but the youngest brother, Lord George, would confound expectations by distinguishing himself in the Crimea and rising later to general.

Torrington and Grey were to accompany Albert overland to the Channel in three carriages sent by Victoria. They had been among the 180 guests at Gotha who had celebrated the Garter investiture at an elaborate dinner that had included toasts, trumpet flourishes, the band of the Coldstream Guards brought over for the occasion to play 'God Save the Queen', and a salute by 101 cannons in the square. At the third and last toast, the windows were flung open as a signal to the artillery and the breeze blew the thin muslin curtains into the candle flames. In an instant they blazed to the tops of the tall windows. The dinner guests, already standing, were trapped between the crowded tables, but the fragile curtains flamed out in seconds. The panelled dining-room survived almost unscathed. Postprandial coffee in the Duchess's apartments was served almost as if nothing had happened, after which the company reassembled to go in state to the new opera house. (It had opened three weeks earlier with a gala production of Giacomo Meyerbeer's *Robert le diable*.)

In Carl Maria von Weber's *Der Freischütz*, the staged operatic shooting seemed anticlimactic. 'With the opera', Grey understated in his journal, 'ended a most exciting and interesting, if somewhat fatiguing, day, but the hours kept are so much better than those in England, that all was over between ten and eleven.'

A plethora of luncheons, dinners and state balls filled the final week. On the Monday evening before Albert's departure, the last banquet was followed by a concert. At its close, as the musicians put away their instruments, the ladies and gentlemen of the duchy, and invited German guests, many of them in tears, passed before the Prince to bid him *auf Wiedersehen*. On Tuesday morning, 28 January, the journey began. 'Every window', Grey recalled, 'was crammed with heads, every housetop covered with people, waving handkerchiefs and crying with each other in demonstrations of affection.' At the home of the dowager duchess of Gotha, the late Duchess Louise's aged stepmother, the carriages halted long enough for her to come to her own window to raise her arms and, weeping, twice shout Albert's name. Too frail to descend and join the family in still another farewell, Duchess Caroline permitted her attendants to help her away. Others, in twenty carriages, gathered at The Last Schilling, a small tavern just north of Gotha, where there were further embraces and handshakes. Finally, in the snow beneath an arch of fir trees erected at the ducal frontier, garlanded girls in white dresses, accompanied by a band, sent him off with a farewell hymn which steamed into the frosty air.

With the Queen's carriages were five of Duke Ernest's, carrying his own entourage that was to attend Albert at the wedding on 10 February. At one o'clock the party stopped by arrangement at Birschhausen for lunch, and at eight they put up at an inn at Kassel for the night; but before dining, the duke and his sons paid a courtesy visit to the Elector of Hesse, whose seat it was. The following morning at nine the carriages clattered east to Arnsberg, arriving at ten in the evening and going on the next day to the Rhine, which they had to cross near Köln (Cologne) by ferry in cold, heavy rain. By three in the afternoon the sodden, exhausted party reached Aachen (Aix-la-Chapelle), where messages awaited Albert, among them the disagreeable news that Parliament had refused to vote him a stipend equal to that secured by his uncle in 1816 as husband of Princess Charlotte, whose death in 1817 had opened the succession to the yet-unborn Victoria.

Having turned down the new throne of turbulent Greece, Leopold had been made King of the Belgians when the nation was formed from the secessionist lower provinces of the Netherlands in 1831. Yet, to the outrage of the House of Commons, he had failed to relinquish his lifetime parliamentary grant of an annual £50,000; and Albert was the second Coburger consort for whom funds had been requested by the Court in little more than two decades. The allegation was at least in part unfair. On the day Leopold left London for Brussels, 16 July 1831, he renounced his full £50,000 stipend. He continued to deduct from it, however, the upkeep of his English estate, Claremont; of the horses and carriages and servants he retained in England; his donations to English charities and subscriptions to English clubs; and the funds he diverted for a time to his nearly penniless sister Victoire for the upkeep of her establishment, including Princess Victoria. These English expenses he computed as about £20,000. The £30,000 he returned was, perhaps not by coincidence, the amount offered by Parliament to his nephew Albert. A younger brother to Duke Ernest, Leopold had been a prince of Saxe-Coburg-Saalfeld, the title into which Albert was born, three months after his cousin Victoria, on 26 August 1819. Leopold at twenty was in the Russian army fighting Napoleon. By Waterloo he had become a senior officer, and had met Princess Charlotte when in London after the war in the suite of the Tsar. To Parliament, Albert was little more than a child, a university student called from his class-room in Bonn.

To Albert, his parliamentary rebuffs suggested that England was now weary of foreign spouses for royalty – especially Coburgers. Parliament had been forced after the death of Charlotte and her stillborn child to pay the debts of, and provide stipends to, George III's spendthrift and often dissolute sons, some already in illegal marriages, to press them into begetting legal heirs. Leopold's stipend now seemed to MPs an expensive anachronism.

It was into the Belgian domains of his uncle that Albert arrived by early evening on the last day of January. By ten his entourage was ready, wearily, to settle down in Liège for the night. Instead, they found the provincial governor and his party waiting to escort them in state to the Pavilion Anglais, where a brass band assaulted the tired travellers until midnight. 'Nor was it all quiet when they ceased', Grey wrote. 'About one o'clock a large company of peasants took their place, and serenaded the Prince with vocal music till nearly two in the morning.'

The next day Albert reported from Brussels via the courier that he had arrived safely in the capital that afternoon. To his 'Dear Beloved Victoria' he poured out his frustration that their ill-treatment was coming not only from the lesser classes elected to the lower house, but from the peers who might rather have applauded the dynastic stability his presence would promise. 'You can imagine how annoyed I am at the news of the really most indecent vote in the Commons about my income,' he wrote. 'We saw it in the paper when we dined at Aix. Even in the House of Lords they are making themselves unnecessarily unplea-sant. I must stop, and only can tell [you] that if your love remains, they cannot make me unhappy.'

Awaiting Albert in Brussels was Thompson, the Queen's tailor, with the uniform that the Prince was to wear at the altar. He had left his Coburg court dress at Windsor to be used as a pattern, and the fitting would take place in a third court – Leopold's. (Innocent of military experience, Albert would be caricatured in his field marshal's regalia astride a rocking-horse.) A letter from Victoria also awaited him in Brussels, cautiously making no mention of the pared stipend, which Albert continued to see as an index to his likely status in England. He was too innocent of the world to be restrained about it, even to the bride to whom he would owe everything but his few Ernestine florins. 'I am surprised', he confessed on 4 February, 'that you have said no word of sympathy to me about the vote of the 28th, for those nice Tories have cut off half my income (that was to be expected), and it makes my position no very pleasant one. It is hardly conceivable that anyone could behave as meanly and disgracefully as they have to you and me. It cannot do them much good, for it is hardly possible to maintain any respect for them any longer.'

Alarmed by the resentment Albert found no reason to conceal during his pause at Brussels, Leopold rushed a letter the same day, 4 February, to the Queen at Windsor. The wedding was only six days away. Albert was 'much irritated', Leopold warned. 'He does not care about the money, but he is much shocked and exasperated by the disrespect of the thing.' He was 'pretty full of grievances'. Albert would have been even more outraged had he known that the Queen had given in to the army of old men in the Privy Council and in Parliament without much of a fight, but the royal cachet had sunk as close to worthlessness as it seemed able to fall, and she was hardly more than a girl.

Albert still assumed that royal regard meant something to a Parliament that had been exasperated by the worthless sons of George III, two of whom had succeeded to the throne, and had been further disillusioned by the young queen, child of another of the embarrassing royal dukes. Victoria had disappointed expectations by her personal failings and appeared flighty and foolish – in need of a mature, sophisticated husband at her side. Yet Albert was even three months younger than the Queen.

Overruled earlier about the staff of his own Household, Albert, already in Belgium, discovered yet another rebuff, this time from his future spouse. Victoria's letter awaiting him had responded to Albert's appeal for a honeymoon, even if only at Windsor Castle, long enough to afford some privacy. He hardly needed to remind Victoria that they had been permitted little experience of each other by Court etiquette. The Queen admonished him loftily, her affectionate interpositions notwithstanding,

You have written to me in one of your letters about our stay at Windsor, but, dear Albert, you have not at all understood the matter. You forget, my dearest Love, that I am the Sovereign, and that business can stop and wait for nothing. Parliament is sitting, and something occurs almost every day, for which I may be required, and it is quite impossible for me to be absent from London; therefore two or three days is already a long time to be absent. I am never easy a moment, if I am not on the spot, and see and hear what is going on, and everybody, including all my Aunts (who are very knowing in all these things), says I must come out after the second day, for, as I must be surrounded by my Court, I cannot keep alone. This is also my own wish in every way.

Whatever Albert's ambitions for himself, marriage with an obscure but appropriately born lesser heiress from Hesse or Saxony or Württemburg may have seemed, then, an opportunity for which he should have waited. He could have completed his university degree or, like Ernest, apprenticed himself to a military career in Saxony. At twenty he would have, at Victoria's order, the uniform of a field marshal, but it would only be a costume in which to be wed.

In London, balladeers hawked broadsheets, mocking 'Saxe-Coburg's pauper prince' and 'the dozen cowboys who compose his court'. In another, the Prince proclaimed, in card-playing metaphor,

> They say I'm a ninny,
> and not worth a ginny,
> But Vic, she declares
> I'm a trump.

The Coburg delegation was to leave Brussels for Calais, Albert wrote to Victoria, early on the fifth – 'and then there awaits us that sad time on the sea, which, I fear, will be bound up with great sacrifices! The public, who will probably be assembled at Dover, will obtain a pleasant vision of me!' Melbourne's view of Albert remained unsatisfactory, but not because of his susceptibility to seasickness. On the same day, at a dinner for the Cabinet given by Lord Palmerston, Melbourne had remarked that the Queen was 'very angry' with him, and the Earl of Clarendon asked why. 'The Queen was talking with him about Prince Albert', Lady Clarendon reported, 'and remarking that one thing that pleased her very much was that he never paid any attention to any other woman. Lord Melbourne *inadvertently* (as he called it) answered, "No; that sort of thing is apt to come later"; an odd remark to make to any woman on the eve of marriage – let alone *the Queen*. She said, "I shan't soon forgive you that!" Lord Melbourne rubbed his hands...and chuckled over it amazingly.'

Registry of Albert's marriage and his exchange of vows with Victoria would lift him on 10 February from Serene Highness to Royal Highness. Their essential preliminary, the Naturalization Bill, cost the Queen and Prince agonies of waiting. It passed on 4 February, the day before he left Brussels by the new railway for Ostend *en route* to Calais. Embarrassingly, the bill guaranteed him no precedence after the Queen. The seemingly harmless precedence clause had been withdrawn in order to get it by its third reading.

All that Melbourne had managed was to prevent Colonel Sibthorp, the architect of the Prince's reduced stipend, from amending the bill in the Commons to cease Albert's annuity if the Queen should die and he did not afterwards remain at least six months every year in England. It was an unveiled slap at King Leopold, and even the Leader of the Opposition, Sir Robert Peel, asked the cranky colonel to withdraw his paragraph. At five in the morning after four nights of debate the Government's slender majority was only twenty-nine. Albert was on his way to becoming a subject of his Queen.

Leaving Buckingham Palace, Albert's emissary Baron Stockmar encountered Melbourne. Long confidential agent for the Coburgers, especially for Leopold, now King of the Belgians, the prematurely wizened Stockmar, by profession a medical doctor, had become a physician of souls, a discreet counsellor to the next generation of ambitious Ernestine princes. He observed unhappily that some members of the Whig Cabinet had evaded voting on the bill. 'The Prince will doubtless be much irritated against the Tories', the Prime Minister conceded. 'But it is not the Tories alone whom the Prince has to thank for the curtailment of his appanage. It is the Tories, the Radicals, and a good many of our own people. I hope you will yourself say this to the Prince.'

Stockmar penned his memorandum, which would reach Albert as he disembarked in England, on 6 February. Stockmar understood that Melbourne felt too weak as minority Prime Minister to demand party loyalty, and did not want misplaced rancour to make a political partisan of the Prince. The problems in accepting the young and inexperienced foreigner as consort to a young and wilful queen were more complicated than simple loyalty to the sovereign.

Albert's party reached Calais on the evening of 5 February and remained overnight. Channel crossings were rightly dreaded, especially in winter, and they were to sail in the morning, to cross in daylight. The two best vessels in the service had been ordered to Calais by the Queen, the steam packets *Ariel* and *Firebrand*, but the wind was at half gale force as the party arrived at dockside on the sixth. It was impossible to board the pitching *Firebrand*. Everyone crowded aboard the *Ariel*, and as the packet weighed anchor at noon, the *Firebrand* followed, nearly empty. Helpless on deck was Victoria's personal representative, Lord Clarence Paget.

Buffeted by high seas, the packets struggled across the Channel, His Serene Highness hanging on to a staircase rail below for most of the voyage. At 4.30 p.m. the white cliffs hove into view. As the ships docked, awaiting crowds shouted, 'God save the Queen!' and 'Hurrah for the Prince!' Weak with seasickness, the tottering Coburgers, accompanied still by Lord Torrington and Colonel Grey, wanly received salutes from a guard of honour from the 90th Regiment, which guided them in the drizzle to open carriages-and-four. The crowds parted to let them through to Payne's York Hotel, where the mayor of Dover and his delegation were to offer a formal address of welcome. Albert was too seasick to receive it. The mayor, magistrates and town councillors offered to return in the morning.

On the banks of the Thames beyond Barking Reach in the direction of London, gawkers and greeters remained waiting for some sign of the Prince's party. People had gathered at Woolwich and Greenwich on the basis of mistaken information in the afternoon papers, expecting Albert to disembark at the docks near the Royal Arsenal rather than at Dover. With disappointment and frustration increasing, the crowds thinned. Some die-hards set off, as dusk fell, toward Shooters Hill overlooking Woolwich Common and the town of Greenwich. They were still hoping to catch a glimpse of the Prince if indeed he were taking the road to London. Instead, at seven the party dined, cautiously under the circumstances, upon a repast on which the landlord of the York had spared little expense. Wobbly, Albert postponed writing to Victoria until the next morning.

Early on Friday a courier took his message to the Queen, anticipating the following day – the eighth – when 'I shall be looking into your dear eyes'. The crossing, Albert confessed, had been 'terrible', with the decks of the *Ariel* 'crammed with sick people'. He could not recall ever 'having suffered so long or so violently. Papa and Ernest too were in miserable condition. When we landed our faces were more the colour of wax candles than human visages.' Yet he saw their tumultuous reception as recompense for the shabby treatment by Parliament. 'Thousands were standing on the quay, and greeted us with loud and continuous cheering.'

Effectively now an Englishman as he set foot on Kentish soil, he awaited the reappearance of the Dover dignitaries and his next leg of the ceremonial journey to London. 'Papa and Ernest lay themselves at your feet', he closed in the courtesies of the occasion. 'I lay myself higher – right up to your heart, hoping to find it open to me, and remain with unchanging love and attachment, my own dear bride's ever faithful, ALBERT.' Thus ended the first full day of the lifetime vocation to which he had been born and bred.

II

Silver Spoon

1819–1831

I N THE SCHLOSS called the Rosenau in Coburg, a 'Pumpernickel State', W.M. Thackeray would joke anonymously in *Punch* in 1845, was exhibited the actual silver spoon, embossed with the English royal arms, which Prince Albert had in his mouth when he was born. Awed, 'the correspondent of the *Morning Herald* fainted when he saw this admirable relic'. The notion that Albert's birth as a younger son to the ruler of a small Saxon duchy might place him in line to be consort to the queen of a great world power could not have been held by many on 26 August 1819. Still, a connection existed. His first cousin, Alexandrina Victoria, had been assisted into life at Kensington Palace three months earlier via the services of the same *accoucheuse*, Dr Marianne Heidenreich von Siebold. The Princess's mother, the Duchess of Kent, born a Coburger herself, was a sister to Duke Ernest, the boy's father.

For years there would be little likelihood that the infant princess would be queen in England. She was merely the first in her generation to be born after the death of Princess Charlotte of Wales, heiress to the future George IV. The corpulent 'Royal George', who would succeed to the throne early the next year, was the eldest of a brood of odious brothers each eligible by accident of death or birth of an heir to be, or to sire, the next king – or queen. Several of the ageing royal dukes would jettison ineligible mistresses and illegal wives to marry and beget, hoping to find in the sorry lottery a means, at worst, of having a grateful Parliament reward such duty to the succession by paying off their substantial debts. Only as the Princess survived what was almost a royal tontine did she appear in political need of a husband, and there were greater princes in Europe than one whose father reigned over what seemed hardly larger than a royal park in England.

Aside from his dubious prospects as little more than an insurance policy upon his elder brother, Ernest, born a year earlier, on 21 June 1818, Albert's life looked cloudless. The little dukedom on an edge of the sprawling Thüringer woods was peaceful and idyllically beautiful. Albert's ducal father was secure in the rule of his mini-state, one of the less significant of the thirty-nine sovereignties in the jerrybuilt jigsaw of the German Confederation. Albert's mother, formerly Princess Louise of neighbouring Saxe-Gotha-Altenburg, born on 21 December 1800, was young, clever and beautiful. No silver spoon of English design was in sight.

Sixteen at her marriage to the worldly thirty-three-year-old Duke Ernest, Albert's mother was eighteen at his birth. Although her elder son had been born in Coburg itself, at the sooty yellow, sham-Gothic Ehrenburg Palace, her *Alberinchen* arrived at the Rosenau, four miles north of the walled town. Unpretentious but for its squat round tower and set amid rolling green hills, its remodelling, with added English gardens, had been financed by Ernest I after the Napoleonic armies receded, through credit advanced by the Frankfurt Rothschilds. Albert's elaborate christening ceremony there, utilizing water from the Itze, which flowed below the rise of the Rosenau, may have been the last happy public event in the doomed marriage. Proudly, the publishers of the *Almanach de Gotha* issued for 1818 a Wedding Edition, with frontispiece portraits of the ducal pair. Since sovereigns awarded each other gaudy Orders as compliments, Ernest's high-collared uniform was weighted down with them, and the young Princess of Gotha, now a duchess, wore her hair in coils atop her head, crowned by a diadem of pearls. There were also views of Gotha and of Coburg, and an ornate dedication, inevitably in French. No king or queen could have been better served by the modestly sized but magisterial book of blue bloods.

On the arrival of the couple in Coburg after the wedding in Gotha, their greeting punctuated by the booming of thirty-six guns, happy townspeople unharnessed the horses from the couple's coach-and-four and in a traditional demonstration of enthusiasm pulled the carriage the rest of the way to the castle. That evening at a concert in their honour a choir sang, 'Hail, Duke! Hail, Duchess! Soon you will be rocking princes in your lap!' Louise was enchanted, but not for long. After the first post-nuptial sermon in the royal chapel, she carped to Augusta von Studnitz, her closest friend in Gotha, she heard only praise of Duke Ernest, and 'not one religious thought'. Her life, with few responsibilities other than to fulfil the hopes of the Coburg choristers, would become one of ordering Paris fashions, accompanying Ernest to the chase with wives of the other huntsmen 'to hear the calling of the stags', and entertaining neighbouring serene highnesses.

An early shadow over the marriage was Louise's visit with her 'beloved husband' to the fortress of Leutenburg, east of Saalfeld, where seventeenth-century Duke Johann Casimir of Coburg had kept his wife, whom he accused of adultery with a young knight, Ulric von Lichtenstein, and whom he had had imprisoned and divorced. She had died in captivity in 1613. A portrait of Duchess Anna and another of her vengeful husband still hung in the gloomy vaults, and were pointed out to Louise by the Duke in the manner of a dramatic monologue by Robert Browning yet to be written, 'My Last Duchess'.

'I thought I could still hear the weeping of the unhappy Anna, and see the flowing blood of the perfidious Lichtenstein', Louise confided to Fräulein Augusta. 'I clutched the Duke's arm and looked anxiously to see if there was, perhaps, any likeness in his beautiful dark-brown eyes to this terrible ancestor, but I don't believe it. Anna was miserable because she was unfaithful. Posterity will never be able to say that about me.'

In Louise's own marriage, the infidelities at first had all been Duke Ernest's, but Louise had no knowledge of his profligate past, nor that he had not relinquished wenching when he pledged his vows. Early in their union, it seemed to the Duchess, they were seldom apart for long. They were together in Vienna, their children left with nursemaids, when, on 23 January 1820, the Duke of Kent, the infant Victoria's father and Ernest's brother-in-law, died suddenly in England. When the dread news reached Ernest's shocked entourage, Louise wrote, 'We...became ill, all of us.' That distant thunderbolt was as nothing, however, to the damaging gossip of her stepmother's lady-in-waiting. Charlotte von Bock claimed to *Grossmutter* Gotha – to whom one had to shout, as she was very deaf – that a courtier, Count Solms, was in love with the flirtatious Duchess Louise. Alexander Solms, a chamberlain, Louise confided to Augusta, laughed at the canard, but also 'felt quite proud, because of the honour of such a likelihood'. It was much less of a lark when the 'boundless stupidity' was brought to the Duke. 'If he had been sensible', Louise explained, 'he would have laughed also, but he took it seriously and was angry with me. Finally, we had it out; all ended in [my] tears. Now he watches me, which he never used to do, and he misconstrues everything.'

Yet for the moment, with an heir in place and another in reserve, and 'well and jolly', Duke Ernest was content, and Louise's stepmother, the Dowager Duchess of Gotha, kept the children's Coburger aunt in London apprised of happier developments. Albert 'looked like a little squirrel with large black eyes', but soon they had become blue and he was 'pretty as an angel'. Duke Ernest's own mother Augusta, *Grossmutter* Coburg, also kept her twice-widowed daughter in England informed that *Alberinchen*, while 'not a strong child', before he was two (21 July 1821) could 'say everything'. Although 'too slight for a boy', unlike his sturdy elder brother, he was 'lively, very funny, all good nature, and full of mischief' (11 August 1821).

Albert and Ernest were not the Duke's only sons, but Coburgers were cautious about open references to his illicit amorous life, even after Pauline Panam, one of his discarded mistresses, published her *Mémoires d'une jeune Grecque* in Paris in 1824. At fifteen she had been slipped into Coburg dressed as a boy. (Among the paintings which had been commissioned for the refurbishment of the Rosenau, Louise would note, was one 'of a Knight who has discovered that his supposed page is really a beautiful girl'.) At sixteen, in March 1809 – Ernest had been Duke since his father, Francis Frederic, had died in 1806 – Pauline had given birth to his son, an earlier Ernst, in Frankfurt, where she had been sent. Leopold had given her some money, and the Dowager Duchess offered her a pension if she refrained from identifying herself with the Duke and named her child Pauline if a girl, and eschewed Ernest if a boy. She ignored the injunction. The Duke's adjutant, Johann Maximilian von Szymborski, offered a settlement if she 'quit' Saxe-Coburg territory. In Dresden and Frankfurt, she received small sums grudgingly given, then went to Vienna and, finally, Paris, where – as *la belle Grecque* – she somehow supported herself, very likely through the 'special protection' of titled admirers and further blackmail of the Duke. The illegitimate Ernst led a dissipated manhood, and persisted in calling himself a Prince of Coburg until his death at thirty.*

Long before Pauline Panam's tell-all book, Louise had become aware of the Duke's proclivities, which may have justified her enjoyment of undisguised male admiration at the tiny court, if at first nothing more. Louise wrote anxiously to her friend Augusta when the *Landgraf* of Hesse-Cassell was expected for a visit that he would be accompanied by his young sister. 'She will make a sensation with her beauty', the Duchess explained. 'I am frightened for the Duke when he sees her.' Once, taking the waters at Franzensbad, she confided to Augusta about the eighteen-year-old Countess Marie of Klebelsberg that she was 'loved by all'. She had accompanied Louise as lady-in-waiting, 'and God knows what will come of it!' Yet her own admirers at the time ranged from *Kammerherr* Thankmar von Munchhausen, twenty-eight, who was 'hopelessly in love' with her, to 'good-looking Baron Stillfried', a Cherubino at only seventeen, who climbed apple trees to look into her windows, and 'did a thousand pretty, amorous things, which amused me'. There was even 'an Austrian *Rittmeister*' who 'lay at my feet, sighed and languished like a turtle dove'. Mozart might have made an opera of it.

At least into the first months of 1823 Louise shut her eyes to Ernest's straying and pretended as well that her own flirtations were harmless acknowledgements of her charms as an adornment to the duchy. Court life had its quota of make-believe, and some small price had to be paid to sustain it. On 16 December 1822, the Duke held a masked ball, with participants garbed as characters from Sir Walter Scott's *Waverley*, an enormous success on the Continent as well as in Britain. Louise came as the beautiful heroine Flora MacIvor, who ominously retires to a convent at the end of the novel. On the twenty-first was another ball, concluded by a sleigh-ride, and the festivities of the holiday season continued into the new year with scarcely a thought for young Ernest and Albert, who were better cared for in any case by their *Kindermädchen*.

---

* Just as Ernest and Albert had a half-brother with a familiar name preceding them, so Victoria had an illegitimate half-sister unknown to her and carrying her name. Adelaide Victoire was the product of the Duke of Kent's early wild oats, born to a Frenchwoman who died in childbirth in Geneva in 1789. He supported her indirectly via Coutts Bank until 1832, when she faded from history.

Balls, especially masked ones, furnished transparent cover for trysts, and Louise appeared guilty only of evoking ducal jealousy. A later invention, a pamphlet of 1915, however, alleged her involvement with yet another court chamberlain, Baron Ferdinand von Meyern, claiming that 'without contradiction' the affair made Albert 'a half-Jew'. In his bitchy fashion, Lytton Strachey in 1921 would repeat this canard as true. The baron's daughters, Bertha and Malvina, were close friends of Louise. But while the posthumous allegation had no substance, at least one obvious relationship seemed to go too far for the Duke. In 1822 Louise had met Lieutenant Alexander von Hanstein, but she did not mention the 'good-looking' officer with 'black, curly hair' and 'shining bright eyes' to Augusta until March 1824. 'Now comes the worst', she finally confessed; 'don't damn me completely... I have sacrificed everything, but don't also let me lose your friendly heart.'

Expecting the worst, Louise was not surprised when it came. With sanctimonious hypocrisy, given his own lifestyle, the Duke had a letter delivered to her insisting that henceforth they were to live apart. 'You have dreadfully deceived me. I can affirm before God that you have had my heartfelt love...' And he went on about her 'blackest betrayal and ingratitude'. She was ordered to remain at the Rosenau until he received a letter he had requested from her stepmother recalling her to Gotha 'or wherever else she wants to send you'. He was too affected, he closed, by his sense of hurt to continue the letter further. 'We shall hardly see each other again. May you not become so unhappy as you have made me.'

Hanstein was later identified in the Duke's formal petition for legal separation. Ernest sent Szymborski, now a colonel, with stipulations for the Duchess. She was to sign away any remaining rights in Gotha, then leave quietly or be expelled. 'If you will have a divorce,' Ernest wrote, 'I will not withhold my consent for a complete parting.'

The news surfaced quickly. Coburgers, she would claim to Augusta on 24 September 1824 (the last letter that has survived), thought she had been betrayed, and gathered at the Rosenau to wish the Duchess well as she departed into exile on the last Sunday in August. As Louise emerged to step into her carriage, townspeople burst through the hedges, unharnessed her horses, and with choruses of loyalty to her, 'pulled me from the Rosenau, through the town to the [Ehrenburg] Schloss, cheering and shouting all the way.' Cries of '*Die Herzogin kommt!*' echoed through the narrow streets, '*die Burger und die Bauern*' – the towns-people and the farmers, as she put it – joining each other.

'At each village a fresh lot took up the harness. Everywhere was black with people. Their love was touching, but very frightening, too, for they were all armed.' When they reached the castle the throng, which had been increasing all the way, discovered that the Duke was away at his mother's residence. From the balcony of the schloss Duchess Louise offered her gratitude to the crowd 'for their love'. They cheered her, sang 'Now thank we all our God', and set out for Ketschendorf to find the duke, 'and brought him and my children here. They wanted to unite us by force. Poor deluded people!...They felt themselves to be power-ful, and rushed wildly into the Schloss, demanding that Szymborski should be given up.' Thousands cried for ousting of 'the foreigner', assuming that the alleged 'grinder of peasants' was the real authority in the duchy. Intervening, a courtier sympathetic to Louise, Moritz von Thümmel, kept the peace, but not without threats from the Duke, who vowed to summon Austrian cavalry to disperse them by force.

It was an empty threat. A villager, recalling the scene nearly forty years later, remembered that Ernest, in white top hat and long green coat fastened up to the neck, rushed down to reprimand the obstrep-erous Coburgers, then hastened inside. The ducal regiment, com-manded by Major Wilhelm von Wangenheim – his son was a playmate, at the Rosenau, of the princelings – had already been called for assistance, but Wangenheim had objected to using the military against the people. Execrations of Szymborski were becoming more violent, and several clergymen, summoned to pacify the crowd, appeared in their vestments, exhorting their parishioners to go home. They were met with insults. Then the throng saw a closed chaise drawn by four horses arrive at a gate of the Ehrenburg. They rushed toward it, assuming that Szymborski was trying to escape, but a castle functionary appealed to them to make way for the Dowager Duchess. Respectfully, the people moved back, and Szymborski leaped in and was driven away at a rapid gallop. By then the Duke had succeeded in summoning the municipal fire brigade and the ceremonial company of archers to shore up the castle entrances. The crowd dispersed, and Louise was sent back to the Rosenau.

In her last surviving letter to Fräulein von Studnitz, Louise wrote, 'I stayed several [further] days in Coburg...I signed the deeds of separation...I often went for drives, being greeted with shouts and hurrahs.' On Friday, 4 September, two days after she had signed away everything, she left Coburg 'at the stroke of midnight' – to evade more loyal demonstrations. Coburgers still knew nothing about her expulsion. Louise's carriage went westward toward Brückenau, on the high road half-way to Frankfurt. She was permitted to take 'a Court Household of my own choosing, and go to a Schloss belonging to my uncle'. The arrangement with the Duke of Gotha would not work out – he would lend her nothing – but she had with her, temporarily, the von Thümmels and a few others, and settled at St Wendel, Ernestine property in the Saar.

'Parting from my children', she wrote to Augusta, 'was the worst thing of all. They have whooping-cough, and they said, "Mamma is crying because she had to go away while we are ill." The poor little mice, may God bless them!' Ernest was six and Albert five. 'Oh, misery!' she wept by letter to Augusta. 'Oh, measureless misfortune!' Louise may never have seen her sons again.

An official notice was printed in the Coburg newspaper: 'On September 2, 1824' – the day she had signed away her rights – 'Duchess Louise left for St Wendel in the Lichtenberg jurisdiction.' It would be a hermitic existence. Propriety kept Hanstein distant. To her sister-in-law Sophie Mensdorff-Pouilly she lamented, 'I live here lonely as ever; each day resembles the last, so that I have no idea of the passage of time.'

In responding to the divorce action, which took eighteen months before it became final – and was never acknowledged in the *Almanach de Gotha* – she neither admitted nor denied the charge of adultery, but on 31 March, 1826 she married Hanstein, who three months earlier had been created Count von Polzig-Baiersdorf by the sympathetic Duke Frederick of neighbouring Saxe-Hildburghausen. 'Speak sometimes with Prince Leopold about me,' she appealed in a letter to Baron Stockmar, Coburg physician and confidant to all the brothers, Ernest included. 'I would not like him to forget me completely.'

Leopold and Stockmar, she guessed correctly, could be conduits to the children. And her stepmother, who had not been without guilt in harming the Duchess's reputation, would once (31 July 1831) write to Duke Ernest of the 'sad condition' of 'poor' Louise. 'The thought that the children have quite forgotten her worries her deeply. She wishes to know if they talk about her. I told her that it was impossible for them to forget their mother, but they were not told how much she suffered, as that would make them suffer too.' A tale almost too poignant to be true, told by Max Müller, is that Louise caught a glimpse of her sons only once, when she heard that they would be at a harvest festival, and slipped into the crowd in the guise of a peasant woman.

Louise was indeed in a sad condition, and on 16 February 1831, she went with her husband to Paris to consult the eminent gynaecologist Dr Antoine Dubois. On 6 March, while watching the celebrated ballerina Maria Taglioni at the Opera, she haemorrhaged and was carried unconscious from the theatre. She was suffering from uterine cancer. On 8 August she dictated her will to her maid, Anna Metz, asking that she be buried in Germany unless her husband chose to live elsewhere. 'If death is going to part us, I want my body at least to be near him.'

In November 1822 she had experienced in Coburg what may have been a miscarriage, described to Augusta von Studnitz only as constant stomach pains and an 'inflammation of the bowels', leading to a haemorrhage. She may have experienced then the first signs of cancer. Still in Paris on 30 August 1831, she collapsed and died before her husband, in the next room, could rush in. On 13 December 1832, she was reburied in the churchyard at Pfesselbach, near St Wendel. Fourteen years later, after their father's death, Ernest and Albert, flouting her will, had Louise's body removed to the ducal tomb in the Church of St Moritz in Coburg where Duke Ernest lay, violating her spirit but satisfying Coburgers as well as the marital ideal that had eluded both their parents.*

By the time of the divorce, the duchy and the princelings had acquired new names, as the deaths of Louise's father, Augustus of Saxe-Gotha-Altenburg, and then his brother, both without male issue, had required a rearrangement of Thüringian mini-states. Duke Ernest added Gotha in exchange for non-contiguous Saalfeld, which went to the Duke of Meiningen, creating the hyphenated title by which Albert was known thereafter. Since ducal dignity was often a reflection of the size of the state, Ernest had achieved, just before the breakup of his marriage might have made the accession of territory impossible, the opportunity for the grander style his children would know, but Albert –

---

* Count Polzig had by then remarried. His second wife died in 1845 but he lived on to become Personal Adjutant to Frederick William IV of Prussia.

unlike his brother – would always prefer countrified Coburg to bourgeois Gotha.

Other than for their visits to one or another of the fond *Grossmut-
terin*, no female presences replaced the vanished Louise in the boys'
lives. Despite the circumstances of her departure and the void left in
his life, Albert never doubted his mother's affection, and he would
name one of his daughters after her. The very years in which his
formal learning began were melancholy ones. Education in real life
had already preceded the tutors and the books. Certain things, both
boys understood, were unmentionable, and certain questions were not
to be asked.

Immediately following the exile of the Duchess, the self-indulgent
Ernest left on a shooting holiday with his still-footloose brother Leopold. As late as the Duke's birthday, on 6 January 1825, an event
celebrated locally since his accession, he had not returned to Coburg.
It was a desolating time for the children, but his heir later imagined a
humane and heroic father. The second Ernest wrote of 'the earnest
mildness' of the Duke, of his 'delicacy of feeling' and his unfeigned
'attention to custom of every kind'. Albert's brother could not recall,
forty years later, ever hearing 'a harsh or ugly word from his lips', and
'never saw an action of his which would not have satisfied every idea[l]
of good breeding'. As children, he and Albert 'looked upon him – and
with right – as the ideal of perfection, and although he never spoke a
stern word to us, we felt for him not only love and adherence, but a
degree of respect which bordered on fear'.

The Duke, Ernest contended, 'seldom blamed, [or] praised unwillingly', yet 'we exerted ourselves more than if we had been blamed or
praised'. When asked – possibly by Leopold – whether the boys studied
diligently and were well behaved, the Duke allegedly answered, 'My
children cannot misbehave, and they know of themselves that they must
learn something in order to become able men, so I don't trouble myself
further about them.' Yet he did, although seldom about learning from
books. 'He never allowed a negligence in dress or carelessness of
demeanour; any transgression was punished by a look alone, but a look
that was so grave that it said more than a long lecture.' The portrait of
Duke Ernest as a genial, loving and indulgent father seems largely
fiction, not only from what emerges between the lines of purported
memory, but from the record itself.

From the start, Albert and Ernest were schooled together as if twins. Intellectually ahead although fourteen months younger, Albert was physically and emotionally less mature. As Ernest would put it, 'His physical development did not keep pace with the quick unfolding of his remarkable mental powers; he . . . had the physical leaning of the weaker toward the stronger.' He was only three – in May 1823 – when the duke assigned Christoph Florschütz of Coburg, an experienced tutor although only twenty-five, to educate both boys. Ernest, whose marriage was already under strain, was eager to remove the boys from the care of their mother and nursemaids and put them under male supervision. Summoned for advice, Count Stockmar recommended young Florschütz.

Christoph Florschütz was the tutor of Alexander and Arthur Mensdorff, the younger sons of Ernest's sister Sophie and her husband, the Count of Mensdorff-Pouilly. Relinquished to the Duke's sons, Florschütz would remain with them for fifteen years. Albert was 'so young and little', Florschütz recalled, that at the start he willingly allowed his tutor to carry him up and down the stairs of the Rosenau, which became schoolroom as well as home for the boys. Set in unspoiled forested hills, it came to be what Albert would recall as 'the paradise of our childhood'.

Well aware of the manly and female-free regimen that the Duke intended for his sons, Florschütz loyally deplored the deficiencies of their upbringing prior to his summons to rectify it. 'Endowed with brilliant qualities, handsome, clever and witty, possessed of an eloquence and a lively, fervid imagination,' he conceded, 'Duchess Louise was wanting in the essential qualifications of a mother. She made no attempt to conceal that Prince Albert was her favourite child. He was handsome and bore a strong resemblance to herself . . . The influence of this partiality upon the minds of the children might have been most injurious.'

However 'sad' the expulsion of the Duchess was, Florschütz claimed, it remained a 'satisfaction' to him that it did not 'interfere permanently with the happiness of my beloved pupils', who retained 'the cheerfulness and entire innocence of childhood. Deprived of a mother's love and care, the children necessarily depended more entirely on that shown by their tutor.'

Often in his early years with Florschütz, Albert cried, his own record of the melancholy time contradicting nostalgic memories he found appropriate to relate afterwards of a childhood Utopia. In the candour of a precocious early boyhood he confided in a journal he kept from January to May 1825, when he was only five, the ups and downs of his unsteady emotions only months after his mother had gone. (In the evenings, before prayers, he and Ernest would write in their obligatory diaries.) On 21 January he was happy. 'Dear Papa' – who had finally returned to Coburg – fetched them for breakfast and took them after lunch on a shooting party. On 23 January Albert awakened ill, with a cough. 'I was so frightened that I cried.' He left his bed only at three in the afternoon – to draw, to build a castle, to do his lessons, to paint a picture and to play with a Noah's Ark. On the 26th he cried because he could not repeat his lessons to Florschütz, 'for I had not paid attention'. When his punishment for crying was a ban from play after dinner he cried yet again, and was permitted to draw with 'black chalk' – probably charcoal. Ordered by 'the *Rath*' – Florschütz was officially a Coburg councillor – to put away lesson books he had left lying about, Albert again dissolved into tears. One detects more tutorial impatience than ingenuity in Albert's notation that February, 'I cried at my lesson today, because I could not find a verb: and the *Rath* pinched me, to show me what a verb was. And I cried about it.'

At first Albert fled from strangers, often retreating into the arms of his brother, who shared an affection not reciprocated by a cold, aloof father. His summons to share breakfasts and dinners, always at the wrong time of day for children and an intrusion into study or play times, were stiff occasions. Even before the illness and death of Louise, about which he knew little, Albert was obsessed by thoughts of sickness and death. He also rejected other women brought into the household, and Theodore Martin, who later wrote a five-volume official biography under Queen Victoria's supervision and with her recollection of Albert's memories, noted cautiously that the Prince had 'even as a child shown a great dislike to be in the charge of women'. In a memorandum to her aide, Charles Grey, in 1864 when he was writing at her assignment *The Early Years of HRH the Prince Consort* (1867), the Queen observed that her husband 'spoke with much tenderness and sorrow of his poor mother, and was deeply affected in reading, after his marriage, the accounts of her sad and painful illness'. In his childhood journals and letters, however, Albert very likely felt too vulnerable to mention his mother at all.

Florschütz was to supervise the studies of both boys in ducal residences in which their father was often absent. Sometimes he took them,
at Baron Stockmar's suggestion, for lengthy stays with a *Grossmutter*.
With the physician's art of making bad news palatable, the shrewd
Coburger never let their father suspect that his sons were being removed,
as often as possible, from the contaminated ambience of the ducal court.

The references to a kindly, caring father in the boys' journals reflect
their awareness that he had access to them through Florschütz. While
complaints about 'the *Rath*' abound in the daily entries – he was
expected to ensure discipline – there was not a hostile murmur about
the feared, authoritarian Duke. On a good day in April 1826, for
example, the boys visited *Grossmutter* Coburg at Ketschendorf, where,
with 'dear Papa', they 'drank beer, and ate bread and butter and cheese'.
Soon, however, accounts involving their father dealt with tests of
manliness more arduous than acquiring a taste for beer.

Some of the early journal entries confess to unremarkable fights with
Ernest, or report sequences of lessons or excursions for rock collecting –
a favourite teaching device for Florschütz. Albert also reported going to
see a play, Friedrich Schiller's *Wallenstein's Camp* – where 'they carried
out a monk'. Florschütz was extremely wary at what he recalled in
writing, as he remained in the service of the duchy all his active life, yet
he remembered escorting the boys to breakfasts with the Duke at so
many locations – 'the Hof Gardens, at the Festung, the Kallenberg, at
Ketschendorf, or in the Rosenau – and from Gotha in like manner at
various places – [that] the greater part of the forenoon was inevitably
wasted, to the interruption of useful studies . . . The Duke, however, was
indifferent to this, and we can only wonder that the Princes, notwithstanding, retained their love for study.'

Albert's distaste for his father, whom he had good reason to blame for
a lonely and insecure childhood, was blunted by time, as were his
impressions of his severe upbringing and his feelings toward Florschütz,
who became, as Albert grew up, a kind companion and devoted teacher.
Dinner (until the boys were much older) was invariably with their tutor
in the early afternoon. If the Duke were in residence, or either grandmother, appearances before them were required later in the afternoon,
followed by supper with Florschütz at seven, after which Albert 'was glad
to retire to bed as soon as possible. An irresistible feeling of sleepiness
would come over him in the evening, which he found difficult to

resist... and even his most cherished occupations, or the liveliest games, were at such times ineffectual to keep him awake.' Despite his often staying out, and awake, beyond ten, and his beginning each day at six, Albert remembered later only the childhood urge to sleep. So did Florschütz, recalling his earliest days with the boys. 'If prevented from going to bed', he wrote about Albert, who was kept on the regimen of his elder brother, 'he would suddenly disappear, and was generally found sleeping quietly in the recess of the window... On one occasion – the first time I was present at his supper – the young Prince suddenly fell asleep and tumbled off his chair, but he was not hurt, and continued to sleep quietly on the ground.' Albert was three.

Early in their acquaintance with books, Albert discovered one with pictures that explained to him his name. 'Our boys', the Dowager Duchess had written to her daughter Victoire in London, 'are called after the sons of the Elector Frederick the Gentle, who were stolen by Kunz von Kaufungen: Ernest and Albert.' Each prince had a handful of baptismal names, but she meant the names by which they would actually be known, and most Coburg schoolboys knew the story of the brothers from whom two lines of Saxon sovereigns would come. The Chamberlain of the Elector of Saxony, von Kaufungen, seeking revenge after a lost dispute over property rights, had kidnapped the boys, on the night of 8 July 1455, from Schloss Altenburg. Albert almost evaded abduction by hiding under his bed, and the Chamberlain's henchmen snatched another boy by mistake. Kaufungen, however, recognized the error, went back himself, and found Albert.

Because of the delay, the kidnappers had taken different routes into the forest. It was day, and the sun was hot, when Albert had begged for a drink and the Chamberlain dismounted to find water. When a charcoal-maker unexpectedly appeared with his dog, Albert cried for help. The labourer went after Kaufungen with his staff while the dog barked excitedly, attracting other charcoal-burners, and the culprit was overpowered. The kidnapper holding Ernest hid in a cave on hearing of the capture, but soon surrendered on condition that his life be spared. It was, but Kunz von Kaufungen was executed and his nemesis, the charcoal-maker, was rewarded with a farm – perhaps one confiscated from Kaufungen.

The story suggested something told by the brothers Grimm, to whose stories Ernest and Albert were introduced early in their schooling. Jacob and Wilhelm Grimm, writing their tales in Kassel, had produced the first volume of *Kinder- und Hausmärchen* in 1812, and in ten years added two more, and Ernest and Albert could recognize settings in Grimm much like their own villages of ornately decorated, steeply gabled wooden houses and small farms ploughed by plodding oxen. Happenings resembling Grimm tales could still occur in the little-populated but tradition-laden duchies. Although the Coburg princes did not know their own mother's history, that too could have been written by Jacob and Wilhelm Grimm.

The great event of Albert's early childhood was the formal accession to Coburg of Louise's home duchy late in 1826. After her father's death, in his late forties, Louise's bachelor uncle Frederick, the last male heir, became Duke of Gotha, and, shopping for a wife who might bear a successor, lighted upon Augusta von Studnitz, who refused him. After Frederick's own death, childless, in 1825, Gotha went to Louise's heirs. Her divorce was still pending. The redivision of the Thüringian *Staaten* had required some petty diplomacy, none of it leaving Coburgers content, as Gotha would become, immediately, the major political factor within the reconstituted borders. Despite the relative insignificance of Coburg, Duke Ernest was determined to receive the homage of his new subjects with all due ceremony. The younger Ernest recalled in his memoirs 'the two cold November days on which we journeyed from Coburg to Gotha, my father in front with the Prince of Leiningen,* and my brother, myself, and Florschütz in the second carriage'. To demonstrate permanency of occupation, Ernest's entire household was moving north to take possession of ducal properties, the carriages assembling below the city, at Siebleben, for a grand procession into the capital. 'My father was on horseback [now]; my brother and I drove in an open carriage, drawn by six horses, with Chamberlain [Ferdinand Hartmann von] Erffa and Councillor Florschütz, while a second empty six-horse conveyance followed behind.' Two further carriages held courtiers, and to further give the impression of substance, mounted gendarmes, post office officials, postilions, minor officeholders, militia volunteers and ducal huntsmen followed, with soldiers closing the ranks. Hardly a male of any status had been left in Coburg.

* Emich Charles of Leiningen was a cousin, the son by her first husband of Victoire, Duchess of Kent and mother of Victoria.

'My monarchical principles', Gotha-born historian Frederick Perthes, of the *Almanach* family, remarked, 'have gained new followers, for everything suddenly devolves to the new Prince; he is indeed, like King Saul, a head taller than everybody else.' Everyone, he thought, was 'enchanted' with Ernest, and even republican-minded Gothaners 'have acquired a ducally inclined heart overnight'. To make certain of that, the Duke's festivities lasted a week, with Ernest prominent at all of them, uniformed and impressive, the very model of a magistrate.

After the week of homage and the wintry ride back to the Rosenau, the tutorial regimen resumed with little sign of the duke. Florschütz in any case had relative freedom to plan a course of study for the brothers that included French and English – and eventually Latin – as well as German. As the hours of instruction expanded with their years, the princes were introduced to basic mathematics (through a visiting teacher) and rudimentary natural science – especially geology.

And as always, the instructional schedule was subject to summonses to leisurely ducal breakfasts and dinners. Further, the Duke did more than encourage outdoor play. Even his meals taken with his sons were often *im Freien*. The November ride to Gotha in an open carriage had been part of the disciplined toughening of body expected of Saxons as well as Prussians. 'Hunting, fishing, riding, driving', the younger Ernest recalled, 'were allowed us' – perhaps *required* would have been more accurate – 'from our ninth year. On the other hand, he would never tolerate the least complaint of bodily inconvenience, even of pain; we were hardened in every way. I remember that we once rode in the depth of winter over the mountain road from Coburg to Gotha, and suffered fearfully from the intense cold. On such an occasion my father expected us to show the self-command of grown men, and we had to behave in a manly way in every such uncomfortable situation.'

Through precept and chronicle, story and ceremony, Ernest and Albert acquired the essentials for adult behaviour. Their cousin Arthur Mensdorff remembered, more than thirty years later, playing at the Rosenau with other boys, some of them Coburg cousins,

and some of us were to storm the old ruined tower on the side of the castle, which the others were to defend. One of us suggested that there was a place at the back by which we could get in without being seen, and thus capture it without difficulty. Albert declared that 'this would be most unbecoming in a Saxon knight, who should always attack his enemy in front', and so we fought for the tower so honestly and vigorously that Albert, by mistake, for I was on his side, gave me a blow upon the nose, of which I still bear the mark. I need not say how sorry he was for the wound given me.

Albert also learned to temper magnanimity with pragmatism. Mensdorff once saw him 'give a beggar something by stealth'. He wondered why, until Albert explained that it was prudent to avoid being overwhelmed by seekers after money. 'When you give to the poor, you must see that nobody knows of it.' Once he was voted a stipend by Parliament, however beneath his expectations, it was clear that he had a guaranteed income, and even his father, extravagant and selfish in his ways, would attempt to cadge money from his son. A few months after his arrival in England, Albert had to write to his brother, 'If you could restrain Papa from constantly asking for money I should be grateful.' Sometimes charity did not begin at home.

Despite Albert's looking back nostalgically at his earliest years in letters to Ernest, Vicky, the Princess Royal, remembered her father saying 'that he could not bear to think of his childhood [as] he had been so unhappy and miserable, and had many a time wished himself out of this world'. Yet always the exception, the Rosenau seemed to Albert a place apart – remote from the selfish, sordid reality. On a knoll above small villages, woods of poplar and pine, and the winding Itze, and out of sight of Coburg, it was school and dormitory and refuge from court and city. There Florschütz lived with his charges, shared meals with them, and kept vigil at night as well. He had no other life than that of the princes.

Their study schedule, which on paper appeared relentless, was often dislocated by the Duke's whim, and broken for play, which Florschütz called exercise. For the less studious Ernest, the regimen had a purpose – to prepare him as heir. For Albert, purpose unfolded less easily. He was a younger son without guaranteed occupation. In the back of the Duke's mind may have been a future for Albert as husband for Victoire, his first cousin and daughter of Ferdinand, Ernest's younger brother by a year, and his wife, Antoinette, heiress of Prince Joseph of Kohary, Chancellor of Hungary, who possessed vast Hungarian estates. For Albert, purpose manifested itself more slowly. The year of change was 1831, in the

Prince Albert and Prince Ernest in Coburg, 1831. Drawing by Sebastian Eckhardt. (From the Veste, Coburg)

crowded months before his twelfth birthday. Prince Leopold, the youngest of his uncles and the one he knew best, had been searching for a role in life since his opportunity to be consort to a queen had vanished with the death of Princess Charlotte of Wales. As one of the candidates proposed by the great European powers, he had been in the running to become king of tumultuous and leaderless Greece, independent from Turkey only since the mid-1820s. Then an alternative opportunity emerged, to be first king of the Belgians, who possessed a precarious small state wrested from the lower provinces of the Netherlands, which had misruled them. First considering Greece, but realizing that the situation might turn out badly for him, Leopold had made his terms unacceptable. Belgium was more civilized, less remote, possessed of a workable constitution and at least a promise of secure borders.

British governments disliked the ambitious, avaricious Leopold, but heading off the French candidate for Belgium, the duc de Nemours, appeared as useful an aim as getting Leopold out of England for good. As soon as Leopold was settled in Brussels, he invited his ducal brother and nephews to visit. Albert had written in his journal at eleven, 'I intend to train myself to be a good and useful man.' Brussels would afford him both reason and purpose for what was still a vague, if worthy, goal. That Leopold could become a king suggested that there could again be a gilded future for younger Coburg sons.

III

The Student Prince

1832–1838

COBURG BOASTED THE *Gymnasium Casimirianum*, an academy which furnished a curricular model for Ernest and Albert, but Florschütz dispensed with its studies in Greek, substituting mathematics and the natural sciences. Latin was taught almost as a second language, but only German was spoken in their father's presence. French and English came later. Florschütz also honed their debating skills. Unenthusiastic but dutiful about 'the business of shooting', which required 'going out for the whole day', Albert preferred riding his English pony into the woods among the larch and pine trees, and searching for geological specimens to add to their cabinet at the Rosenau. Proud of their outdoors hardiness, on 30 January 1831 he wrote to his father, who claimed to be spending long periods in grander Gotha although he may have been wenching elsewhere, 'It snowed without stopping for three or four days, and the snow is very deep. The drifts are six feet high at the Festung, as we found out ourselves yesterday. We walked to Ketschendorf, and thence through the snow, by an unbeaten track through von Schauroth's garden, [back] to the Festung, and sank several times up to our middle...'

Since they were granted student privileges at the Academy, Albert added that he was offering a poem to the Academy poetry competition '[so] that I may get the prize this afternoon'. He radiated confidence in his abilities. Later in the year – in July – he wrote to his still-absent father that both boys had driven to the Gymnasium for its summer fête 'and heard a beautiful speech from Professor Troupheller. I am sure it would have pleased you.' The brothers strained to please the Duke. Albert would have been horrified, later, by the thought that his attitudes were already being formed by quiet rebellion against everything his father was, for his responses on the surface seemed lovingly dutiful. He was a month short of twelve. Although he would not learn of it then, that was the month his mother died.

Since July was the natal month of their *Grossmutter* Coburg, the boys rode to Ketschendorf to offer the Dowager Duchess Augusta 'two little poems that we made for her'. It was the last time they would see her. She died that November, but had lived long enough to visit her son Leopold, King of the Belgians, in Brussels.

In the summer of 1832 the young princes, accompanying their father and overseen by Florschütz, had the opportunity to visit their uncle and bask in the pride of his new status. Brussels, with a population of a hundred thousand, was the seat of government and focus of intellectual life in the new kingdom. It was the grandest city the princes had yet encountered, sophisticated beyond anything in the duchies. At Baron Stockmar's suggestion – he kept a house and family in Coburg but spent most of his time as confidential secretary to Leopold in Belgium – the boys were offered a return visit, to widen their world and (a private understanding between the King and the Baron) to separate them from the contamination of their father's life, about which they knew nothing.

The Duke remarried late in 1832. The event came as a surprise to Albert. In a letter to him – his father was again, ostensibly, in Gotha – on 21 September 1832, the Prince made no allusion to the imminence of a stepmother, who would have been offered, if the betrothal were known, a dutiful closing greeting. The new duchess was Duke Ernest's own niece, the Princess Mary of Württemberg, daughter of Ernest's sister Antoinette. At thirty-three she was fifteen years younger than the Duke. The boys travelled with their father to the Castle of Thalwitz in Saxony to await the arrival of their new stepmother and to accompany her to the duchies, but they saw little more of her. The marriage proved quickly to be less than a success, and the Duchess lived largely apart from their father, who was himself seldom at the Rosenau, where the boys remained. From the letters of Albert to Duchess Mary, one would not guess the emotional and physical distance, as, diplomatically, the prince always addressed his letters to 'Dear Mama', and closed them as effusively as they began.

When the boys were confirmed together on Palm Sunday 1835 in Coburg, the Duchess wrote that the weather remained too inclement for her to attend. She was not close to their affairs any more than she was, but for the title, part of the Duke's life. Still, it was a major occasion for the princes, who were nearly seventeen and sixteen. They had determined to make their ceremonial profession of faith together although Albert was the younger – and the fact of jointly lived lives would even be legislated later when the Hereditary Prince came of age at eighteen. Later it became diplomatic for Florschütz to stress, in his memoir for Victoria, the 'singularly earnest and thoughtful' preparation Albert made for his confirmation, and Charles Grey, in his early life of Albert written for the Queen, emphasized Albert's 'conviction of the great truths of Christianity'. For English publication, such professions were essential.

A worldly Coburg clergyman, Karl Gottlieb Bretschneider, fifty-six, was, to the younger Ernest, 'like a friend of the family. His extraordinary learning and . . . his important scientific services, as well as his easy, companionable ways, shielded both him and us from the reproach of taking too light a view of religious things and the historical puzzles of dogmatics; but our Christianity lay in Bretschneider's hand . . .' Although he enabled the brothers 'to look forward cheerfully to our confirmation, being neither too alarmed by the indiscoverable . . . nor too much hemmed in by the ideas of a bigoted church', the rote preparation was overseen by a very different breed of theologian, a Revd Jakoby, Court preacher at Coburg and former director of the Gymnasium at Rinteln, who had an 'encyclopaedic' knowledge of church history.

For the public in the duchies on 11 April 1835, assembled in the Giants' Hall in the castle in Coburg, the ceremony that Saturday, with each prince responding to theological questions with a scrupulous correctness coached by a local cleric, was a satisfying event, reinforcing the pieties. 'St Paul's doctrine was kept here', Albert's brother wrote, looking back on their confirmation, 'as in an impregnable fortress. People took an interest in the often unspeakably prosaic and sometimes absurd explanations of the biblical wonders.'

Ernest recalled his pleasure that 'no formula' or 'strict confession of faith' was forced on them: they responded to their examiner, instead, 'with a surprising amount of familiarity with church questions'. As for the 'natural piety' ascribed later to Albert, his brother noted wryly, 'it was probably on account of the English public, for this description suited him certainly even less than it me'. The rite required closing with the question as to whether the confirmants intended to remain true to the Evangelical Church, which meant the Augsburg Confession of 1530, endorsed by Martin Luther. 'I and my brother', Ernest declared for both, 'are determined to remain faithful to the acknowledged truth.'

On Palm Sunday the princes celebrated their success in the Cathedral of Ehrenburg, where, in 1818, with the benedictions of the same Pastor Genzler, the Duke of Kent had married Ernest's and Albert's aunt Victoire. The next day at a banquet in the Giants' Hall, *Rath* Florschütz was presented with a diamond ring to acknowledge service to the princes that was not yet over, although Ernest was nearly seventeen and Albert approaching sixteen.

Since his presence would have been inappropriate as king of a largely Catholic state, their uncle Leopold wrote from Brussels to congratulate them, adding that he had 'a fatherly affection' for the brothers and felt that their 'home education' had gone far enough – that it was time 'to prepare for the affairs of life'. The invitation to continue their studies in Belgium would be repeated – and accepted. First, however, came a Saxon version of the traditional Grand Tour offered well-born young men on the brink of adulthood. Duke Ernest was to initiate a tour of central Europe.

Their first journey was to Mecklenburg, to visit the venerable Grand Duke of Mecklenburg-Schwerin, grandfather of their late mother, on the fiftieth anniversary of his accession as *Grossherzog*. Then they went on to Berlin, where, once they were again presented, Duke Ernest left them to Florschütz for the remainder of the itinerary – Dresden, Prague (where their uncle, Count Mensdorff, now commanded the Austrian garrison), Vienna and Budapest. From Berlin, Albert wrote to his step-mother, with the tour hardly begun, 'It takes a giant's strength to bear all the fatigue we have had to undergo. Visits, parades, *déjeuners*, dinners, suppers, balls and concerts follow each other in rapid succession, and we have not been allowed to miss any of the festivities.' Travel was difficult enough by horse-and-carriage on rutted, often muddy if not dusty, post roads on which moving five miles in an hour was expeditious. It was exhausting then to march through a formal schedule in appropriate garb. Yet following the circuit came another required visit, to *Grossmutter*

Gotha for her birthday, after which Florschütz, unwilling to have their studies further interrupted, returned them to the Rosenau.

As a transition to external education they were soon transplanted to Gotha, but from a distance their studies were now overseen as well by Dr Seebode, the director of the Gymnasium at Coburg, to whom they sent completed papers for review. Albert worked on a naïvely ambitious essay on German philosophy concluding, he explained, with 'a retrospect of the shortcomings of our time, with an appeal to everyone to correct those shortcomings in his own case and thus to set a good example to others'. By March 1836 he was also working on a history of German literature which 'gets on but slowly, owing to our Gotha engagements'. (Seebode would later respond to Albert that he had omitted Friedrich Gottlieb Klopstock, an epic and lyric poet who had influenced Goethe and the *Sturm und Drang* movement as well as song cycles by Gluck, Beethoven and Schubert. Albert in turn would write from Brussels – where Leopold's educational programme for him was about to begin – 'It is painful to see the mean idea which the French and Belgians, and even the English, have of our German literature.')

The world began to open to Albert in May 1836. Earlier in the year, King Leopold sent Stockmar to furnish a confidential assessment of Albert. Ernest's place was assured. He would, when of age, be commissioned into the army of Saxony or Prussia to mature and to wait out his inheritance of the duchies. Albert's prospects as he passed sixteen were less clear, yet whatever they were depended upon his suitability as future mate for some desirable aristocratic or noble heiress. Earlier, his father and Leopold had contemplated a Kohary cousin. Although her Roman Catholicism was a technical obstacle to a professed Lutheran, Victoire Kohary was heiress to a Hungarian fortune and, even as early as 1831, when the Kohary children resided temporarily at the Rosenau in refuge from a cholera outbreak at home, she was on her way to becoming a beauty.

By 1836 other alternatives had appeared. It seemed then certain that another Victoire in the Coburg cousinhood – Princess Victoria of England – would, if she lived into her own inheritance as child of the eldest, though deceased, royal duke, become Queen. Her aunt Adelaide, William IV's queen, had suffered a succession of miscarriages and deaths in infancy. The King was seventy-one and seriously ailing. Adelaide and William loved Victoria almost as a daughter, but Victoria's ambitious mother (she was, after all, a Coburger) and her even more ambitious aide, Sir John Conroy, whom no one but the Duchess trusted, were anathema to the King, who hoped to remain alive until Victoria was of age if only to forestall a regency under the Duchess.

To Victoria, fatherless before her first birthday, Leopold was the '*dearest* of uncles', a paternal figure she relied upon, if only as occasional visitor and regular correspondent. Might Albert be up to the role of consort to a future queen? Leopold asked Stockmar to report to him. If the potential existed, their mutual uncle would attempt to educate Albert into the role and commit Victoria to the arrangement. Let in on the secret, Florschütz was enthusiastic, but conceded his charge's diffidence and unsophistication. Leopold's agent arrived to check for himself. At sixteen the young prince, Stockmar reported, was handsome and 'tolerably developed' for his age. With maturity, he would acquire a 'distinguished bearing', and was likely to be attractive to women. 'It may also be considered a fortunate circumstance that he has already a certain English look about him.'

Albert, Stockmar advised, had little understanding of contemporary European affairs but was otherwise well educated for his years. The Florschütz regimen excluded post-Napoleonic history, and the relapse into eighteenth-century authoritarianism that ignored the cautionary lessons of the French Revolution and its aftermath. Classical Greece and Rome were studied, as well as a sentimentalized national history that glossed over German fragmentation. Beyond the limitations of tutoring, Stockmar saw Albert as painfully prudent – in need of a seminar in striving from his uncle Leopold, who had vaulted from Coburg to serve a Tsar, wed (however tragically) a likely queen, and become a king. Wits and wariness were 'not enough. He must not only have great capacity but true ambition, and a great strength of will. To pursue so difficult a political career a whole life through requires more than energy and inclination.' It required, he thought, a readiness 'to sacrifice mere pleasure to real usefulness. If simply to fill one of the most influential positions in Europe doesn't satisfy him, how often will he feel tempted to regret what he has undertaken?' Further, Stockmar saw nothing in the late Duchess Louise's flightiness or in Duke Ernest's amorality to suggest that Albert might have inherited any strength of character. But nor had Albert acquired anything negative from 'such a father and such a brother, both equally unprincipled'.

What Stockmar had already perceived in the younger Ernest to worry him was left unsaid, but Leopold apparently understood. There was mettle in Albert to be cultivated – and protected. Besides, young Victoria might be coerced into an early marriage by courtiers not susceptible to Leopold's influence. His sister, the Duchess of Kent, might seek someone she and Conroy could control, while English politicians might want a much older husband who could control the future queen for them.

Leopold also worried that further immersion in Coburg and Gotha would tarnish the Prince as well as impair his chances. Stockmar agreed that 'an endless amount of good can be done, and an equal amount of evil be prevented. The Prince ought to receive the education which the consort of an English Queen requires.' He could not be sent to England, and the 'petty circumstances' of the duchies were 'impossible'. Limiting the alternatives to the universities at Berlin, Vienna and the smaller German states, the Baron ruled out Vienna as 'not at all a suitable school for a German prince'. The only subjects about which Albert would 'gain anything' in the Prussian capital were 'political administration and military organization'. In Berlin, the Prince would 'hear everything about politics but the truth', and 'a certain dissoluteness is as epidemic in Berlin as the influenza'. Stockmar would look into a more advantageous arrangement while both brothers, he suggested, should pursue preparatory studies under Leopold's 'superintendence' in a 'constitutional country' – Belgium.

On 16 April 1836, Stockmar suggested that the immediate essential was a letter from the Duchess of Kent, as Duke Ernest's sister, suggesting that he and his sons visit Kensington Palace as her guests. 'If the first favourable impression is now made, the foundation stone is laid for the future edifice. But it must be a *conditio sine qua non* that the real intention of the visit should be kept secret from the Princess as well as the Prince, that they may be perfectly at their ease with each other.'

Leopold quickly arranged for the invitation – and a further one made on his own. After the stay in England, both princes would remain in Brussels under tutelage that would lead to matriculation at a German university. To preserve the necessary ambiguities of purpose, the strategies had to involve, at every stage, Ernest as well as Albert.

Duke Ernest began the journey to England separately from his sons, possibly to revisit his former Rhenish principality – actually on the

Nahe – of Lichtenberg, just incorporated into the Prussian district of Trier. Once in the Napoleonic department of the Sarre, it had been awarded by the Congress of Vienna to Ernest for services rendered in the war, and included St Wendel, where the body of Duchess Louise lay. Named for an old Palatine castle, the territory, distant from Coburg, was useless to the Duke, who had tried for years to trade it for detached Prussian properties in Saxony. Germany was a patchwork of *Kleinstaaterei*. In 1833 he thought he had succeeded, and reported as much to Prince Clemens Metternich in Vienna, as Austria dominated the confederation, but the wily foreign minister retorted that governments had difficulty in keeping order in 'far removed territories, especially when they lie in a bad tract of land as on the left bank of the Rhine'.

What Metternich reported to Berlin is unknown, but Ernest, assuming the exchange as settled, 'made the mistake', his elder son recalled, 'of inspecting the domains in … Saxony which he thought would be his, and thus arousing [local] attention'. The arrangement lapsed, and the next year Ernest transferred his burdensome sovereignty to Prussia for a landless annuity of 80,000 thalers. Every hectare added in the Rhineland shifted the fulcrum of Prussian power in Germany further toward France, exacerbating the problems created by the Congress of Vienna in expanding Prussia substantially westward. Ernest's acres were few, but they would contribute to Prussia's future hegemony, and to concerns inherited by his sons.

Jolting overland day and night, Albert claimed to his stepmother from Rotterdam on 17 May 1836 that he and Ernest – without Florschütz – had made the carriage journey from the duchies to Mainz, on the Rhine, in twenty-two hours. At Koblenz they boarded a Rhine steamer. Having conducted business or assignations, or both, the Duke met the boat at Rüdesheim. At Cologne they changed for another steamer to Rotterdam, where they waited impatiently for a North Sea packet. 'We have to thank some Dutch speculators', Albert fumed, 'whose object it is to detain travellers as long as they can.'

On board the Rhine steamer he practised his English on several returning Londoners, to whom they remained 'incognito, which succeeded perfectly, till the chamberlain of the Princess of Orange, saluting us with a malicious smile, unmasked us'. Only then did it occur to Albert that he had been entered, rather prematurely, in a matrimonial competition for which the stakes were high. It was already news in the Netherlands that the Prince of Orange and his two eligible sons* and the young Duke William of Brunswick had been invited by an ill-tempered William IV at the same time. The King intended to foil the Coburgers, a family he detested and had not summoned. Before Ernest and Albert had even embarked for England, to the Prince's embarrassment everyone knew why they were coming, although ostensibly it was to visit 'Aunt Kent'. As far as her brother Leopold was concerned, only one of them – and he hadn't told that one as much – was fit for the office of royal consort, and he had every intention of bringing off the betrothal. Victoria knew very well why, as she approached seventeen, young men of high birth were being pressed upon her. Understanding King Leopold's wary game, Victoria responded with cautious indirection until he sent her a warning in a letter of 13 May delivered via confidential messenger. Was she aware, he asked, that she was being imposed upon by the King?

> Really and truly I never heard or saw anything like it, and I hope it will a *little rouse your spirit*; now that slavery is even abolished in the British Colonies, I do not comprehend *why your lot alone should be to be kept, a white little slavey in England,* for the pleasure of the Court, who never bought you, as I am not aware of their having gone to any expense on that head, or the King's even having *spent a sixpence for your existence.* I expect that my visits in England will also be prohibited by an Order in Council...
>
> I have not the least doubt that the King, in his passion for the Oranges, will be *excessively rude to your relations*; this, however, will not signify much; they are *your guests* and not *his*, and will therefore *not* mind it.

Victoria knew of the schemes to attach her to someone, and had already entertained her own ideas, soon discovering that they were not permitted. Knowing that the Duchess of Kent read her daughter's diaries every evening, Victoria does not mention John Elphinstone, the thirteenth Lord Elphinstone in the Scottish peerage (1807–1860), since 1826 in the Royal Horse Guards. He rose to captain by 1832 and then

---

* The elder, two-and-a-half years older than Albert, would become King of the Netherlands in 1849, reigning until 1890.

became Lord-in-Waiting to King William, affording Victoria the opportunity to make his acquaintance. The Princess, so Court gossip had it (and it was repeated by Robert Browning), was 'bent on marrying nobody but Lord Elphinstone'. Suddenly, just before the parade of potential suitors began arriving in England, Lord Elphinstone was posted, at twenty-nine, to India, to become governor of Madras, a remarkable appointment for a young man.

If his removal was to distance him from contention, his exile to India hardly improved Victoria's estimate of her supplicants. Early among them were the two sons of Duke Ferdinand of Saxe-Coburg-Kohary. The ineligible one, also a Ferdinand, and twenty, was on his way to Lisbon to marry Queen Maria da Gloria, sixteen, whom he had never met. The other, Prince Augustus, only eighteen, Victoria noted in her diary on 17 March, 'is a dear good young man, and is very handsome', but 'extremely quiet and silent'. What remained unspoken was the Kohary religious disability. Uncle Ferdinand had married wealth and property, but a Roman Catholic ceremony had made his opportunities possible. The throne of Portugal also required a Roman marriage. Augustus, his father assumed, would accept whatever benedictions were required for proximity to a throne. The Coburg clan's religion seemed to be simple pragmatism.

The next day Victoria described – and dismissed – Augustus as 'a dear boy . . . so extremely good, kind and gentle'. When the brothers left, she was sorry only to see the balls and other entertainments arranged for her cease. She was starved of companionship from her own generation, but her professions of affection for the Kohary brothers suggested little more. Uncle Leopold in any case had another brace of Coburg nephews ready.

King William's instructions to Palmerston were to 'turn back' Ernest and Albert, and the Foreign Secretary did send Leopold a message that it would be 'highly desirable' that the princes put off their visit for another year. But the Coburgers were not travelling through Belgium, and Leopold would not see them until the return leg of their journey. Given the subtleties of Palmerston's machinations, it is at least possible that the delay in Rotterdam may have been occasioned by some discreet bribes which made a clear field possible for the Dutch aspirants.

On 13 May 1836, William gave a ball in honour of the Princes of Orange, William and Alexander. Since her cousin Prince George of Cambridge, Victoria's own age and heir to Augustus Frederick,

George III's seventh son, was also present, three aspirants for espousal were on view. ('She must marry somebody', Palmerston would urge the King. 'Why not the Prince of Cambridge? He has been educated here and we know him.') Leopold was relieved when Victoria wrote on 17 May, 'The [Netherlander] boys are very plain and have a mixture of Kalmuck' – Mongol – 'and Dutch in their faces, moreover they look heavy, dull and frightened and are not at all prepossessing. So much for the *Oranges*, dear Uncle.'

The confident dismissal of the Dutch princes belied her concern that a husband might be imposed upon her. The unspoken pressure she sensed, Victoria recalled nine years later, was so intense that she felt 'extremely crushed and kept under, and hardly dared say a word'.

For two frightening days in turbulent waters, the Dutch paddle-wheeler ploughed across from Rotterdam. His stomach churning with the swells, Albert declared 'a disgust of the sea'. Unsteady on English soil, the Coburgers arrived on the eighteenth to a surfeit of levées, balls and other after-dark entertainments originally arranged for the disappointed Netherlanders, who had left earlier than planned, and into whose schedule Ernest and Albert were introduced. (Once her cousins arrived, the Dutch aspirants were of increasingly diminished interest to Victoria.) Albert struggled at first to stay awake, then to keep down the heavy English meals always served too late.

Recording their first meeting, at a quarter to two in the afternoon, Victoria wrote, 'Ernest is as tall as Ferdinand and Augustus; he has dark hair, and fine dark eyes and eyebrows, but the nose and mouth are not good; he has a most kind, honest and intelligent expression in his countenance, and has a very good figure.' Clearly she was assessing the genetic as well as the companionable qualities in her possible suitors. 'Albert, who is just as tall as Ernest but stouter,' she noted, 'is extremely handsome; his hair is about the same colour as mine; his eyes are large and blue, and he has a beautiful nose and a very sweet mouth with fine teeth; but the charm of his countenance is his expression, which is most delightful.' He also seemed 'full of goodness and sweetness, and very clever and intelligent'.

Further, the brothers spoke English competently, and she could converse as easily with them as she could with her sophisticated uncle Ernest. To her delight, he brought as a gift 'a most delightful Lory' – a brightly plumaged parrot – 'which is so tame that it remains on your hand, and you may put your finger into its beak, or do anything with it, without its ever attempting to bite'. Had the duke brought a symbol of what her future husband should be like?

A formal dinner at St James's Palace, following a royal levée and preceding a concert that ran until two in the morning, left Albert barely able to remain on his feet. Before long, he was running what he described in a letter to his stepmother as a 'bilious fever'. Summing up his dilemmas he explained unhappily, 'The climate of this country, the different way of living, and the late hours, do not agree with me.'

The afternoon following, he and Ernest had to be upright for a drawing-room reception with a receiving line of nearly four thousand guests, which itself was only a prelude to another long night. On 23 May, at a grand dinner at Kensington Palace hosted by the Duchess of Kent, Albert, having reached the end of his endurance, excused himself and went to bed. The next day, Victoria's seventeenth birthday, was occasion for a state ball hosted by the King at St James's Palace. Albert could not miss it without damaging his prospects, for he understood that he was only one of many to be set before the future queen. 'Poor, dear Albert', Victoria sympathized in her diary '...looked very pale and felt very poorly.' After two quadrilles he 'turned pale as ashes; and we all feared he might faint; he therefore went home' [to Kensington Palace].

Again Albert recovered. 'We took them to the Opera on Friday,' Victoria wrote to Leopold, 'to see the *Puritani* [by Vincenzo Bellini], and as they are excessively fond of music, like me, they were in perfect ecstasies...' Both brothers also played the piano, composed, and drew 'very well' ('especially Albert'). Exhaustion then left Albert with what Victoria described in her journal as 'a smart bilious attack', but after a day in bed, and 'by dint of starvation, he is again restored to society, but looks pale and delicate'.

A few days of lessened activity brought the Prince around. He played piano duets with Victoria and managed to stay up 'until 10 minutes past 10'. He told Victoria about his plans to be prepared at Brussels, under their uncle's guidance, for university studies, and to travel with Ernest to Italy to see more of the world. He had no idea that Victoria already knew – from Leopold – more than he did of his future.

Despite King William's objections, she had been well prepared, Leopold having written on 1 May to her one-time nurse and tutor, and now confidante, Louise Lehzen, 'I talk to you at length and through you speak to Victoria.' Though the Princess and her cousin had never before met, Leopold was now certain that the small and rather plain future queen would see her best possible destiny in Albert. However, any 'immediate alliance' was impossible as Victoria was not yet in control of her future. At her eighteenth birthday, he explained, 'the possibility of a Regency vanishes like an evil cloud'. And no potential consort of 'riper years' existed 'to whom we could entrust the dear child without incurring the gravest risk'.

On the last day of May, Albert felt up to an evening of dancing at Kensington Palace, but quickly pleaded illness. Victoria left with him until he was able to return, and she recalled, half a year later, in a letter to Leopold, 'The last ball *I* was at was our own, and I concluded that very ball at half-past three in the morning with a country dance, Albert being my partner.' At the time she noted that it was 'broad daylight when we left the room', and, as she confided to her uncle early the next year, 'I *often* think of that night'.

When only a few more days remained before the princes were to leave, Victoria called their father in for a private meeting at which she gave him a letter to Leopold, whom they would visit *en route* home.

By the time of the princes' departure, even King William had warmed to Albert, yet the King was in such failing health that he was given only a small chance of surviving until Victoria's eighteenth birthday. Conroy and the Duchess still loomed – Leopold's 'evil cloud'. Victoria hoped for the best in a letter to Leopold which she framed carefully to evade any direct commitment:

I must thank you, my beloved Uncle, for the prospect of *great* happiness you have contributed to give me, in the person of dear Albert. Allow me, then, my dearest Uncle, to tell you how delighted I am with him, and how much I like him in every way. He possesses every quality that could be desired to render me perfectly happy. He is so sensible, so kind, and so good, and so amiable too. He has, besides, the most pleasing and delightful exterior and appearance you can possibly see.

I have only now to beg you, my dearest Uncle, to take care of the health of one, now *so dear* to me, and to take him under *your special* protection. I hope and trust that all will go on prosperously and well, on this subject of so much importance to me.

On 10 June, Victoria breakfasted with the princes for the last time before they departed by carriage to Dover. She could not restrain her tears. 'I feel this separation . . . deeply', she told her diary, but, after the pressure of earlier princely attentions – they had begun when she was barely fourteen – the tension had eased. Her nerves had not been as 'strong' as they now were. 'I can bear more now.'

Duke Ernest could not put off his need for less genteel entertainment, delaying the family visit to Brussels and Leopold until he could sample the pleasures of Paris. Prince Ernest was already under his tutelage, and as early as the post-confirmation Grand Tour, to Albert's horror and shame, had sampled the underside of Berlin with his father. Kept awake at the Hôtel des Princes in the rue Richelieu by the noise that seemed never to leave Parisian streets, and worn by illness and exhaustion after his introduction to English court life, Albert indulged, when he could, in sleep.

A month later, dandy and failed merchant Thomas Raikes, distant from his creditors in Paris, was told by the Dutch Minister to France, General Fagel, that the chances of the princes of Orange were nil – 'fine young men, but stiff and formal'. The Coburg brothers, Fagel and Raikes recognized, had the advantages of an aunt at Kensington Palace, yet that might not produce results at Buckingham Palace. 'The son of the Duke of Cambridge would be the most popular match . . . in the eyes of the English people.'

The life of the court of Louis-Philippe meant nothing to Albert, although his father and brother were delighted by invitations to meet the King and the younger generation of the House of Orléans. The Queen of the Belgians, Marie-Louise, was a daughter of the French sovereign, and the Coburgers found that their uncle Leopold was also a guest at the Tuileries. Later, in Belgium, Ernest learned that he had been looked over in Paris as a possible husband for Louis-Philippe's daughter Clementina, a union that would have required his conversion to Rome. Seven years later the Princess would marry his Kohary cousin Augustus. To his stepmother, Albert reported that they had been received by the royal family 'with the greatest kindness and civility', but he was more interested in the places in which history had been made – Versailles, the Trianon, Meudon, Neuilly. He was also in a quiet panic arising from his naïvety when in England. He had little idea then how seriously he was being considered as Victoria's consort, although he was not yet seventeen. In Paris, his father explained that the Duchess of Kent accepted the family strategy that 'some time in the future' the sixteen-year-old Albert would marry the future queen. Victoria had been privately warned that her uncle William was trying to treat her like a white slave; Albert now realized that his Coburg aunts and uncles were not seeking his permission to offer *him* into a possibly splendid foreign slavery.

Brussels emerged as an oasis for Albert. His father left almost immediately, although Leopold had not yet returned to his capital from Paris. The King, however, had arranged everything. 'Nothing disturbed us', Ernest recalled; 'everything seemed formed to help us to gain the end in view' – which was preparation for an appropriate German university. They occupied a house with garden that was, Albert wrote to his stepmother with relief, 'perfectly insulated from the noise of the streets' although just off the bustling Boulevard de l'Observation. There they were overseen by the ubiquitous Florschütz and, for logistical matters, Baron von Wiechmann, a colonel who had served under Wellington at Waterloo in the German English Legion.

No tutor, however eminent, was likely to turn down a royal request to furnish expertise. Among the visitors to offer instruction was the director of the Royal Observatory, the mathematician and astronomer Laubert Adolphe Jacques Quételet, who became a godlike figure to Albert. Quételet was a founder of the science of statistics – what Albert would call 'governing laws . . . which can only be approached by the accumulation and reduction of statistical facts'. The Prince's orderly mind responded gratefully to what Quételet offered, and as Ernest would put it, the Belgian's influence upon Albert 'was one which formed his whole manner of viewing the world. During his entire lifetime he preserved the statistically mechanical grasp of social and political questions.' Quételet himself later quipped that Albert never thought enough of his own talents, while the King of the Belgians never forgot his.

As tutors in economics and politics, Leopold assigned Charles and Henri de Broukere, Members of Parliament and men of ability. Charles de Broukere had already been Minister of the Interior and Minister for

War, and was a future prime minister. For instruction in French and English literature, Leopold chose Dr Pierre Bergeron, Professor of Rhetoric at the University of Brussels, and Dr Henry Drury, a minor poet once a friend of Lord Byron. Sir Henry Lytton Bulwer, Secretary of the English legation, then at the beginning of a distinguished diplomatic career, was brought in for history and foreign affairs. Leading Belgian painters invited the princes to their studios for instruction, and Leopold's Cabinet Secretary visited to explain governmental administration.

Since the Dutch had refused to sign the Treaty of London under which the Belgian provinces were detached as a separate nation, both countries remained on a war footing. With Leopold's army actively mobilized, in early August the King took Ernest and Albert to the plain of Beverlo where his troops were encamped overlooking the southern finger of Holland at Maastricht, and both young men were assigned as staff officers to generals for manœuvres. The experience would lead, later, to Albert's proposal for a permanent English site for military exercises. The outcome would be Aldershot.

In mid-October, as another break from studies, Colonel von Wiechmann took the young men to Waterloo, where, Albert wrote to his father, they 'went on foot all over the field of battle'. Other explorations opened more of the real world. Politicians and thinkers of every persuasion, even exiled revolutionaries from other countries, were permitted entry at the cul-de-sac off the Boulevard de l'Observation. In turn Ernest and Albert even visited the house in the Brussels suburbs where Italian fugitives involved in the secret society of the *Carbonari* awaited their call to action. In Coburg the Duke worried about what sympathies his sons would ingest in the heady atmosphere of Brussels, and invited – commanded – them home for an extended Christmas stay. Unhappily, Albert brought the letter to his uncle, who recommended a 'reasoned and calm' explanation why returning would be unwise.

'We should be so glad to accept your invitation', Albert responded on November 29, 1836, '... But if we are to profit from our stay here, I am afraid we must deny ourselves that pleasure. Such an expedition would require five or six weeks, and our course of study would be quite disturbed by such an interruption. We told dear uncle the purport of your letter, and he said he would write to you on the subject.'

The King duly wrote, and the brothers remained until matriculation time neared at a university chosen for them. Consulting Stockmar further, Leopold had ruled out Munich ('formal and priggish'), Göttingen, Jena (although founded by the early Ernestines), and Heidelberg, settling upon the newer University of Bonn, already recognized for the quality of its professoriate. To alleviate Duke Ernest's anxieties that university life would reduce his sons to the level of ordinary Germans, they were to be enrolled as noblemen rather than as normal students. Leopold even offered to pay half the fees.

Although, as the younger Ernest explained, 'the Head of no reigning house would be too willing to see his sons allowed to follow a public course of study at a university', German princelings were beginning to sample higher learning, and the Duke pronounced himself satisfied. From London, Victoria wrote to her uncle Leopold that she missed 'both young gentlemen'.

In April 1837 Ernest and Albert left Brussels for Berlin, where they were to meet their father, then return with him to the duchies before leaving for Bonn, on the Rhine fifty miles south of Cologne. With the new term to begin on 3 May, thoughts of Victoria were put aside.

The number of princelings, overt and covert, out to win Victoria during what would prove to be the last year of William IV's reign would have been far higher had the King and the Duchess of Kent not discouraged some of them and forbidden others. Warding them off required every means from diplomacy to lies. On the very day that Albert was beginning studies at Bonn, the English Minister in Berlin, Lord William Russell, appealed to the Duchess of Kent, 'Would it be agreeable to your Royal Highness that Prince Adalbert of Prussia, the son of Prince William, should place himself on the list of those who pretend to the hand of HRH the Princess Victoria?'

Five days later, on 8 May 1837, the Duchess parried the plea by recommending that Prince Adalbert, who was twenty-six, apply to William IV: 'But if I know my duty to the King, I also know my maternal ones, and I will candidly tell your Lordship that I am of opinion that the Princess should not marry till she is much older.' When Russell explained the Duchess's objections, the King of Prussia withdrew his request for a visit, and Russell apologized to Kensington Palace, commenting it was 'only proposed to admit Prince Adalbert to the list of suitors for the hand of Princess Victoria, to which he was to

*The Electoral Palace (*Residenz*) was given to the University of Bonn for its new site. Albert knew it in this form.*

win his claim by his character and personal attractions'. The Prussian prince hoped only for a place on a rumoured but non-existent roll, yet Victoria's mother admitted neither Adalbert nor the list. Nor, in future years, would the suits of the duc de Nemours, Louis-Philippe's second son, or Prince Christian of Schleswig-Holstein, the future Christian IX of Denmark, or other serene or royal highnesses, be entertained.

Bonn had boasted a university as early as 1786. It had been suppressed by Napoleon, remaining, however, the seat of many learned societies. In 1818, awarded the buildings which had belonged to the Electors of Cologne, the university reorganized, and under the rectorship of Wilhelm Wutzer was, for Germany, a liberal institution with eighty professors and seven hundred students.* At the head of the *Sommerhalbjahr* matriculation register, in rigid aristocratic tradition, was Friedrich Wilhelm, the young Grand Duke of Mecklenburg-Strelitz, followed by August Ernst, Hereditary Prince of Saxe-Coburg-Gotha, and Albrecht Franz, identified as a duke of Saxe-Coburg-Gotha, all listed as studying jurisprudence. Lesser students pursued medicine, agriculture, theology (Catholic or Evan-

*At the same time Göttingen also averaged seven hundred students, while Heidelberg had five hundred.

gelical), philosophy, classics, natural science. Almost all were from the German states, but one, Gustav Ferreira Bandeira, listed his home as 'Bahia in Brasilien'.

In Bonn, Florschütz remained in attendance, assisted by the brothers' valet, Cart, while Baron von Wiechmann continued in charge of non-academic matters. (A French-speaking Swiss also fluent in German, Isaac François Daniel Cart had been with the boys since Ernest was eight and Albert seven.) The entourage required for Ernest and Albert ruled out common undergraduate digs. Other minor nobility resided apart as a matter of course, and in the case of the Coburgers there was the matter – left unspoken but hardly unknown – of what was fitting for the rumoured consort of the Queen of England. Despite their rented, semi-detached house, with servants and a major-domo, the princes tried valiantly to mix with other university students. That they managed to blend in, although Bonn did not subscribe to the forced equality of academic dress, made Albert's experience, even when interrupted, an idyll.

During their first *Sommerhalbjahr*, the brothers attended lectures by Moritz Arndt von Bethmann-Hollweg on Roman and on Prussian civil law, Clemens Perthes on German law, Johann Wilhelm Loebell on ancient history, Peter Kaufmann on finance, and Edward d'Alton on art history. 'With all our conviviality,' Ernest recalled, 'we were all nevertheless very diligent and possessed a kind of reading rage, which caused us to devour a huge quantity of books.' At lectures they filled their 'beloved notebooks' – which they then reviewed 'with the greatest conscientiousness'. Some professors held '*conversaziones*, in which there was a great deal of ardent discussion'.

Six weeks into the term came the news from England that William IV had died and Victoria was queen. She was one month past eighteen. Albert wrote to his 'dearest cousin' on 26 June to offer his 'sincerest felicitations on that great change which had taken place in your life'. It was a difficult letter to compose. Now that she was 'Queen of the mightiest land of Europe', he went on, 'the happiness of millions' lay in her hands, and he trusted that Heaven would assist her in 'that high but difficult task'. He hoped for a long and happy – and glorious – reign, in which she would achieve the 'thankfulness and love' of her subjects. He wished neither to be indiscreet nor to 'abuse' her time, but, he closed, 'May I pray you to think likewise sometimes of your cousins in Bonn, and to continue to them that kindness you favoured them with till now.' And he signed it as 'your Majesty's most obedient and faithful servant, Albert'.

Further bulletins came from his aunt in London and his uncle in Brussels, keeping him informed, and he wrote to his father in Coburg, 'Cousin Victoria is said to have shown astonishing self-possession. She undertakes a heavy responsibility, especially at the present moment, when parties are so excited, and all rest their hopes on her.' Leopold continued to furnish news, which seemed to picture England in the new reign as 'a network of cabals and intrigues', with political parties arrayed against each other 'in the most inexplicable manner'. Knowing almost nothing of the English party system, and of the mysteries of the English unwritten constitution, for which there was no parallel in Germany, the young prince was mystified.

With Victoria now queen, rumours circulated that Albert would soon be marrying her. Deflating them, Victoria announced, both to deflect matchmakers and to furnish herself with time to enjoy her elevated new status without domestic hindrance, that she had no present interest in matrimony. That put no quietus on the rumours in Britain and abroad. One circulating across the Atlantic was that the widower President of the United States, Martin Van Buren, who was the same age as Viscount Melbourne, 'thinks seriously of making an offer' to the young queen. Commenting on the report in the Salem, Massachusetts *Register*, the Boston *Daily Advertiser* observed that Victoria was 'at liberty to marry whom she chooses, *except a Papist*'. Since Van Buren passed that test although 'everything by turns and nothing long', the *Daily Advertiser* saw 'no reason why he should not *offer*, or why he may not stand as good a chance as the namby-pamby princes and kinglings of Europe'.

Albert's situation in Bonn was compromised by the reports and the gossip, and Leopold advised him to 'disappear' into unpublicized but useful travel. Albert concurred that the reasons were 'imperative and conclusive'. Leaving Bonn at the close of term on 28 August 1837, Ernest, Albert and Florschütz journeyed south into Switzerland, Austria and Italy, going as far as Venice and returning to Coburg through Munich. Whatever their condition, many roads required payment of tolls. In pre-railway days – and there was little trackage then, only between a few industrial sites – travel without one's own conveyance and horses was by stage from inn to inn. It would be four years before the first international line for steam locomotives was operating, from Strasbourg to Basel. In Germany the first line had already opened in December 1835, between Nuremberg and Fürth.

In days of large families and dynastic marriages, hardly a place in Europe was without a Coburg relative, and in the grand Elfenau *Gut* (Estate) overlooking the Aar in the suburbs of Bern, Ernest and Albert found their aunt Julia, known in Russia still as Grand Duchess Anna Feodorovna although she had been divorced fourteen years earlier from the dissolute second son of Tsar Paul, Grand Duke Constantine, who had died in a cholera epidemic in St Petersburg in 1831. (Contrasting his huge country with Julia's native duchy, Constantine had once scoffed that her brother 'reigns over six peasants and two village surgeons'.) Leaving their aunt on 9 September, Ernest and Albert set out on foot. As much as was possible – and it was often necessary in Alpine terrain – they walked. Beginning in incessant rain along the Rhine, they trudged into the Swiss cantons as far as Lucerne, took a boat across the lake, and saw the next sunrise from a snow-covered mountain-top, descending then on foot to the glacier of the Rhone. Ponies accompanied the party through the Alps, but wherever possible Albert refused them, intending to keep to his purpose of a walking tour. They crossed through the Simplon Pass into Italy, then through the lakes region into Milan, and, by 12 October, across the top of the boot to Venice. 'Milan, and still more, heavenly Venice', Albert wrote to his father, 'contain treasures of art that astonish me'.

Once home, Albert prepared a small album of scenes he had drawn on the journey, a dried '*Rose des Alpes*', and a scrap of Voltaire's hand-writing he had obtained from an old servant of the philosopher at Verney, and posted the souvenir to Victoria. Years later she attested it was 'one of her greatest treasures', but her acknowledgement at the time only expressed envy that he could travel to such places while she – as Victoria innocently assumed – could no longer, as monarch, go abroad. 'I fear now I shall never do so.'

The brothers returned to Bonn in early November to resume studies while Albert, as he wrote to his father, began to contemplate 'the arrangement of my mode of life'. He was only nineteen, and whatever arrangement had been contemplated for him with Victoria now seemed uncertain at best. 'The last term really ended before we had time to collect our thoughts about it', he explained in a letter to Duke Ernest on 12 November. 'We have already plunged into the midst of the new one.'

In the *Winterhalbjahr* they were 'overwhelmed with lectures, papers, exercises...' As before, they studied Roman law, German law, political science, the principles of finance and, with d'Alton, the art of ancient Greece. They also attended lectures on literary history by A. W. von Schlegel, and on anthropology as well as philosophy by Immanuel Hermann von Fichte. Schlegel was privately derided by students for his vanity and his pandering to nobility. When Schlegel learned, Ernest wrote, that the Hereditary Prince of Lippe-Bückeburg would be present, he had a beadle set apart a chair for the Prince, and, as Friedrich Wilhelm of Mecklenburg arrived, 'the Professor opened his address by solemnly welcoming the Grand Duke, and then turned to the rest of the audience', and 'an unexampled uproar ensued, so that Schlegel had trouble in making himself heard'.

Still, Ernest conceded, 'old Schlegel' was 'brighter than all the star professors', and Bonn had a distinguished faculty. In Schlegel's own house 'we shared in the...pleasure of hearing him read Shakespeare. His clever and brilliant delivery made one forget his incredibly senile manner and problematical character. His delineation in his "History of Literature" of modern German poetry since Schiller, in which he enlarged particularly on the romantic style, forms one of the most unfading impressions which I ever received. These lectures were public, and immensely sought after. My brother and I attended them like other students, and were looked upon as such by everyone.' But not by Schlegel, who told the equally elderly William Wordsworth in Bomal, a Belgian town east of Brussels, of Albert's 'promising habits and dispositions, wh[ich] he was prompted to do by the then already talked of probability that the Prince would become the husband of our young Queen'.

More than lectures occupied the princes. Museums, a riding school, botanical gardens, and a well-stocked library of 150,000 volumes were attached to the university. Bonn offered fencing, theatricals, singing and drinking clubs, and the shops that enabled Albert to begin an art collection. In walks down the Rhine to nearby towns, he bought a Dürer drawing and a portrait by Van Dyck, and sketched landscapes and riverscapes. When lectures began to bore, he drew heads of teachers and students. He composed music for the university organ and bought a cheap piano that seemed to require the continuous services of a tuner. It was a vain attempt by Albert to put at bay, by activity, speculation about a future over which he had little control.

On 17 November Ernest and Albert were asked – in effect, commanded – to spend Christmas week, when there would be no lectures, with King Leopold in Brussels. 'We shall then have an opportunity', Albert explained to his grandmother in Gotha, 'of learning more distinctly what Uncle thinks of the coming separation, next spring, of our hitherto united lives, and also of giving him . . . our own views of it'. (The plans set out for them had been to leave the university after the *Sommerhalbjahr* of 1838, with Ernest becoming an apprentice officer in the Saxon army at Dresden.) But Albert injured a knee just before Christmas when a horse from the riding school refused to take a jump and crashed into a wall. He broke no bones but would retain a deep scar. The holiday in Brussels was cancelled, and Albert limped about Bonn into the new year.

The delay in consulting with Leopold meant a trip to the Belgian summer palace at Laeken for Easter. By then, Stockmar had visited Victoria and found her rejecting all thoughts of marriage, even startling the Baron with the remark that she was unsure whether Albert was experienced enough for the role they had contemplated for him. For her coronation scheduled for June, an elaborate event with thousands of guests, she had invited Duke Ernest but not his sons – possibly a signal to Albert. At Laeken, the King explained that he would consult Victoria confidentially, but continued to find it awkward to be in England and would absent himself from the coronation festivities. He advised Albert to keep a low profile and to use his time in waiting for study and travel. Explaining the situation to Stockmar, Leopold wrote, 'He looks at the question from a most elevated and honourable point of view; he considers that troubles are inseparable from all human positions and that, therefore, if one must be subjected to plagues and annoyances, it had better be for some great and worthy object rather than for trivial and paltry ends.'

Leopold followed up his understanding with Albert with a letter to Victoria so blunt and businesslike as to suggest that it must have been hand-carried by Stockmar who, she had written to her uncle, 'knows best my feelings and wishes on that subject'. Both uncle and niece had been discussing Albert as a commodity for which the Queen was not ready to accept delivery. She referred to 'the finishing of Albert's education' as equivalent to the finishing of a painting in oils or a piece of cabinetry – and as if he were not far better educated than she. Victoria was Queen: formal learning seemed now superfluous.

'Concerning the education of our friend Albert', Leopold wrote to Victoria on 13 April 1838, 'it has been the best plan you could have fixed upon, to name Stockmar your *commissary-general*; it will give *unité d'action et de l'ensemble*, which otherwise we should not have had.' Stockmar, he agreed, would be their joint intelligence agent, reviewing the finishing of Albert, which would include, at the Baron's recommendation, further guided travel, 'as nothing enlarges the mind so much'. (Victoria herself had journeyed only to a few country houses of the aristocracy in the Home Counties, and as a child had visited the seaside at Ramsgate.) 'On one thing you can rely', their uncle promised, 'that it is my *great anxiety* to see Albert *a very good and distinguished young man*, and *no pains will be thought too much* on my part if this end can be attained...'

While the prince was being packaged, with no guarantee that something might intervene to preclude acceptance of the finished product, Albert knew that Victoria continued to receive aspirants for her hand, including elevated and dashing ones like the Grand Duke Alexander of Russia, a year older than Victoria and a future Tsar. As Mary I had discovered with Philip of Spain, becoming the bride of a reigning monarch of a great nation – the Grand Duke would become Alexander II – was a practical impossibility. The hospitality which the Queen continued to offer to suitors suggested that Victoria was resisting Coburger matchmaking. 'My intentions are still the same', she would assure her uncle, Duke Ernest, when he came for the coronation, 'but that could not happen before two or three years'. Albert could only do the possible, which was to begin the new *Sommerhalbjahr* and to occupy himself in student pursuits. He practised with the broadsword, won a fencing match, and emptied cartridge cases in target-shooting.

As the Queen readied herself for her coronation, Albert walked his black greyhound, Eos, along the banks of the Rhine, and had long, impassioned talks with one of the serene highnesses who had been attending the same lectures, Paul Wilhelm, Prinz von Löwenstein-

Werthheim-Freudenberg, with whom he had been close since the winter term. Without Ernest, who had other preoccupations, they hiked into the nearby Siebengebirge, and along the valley of the Aar to the Walportzheimer vineyards. Perhaps because he was a crucial year younger as a child when his mother was banished, perhaps because he was always under strain to keep up physically and intellectually with his more mature brother, Albert was a very different young man as he neared seventeen than was Ernest at eighteen. Brought up like twin brothers, they might have developed, but for such formative contrasts, in the same ways.

Professions of intimacy with his brother would remain vocal and zealous, and Albert remained excessively loyal all his life, but Ernest was busy demonstrating his own maturity, which went well beyond Albert's in seductions of servant girls and other evidences of manliness that recalled his father's lifestyle. Leopold's careful housing arrangements failed to deter Ernest. The brothers were lodged in a house rented from Dr Bischof, a professor of medicine at Bonn. On a slope overlooking the Rhine, it was set in a small courtyard enclosed by an iron railing. Until their household, from tutor and *Stallmeister* to domestics, was complete, meals were sent in from the Star Hotel, Bonn's best establishment. Still, Albert and Ernest attempted to blend in as much as did the other young noblemen whose lives were set apart by rank. Somewhat stiffly, Albert would recall to Prince William later in the year, when Löwenstein remained at Bonn but his Coburger crony had gone, 'I believe that the pleasant days which we spent together, partly in useful occupations, partly in cheerful communion, will ever appear to me as the happiest of my life ... How pleasant were our winter concerts – our theatrical attempts – our walks to the Venusberg – the swimming-school – the fencing-ground!'

The useful occupations were the lectures on Roman law, German civil law, public administration, modern history, property law, finance, policy studies, fine arts theory and the archaeology – to be revised by Schliemann – of Homeric Greece. Curiously, given Albert's great interest in music, he attended no lectures on music theory, although studies in music were available. He may not have had time.

Few anecdotes exist about Albert at Bonn. He recognized the necessity for a low profile. Even if apocryphal, one suggests his personality. A student with whom he had become friendly came from Andernach, on the Rhine below Bonn. When his mother, a well-to-do widow, remarried, and the new husband drastically curtailed the free-spending ways of his stepson, three undergraduates on a river ramble who recognized the 'old gentleman' embarrassed him with a public tirade about his miserliness. Angered, the man from Andernach offered money to some passing peasants if they would pursue the students, give them a thrashing, and throw them into the river. Overpowering the boys, the farmhands performed their office and boasted about who had paid them to do it.

Drenched and soiled, the undergraduates returned to the campus and recruited volunteers to avenge them. As they gathered on the riverbank, still in their academic gowns, to plot stern punishment at least equal to the offence – retaliation which they failed to realize might prompt their expulsion – Albert turned up. Moving to the head of the mob, he exhorted them to behave with moderation. 'The circumstances connected with this affair', he reportedly said, 'require some particular mark of our determination to defend and avenge each and every one who had been abused; but I hope that in chastising the offenders no one will overstep the bounds of prudence, or use any uncalled-for violence. Remember, we belong to Bonn University, and any misdeeds of ours will throw odium upon one of the finest institutions in the kingdom. Convince the aggressors that you will not let them escape with impunity, but do so in a manner that will be equally creditable to yourselves as it will be efficient in its object.'

The students cheered, then went off to hunt down the culprits, whom they 'paraded through Andernach amid deafening shouts'.

At his Easter tête-à-tête with Leopold, Albert had been spared none of the realities of his position, which remained awkward both publicly and privately. At best, no rival had materialized. Enjoying power, status and the freedom both afforded, Victoria appeared to have no intention of marrying, and had even begun to complain coldly that uncle Leopold was attempting to rule her 'roost'. The Prince's situation as he was completing what was to be his final term in Bonn was precarious. His inherited income was small. Even his potential as Protestant spouse in a lesser court was hostage to his marital limbo in England. He had agreed that Leopold could confide to Victoria after the coronation that he – Albert – was willing to submit to reasonable delay 'if I have only some assurance to go upon'. If, after waiting for three years, 'I should find that the Queen no longer desired the marriage, it would place me in a very ridiculous position, and would, to a certain extent, ruin all the prospects of my future life'.

As the *Sommerhalbjahr* came to a close, Albert returned to Coburg without even a tourist's look at the coronation. His student years were over, and perhaps his useful life. He had no status and no role. In the Queen's letters to his family he went unmentioned. His few cautious letters to her went unanswered. To his grandmother in Gotha he would confess, in boredom, a few months later, 'when a man is sunk in idleness, it is difficult to get out of it'. He was crammed with facts, but having gone to the University of Bonn with the half-promise of Windsor Castle to follow, his life as a student had to be more guarded and more remote from scandal than the ordinary playboy prince. Not that it was in his nature to follow the profligate examples of his father and, now, brother. As a later observer would put it, 'His virtue was, indeed, appalling; not a single vice redeemed it.'

IV

Courting a Husband

1838–1839

FOLLOWING THE CORONATION to which he was not invited and the close of the final *Halbjahr* which the brothers were to spend at Bonn, Albert expected his life to be one of waiting for something to happen. What happened first was a fire. The ducal palace at Coburg was heated by wood stoves. While Ernest and Albert were at the Ehrenburg Palace overnight, a servant lit a fire in a seldom-used stove that was piled high with books and prints and against which were more maps and prints. They awakened to billowing smoke and darting flames. Albert shouted 'Fire! Fire!' and with the aid of Ernest and their valet, Cart, battled the blaze with two jugs of water and another of camomile tea. 'Ernest took my cloak and his own', Albert wrote to their grandmother in Gotha the next day, 18 October, 1838, 'and threw them upon the flames, while I dragged all my bedding there, and pressed the mattresses and large counterpanes against the burning wall. Cart lifted a marble table with incredible strength and threw it against the bookcase enveloped in flames, causing it to fall down ... The heat and smoke were so powerful that all the windows had fallen out; even the glasses of the framed pictures [on the walls] were cracked, and the pictures shrivelled, and the paint of the doors is quite charred.'

Aside from the material damage, Albert and Cart scorched the soles of their feet by repeated barefoot dashes into the cinders. 'The only picture that is not injured', he summed up to Dowager Duchess Caroline, 'is the one of the fire at the Palace of Gotha.'

Two partings altered Albert's life in the closing months of 1838. Florschütz became betrothed to the daughter of Pastor Genzler, ending his close association as the princes' *Rath*, and Ernest took up his military apprenticeship in Dresden. The Duke and Albert travelled north-east from Coburg to meet the younger Ernest at Lobenstein for another round of farewells, driving, in the Duke's hardy manner, in an open carriage in freezing late-November weather.

Stockmar had recommended that Albert, who had sampled Italy only from Milan to Venice, spend the winter and early spring in Florence and Rome absorbing history and the arts – that it would be a more pleasant atmosphere than Berlin or Vienna or Brussels in which to wait out the winter, and Victoria's hoped-for change of mind about matrimony. With Florschütz no longer available as mentor, the Duke offered to conduct Albert as far as Munich, and then leave him to such arrangements as Stockmar might work out. The *Rath* had become suspect in any case as possibly a bad influence, the Duke's militia chief, von Wangenheim, having reported on 11 April 1838, 'as a faithful Gothaner', his suspicions that the Prince had 'imbibed liberal principles' from Florschütz. Both he and the Prince admired Leopold's constitutional monarchy. The sooner Albert was distant from such influences the better.

In early December the ducal party set off southwards. The fiftyish physician was not the ideal companion. Stockmar suffered from chronic indigestion and general hypochondria, and could not manage many miles each day, but at least he preferred travelling in a closed carriage. In bitterly cold weather, often on snow-covered roads, they jolted through Innsbruck, the Brenner Pass, Verona, Mantua, Modena, Bologna, Conigliano and, finally, Florence, which they reached on 29 December. 'The whole of north Italy', Albert wrote to his father, 'is covered with snow three feet deep. We found so much snow in the Apennines that we took five hours to accomplish what should have been less than three, though we had six horses and two oxen to the carriage.' Just short of Florence they had to be dug out of a snowdrift and move at walking pace. On 9 January 1839, he wrote again, confirming that they had established themselves in a 'well situated' house belonging to the Marquis Cerini. Albert would remain in Florence with Stockmar until early March.

Life for well-placed expatriates in Florence was crowded with balls, concerts, exhibitions, dinners and sightseeing, all opportunities for Albert to become more socially sophisticated – yet there is no hint of any involvement with young women of his class. For diplomatic reasons, perhaps, he did attend a ball given by Henry Fox, Minister Plenipotentiary in Florence, in January, to celebrate Her Britannic Majesty's forthcoming coronation. Fox was the son of Lord and Lady Holland, social lions and great friends of Viscount Melbourne. Very likely Albert understood that his presence would be reported to London, and indeed Fox wrote to his mother that young Prince Albert was handsome and pleasing, 'and so unaffectedly gay and amused'.

It would take some weeks, until the atmosphere of Florence altered in anticipation of Carnival, for Albert to feel its contagion. To Florschütz he wrote, 'Every morning by five o'clock I sit down by my little student's lamp' – and he did study English and French most mornings, and practise on the organ and piano in the early afternoons, after which he often took long walks round what had been, since medieval days, a city with attractive architecture and striking views along the Arno and from the nearby hills. To Prince William, a far different audience for his activities, he wrote, 'I am often quite intoxicated with delight when I come out of one of the galleries...I have lately thrown myself entirely into the whirl of society. I have danced, supped, paid compliments, have been introduced to people, and had people introduced to me; have spoken French and English – exhausted all remarks about the weather – have played amiable...You know my passion for things, and must therefore admire my strength of character, that I have never excused myself – never returned home till five in the morning – that I have emptied the carnival cup to the dregs.' If true, during Carnival week at the least, he was not burning his student's lamp at the usual pre-dawn hour.

On 10 March, he and Stockmar left for Rome, where they expected to remain for three weeks and then go on to Naples until the heat of late spring would drive them back toward the Alps, and home. From the cultural standpoint he enlarged his view beyond German, Dutch and Flemish painting and Romanticism in general, thanks largely to young Ludwig Gruner, brought along by Stockmar, who knew little about such things. Gruner was especially drawn to the accomplishments of the early Renaissance, then little appreciated in England.* Albert wrote to Florschütz with cautious understatement that he had made his peace 'with the Antique'. He would also learn to love Italian 'primitives' like Giotto in the most convincing way of all – by purchase.

In Florence one of his friends had been the duc de Nemours. Another was Lieutenant Francis Seymour of the English 19th Regiment, who joined the Prince early in February on leave of absence from his unit. Seymour, like the crotchety but well-meaning Stockmar, was there at the behest of King Leopold, to rein in any possible defection from the straight and narrow by Albert – hardly a real concern in his case – and to be Leopold's, and therefore Victoria's, spy. (Seymour's parents lived in Brussels and were known to Leopold.) Seymour continued with the party into Rome for Holy Week, and the Prince – six years his junior – was delighted to have a young companion. Seymour – later Lieutenant General Sir Francis, and a future Crimean War hero – would have links with the English Court that outlasted Albert, and a daughter, Victoria, to whom the Queen would be godmother. Seymour wrote home that Easter, 'The Prince danced the Cottilion with Lady Augusta Fox,[†] which lasted until five o'clock in the morning... Tuesday went to the Bal Masqué with the Prince...'

Even in Italy, Seymour reported, the Prince, who 'has grown very handsome and distinguished in his appearance... is talked of in public... as the husband of our young Queen. I accompany him everywhere, because the Baron is too unwell to go out...' Regularly, however, Stockmar would report to the Queen about their progress, to remind her that Albert's education on her behalf was progressing favourably; and from Naples on 16 April, once they had left Rome, he sent her what he described as 'a further account of our crusades'. Of the visit to Gregory XVI he said little more than 'We paid our respects to the Holy Father.' Albert, he added, made an 'admirable' sketch of the Pope.

---

* Ludwig Gruner, who became Lewis in England, would advise Albert on art matters from 1841 to 1856. Beginning as an architectural historian, he became an expert on northern Italian terracotta and ornamental art with books to his credit which he dedicated to Albert and to the Princess Royal. The Italianate aspects of Osborne House would owe much to Albert's consultations with him, and he would design the Royal Mausoleum at Frogmore, Windsor, in 1862.
[†] Wife of Sir Henry Fox.

On 31 March they had gone to observe the Pope's Easter blessing of the crowds in St Peter's Square 'from the balcony, amidst the ringing of bells, firing of cannon, and military music'. It was, Albert wrote to Lowenstein, 'really a most imposing scene', although it 'savoured strongly of idolatry'. Nevertheless he arranged an interview with Pope Gregory, and 'The old gentleman was very kind and civil. I remained with him nearly half an hour, shut up in a small room. We conversed in Italian on the influence the Egyptians had on Greek art, and...on Roman art. The Pope asserted that the Greeks had taken their models from the Etruscans. In spite of his infallibility I ventured to assert that they had derived their lessons in art from the Egyptians.' In the arrogance of youth, bolstered by scraps of newly acquired knowledge, the nineteen-year-old foreigner, new to Tuscany (pre-Roman Etruria), had committed the high solecism of challenging the Pope. And although only partially correct, Albert was less wrong than the venerable Gregory XVI. Much of Etruscan art seemed of Greek origins, while its funerary culture, with tomb provision for ultra-terrestrial life, appeared linked to the Egyptians. Some Etruscan writings would be found with mummy wrappings.

His Lutheran training at odds with Roman ritual and trappings, Albert also thought – so he wrote to Florschütz – that the Pope looked 'like a Pagoda'. Another German who had obtained an audience, a Herr Plattner,* Albert reported irreverently, flung himself on his knees to kiss the Pope's foot. 'He had already brought his lips within reach of the shoe when the Pope took a step backwards and turned round to pull the bell for the door to be opened to us. Thereupon P[lattner] lost his balance and fell on his face. Nevertheless he crawled after His Holiness on his stomach and grasped his raised foot. The Pope, a very stout, heavy man whom one foot only could not support, began to stagger and made violent efforts to free himself, which made him kick Plattner's mouth, outstretched to kiss, ten times at least.' In the background, struggling to keep from laughing, were Seymour and Stockmar, who

---

* The obsequious German who shared Albert's audience was very likely Ernst Zacharias Platner (1773–1855), an art historian from Leipzig who had painted piously biblical subjects before settling in Rome, and turning to art criticism, in 1804. He doubled as the King of Saxony's agent, then chargé d'affaires, to the Holy See. (Only *hearing* the name, Albert apparently doubled the 't'.)

pushed Plattner out the door as he mumbled thanks to the Pope for his 'graciousness'.

Later the Prince would be faulted for failing to evidence a sense of humour, but his public manner had to conform to his aspirations. Even now, with his unconfirmed future accepted as fact wherever he went, he was cautious to a fault. A public embarrassment might doom his chances. Stockmar reported as much to Leopold, observing that Albert, however amiable to everyone, showed no interest in women, and that the Prince, who had a passion for ideas, nevertheless did not discuss politics. (Earlier, Stockmar had noted that in Coburg Albert seldom looked at any newspaper other than the *Augsburger Allgemeine Zeitung.*) 'On the whole,' the Baron concluded, 'he will always have more success with men than with women, in whose society he shows too little *empressment,** and is too indifferent and retiring.' Since the public world in which Albert hoped to move was entirely male, and the only woman whose favour he required was Victoria, the Prince appears to have been aware of his priorities.

That he needed to project a maturity and sagacity beyond his few years was becoming evident as his Italian experience was coming to a close. The Queen at twenty – her birthday in May was in the month that Albert returned home – had become a problem even to herself. Dazzled by her position and inadequately trained for her role, she was imperious, unsophisticated and wilful. With the suave, widowered Prime Minister, who had already weathered extra-marital scandal, at her side afternoon and evening, mentoring her in his easy, avuncular manner, Victoria's obstinacy about being limited by a husband intensified. Malicious gossip reached her only through the rude crowds that occasionally jeered 'Mrs. Melbourne!' as she cantered in London parks with him or showed herself to the public in her carriage. All such signals were ignored, although much later she confessed, 'I was very young then, and perhaps I should act differently if it was all to be done again.' Charles Greville confided to his diary that the young queen's feelings toward Melbourne were 'sexual though she does not know it'.

That Victoria was queen of the Whigs rather than sovereign of England was a perception seemingly confirmed by the 'Bedchamber

* Eagerness.

Crisis' in which she was adamant about retaining her 'ladies' after a confidence defeat in the Commons had apparently unseated Melbourne. 'They wished to treat me like a girl,' Victoria exploded indignantly to Melbourne, 'but I will show them that I am Queen of England.' Largely the wives and daughters of leading Whigs for whom the appointments were political perquisites, they were, Peel patiently pointed out, holding public offices with stipends authorized by Parliament. But when Victoria insisted, in a misunderstanding of constitutional principle, that Peel was deviously attempting to dominate her Household, which she claimed was exempt from ministerial control, he refused office, restoring Melbourne's untenable government – exactly what the Queen wanted.

The embarrassing Lady Flora Hastings affair had already shown Victoria as petty and precipitate. In her haste to worsen the none-too-good reputation of Sir John Conroy, who she privately suspected was her mother's lover, Victoria had accused Lady Flora, a sister of the Tory Marquess of Hastings and lady of the bedchamber to the Duchess of Kent, of being pregnant out of wedlock, and hinted that Conroy had been responsible. The questionable swelling proved to be cancer, and the innocent Lady Flora died. The press fanned public outrage, revealing the Queen to be much in need of counsel she did not have. And looming over the North Sea was her allegedly wicked uncle, the Duke of Cumberland, and also now, since a provision much like Salic Law* prevented her own succession there, King Ernest Augustus of Hanover. Should the young queen die without issue, the Hanoverian king would wear the English crown as well, as had his brothers George and William.

Someone with an appropriate bloodline, preferably of mature years, was needed to rescue the girl-queen from herself – and sire the succession. Early in 1839 the problem was to persuade Victoria, who now preferred to put off marriage, that a consort was preferable sooner rather than later. Into that breach – and in Albert's interest – Leopold

---

* Since George I had succeeded Queen Anne in England, the sovereigns of Hanover also reigned in England. The Electorate of Hanover had been raised to kingdom status in 1814 after the post-Napoleonic powers decided not to restore the dismembered Holy Roman Empire. Salic Law eliminated females altogether from succession. A woman could not succeed in Hanover as long as male members on the paternal side of the family survived.

directed Stockmar to negotiate not with the Queen, but with Louise Lehzen. Daughter of an Hanoverian clergyman, Lehzen had come to England in 1818 as governess to Victoria's half-sister, Princess Feodora of Leiningen, transferring her functions to Victoria in 1824, when she was five. To afford Lehzen some status, Princess Sophia, the elderly unmarried daughter of George III who, like Victoria's family, had apartments in sprawling Kensington Palace, persuaded her brother, George IV, to raise Lehzen to Hanoverian baroness. As such, she performed Household administrative duties for Victoria, and was Stockmar's conduit for strategies to bring Albert and Victoria together. Stockmar wrote to Lehzen in the direct language of one private secretary to another, and neither showed their texts to the person for whom each was acting. The conspiratorial method would prove its necessity.

Late in May Albert's entourage began returning northward through Pisa, Leghorn, Genoa and Milan, crossing through the St Bernard Pass to Lausanne and then to Bern. At Milan he was met by his father and his cousin Count Hugo Mensdorff. Stockmar returned home to his family, and to covert correspondence with Brussels and Windsor. From Geneva, where Lieutenant Seymour parted company for London, Albert and the Duke began their return to Coburg, where, by act of its assembly on 21 June, the coming-of-age day of Prince Ernest, both brothers were declared, simultaneously, to be of legal age. Albert was still two months short of twenty.

On 13 July, Albert accompanied Ernest to Dresden, planning to remain for two weeks. 'Then', he wrote to his friend Löwenstein, 'I must go to a place that I hate mortally, that charming Karlsbad, where Papa is taking the waters, and much wishes me to be with him. I hope this campaign will be over by the middle of August.' Albert had dreaded the Duke's plans for months, and hoped they would fade away. His father wanted him to 'accustom himself more to society', and 'pay more attention to the ladies', which 'as an occupation' Albert disliked. The fashionable Bohemian spa, frequented by females among whom might be some who would see to it that the Prince came of age in other ways then by legislative fiat, seemed to the Duke the appropriate place to further Albert's education. 'I had, on the contrary', Albert recalled, 'formed the finest plans for the study of the English language and history, for which the quiet of the Rosenau would have been particularly well suited.'

As far as Victoria was concerned, Albert's immersion in things English was premature. In her diary for 12 June she recorded a discussion with Lord Melbourne in which she 'talked of my cousins Ernest and Albert coming over – my having no great wish to see Albert, as the whole subject was an odious one, and one I hated to decide about; there was no engagement between us, I said, but that the young man was aware that there was no possibility of such a union; I said it wasn't right to keep him [hanging] on and not right to decide before they came; and Lord M. said I should make them distinctly understand anyhow I couldn't do anything for a year.' Privately, she felt that she could think of no marriage at all for at least four years. In the meantime she wrote to Albert rather coldly that although she looked forward to seeing both brothers at Windsor again, she hoped that neither would be ill as he had been in their only previous visit nearly three years earlier.

Melbourne, who preferred matters as they were, without unpredictable spousal intrusion, offered no objection. He seldom said 'no' to Victoria. Since it was her pushy uncle in Brussels who kept reminding her of Albert, she wrote to Leopold three days later as if nothing were happening in England to erode public confidence in her as queen. Airily, she assumed – and she appeared to have the Prime Minister's concurrence – that she could go on indefinitely in her wilful independence, and that 'the young man' could be kept waiting, or perhaps fobbed off on someone else. Most surprising of all to Leopold, who knew that she did not want to be reined in, was that she had no sense of the dissatisfaction about her. No one close to the Court was willing to tell her the truth.

She was sending her letter by courier, she began, as the content was sensitive. Talk of a visit by Ernest and Albert was to cease: 'I am desirous [it] should not transpire.' Further, she went on, imperiously,

I wish to know if *Albert* is aware of the wish of his *Father* and *you* relative to *me*? Secondly, if he knows that there is *no engagement* between us? I am anxious that you should acquaint Uncle Ernest, that if I should like Albert, that I can make *no final promise this year*, for, at the *very earliest*, any such event could not take place till *two or three years hence*. For, independent of my youth, and my *great* repugnance to change my present position, there is *no anxiety* evinced in *this country* for such an event, and it would be more prudent, in my opinion, to wait till some such demonstration is shown, – else if it were hurried it might produce discontent.

Though all the reports of Albert are most favourable, and though I have little doubt I shall like him, still one can never answer before-hand for *feelings*, and I may not have the *feeling* for him which is requisite to ensure happiness. I *may* like him as a friend, and as a *cousin*, and as a *brother*, but not *more*; and should this be the case (which is not likely) I am *very* anxious that it should be understood that I am *not* guilty of any breach of promise, for *I never gave any*.

As Leopold paused to wonder what he could do, Albert was writing to Stockmar about his premature – but legal – majority, 'I am now my own master, as I hope always to be, and under all circumstances.' Yet even then he was not, as the Duke was bent upon keeping him away still longer from the Rosenau. He was 'almost dying of boredom' in Karlsbad, he wrote to Ernest; 'yesterday I nearly hanged myself in desperation when I heard that the reward for all my sufferings is to be a stay at Reinhardsbrunn.' The Thür-inger Wald family castle was certain to be even more dull than Karlsbad. But his father had given up on Victoria and was eager to make connections for Albert although the benefactor of his industry showed no enthusiasm for the scheme.

Without warning, the Duke's plans were altered and a reprieve won for his son. Leopold had summoned Ernest to England. Unable to spurn a delegation of her Coburg uncles, Victoria had conceded, with some exasperation, to a visit. In the last days of August, Duke Ernest travelled to Windsor with Prince Ferdinand of Saxe-Coburg-Kohary. On 6 September, King Leopold, who had pressed for the meeting, arrived with Queen Louise, whom Victoria considered a friend. The business was briefly dispatched. The Queen again declared her misgiv-ings about marriage but agreed, so long as no understanding was read into their presence, to see the princes.

Duke Ernest returned to Coburg to report that the Queen had insisted that she had settled on no spouse, had no intention of marrying very soon, and was quite content the way things were – and that the lax Prime Minister, whose Downing Street lease had been extended by the Bedchamber fiasco, was of similar disposition. Victoria's subjects felt otherwise, the Duke conceded. She enjoyed entertainments that went on into the small hours, and then sleeping late. She loved pomp and display, and was more stubborn than ever. She 'might as well marry George of Cambridge, since no one else will have her'. And the Duchess of Cambridge, the former Princess Augusta of Hesse-Cassel, imagining such chances, was unsubtle in pressing the claims of her son, whose bad complexion, at nineteen, was concealed by fresh whiskers. 'Infamous woman', Victoria snapped in her journal.

Twenty on 26 August, Albert had written to his brother, as Ernest was hurrying to Windsor, 'Our childhood is over ... yet I can say that I retain my childlike soul, and this is the treasure that everyone should take with him into his future life.' Ordered about by his peremptory father, he may have felt more of the powerlessness of the child than the ideal of innocence and wonder he fantasized. The days leading up to his birthday, for example, had to be spent, unwillingly, in Gotha, in which he never felt at home. But he was back in Coburg to read Victoria's invitation which reopened the question of his future yet left him in the position of a child. His life was still being discussed and determined without even his presence.

To make her position clear, Victoria had drawn up an invitation that was little short of a cold dismissal. Its language suggests that she intended to evoke either an outright rejection or a humble acceptance of conditions set by a sovereign understood as having her way then and thenceforth. Ernest and Albert were each to bring only one accompanying person, neither of whom was to be the suspect Stockmar, and they were to arrive by 28 September. Albert's move in the chess game of wills was to make the tactless Queen wait. The King of Saxony planned a state visit to Coburg beginning on September 30, and the presence of both brothers, Albert claimed, was mandatory. Ernest was, after all, serving in the Saxon army.

When Leopold urged that one didn't keep the queen of a great nation waiting, Albert, intending exactly that, explained to his uncle, 'We really have no option, and we shall not be able to leave before the fourth [of October].' It would take nearly a week after that, by carriages overland and then by the wretched Channel boat, to make it to England. He hadn't lost interest in being consort to a queen, but he was having gloomy second thoughts about the price. (In a letter dated 6 December, Albert would confide to Prince William of Löwenstein that he had determined to go only 'with the quiet but firm resolution to declare, on my part, that I also, tired of the delay, withdraw entirely from the affair'.)

Since two could play the stalling game, Victoria rushed off a request to Leopold that he hold the brothers in Belgium longer than their planned overnight stay. 'You will think', she told her uncle, 'I only mean to employ you in *stopping* my relations at Brussels', but she alleged need for a delay to afford her ministers, who were coming to Windsor 'on affairs of great importance', time to leave – as, if Ernest and Albert arrived before the Cabinet departed, 'people would say – it was to *settle matters*'. Besides, she added, with more than a little arrogance, 'I think indeed a day or two at Brussels will do these young gentlemen good, and they could be properly fitted out there for their visit.' The ungracious aside suggested that 'these young gentlemen' from the forests of Thüringia (otherwise 'my relations') might be planning to arrive in *Lederhosen*.

On October 1 she pouted to Leopold, 'The *retard* of these young people puts me rather out...I had a letter from Albert yesterday saying they could not set off, he thought, before the 6th. I think they don't exhibit much *empressement* to come here, which rather shocks me.' But she would send 'a gentleman and carriages to meet my cousins, either at Woolwich or the Tower, whichever place you inform me they land at.'

Sailing from Antwerp, Ernest and Albert – and the uninvited four-legged Eos – arrived at the Tower of London dock in the Thames on 10 October, a Thursday. Since the rough overnight voyage had left both brothers in agonies of seasickness, they failed to notice that their trunks were not stowed onto their carriages, which guaranteed that whatever they had been fitted out with, they would begin the visit without acceptable clothes.

At Windsor the day had mellowed into a beautiful autumn evening before the sound of hooves and wheels sent a servant scurrying to report that the princes were arriving. The Queen had been walking with her guests on a terrace edged by what Lady Granville described as an 'embroidered garden'. Returning indoors, Victoria awaited Ernest and Albert at the top of the broad stairs in the upper quadrangle. She had lost the pounds she had put on when, to allay her gathering anxieties, she had eaten and drunk to excess, and Harriet Granville thought she appeared 'lovely, much more delicate without looking ill'. Victoria had chosen her vantage to suggest a height she did not have. Just under five feet, she intended to look queenly.

As the brothers ascended, erotic lightning struck. 'It was with some emotion', Victoria confided to her journal, 'that I beheld Albert – who is beautiful. I embraced them both and took them to Mamma.'

Amid the initial presentations, Victoria learned that they had arrived not with inappropriate clothes but with no trunks at all. Although protocol demanded formal attire for dinner, the Queen failed to recall the lines which Shakespeare had given to Henry V in wooing Katherine of France – that 'nice customs curtsy to great kings', who are 'the makers of manners'. Dining apart, the princes joined Victoria in her spacious drawing-room *'in spite of their negligé'*, as she would write, and she presented them to Melbourne, who sat with her on a sofa as usual. Albert was offered a chair opposite the Queen, who found it difficult to keep her eyes off him. 'Lord M.' took due note, and when Victoria managed to turn away to ask him in a whisper whether he saw any family resemblance, the Prime Minister answered gallantly, 'Oh! yes. It struck me at once.'

The Queen's postprandial guests sat through the evening, Lady Granville wrote to the Duke of Devonshire, 'with much to look at . . . Prince Albert the youngest is charming. Ladies Sandwich, Clanricarde and I are won. It remains to be seen who else will be.'

As was customary, they broke up into small groups, and Albert chose chess over cards. The emotional pitch was high. Lady Clanricarde commented, *sotto voce*, 'The trial is too great; if he wins he has a master mind.' He lost. Her Majesty bent over the velvet-gowned Lady Clanricarde to ask, 'Do you think my cousin [looks] like me?' 'Yes', she said.

Harriet Granville and the other transfixed ladies, having had 'all our eyes on', came away thinking that the Queen evidenced 'much attention but no liking', which if so, demonstrated the Queen's public manner as more disciplined than her pen. She was besotted. Her journal for the next day included as much of a physical description of Albert as clothing permitted. He was 'quite charming, and so excessively handsome, such beautiful blue eyes, and exquisite nose, and such a pretty mouth with delicate moustachios and slight but very light whiskers; a beautiful figure, broad in the shoulders and fine waist; my heart is quite going . . . '

On the twelfth she wrote to Leopold in terms that made clear that the uncles' strategy had worked. She and Albert rode into Windsor

Forest together, danced after dinner, played at cards, and as Eos
stretched and yawned, talked into the night. In her journal for the
thirteenth her cousin was now 'dearest Albert', and she confided to
Lord M. that she had changed her opinion about marrying and felt that
she had to decide 'soon'.

'You could take another week', said Melbourne, agreeing in effect
that little further consideration was necessary. Albert, he conceded, was

Victoria's proposal to Albert on 15 October 1839, in a contemporary lithograph.

'a very fine young man'. The next day – the fourteenth – she told Melbourne that she had made up her mind, and the Prime Minister wrote to Lord John Russell, 'I do not know that anything better could be done.' To the Queen he ventured, 'I think it'll be very well received; for I hear there is an anxiety now that it should be; and I'm very glad of it; for a woman cannot stand alone for long, in whatever situation she is.'

They discussed how 'such things were done' when the gender situation was reversed, and Victoria decided to send Baroness Lehzen to Albert's equerry, Captain Buffo von Alvensleben, to inform him that a personal declaration from the Queen was forthcoming.

On the fifteenth, a half hour after noon, Victoria sent for Albert. She was alone and tried to restrain her trembling. 'I said to him', she wrote in her journal, 'that he must be aware *why* I wished [him] to come here, and that it would make me *too happy* if he would consent to what I wished (to marry me); we embraced each other over and over again, and he was so kind, so affectionate. Oh! to *feel* I was, and am, loved by such an *Angel* as Albert was *too great a delight to describe!* he is *perfection*; perfection in every way – in beauty – in everything! I told him I was quite unworthy of him and kissed his dear hand – he said he would be very happy "*das Leben mit dir zu zubringen*" and was so kind and seemed so happy, that I really felt it was the happiest brightest moment of my life, which made up for all I had suffered and endured. Oh! *how* I adore and love him, I cannot say!! *how* I will strive to make him feel as little as possible the great sacrifice he has made; I told him it was a great sacrifice, – which he wouldn't allow...'

It would be a sacrifice in many ways, Albert knew, but at the moment he was loved, and he was on the verge of being extricated from the claustrophobic court of Coburg, where he was a superfluous son in a statelet of little consequence. He had been offered the career for which he had been groomed.

Returning to his rooms to get his emotions under control, Albert penned a note to Victoria, in effect to confirm the betrothal. 'How is it that I have deserved so much love, so much affection?' And he signed it, 'In body and soul ever your slave, your loyal Albert'. In circles where courtship followed the engagement rather than created the conditions for it, they were about to begin the next phase of their lives.

Later in the day Victoria hurried a message to Leopold completely at variance with the chilly hostility her uncle had learned to expect. 'My feelings are a *little* changed, I must say, since last Spring,' she confessed. Her mind was 'quite made up' – and she had told Albert as much.

'*If you love him, and are kind to him,*' the King responded, 'he will easily bear the burden of the position.' It would be a burden; the career of consort to a reigning queen at any time or place had seldom, if ever, been a source of satisfaction. For the next few weeks, however, as Ernest and Albert lingered on at Windsor at Victoria's request, the couple were in a state of complete bliss. Alone, they kissed 'again and again', and Albert called her '*vortrefflichste*' – superb one. Still, Albert was uneasy in England. He was uncomfortable with the language, the climate, the food, the prospect of alienation, the likely frustrations of his occupation. To Stockmar he wrote, nevertheless, with deep feeling, lines from Schiller's *Lied von die Glocke,*

> *Das Auge sieht den Himmel offen,*
> *Es schwimmt das Herz in Seligkeit –*

One's eye sees heaven open, the heart floats on a sea of blessedness.

Yet the announcement, Albert warned, was to be withheld, for reasons of state, until Parliament met in mid-November. What particularly grieved him, he confided, was that Victoria's mother – his own aunt – 'is not to know of it. But as everyone says, she cannot keep her mouth shut and might even make bad use of the secret if it were entrusted to her.'

Secrets were difficult to keep at Windsor, where servants blended into the furnishings. Having been present when the princes arrived, and with lines of communication to Windsor open, it was only the day after Victoria's proposal that Harriet Granville reported to the Duke of Devonshire the latest gossip from the Dowager Lady Sandwich – that 'Prince Albert has been flirting the last two days, she was not sure, but thinks with Miss Cocks. An odd distraction I think.' Lady Caroline Somers-Cocks was a maid of honour to the Queen, and it is quite possible that a young Saxon prince, bored with inactivity, was distracting himself in his habitual manner. But it would have been Ernest – a case of mistaken identity which at least kept the betrothal under wraps a little longer.

Two days after Victoria and Albert became engaged, they attended a musical evening at Windsor. His standard for music being high, and bored by the waltzes and galops, Albert covered his handwritten programme with doodles and caricatures. The Queen treasured it, keeping it all her life.

The fleeting days before the public announcement of the engagement were spent in work and play. With Albert her imperious surface vanished, and she was the vulnerable young woman who had craved affection all her life. Having arrived to be interviewed by his prospective employer, the Prince succumbed to her passion. She asked for a cutting of his 'dear hair' to wear in a locket, and gave him a ring 'with the ever dear to me 15th engraved in it'. Radiant in her new happiness, she understood, nevertheless, that she was no beauty, and Albert confided his impatience with society beauties. Alone, afterward, with Lord Melbourne she innocently told him of the exchange and he grumbled, disapprovingly, with what he thought was political wisdom, 'Ought to pay attention to the ladies'.

Between kisses in the Queen's blue sitting-room one day, Victoria signed a sheaf of papers and warrants, Albert at her side, 'and he was so kind as to dry them with blotting paper for me'. It was symbolic of the official role intended for him, but such concerns remained far from his mind. His life had taken on an unexpected emotional dimension, and the couple returned to reality only when such business as setting a wedding date came up – it would be 10 February 1840 – and what other arrangements had to be made for Albert – an income, a staff, a rank or title, even such an essential as citizenship.

With much to do to wind up his affairs in Germany and to proclaim the nuptials there officially, he soon had only eight weeks left for all of it, including the journeys back and return. He left with Ernest, via Belgium, on 14 November. 'We kissed each other so often, and I leant on that dear soft cheek, fresh and pink as a rose . . .', Victoria gushed in her journal for the day. 'It was ten o'clock and the time for his going . . . I gave Albert a last kiss, and saw him get into the carriage – and drive off. I cried much, felt wretched, yet happy to think that we should meet again so soon. Oh! how I love him, how intensely, how devotedly, how ardently! I cried and felt so sad. Wrote my journal. Walked. Cried.'

Since Albert had been secluded at Windsor, few knew but many guessed at the outcome. Ordinary visits, however important the guest, did not lengthen into weeks. Even so, Victoria's mother – Albert's aunt Kent – had not been called in to be told of the betrothal until 10

Victoria's watercolour sketch of Albert made at Windsor when he was twenty shows far more honestly than the idealized portraits by Court painters how young he was. (Royal Collections)

November. Although she wept then with happiness, second thoughts quickly intervened. The next day, to consolidate her position at Court she began urging upon Albert appointments of her friends, and insisting that she would live with the couple after their marriage – 'which we agreed *never* to do', Victoria noted. Once Albert left, the Duchess began complaining about her imminent separation from her daughter, who offered no consolation. Instead, Victoria consulted with Melbourne, who urged that her mother be moved 'out of the house. There must be no harshness, yet [be] firm.'

Albert's departure was only hours old when Victoria began, in her sudden physical loneliness, to pour out her passion for him in letters interspersing English and German, the first sent via her uncle, so that the Prince would receive it *en route* home. Confident that Melbourne, as he guaranteed in his usual accommodating manner, could fix all the details of the marriage to mutual satisfaction, Victoria promised to have Albert invested with the Order of the Garter before he left Coburg, to have him made a field marshal, and to have a simple marital declaration approved by Parliament. 'Everything will be very easily arranged.' Yet even in the very first of many messages to be exchanged between November and February a dark foreshadowing of difficulties emerged: '*Lord Melbourne told me yesterday that the whole Cabinet are strongly of opinion that you should not be made a Peer.*' The crucial word was 'yesterday'. She had known that Albert would have to be married in his trivial and un-English title of Prince of Saxe-Coburg and Gotha, but could not bring herself to tell him and spoil their leavetaking.

Because of winds and tides, the Channel crossing to Calais had to be delayed until 2.30 in the morning. Even then the *Firebrand* could not dock at the quay and passengers had to go ashore in a small boat just after dawn. The entire party, Albert wrote to Victoria, was fearfully ill. 'I have hardly recovered yet.' But his letter closed with all the endearments she could have wished for. 'Your image fills my whole soul. Even in my dreams I never imagined that I should find so much love on earth.'

After Brussels they travelled by way of Aix la Chapelle and Bonn, where the brothers hosted 'a great luncheon for one of the professors, who was our old tutor', and met their father, the Duke, at Wiesbaden, for a formal escort home. It was there that Albert answered, with tact and shrewdness, his future mother-in-law's parting request to give her as a token something he had worn. 'I send you the ring which you gave me at Kensington [Palace] on Victoria's birthday in 1836. From that time it has never left my finger. Its very shape proclaims that it has been squeezed in the grasp of many a manly hand. It has your name upon it: but the name is Victoria's too . . .'

At Coburg, Albert met Stockmar, whom he would send to England as his representative in negotiations about his status. Awaiting him from Victoria was a book never part of his law studies at Bonn – Sir William Blackstone's *Commentaries* (1765–69) on the laws of England. He promised that the volumes would receive 'a thorough study', but it was much later before he discovered that the unwritten English Constitution, a body of precedent, conceded him 'just as much space as I could stand upon'. Although English marriage laws left a wife as little more than a chattel of her husband, the Constitution was 'silent as to the Consort of the Queen; – even Blackstone ignores him'. But that was years afterward. Legal English was a more complex matter than ordinary language, which was trying enough despite his schooling. He should have responded in English, he conceded, 'but German runs more easily with me, and as we always spoke in German together during that heavenly time together at Windsor, it does not sound right to me at all to address you in English'. Their private interchanges in all the years of their marriage would follow the same pattern. In public an English prince, at home he and Victoria spoke German.

By the time that Albert informed his friend Prince William, in early December, of the royal engagement, difficulties were emerging about his English status. He expected to be happy in his marriage, he confided, 'for Victoria possesses all the qualities which make a home happy', but his role beyond that of husband was another matter. 'My future lot is high and brilliant, but also plentifully strewed with thorns.' Frank, too, was his assessment to the Duchess of Kent, to whom he described, the same day (6 December 1839), the 'multitude of emotions' that overwhelmed him as he prepared to leave Coburg – 'hope, love for dear Victoria, the pain of leaving home, the parting from very dear kindred, the entrance into a new circle of relations ... prospects most brilliant, the dread of being unequal to my position, the demonstrations of so much attachment on the part of the loyal Coburgers, English enthusiasm on the tip-toe of expectation, the multiplicity of duties to be fulfilled, and to crown all, so much laudation on every side that I could sink to earth with very shame. I am lost in bewilderment.'

The praise in England, except from those close to Victoria, was already diminishing as others were redefining him as alien and parasite. It would be impossible for Victoria to keep that from him. Meanwhile, he told his aunt, while outside the countryside was deep in snow and he struggled with a heavy cold, 'I pack, arrange, give directions about pieces of property, settle contracts, engage servants, write an infinitude of letters, study the English Constitution, and occupy myself about my future.'

The formalities for that future, social as well as legal, were far more complex than either had anticipated. Before the Privy Council, and Parliament, knew, the Queen had to inform, confidentially, if the delicious confidences could be kept, Queen Adelaide, her royal uncles, and those of the Cabinet not already knowledgeable. On 18 November she invited the Cambridges – including Prince George – to acquaint them with her betrothal. Her cousin, she told Melbourne, was 'evidently happy to be *clear* of me'. Melbourne's sister, Emily Cowper, long Palmerston's mistress and now that she was widowed, to be married to him in a month – which amused Victoria, since the elderly lovers were in their fifties – had been to Windsor to meet Albert. 'Nothing openly stated', Lady Cowper wrote to Dorothea de Lieven in Paris, but 'with a good figure and well built'. Albert possessed 'everything which is likely to engage a young girl's affections'. Marriage, the future Lady Palmerston predicted, would come 'sooner or later, and I do not think she could find anyone more suitable. They say he is as sensible as his uncle [Leopold] and has great learning.'

Soon after Albert returned to Coburg a letter arrived from Victoria, dated 22 November, with more disconcerting news. Melbourne had been asked in the Cabinet about confirming the Prince's Protestantism. He had assumed that it was understood and had not been necessary in the Declaration. Now Victoria required a history of the ducal house and its religious ties, '*for a few stupid people* here *try* to say you are a Catholic...'

Her next letter to Albert would describe the ordeal of announcing her own betrothal. As Lord Holland put it in his diary, 'A modest girl of twenty, unaccompanied by any one of her own sex, had to announce to a grave and observant assembly of 85 men her *determination* to take as bedfellow a young man who had lately left her palace.' Asked afterwards by the Duchess of Gloucester if the prospect of the ceremony alarmed her, Victoria said, 'A little, but not much, for I had to propose it to Albert himself and had gone thro' that much more awkward ceremony before I mentioned it to the Privy Council.'

The Privy Council met in Buckingham Palace at two in the afternoon on 23 November. Victoria had come in from Windsor for the session, and a crowd had begun gathering, recognizing that the marital rumours were about to be confirmed. When the folding doors of the council chamber were swung open, the Queen entered alone, wearing a simple morning gown. Her only jewellery was a bracelet containing Albert's portrait in profile – a miniature by Sir William Charles Ross. 'I had to read the Declaration,' Victoria wrote to Albert. '*It was rather an awful moment, to be obliged to announce this to so many people, many of whom were quite strangers.*' Charles Greville, as Clerk of the Council, saw her hands quiver as she held the folded sheet with the statement composed by Melbourne, but, Tory stalwart John Wilson Croker wrote to Lady Hardwicke, 'I cannot describe to you with what a mixture of self-possession and feminine delicacy she read the paper. Her voice, which is naturally beautiful, was clear and untroubled; and her eye was bright and calm, neither bold nor downcast, but firm and soft.'

As the Queen's carriage passed through the gates *en route* back to Windsor on the cold, overcast day, smoke as usual hanging low over London, crowds, now larger and aware of the news, cheered Victoria lustily. 'Radiant and bowing' according to press accounts, she responded happily. The public, however, appeared more delighted with the betrothal than would Parliament, already less than enthusiastic about providing a purse for yet another penniless German princeling, especially as political agitation burgeoned. Farms and factories were both subject to market forces, and machines also seemed to take jobs from the able-bodied. When consumption declined, the work-force fell even further, although not the fertility of the exploding population. Since Parliament feared that economic distress would increase discontent, which in turn would feed revolutionary fervour, its members, more middle-class since the Reform Act of 1832 enlarged the electorate, sought expenditures for police and poorhouses and public works. The unemployed got little help indeed from Parliament, and its largesse towards Albert seemed, if anything, overly generous. Looking back at precedent, Victoria complained to Melbourne that the 'very stupid and insignificant' Danish prince who became Queen Anne's husband was made Lord High Admiral and presented with a £50,000 stipend. Yet their failure to assure the succession – no child survived infancy – had brought the despised Hanoverians to England, including the uncles of the Queen, Princes of the Blood Royal, who even now disputed raising a mere Serene Highness to precedence over them. Albert's hypothetical sons – the very reason for his importation – would be born to precedence over their father, a problem of little concern to the people in the streets, but of great moment to the rank-ridden classes that still ruled.

Lord Shaftesbury recalled nearly forty years later being told by Melbourne that the Queen was eager to have Albert made, by parliament, King Consort upon his marriage. Cautiously evading a direct answer, the Prime Minister was very pressed for one, and determined that it was his duty to be 'very plain' about it. 'For God's sake', he said to Victoria, 'let's hear no more of it, ma'am; for if you once get the English people in the way of making kings, you will get them into the way of unmaking them.'

Whether on religious or national grounds, the undercurrent of hostility towards another imported sovereign or consort was real. England had endured five Hanoverian kings and their German brides. Also forgotten was Leopold. And now, a malicious broadsheet, *The German Bridegroom*, mocked,

> Saxe-Coburg sends [Albert] from its paltry race,
> With foreign phrases and a moustachio'd face,
> to extract treasure from Parliament by wooing
> The hoyden Sovereign of this mighty isle[, who]
> Welcomes her German with enraptured smile.

Debate on the Naturalization Bill had thrown Victoria's precedents back at her. Prince George of Denmark had been awarded all the pocket money the Queen had claimed, but it had come from the future Queen Anne's own pockets, and the Coburger Leopold had indeed received a parliamentary stipend, yet on departing for another throne had continued taking Parliament's money. The climate for German bridegrooms had changed.

Since Parliament was determined that Albert should play no political role, he was also to have no rank in the army, and no English peerage. 'It needs but the stroke of your pen to make me a peer and to give me an English name,' Albert had appealed from Wiesbaden *en route* home. He had no idea what an unpopular and even illegal act that would have been. From status-conscious Vienna, Prince Metternich would scoff that one could no more make a man royal who was not so, than make him eight feet tall. Victoria was furious at the outcry. Parliament was not merely legislating, mean-spiritedly, the lives of two twenty-year-olds about to be married; it was attempting to diminish the powers of the sovereign. Was Albert, she asked Melbourne, worth less than Queen Anne's consort, 'stupid old George of Denmark'?

The votes against comparable arrangements for Albert were actually less a rebuff to Victoria than to the weak Melbourne Ministry that she had, through her own wilfulness, kept too long. Albert was paying the price. It did not augur well that his only legal position in England was to be that of a minor foreign princeling who happened to be the Queen's husband. Even his arms were to be quartered with the royal arms in the inferior position, as if he were a woman. As for his role in politics, he could continue to wield the blotting paper. The functions for which he was imported from Coburg would have to be performed in bed.

V

Serene Highness to Royal Highness

1840–1841

A T NOON ON 7 February 1840, now recovered from seasickness, the Coburgers departed Dover for Canterbury. Despite the cold February rain they rode in open carriages under darkened skies to accept loyal English cheers. Exposure to the elements was a hazard of rank Albert had experienced at home.

The escort changed as they clattered closer towards Canterbury. Now it was the crack 11th Dragoons, commanded by James Thomas Brudenell, 7th Earl of Cardigan, a lieutenant-colonel who had inherited a peerage and vast income in the year Victoria succeeded to the throne. Spoiled beyond efforts at discipline from his superiors, at forty-two he had already been the beneficiary of a commission and a seat in the Commons, both purchased for him; and he used his private purse to promote the swagger of his men and mounts. Only the best equine breeds were good enough for the 11th. On a costly Arab charger, Cardigan greeted the Prince's party at the head of two files of just over one hundred smartly accoutred troops. As cathedral bells pealed, the Dragoons accompanied the future consort into Canterbury.

Following divine service, the weary Saxons dined at the Royal Hotel with Cardigan and two majors from his regiment. Canterbury was illuminated as never before. Defying the drizzle, crowds outside the hotel shouted for the Prince and hailed him when he appeared on a balcony. Learning about the enthusiasm the next day, Melbourne advised Albert wryly not to become intoxicated by adulation.

A contemporary lithograph, by G.F. Bragg, of Albert's carriage being escorted from Dover early in February 1840, by the Earl of Cardigan's 11th Light Dragoons.

On Saturday morning – it was now the eighth, with the nuptials set for Monday – the entourage set out for London, the Dragoons leading the way along the road toward Sittingbourne, on the south bank of the Thames. The balding, bewhiskered Earl was in his glory. His men were in their finest plumage and efficiently doing what he had trained them to do while garrisoned in Cork. Even his enemies, of whom there were many, conceded that he had the makings of an excellent sergeant-major.

Young Albert was impressed. Not long after the wedding Cardigan was informed by the Adjutant-General, Sir John Macdonald, 'My Lord, I have the honour to acquaint you . . . that Her Majesty has been graciously pleased to direct that the 11th regiment of Light Dragoons shall be armed, clothed and equipped as Hussars, and styled the "Eleventh" or "Prince Albert's Own Hussars".' A dragoon in the British army was a mounted infantryman armed with a short musket; a hussar – a term originally in use in Hungary for a light cavalryman, and a variant of the Italian *corsaro*, or corsair – was the same soldier decked out in flamboyant uniform, exactly to the taste of the Earl. Cardigan, who spent at least £10,000 a year of his personal fortune on tack and tailoring for his troops, quickly employed fifty fitters to fashion brilliant new plumage. It was more appropriate to *Mitteleuropa* than to an army that needed to learn all over again, long after Waterloo, how to fight. The Earl was a patrician parader of post troops, unable to hear above the splendid din of drum and trumpet any orders from nominal superiors. Blundering in 1854 at Balaclava, he would inspire a poem by Tennyson.

Albert's personal escorts were rewarded in a different manner. Lord Seymour, a companion in Italy, would spend much of his subsequent career as a courtier, as would George Byng, the 7th Viscount Torrington, who would be Lord-in-Waiting to Albert and then to Victoria, while Charles Grey would rise to general in the royal administrative retinue.

The escort of the Prince brought him to London by mid-afternoon on the eighth, using a route again different from advance prognostications in the press. Albert offered no complaints but his brother, peeved at the futility, recalled, 'The bridegroom, in the most incomprehensible manner, was driven through side streets, while people vainly awaited him in another part of the city.'

At four-thirty the Prince's carriage and escort arrived at Buckingham Palace through the centre gate. 'I stood at the very door,' Victoria wrote, evidencing her eagerness; '1st stepped out Ernest, then Uncle Ernest, and then Albert, looking beautiful and so well; I embraced him and took him by the hand and led him up to my [sitting] room . . . ' No privacy was possible; her mother, uncle, cousin and the Prime Minister followed them. Gifts were exchanged – the Star and Badge of the Garter in diamonds for Albert, a sapphire brooch set round with diamonds for Victoria. Within half an hour the Lord Chancellor had administered the formal oath of naturalization to Albert. He had now left Germany legally as well as physically.

At dinner Albert claimed to be still giddy from seasickness, but the ailment was more likely the tension that was inevitable in his situation. The next day, a Sunday, was left to him to recover, but by early afternoon he was again in Victoria's sitting-room, this time to accept, however sulkily, the staff appointed for him, including George Anson as his private secretary and treasurer. What confidentiality was he to have if Melbourne's own secretary were to become his? 'We had some little misunderstandings', Victoria understated in her journal, 'and he was so dear and *ehrlich*' – honest – 'and open about it; he will appoint him. I embraced him again and again.' They went over the wedding responses, and even practised placement of the rings.

When Albert drove away toward Kensington Palace, his guest quarters, the Queen saw throngs out in welcome – Londoners caught up in the romance and unimpressed, if aware at all, about higher-level misgivings that Victoria needed a more experienced, more mature, spouse at her side.

Upper-class concerns about the Prince often followed party lines. The Tory John James Ruskin, a prosperous wine merchant (and father of the critic), carped that the Queen's choice augured badly for Britain: 'I wish the Boy may grow into something better. It is a poor prospect for the Country.' The Earl of Aberdeen, a Peelite Tory and future Prime Minister, expressed no enthusiasm to Princess Lieven, whose lover, French politician François Guizot, was about to move to London as ambassador. 'The affair had excited no great interest', he scoffed, seeing Victoria as queen only of the Whigs; '... the Government have been unwise in giving a party character to the proceedings. It is said that the Duke of Wellington has only been invited at the last moment, and after much difficulty.' Assuming that it was Melbourne's decision to snub the Tory icon, rather than Victoria's, Aberdeen offered a scenario that suggested a more authoritarian Melbourne than was the case. 'Had they persevered in the omission, I really believe that publick indignation would have been so strong as to have endangered their places.' Still, 'Everything we hear of Prince Albert is favourable; he will have much in his power, and if he possesses sense and discretion he may be eminently useful to the country.'

Monday began miserably. Gusts of rain made travel unpleasant for the hundreds of wedding guests in elaborate finery. Since the venerable Chapel Royal, St James's Palace, could not seat everyone required by rank, relationship or diplomatic representation, invitees were seated everywhere some glimpse of the royal couple was possible, even on the staircase. As carriages queued up, Victoria – who had to travel to the chapel like the others – saw Albert 'for the last time alone, as my Bridegroom' – a flouting of tradition. The sky was clearing as the Prince, in his field marshal's uniform, left for St James's. As Victoria, accompanied by the Duchess of Kent and the Mistress of the Robes, the Duchess of Sutherland, who had become the Queen's closest friend, squeezed her satin gown with its lace flounces into her carriage, the rain persisted. It was twelve-thirty. A guard of honour opened a path for the short distance across Green Park: 'I never saw such crowds of people as there were in the Park', Victoria wrote, 'and they cheered most enthusiastically'.

Victoria's revenge upon the Tories for their treatment of the Prince was observable in the presence of only two Conservative peers, Lord Liverpool and the Duke of Wellington, both former Prime Ministers, and the Duke would not be invited to the wedding breakfast. Albert entered with his father as the organist played, incongruously, 'See the Conquering Hero Come'. The Queen's procession included twelve train-bearers. She was led in by the Lord Chamberlain and given away by her uncle the Duke of Sussex, who was 'always ready to give away', *John Bull* quipped, 'what does not belong to him'. The most awkward moment in the ceremony came, according to Sallie Stevenson, wife of the American Minister, when Albert had to profess endowing Victoria with all his worldly goods, yet he responded strongly when asked whether he would take 'this woman' for his wife – and the Queen looked into his eyes as he said 'I will'.

'The idle portion of the Town', Thomas Carlyle wrote crankily the next day, 'was in a sort of flurry owing to the marriage of little Queen Victory. I had to go out to breakfast with an ancient Notable of this place, one named Rogers, the Poet and Banker; my way lay past little Victory's Palace, and a perceptible crowd was gathering there even then, which went on increasing till I returned (about one o'clock)...' The sage of Chelsea had been on his way to 22 St James's Place, to which the elderly bachelor banker and sometime poet, bald, gnomelike Samuel Rogers, now seventy-seven, had retired in 1803 to cultivate his muse and the art of conversation. 'Streams of idle gomerils' – Carlyle was employing an obscure Scots word for *simpleton* – '[were] flowing from all quarters, to see one knows not what – perhaps Victory's gilt coach and other gilt coaches drive out, for that would be all! It was a wet day, too, of bitter heavy showers and abundant mud.'

Over breakfast, Rogers had defended the Queen against Carlyle's acerbities – 'her fooleries and piques and pettings' – and the Sage withdrew into ironic sympathy for the royal couple. 'Poor little thing, I wish her marriage all prosperity too...As for him they say he is a sensible lad; which circumstance may be of much service to him; he burst into tears on leaving his little native Coburg, a small, quiet town, like Annan [in south-west Scotland], for example; poor fellow – he thought, I suppose, how he was bidding adieu to *quiet* there, and would probably never know *it* more, whatever else he might know.'

The bridal party and guests had to return through the rain for the wedding breakfast at Buckingham Palace. Although chroniclers have written of 'Queen's weather' – sunshine – breaking through, Lady Charlotte Guest, future translator of the *Mabinogion* and wife of a Welsh ironmaster, noted in her diary (she was in a carriage directly behind Victoria's party), 'The rain was pouring in torrents, but it did not damp the hearty expression of feeling which burst from the enthusiastic crowd.' Few of the drenched onlookers had missed seeing newspaper descriptions of the wedding cakes, but the confections would elude ordinary Londoners although over a hundred were ordered. Gunter's of Berkeley Square baked fourteen – for royals and the Cabinet. One was for a banquet for élite guests after the bride and groom had departed. The primary wedding cake was a nine-foot circle on which another layer rested on pedestals, with Britannia observing the royal pair pledging their vows, Cupid apparently recording it on tablets, watched over by masses of turtle doves.

At twenty minutes to four – the couple were to leave for Windsor on the hour – Melbourne came to bid farewell to the Queen, who had changed into white silk travelling clothes. 'Nothing could have gone off better,' he crowed. Wearing a dark coat, Albert joined her, and as their carriage departed they again accepted the cheers of what Sallie Stevenson called 'her sight-loving subjects who took the rain as quietly as if it had been a passing April shower'. Fashionable London then separated into smaller celebratory parties – Lord Palmerston gave a diplomatic dinner for forty – while the newly-weds clattered toward Windsor in what Charles Greville called 'a very poor and shabby style. Instead of the new chariot in which most married people are accustomed to dash along, they were in one of the old travelling coaches, the postilions in undress liveries.'

Not only was it to be an inelegant wedding trip; it would be more abbreviated than that of many lesser folk. Albert had appealed from Gotha for some private time with Victoria at Windsor. 'It is usual in England, is it not, for newly married people to stay up to four to six weeks away from the town and society...?' He had been willing to settle for 'at least a fortnight – or a week'. Even then he had been rebuffed, the Queen having declared that her presence when Parliament sat was needed 'after the second day'. In reality their absence would encompass the working week, with the couple departing for Buckingham Palace on Friday after arriving at Windsor on Monday evening. Victoria could well have remained into Sunday, but then would not have had her way. As one lampoon put it,

> She's lovely, she is rich
> But they tell me when I marry her
> That she will wear the *britsch.*

It seemed an inauspicious beginning, and the first months of marriage would be a roller-coaster of emotions for Albert, but he saw some positive signs. The Queen, not Parliament, signed army commissions, and he had become before the wedding a field marshal with no duties, but formally more than a wearer of a dress uniform. Leaving the Palace, the couple were followed by three coaches as escort, and Albert was surprised and pleased to discover as they continued on towards Windsor that they picked up an informal additional escort of well-wishers on horseback and in gigs and carriages which scattered happy throngs in their path. Approaching Windsor in early evening darkness, they saw homes brightly lit in welcome and crowds out with lanterns.

Almost in the shadow of the Castle, masters and students at Eton waited impatiently to receive the royal couple, and the boys followed the carriage up the hill, cheering and shouting. As Victoria and Albert alighted at the quadrangle, Etonian merriment echoed off the venerable walls.

While elsewhere in the town three public banquets, one of them chaired by the mayor, celebrated the wedding, in their private suite in the Castle the Queen ordered dinner brought but could not touch it. She blamed 'such a sick headache', and was 'quite deaf' from the lusty cheering over the route from London. With Albert at her side, she spent the evening on a sofa, 'and his excessive love and affection gave me feelings of heavenly love and happiness I could never have *hoped* to have felt before. He clasped me in his arms, and we kissed each other again and again. His beauty, his sweetness and gentleness – really how can I ever be thankful enough to have such a *Husband*!' In her journal she confided that 'to be called by names of tenderness I have never heard used to me before – was bliss beyond belief!'

'*Counting the Chickens*'. *Broadside cartoon, 1840, in which Victoria expounds to Albert on possible names for their future children, largely compliments for their uncles and aunts, from Leopold to Sophia. The Prince's shocked reaction shows in his posture. (Collection of the author)*

A London cartoonist, in a broadside sold on the streets, depicted the newly-wed couple 'Counting the Chickens' at their dining-table, perhaps the morning after. 'I have decidedly made up my mind, Al', says Victoria, 'to have our first Boy named after my much respected Uncle Leopold, the next in honour of my Uncle Cambridge, Adolphus Frederick; then we must have one [named] Augustus Fred for Uncle Sussex; and then, Al, in case of twins, Albert and Edward, we will call them; there's my cousins of Hanover and Cambridge [both named George]; we mustn't forget them, you know...' In case of girls, she adds, they might use Mary, Caroline, Sophia, Wilhelmina, Louisa, and Adelaide. Albert is given no response.

'When day dawned (for we did not sleep much)', Victoria wrote of her first night as a bride, 'and I beheld that beautiful angelic face by my side, it was more than I can express! He does look so beautiful in his shirt only, with his beautiful throat seen.' Greville got it wrong when he guessed that the relationship at the start, especially on Victoria's part, was not passionately physical. 'It was much remarked', he noted, 'the Queen and the Prince...were up very early on Tuesday morning walking about, which is very contrary to her former habits. Strange that a bridal night should be so short; and I told Lady Palmerston that this was not the way to provide us with a Prince of Wales.' To Melbourne that morning after, Victoria scribbled an ecstatic message about her 'most gratifying and bewildering night'. She never thought she 'could be so loved'.

The Queen's frankness was as nothing to the *risqué* 'club wit' going the rounds about the marriage of that rare pairing among the high-born, two virgins. Richard Monckton Milnes, MP, littérateur and collector of pornography, would receive a letter from his Scottish crony Robert Monteith acknowledging 'notelets from you containing the last indecencies on the subject of Royal venery; I burn with chaste and loyal indignation, shout with laughter & end by showing the documents right and left'. In contrast was the 'simple provincial spirit' of the folk on his demesnes, Monteith gibed. 'How sincere was the mighty bonfire I raised on a hill top – how spontaneous the gush of ale & porter which it cost 9 men's toil to distribute, how cordial the vibrations of the [fiddle] catgut to which 800 people danced & reeled like Baal wor-shippers round the blazing summit...How our poor villagers lit their windows – every pane in a glow!' At the same time, he scoffed, Milnes's people in England, 'with your hearts shrivelled with meanness and envy & hate & ...debauchery[,] could only make bawdy charades on this solemn sowing of a new Royal [family] tree. Do you mean to insinuate he has dared to touch her?'

At polar opposite were Elizabeth Barrett's chaste verses, 'The Crowned and Wedded Queen', in the *Athenaeum* of 15 February 1840. Sentimentally the future Mrs Browning looked beneath the regal pageantry and celebrated 'uncrowned womanhood':

> SHE vows to love who vowed to rule –
>   (the chosen at her side)
> Let none say, 'God preserve the queen!'
>   – but rather, 'Bless the bride!'
> ...She is a *woman*, and *beloved*! – and 'tis
>   enough but so.

> Count it enough, thou noble prince, who
> tak'st her by the hand,
> And claimest for thy lady-love, our lady
> of the land!

From the start, tables were set up in the Queen's room so that they could work side by side, but the work was Victoria's. Albert could make small talk or write personal letters. Sometimes she involved him enough to record a journal entry like 'rested and read Despatches – some of which I read to Albert'. What she wanted during the first days of marriage was closeness to Albert. She would watch him shave – an occasion dramatized with great charm by Laurence Housman in his play *Victoria Regina* (1934). 'How strange it looks!' Housman had his Victoria exclaim, '. . . and how interesting! – fascinating! . . . Is it dangerous?'

'Not if you don't talk to me,' says Albert.

When Victoria dressed, in those first idyllic days, Albert would help her put on her stockings – assistance unstageable in days when the Lord Chamberlain's censor guarded theatrical propriety so rigidly that even Housman's most circumspect scenes were first forbidden because 'her near kin' were alive.

Victoria's own reaction is clear enough from a letter she would write to their cousin 'Victo' (Victoria Augusta Antoinetta). The daughter of Uncle Ferdinand was about to marry the duc de Nemours. Only weeks after her own wedding, Victoria rushed to offer such advice as 'Love him with all your heart always and then you will be happy. YOU CANNOT IMAGINE HOW DELIGHTFUL IT IS TO BE MARRIED. I COULD NOT HAVE DREAMED THAT ANYONE COULD BE SO HAPPY IN THIS WORLD AS I AM.'

Eager to show Albert off to her contemporaries, Victoria ordered Lord Clarence Paget to organize a dance for her second evening at Windsor, and had high-spirited young people in for galops and quadrilles. Privacy was in any case impossible. By their second day as husband and wife, the Duchess of Kent, Duke Ernest, the younger Ernest and their attendants had come to Windsor. Another ball followed, and on the fourteenth the Court returned to London so that the Queen could receive, with Albert, formal addresses from both Houses of Parliament, and begin a series of levées at Buckingham Palace which introduced the Prince to the many who counted in government, business and society left out of the limited list for the wedding. On each occasion Albert led in the Queen at her left hand, the place he would continue to occupy. Every visit to the theatre or to divine services became an event, as Londoners vied to glimpse the royal couple.

For Albert, a melancholy post-wedding inevitability was the departure of his father – and soon after his brother – his last links with home. Yet he knew that the tender family feelings which he professed concealed realities he could not confide to Victoria. 'He said to me', the Queen told her journal, 'that I had never known a father, and could not there-fore feel what he did. His childhood had been very happy.' If she continued to love him, he added, 'I could make up for it all'. He 'never cried', he insisted, but Coburg aides who had to part from him 'had cried so much that he was quite overcome. Oh, how I did feel for my dearest, precious husband at this moment! Father, brother, friends, country – all he has left, and all for me. God grant that I may be the happy person, the *most* happy person, to make this dearest, blessed being happy and contented! What is in my power to make him happy I will do.'

Some things the Queen could not do, and others at which she hesitated tore at older if now less tenacious loyalties. Albert was immed-iately lonely in an environment where no one else spoke English in his heavy, accented fashion, and it helped little that Victoria continued in the privacy of their domestic suite to speak in German, which kept his English more that of the written or printed page. As Ernest left for Dresden, Albert was compelled to recognize that the Saxon officer and Hereditary Heir (in the German usage) who had been almost a twin brother would not only be living a very different life, but had already done so. The symptoms of venereal infection had emerged, and Albert felt unable to speak to Ernest about his anxiety for him. At court, Victoria seemed too imprisoned by her veteran courtiers to initiate changes in her husband's favour. Louise Lehzen even questioned Albert's right to ride with the Queen in the State Carriage. Appointees through Melbourne's influence seemed to share the Prime Minister's indefinite tenure, and socialite courtiers appeared to encompass entire families, like the Pagets or the FitzClarences – the illegitimate but titled brood of William IV.

The Prince began discovering his silken bonds immediately on return from the non-honeymoon, and was not always assisted by the persistent intrusions of Stockmar, who seemed nearly as ubiquitous as Lehzen.

His bureaucratic and domestic advice, hammered at Albert in long Teutonic memoranda, urged boldness where caution was called for, and offered inapplicable remedies to peculiarly English problems. For Albert it was nevertheless not enough that his cage was gilded. Buckingham Palace had been sumptuously decorated for Victoria when she became Queen, and early in 1840 many of the rooms were equipped with gaslight. The modern lighting eased paperwork, but there was still no work for Albert to do. Making fun of his apparent uselessness, a spoof Court Circular would announce the appointment of a Toothbrush in Ordinary and a Shaving-pot in Waiting to his Royal Highness, adding, 'There is no foundation for the report that there is to be a Lord High Clothes-brush.' At first Melbourne, characteristically cynical, approved. 'The Prince is indolent,' George Anson noted Lord Melbourne as remarking, '& it would be better if he was more so, for in his position we want no activity.'

Already loyally taking the Prince's side, Anson countered that there was 'no scope' for Albert's energy. 'If you required a cypher in the difficult position of Consort of the Queen you ought not to have selected the Prince; having got him you must make the most of him, & when he sees the power of being useful to the Queen he will act.' In the early months of the marriage the Queen still confided in him only after she had consulted with Melbourne and Lehzen. Lehzen even retained her private passage into the couple's bedroom, and controlled the Queen's personal expenditures, no bill being authorized for payment until the Baroness had signed.

How the public viewed Albert's status was evident in dozens of sardonic jingles and verses making the rounds. When a paper reported that sometimes at Windsor the Queen drove her husband out in their pony carriage, another joked,

> *Why* Vic drives the Prince is plain
>   To any common view –
> The Sovereign who holds the rei[g]n
>   Should have the whip hand too.

Melbourne predicted to Greville, although it did not appear that way at the start, that the Prince would acquire 'boundless influence'. Possibly because he did not want the next – almost certainly Tory – Prime Minister to have his own influence with the Queen, Melbourne urged

Victoria to show her husband all the state papers he wished to see. Albert, he knew, would be above party. To help the process along, Melbourne began discussing public matters with Albert, and since Albert's background suggested that his interest might lie in foreign affairs, the Prime Minister urged that the Prince forward his views. 'He seldom answers me', Albert would write to his father, 'but I have often had the satisfaction of seeing him act entirely in accordance with what I have said.' For Albert, any discussion with someone as easy with words as Melbourne was painful, as his own English was awkward, and that realization, combined with his natural shyness, left the impression of a frigid reserve. Newspapers made the most of it. Victoria corrected his spelling in drafts of his letters, but even there his prose retained a rigidity that paralleled his public persona.

Albert's initiation into public life progressed slowly. When François Guizot dined at Windsor, he was looking forward to more than a social call. Palmerston was present, and Guizot, a power in the July Monarchy of Louis-Philippe, wanted to gain assistance for Turkey against the ambitions of Russia. Guizot was left to a postprandial chat with Lady Palmerston. The Queen sat on a sofa, sewing, while others gossiped round her small table. Albert played chess. Guizot was glad to be recalled in a few months to become foreign minister.

On 21 March the Queen awoke feeling unwell; recognizing the symptoms as possibly the first signs of pregnancy, she cried bitterly. Two months before the wedding she had confided to her journal how much she looked forward to marriage, and how little to childbearing – 'the ONLY thing I *dread*'. Years later she would describe pregnancy to her firstborn as 'an unhappy condition' that replaced 'happy enjoy-ment'. She was then, she confessed, 'furious'.

Whether or not Victoria blamed Albert, the satiric papers, even before the news was out, printed tales that she had begun directing her virago temper against him. One allegation was that he had, at tea, contradicted her on a trivial matter, whereupon 'the Queen sprinkled the contents of her cup over his face, which led to an estrangement for the whole evening'. Another report had Albert admiring a bouquet brought in by a pretty Maid of Honour. Allegedly Victoria dismissed Miss Pitt, then 'seized the bouquet and scattered its fragments over the room'. Whatever the truth of such gossip, the gutter press relished rumoured quarrels, common to all newlywed couples and difficult to conceal in a palace atmosphere where there was very little privacy. 'Is your Queen so much in love with her husband as to be already jealous of him?' Princess Lieven asked Lady Palmerston from Paris. 'What is to become of Prince Albert; will he always remain at his wife's side? It will be a dreary situation.' Such canards quickly crossed the Channel, as did the intelligence that the Queen was expecting, which seemed to reach Dorothea Lieven immediately after Victoria's consultation with her physician. 'Is the Queen pregnant?' she queried Lady Palmerston on April 5. 'And is her husband attempting to acquire some political influence?'

An inquiry about Albert's relations with the Queen even came, hardly more than a month after the marriage, from as far away as Rome, from the Scottish wife of the Comte de Flahault, the former Margaret Elphinstone, 'The Queen and Prince', Emily Palmerston protested, 'are very happy in their marriage, and there is no truth in any of the foolish stories that have been invented to the contrary. He is very good looking and amiable and charming, and pleases every body that approaches him. Even the mob, who are much taken with his looks and agreeable expression . . . ' Royals, however, seemed to create gossip merely by existing – almost, to the mob, a reason for their existence.

Victoria's frustrations about her pregnancy and its discomforts were for Albert's ears alone, and since she appeared to be in glowing health, the reason first went unsuspected. Lord Melbourne's advice, when the Queen confirmed that she was expecting, was to eat and drink heartily, for which she needed little prompting. Albert tried to reduce her involvement in public business, but she insisted that she was Queen, and had responsibilities uniquely her own. While shut out of her working routine and seeking things to do on the fringes of official life, he remained the focus of gossip very likely gleaned from, or invented by, Household staff. 'They say', Disraeli would prattle to his sister, Sarah, 'that Prince A[lber]t does nothing but eat[,] sing, and learn to ride* – speaks little and never but on the most trifling subjects, – very bored by his wife who is fearfully jealous. This is a Whig acc[oun]t – the Tories on the contrary maintain that he is a good Conserv[ativ]e and will make [out] all right. Fudge.'

That May, Albert wrote to Löwenstein that in his home life he was 'very happy and contented', but that he had difficulty outside it in

* In the English fashion, as opposed to German equestrian style.

finding any dignified role for himself. 'I am only the husband, and not the master in the house.' It was an awkward business to approach Victoria directly about his being left out of things, especially as he realized that her pregnancy, which she despised, would in time limit her independence, but he was only twenty, and impatient. He left it to Stockmar to approach Melbourne, who saw the Queen daily, and the two men met with Anson on 28 May after the Prime Minister brought up the subject with Victoria. The Queen conceded, Anson minuted, that Albert had complained of 'a want of confidence' both in 'trivial matters' and in 'matters connected with the politics of this country'. She blamed her own 'indolence', then confessed her belief 'that domestic harmony is more likely to follow from avoiding subjects likely to create difference'.

Albert, she did not need to say, had little knowledge of domestic English politics and had come only recently to any interest in Continental matters. Three months of residence on the other side of the Channel had not made him an expert in either realm. Still the Prince, Melbourne understood, intended to apply himself with Germanic discipline to both tasks, and he suggested tactfully that Victoria 'by degrees impart everything to him' and discuss with her husband 'any subject she pleased'.

Suspecting that Victoria's withholding royal business from Albert arose at least in part from Lehzen's attempts to retain what she recognized as a fading influence, Melbourne spoke, as he told the Queen, 'most seriously' to the Baroness, warning her that if she created dissension between husband and wife she would 'draw down ruin on herself'. Biology was against her. It was a power rivalry which Lehzen could not win. The Queen's condition not only drew husband and wife closer emotionally, but inevitably, as Victoria gradually relinquished more of the day-to-day details she had always insisted upon knowing, she threw more responsibility on to the husband. The red dispatch boxes arrived whether or not the Queen was up to them, and Albert read the contents, often to Victoria. As pregnancy increased the Queen's lassitude and the selection from the red boxes became his, Albert's informal authority and influence grew.

Without official status – he was only a recently naturalized subject of the Queen, although married to her – he had to become formally useful in other ways. One of his first ventures was to accept the presidency of the Society for the Extinction of the Slave Trade and for the Civilization of Africa. 'Civilizing' Africa meant Christianizing the continent: slavery was already illegal in the Empire. Ending the slave trade was far more difficult so long as there were markets for working bodies. France would permit slavery in its colonies until 1848; it remained lawful in the United States. Still, the international meeting was high-minded, with dozens of impassioned American abolitionists, especially women, setting the tone.

Albert found his role in the chair in keeping with the public posture he wanted to display. He wrote his own brief address – only about two hundred words – in German, then translated it with Victoria's help. Nervously he memorized it, trying out on Victoria his ringing phrases about the slave trade as 'repugnant to the spirit of Christianity' and 'the blackest stain upon civilized Europe'. Then, on 1 June 1840, he spoke before 'five or six thousand people' (in his estimate), at Exeter Hall in the Strand. Propping his remarks on the brim of his upturned hat, he opened the proceedings in his halting English, distracted only a little when his papers fell into the crown of the hat. On his conclusion, he reported to Victoria, there was 'great applause'. To attempt the address at all was an act of courage for a twenty-year-old to whom English was a foreign tongue.

'All the world has been this morning to Exeter Hall to see Prince Albert in the chair,' Disraeli wrote to Sarah. After the address Sir Robert Peel moved a vote of thanks to the Prince, and went on to describe emotionally how two slave ships in a recent storm on the high seas had battened down their hatches and caused seven hundred slaves to die from suffocation. He called for action to suppress the trade in humans. Disraeli observed 'a great effect on his Highness'. But after two hours of orations Albert slipped out, as he would learn to do on hundreds of occasions when he represented the Crown, often several times on a single day. (The chair was taken by the Earl of Ripon.)

One outcome was to support the fitting out of three vessels – one christened the *Albert* – to make contacts with the inhabitants of inland West Africa, and induce them to cease co-operation with slave traders. On 14 April the expedition sailed off, eventually to probe three hundred miles up the Niger. Of the 301 crewmen, forty-one, including one of the captains, would die of fever. The well-intentioned enterprise ended in failure.

Another gesture of Albert's would be to become a patron of the newly established London Library, which Carlyle called 'a democratic institution . . . where all men, on payment of a small annual sum, can now borrow Books . . . which in such a city as London, appetite growing by what it feeds on, may well become by and by one of the best Libraries extant . . . Prince Albert, good youth,' he added to Karl Varnhagen von Ense in Germany with unaccustomed if condescending praise, 'is Patron, by his own free offer; has given 50 pounds of money, and promises "a stock of German books".'

Ten days after the Exeter Hall baptism into public life, as the Queen and Prince drove up Constitution Hill, just above the Palace, beginning an early evening outing in the long summer light, 'a little mean-looking man' (in Albert's description), a pistol in each hand, fired a shot at them from about six paces away. Although the open phaeton made them an easy mark, the gunman missed. As he fired again, Albert drew Victoria down out of view. His reaction would have been too late for an accurate marksman, but young Edward Oxford, a waiter in a 'low inn', was slow-witted and equally slow of foot. (He would be judged guilty but

EDWARD OXFORD FIRING AT THE QUEEN AND PRINCE ALBERT ON CONSTITUTION HILL, JUNE 10ᵗʰ 1840.

A lithograph printed in June 1840 to celebrate the escape of the Queen and Prince from an assassin near Buckingham Palace.

insane.) Onlookers who had cheered the Queen and Prince seized him, and the royal couple called to the postilions to go on. They visited 'Aunt Kent' – who had been moved to Ingestre House, Belgrave Square – and took a drive through Hyde Park, Albert wrote, 'to show the public we had not... lost all confidence in them'.

The attack had no adverse effect on Victoria's pregnancy, then four months along, and now common knowledge. As the news of the attempted shooting spread across London, crowds gathered on horseback, in carriages and on foot, to hail the Queen as her carriage made its way back through the gates and Marble Arch, then still before the Palace. For days afterwards, wherever the couple went they were applauded enthusiastically, with special cheers for Albert, whose coolness was much admired in the newspapers. Spontaneous choruses of 'God Save the Queen' were common, even at the opera, where formality usually prevailed.

Addicted since her teens to opera and ballet, Victoria under Albert's tutelage also began regular playgoing, with an emphasis on Shakespeare that Professor Schlegel would have applauded. Covent Garden, under the direction of Madame Lucy Elizabeth Vestris and her husband Charles James Mathews, was then producing Shakespeare with Charles Kemble as leading actor. With Albert devoted to music, Victoria had begun going to concerts of more serious fare then heretofore. She first heard Mozart's *The Magic Flute* on 12 June 1840, when excerpts were performed at an amateur palace concert arranged by the Prince, at which he and Victoria sang a duet from Luigi Ricci's opera *Il disertore de amore*, 'Non funestar, crudele' ('Don't afflict me, cruel one!'). Luigi Lablache also took part – Albert knew he was one of the Queen's favourites – as did Battista Rubini and a lesser-known singer, Michael Costa, whom Victoria later knighted for his eminence as a conductor; and other roles were taken by the ladies and gentlemen of the Court. Even earlier, in March 1840, Albert had become a director of the Ancient Concerts, which attempted to keep alive such neglected composers as Handel.

Albert was only twenty-one that August, and too inexperienced to promote his larger ambitions. Nevertheless, he was exploiting the cultural opportunities that came his way, and Parliament registered its confidence before his birthday came, and with it his legal majority in England. He was designated Regent in the event of Victoria's death while their child was still a minor. Stubbornly, the old Duke of Sussex, the King of Hanover's brother, cast the only negative vote in the upper house. Until then, every parliamentary division had served to diminish him, as had the measure just before his marriage which stipulated that he could not possess any property that had been acquired by the Queen.

Stockmar's political efforts had made the Regency Bill possible, and on that success he quietly returned to Coburg (where he spent his summers with his family), briefing Anson before departure. The Baron's concerns about the royal couple's immaturity were still acute, but he realized that every German at Court after Albert was one too many, and that both he and Lehzen had to go. She was the conspicuous presence, relishing her Palace perquisites. Stockmar had kept a low profile from his earliest days in England, slipping in and out of Court and maintaining a residence few could locate. Albert labelled Lehzen 'the House Dragon'. He saw her removal – at minimal pain to Victoria – as his personal priority. But he had to work imperceptibly, increasing his pressure by degrees.

Lehzen even arranged who sat at dinner with Albert, for she controlled Household affairs, and Albert intervened fruitlessly with Melbourne to suggest that the Queen might be educated indirectly about practical matters by having men distinguished in scientific and cultural pursuits invited to the palace. The Prince had been bored by the courtiers, socialites, and occasional diplomats at the table, and the Prime Minister's 'She'll come round to it by and by' prompted Albert to consult Leopold. The result was that Sir John Cam Hobhouse, an MP who had been friendly with the Belgian king in his London years, came for dinner at Victoria's invitation, and through Hobhouse, once a crony of Lord Byron, Albert was able to invite Englishmen who could improve the quality of conversation as well as furnish him with useful contacts.

Altering the pool of dignitaries for whom 'covers were laid' at the Queen's table would often be a futile effort, and the Prince had to meet the people he wanted separately, and at other times. While much was made of the occasional intellectual at dinner, most guests were 'illustrious by courtesy' rather than 'illustrious by deeds', as *Punch* put it, inventing 'covers laid for forty', including authors, astronomers, sculptors, painters, geologists – 'princes of the realm of thought' – in a mock Court Circular that included authoress Joanna Baillie, painter Edwin Landseer, architect (of the new Houses of Parliament) Charles Barry, playwright Sheridan Knowles, physicist Michael Faraday, and Astronomer Royal George Airy.

A symbolic political success came when on 10 July Albert could write to Palmerston, 'The Queen thinks you might like to see the accompanying letter from the King of Portugal giving an account of proceedings at Lisbon...' It was a beginning of his personal involvement in world affairs – which was not to the foreign minister's liking – and a beginning, as well, of his acting for Victoria. There were now, also, dinners and meetings for the Prince outside the Palace, including his involvement with the medieval survival of membership in a company or guild, which had become a distinction precious to Londoners. In the City on 28 August 1840, according to the goatskin-bound New Testament on which he was sworn, His Royal Highness was 'admitted to the Freedom of the Fishmongers' Co[mpany]...the oath administered to him in their Hall on this book. A copy of the Freedom was presented in a Gold Box.'

Unfortunately, some honours recognizing the Prince's position were complicated by the rankling issue of royal precedence that failed to vanish and which Victoria and Albert felt they could not ignore. Both were furious that August when, at a banquet given for Victoria by the dowager queen, Adelaide, the Duchess of Cambridge – before her marriage only a Serene Highness herself, as the third daughter of the Landgrave of Hesse-Cassel – remained seated when Albert's health was toasted. The Queen retaliated at her next ball, when no Cambridge was invited – a marked public insult. Then Albert was invited to receive the Freedom of the City of London, the ceremony to be followed by a banquet at the Guildhall. The venison and turtle soup, the Lord Mayor promised, 'would be such as to startle the company'. But the Duke of Cambridge was present, and rather than, by protocol, sit next to him, Albert announced that he could not remain for dinner because of the illness of the Queen's aunt, the Princess Augusta. (She died on 22 September, a month later.)

Augusta, the Duke observed loudly, was his own sister, and he had heard no news so urgent. If he could stay, the Prince could also. But Albert left anyway, which meant that the Duke had to reply to the toast to Albert, the absentee that the company had assembled to honour. That the illustrious Prince could not remain, the Duke declared, was everyone's disappointment, but he thought that all would understand the validity of His Royal Highness's excuse. 'The Prince had lately married a very fine girl, and they were somehow or other very fond of each other's society.' There was loud cheering. Then the Duke added broadly that he thought that no one present would deny the Prince credit for his 'performances' to date – a smirking reference to Victoria's pregnancy that provoked more laughter and cheers.

The Queen read, to her outrage, an account of her uncle's response in the newspapers the next day. Someone had fed it to the press. Her relatives, Victoria later told her eldest daughter, 'behaved shockingly to dearest Papa. . . . I was always in a state of feud about it.' Still, the elderly dukes of the Blood Royal were taken less and less seriously. As was the Baroness Lehzen. When Parliament was to be formally closed for the session that August, Albert boasted to his brother, 'In spite of Lehzen and the Master of the Horse, I shall drive *with* Victoria in a carriage to the House of Lords, and sit beside her, on a throne especially built for me. As Lord Albemarle will not feed all the horses sent by the Shah of Persia, Imam of Muskat, Princes in India, etc.,* Arabian, Persian and Indian horses (which cannot be ridden) at his expense, I induced Victoria to make me a present of them. So I will have a stud at Windsor. V. will give me the money to keep them and I shall have the sole control over them.'

As Victoria's pregnancy advanced, Albert's control of other aspects of their lives was enhanced. At a Privy Council meeting on 11 September at Windsor, the Queen introduced Albert, implying an active role for him now that the Regency Bill had afforded him status, and Palmerston began to receive letter after letter from the Prince on the subject of confronting French ambitions in Syria and Egypt. He began to look into the ways in which Lehzen ran the Household, and the Queen's life. And an apparent prudery began to take hold at Court that observers attributed to the Prince's rigid imported morals. Yet Albert had brought with him from Germany only a distaste for what he saw, which coincided with the expansion of Wesleyan Methodism in Britain. 'Nobody is gay now', Melbourne had mourned to Victoria in the year of her accession; 'they are so religious'.

---

* Wedding presents to the pair. Albemarle, Master of the Horse, was a Whig appointment.

Evangelical religion emphasized religious revival, but also serious-ness of behaviour, respectability and the work ethic. Since the human body was the temple of the spirit, looseness in sexuality was deplored despite the awareness that economic need drove women into prosti-tution, couples into irregular unions and children into working naked deep in dark sweltering mines. Methodism was especially tainted among the upper classes by its attractiveness to the lower ones, but that appeal was strong, and the first Reform Parliaments included more and more of its adherents and sympathizers. Albert's un-English seriousness and strictness had found its time and place as the balance of political power was beginning to shift away from the ruling classes of the Regency.

People welcome at Court began to bear different histories than heretofore. The Prince's prudery, if it was that, represented what he wanted the public's perception of Victoria's court to be. He knew what it had been during the raffish reign of the Queen's uncles. And he knew the sleazy sexuality of the Coburg court under his own father, and what had happened to his mother – and what appeared to be happening to his brother. Albert had only to look around him every day for evidence of what he had escaped. Soon he would have with him not only Isaac Cart, who had been with him since childhood, but a second personal attendant, Rudolf Löhlein. The Queen later described Löhlein as the son of a forester of Füllbach, near Coburg, but her courtiers were convinced that he was a by-blow of Duke Ernest, whom he closely resembled. If so, Albert had imported his unacknowledged half-brother. He appealed to his brother to marry, and soon, without regard for the prestige or wealth of the bride – although the elder Ernest was seeking a match with the Grand Duchess Olga of Russia, rank and riches having more to do with the choice than religion or nation. Such an elevated alliance, the younger Ernest suggested, envying his brother's new prestige, would mean that he would hardly feel his marital chains.

'Chains you will have to bear in any case,' Albert warned, 'and it will certainly be good for you . . . The heavier and tighter they are, the better for you. A married couple must be chained to one another, be insepar-able, and they must live only for one another. I wish you could be here and see in us a couple united in love and unanimity.' Each, he said with evident pride, gave up things for the other, and he was ready 'to give up everything for her sake'. But, he insisted, he was not leading 'a submissive life'. He was, in the marriage, in 'the lawful position of the man'.

Ernest was offended and so was their father, as both their responses made clear. Albert, his junior, was issuing orders to the heir to the duchy, and even advising him – although Ernest had brought up the subject – not to move from Coburg to more sophisticated Gotha when his military apprenticeship to Saxony ended. Aside from the expense of 'building new houses', Albert explained, 'I should consider it a sin'. Meanwhile he recognized that both his father and brother wanted hand-outs from their rich relative, who, despite Parliament's penuriousness, had access to Victoria's capacious purse.

Victoria's love, however angry she was with herself for her pregnancy, was at least as capacious. She and Albert, whatever their lack of sexual experience, had quickly discovered a compatibility between the sheets that would last. Despite carping from outsiders about the Queen's plainness, Albert would write to his brother (22 August 1840), 'Victoria has changed much to her advantage. . . . She was lovely to look at yesterday at dinner. She had a very low-necked dress, with a bunch of roses at her breast which was swelling up from her dress.' Some of the change was the radiance of her despised pregnancy, and the bust enlargement which resulted, but Albert's pleasure was obvious.

Whether the press guessed from the results, or learned from Court gossip, the assumption was that Victoria, at least, had a Hanoverian libido. Circumstances failed to inhibit it. The Queen required a maid or dresser to sleep nightly on a sofa outside her bedroom. 'I never do otherwise', she later confided to her eldest daughter, ' . . . wherever I go – even if Papa is with me.' Further, she confessed, Albert, who was always as cold as Victoria was warm, slept 'in long white drawers, which enclosed his feet, as well as his legs, like the sleeping suits worn by small babies'. Whatever the conjunction of opposites, a published rhyme early in the marriage suggested only marital bliss, with the royal pair sipping nightcaps

> Before, like honest man and wife,
> Withdrawing into private life,
> Or, in the phrase we often hear,
> Retiring into *Bed*-fordshire . . .

With her pregnancy uneventful and Parliament prorogued, the couple remained at Windsor as long as Victoria's doctors permitted, returning on 13 November to what Albert called 'the smoky town'. Labour began in the morning darkness of 21 November, three weeks early, and lasted twelve less-than-difficult hours. The Queen remembered, forty-four years later, 'a dark, dull, windy, rainy day with smoking chimneys, and . . . Papa's great kindness and anxiety'. When Dr – later Sir Charles – Locock had first examined her and asked about her likely need for sedatives, she had insisted, 'I can bear pain as well as other people.' On his way out, he also asked Albert, who scoffed and predicted 'a great *Rompos*'.

With a shifting population of Cabinet ministers and clergy in the next room as potential witnesses by tradition, Victoria was determined to be queenly to the end, and was. 'Oh, Madam,' the dignitaries could hear Locock say before the naked baby was brought out for their inspection, 'it is a Princess.'

'Never mind', said the Queen, 'the next will be a Prince.' But her husband wrote to his brother in Dresden, sheepishly, 'Albert, father of a daughter; you will laugh at me'. Both parents, Lord Clarendon wrote to Lord Granville in Paris, 'were much disappointed at not having a son . . . but what the country cares about is to have a life more, whether male or female, interposed between the succession and the King of Hanover'.

On one of Locock's visits after the delivery, the Queen asked whether Prince Albert might read to her. When the doctor objected that a novel would be too exciting in her condition, she explained, 'No, he would read to me the lessons for the day, and as he has done so ever since we were married, it would be particularly gratifying to me now.' In an age when religion permeated the home, from morning prayers to bedtime, Locock found no way to refuse.

For the celebratory banquet following the christening on 10 February 1841, Albert composed a chorale. After writing songs as a student – a '*Reiterlied*', a '*Winterreise*', and '*Abendruhe*', and more than a dozen others – and music for piano, organ and violin, he would find less time now for composition and produced little following his marriage. But his firstborn was something special: she remained alert during the ceremonies and her father concluded proudly that she was 'very intelligent and observing'.

From the beginning, Albert was as devoted to the Princess Royal as he was to the Queen, and a rapport would grow between them unlike that with any of the later children. But Albert's solicitude for his wife was tender beyond anything she could have expected, and as she indulged in the lassitude of postnatal recovery, which physicians then preferred to prolong, she became more and more dependent upon him than she had intended. As her pregnancy had progressed, she had approved setting up writing-tables side by side in Buckingham Palace, like those in use at Windsor, and from there Albert began sending almost daily notes to Melbourne, as well as Palmerston, usually on foreign questions. Mehmet Ali, Ottoman viceroy in Egypt, had used the death of the Sultan and the succession of his sixteen-year-old son, Abdul Mejid, to attempt to break away from Turkey, exacerbating great power rivalries in the Middle East. Albert argued for the politics of conciliation rather than confrontation with France and Russia. Melbourne and Palmerston did much as they wished, but were pulled back into more temperate language by the Prince's intervention. Carefully, however, Melbourne's messages went to Victoria, with reference to 'the Prince's observations'. More and more, even the letters in Victoria's hand would be based on Albert's 'observations'.

The Court returned to Windsor for Christmas, which was celebrated in German fashion. Gifts were placed on tables under small Christmas trees, with each table and tree, decorated with candles, sweetmeats, and cakes hung by ribbons and paper chains, intended for a different recipient. Introduced from Germany earlier in the century, credit for their popularity is sometimes given to Queen Adelaide, and even to George III's Queen Charlotte, who had set up a tree of yew branches at Windsor. But Albert imported small trees from Coburg, and turned the royal family's Christmases into semi-public events. The fashion caught on, popularized by the new illustrated papers.

Not intended as a Christmas present to Albert, but timed almost as such, was Albert's own key to the prized red boxes in which Cabinet papers were delivered. During the last weeks of Victoria's pregnancy he had handled all her business, and become, as Anson put it, 'in fact, tho' not in name, Her Majesty's Private Secretary'. Since authority gravitates to its user, Albert quickly took advantage of an incident several weeks before Christmas when 'the Boy Jones' was discovered lolling about in Buckingham Palace. Edmund Jones had climbed a wall and crept through a window, 'sat upon the throne', he said, 'saw the Queen and heard the Princess Royal squall'. Home Office interrogation revealed that he was seventeen, stunted in growth, and the son of a tailor in Cannon Row. A chronic intruder, he had been declared insane the first time, and discharged; this time he was sentenced to three months for vagabondage, after which he returned once more, and following three more months on the treadmill at Tothill Street he was sent to sea.

The royal couple had known little about the lax security that had encouraged the curiosity of 'Boy Jones' and an even earlier 'Boy Cotton'. Now, Albert had a reason to reform the slipshod administration of the palace. To accomplish that meant removing the stewardship reins that Lehzen had been accumulating from her hands, but Albert was determined to end the palace inefficiencies as well as the Baroness's powers. For both he needed some further pretext, and he began to look for one.

One area of the Queen's life he could begin to organize was the business of the Duchy of Cornwall, which furnished hereditary income in 1840 of £36,000. One-third of that, Albert discovered, disappeared in administrative costs. He began cutting expenses and raising revenues, furnishing the royal couple with more discretionary funds. He also began organizing the Queen's day, which before marriage had begun so late that much of it was wasted. They began to breakfast regularly at nine, then took a walk, and worked on incoming and outgoing correspondence immediately after. Relaxing after their business, they drew or etched together.

When at Windsor or at Buckingham Palace, they would lunch together at two, after which Victoria, often now accompanied by Albert, would meet with one or more of her Ministers, usually Melbourne. (When the Queen was at Windsor, 'Lord M.' usually lived there unless Parliament was sitting.) Then the royal couple would drive in the park in a pony phaeton, the Prince at the reins. (If the Prince was away on his own or the Queen's affairs, as became increasingly frequent, she went for a drive with her ladies-in-waiting, or her mother.) Dinner was at eight, usually with guests. Before or after dinner one often read to the other, Albert reading 'serious' works, Victoria reading fiction.

Sometimes they went over albums of their own drawings, or of engravings and etchings they had begun to purchase. The Prince's art interests had been quickly recognized in London, and later in the new year Peel would appoint him chairman of a royal commission (at first a

select committee) 'to take into consideration the Promotion of the Fine
Arts of this Country, in connexion with the Rebuilding of the Houses
of Parliament'. At the studio of John Lucas, a portrait painter and
engraver for whom Albert would sit, Elizabeth Barrett visited and
talked, she wrote to her friend Miss Mitford, 'of Prince Albert & his
talents', quoting Lucas as saying, 'If he had studied five years under
Raffael, his remarks could not have been acuter.' Lucas, she added
cattily, thought the Prince 'very handsome, & the Queen charmless if
you except the pleasant countenance & youthful freshness'.

At Windsor during the holidays Albert received a letter informing
him of his brother's 'severe illness' – a recurrence of a venereal infection,
he realized. 'I am deeply distressed and grieved . . .' he wrote to Ernest
on New Year's Day. 'I have to infer that it is a new outbreak of the same
disease which you had here.' As a 'loving brother', he urged Ernest to
give up thoughts of marriage until his health was restored, as 'to marry
would be as immoral as dangerous . . . for you. If the worst should
happen, you would deprive your wife of her health and honour.'
Further, he might sire 'a sick heir'. Neither prudery nor shame got in
the way of Albert's candour. 'For God's sake,' he appealed, 'do not trifle
with matters which are so sacred.'

Returning to Buckingham Palace early in January for the resumption
of Parliamentary business, the royal couple learned of a controversy
about them in Paris that had already reached London – yet which
afterwards vanished from history. Lord Granville, Palmerston's envoy
to France, had objected to a farce due to open on 9 January at the
Théâtre de Renaissance, *Il était une fois un roi et une reine* – 'Once upon
a time there was a king and queen'. Rejected seven times by the Board
of Censorship of the Department of Fine Arts, it had been finally
approved for performance in 'mutilated' form (according to the Paris
press). The author, Léon Gozlan, was a novelist whose only previous
play had been a failure. His new work was set in the English court, and
Granville objected vigorously to its alleged slanders on Victoria and
Albert, who according to the play was 'a husband who is not a king'.

Granville's charges of questionable references to the Crown had been
lodged before, and the sanctioned text allegedly contained no identification of the rulers or nation, yet the two principal characters were still
in positions equivalent to that of Queen and husband. On the day
before the opening, with handbills distributed and posted, the censor-

ship office learned that political radicals, many of them students, planned to fill the theatre, cheer every reference that could be construed as anti-English (as Palmerston's policies were considered hostile to French interests), then exit toward the British embassy, where they intended to break all the windows. Guizot, now Minister of the Interior, consulted with King Louis-Philippe and decided against risking a rupture with London. At four o'clock on the afternoon of the ninth, a few hours prior to performance, a police commissioner with his deputies ordered the playbill removed and replaced with an *affiche* reading '*Relâche par ordre*'.

The opposition French press was apopleptic about the slight 'to the honour of France'. *The Times* responded with an attack on the mob spirit of Paris, and praised the French government's 'desire not to subject a young Queen and the Prince her consort to allusions, and perhaps to ridicule'. Although rebuffed, Gozlan briefly became a local hero. Prudently, some months later, he transferred his locale to Sweden and on 24 December 1842, the play began a run of sixty performances, after which it was never heard of again.

A month to the day after the suppression of Gozlan's farce, Albert had a more local embarrassment. Winter temperatures had been bitter, and the pond in Buckingham Palace Gardens had frozen over enough to tempt him into ice skating, an accomplishment in which he took pride. 'I was making my way to Victoria, who was standing on the bank with one of her ladies,' Albert wrote to *Grossmutter* Gotha, '...when within some few yards of the bank I fell plump into the water, and had to swim for two or three minutes in order to get out. Victoria was the only person who had the presence of mind to lend me assistance; her lady [in waiting] being more occupied in screaming for help.' The shock from the chill was 'painful', as he had gone in over his head, but he had no more than a cold thereafter, which fortunately held off until after the christening of Victoria Adelaide Mary Louisa the next day.

Recognizing the imminence of political change and attempting to keep the Court above politics, Albert prevailed upon Victoria to invite the old Duke of Wellington, so recently considered her bitter enemy, to stand in at the christening for the designated godfather, Albert's ailing brother Ernest. 'The Duke is the best friend we have', Victoria assured herself in her journal. Albert was pleased that the infant's heraldic device would bear the Saxon arms 'in the middle of the English'.

The Saxon 'in the middle of the English' suggested something of Albert's trials with his adopted tongue, although he worked at it assiduously, writing his English in large, almost childish, hand to get it right. Carlyle, never happier than when dispraising someone, would refer to him (to Monckton Milnes on 9 March) as 'His Serene Highness the Incarnate-Solecism Prince Albert'. Almost at the same time Albert was writing to his brother to anticipate more christenings: 'It will interest you to hear that we are expecting an increase of our family. Victoria is not very happy about it.' The Queen had herself, as well as the state of medicine, to blame. Since the only respectable method of birth control was abstinence, the passionately fond young couple, both only twenty-one and even more ignorant of contraception than their doctors, had to take for granted that biological roulette was the mandate of Divine Providence. Artificial methods of birth control were condemned by the Church; and most nineteenth-century physicians who had the temerity to recommend the semi-abstinence of a rhythm method (would a Queen's gynaecologist have had the courage?) were confused about the menstrual cycle. Assuming that women were like animals in heat, many recommended against intercourse immediately after the menses and considered it safe in mid-month.

Seventeen years later Victoria would write to her eldest daughter, 'I had constantly for the first 2 years of my marriage...aches – and sufferings and miseries and plagues – which you must struggle against – and enjoyments etc. to give up – constant precautions to take...' It was 'the yoke of a married woman' that no queen who desired a spouse could evade – yet 'certainly it is unbounded happiness – if one has a husband one worships! It is a foretaste of heaven.' Albert's solicitude in her pain was enormous, leading the insensitive Stockmar to warn that the Prince could be setting an inescapable pattern of docility that would erode the powers already accruing to him. A change of ministry was inevitable, and Stockmar wanted Albert to gain by it as Victoria was certain to lose the personal relationship she had enjoyed with the avuncular Melbourne. 'Be you, therefore,' Stockmar enjoined Albert, 'the Constitutional genius of the Queen.'

Stockmar's letter from Coburg was dated 18 May. On 8 May, Albert had already sent Anson to Peel, who seemed certain to succeed Melbourne, to consult about the Queen's ladies. Sir Robert's 'doggedness', Melbourne had warned Anson, might cause the Bedchamber once more to become a battleground of principle. Albert felt that both sides had to yield. Without informing Victoria, he had Anson recommend a compromise whereby the Queen would announce the 'resignations' of her three most politically visible ladies.

A stickler for protocol, perhaps because he was born into the acquired purple of manufacturing wealth rather than the aristocracy of land, Peel countered that Albert should furnish him with a list of ladies acceptable to the Queen from whom he would make, and announce, a selection. The appointments were to be perceived as his. Victoria was furious. Peel could select and *she* would appoint. Seeing that his future in political accommodation required some sort of initial success, Albert sent Anson back. This time the Prince's formula was that Peel could inform the ladies of the Household as to the Queen's intentions for them, while Victoria would offer each personally the actual appointment. Consulting Wellington, Peel discovered a convert to the Crown. 'The truth is,' he wrote to Peel, 'that all I desire is to be as useful as possible to the Queen's service – to do anything, to go anywhere...'

Although the compromise was settled, Melbourne's fall did not take place in May, or even in June. Division after division in the Commons went against the Whigs, with a vote of no confidence on 4 June – actually three in the morning on 5 June – failing by only one vote. Change was certain, however, and both Albert and Peel understood that they would get along but that it would take Albert to bring along the Queen.

As the elections approached to which Melbourne looked forward as his only hope of remaining in office, the Queen agreed to a round of Whig country house visits to help prop up the party's chances. Unhappily, Albert accompanied the Queen as was essential, visiting the Palmerstons at Pansanger and Woburn, and Melbourne at Brocket. Emily Palmerston described the multitude of Victoria's subjects looking on at Brocket (where she was also hostess for her brother) as 'an ampitheatre of heads' while Melbourne 'with his grey hair floating in the wind and the Queen on his arm... walked her round the lawn'. Afterwards there was a dinner for thirty-six in the ballroom. 'Albert', she added in her letter to Elizabeth Huskisson, widow of the one-time Colonial Minister, 'is like the Prince of a fairy Tale, all perfection'.

*

The royal reception was very different when the Prince's turn at centre stage came at Oxford, where he was awarded an honorary doctorate. In the Sheldonian Theatre the Queen was cheered, as was Albert, but, Greville wrote, 'her Ministers, individually and collectively, were hissed and hooted with all the vehemence of Oxonian Toryism. Her Majesty said she thought it very disrespectful to the Prince to hiss her Ministers in his presence; but she must learn to bear with such manifestations of sentiment, and not fancy that these *Academici* will refrain from expressing their political opinions in any presence, even her own.'

Unused to the electoral system, Albert observed the turmoil with amusement. He had heard the Whig arguments for Free Trade and the rejectionist arguments for Protection from the conservative wing of the Tories, yet realized that seats in the House of Commons were being won less on the price of bread than on the price of a vote. He was less amused on learning that Lehzen, an outspoken Whig, had given £15,000 of the Queen's money to the party coffers. When Albert confided his horror to Melbourne, the Prime Minister shrugged off the complaint, observing that the few thousands were nothing compared to what George III used to spend on elections. Bribery and corruption were widespread; the Reform Bill, despite its merits, had also increased the number of new voters whose ballots candidates, inured to bribery, attempted to purchase, and many non-voters also expected something for their vocal support, something that Albert – and the Queen – did not realize when they were greeted at Ascot with prearranged cheers and loud cries of 'Melbourne for ever!' Even so, it was clear that the Whigs were unpopular and that the Tories would get their chance.

Victoria dissolved Parliament on 29 June. The Whigs were smashed, and despite second thoughts about resignation by the Duchess of Bedford, she and two other ladies were replaced. Victoria's initial feeling (according to Anson) 'that she had been hurried and compromised by the Prince and Lord Melbourne', was quickly over, but not before a scene that Anson watched with dismay. 'The Q[ueen] ... burst into tears which could not be stopped for some time – & said that she could Not force the Duchess [of Bedford] to resign – they could not make her do that & she would never appoint any Tories ...'

'The P[rince] said, in this moment all shd be done to quiet you & get you over difficulties & it was shameful on the part of those who attempted to convert her mind...'

Albert was clearly accusing Lehzen, behind the scenes, but the Queen's summons to Peel on the evening of 29 August was Whiggishly frigid. Still, he understood that Albert and Anson would prevent the embarrassments of 1839. At half past twelve noon the next day, the new Prime Minister kissed hands and spent twenty minutes assuring Victoria that he was anxious to do whatever was agreeable to her, and would not even press ministerial recommendations upon her on their first interview.

The three principal Whig ladies at Court had already offered their resignations, as recommended; and Albert, the Queen learned, had asked his two leading Household officers, both Whigs, to resign. Anson remained the intermediary for Albert in choreographing mutual concessions, and on 1 September Peel told Lord Ellenborough, who was riding in a carriage with him from the railway station at Slough, 'Prince Albert is altogether with us'. It was already evident, even outside officialdom, that the Prince, who had just passed his twenty-second birthday, was an assiduous planner and did not intend to be a political cipher. Writing to the actor William Macready on 24 August, Charles Dickens observed of one of their friends that he had 'gone into his case as if he were Prince Albert, laying down all manner of elaborate projects...' For better or worse, Albert had established that reputation.

Victoria had remained prone to depression through her entire second pregnancy. She was in her seventh month when she had to preside over the ceremonial changes of the ministries on 4 September 1841. The Privy Council was summoned to Claremont, Leopold's former estate near Esher, where Victoria and Albert had retreated for privacy. Greville, the Council's secretary, found the Queen there 'with the Prince, and the table covered with bags and boxes' – the seals of office just relinquished by outgoing Whig ministers, and their dispatch boxes. Recognizing Victoria's emotional and physical burdens, the new Tory appointees praised her dignity and fairness in the proceedings. 'This struck me', Greville wrote, 'as a great effort of self-control, and remarkable in so young a woman. Taking leave is always a melancholy ceremony, and [those] whom she thinks are attached to her, together with all the reminiscences and reflections which the occasion was

calculated to excite, might well have elicited uncontrollable emotions.'
Peel told Greville that she had behaved 'perfectly'.

What Peel did not know at the time was that at her emotional
parting with Melbourne she had asked him, unwisely, to continue
contacts. Their emotional bonds were too great to be severed at once,
and it would require both Anson and Stockmar to ensure that Melbourne kept his political distance. Sensing his opening, Albert also
urged Melbourne, through Anson, to suggest to the Queen that her
husband be her future guide on political questions. Melbourne duly
wrote that he had 'formed the highest opinion of HRH's judgement,
temper and discretion', and that the Queen 'cannot do better than have
recourse to it'. That, too, was a changing of the guard as great as the
ministerial one, and it would be even longer-lasting. While the Queen
was lying-in for the birth of her second child, Peel sent Albert nightly
reports of debates in the Commons and discussions in the Cabinet. A
year earlier, Albert had not even had his own key to the boxes.

VI

Taking Hold

1841–1843

A 'PRIVATE LETTER' FROM Hanover, *Punch* joked, revealed that 'precisely at twelve minutes to eleven in the morning on the ninth of the present November, his majesty King Ernest was suddenly attacked by a violent fit of blue devils. All the court doctors were immediately summoned, and as immediately dismissed, by his Majesty, who sent for the Wizard of the North (recently appointed royal astrologer), to divine the mysterious cause of this so sudden melancholy. In a trice the mystery was solved – Queen Victoria "was happily delivered of a prince"! . . . There are now two cradles between the Crown of England and the White Horse of Hanover. We have a Prince of Wales!'

'From some crotchet of Prince Albert's,' Greville complained, 'they put off sending intelligence of her Majesty being in labour till so late that several of the Dignitaries, whose duty it was to assist at the birth, arrived after the event had occurred, particularly the Archbishop of Canterbury and the Lord President of the Council.' The actual reason was a series of earlier false alarms, but it was now predictable that the young father of the newborn prince would be blamed for anything that made bureaucrats unhappy. Yet it did not displease male officialdom that Albert had accrued authority as Victoria had relinquished it to childbearing. The Queen's womanly role better suited her sex, and Albert was unexcitable and businesslike.

The Queen and Prince fitted the figurehead conception many in government had of post-Reform Bill constitutional monarchy. John Stuart Mill would visualize the system as one in which 'the so-called sovereign does not govern, ought not to govern, is not intended to govern; but must yet be held up to the nation, be addressed by the nation, and even address the nation, as if he or she did govern'. On the day of the birth of Albert Edward, the future Prince of Wales, the crowds that enthusiastically sang 'God Save the Queen' wherever Victoria's subjects gathered, were acclaiming a sovereign who reigned rather than ruled. But behind the royal façade Albert would seek a more influential activist role for the sovereign and, indirectly, for himself.

Recognizing that some powers required position and opportunity rather than parliamentary sanction, Albert acted for the Queen during her lying-in and even beyond the christening on 25 January. His relationship with Peel flowered, and the Prime Minister, eager to have the Palace friendly rather than frosty, accepted Albert almost as a surrogate son. They discussed German literature, which Peel admired, and the Prince presented him with a lavish new edition of the *Nibelungenlied*, warmly inscribed. They discussed Dutch paintings, and the state of the arts in England. They hunted for pheasant and hare in Windsor Great Park on mornings when the Prime Minister was in residence, Peel in his town clothes and with borrowed gun. And Peel and his foreign minister, Lord Aberdeen, condoned Albert's communications in the Queen's stead with Continental monarchs.

Once Parliament resumed its sittings in February 1842 Peel began sending Albert confidential memoranda on proposed amendments to the Poor Law of 1834 that had established coldly economical workhouses separating even spouses by sex, and to the Corn Laws establishing import duties on grain, which the Prime Minister, despite fierce opposition from die-hard Tories, hoped to eliminate. If the Prince were interested, he would continue the practice. Albert, it appeared, was interested in everything. He began signing his letters to Peel 'always, my dearest Sir Robert'. The tall, commanding, workaholic Peel was something new for Albert – an English father-figure who sought the role and fitted the Prince's needs. Rarely able to expose his emotions – Irish MP Daniel O'Connell described Peel's forced smile as 'like the silver plate on a coffin' – he was honest, honourable and businesslike, with an encyclopaedic grasp of past legislation and parliamentary studies. Between Peel and the Prince the smiles were genuine.

With assistance in drafting responses from Anson and Stockmar, who shuttled between Coburg and London, Albert put further distance between Victoria and her out-of-office father-figure, the amiable Melbourne. The Duke of Kent had died when his daughter was eight months old. Only Leopold had replaced him – until Melbourne. A quiet contest for power was inherent in the move, but Albert insisted that continued political contacts with the former Whig leader might injure her relations with the Tory ministry. Both Melbourne and the Queen were peeved, but the former Prime Minister kept to friendly gossip and Peel was appreciative.

Claiming postpartum fatigue, Victoria argued that some levées could be conducted with Albert and without her, but the experiment was not a success. However curious her subjects were about Albert, they wanted only to *see* him, but to kiss the ringed hand of their Queen. Actress Fanny Kemble recalled a drawing-room reception in 1842 at which the Queen presided, and where, 'in great uncertainty of mind' as to whether she should look at Victoria, she lowered her eyes and kissed 'a soft white hand which I believe was hers'. Eyes still down 'I saw a pair of very handsome legs, in very fine silk stockings, which I am convinced were not hers, but am inclined to attribute to Prince Albert'.

Victoria would suffer from more than postpartum fatigue following each accouchement. As her pregnancies would advance, and into the months following each birth, she resented her condition, however unavoidable, and would lash out at her husband, who could no more prevent the circumstances than could the Queen. And their turbulent exchanges could not be private where servants were ubiquitous. Pained, Albert learned to respond quietly, in handwritten notes.

Taking control in the Household became easier for Albert after the birth of the Prince of Wales. Without consulting Lehzen, he appointed Lady Lyttelton in April to take charge of the royal children. Born Lady Sarah Spencer, she was well connected and a widowed mother of five. Her appointment accelerated the erosion of Lehzen's domination, which the Baroness herself hurried on by proposing that she oversee the Duchy of Cornwall revenues, usually linked with the Prince of Wales, and that nursery expenses be drawn from them. Since Anson's authority came in part from being comptroller of the Duchy's revenues, he and Albert perceived Lehzen's bid as a test of strength.

Whatever the Baroness's credits with the Queen, and they were many and well-earned, she had outlived her role. Victoria, in her lack of experience, had depended upon Lehzen. Although the Baroness had

CUPID OUT OF PLACE.

Punch in 1843 observing Albert's apparent lack of any employment but his siring of the succession.

no official title, and was innocent of administrative detail, she had been given a proliferation of duties and responsibilities. While her interests were focused upon the Queen, sinecures and perquisites flourished. Courtiers, from titled officials to humble attendants, lived and dined on Victoria's purse; tradesmen furnished supplies that went elsewhere than Buckingham Palace or Windsor; and horses and carriages were ordered by anyone willing to sign someone else's name. While few of the figures presented for inspection were verifiable, no one had ever been concerned about that before.

Unsophisticated about the costs of anything, Victoria entertained often and lavishly, and gave expensive gifts. In 1839 alone – her last year without Albert – she spent £34,000 from her Privy Purse on pensions and charities, and £600 on her box at the opera. In the first three months of 1840, when royal guests had come for the wedding, inflating normal expenditures, 24,600 dinners were served at Buckingham Palace. At Windsor Castle the year before, 113,000 dinners were served, not including the grand ball suppers. Even when the Court was not in residence, more than a dozen large joints of meat were roasted daily for the servants permanently present. The statistics also included people who elected to dine at the Queen's expense because it was easy to do. Many of the meals billed for may have never been served, with someone pocketing the funds. The christening of the Prince of Wales cost the Queen's purse £4,991 16s. 5d. Yet this was an age when the pound sterling was so sturdy and inflation so low that a shilling – a twentieth of a pound – could purchase a dinner, and a penny – a twelfth of a shilling – could post a letter.

Laurence Housman's stage-Albert explains to Victoria, 'One of the things I discovered was that anything once ordered always goes on being ordered. The thing is sent in and paid for, but it is not used.' It was very nearly like that. In the palaces, Albert observed, hundreds of candles were placed in chandeliers and candelabras daily, then replaced even if never lighted. He discovered – the Queen had never noticed – that since Queen Anne's day the privilege of selling 'Palace ends' for pocket money had been that of the servants. Similar sinecures existed at Windsor Castle, such as the thirty-five shillings that a half-pay officer received annually for 'Red Room wine' meant for a captain of the guard last on duty in the reign of George III.

Getting Court management under control would be a slow process. Too many absentee authorities officially oversaw such matters. In Lehzen, however, Albert had someone to blame for at least part of the chaos. He had already enlisted Stockmar to do research on the problems and possible solutions, all of which would make many more besides the Baroness unhappy. Still, consolidating administrative functions and powers, as much as he could within existing traditions and regulations, in his own hands and those of George Anson as his deputy, required pushing Lehzen aside. Since all her powers were informal, Albert needed only Victoria's acquiescence. He confronted the Queen with a litany of Household waste and inefficiency detailed in Stockmar's memorandum. When Victoria refused to see Lehzen as obsolete, or the relationship with the Baroness as dangerous, Albert explained to Stockmar, Victoria 'has never been away from her, and like a very good pupil, [she] is accustomed to regard her governess as an oracle. Besides this, the unfortunate experience they went through together at Kensington had bound them still closer, and Lehzen, in her madness, has made Victoria believe that whatever good qualities she possesses are due to her.' He saw 'the welfare of my children and Victoria's existence as sovereign' at stake if Lehzen remained, and through the first weeks of 1842 there were bitter words exchanged between husband and wife, each writing to Stockmar in Coburg as intermediary.

'Victoria is too hasty and passionate...' Albert explained. 'She will not hear me out but flies into a rage and overwhelms me with reproaches of... want of trust, ambition, envy, etc., etc. There are, therefore, two ways open to me: (1) to keep silence and go away (in which case I am like a schoolboy who has had a dressing down from his mother and goes off snubbed); (2) I can be still more violent (and then we have scenes... which I hate, because I am sorry for Victoria in her misery, besides which it undermines the peace of the home)...'

The Queen insisted to Stockmar that Albert exaggerated the Baroness's influence. 'I have often heard Albert own that everybody recognized Lehzen's services to me and my only wish is that she should have a quiet home in my house and see me sometimes... about papers and *toilette* for which she is the greatest use to me... Dearest Angel Albert, God only knows how I love him. His position is difficult, heaven knows, and we must do everything to make it easier.' In a later letter to Stockmar, on 20 January 1842, Victoria acknowledged that she was 'so passionate when spoken to', an impulse she feared was 'irremediable', and made her say 'cross and odious things which I don't myself believe and which I fear hurt A., but which he should not believe'. Their position was 'very different to any other married couples. A. is in my house and not I in his. – But I am ready to submit to his wishes as I love him so dearly.'

Submission came when the Princess Royal became seriously ill and Albert blamed 'Pussy's' condition on Victoria's toleration of Lehzen's mishandling of the nursery and Sir James Clark's continuing incompetence. Dr Clark, Albert told the Queen in a note, 'has mismanaged the child and poisoned her with calomel, and you have starved her. I shall have nothing more to do with it; take the child away and do as you like, and if she dies you will have it on your conscience.'

The war was over, although more battles would be fought – delaying actions by Lehzen. Had she made any conciliatory gestures toward Albert, she might have rescued her place in the palace. Instead, the Baroness discovered that her departure was the price of the Queen's future happiness. As with Peel and the ladies of the Court, Albert took the initiative when he saw his opportunity. By then, anticipating her expulsion, she had quietly passed on her responsibility to make copies of Victoria's outgoing correspondence in a letter-press to the Queen's loyal dresser, Marianne Skerret. The niece of Queen Charlotte's sub-treasurer, she had entered Victoria's service in 1837, and would remain into 1862, largely writing letters to tradespeople.

On 25 July, Albert informed Victoria that Lehzen had decided to retire because of her health. Since the Baroness was a vigorous fifty-six, Victoria understood that it was a move 'for our & her best'. Lehzen was presented with a carriage and a pension of £800, an annual income which would enable her to live in comfort in Germany. At the end of September she slipped out of London without any farewells – a gesture to spare Victoria's tears – and went to Bückeburg, a quiet town west of Hanover. Lehzen's sister, with whom she intended to live, died unexpectedly three months later. The Baroness remained alone, in a house filled with royal memorabilia, until her own death at eighty-six, in 1870.

It was Lehzen, Albert claimed to Anson, who was responsible for the Queen's fears of intellectual inadequacy. She had overseen Victoria's education and had kept it at an inferior level. It was true that Victoria knew little about science and technology, Albert's chief passions, and was reluctant to bring them into her conversation. She knew more about art and music, interests he shared, but her tastes were rather conventional. She knew still more about history and politics, and understood their direct importance to her; but Albert saw that as only a beginning, and had set to work to become her Stockmar as well as her university. When she began to lean more and more on her husband's competencies, and later, when she would have to work alone, her ministers would confront a shrewd mind and a sharp writing style. At twenty-three, Victoria did not have some of the sophistication that might have been useful during country-house weekends, but she had survived her upbringing well. Further, few people would dominate her intellectually, if only because as Queen she could select her conversation topic or dismiss it.

Whatever the external frustrations in his own position, Albert could see growth in Victoria's grasp of her role, and could preen himself for having added a dimension to it. When Victoria was having her hair done, she read *Cornwallis on the Sacrament* or Guizot's *Révolution de l'Angleterre.* When Felix Mendelssohn came to England in June 1842 to conduct a performance of his new A minor (*Scottish*) Symphony, Victoria invited him and his wife Cécile to Buckingham Palace. On June 20, the composer, thirty-three but small and boyish under a mass of curly black hair, arrived to play for the royal couple, giving them a recital of his *Songs Without Words.* Afterwards, he and Cécile were taken to tea in the Grand Gallery. Before they left, Albert invited the Mendelssohns back the following Saturday so that Felix could try the palace organ; and he returned to play 'How Lovely Are the Messengers' from his *St Paul,* with Albert assisting with the stops.

The musical capacities of Victoria and Albert, Mendelssohn discovered, went beyond any social requirements. First, Albert played a chorale, 'by heart, with the pedals, so charmingly, clearly and correctly, that it would have done credit to any professional ... and then all the music sheets going all over the floor, and being picked up by the Queen'.

Finding the pages she wanted, Victoria sang the lyrical '*Italien*', and then with Mendelssohn at the piano she tried his '*Lass dich nur*' – 'really quite faultlessly, and with charming feeling and expression', the composer wrote to his mother.

Then the Prince sang the '*Erntelied*', also from the *Pilgerspruch*, and finally Mendelssohn improvised happily on the piano from musical themes the couple recognized, then took his leave. It seems likely that in conversation the forthcoming royal trip to Scotland came up, for once back in Germany Mendelssohn wrote to the Queen to obtain her permission to dedicate his symphony, inspired by Scottish airs and dances, to her.

For royal travel, the Great Western Railway Company had designed a State carriage, short (even by 1840s standards) and ornate, with a small crown on the roof, its interior suggesting a small but opulent parlour. On 14 June 1842, the Queen and Prince made a trial journey in it, on the new line from Slough, near Windsor, to Paddington Station in London. The Queen announced herself 'quite charmed', but Albert worried about dangerously excessive speed – fifty miles an hour. (It was the year that J. M. W. Turner was painting his brilliantly impressionist 'Rain, Steam and Speed – the Great Western Railway'.)

For the trip to Scotland the Court proceeded on 29 August, in a convoy of carriages, to Slough, where they boarded a special train of engine, luggage tender, royal saloon, and two carriages for attendants and railway officials. (Twenty-seven royal horses and five carriages went on in advance.) The party would change to carriages at Paddington, crossing the city to Woolwich, where they embarked on the antiquated yacht *Royal George*.

The voyage was unpleasant. The *Royal George* had ferried the eight-months-pregnant Duchess of Kent from Calais to Dover in 1819 and was a cumbersome sailing ship in the new age of steam. Lurching to Scotland, it was towed by two steamers, and the uneven strain on the tow ropes, combined with the North Sea swells, left the royal party severely seasick. The planning had been meticulous, except for the obsolescence of the *Royal George*.

Yet the royal tour went well. 'The Highlands and the mountains are too beautiful', Victoria wrote to Melbourne from Taymouth on 10 September, 'and we *must* come back for longer another time.' (She was still corresponding with Melbourne, but neither Peel nor the Prince was concerned any more, as the letters now exchanged felicities and trivialities.) Besides, Peel had accompanied her on the voyage, and was working at winning her confidence. He was 'very nervous', Peel later told Greville, for the tour went through 'disturbed districts' where there had been unrest among the working class, but the outpouring of loyalty to the Crown impressed Victoria and Albert.

Scottish devotion remained high for the full fourteen days. Few English sovereigns spent any time north of the Tweed. For Scots, the Prince had been little more alien than the Queen. Accompanying newspapermen leaped at Albert's failure to comprehend the Scottish 'Ben' (from the Gaelic *beann*) for 'peak'. An equerry had observed that

Ben Lomond held his head particularly high during their visit. 'Benjamin who, did you say?' asked the Prince.

'Ben Lomond,' explained the equerry.

'Oh, Benjamin Lomond,' Albert insisted with studious Germanic formality

Recognizing, however, their forests that reminded Albert of Thuringia, the *Caledonian Mercury* predicted happily 'no long absence of the royal pair; and perhaps . . . the formation of a more permanent tie with Scotland'. It might have been initiated even then, as they refused to return on the heaving *Royal George*, waiting instead for the steamship *Trident*. A paddle-wheeled royal yacht would be ordered for future progresses by sea. 'Utilitarianism must prevail over the Romantic and Picturesque even in the case of Royal Voyages', Peel would explain to the Earl of Haddington at the Admiralty. 'Towing, after all, is but an ignoble process.' He had been aboard, and he knew.

Once back with their red boxes, the Queen and Prince recognized the extent of the foreign policy concerns that their domestic affairs had put out of mind. The press made much of disputes with the United States, a major unfriendly power, over Canada's border with Maine and over the Admiralty's right to search ships suspected of slave trading; and new British interventions in Afghanistan, India, Persia and China – where Hong Kong had been seized as a base for trade. From Paris, the government of the bourgeois monarch, Louis-Philippe, was intriguing in adjacent Spain, where England supported the weak regency of a child queen under her mother, Maria Cristina. The Regent, Victoria wrote to Aberdeen, 'is thoroughly attached to England'. That would always be the index to her policies. After reading a draft of a message to her ambassador in Portugal, she returned it to Aberdeen with the suggestion 'to *soften* the words under which she has drawn a pencil line'. The matter was not as important as the conciliatory intent and the continuing intervention with her ministers. It made no difference that Albert may have drafted the original of a memorandum that Victoria then rewrote in her own hand. It was in the Queen's name that both then insisted on being informed, and on making their views known.

Among Albert's appointments, arranged by Peel, was to preside over the committee to oversee the internal decoration of the new Houses of Parliament. Such chairmanships were usually honorific, but the Prince went to the meetings, Lady Holland wrote on 19 April, and 'shews not only taste but considerable knowledge. One great question is how the walls are to be treated. Fresco paintings are proposed.' The subjects suggested were incidents from British history and from works by major poets, and when Milton was named, Albert turned to Lord John Russell, a widower who had recently remarried, asking, 'Perhaps you would approve of passages from *Paradise Regained*?' Lady Holland was impressed. 'This was very well for a Royal joke, & in a foreigner.'

Three weeks later, Albert presided over the annual dinner of the Literary Fund, his willingness surprising Irish poet Tom Moore, who observed in his journal, 'this is indeed meeting the spirit of the times more than half-way – the King-Consort taking the chair at a Free-Mason* Tavern Dinner!' On 11 May Albert duly arrived, and his remarks, Moore noted, 'were delivered with much grace and in what the ladies call "very pretty English".' Washington Irving, a London Yankee, returned the company's thanks, and Scottish poet Tom Campbell, doddering at sixty-six, followed with an oration, Moore noted, that broke down 'from sheer tipsiness in the middle...' Yet it was a 'grand show', and everyone left late, in pelting rain.

The next day promised a more stately occasion. 'Your *fête* I believe', King Leopold would write to his niece, was 'probably one of the most splendid *ever* given. There is hardly a country where so much magnificence exists; Austria has some of the means, but the Court is not elegant from its nature.' Even the most high-minded intentions can have contrary results, however, and the Plantagenet Ball on 12 May was a painful example. Since Sir Robert Peel had emerged from a wealthy cotton-spinning family in the Midlands, his background had helped focus the royal couple's minds on the vast and crucial English textile industry, then beset by foreign competition and falling demand. Why not, Victoria and Albert thought, create what would be described more than a century later as a 'media event' to focus attention upon English goods? Specifically, they had the Spitalfields silk-weavers in mind in planning a ball in fourteenth-century guise, and after some research they determined to dress as Edward III and Queen Philippa, in costumes copied from their effigies in Westminster Abbey. Intended as a

---

* The name of the tavern.

tribute to English history as well as to domestic industry, the ball fell victim to a practical joke.

Richard Monckton Milnes sent the *Morning Chronicle* what he purported was the text of a debate in the Chamber of Deputies in Paris about the intentions of the *bal masqué* to reawaken 'the long-buried griefs of France' about their defeats by the English at Crécy, Poitiers and Calais. The Home Secretary rushed to Sir Robert Peel, crying, 'There's the devil to pay in France about this foolish ball!' And in Paris a newspaper suggested holding a similar ball at which the duc d'Orléans should attend, costumed as William the Conqueror.

Controversy increased interest in the ball but twisted its focus. The display of the Queen's gown in Hanover Square drew crowds to gaze at its magnificence, but also caused London newspapers to decry the extravagance at a time when the unemployed were hungry. *Punch* published verses in which aristocratic 'revellers', in 'purple dress'd', were contrasted with the poor, whose 'only swathing was The cere-cloth of the dead.' Instead of promoting the weaving industry, the Plantagenet Ball created discord, but the Queen stubbornly commissioned Edwin Landseer to paint her and Albert in their regalia. By a stroke of good luck, it was only days later that John Francis tried to assassinate them; the attempt stirred a new wave of public good feeling. The royal pair would regularly ride the roller-coaster of rejection and acclaim.

On 29 May, they had been shot at again while out in an open carriage near Buckingham Palace. When the gunman was not apprehended, Victoria worried over being 'shut up for days' because of the threat of a renewed attempt. Such fears were not empty. Peel's private secretary, Edmund Drummond, had been killed early in 1843 by a gunman who thought he had shot Peel. Some shootings were the work of political radicals targeting a scapegoat for hard times; others were copycat crimes committed by the mentally deranged. Attacks on political figures had been a hazard of office since Spencer Perceval, the Prime Minister who was the younger William Pitt's successor, was assassinated in 1812.

As if nothing had happened, the royal couple drove out again the next afternoon, this time without a lady-in-waiting but with their usual 'gentlemen', to try to draw the gunman's fire. 'You may imagine', Albert wrote to his father, 'that our minds were not very easy. We looked behind every tree, and I cast my eyes round in search of the rascal's face.' From five paces, Francis fired again and missed; this time he was arrested. (John Francis was condemned to death; then, on 1 July 1842, hardly a month after the incidents, he was reprieved.) Two days later, John William Bean, a stunted young man barely four feet tall, fired a pistol at the Queen. When it proved to be loaded with more tobacco than gunpowder, he was released as insane. The public applauded the royal couple's courage. A later age may marvel at their youthful folly. The Queen's birthday had just passed. She had already reigned for nearly five years, and was just twenty-three. Albert was still twenty-two.

The Prince's responsibilities were staggering for a young and inexperienced man, and his status was only what he could make of it. Fortunately for Victoria, he submerged much of his ego in tireless work behind the scenes to extricate her from the intermittent despair that had overtaken her euphoric first years as Queen. The Bedchamber imbroglio, the battles over Conroy, the Lady Flora embarrassment, the defeats over Albert's position and stipend, the loss of Melbourne, the expulsion of Lehzen, the unwanted pregnancies (with fear of more), had proved Victoria to be less than she seemed. With her ministers she was assured; in her correspondence she was confident; at Court ceremonials she was queenly. Yet Anson had already written at Christmas 1841 that 'Her Majesty interested herself less and less about politics' – because, he knew, Albert was discreetly maintaining the monarchy's business while Victoria struggled through a prolonged depression about which few were aware.

Albert bore his matrimonial trials with patience and grace, but he realized that if he did not assert himself as husband, Victoria's Hanoverian hauteur could unravel the monarchy as well as their marriage. Sallie Stevenson recalled a tedious evening at Buckingham Palace when, after she complimented Albert on his English and he said, realistically, 'Oh, no; it is just tolerable. I hope to improve', a group sat down at tables with the Queen to play whist, as usual. The Prince, who despised cards, sat separately with several others over four-handed chess, a curious nineteenth-century version of the game, played with partners and two sets of chessmen of different colours on a board of 160 squares. Finally the whist players rose, at the Queen's lead, to retire. Since the Prince 'was still intent on his game', the Queen 'leaned over to him and said in the softest, sweetest tones, "Albert!" But as His Royal Highness was too much employed to hear these soft and silvery accents, she repeated his name again and again, each time modulating her voice to greater earnestness, without losing any of its sweetness or tenderness. They do say, however, that, Queen though she be, he will not allow himself to be, in matrimonial phrase, "managed", – that when it is necessary, he resists her firmly, though kindly, and I think it is the best security for their future happiness.'

The painter E.M. Ward remembered one such moment when the Prince had gone to dine with the Council of the Royal Academy. Before dinner had proceeded very far, a messenger arrived to announce that the Queen desired Albert's presence at Buckingham Palace. The Prince nodded, and sent the messenger off. Soon a second messenger turned up with a message that the Queen was still waiting. Albert again nodded and waved the emissary off, only to find a third messenger at the door with a peremptory 'The Queen *commands* your Royal Highness's immediate return to the Palace'.

Dismissing the servant, the Prince remained with the company the rest of the evening. When Ward escorted him to his carriage he heard the coachman instructed to drive to Claremont, where, undoubtedly, Albert slept soundly while Victoria learned once more that even sovereigns made up only half of a marriage.

Albert's assertiveness and Lehzen's departure combined to bring stability to the marriage. It did not take Victoria long to recognize that. The night following Lehzen's exit, Victoria dreamed that the Baroness had come back to say good-bye, and the Queen awakened only to the reality of her loss. The next day she pulled down some of her old diaries, perhaps to recall Lehzen's part in her life, and came to a passage in 1839 where she had written of her 'happiness' with Melbourne. Now, with both Melbourne and Lehzen gone, she noted, '1st October. Wrote & looked over & corrected my old journals, which do not now awake very pleasant feelings. The life I led then was so artificial & superficial, & yet I thought I was happy. Thank God! I now know what real happiness means.'

On 13 December 1842, musing over the departure from their lives of Melbourne and Lehzen, Victoria and Albert wondered what had caused her 'unbounded admiration and affection' for Melbourne, which already was beginning to seem puzzling, given their satisfaction with each other and the rapid emergence of their confidence in Peel. In her journal, Victoria blamed her 'very warm feelings', which had nowhere else to go, but, she added, 'Albert thinks I worked myself up to what really became, at last, quite foolish.'

After the discordant notes recorded by Anson at the close of 1841, the ending of 1842 echoed with harmonies that Victoria and Albert hardly dared anticipate only a few months earlier. Even the Queen's less than welcome third pregnancy caused little alarm, and she could respond to Leopold's congratulations, 'My poor nerves, tho' thank God! nearly *quite* well *now* were so battered last time that I suffered a *whole year* from it... Still those nerves were incidentals and I am otherwise so strong and well, that if only my happiness continues I can bear anything else with pleasure.' At the same time – actually 27 December 1842 – Albert was writing to Stockmar, again in Coburg, that when he had left his parting words had been, 'When you really want me, write, and I will come.' Again Albert wanted him. Having managed 'a host of trifles', he wanted to deal with 'higher and graver things'.

It was no trifle, however, that Albert had furnished the nation in less than two years with two heirs to the throne and a third on the way. The fact lent itself to much punning in the press, especially after Albert, so *Bell's Life* reported, secured 'a large number of hares' from the Earl of Leicester's game preserve for his own at Norfolk Farm, 'to be let loose for breeding against the ensuing season'. *The Satirist* had Albert explain the acquisition to Victoria as a method to improve the breeding stock, and the Queen responds,

> If clever, thus, in the *hare* line,
> Why not, Albert, improve mine?

Determined 'to outstrip all competition', *Punch* forecast 'the Royal Family ten years hence', listing further, one a year, Augustus Leopold (Duke of Brompton), Sophia Maria, Elizabeth Leonora Jane, Henry Philip William (Duke of Lambeth), Mary Alexandrina, John Charles Peter (Duke of Chelsea), Timothy Theobald Thomas (Duke of Kensington), Matilda Seraphina, Richard Stephen (Duke of Deptford), Ethelred Guthrum (Duke of Battersea), and Seraphina Susan Cecilia. 'The above will be thought by any reasonable person enough for the present.'

Under Peel's ministry and with Lehzen's departure, and abetted additionally by royal confinements, Albert had become Victoria's unofficial private secretary and confidant, acquiring the informal power possessed by all efficient private secretaries. Everything the Queen was to see passed through his hands, and papers that went on to her usually bore comments and in some cases a draft reply, which she would revise, improving his English into something more Victorian. With Germanic thoroughness, he organized and filed documents, kept minutes of the Queen's conversations with ministers – which he attended – and gave each record a subject title in red ink. He read newspapers she would not see, cut out and marked articles for her attention, and prepared memoranda on topics he deemed of current or future importance. While simplifying her work, he was carefully forming Victoria's mind. He also hoped that the volumes of paperwork he was compiling would some day be of use as reference to the Prince of Wales, whom he viewed not as a pretty child just learning to walk, but as a future Albertine king.

Victoria's relationship with Peel, thanks to Albert and to her own maturity, was very different from that with Melbourne. She was less malleable, more inquiring, and willing to accept, or assent to, ministerial decisions once Peel had given her (and Albert) an opportunity to register their reactions. Theoretically unfettered by a written constitution, the Queen was nevertheless bound by the unwritten one of legislative precedent and the accumulating restraints of Cabinet democracy. She had the right to be informed – a right that she and Albert insisted upon – and to be heard. The sovereign, as the continuing instrument of government, possessed moral authority beyond that of elected officeholders, and technically, royal assent was needed for a host of government appointments and operations; nevertheless, an expanding electorate had left few initiatives to the monarch and little more than what Walter Bagehot would describe, in the later years of Victoria's reign, as the right to be consulted, the right to encourage, and the right to warn. Used shrewdly and cautiously, these 'rights' remained powers that could make the sovereign more than a symbol. And not only the sovereign but, in Victoria's case, her consort. However he effaced his traces from her official actions, she knew how much of her authority emanated from Albert's preparation and from his reshaping of her personality. She recorded in her journal how she once told the Prince, 'It is you who have entirely formed me.' The sweeping adverb was far from accurate, as she was too strong a personality to be so diminished, but Lord Brougham, once a Whig Lord Chancellor and a combative law reformer and parliamentary debater, recognized the reality and called her privately 'Queen Albertine'.

Henry Brougham had always been short on civility, and his acerbic aside was gossiped about until it got to Albert, who made sure that pamphlets which the noble lord had sent to Buckingham Palace – his miscellaneous publications alone would number 133 – were acknowledged cordially by both Queen and Prince. To Brougham's surprise, he was entrusted to carry some important Court documents to Paris – he travelled often to Nice, where he resided out of session. Albert explained to his brother, 'A little attention towards a man like Brougham is never thrown away.'

VII

The Goldfish-bowl

1843–1844

IN THE EARLY years of her reign, Victoria had enjoyed the goldfish-bowl of public attention in which she lived from morning to night. Royal levées and drawing-rooms remained the formal entrée into Society; levées held on an occasional morning to introduce gentlemen to Court, drawing-rooms in the afternoon for ladies. Rigid in dress and protocol, emotionally arid and only momentary in contact, the opportunities to brush one's lips upon the sovereign's hand and to exchange fleeting words with the Queen and Prince were, nevertheless, essential credentials for the privileged. Yet the first years with Albert saw a gradual withdrawal by the Queen, as much as was possible, into reserved hours of privacy. Since Albert was uncomfortable with the demands and preoccupations, as well as the denizens, of upper-class society, Victoria soon disappeared as the focal point of high life in London. As the monarchy became more bourgeois, in public as well as in private, it would lose much of its attractiveness to the aristocracy, traditionally a counterweight to the fickle public mood. Although peerages and perquisites remained in the sovereign's gift, in the diminished modern monarchy these were far more often her Prime Minister's selection than her own.

Change came at first imperceptibly. The most private part of their lives, apart from the large bed in which Victoria and Albert slept, was their morning. The romantic pair of writing-tables, side by side, had soon given way to the more efficient practice of using separate rooms. At the close of the morning's work the Prince would come to the Queen to discuss business, or they would read to each other from books as various as Hallam's *Constitutional History* and Scott's *The Lay of the Last Minstrel.*

After a luncheon, usually with guests, appointments often filled their afternoons. When there was leisure time, they still played piano duets, sketched, or painted. Despite Albert's seriousness in public, a result of his continued grappling with English language and manners, when he was with Victoria, as with his young children, he was playful and eager to shed restraints, crawling about the floor with Pussy and Bertie, delighting Victoria by making her an 'April Fool'. Only their walks and their guests would make the uninformative Court Circular offered to the press.

All of the Princess Lieven's visitors in Paris, she wrote to Lady Palmerston, reported 'that Prince Albert is exceedingly unpopular, the Queen also, and that both of them are extremely rude'. They were not so much rude as ungracious – the acquired arrogance that often came with elevated position. Whatever small courtesies Victoria had been taught as a child, protocol, even among the most privileged, limited her intimacies as Queen. Albert bore himself stiffly and shook hands awkwardly – more, perhaps, a sign of insecurity than *Hochmut.* At Court there were murmurs of resentment that the pair, for privacy, often exchanged comments in German. Albert even made comments in English that suggested unweaned loyalty to Germany. His 'No tailor in England can make a coat' caused as much outrage on one island as his 'The Poles are as little deserving of sympathy as the Irish' did on the other.

Early in the royal marriage the Boston artist G.P.A. Healy, newly married to an English girl, Louisa Phipps, and struggling to make a living, petitioned for permission to copy several portraits at Windsor for King Louis-Philippe. Healy was already at work before the much admired Sir Thomas Lawrence canvas of Earl Bathurst when the Queen and Albert happened upon the Yankee painter, only a few years their elder. Citizen of a socially egalitarian realm, he did not realize that what happened next was a result of a young sovereign's training that one spoke to the lower orders only indirectly. Wondering what Healy was doing, Victoria turned to her husband and said, 'Ask Mr Healy if – ', and the Prince put her questions to him 'as though he had been translating from a foreign tongue' and the Queen were somewhere in another dimension.

The interrogation over, she exclaimed, looking at Healy's copy rather than at him, 'It is extremely like!' – and with an almost imperceptible 'bend of the head' strode off with Albert, neither offering another word. 'I own', Healy recalled with indignation decades later, 'that my American blood boiled in my veins.' However unkind he thought the royal couple were, in their rarefied sphere they were merely being, as always, correct.

The public prudery by which they continued to protect the Court reflected a similar unworldliness, a rule-book reign. But Albert had little need to persuade Victoria that her Court, its recent past tarnished, had to earn respect by example and be impenetrable to scandal. 'On the Queen's accession,' Albert noted in a memorandum in 1852, 'Lord Melbourne had been very careless in his appointments, and great harm had resulted in the Court therefrom. Since her marriage I had insisted upon a closer line being drawn, and though Lord Melbourne had declared that "damned morality would undo us all", we had found great advantage in it and were determined to adhere to it.' Albert recorded an instance that year when Lord Derby, as Prime Minister, appealed unsuccessfully to have the wife of the new Lord Chancellor, Lord St Leonards, presented at Court 'although she had run away with him when he was still at school, and was now nearly seventy years old'. The transgression had occurred a half-century earlier, and the couple had since lived respectable lives, but the Queen 'said it would not do to receive her now...although society might do in that respect what it pleased; it was a principle at Court not to receive ladies whose characters are under stigma.'* With the most succulent gossip barred from conversation, Victoria ran out of things to say after family talk and empty pleasantries, even with her closest friend in the Household, the Duchess of Sutherland. Almost the only time the Prince came alive at

---

* The highest society deplored the strict morality as out of touch with reality. Even the cautious Albert was caught up in early 1843 as a sponsor of the Society for Ancient Music. The 'prudish ladies' who attended, Lady Holland (who did not) wrote acidly to her son in Naples in May 1843, 'are scandalized at the *immoral* life of [Giulia] Grisi; & have remonstrated with Prince Albert & [the] Duke of Wellington at her singing here. Can you believe such canting folly?' The soprano, then thirty-two, was famed for her roles in operas by Bellini and Donizetti, but would not marry tenor Giuseppe Mario, with whom she travelled and performed, until 1856. Yet the concert-going ladies kept to the double standard and deplored only his partner.

dinner was when he could discuss problems of drainage and heating, or the royal farm animals.

Dinner for Victoria and Albert, whether in London or at Windsor, was often solemn and seldom private. With rare exceptions, courtiers, however much they dreaded the duty, were present, even when no formal evening entertainment was scheduled. The cycle of ladies-in-waiting and gentlemen-in-waiting might change the names of the company at the table, but each was expected to remain in nominal attendance until the Queen and Consort elected to retire for the night. The Queen was, by protocol, last to arrive at dinner, Albert preceding her but first looking in at her preparations. Then came Victoria, often a quarter of an hour later, her doors opened by two courtiers who bowed deeply as the bejewelled Queen made her entrance with a nod or a smile at the Prince.

Dinner was over as soon as the Queen finished her portion. Since she was served first, and never toyed with her food, small talk could leave a guest hungry. The knowledgeable kept their remarks animated but brief. An intimate family meal with a rare German visitor was more relaxed, Victoria noting how her husband was 'always so merry' on such occasions. To King Frederick William IV of Prussia, who had come to London to be godfather at the Prince of Wales's christening, Albert wrote of the 'deep pleasure' he had felt when his 'old friend' from Bonn University, 'Fritz Strelitz' – then, as since, the Grand Duke of Mecklenburg-Strelitz – visited; and he was delighted to entertain 'Uncle Mensdorff' and talk over old times. When Frederick sent an aide to study English agricultural practice, Albert took him round the parks and public gardens, 'which we may say without exposing ourselves to a just reproach of Anglomania, are more numerous and more artistically designed and kept than anywhere else'. While happy to have another guest with whom to speak animatedly in German, it was clear that the Prince had taken an Englishman's pride in what they saw.

Sometimes during domestic, but rarely private, evenings, Albert was even diverted from chess to cards, one of his intellectual sacrifices to keep the Queen content; but by 1845, when the new American Minister, Edward Everett, visited, some subtle changes were apparent. Court elegance awed Everett, a Massachusetts politician already renowned at home as an orator, almost into speechlessness. At dinner Victoria chatted over 'a range of topics' with 'no stiffness or reserve', and in the drawing-room over coffee 'several quiet games – not cards – were played ... The Prince and I played a couple of games, also new to me, about halfway between chequers and chess. The Queen gave out ivory letters to put together into words.' Had the Minister encountered an early version of Scrabble, more than a century before it became an American board game? Whatever it was, it was 'not cards', and the Queen's intellectual world, under Albert's tutelage, was widening.

Indulging gentlemen to linger at table for hours over brandy, coffee and cigars, while the women had to leave, ended under the Prince. The tradition emphasized that though the Queen might be sovereign, she was a woman, and as such remained in second-class status to the men. *She* had to leave her own table. Albert abbreviated the routine, leaving the men as a signal to break up, then joining the ladies. Often he sang duets with Victoria, who preferred not to perform before gentlemen. Unless there were family members visiting, or a period of formal mourning intruded, evenings were lost to other pursuits, and Albert, a compulsive reader, had to catch up late into the night or very early in the morning.

At Windsor, where invitees had to come by carriage and by rail, and Buckingham Palace, which was easier of access for guests, it was expected that Victoria and Albert, despite her young family and now frequent pregnancies, would entertain daily, at least at dinner, which began, and ran, late. For privacy there was only Claremont, for another residence that the Queen acquired at her accession remained uninviting. Much as Victoria enjoyed the seaside, the Royal Pavilion at Brighton, so loved by George IV, was uncomfortable and orientally ornate – 'a strange Chinese looking thing, haunted by ghosts best forgotten'. The town had grown around it, leaving little privacy. 'I only see a little morsel of sea from one of my sitting room windows', she objected. When she and the Prince walked along the crowded seafront, they were 'mobbed by all the shopboys in the town, who ran and looked under my bonnet, treating us just as they do the Band, when it goes on parade'. A cat may look at a king, but pawing by mongrels was another matter. Before the year had ended, she and Albert had determined to investigate alternative places by the sea. The 1840s were a boom time for railway entrepreneurs. New trackage had enlarged the range of accessibility for royal travel within England and made it possible to think beyond Brighton. Albert promised to look into it.

Princess Alice Maud Mary was born on 25 April 1843. Parliament had convened two months earlier without the Queen, Dr Locock having forbidden her appearance 'in consequence of her present state'. Her speech from the throne, written by Peel and read for her, referred to the successes of military operations in China and in Afghanistan, the burgeoning of the Empire continuing until there would be places named or renamed after Victoria and Albert in every populated continent. As usual Albert filled the long gap in the Queen's calendar, including that of the lying-in. 'I have endless letters to write, to all parts of the world', he wrote to his brother. He also stood in the next week, in mourning habit he thought ridiculous – a wide-brimmed black hat and long black cloak that required a page to carry his trailing train – for the funeral of their uncle, the Duke of Sussex, whom both Queen and Prince had scorned almost as much as they did their other surviving uncles, Augustus of Cambridge, who played petty games of precedence with Albert, and Ernest of Cumberland, who remained troublesome even from Hanover.

With the death of the Duke of Sussex, the presidency of the Society of Arts fell vacant and brought to an end, an historian of the Society has written, 'a long period of happy-go-lucky Hanoverian buffoonery at its public ceremonies'. There was no requirement in its by-laws for a royal patron, but Albert had been a member since June 1840 and a vice-president since 19 April, a week before the Duke's death. A nomination committee composed of two dukes and a marquess asked him to accept the presidency, which he did on 31 May, presiding over its prize-giving ceremonies for the first time on 19 June. Since the Society's claimed interest was in arts in the broadest sense, including manufactures, it would have special importance for Albert in the later 1840s as it fostered annual shows that would lead to the Great Exhibition of 1851.

Always an activist in the organizations in which he consented to be involved, Albert appears to have promoted Act 6 & 7 Vict. c. 36, the Scientific Societies Act of 1843, which exempted from Rates – local property taxes – 'Land and Buildings occupied by Scientific and Literary Societies' if they were 'supported wholly or in part by annual voluntary contributions'. It became known as 'the Prince Consort's Act'.

Although the couple's uncle Ernest Augustus did not attend his brother's funeral on 6 May, four weeks later he turned up at the christening of Princess Alice, determined to make his visit across the

Channel as unpleasant as possible. Bent and thin, using his deafness to advantage where he could, the King deliberately materialized at the baptismal font, Victoria fumed to Leopold, '*just in time* to be *too late*'. He also made a scene over rights to the late Princess Charlotte's jewels, which Victoria wore although he insisted they belonged to the Crown of Hanover. She was 'loaded with my diamonds', he claimed to a friend.

The wedding in July of 'Fritz Strelitz' to Princess Augusta of Cambridge found the King of Hanover still in England seeking ways to air his rancour. He took his controversial seat in the House of Lords, claiming dual citizenship as Duke of Cumberland. At the wedding, Albert wrote to his brother, 'He insisted on having the place at the altar where we stood. He wanted to drive me away and, against all custom, he wanted to accompany Victoria...I was forced to give him a strong push and drive him down a few steps, where the First Master of Ceremonies led him out of the chapel.' After the wedding he pushed his way inside again to prevent Albert from signing the register with the Queen. 'He laid his fist on the book. We manœuvred round the table and Victoria had the book handed to her across the table. After a third trial to force Victoria to do what he commanded...he left the party in great wrath...and, happily, he fell over some stones in Kew and damaged some ribs.'

In August he was still in England, threatening to remain until the matter of Princess Charlotte's jewels was settled in his favour. Worried about the potential embarrassment, Peel queried Victoria for advice. 'The Queen is desirous that whatever is right should be done', she responded on 13 August, 1843, 'but [she] is strongly of opinion that the King of Hanover's threat (for such as it must be regarded) not to leave this country till the affair is decided upon should in *no way* influence the transaction, as it is quite immaterial whether the King stays here longer or not'. It was clearly a letter in which Albert had no hand.

A commission consisting of Lord Lyndhurst, Lord Langdale and Chief Justice Tindal was appointed to review the dispute. All three died before deciding the award. Only in 1857 was a settlement made, substantially in favour of Hanover. By then Victoria, who had come to the throne with little jewellery of her own, had acquired more than she needed.

In the final days of the King's visit, he proposed, according to Greville, that Albert take a walk with him. The Prince made some excuses that walking in city streets would expose them to inconvenience from the London crowds. 'Oh, never mind that', said Ernest. 'I was more unpopular than you are now, and used to walk about with perfect impunity.' With that story about, he could return to Hanover with some satisfaction.

On 24 August the Queen ceremonially closed the parliamentary session and readied herself for her state visit to King Louis-Philippe of France. It would be the first major test of the royal yacht, which Greville had inspected a few days before and pronounced 'luxuriously fitted up, but everything is sacrificed to the comfort of the Court, the whole ship's company being crammed into wretched dog-holes, officers included'. The Queen and Prince never noticed.

En route, the new steam paddle-wheeler docked at Falmouth, lowered the royal barge, and permitted Victoria and Albert to glide through a glassy sea amid a throng of nearly five hundred small boats out in greeting. On their return the mayors of Falmouth and Penryn, so the Quaker Barclay Fox wrote in his diary on 1 September, 'presented addresses from their respective corporations and inhabitants. It was explained . . . that [Tom Fox] the mayor of Falmouth was a Friend & therefore [his head] remained covered. The unfortunate H[enry] Lamb, mayor of Truro, in the excitement of the moment, lost his balance & tumbled into the water & as there was not time to hang him up to dry, he lost the chance of an introduction.'

For diplomatic reasons, Albert described the voyage across the Channel to France, in a letter to Frederick William IV of Prussia, as incidental to a longer voyage, now curtailed by events: 'Owing to Mr O'Connell's agitation' – the fiery nationalist Daniel O'Connell had been drawing excited crowds – 'we have been obliged to give up an earlier plan of visiting Ireland this autumn, and shall have to limit our cruise to the Channel.' The royal houses of Europe treated Louis-Philippe coldly because he was considered a usurper and because he had initially courted popularity as a bourgeois king, thus becoming a traitor to the class into which he had forced himself. Since the Queen's visit to France early in September 1843 was the first by an English sovereign since that of Henry VIII to a country often considered its hereditary enemy, enthusiastic receptions were worked up for Victoria at Le Tréport, *en route* to the Château d'Eu, and she was not displeased at having conveyed some semblance of respectability to the King. 'The

Emperor of Russia will be very much annoyed,' she wrote in her journal, 'but that is neither here nor there.'

For some reason Peel's ministers also looked upon a stop by the *Victoria and Albert* at Ostend as a matter of delicacy, although it was little more than a visit to a favourite uncle. Peel assured the Cabinet that it was not a matter of state, and 'they will be as reasonable as possible – but it does not do to thwart them. I know how to manage them – the way is to receive the proposals [for foreign travel] without objection and show a willingness to meet their desires. Then as difficulties appear they will grow cool.'

Aberdeen accompanied the royal party only to France, and had his own meetings with Guizot, an old friend, but the wily minister no longer had the confidence of the French Chamber, which could see change approaching. The King was old and failing, and the target of repeated assassination attempts – something with which Victoria and Albert had direct acquaintance. His eldest son and heir, the duc d'Orléans, immensely popular and liberal in his views, had been killed in a carriage accident the year before, prompting Alexandre Dumas to remark, 'God has removed the only obstacle which existed between the monarchy and the republic.' Louis-Philippe was emotionally grateful for the royal visit, but the French still resented the nation they saw personified by Palmerston. The King could make only cosmetic com-promises on foreign policy with England that kept the chances of his remaining sons intact.

In an age when marriages among the propertied and the politically influential were often arranged for other reasons than affection, Albert had already seen many such alliances contracted by the ambitious Coburgs, including that with the Queen of Portugal. One of the most contentious issues with France was the desire of Louis-Philippe to bind Spain to France through the marriage of one of his sons, if not two of them, to the very young queen of Spain, Isabella II, then thirteen, and her younger sister, the Infanta. If Isabella – declared of age in 1843 despite her years – produced no heir, France would then have an insurance policy on power through her sister. While Albert was busy promoting the cause of his Coburg cousin Leopold, younger brother of the King Consort of Portugal, he and the Earl of Aberdeen were claiming that the marriages were a matter for the young queen and the Spanish people – a polite way to deflect France.

Neither side would win, because Spain and Portugal, once great colonial powers, were becoming too weak and divisive internally to matter, and a pre-emptive betrothal desired by Louis-Philippe for the duc de Monpensier would lead to nothing. There were also fears that Catholic France was once again intriguing to stir up Catholic Ireland. Intrigues, real and imagined, propelled some foreign affairs, and Albert would write to Peel about the King of France, 'Let us show that we are neither afraid of him nor prepared to be made dupes of.' There would be little reality to the Earl of Aberdeen's hopeful coinage, '*Entente Cordiale*', but Peel would insert a reference in the Queen's Speech from the Throne at the opening of the 1844 Parliament to the 'good understanding happily established'. In reality the two countries were rivals for influence not only on the Continent but as far away as the southern Pacific.

Since October was considered a good travelling month within England, Albert accepted an offer of an honorary LL D from Cambridge University to be awarded as part of a visit under the auspices of Trinity College. (On the return journey, the Queen and Prince were to be guests of Lord Chancellor Hardwicke at Wimpole and Lord De La Warr at Bourne.) Only the journey from Slough to Paddington was made by rail; the royal coach-and-six was met south of Cambridge, in the rain, by three thousand mounted yeomanry, all splashed with mud while accompanying the royal carriage along hedges and ditches for a dozen miles.

At the Cambridge Barrier a master-tailor among the horsemen halted the splattered honour guard with a bright red flag scissored from what Adam Sedgwick, Woodwardian Professor of Geology since 1818, described as 'the nether-garments of a livery-servant'. The October weather was gloomy despite the sunny forecast of the Astronomer Royal at Cambridge, but the pageantry of addresses and parades and inspections went on as scheduled, concluding late the next day.

It was already dark when, by torchlight, Victoria and Albert arrived at the steps of Trinity College Chapel, where, in the rain, a red carpet was unrolled. 'But alas! it was too short to serve its purpose; and while the Master and Seniors were conducting her across the Court, there was, for about half a second, a horrible conviction that the royal footsteps would be brought in most unseemly contact with the dusty pavement. But our undergraduates, who lined both sides of the path,

saved our credit by a Sir Walter Raleigh movement. They simultaneously pulled off their gowns, and spread them two or three deep
under the royal footsteps. We had a splendid Levée in the evening.'

The state bed for the overnight stay, Sedgwick added, had imperial
associations. In lieu of the usual featherbed cover was the former prayer-
rug 'of a great Mandarin, and [which] was snatched from the fingers of
his wife at the storming of Ningpo*...It was of bright scarlet, and
adorned with golden dragons. Their claws were symbolical of power,
and their wings of swiftness....'

On the Thursday morning of degree-granting, a sunny day, Victoria
and Albert visited the animal and fossil collections before the ceremonies
in the Senate House. Sedgwick, explaining as he preceded them, 'went
through every kind of backward movement to the admiration of all
beholders, having only once trodden on the hinder part of my cassock,
and never once having fallen on my retrogradations...In short had I
been a King Crab I could not have walked backwards much better.'

After the election-eve awkwardness of the reception at Oxford, the
enthusiasm at the sister university was a relief. Albert, observed Sedgwick,

was looking well and happy. He has, you know, a noble figure, and
he seemed well-fitted for his place beside the Queen. Far better than
all this, it is plain that the royal pair love one another. They went
together to every place she wished to see, and when she required
some moments of rest he started on some expedition of his own, so
that he lost not one moment from his entrance at our gates till the
hour of his departure. As a proof of this I may tell you, that while the
Queen was putting on her travelling dress just before she left us, he
started on foot privately with our Master,† and went on to the top of
King's College Chapel to have a parting bird's-eye view from its
battlements. In short, everything went on brightly and gloriously
from first to last, and the Queen and Prince have carried off all hearts
with them from the highest to the lowest.

* Ning-po, now Yin-hsien, is south of Shanghai and south-east of Hang-chou.
† William Whewell, a recent royal appointment at the recommendation of Albert
and Peel.

Then, with the excitement over and the travelling carriage off to meet the train, the Woodwardian Professor of Geology returned to his 'ill-arranged papers, sometimes listening to the clock, at other times... to the melancholy murmur of my dirty tea-kettle'.

Once Parliament ceased sitting, the Queen and Prince as a sign of royal favour also visited Peel and his wife, Julia, at Drayton Manor, depoliticizing the occasion as part of a round of appearances at other great country houses. Much of the trip north was made by rail, in which travellers now reposed great confidence. While Victoria remained at Drayton, Albert entrained for Birmingham, the burgeoning industrial city and Radical stronghold where the mayor – a hosier – was an outspoken Chartist. The Prime Minister considered it as hazardous a setting for the Queen as Dublin, but Albert was impressed by the cheering throng of nearly a quarter of a million, the mayor assuring him of 'the devoted loyalty of the whole Chartist body'. It would match in memory Albert's experience soon after of the great conservatory at Chatsworth, although no paradox would ripen in the princely mind between the Radicalism of the urban industrial masses and the political conservatism of the bachelor squire of Chatsworth, whose income very likely exceeded that of all the labourers of Birmingham and went into the lavish ornamentation of his land-holdings.

The year before, the Queen and Prince had visited the Horticultural Show at Chiswick and lunched with the Duke of Devonshire, President of the Society, who wrote afterwards to Lady Granville, 'Prince Albert was charming, and may be as popular as he pleases.' A visit to Chatsworth, the ducal estate, was considered, but it took until December 1843 to arrange; however, the immensely wealthy grandee did not worry about winter weather. His gardens were indoors as well as outdoors.

The Duke met Victoria and Albert at Chesterfield station with a coach and six, and eight outriders. As they entered Chatsworth Park, a royal salute (prearranged with local military authorities) thundered from the Hunting Tower. After dinner the royal guests thrilled to outdoors illuminations observed from the drawing-room windows – waterfalls and fountains bursting into blaze from gas jets placed by the Duke's ingenious superintendent of gardens, William Paxton. Paxton's Great Conservatory, hung with thousands of lamps, was an enchanted tropical forest under a crystal roof, heated by seven miles of pipes. It was, Victoria would write to Leopold, 'out and out the finest thing imaginable of its kind. It is one mass of glass, 64 feet high, 300 feet long, and 134 feet wide.' There was also the Great Stove and special glasshouse that Paxton had built to house the Duke's gigantic water lilies, christened loyally the *Victoria regia*. A steam pump sent a hot spray fifty feet high, and twelve thousand gas lamps warmed and lighted the huge space. Albert would be reminded of the visit when, seven years later, his plans for a great exhibition of arts and manufactures in London were in trouble.

At Belvoir Castle, he went fox-hunting with the Duke of Rutland's hounds with relaxed éclat, which for Victoria was the high point of the royal progress. 'One can hardly credit the absurdity of people here [in England],' she wrote to King Leopold, 'but Albert's riding has made such a sensation that it has been written about all over the country, and they make more of it than if he had done some great act! It rather disgusts one, but still it had done, and does, good, for it had put an end to all impertinent sneering about Albert's riding. This journey had done great good, and my beloved Angel in particular has had *the greatest success...*'

'People are very strange,' her uncle responded on December 15, recognizing the pettiness of aspersions upon the Prince's reputed Prussian stiffness in the saddle; 'and their great delight is to find fault with their fellow creatures; what harm could it have done them if Albert had *not* hunted at all? and still I have no doubt that his having hunted well and boldly has given more satisfaction than if he had done Heaven knows what praiseworthy deed...'

Praise for Albert came hard to Englishmen. When the Duke of Wellington took him under his wing and the Prince responded with recommendations for the Army – Albert took everything under study and always emerged with suggestions – even the valuable advice earned no credits. In January 1844 he proposed that, as in Austria, duelling in the military be ended, and that, since 'a man whose honour... has been insulted must possess some means whereby he can recover the treasure that has been taken from him and reinstate himself in the opinion of the world', such grievances be taken for satisfaction to the law. Wellington would ban duelling, but the public would first see Albert's involvement as interference. Even earlier, thinking in *mitteleuropäisch* fashion, the Prince, who was interested in weapons and uniforms, designed a shako (Hungarian for a stiff military hat with a high crown) for army use. The prototype for the Household Cavalry was conical, but flat on top, and with a brim, and was derided as tasteless in the *Illustrated London News* and lampooned by *Punch*, which described it 'as a decided cross between a muff, a coal-scuttle, and a slop-pail'. In unsigned spoof-German W.M. Thackeray chaffed, 'Ven de hat grow old (or vat you call zeedy), Brinz Albert has arranged so dat it vil make a beawdiful and ornamendal flower-bot for a drawing-room vindow.' The hat was adopted and worn until 1855. Caricaturists loved it.

Albert's father died on 29 January in his sixtieth year, a victim of his dissipations. When the Prince determined to return to Coburg, although not for the funeral, to pay his respects to his brother and stepmother, Princess Lieven carped to Lady Palmerston from Paris, and was very likely not alone in thinking, 'I imagine that Prince Albert is to receive a big inheritance; she' – the Queen – 'would not have allowed him to leave her for any trivial reason.' It was, however for the trivial reason of grief – guilty grief, perhaps, for his affection for his father had not been all that ties of blood required.

Both Victoria and Albert mourned as if Duke Ernest had been a paragon cut off in his prime. 'Here we sit together, poor Mama, Victoria, and myself, and weep', Albert wrote to Stockmar from Windsor, 'with a great cold public around us, insensible as stone.' Victoria was a 'consoling angel', he added, and indeed her desolation was excessive in the manner of the time, which exploited the event to create a *frisson* of woe. More revealingly than she understood, Victoria wrote to Leopold, the dead Duke's younger brother, 'One loves to *cling* to one's grief.' Although she hardly knew her father-in-law, he was 'our dearest Papa', and the Court was commanded into deep mourning. The royal notepaper was heavily bordered in black; courtiers dressed in black; official gloom pervaded royal residences already known for a surfeit of solemnity.

Most appalling of all to Victoria – the reality of what was otherwise a distant and overdramatized death – was that it forced Albert into a return to Coburg. In part it was to pay his respects at his father's grave; more significantly it was to caution the new Duke Ernest, his brother, about his excesses, and to secure insincere pledges of good behaviour. Besides, Albert ached for the sights and smells of what Victoria called his '*dearly beloved Vaterhaus*'.

The thought of the empty bed (although she was again pregnant) filled the Queen with alarm. 'I have *never* been separated from him for even *one night*', she confided to Leopold, 'and the *thought* of *such* separation is quite dreadful.' That she meant it, and more, is evident from her later letter to Vicky, recalling being 'clasped and held tight in the sacred Hours at Night when the world seemed only to be ourselves'.

Even before his Channel crossing had begun, Albert wrote to her from Dover, expressing his hope that although his place at the table would be vacant, his place in her heart would not be. By the time she received his note, he assured her, one of the fourteen days he would be away would already have passed – 'thirteen more, and I am again within your arms'. 'The Queen cried all day long after Albert departed', Lady Granville tattled to the Duke of Devonshire on 29 March, irritated at what she saw as self-indulgent immaturity. 'How rare it is for royalty to have such pleasant sorrows.'

By the time Albert arrived in Gotha – where Ernest II preferred to reside – the new duke had already taken hold. The brothers would differ on everything. Albert, so Ernest would write in later years, 'was by no means inclined to consent to an energetic rule such as I adopted immediately afterwards for the perfection of the constitutional system ... His mild amiability really went hand-in-hand with a critical severity ... The greatest warmth and self-sacrificing love would sometimes change to painful coldness ...' Ernest II was not about to take advice about his personal life or his political absolutism, and Albert had to console himself with the treasured past before he returned, through snow in northern Germany, to an England that looked better than ever. Yet, while at the Rosenau in Coburg, he wrote, full of nostalgia for a boyhood that memory had enhanced, 'How glad I should be to have my little wife beside me, that I might share my pleasure with her.' Nevertheless, his diary for 11 April 1844, noting his arrival back at Windsor that evening, ended with the two words 'Great joy'. They suggested much more.

Royal travel on state visits, rare before the age of rail and steam, had almost become commonplace as rulers began using such opportunities for political advantages once left to arranged marriages. As Victoria waited out her fourth pregnancy, she expected the sovereigns of Russia, Saxony, France and Prussia. Thoughts of lengthy mourning for Ernest I were pushed aside by frenzies of preparation. Tsar Nicholas I had become concerned about England as a result of the state visit of Victoria and Albert to Russia's historic enemy, France. Both had designs upon the Middle East, hoping to appropriate some of the territories of the crumbling Turkish empire. The Queen was prompted to respond to anxieties emanating from France by writing to Leopold, her informal conduit to Louis Philippe, 'If the French are angry at this visit, let their dear King and their Princes come here.'

When Nicholas arrived on 1 June – the same day as King Frederick Augustus II of Saxony – Victoria was seven months pregnant; yet she went to Ascot with the Tsar and to the opera, held a review of troops for him in Windsor Great Park, gave huge dinners for him every evening in Buckingham Palace's Waterloo Room, and listened to his undiplomatic bellowing, carefully directed toward the Prince and Prime Minister – since she was a woman – on European politics, particularly his loathing of France and his contempt for Turkey. Autocratic and severe at home, at forty-eight he had travelled little and was unversed in the niceties of Court behaviour abroad.

Victoria was charmed by his rugged handsomeness (he was six feet two), his 'melancholy' eyes, his stern honesty, and his claim at Windsor that he needed some straw from the stables on which to sleep. Besides, she wrote to Leopold, the Tsar 'spoke in the highest praise of dearest Albert'.

When the King of France rushed to London afterwards, following a suitable period for Victoria's recovery from the birth of Prince Alfred Ernest Albert on 26 August, he also had words to describe Albert that Victoria relished – that '*le Prince Albert, c'est pour moi le Roi*'. The renewal of amity on the highest level between the traditional rivals suggested one dimension, the value of family links. Louis-Philippe's daughter Marie Louise was Leopold's spouse and Belgium's queen. His son, the duc de Nemours, was married to a Coburger cousin, Victoire. When Victoria and Louis-Philippe had met at Eu, they had kissed as family. When the King paid his return visit via Portsmouth, he was greeted by such an array of boats in informal escort, from great vessels to cutters and skiffs, that the *Gomez* had to slacken speed. There seemed to be national joy at the apparent end to hostility from across the Channel.

Since the King was not going beyond Windsor, the Lord Mayor and a delegation of dignitaries from London came to present a formal address to Louis-Philippe, and in expectation, Guizot recalled, 'I had written [a response for the King] in the morning and had it translated by M. de Jarnac . . . The Queen and Prince Albert spent half an hour in the cabinet of the King, reading and correcting the translation. It is like a family intimacy.'

Louis-Philippe's praise of Albert as '*le Roi*' remained far from possible in reality. The MP for Evesham, Peter Borthwick, early in the next year upset any expectations which Victoria might have had for renewing her attempt to secure for Albert an English title. A paragraph had appeared in the *Daily Chronicle* in February rumouring that the Prince would be named King Consort, and Borthwick, in the Commons,

Setting a hoped-for example, Albert had established a model farm at Windsor. Punch mocks it as a dilettantish operation, but the Prince was serious, and won legitimate livestock prizes at agricultural shows.

raised the question with Peel. When the Prime Minister correctly denied that any title was being considered, Victoria, embarrassed by the speculation, quickly picked up by provincial papers, wrote to Peel that she was 'positive that something must at once be done to place the Prince's position on a constitutionally recognized footing, and to give him a title adequate to that position'. But Albert's claims to public recognition often took an unexpectedly perverse turn. In December 1844 the press was pleased, as Jane Carlyle wrote to Lady Harriet Baring, that at the annual Smithfield Club Cattle Show of farm animals, 'our poor Prince gained the prize for pigs'. Much was made of Albert's having received *second* prize for his Windsor porker at the show, held at the Horse Bazaar, Portman Square. Albert also exhibited, according to the *Examiner* on 14 December, 'a fine polled ox, of the Scotch breed, which has been highly commended by the judges, although it has not obtained a prize'. That 'fortunate animal', according to the *Examiner*'s 21 December edition, instead of being released to the butcher who had purchased it, was, on the Queen's order, conveyed to Windsor Park, 'where in future it will be kept'. 'Our dear little Queen', Lady Holland gossiped to her son, 'must have imbibed some German sentiment from her two connexions, by sparing the life of the ox, because it licked the hand of Prince Albert at the Cattle Show'. The press made much of Albert's ox.

Emotionally, Victoria had already left such society for private life with her growing family, but the death of Duke Ernest early in the year had diverted Albert from his search for homes remote from Windsor and London. While Parliament sat, Victoria saw need for a retreat that was accessible by rail from Westminster. Some months earlier, Peel had learned of a potential royal seaside residence for sale, in one of Victoria's favourite places, the Isle of Wight. Negotiations faltered when the Prince went to Coburg; they dragged on during the Queen's confinement. The asking price for the two hundred acres at Osborne was £30,000, later reduced to £28,000, including furniture, but that figure was reasonable only if the purchaser planned to use the existing structure. For the royal family the house was far too small, and the furniture of little but temporary use. Whatever was there would have to be replaced.

Peel had warned Victoria and Albert that no Parliamentary grant could be expected, and that there would even be resistance – the times were hard – to the renovation and repair of Buckingham Palace. Expecting no help with Osborne House, they planned to sell the obsolete Pavilion at Brighton, and use the proceeds to compensate the government for any expenditures to improve Buckingham Palace.*

The Privy Purse, in which Albert and Anson had made substantial economies, would pay for Osborne, which became private property, as Victoria put it to Leopold, 'a place of *one's own*, quiet and retired, and free from all Woods and Forests, and other charming Departments who really are the plague of one's life'. Settlement was made on 1 May at £27,814 18s. 5d. When the Prince decided that more land was required for privacy and guest accommodations, a further £18,000 was spent. It was impossible to imagine a prettier spot, Victoria wrote enthusiastically to Lord Melbourne. It reminded the Prince of the bay at Naples.

Even before settlement, Albert sent for his proposed builder – Victoria was quite willing to leave renovations of the existing property to him. Albert's intention was to enlarge and repair the mansion, which already had sixteen bedrooms, but not nearly enough service area. He consulted not an architect, but an imaginative and successful London builder, Thomas Cubitt, who had made a fortune out of developing the district now called Belgravia. Cubitt, then in his late fifties, had first been called upon at Christmas 1844 to prepare a survey of the house. His report recommended a new structure as 'less expensive in the end than the repair of the present one'. Victoria and Albert had agreed, but wanted to live there as soon as possible, and directed that the old house be repapered and painted for occupation while plans went ahead to design and build a new house. Architects grumbled at the slight to their calling, but the self-taught Cubitt went ahead with the Italianate structure Albert outlined with the expert assistance of Ludwig Gruner. After Easter, Cubitt walked around the property with the couple, explaining his ideas for the new house as well as his plans for immediate

---

* The Queen ordered the stripping of the Pavilion begun in 1846, and by 1848, 143 van-loads of furniture, decorations, porcelain, pictures, clocks, and carpets had been removed to Buckingham Palace, Kensington Palace and Windsor Castle. In 1847 a sale of many of the objects was held; in mid-1848 the remaining items were sold. On 7 June 1848, the doors of the Pavilion were locked and the keys given to the Lord Chamberlain. However, demolition by the government met with opposition from the town councillors of Brighton, who bought it in 1850 (for £60,000 – but not before the fixtures had been removed by the Board of Woods and Forests, which wantonly destroyed much of the interior in the process).

improvements to the existing one. He would become one of Albert's few real friends in England.

The next year, once Victoria and Albert moved into Osborne House, Cubitt was also given the task of rehabilitating Buckingham Palace, most parts of which, the Queen had told Peel in February 1845, 'are in a sad state'. A large sewer had been discovered under the forecourt, which explained why substantial portions of the palace were, in her words, hardly '*decent* for the occupation of the Royal Family or any visitors'. There were also too few rooms for formal or family use. A study commission representing the rival bureaucracies was appointed, and the Commons, on receiving its report, voted to add £150,000 to funds available for what was called the enlargement of the palace; but plans for the project were not unveiled until 1847.

Even then there were some things the managerial Prince could not do. By 1846 gaslight would penetrate the public rooms at Windsor, and then at Buckingham Palace, but in private Victoria would insist upon candlelight all her life. Disliking the smell of coal, she would insist upon beech logs in her fireplaces, and however much Albert complained of the cold, Victoria kept thermometers in ivory obelisks in most rooms to ensure that they remained invigoratingly chill. About him were constant reminders that he was the Queen's husband.

A contemporary ballad by the pseudonymous 'Bon Gaultier'* put Albert in his proper place:

> The Queen she kept high festival in Windsor's lordly hall,
> And round her sat the gartered knights, and ermined nobles all;
> There drank the valiant Wellington, there fed the wary Peel,
> And at the bottom of the board Prince Albert carved the veal.

* William Aytoun and Theodore Martin.

VIII

The Queen's Business

1845–1848

H UNTING AT BAGSHOT with the Duke of Bedford, Albert spoke openly about problems facing Britain, including 'the long course of misgovernment [in Ireland], and the necessity of doing something'. Peel's administration, faltering yet not falling, had become hopelessly divided by the issues of Ireland and Free Trade. Famine was worsening – the potato blight of 1845 struck at the dietary staple of the chronically impoverished – but Protectionists representing the landed interest were more concerned about cheap grain from abroad than feeding hungry Irishmen. Albert felt helpless to interfere; but despite a sense of futility, he continued, with Victoria, to meet with her ministers, ask questions that pointedly revealed royal attitudes, and listen. Their efforts to remain above party politics limited their freedom to speak out, yet in private the Prince's Peelite sympathies were undisguised.

For Albert, the dilemma was that he had no privacy in which to operate. Little that was said and done at Court remained confidential, he deplored to Bedford. Somehow, he charged, governments on the Continent knew through their agents and informers whatever was discussed and done at the highest levels. Also, indiscretions of any sort found their way quickly into public currency, as when the new Bishop of Oxford, 'Soapy Sam' – for his charm, rather than his theology – Wilberforce wrote to Albert to ask the Prince's views on his position as a bishop in the House of Lords. 'A Bishop', Albert would pontificate on 19 October 1845, 'ought to abstain completely from mixing himself up with politics of the day, and beyond giving a general support to the *Queen's government*, and occasionally voting for it, should take no part in the discussion of State affairs...' The concept of neutrality in an essentially honorific situation was Albertine to the core, but religious practice then was inextricably involved in politics, and Wilberforce could not keep a confidence. The Prince would be embarrassed.

Earlier in the year the Duke of Bedford had shrugged off the royal dilemma about privacy as 'the tax they' – Victoria and Albert – 'paid for their situation; that the world was curious to know and hear about them, and therefore the press would always procure and give the information... All conspicuous people were brought into public notice in the same manner.' It was 'the misfortune of princes'. Albert had been referring to matters of policy, but the Duke interpreted the complaint as about the exposure of gossip. In either case the functionaries who came and went at Court and were faceless presences whose eyes and ears might be bought were, indeed, the tax paid to keep the royal residences running. Acquiring Osborne would limit their numbers and their access to a few dozens rather than Brighton's thousands.

Writing to her husband's sister, Sarah, on 20 January 1845, just about the time of Greville's journal entry, Mary Anne Disraeli gossiped of the Royal visit to Stowe, the sprawling seat of the Duke of Buckingham and Chandos. A few grandees had personal railway sidings on their estates, with facilities that were almost regal. For the Queen, the platform 'head woman' told Mrs Disraeli (a palm extended, probably, for a coin), 'a large red curtain' was hung across the staircase 'when her Majesty went to the Cabinet'. On her return 'the Queen asked the woman, *Where the Prince could go* – but there was *no second convenience*'. Despite a lavishness that concealed the Duke's financial straits, there were curious limits to privacy.

In the immensity of Stowe, a great political conclave discussed possible alterations to the Corn Laws, and most Tory leaders were present. Despite the political nature of the event, the Queen and Prince were there ostensibly for its social aspects. With the issue of domestic precedence for Albert having died with the Duke of Sussex, what pleased Victoria was the respect afforded the Prince, a result of his increasing, if informal, authority rather than recognition of her desire. A 'trifling instance', she explained in a letter to Leopold, was 'the Duke of Buckingham, who is immensely proud, bringing the

cup of coffee after dinner...to Albert himself'. But, in no public
relations boon, *The Times* reported that the Duke's game preserves, in
expectation of the visit, had been off limits for other hunting so that
sixty beaters could drive enormous numbers of hares before the
sportsmen. 'The ground immediately in front of the shooters became
strewn with dead and dying; within a semicircle of about 60 yards
from his Royal Highness, the havoc was evidently greatest. The gun
was no sooner to his shoulder than the animal was dead. In other
cases' – the aim of other gentlemen was less than unerring –
'wounded hares vainly endeavoured to limp away, but every provision had been made to avoid the infliction of prolonged torture.
Keepers were in readiness to follow up and kill such as were
maimed.' With the proliferation of London newspapers, each appealing to different classes and parties, it was to Albert's advantage that
few carried the story in as much detail.

While publicly the Prince remained politically neutral, privately he
supported the economic liberalism of Peel. As others – including Whigs
who actually liked the legislation – attacked the extension of the income
tax as inquisitorial and intrusive, Albert wrote realistically to the Prime
Minister, 'It is evident that everybody wants you to bear the abuse of it
and still have the 5 million in case of getting into office.' Peel found the
votes for his taxes and tariffs. He did not have his own right wing with
him but he had nearly everyone else.

On 3 April 1845, Thomas Cubitt was authorized by Albert to
proceed with a new residence at Osborne while his workmen were
still making Lady Isabella Blatchford's 'Old Osborne House' temporarily habitable. Walls were papered – still a rather new extravagance –
a new water-closet was added for Victoria's bedroom; new stoves and
chimney-pieces were installed. 'It does one's heart good', the Queen
wrote in her journal after yet another exploration of their grounds at
their springtime best, 'to see how my beloved Albert enjoys it all, and
is so full of all the plans and improvements he means to carry out. He
is hardly to be kept home a moment'. On 15 May they took a last look
before some venerable trees obstructing the builders were cut down,
and by 23 June they were able to return to take the children into the
newly laid foundations to place a box of coins of the realm, each
bearing their mother's profile, along with the names of the participants
in the ritual. It was Victoria's ceremony, but the house in almost every

way would be Albert's. Within months the Italianate tower would be rising.

Between events on the Isle of Wight was the royal *bal poudré*, again in period, the 'powder' motif to suggest the 1740s. Society was ecstatic. As the royal family withdrew into family pleasures, a Buckingham Palace extravaganza was now rare. The élite hairdressers were rumoured to be asking ten guineas *par tête* and were so busy that women had to be prepared days ahead and hope for the best. The Queen and Prince would come in costumes of the court of George II, and invitees researched the prints of Hogarth for ideas.

To free the fortunate for the event, the Lords did not sit that evening, prompting abuse the day before from Lord Brougham, who grumbled something *sotto voce* and unheard by *Hansard*. Lady Holland claimed it was about 'Albert & his *ugly* wife'. Yet, she added, 'Strange to say, all' – but Brougham – 'were pleased, young & old; & even those who did not go enjoyed the success. The streets were crowded; large groups assembled at the doors of those invited, to catch a glimpse of their costume; & many persons in their strange fashions stopped to shew themselves to the assembled crowd[s] & got cheers for their obliging-ness.'

By then, to mark the move to Osborne, the Privy Council had met there, the first of hundreds of voyages across the Solent that members of the government would have to make over the years. A more important concern for officials accompanying the Queen was the forthcoming journey to Coburg that she and Albert had planned. So that no regency need be declared in the Queen's absence, a Minister of State would join the party. The arrangement was a sign of the revolution in commu-nications. The steamship and the railway had been followed, in the year of her accession, by the first practical electric telegraph. By 1845, tele-graphy was operational in America and England, and on much of the Continent. If necessary, an Act of State could now be performed abroad.

Anticipation of the August journey to the cradle of her family excited the Queen. Her first impression, as she crossed into the conglomeration of states east of the Rhine, was of the singularity of hearing 'the *people* speak German'. At Bonn, the seventy-fifth anniversary of the birth of Ludwig van Beethoven was being celebrated on 12 August by the unveiling of a statue and an outdoor concert conducted by Franz Liszt.

The King and Queen of Prussia had promised to attend, and to bring with them Queen Victoria and Prince Albert.

The last day of the festival opened with a memorial concert in the *Festhalle*, featuring Marie Pleyel, Jenny Lind, and Liszt himself. The programme began without the exalted guests. When Liszt approached the rostrum to conduct the cantata he had composed for the occasion, the King's party was still absent. He held his baton until the restlessness of the crowd forced him to begin, and he was at the closing bars of the long, lugubrious work when the royal guests finally arrived. For them, Liszt conducted a second full performance, although the audience evidenced unmistakable signs that one had been enough.

Victoria was less concerned about the King of Prussia's lack of interest in music than about his failure to accord Albert the precedence at official functions 'which common civility required', she recalled in a memorandum in 1856, 'because of the presence of an Archduke, the third son of an uncle of the then reigning Emperor of Austria... whom the King would not offend'. But her uncle, the King of Hanover, was delighted, writing to a friend in England that the behaviour of Victoria and Albert was 'childishness'. He pretended to be 'mortified' by the 'complete failure' of the Prussian visit – that Victoria was allegedly 'cold and uncivil', while Albert 'was represented as being full of pretensions, and ignorant of the common usages of the world'. He had appeared at a military parade at Mainz 'in a great frock coat and round white hat, looking more like a tradesman or *garçon de boutique* than a prince'. And he failed to wear his Prussian insignia of the Order of the Black Eagle – an alleged discourtesy to his royal host. It was Victoria who was mortified, blaming Prussian pettiness on Albert's lowly rank. English law 'does not know of him'.

Albert's forebodings about Coburg caused him to question coming at all. Ernest resented his brother's intrusive advice, and Albert had responded, unrepentant, 'The worm that is gnawing at your heart and which often robs you of pleasure in life is *mistrust*. Those who really love you must have the sincere wish to lift this veil from your soul... You might think we are coming to govern you or to do you some damage.'

The London press followed the royal couple to Coburg, filing reports that made the Queen's indignation about mere title appear mild. Albert had written to his brother about appropriate entertainment for the

Queen, who wanted nothing arranged on a 'grand' scale, and because of the 'English way of keeping Sunday and the scruples belonging to it', nothing but a family assemblage on the Sabbath. She hoped to see German plays, participate in small folk dances and attend a children's festival. 'You needn't arrange a chase, as Victoria does not like such pleasures, and *I* prefer to stay with her.' Ernest however had managed a way for gentlemen to shoot without leaving their ladies. Albert found himself in a Germanic liquidation of deer.

The Continental *battue* did not merely employ beaters to drive game toward marksmen but herded targets into a broad enclosure which made chase unnecessary. To English newspapermen reporting home on the new telegraph, that was murder rather than sport. Reading press accounts, Greville dismissed the 'clumsy (and false) attempt to persuade people that she' – Victoria – 'was shocked and annoyed. But the truth is, her sensibilities are not acute, and though she is not at all ill-natured, perhaps the reverse, she is hard-hearted, selfish and self-willed.' A Leech cartoon in *Punch*, in two panels, compared bear-baiting in Elizabeth's time with dead and dying stags piled up before the royal tent, and verses by 'Jeams' (Thackeray) scoffed at 'Halbert Usband of the British Crownd' and his 'pore Germing sport' which was nothing less than a 'massyker'.

Rather than one massacre, unfortunately, there were two, the second when Victoria and Albert were guests on an elevated stand in an enclosure where thirty wild boar were released to be speared, or shot. According to her journal the platform for the audience was 'charmingly arranged' – curious words in the aftermath of a butchery. 'After this,' she concluded, without confessing any lacerated feelings, 'we walked away & then got into our carriage & drove home.'

The German entertainment arranged for Albert proved a public relations embarrassment in the English press. 'We understand', went one pseudo-report, '[that] several of the Civic Companies have invited Prince Albert to a day's sport in the City. They have offered to collect in the area of the Stock Exchange all the bulls and bears that are in the habit of prowling about the neighbourhood.'

Hunting would continue to be a public relations cross for Albert to bear. To hobnob with powerful peers on the informal terms necessary to conduct his extra-legal business, he needed to be with them as he was at Bagshot with the Duke of Bedford. That meant the hunt and chase.

SPORT! OR, A BATTUE MADE EASY.

Another in Punch's *campaign against bloodthirsty gunnery. Although the Prince was the captive of his hosts on such occasions, attacks like this one in 1845 were unsparing.*

Yet invariably that would lead to abuse from other quarters. 'Didst thou see in any of the papers that account of the battue at Lord Salisbury's,' Radical MP John Bright wrote to Elizabeth Leatham, 'when Prince Albert, the Duke of Wellington, Lord John Russell and others were present? . . . I think the Queen, as patron of the Society for the Prevention of Cruelty to Animals, should counsel her "subject" husband against such barbarous slaughter of defenceless animals for amusement only . . .'*

---

* Albert's eldest son would 'hunt' no differently, especially when out of England; and his heir in turn would take shooting as target practice. When in India in 1911, George V would bring down thirty-nine rare tigers and eighteen rhinos beaten, at his request, into his range.

The attacks on Albert in *Punch*, which had especially glorious fun with Albert and hunting, became so vicious in 1847 that a rival comic miscellany, *The Man in the Moon*, published an attack by Shirley Brooks in its November number, misidentifying the chief culprit at *Punch* as Douglas Jerrold, whose hands, too, were not clean:

> We'll clear thy brain. Look westerly [from Fleet
>   Street]. See where yon Palace stands;
> Stains of the mud flung there by thee are on thy dirty
>   hands . . .

Realizing that the lines were meant for him, Thackeray declared his loyalty to, and admiration of, the Prince, claiming to have composed more chaff than rebuke. Significantly, one line by Brooks – certainly no accident – had referred to honouring 'the King'.

Aside from the public slaughter of deer and boar, in which his brother had literally met Albert's wishes (as he was not separated from the Queen), Ernest unexpectedly proved a genial host. Albert gloried in the *Gemütlichkeit*. Uncle Leopold and Aunt Louise had arrived even earlier for the family reunion, as had Victoria's mother and half-sister, Feodora, and even Albert's stepmother Marie. At the ducal palace on 19 August, Victoria's journal records, 'The staircase was full of cousins.'

In the Rosenau, where Albert had spent his boyhood, the royal couple used three rooms atop winding stairs which overlooked the sparkling Itze and the tree-shaded *Eremitage* in a bend of the stream where the Prince, as a boy, once slipped off with his books. 'I felt', she wrote, 'as if I should always like to live here with my dearest Albert, and if I was not what I am – this would be my real home . . . It is like a beautiful dream.'

The presence of Lord Aberdeen and Lord Liverpool were reminders of reality, yet the days passed in a fairy-tale atmosphere suggesting that time had bypassed Duke Ernest's mini-state. On a quiet Saturday afternoon she 'sent for Bratwürste which is the national dish of Coburg – from the Markt & ate them & drank some of the excellent Coburg beer – they were so good'.

On August 26, Albert's twenty-sixth birthday was celebrated at his birthplace – '*more than I ever hoped for*', Victoria wrote. Her gift, brought from London in the couple's voluminous baggage, was a painting, with an abundance of warm flesh, by Thomas Uwins, *Cupid and Psyche.* Albert knew Uwins and liked his work. Also among Victoria's gifts were a walking stick and a snuffbox. (At Osborne, reflecting the Queen's distaste for tobacco, the only room not to be monogrammed above the doorway with a 'V & A' was the smoking-room. Only an 'A' identified it – although Albert did not smoke and intended the convenience for male guests.)

'From Mamma,' Victoria added scrupulously in her journal, 'he got trifles, and from Ernest a beautiful chessboard.' Albert's health was drunk at dinner, after which the family adjourned to a concert in the trompe l'oeil *Marmorsaal* (Marble Hall), where two of the pieces performed were compositions by Albert and Ernest.*

'God grant that we may come here again ere long!' she wrote. The next morning, they left in carriages for the long ride to the nearest railway station. Fifteen years later, when finally they were able to return, there were tracks laid all the way. Modernity would creep up even on Coburg.

Although, for Christmas and birthdays, Victoria and Albert often gave each other pictures innocent enough to hang in public view in any Evangelical home – children and angels and domestic scenes – the art in which they delighted and would display in their private chambers, especially at Osborne, revealed their pleasure in the nude, male and female. In all sizes from grand to miniature, these reflected fashion much less than preference. It may have been the Italianate quality of structure and setting of the Albert-designed Osborne House which would replace the original structure which suggested to Victoria and Albert commissioning statues of themselves in Roman dress. One by the German sculptor Emil Wolff shows the barefoot Prince in a warrior's short-skirted tunic, shield at his side, left arm resting on his belted scabbard. A Victoria by John Gibson shows a Roman queen, crowned and sandalled, in bare-shouldered dress and cloak, scroll in one hand, wreath in the other. Both are at Osborne House still, where the Queen and Prince accumulated a long corridor of classical reproductions as well as new works in Roman style.

---

* Albert wrote thirty-seven *Lieder* as well as pieces for organ and piano – 'pleasant music without presumption', according to Yehudi Menuhin. Ernest also dabbled in opera, producing several at his own opera house and even singing in them.

Bought at the Great Exhibition of 1851 and given by Albert to the Queen as a Christmas gift was William Geefs's heroic and half-nude *Paul et Virginie*. John Bell's neo-classical nude and erotically posed *Andromeda*, exhibited by the sculptor ostensibly as an example of modern bronze casting, was purchased by Victoria in 1851 for Albert. Still another was William Theed's neo-classical *Narcissus*, totally nude in the original but fig-leafed in Victoria's copy, perhaps because the exposure of male genitals would have made guests uneasy: Victoria and Albert demonstrated few qualms about flesh in art. The Queen even bought a marble, nearly life-size, *Venus Anadyomene*, an authentic Roman nude found in the baths of Caracalla. It had been in the Duke of Buckingham's collection at Stowe, where it had been admired by Albert. When the Duke, in bankruptcy because of the royal state in which he lived and entertained, had to dispose of his art, Victoria presented the statue to the Prince on his twenty-ninth birthday.

Perhaps the last of the suggestive statuary purchased for Albert was his birthday gift for 1857, when both Queen and Prince were thirty-eight. Designed by Emile Jeannest, it was a gilded silver Lady Godiva, wearing only her hair, and sitting side-saddle on her horse. In art, at least, Victoria offered continuing access to fleshly attractions while her own physical appeal diminished with poundage and pregnancies.

Possibly the most intriguing painting to be hung at Osborne House was one not publicly visible – a startling, sensual, well over life-size *Omphale and Hercules*, by Anton von Gegenbaur that covered much of the wall opposite Albert's bathtub in the couple's private apartments. The canvas, which would be astonishing in the household of a truly prudish pair, confirms that Victoria and Albert were not. But perhaps *Omphale and Hercules* is also an index to Albert's subconscious. The seductive young woman, dandled on the broad thigh of the muscular god and clad only in alabaster flesh and a head scarf, is in Greek myth the Queen of Lydia, who once kept Hercules as her sex slave. Omphale, Greek for the navel, seems to have acquired her name not only from her exposure of it, but because the umbilicus was considered the seat of the passions. Foreshadowing Albert's public role, the Omphale–Hercules relationship also represented a stage in the shift from matriarchy to patriarchy, for as the Queen's consort Hercules often ceremonially deputized for her. Dated Rome, 1830, it was bought by the Prince in

1844, when furnishings were being acquired for Osborne. It hangs there still.

Albert was not unaware of what he was doing, although such pictures contrasted oddly with the early Italian masters he bought for their design values rather than their naïve piety. Out of keeping with Christian piety but reflecting Albert's interest in fresco was a scene he commissioned in 1847 from William Dyce. Is there a message in it? In the panel a nude Neptune, king of the seas, offers his crown to a modestly clothed Britannia. The head of a rearing horse conceals the god's genitals, but the stallion's dark forelock itself strikingly suggests, in the anatomically appropriate place, luxuriant pubic hair. All Neptune's sea-maidens are nude, as are several sinewy males in his ranks.

Paintings remained a private language to Victoria and Albert. The year before Albert had purchased the *Hercules and Omphale*, each had Sir Charles Eastlake do a birthday present for the other, with the artist charged to keep the secret. Daniel Maclise, whose pictures often had an erotic edge, was also kept busy. 'He is in great favour with the Queen', Dickens gossiped to Cornelius Felton, 'and paints secret pictures for her to put on her husband's table on the morning of his birthday, and the like.'

The impression left by some of the Queen's choices is that if suggestive nudity in art stirred the libido, it had rewards beyond purely aesthetic ones. The pastel male nude she secured from William Mulready for the Prince seemed more a reflection of her own taste than that of her husband. Its seated subject, legs stretched out, looked thoughtfully upward, hoping perhaps for release from the pose. Victoria admired Mulready's nudes of both sexes (while Ruskin called them 'degraded and bestial'), yet Albert sought unsuccessfully to have Mulready copy his quite innocuous *Choosing the Wedding Gown* (1846) for the Queen.

Victoria even recruited Franz Xavier Winterhalter, the favourite Court painter of family scenes. As late as 1852, when both the Queen and Prince were thirty-four, she commissioned from the usually decorous Winterhalter a sensuous *Florinda* for Albert's birthday. Ostensibly a scene from literature, the canvas displayed a bevy of bare-breasted young women, the sun dappling their generous flesh. It was hung in Victoria's private sitting-room, where the couple often worked together. An even earlier queenly birthday present to Albert was William Frost's

L'Allegro (1848), from John Milton's poem. The grave poet would have been appalled by the treatment – three dancing girls, two of them bare-breasted. Frost also painted, for Albert, a *Disarming of Cupid*, again with warm nudes and semi-nudes. An earlier birthday gift, this time from Victoria to Albert, in 1843, had been Maclise's *A Scene from Undine*. The subject came from a romantic German novel, possibly the reason Victoria chose it, but despite the proper young lovers who are the central images, the painting bursts with unclothed goblins and sensual, nude, water-nymphs.

Albert's chairmanship of the Fine Arts Commission, dedicated to the cultivation of the arts but largely focused upon internal decoration at Westminster, had put him in regular contact with major English artists and demonstrated as well his artistic pragmatism. An exhibition of the prize cartoons – the sketches of the winning pictures – in Westminster Hall in the early summer of 1843, managed by the secretary of the commission, Charles Eastlake, drew large crowds at a shilling a head after Albert brought the Queen and gave her a guided tour. The Prince favoured the fee, and made the exhibition fashionable enough that from the proceeds the Commissioners could award ten additional competition prizes. Although some artists found Albert's tours of inspection distracting and even demeaning, he was putting a useful imprimatur on their work by openly caring about it.

No art scholar, he also added a touch of simple pragmatism when the committee looked at interior niches as suitable for statuary. Summoning a mason, Albert asked him to stand inside a questionable space so that viewers could assess the effect.

Often artists found that a royal purchase or commission resulted from the parliamentary competition, sometimes a work less close to history – and less clothed. For the Palace of Westminster, J.C. Horsley, later derided as 'Clothes Horsley' because he had become so prudish, offered to paint a combination of 'L'Allegro' and 'Il Penseroso', but T.B. Macaulay, one of three historians on the Commission, insisted – as if it were true history – that no topic could illustrate Milton unless it were from *Paradise Lost.* Horsley painted, instead, *Satan Touched by Ithurie's Spear while Whispering Evil Dreams into the Ear of Eve.* Albert, impressed by the artist's semi-nudes, had him do his Milton for Osborne.

Hardly a birthday went by without the Queen's presenting an image of herself, and soon of the family. So many portraits and statues of

Albert were commissioned in so many attitudes and costumes that the press joked it was the primary subsidy for the arts in Britain. Art dealers were also patronized, as Albert had Ludwig Gruner alerted for early Italian pictures. Albert even commissioned a painting in pre-Raphael* style, a *Virgin and Child* by William Dyce (1846). Albert also had Gruner watch for works by the sixteenth-century Saxon painter Lucas Cranach, his favourite among German artists. (One Cranach purchased in 1846, an *Apollo and Diana*, was a double nude.) But for the sculptures of Carlo Marochetti and the paintings of Franz Winterhalter, most royal commissions were from English painters. Masterpieces of their time, J.M.W. Turner's impressionistic waterscapes and landscapes moved neither Victoria nor Albert. Turner's bid for Court recognition failed. Instead, recognizing Albert's admiration of George Eliot's *Adam Bede*, Victoria commissioned two scenes from the novel to be painted by George Henry Corbould.

Birthday pictures had been important to the Queen and Prince from the beginning. When they had been married only eighteen months, Victoria had asked Edwin Landseer, one of the great animal painters of his day, to do a portrait of the infant Princess Royal with Albert's greyhound Eos in time for his birthday on 26 August 1841. A birthday present was no vaguely deadlined commission. When it had not arrived by eleven in the evening on the twenty-fifth the Queen sent a footman from Windsor in a carriage with instructions to return with the painting, 'done or not done'. He awakened Landseer at two in the morning and was back at six with the picture wrapped in a tablecloth.

Twice Albert found himself as purchaser of art collections he had not bargained for and which did not represent his own taste. In April 1847 his brother, short as usual in spending money, attempted to sell family portraits from the castle in Coburg. It evidenced, Albert appealed, a 'want of feeling' which would embarrass 'the whole family'. The publicity 'must damage your reputation in your own country and abroad', he warned. 'I cannot imagine how anyone could think of such a thing.'

---

* But not 'Pre-Raphaelite'. The self-anointed 'PRB' fellowship organized by Dante Gabriel Rossetti, Holman Hunt and John Millais to promote their pre-Renaissance ideals of simplicity, sincerity and fidelity to nature in 1848, first exhibited in 1849, and announced their goals in the short-lived Pre-Raphaelite Brotherhood journal *The Germ* in 1850.

In Gotha, where he now spent most of his time, Ernest was unmoved. Albert bought them.

More complicated and more expensive were the affairs of a remote, and hard-up, relation, Prince Ludwig Kraft Ernst von Oettingen-Wallerstein, who had visited Windsor in November 1843, when he was characterized by Victoria as 'gentleman-like and clever but slightly effeminate'. While in Bavarian government service, he fell into serious debt and asked Albert to co-sign a note with the London Rothschilds for three thousand pounds, then a substantial sum, against which he would deliver as surety to Albert a collection of early Italian, German, and Netherlandish pictures. Lionel de Rothschild came to Buckingham Palace on 13 May 1847 to explain what Albert's risks were, and he hesitated for three further weeks, finally signing a letter to N.M. Rothschild & Sons guaranteeing that if any of the three promissory notes, each for £1,000, were not paid, with five per cent interest, on time, he would, 'immediately after default', make the sums good.

By the first due date a year later it was already clear that his cousin, now fifty-seven, had neither the intention nor the wherewithal to clear his loan, and Albert, hoping to attract a buyer, put the collection of a hundred paintings on display at Kensington Palace.

When no purchasers emerged, Albert tried vainly, through the dealer Henry Mogford, to interest the National Gallery, which, had it the gift of foresight, would have recognized that among the mediocrities were individual works worth the total asking price. When that ploy failed, Albert became the poorer, as well as the possessor of the lot, while the press carped 'that the Prince was forcing the nation to buy the possessions of his German relatives'. Some, then, were what Peel would have called 'curiosities', including a portrait of Cosimo I of Tuscany by Angelo Bronzino, and works by or attributed to Jan van Hemessen, Bernard van Orley, Martin Schongauer, Hans Memling, Gerard David, Jan Provoost, Adriaen Isenbrandt, Quintin Metsys, and Giusto de Menabuoi. In the 1930s, a restorer discovered that the haloes of some of the saintly personages in the fourteenth- and fifteenth- century paintings had been 'improved' by spiky pseudo-Gothic ornament. Albert probably never knew.

Eventually the Queen, in Albert's memory, would present twenty-five Wallerstein paintings to the National Gallery – five German, sixteen Dutch and Flemish, and four Italian. Many now hang in the

Sainsbury Wing of the Gallery; the rejected canvases are at Hampton Court and Buckingham Palace.

Although Albert influenced English art largely by patronizing English artists, the Italianate Osborne House he designed with Gruner had real architectural influence from the moment the royal family moved into it. Not only was it pictured regularly, inside and out, in the illustrated magazines; it could be admired, even when under construction, from ships arriving at or departing from Southampton. Stucco became more fashionable, as did the short towers and the avoidance of exact symmetry. Suburban villas on both sides of the Atlantic echoed aspects of Osborne for decades and, despite its red brick, the Smithsonian Institution in Washington has an Osborne look, as do many American college buildings of mid-century and after.

Among the problems which Peel brought to the royal couple on their return from Coburg was his government's continuing inability to repeal the Corn Laws. Hunger in Ireland was worse than ever, causing wholesale emigration into Liverpool, where tens of thousands who could not afford steerage to America remained in teeming slums. Protectionists in Peel's party, even the revered and godlike Wellington, would deprecate the 'fright' given to Peel over 'rotten potatoes', and vote with the squirearchy. While the royal family was at Osborne in December, Peel announced his intention to resign.

'We were, of course, in great consternation', Albert noted in a memorandum. While he conducted much of the Queen's business, it was often now in both names. His notes of meetings with her ministers almost always employed 'We' rather than 'I', but Peel usually consulted Albert before going to the Queen. As 1845 wound down, it was clear to officialdom, as Greville observed, that Albert had been 'so identified' with the Queen 'that they are one person, and as he likes and she dislikes business, it is obvious that while she has the title, he is really discharging the functions of the Sovereign. He is King to all intents and purposes.' Even had he been the king he would have had no constitutional means but to persuade privately, and Albert wondered in his memorandum why measures similar to those adopted by other European countries affected by the potato blight could not be enacted – opening Irish ports and otherwise taking 'energetic means' to replace the 'usual food' of the 'poorer class'. The poor, however, had few votes in Parliament, and peers who preferred price stability whatever its consequences could block compromise.

All that Victoria and Albert could do, and then only when the founding of the charity made it possible, was to contribute to the British Association for the Relief of the Extreme Distress in the Remote Parishes of Ireland and Scotland, created by Lionel de Rothschild and Abel Smith. Even that was kept low-key. Legend had it that the Queen subscribed a mere five pounds; in fact, in the subscription list preserved in Dublin the first three names are 'HM The Queen, £2,000; Rothschilds' £1,000; Duke of Devonshire, £1,000'. Albert contributed £500 on his own.

It had been easy for Victoria and Albert to believe, confident as they were of Peel's efficiency and integrity, that he would go on for ever. Each reorganization of government further demonstrated the instability of electoral office and the continuity of the sovereign, political realities that Victoria would not allow herself to forget. Less concerned about distress in Ireland than about relations with France if Lord Palmerston, as seemed inevitable, returned as Foreign Minister, Victoria and Albert hoped that Lord John Russell – the heir apparent as Prime Minister – would be unable to form a government. After a fortnight he did indeed fail to patch a Cabinet together from his split party, and Peel was asked to continue. Meeting with Victoria and Albert at Windsor, according to the Prince's minutes, Peel was 'much moved' by their desire to have him return to office. 'There is no sacrifice that I will not make for your Majesty', he assured the Queen, 'except that of my honour.'

Peel's patched-up Cabinet promised only a delay of the inevitable. Attempting to help him, Albert went to the gallery of the Commons on 27 January 1846, to lend silent moral support at a Corn Laws debate. On the floor, Lord George Bentinck deplored the Prince's presence as giving 'the semblance of a personal sanction of her Majesty to a measure which, be it for good or for evil, a great majority, at least of the landed aristocracy of England, of Scotland, and of Ireland, imagine fraught with deep injury, if not ruin, to them'. Albert would never again make the mistake of going to the House.

More and more, as Peel struggled through the tumultuous last months of his Ministry, Albert was king without a crown. Pregnant again, Victoria left nearly everything but a few ceremonial functions to her husband. 'When politics are chaotic,' Lady Palmerston complained to Dorothea de Lieven, 'evening parties become duller. The Queen is in good health, but her pregnancy is the despair of her dressmakers...' Albert's memoranda of conversations with the embattled Prime Minister more often read, 'I saw this day R. Peel' than the more circumspect but misleading 'We'. Victoria's letters suggest more involvement with affairs than was the case, because she routinely commented in writing on matters brought to her; but tangible evidence otherwise appeared in Emily Palmerston's letter to Princess Lieven early that June: 'Prince Albert has just driven past my window with Ibrahim Pasha, on his way back from a review.' The son of Mehmet Ali, Pasha of Egypt, was visiting European powers as his father's agent, and Albert was acting for the Queen. Pregnancy and postpartum confinement had been the Queen's reasons in the first half of 1846, but Victoria no longer needed to furnish excuses for Albert.

A frank memorandum dated from Buckingham Palace that April – Albert seldom threw any document away – shows the Prince in action as he struggled to keep Peel in office. He had called in the Prime Minister and opened by offering him a six-page summary of their conversation five days earlier. Peel scrutinized it, and after a long pause said, uneasily, 'I was not aware when I spoke to your Royal Highness that my words would be taken down, and don't acknowledge that this is a fair representation of my opinion.' Had he known that his remarks would be committed to paper, he confessed he would have spoken with more caution.

'I was anxious', Albert, who seldom discarded a document, minuted, 'that nothing should prevent his speaking without the slightest reserve to me in future as he had done heretofore. I felt that these open discussions were of the greatest use to me in my endeavour to investigate the different political questions of the day and to form a conclusive opinion upon them. As Sir Robert did not say a word to dissuade me, I took it as an affirmative, and threw the memorandum into the fire...'

Only twenty-six, the Prince was dealing with statesmen who were already in office when he was born – in a different country and political culture under a different language.

As with ministers, Albert attempted to speak frankly to sovereigns, assuring them, as he did (2 April 1847) to the authoritarian Frederick William IV of Prussia – whom *Reichsmarschall* Hermann Göring a century later strongly resembled – that confidences would be treated 'by us both with the strictest secrecy, and to be withheld from every one, including our Governments'. Not only would the exchanges be valuable, he argued, but they would be handed down to 'the Prince of Wales, your dear god-son, as the best endowment for his future kingly office'. Although the King might expect 'a certain excess... of purely British feeling', Albert conceded, because 'I am incidentally the Queen of England's husband, I am also one German prince speaking to another.' Albert sought not only Anglo-German understanding, but democratic evolution in Prussia that might lead to a unified Germany under a constitutional monarchy on the British model. Unreserved about bringing up political reform, he felt it necessary to interject, 'I venture to hope that our correspondence may not come to a close with this present letter.' It almost did. Albert's letters were often emotional and idealistic, stressing his Germanness, yet written as the uncrowned king of another nation. Only political necessity kept Frederick William writing – but not on the terms Albert hoped for.

The family spent the early spring at Osborne while Albert oversaw Cubitt's builders. In May the couple returned to Buckingham Palace, where Princess Helena Augusta Victoria was born on the twenty-fifth. Albert's surrogacy by now was seamless. He managed the Queen's business, attempting to prop up Peel, although Peelites – there was no longer one Tory party – were harassed by Protectionists on both Irish legislation and repeal of the Corn Laws. The rejection of Peel's Irish Bill came as Albert and family were back in Osborne, and the Prime Minister took the train to Gosport and a packet to the Isle of Wight to tender his resignation to the Prince. Ironically, Peel had won on the very issue that had split the Tories, but he needed Whig votes. (The parties were gradually realigning, with Peelites, the liberal Tory wing, largely joining the Whigs, now beginning to call themselves Liberals, while the Protectionists among the Tories were becoming known as Conservatives.)

Peel arrived at Osborne on the evening of 28 June, leaving the next morning to confer in London with his Whig successor, Lord John Russell, for whom he was certain Victoria would send. She and Albert were unhappy at losing Peel, but they had expected the event for six months, and his departure had only depended upon which bill would precipitate it – one to diminish the powers of the Church of Ireland, which had long colonialized Anglicanism, or Free Trade and cheaper grain. Victoria had resisted Peel earlier; now she wrote that she would miss 'a kind and true friend' whose loss was England's. Diminutive Lord John Russell arrived the next day, his interview conducted in Victoria's presence by Albert; and in the first days of July the Queen returned to Buckingham Palace to install the new Ministry.

Almost as great a loss was the replacement of the deliberate Earl of Aberdeen at the Foreign Office by the impetuous Viscount Palmerston, whose francophile sympathies were at odds with the Palace on the long-threatened Spanish marriages. Blocked in having one of his sons marry the adolescent Queen of Spain, Isabella, Louis-Philippe arranged to have him marry, instead, her younger sister, the Infanta Louisa, then fourteen, while the Queen, sixteen, would be provided with a Spanish Bourbon cousin, Francisco, the Duke of Cadiz, who was effeminate and believed to be impotent. In that way, Antoine, duc de Montpensier, might inherit the throne, or at worst a son of his marriage with the Infanta would be heir. With the European power structure still visualized in terms of crowns, Victoria and Albert, to prevent the political levelling of the Pyrenees by a dynastic betrothal, suggested for one or the other of the girls – and they were hardly more than that – their cousin Leopold of Saxe-Coburg-Kohary. Beyond Windsor Castle, that appeared to be the usual Coburger aggrandizement.

No marriages had been settled when Palmerston took office, but King Ernest of Hanover spitefully – yet accurately – accused the Prince of meddling. Meddling in the Spanish marriages seemed the foreign policy pastime of the mid-1840s, and Palmerston was no less involved and no more successful. Montpensier would never achieve any sort of power in increasingly anarchic Spain although he wed Louisa on the same day, 10 October 1846, as Isabella II was married to Don Francisco de Asis. The Queen would console herself with officers and men of the royal guard, among others, causing Albert to write, resentfully, of the marriages in April of the next year, 'The [new] King follows the inspirations of a miraculous nun who is paid from Paris, the Queen has her lovers and at present she is kept a prisoner in the castle... What will Louis-Philippe have to answer for in heaven!'*

* Isabella's house arrest evaporated quickly. She would bear a son, later Alfonso XII, and four daughters, all of questionable paternity. Louisa and Montpensier would have three sons and three daughters. One son, Antonio (1866–1930), survived childhood, becoming the duca di Galliera, an empty title. A descendant of Isabella,

With the new Ministry functioning, although not as Victoria and Albert would have liked it, the next dissatisfaction came with events in Portugal. Another cousin, Ferdinand of Saxe-Coburg-Kohary, was King Consort, and correspondence flowed between Buckingham Palace and both Ferdinand and Donna Maria that furnished royalist points of view very different from those of Palmerston's typically interfering – and liberal-minded – representatives, who took partisan sides in troubled Portuguese affairs. With still another cousin, Count Alexander Mensdorff, Austrian ambassador in Lisbon (later to become Foreign Minister), the family became involved when a revolution arose against what was a despotic but Coburg-related reign. Albert crossed Palmerston again in 1847 when Austria illegally annexed the rump Polish Duchy of Krakow, claiming that it encouraged rebellion within Austria's Galician and Silesian territories. An outspoken liberal on self-determination of peoples, Palmerston was almost always at odds with Albert's desire for stability, whatever the regime. Even the Prince conceded, however, that Austria was no model government. Perceptively ahead of his time, he observed, later, to Lord John Russell, 'The conduct of Austria can only be explained in one way: that it is one of the convulsions of a dying man. Her system is rotten, and conscious of her own disease and weakness, she struggles in despair.'

The volume and bulk of the letters sent and received by Albert, plus those he drafted for Victoria to rewrite in her own hand, suggest an enormous expenditure of time and energy. Many of Albert's exchanges with Peel and Palmerston run to ten or twelve handwritten pages from each correspondent. It was an age of copyists, a major task for clerks and secretaries, but most letters were laboriously penned first by the signer. It is easy to imagine a sleepless Albert writing and reading by candle-light or gas into the early hours of each new day.

A continuing distraction from external affairs was the rising of Osborne House adjacent to and overwhelming Lady Isabella's original dwelling. Throughout the year Victoria and Albert crossed the Solent to supervise the placement of furniture and the hanging of curtains and

however, a great-grandson of Alfonso XII, became King Juan Carlos when the monarchy was restored after the death of Generalissimo Francisco Franco in 1975. An irony which neither Albert nor Victoria lived to see was that Alphonso XIII, Isabella's grandson of dubious lineage, in 1906 married Victoria and Albert's grand-daughter Victoria Eugenie Julia Ena of Battenberg, who became queen of Spain.

pictures in what they called the Pavilion. In a niche on one landing the bare-legged Wolff statue of Albert in Roman garb already looked down on the central staircase around which the rooms were grouped. Finally, on the evening of 14 September 1846, after a lady-in-waiting threw an old shoe into the house for luck, the royal family moved in for their first night in the unfinished structure. Lady Lyttelton, remaining in charge of the royal nursery, oversaw the children scampering about, each attended by a scarlet-clad footman, and Victoria called the occasion 'like a dream to be here now in our own house, of which we laid the first stone only fifteen months ago'.

At their first dinner in Osborne House, everyone rose to drink to the royal couple's health, and Albert responded with a house-warming hymn of Luther's, from the 128th Psalm:

> So shall thy wife be in thy house
> Like vine with clusters plenteous,
> Thy children sit thy table round
> Like olive plants all fresh and sound.

'The windows,' Lady Lyttelton wrote, 'lighted by the brilliant lamps in the rooms, must have been seen far out at sea.'

Cubitt and the Prince had meticulously planned everything down to the height of the furniture, some chairs, desks and tables slightly scaled down to compensate for Victoria's small stature. Despite its formality, even the drawing-room was planned for efficiency, as off to one side was a billiard room separated from it only by open columns so that gentlemen of the Household, technically not in the same room, could sit in the Queen's presence on call. The private suite above the rooms for entertaining guests had splendid views of the sea enhanced by large windows of expensive new plate glass. In the Queen's dressing area her water-closet was disguised as a large wardrobe, and in Albert's bathroom *Hercules and Omphale* already hung. Perhaps the most curious feature of the suite was a mechanism beside their large bed which locked the door to the bedroom without the occupants having to stir from the sheets. For soundproofing and fireproofing Cubitt had insulated the walls with crushed sea shells.

Only a week remained of their scheduled autumn stay when the relocation had taken place, and Lady Lyttelton very likely spoke for the family when she wrote, 'We are miserable at having to leave this

Paradise, with this perfect house, so soon.' For Victoria it was Albert's house, which made it all the more perfect. 'When one is so happy & blessed in one's home life, as I am,' she had written in her journal a few months earlier, 'Politics (provided my Country is safe) must only take a 2nd place.' Home life meant the proximity of Albert rather than the presence of her children, as she confided to Stockmar when, in July 1846, the Prince had gone off on one of his many ceremonial journeys, this time to dedicate the Albert Dock at Liverpool. 'I feel lonely without my dear Master', she wrote, 'and though I know other people are often separated for a few days I feel habit could not make me get accustomed to it. Without him everything loses its interest. It will always be a terrible pang for me to separate from him even for two days; and I pray God never to let me survive him.'

In December, when the family returned,* Cubitt arrived with plans for Household and Main Wings. The old residence continued to be a service structure until the next stages were constructed. (By the time Victoria and Albert were finished building and furnishing Osborne, it had cost them £200,000, all of which they were paying for out of their own income, now efficiently managed.) The plaster walls of the new building were nearly dry, furnaces having been run while the family was away, and more of Victoria's and Albert's personal pictures could be hung. For the dining-room's largest walls, Winterhalter was painting a large group portrait of the royal family, the Queen and Prince seated, the children around them.

Royal differences with the new Whig (Liberal) ministry were not merely with personalities. Albert saw a philosophical chasm. He told Russell that he disagreed 'totally' with the view that the Crown had no activist role. Seeing royal authority in male-pronoun terms although he was ostensibly referring to the Queen, he insisted that the sovereign had 'an immense moral responsibility upon his shoulders with regard to his Government and the duty to watch and *control* it'. Both Albert and Russell understood that leashing Palmerston was close to impossible, but the Albertine doctrine rested on the need for something more than

---

* Albert had written to his aunt Julie (Anna Feodorovna) on 18 December 1846 that leaving Osborne for draughty and poorly heated Windsor would be 'a cold sort of pleasure'.

CINDERELLA; OR, LORD JOHN TRYING IT ON AGAIN.

Lord John Russell was a Prime Minister in waiting, or actually in Downing Street, for more than two decades. Punch satirizes his aspirations, and his diminutive size, in 1846 while openly observing that it was Albert who made the political decisions for the Crown. Victoria is not even in the picture.

historical precedent behind a royal seal or signature. Acting, rather than standing by, for Victoria required confidence that the royal will counted for something more than ceremony. Yet 1847 was the year that political economist Nassau Senior postulated to his friend Alexis de Tocqueville, 'Our Queen is a phantom, put there not to act, but to fill space, to prevent anyone else from being there.'

The risks of royal activism would touch Albert directly, and soon. The Chancellor of Cambridge University died on 12 February 1847. The proponents of Edward Herbert, second Earl of Powis, a former Tory MP and popular 'old boy' from St John's College, immediately put forward his candidacy, but he was regarded with distaste by the Master of rival Trinity College, Dr Whewell, who owed his place to Albert. The Vice-Chancellor, Dr Henry Philpott, Master of St

Catherine's and the real executive of the university – the Chancellorship was ceremonial and honorary – suggested to Albert, possibly at Whewell's bidding, that it was the unanimous wish of the heads of the colleges that the Prince stand. Since that suggested a solid internal base, Albert invited a deputation which waited upon him at Buckingham Palace on 17 February. He was assured of 'lively satisfaction' within the university, Philpott assuming that Powis would step aside.

With his interest in education, particularly in applied science, already established, Albert might have expected enthusiasm for him beyond the Masters of Colleges. He had even attended the previous annual meeting of the British Association for the Advancement of Science, at Southampton, in September 1846. At the mathematical and physical section he listened, with Sir John Herschell on his left and Sir Roderick Murchison on his right, to a paper on instrumentation to measure wind velocity. At the mechanical section he heard an explanation of the weight capacity of tubular construction for railway bridges, and another on methods of deep boring for wells and mine-shaft ventilation. Albert was earnest about enhancing the academic climate for technological change, yet that was a drawback to the many old boys and ageing dons who preferred tradition to innovation and who saw universities as places to prepare clergymen and gentlemen rather than engineers and chemists. Even William Whewell, whom Albert admired for his interests in geology and astronomy and who would promote the 'moral sciences' and 'natural sciences' Triposes at Cambridge, had published, in 1834, a treatise to be expanded into *Of the Plurality of Worlds* (1853), insisting that man was, by faith and fact, an unique creation and that no other life could exist elsewhere in the universe. With Whewell as with so many, science had to be reconciled with theology, not theology with science.

To Henry Reeve of *The Times*, Greville predicted on 21 February that Powis and his High Tory supporters would not back off – that it would be 'a sharp contest, which will, I take it, rather astonish foreigners. The victory will be quite as mortifying as pleasing to the Court...' Greville assumed that, somehow, the Prince would win, but Powis was well financed, and opened a campaign office in a hotel in Cockspur Street, London. Albert thought of withdrawing, which would look like cowardice, while his aides Anson and Phipps – in a memo by Anson –

warned of 'a disagreeable Encounter, & one which those who support YRH ought not to have subjected you to'.

Consulting Peel, whom he trusted above all other Englishmen, Albert asked on the twenty-second whether he should 'stop the possibility of my name appearing in the Contest'. Even if he should win, he asked, should he refuse a tarnished honour? Peel responded tartly the next day that he was 'strongly in favour of permitting the Election to take its course'. Phipps intercepted an election circular sent from Whewell and warned the Master of Trinity that Albert should have no knowledge of the steps taken on his behalf. At the same time, the Master of Clare Hall publicly called for Albert – who knew nothing about it – to withdraw, and Whewell produced another circular contending that Powis would only be 'a Chancellor of St John's'.

Polling was to begin on 25 February. At the end of the first day Albert was ahead, at only 582 to 572, a crowd of Powis voters having arrived on the train from London. Ineligible to cast ballots, undergraduates crowded the Senate House, raising the excitement. The next day, learning of the tight race, Thomas Carlyle wrote to Scots theologian Thomas Erskine with mock concern, 'Poor Prince Albert, it will be an ugly thing if he is beaten in this Inanity.'

At the close of balloting on the second day Albert had drawn ahead, 875 to 789. It had not been easy to vote that Friday, *The Times* reporting that crowds outside the Senate House campaigning for both sides threw 'missiles of all sorts' at people entering with their voting cards, 'and some refrained from voting at all, after having travelled many miles for the purpose, rather than subject themselves to the fury of the storm . . .' The third and last day for voting was Saturday, 27 February. Powis-supporting Cantabrigians struggled in, casting almost as many ballots that day as the Prince's men. The final tally was 953 to 837 – so underwhelming a victory that Albert asked Peel whether the Chancellorship should be accepted.

'The acceptance of the office without reluctance or delay', Peel advised, 'has about it a character of firmness and decision', and he offered the Prince a draft reply in the affirmative. Victoria also advised acceptance, assuring herself in her journal, and, presumably, Albert, that 'all the cleverest men were on my beloved Albert's side'.

Like campaigns for public office, inaugurations of the victors were not unduly delayed in the efficient 1840s. Albert was invested with the

ELECTING A CHANCELLOR AT CAMBRIDGE.

Punch *late in 1847 describing the campaign for Chancellor at Cambridge, and Albert's alleged qualifications.*

seals of the Chancellorship on 25 March 1847, in the Green Drawing-Room at Buckingham Palace in the presence of the Masters of the Cambridge colleges. 'It is my first chance', he wrote to his brother, 'to do something in my own name for my adopted country.' Personally invited by the Prince in a spirit of reconciliation, the Earl of Powis found excuses not to be present. Within a year the Cantabs on both sides found reasons to be grateful for the outcome. In January 1848, while pheasant shooting in Wales on his estates, Powis was accidentally shot and killed by one of his sons. Had he been Chancellor, another election would have been necessary.

Albert would be an activist Chancellor in the best interests of the university. Appealed to by geologist Charles Lyell about Cambridge's forlorn and nearly non-existent coverage of modern science and literature amid its preponderance of classical and theological studies, Albert agreed to look into the problem, and appointed Adam Sedgwick as his on-site Secretary. In preparation for the formal installation, Albert had Charles Phipps write to the aged Poet Laureate, William Wordsworth, to request verses for the occasion, and Wordsworth, a St John's man whose brother Christopher had been Master of Trinity, agreed 'to retouch a harp...which has however for some time been laid aside'. The result was mediocre, describing Albert as 'the chosen lord' of the university. *Punch* parodied it in 'the Laureate's Installation Ode, as (it might have been) originally written', hailing Albert as

> One who, if not a King,
> He can be quite declared to be
> ...the next thing.
> And though thou wearest not a crown,
> (To Majesty alone belongeth that),
> Thou own'st a coronet of high renown,
> Thy memorable Hat.

While pleased with the versatility for satire of Albert's memorable shako, *Punch*'s writers put it aside to suggest other ceremonial offices which he might now fill, from Lord Mayor of London to Ranger of the park at Whetstone and Professor of Hebrew at the University of Houndsditch.

The installation ceremonies, beginning on 5 July, were graced by eminent Continental as well as British academicians, and nobility from Albert's friend Prince Löwenstein to the Duke of Wellington. Upstaging all the recipients of honorary degrees to be awarded by Albert as Chancellor was Sir Harry Smith, who arrived in Cambridge preceded by a regimental band and mounted on the Arabian charger which he had ridden at the Battle of Aliwal in the Punjab the year before. 'Almost covered with diamonds', as Sedgwick described her, the Queen was Sir Harry's chief rival for attention, but as a woman she was ineligible for an honorary degree.

For a couple used to having few private moments in public, the Queen and Prince had to take what opportunities they could, and one evening they walked, an entourage discreetly following, along the Backs – in Victoria's journal, the Cam 'waterside' – Albert covering his formal black-and-gold academic regalia, all but his Chancellor's cap, with a mackintosh, and the Queen a contrast in evening clothes but 'with a veil over my diamond diadem'.

For the Prince, it was the prelude to the real work of reforming the hidebound Oxbridge system and dragging university education in England into the nineteenth century. He began following up Lyell's plea with a request to the Vice-Chancellor for curricular data, intended for comparison to German universities. The British Association for the Advancement of Science had already condemned the university hierarchies as interested in preparing students only for a Church vocation. Albert also asked for suggestions from both Peel and Russell, observing to Peel that Whewell, whom both had admired, felt that no scientific discovery was appropriate for academic instruction until it had been sanctioned for a century. Peel derided the 'absurdity'. To Russell, Albert outlined the antique course of study that omitted history, economics, law, psychology, chemistry, geography, art, astronomy, natural history and modern languages. The Professor of Oriental Languages, he noted, lectured on Sanskrit to one pupil.

Sedgwick would carry proposals to and from Osborne, and in the last days of 1847 Albert at Osborne was working out reforms with Vice-Chancellor Philpott – but not without internal resistance that would last well into 1848.

The winter of 1847 had been too vile for the family to remain at Osborne while work on the new structure continued. With the Irish enduring another year of famine and little government effort at relief beyond inadequate soup kitchens; foreign policy disappointments in Portugal, Spain, France and Austria; and a section of scaffolding collapsing at Osborne on 10 March, killing one of Cubitt's men and injuring several others, Albert had sunk into one of his frequent periods of gloom. 'We betook ourselves here,' he wrote to his stepmother that March from the Isle of Wight, 'in the hope of getting a breath of spring . . . but have found nothing but frost and a parching east wind; the day before yesterday for a change we had a foot of snow.' Finally, April brought real spring; Albert

busied himself overseeing construction work, and Victoria received dispatch boxes from London and planned another Scottish trip. Their
savings from Privy Purse income and other sources raised the possibilities
of leasing or buying property in Scotland, which reminded them of
Albert's Thüringia. The Duchies of Lancaster and Cornwall, income
from which accrued to the royal family until the Prince of Wales was of
age, were now managed by Albert and earned significantly more than the
£3,000 a year he brought with him from Coburg and the £30,000 he was
allowed by Parliament. Albert also anticipated, despite his experience
with Wallerstein, that he could borrow more on the strength of his status
and his augmented income.

With the new Osborne House a reality, Albert remained preoccupied
beyond state business. He was planning formal gardens to emphasize
the Italianate nature of the structure – patios, balustrades, stairways,
topiaries, pathways, lawns, parks, external statuary and urns. He was
ecstatically busy. And he seemed never still.

The Queen and Prince left Osborne Pier for Scotland in the *Victoria
and Albert* once Parliament recessed in August. With them were the
Queen's half-brother Prince Charles of Leiningen and the two oldest
royal children. The convoy, including four warships and the packet
Fairy, steamed up the Welsh coast and past the Isle of Man, into the
Firth of Clyde. The steam yacht continued on with the accompanying
ships to anchor off Strathclyde in the Sound of Jura. Undisturbed by
the incessant rain or the Queen's new pregnancy, the family transferred
to the smaller royal vessel to visit sparsely populated and wilderness
country.

Nosing into the forest-ringed lochs and glens, the *Fairy* disembarked the party at Fort William, just west of 4,406-foot Ben Nevis,
from which they jolted in pony carriages up what Victoria described as
'a very wild and lonely road' to Loch Laggan, just below the southern
end of the long diagonal of Loch Ness. James Hamilton, Earl of
Abercorn, had offered the use of his lakeside home, Ardverikie. Brav-
ing sheets of rain, a band of Highlanders in traditional garb emerged
to guide them over the floating bridge to the Earl's long, isolated stone
house, decorated as a hunting lodge with stags' horns and drawings by
Landseer.

Later in the day, the Earl arrived with his family to be presented
to the Queen and Prince. With his children, he had moved from

Ardverikie for the ten days of the royal visit to their more spartan inland farmhouse. Despite the mist and rain his two girls were wearing their best dresses; the boys were in kilts. Upon being presented, Lord Frederic Hamilton recalled seventy-two year later,

> My two sisters made their curtsies, and my eldest brother made his best bow. 'And this, your Majesty, is my second boy. Make your bow, dear,' said my mother; but my brother [Claud, who was four], his heart still hot within him at being expelled ... instead of bowing, *stood on his head in his kilt*, and remained like that, an accomplishment of which he was very proud. The Queen was exceedingly angry [especially as nothing was worn beneath kilts], so later in the day, upon my brother expressing deep penitence, he was taken back to make his apologies, when he did precisely the same thing over again ... *

Albert especially welcomed the privacy the floating bridge guaranteed. It 'belongs exclusively to ourselves', he wrote to the Duchess of Kent. Frustrated reporters, he added, called Ardverikie 'an un-come-at-able place', as they were 'quartered on the other side of Loch Laggan'. The party remained at the lodge in near solitude until September 17, Victoria observing in her journal that the hills and woods 'reminded us much of Thüringen'. Albert wrote genially to Stockmar on 2 September, 'Whenever we stir out we come home almost frozen and always wet to the skin ... The grouse are wild, and the deer very hard to get at, despite all of which we are still very happy.'

However isolated, Albert remained busy with domestic and foreign politics, taking off at the close of their Ardverikie stay without Victoria to inspect the engineering feat of the Caledonian Canal, which ran north-east from Fort William along the lochs to Inverness. Despite the terrible weather his reception was enthusiastic, with the people of the northern shires, already proud of the accomplishment, further pleased that Albert was willing to grace it.

Looking towards Europe, he wrote on 5 September to Lord John Russell, a weak Prime Minister dominated by Palmerston, who

---

* Years later, Lord Claud Hamilton was an MP and, from 1887 into 1897, ADC to the Queen.

accepted no advice, that it was not England's mission to '*impose* upon any nation' governmental forms alien to its natural development. He did not need to mention Palmerston. England, Albert insisted, had been fortunate in its head start in 'civilisation, liberty, and prosperity' and needed to be the exemplar rather than intrusive activist, for 'the return for all our zeal is hatred'. Italy and Germany, incomplete still as nations, were progressing 'of their own accord'.

While rain pounded the roof at Ardverikie, he penned a long memorandum defining two reasons for the failure of the German states to unite – 'mutual jealousy' and 'sovereign authority', and the resistance of Austria, 'a State composed less of German than non-German elements, whose policy is governed by other than German interests and views, and whose system of government is so wholly based upon stagnation that it cannot hold out a hand to progress of any kind without shattering its own foundations...' Somehow, he felt, Prussia had to take the lead in both unity and in reform. 'If, on the other hand, she declines to undertake the guidance of a moderate and systematic German development, then the vital forces of the nation driven onwards by the pressure of the times will find some irregular vent for themselves, and produce conclusions of all sorts, the final issue of which no human power can foresee.'

Distant from crowds and affairs, Victoria was content. Albert never abandoned business. The Post Office boat brought, and took, the mail, and between deliveries, when not out in the wet, stalking stag, Albert penned further letters and memoranda. On returning to Windsor in October he was full of plans for reform at Cambridge. Also, he intended to prod the King of Prussia gently toward reforms of a different kind, using the bogeyman of a German federation guided by Prince Metternich, who had been trying to keep Europe in stagnation since the Congress of Vienna in 1815.

While the luxuriantly bewhiskered Sir James Clark was attending the medical needs of the royal family in the west of Scotland, his son John was, on fatherly advice, attempting to soothe his weak lungs near Ballater in the drier air of the salubrious east. Young Clark was guest of Sir Robert and Lady Alicia Gordon in a castle – as spacious Scottish country homes, often with decorative towers and turrets, were sometimes referred to – called Balmoral. (The Gordons were brother and sister of Peel's Foreign Secretary, the Earl of Aberdeen.) Although Clark was only forty-five miles away as the corbie flew, he wrote to his drenched and chilled father of one sunny day after another. Impressed, the Queen and Prince asked Sir James to make inquiries about estates in the area which might be rented. A Deeside artist was commissioned to make sketches – which arrived at Windsor just before the news that Sir Robert Gordon had, on 8 October, died suddenly at his breakfast table.

The demise of the lessee of the owner of Balmoral seemed unconnected with its geography, and Lord Aberdeen, who had been brought into the royal search for a Scottish home, suggested that Victoria and Albert take up the unexpired twenty-seven years of the lease. Busy laying out the elaborate terraces at Osborne, Albert authorized James Giles, the artist who had drawn the earlier sketches, to paint watercolours of the whitewashed granite castle and its grounds and bring them to London. Before the close of 1847 he was back, and Victoria and Albert were impressed enough to have a solicitor initiate negotiations with the owner, the Earl of Fife.

Royal accommodations north and south were the chief Court priority that December. Parliament had voted, reluctantly, to rehabilitate and enlarge Buckingham Palace, with its wings to be extended and joined to create an inner court. Thomas Cubitt, now a friend of Albert, refused, as demeaning to his reputation, to bid for the job, but Edward Blore, the assigned architect, recommended to the Commissioners for the Enlargement of Buckingham Palace that Cubitt be accepted unconditionally. The work in London had already begun when Cubitt's crew at Osborne began stripping and disassembling Lady Isabella's former home. Nearby, Victoria and Albert and their children, at the new Osborne House for Christmas, watched. On the last day of 1847, Albert was away on business in London. The Queen was in her seventh month of her sixth pregnancy and leaving affairs to her husband. Alone on New Year's Eve, she went to her diary to reassess her life. 'When one is as happy as we,' Victoria concluded, 'one feels sad at the quick passing of the years, & I always wish Time could stand still for a while.'

The year 1848 was half an hour old when Albert returned by rail and packet and carriage and wished her a '*Prost Neujahr!*' It would be anything but that.

IX

The Violent Year

1848

'T HINGS ARE GOING badly,' Albert wrote to Stockmar in rare panic on 27 February 1848. 'European war is at our doors, France is ablaze in every quarter, Louis-Philippe is wandering about in disguise, so is the Queen; Nemours and Clementine have found their way to Dover; of . . . the others, all we know is, that the Duchess of Montpensier is at Le Tréport under another name; Guizot is a prisoner, the Republic declared . . . ' Exaggerating local unrest, he claimed that radicals 'refuse to pay the income tax, and attack' – he meant verbally – 'the Ministry'. Further, following a litany of troubles, 'Victoria is on the point of being confined'.

European economic crises in 1846–47 prompting widespread unemployment and misery had been mishandled by reactionary post-Waterloo governments that feared 'the spectre of communism' but not enough to liberalize their societies. Secret revolutionary groups and working-men's radical organizations took their frustrations into the streets. The first uprisings, the 'February Revolution' in France, sparked equally uncoordinated and generally futile revolutions elsewhere on the Continent, the discrepancies in aims between bourgeois and working-class leaders thwarting any chances of permanent change. But while regimes were being threatened, and some unseated, it appeared at first that the instability was not sufficiently contagious to cross the Channel.

En route to visit Albert in January, Ernest had stopped first in Berlin and then in Brussels. In Prussia, Frederick William IV assured Ernest that agitation for political reforms could be satisfied by window-dressing changes. In Belgium, Leopold worried that his rather liberal regime might be menaced by the hopeless erosion of the monarchy in France. Paris was particularly explosive. 'My father-in-law', he predicted, 'will soon be driven away, like Charles X. The catastrophe is coming unavoidably over France, and, in consequence, into Germany also.'

Thrones trembled across Europe. As Albert and Palmerston argued over the future of incompetent King Otho, an unpopular Bavarian who had been imposed upon Greece in 1833, other crowns were in even greater jeopardy. As Foreign Minister and most knowledgeable Englishman about external affairs, Palmerston cared nothing for European stability – as did Albert – if the alternative was liberal change. In a long entry on 22 January Greville gossiped in his diary that a Palmerstonian paragraph on the Spanish succession had been taken to the Queen and Prince by Russell with the suggestion that it be expunged. 'It did not become *us*', said the Prime Minister, 'to lay down the constitutional law of Spain.'

The Queen and Prince agreed. 'It was returned (so altered) to Palmerston; but when the despatch was published, it was found that Palmerston had re-inserted the paragraph, and so it stood!' What impressed Greville most was 'that they all *stood* it, as they always will'. The upheavals of 1848 would be responded to by Britain in two voices, the Palace's and Palmerston's, although the domineering Foreign Secretary would close his contrarieties to Albert with 'I have the honour to be Your most obedient Humble Servant'.

As messages flooded in with particulars about risings across Europe, 'Oh!' Victoria recalled to her eldest daughter after Albert's death, 'how much we talked over all those events day by day and hour by hour.' Even at eight, however, Vicky was considered a small adult, her father's protegée, and up to serious talk, while nothing was ever expected of the eldest royal son. As Greville observed, the Princess Royal was already 'very clever' while Victoria considered Bertie at seven 'a stupid boy'. It was 'the hereditary and unfailing antipathy of our Sovereigns to their Heirs Apparent . . . thus early to be taking root'. According to one of the Queen's ladies, Greville added, Bertie confided that during the voyage to Scotland – the episode sounds more like Albert than Victoria – 'he was very nearly thrown overboard'.

Paradoxically, as soon as the *status quo* began to crumble, the King of Hanover blamed both the Prince and Palmerston for the unravelling. It was Albert who was encouraging the King of Prussia to unite Germany under a liberal constitution, yet also tempting his brother to amalgamate the Ernestine statelets into a Kingdom of Thuringia. At the same time Palmerston was encouraging the ethnic fragmentation of authoritarian Austria and the unification, at Austria's cost, of Italy. Even Switzerland was, early in 1848, in the turmoil of further federation. 'What has Palmerston to answer for,' Ernest Augustus wrote to the Tory Lord Strangford on 21 February, 'for his conduct in throwing fire and flame throughout Europe?'

Duke Ernest was with his brother when news arrived from Gotha on 22 February that their step-grandmother, Dowager Duchess Caroline, had died. He rushed back for the obsequies. Albert could not leave the Queen in her ninth month of pregnancy, and was worried, further, about the imminence of trouble, foreign and domestic. Just before five in the afternoon of 25 February the Belgian ambassador to London, Van de Weyer, was in *The Times*'s offices looking for news, as telegraphic and rail communication with Paris had ceased the day before. As he was about to give up, a dispatch clicked in from Brussels with the first reports from travellers of the proclamation of the French Republic. He carried the news himself to Prince Albert, who brought it to Victoria.

On the leap-day of the 29th, Albert wrote to Duchess Marie, his stepmother, that the scattered royal family of France 'have come to us one by one like people shipwrecked'. The portly Louis-Philippe, his whiskers shaved, had managed with the connivance of the British consul at Le Havre to sail from Honfleur. On landing in England he appealed for asylum. Claremont was reopened for the Orléanist refugees. Albert went to see them on 4 March and despite his past hostility toward the Spanish marriages invited them to Buckingham Palace. The King, Queen, and duc de Montpensier came on the seventh, looking, Victoria noted, 'very *abbatu*'. Since they had 'hardly the means of living', she asked Palmerston to arrange for the family's expenses from a secret Intelligence account. (To avoid awkwardness, the ex-king and queen would refer to themselves thereafter as the Comte and Comtesse de Neuilly.)

Other royal refugees arrived. On 6 March, with revolutions in France, Sicily, Austria and, it seemed, additional places daily, Albert wrote with foreboding to Frederick William IV of Prussia that the uprisings of January and February let loose 'the evil spirit of communism, the hereditary foe of all society, and threatens the fall of other states'. Even in conservative Gotha there was unrest, with demands that much of Ernest's property become public – he had a proliferation of palaces and estates – and that citizens be guaranteed constitutional rights. 'My house is like a headquarters,' he reported to Albert on 20 March. '...I thank Providence for not having given me any children, for I should tremble for them.'

Unaware yet of outbreaks in Germany, Albert had written again, on 18 March, to the King of Prussia, this time about the birth that morning of Louise Caroline Alberta. He had no idea that Berlin had boiled over and that the King would be forced by fighting in the streets to mourn the revolutionary dead publicly, concede freedom of the press, and call for the assembly of a representative Diet in April. Scurrying under the umbrella of a liberalism in which he did not believe and a pan-German-ism he distrusted, Frederick William even called for the unity of the German states in defiance of faltering Austria, which was losing control of Lombardy and Venetia to Italian nationalists and seemed likely to unravel further. That France supported Italian unification at Austria's expense troubled Albert. An Italy shaped by France, with its radical republican tradition, he would write to Lord John Russell on 17 May, would be in its neighbour's debt, and France 'is sure to bring only developments of destruction into any matter'. Further, he saw the need for a formidable Austria to offset the ambitions of Russia.

Prince William of Prussia added to Albert's cares in England, arriving on 27 March. Although it was an opportune moment for him to be godfather to the new princess at her christening, when the Foreign Office advised against it, Albert asked Palmerston instead to give the Prince the dignity of diplomatic status – he had settled at Baron Bunsen's Prussian embassy – rather than have him identified as a political refugee. 'The poor Prince of Prussia', Albert wrote to Ernest, still safe in his backwater, 'is much to be pitied. He is very unjustly under a cloud.' He had been accused of ordering troops to fire on the barricades but claimed it was a canard.

In a long memo, in German as usual, and dated the next day, Albert thought out an idealistic plan for which events had now created an opportunity. He envisioned a German 'Federative State' with a strong sovereign, chancellor and parliament which would retain the 'States complete in themselves' with their 'dynastic forms' that embodied 'the Individualities of these People'. Thinking well of it, he had copies made and sent to King Frederick William and to Baron Stockmar, to Duke Ernest and to Frederick Augustus II of Saxony (deposed by revolutionaries but restored a week later by Prussian troops), to Ludwig I of Bavaria (driven to abdicate later in the year in favour of Maximilian II, who was forced to institute domestic reforms), and to the weak-minded Emperor Ferdinand of Austria, who would abdicate before the frenzy of 1848 ended and be replaced by his nephew of eighteen.

The young emperor, Franz Joseph, would be immediately fortunate in his Chancellor. As innocent of government as was Albert on arriving in England, the new sovereign learned quickly how an authoritarian state was run from the sophisticated Prince Schwartzenberg, who had been with General Radetzky's headquarters in Italy. By then the Austrians were turning back the Italians, and had tired of Palmerston's efforts to settle the destiny of their lower Alpine provinces. 'We never pressed on him *our* advice', Schwartzenberg wrote wryly to his Under-Secretary for Foreign Affairs (the Prince had also taken the foreign office portfolio), 'concerning the affairs of Ireland'. He would send, Schwartzenberg went on, an Austrian archduke to every European court but England to announce formally Franz Joseph's accession. No emissary would go to London to be exposed to 'the devoted protector of the Emperor's rebellious subjects' – and he identified Palmerston by name.

The British ambassador in Vienna forwarded a copy to his chief, who dismissed the complaint as 'the outpourings of an enraged woman of the town when arrested by a Policeman in the act of picking a Pocket'. Albert's secretary Charles Grey told the Prince years later that Palmerston had ordered Schwartzenberg's letter to be removed from the embassy files and destroyed.

Later Albert assumed that Prince William's two months of gentle exile in England – and education in politics for the likely emperor of Albert's ideal German government – meant that the Prussian heir apparent had become 'wholeheartedly' for reform. He had even praised English democratic institutions, and his wife, Augusta, to whom Victoria warmed, would vainly remind him of such virtues as William slipped back into traditional Junker attitudes.

More than one convert to constitutional monarchy was needed, however, and Albert also urged his reluctant brother, 'if some important

German prince' – there was flattery in the description – 'fails to under-take the task, it will fall into the hands of clubs, societies, professors, theorists, and humbugs; and if the work is not begun soon, the masses will seize the control of it'. Dragged-out attempts to patch together a new German federation would fail, as would the squabbling revolu-tionaries. At the end of May, it was safe enough for Prince William to return to Berlin.

England expected its own share of instability. Financial panic had cost jobs and savings; speculators caused huge losses in inflated railway stock; wheat prices had plunged to new lows although the hungry Irish could not afford it and would not eat it; unemployment and poverty – even many who worked earned starvation wages – had given new impetus to Chartism; and as a late winter gave way to cold spring, the homeless and the hungry thronged London and other grimy industrial cities. Benjamin Disraeli, the ambitious MP who led the anti-Peel faction among the Tories, privately considered a bounder by Albert, had published a much-discussed novel, *Sybil, or The Two Nations,* in 1845, in which he described England as two nations which had little understanding or even communication with each other – the Rich and the Poor. Their clash seemed inevitable, and Albert, worried about the turmoil, foreign and domestic, asked Peel, whom he trusted more than anyone else in public life, to call at the Palace for a talk on 'the many awful events that are taking place around us'.

Chartist demonstrations in English industrial towns had been grow-ing larger and noisier since the routing of the Orléanists in Paris. To prevent the disaffected from rallying around symbolic martyrs, the government in London shrewdly released radical agitators who had been imprisoned for sedition. Chartist leaders then announced a non-violent mass meeting on Kennington Common, south of the Thames. From there, a procession of tens of thousands of sympathizers would convey a huge petition to the House of Commons, demanding the liberalized enfranchisement spelled out in their charter. Allegedly endorsed by more than a million people, its roll of signers cast some doubt as to the genuineness of the document. The bogus signatures included the Duke of Wellington – seventeen times – and Queen Victoria. Even the reality represented a formidable following of the disaffected. The date set for what could possibly be a peaceable revolu-tion was 10 April.

Alarmed, the Home Office and War Office called up reserve troops to patrol the streets, and across Britain 150,000 special constables were enlisted. 'Every gentleman in London was sworn', Greville wrote. (Among them was an ambitious French exile, Louis Napoleon Bonaparte.) Her child of three weeks with her, Victoria prudently left for Osborne with Albert in the morning of 8 April, Waterloo Station having been cleared by police in advance. Concerned that there would be talk of royal cowardice, Colonel Phipps quietly walked the streets listening for any disparagement of the flight from London, reporting to Albert, 'her reputation for personal courage stands so high, I never heard one person express a belief that her departure was due to personal alarm.'*

In the short run, the Chartists had failed; yet as with many once-radical movements, its aspirations largely became law. Despite the Combination Acts which restricted mass agitation, popular frustration could not be wholly contained, and small demonstrations occurred in parks and squares, all easily put down. 'We have Chartist riots every night', Albert exaggerated to Stockmar from the Palace on 6 May, adding dramatically that they resulted 'in numbers of broken heads'. Another failure was an abortive Irish rising in July, inspired by very different motives. Hunger had led to apathy, and there was no end to the famine.

Most outbreaks on the Continent sought political liberalization or national separatism, and concluded in confusion of leadership and restoration of the absolutism that inspired them. Even in Austria, from which stretched an ethnic hotchpotch of an empire and where Metternich was ousted as the power behind a succession of weak sovereigns who fled to England, the regime survived. Warily, Metternich also returned, but the aged relic of the Congress of Vienna in 1815 would

* Nevertheless, the English radical G. Julian Harney would write to Friedrich Engels – Karl Marx's collaborator on *The Communist Manifesto* (1848), who had been living in Manchester since 1842 – that 'we Englishmen have but a very poor opinion of your German *princes*. We have a noted German prince amongst our field-marshals – well when the Chartists were about to hold their meeting on Kennington Common to *petition* for Parliamentary Reform, the said Prince *bolted* (do you understand the expressive English vulgarism?) from London to the Isle of Wight, and there his princeship remained until he was quite sure the naughty Chartists had gone back to their homes. After all the Prince I speak of was more of a hero than the celebrated Orléans princes. *Our* prince ran away *with* his wife, but the precious sons of Louis-Philippe ran away *from* their wives!' (28 March 1849)

never regain office. Nationalism was also behind the succession imbroglio in the Duchies of Schleswig and Holstein, part-Dane, part-German. The death of Christian VIII, who had declared their union with Denmark inseparable, and his succession by Frederick VII, prompted uprisings by the German population on 18 March. Prussian troops came to their support, driving the Danes out. The situation would fester after the Danes fought back and achieved a temporary truce. The dilemma required a Solomon.

Explaining away what seemed a partisan view of the conflict to Lord John Russell on 1 May, Albert wrote painfully, 'The Schleswig-Holstein question causes me much anxiety as I am afraid that we may be dragged by the Danes and Russians, perhaps even by French insinuation and diplomatic efforts, into an open opposition of Germany. I assure you that I try to divest myself of every particle of German feeling.' British opposition, he cautioned, might appear as hostility towards German 'regeneration and consolidation'.

Fourteen years later, the question would involve the Crown again, and with even greater anxiety.

With the threat of internal upheaval diminished, many in power were content to see a return to the *status quo*, but Albert, out inspecting working-class conditions in April, was appalled by the dank, dark slums, widespread malnutrition and unemployment. Poor relief, he learned, went to four and a half million people out of the thirty million in the United Kingdom, yet had almost no impact upon the poverty and misery. 'Surely', he wrote impatiently to Lord John Russell, 'this is not the moment for the taxpayers to economise upon the working classes!' Albert had been nominal president of the Society for Improving the Conditions of the Labouring Classes since 1844, taking the title at the request of Lord Ashley, the philanthropic future seventh Earl of Shaftesbury, but had done little other than lend his name. When Ashley now asked him to take the chair at a public meeting which would air the abominations, Russell's colleagues objected that the Prince might be exploited by noisy demagogues. As evidence, the Prime Minister showed Albert a pamphlet attacking the royal family for its guilt in the plight of the poor, which only reinforced his determination to speak out. The people, he wrote to Russell on 29 April, had as yet no 'tangible proof' of any interest in their plight on his part or that of the Queen. Despite Cabinet objections, he presided at the meeting on 18 May after an inspection of a model house to lodge the labouring classes.

His recommendations were paternalistic yet his reasoning was radical. 'Wealth should lead the way,' he exhorted. 'Wealth is an accident of society', and those happy possessors of it should intervene to ameliorate 'the evils produced by other accidents'. Those who 'enjoy station, wealth, and education' owed it to the disadvantaged to furnish, without being forced to by legislation, the means of self-help through making land, loans and lodgings available so that 'their poorer brethren' would have opportunities to work toward their own improvement. Further, he exhorted, the increasing prosperity of 'that class of our community which has most of the toil, and least of the enjoyments, of this world' would contribute to the happiness of all classes. 'Depend upon it that the interests of often contrasting classes are identical, and it is only ignorance which prevents their uniting to the advantage of each other.'

'At a time when it is much easier for Royal personages to lose popularity than to win confidence', *The Times* commented the next day, loyal subjects should greet the Prince's address with satisfaction. 'It is thoroughly English in feeling, English in language, and English in sense. Among the many speeches it has been our lot to peruse, we have not seen one which for brevity and plainness, for goodness and truth, would be more worth the reading of every man in these islands.' Widely reported, Albert's words encouraged even the illiterate, and would exert moral pressure upon business into acting in its own interest, and, eventually, even government. The Prince had found an unofficial pulpit.

On the housing issue, Albert proved as good as his words, commissioning out of his own pocket the construction of model working-class flats. Henry Roberts, who had designed Fishmonger's Hall in the City, planned the 'cottage flats' with simple but neo-classical façades and with two levels, each with two living areas divided by a central staircase. In 1851 they were exhibited on the edge of Hyde Park, then re-erected for use in Kennington Park in South London.

One of the first to take the Prince seriously was an elderly American expatriate banker. George Peabody had settled in London in the year of Victoria's accession, aged forty-two. He quickly made a fortune in brokerage and returned his wealth in great measure through philanthropic efforts on both sides of the Atlantic. Setting up trusts later worth tens of millions, he had vast tracts of tenements cleared and low-income housing erected that would be models for the future. (Many Peabody Trust buildings still house low-income Londoners.) Victoria would offer him a knighthood but he chose to remain an American citizen, and instead accepted a miniature of her portrait.

Pleas to Albert to lend his name and prestige to, or to speak or act for, myriad causes and committees and conferences filled his mail and sometimes emptied his purse. His personal Household cost half his allotment from Parliament, and he was always working to make royal lands turn more of a profit while paring the managerial costs that came from the royal family's pockets. Sometimes, although not always – as occurred with Irish relief – there was a public relations as well as a philanthropic benefit. When Albert became head of a fund to purchase Shakespeare's cottage in Stratford-on-Avon, and contributed the first £250, even *Punch* praised him, yet hoped, cheekily, 'that, having helped to buy Shakespeare's house, you will also buy his book'.

Albert also had another house in mind. Even more than her husband, who saw Scotland through a Thüringian lens, Victoria was eager to acquire a permanent home there, unconcerned about its inaccessibility for state business. However difficult it might be for her ministers, one of them would have to accompany the royal party, to represent the government. Despite railway lines that would eventually take passengers as close as Ballater, ministers would dread the assignment, while the distance would further attenuate the Crown's influence on events. Telegrams would not have the effectiveness of talk, and the bracing climate would not buoy up politicians who preferred the smoke and fogs of London to the sunny brilliance of the Solent. But at least the rail terminus at Gosport was only two hours from Waterloo Station, as opposed to the night-and-day journey to the north. Although the Prime Minister warned that Parliament would not finance a private royal home – and a second one at that – Albert went ahead, confident that he could support not only a lease but the unpredictable upkeep.

Two bills to recognize the right of Jews to sit in Parliament failed in the Lords in 1848, as they had failed in previous years. Lionel de Rothschild had been elected overwhelmingly and often by the City of London, but continued to be denied his seat. When the first of the bills in 1848 had again passed the Commons in February, largely with Liberal votes, Nathaniel ('Nat') de Rothschild, working since 1840 in the Paris offices of the firm (it would be untouched by events), suggested to his three brothers in London that in order to ease the bill through the Tory-dominated Lords, 'You should work with the Court party. Get your friend Prince Albert to use his influence and then perhaps it will go through.' Suddenly Albert's negotiations for the Balmoral lease (little escaped the Rothschilds) and the Oettingen–Wallerstein loan for which the Prince had been co-signatory intersected in the fertile brain of one of the brothers at St Swithin's Lane.

Albert's sympathies with Jewish aspirations were known to be stronger than those of the Queen. When legislation opened the path for Jews to sit on governing bodies in the City of London, David Salomons became an Alderman in 1847 (he would be Lord Mayor in 1855), allegedly prompting a liberal bishop to observe to the Prince, 'Thank goodness we've got a gentleman in the civic chamber, at last.'

'Yes,' Albert agreed, 'but you had to go beyond the pale of Christianity to find him.'

Working the Court party meant little more than having Albert or his surrogate, possibly Peel, attempt to sway peers closest to the Prince. The carrot suggested by the brothers in response to Nat was, apparently, the waiving of the £3,000 Wallerstein loan through accepting his worthless pictures held by Albert, and the offer of a further loan of £15,000 for a Scottish lease or purchase. But Nat turned bluntly negative. Conditions had become unpredictably chaotic. Further loans to royalty were unsafe. On 10 May, as Albert was close to agreement on Balmoral, Nat responded to 'My dear Brothers' – Lionel, Anthony and Mayer – to put all ideas of a *douceur* aside:

> You ask my advice respecting a loan of £15,000 to P[rince] A[lbert]. I think there is not the slightest occasion to consent to it. You will find yourselves in the same position with regard to him as we are with L[ouis-] P[hilippe]. If I do not mistake, my dear Brothers, he already owes you £3,000 which we paid here to the Bavarian minister. I really do not think you are authorised to advance so large a sum considering the state of things, and you should in my opinion tell him so. There is not the slightest reason to make compliments with him & I am convinced that whether you give the cash or not it will not make

the slightest difference in the fate of the Jews Bill. I can only repeat that I am decidedly against the advance & under the present circumstances I do not think you are authorised in consenting to it.

Nat's reply was more than a veto – it suggested that one of the brothers in London had already made quiet soundings with the Prince. Given the already legendary Rothschild secretiveness, confidences could have been exchanged in such an informal setting as a hunt – a favourite pastime of both Anthony and Mayer. Yet within a fortnight Albert had Balmoral. Sight unseen, and through a solicitor, he arranged to purchase the remaining twenty-seven years of the Gordon lease, including 10,000 acres of forest, for £2,000. On 20 May 1848 in the Tory bastion of the Carlton Club on Pall Mall, Captain Alexander Wharton Duff, acting for the Fife Trustees, signed after adding a clause that exempted them from any claim 'on account of additional buildings' put up by the Prince. Both Osborne and Balmoral would be Albert's properties, unconnected with the Crown.

At the time of his twenty-ninth birthday, he and Victoria were preparing to establish themselves on Deeside. Furniture, pictures and personal belongings had already been shipped and placed according to instructions. In time to mark the Prince's birthday on the 26th, King Leopold had sent greetings, and three days later, from Osborne, Victoria responded to him that the '*dearest* of days' was to her one of 'eternal thankfulness, for a purer, more perfect being than my beloved Albert the Creator could *not* have been sent into this troubled world. I feel that I could *not* exist without him, and that I should sink under the troubles and annoyances and *dégoûts*' – disgust – 'of my *very* difficult position, were it not for *his* assistance, protection, guidance, and comfort. Truly do I thank you for your *great* share in bringing about our marriage.'

Victoria and Albert saw Balmoral for the first time on 8 September, after a voyage north to Aberdeen. The railway from London had not yet extended that far into Scotland. The land around the castle that was part of the lease included bothies in which peasants lived in near-feudal simplicity – two-room hovels of unhewn stones closed up with a mortar of mud and thatched with heather. Light came through small sealed windows and a wide fireplace sometimes gave out enough heat to keep the earthen floor dry. For the occupants, a nearby royal residence meant prosperity of a sort – year-round and part-time jobs for footmen and housemaids (supplementing staff brought from the south), gillies and gardeners, keepers and coachmen. By comparison with even the finest cottages in the area, quickly requisitioned for retinue who could not fit into the castle, the structure called Balmoral was regal, with mullioned windows, gables, turrets and round towers with conical roofs. The Household would dread its chill and loneliness, on both of which the Queen thrived. In the violent year of 1848 her journal entry was especially meaningful: 'All seemed to breathe freedom and peace, and to make one forget the world and its sad turmoils.'

The excitement surrounding the rare residence of a British sovereign in Scotland was such that even on Deeside the Queen and Prince could not shut out the world. In the form of press coverage the world arrived in advance of the royal family, and illustrated papers were rushed drawings as soon as the principals could be penned into them. One in the *Illustrated London News* showed the Queen, Prince and a kilted Bertie rushing across a bridge into beflagged Ballater. Press efforts to bribe backstairs maids and brawny ghillies would become such a nuisance that even the irreverent *Punch* would publish a John Leech cartoon of a reporter-artist at a keyhole – 'Gross Outrage: or, Paul Pry in the Highlands, making a sketch'. Once the stays in Scotland became routine, newspapers lost interest.

As with Osborne, the original structure and outbuildings were insufficient for the Household and such visitors as the Minister-in-Residence, and at first much of the adjacent land could be leased but not purchased. Eventually the royal estate would encompass 24,000 acres, and miles along the Dee. All farmers and cottagers on the estate would be forbidden to let their houses or to receive lodgers – a drastic protection of the Queen's privacy. The funds needed for the acquisition came unexpectedly in 1852. Even by English standards, James Camden Nield of 5 Cheyne Walk, Chelsea, was an eccentric, the uncharitable child of a wealthy amateur sociologist who had visited English and Scottish prisons in fifty-nine counties, gathering material for a book, *The State of Prisons* (1812). His son inherited only the elder Nield's frugality and his fortune in Home Counties properties. When 'Miser Nield' died in a nearly empty, cobwebbed house that might have excited the admiration of Dickens's Miss Havisham, there was little more to tally of his possessions than a bed made of a board, a few shabby sticks of furniture, a tallow candle, and a cat. But Nield also had holdings that would realize more than £250,000, then fifty times the annual salary of the Prime Minister. Having no family, he left it all to the Queen. Nield knew, Victoria observed, that she 'would not waste it'. Leased lands could be purchased, and a grander Balmoral built. Nield's largesse also went into the improvement and expansion of Osborne.* Stockmar wished Nield 'a joyful resurrection'.

Before the expansion of Osborne and the rebuilding of Balmoral, family life for Victoria's brood in both settings was *gemütlich* in the extreme. Limited as the facilities were, especially at Balmoral, Victoria preferred being away, in conditions far from royal, to the gloomy grandeur of Windsor and the city seediness of odoriferous drain-clogged Buckingham Palace. Charles Greville, who visited Balmoral with Lord John Russell, was amazed at the limitations of the Scottish house and the lack of 'any state whatever':

> They live not merely like private gentlefolks, but like very small gentlefolks, small house, small rooms, small establishment. There are no soldiers, and the whole guard of the Sovereign and the whole Royal Family is a single policeman, who walks about the grounds to keep off impertinent intruders or improper characters. Their attendants consisted of Lady Douro and Miss Dawson, Lady and Maid of Honour; George Anson and [John] Gordon; [Henry] Birch, the Prince of Wales's tutor; and Miss Hildyard, the governess of the children. They live with the greatest simplicity and ease. The Prince shoots every morning, returns to luncheon, and then they walk and drive. The Queen is running in and out of the house all day long, and often goes about alone, walks into the cottages, and sits down and chats with the old women... We were only nine people, and it was all very easy and really agreeable, the Queen in very good humour and talkative; the Prince still more so, and talking very well; no form, and everybody seemed at their ease. In the evening we withdrew to the only room there is besides the dining-room, which serves for billiards, library (hardly any books in it), and drawing-room. The Queen and Prince and her ladies and Gordon soon went back to the dining-room, where they had a Highland

* The Queen and Prince put aside some funds for a window in Nield's memory at his church.

dancing-master, who gave them lessons in reels. We (John Russell and I) were not admitted to this exercise, so we played at billiards. In the process of time they came back, when there was a little talk, and soon after they went to bed...

The Queen and Prince travelled without the burden of the youngest children, who were left at Osborne. Albert loved his brood with real affection and enjoyed playing with them, unlike the remote Victoria, who disliked children, especially small ones, almost as much as she abhorred the pregnancies that produced them. Nevertheless, she left them with morning and evening prayers by which to recall their mother and father. For Alice, the Queen inscribed on her gold-embossed and crested letter paper

Evening
O kind and good God, I thank thee for this happy day; pray keep me, and dear Papa & Mama, & my dear Brothers and Sisters & Relations Safe this Night.
Morning
O heavenly Father I thank thee for this quiet night; – pray make me a good little child, & keep me, & dear Papa & Mama & my dear Brothers and Sisters & Relations, safe through this day.*

Left at home with her prayers while Alfred, at four a year younger but required to keep Bertie company, went along, Alice was rewarded by a letter from her father, which he penned, in large print, on 16 September from Balmoral. 'You have written me another very nice little letter,' he complimented the precocious Alice. '...We hope soon to be with you again. ...Affie is grown still fatter and wears a cap, "who goes over my eyes" he says. Mama embraces you and I am your affect[ionate] Papa, Albert.'

Three days after the royal party's arrival in Balmoral, Albert wrote to his stepmother in Coburg, Dowager Duchess Marie, 'We have withdrawn for a short time into a complete mountain solitude... where the snow already covers the mountain tops, and the wild deer come creeping stealthily round the house. I, naughty man, have also been creeping

* Victoria actually wrote the prayers for Alice's fourth birthday, on 25 April 1847; presumably they were for general use thereafter.

1. Prince Albert and Prince Ernest in 1829 as painted in Coburg by Louise Leopoldine von Meyern, daughter of Baron Ferdinand von Meyern, a Court chamberlain, who was herself only fourteen at the time

2. Duchess Louise, first wife of Ernest I of Coburg, with her children. The future Ernest II is on her left, Prince Albert on her right. Painting in oils by Ludwig Doll, Gotha, 1823–4, Schloss Ehrenburg, Coburg

3. Schloss Rosenau, as it appeared in 1857 to the camera of Francis Bedford

4. Schloss Ehrenburg in Coburg in 1857 as background to the recently erected (1849) statue of Ernest I, Albert's father, by Ludwig Schwanthaler. Photo by Francis Bedford

5. The Royal Marriage, engraving from a painting by George Hayter, 1840

6. Edwin Landseer, *Queen Victoria and Prince Albert at the Bal Costumé of 12 May 1842* attired as Queen Philippa and Edward III

7. The baptism of the Prince of Wales, 25 January 1842. Engraving from a painting by George Hayter

8. Edwin Landseer's *Windsor Castle in Modern Times* shows the young married couple in the early 1840s with their first-born, the Princess Royal, dressed as an angel. Albert has just returned from shooting, and the results are spread out to admire. The Queen seems to be admiring her husband's handsome figure

9. *Omphale and Hercules* (1830), purchased for Osborne House by Albert in 1844. Joseph Anton von Gegenbaur shows Hercules holding weaving implements to emphasize his having been purchased by the Queen as her slave for domestic duties, including, as is obvious from their unclothed state, siring her children

10. Albert's portrait by Alexander de Meville, 1845, Schloss Friedenstein, Gotha

11. Albert
presiding at a
German-style
table-top
Christmas tree,
in an 1848
lithograph

12. Albert and Victoria sitting in the royal railway carriage with King
Louis-Philippe, late in 1844. From a contemporary lithograph

13. *Punch* in 1843 satirizing Albert's design of military paraphernalia, especially the shako hat

PRINCE ALBERT'S STUDIO

A CASE OF REAL DISTRESS

14. *Punch* in 1846 taking note of the royal family's alleged needs as its numbers burgeon. The waifs in the foreground represent widespread public distress

PRINCE ALBERT "AT HOME."
WHEN HE WILL SUSTAIN (NO END) DIFFERENT CHARACTERS

15. *Punch* in 1847 displayed a plethora of Alberts. The Prince was soldier, statesman, academic administrator, sportsman, designer of army regalia, courtier, and whatever else was needed

16. When Albert was admitted to the Guild of Merchant Tailors in 1845 – many City guilds so honoured him – *Punch* put him in his Field-Marshal's uniform for the investiture, doubling the satire by turning the tailor's iron into the torso of a rocking-horse

This is the Palace the Prince had built.

17. Opening page of an 1851 children's book in the 'Aunt Busy-Bee's' series (London), showing Joseph Paxton offering his plans to Prince Albert

And this is the Man submitting his plan
To the Prince who approved, and said it was good,
That a Palace of Glass should be built on the grass,
For the great World's Fair, which has since been held there,
And that Palace so famed, is everywhere named,
    The fine Crystal Palace the Prince had built.

18. Charles Phipps, F.W. Gibbs, tutor to the Prince of Wales, Bertie, Albert, Baron Stockmar, Dr Ernst Becker, Albert's German librarian, and Stockmar's son, Ernst. Windsor Castle, April 1857. Photograph by L. Caldesi

19. Osborne House in its completed sprawling state

20. Balmoral Castle, with the River Dee in the foreground

21. The Royal Family at Osborne, May 1857. *Left to right* : Princess Alice, Prince Arthur, Prince Albert, the Prince of Wales, Prince Leopold, Princess Louise, Queen Victoria with Princess Beatrice, Prince Alfred, the Princess Royal and Princess Helena

22. The Royal Family assembled for the marriage of the Princess Royal (*right*), 25 January 1858. Engraving from a painting by John Philip. Standing kilted in front of his father (*left*) is the Prince of Wales. Behind Victoria's left shoulder is her mother, the Duchess of Kent

23. Prince Albert, idealized in his uniform as Colonel of the Rifle Brigade, in 1859. Painting by Franz Xavier Winterhalter

24. Queen Victoria and
the Prince Consort,
Osborne, July 1859.
Photograph by Miss Day

25 Victoria and Albert, 1860,
from a *carte-de-visite*

26. Albert in his last years, in a lithograph from a watercolour by Edward Corbould, in his sitting-room at Windsor. His need for fireplaces and warmth is obvious, as is his balding, revealed in the mirror

27. An artist's conception of the death of Prince Albert, December 1861. The room is dramatically enlarged, and solicitous personages not actually present are added for effect. The artist may have been Octavius Oakley, but attribution is uncertain

28. The funeral of the Prince Consort in the Chapel Royal of St George's, Windsor, 23 December 1861, *Illustrated London News*

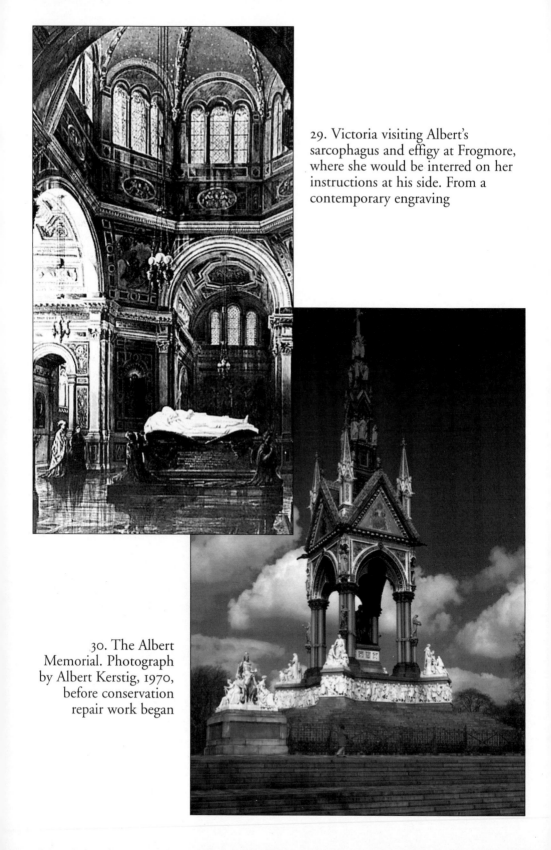

29. Victoria visiting Albert's sarcophagus and effigy at Frogmore, where she would be interred on her instructions at his side. From a contemporary engraving

30. The Albert Memorial. Photograph by Albert Kerstig, 1970, before conservation repair work began

stealthily after the harmless stags, and today I shot two red deer – at least I hope so, for they are not yet found [by the ghillies], but I have brought home a fine roebuck...' The self-reproaches are of great psychological interest. He knew his behaviour was morally dubious, yet compulsive. That recognition would change nothing. Something pent up in him needed violent release, which could emerge from the end of a double-barrelled shotgun.

Although Victoria and Albert received daily messages about the state of the Continent and the condition of Britain, nothing but urgent business would keep them long in London. On 28 September they left for Buckingham Palace, where they stayed overnight, then departed for Osborne. On 9 October they returned – to Windsor.

Even in Scotland, Albert had worked on his reforms for Cambridge, and over the months since his election had Sedgwick and Philpott come to Osborne to discuss the necessary university rules changes. As a dramatic gesture in the direction of modern ideas, he had the most distinguished scholar at Cambridge, Charles Lyell, visit Balmoral. He was knighted there by the Queen. Lyell's 1,600-page *Principles of Geology*, published in 1833 to the dismay of biblical fundamentalists, demonstrated, as Disraeli would write to a friend, 'that the great changes which have taken place in our globe are not the consequence of fast, sudden, and spasmodic changes but the result of that continual change, thro' countless ages, which is now, as it always has been, going on'. Darwin's work in the same spirit would not appear until 1859. Since Albert's boyhood explorations with Florschütz in Saxony, he had been fascinated by geology. Excursions with Lyell to nearby Scottish crags not only tapped that interest but demonstrated that the Prince would not be a merely ceremonial Chancellor.

On 31 October the Senate of the University carried the Albertine reforms although a considerable minority vote evidenced donnish antipathy to change. A new Moral Sciences Tripos included philosophy, political economy, modern history and law; a Natural Sciences Tripos, dear to Albert's heart, included anatomy, physiology, chemistry, botany, and geology. 'Some men will cling to their ignorance with their hands and feet,' Albany Fonblanque wrote in the *Examiner* of the reluctant minority. 'The student of Saxe-Gotha', he went on, had 'weighed Cambridge in the balance', and found what it called

H.R.H. FIELD-MARSHAL CHANCELLOR PRINCE ALBERT TAKING THE PONS ASINORUM.

Punch in 1848 saluting Albert's victory in modernizing the Cambridge curriculum.

university education only 'a sham'. *Punch* published a Leech cartoon, 'HRH Field Marshal Chancellor Prince Albert taking the Pons Asinorum' – Bridge of Asses – 'after the manner of Napoleon taking the Bridge of Arcola'. Oxford would be forced by the example into its own reforms.*

Albert legitimately resented the action of Lord John Russell in 1850 in establishing a 'Royal Commission' on universities without consulting the Chancellor of Cambridge. It was still another signal of the reluctance of the English power structure to move quickly and decisively into

---

*Punch – and John Leech – were counting upon their educated audience to recognize an additional inference in *pons asinorum*, which was a satirical allusion to the fifth proposition from the first book of Euclid, representing something difficult for beginners to get over. Tobias Smollett had employed the expression in his still-read novel *Peregrine Pickle* (1751). Albert, *Punch* was suggesting, was a political beginner, but a success at it.

the new world of science and technology. Albert would look for other and more visible means to educate a society that preferred to be left alone.

As the difficult year dragged to a close, Albert even found himself – through his affidavits and attorney – dragged into a court of law. Almost since the first days of their marriage, the Queen and Prince had been enthusiastic etchers of family, friends and domestic scenes. From October 1840 through November 1847 they sent their copper-plates to a Windsor printer, J.B. Brown, who had his journeyman, Middleton, make the impressions, dutifully returning all the paper, perfect and imperfect.

Before he returned the plates to the Castle, however, Middleton quietly ran off copies on card or common paper. When it became known 'in the street' that the copies existed, he was approached by Jasper Tomsett Judge, now arraigned, and the etchings, many signed in the plates, turned up in Paternoster Row in the publishing firm of William Strange, also charged. Strange had produced for sale, to the embarrassment of the Crown, *A Descriptive Catalogue of the Royal Victoria and Albert Gallery of Etchings* for an exhibition of sixty-three of them, ranging from heads of terriers to portraits of Vicky and Bertie. 'Every purchaser of the catalogue', the preface promised, 'would be presented (by permission) with a *facsimile* of the autograph of either Her Majesty or of the Prince Consort, engraved from the original, the selection being left to the purchaser'.

In the Vice-Chancellor's Courts the case was first heard on 6 November, with Albert's attorney, W.M. James, requesting that the defendants be enjoined from exhibiting the works or selling or other-wise distributing the catalogues, and that all impressions be delivered up to the Queen and Prince. In this they were joined by the Attorney General, Serjeant* Thomas Talfourd. The case was taken up on 6 December in the court of Sir J.Knight Bruce in Lincoln's Inn amid a flurry of affidavits from Brown's barristers and the formalities of appointing counsel to represent Jasper Judge, who claimed to be *in forma pauperis*.[†] A temporary injunction was granted and the case

---

* A serjeant at law was a member of a superior order of barristers. The term has fallen into disuse.
[†] 'in the character of a pauper', i.e. granted exception from court fees.

continued. On 13 December a barrister for William Strange claimed
that the printer, rather than committing 'wilful misconduct', had
offered 'a voluntary tribute of loyalty to Her Majesty, and of respect
to her illustrious consort'. Nonetheless, the Prince had 'no right of
property in any of the drawings or etchings, or impressions from the
same, which have been done or executed by Her Majesty... and no
right in this suit to restrain the exhibition or publication of the same'.
The Queen chose not to be a party to the action. Further, descriptions
of private works did not constitute reproduction of them. 'The plaintiff
was bound to show that he had a property some injury to which was
now sought to be restrained.'

Serjeant Talfourd responded that he supported the Crown not on
grounds of the questionable morality or propriety of the plaintiff's
'adventure' but on the more limited issue of property. Could anyone
doubt the profitable return to the adventurers who wished to utilize
property in its 'tainted state'? Albert, it was argued, had legal standing as
the Queen's husband to act on behalf of his wife because the property
involved was marital rather than royal. That the Queen's husband had
to go to the courts like any common citizen for a redress of his and
Victoria's grievances said much about the independence of the British
judiciary.

The end, after many defence postponements, was not reached until 1
June in the next year, when the injunction was made permanent and the
catalogues ordered to be destroyed (although their entire contents had
already appeared in *The Times* as a matter of court record). In a
conciliatory gesture, the Solicitor General observed of the defeated
printer that he was 'happy to state that the advisers of Her Majesty and
the Prince felt it consistent with their duty to take a decree against him,
but without asking any costs against him, because he might have been
misled [by the seller]'. The barristers for Strange accepted the decree
with gratitude that forgoing costs relieved their client 'from the impu-
tation that had rested on him'. The counsel assigned by the Court to
represent Jasper Judge was eager to argue his client's side further, but in
effect the case was over at the 1 June hearing. The hapless Judge had
already spent some days in Reading Gaol the previous August for
contempt, having failed to pay a judgement of £181 1s. 8d. in costs to
Albert, and wrote to the press from confinement, 'I have been compelled to pawn the very blankets off our beds.' It had been an embar-

rassment to the Crown, but the Royal art was safe from commercial contamination. *His Royal Highness Prince Albert* v. *Strange* was over.

Many who perceived the case only as the harrassment of insignificant men of business rather than the invasion of privacy, considered Albert a troublesome foreigner, meddling, as the Queen's husband, in matters beyond his place. The Prince seemed to intrude at every level. Always reluctant to delegate authority, had he been qualified to plead a case he might even have represented the Crown.

Even from Balmoral, as Victoria began making what would be continuing demands that the arrogant Palmerston be replaced at the Foreign Office, it was clear that whether messages to Russell or to Palmerston were from the Prince under his own signature or from the Queen under her own, they were all drafted by Albert. In communications to other governments, Palmerston was committing the nation to actions in the Queen's name about which she knew little or nothing, as he either omitted to inform her or deliberately altered messages she had seen without asking her. Some of the Queen's letters on the controversy were composed on the *Victoria and Albert* on the voyage to Aberdeen or on the return trip, and others followed in October from Osborne. The Queen in one draft by Albert was 'highly indignant at Lord Palmerston's behaviour', and both would continue to be outraged into 1849 as many of the revolutions on the Continent were flickering out and the Foreign Secretary tried every diplomatic means to keep them going. Radetzky's Austrians had overwhelmed the poorly led and poorly equipped Italians in Lombardy and Venetia, and – taking sides as usual – Palmerston pressed for Austria to make good on concessions offered when it was losing. Palmerston was also at odds with the Crown on Greece, on Schleswig-Holstein, and on France, while the Queen pressed Russell – since she was ignored by Palmerston – 'to keep a watchful eye upon our foreign relations, in order to prevent any other gradual deviation from the line of justice and impartiality which alone befits the dignity of the British Government'.

To rein in Palmerston's independent foreign policy, Albert asked Russell directly to require that all Foreign Office drafts be sent first to the Prime Minister for his reaction and then to the Queen for her approval. When Russell caved in and instructed Palmerston accordingly, the Foreign Secretary gave lip service to the command while establishing his privilege to claim extenuating circumstances – 'that her

Majesty should give every facility to the transaction of business by attending to the drafts as soon as possible after their arrival'. John Henry Temple, 3rd Viscount Palmerston, sixty-four, had his own cause for indignation. He had been in the Cabinet as early as 1809, ten years before the Queen and Prince were born, and he was schooled in a great nation numbering more than a hundred times the population (even excluding Britain's many colonies) of Albert's puny and backward duchy. Consultation with comparative children was not his style.

Albert's foreign policy arguments in the violent year of 1848 carried as little weight with blood relations. At odds with him on Germany was his brother, who preferred as little reform as possible, and also his cousin, Victoria's half-brother (by her mother's first husband), Prince Charles of Leiningen. By virtue of his powerlessness as heir to a mediatized, formerly sovereign, principality, the Prince had been named in August – he did not last long – President of a Reich Ministry set up in Frankfurt as a façade for nominal German unity while the individual states retained all former authority. Attempting to have it both ways, Albert protested that unity without impotence could only come about by strong Prussian leadership, and he protested against Leiningen's radicalism in relinquishing his own estate – his lordly prerogatives – as *Standesherr* for his family. Albert reminded him of the duc d'Orléans in the French Revolution, who 'forswore his estate' and was then sent to the scaffold anyway. But implicit in Albert's argument was his own family standing in Coburg. With Ernest childless, he wanted to reserve ducal sovereignty for one of his own sons. And he wanted to protect his German property and annuity, which the ducal financial administration, hard pressed in difficult times, had just taken away. 'It is my private fortune to which the *Kammer* is not entitled in any way,' he protested to Ernest. 'If it is bankrupt, it has to declare this...' He 'could not afford to loan out' his income.

It was a very bad year.

X

Master Mason

1849–1851

THE NEW YEAR of 1849 opened with the colour, tradition and serenity which only masked the unsolved problems of 1848. At Windsor there were nightly theatricals with imported London casts. One farce, only the tailpiece to a long-forgotten comedy, *Used Up*, remains memorable – *Box and Cox*, a single-act 'Romance of Real Life' by John Maddison Morton. Once Lord John Russell's clerk, Morton had become one of the most prolific writers of burlesques, many adapted from the French, complete to the *double entendres*. Produced at the Lyceum late in 1847, *Box and Cox*, the story of the complications of John Box, a journeyman printer; James Cox, a journeyman hatter; and Mrs Bouncer, a lodging-house keeper, would become the most often-revived farce of the century (and set to music as *Cox and Box* by Arthur Sullivan). Refreshments were served in the Throne Room and the Castle's private band played.

Two evenings later Twelfth Night was celebrated with a superb, crown-shaped cake thirty-inches in diameter, on top of which were sixteen figures in eighteenth-century costume, dancing alfresco under several edible trees. Even their miniature picnic, designed by the royal *confiseur*, Mr Mawditt, appeared real. Yet the same day, 6 January, reality itself had intruded, Albert imploring Prince William of Prussia to seize the opportunity of the eclipse of revolutionary zeal to return sufficient power 'to the princes and Governments' to enable them 'to undertake the shaping of the future'. And in that tomorrow he still saw Prussia, freed from Austrian backwardness, unifying Germany in a manner that would preserve regional sovereignties. 'I sing you the song of Cassandra,' he appealed, 'to get you to help in preaching energy, unity and patriotism to all whom you are in a position to influence.' A few weeks later Albert would encourage William, who seemed more forceful than his elder brother, the King, not to 'give up German unity'. He wrote similarly to Frederick William IV, but the pleas were futile. The Frankfurt Assembly would decide in March to offer the title 'Emperor of the Germans' – rather than Germany – to the King, a splendid title he declined for its emptiness.

Albert urged exploiting the illusory unity to accomplish larger goals – an empire of *immediate* territories under Prussian rule and *mediate* territories made up of other states in the *Bund*, with all international powers – diplomacy, peace and war, post, customs – under the Emperor. Trying to have it both ways, he was playing the part of a Saxon duke while a royal outsider in England. At the same time he and Victoria were busy attempting, one more futile time, to rein in the personal diplomacy of Palmerston – 'Pilgerstein' to the indignant Queen and Prince – who was representing the British Empire all by himself, especially in encouraging the breaking away of Austria's Italian provinces. Aside from instinctive loyalties toward a monarchical system under threat of nationalist implosion, the Queen and Prince saw detestable Austria as a crucial bulwark against expansionist-minded Russia. Albert explained to King Leopold of the Belgians, 'We . . . have incessantly waged war . . . with Pilgerstein, in which he got many an ugly poke, as it says in the White Cat.'* What he meant is that they constantly badgered the Prime Minister, Lord John Russell, to keep his Foreign Minister from acting independently, calling him to Windsor on 24 January for two hours of exhortation. Albert meticulously recorded the gist of the audience in just over a thousand words, explaining that it was only an extract. The key line was their contention that Palmerston had been 'careful not to place anything in writing before us'.

The Earl of Clarendon, a once and future ambassador close to Palmerston and now Lord Lieutenant of Ireland, was also summoned, and Russell sighed sympathetically, 'Oh, so you've had that, too'. Palmerston, both knew, habitually altered the texts of messages, even

---

* One of the *Fairy Tales* of the Comtesse d'Aulnoy. *Pilger* is the German for palmer, or pilgrim, while *Stein* means stone (ston).

when already approved by the Prime Minister or the Palace. The Foreign Minister, Russell confided to Greville, would have to go – but only after the parliamentary session was over. Until then, Albert wrote to Russell, if the Queen had 'any remark' on foreign affairs, 'she will make it to you'. And, obviously, the Prince would draft it.

Recognizing that the ground was shifting under him, Palmerston became, at least outwardly, more conciliatory toward Albert, responding to one of the Prince's many messages (this on 19 June) that he agreed that Germany 'under one body politic' – at least for foreign affairs – would be desirable. But as far as the various formulas proposed for unity, the government of Britain 'would, I think, be stepping beyond its legitimate or its safe grounds, if it were to become the partisan or the advocate of any particular scheme *or of the views of any particular German Power*'. When he spoke of the dangerous practice of becoming champion of a policy not thoroughly understood, he may have implied irresponsibility on the part of the Prince, but cagily confessed failure to 'comprehend the Plans' himself, or to 'foresee the consequences'. The Prince knew his own objectivity in German matters was at risk.

Although Albert's brother was leading a Thüringian contingent against the Danes in politically unsettled Schleswig-Holstein, Albert saw his own prejudices as unfamilial. Germany represented something unpolitical for Albert, an energetic people who in the most advanced of its states were in the vanguard of modern science – a model in that sense for his adopted country. Tirelessly keeping his hand in domestic affairs, he was determined to coerce what he saw as a reluctant England into the technological and industrial competition certain to dominate the economy of the second half of the century. He was pushing Cambridge University, as his example, into recognizing the need to educate the next generation differently.

Utilizing his various pulpits, such as the presidency of the Society of Arts, Albert was pressing for the increased visibility of British manufacturing. He regularly demonstrated his interest in new industrial techniques by visiting factories, going on 24 February with Lieutenant-Colonel (as he now was) Seymour to Minton & Company in Blackfriars, best known for its porcelain, to examine its new processes for making encaustic pavement tiles. Victoria, with Albert, went only to the Drury Lane Theatre that evening. Science and technology were the province of the Prince.

Carefully choosing his exemplars, Albert had already established friendly relations with Michael Faraday. Described by *Punch*, not noted for its enthusiasm for technology, as the man 'who can freeze water for you in a red-hot crucible', Faraday, then fifty, was at the acme of his reputation. A blacksmith's son once apprenticed to a bookbinder, he had acquired his science as a part-time assistant to Sir Humphry Davy at the Royal Institution, to whose Chair of Chemistry he succeeded in 1832. 'The prince of scientific expositors' (to Thomas Huxley), Faraday, when asked 'How much may a popular lecturer suppose his audience knows?' answered, emphatically, 'Nothing.'

For a country which prized church-going, Albert recognized the appeal of Faraday's devout Christianity, which remained unaffected by his discovery of electromagnetism. His view of the physical world was strongly theistic – that the properties of matter and the state of the physical universe emanated from divine creation – 'established from the beginning'. To bring to the English establishment the sense that supporting science was the highest – even the godliest – of undertakings, Albert asked Faraday to speak to an invited audience at the Royal Society on 26 February, a Monday afternoon. Court sponsorship made it an event. The audience was a non-scientific one, and included women as well as men – one of the ladies was the banking heiress and philanthropist Angela Burdett-Coutts. Electromagnetism, Faraday explained, utilizing what the *Illustrated London News* called 'ingeniously arranged machinery' to demonstrate effects on metals, flame, smoke and gases, was not a theory but a cosmic reality. 'What its great purpose is, seems to be looming in the distance before us . . . and I cannot doubt that a glorious discovery in natural knowledge, and of the wisdom and power of God in the creation, is awaiting our age.' The interest of his Royal Highness, Faraday closed, would be 'an additional incentive' to investigators of forces likely to benefit man.

'On the termination of the address,' the *Illustrated London News* reported, 'his Royal Highness approached the lecturer's table, and himself performed, under the superintendence of Dr Faraday, several of the experiments which had been exhibited. The Prince retired amid the loud applause of all present.'

Like the study of science, the professional study of history lagged behind Germany. Only eight of Oxford's 1,600 students enrolled in modern history – which meant anything beyond medieval studies.

Cambridge offered no lectures in modern history. Albert tried to interest T.B. Macaulay in accepting a chair in history at Cambridge, but when he declined, settled on Sir James Stephen, who had retired from the Colonial Office and now wrote for the distinguished *Edinburgh Review*. It was an unappreciated appointment, as Stephen had made many enemies in both incarnations, but Albert was Chancellor. 'Never have I seen an Englishman with a mind more open and free from prejudice', the Prince explained to Stockmar. 'I understand now why he was unpopular; for he hits hard at the weak points of his countrymen.' Cautiously, Albert had omitted the chief detail. Sir James's public scepticism about the existence of hell-fire had outraged the devout, who charged Albert with encouraging a heretic. Stephen, nevertheless, owes his being remembered at all to having been the grandfather of Virgina Woolf.

Not only *higher* education was on Albert's mind. Bertie, the Prince of Wales and future King of England, was now a few months past seven and, Lady Lyttelton reported, doing lessons out of the same book as his younger sister, Alice. He was handsome and polite, but backward in his studies. His father, who doted on the clever, articulate Vicky, put pressure on Albert Edward to approach her standard. Bertie responded with disobedience and tantrums. On 10 April, Albert wrote to his stepmother, 'Bertie will be given over in a few weeks into the hands of a tutor whom we have found. He is a Mr Henry Birch, a young, good-looking, amiable man, who was a tutor at Eton, and who not only himself took the highest honours at Cambridge, but whose pupils have also won especial distinction. It is an important step ... '

No pupil of Birch's would achieve greater distinction, as Bertie would become King Edward VII. But Birch would never again undertake so difficult and distasteful a task, one that he eased by combining Bertie's lessons with those of Prince Alfred, who was even younger than Alice. It enabled Birch to survive into 1852, when he escaped to the Rectory of Prestwich, near Manchester, promised to him earlier by Lord Wilton.* However distasteful to Birch's Puseyite predilections, when at Balmoral

---

* Young Birch would receive a living worth £3,000 a year plus the assistance of four curates – an astounding emolument that would put him immediately into the ranks of the well-to-do. Anthony Trollope would write scathingly of moneyed clergymen who would take their cabinet minister salaries and move to gentlemanly leisure in Italy while poorly paid curates tended the flock.

with the Prince of Wales he had to attend Presbyterian worship at Crathie Church, and at the Queen's further insistence, observe with Bertie such 'innocent amusements' as dancing, theatricals and shooting. Albert Edward would never become the intellectual counterpart of his father, which was not the fault, either, of Birch's successor, Frederick Gibbs, recommended by none other than Albert's Cambridge appointee Sir James Stephen. With Gibbs, the Prince of Wales's lessons would be extended to six days a week, from eight in the morning to six in the evening. The regimen would not improve the heir's ungovernable temper, nor accelerate his learning.

Albert would see to it that the future king's tutoring would not flag as he travelled with his parents to Ireland and Scotland. But before the journey to Ireland, which was anticipated with alarm by Whitehall, Albert had still further gestures to make on behalf of British technology. He had become so ubiquitous at laying foundation-stones that *Punch*, in a piece entitled 'the Prince of Bricklayers', observed that he had even set the first stone of the Ladies' wing to be added to the Licensed Victuallers' Asylum. 'His Royal Highness is now always laying the foundation of some charitable institution or other, and we congratulate him on employing his time...in this praiseworthy occupation of dabbling in bricks and mortar... *Punch*, in order to reward him in kind, hereby spreads the mortar of approbation, with the trowel of sincerity, upon a Prince who really appears to be coming out like a regular brick.' It was a long way from the vicious attacks of only a few years before. *Punch*'s gibes were now good-humoured. The Prince – for the moment, at least – had earned acceptance.

Albert's most newsworthy trowelling required rail passage to Lincolnshire in mid-April to the Great Grimsby Docks at the mouth of the Humber. There, shipments from the Continent could be transferred by rail to the manufacturing districts of Manchester, Sheffield and Birmingham, or to the port of Liverpool for the Atlantic trade. The banquet to celebrate the event, Lord Yarborough observed in introducing the Prince, would be held in a spot once nineteen feet below sea level. Into the eleven-ton 'stone', Albert placed a glass vessel containing the current coins of the realm; then he sealed the opening, using a silver trowel displaying the prow of a ship, a Triton figure, a young man representing dockyard labour, and a shield with the arms of England

*Prince Albert dedicating the new docks at Great Grimsby in April 1849 (*Illustrated London News, *21 April 1849)*

quartered with the Saxon emblems of the Prince. He was acquiring perhaps the largest collection of ceremonial trowels ever earned.

Here, the Prince predicted, would be 'a great commercial port. This work, in future ages, when we shall long have quitted this scene, and when, perhaps, even our names shall be forgotten' – here there were shouts of 'No, no, never!' – 'will, I hope, become a new centre of life, with the vast and ever increasing commerce of the world, and a most important link in the connexion of east and west.' After another burst of cheering faded he went on, linking two of his major themes in opposing the revolutionary spirit abroad. 'This work has been undertaken, like almost all great enterprises in this great country, by private enterprise, private capital, and at private risk; and it shares also in that feature so peculiar to the enterprises of Englishmen, that, strongly attached as they are to the institutions of their country, and gratefully acknowledging the protection of the laws under which those enterprises are undertaken and prosper, they love to connect them with the authority of the Crown and the person of the Sovereign.' There were loyal cheers as he went on to note that the Queen reciprocated their feelings. But she was far off at Windsor, where a messenger took a letter to his 'Dear Wife' reporting that he was still alive after a late snowstorm that had blown in from the North Sea, that in the circumstances the new North Pole seemed to be the spire of Lincoln Cathedral, and that he had icicles at the end of his nose.

Recuperating briefly under his own roof, Albert went off again in early May as an informal member of the Guild of Masons, this time to a hamlet south-east of Barnet that has given its name to the language.* At noon, on an elevated plot near the Great Northern Railway, in the presence of the magistracy and leading gentlemen of the country and using a silver trowel with a miniature crown on the handle and a scoop shaped like an oak leaf, Field Marshal His Royal Highness Prince Albert, Her Majesty's Consort, as the foundation stone inscribed him, raised a bricklayer's level vertically and horizontally, declared the stone well placed, and spread the first mortar for the Middlesex New Pauper Lunatic Asylum at Colney Hatch.

From there the Prince, having time only to take coffee from the luncheon spread for the guests by the Messrs Staples of the Albion Tavern, rushed back to Buckingham Palace by carriage. There he and Lt.-Col. Seymour left with the Queen's party for the annual visit by the sovereign to the Royal Academy on the Thursday prior to the opening of its annual Spring Exhibition. With the Queen and Prince at Trafalgar Square were, to the delight of the Academicians, the Prince of Wales, the Princess Royal, and Princess Alice. Greeted by the officers of the Academy, they were shown paintings squeezed frame to frame and reaching nearly to the high clerestory windows. At a quarter to five the royal party left in several carriages, with Albert's only remaining duty the usual formal dinner for distinguished guests. His days were often far more crowded than the bland descriptions in the Court Circular suggested.

Early the next morning he was busy writing to Lord Palmerston to set up a meeting to discuss, once more, the future of Germany. Some states were still chaotic. Baden was, for the moment, a republic as the contagion from France spread. 'If Germany is not yet constitutionally organised, if Prussia has not assumed the leadership of German affairs legally and according to contract', Albert would write to his brother, 'the poor Fatherland will have but poor prospects!'

---

* For institutions for the insane.

Despite Albert, England's priorities remained internal, with Ireland still on the edge of insurrection, and many of its poorest and most hungry flooding across to Liverpool, now the worst slum in the United Kingdom. Yet Victoria remained determined, whatever the security problems, to visit Ireland and demonstrate royal concern, although her government demonstrated little interest. From Dublin, Lord Fitzwilliam warned that a visit in ceremonial splendour, after the failure of another annual potato crop, would be an act of stupidity. 'A great *lie* is going to be acted there... I would not have her go *now* unless she went to Killarney workhouse... Galway, Connemara and Castlebar. That would have been *my* tour for her.' The Queen and Prince asked the Lord Lieutenant, the Earl of Clarendon, and the Chancellor of the Exchequer, Sir Charles Wood, to work out an unostentatious tour that could be accomplished as the *Victoria and Albert* steamed toward Scotland and their Highland retreat. Referring to the still-endangered vegetable of the Queen's other island, *Punch* quipped that on her austere arrival in Dublin, 'The Queen will... proceed to the [Viceroy's] Lodge, where she will be met at the door by the Countess of Clarendon with a dish of buttermilk and potatoes. Upon this the Queen will lunch; and, afterwards, in a thimble-full of regal punch, drink [a toast to the] Prosperity of Ireland.'

Albert, meanwhile, had become involved with the most formidable and frustrating task of his life, a project that had been germinating since the previous year. Science and technology had always fascinated Albert, but as consort to the Queen they became his mission in England's interest. In a speech later in 1849 he linked them to destiny. 'No human pursuits make any material progress', he declared, 'until science is brought to bear upon them.' Some cultures had slumbered for centuries, 'but from the moment that science has touched them with her magic wand, they have sprung forward... Look at the transformation which has gone on around us since the laws of gravitation, electricity, magnetism, and the expansive power of heat have become known to us. It has altered our whole state of existence... We owe this to science, and science alone; and she has other treasures in store for us, if we will but call her to our assistance.'

Such attitudes were not easy to impose upon the squirearchy, which preferred things as they were, and still dominated the House of Lords. When the renowned German chemist Baron von Liebig had visited from the University of Giessen in 1842, merchants and industrialists were impressed by his concepts of the future, but he left with the unpromising appraisal, 'England is not the land of Science.' Albert was eager to use the impetus of Liebig's visit to found a Sir Humphry Davy College of Practical Chemistry within the Royal Institution. When the school's hierarchy resisted change, in 1845 Albert (with Royal Physician Sir James Clark) was instrumental in the founding of an independent institution, the Royal College of Chemistry, in Hanover Square. Through Liebig's recommendation, the Bonn chemist A.W. Hoffmann was imported as director, contributing to the beginnings of the organic or aniline dye industry, which became crucial to English textile manufacture.

Through the Society of Arts, which Albert had joined in 1842, other means of encouraging technology were explored, and in 1845, the year he assumed the presidency, the Society promoted the idea of annual exhibitions of British manufactures on the model of France and Belgium. Albert asked to be informed when sufficient support made the idea practicable. Although a committee was formed to raise immediate expenses, the attempt, they reported, failed. Even manufacturers were lukewarm, some of the most eminent among them hostile to the idea of competition for prizes. One might not win, and then... In 1846, some came forward, and the Prince distributed a few prizes, acknowledging that although English manufactures excelled 'in solidity and excellence', they were 'outdone in beauty of design' by other countries. He suggested expanding the series of products to be open for prizes.

The 1847 exhibition, the first of any magnitude, was held in the Society's Adam-designed building – which it still occupies – in the Adelphi. To the astonishment of the manufacturers, twenty thousand people came. Twenty thousand people learning how to separate the good from the bad were a spur to the next competition, in March 1848. Seventy thousand came, crowding the Society's exhibition rooms daily. The success led Albert to propose two new prizes for the 1849 exhibition – for the encouragement of art in the colonies and for 'the improvement of an important Art'. The Queen contributed objects for display, as did the Duke of Richmond, the Duke of Bedford, and even Mr Henry Greville. Exploiting the momentum, the Society in March 1849 asked the Commissioner of Woods and Forests, who also had Windsor Castle and Buckingham Palace in his purview, to furnish a London site for periodical exhibitions of British industry. The Society also asked for the co-operation – which meant financial support – of both houses of Parliament. For the Prince, whose philosophy emphasized the private sector, seeking public funding was a recognition of the scale of the undertaking. Neither House, however, would be willing to spend anything.

On Saturday, 30 June 1849, Henry Cole, Francis Fuller, and John Scott Russell of the Society met at the Prince's invitation in Buckingham Palace at noon to discuss a more ambitious exhibition. Because a hall of large dimensions would have to be erected or acquired, Albert also summoned Thomas Cubitt, who, although a friend, proceeded to scotch the Prince's idea for a permanent building in Leicester Square – or any public square. 'Your Royal Highness proposes to accomplish a great public good by the Exhibition,' Cole quoted Cubitt as explaining, frankly, 'but if you build on a square on which the public had a moral, if not a legal, right, you will do a great wrong, and set a bad example.'

Albert did not see the loss of his easy solution as the end. Putting the site problem aside, he proposed four exhibition divisions – 'Raw Materials', 'Machinery and Mechanical Inventions', 'Manufactures', and 'Sculptures and Plastic Art'. The deputation assumed that he was thinking of encompassing all of Britain, but Albert had grander ideas. 'Whilst it appears an error', he proposed, 'to fix any limitation to the productions of Machinery, Science, and Art, which are of no country, but belong as a whole to the civilised world, particular advantage to British Industry might be derived from placing it in fair competition with that of other nations.'

The Society accordingly undertook an 'Industry of All Nations' exhibition for 1851, and recommended, for oversight, a Royal Commission. With the Prince at the head, financial guarantees might be secured and land made available. They expected the venture to be self-supporting.

The Prince took the enterprise under his personal purview, and asked John Scott Russell to visit at Osborne on 14 July to go over a proposed announcement, and to discuss the composition of a Royal Commission. Albert also proposed sending members of the Society as his deputies across the kingdom (as the credentials prepared put it) 'to collect opinions and evidence with reference to the expediency of forming a great Exhibition of the Industry of all Nations . . .' In effect they were to solicit support. Henry Labouchere, then President of the Board of Trade, was also present, and the three went over a plan of operations, from invitations to other nations and the values of prizes to the means of financing construction. Since the Society had no appreciable funds, its Council employed its solicitors, Tooke, Son, and Hallowes, to work out an arrangement that would give the contractor a substantial share of profits after expenses if the firm guaranteed a prize fund and built the exhibition hall, much of that cost presumably defrayed by sub-scriptions.

During the trip to Ireland and Scotland, the first an unexpected popular success for the Queen in the face of dire predictions, Albert never lost sight of the Exhibition. At Queenstown (now Cobh) on 3 August he arranged for Scott Russell to have princely letters of intro-duction to foreign ministers. At Balmoral on 3 September the signatures of directors of large manufacturing firms willing to support the Exhibi-tion were delivered to him. 'I do not lose patience', he told Stockmar on 10 September. The direct reference was to ill luck in hunting, but in a birthday summing-up on 26 August, as he reached thirty, he had confided to the Baron his contentment 'with everything', wanting only 'more energy and perseverance'. He had much on his mind. With Peel and Clarendon, he was pressing for university education in Ireland that would not (as he put it to Peel) 'degenerate in the South into Roman Catholic Seminaries, and in the North into a Presbyterian School'. He was still promoting better homes for the poor, 'and the boon will tell in improved health, sobriety, and domestic peace'. He was constantly – from whatever distance – attempting to rein in Palmerston on foreign affairs. And he was keeping watch on Exhibition matters, as the con-tractors, worried about the large advance expenditures, wanted their agreement renegotiated.

Much of Albert's business, especially when remote from London, had to be transacted through his secretaries Anson, Phipps and Grey, and it was while the Queen and Prince were travelling from Balmoral to Osborne that they received word of Anson's sudden death. He was only thirty-seven. His wife, whose previous children had died in infancy, was expecting a baby in two months. (It would be a healthy daughter.) Anson had been experiencing severe headaches for more than a year and seemed to have suffered a stroke – possibly an aneurysm. The Queen's journal on 8 October recorded her grief and Albert's woe. 'To see my poor dear Albert's deep distress made me wretched, for he loved and valued Anson who was almost the only intimate friend he had in this country, and he mourns for him as for a brother.' Anson's adroit balancing of the strong personalities of the Prince and the Queen was one of the least-kept secrets at Court. On 13 October 1849 *The Satirist* cautiously ventured that Anson's 'dexterous management often warded off a "blow-up" from his Royal Highness, when *the wind lay in the wrong direction*, in the *highest quarter*.'

Needing someone to lean on in his grief, Albert again turned to Stockmar. 'If you could come to me now', he wrote, 'I should regard it as a great act of friendship.' Because George Anson had been failing in ways no one wanted to notice, some of his work had been quietly taken over by Charles Phipps, who now took the secretaryship, while Charles Grey moved up to Phipps's place. Shaking off his despondency, Albert presided on 30 October over the opening of the New Coal Exchange in the City in place of the Queen, who had caught chicken-pox from one of her children. In state, the Prince travelled from Westminster Pier with his two eldest children in the royal barge, rowed by twenty-seven watermen. Bands played and bells pealed, and the Tower guns shook the air. At the Exchange not only was Albert introduced, but also the Prince of Wales. The Lord Mayor described him as 'the pledge and promise of a long race of kings'. Lady Lyttelton, accompanying the children, wrote to Catherine Gladstone, 'Poor Princey did not seem at all to guess what he meant.'

Albert's major anxieties into the new year of 1850 were the siting and financing of what was already being called, with derision in some cases, the Great Exhibition of 1851. A *Punch* cartoon showed the Prince, hat in hand, as 'The Industrious Boy' seeking donations:

> This empty hat my awkward case bespeaks,
> These blank subscription-lists explain my fear;
> Days follow days, and weeks succeed to weeks,
> But very few contributors appear.

Failure was widely forecast, but under Her Majesty's warrant an Executive Committee was appointed, and a full Royal Commission announced on 3 January 1850, each name preceded by such elaborately formal language as 'Our right trusty and well-beloved...' Bankers, brokers, scientists, engineers, architects, artists, merchants, and Mem-

THE INDUSTRIOUS BOY.

"Please to Remember the Exposition."

Since Albert in 1850 had to raise the money for the Exhibition as well as oversee it,
Punch shows him as refusing no donation, however small.

bers of Parliament appeared in the list, along with a few of the socially
eminent. Among the Treasurers, for public reassurance, were Arthur
Kett Barclay and Lionel de Rothschild. At its first meeting, in the still-
unfinished new Houses of Parliament, presided over by Prince Albert
on 11 January, the financially risky contract with Messrs Munday was
cancelled. At a second meeting on 18 January, a fundraising scheme
was developed, and at a third, six days later, subcommittees for each of

the exhibition areas were named, the ten members for Machinery and Mechanical inventions including such technological luminaries as mathematician Charles Babbage, inventor of the first calculating machine; Isambard Kingdom Brunel, designer of great ships, docks, railways and bridges; and Robert Stephenson, railroad and bridge engineer and son of the builder of the first locomotives. The meetings continued weekly – and almost always with Albert in the chair.

The day after the third session a public meeting was convened at the Mansion House by the Lord Mayor, Thomas Farncomb, to pass a resolution by City bankers, merchants and manufacturers 'That the proposal of His Royal Highness the Prince Albert to open an Exhibition of the Works of Industry of all nations in the year 1851, in this metropolis, is a measure in harmony with public feeling, and entitled to the general support of the community and is eminently calculated to improve manufactures, and to end in diffusing the principles of universal peace'. It carried unanimously.

A second resolution, moved by Lord John Russell in his private capacity rather than as Prime Minister, and seconded by Lionel de Rothschild – listed in *The Times* as MP from the City of London although still refused his seat because he would not take a Christian oath* – concurred in the cancellation of the Munday contract and declared that 'the large funds requisite for this purpose ought to be provided by the voluntary contributions of individuals, rather than from the public revenue'. It passed unanimously, whereupon the first announcement of subscriptions, in anticipation of the move, was released, beginning with a thousand pounds from the Queen and five hundred from the Prince. Lord John Russell was listed at £100 and his Chancellor of the Exchequer, Sir Charles Wood, also for £100. Bankers Joshua Bates, Thomas Baring, Lionel de Rothschild and Anthony de Rothschild each subscribed £500, as did several other financiers. The Governor of the Bank of England, H.J. Prescott, offered a paltry fifty pounds, while Charles Chubb and Son, the prosperous safe and lock company, managed only £25. Albert's hat would remain extended for many months, his sleep disturbed by funds worries and the increasing controversy over the proposed Hyde Park site.

---

* Rothschild was seated in 1858, after other re-elections, when the Lords gave in and permitted the Commons to prescribe its own oaths.

A *Punch* cartoon, 'London in 1851', predicted mobs from the lowest classes descending upon London for the Great Exhibition. It also forecast the destruction of the south-east corner of Hyde Park, 'the lungs of the metropolis', by massive crowds, the grassy expanse 'pulverised'. Why, *Punch* asked, should the park's turf be wasted? 'As it must inevitably be walked off, why not sell it, and let the proceeds go in aid of the Exhibition, which, we fear, is not supported with the liberality a project so laudable indeed deserves.' One issue cartooned the Queen 'interceding' with Albert, who stood adamant, arms crossed and stern face under his lampooned army shako, before an attendant displaying a rolled-up plan 'for spoiling Hyde Park', while a plaintive Belgravian lady representing socialite inhabitants threatened by the Exhibition site, watched workmen lowering ugly building cranes. Another cartoon showed a 'simple design' suggested for the Exhibition hall – a Brobdingnagian (and Albertine) shako. A verse began, 'Albert! Spare those trees...'

The Hyde Park elms were no joking matter, as Members of Parliament began to demand that no heretofore-ignored tree be felled to create exhibition space. In the Lords, the inevitable Baron Brougham

Punch *in July 1850 satirizing designs for the Exhibition building by devising one in the shape of Albert's shako* hat for the army.

made a fiery speech condemning the use of any West End park and suggested instead one to the east, as few who counted lived in such benighted locations as Spitalfields. 'The opponents of the Exhibition', Albert wrote, 'work with might and main to throw all the old women here into a panic and to drive myself crazy. The strangers, they give out, are certain to commence a thorough revolution here, to murder Victoria and myself, and to proclaim the Red Republic in England; the plague is certain to ensue from the confluence of such vast multitudes, and to swallow up those for whom the increased price of everything has not already swept away. For all this I am to be responsible, and against all this I have to make efficient provision.'

'An absolute prostration of the understanding takes place even in the minds of the bravest', Brougham asserted in the House of Lords, 'when the word "Prince" is mentioned in this country.' He displayed a petition against the desecration of any part of Hyde Park for exhibition purposes. *The Times* kept up the pressure by publishing a report on 16 March that according to rumour, four secretaries working for the Exhibition commissioners were each being paid £800 a year, then a very large salary, and that such extravagances were harming subscriptions. Not yet done with Albert, *The Times* on 25 June warned that the Exhibition would turn Hyde Park into 'the bivouac of all the vagabonds of London', and that the Exhibition building – predictably an oversized brick warehouse that would cost almost as much to disassemble as to erect – would be a 'vast pile of masonry' that would for ever destroy the character of 'our pleasant Park, nearly the only place where Londoners can get a breath of fresh air'. The Prince blamed the editorial turnabout on the recent purchase by *The Times*'s solicitor of a house near the Park.

Three days earlier – and very likely the reason for the outburst in the press – the *Illustrated London News* had published a drawing by commission member Isambard Kingdom Brunel, who had just constructed Paddington Station, of the building committee's likely design, a hybrid of ideas lifted from some of the entries. A series of connected, barn-like structures, it had at its centre a huge dome unrelated to anything else.

The Exhibition executive committee stubbornly laboured on, its meetings largely chaired, as in earlier months, by Albert. He spoke at one fundraising dinner after another, promoting his vision of the Great Exhibition of All Nations, 'We live in a period of most wonderful transition', he would say, 'which tends toward that end to which all history points – the realisation of the unity of mankind.' He felt confident that the application of new technologies was the key to a better future.

There could be no public sign of turning back. The location was firm, and cancellation or even delay risked national and royal embarrassment. Earlier in the year the Prince had reported that, despite public outcry, the Commissioner of Woods and Forests would lend no other site in London but that east of the cavalry barracks in lower Hyde Park, and extending to Rotten Row, above Knightsbridge. The mandate failed to silence objections, which were made more shrill by attacks on proposed building designs and materials. Yet amid the agitation, the Commissioners went ahead with plans for managing a huge international show without any practical concept of an acceptable structure. Despite Brunel's protest to Albert that prizes were 'mischievous as conferring undue advantages upon a thing well displayed... The opportunity of exhibition will be quite sufficient to induce all the competition we can desire', rules for exhibiting and standards for prizes were adopted, and communications sent and received for exhibitors and exhibits – even one from Berlin about showing a steamship. The announced opening date of 1 May 1851 somehow had to be met.

Sleep came less and less to Albert as other dilemmas and controversies kept him agitated. With the grand dream in jeopardy, he continued his running warfare with Palmerston, and involved himself – but cautiously, from the outside – in the anti-papal debates in Parliament which had followed the naming by the Vatican of Nicholas Wiseman as Cardinal and Roman Catholic Archbishop of the See of Westminster – the first such appointment in England since the Reformation. Both Church and State had condemned the designations as encroaching upon British sovereignty. The empty and unenforced Ecclesiastical Titles Act would follow. Another prospective appointment both teased and anguished Albert. The aged Duke of Wellington understood that he could no longer function as Commander-in-Chief of the Army. In the ten years he had known Albert, who had arrived for his marriage with an honorific and much derided title of Field Marshal, Wellington had learned to appreciate the Prince's efficiency and ability, and suggested on a visit to Windsor that he was the best man in England to succeed the hero of Waterloo. Despite rumours in the press since early in 1848 that the Queen herself wanted to have Albert in command at the Horse Guards in Whitehall, he had not been approached by the Duke before, and professed to be taken by surprise. Flattered, he agreed to consider the prospect.

It was an even grander dream than the Great Exhibition, which might come once in a lifetime and, if successful, be only the model for another place and time. To sit at Wellington's historic desk and command the army of the burgeoning empire – even the temptation was worth some sleepless nights. Yet Albert knew the impossibility of it all. Candidly, at Wellington's annual Waterloo Dinner at Apsley House in June 1849, Albert had responded to a toast proposed by the Duke that he appreciated the honour of being able to participate in an occasion to which 'no merit of my own could entitle me'. There had already been talk of how 'English' troops would respond to the command of 'the German husband of Her Majesty'. Aside from public reaction to what assuredly would be considered an act of gross nepotism rather than the thoughtful judgment of the exalted Wellington, the post would compromise Albert's already overwhelming duties as consort to the Queen. He had 'anxiously weighed' the question, he responded to the Duke on 6 April, and concluded that he had to be guided by 'whether it would interfere with or assist my position of consort to the Sovereign, and the performance of the duties which this position imposes upon me'.

He recognized his situation as 'peculiar and delicate'. If he were successful in his present duty, the Queen might be in an even stronger position than a male sovereign – 'But this requires that the husband should entirely sink his *own individual* existence in that of his wife – that he should aim at no power by himself or for himself – should shun all contention – assume no separate responsibility before the public, but make his position entirely a part of hers – fill up every gap which, as a woman, she would naturally leave in the exercise of her regal functions.' He listed a litany of functions he had assumed, from 'natural head of her family' to 'her permanent minister'. Wellington's proposal was 'a tempting idea' which he 'must discard'.

In some ways Albert had already violated the ideal. He had become, in a competition, an activist Chancellor of Cambridge University. He was also far and away the visible symbol and guiding force of the Great Exhibition. Even so, these were small matters in contrast to

Wellington's succession. And he had his role as sovereign surrogate much in mind in April 1850 as the Queen was again pregnant. Overworked as usual, the Prince had more than the usual demands on his energies as her confinement approached.

A year to the day before the planned opening of what appeared to be Albert's folly, 1 May 1850, Victoria was delivered of her third son and seventh child. The date was also the eighty-first birthday of the Duke of Wellington, and the child was named Arthur, after him, with the Duke standing as godfather. The delivery had gone well; the Queen was soon up and able to recuperate at Osborne, where she remained until Prince Arthur's christening. With Victoria largely out of the picture because of her confinement, Albert's supervision of the Household had again become almost total. Although he was willing as a matter of public display to have as elaborate a christening as the Church of England offered, only the month before he had admonished the Prince of Wales's tutor Henry Birch, who was suspected of 'Puseyism', to be less aggressive in his religiosity, and to cease resisting, when in Scotland, the Sundays at the kirk, as the Queen was Defender, as well, of the Scottish, or Presbyterian, Church. Birch offered to resign unless his charge could be taught the proper catechism.

Not needing another Household problem, Albert had relented despite his feelings, which Victoria shared, that all churches were alike but for the ecclesiastical formulas for which neither had much use. Birch finally resigned in January 1852 in favour of his rectorship. The young prince had become attached to him and was unhappy at the loss; his parents were relieved.

Attacks upon Albert's Anglican commitment were unrelenting over the years. His recommendations of knighthoods for scientists put him in bad odour with the clergy, and his and Palmerston's proposal, after *The Origin of Species* was published, that Charles Darwin be knighted was scotched when Samuel Wilberforce, the Bishop of Oxford, advised Victoria not to recommend it. Later, Dean Arthur Wellesley assured Bertie's second tutor, F.W. Gibbs, that it was not the Prince Consort who forbade the Athanasian Creed, with its hell-fire and damnation, to be recited in the chapel at Windsor but George III, 'because I won't allow my subjects to be damned in my own chapel!'

Hardly had the Queen been out in public again after Arthur's birth when, in London for his christening, she was fired at by William

Hamilton, a visiting Irishman, as she drove up Constitution Hill. Although the pistol proved to be loaded only with blanks, the shock was considerable. Eight days later, on 27 June, Robert Pate, an insane ex-officer whose surname was grotesquely appropriate, struck her viciously on the forehead with the brass knob of his cane as she left Cambridge House after visiting her elderly uncle. Fortunately addicted to unflattering bonnets, the badly bruised Queen was less hurt than she might have been. The old Duke of Cambridge died on 8 July, the day before the burial of Sir Robert Peel, whose horse had slipped while trotting up Constitution Hill and fallen on the former Prime Minister. (A broken rib penetrated Peel's lungs, and he had suffered three days of great agony.)

Peel's last speech in the Commons had been on the imbroglio which the reckless Foreign Minister had raised by his gunboat diplomacy against Greece. The Queen and Prince had once more urged Russell to remove Palmerston, but the Prime Minister weakly suggested the alternative of moving him to the leadership of the House of Commons, thus increasing his influence. 'Pilgerstein' had backed the claim of a Gibraltar-born merchant, Don David Pacifico, for alleged damages when his house in Athens was sacked, even insisting on reparations for large unprovable losses. Greece elicited support from France and Russia while Palmerston threatened naval action in a show of brinkmanship. His 'mode of doing business', Albert wrote sharply to Russell, causes Britain, which should be at the height of its influence, to be 'detested, mistrusted, and treated with indignity...'

The Tory leader Lord Stanley (the future 14th Earl of Derby) had offered a censure motion in the Commons on 17 June, and a week of spirited debate followed in both Houses on how foreign policy should be conducted. Gladstone, Disraeli, Cobden, Peel, Roebuck and Cockburn spoke brilliantly, and Palmerston responded with a speech four hours in length, accusing his detractors of abetting foreign conspiracy (in which by implication he included Albert) and 'domestic intrigue'. 'As the Roman in days of old', he defended himself in his peroration, 'held himself free from indignity when he could say *civis Romanus sum*, so also a British subject, in whatever land he may be, shall feel confident that the watchful eye and the strong arm of England will protect him against injustice and wrong.' The motion of censure failed.

Punctuated frequently by cheers, the greatest speech Palmerston ever declaimed 'made all of us proud of the man who had delivered it', confessed Peel, who had been on the other side. Albert wrote tartly to Russell that the Queen 'has no more confidence in Lord P. now than she had before'. He saw no likelihood that Palmerston in his sixty-seventh year would change his nature. The vote would only 'gratify his vanity and self-esteem'. Later in the year, while Palmerston remained above criticism, Greville would observe of the Queen and Prince, 'I find their aversion to Palmerston is rather greater than ever, for to his former misdeeds is now added the part he takes in German affairs, on which Albert is insane; so they hated him before for all that he did that was wrong, and they hate him now for doing what is right. However their love or hate makes no difference to him.' Albert could not resist the compulsion to meddle in what were essentially German domestic affairs, although the states and statelets were each essentially sovereign, and Palmerston, with the increasing arrogance of real power in foreign affairs, found less and less reason to exercise diplomacy toward his own Court.

Mutual animosity led Albert to a rare ethical lapse. He had learned nearly ten years before from Stockmar about Palmerston's attempt to seduce one of the Queen's ladies at Windsor. Mrs Brand was now Lady Dacre, and the potential scandal then had been suppressed in her interest as well as that of the Foreign Minister. Under great anxiety that the Great Exhibition might have to be cancelled, Albert lost his moral compass and tattled to Lord John Russell in hopes of swaying him toward dismissal of Palmerston. The matter simmered into August, Russell informing Palmerston only that the Court was seriously unhappy with him. From Osborne, Victoria then sent Russell a memorandum written for her by Albert and Stockmar laying rigid rules for Palmerston's future communications with her.

Realizing that Albert was behind the backstairs intrigue to oust him, the Foreign Minister requested an audience. The meeting on 14 August was a dramatic affair. A master performer, Palmerston had tears in his eyes; his voice trembled as he expressed his pain and regret at the remonstrances he had earned. What remained intolerable, Albert told him coldly, was not their disagreement on issues, but that the Queen, who had the right to be informed, was being treated evasively. They moved cautiously to discussion of cases like Schleswig-Holstein, which Albert worried might lead to further instability in Europe, and adjourned.

Since Palmerston controlled the editorial policies of several London papers, he saw to it that gossip about malign Court influence upon the conduct of foreign affairs surfaced. Again incorrigible in his behaviour, he challenged Russell to prove that his government could survive without 'Pam'. Russell accepted his resignation and replaced him with Earl Granville. Contemptuously, Palmerston refused to go to Windsor to relinquish his seals of office, and that December, Russell, in embarrassment, had to perform the ritual. It would not be the end of Palmerston, as the Queen and Prince hoped, but the beginning of the end for Russell's Ministry.

When a long and anonymous article appeared in the Palmerstonian *Westminster Review* condemning the sovereign's inability to look with 'passive indifference' on foreign affairs because the 'high interests' of the Coburg family prevented objectivity, Albert recognized the authorship and set out his response in a long but private memorandum. In effect it was a debate with himself about the legal and moral responsibilities of the Crown:

> Nowhere does the Constitution demand an indifference on the part of the sovereign to the march of political events, and nowhere would such indifference be more condemned and justly despised than in England. There was no interest of the House of Coburg involved in any of the questions upon which we quarrelled with Lord Palmerston, neither in Greece nor Italy, Sicily, Holstein, Hungary, etc.
>
> Why are Princes alone to be denied the credit of having political opinions based upon an anxiety for the national interests and honour of their country and the welfare of mankind? Are they not more independently placed than any other politician in the State? Are their interests not most intimately bound up with those of their country? Is the sovereign not the natural guardian of the honour of his country; is he not *necessarily* a politician? Has he no duties to perform toward his country?

In the months since the Don Pacifico debates, Albert had been on an emotional roller-coaster not only regarding foreign policy, but about the future of the Exhibition, which had become identified with him personally. Soon after the last of the last of the debates, on the afternoon of 29 June, Peel had left a meeting of the Exhibition Commission, his last official act, for his fatal horseback ride. Setting the accident against that context, the Prince had been plunged into agonies of guilt. A father figure to Albert who had meant much more to him than his unworthy actual parent, Peel was a devastating loss to a still-young man whose position made achieving intimacy with anyone other than his spouse almost impossible. And Peel only followed Anson. Nothing was going right. Even before Peel's fall, deeply depressed because it appeared that the Exhibition might have to be abandoned for want of a structure and the lead-time to build one, Albert had urged the avuncular but now hypochondriacal and doddering Stockmar, 'If you can come' – his usual appeal to the Baron when unhappiness seemed too much to be borne – 'pray do so, as we have need of you.'

Of her own accord, Victoria added her plea to Stockmar: 'It will do you good to be with my *beloved prince*. He *longs* for you.' To Leopold, the Queen wrote that Albert 'felt and feels Sir Robert's loss dreadfully. He feels that he has lost a second father.' Peel dead would have more impact upon the Exhibition's future than Peel (only a former Prime Minister) alive. Many in Parliament knew how much he had wanted the project to succeed, and that he favoured the Hyde Park site. Albert would soon eulogize Peel as 'liberal from feeling but conservative upon principle', and in an indirect Exhibition reference as 'the true type of the English character, which is essentially practical'.

Political opposition began to fade even before Peel's funeral. He had died on the night of 2 July. Two days later the motion in opposition to the Park site was defeated in the Commons by a large majority. It was then withdrawn in the Lords. Yet subscriptions, Albert deplored in his diary, remained 'very backward'. He was forced to recommend raising a guarantee fund, and £200,000 would be collected. Opposition now focused upon the huge masonry edifice everyone assumed would be necessary. Estimates based upon the composite Brunel plan drawn from the 233 designs submitted were that fifteen million bricks would be required. If indeed a structure larger than St Paul's were erected, what were the expectations that it would be torn down after a season's use? On that reasonable suspicion, no specific plan stood a chance of being erected, although 13,937 applications to exhibit had been received and financing was now assured.

A rescuer for the Exhibition, however, stood in the wings. The sideburned, dapperly dressed guiding genius of the Duke of Devonshire's conservatories, Joseph Paxton, had been in London early in June to look over the rebuilt Houses of Parliament, now almost ready for occupancy. The spacious chambers were being tested for sound, with unsatisfactory results. When Paxton commented to his companion John Ellis, the new chairman of the Midland Railway, that he hoped the Exhibition structure would be less of a mistake, Ellis challenged him, although specific plans for estimating contractors' bids had to be ready within a fortnight, to enter the competition. Intrigued, he went with Ellis to Lord Granville at the Board of Trade. Granville introduced them to Henry Cole.

According to Cole, all plans had to meet a basic design on which the Committee insisted in order to house the expanse of exhibits. If it could be done another way, said Paxton, could I submit a proposal? There wasn't much time, said Cole, and the deadline had to be firm, but he would arrange that the Executive Committee would permit review of an alternative design.

'Well, if you will introduce such a clause,' Paxton offered, 'I will go home and in nine days hence will bring you my plans, all complete.'

With nothing to lose, Cole agreed. Before hurrying westward, Paxton took a hansom cab to the Hyde Park site and walked about the twenty-six acres allotted to the Exhibition to get the breadth, length, and tree obstacles in mind. With his weekend already fixed – he had to supervise some work on the Britannia (now Menai) Bridge being built near Bangor in Wales – Paxton could not work on the Exhibition design until the next Tuesday, when he was seated in the boardroom of the Midland Railway for a business meeting. A large sheet of blotting paper lay on the table for each participant, and Paxton used it to pen a plan for Hyde Park based upon the *Victoria regia* greenhouse at Chatsworth. Before he returned to Chatsworth himself, he took his blotting paper to the Midland's chief engineer to ask about calculating the strength of columns and girders. On 21 June he returned to London.

At Derby Station, *en route*, he encountered Robert Stephenson, one of the Royal Commissioners, on his way to a meeting about the Exhibition. Paxton explained what was in his roll of plans, and the engineer scoffed, 'You can't be serious; besides, you're too late – the whole thing is settled and decided.'

By the time the train reached London, Stephenson, having examined the designs, was a convert. The next day Paxton saw Granville again, and afterward brought his plans to a Commission meeting. On the 24th he had a long, private meeting with Prince Albert. When the Commission met again on the 29th, Peel, in the last business meeting of his life, spoke in favour of Paxton's design. Yet the Commissioners, as Stephenson had warned, were largely resigned to the composite, and had already ruled out as unsound a five-domed glass-and-iron model submitted by Dawson Turner, who had designed a palm building for Kew Gardens.

Paxton remained convinced that his 'palace of glass', in effect a long, elegant greenhouse that promised ease in erection and equal dispatch in disassembly, combined vastness with strength. Albert's committee worried, nevertheless, that it could be dangerously flimsy in storm and wind. It might create its own climate indoors and produce rain and fog. With many thousands inside, the air might become intolerably noxious. The best that Albert – and Paxton – could achieve was avoiding a formal negative vote. After the meeting adjourned, Paxton offered his drawings to the *Illustrated London News*, which published a dramatic depiction of a sweepingly elegant building in its issue of 6 July 1850. Editorially, the *News* supported Paxton's design, for it 'has been considered and planned with a view to its fitness for the objects intended, as well as for its permanent occupation or removal to another site for a winter garden'. Further, it would 'form a peculiar novelty in mechanical science' while being much more attractive than the 'official' composite design. Public admiration was instant. The Commissioners' building committee retracted its disapproval to the extent of advising Paxton that if he submitted a detailed tender – a bid for a contract – his design would be reconsidered.

By the time Paxton returned from London he had revised his clean roof line to accommodate rounded transepts creating space for the tops of the big elms. In one section to the rear of the building, an angle from which drawings and photographs were seldom made, trees projected through an opening in the roof – this being the refreshments area. The aesthetic compromises were a practical solution to political necessities.

Confidently, Paxton had already consulted the builders Fox and Henderson, and had secured estimates from suppliers of iron and glass. Now he telegraphed requests for particulars. The following Monday, representatives from manufacturers in Warwickshire and Staffordshire took the train to London to meet with Paxton at the City offices of Fox and Henderson. Within the working week they had detailed drawings and specifications, and a cost estimate for the first building to involve mass production of parts – gutters, sash bars, girders, columns, windows, doors, pipes, flooring – on a large scale. Relieved, the Committee on 15 July accepted Paxton's plan.

With Hyde Park protected and a design which seemed affordable, there was little question that Fox, Henderson and Company of the London Works, Smethwick, would be given the contract for erection. For the Royal Commission, Henry Cole was appointed overseer of the project. The actual overseer proved to be the embattled Prince, as he was concerned with the exhibiting nations, the exhibits themselves, and the exhibit space. Once hostile, the press became an ally. Caught up in the reality of what would become the first World's Fair, even *The Times* was enthusiastic. *Punch*, which earlier had satirized building ideas for the Great Exhibition with its drawing of the 'Albert helmet', christened Paxton's concept a 'Crystal Palace'.

'I dreamt that the Exhibition', went a 'Mrs Mouser' letter to Mr Punch, 'which wasn't in Hyde Park after all, though, being awake, I can't be sworn where – was, as it ought to be, a palace of very crystal, the sky looking through every bit of the roof upon all nations under it'. And Mr Punch himself suggested, in a mock letter to Paxton, that the new Palace of Westminster about to shelter the Houses of Parliament after years of rebuilding, be replaced by a similar glass house. 'Here and there you can insert a pane of magnifying power to make any favourite Minister look a greater man than he is.'

'Crystal Palace' caught on, quickening the excitement of the curious who came to gape at the preparation of the site, the delivery of enormous quantities of parts, and the assembly of the structure, each rising section a small drama. The climax would be the bridging of the great transept late in the year by huge wooden ribs painted black to look metallic and stretching higher than the tallest elms. Before railways, the efficiency of the operation would have been impossible. Iron segments forged in the Fox and Henderson factory west of Birmingham went via the North-Western Railway Company to London and often within eighteen hours after manufacture were fixed in place at Hyde Park.

A secondary enterprise materialized close to the grounds – the sprawling wagons and carts of vendors of every conceivable comestible a gawker might ingest. Each observer was a potential visitor afterwards, and the crowds which thronged Knightsbridge and the Park grew daily;

many attracted by the constant inspections by the Prince, sometimes accompanied by the Queen. More than two thousand workmen laboured at the site, with thousands more fabricating elements of the building elsewhere, and still more thousands engaged in developing and shipping exhibits from as far off as Australia and India. On the site Charles Fox, the managing director of the construction firm, often put in eighteen-hour days and complained that each royal visit cost him pounds in lost work-time.

Exhibitors were encouraged by rules charging them no rent – but they would have to deliver and remove their exhibits as well as maintain them at their own expense. There was plenty of room for them. In scale, nothing like the Crystal Palace had ever been built. The structure was 1,848 feet long* – more than a third of a mile – and 408 feet wide, one of the great engineering achievements of the century.

The ever-malicious uncle of the Queen, the King of Hanover, now becoming senile, warned Frederick William IV that it would be unsafe to attend 'this rubbishy Exhibition' because 'the excommunicated of all lands' were in London and constituted a threat to visiting eminences. According to his informants, 'Ministers will not allow the Queen and the great originator of this folly, Prince Albert, to be in London while the Exhibition is on.' Other forecasts warned that the mammoth structure would collapse in a gale, or cause epidemics because of the masses of people spreading contagion, or, as Albert put it to the worried King of Prussia, 'that his second Tower of Babel would draw upon it the vengeance of an offended God'. But the work went on and the public was awed.

The Crystal Palace, and the preparations for the Great Exhibition, helped alter the face of London. Victoria Street was opened, ploughing a path through Westminster's worst slum. The Marble Arch was moved from the palace grounds to anchor the north-east ('Speaker's') corner of Hyde Park. Trafalgar Square was finally completed, although without Landseer's lions, which were added in 1868. Little-populated areas around new railway junctions underwent building booms, expanding living space, a crucial matter as in 1851 2,362,000 people lived in a far smaller London where open sewers still flowed into the Thames. Kensington, abutting Hyde Park to the west, became citified, and in

---

* Paxton wanted a symbolic 1851 feet, but the dimensions would not work.

Knightsbridge, even closer to the Exhibition grounds, a tea merchant, Charles Harrod, opened a grocery with a large range of merchandise opposite the village green. His trade thrived. To the south-west, Old Brompton lost its fairground, villas and market gardens to urban expansion. Only some of the metamorphosis was related to Crystal Palace expectations, but London was reaching into former suburbs and villages.

Despite the demands of the Exhibition, when Victoria insisted upon her now annual autumn retreat to Balmoral, Albert dutifully accompanied her to Scotland, from which he fired off letters and telegrams to London and foreign parts, and received visitors who undertook the gruelling day-and-night rail journey to Ballater. On Wordsworth's death, he exhorted Russell to name Tennyson for the Poet Laureate's chair. 'There are three or four authors of nearly equal merit,' Russell responded by form to the Queen rather than the Prince, 'such as Henry Taylor, Sheridan Knowles, Professor Wilson, and Mr Tennyson, who are qualified for the office.' Although Alfred Tennyson had become the most respected poet in England with his *Poems* of 1842 and sealed his reputation with the newly published *In Memoriam*, the Prime Minister had hardly heard of him.* Albert had to intervene once more to keep Duke Ernest's debts from causing the confiscation of a castle in Coburg and embarrassment to his brother. Without asking how many women Ernest kept, Albert wrote from Balmoral, 'I must remind you that you are still one of the richest of the small sovereigns in Germany. Besides, you have no family to keep, no brothers or sisters, nor any children.' By 21 October Albert was speaker at a dinner given by the Lord Mayor of York, using every possible occasion to talk up the Exhibition.

In November, as the Crystal Palace was rising spectacularly over Hyde Park, Albert materialized everywhere. Overwork seemed a compulsion. He appeared more aged than his thirty-one years. Thickening sideburns compensated for a thinning pate, and his increasing heaviness of body

---

* John Wilson as 'Christopher North' contributed essays and verse to *Blackwood's* magazine and since 1820 held the Chair of Moral Philosophy at the University of Edinburgh. James Sheridan Knowles, a playwright known for *William Tell* (1825) and *The Hunchback* (1832), had become a Baptist minister in 1845. Henry Taylor, a minor poet and dramatist, wrote the tragedy *Philip van Artefelde* (1834), and the comedy *The Virgin Widow* (1850). On 21 October, six weeks later, Russell conceded that Tennyson was a 'fit person'.

suggested too much desk-work and too many fundraising dinners. Thackeray thought the Prince looked ill, and while impatiently watching William Macready in *Hamlet* at the Haymarket, and wishing himself elsewhere, Thackeray imagined Albert in 'that absurd play'. Not as the Prince of Denmark but as the ghostly dead king. 'Suppose', he mused, 'our beloved monarch were to lose Prince Albert & marry his brother the Duke of Saxe-Coburg? 2 months after Albert's death suppose I saw a company of actors going to Windsor & acting a play full of the grossest allusions to widows marrying, to marriage with a deceased husband's brother & so forth – what a noise there'd be!'

Unable to slow down, Albert spent some early winter weather at Windsor writing memoranda on how a federation under Prussia and without Austria, both of which were threatening war to secure their rights in Germany, might be developed under clauses of the 1815 Treaty of Vienna. Austria, he warned Frederick William IV, was a Jesuit despotism, while Protestant Prussia could prosper as a constitutional monarchy, winning thereby England's support and ensuring (as the fifth and balancing Great Power with England, France, Austria and equally despotic Russia) 'universal peace'. But Albert's concepts were too large for the King, who was busy with more immediate problems. Almost without pause, Albert then wrote to Prince William, the designated successor, pressing him not to permit Prussia's humiliation by Austria. 'I have poured out a flood of considerations', he apologized on 29 December, 'as is bound to happen when one has had to dam the stream for so long . . . ' But he closed with better news. 'The Exhibition is well forward, and its originator still hopes most earnestly it may be possible for you, the Princes, and your son, to be present at the opening. The building was started on November 1st, and will be nearly ready in a few days. It is a real work of art.'

The Crystal Palace was that, and more. The vast building was a technological marvel. None of its iron and glass had been anything but ideas on paper when the contractors accepted the assignment on 26 July 1850. Yet in his enthusiasm Albert exaggerated the frenetic pace of construction. Not a column had been raised until 26 September. Each vertical column was hollow, to act as a pipe to carry away rain and external moisture from the roof. A groove in the topmost gutters was designed to carry condensation from inside the building into the same pipes – part of the thirty-nine miles of piping in the building and foundation – and away from the building. The girders, each seventy-two feet long and intended to support the width of a section of the central aisle, were raised by a hoist powered by a team of six horses. Each girder was first tested on a hydraulic press to support fifteen tons, exceeding any predictable strain.

Raising the ribs of the transept roof, Illustrated London News, *14 December, 1850.*

Despite a brief strike – workmen demanded five shillings a day rather than four – they laboured as if they were being paid on a piecework basis. For laying the glass panels from Messrs Chance and Company of Birmingham, Paxton designed trolleys which were propelled backwards on tracks as each pane was placed. In one week in December, eighty men set 18,932 panes in the vast roof, one fixing sixty-eight panes in a single day.

When, two weeks earlier, the sixteen ribs of the transept were lifted into place, Albert had been there to look on, competing for attention with a brewer's dray bringing 250 gallons of beer for the 2,000 men. Both beer and Prince were lustily cheered.

Assembled on site from prefabricated parts and covering eighteen acres of parkland, including the politically precious elms, the glass palace was completed externally (but for painting) on 31 December. The Queen, with Albert, took the children to see it for the first time on 18 February 1851, and described it in her diary as 'one of the wonders of the world, which we English may indeed be proud of'. To Prince William, Albert had scoffed about rumours that the Court would flee London because of all the dire things likely to happen during construction and after. All of them were 'the inventions concocted by the enemies of our artistic and cultural venture and of all progress in civilisation . . .' In actuality it would prove difficult to keep the Queen and the older children away.

XI

The Palace of Glass

1850–1851

E VEN AFTER COMPLETION, the Crystal Palace remained a huge
problem for Albert. In matters small and large, his responsibilities
had hardly begun. The Commissioners were a scattered group, some
living very far from London. Until 3 October 1850, Fox and Henderson
had not been able to secure an official order from the Commissioners
authorizing payment for the work already accomplished and the materials purchased, yet the contractors had already spent more than £50,000
– an enormous sum by nineteenth-century calculation. Even Paxton
blundered, intruding with a letter to *The Times* urging the Prime
Minister to have the government pay for the construction and open the
Exhibition to all-comers free of charge. It was interpreted erroneously as
a confession of bankruptcy, which pained the Prince as much as did the
concept that private enterprise was not up to the challenge. Once the
building was enclosed, it was discovered that sparrows in large numbers
nested in the elms under the transept. Worried about what they might
do to exhibits and to spectators, the Commissioners brought the difficulty to one of Albert's favourite people, the Duke of Wellington. Hard
of hearing and dim of sight, his wits were still sharp at eighty-one. As
Ranger of Hyde Park, he allegedly arrived for an audience with the
Queen and Prince and advised, 'Try sparrow hawks, Ma'am'. She did
not, but somehow the sparrows were ousted.

Albert anguished over larger problems, including the perennial one
of money. Additions, alterations, and overtime labour made a subsidi-
ary contract for an additional £27,980 necessary; and then another for

£35,000. Internal costs brought the total higher. The final figure, including fittings – shelving, lighting and decoration – and re-landscaping the site once the construction crews were withdrawn, came to £169,998, many millions by later calculation. Yet income would cover all costs and leave a large surplus.

When public carping continued at each stage in the project, Paxton turned on the detractors and declared, 'It is a grand period in our history when a Prince ... is engaged in doing all he can to foster the arts of peace, instead of lending his name and the bad example of his influence in fomenting petty distractions, and stirring up passions which tend to perpetuate strife, ill-blood, and the destruction of human life. To foster the arts, to promote the extension of industry and commerce, to knit nation and nation in the bonds of universal brother-hood, was a noble object for Prince Albert to engage in.'

Unconvinced, Colonel Thomas Sibthorp, MP for Lincoln, arose on the first day of the parliamentary session to decry the completion of the Crystal Palace. 'They might call it success,' he insisted of the alleged desecration of Hyde Park, 'but I call it failure. I do not wish to see that building destroyed by any acts of violence, but would to God that some hailstorm, or some visitation of lightning, might descend to defeat the ill-advised project.'

By 12 February – only two weeks after the interior was ruled accep-table for occupancy – goods were arriving. Once cleared by customs officers, objects were escorted to spaces allotted to each country by soldiers of the Royal Sappers and Miners, loaned to Albert by Well-ington for the duration of the Exhibition. Given their speciality, they were expected to have some technological know-how. Engineers might have been the better choice, as the press aired public anxieties about the safety of the building when crowded with heavy machinery and sub-jected to the tread of thousands of visitors. Wellington sent soldiers to march over the wooden footways, and workmen built a test gallery for walking, running and jumping upon, to ensure the sturdiness of every portion of the Palace. The experimentation was deliberately public, satisfying everyone but committed doomsayers.

Almost everything relating to the Exhibition went to Albert for advice or approval. He had to authorize the artists for the *Illustrated London News* to make drawings – 'with the consent of the manufac-turers'. He even checked to see that the exhibits were labelled properly.

Meanwhile the business of government became a major distraction. On 22 February Lord John Russell's ministry was defeated on an electoral bill and promptly resigned, forcing the Queen to send for Lord Stanley, whose minority Tories could only govern with external collaboration. Stanley (who succeeded his father on 30 June as 14th Earl of Derby) found, as expected, the Queen and Prince together at Buckingham Palace. 'The Queen said little', Stanley's son Edward reported in his diary, 'but listened with profound attention'. Albert wanted to know whether the Tories had enough talent to form a government, and Lord Stanley emphasized the veteran Herries and the rising Disraeli. One had a 'considerable knowledge of routine [but] was not possessed of distinguished ability'. The other 'had extraordinary talent, but no practice in official duties'. He would have problems, Derby added, in maintaining office, as it would require 'retraction of avowed opinions' – a reference to Tory policy in favour of protectionist tariffs. The Corn Laws had been repealed by Peel's ministry in 1846 at the cost of Conservative unity. Now the Peelite faction was melting into the Liberal (Whig) Party, leaving only the minority Rightists, whose goal to restore some restrictions elicited no sympathy from Albert.

'The Prince seemed inclined to press this subject and enter into argument, but my Father saw that the Queen wished to change it, and hinted that the details . . . would be better discussed bye-and-bye.' Clearly, Albert saw the year of a world fair keyed upon world manufactures as the wrong time for Tory trade ideology, but it was obvious that Stanley could find no coalition partners anyway. By early March, Lord John Russell, a perennial survivor, was reconfirmed in office after Lord Aberdeen and Sir James Graham had also found no workable combinations and Wellington advised settling once more for Russell. At each session Albert asked most of the questions and afterwards penned memoranda of the exchanges without identifying himself as anything but an observer, noting that with Stanley the Queen had pointedly warned that he would have to be responsible for Disraeli's conduct – neither she nor the Prince trusted the ambitious upstart. With Russell on 3 March she warned that she did not want Palmerston back, a matter she could not finally block, as (in Albert's words) 'Lord John . . . was in fact the weakness and Lord Palmerston the strength of the Government from his popularity with the Radicals'.

That the public understood how the monarchy was being administered was evident from a clever *Punch* cartoon, 'Cinderella; or Lord John Trying it on Again'. The scene, with a wonderful old crone with a cane – a fairy godmother in disguise – a frowning stepmother, various hangers-on in Court dress of a bygone age, and a diminutive Russell in a chair trying on the slipper of state once more, has at its centre to oversee the proceedings a cautious Prince Albert. Victoria is not even in the picture.

Two days later, while the Exhibition Commissioners met, Albert called Lord Stanley aside for a conversation on politics. Edward Stanley noted after talking with his father 'that the Prince's mind appeared to have been formed by Sir R. Peel, whose sayings and acts he continually quoted'. But Albert's mind was moulded more by the men he had encountered in working on the Great Exhibition, for 'He talked much of the necessity of a Conservative policy, expressed alarm at the [Radical] policy of Manchester, but said "What is to be done? Here are your rising men, sons of the aristocracy, educated in the best schools and universities, and among them there is not one that can compete with the self-taught middle-class manufacturers." Unluckily, this is true...'

Albert's concerns about the Exhibition were focused, by April, upon internal arrangements and the arrival and placement of the exhibits themselves. Could London's streets handle the traffic, and its police cope with security and crowd discipline? A *Punch* cartoon showed Albert bursting into the Crystal Palace, coat and shirt awry in his haste, confronting Britannia still trimming candlewicks. 'Here's a to-do!' he shouts. 'Here's all the Company come, and the Street's full of Carriages and Brooms – and there's such a Row! – and the Candles arn't Lighted, nor the Supper Ready, nor the Man dressed who's to Wait, nor the Music – nor Nothing.'

As opening day neared, Lieutenant Henry Tyler, an engineer and much later (as Sir Henry) Chairman of the Grand Trunk Railway Company of Canada, made a very likely modest estimate for Albert of the value of the objects in the Exhibition, excluding Victoria's acquisition from Kashmir, the Koh-i-noor ('mountain of light') Diamond, expected to magnetize visitors. Those of the United Kingdom were valued at £1,031,607 4s. 9d; of the Colonies – largely raw materials rather than manufactures and equipment – at £79,901 15s. Foreign countries had

BRITANNIA'S GREAT PARTY.

Early in 1851, Punch *observes Albert's concern that the exhibitions in the Crystal Palace may not be in place for the opening on 1 May.*

brought in objects estimated at £670,420 11s. 7d. How to protect the property at night engaged the minds of the Prince, the Commissioners, and the Police. Colonel Reid of the Metropolitan Police suggested a barbed-wire entanglement with upright iron railings eight feet high, a prison-like vision which Albert reduced to an ornamental iron railing, and a force of four inspectors, twenty-five sergeants and 334 constables. The fire watch would consist of two hundred Royal Sappers, twenty-four of whom would begin night duty at eight each evening.

There would be no disorder, even when, on 7 October, there were 109,000 visitors in the building – a daily record. The only fire was a small blaze of cotton waste, easily extinguished. The myriad of detail left the Prince, he wrote to his stepmother in Coburg, 'more dead than alive from Overwork'.

'My poor Albert', Victoria wrote in her journal the day before the opening, when she visited the site for a preview, 'is terribly fagged. *All* day some question or other, or some difficulty, all of which my beloved one takes with the greatest quiet & good temper.' Even the Exhibition's motto, at the head of the catalogue, was chosen by the Prince – '*The earth is the Lord's and all that therein is.*' That too would inspire controversy, as the president of the Bible Society complained that Albert had used the Prayer Book version of the line rather than that of the King James Bible. There could also be too much religion. Augustus Pugin, an ardent Catholic, had designed a Medieval Court that would become one of the most popular exhibits, but he was required to remove the large crucifix overlooking his medieval fantasies. On the eve of the opening Albert wrote in his journal, '*Entsetzliche Unruhe durch die Arrangements für die Eröffnung*' – irresistible anxiety during the arrangements for the opening. Yet Victoria would have had good reason, as she entered, to recall what she had written in her journal more than a year earlier: 'I *do* feel proud at the thought of what my beloved Albert's great mind has conceived.'

Nothing went awry – except that a Chinese trespasser in traditional robes, actually the proprietor of a junk moored in the Thames, was mistaken for be an emissary from the Celestial Kingdom and placed in the procession between the Archbishop of Canterbury and the Duke of Wellington. Ecstatically, the Queen recorded in her journal one of its longest and most vivid entries. The bustle, the crowds, the excitement – even her own dread – reminded her of her coronation day. With Vicky and Bertie and the Prince in her carriage – one of nine state coaches – they arrived in 'Queen's weather', the light rain that fell as they left having stopped. 'The sun shone & gleamed upon the gigantic edifice, upon which the flags of every nation were flying... The glimpse through the iron gates of the Transept, the moving palms & flowers, the myriads of people filling their galleries & the seats around, together with the flourish of trumpets, as we entered the building, gave a sensation I shall never forget, & I felt much moved.'

The spectacle was 'magic and impressive' as light danced about the dazzling interior, sunlight streaming through its 293,655 panes of glass and reflecting off the facets of a twenty-seven-foot crystal fountain that was the structure's centrepiece. The four faces of the clocks on the building were about to record noon when Albert escorted Victoria in, Vicky at his right hand, Bertie (in Highland dress) holding his mother's hand. 'The tremendous cheering, the joy expressed in every face, the

The Queen, Prince and their older children visiting the Machinery Department of the Great Exhibition in May 1851. From the Illustrated London News, *which advertises itself on the signboard, centre left.*

vastness of the building, with all its decorations & exhibits, the sound of the organ (with 200 instruments & 600 voices), & my beloved Husband the creator of this great "Peace Festival", uniting the industry & art of *all* nations of the earth, *all* this, was indeed moving, & a day to live forever. God bless my dearest Albert, & my dear Country which has shown itself so great today...'

To Leopold, Victoria called the Crystal Palace 'astonishing, a fairy scene. Many cried, and all felt touched and impressed with devotional feelings.' It was a reaction that united onlookers. The historian and politician Thomas Macaulay, cautious with his words, in his diary called the interior 'a most gorgeous sight; vast; graceful; beyond the dreams of the Arabian romances'. Greville marvelled at 'no soldiers, hardly any policemen to be seen, and yet all so orderly and good humoured' – and although 6,063,986 visitors, equal to a third of the kingdom, poured through the Crystal Palace over 140 days (no Sundays), there would be no damage and no violence. 'The *frondeurs* are all come round', Greville wrote on 10 May, 'and those who abused it most vehemently now praise it as much.'

A rare complaint about the opening was John Bright's dismissal of Court dress as 'absurd', but for the tens of thousands at the opening such colour added to the spectacle. The vista had been everyone's realization of fairyland. 'Such a beautiful scene', Harriet, Countess Granville, wrote, 'never was seen in the world before, for there was never a place to show it. The bright, fairy-like decorations of the place altogether, visible in its whole length and breadth, filled below and lined above with thousands of well-dressed people, was the prettiest and most imposing sight I ever saw; and when one saw that it was formed of a combination of all nations, all classes, and almost of all times, from the last inventions of the present day to the old Beefeaters of the thirteenth century, it caused one's pleasure to consist of a mixture of feelings and sensations almost impossible to define to oneself.'

Lady Charlotte Guest, wife of a Welsh iron-and-steel baron and a writer and translator, watched the Queen and Prince arrive with their children to stand on the broad, raised dais, their Court surrounding them, and watched by thousands of renowned and the loyal subjects, and recognized that 'all this pomp and panoply were called together to do honour to the industry of millions, whose toils, erst scorned upon, seemed suddenly ennobled.' It was an enterprise unlike anything anyone had ever known. 'I am lost in thronging thoughts, I cannot fitly express what I would say. But as the wife of the largest manufacturer in the world I could not but feel this to be a most impressive sight. Parts of the ceremony were to me most touching, and many times I found the tears starting from my eyes. I need not describe what any newspaper of the day will tell more accurately. I only know it was the most dazzling sight I ever beheld . . .'

Charlotte Brontë, visiting London for the Exhibition, would go five times, writing to her father, gloomily living that June in her house in Yorkshire, that its grandeur did not consist in one thing, 'but in the unique assemblage of *all* things. Whatever human industry has created, you find there, from the great compartments filled with railway engines and boilers, with mill-machinery in full work, with splendid carriages of all kinds, with harness of every description – to the glass-covered and velvet-spread stands loaded with the most gorgeous work of the gold-smith and silversmith, and the carefully guarded caskets full of real diamonds and pearls worth hundreds of thousands of pounds.' To the author of *Jane Eyre*, the awed multitude thronging the long aisles was subdued beyond ordinary explanation. 'Amongst the thirty thousand souls that peopled it the day I was there, not one loud noise was to be heard, not one irregular movement seen – the living tide rolls on quietly, with a deep hum like the sea heard from a distance.' On 13 June she was rewarded by the sight of the ex-royal family of France venturing down the transept – the former queen and her daughter-in-law the duchesse d'Orléans with her two sons.

Also there, fictionally, were the Sponges of Robert Surtees's *Mr Sponge's Sporting Tour*, the last instalment of which appeared in the *New Monthly Magazine* only a few weeks before the Great Exhibition opened. Miss Howard wonders about 'the sliding-scale of children' she sees thronging outside a shop window, and Miss Glitters explains, 'They must be on their way to the Great Exhibition of National Industry to show' – compete – 'against the Prince's little people'.

'There you go again, Miss G', exclaims the mortified Captain Cutifat while the lady, 'looking quite innocent' about her jest, claims, 'I said nothing'.

Victoria and Albert had already produced seven children since 1840, and the *double entendre* about Prince Albert's industry was so easily apprehended that when Surtees's one-volume edition appeared in 1853 the witticism was withdrawn. Although Albert's productivity as a stud was in the tradition of George III and at least two of his sons (whose children were almost all illegitimate), Prince Albert's brood with Victoria may have also recalled the last reigning queen, although of Anne's eighteen pregnancies most miscarried. In boisterous circles, jokes were not uncommon about Prince Albert's parenting efficiency, the Queen usually unmentioned out of respect for the Crown. At much the same time as the Surtees story, T.W. Booker, MP, later Booker Blakemore, spoke to the Herefordshire Agricultural Society (reported in *The Times*, 20 October) in praise of the fecundity demonstrated in their county. 'It would be a libel on the buxom, rosy-cheeked women of Herefordshire', he smirked, 'to say that at least they were not as good breeders as their own cows, or that their qualifications were not superior to those of the half-starved creatures in the overcrowded alleys of the towns, called women, but who had none of the "points" of a woman, either before or behind; and it would be a libel, too, on the broad-shouldered men of Herefordshire to say that they were not as sure foal-getters as the men of any other county, or even as Prince Albert himself.' There were exclamations of 'Oh! Oh!' heard from the audience, and the next day *The Times* printed a letter to the editor deploring 'the most indecent manner' in which the Prince's name had been used.

The Times on 2 May 1851 published an unprecedented three pages and thirteen columns of description of the opening events, plus a plan of the building and catalogue of exhibits, country by country, with a last line, 'To be continued'. The contents of the Crystal Palace had overwhelmed even the newspaper of record. 'Certain it is', *The Times* began, 'that people who had never before seen the sun rise, except through a ballroom window, were in full activity soon after dawn, impelled by the impulse which seemed to lend life and energy to the whole substance of the great and somewhat lethargic metropolis.' In grand hyperbole, *The Times* went on, 'Never before was such a vast multitude collected together within the memory of man. The struggles of great nations in battle, the levies of whole races, never called forth such an array as thronged the streets of London on the 1st of May; ... but here was an occasion which might be celebrated by the whole human race without one pang of regret, envy, or national hate.'

Perhaps the greatest tribute came from Thackeray, in the person of Mr Punch himself, who was shocked into sentimental awe, an unusual if not unprecedented condition:

I remarked that the scene I witnessed was the grandest and most cheerful, the brightest and most splendid show that eyes had ever looked on since the creation of the world; – but as everybody remarked the same thing, this remark is not of much value. I remarked, and with a feeling of shame, that I had long hesitated about paying three guineas – pooh-poohed – said I had seen the Queen and Prince before, and so forth, and felt now that to behold this spectacle, three guineas, or five guineas, or any sum of money (for I am a man of enormous wealth) would have been cheap; and I remarked how few of us know really what is good for us – have the courage of our stations, and what a number of chances in life we throw away. I would not part with the mere recollection of this scene for a small annuity; and calculate that after paying my three guineas, I have the Exhibition before me, besides being largely and actually in pocket.

I remarked that a heavy packet of sandwiches which Jones begged me to carry, and which I pocketed in rather a supercilious and grumbling manner, became most pleasant friends and useful companions after we had been in our places two or three hours; and I thought to myself, that if I were a lyric poet with a moral turn, I would remark how often in the hour of our need our humble friends are welcome and useful to us, like those dear sandwiches, which we pooh-poohed when we did not need them.

I remarked that when the Queen bowed and courtesied, all the women about began to cry.

I remarked how eagerly the young Prince talked with his sister – how charmed everybody was to see those pretty young persons walking hand in hand with their father and mother, and how, in the midst of any magnificence you will, what touches us most is nature and human kindness, and what we love to witness most is love.

The opening of the Great Exhibition in the Crystal Palace was indeed a love feast.

Season tickets were three guineas for men and two for women. (Albert held Season Ticket No. 1, his signature at the bottom as 'Proprietor'.) After the first two days at £1, admission until 24 May was five shillings. After 26 May, admission Monday through Thursday was one shilling and on Friday and Saturday two-and-sixpence. Cheap tickets enabled the working classes to visit the Exhibition, and employers released labourers to attend with their families. On one excursion day the Great Western Railway ran a train with 151 coaches carrying five thousand ticket-holders. (People paid a few pence weekly to a savings fund for the trip.) No alcohol was sold in Exhibition restaurants, and while the press complained about the public necessity to drink ginger beer, sobriety was a crucial element in an orderly flow of visitors. The cuisine was deliberately limited: 1,092,337 bottles of soft drinks were sold, 934,691 fluffy, currant-filled Bath buns and 870,027 ordinary sweet buns. In a pre-deodorant society, the Commissioners arranged to distribute 270 gallons of eau-de-Cologne and other scents through the building.

As befitted a design extrapolated from a greenhouse, the interior was colourful in objects and people and decoration. Paintwork in red, blue, yellow and white, with crimson banners identifying the exhibit areas, accentuated by light streaming from the glass walls and roof. Crowds grew daily but exhibited Sunday decorum, belying Colonel Sibthorp's cranky prediction of mass criminality and sexual licence. The forecast of the Astronomer Royal, George Airy, that the building would collapse under the strain of wind and storm, equally proved false, as did the dire prognostications by King Ernest Augustus of Hanover. For many, the Exhibition was an opportunity for a first railway experience, as excursion trains brought hundreds of thousands of sightseers (the word dates only from 1847) to London, while tens of thousands more came by boat from the Continent and from America. For exhibition-goers, the odds were good that they would see the Queen and Prince. Albert was there almost daily when he was in town. Victoria herself visited often until

THE SHIPWRECKED MINISTERS SAVED BY THE GREAT EXHIBITION STEAMER.

The government is rescued from public wrath about its legislative failures by the distractions of the Great Exhibition. In the background, Punch *shows the Crystal Palace with a steamer's funnel.*

the formal closing in mid-October, inquisitive about everything and unconcerned about security.

In June, *Punch* would print a cartoon of a shipwrecked Lord John Russell government saved by a steamer labelled *Exhibition*, which was substantially true, in that the marvels of the Crystal Palace were a distraction for both Parliament and the press. 'It was such a time', Victoria wrote in her journal (18 July 1851), 'of pleasure, of pride, of satisfaction & of deep thankfulness; it is the triumph of peace & good will towards all, – of art, of commerce, – of my beloved Husband – & of triumph for my country.' For many who came, it was their first glimpse of the new realities of mechanical invention and accomplishments in arts and crafts, a revelation of the technological future and of an English pre-eminence in mass-produced industrial goods that, ironically, the spread of know-how afforded by the Exhibition would soon threaten.

Victoria was not the only ticketholder who would come again and again. 'A very fine thing,' said Gustave Flaubert, 'despite being admired by everyone.'

With rare exceptions, enthusiasm for the Exhibition ran high and across the classes. Cantankerous Thomas Carlyle had 'no patience' with the Prince and 'that Cole', who had contrived to bring so many out-siders to London. He told *Westminster Review* publisher John Chapman that he had been 'worn to death with bores all summer, who present themselves by twos and threes in his study, saying "Here we are".' A few were as surly as Carlyle. Herman Melville dismissed it as a 'vast toy, . . . overdone', but his pastor at All Souls' in Manhattan, Henry Whitney Bellows, perceived 'a noble & unmistakable tendency to unite man with God', and described the Crystal Palace as 'the digest of the universe'.

Charles Dickens complained that the Exhibition complicated his life, and visited only twice, but he had already received a private tour of the frigid, nearly empty, building from Joseph Paxton himself in February, and since April had been busy managing and performing in amateur theatricals to raise funds for creative fellowships for artists and writers. The Queen and Prince had even agreed to attend the première perform-ance of the first benefit production, Sir Edward Bulwer-Lytton's costume piece set in the reign of George II, *Not So Bad as We Seem.* Paxton's patron, the Duke of Devonshire, had offered use of the picture gallery in his mansion, Devonshire House, and the price had been set steeply at five guineas. At Victoria's suggestion, the date fixed was 30 April, the eve of the opening of the Crystal Palace, to capture the aristocratic élite in London for the Exhibition, but the sudden death of eight-month-old Dora Annie Dickens on 14 April postponed the play. 'Queen's Night' – Albert did not reign and did not count – became 16 May. Special care was taken to have a character smoking a clay pipe only feign the act, with the smoke merely whorls of cotton on fine wires. 'The Queen can't bear tobacco', Dickens had warned.

When the Queen and Prince attended a ball at the Guildhall on 9 July, 1851 to celebrate the success of the Exhibition, excitement about it seemed to have been reached flood stage. The royal party left Buckingham Palace at nine, travelling through the city in state carriages to swelling acclaim from Londoners lining the streets. Rather than dispersing, the crowds continued to grow, awaiting the return of the Queen's carriage. Since the ball was a brilliant extravaganza, the Queen stayed late; but so did the waiting crowds. As Albert wrote to Stockmar, 'A million of people remained till three in the morning in the streets, and were full of enthusiasm towards us.' It was an occasion without precedent.

More than ever, Albert seemed wanted everywhere to make an occasion memorable, but he was wearing down. Before the Guildhall event he had presided at the close of the academic year at Harrow, and his appointment calendar was full. At the annual Royal Academy dinner he spoke of the rapport that the artist must seek with some audience, for no creation truly existed without welcome response. 'Gentlemen,' he put it, 'the production of all works in art or poetry requires, in the conception or execution, not only an exercise of the intellect, skill and patience, but particularly a concurrent warmth of feelings, and a free flow of imagination.' In the increasing gulf between creator and critic he saw potential problems for artists even as the consumers of art were increasing. There was now 'as judge, a great public, for the greater part uneducated in art; and thus led by professional writers, who often strive to impress the public with a great idea of their own artistic knowledge, by the merciless manner in which they treat works which cost those who produced them the highest efforts of mind and feeling'.

Painter Thomas Uwins was ecstatic at Albert's perspective. 'The speech of this accomplished prince', he wrote to his friend John Townshend, 'beat all the dukes, and lords, and ministers of state. The whole was much beyond anything of the kind I ever witnessed.' Every critic, *Art Journal* advised, should take the Prince's words to heart, but Thackeray called his appraisal 'mistaken benevolence': 'Art, like a foot-ball, bounds the higher the more you kick it.' Pleasing a public would turn art 'effeminate'. He preferred critical tension. 'No, no; let us still dab mud on the pallette of the painter; let us still mix dirt in the ink of the writer.'

Albert's plate was varied. At a cattle show in July, he wrote to his brother, 'I had a dinner . . . with two thousand farmers, and I had to give a long address. The dinner lasted five hours.' Later in the month the family left Windsor for Osborne, 'the haven of peace and rest', from whence Albert deluged Whitehall and other London venues with business mail; and when they retreated further to Balmoral for six weeks, he was preoccupied at a distance with winding down the Exhibition and with foreign affairs, which meant the continuing exasperation of dealing with Palmerston. Feeling among Liberals was still heated about Austrian suppression of independence movements in northern Italy and in Hungary. Among the foreigners attracted to London at Exhibition time was Baron Julius von Haynau, the general who had put down the rebels with what most English considered savagery. When 'General Hyaena' arrived and was recognized by his trademark moustachios, he was roughed up by a crowd and Victoria wrote to ask Palmerston to apologize on behalf of the nation 'at the brutal outrage on one of the Emperor's distinguished generals'. Palmerston duly penned his regrets, but tactlessly added that someone of Haynau's notoriety risked such a reception. The imbroglio continued into the Balmoral weeks and after, souring the good feeling about the Great Exhibition.

Good feeling, in any case, Dickens forecast, sceptically, would be the inevitable outcome, rather than enlightenment. The public was bewildered by the profusion of the unfamiliar, he explained to W.H. Wills. 'My apprehension – and prediction – is, that they will come out of it at last, with that feeling of boredom and lassitude (to say nothing of having spent their money) that the reaction will not be as wholesome and vigorous and quick, as folks expect.' Yet Albert's perennial adversary, Lord Brougham, spoke in the Lords in favour of Paxton's petition against dismantling the Crystal Palace – Albert stood by his guarantee to take it down – by declaring it 'not only a work of great national utility, but of European usefulness'.

At her final visit to the Crystal Palace on 14 October, arriving with Albert, Victoria found the building, still filled with eager visitors, in the process of being dismantled. A huge brass organ, labelled a Sommerophone, was playing, and the booming notes, she wrote, 'nearly upset me'. The glass fountain was already removed, and exhibits being taken down. 'The canvas is very dirty, the red curtains are faded, and many things are very much soiled, still the effect is fresh and new as ever, and most beautiful.' So much remained beautiful, she noted, 'I could not believe it was the last time I was to see it . . . It made us all very melancholy.' There at the close, in the crowd, was an old Cornishwoman, Mary Kerlynack, 'who had walked hundreds of miles to see the Exhibition'. A 'most hale old woman', she was 'at the door to see me', and was 'near crying at my looking at her'.

The next day saw the official closing, and the Queen regretted not being there. (It was 'not to be in state'.) Albert left at ten for the ceremonies, where an estimated fifty thousand people crowded inside, despite dripping skies, for a last look. The only formalities were Albert's address to the prize juries, and their reports. The high dignity of the opening was impossible in the already disassembled state of the interior.

'Albert was right', Victoria confided to her diary. ' . . . I could hardly have been there as a spectator . . . How sad and strange to think that this great and bright time has passed away like a dream . . . I feel as if it were doing my dearest Albert an injury that it should be gone by . . . '

Some of the ideas, devices and products exhibited would lead to real change, as Albert had hoped, and the traffic was not all *from* Britain to overseas markets. For example, John Sutton Nettlefold, a Birmingham manufacturer of wood screws (and uncle of Joseph Chamberlain, the future apostle of British imperialism), came upon an American-patented machine which fully mechanized the screw-making process. Birmingham screws were made laboriously by hand, a costly method that also prevented uniform quality. Thomas J. Sloan's machinery had afforded small metal goods from America technological superiority and competitiveness in cost, and Nettlefold adopted the process, boosting Birmingham's economy.

To avoid chaos, exhibitors displayed, rather than sold, their wares at the Palace, but were permitted to dispense leaflets and other hand-outs –

the chief means of creating markets for them. Souvenirs were plentiful, ranging from models of the building and peepshows (with an eyepiece) of the interior, to coloured lithographs ('from the originals painted... for HRH Prince Albert'), of which fifty-five scenes were printed. Among the handbills sold were songs and ballads related to the Exhibition, one of them, 'How's Your Poor Feet?' – its subject a tourist who came by train – typical of what visitors took home with their sore feet.

> I, the Exhibition came to see,
> and gaze at London town;
> I really was amazed...

There was even a children's illustrated book, beginning,

> And this is the man submitting his plan
> To the Prince who approved, and said it was good,
> That a Palace of Glass should be built on the grass,
> For the great World's Fair, ...
> The fine Crystal Palace the Prince had built.

A silent success of the Exhibition was the operation of 'Public Waiting Rooms', as reported afterward to the Society of Arts. For tuppence admission, a person secured lavatory privileges, and for fourpence also a clean towel. Two 'sets of rooms' were set up 'by way of experiment', one for ladies at 51 Bedford Street, near Coutts's Bank, and one for gentlemen at 95 Fleet Street. They were a long walk from the Crystal Palace, and the accommodation was 'of so novel and delicate a character' as to be difficult to make widely known, but the facilities turned a large profit. On expenses of £680 during the five months of the Exhibition the 'Waiting Rooms' earned £2,470. Of all the innovations of the Great Exhibition, clean public lavatories at nominal cost may have been the most civilized.

Among Albert's aggravations were the choices of medals, which became a diplomatic nightmare, especially as the French jurors, to the dismay of Stafford Northcote, claimed that most major prizes should go the French exhibits, putting forward a list of twenty-five claimants. To allay trouble, five had to be awarded to France. In general the policy of the Commissioners was to award medals to international exhibitors. As much as national rivalries permitted, it was to be a fair of good feeling.

For Albert, who was barely thirty-two at the close of the Great Exhibition, and still held no British rank or title, the most immediate result was a prestige he had never known and which would never be higher in his lifetime. Many of his collaborators would earn royal honours. Paxton would even be awarded a bursary of £5,000 by the grateful Commissioners once they recognized that even with shilling admissions the fair had accumulated a sizeable profit. Matthew Digby Wyatt, architect and art critic, and secretary to the Exhibition Committee, received a special gold medal from Albert for his services, after which the Prince promoted him for government posts as 'industrious, upright & amiable'. Cole and Northcote each became Companions to the Order of the Bath, with knighthoods going to Fox, Cubitt, Paxton and the Exhibition Commissioners – except for the reluctant Cobden. He wrote to a friend that the Exhibition was 'truly a spectacle that will make your heart expand ... Description is powerless, and the imagination fails to picture the beauty and variety of the glass palace'. Yet the strict Radical principles that kept him from appearing at the opening in Court dress also kept him from accepting any royal honours.

The summit of Albert's public career came at a cost. He had regularly complained of a 'weak stomach', and was increasingly subject to severe stomach cramps which he blamed on the tension of his crush of activities and which were assumed afterwards to be the price of his conscientiousness about detail. On 10 October, when he was involved in planning the elaborate closing ceremonies at the Crystal Palace, he was ill through the night that followed with what Victoria described as another stomach 'attack'. Now balding and paunchy, he looked prematurely old. But not to George Eliot who, at Covent Garden to hear *La Juive*, claimed to have fallen in love with the Prince, 'who was unusually animated and prominent. He had a noble, genial, intelligent expression and is altogether a man to be proud of. As for the Queen, she is deplorable – worse and worse the more one looks at her – so utterly mean in contour and expression.'

As it became accepted that the Crystal Palace would indeed have to be removed from Hyde Park as promised, press speculation burgeoned as to what would happen to it and to what uses it would be put. The formal vote for its removal did not come until 30 April, 1852, after which a Crystal Palace Company for its dismantling and reassembly was formed by Samuel Laing, Chairman of the Brighton and South Coast

Railway; John Scott Russell, a Millwall shipbuilder and a power in the Society of Arts; Charles Geach, an ironworks owner and Chairman of Midland Bank, and several others who had been associated with the Great Exhibition. It would cost nearly £200,000 for its purchase and reconstruction at Penge Park on Sydenham Hill in the Kent countryside.

The reopening would attract vast crowds. The new art and science of photography, which fascinated Albert, an early *aficionado*, recorded the dismantling and the reconstruction with a new roof line; and the opening ceremonies at which Victoria and her family participated amid choruses, orchestras, and audiences of thousands provided history's most populous daguerreotype. Shortened and slightly heightened by a barrel-like roof, the new Crystal Palace prospered as a concert and exhibition centre until it was destroyed by fire in 1936.

Sale of the building in 1852 added to the Commissioners' parallel problem by supplementing a surplus that had already reached £200,000. Disposing of the largesse was a politically sensitive matter. The Prince's scheme was to purchase eighty-seven acres in South Kensington to continue the goals of the Great Exhibition. With the help of Disraeli, then Chancellor of the Exchequer, the Commission paid £342,000 for the site, nearly half of which (£165,000) came from Crystal Palace earnings. Sceptics would label the idea 'Albertopolis', but the educational, cultural, and scientific institutions initiated by Albert's energy and foresight would materialize into a great South Kensington complex of museums, colleges, and concert halls, keeping Victoria busy at dedications for decades. Overlooking them from the southern edge of Hyde Park, within the neo-Gothic Albert Memorial, the Prince, in John Foley's bronze statue, holds on his right knee one of the volumes of the Great Exhibition catalogue, his forefinger slipped into its pages as if he is anxious not to lose his place, and looks over his legacy.*

---

* The Royal Commission for the Exhibition of 1851 operates still, now under the presidency of another queen's husband, Prince Philip, Duke of Edinburgh. The interest from the unexpended surplus remaining after the establishment of the educational and cultural estate in South Kensington amounted annually by the 1990s to more than £900,000. Much of this income has been used for fellowships and other grants for advanced study and research in science, engineering and the

In the aftermath of the Exhibition, with its effervescence evaporated, Albert returned to the routine tasks of the Court only to find that Palmerston's handling of the Foreign Office had become even more irksome while royal attention was elsewhere. Haynau's visit had been followed by his opposite number, Lajos Kossuth. The Hungarian revolutionary, although ousted at home, was the darling of Radicals and Liberals alike. As the Queen's government maintained friendly relations with imperial Austria, any official acceptance of Kossuth would be awkward, and Victoria wrote a cautionary letter to Palmerston, who had declared his enthusiasm for the resistance hero. Also in December the 'Prince-President' of France engineered a *coup d'etat* and named himself Emperor Napoleon III. The Queen and Prince were outraged, but Palmerston was an admirer of Louis Napoleon and embarrassed the Court by avowing it. Victoria and Albert appealed to Lord John Russell to keep Palmerston in bounds, both of their letters very likely drafted by Albert, as was the royal manner. Kossuth was not to be received by Palmerston publicly or privately, as his position made any gesture public.

Intemperately, Palmerston replied to his Prime Minister, 'I have just received your letter ... I am told, your messenger waits for an answer. My reply then is immediate and is: That there are limits to all things, that I do not choose to be dictated to as to whom I may or may not receive in my own house and that I shall use my own discretion on that matter. You of course will use yours as to the disposition of your government. – I have not detained your messenger five minutes.'

The contretemps kept Victoria and Albert at Windsor, rather than Osborne, during Christmas, and at a Privy Council meeting the next day Palmerston failed to arrive to deliver up his seals of office, writing to Lord John instead of his 'just indignation'. In due course the seals went to his former deputy, Lord Granville. The Queen and Prince considered ousting 'Pam' a victory, and saw the old year out happily. 'And now the year is ending', Albert wrote to his brother, 'with the

arts. Among Exhibition Awardees have been eleven future Nobel Prize winners, six future holders of the Order of Merit, and three Presidents of the Royal Society. Such opportunities had been foreseen in the Commissioners' Second Report (1852), under the leadership of the Prince Consort, which recognized the inadequacy of both public and private support of science and art, and suggested judicious investment and application of Exhibition funds.

lucky circumstance for us that the man who has been embittering our whole lives by setting us the shameful alternative of endorsing his misdeeds throughout Europe, or of raising the Radical Party here to power under his leadership... – that man has cut his own throat'. Yet Albert realized in his rush to gloat that 'Pam' was far from dead, and that his incised gullet would mend. 'We shall have plenty of trouble with Palmerston, who is raging', he predicted. Palmerston would become the most courted politician in Britain, the sought-after saviour of every party, while John Russell's government, bereft of its strongest member, was destined to drift into dissolution.

Among other misdeeds, Palmerston had become, Albert wrote to Prince William of Prussia early in 1852, 'Louis Napoleon's accomplice... There is no doubt that now he is thinking solely of revenge, but I think him less dangerous in opposition than he would be in power, for there are not at his disposal those vast possibilities of doing harm, which the Foreign Office gave him.'

Albert had already made his feelings known as to where to apply the surplus left by the Great Exhibition and the prospective sale of the building, yet early in the new year he was still receiving proposals. One, from Lord Seymour of the Office of Works, had behind it the desire to move the Royal Society out of its rooms in Somerset House, needed for other government uses. The Society had once been a progressive scientific body, but the Prince viewed it now as an anachronism. 'To give the surplus away however,' he responded testily, 'in order to provide with better accommodation a Society, which as at present constituted has forfeited the sympathy of the generality of the Public, by its lethargic state & exclusive principles, could not, I am sure, be thought of for a moment.'

Seeing for himself 'hardly... any time for peace' in the aftermath of the Exhibition, and the political instability occasioned by Palmerston's exit, Albert, and Victoria as well, worried that Napoleon III might look for a war to deflect any opposition to his seizure of power. Early in February, as the Queen waited to drive off to the Lords to reopen Parliament – the moment was only two hours off – she used the pause in schedule to write to her uncle Leopold, who was anxious about possible French designs on his small and weak country. 'With such an extraordinary man as Louis Napoleon,' she conceded, 'one can never be for one instant safe. It makes me very melancholy; I love peace and quiet – in fact I *hate* politics and turmoil...' Fortunately, she thought,

Albert loved both. 'Albert grows daily fonder and fonder of politics and business, and is so wonderfully *fit* for both – such perspicacity and such *courage* – and I grow daily to dislike them both more and more. We women are not *made* for governing – and if we are good women, we must *dislike* these masculine occupations; but there are times which force one to take *interest* in them *mal gré bon gré*, and I do, of course, *intensely.*'

So she concluded, as it was time to dress and go off with Albert to Parliament.

XII

From Glory to Gloom

1852–1853

S AILING IN THE arctic north-west of Canada, Captain Edward
Augustus Inglefield indulged in the contemporary practice of
christening geographical features he encountered, whatever natives may
have already named them, to satisfy his own whim. Thus Victoria
Island had its Prince Albert Peninsula and Prince Albert Sound, while
to the east was the smaller Prince of Wales Island. On the east side of
Smith Sound, 'some extraordinary table-topped cliffs attracted our
notice', he wrote, 'and so perfectly even and marked into galleries did
they appear, that my mind associating them with the glassy sides of the
Great Exhibition, I named them the Crystal Palace Cliffs.'

In his years with Victoria, Albert travelled to no setting more exotic
than Coburg – and Inglefield duly named an expanse south-east of
Ellesmere Island in the Prince's honour (although spelled in un-
German fashion) Cobourg Island – but in June 1852 Albert ventured
vicariously, without leaving London, into Continental mountain
climbing. Another Albert, surnamed Smith and a proprietor of
dioramas, had opened an 'Ascent of Mont Blanc' exhibition at the
Egyptian Hall in Piccadilly. At a command performance, Prince Albert
brought his sons Bertie and Alfred. Other than escaping to the royal
retreats at Osborne and Balmoral, Albert was too busy for holidays.

Among his reasons to be close to home was the liability of Lord John
Russell's lame ministry, which failed within weeks of Palmerston's exit.
Back came the Earl of Derby, who had failed to cobble a Tory ministry
a year earlier. This time he succeeded, with Disraeli as Chancellor of the

Exchequer and Leader of the House of Commons, although he could never balance his cheque-book at home. With few experienced hands, Derby promised the Queen and Prince little more than to weather out the parliamentary session and ask the Crown for Dissolution and a General Election before the year was out. As usual, Albert sat in on meetings with the Queen's ministers, asked probing questions, and kept memoranda which deliberately suggested that he did little more than secretarial duties.

Palmerston's former post went to James Howard Harris, 3rd Earl of Malmesbury and Tory whip in the Lords, who was forty-five. His most persuasive claim to the job was that his grandfather and father had both been diplomats and that he had edited, despite a reputation for execrable grammar, his grandfather's *Diplomatic Journal and Correspondence*, which taught him 'all the verbiage of the profession'. His interest in foreign affairs also extended to his having married a Frenchwoman with social cachet, but that was hardly enough, and he was handicapped by Derby's appointment of his son Edward Stanley as Under-Secretary for he was, Malmesbury recalled, far off 'in India for his pleasure'. Fortunately there was a Permanent Under-Secretary who had been Minister in Washington, and there were 'the Queen and Prince, who, in the kindest and most gracious manner, gave me a great deal of private information of which I could know nothing as to foreign, especially German, Courts'. Although Malmesbury basically endorsed Palmerstonian policies, they were both grateful not to have Palmerston at the Foreign Office.

Among other moves his larger-than-life predecessor would have taken, Malmesbury accepted the reality of an another imperial Bonaparte, first satisfying himself that Napoleon III was the correct numeral. Louis Napoleon had bypassed the 'II' which the unlucky young son of the first Bonaparte would have had. It was not long before Victoria began addressing the new emperor formally as 'brother'. 'With us he has become *mon frère*,' Albert remarked, 'but he must not become *frère* Cain.'

Less well received at Court were Derby and Disraeli, both regarded with distrust. Derby seemed too cautious, his lieutenant too much the reverse. Yet Disraeli's memoranda on Cabinet and Commons matters, witty and colourful in characterization as befitted the successful novelist, won over the Queen and softened the suspicions of the Prince. 'Disraeli appears to have a certain degree of influence over Prince Albert's mind', Edward Stanley noted in his diary, very likely from Disraeli's boastful confidences that spring. 'Disraeli describes him as one of the best educated men he knows, indeed over-educated, something of a pedant and theorist, but a man of talent nevertheless.' One reason for the change in Albert toward Disraeli, however inefficient the minority ministry seemed, was that the Tories had all but abandoned protective tariffs as principle, while the opposition appeared to employ religion for the votes it might draw. Anti-Catholic agitation was running high as a result of the Vatican's efforts to reorganize the Church in England, its adherents having grown in numbers with the exodus of the hungry from Ireland into the industrial Midlands and London. 'Mr Gladstone', Albert had written to his brother that March, 'pursues bigotry'.

'We are at the point of breaking up Parliament', he added to Ernest in June. '. . . Then we shall have General Elections. In October the new Parliament will assemble and then we shall see how the parties will be formed. I will not try to prophesy more than that there will be an end to Protection. The Protectionists are already going to the elections as Free Traders.' Albert hoped to be able to stay remote from the campaign while in Osborne, then to entrain for Balmoral in August before the new Parliament sat.

Much as Albert loved Osborne once it was built, landscaped and occupied, it lacked the useful distractions of Balmoral. No hunting, no climbing, no activities that distanced him from the burdens and anxieties of his position. And so he worked, which often meant dictation to his secretariat, convening consultants summoned to Osborne. One who came in July was Adam Sedgwick of Cambridge, to discuss the Oxford Commission recommendations on university reform. Albert wanted to experiment with a combination of Continental and English systems, and was disappointed when Sedgwick felt that the two could not mix. As for the Oxford report, he said, 'We have not half so much to reform as they have.' Albert, he discovered, had studied the report 'from end to end . . . [although] I read it the way Jack Horner ate pie'. The Prince was less smug. Further changes would be mandated at Cambridge, with Sedgwick doing much of Albert's on-the-scene work. At Osborne, however, he remained far more interested in how little ostentation there was in day-to-day life. The Queen and Prince cantered out most mornings, 'followed only by one lad on horseback to open gates

... There is a policeman at the gate of the Park, and at the landing-place; with this exception there is nothing here that much differs from a private gentleman's house.'

The Prince was still at Osborne for his thirty-third birthday, which Victoria made an occasion for the servants, soldiers and sailors on duty in the vicinity. To the strains of a band playing 'The Roast Beef of Old England', several dozen sailors and marines carried kegs of beer and bowls of plum pudding to tables set on the Osborne green, and the royals walked among them greeting their guests, then sat under their marquee to watch young ladies in their beribboned Sunday best, with white stockings, dance with the blue- and scarlet-coated men. When at seven, the band struck up 'God Save the Queen', Victoria and Albert rose and withdrew indoors.

On 16 September 1852, the royal family learned by telegram at Balmoral that the Duke of Wellington, eighty-three, had died two days earlier. 'A gloom cast on everything!' the Queen wrote in her diary. 'Albert dreadfully sad at the news.'

Rushing back to London seemed unnecessary. The nation clearly expected a grand funeral for the greatest Englishman of their time, and such planning necessitated refrigerating the Duke's cadaver as effectively as circumstances permitted. While Albert contributed ideas for the occasion, which would become a funereal orgy for a generation that indulged itself in death, he could continue, with Lord Malmesbury, the Minister in Residence, to pursue stags, and to plan the rebuilding of Balmoral, no longer a rented estate but the property of the Queen and Prince.

At first, Malmesbury's education in foreign affairs had been conducted by the Queen and Prince, but in ensuing months he and Derby began to complain to each other about Albert's 'interference...in matters of foreign policy', largely through bypassing the minister to consult directly with an envoy abroad. His exchanges with family and assumed friends in high foreign places would amount to a *Papierberg* – a paper mountain. While he had every right to personal communication with his brother, his uncles and his cousins, and rulers called *cousin* by royal courtesy, Albert seldom composed an unbusinesslike sentence. Ministers had little idea of the extent of his network, and for how long his and the Queen's private correspondence had been going on, for their most confidential letters were carried by couriers for N.M. Rothschild and Sons. A thank-you note from Albert's secretary George Anson for such services dated 4 January 1845 still exists in the Rothschild Archive, and other documents indicate that the couriers were busy into 1861.

An indignity which went on before ministerial eyes, according to Edward Stanley, was that Albert was 'constantly in the habit of expressing to Lord Derby and his colleagues what he states to be the Queen's wishes on this and that point'. While they took that as high-handed and dictatorial, soon they accepted that the Queen wanted it that way, and reinterpreted Albert's style as 'friendly and confidential'.

By the time that Malmesbury paid his first ministerial visit to Balmoral he had become used to consulting with Albert in Victoria's presence, but he could not get used to what they called a 'castle'. It was, he noted in his journal, 'in bad repair, and totally unfit for royal personages'. Also for lesser ranks, he thought. 'The rooms are so small that I was obliged to write my despatches on my bed and to keep the window constantly open to admit the necessary quantity of air.' His private secretary, for whom there was no room, had to lodge three miles away. 'We played at billiards every evening, the Queen and [her mother] the Duchess being constantly obliged to get up from their chairs to be out of the way of the cues.' Still, 'Nothing could be more cheerful and evidently perfectly happy than the Queen and Prince, or more kind to everybody around them. I never met any man so remarkable for the variety of information on all subjects as the latter, with a great fund of humour *quand il se déboutonne*.' It would have surprised many to have unbuttoned humour ascribed to Albert, who remained Germanically stiff in public appearances.

To mark Balmoral's possession, the Queen noted in her diary for 11 October 1852, most of the Household set off mid-morning to climb to the top of Craig Gowan to build the traditional cairn establishing claim to the site, the former pile having been pulled down by the servants. 'I then placed the first stone, after which Albert laid one, then the children according to their ages.' Then, in turn, the ladies, gentlemen, servants, and tenants, including spouses and children, each placed stones on the cairn, while a piper played and whisky was 'given to all', and 'some merry reels were danced'.

When the cairn reached its final height – about eight feet, Victoria guessed – 'Albert climbed to the top of it, and placed the last stone, after which three cheers were given.' She was touched by the event and the setting, and 'felt almost inclined to cry. The View was so beautiful over the dear hills; the day so fine; the whole so *gemütlich*. May God bless this place, and allow us yet to see it and enjoy it many a long year.'

Reluctantly they left for London. Once, Victoria had wanted to exclude the Duke of Wellington from her wedding. Now he was, she announced, 'Britain's pride, her glory, her hero'. The mourning period had already reached royal dimensions, and the lying-in-state had become one of legendary length, 65,073 persons filing by the sable catafalque surrounded by rows of colossal candelabras.

For the final procession on 18 November, the Prince designed a huge funeral car so awkward and heavy as to give the horses and men dragging it extraordinary difficulty. Prevented by protocol, the Queen was not present at the final ceremonies at St Paul's where 'the Car', as Greville sneered, 'tawdry, cumbrous and vulgar . . . contrived by a German artist attached to the School of Design, and under Prince Albert's direction', was met by the Prince at the cathedral steps. The ceremonies within were tedious and exhausting. Even reading newspaper accounts, overwhelming in their detail, was exhausting. Victoria remained at Buckingham Palace. She was again pregnant.

The Duke had worked until close to the end, reporting regularly to Albert, whom he regarded as his moral if not his actual successor,* and the Prince took the old soldier's pride in his troops to be an index to their readiness for a modern war. 'It is stated', the Duke deplored, 'that the British Infantry cannot march, that the Cavalry cannot ride, that the Officers are ignorant, that the Soldiers do not know the use of and cannot use their Arms!' He did not want Albert to believe that, and the Prince's veneration of Wellington ensured that the armed services, beset by parliamentary parsimony and purchase of commissions, would go into the unstable 1850s able to defeat bands of alleged savages in petty colonial skirmishes, but little more.

Although Albert was not blind to shortcomings in the services, Wellington had been untouchable and unapproachable. Now, the day after the Prince learned about the Duke's death, he penned a memorandum to himself, based upon his immediate exchanges with

---

* Wellington's actual successor as army chief would be Viscount Hardinge. General Henry Hardinge, already sixty-seven, was a hero of the Napoleonic wars, a veteran of parliamentary life and a governor-general of India.

the Prime Minister, Lord Derby, observing that the loss had been one of '*authority*' rather than '*efficiency*'. When Derby had proposed Victoria's cousin George, the Duke of Cambridge, prematurely at thirty-three a major-general, as the new commander-in-chief, Albert brushed the suggestion aside. 'He would have carried no weight with the public, and we must not conceal from ourselves that many attacks on the Army which have been sleeping on account of the Duke will now be forthcoming.' But Albert had a list of titles and duties belonging to Wellington to be parcelled out to successors, from Constable of the Tower of London to Chief of Ordnance, effectively the second most important job. For that he proposed a popular general, Fitzroy Somerset, with a step up in the peerage, and when Somerset, younger son of a duke, claimed that he could not afford the expense of an elevated title, Albert told Derby in confidence on 22 September that the Queen would pay the fees, and – to spare the general's feelings – 'you could easily manage it so that he need never know from what source the £500 came.' At sixty-four a desk officer who had been Military Secretary of the Horse Guards for twenty-five years, and close to Wellington for forty, Somerset had lost his right arm at Waterloo, which gave him a special cachet. He became Lord Raglan.

Greville privately carped that the Prince had 'shown little judgement' in the new military appointments, and had effectively made 'himself the Heir', which was 'ridiculous as well as odious', but he had no knowledge of Albert's actual refusal, in Wellington's lifetime, to become his chosen successor, nor that Somerset – Greville's favourite – had nearly, but for Albert's intervention, declined his own promotion. However the Prince did set himself up for trouble by reserving one of the relinquished appointments for himself. He informed Derby that he would take the colonelcy of the Grenadier Guards, with which came an annual emolument of £3,000, exchanging that for the Coldstreams, and £2,000, which would go to cousin George. When that became publicly noticed through debate on the Army estimates on 28 February 1853, press reaction was unkind, and it triggered what would be a year of indignities for Albert just as new causes for rearmament were emerging.

Although Albert's lifelong need for a father figure caused him repeatedly to summon Stockmar, who now largely kept to Coburg and when in England was regarded with suspicion, the ageing Baron was more out of touch with England than ever, and his advice often ranged from bad to dangerous. After Wellington's death he wrote to advise Albert to use the opportunity of the vacuum left by the Duke to become 'the idol of the people'. The Prince's popular success with the Great Exhibition may have prompted the suggestion, but the Prince understood that he could not and should not attempt anything of the sort. When he had responded to Wellington's offer of succession in the army that his primary responsibility was to submerge himself in his wife's position, he had recognized a role that was as crucial as it was difficult to perform. Irresistible temptations were always surfacing, as with the Grenadier Guards, or acting politically on his own. But he told Stockmar that much as his role as 'merely the wife's husband' was a presupposition of 'inferiority', he would keep to it. 'Now silent influence is precisely that which operates for the greatest and widest good, and therefore much time must elapse before the value of that influence is recognised by those who can take cognisance of it, while by the mass of mankind it can scarcely be understood at all. I must content myself with the fact that constitutional monarchy marches unassailably on its beneficent course, and that the country prospers and makes progress.' Yet it was hard to be silent or to appear nearly invisible.

Among the myriad of vacancies created by the death of the Duke was the Mastership of Trinity House, a charitable corporation under the sponsorship of the [Harbour] Pilots Guild which maintained good works from almshouses to lighthouses. Albert had been an Elder Brother, an honour open only to leading members of the establishment, and on his moving upward he arranged for the Prime Minister, the Earl of Derby, to become an Elder Brother to fill the emptied office. As with everything the Prince undertook, he carefully studied the rules and goals of the corporation and recommended reforms to rectify the failing Wellington's lack of oversight, such changes requiring parliamentary action. The annual banquets of the Trinity Brotherhood at its grand building just north of the Tower of London were events, and Albert would use his first as Master (4 June 1853) to press for an end to the penury which hobbled the armed services. Proposing a toast to the Army and Navy, he hoped that Britain was not 'so enervated by the enjoyment of riches and luxury, or so sunk in the decrepitude of age, that, from a miserable eagerness to cling to our mere wealth and comfort, we should be deaf to the calls of honour and duty'.

The coded message was easy to interpret. The riches and luxury had been secured at someone's cost. India was a collection of fiefdoms which benefited few Indians. The Opium Wars that opened China to commerce had an incalculable moral cost. The colonization of more and more of Africa had made the continent more accessible to missionaries – and slavers. Few Africans were the better for it. The armed services which had planted the Union Jack worldwide and could win an occasional colonial war were in no condition to defend Britain itself.

Albert's applause was less enthusiastic than polite. Ornaments of the class whose interests they thought he represented felt badly served by such badgering, and had he not already explained to Baron Stockmar that such populist declarations were not made in purely Albertine interest, the Baron would have assumed that his mentoring was being heeded.

With Louis Napoleon about to formalize his Second Empire with a pompous coronation, sabre-rattling from France increased as a symbol of new imperial assertiveness, and renewed fears of invasion obsessed the English. Malmesbury even learned from the excitable Lord Raglan on 30 October of alleged plans not only to invade England but to 'carry off the Queen from Osborne by a *coup de main*'. Lord Hardinge claimed to be anxious about the obsolescence of his artillery, which used gun carriages manufactured before Waterloo, and Albert suggested a huge rise in expenditure for the Army and Navy, including two thousand additional artillerymen, a thousand horses and five thousand seamen, which alone would add £230,000 to Disraeli's straitened budget.

'We are cleaning our rusty cannons and building fortifications,' Albert wrote to Ernest on 2 November. 'We have 80,000 men ready and we are improving our weapons.' For that he asked his brother to procure a 'Prussian needle gun' which the English might copy. '*We are quite unprepared*', he emphasized to Hardinge on 8 November, underlining his words. Comparing slow Wellington-era muzzle-loaders to the breech-loading, rapid-fire gun when it arrived from Gotha, Hardinge worried to Albert about 'expense', but the Prince insisted it was worth a trial. Only invasion scares from France, however unfounded, prompted any efforts to bring the army closer to Continental standards.

Whatever the resistance from within the armed services and from supporters of the *status quo* in the press and in Parliament, the Prince was one of the few possessors of influence to press for continuing modernization. In later years he would badger the Cabinet to equip the army with breech-loading arms while the generals insisted, still, on obsolete muzzle-loading guns abandoned by European armies. *Punch* would make fun of his shako, but thirty years after Wellington's obsequies, General Sir Garnet Wolseley, whom Disraeli would call 'our only soldier', wrote to the Queen's private secretary 'that we have never had any substantial reforms in the Army since the Prince Consort died, and that were he living now, Army Reform would be in a very different position . . . Prince Albert was a very sensible man.'

The new Parliament had opened on 11 November, a week before Wellington's state funeral, and limped into December 1852 still under Tory leadership; but a budget bill in December, attacked passionately by Gladstone, was defeated by 305 to 286, and Derby, the next day, took the train to Portsmouth and the ferry across the Solent to the Isle of Wight. Victoria and Albert were spending their Christmas at Osborne, and the Earl's duty was to resign in person. On returning Derby described the meeting to his son, and Edward entered the details in his diary:

> The Queen received him cordially: she seemed grave and anxious: the Prince entered into confidential discussions on many subjects, appearing desirous to take upon them the last opinion that he could receive from his ex-minister. He spoke often of Disraeli, extolled his talent, his energy, but expressed a fear that he was not in his heart favourable to the existing order of things. My Father defended his colleague: said he had been unnaturally kept down for several years, and then suddenly raised to the highest position. 'He has better reason than anyone to be attached to our constitutional system since he has experienced how easily under it a man may rise.' The Prince was glad to hear it, but still thought Disraeli had democratic tendencies 'and if that is the case, he may become one of the most dangerous men in Europe'.
>
> My Father, with his accustomed frankness, related the substance of this conversation to Disraeli.

The Prince feared, Derby added, that Disraeli's example might 'raise up a host of inferior imitations'. Albert may very well have dreaded a potential Louis Napoleon arising on English soil, and noted, when the outgoing ministers returned their seals at Windsor Castle on 28 December, 'Mr Disraeli seemed to feel most the loss of office.' Yet a curious metamorphosis in his relationship with the Court was already in progress, with Disraeli returning to Albert a state paper late in December with the awkward if fulsome parting words, 'I may, perhaps, be permitted to say that the views which your Royal Highness has developed to me in confidential conversation have not fallen on un-grateful soil. I shall ever remember with interest and admiration the princely mind in the princely person, and shall at all times be prepared to prove to your Royal Highness my devotion.' And at Windsor, as the opposing sides gathered for the transfer of seals, Disraeli, according to a later Cabinet member, John Morley, 'with infinite polish and grace asked pardon for the flying words of debate, and drew easy forgiveness'. Prince Albert's minute remarked, 'We owned that we had been astonished to find them all so *well bred.*'

The Tory ministry had been brought down by a combination of Whigs, Peelites, Radicals and Irish who had no common interest but to drive Derby and Disraeli from Downing Street, and for the Queen and Prince the dilemma was to find a Prime Minister from among them acceptable to the Crown. Without being asked for advice, Derby recommended Lord Lansdowne, and was dressed down for his intervention. The 3rd Marquis of Lansdowne, seventy-two, was a cautious Liberal and a veteran of Cabinets since 1806: too old, they felt, for the job. He was invited to Osborne with the safe and unremarkable 4th Earl of Aberdeen, only four years younger, but a Peelite. But Lansdowne fell ill. Aberdeen came alone, and was offered the Ministry, less on his own long experience, largely in foreign affairs, but because he was neither Russell nor Palmerston. And Albert handed the Earl a list of persons whom the Crown preferred to see named to his government. Politely, Aberdeen thanked him for 'these valuable suggestions', but the Cabinet remained his to propose and the Queen to review, and he departed inconclusively.

To settle the transition, the Queen and Prince interrupted their usual Christmas at Osborne, leaving by packet and rail early on December 28 to meet Aberdeen that afternoon in Windsor. The Earl was in difficulties, Albert recorded in one of his many memoranda, which by now filled dozens of volumes. No one expected the government to survive unless a place could be made in it for Palmerston, to whom Aberdeen, a friend of sixty years' standing, since they were boys at Harrow, had offered any post but the Foreign Office. To emphasize how indispensable he was, Palmerston was biding his time. To keep him out, Victoria and Albert were even willing to accept Lord John Russell, who was not interested and kept the Foreign Ministry only briefly, turning it over early in 1853 to the Earl of Clarendon. With the only portfolio to which Palmerston aspired (other than that of Prime Minister) foreclosed, to keep his hand in he accepted the powerful but ponderous Home Office. Albert was pleased, he told the new Prime Minister. Since the Home Office 'is a department where he has to work like a horse, he cannot do any mischief'. Meeting Palmerston two days later, Albert was even more satisfied, observing, hopefully, 'He looked excessively ill, and had to walk with two sticks, on account of his gout.' That augured to the Prince the end of Palmerston's ambitions, but at sixty-nine the wily 'Pam' was far from finished.

On the final day of the former Ministry, Lord Malmesbury had been at Windsor with all his colleagues but Derby (who had taken his leave earlier), to give up their seals. During a private half-hour the Prince, who respected Malmesbury's inside knowledge of France, read a surprising letter from the distrusted usurper who was now calling himself Napoleon III to Prince Hohenlohe, the husband of Victoria's half-sister, Feodora. Seeking to found a dynasty and in need of an appropriate bride, he was interested in Her Serene Highness Princess Adelaide of Hohenlohe, aged seventeen. Her father raised objections about religion and morals, and 'was not sure of the [financial] settlement being satisfactory'. He was a pragmatic German who was short in ready money, and just as Albert regularly and usually covertly paid Ernest's debts, so had Victoria regularly rescued the Hohenlohes.

'The Queen and Prince', Malmesbury wrote, 'talked of the marriage reasonably, and weighted the pros and cons.' There were more of the latter, but they were 'afraid the Princess should be dazzled if she heard of the offer'. It could not be concealed from her, and Napoleon's envoy to London, Alexandre Florian Walewski, was prepared to convey the Emperor's bid in person. Ironically, Count Walewski, an illegitimate son of the first Napoleon, was the complaisant husband of one of the Emperor's mistresses, Maria, Countess Walewska. The élite of the Second Empire never confused marriage with sex, or politics with passion. By 1855 the Polish-born Walewski would be Foreign Minister.

To many Englishmen, Charles Louis Napoleon, forty-four, was a charismatic figure. He was not only the nephew of a legendary hero but a man who had survived by his wits and accomplished the impossible. He had lived in conspiratorial exile in England, had English friends in high places, and even a wealthy English mistress, Elizabeth Howard, whom he was now prepared to discard. Both Victoria and Albert despised him as a vulgarian and immoralist, but neither disability ruled him out any more than his politically necessary Roman Catholicism, as husband for their niece less than half his age, if he were the means of making 'Ada' an empress and creating yet another rapprochement with historically inimical France.

That the sleazy bargain was taken seriously by the rigidly moral Queen and Prince suggests the power of pragmatism, for it was easy for Victoria to recall the disgust of her own mother at the possibility that Feodora – Adelaide's mother – might have been taken as wife by the wicked and gross – and aged – George IV. Paradoxically, however physically unhandsome Louis Napoleon was, in the popular mind in England he was more dashing and attractive than the cramped foreign intellectual who was the Queen's consort. Feodora might have looked on the match as a way out of the difficulties that had dogged her since 1848. Although her husband had rescued his principality when revolutionary fervour receded, they had been living 'a new existence of privations' (as she wrote to Victoria) that was alleviated largely by 'loans' from her sister and mother, and frequent residence for her daughters in England. 'Ada' was even with Victoria when the marriage offer was transmitted. Indirectly through her ministers, Victoria replied that the proposal was a matter for the girl and her parents. Feodora considered the bargain 'disagreeable', not because of the religious *mésalliance*, but because of her daughter's immaturity and the Emperor's morals. Yet she thought that Ada would 'rather like' the dazzling marriage, a misunderstanding of her daughter, who rejected 'a position as elevated as it is perilous'.

By the time Princess Adelaide of Hohenlohe had written her refusal, the question was moot. Expecting otherwise, the Queen had said frankly to Lord Derby, 'You know *our* family [the Coburgs] have always been accused of being too ready to pick up any crown that had tumbled in the dirt.' Anticipating a rebuff, however, the Emperor remained susceptible to signals from other marriageable women, even those only on the fringes of acceptability. On 31 December 1852, Count Walewski arrived from London to report on the likely failure of his mission, and was greeted to his surprise with '*Mon cher, je suis pris!*' Louis Napoleon had met and been captivated by the beautiful, ambitious Eugénie di Montijo, who was appropriately Catholic, a mature twenty-seven, and ostensibly the daughter of a Spanish count. The ambassador reminded him that his engagement announcement was premature; he could not jilt Queen Victoria's niece. He would not have to. Ada's letter would arrive the next day.

The sordid business of government, from political marriages to cynical foreign-policy machinations, left Victoria feeling very different from the way she had when she stood on the dais in the Crystal Palace and felt at one with what she visualized as the aspirations of human-kind. Napoleon III had only personal aspirations, identifying them with France. His reign needed the sense of continuity only a legitimate heir could create, and it needed continuing instability elsewhere on the Continent because such distractions further coalesced support for his throne. In that he was inadvertently assisted by Austria's heavy-handedness in Italy, where new insurrections flared, and France declared its sympathies with Italian aspirations. Another opportunity arose from Russia's territorial greed in eastern Europe, Tsar Nicholas I seeing gains to be made at the expense of mismanaged Turkey, a sick octopus losing its tentacles to ethnic risings and opportunism. Even there Napoleon found a cause – the protection of Roman Catholics in the Turkish-held Holy Lands. In every foreign crisis area Prince Albert was seen as interfering. The exposure of his Grenadiers sinecure, and two caustic leading articles that followed in *The Times* on 1 and 2 March, raised his ire and that of the public. Incautiously his private secretary Charles Grey told Greville that 'he never saw the Prince so riled at anything'.

Although the pinnacle of esteem that was the Crystal Palace could not have been permanent, Albert was seeing his reputation begin to unravel often for no fault of his own. The *Spectator*, in Palmerstonian terms, even viewed his German origins as dangerous for the times. 'It is evident', it wrote, 'that a serious disturbance in Europe might be very inconvenient to the minor German Powers; and that fact has perhaps suggested that rough guess that a Prince bound up with German interests by family relations, has used his position near the British

Sovereign...' The implication of 'officious meddling with affairs which are not his' would appear in the press often through the year, sometimes by raising the charge and then piously but weakly denying its truth. Even Lord Aberdeen's keeping England aloof from Continental quarrels was interpreted as a policy of permissiveness.

With Palmerston as a very activist Home Secretary, Albert could not evade further involvement with the man he disliked more than anyone else in England, for 'Pam' had responsibility for the militia. Late in March the Prince was writing to the Home Office about professionalizing amateurish militia leadership. Albert also promoted the purchase of a permanent training site at Chobham in Surrey, an idea he had unsuccessfully offered to Wellington, based upon his youthful visits to King Leopold's manœuvre area at Beverlo. Like the 'Albert hat', such innovations were derided in the press as his 'army mania'.

Fuelled by popular francophobia, the Chobham Heath 'camp of instruction' was established, with troops quartered in a vast tent city.

In a mock medallion, Punch *shows the Queen and Prince at the Chobham military exercises.*

(The experience would lead to the establishment of Aldershot.) An elaborate review was planned for 21 June 1853, with the Queen present on horseback to take salutes. Regiments of the home garrisons were under Lieutenant-General Lord Seaton. John Colborne had served under Wellington at Waterloo and Hardinge at Quatre-Bras. The Earl of Cardigan was there with his smart 11th Hussars, and Albert was present as colonel of his own Grenadier Guards.

Large crowds of the curious, the colourful uniforms of élite units, and the presence of foreign observers from the King of Hanover to Prince Lucien Bonaparte, created a holiday atmosphere akin to Derby Day. The cavalry charges, with ten thousand horsemen brandishing swords over the heath, and the infantry sweeps, with foot soldiers holding their weapons at the ready, were dramatic. From the adjoining height where Victoria watched, Duke Ernest and his German party scoffed privately at the 'few tactical evolutions, which appeared to be rather childish'.

Favoured guests, including ladies, then retired to tents for a six-course luncheon, with sherry and champagne, until a storm materialized. When the rain and wind lifted the canvas, officers and guests had to flee to the cavalry stables before breaking camp. But the press had covered the event, and military attachés were present, so that potential foreign adversaries might be impressed by the state of English prepared-ness, which in actuality was poor for anything but a very small war.

Three days later, Albert returned for another look. Rain had becalmed the camp. Tents were blown awry by the wind, and mud was everywhere. Food for the ranks was bad and facilities at best were inadequate. In the afternoon his own brigade had polished itself up for his inspection, but he knew that beneath the spit-and-polish they were as unready for warfare as were their Waterloo-era guns.

While preparations had been underway for the Chobham Heath review, which Albert left feeling ill – two days later he was in a sick-bed – he had problems close to home as well. In Victoria's last month of her eighth pregnancy there was a serious fire at Windsor Castle. She was, Albert wrote to his stepmother on 23 March 1853, 'quite well, and has suffered absolutely nothing from the agitation into which we were naturally all thrown by the danger. We had to battle with the flames from ten at night till four in the morning before we got them com-pletely under [control]; nevertheless the injury was confined to one tower of the Castle, which has been gutted by the flames through four stories.' The chief loss had been 'the beautiful dining-room'.

Two weeks later, on 7 April, the Queen gave birth to her fourth son, Leopold, with the assistance, for the first time, of 'blessed chloroform'. Two weeks later, in her journal, she recalled its effect as 'soothing, quieting and delightful beyond measure'. Yet she had not been quieted long, for there were problems with the new baby. Victoria was suffering again from postpartum hysterical crises, which went on to become intermittent bouts of depression and recrimination, embittering her relationship with Albert.

It was a matter of class and rank as well as of sheer lack of interest that the Queen and Prince quickly turned over to their attendants all parental involvement with their infants, short of formal social occasions. They had often seen Vicky and Bertie bathed and put to bed. Now that they had less time for that, the Queen confessed, she saw the 'younger ones' on such occasions 'once in three months perhaps'. But she was able to tell her uncle, after whom Leopold was named, that he seemed 'a jolly fat little fellow', belying his diagnosis as a haemophiliac, which added to Victoria's anxieties. She sent vicious, accusing notes to Albert, usually about alleged affronts too trivial to suggest anything but emotional breakdown, and her surviving official correspondence of the period is so slight as to suggest unusual inattention on her part.

Albert would respond in notes addressed to 'Dear Child', once calling attention to a 'distressing scene' caused by a 'miserable trifle', yet realizing that he only increased her distress by referring to the 'groundlessness and injustice of the accusations'. Pregnancy always increased her hostility to her husband because she brooded over the injustice of woman's lot in suffering disfigurement and discomfort. The baby's poor health – Albert blamed the difficulties on her insistence upon a wet nurse from the Scottish Highlands whose milk seemed to disagree with the child – aggravated her feelings about the futility of repeated pregnancies. The Queen's testiness – a recurring agony to Albert – would continue off and on for years, into and beyond her ninth and last pregnancy in 1857. When she told her eldest daughter in 1859 that too many pregnancies too soon had made life 'wretched' for years – 'one becomes so worn out and one's nerves so miserable' – the lesson was from still fresh and painful experience.

Few husbands in history can have tried as hard as Albert to maintain the emotional equilibrium as well as the professional effectiveness of a wife. His love survived the trials of his inferior position and his continued unacceptability as an alien, and it survived the pendulum swings of Victoria's almost helpless doting upon him and her using him to vent frustrations of which he was victim rather than cause. He thought constantly of her emotional and physical needs, writing from Chobham that he was happy that she had got through her day without needing him, and signing off with the familiar German love song,

> *Du, Du liegst mir in Herzen,*
> *Du, Du liegst mir im Sinn,*
> *Du, Du machst mir viel Schmerzen,*
> *Weisst nicht wie gut ich Dir bin.**

One matter that continued to mar their domestic happiness, and remained a matter for mutual accusation, was the apparent backwardness of the Prince of Wales. While Vicky was rapidly growing into a miniature of Albert, all that Bertie seemed to have in common with Vicky was Hanoverian obstinacy. No study regimen, however meticulously devised by Albert, made any impression upon the Prince of Wales. Whether he would have been a better scholar had the pressure upon him been less intense is idle speculation. Victoria sensed that Albert was requiring too much of the child and asked Lady Lyttelton to see that Bertie was not 'overworked'. But Bertie remained overworked for his capacities. He would take out his frustrations in Hanoverian blind rages at his tutors, and occasionally at his parents, who perceived nothing of the potentially effective ceremonial sovereign in the amiable young man already at social ease with adults. With their hopes for the future of the monarchy invested in him, they saw only a vacuous future king. The other children were unimportant. The girls would have to be found appropriately arranged marriages, perhaps with a diplomatic intent; the other sons were only insurance.

---

* You, you are in my heart,
You, you are in my thoughts,
You, you give me heartache,
Don't you know that I love you?
Popular English adaptations of the folk song appeared in the 1940s and 1950s as 'You, you, you are the One'.

'The Queen and Prince Albert at Home' – a contemporary lithograph, dated possibly (from the existence of only three royal children) as late in 1843.

Such attitudes suggest an insensitivity to their children that contradicts the *gemütlich* image that has come down to us of family picnics and outings, Albert on a sledge in the snow with a child, or crawling about on the hearth rug at Osborne playing children's games, Victoria sketching outdoors with the girls. At Osborne and Balmoral there was more togetherness, but the royal parents were like other rich parents of their time except that they had a far busier social and official life. The doting, devoted, and cosy family of the illustrated papers and the gossipy articles was largely mythical, yet the illusion of domesticity seemed to democratize the crown. When the royal children were small, they seldom appeared at the table, or anywhere else where their parents happened to be in the servant-saturated households. Except on holiday or ceremonial occasions, they were overseen rather than seen.

But for Prince Leopold's christening, the Chobham appearance had been Victoria's re-introduction to public life, but her activities were cut short the next month by measles, which had been running through the family. Bertie was first to be sick, and recovered quickly. The others were treated – incompetently, as usual – wherever they happened to become ill, Helena and Louise at Windsor, Vicky and Alice at Buckingham Palace, Victoria and Albert at Osborne. Even Albert's valet, Löhlein, kept to his bed, and Cart oversaw both him and the Prince, who, run down from overwork and lack of sleep, had the worst case – a high fever that left him delirious, and with temporary weakness that required him to walk with a cane. Sir James Clark, his physician, saw no cause for alarm. But only in August was he up again, prompted largely by preparations for the great naval review at Spithead, the area of the eastern Solent between Portsmouth and Ryde.

Spithead was to be a nautical Chobham. Among foreign invitees were Prince Adalbert and a Prussian naval contingent, part of Albert's continuing effort to establish a special relationship with Prussia – to influence its foreign policy and to have an indirect role in inevitable German unification. (He would be frustrated in both.) Spithead was a showplace to demonstrate to Europe the screw-propelled, 131-gun, three-decker *Duke of Wellington*, new pride of the Royal Navy. On 16 August, in a letter to Stockmar, Albert boasted that the fleet now had sixteen steamships, with ten more under construction, and that at Spithead '300 ships and 100,000 men must have been assembled in one spot', with the Navy itself carrying '1,100 guns and 10,000 men'. In his enthusiasm for the apparent efficiency of the fleet, Albert shut his eyes to the fact that even the new *Wellington* had been designed and launched, decades after steam propulsion, as a sailing ship, and only fitted afterwards with retractable funnels and screw. The Royal Navy was far behind France in modernization – and imagination. It was still considered unseamanlike to use steam except in a flat calm, and a mixed fleet of screw-propelled, paddle-wheeled and sailing frigates was considered appropriate. Most ships were obsolete hulks unfit for battle or for ferrying troops, and in the highest Admiralty positions were dodderers who dated back to Trafalgar.

A major problem in modernizing the services remained money, and Gladstone, as Aberdeen's Chancellor of the Exchequer, reluctant over a long lifetime to furnish funds to the military, did push through for the first time an inheritance tax on property while extending income tax for two further years. Knowing what uses the funds might have, Albert wrote, to Gladstone's surprise, a congratulatory letter. It was probably improper for Albert to do it, out of keeping with ostensible party neutrality, but the Prince found it difficult to be uninvolved.

Through the spring and summer, as Victoria and Albert moved to Osborne and then to Balmoral on what had become the Queen's annual cycle, Albert was unable to remain because of military preparations, yet he managed to oversee the rising of a new Balmoral Castle, which by early September was 'up one story' and faced with granite. But, he wrote to Stockmar on 12 September, 'the workmen, who have to be brought here from a distance and to camp in wooden hutments, have already struck several times, which is now quite the fashion all over the country'. He attributed that not to the 'terribly hard' work and the terrible living conditions, but to the shortages of labour caused by emigration.

Even before Spithead, it was clear that Europe would soon be at war. It was merely uncertain who the opposing nations would be, and who could safely remain neutral. Briefly Foreign Minister before transferring the seals to Clarendon, Russell, who was anti-Napoleon, sought accommodation with Tsar Nicholas by conceding Tsarist claims to be the protecting power on behalf of adherents to the Orthodox Church in the Eastern Holy Places. Albert warmed to the idea as a reasonable parallel to powers granted to the French. Tsarist ambitions, however, were more than spiritual, and the privileges claimed by Napoleon III, whose forces were distant, were looked upon at Constantinople far more favourably than those of adjacent and overwhelming Russia. When it became obvious that the hardly covert aim of St Petersburg was to establish a protectorate over millions of the Sultan's Orthodox subjects wherever they were, Victoria – in a memorandum written by Albert – declared to Lord Aberdeen that the claims of Nicholas I were inadmissible. 'We must take care not to become the dupes of Russian policy,' Victoria wrote on 4 May.

With the Palmerston wing of the government for a hard line against Russia and the Russell–Clarendon wing less than eager to drift into war on Turkey's behalf, Aberdeen, agreeing to station warships in the Black Sea area for their symbolic value – and to keep his Cabinet from collapse – dithered. Russia exploited the time to move up troops to the Turkish borders, then invaded the Danubian provinces. Turkey then recognized a state of war with Russia on 4 October 1853, and the news of both events spread quickly in the new age of telegraphic transmission. Stratford Canning, recently elevated as Viscount Stratford de Redcliffe, had, as ambassador, encouraged Turkish resistance, putting his country on a side opposite from the one Russell had taken in January, and Albert wrote wryly, although alarmed, 'Lord Stratford fulfills his instructions to the letter, but he so contrives that we are getting deeper and deeper into a war policy.' Weak within his own Cabinet, the Earl of Aberdeen could do little more than deplore. What were the limits of Russian expansion which England and its empire could safely countenance? Without outside help, the Turks would lose, and Russia would emerge into the Mediterranean.

Aberdeen's ministers were divided. For imperial reasons, and to keep Russia from dominating Europe, the Tsar's imperial ambitions had to be curbed, and Turkey propped up, however much the Sultan might have to relinquish in Europe to ethnic aspirations and Russian greed. The Cabinet ranged from Gladstone's pacifism at almost any cost to Palmerston's bellicosity.

With a sense of despair Aberdeen wrote to the Queen on 6 October, 'No doubt it may be very agreeable to humiliate the Emperor of Russia; but Lord Aberdeen thinks that it is paying a little too dear for this pleasure, to check the progress and prosperity of this happy country, and to cover Europe with confusion, misery, and blood.' The Queen and Prince would have preferred to see truculently Palmerstonian Stratford de Redcliffe replaced at Constantinople, and ethnically un-Turkish Wallachia and Moldavia fly whatever colours emerged from the confusion. The fraying Ottoman Empire was too weak to maintain them anyway. Yet squadrons flying the British White Ensign were already at the Dardanelles, a commitment to check Russia somewhere.

That the Tsar was willing to acquire segments of European Turkey one at a time had already been clear from his acceptance of a diplomatic 'Note' from England, France, Austria and even Prussia that implicitly only slowed Russian expansionism, for the message had been rejected by Turkey, which had everything to lose from appeasement of Russia. Turkey, then, held moral hostage the English and French flotillas in its waters, which had not cowed Russia, and on 8 October 1853, Aberdeen wrote to Sir James Graham, sending a copy to the Queen, that he preferred, if possible, a 'defensive war' on behalf of Turkey with 'a French army, and perhaps English money'. To Nicholas I, England and its accidental ally, France, seemed too remote to matter militarily, and Austria and Prussia saw something to gain at virtually no expense in the further dismemberment of European Turkey. 'The Queen', Albert wrote helplessly in a memorandum at Balmoral on 10 October, 'might now be involved in war, of which the consequences could not be calculated, chiefly by the desire of Lord Aberdeen to keep his Cabinet together; this might then break down, and the Queen would be left without an efficient Government, and a war on her hands.' And Albert knew from the experience of Chobham and Spithead, whatever his apparent boastfulness, that England was unready.

From Balmoral, the wrong place at the wrong time because the Court had little influence on events from there – yet Victoria stubbornly stuck to her Balmoral cycle – Albert admitted in a memorandum of 16 October that to prevent Constantinople and the Dardanelles from falling into Russian hands it might even be 'right and wise' to go to war. However, the peace that inevitably would follow had to include 'arrangements more consonant with the well-understood interests of Europe, of Christianity, liberty and civilisation, than the reimposition of the ignorant barbarian and despotic yoke of the Mussulman over the most fertile and favoured portion of Europe'.

Albert was hoping to have it both ways, but there was little to choose between Tsarist oppression and Ottoman oppression, and meetings at Balmoral and then Windsor, each carefully recorded by Albert, complete with snatches of memorable dialogue, evidence of how much the decisions on behalf of the nation about war or peace were subject to the rivalries of Liberals, Radicals, and Peelites, and to individual ministerial aspirations. Even parliamentary reform (which Palmerston opposed under any conditions) was hostage to war, and Lord John Russell claimed that he had a bill ready but under the 'present circumstances' it had no future. 'You mean unless you sit in the chair which I now occupy?' asked Aberdeen. Russell laughed.

Several Ministers hoped to exploit Aberdeen's weakness into a turn at Downing Street, and the 'Eastern Question' offered an opportunity. Graham, Palmerston, Russell and even Gladstone made little secret of ambitions for higher office. Gladstone's pacifism was the closest to a pro-Russian stance of any minister, but based upon his desire (not uncommon since the days of Peel) to spend as little as possible on the military budget, and on his Christian fervour, which accepted Russian domination in the east as preferable to Islamic rule, however benign.

Recognizing that sooner rather than later, they might have to accommodate themselves to Palmerston, the Queen and Prince even agreed to have the Home Secretary take a one-week tour of duty as Minister-in-Residence in the close confines of Balmoral. It was not a success. He would discuss no business, and seemed interested only in playing billiards with Albert, who was drawn away from overseeing the start of new construction. As he had helped to design Osborne with a builder, Thomas Cubitt, at his side, Albert worked in Scotland with William Smith to reshape the land as well as to give the structure character. Two terraces were to descend from the ground floor to the bank of the Dee, and pepper-box turrets and a nearly detached tower were to suggest a larger castle. The granite from a quarry in Kemnay was to be crystalline and almost white. Victoria's diary contains an account of Albert's modelling for Smith's men a sand-castle and terraces to realize his vision.

Not only was a new and larger residence going up, but also new living quarters for the workmen. A fire had gutted the row of huts, which had to be rebuilt. Albert paid out £318 11s. 7½ d. for workmen's belongings also destroyed.

The losses in Aberdeenshire were only inconvenient; in the East there were debits about which he could do nothing, but for which Albert would have to pay. Late in November, with the Eastern Question having turned from threats to war, the unprepared Turks suffered a Black Sea disaster at Sinope (modern Sinop), on their central coast, which turned the newspaper-reading public in Britain furiously Russophobic. While the Turks were resisting incursions on their Danubian fronts, a Russian fleet had surprised Turkish ships under anchor and burned them to the waterline, with four thousand dead. Although a victory of Russian enterprise over Ottoman somnolence, the London press declared the catastrophe 'a crime', and called for revenge. While

Aberdeen's government vacillated about a response, Albert was targeted as the pro-Russian, power-hungry villain emboldening the Tsar.

A series of blunders, some Albert's own, had focused public attention on him anew. Reports surfaced that his admirers were lobbying for a statue of the Prince in Hyde Park on the former site of the Crystal Palace. Rumour had it that statues of George III and George IV, and a pillar memorializing the little-lamented Duke of York, Victoria's insolvent uncle, would be melted down for their bronze. The basis for the allegations was that Thomas Challis, a hide-and-skin merchant and Lord Mayor of London, late in 1853 had also proposed that it was time for a statue of Prince Albert to be erected in the City. *Punch* made fun of the idea with a column, 'The Albert Statue Movement', accompanied by a cartoon, in which 'the principal metropolitan Statues' reportedly met to consider adding to their number one of the Prince, to watch over Temple Bar at the Strand entrance to the City rather than at Hyde Park Corner, 'to conciliate the protection of Royalty for the City'. Rising together, 'Gog and Magog . . . loudly expressed their approbation of this view; the adoption of which would tend to secure themselves in their own places, which they wished to retain as long as they were able, like all others holding comfortable situations in Guildhall.'

Embarrassed by the proposal, and even more embarrassed by its reception, the Queen and Prince quashed such ideas. Writing to Earl Granville on 3 November, Albert attempted to deride the idea of a statue in Hyde Park with humour. 'I can say, with perfect absence of humbug,' he claimed, 'that I would much rather not be made the prominent feature of such a monument, as it would both disturb my quiet rides in Rotten Row to see my own face staring at me, and if (as is very likely) it became an artistic monstrosity, like most of our monuments, it would upset my equanimity to be permanently ridiculed and laughed at in effigy.'

Seeking causes for governmental unwillingness to confront the Eastern Question, which had implications for British pride, British trade, and British imperial security, the press found an explanation in Albert's alleged aggrandizement of power, symbolized now by the statue imbroglio. He was known to intrude into foreign affairs, but rumour reversed his position. When Prince William of Prussia was in London for the christening of Leopold, Albert had encouraged him to have his brother, King Frederick William IV, join other Western nations in urging restraint upon Russia. The King, however, refused to intervene with his brother-in-law, the Tsar, or expose, he claimed, his country's eastern frontiers to instability. Albert fumed about Prussia's 'wicked policy' – which seemed to him 'fish[ing] in troubled waters'. Yet, trying to have it both ways later, he had written to Stockmar on 7 November, 1853 that Prussia's position – it had agreed to be a party to the innocuous Vienna 'Note' accepted by Russia – had become 'very useful for the maintenance of peace' because Berlin's neutrality meant that Nicholas could not count upon Frederick William as ally.

To Aberdeen, who sent Albert's memorandum to Palmerston for comment, the Prince proposed keeping Russia out of the Balkans by creating an imperial Greece at Turkey's expense – a Greek Orthodox state in Europe that would protect all Christian denominations and holy places in the Ottoman provinces. Scoffing at the idea, Palmerston wondered, then, why Albert failed to support Russia against Turkey, as the result would be the same. To Palmerston, Britain's goals were, simply, 'the Relinquishment by Russia of inadmissible Pretensions and her Retirement from Turkish Territory'.

Aberdeen showed Palmerston's objections to the Queen, and Albert urged the Prime Minister to use Palmerston's bellicose tendencies to get rid of him, but to fashion a Home Office excuse – perhaps differences over Reform.* But while the Eastern Question simmered at home, news arrived in London on 11 December of Russian 'treachery' at Sinope. The press wrote of England's 'shame' – and blamed timidity in Whitehall about sending the Royal Navy into the Black Sea. Palmerston, popular feeling went, would not have permitted the massacre to happen.

Adopting Albert's strategy, Aberdeen wrote at length to Palmerston on 14 December to disagree about a Reform bill and to suggest that as the ostensible reason for him to leave the Cabinet. The Home Secretary had no doubts as to the source of the suggestion and responded curtly, 'My dear Aberdeen, I have received your note of this Morning and in Consequence I have to request you to lay before Her Majesty the Resignation of my Office. I shall be ready to give up the Seals at any Time that may best Suit your Convenience. Yours sincerely, Palmerston.'

* Palmerston had no Cabinet role in foreign affairs but his stewardship of the Home Office gave him a voice in internal reforms.

Newspapers the next day published the text, which Palmerston was quick to supply. The *Morning Post* added the observation, almost certainly also from Palmerston, that although disagreement over Reform was the supposed grounds for the resignation, the actual reason was his disgust with the Ministry's craven behaviour toward Russia, which had led to the disgrace in the Black Sea. Word got about quickly as to who appeared responsible for driving him out of the government. If foreign intrigue was involved – someone with a key to diplomatic red boxes – who was the only foreigner in the highest circles? Hadn't that ambitious eminence also driven Palmerston out of the Cabinet only two years earlier? 'The public had graciously selected me as its scapegoat', Albert would write more dismissively than he should have to his brother, 'to answer for its not yet having come to war, and says "logically" that the interest of the Coburg family, which is Russian, Belgian, Orleanistic, Fusionistic, is preferred to the alliance with Louis Napoleon. The Emperor of Russia now governs England. He telegraphs to Gotha, to you in Brussels, Uncle Leopold to me, I whisper in Victoria's ear, she gets round old Aberdeen, and the voice of the only *English* Minister, Palmerston, is not listened to – ay, he is always intrigued against, at the Court, and by the Court.' Reflecting insider understanding, Edward Stanley observed in his diary on Christmas Day 1853, 'The more probable version [of events] is, that Lord Aberdeen and Albert jointly have contrived the affair, the latter being the prime mover, the former only his tool. This . . . is certainly the idea commonly received out of doors: and has led to loud and growing complaints of the secret influence exerted by the Prince Consort.'

Newspapers in Palmerston's web led denunciations of the Prince as the agent of Russian interests who operated through German connections related to the Tsar. A conglomerate of little-related suspicions and antipathies had finally converged. Albert was in trouble.

XIII

Impeaching the Prince

1853–1855

O N CHRISTMAS DAY 1853 Palmerston was back. At Windsor the day before, in audience with the Queen and Prince, Aberdeen reported that not only had his Cabinet been eager to have Palmerston return, but that he had been under pressure from Emily, his wife, 'to have his resignation', as Albert reported it, 'considered as not having taken place'. Emily Palmerston, the late Viscount Melbourne's sister, was too politically astute to let her husband burn his bridges to Down-ing Street. He was the only alternative to Aberdeen's motley Ministry. Thus the day after Christmas the Prime Minister disclosed Palmerston's letter avowing that he had misunderstood the details of the 'intended Reform Bill' and was withdrawing his resignation. The entire affair had been dishonest, and everyone in politics could decrypt the language.

The failure of Albert's scheme, however, only sank him deeper into trouble. No amount of exposure to English ways seemed to make Albert more acceptable; if anything, the Queen was becoming more German. Blindness to the symbolism of small things did not help. Albert, for example, had brought small green German table lamps with him when he first arrived in England, and he still used their successors in his study, whether from nostalgia or a feeling that they were more efficient than domestic counterparts. He often wore, for hunting or stalking, thigh-high leather boots from Germany and an open-necked shirt, which to one gossip made him look like a *Heldentenor*. He not only spoke English slowly, but was not 'fast' in accepted upper-class recreations like betting, swearing and wenching. 'They call him slow', a letter to

The Times defending him went, 'because he does not gamble, does not use offensive language, and does not keep an opera dancer.'

Whatever he did seemed to call attention to his origins. He kept his diary in German. He spoke German within the family – when he would wake Victoria at eight, it would be with '*Es ist Zeit, steh' auf!*' ('It is time, get up!') – and he would always feel insecure with his English correspondence, giving much of his mail to Victoria or his secretaries to read, to reassure himself about his understanding. To Anson, earlier, Victoria had explained, 'The Prince and Queen speak English . . . quite as much as we speak German.' That was hardly enough.

The strain affected both Queen and Prince, who felt that they had no one on English soil with whom to share their misery. 'If our courage and cheerfulness have not suffered,' Albert confided to Stockmar in Coburg, 'our stomachs and digestions have, as they commonly do when feelings are kept long on the stretch.' On 27 December he was less restrained in reporting what appeared to be a newspaper campaign to drive him out. 'The stupidest trash is babbled to the public, so stupid that (as they say in Coburg) you would not give it to the pigs to litter in.' Had Albert waited two more days he could have included an issue of the *Morning Herald*, in which a letter under the initials 'M.P.' – actually young Edward Stanley – reported without attribution his gossip from Malmesbury and from the pro-Russian diplomat Lord Howden (he had married a great-niece of Prince Potemkin) about Albert's allegedly unconstitutional role in ousting Palmerston. 'It was too bad', the diatribe charged, 'that one man, and he not an Englishman by birth, should be at once Foreign Secretary, Commander-in-Chief and Prime Minister under all administrations.' In his diary for 3 January 1854, Stanley 'expressly decline[d] vouching for' the 'rumour', but it did Albert further harm when provincial papers reprinted the charge.

The new year had begun very badly, contributed to by Victoria, who wrote heatedly to Aberdeen on 4 January that she intended, on her own authority, to legitimize 'Prince Consort' as her husband's title, as he was known by it anyway. If that gesture were to cause further attacks on Albert and convince her that these represented the popular will, 'she would LEAVE a position which nothing but her domestic happiness could make her endure, and retire to private life – leaving the country to choose another ruler after their own HEART'S CONTENT'. Although she did not 'think so ill of her country' to believe that her subjects would prompt her to abdicate, she claimed '*very bitter* feelings in her breast, which time alone can eradicate'.

Although she did not test public sentiment with a title for Albert, the attacks continued for other reasons. By extrapolation, German connections meant Russian ones, and on 7 January the *Daily News* charged, absurdly, 'Above all, the nation distrusts the politics, however they may admire the taste, of a Prince who has breathed from childhood the air of courts tainted by the imaginative servility of Goethe.' One cause for hostility, Albert felt, was popular frustration that war fever against Russia had not yet exploded into actual war. Allegedly, he had blocked all efforts to curtail Russian ambitions in Europe and Asia. Another adversary he identified in a letter to Stockmar was the army faction under Lord Raglan – 'the Senior United Services Club, with all its grumblers'. Raglan loyalists felt that the former Fitzroy Somerset's military secretaryship to Wellington over thirty years should have earned him succession to the Duke over the more senior Lord Hardinge, who had the advantage of 'confidential intercourse . . . with myself in all military matters'.

As attempts to embarrass the Prince multiplied, Edward Stanley noted in his diary, evasively, 'I did not follow up the attack [on Albert] farther than by a single letter under a different signature, and that rather in defence of M.P.' – himself – 'than with any intention of rousing further passion'. And via the *Daily News* of 11 January, the Radical MP John Arthur Roebuck announced that he would demand explanations in the Commons from ministers about the improper interference of the Prince in government business. *Punch*'s most striking cartoon as 1854 opened had no humour in it. Long familiar to the public as an ice skater, Albert appeared, to the horror of watchers, skimming into an area marked off as thin ice and posted with a warning, 'FOREIGN AFFAIRS. VERY DANGEROUS'.

In London on 12 January a curious letter in Albert's defence appeared as news in the *Morning Chronicle*, which had taken it from the Dublin press. Newspapers in both British isles were evidencing how much the Prince's alleged intervention in political affairs had become a matter for public debate, and he knew it as well from his own mail, as writers would often rush off to a local newspaper a copy of a letter to Windsor Castle. Thomas Mulock 'of Killiney, near Dublin', had waited until he received a courteous but innocuous note from Charles Grey acknowledging the 'kind consideration' before sending both letters to the *Freeman's Journal*. Despite evidence to the contrary, the *Chronicle* described the correspondence as looking 'very like a hoax'. Mulock, however, was authentic, listed in *Thom's Directory* of Dublin as 'Esq.' – and therefore a gentleman.

When a writer impugned the genuineness of the reply from Albert's secretary the next day, Mulock responded in print that he had 'exhibited . . . the respective autographs' to the editor prior to publication; however the London story carried only the negative bias. Nevertheless there were many who felt, with Mulock, 'pain and indignation' at the 'unjust and anti-Christian accusations' that there was something wrong in a husband's offering advice to his wife even when she was the Queen, or that 'your Royal Highness is invariably present when her Majesty grants audiences to her Ministers'. Although the Prince, Mulock contended, 'cannot act as the political head of the State, . . . when the Queen voluntarily selected your Royal Highness to be her consort, you became her head by sacred rite of marriage. What object can your Royal Highness have in view but that the best interests of the British Crown may descend to your royal posterity?'

It was difficult to see how Mulock's argument could assist Albert, and his second point may have been even less helpful. 'The peculiar position of a female Sovereign', he argued, 'renders it highly decorous and eligible that, in all interviews with her Ministers, the Queen should enjoy the protective presence of your Royal Highness . . . as an effectual safeguard against even the surmised exercise of sinister influences'. That the ministers of the Crown could be malign was a suggestion unlikely to bolster the Prince's credit.

Since charges often convert themselves in the public consciousness into proven guilt, rumours raced across London in mid-January that Albert, having acted as the Queen's ventriloquist and run the Empire in her name, had been arrested for treason. 'It was like the man in *Martin Chuzzlewit*', Julian Osgood Field later wrote, 'who absolutely refused to believe that Queen Victoria did not live in the Tower of London, since he felt sure she ought to live there and therefore did live there.'

'One word more about the credulity of the public', Albert wrote to Stockmar on 24 January. 'You will scarcely credit that my being committed to the Tower was believed all over the country – nay, even "that the Queen has been arrested!" People surrounded the Tower in the thousands to see us brought to it!' Laurence Housman dramatized the episode in *Victoria Regina* by having the Prince read to the Queen from one of the more circumspect newspapers:

'We learned on what we believe to be good authority, that at a late hour last night two Personages of the highest rank' – ('Personages of the highest rank' can only be you and me, Vicky) – 'were secretly conveyed to the Tower, under a military guard, by order of the Government, and have there been lodged in safe custody to await their trial on a charge of high treason for conspiring against the safety of the Realm.' There, Vicky, what do you think of that? 'This news, which it was not intended should at present be made public, will be received with the greatest satisfaction by all who have been aware of the danger to which our Country has lately and increasingly been exposed by the machinations of a certain powerful foreign influence behind the Throne.' (That means me, Vicky.)

The suggestion that Albert was a Russian agent seemed logical enough to Englishmen of anti-German persuasion, and that he had somehow given cause to be marched off through the Traitor's Gate into the Tower, seemed to some appropriate justice. The inevitable ballads giving spice to the rumour were sung in London streets, 'Lovely Albert' suggesting that the impatient Queen had ceased to tolerate the Prince's obstruction of the laws, his 'mingling' in politics, and his outright treason. 'Little Al, the royal pal, They say has turned a Russian', the ballad went, and the chorus included the line, 'We'll send him home & make him groan'. When he had come to England

> He brought with him no riches,
> He had scarce a rag upon his back,
> And great holes in his breeches;
> Oh, England on him pity took,
> And changed his sad condition,
> And soon he planned you understand,
> The National Exhibition.

But he had gone 'a begging for the Russian bear', which he had led 'to [a] massacre [of] the innocent Turks', an outcome exasperating

Victoria, who tumbled him out of bed 'and wopped him with her night-cap'.

> There with the bolster round the room,
> Vic gave him dreadful lashes,
> She scratched his face and broke his nose,
> And pulled out his mustachios;
> You German dog, you shall be flogged,
> She hallo'd like a Prussian,
> How could you dare to interfere,
> And turn a cursed Russian?

The verses interrupted the vilification of the royals with an anti-Tsarist exhortation,

> You jolly Turks now go to work
> And show the Bear your power,
> It is rumoured over Britain's isle,
> That A— is in the Tower...

Once the vilification reached inane proportions, reason began to surface. An article in the *Morning Chronicle* on 16 January took 'quite the *right line* upon the infamous and *now* almost ridiculous attacks', Victoria wrote to the Prime Minister. 'Has Lord Aberdeen any idea who could have written it?'

The author, he responded, was W.E. Gladstone, 'although he would not wish it to be known'. There were further loyal rejoinders, he observed, suggesting a disposition on the part of some of the 'scurrilous' papers to change course before the opening of Parliament, when airing of the matter might quiet the hysteria.

Albert could hardly wait for Parliament to sit. 'All the gossip and idle talk of the last fourteen years', he wrote to Stockmar, 'have been brought to light by what has occurred. Everyone who has been able to express or surmise any ill of me has conscientiously contributed his faggot to burn the heretic... It was anything but pleasant to me amidst it all, that so many people could look upon me "as a rogue and traitor", and I shall not be at ease until I see the debate in Parliament well over; for it is not enough, that these rumours should be dispelled for the time; they must be knocked on the head, and the disease radically cured.' Another portent followed Palmerston's letter of 25 January to Peter

Borthwick, since 1850 editor of the *Morning Post*, instructing him, 'I think it would be useful if you were to put into the Post the following paragraph: We have observed that some of our contemporaries have endeavoured to connect the resignation of the Home Secretary with some proceedings on the part of the Court. Now we believe we may confidently affirm, without the slightest fear of contradiction, that the resignation of the noble Lord was the result of some misunderstanding between himself and some of his colleagues, and had not the remotest connection with anything on the part of the Court.'

Palmerston's instructions to Borthwick signalled that an end to the crisis was coming. His move had followed publication in the *Morning Advertiser* on 20 January of a letter by William Coningham, a failed candidate for Westminster in 1852, describing a pamphlet demonstrating the Court's interference which he had helped produce after Palmerston was dismissed in 1851. It had been based, Coningham alleged, on documentary evidence involving the Court, but was suppressed when the author was bought off. Greville 'fancied it was all moonshine', but queried the editor of *The Times*, John Delane, who knew almost everything unfit to print. He knew all about it, Delane confided. Palmerston at the time had sought revenge and had procured a journalist who had written leaders for the *Morning Herald*, Samuel Phillips, whom Tory leader Lord George Bentinck called 'that circumcised renegade' (Phillips was a converted Jew), and offered him £100 for the job. Phillips 'went down to Broadlands, where he was instructed by P[almerston] (who Delane said, gave him heaps of papers to read, though there is no proof of this), and he composed the pamphlet and had it printed. Before it was published P[almerston] thought the better of it... The copies were all bought up and destroyed, but a few remained behind, and one of these Phillips gave Delane.'

On the evening following the publication of Coningham's letter, Delane showed the pamphlet to Greville and Earl Granville, 'and we found it a very harmless production. It would not harm the Prince if it should appear; but... would be immensely damaging to Palmerston.' A deal was arranged with Delane, and Greville dashed off a letter, signed 'Juvenal', which *The Times* published the next morning, describing the *Advertiser* as unworthy of credit. And on 24 January, *The Times* published large extracts from 'Letters by William Coningham', which alleged that the turning out of Palmerston in 1851 was 'a *coup d'état*' arranged by Albert through Lord John Russell. Further, it claimed, Blackstone's *Commentaries* did have something appropriate to say about a Prince Consort: 'The husband of a Queen Regnant, as Prince George of Denmark was to Queen Anne, is her subject, and may be guilty of high treason against her.' The intemperate allusion to another consort of a Queen Regnant was a potential embarrassment to Palmerston, who had been identified as the pamphlet's sponsor.

The day before the reassembly of Parliament, gullible crowds gathered on Tower Hill to see Prince Albert and the Prime Minister committed to the Tower. Both were burned in effigy. It was obvious that the shift in attitude by the more respectable press had not yet made a difference. 'It was actually hinted to the Queen', Baron Vitzthum von Eckstaedt, Saxon Minister to England, recalled, 'that she would do well to open Parliament alone, as the presence of the Prince might expose her to the insults of the mob. The Prince behaved admirably... He refused to be intimidated, and on the morning of the day when Parliament was opened, 30 January, rode, accompanied only by a groom, through the most restless quarters of London, as if to say to the masses, "I am not afraid; here I am, if you have anything against me, speak out." '

The bold morning ride through the Strand and Fleet Street, beyond St Paul's into the teeming East End, either created the changed climate or confirmed it. When, that afternoon, seated beside the Queen in the State carriage drawn by eight cream-coloured horses, Albert drove to Westminster, 'an immense concourse of people', Victoria wrote to Stockmar, was 'very friendly'.* Yet the crowds reserved their greatest enthusiasm for the Turkish Minister, foreshadowing the war to come.

In the Lords, Aberdeen scoffed that unseemly allegations had led thousands of Londoners 'to attend at the doors of the Tower to see His Royal Highness go in'. Further, many expected to see the Queen imprisoned as well, as they had heard that she had 'announced her intentions to go with him'. The Prince's 'unimpeachable loyalty to the Crown and to the Country' should put to rest such calumnies 'at once and for ever'.

In the Commons, Lord John Russell ridiculed 'these delusions, blind as they have been', which, now exposed, 'will...attach the Crown still

---

* Lady Charlotte Guest, nevertheless, reported hearing Albert 'hissed'.

more strongly to the realm'. The 'abomination', Greville concluded, 'may be considered to be destroyed altogether, and we shall probably hear no more of it'.

Despite the publication of the 'Suppressed Pamphlet', with additional material by William Coningham, early in February by the printer Effingham Wilson at the Royal Exchange, talk of impeachment of the Prince faded into anti-Russian sentiment as the Queen and Albert returned to Windsor to celebrate the fourteenth anniversary of their marriage. Among the guests, on the afternoon of 13 February when the royal children put on an entertainment based upon recitations of James Thomson's once-popular *The Seasons*, were the Prussian ambassador, Baron Bunsen, and his wife. 'A red curtain was let down', the Baroness wrote to her granddaughter Lilla, 'and we all sat in the dark, till the curtain was drawn aside, and the Princess Alice, who had been dressed to represent Spring, recited some verses... enumerating the flowers which the Spring scatters around'. And she did it, the Baroness added, in 'a tone of voice like that of the Queen'.

Once the curtain was drawn and reopened, Princess Vicky appeared as Summer, with Prince Arthur, not yet four, 'lying upon some sheaves, as if tired with the heat and harvest...' After the Princess Royal's verses there was another change of scene, and Prince Alfred, nine, 'with a crown of vine-leaves and a panther's skin, represented Autumn, and also recited verses'. Lastly, the scene represented snow, and the Prince of Wales appeared as Winter, 'with a white beard and a cloak with icicles or snow-flakes (or what looked like such), and the Princess Louise warmly clothed, who seemed watching the fire: and the Prince also recited well...' Again the curtain closed and reopened to disclose all the participants, 'and far behind, on high, appeared the Princess Helena, with a long veil hanging on each side down to her feet, and a long cross in her hand, pronouncing a blessing upon the Queen and Prince, in the name of all the Seasons'.

Although that was the formal close, Victoria asked that the curtain be reopened, 'and the Baby Prince Leopold was brought in by his nurse, and looked at us all with big eyes, and wanted to go to his papa, Prince Albert'.

The family festival was the last in peacetime. War had not yet been declared but the Russian ambassador had left London on 7 February. The British envoy in St Petersburg departed the next day. In the new age of telegraphy it was possible – where wires were strung – to communicate more quickly, but not to prepare for war or to prosecute it at long distance. There was no direct wire link to Constantinople.

If the national blood was indeed up, it was not because Victoria and Albert had encouraged a diversion from their own problems. At the Sublime Porte, Stratford de Redcliffe had taken advantage of the semi-primitive communications with Turkey by conducting personal diplomacy, which meant reading the worst intentions into any Russian communication – an easy enough task – and frowning at his own instructions. If there were opportunities for compromise, he ignored them.

It would take weeks to learn that in London, and to send him fresh dispatches. The Cabinet was divided. To her Foreign Secretary, the Queen (almost certainly in conjunction with Albert) had written a candid warning that Stratford's actions in Constantinople 'exhibit clearly a *desire* for war, and to drag us into it', and she wondered how long he should be permitted 'to remain in a situation which gives him the means of frustrating all our efforts for peace'. Had her Government wanted the ambassador to do otherwise, Stratford long before would have been ordered home.

As with most wars, popular expectation was for a short and victorious affair. It was easy to ignore the reality that Britain had fought no war for forty years and was not ready to fight one now.

On 21 February Albert inspected his battalion of Guards. Cousin George, Victoria wrote to her uncle, the King of the Belgians, about the Duke of Cambridge, 'is quite delighted to have a division'. Five days later the government drafted an ultimatum to be sent by Lord Clarendon, the Foreign Minister, to his counterpart in St Petersburg, Count Nesselrode, demanding that Russia evacuate the Danubian principalities. A similar message was to be sent by France. The bearer would be directed to wait six days for an answer. Refusal, or silence, was to be considered as equivalent to a declaration of war.

The official courier delivered the message to Nicholas I on 14 March. The Tsar's decision that it was not fitting to reply became known in London only on 24 March, however early in the month of limbo between peace and war – on 23 February – an initial force of 12,000 men with 30 cannon left for the war zone via Malta. '*Until now*', Albert wrote to his brother, exasperated with the inaction of Prussia and other German states, 'Napoleon has behaved loyally, peacefully, justly and reasonably on all points. Our alliance will, we hope, keep him so. How Russia can accept a war in these circumstances, the Gods only know. The Czar must be mad if he does it. But whether he does it or not, the wand with which he ruled Central Europe is broken. We can only pity the poor German Kings who considered it an honour to clean his shoes.'

Despite Albert's words about Louis Napoleon, the Queen and Prince were still so markedly concerned about how much trust to put in him that Duke Ernest, on a visit to Paris, was entreated by the Emperor to help thaw relations. Pre-Waterloo animosities persisted on the military level as well, making co-operation awkward and ineffective. Lord Hardinge was sixty-nine, and his deputy, the one-armed Lord Raglan, whom he appointed commander of the expeditionary force to the East, was sixty-five. Most senior generals and admirals were veterans of the wars against the first Napoleon, and physically unfit for the rigours of

GRAND MILITARY SPECTACLE.
The Heroes of the Crimea Inspecting the Field-Marshals.

At the beginning of the Crimean War, Albert was the only non-doddering Field Marshal. At the close, he was the only Field Marshal.

combat service. Recognizing that, *The Times* had already quoted Lord Chatham's wry remark about the senior officers ordered off to put down the American revolution, 'I do not know what effect these names have on the enemy, but I confess they make *me* tremble.'

A case in point was the admiral of the battle fleet assembled at Spithead, which the Queen and Prince reviewed on 10 March. Sir Charles Napier, sixty-eight, had captained the *Thames* in battle against the French in the Mediterranean in 1811, and led ships up the Potomac against the young United States in 1814, landing near Baltimore. He was to command a fleet to move into the Baltic against Russia.

Few in Britain worried. War fever had seized the nation. All generals and admirals associated with past victories, however remote in time, were again heroes. Crowds cheered troops marching off, equipped for the last war, and no one felt more helpless than the Prime Minister, Lord Aberdeen, who could carry few of his Cabinet with him when he expressed grave doubts about the outcome. As Albert explained to King Leopold, the masses *felt* even when they failed to think. 'In the present instance their feeling is something of this sort: "The Tsar of Russia is a tyrant, and the enemy of all liberty on the Continent... He wanted to coerce the poor Turk. The Turk is a fine fellow; he has braved the rascal. Let us rush to his assistance."'

With the ultimatum to Russia about to expire, most newspapers fanned the excitement, and Albert, at least in his messages to his brother, intended indirectly for Prussia, appeared enthusiastic about reducing the 'Russian Colossus'. The Baltic fleet, he predicted, 'will be magnificent, unless it be too heavy for that shallow sea. The 25,000 men for Constantinople are organized; 10,000 of them have already arrived in Malta; the artillery has left; and the calvary will go by way of France, and march through Paris, at the Emperor's desire! Who could have imagined such a thing a year ago?'

Much had gone beyond Albert's own imagining since his idealistic words opening the Crystal Palace only a few years earlier. The Utopian vision of unity and progress and peace had become Prospero's 'insubstantial pageant faded'. Greed, hate and violence were proving the more natural condition of humanity. If, too, his unremitting industry, subsuming all personal ambition into others who represented the present and future for his adopted country, led only to popular eagerness to see him committed to the Tower, where was the democratization of monarchies leading? Albert was hard put to fend off dismay and depression, which he tried to do by longer hours and harder work.

On 27 March the Queen's war message was read in the Commons, and war was declared the next day. The paradoxes of power politics set the Christian British and French on the side of an Islamic empire against other Christians, leading to Disraeli's wry summing-up that his nation was going to war in order to prevent the Tsar from protecting the Christian subjects of the Sultan. And by 6 April, with the Queen's forces landing in Turkish areas bordering the Black Sea baffled and helpless in the local squalor, heat, and disorganization, questions began to be asked in the Lords about conditions in which Her Majesty's troops would operate. Heartsick about the war, which seemed to him stupid and unnecessary, if inevitable, the Earl of Aberdeen watched his second son, Alexander, leave the same day to join his regiment, taking with him a fine horse that was a parting gift from Prince Albert.

The western allies planned to take the war to Russia by landing in the Crimea, and the Duke of Cambridge, his infantry division designated for the mission, went via Vienna by rail. While hastily assembled troops crowded on to obsolete ships bound for Black Sea ports, the war at home was a skirling of pipes and a flashing of uniforms on parade grounds, bellicose editorials in the press, and confusion and disunity in the Cabinet. 'The Ministry causes us much trouble', Albert confided to Ernest. 'Aberdeen is still in 1814, Palmerston in 1848, and Lord John [Russell] in 1830. Parliament and the Press are, one and all, suddenly born generals...' Cholera and dysentery would soon begin to travel with the army to the war-zone even when modern ammunition and guns did not. Mismanagement of sanitation, supplies and soldiers by both the British and the French was easy to perceive in the collection areas on the Bulgarian coast, but disconcerting disclosures were filtered home through a haze of slow and inadequate communications and deliberate obfuscation.

For the public, few events could distract attention from the war. One, briefly, was the reopening of the Crystal Palace on a brilliantly sunny 10 June 1854 on a hill south of London in Sydenham. Unlike its original, it had taken two years and the lives of twelve workmen – and the promised railway to the site was unfinished, like the huge structure itself. But Victoria and Albert came; 1,500 singers featuring soprano Clara Novello and under the direction of Michael Costa sang the

'Hallelujah Chorus', and an orchestra augmented by two hundred brass instruments failed to shatter the glass.

The Queen also went to Woolwich Dockyard to launch the new warship *Prince Albert*, one of the enormous new military expenditures which required politically painful new taxes, few of which Parliament cared to extract from landed wealth. Suddenly the war took a new turn when the denizens of drinking establishments had to pay for it, and *Punch* quipped, 'Owing to the imposition of the malt tax, the Marquis of Westminster and Baron Rothschild are the only persons in the country besides the Queen and Prince Albert who can afford beer: and consequently all the cab-drivers and coalwhippers are in a state bordering on revolt.'

In France, Napoleon III was in a spendthrift frenzy that had few connections to the war but many to his sense of power and status. His subjects would be burdened by debts they hardly knew then existed as they basked in the splendour of his state. He intended, with Baron von Hausmann's planning, to transform Paris into Europe's most awesome capital, and to live palatially wherever he and his empress pleased. In the summer of 1854 he was also having the sumptuous Villa Eugénie built as a holiday estate in Biarritz, leaving there on 27 August to observe manœuvres of 70,000 troops near Boulogne. Both King Leopold and Prince Albert had been invited, *Punch* marvelling at the ironies of history,

> I wonder what his thoughts were – that sad-eyed, silent man,
> As alongside Boulogne's jetty England's royal steamer ran;
> While with a King beside him, that adventurer was seen
> Greeting, as Emperor of France, the Consort of our Queen?

As Albert was not Head of State, but only the husband of one, he fulfilled his diplomatic obligation once he entered Napoleon III's carriage by handing the Emperor a letter from Victoria. It prompted *Punch*, on another page, to remark that he thereby 'infringed the rules of the French Post Office, and subjected himself to a rather heavy penalty. It is against the law to carry a sealed letter from England to France, though it may perhaps be urged on behalf of the Prince, that the letter was in fact stamped, for the Queen had given her head to it.'

The Anglo-French alliance seemed a reality during the four days of the Prince's visit, more carnival on the surface than military conference.

THE ENTENTE CORDIALE.

Albert, according to Punch *in 1854, acting as actual sovereign in his meetings with Emperor Napoleon III.*

Cheap excursion trains from Paris brought thousands of sightseers, and the streets were beflagged by day and illuminated at night. The letters *V.N.A.* were inscribed everywhere, for Victoria, Napoleon and Albert. (Some said they also stood for *Vive notre amitié.*) Despite the unbusinesslike air, the Emperor and Prince arose each day at six for the military exercises, and conferred at length over breakfasts and lunches, sometimes with military and diplomatic advisers, the uncrowned king an equal with the self-appointed emperor.

On a holiday from editing *Household Words* and yet to begin *Little Dorrit*, Charles Dickens was also in Boulogne, indulging in escapist reading and dozing against a haystack in the sun, and seldom going into the town, 'which looks like one immense flag', he wrote to John Forster. On the day of the culminating review Dickens went off on his daily country walk along the Calais road, only to be showered with dust as Napoleon and Albert cantered toward him, accompanied by mounted guardsmen and grooms. Dickens loyally removed his hat, and the

Emperor and Prince, both of whom recognized him, raised their cocked hats. Louis Napoleon had been a Gore House crony* in his conspiratorial London days, and Albert was devoted to Dickens's novels and theatrical ventures. Determined that evening to join in the festive illuminations of Boulogne, Dickens set up a hundred and twenty wax candles in the windows of his rented cottage.

To the Queen the rare absence of her husband was trying, and she did not conceal that, prompting Greville to write that 'H.M. thinks nothing' of absenting her Ladies from their husbands during her holidays to Osborne or Balmoral – or ordering their husbands to Baltic or Black Sea regions from which their absences could become permanent. From Boulogne, Albert wrote to Victoria several times daily during pauses in military business, addressing her as 'Dear little Wife' and 'Dear Child'.

The French command made no secret of its dissatisfaction with gerontological British leadership in the Crimea, to which Albert had explained that 'to carry public opinion with us is the main point'. Popular generals and admirals had to remain until they were less so, or confirmed popular, if unrealistic, expectations.

On 5 September he wrote to Victoria before retiring for the night, 'The Emperor thaws more and more. This evening after dinner I withdrew with him to his sitting-room for half an hour . . . in order that he might smoke his cigarette, in which occupation, to his amazement, I could not keep him company.' Nevertheless, newspapers reported as a favourable omen that Louis Napoleon and Albert 'are said to have smoked cigars together'.

An even more unusual tête-à-tête for Albert occurred in November when on the 8th, on returning from business in London, he was told that Thomas Carlyle, then working on a life of Frederick the Great, was in one of the Windsor galleries examining prints and engravings of the King. It was four on a darkening afternoon when the Prince entered to chat with Carlyle, who may have felt awkward about his appearance as, at fifty-nine, he had just begun to grown a beard the month before. Albert put him at ease – 'civility itself', Carlyle wrote to his sister, Jean Aitken, two days later. He was impressed by the 'strong steady eyes', and

---

* Marguerite, countess of Blessington, and her lover, Count Alfred D'Orsay, hosted high Bohemian soirées at Gore House until their debts – and illnesses – forced them into French exile.

Albert's 'briskness'. They 'talked first of Frederick's portraits; then went, by a step or two, into the Saxon genealogy line', especially Albert's ancestors, with 'abundant scope of talk'. A hour passed before a servant came to inform the Prince that the Queen was on the Terrace, and he bowed himself out with a reference to his pleasure with 'your Works'. The usually morose Scot was charmed.

Carlyle lost no time, once back in Chelsea, in preparing, with many semi-colons, 'The *Prinzenraub*', about Albert's line, focusing upon the story of the young Saxon princes Ernest and Albert, abducted from Altenberg on 7 July 1455 by Kunz von Kaufungen. Describing the article as 'pearls of memory', he sent it off to the *Westminster Review*, which published it that January, when he explained the title to Mrs Aitken as ' "Prince *rob*", or the stealing of Princes'.

The war in the Crimea heated up further in October and November. Accounts arrived of severe losses accompanying glorious victories which were only victories in that the allies kept a foothold in Russia that was equally exhausting to the enemy. To Colonel Francis Grosvenor Hood of the 1st Grenadier Guards the Prince wrote, on 17 October 1854, of his 'admiration of the manner in which the battalion of my regiment under your command bore itself in that desperate fight at the Alma, and my pleasure and satisfaction at the fact, that upon the whole it suffered less in action than the other battalions of our noble Brigade of Guards'. It was an index to the realities not only that Albert wrote in relief that his troops experienced fewer casualties – rather than rewarding triumphs – but that before his letter arrived, Colonel Hood was killed in the trenches near Sevastopol.

Not long after, the Member from Lambeth complained in the Commons that the Prince was collecting £3,000 for the colonelcy of a battalion he was not leading into battle while others of similar rank were risking their lives for half his stipend. Another MP, Lieutenant-Colonel Brownlow William Knox, responded, 'If the honourable gentleman would look at the number of battalions commanded by his Royal Highness, he would find that the increase was a perfectly just one...' Although the implication was that Albert had a major role in the prosecution of the war, *Punch* felt that the defence rested upon the wrong grounds. Would it not be better, it asked, to recognize him for 'what he does, than for what he cannot do; for value received rather than value irreceivable? His Royal Highness cannot discharge the functions of a Colonel... You will not permit him to go to the wars, very properly. Of course it would never do to have the husband of our Queen returning from the field of glory [preserved] in a cask of rum, or curtailed by the loss of an arm or a leg, or of his fair proportions. He, doubtless, would be too glad to go, and be instrumental in scattering the enemies of his August Lady. But you won't let him...'

Whatever Albert's efforts, which included liaison with the Emperor of France, the 27,000 men shipped from England to the Black Sea in 1854 had almost no reserves behind them, and carried weapons that Wellington's soldiers had used decades before. There was almost no system for the care of sick and wounded, and it took a letter to *The Times* from Sir Robert Peel, the late Prime Minister's son, to raise £25,462 for medicines by popular subscription. As there was no provision for widows and orphans of war dead, Albert arranged to be head of a royal commission, soon known as the Patriotic Fund, for such war relief. It would raise more than a million pounds. Parliament had voted little support for military chaplains – who were often little more than nurses, and then undertakers. Soon another subscription drive was begun to send more men of the cloth to the Crimea. Finally, a lady with a bent for hospital work and a genius for organization, Florence Nightingale, recruited thirty-seven lady nurses for service, and, with several chaperons of appropriate dignity, embarked for Scutari (on the Asiatic side of the Bosphorus), reaching there on 5 November, in time to succour the surviving wounded from the battle at Balaclava.

Governmental stinginess, inflexibility, and absence of compassion were not partisan matters. Whigs and Tories had been of similar penurious mind for decades, happily accepting a military policy that made generals of gentlemen from good families who liked colourful parades, dashing uniforms, champagne with lunch, and remoteness from action. Undrinkable green coffee was the least of the hardships of hastily trained soldiers who had no fires in winter, huddled in wet blankets when they had any at all, died of pneumonia and dysentery by the thousands, had no ammunition for their obsolete weapons, and, if able-bodied, were thrown into combat in textbook drill formations that were little short of suicidal. Only the enemy's equal incompetence kept the war at stalemate.

As the bad news continued, and was received at home with indignation, especially the disaster of Lord Cardigan's Light Brigade, committees of inquiry were called for in the Commons, and there were private investigations by the Queen and Prince.

Matters would get even worse in November. Of the men who came to the Crimea, six thousand, including three generals, were killed in action in October and November, and a further eight thousand were wounded or desperately ill with cholera. Half the original English force was gone, and Louis Napoleon offered twenty thousand more Frenchmen if London could send ships to convey them. But there were no ships available, as every Navy bottom that was seaworthy – even obsolete sailing ships were resorted to – was being used to send supplies, including winter clothing, to the Black Sea.

Exasperated, Albert fired a long memorandum to Aberdeen on 11 November that failed to include the friendly language that had long been exchanged between them. 'The Government will never be forgiven, and ought never to be forgiven', he warned, 'if it did not strain every nerve to avert the calamity of seeing Lord Raglan succumb from lack of means.' Prosecuting the war in any case was beyond the general's abilities, but troops were badly served in every way. A battle at Inkerman had been fought on 5 November, and it took ten days for news to reach England of an expensive victory that settled nothing but that Sevastopol would eventually fall, and with it, probably, the Russian government. Yet the siege would outlast Aberdeen's faltering Ministry, and the Prime Minister, a compromiser rather than a leader, was distracted with anxiety about his son Alex, and only able to find out about him when a list of dead and wounded was telegraphed to London on the evening of 22 November. Alex's name was not on it.

Later, Colonel Gordon's letters from the front arrived. His troops had been successful 'but with a loss which we can ill afford'. Also, the charger given to him by Albert had been shot from under him, while most other horses 'are fast dying of starvation and cold'.

Aberdeen called for a special session of Parliament early in December to vote funds for reinforcements. With the mood in England turned ugly, enlistments were not filling the army's needs, and Albert suggested hiring mercenaries from Switzerland and the German and Italian states. Palmerston liked the idea, especially as it would promote his idea of a unified Italy, and Victor Emmanuel, King of Sardinia and ambitious to be more than that, offered 15,000 Piedmontese troops if British ships could transport them. Napoleon, who preferred the glory of using Frenchmen, recognized reality, and approved.

Parliament was to meet on 12 December 1854, to pass a Foreign Enlistment Bill, authorizing the financing of 15,000 recruits to be trained in England. In a meeting at Windsor, Lord Aberdeen went over the legislation and confided the turmoil in his Cabinet over the domestic sacrifices being made to pursue the war. Offering to resign, he pointed out to Victoria and Albert that no new Cabinet could be formed under the ubiquitous but divisive Lord John Russell. It would have to be Palmerston, and early in the new year the unspeakable would happen.

A watered-down version of the Foreign Legion Bill would survive, but not before an unlikely opposition of Tories and Radicals raked over old allegations against Albert. Popular feeling, he wrote Ernest, was that mercenaries represented 'ingratitude against the brave army in the Krim [Crimea]. They say it is a foreign idea and that it must have come from me.'

Three German battalions and a Swiss battalion would be formed, and a Sardinian division would actually exchange fire with the Russians, but the discomfort of needing foreigners to fight British battles was repugnant enough to hasten the demise of Aberdeen's government. The influential *Times*, bolstered by W.H. Russell's dispatches, raged on the day that Parliament again rose, just before Christmas, that 'the noblest Army England ever sent from these shores has been sacrificed to the grossest mismanagement. Incompetence, lethargy, aristocratic hauteur, official indifference, favour, routine, perverseness and stupidity reign, revel and riot in the camp before Sevastopol, in the harbour at Balaklava, in the hospitals at Scutari, and how much nearer to home we do not venture to say.' The day after Christmas *The Times* added that it was 'disgraceful that England, so wealthy, so mechanical, and with such an infinity of resources', should waste its soldiers 'wholesale' out of a lack of 'military science, not to say common sense'. In an image out of the Crusades, Albert's brother deplored British tactics as 'quite as imprudent as those of Louis the Holy against the Mamelukes'.

Aberdeen's coalition fell on 29 January 1855, after a vote of censure carried by a large majority, and the wily Palmerston became Prime Minister for the first time. With both reluctance and relief, Albert closed the hostile files on Palmerston which he had been keeping in mistrust of his machinations since 1848.

In Paris, Louis Napoleon could evade the parliamentary fate of Aberdeen, but seemed left with only one public defender of his conduct of the war, the Turkish ambassador, Vely Pasha. Yet fortune soon rescued both Palmerston and the Emperor. Early in March, Nicholas I died unexpectedly. His son and successor, Alexander II, only a year older than Victoria and Albert and once thought of as a possible husband for her, was eager to end the war, but no one expected a resolution very soon, as he would have to extricate Russia with some perceived dignity.

As the Tsar already realized, Russia's defeat would mean a gain for someone else, and an Anglo-French bargain had already been struck with the Victor Emmanuel II of Sardinia. In exchange for a loan of a million pounds from England and a joint guarantee of his borders, the King's Piedmontese troops would fight in the Crimea. To furnish shipping for that and other war needs, the government hired Samuel Cunard's passenger steamers, embarrassing the already abashed Admiralty.

The Queen's ire about the press would continue through the war, and into the new Ministry, a draft from Balmoral to the Prime Minister, in the Prince's hand, declaring that the Queen was 'much disgusted with the late atrocious articles in *The Times* on the Army in the Crimea...' The Prince's opinion was that 'soon there will not be room enough in the same country for both the Monarchy and *The Times*'. The Queen's feeling was that 'repressive laws' against the press would only 'aggravate the evil', but she wondered to Palmerston 'whether it is right that the Editor, the Proprietor and the Writers of such execrable publications ought to be the honoured and constant guests of the Ministers of the Crown'.

Delane of *The Times* paid no attention to threats and social disapproval. 'Continue as you have done, to tell the truth', he wrote to William Russell, 'and leave such comment as may be dangerous to us, who are out of danger.'

Russell did exactly that, although Albert was unrepentant about condemning what he described to Clarendon as 'mischief which the gaining of three pitched battles could not repair'. With Parliament following the press in criticism, J.A. Roebuck, MP, was busily seeking goats and scapegoats via an investigating committee on conduct of the war. In March 1855 he asked the former Secretary for War, the 5th Duke of Newcastle, whom Palmerston had not kept on, whether he objected to being examined, for the key to the Crimean 'mysteries' could only be found in high quarters. 'Now I must be careful how I talk further with you', said the Duke. 'I see you are laying the ground for an impeachment, as you can only mean me by a *high quarter.*'

'Oh, no!' said Roebuck, 'I mean a much higher personage than you; I mean Prince Albert.'

XIV

Albert's War

1855–1856

A S ALBERT WAS drawn more and more into the prosecution of
the Crimean War, he had to consider his every public move. The
accusations of unconstitutional interference might revive. Because Prussia and the lesser German states could not be drawn in on the Western
side, and he remained, in English perception, a German, his reluctance
on purely military grounds had appeared to some as pro-Russian.
Russia, however, was not only distant and difficult of access, but
possessed what seemed to be infinite manpower and infinite space. Yet,
because Napoleon III often interfered with his generals, a royal dimension to British involvement became necessary. English generals could
negotiate on even terms with their French counterparts, but the intrusion of Napoleon III, who fancied himself to be above mere military
rank, made the presence of the Prince essential. Ceremonially, the
Queen represented the Crown. Where war strategy was hammered out,
she remained only a woman.

With an entourage of ministers and military men, Albert had thus
gone to the Boulogne encampment the previous summer. There he
achieved a wary rapport which the Emperor, possessed of a throne that
as yet lacked external dignity, attempted to build upon. Eager for a
State visit to England to add cachet to his position, he had poured on
the compliments about the Prince to '*Madame et bonne Soeur*' and, at
greater length, to the Earl of Clarendon (via Count Walewski) for
transmission to the Queen. 'In all his experience', the Count quoted
his master as gushing, 'he had never met with a person possessing such

various and profound knowledge, or who communicated it with the same frankness... He had never learned so much in a short time, and was grateful.'

Clarendon and Granville, accompanying Albert, had suggested that following the hard Crimean winter and an expected stalemate in early 1855, the Emperor pay a visit to Windsor, which would add a Royal imprimatur to his reign, and during which the war situation could be reassessed. Albert proposed that Napoleon visit with his Empress in the early spring. Delighted, the Emperor suggested a reciprocal visit to Paris, and the meetings ended warmly although no quick military results were expected. In fact, there were further disappointments, and to reverse them as well as retrieve some military lustre for the Bonaparte name, Louis Napoleon proposed going to the Crimea himself. That was a more impelling reason for a person-to-person meeting, this time in England, a better venue in which to dissuade him. To Prince William of Prussia, Albert joked, 'I shall have to have precautions taken in the Crypt of St George's Chapel, to see to it that George III does not turn in his grave!'

The Emperor had every reason to go to the Crimea except one. He might have no crown when he returned, if he could return at all. Further setbacks might endanger his regime, and he was no Napoleon I. Yet he recognized that British generalship and disorganization in the Crimea were contributing to his problems. Whatever his censorship at home, the freer press in London was reporting every embarrassment, and bad news crossed the Channel. Albert had tried his best to establish some efficiency at the Horse Guards and beyond, but each intrusion risked his regained reputation as above politics. On the last day of the old year of 1854 he had warned the obviously outgoing Minister for War, the Duke of Newcastle, of 'the want of system and order in our army before Sebastopol', which caused confusion and suffering to the troops, and 'painful uncertainty' at home. Both to him and the succeeding Minister, Fox Maule, 2nd Lord Panmure, Albert pressed the urgency for regular and honest reports from the field on the conditions troops faced – the state of rations, forage, clothing, sanitation, fuel, quarters, ordnance. The language of Panmure's orders to Lord Raglan followed closely Albert's memoranda, complete to the complaint that Panmure was 'at present compelled to rely on reports of unofficial individuals' – a euphemism for the press.

The bungling and blundering revealed by the war had exposed the cumbrousness of military administration. The problem for would-be reformers before 1852 had been the continued immunity of Wellington from criticism. He had seen little reason to alter the system that won at Waterloo and Trafalgar. No authority remotely so overwhelming, civilian or military, had succeeded him. When an Army Board had finally been set up in Newcastle's last days to co-ordinate fiefdoms, Albert drafted a request for the Queen that she be sent minutes of its weekly meetings. It was another way he could keep his hand in events. A further opening came when Panmure, on the eve of taking office, alleged to Albert, 'The lamentable results which have attended to our present expedition ... are solely to be attributed to the want of proper control by a single Minister of every department of the Army.' Albert had, then, his opportunity to prepare a 'Paper on the organisation of the Army' for Panmure, and would not only offer military advice throughout the war to Panmure and Palmerston but be asked for it.

Publicly, the Queen supported the incompetent Lord Raglan, whose position Roebuck attributed to Albert. Yet she and the Prince knew the disconcerting truth about command failures in the Crimea. So did the outgoing Prime Minister, the Earl of Aberdeen, whose son, Colonel Alexander Gordon, wrote to Albert's secretary, clearly for the Prince's eyes, that toward the end of January, in the mud and cold before Balaclava 'our effectives today are only 10,362!' The Palmerston government that replaced Aberdeen had almost the same personnel but promised more vigorous prosecution of the war, which was likely as winter left the Black Sea and further reinforcements arrived. The new Ministry was also goaded by the Roebuck investigatory committee and the forthcoming Imperial visit. If matters did not improve, the government faced the additional shame of having Napoleon III, only seven years earlier a penniless exile in London living on the purse of an English mistress, and a volunteer special constable on the day of the failed Chartist demonstration, go out to command the Allied armies against Russia.

As preparations were hurried for the arrival, Albert also managed time for other matters. On 28 February, at the end of the first month of Palmerston's Ministry, he again presided over the Exhibition Commission, which met regularly to disburse its funds, and drew up a proposal to purchase, for £50,000, a major portion of the Bernal Collection – as the government would not participate in buying it outright. Ralph Bernal, the father of MP and wit Bernal Osborne, had died the year before, leaving a vast collection of glass, plate and miniatures. Of Sephardic origins and with lucrative inherited West Indian properties, he had abjured his faith to matriculate at Cambridge and, as was then possible, buy a parliamentary seat. Albert's purchase was the foundation of what would be the South Kensington Museum of Art and Manufactures, later the Victoria and Albert Museum.

A few days later, Albert's secretary wrote to John Scott Russell of the Eastern Steam Navigation Company asking whether the Prince could visit the 'Great Ship' under construction while he was there inspecting a floating siege gun being built for the Crimea. The shipyard on the Isle of Dogs in a loop of the Thames was building a colossal iron vessel 693-feet long, 'the Crystal Palace of the sea'. Designed by Isambard Kingdom Brunel, it would be christened *Leviathan* (then altered to *Great Eastern*). Beneath its five funnels it would displace 22,500 tons – five times the size of anything afloat – and for insurance it would carry masts and 6,500 yards of sail. Its proposed engines for paddlewheels could power all the cotton mills in Manchester, and battalions of recruits could be drilled on its 120-foot-wide deck while steaming to war. Noah's Ark, it was estimated, had been only two-thirds the size of the new behemoth. The ship, which would have a chequered history after its launch in 1858, was considered the 'child of the Mechanical Section of the British Society for the Advancement of Science'.

Albert's siege gun was another such child. He had envisioned prototype 'floating cupolas' – partly submerged floating gun turrets – for bombarding shore fortifications, hoping to have one ready for use against the Russians. Albert was always designing something. But the Scott Russell cupola would be gutted by fire in May, on the night before it was to be launched. The £45,000 investment was only partly covered by insurance but rumour had it that the fire retrieved what was possible of an investment expected to fail. The war would have to be won some other way.*

* Another abortive victory weapon was Robert Mallet's 42-ton monster mortar, intended also to break the siege. With its thirty-six-calibre bore, it was designed to launch a 2,395-pound projectile 1.56 miles. The first of two was not ready until the war was over. When it was tested and proved to cost £675 per shot, the War Office rejected both guns.

By then Napoleon III had come and gone, and the matter of his leading troops in the Crimea had been solved. His ship delayed and his waterside greeting muted by heavy fog, the Emperor, with Eugénie, arrived at Dover at noon and was met by Albert, who conveyed them by rail and then by procession through Lambeth and London to Paddington for the special train to Windsor. In passing from Pall Mall to Piccadilly, as they went up St James's Street, Louis Napoleon pointed out King Street, to show Eugénie where he had lived in less grand days.

At Dover a telegram had awaited the Emperor – that allied batteries, four hundred guns in all, had opened fire on Sevastopol on 10 April, the very anniversary of his constable duty as exile in 1848. He gave the bulletin to Albert, who kept it among his prized papers.

Since conferences that had gone on in Vienna for a month to discuss a settlement had been going nowhere, the English visit was one of military conferences sandwiched between concerts, operas, parades and presentations. To allay sensitivities, the Waterloo Room at Windsor was renamed the Picture Gallery for the duration of the visit. In it the Queen danced a quadrille with the rather short, swarthy, moustachioed Emperor, whom she found magnetic and charming – 'as if he had been born a king's son'. When they left for London on the nineteenth, Napoleon voiced regret at leaving. She had heard, Victoria noted in her diary, 'that the Empress was equally sad at going away from Windsor... Altogether I am delighted to see how much Albert likes and admires her, as it is so seldom I see him do so with any woman.' It may have assuaged the Queen's sense of having been charmed too easily by Louis Napoleon to feel that Albert had been smitten with the beautiful Eugénie.

Planning to emulate Albert's Great Exhibition with a Parisian one, the Emperor was eager to inspect the Crystal Palace in Sydenham, which they visited on 10 April, Napoleon's forty-seventh birthday. The next day, after further meetings in Buckingham Palace, the French party left. It had all been, Victoria confided to her journal, like 'a dream, a brilliant, successful, pleasant dream'. The success had come not only in the '*amitié*' which the Emperor had signed into the Queen's visitors' album, but in the military decisions reached. Rarely had Victoria sat in with Albert on military discussions, but now she did, claiming 'stirring times'. Further, at meetings of the monarchs and their entourages, including Maréchal Jean-Baptiste Vaillant, Ministre de la

Guerre, Napoleon had been persuaded – although he had not yet confessed as much – to leave the prosecution of the war to the generals. His eagerness to lead troops into battle had been blunted by reports reaching London that the Russian artillery answering Allied fire was numerous and effective, with every sign of developing into a long and indecisive siege. Further, as Albert pointed out diplomatically, there was great danger to France in the Emperor's absence. Confirmation came in a letter to the Queen dated 25 April 1855, in which Napoleon reluctantly conceded that he could not leave France, and which closed with appreciation for Royal hospitality. '*Le Prince votre époux a été bien net*' – 'The Prince your husband has been very definite', Vaillant, intimating the outcome, had told Victoria on parting.

Speeches for and against continuing the war stretched into the summer as Roebuck's revelations in the Commons of gross military incompetence were corroborated by the newspapers. Early in June the Prince, in presiding over the annual Trinity House dinner, used his forum to charge the press with irresponsibility in sowing despondency and in revealing information to the enemy of a nature which the Allies could only glean from spies and deserters. Britain had to contend with a less-than-civilized adversary operating under despotic conditions, Albert maintained, 'whilst we have to meet him under a state of things intended for peace and the promotion of that very civilisation – a civilisation [which is] the offspring of public discussion, the friction of parties, and popular control over the government of the State'. Constitutional government, he insisted, was under its heaviest trials in wartime, and it required some voluntary sacrifices of the right to know so that operations – and negotiations – could proceed with secrecy and surprise. Undisciplined liberties could incapacitate governments.

A military strike planned by the Prince (according to Baron Vitzthum, the Saxon ambassador) gave him further cause for leaving the press in the dark. While envoys in Vienna haggled over how to keep the Russian fleet in the Black Sea from becoming a continuing post-war threat to Turkey, requiring the permanent presence of Western navies, Albert devised a surprise attack on the supply base at Kerch, on the eastern tip of the Crimea, where a strait links the Black Sea with the lake-sized Sea of Azov, to the north. On 24 May the expedition, commanded by Captain (later Admiral Sir) Edmund Lyons, struck, landing troops who destroyed installations, beached and burned four warships, and captured Russian stores of grain intended for Sevastopol. No newspapermen knew it had happened until it was over, and no one knew Albert had a hand in it. The vast loss in rations destined for the defenders of Sevastopol would have an impact on the siege.

Lord Raglan, who blamed the French for dragging their feet in the Crimea – for insisting upon delays in joint operations when he was allegedly ready and they were not – died of dysentery at his head-quarters on 29 June. Eleven days earlier the French had suffered another defeat, and the outnumbered British, coming to their aid, had been driven off with heavy losses. Since only ten percent of the 188,000 Allied effectives were British, while half were French (and the rest Turks and Sardinians), Raglan had seen his authority erode with the numbers, and his last days were embittered. Entirely a desk general, he had been the wrong man in the wrong place, but the Crimea may have been the wrong place for any soldier. Lieutenant-General James Simpson, another relic of Wellington's army, replaced Raglan.

The royal return visit to Paris was far more necessary to Napoleon III than to Victoria and Albert. In the aftermath of reverses in the Crimea which could lead to instability at home, the Emperor needed internal spectacles to distract his subjects from external anxieties. Coincidentally, on 16 August 1855, just as the Queen and Prince were due to arrive, a force of largely French troops were victorious at the river Chernaya, beating back an estimated sixty thousand Russians struggling to relieve Sevastopol. It was a good time for Victoria and Albert to appear with the Emperor and Empress at the Grand Opéra to see an overlong ballet which included a scene with a view of Windsor. 'God Save the Queen' was sung, and enthusiastically cheered. After the performance the monarchs returned to the palace at St Cloud, where Louis Napoleon – once a student in Augsburg – and the Prince sang (according to Victoria's journal) 'all sorts of old German songs'.

The needs of the times had overturned centuries of cross-Channel enmity. As late as May 1854, however, the Cabinet had boggled at the expenditure of £50,000 for a major British presence at the *Exposition Universelle*, from arts to manufactures. Intervening, Albert hoped that 'as we were spending so much in destruction (in the Crimea), we ought to spend some in construction'. The government was shamed into supporting British participation, and Albert supported the exhibition further by going to a preview of the paintings to be shown at the new

Palais des Beaux-Arts and seeing to it that a 'sold' notice was put on one. 'Albert was so enchanted with it – so much so', Victoria recorded in her diary about Frederick Leighton's *Cimabue's Madonna Carried in Procession through the Streets of Florence* – it was the artist's first appearance at the Royal Academy – 'that he made me buy it'. Albert had not been in Florence since his student days, but retained an affection for it, and for the early Italian painters Cimabue represented. Stopping to greet W.P. Frith, whose populous *Ramsgate Sands* Victoria and Albert had bought out of her affectionate childhood remembrance of seaside holidays there, the Prince congratulated him on his 'marvellously light and elegant', and equally crowded, canvas, *At the Opera*, which seemed appropriate for Paris. At the Exposition itself, Albert would tour the Palais de l'Industrie and make purchases he thought would be useful for England.

In Paris, Victoria and Albert were greeted everywhere with frenzied acclaim, and were awed by the profound yet rapid alterations in the face of the capital, which Albert remembered as a city of seedy, narrow streets. Broad, tree-lined avenues beautified areas where slums had been cleared, and the Bois de Boulogne, Albert wrote to King Leopold, vied 'with the finest English parks. How all this could have been done in so short a time no one comprehends.' Further, as an electrical storm crackled outside, the Emperor had escorted Victoria and Albert by torchlight into the still-unfinished tomb of the first Napoleon, whose ashes had been returned from St Helena in 1840, 'while the organ of the Church of the Invalides played "God Save the Queen". So numerous were the strange impressions wrought by the contrast of past with present, that one could often only wonder.'

At the coffin, covered with black velvet in a side chapel, the Queen, according to Marshal François Canrobert, broke the silence by turning to the awed Prince of Wales, not yet fourteen, and directing him, 'Kneel down before the tomb of the great Napoleon.' Peals of thunder were shaking the windows, and the event could not have been better staged by his imperial nephew.

As Prussian minister to the *Bundestag* in Frankfurt, the most influential post in the kingdom's diplomatic service, Otto von Bismarck was in Paris at Eugénie's ball for Victoria and Albert, to reconnoitre the couple who had been pressing Frederick William IV to intervene in the war on the side of the West. (Bismarck would be the ambassador to

St Petersburg from 1859 into 1862.) 'The Prince', he wrote much later with undiminished hostility, 'handsome and cool in his black uniform, conversed with me courteously, but in his manner there was a kind of malevolent curiosity from which I concluded that my anti-occidental influence upon the King was not unknown to him ... In the eyes of the Prince ... I was a reactionary party man who took up sides for Russia in order to further an Absolutist and "Junker" policy. It was not to be wondered at that this view ... descended to the Prince's daughter ... '

Vicky and Bertie, both with their parents in Paris, were charmed by the exotic Emperor and his beautiful consort. 'You have a nice country', the Prince of Wales told the Emperor after Napoleon had taken the carriage reins himself, followed agitatedly but discreetly by security men, to show Paris to the children. 'I would like to be your son.' Later he asked Eugénie whether she could intercede with his parents so that he and Vicky could stay a little longer. Diplomatically she explained that the Queen and Prince could not do without them. 'Not do without us!' Bertie exploded; 'don't fancy that, for there are six more of us at home and they don't want us.'

Sevastopol seemed about to fall. An indecisive conflict would follow until peace terms could be settled. In the Crimea, Albert's friend since his Italian winter of 1839, now General Sir Francis Seymour, had been wounded for the second time, a grenade fragment grazing the back of his head. There were now 35,000 English troops on the peninsula, along with 110,000 French, 54,000 Turks and 12,000 Sardinians, most finally equipped with viable weaponry. Artillery fire was demoralizing the supply-short Russians, especially the cannonading of heavy mortars, and finally, on 10 September, when Victoria and Albert were back from France and at Balmoral, news came that the siege had been broken.

'Albert said', Victoria wrote, 'that they should go at once and light the bonfire which had been prepared when the false report of the fall of the town arrived last year ... In a few minutes, Albert and all the gentlemen, in every species of attire, sallied forth, followed by all the servants, and gradually by all the population of the village – keepers, ghillies, workmen – up to the top of the cairn.' The young princes were awakened to watch the blaze, which flared as the Queen's piper played. Ghillies fired their guns in the air. Prudently, Victoria remained distant, but 'about three-quarters of an hour after, Albert came down, and said that the scene had been wild and exciting beyond everything. The people had been drinking healths in whisky, and were in great ecstasy'.

The Queen ventured out to watch, remaining until close to midnight, 'and just as I was undressing, all the people came down under the windows, the pipers playing, the people singing, firing off guns, and cheering – first for me, then for Albert, the Emperor of the French, and the "downfall of Sevastopol".' Noting that whisky was drunk round the Balmoral bonfire – such news travelled fast – *Punch* warned wryly that the 'sad example' of the Prince's participation would cause outrage in the 'Sackcloth Sunday Society'.

The Victoria Cross would emerge from the war. The Queen wanted a medal for extraordinary bravery in battle that could be awarded regardless of rank. The methodical Albert designed it and composed the language of the Royal Warrant, which referred to 'officers or men who have served Us in the presence of the enemy and then shall have performed some signal act of valour or devotion to their country'. *The Times* fussed, 'Never did we see such a dull, heavy, tasteless affair... There is a cross, and a lion, and a scroll worked up into the most shapeless mass that size admits of.' Valour, it concluded, would have to be its own reward; had the medals been on sale at a penny, 'hardly a dozen would be sold in a twelve-month'. The Queen liked it, but objected to the initials 'V.C.' to appear after the recipient's name, preferring 'B.V.C.' – the initial letter for 'Bearer'. After Albert's role at Cambridge she thought of 'V.C.' only as Vice-Chancellor. The abbreviation had to parallel other awards, however, and it was a battle she could not win.

The Crimean War, in which all the major combatant parties lost more than was gained, would not be the last Victorian small war, but it would be the last in which Albert had a principal hand. Only indirectly did it promote one of his greatest desires, the unification of Germany. By breaking the long ties of mutual interest between Austria and Russia it exposed, as never before, the rivalries for control of the buffer principalities between them, and left Austria without a military ally looming over Prussia. That was not the Prince's intention. He had a more peaceful strategy in mind, one that would foreshadow a liberal, rather than a militaristic, united Germany, Albertine at the top. Although dynastic marriages were fading out as grand gestures of international amity, he hoped to bring off the last and greatest of them.

He would marry his most beloved daughter, Vicky, to the future emperor of a future Germany.

The idea had surfaced when Prince William of Prussia had come with his family to the Great Exhibition in 1851. His eldest son, Frederick William, already nineteen, was tall and fair. Princess Victoria, only ten, was pretty and intellectually advanced beyond her years. While Vicky's German was faultless – it was spoken within the privacy of the family – the Prince's English was awkward, and he had no experience of travel beyond the university at Bonn. Privately, Albert explained how inadequately 'Fritz' was being prepared for kingship in the claustrophobic atmosphere of the Prussian court, and Frederick William asked Albert to help him with reading suggestions, and with occasional letters and memoranda. When he left for home, the young prince asked Albert to sign his autograph book, and Albert, never slow to proffer advice, prefaced his signature with 'May Prussia be merged in Germany, and not Germany in Prussia'.

Little correspondence between the Queen and Fritz's mother, Princess Augusta, was exchanged during the Crimean War, and Albert's to her husband, Prince William, was businesslike but unsympathetic. As the war, after Sevastopol, muddled toward peace, both the Prussian and English courts quietly broached the possibility of an eventual marriage although Vicky was not yet fifteen. On 29 August 1855, on the family's return from Paris, Albert sent a note to his mother-in-law, the Duchess of Kent, 'We shall probably have Fritz of Prussia visiting us ... for a few days. He has been taking the baths at Ostend, and will come to England. He wishes to see Scotland.' Another and less understated letter went to Baron Stockmar, who had been consulted earlier.

From Balmoral on 20 September Albert wrote to Stockmar, 'The event you are interested in reached an active stage this morning after breakfast. The young man laid his proposal before us with the permission of his parents, and of the King [of Prussia]; we accepted it for ourselves, but requested him to hold it in suspense as regards the other party till after her Confirmation. Till then all the simple unconstraint of girlhood is to continue undisturbed. In the Spring the young man wishes to make his offer to herself...' The marriage, Albert added, would not take place before Vicky was seventeen.

In the relative seclusion of Balmoral, the romance, even under ostensible chaperonage, prospered. In a further bulletin on 29 September, Stockmar was informed, 'The Prince is really in love and the little lady does her best to please him.' In her journal that day the Queen put it more explicitly. Vicky was 'engaged'. She and Albert had been 'uncertain, on account of her extreme youth, whether he should speak to her himself, or wait till he came back again'. However, during a ride they took to Craig-na-Ban, Fritz picked a sprig of white heather, a Scots symbol for good luck, and gave it to Vicky, enabling him 'to make an allusion to his hopes'. Since it had been clear a week earlier that the betrothal would happen, Albert had already informed the Earl of Clarendon, the Foreign Minister, so that official confirmation could go to the Prince of Prussia, Fritz's father, and to Viscount Palmerston.

The departure of Frederick William on 1 October enabled Albert to return to the pressing problems of the Russian war. Although what was diagnosed as rheumatic pains in his right shoulder and arm had left his nights nearly sleepless for a fortnight, and kept him from holding a pen for long, his correspondence went on. Unwisely he informed his brother Ernest of the engagement, which ensured leakage of the news. Whatever the source, *The Times* was out with the story on 3 October. With Prussia's leaning toward the Tsar's interest during the war still embittering the papers' editorial tone, Fritz's family was called a 'wretched German dynasty' which 'would not survive the collapse of Russia's influence'. While the war continued with Frederick William IV's passive support of his brother-in-law, the exasperation of the press was as inevitable as Albert's anguish.

Albert had engineered a marital *coup* planned to bind Britain to the Continental power of the future, but he had not anticipated the continuing undercurrent of anti-German feeling that had been a personal misery to him since his own betrothal to Victoria, and would outlast them both. Theodor Fontane, the Berlin novelist born in the same year as the Queen and Prince, and then visiting England, noted in his diary a scrap of street ballad invective that demonstrated the persistence of that paranoia:

> Bad luck they say both night and day
> To the Cobugs and the humbugs,
> The Wirtembugs, the Scarembugs,
> And all the German horse-rugs ...

The elation and the anxieties of the matchmaking could not shut out the reality of the war. In the Crimea itself, Raglan's timid replacement, General Simpson, was not a success, and nearly invisible. For internal political reasons, Louis Napoleon was planning to return home a hundred thousand of his troops, who were bogged down anyway beyond Sevastopol. Russian inefficiency contributed to the favourable Allied position, as there was no rail link to the Crimea, and reinforcements and supplies had to move the final 230 miles by animal and human transport. 'At Sebastopol', Albert wrote tartly to Stockmar, 'our Generals appear to be suffering from a remarkable lack of brains.' By 29 October he had worked out, due to lack of initiative at Whitehall, a reorganization of the army in the Crimea 'into two *Corps-d'armée*', under one chief, which has been adopted by the [War] Ministry ... Sir W[illiam] Codrington becomes Commander-in-Chief, Sir Colin Campbell and Sir W[illiam] Eyre take the Divisions, General [C.A.] Windham becomes Chief of the General Staff ...' Among those to return was the relieved commander, General Simpson. Both he and Raglan, Albert told Stockmar irritably, 'declared their inability to trouble themselves much about plans of campaign, while their whole time was taken up with writing and correspondence'.

'I and all the other members of the Cabinet', Albert's former *bête noir*, Lord Palmerston, wrote to him, 'feel greatly obliged to your Royal Highness for having suggested an arrangement which had not occurred to any of us, but which when proposed and explained at once obtained the assent of all those whose duty it was to take it into consideration.' The Prince by his own decision had declined to replace Wellington, but informally he found himself overseeing the winding down of the war. Ironically, at the time, despite years of jokes at his expense about his exalted military rank, he was, through attrition, the only Field Marshal in the army. Since that seemed to Victoria and Albert impolitic, three active generals were promoted, including Lord Hardinge.

Albert now carried on a regular exchange with Palmerston on the war, planning to resume naval operations in the Baltic in the spring of 1856 if necessary, to pressure the Russians further into signing a peace treaty. 'We might have struck home at Cronstadt and St Petersburg in the first year of the war', he confided to Baron Vitzthum, 'had our fleet been managed by a more resolute man than Sir Charles Napier.'

Methodically looking farther ahead, the Prince worked out an agenda, once peace came, for transferring equipment and stores stockpiled in the Black Sea region to Malta and Gibraltar.

While the war remained Albert's chief concern, its political, economic and social dislocations far out of proportion to the manpower committed to the Crimea, he put in many more hours on the future. He was preparing an address, he explained to Stockmar, on 'the influence of Science and Art on our Manufactures', for delivery on laying the foundation stone of the Birmingham and Midland Counties Institute. He was working on reform of the examinations for aspiring diplomats, and was still working, as Chancellor, on further academic reforms at Cambridge. And while he managed to see his other children only briefly, and to consult with Henry Birch about Albert Edward's lack of progress and developing stammer, he set aside an hour every evening to tutor Vicky on German history, on politics and law, and on other matters which he felt might prepare a future queen. To Fritz, she wrote, 'from dear papa I learn more than from anyone else in the world'. A demanding tutor, he gave her, nearly a year later as their lessons continued, a pamphlet to translate, *Karl August und die Deutsche Politik*, by Johann Gustavus Droysen. Since it dealt with Fritz's grandfather it was doubly useful as preparation for her new position. Pleased with the result, Albert sent her manuscript to Lord Clarendon to examine. Praising father and daughter simultaneously, the Foreign Minister described the translation as 'the reflection of a highly cultivated intellect'. It was no exaggeration. The Princess Royal was very likely the brainiest royal offspring to be born in Britain, and Albert described her to her future bridegroom as having 'a man's head and a child's heart'.

The Queen had far less interest in her firstborn. To Victoria, only the hours with Albert were crucial; hours with the children were dispensable. 'When Albert is often away all day long', she confided to the Queen of Prussia, Fritz's aunt, 'I find no especial pleasure or compensation in the company of the elder children.' She was only '*à mon aise*' when Albert was with her, for she had grown up without the company of other children and always knew adult society. 'Lastly I cannot get used to the fact that Vicky is almost grown up. To me she still seems the same child, who had to be kept in order and therefore must not become too intimate.'

Albert may have expected too much of his children. The eldest ones represented to him the future of England and Germany. Even Alfred was expected to succeed his childless uncle as Duke of Coburg – if Coburg survived. All the children but Vicky, whom he adored, were afraid of him as master of the family, but except for Bertie they could penetrate his Germanic reserve and enjoy his company. Victoria merely summoned them on occasion, Albert once writing to her (1 October, 1856), preferring to offer bad news in notes rather than quarrel in person, 'It is indeed a pity that you find no consolation in the company of your children. The root of the trouble lies in the mistaken notion that the function of a mother is to be always correcting, scolding, ordering them about and organising their activities. It is not possible to be on happy friendly terms with people you have just been scolding.'

Vicky's husband-to-be, Albert dreamed, would be another child to be moulded, like his eldest daughter – a son more than son-in-law. In that he failed to reckon with the conservative Prussian milieu in which Fritz's future rested. Still, among the additions to Albert's *Papierberg* of correspondents was Prince Fritz, who was showing, happily, clear indications of political liberalism. What was Fritz to do in response to reactionaries who were pushing the monarchy, despite the lessons of 1848, back toward the past? Albert considered his future son-in-law's sensitive position and suggested that he defend individual rights – 'those of my country and my people' – but in order 'that my conduct might be divested of every semblance of being dictated by a spirit of opposition or desire for popularity – and in order, it may be, to make the step itself unnecessary – I should in all confidence make those who are contemplating the wrong aware, that if it were persisted in, I should feel myself compelled to adopt this course'. Stepping even more gingerly, Albert added, 'this done, I should certainly entertain no animosity towards my friends, but, on the contrary, should live upon terms of peace with the reigning powers'. Some guarded measure of activism, he felt, was necessary 'to keep the nation from losing all hope, and there is no such solid basis for patience as hope'.

It was clear that Albert saw Prussia as slipping backward into traditional authoritarianism, and that the hope he had borne for a liberalized monarchy under Fritz's father was no longer to be counted upon. 'The German', he explained to his future son-in-law, 'stands in the centre between England and Russia; his high culture and his philosophic love of truth drive him towards the English conception, his military discipline, his admiration of the Asiatic greatness...which is achieved by the merging of the individual into the whole, drives him in the other direction.'

Vicky, he told Fritz, 'comes to me every evening from six to seven, when I put her through a kind of general catechizing, and in order to give precision to her ideas, I make her work out certain subjects by herself, and bring me the results...Thus she is now engaged in writing a short Compendium of Roman History.' Like her father, she promised to be an activist consort, one to be dreaded by Prussian rightists who might have already arranged to have Fritz's mail secretly opened and read. When Otto von Bismarck came to power as Minister-President of Prussia in 1862, such spying became routine.

The pressure within France to end the war was straining the still fragile relations between England and its unlikely ally. The Emperor had borrowed as well as cadged money for both grandeur at home and glory abroad, and was riskily close to financial embarrassment. Bringing home most of the French troops and releasing them into the work force was of less anxiety to Albert than Napoleon's willingness, for a quick accord, to readjust the map of eastern Europe and win the peace, if not the war, for Russia. Palmerston conceded, despite his long francophile sympathies, that Louis Napoleon's problems, which were not unknown to the Tsar's informants in Paris, weakened the English bargaining position. To bolster it by a dose of John Bullish stubbornness, Albert drafted a blunt letter to the Emperor, for Victoria's signature, pointing out that Napoleon could do what he wanted as absolute monarch, but for the Queen, 'the peace must be supported by Parliament and acceptable to the nation'. The Emperor was 'answerable to nobody'. She was bound by 'the advice of a Council of Ministers'.

A sticking point in negotiations was the openness and the neutrality of the Black Sea. Another was the disposition of disputed territories. Little was said about the pretexts responsible for the war. To England the issues were the viability of Turkey, the 'Sublime Porte' now only in name, as a buffer to Russian expansion, and the fencing of Russia away from the Mediterranean. Despite the Roebuck investigation into the war, England, as a free and dynamic society, was emerging from the conflict stronger than any of the other belligerents – with the rather small exception of Sardinia, whose bluff king paid a call upon Victoria and Albert toward the end of 1855 and aspired to be monarch of a future united Italy, largely at the expense of Austria, which no longer had a staunch friend at Windsor Castle.

The allies had no idea how desperately Alexander II needed peace for exhausted Russia until the Queen received the professedly secret news on the night of 16 January 1856, in a telegram, puzzlingly sent *en clair*, by the secretive and unstable King of Prussia. Although the message that Russia was ready to discuss peace came by commercial telegraphy, uncoded, the excited Frederick William IV begged that his name be concealed. Albert forwarded the 'telegraphic curiosity' to Lord Clarendon, noting that the Queen wanted him to be aware of the sender as well as the message, since 'the whole line of the telegraph' already knew.

Because of Louis Napoleon's internal needs, the peace conference, preparations for which had long simmered in Vienna, was held in Paris. The Prussian king asked to be seated at it, but Paris and London turned him down, even after King Leopold of the Belgians interceded with Albert. To his uncle, the Prince replied that England's position at the table would be difficult enough with Emperor Napoleon on its side, as anti-German feeling was strong in France, and that went for Austria as well, which was 'as selfish and as little to be relied upon as ever'. To have Prussia in the conference would only bolster the Tsar, Albert contended. 'Russia will not yield one hair's breadth more than she is *forced* to yield.' It was, he felt, 'a perilous precedent for the future to admit the principle, that a Power may take a part in the great game of politics, without having laid down their stake'. Even Vicky's future father-in-law, Prince William of Prussia, failed to budge Albert, but in the interests of giving a settlement broader acceptability, plenipotentiaries from Berlin were seated on 18 March. On 10 March, the English delegates had already yielded to French desires to be easy on the Russians. All the Prussian delegate had to do was sign.

Recognizing gloomily that the results of the war would not be worth the sacrifices, Albert had already agreed to an audience with Baron Vitzthum to vent his exasperations to the Saxon envoy in the hope they would travel farther. He wanted, he insisted, a 'sound peace' or the further prosecution of the war – which he knew would not happen. But, suggesting that alternative, he warned, 'English indolence has taken several years to get [us] ready. Our preparations are now complete, and we can show that England is not made up only of cotton spinners and shopkeepers, as we are told.'

The Treaty of Paris was signed on 30 March 1856. By it, Russia rescued much of the Black Sea territory it expected to be forced to cede, but did return some seized Turkish lands on the eastern shore. The delta of the Danube remained Turkish territory but the Danubian provinces of Wallachia and Moldavia, core of a future Romania, would remain only nominally under Turkish sovereignty. Free navigation of the Danube was mandated, as was the neutralization of the Black Sea. The religious issues that had precipitated the conflict were shelved for Turkish promises to protect Christians.

Albert, who had no role in Paris, was dissatisfied with the terms, which left the 'Eastern Question' unsolved and further partition of European Turkey inevitable. His personality dominating the delegates, Napoleon III got his way on most issues, the unspoken one his desire to make an ally of Russia as his counterweight to the Germanic powers in the European centre. The Prince had hoped that Lord Clarendon and Count Buol* would be able to deal with 'the finessing of the Russians', but biology intervened on 16 March, when the Empress Eugénie, after a difficult pregnancy, gave birth to Prince Eugène Louis Jean Joseph, the future Prince Imperial. A salute of 101 guns shook Paris, and Lord Clarendon observed, 'The Emperor is enchanted with his son ... [and] does not care sixpence for the terms.' He had founded, he thought, a new Napoleonic dynasty, and events could thereafter be managed from the perception of imperial continuity.

The treaty left England largely isolated. Russia was, and would be, hostile for decades, and Austria and Prussia had not, as Albert put it, laid down their stake. Further, England's sole major-power ally, excepting disintegrating Turkey, was an unstable France only as reliable as its unreliable Emperor.

For the Queen and Prince the Treaty of Paris did not end the Crimean agony. There would be another year of visits to the grievously wounded, the laying of foundation stones for military hospitals, the reviews of returning troops, the awards of the first Victoria Crosses, the

---

* Count Karl Ferdinand von Buol-Schauenstein was the Austrian Foreign Minister who had chaired the preliminary Vienna conference, and saw gains for Austria in a weakened Russia.

The royal family, with Albert in top hat, Victoria wearing a bonnet, and Vicky and Bertie at their sides, visiting Crimean War wounded at a London hospital. (From a contemporary lithograph)

audiences with Crimean heroes – and heroines. One would be Florence Nightingale, who met twice with the Queen and Prince in Scotland, and conversed privately with Albert on metaphysics and religion. The emotional end came on 8 July 1856 when, at Aldershot for a review, the Queen received from Field-Marshal Lord Hardinge the report of the Military Commission on the Crimea, a watered-down rebuke to the military. As he began explaining its findings, he toppled against the table at which he had been standing, felled by a paralytic stroke. Albert assisted him to a sofa, where (the Prince wrote to Stockmar) Hardinge 'at once resumed what he was saying with the greatest clearness and calmness, merely apologizing "that he had made such a disturbance".' Yet his right leg and arm were useless, and he had to be lifted into his carriage. Albert realized, he told Stockmar, that Hardinge, however 'courageous and composed', would have to be replaced. Two days later came Hardinge's resignation. He died on 24 September, a belated casualty of the Crimea.

Victoria preferred to have Albert remember the war through a darkly lit anecdotal canvas they had admired at the Royal Academy show the year before. Joseph Noël Paton's *Home* depicted with Pre-Raphaelite attention to domestic detail the return from the war of a bearded Scots corporal in the Fusilier Guards. A bandage covers a head wound, and his left sleeve is empty. The Crimean Medal, awarded by the Queen to all who fought in the war, is conspicuous on his uniform, and on the floor next to his chair before the fireplace is a trophy – a Russian helmet. Leaning over his shoulder, his bonneted mother weeps; at his knees he is embraced by his anguished young wife. In the background a child sleeps. On a small table in the foreground is an open Bible. In the picture, the glory (the medal, the trophy) is vastly overshadowed by the price. The canvas had a profound impact upon a public disenchanted by the Crimean experience. The Queen commissioned from Paton a reduced-size replica as a Christmas gift for Albert.

XV

Managing Destiny

1856–1858

T HE TREATY OF Paris ending the Crimean War was received in London, Albert wrote, 'with moderate satisfaction: in Paris with exultation'. Ten days earlier Vicky's confirmation, the essential preliminary to her marriage, should have been an occasion for parental exultation but generated only moderate satisfaction. Rigid Prussian court protocol required official publication of the forthcoming nuptials, which Victoria and Albert considered premature. Also, the acrimony between the ruling houses about permitting a traditional German ceremony of betrothal was threatening to blight the engagement. 'At present', Victoria wrote to the Prime Minister, 'not even our other children are acquainted with it, which puts the Princess to great trials.' Albert, she added, would write to Fritz's father 'and ask him to consider the German part of the question, whilst the Queen asks Lord Palmerston to consider our own'.

Victoria had hoped that with peace, and the dynastic *coup*, the time had finally come to grant Albert the title of Prince Consort. It was already informally in use. Yet any parliamentary action was hostage to the failure of anti-German feeling to abate. Anything that could remotely be complained of as a German evil remained attributed to Albert. In the first season of victory, Sir Benjamin Hall, the Commissioner of Works, whose purview included public parks, thought that it would promote a festive atmosphere among the masses if military bands were to play on Sunday afternoons. Both the Cabinet and the Court approved, and the concerts drew large crowds when they began in May.

Leaders of the movement for strict Sabbath observance were outraged that the working classes might be drawn away from prayer, and promoters of penitential Sundays also objected to the bands as a German sacrilege introduced by Prince Albert.

Few circumstances earned him credit. Among his plans for a cultural and scientific district in South Kensington with seed money from Great Exhibition earnings was the transfer of pictures from the National Gallery in Trafalgar Square to the less polluted atmosphere of Kensington, where an efficient new edifice was to rise. Again there was an outcry. The Prince was tampering with the national heritage, and *Punch* depicted Albert trying to slip out of the Gallery with a framed canvas under each arm, while a policeman confronts him with the charge, 'Only moving the pictures to Kensington Gore! Suppose you leave them where they are, eh?'

He had no business lamenting his ill fortune, *Punch* cautioned:

> Never mind, noble Prince, we our crosses have all,
> Your great matters if I may compare with our small;
> But when you complain of your bad luck, you should,
> I would humbly suggest, also think of your good.

At about the same time, the successor to Hardinge at the Horse Guards was appointed, Victoria insisting upon her cousin George, Duke of Cambridge. An undistinguished general in the Crimea, he had arrived, splendidly accoutred, and pleaded illness when conditions at the front were not up to those at his clubs. No exhortations from Victoria could induce him to return. Still, nepotism remained the first rule of the army, and the Queen had the right of appointment. Again, Albert was blamed, and a *Punch* cartoon that July showed the Duke hurrying to the Horse Guards on Albert's bowed back.

In that inauspicious climate the Queen wrote confidentially to the Earl of Aberdeen, no longer at Downing Street but still a royal favourite, and then to Viscount Palmerston, to broach the matter of an English title for her husband. 'Oh! if I only could make him King!' she had written in her diary in 1845. Victoria had long since reduced her expectations, explaining now to Palmerston (5 June 1856), 'It is a strange omission in our Constitution that while the *wife* of a *King* has the highest rank and dignity in the realm after her husband assigned to her by law, the *husband* of a *Queen regnant* is entirely ignored by the law.'

THE NEW COMMANDER-IN-CHIEF.

*Although Albert was blamed for the nepotism involved in the appointment of the incompetent Duke of Cambridge as commander-in-chief of the Army, it was actually Victoria's favouritism that sent him to the Horse Guards in 1856. Here the Duke rides on Albert's back to get there. (*Punch*)*

She wanted 'to put this question beyond all doubt . . . for *all future Consorts of Queens*'. It made her position as well as that of her husband 'humiliating' to have him recognized in English law only as 'her foreign husband'.

Palmerston's political advice was to postpone the matter further. Aberdeen fussed that a title might grant Albert the right to sit in the House of Lords and the Privy Council, giving the Crown legislative powers. Derby worried that by the time the matter was considered by

Parliament, enough months would have elapsed for opponents to mount a negative press campaign. Dragging its feet in hopes that the Queen would withdraw her request, the Cabinet would not consider a Prince Consort Bill until March 1857, when, via the Lord Chancellor, a further complication was raised. In English usage a wife received her husband's rank, suggesting that the spouse of a Queen Regnant would become King Consort, which would not sit well with the people. Further, if the King Consort then survived his wife and remarried, could he communicate his rank to his wife, making her in style, at least, a queen? Nit-picking further, the Cabinet saw a new legal rank as interposing someone not in the line of succession between the sovereign and the Prince of Wales.

The Queen had to coax a response from Palmerston, and when she received it she huffed that he 'will not be astonished when she tells him that the perusal of this document has caused her much surprise...' Having had no success since 1840 in legalizing even the modest dignity afforded Queen Anne's mediocrity of a husband, Victoria determined to do 'merely as much as her Prerogative will enable her'. By Letters Patent she would give Albert the title of Prince Consort, which the Privy Council approved, finally, on 25 June 1857. Long public usage was ratified.

Despite the Sabbatarian frowning at bands on Sundays, the popular relief, and even joy, that troops were coming home made the spring and summer of 1856 a happy one, and a propitious time for balls and banquets to celebrate the Princess Royal's still-informal engagement. Since she was only fifteen, the wedding remained nearly two years away, but her coming-out inaugurated the new concert gallery and ballroom at Buckingham Palace, designed, inevitably, by the Prince Consort. The prospects were not nearly so pleasing to conservatives in the bridegroom's country, where Bismarck, Prussia's representative to the Bundestag at Frankfurt, carped to a colleague about the future 'English marriage' that the 'English' in it failed to please him but 'If the Princess can leave the Englishwoman at home and become a Prussian, then she may be a blessing to the country'. Under Albert's tutelage she was learning how to be a German rather than a Prussian.

With Vicky's grand marriage pending, the Consort Bill in the hands of the Prime Minister, England (with the Prince a primary if mostly silent factor) successful in the now-concluded war, the redesign of Buckingham Palace completed, Osborne finished, and the new Balmoral Castle now occupied, all the portents seemed favourable for Albert. While at Osborne in May 1856, leaving his reputed stuffiness behind, he even visited, informally, Alfred Tennyson, the Poet Laureate, who had just moved to nearby Freshwater. 'Prince Albert called on me the other day here', Tennyson wrote in surprise to Elizabeth Russell, his favourite aunt, 'and was very kind in manner shaking hands in quite a friendly way. We were in the midst of a packing bustle, things tumbled about here and there ... he stood by the drawing-room window admiring the view which was not looking its best, and on going away said ... "I shall certainly bring the Queen – it's such a pretty place."' Yet, still another of a proliferation of pamphlets about his failure to find a welcome in England had just appeared, *Prince Albert. Why is he Unpopular?*

A political rarity, the tract took his side. Although his unpopularity seemed 'a feeling shared by almost anyone', it observed, 'no one can give a rational cause for its existence'. Inexplicably, 'the consort ... of the most amiable and beloved Sovereign that has ever sat on the throne of these seagirt isles, is the most unpopular man in them'.

One of the most admired, returned from the charge in which so many of his cavalrymen were slaughtered, was Lord Cardigan (of Balaclava fame), whose surviving troops were reviewed in Hyde Park on 9 July by Victoria and Albert. A 'halo of heroism' (said a sarcastic newspaperman) hung about him. Among the curious residual problems of the war, relating to officers who did not return, was that some had been gazetted Knights Commander of the Bath but had died before being invested with the title. Panmure and Palmerston brought the matter to Albert. It might be prudent, they suggested, 'to ascertain which of [their widows] are desirous of having the title of Lady, which they would have had if their husbands had lived; it is possible that to some of them the title might with reference to their pecuniary means be an inconvenience'. The honour was monetarily empty. The Prince agreed that they should be offered titles rather than awarded them.

In September and October the Queen and Prince escaped to the 'bracing' climate of Balmoral, where Victoria claimed 'half her heart' was in the 'great loneliness'. Despite her learning to her surprise there that she was again, at thirty-seven, pregnant, she escaped the depression that often followed such tidings. It was the risk run for the pleasure she would not deny herself. Albert's alternative amusements were unavailable to her. While in the Highlands she reported to Fritz's mother, Augusta, in Berlin, the Prince had shot 'twenty-nine very fine stags', delayed compensation, perhaps, for the frustrating Peace of Paris.

Again Albert had taken over all but epistolary functions for Victoria as her pregnancy advanced. Always in charge of the family, he confronted a new problem. The childless Duke Ernest had complained about the seafaring education of Prince Alfred, the nephew already designated to succeed him. 'Affie' might find his enthusiasm for a naval career at odds with residence in a small, landlocked German duchy. Reminding his brother that Alfred was also succession insurance in England, Albert noted that there were 'only two eyes' – those of the Prince of Wales – between Affie and the throne.

Although the Prince promised that Alfred would visit his likely inheritance, and he did travel to Coburg and Gotha in the spring, he was given no special German education for his future, as Vicky was receiving. 'If we make a German of him', Albert explained, 'it might be very difficult for him and for our country.'

Following the journey, the Prince wrote to thank his brother for the two weeks of hospitality for Alfred, and to regret that he could not share, with his son, 'our beloved quiet Rosenau' – 'the paradise of our childhood'. His spirit had been 'lost in the dear memories', but 'the plagues and serious business of which every day brings me plenty' returned him to reality. The confession, he admitted, was an uncommon lapse into nostalgia. 'Sentimentality is a plant which cannot grow in England, and an Englishman, when he finds he is being sentimental, becomes frightened at the idea, as of having a dangerous illness, and he shoots himself.'

As Albert wrote of the loss, some day, of his second son to a German destiny, the Queen was having the birth of their ninth and last child made tolerable by the intervention of chloroform. Princess Beatrice – 'Baby' for much of her life with Victoria – was born on 14 April 1857. While she was still recuperating at Osborne, Albert, on 23 April, asked for a meeting with Palmerston and his Chancellor of the Exchequer to arrange for a request to the Commons for funds for their firstborn, who required the customary dowry. Surfeited with the discomforts and distractions of pregnancy and babies, the Queen was aware that as each child reached maturity there would be more money-grubbing from Parliament and matchmaking on her part (an activity that would consume her later years). She and Albert, Victoria told Vicky twenty years later, considered 'many Princes a great misfortune – for they are in one another's and almost everybody's way ... Papa felt this so much that he was always talking of establishing if possible one or two of your brothers and eventual grandchildren ... in the colonies'. Nearly thirty-eight when Beatrice was born, and possibly embarrassed by the prospects of further motherhood – she had called even more fecund women 'rabbits' – Victoria raised the issue delicately with her *accoucheur*. Even more discreetly, he apparently suggested that the only legal and moral solution was abstinence. 'Oh, doctor,' she is reputed to have exclaimed, 'can I have no more fun in bed?' The remark seems too unqueenly to be literally Victorian, but in substance may have represented something of her sexual innocence, even after seventeen years of marriage. Still, recognizing that the Queen feared further pregnancies, and was prone to severe postpartum depression, Dr Clark warned Albert that a tenth pregnancy might threaten Victoria's mental stability.

Many Royal functions had become Albert's because the Queen was either unavailable or uninterested. They also seemed his province because of authentic interest or the realization that something had to be done, and no progress could come without a proposer or initiator. In every case he did his homework, not only to appear prepared, but to *be* knowledgeable. His original need for one secretary-assistant had expanded to three as responsibilities burgeoned – Sir Charles Phipps, General Charles Grey and Sir Thomas Biddulph. It was Phipps who recalled 'a great glass manufacturer' who, once the Prince had left the room, told Sir Charles enthusiastically, 'That is wonderful! He knows more about glass than I do!'

Clearly the Prince did not, but he had readied himself for the audience, and was also a good listener. And just as he learned the rudiments of experimental science from men as accomplished as Faraday and Lyell, he learned about the arts not to exhibit his results or parade his expertise, but to understand their values. Once, at a dinner at Windsor Castle, he explained to Lady Bloomfield – her husband was Minister to Berlin – that he realized 'that persons in our position of life can never be distinguished artists'. Those in his situation had 'too many other duties'. Their business was 'to learn to appreciate and understand the works of others, and we can never do this till we have realised the difficulties to be overcome. Acting on this principle myself, I have always tried to learn the rudiments of art as much as possible. For instance, I learned oil-painting, water-colours, etching, [and] lithography... and in music I learnt thorough bass, the pianoforte, organ, and singing.' He also learned composition – but always 'to enable me to judge and appreciate the work of others'.

For Albert, too, a cultural event had to be purposeful. Dickens's theatricals, while exploiting the snobbery of wealth and position, had a social and charitable function beyond their values as entertainment. Similarly, the Manchester Art Treasures Exhibition which opened on 5 May 1857 was able to borrow from royal art as an example to more reluctant possessors because Albert emphasized its potential for art education, which hardly existed in England. An illustrated catalogue could reach many unable to entrain to Manchester. To give the opening further cachet, he invited all envoys accredited to the Court – 'summoned', the American Minister, George M. Dallas, explained to his Secretary of State, Lewis Cass. And on the appointed day, Albert made the rail journey to Manchester, although already 'half-dead' with a bad cold, and delivered, in a 'quite cracked' voice (so he wrote to Victoria, then lying-in), the main address and officiated at a procession in which Sir Harry Smith again rode his Arab charger to great cheers. After an elaborate dinner at neo-Gothic Abney Hall, he managed to get to bed.

At eight the next morning he was on his way to Peel Park at Salford to visit the Museum and Public Library, and reply to an address. Then there was an exhibition by Manchester local artists, and the unveiling of a statue of the Queen – there would be thousands in the United Kingdom and the colonies – subscribed to by eighty thousand Sunday School teachers and their students. He had almost lost his voice by then, yet struggled to say something fitting for his audience. Art and Manufactures were indivisible, he claimed. All forms of beauty and utility were governed by the same laws of order that govern the universe and give delight to its inhabitants. The feeling and the thought that should go into all kinds of creativity need not be cheap and superficial.

As for the statue of Victoria, the figure was not merely a person: the Queen was 'the representative of the institutions of the country'.

Off, then, he went, to the railway station at Birmingham for the return to Paddington, and then Windsor, and Victoria's retreat the next day, with their expanded family, to Osborne. There, between visits by grand dukes and archdukes, princes (his future son-in-law) and kings (his uncle, Leopold), Albert would find time to plan a European tour for Bertie to help him grow up, to organize the first Handel Festival at the new Crystal Palace, where 2,500 singers and instrumentalists would perform *Judas Maccabeus* (in his diary he would call the event '*ganz vortrefflich*' [quite splendid]), and to prepare for still further occasions. He was particularly worried, he confided to Stockmar, about presiding and speaking at the annual Educational Conference. Given 'all our political and theological antagonisms', he explained, the challenge was 'an extremely ticklish one, and my address, I regret to say, will be very long. One's nervous system, therefore, has something to endure.'

On 16 May, the Princess Royal's engagement was formalized in the Prussian *Official Gazette*. Three days later, on 19 May, the Queen sent a request to Parliament for a dowry for Vicky, with Albert hoping that some precedent for provision for all the royal children might result, to avoid degrading appeals for each of their progeny. The Commons would only take up the issue at hand, but voted 328 to 14 to settle £40,000 on Vicky, with a further annuity of £8,000. Attitudes had changed since the debate on Albert's annuity. Since the annual stipend itself was far more than the salary of the Prime Minister, Albert saw it as a gesture 'of respect for the Queen'. The Princess Royal's allowance was 'not large, but it makes her independent, which is most important for her'. Whatever the considerable sum, the idea that Vicky as a Prussian wife could have any independence save as the daughter of a prestigious monarch with whom Prussia needed to remain on good terms was Albert's wishful self-delusion.

Since Fritz was a future sovereign, there was talk in Prussia of a grand marriage in Berlin rather than, as customary, at the bride's venue. Victoria instructed Clarendon to caution his ambassador 'not to *entertain* the *possibility*'. It was 'too *absurd*, to say the least'. With none of Albert's diplomacy she added, 'Whatever may be the usual practice of Prussian Princes, it is not *every* day that one marries the eldest daughter of the Queen of England. The Question therefore must be considered as settled and closed...'

The other question settled and closed was Albert's royal style. As Clerk of the Privy Council, Greville could not 'see the use of it', as the Queen's order conferred on the Prince Consort 'neither title, dignity, nor privileges' and would give him 'no higher rank abroad, where our acts have no validity'. When Albert expressed relief to his brother about being able to write in the new guise, Ernest remarked, 'Of course it should have been done long ago'. *The Times* agreed, observing that in practice the title had been adopted many years before. Even Greville conceded, after Albert attended a royal wedding in Belgium, that the 'Consort' title did have some effect, as the Prince 'signed the marriage contract immediately after Queen Marie Amélie, and before an Austrian Archduke who was present'. In John Bullish fashion *Punch* dismissed the episode. 'We should have supposed it better to be "Serene" in England, than "Royal" on the Continent – as Continental Royalties go.'

Issues of precedence and protocol still mattered a great deal in mid-century. Grand Duke Constantine, uncle of the Tsar, was an example. With French rapprochement in progress, and a mission to woo Western funding for railway construction in the Russian hinterland, Constantine invited himself to Osborne House. The Queen and Prince felt obliged to send their yacht to Cherbourg to fetch him, and were not pleased that ceremony required it to fly the former enemy flag when it returned to English waters on 30 May. Although the visit was supposedly informal, Palmerston rushed to greet Constantine, a guard of honour materialized on the lawn, and the Grand Duke debarked in full military uniform, a preface to his arrogant and absolutist remarks at dinner (not 'well-bred', the Queen concluded), where he also tried to conduct business with ministers.

The next day, again flying the Russian flag, they sailed out briefly in the new *Victoria and Albert* to show Constantine the fleet at Spithead, and naval guns saluted the Grand Duke's welcome departure.

On 26 June 1857, with levées and drawing-rooms in the wake of Ascot week over, and her Order in Council the previous day about Albert's title creating little stir, the Queen decorated Crimea veterans with the first Victoria Crosses at a review in Hyde Park. Even at ten that morning the summer heat had the oppressive feel of India. Gentlemen in the seats reserved for the élite put dignity aside to fan themselves with the tails of their coats; their ladies improvised fans from newspapers and flapped handkerchiefs. Beneath the drooping Royal Standard at the

Queen's dais, Victoria, bonneted and implacable under the broiling sun, pinned sixty-two medals upon the men on parade, one now in the uniform of a police constable and another in the dress of a park keeper, all heroes of Inkerman and Redan.

Returning from the ceremony, Victoria and Albert learned of the 'Sepoy Mutiny' near Calcutta. The news, followed by the 'cruel suspense' (as she put it) of weeks of delay in the convoluted sea-and-land communications from India, came in the aftermath of post-Crimea military retrenchments. Suddenly, Cabinet penny-pinching was abandoned. The Commander-in-Chief of forces in India, General George Anson, was reported dead. Palmerston rushed a replacement, Sir Colin Campbell, who left the next day on the long voyage around the Cape to a situation which was bound to be very different when he arrived from anything he knew as he embarked.*

To the long history of mismanagement, incompetence, penuriousness, confused responsibility and indifference, already the source of embarrassment in the Crimea, were added, in India, guilt on the scale of the subcontinent. Ever since the reign of Elizabeth I, under the transparent cloak of a merchant company, Britain had exploited teeming subject races occupying vast tracts of southern Asia. The East India Company, prospering under a feudal royal charter and gradually relinquishing its political powers to the Crown, was still landlord and tax collector, and paid the bills for the British-officered army that maintained order. By the 1850s a Cabinet minister in London was overseeing the directors of the Company. The Governor General, ostensibly its appointee, was in fact designated by the government.

Beneath the unrelenting sun, Indians toiled for a few farthings a day, under Company and civil-servant employers for whom India was largely the safety valve for British excess population, from younger sons to superfluous daughters. Sepoys – Indian infantrymen serving under British officers in regiments supported by Company funds – represented five-sixths of the quarter of a million troops in India. The rest were in Queen's regiments, British in origin but in effect hired out to serve an Indian tour of duty.

---

* Although Albert's involvement in the suppression of the mutiny would always be indirect, Campbell had proved himself in the Crimea after the Prince had recommended him for the assignment.

Early in 1857 a rumour had raced among sepoy troops that the new rifles, lighter-weight Enfields, required greased cartridges, for which the manufacturer had used beef fat or – even worse – pork fat. Contact with either meant defilement for Moslems as well as Hindus – even rejection from the marital bed. (A related rumour – one that surfaced in Calcutta – was that at Queen Victoria's command, all sepoys would be baptized.) The concern about pollution with unclean grease was real; to save a few pennies, some British weapons manufacturers had substituted for the prescribed mutton fat (acceptable to Indians of any religion or caste but the strictest vegetarians) bullock's or hog's fat.

When, in April, some troops began to reject the defiled cartridges, eighty-five sepoys at the Meerut encampment near Calcutta were court-martialed for insubordination. Their sentences were ten years' hard labour – in chains – on roadbuilding crews. In the heat and dust of India it was, in effect, a death sentence, but there was never any doubt that General George Anson, commander-in-chief of the Indian Army, would confirm the verdicts. Yet Anson had already written to Charles Greville of his forebodings – that, according to Greville's diary, 'there is a strange feeling of discontent pervading the Indian Army from religious causes, and a suspicion that we are going to employ our irresistible power in forcing Christianity upon them. It is not true, but the natives will never be quite convinced that it is not, as long as Exeter Hall and the missionaries are permitted to have *carte blanche* and work their will as they please in those regions.' Exeter Hall was the London meeting place of Bible, religious tract, and missionary societies. The Liberals owed their majority to the evangelical vote.

How much of Anson's concerns were known in Whitehall made little difference until it became too late. And once Anson sanctioned the sentences, and the men were publicly fettered to warn off further dissidents, mutiny flared up – first as an attempt to free the prisoners. Violence spread across India.

In what seemed poetic justice, from the Indian standpoint, one of the first deaths – albeit from cholera – was that of General Anson. Epidemics and massacres would take more lives on both sides than conventional skirmishes, but at the start the British were losing the shooting war as well as the silent one. Through the early months of the uprising, as all the belated news from India remained bad, and as

Victoria feared for the lives of her subjects (Palmerston had once preached that the harming of a single British subject was *causus belli*), she vented her fury on her Prime Minister. 'The Queen must say', she wrote to him in exasperation on 25 August 1857, 'that the Government incur a fearful responsibility towards their country by their apparent indifference. God grant that no unforeseen European complication fall upon this country – but we are really tempting Providence.' To Leopold she confided that the affair was 'so much more distressing than the Crimea – where there was *glory* and honourable warfare, and where the poor women and children were safe ... There is not a family hardly who is not in sorrow and anxiety about their children, and in all [social] ranks – India being *the* place where everyone was anxious to place a son!'

Ironically, Albert's promotion of a German Legion for Crimean deployment now proved useful. The East India Company had wanted four of its regiments, but negotiations faltered and the men not eager to return home with the promised £20 in discharge pay were shipped to South Africa. Thanks to the Legion's presence in Cape Colony, it became possible to rush British troops there, five thousand strong, to India.

The Queen considered herself 'a soldier's daughter', and from Osborne fired off to Palmerston memorandum after memorandum deploring the relapse in readiness which required sending troops just returned from 'most trying climates' back into action and urging the raising of additional battalions in England. The detailed messages revealed Albert's organizing hand. In his diary for 22 July he recorded, 'The Cabinet has at last adopted our suggestions for an increase in the army.' His first-person plural is revealing. As Albert wrote to Prince William of Prussia, the English public remained too smug about what was happening, largely because they knew too little, and 'the Ministry [was] *too* calm for my notions, and therefore we are constantly digging our spurs into their sides'. Not only did Albert want the desperate situation in India reversed; he wanted no perception of weakness to be exploited by governments on the Continent. The 'European complication' alluded to in Victoria's memorandum to Palmerston implied, in particular, the regime of her unreliable Crimean ally, Louis Napoleon.

India was more of a calamity than most outside India realized. As the carnage escalated – the British civilian population of East India

Company and Indian Army dependents were at risk · – a visit by Napoleon III to Osborne was imminent. The Isle of Wight seemed a safe spot to rendezvous for a monarch who felt under constant threat of assassination, and he had requested the locale. Since Albert as a matter of policy kept state visits away from Osborne, he arranged an informal greeting at the dock with only the Queen and Prince and their children. As American Minister Dallas reported to Washington, 'prodigious pains' were taken to secure the 'personal safety' of Napoleon and Eugénie. 'Nothing was allowed, on the water, to approach within two miles of them. A body of Parisian detectives formed a cordon round them at a distance. And yet the eagerness of his Majesty to greet Prince Albert, when near the landing, led to his stumbling . . . and falling heavily on the deck [of the *Reine Hortense*], thereby, as it is said, "grazing his face and shaking himself considerably".' Officially he had a bad fall 'on board' and was 'rather lame' on disembarking on 6 August.

For most of the 'private' visit Lord Clarendon was present for discussions, but before the Emperor returned on the tenth he had a private exchange with Albert. The Prince recorded its substance in a long memorandum which he sent to Stockmar, still his chief confidant, dictated to Princess Vicky 'as a lesson', his authorized biographer, Theodore Martin, later put it, 'in the political studies in which he had for some time been educating her'. The Emperor's unburdenings had disturbed Albert. From Napoleon's conspiratorial standpoint, all other Continental powers were duplicitous toward France, and he was worried most, he claimed, by hostile combinations seeking advantages. He wanted territorial revisions which would satisfy national appetites short of further war.

'If everybody were to get great advantages, where were they to come from?' Albert asked. 'Certainly not from within Europe.'

'That is why I always thought better means "*pour rendre de grands bienfaits au monde*" could be found out of Europe than within.' The Emperor would make '*un lac Européen*' by awarding countries segments of Africa and Asia fronting the Mediterranean made 'useless to humanity and civilization by their abominable governments. France herself wanted an outlet for her turbulent spirits.'

Diplomatically, Albert agreed that was 'a great improvement' over interfering with '*le vieux monde et la vieille société*', but he was disturbed by the inevitable impact of such ambitions on the Old World.

Napoleon III, he realized, could remain in power only by pandering to what the Emperor called the '*esprit de la nation*'. He claimed to prefer the more placid internal state of England, 'but it could not be imitated in France'. And he offered as a guarantee (Albert later told Baron Vitzthum) an offensive and defensive alliance which England's need for freedom of action would not allow. Albert was playing on a large stage, and knew he should not. Accordingly, he informed Palmerston of all the details, having committed England to nothing. Pleased, the Prime Minister conceded to Victoria, 'The Prince can say many things that we cannot.'

Departing, the Emperor bestowed gifts on servants, officials, and the royal children. Vicky and Alice received rings and bracelets, and the younger children were given lockets with wisps of Eugénie's carefully coiffed hair – a nineteenth-century practice now long lapsed. Tears flowed as a band played '*Partant pour la Syrie*' and the imperial guests – much like family, the Queen thought – were ferried back to the *Reine Hortense* in the early afternoon of 10 August 1857. Napoleon's guards and secret police quietly melted away.

They would be needed in Paris. Early the next year came an attempt on the Emperor by four Italian radicals who employed three bombs found to have been made in Birmingham. Ten bystanders were killed, 156 wounded. Napoleon and Eugénie were only slightly injured but two of their carriage horses died. The assailants had been exiles in England on friendly terms with such Liberal leaders as Gladstone. Although Palmerston cautiously did not reply to a French request to expel political fugitives, he prepared a bill to strengthen the conspiracy laws. Anti-British outrage orchestrated in the Parisian press, however, stiffened resistance in the Commons, and on a second reading the bill failed. To the unhappiness of Victoria and Albert, Palmerston would resign in February 1858, and a minority Ministry led by the diffident Derby and the distrusted Disraeli came in.

Early autumn in the Mutiny year of 1857 was a period of continuing calamities in India, of battalions sent too late to save Cawnpore and Lucknow, and of the spread of the uprisings. The Queen and Prince received the doleful tidings in the fastness of Balmoral because Victoria would not alter the calendar of her rounds. 'We are tortured by the events in India', Albert confided to Stockmar. '...The distance and the double government of Crown and Company make all remedial measures extremely difficult and slow. Our first considerable reinforcements will not arrive in India before the middle of October; our latest intelligence is dated August. What may not have happened in the interval!'* Friendly relations with France, however, speeded the task, as troops were permitted to debark in French-controlled Egypt and re-ship on the Red Sea side to continue into the Indian Ocean. Construction of the Suez Canal would only begin in 1859.

Realizing, as did Victoria and Albert, that overwhelming firepower would inevitably prevail, the Governor-General, Lord Canning, was already attempting to ensure tranquillity in reoccupied areas by conciliatory administration, although pilloried by newspapers at home as 'Clemency Canning'. The public wanted retribution for barbarism. The Queen and Prince preferred an end to the East India Company, and an efficiently organized new government, while Palmerston was unready to cross business interests, at least until the violence had subsided. But he was, Greville claimed on 8 October, having listened to Cabinet confidences from Earl Granville, Lord President of the [Privy] Council, 'on good terms with the Court, and behaves very well to the Queen, even with extraordinary deference, and she likes him well enough. The Queen is not clever, and everything is done by the Prince, who is to all intents and purposes King. She acts in everything by his inspiration and never writes a letter that he does not dictate every word of.'

Greville's litany of prejudices, fed from his listening posts at Court, both underrated the Queen's shrewdness and overestimated Albert's overtaxed capacities, which could not have been as prodigious as he and Lord Granville admiringly imagined them. The Prince remained human. Yet, Greville wrote, 'His knowledge and information are astonishing, and there is not a department of the Government regarding all the details and management of which he is not much better informed and more capable than the Minister at the head of it.'

* Greville noted on 2 November 1857, when the recapture of Delhi was telegraphed, 'All the advantages of the electric telegraphy are dearly paid for by the agonies of suspense which are caused by the long intervals between the arrival of general facts and of their particular details.'

Lord Clarendon, Greville noted on 19 October, was of much the same opinion. According to the Foreign Minister,

> the manner in which the Queen in her own name, but under the inspiration of the Prince, exercised her functions, was exceedingly good, and well became her position and was exceedingly useful. She held each Minister to the discharge of his duty and his responsibility to her, and constantly desired to be furnished with accurate and detailed information about all important matters, keeping a record of all the reports that were made to her, and constantly referring to them, e.g. she would desire to know what the state of the Navy was, and what ships were in readiness for active service, and generally the state of each, ordering returns to be submitted to her from all the arsenals and dockyards, and again weeks or months afterwards referring to these returns, and desiring to have everything relating to them explained and accounted for, and so throughout every department. In this practice Clarendon told me he had encouraged her strenuously. This is what none of her Predecessors ever did, and it is in fact the act of Albert, who is to all intents and purposes King, only acting entirely in her name. All his views and notions are those of a constitutional Sovereign, and he fulfils the duties of one, and at the same time makes the Crown an entity, and discharges the functions which properly belong to the Sovereign. I told C. that G[ranville] had told me the Prince had upon many occasions rendered the most important services to the Government, and had repeatedly prevented their getting into scrapes of various sorts. He said it was perfectly true, and that he had written some of the ablest papers he had ever read.

The insurrection in India was not yet put down when a financial panic erupted from the contagion of bank failures in the United States. Yet despite the proliferation of bankruptcies and bank closings across Britain, the panoply of the emergency recall of Parliament was as lavish as usual. On 3 December, wearing her crown and a velvet cloak trimmed in ermine, the Queen was escorted to the Lords by the Prince Consort, who then occupied a secondary throne to her left while Victoria read an address prepared by Palmerston's Ministers. On the twelfth, having enacted some stopgap measures, Parliament set itself free without having done anything about reordering the affairs of India, also mentioned in the Queen's Speech, and discussed at length earlier, at Windsor, with Victoria and Albert. By the time that Palmerston sent his draft for a future government of India to them, the Court had adjourned to Osborne for the Christmas season.

At Osborne, too, Albert worked further, no longer with his former enthusiasm, on the preparations for the royal wedding. Aware that Princess Vicky wept often about leaving home, he did not know that the doleful fact was known beyond the Court. Inwardly he wept himself, but he was outwardly optimistic about her brilliant expectations. Early in 1858 he wrote to his stepmother, the Dowager Duchess of Coburg, 'the last year has again brought so much trouble with it that one is glad to leave it behind. The new year begins for us with the separation from a beloved daughter, which will be especially painful to me. I do not, however, let any hint of this be seen, and I rejoice for her in the prospect of a happy future.'

Nearly a year after the marriage the Queen recalled, in a letter of 20 April 1859 to Vicky, 'that last night when we took you to your room, and you cried so much, I said to Papa as we came back "after all, it is like taking a poor lamb to be sacrificed" ... I know that God has willed it so and that these are the trials which we poor women must go through; no father, no man can feel this! Papa never would enter into it all! As in fact he seldom can in my very violent feelings.'

After a festive fortnight of balls and levées, concerts and dinners, the wedding took place at St James's Palace on 25 January 1858. In the first carriage to leave Buckingham Palace were Prince Albert and King Leopold, both in the uniforms of English field marshals, with Princes Bertie and Alfred. The bride would walk in procession between Albert and Leopold as Fritz waited at the altar. After the ceremony, Prince and Princess Frederick – as they now were in Prussian style – proceeded from the chapel, arms linked, while Mendelssohn's Wedding March was played for the first time at an actual marriage.

Following a honeymoon of only two days – even more abbreviated than that of Victoria and Albert – the Court gathered at Windsor, where Frederick William was invested with the Garter. On 1 February, a snowy day, the Prince Consort and his two eldest sons accompanied Vicky, barely seventeen, and her husband to Gravesend, on the south bank of the Thames, from which they were to sail for Germany. Only an hour after they left, the Queen wrote the first of what would be 3,777 letters to her daughter, confessing how 'trying' it was to 'give up' a beloved child. The letters would be full of the trivia of everyday life, and Court gossip; and the Queen also warned her of the 'yoke of a married woman' – the 'sufferings and miseries and plagues – which you must struggle against – and enjoyments etc to give up – constant precautions to take . . . ' But 'with a husband one worships' the married state was a 'foretaste of heaven'. The price, nevertheless, was that she had '9 times for 8 months to bear with those above-named enemies . . . and I own it tried me sorely . . . I think our sex a most unenviable one'. Cautionary words, however, had little impact in Vicky's bedroom, and she was soon pregnant. 'I hope Fritz would not bear for a minute what we poor slaves have to endure', the Queen would write unhappily.

From Albert, who always made an effort to conceal his feelings, would come an agonized letter to Vicky about their farewells at Gravesend. 'My heart', he confessed, 'was very full when yesterday you leaned your forehead on my breast to give free vent to your tears. I am not of a demonstrative nature, and therefore you can hardly know how dear you have always been to me, and what a void you have left behind in my heart: yet not in my heart, for there assuredly you will abide henceforth, as til now you have done, but in my daily life, which is evermore reminding my heart of your absence.'

From the royal yacht, already in Continental waters, the Princess confided to her father, whom she idolized,

> My beloved Papa,
> The pain of parting from you yesterday was greater than I can describe; I thought my heart was going to break when you shut the cabin door and were gone – that cruel moment which I had been dreading even to think of for two years and a half was past – it was more painful than I had ever pictured it to myself.
>
> Yesterday evening I felt weighed down by grief, today though very melancholy I am able to think with more composure of all that has passed – and of all that is to come.
>
> I miss you so dreadfully dear Papa, more than I can say; your dear picture stood near me all night, it was a comfort to me to think that I had even that near me. I meant to have said so much yesterday, but my heart was too full for words. I should have liked to have thanked

you for all that you have done for me, for all your kindness. All your love etc. I shall most earnestly endeavour to deserve. To you, dear Papa, I owe most in this world. I shall never forget the advice it has been my privilege to hear from you at different times, I treasure your words up in my heart, they will have with God's help an influence on the whole of my life. You know dear Papa, how entirely you possess the deep confidence, reverence and affection of your child, who is proud to call herself such; and I may say of my husband too; and we feel secure and happy in the thought that you will never refuse us your precious advice, in anxious moments.

I feel that writing to you does me good, dear Papa, I feel that I am speaking to you, and though the feeling that I cannot see you or hear your dear voice in return makes the tears rise to my eyes, yet I am thankful that this is left to me. Goodbye, dearest Papa – I must end. Your most dutiful and affectionate daughter, Victoria

Duke Ernest would write coldly that 'with the Princess [gone] ... my brother lost also a pedagogic occupation which had become dear to him, and which had exercised an extremely refreshing influence on his mind'. Ernest was without any perspective to measure the deprivation, which to Albert, who had managed his daughter's destiny, was a bereavement. For that, and other reasons farther into the year, the Prince began to feel that his life was over.

XVI

Royal Enterprises, Ltd

1858–1860

IN THE EARLY weeks of 1858, at the time of the royal wedding, the
Prince Consort's status under the Crown had stabilized at a very
high level. The monarchy had become the corporate personality of
Victoria and Albert, and with rare, and increasingly fewer, exceptions,
maintained itself above politics. Although common law granted a wife
the style and status of the husband, and the Queen had long battled for
the gender equivalent for a husband in the Prince's case, both had
settled for the 'Consort' title, and found it easily accepted. Albert
recognized that whatever titular glory he lacked was more than balanced
by his actual power. The xenophobia that had reared up as recently as
the Crimean War was gone, and the succession nightmares of past
reigns were, to the subjects of the sovereign, non-existent through the
insurance of four princes of the blood royal. George Mifflin Dallas, the
American Minister, would write to Washington that the Queen was
preparing a bill to make Albert King Consort, but that rumour lacked
credibility. He had a far more substantial role, and influence, and title,
than the husband of a later queen and great-great-grandson of Victoria,
would ever have.

That the one authentically Albertine royal sibling in the next gen-
eration could never reign in Britain was hardly realized outside the
Royal Household. In the first month of the new year she was gone.
Hardly had Princess Vicky left for Berlin before both Victoria and
Albert recognized that her marriage would be to both a self-inflicted
wound. A letter from the Queen to go to Vicky by messenger on 17

February 1858 noted at the start that it would contain matter 'which I do not wish to confide to the post'. Victoria had already been scolded by Albert for quoting him about the Prussian royal family in a letter which had gone by ordinary mail – 'an imprudent remark to go by the post', he warned, opening up vistas of spies and informers that were the natural condition of life in the militarist state to which they had consigned their daughter for her lifetime.

More self-inflicted pain followed on the heels of Vicky's departure. Arrangements were under way for Prince Alfred to go to sea on the *Euryalus*, to learn a midshipman's life. Born on 6 August 1844, he was well short of fourteen, but would not be needed unless something happened to his uncle in Coburg or to his elder brother. Prince Albert Edward, sixteen, desperately wanted to evade the navy, and requested learning the rudiments of officerdom in the army, although he knew he could not actively serve. He was promised some military experience, but Coburg-style education had to come first – and his confirmation.

Victoria had already urged upon Bertie the necessity of his becoming the first Albertine king. 'You may well join us', she wrote to him on his father's previous birthday, 'in thanking God for joining to us all your dearest, perfect Father ... *None* of you [his offspring] can *ever* be proud enough of being the *child* of SUCH a Father who has not his *equal* in this world – so great, so good, so faultless. Try, all of you, to follow in his footsteps and don't be discouraged, for to be *really* in everything like him *none* of you, I am sure, will ever be. Try, therefore, to be like him in *some* points, and you will have *acquired a great deal*.'

It would not have been easy for any son to bestow affection and obedience on a father so beatified, and the fault here was Victoria's own, although Albert contributed by raising expectations that were beyond Bertie's capabilities. Even at Osborne and Balmoral, his lessons continued unslackened, and when his father entertained learned eminences, Bertie was brought forward to acquire, if only by osmosis, something from their conversation. And as Vicky was receding from life in the family orbit, Bertie was being prepared not only for confirmation but life apart – with tutors and managers – in White Lodge, Richmond Park, refurbished for him now that its occupant, George III's last surviving child, the Duchess of Gloucester, had died. Vicky had gone her own way after confirmation; it was now Bertie's destiny.

While he recoiled from Albert's carefully planned grooming, Victoria and Vicky were congratulating each other on the good fortune of having the Prince Consort for husband and father. But Vicky was almost a clone of her father – an unfortunate piece of ill-luck for a married woman in Prussia. 'You know, my dearest,' the Queen would write to her, 'that I can never admit any other wife can be as happy as I am – so I can admit no comparison for I maintain that Papa is unlike anyone who lives or ever lived and will live.' And Vicky would respond, 'I do not like to write all the foolish, mischievous things that are said and done [in Berlin]. I wish Papa could just be here for a little, he would see the whole thing in a moment.' To her father she expressed hope that she might surround Fritz and herself 'with good and useful people', for 'scales have fallen from my eyes on so many subjects'. She longed for a visit from him, to talk over 'a store of things'. She trembled to 'think of the awful scrapes I might get not only myself but my husband and mother-in-law into, if I had not your advice, dearest Papa...'

From Osborne on 4 March, while Victoria, who was seldom cold, shivered as a late winter wind off the Channel battered the windows and kept temperatures indoors to fifty, Albert posted Vicky's translation of the Prussian political monograph to Palmerston, who had just relinquished Downing Street to Derby's minority ministry. Now that he had 'a moment's leisure', the Prince wrote, there might be opportunity to read the 'peculiarly interesting' work. When it came to Vicky, Albert was a very proud Papa.

At Osborne and then Windsor, Bertie lacked no advice as the confirmation date approached. Examined by the Dean of Windsor in St George's Chapel on 31 March, the day before, he stolidly responded, and Albert was pleased, so he wrote to Stockmar, that the Dean 'prolonged' the questioning for 'a full hour'. Other than for its public demonstration of fidelity to the official faith, the ceremony remained meaningless for Albert. 'Love' for the God of clerical sermons, he told Victoria, who later (7 February 1862) told Vicky, was 'most preposterous'. For him 'the love for God was quite of a different kind – it was the trust and confidence in and adoration of a great, incomprehensible spirit'.

Following the post-confirmation reward of a fortnight's holiday with his tutor in Ireland, the Prince of Wales was established at White Lodge with three companions in their twenties, all 'distinguished' and 'moral' and 'accomplished'. Two had won Victoria Crosses in the Crimea. They would rotate monthly residence with Bertie, based upon a confidential memorandum from Albert about instructing his son in 'Appearance, Deportment and Dress', 'Manners and Conduct towards Others', and 'The Power to Acquit Himself Creditably in Conversation, or whatever May Be the Occupation of Society'. Bertie was to eschew gossip, cards and billiards, and devote some of his leisure time to music and the fine arts. In dress he was to avoid 'the frivolity and foolish vanity of dandyism'. In manners the primary attribute would be 'the absence of selfishness'. And he was to be 'scrupulously courteous, attentive, punctual . . .'

Albert was a model of efficiency. If high-minded rules and clockwork organization could transform the Prince of Wales into what a king should be, the result would have pleased Plato. And Albert, despite the slings and arrows of nearly two decades in public life, remained high-minded. When his brother offered to send him some writings by Machiavelli, Albert replied (10 July 1858) that he would read them but expected to dislike them. 'He who attacks the eternal laws of morality or who divides them, some for the subject, some for the state, and some for personal use, is the enemy of God and mankind and I should like to kill him.'

In Vienna, Prince Metternich, a disciple of Machiavelli now in enforced retirement, was discussing Albertine politics with Baron Vitzthum of Saxony, the ambassador observing that Albert had questioned whether Napoleon III could 'owe his crown at once to hereditary succession and universal suffrage. This contradiction is bound to be the ruin, I don't say of himself personally – perhaps he is destined to die an Emperor in his bed – but of his system, his dynasty. He has built nothing lasting; he is only a meteor – no fixed star.' Albert, said Metternich, had learned how to exploit for the monarchy the English system of an unwritten constitution, which he compared to a game of whist. 'The Crown's hand', he conceded, 'has not been played so well for a long time as it has been of late years.'

Vitzthum would visit Albert on a confidential matter and see his political pragmatism in action. The Saxon envoy had received a telegram from his sovereign asking whether the Queen could receive a visit from Prince George. 'Tell me honestly', Albert asked, 'what brings

Prince George here? Does he wish to see us or London?' Vitzthum attempted ambiguity, but Albert lacked little information, and rang for a calendar. He understood, and the Minister confirmed, that the Prince wanted private background information about the Portuguese Infanta before he agreed to an arranged marriage. (There was a Coburg connection. The Princess's father was Albert's cousin.)

'Then he will be in Paris at the end of March? On the 2nd of April is the confirmation of the Prince of Wales.* It is no use inviting a Roman Catholic Prince to that. On the 9th, you say, the Brazil steamer goes to Lisbon. That suits admirably. Please telegraph that we should be glad to welcome the Prince at Windsor from the 5th to the 9th of April...'

'All was, therefore, practically settled in three minutes. The way and manner of doing it was characteristic of the Queen's husband. He was completely master of the house, however much he concealed it from the public.'

At the Queen's dinner table nothing would be said to embarrass Prince George. Instead, Victoria and Albert offered the information desired – largely about any possible hereditary problems – to Vitzthum, and the Minister spoke privately to the Prince. 'We like the Prince extremely', said the Queen, an opinion that no doubt was transmitted to Portugal, 'and his noble bearing will certainly not fail to create an equally good impression in Lisbon'.

On the fourth morning after the departure of the Baron and Prince from Southampton on 9 April 1858, the steamer *en route* to Brazil docked in Lisbon harbour. The betrothal followed on the 17th.

Albert's efficiency, intellectuality and conscientiousness had fixed English attitudes toward him at the level of grudging respect. He had also earned esteem, but having never embraced the values of the English gentleman, that seemed denied him. The Royal Literary Fund dinner in the month of Prince George's visit was a case in point. Albert had chaired the event in the past, and was now a distinguished guest. The cause – to grant assistance to needy authors – was one he appreciated, and he looked forward to such literary occasions. Another place was set for a distinguished visiting author, Ivan Turgenev, who described the event in a St Petersburg paper.

---

* The Baron's memory was off by a day.

The once and future Prime Minister, Viscount Palmerston, presided in dignified fashion, proposing, at the start, the Queen's health, which was greeted by literally thumping cheers, as the attendees enthusiastically banged their plates and cutlery. Palmerston's address paid the expected tribute to literature, and noted that Victoria enjoyed reading books – a remark greeted by further cheers from an audience that, except for Albert, did not know that she seldom read a book, but had Albert or one of her ladies-in-waiting read to her. When Palmerston then referred to the Prince Consort, observing that no one could converse with him without having his mind improved as a result, the statement, meant in genuine regard, was received in utter silence. The Russian novelist took that as a sign of Albert's unpopularity, but it was more an indication of unease with his alien sensibility.

Despite Albert's foreign profile at home, he was seldom seen across the Channel except for rare family visits to Germany and the series of diplomatic journeys to France that would culminate with yet another, to Cherbourg, in August. When the Prince had last met with Napoleon III, General Aimable Jean Jacques Pelessier, who had stormed the fortress of the Malakoff at Sevastopol, was still in the Crimea. Since a role recognizing his reputation had to be found for him in peace, the Emperor had decided to impress London by making him ambassador there. The week after the Saxon ambassador left England for Portugal with his princely charge, Lord Malmesbury, again Foreign Minister under the Earl of Derby, escorted the short, plump Pelessier, who lacked all the social graces but was now ennobled as the duc de Malakoff, for an introductory audience with the Queen. 'He had never seen Prince Albert', Malmesbury noted in his diary for 16 April, 'and, as the Queen did not present him, he evidently took him for some lord-in-waiting, for he turned his back upon him whilst talking to the Queen. Suddenly it seemed to occur to him who the Prince was, for he turned towards him and exclaimed' "*Comment! c'est vous!*" and made a low bow. The Queen and Prince were much amused.'

Albert left for Coburg and Berlin immediately after Victoria's birthday in late May. He was inured to long rail journeys – to inspect factories and bases, or to open exhibitions or lay foundation stones – but May 1858 saw his first rail travel almost to the city of Coburg itself, as he changed trains at Bamberg for a special carriage to Lichtenfels, bringing with him a larger retinue than accompanied his day-trips in

England. Colonel Ponsonby and Dr Becker – his English and German secretaries, a courier, a valet, and three servants made the trip, which Albert promised to repeat with Victoria as soon as possible.

In Berlin he found that Vicky, who knew no more than her mother did on her marriage about postponing motherhood, was pregnant. No paragon of bedroom caution herself, the Queen was nevertheless appalled, writing to Vicky from London that it was 'horrid news', but to Vicky's mother-in-law, Crown Princess Augusta, Victoria lied that she was 'very happy'. Chastising Vicky for her professed pride in giving life to an immortal soul, the Queen, in a letter of 15 June which Albert did not see, described 'such moments' as 'our being like a cow or a dog'.

To be in London then, as was necessary for the parliamentary sessions, was to be immersed on the edge of a vast cesspool, which stank even more in sultry summer heat. The Household's month-long stay on the Isle of Wight in July was almost a flight. 'London', she explained to Augusta, 'is very unhealthy on account of the dreadful state of the Thames which smells so frightful that hardly anyone can live nearby.' The day before, the Queen and Prince, with Bertie, had braved the river at Deptford, an open drain now additionally malodorous, to inspect Brunel's still-unfinished *Leviathan*, the world's largest ship. She was 'longing for a rest' from public affairs, she told Augusta. Were it not her duty, she 'should like to retire to the country with my husband and children'. Confessedly, 'everyone has their duty and this of mine is not the hardest!' Albert, she did not add, performed many of the ceremonial aspects of the Crown for her.

Before departing for Cherbourg, Victoria had sent her daughter, who was attached to her Church of England faith, which she found less grim than Prussian Lutheranism, a book by George Combe, a non-believing phrenologist who had died the year before. That Combe had given lectures at Heidelberg only confirmed to Albert that analysis of the contours of the skull to determine a person's dispositions and talents was indeed a science. Albert was open to all advances in science.

Despite his passion for organization and control, in the summer of 1858 matters seemed to be flying apart. He had always experienced difficulty in delegating responsibilities, and now had too many of them. Nothing was done at Court without him, and the weak Derby government consulted him even more than did the fractious Palmerston ministry it succeeded. His red dispatch box went along with him everywhere, and a staff of secretaries and servants. Victoria's demands increased with his absences. She could not finish *Jane Eyre*. He had to read it to her. She attempted in turn to read *Barchester Towers* to Albert but found insufficient romantic interest, she explained to Vicky, to keep going, and disliked the emphasis on clerical characters.

Neither the Queen nor the Prince saw anything positive likely to emerge from the long-scheduled reciprocal visit to the self-aggrandizing Emperor of the French, yet to call it off would further fan anti-English feeling. 'But we are pressed by the Emperor and our Ministers', Albert explained to Ernest on 10 July, 'to go to Cherbourg. As the festivities there, in reality, include a glorification of the army and navy against England, we do not intend to take part in them. We shall leave before they begin and only pay a personal visit.'

The visit became more than that because the government could not be seen as alarmed at a time when Napoleon III was plotting with Prime Minister Cavour of Sardinia to liberate northern Italy from Austrian domination, while sabre-rattling to keep England and Prussia timid and neutral. Ostensibly the French festivities were to open the new rail link between Paris and Cherbourg, the potential military significance of which was obvious. The Emperor was also to unveil a statue to the first Napoleon. Representing their government, Malmesbury and Disraeli were present, Derby being again ill with gout. The Duke of Cambridge and Admiral Lord Lyons represented the military, and thirty MPs the people. To promote Anglo-French friendship, 140 private English yachts crowded Cherbourg harbour as Victoria and Albert steamed across the Channel on 19 August, the Prince reading *Jane Eyre* to the Queen below decks until the low clouds lifted. Toward sunset the skies cleared and turned golden, illuminating the naval fortifications, some still under construction, which gave the scene a more unpleasant look than the Isle of Wight. In the spirit of Osborne, the royal family had brought their eldest children, who did, indeed, sightsee picturesque farmhouses and châteaux, but Napoleon was eager to show off battle-ships and fortresses, and Eugénie contributed a complaint about the hostility of English newspapers. Albert tactfully explained the lack of constraints upon a free Press, which was a bulwark of English liberties.

Despite discussions of furthering the *bonne entente*, Albert noted in his diary, 'I am conscious of a change in the Emperor'. The attempted assassination – by Italians – had reinforced Napoleon's conviction that

Italy had to be united if only to defuse one source of anti-Bonaparte hostility. If that undermined Austria, which clung to its Italian provinces, both Prussia and Russia would be pleased. Albert recognized that England, as a naval power, faced problems with an expansionist Italy. Malta lay within the likely ambitions of Victor Emmanuel and, like Gibraltar, was a non-negotiable base for the Royal Navy in the Mediterranean.

Warm toasts of friendship were exchanged with Napoleon aboard and on shore, and the parting would again be friendly, but now only ostensibly so, with the Emperor assuring France's 'unalterable devotion to the English alliance'. If so, Albert wondered, what was the reason for such formidable and unpacific investment along a coast opposite which was only England? Writing to Stockmar on 21 August 1858, he described Cherbourg as 'a gigantic [military] work that gives one grave reflection'. The visit dramatized disturbing inadequacies at home almost inevitable in a liberal state that armed only in emergencies, and refused to tax itself in order to maintain a constant state of preparedness, or to reform its outmoded administration of the army and navy. England considered itself a first-rate military power, as Cecil Woodham-Smith would put it, 'on the memory of Trafalgar and Waterloo'.

The Queen and Prince returned to Osborne only to prepare to leave again to visit Vicky in a Berlin changing as a result of the mental breakdown of the Prussian king, and his effective replacement in the business of government by Fritz's father, Prince William. Reflecting more and more the conservatism of the Prussian ethos, he no longer seemed an improvement, while Frederick William IV, Albert wrote to Ernest, was a 'ruin' although 'he behaves as a King'. Berlin was, to the Queen, 'sickeningly' hot every day, but there was no allowance for that in the proliferation of parades and reviews in stiff military dress, ostensibly in their honour.

The 26th August, the Prince Consort's thirty-ninth birthday, was celebrated in Potsdam. Victoria gave Albert all the children's birthday letters prepared before they had left Osborne. 'Blessed day!' the Queen wrote in her journal. Both Ernest and Stockmar arrived for the event, and Vicky brought a cake with as many candles on it as years, as was the Prussian custom. The Glienecke Bridge was illuminated, salutes fired, and healths drunk.

'*Der Abscheid sehr schmerzlich*,' Albert noted the next day in his diary – 'the parting [was] very painful'. He kept to himself his anxieties that he might never see Vicky again. The prospect of childbirth was disquieting – she was small and still seventeen – and he was sensing signs of mortality in himself, these apparent to no one but Stockmar, who was not only a father figure but a former physician. His unease predated Cherbourg and Potsdam but it was in Cherbourg, on 12 August, Victoria wrote, that 'While I was dressing, Albert came in, quite pale, with a telegram [from London], saying "My poor Cart is dead, having died quite suddenly."...I turn quite sick now writing about it...I burst into tears. All day long the tears would rush every moment to my eyes.' Isaac Cart, long devoted to Albert's service, 'was the only link my loved one had about him which connected him with his childhood...I cannot think of my dear husband without Cart...We had to choke down our grief all the day.'

Albert's disappointments in the failure of his eldest son to be Albertine were more than balanced by the frustrations of Albert Edward in failing, even, to want to live up to expectations. He had no intellectual interests, and would have preferred the military career his new brother-in-law in Prussia had managed. That the cultures were different was never explained to Bertie, although his father understood, writing to Ernest (22 April 1858) that it was 'to be regretted' that Fritz had 'taken up the game of soldiering'. It was 'not astonishing in a member of his family and a subject of his country. A good feeling lies at the bottom of this inclination, that of a longing for a manly occupation, duty and self-sacrifice, in the service of the state.' Otherwise the Prince had 'absolutely nothing to do and as affairs are at present, I do not know what [else] he should do'.

Prince Frederick William, however, was as old as the combat-tested officers seconded to Bertie, ambitious young men whose careers were being interrupted at Albert's order. Bertie was still half a child, and Albert sought for signs of maturation that would renew hope for the monarchy. Lessons and lectures, concerts and exhibitions bored him, however, as much as they did his escorts, but since his sister was married when hardly past seventeen, he looked forward to his birthday on 9 November, when he expected some further allocation of freedom, and to a promised visit later in the month to Vicky in Berlin. In London, vast Marlborough House was being refurbished to become his London home. Ironically, it had been a private picture gallery.

On 9 November he received a birthday letter from his parents, written by Albert, which ostensibly emancipated him from their authority. He was to have an annual income, to start, of five hundred pounds beyond all necessary household expenses. It further explained that however severe he thought his education had been, its only object had been his growth into a proper heir apparent. His tutor, Frederick Gibbs, was to be replaced by a governor, Colonel – soon General – Robert Bruce. ('Poor Mr. Gibbs', the Queen wrote to Vicky, 'leaves tomorrow. He has failed completely the last year and a half with Bertie.')

Bertie's military aspirations were to be fulfilled by gazetting him a lieutenant-colonel (unattached) without duties. On ceremonial occasions he could wear a uniform. It was an unearned push that he would resent, but the Queen had a morbid fear of mortality, and would confide in Vicky early the next year, 'Oh dear, what would happen if I were to die next winter! One trembles to think of it. It is too awful a contemplation.' The problem as she saw it was Bertie's 'laziness'. Even 'the greatest improvement, I fear, will never make him fit for his position. His only safety – and the country's – is his implicit reliance in everything on dearest Papa, that perfection of human beings!'

Yet Albert Edward resisted any reliance on his father, whose freedom document enjoined the Prince to liberate himself 'from the thralldom of abject dependence' upon servants, and to become 'a good man and a thorough gentleman', goals which he would find at odds with each other. He was 'to do unto men as you would they should do unto you'. And it concluded in true Albertine fashion, 'Life is composed of duties', which were to be performed in a 'punctual and cheerful manner'.

Bertie took the letter to Gerald Wellesley, the Dean of Windsor, thrust it at him, and burst into tears.

On 17 November, three days before the Prince of Wales was to leave with Colonel Bruce and Major Teesdale for Prussia, Albert wrote to Vicky, 'Do not miss any opportunity of urging him to hard work... Unfortunately, he takes no interest in anything but clothes, and again clothes... I am particularly anxious that he should have some mental occupation in Berlin. Perhaps you could let him share in some of yours, lectures, etc...' However, he returned three weeks later recalling happily only a round of parties and balls, an atmosphere in which he thrived. 'Bertie has a remarkable social talent', Albert conceded to Vicky while her brother was still visiting. 'He is lively, quick and sharp when his mind is set on anything, which is seldom . . . But usually his intellect is of no more use than a pistol packed in the bottom of a trunk if one were attacked in the robber-infested Apennines.'

The Apennines were on the Prince Consort's mind as he intended to send Bertie to Italy on his return to study art, archaeology, and the affairs of troubled parts of Europe. He was to keep a journal for Albert's perusal, and it was predictable that both his parents would find it uninspired and error-ridden. 'I am very sorry that you were not pleased with my Journal', Bertie apologized to his father, 'as I took great pains with it, but I see the justice of your remarks and will try to profit by them.' Albert was left with nothing further to admonish, and Bertie would go on into north Italy in 1859 only to encounter war between misnamed Sardinia and Austria, and the expected intervention of France on the side of King Victor Emmanuel, who reigned over Piedmont from Turin. The British warship *Scourge*, sailing from Malta, would evacuate Bertie and his party to Gibraltar, where he confessed – but not to his father – 'plenty of larking', and then to Lisbon, where the king, Pedro V, was a young cousin.

Not ready yet to give up on moulding Bertie into a proper heir apparent, Albert had further plans for him – a summer (1859) stay at the University of Edinburgh to cram for Oxford in the autumn, where he would enter in the undemanding category of 'nobleman'. Only one thing was certain, Albert told his brother on 18 November 1858 – that the Prince of Wales 'is not to be in London during the [social] Season, as long as he is neither fish nor flesh, as the old saying is. It would not be good for him.'

With mortality on his mind, Albert became more searching about religion, reading, in November 1858, Charles Kingsley's *Two Years Ago*, and praising to Vicky its 'insight into the relations between man, his actions, his destiny and God'. The next year he had the Queen appoint Kingsley as one of her chaplains, and arranged to have him tutor Bertie on history. Albert also read *On the Mind*, by Richard Whately, Anglican Archbishop of Dublin, a near-agnostic who minimized theology and emphasized morals; and he was drawn to the religious questioning in Anthony Trollope's *Barchester Towers* and George Eliot's *Adam Bede*. He awaited with some dread the accouchement of Vicky in January, for she had caught her foot in a chair in September in the old Schloss in

Berlin, and fallen hard to the parquet floor. She would not tell 'dearest kindest Mamma' but she did inform her father.

Confiding in her mother was a risky matter in any event, and Stockmar delicately raised the matter of the Queen's attempting to dictate to a married daughter who was in a delicate condition and sensitive position. Albert cautiously raised the issue with Victoria, and it emerged that Stockmar had intervened with the Prince. The Queen was furious, and Albert left the room to avoid a scene certain to be overheard, and to write his response:

> You have again lost your self-control quite unnecessarily. I did not say a word which could wound you, and I did not begin the conversation, but you have followed me about and continued it from room to room. There is no need for me to promise to *trust* you, for it was not a question of trust, but of your fidgety nature, which makes you insist on entering, with feverish eagerness, into details about orders and wishes which, in the case of a Queen, are commands, to whomever they may be given. This is your nature; it is not against Vicky, but it is the same with everyone and has been the cause of much unpleasantness for you. It is the dearest wish of my heart to save you from these and worse consequences, but the only result of my efforts is that I am accused of want of feeling, hard heartedness, injustice, hatred, jealousy, distrust, etc. etc. I do my duty towards you even though it means that life is embittered by 'scenes' when it should be governed by love and harmony. I look upon this with patience as a test which has to be undergone, but you hurt me desperately and at the same time do not help yourself.

Victoria had little idea why, at thirty-nine, Albert looked like a man of sixty. At Balmoral that autumn he seemed paunchy and overweight. His hair had receded, and his sidewhiskers had grown heavier, and he took to wearing a wig on chilly mornings. Her zealous policing of fireplaces added to his miseries, and he confessed to his daughter early on one cold morning, 'Mama will be much hurt when she gets up and finds I have a fire lit.' Yet he loved his work, and knew he was doing his job well, the job he had created for himself. '*Lese recht aufmerksam, und sage wenn irgend ein Fehler da ist!*' he would instruct the Queen about draft memoranda – 'Read carefully, and tell me if there is any fault in this!'

Or '*Ich hab' Dir hier ein Draft gemacht, lese es mal! Ich dachte es wäre recht so*' – 'Here is a draft for you; read it. I should think this will do.'

Her 'beloved and perfect Albert', the Queen wrote to Leopold, forgetting her occasional rages at her husband, 'had raised monarchy to the *highest* pinnacle of respect, and rendered it popular beyond what it *ever* was in this country'. More wishful thinking than reality, it was nevertheless a reflection of the upward swing of the pendulum of popular appeal to which a foreign war, a colonial insurrection and a dynastic marriage had contributed.

The early winter was a time of waiting for news from Berlin, which came on the morning of 27 January 1859, when a telegram arrived that the Princess Royal 'had been for some time indisposed'. That afternoon came the news that 'the young Prince' had been born, and toasts were drunk across England as well as Prussia.

No one in England sensed a catastrophe. Vicky's pregnancy had been difficult, and in her final months, when, barely eighteen and away from home, the Princess was sunk in gloom, the Queen sent her own midwife, Mrs Innocent, to restore some confidence and to be available if labour came unexpectedly early. It did, but the doctors in attendance failed to get an urgent message to Professor Eduard Martin in Berlin, who was on call, about the prolonged, exhausting labour that began in the first hours of 26 January and did not end until the next day. By the time that Martin arrived, mother and child appeared to be dying.

It was a breech birth; Vicky was in great agony. To the distress of the Court physicians, Martin applied chloroform. Both mother and infant came through the ordeal, but only the next day did Mrs Innocent notice the state of the baby's left arm, which had been torn loose from its socket during the bungled delivery. Although the doctors assured Vicky that the damage was temporary, Prince Frederick William Albert Victor (in 1888 he would become Wilhelm II) would have a withered arm, a defect that would warp his personality. Since he was immediately known as William, and inevitably Willy, to avoid confusion with his father and with the King, Albert speculated to Fritz about what posterity 'will attach to his name'. He hoped for 'the Great' – as 'there is none with this designation'.

Victoria and Albert could not attend the christening. Parliament was to open with the Queen's Speech on 3 February 1859. Reports from France suggested an imminent war with Austria to assist Italian unification, and, if Prussia came to Austria's aid, an attempt to occupy its Rhenish provinces. The Speech appealed for 'preservation of the general peace', but included the Cabinet's request for large expenditures to put the navy entirely under steam. Albert noted his apprehensions in his diary; Victoria, writing to Leopold in Brussels, predicted that a Prussian war would cost Napoleon his crown.

On 9 February, Albert visited the new public school named for the late Duke, Wellington College, to present the school with a gift of books for its library. Although its charter permitted admission of boys from all walks of life, it was intended particularly for needy sons of army officers who had died in the line of duty. Albert was chairman of the governing board and had, characteristically, designed the school uniform, which E.F. Benson, son of the young first headmaster, E.W. Benson, claimed, 'remarkably resembled that of the porters and ticket-collectors of the Southern Railway – then the Reading–Reigate line – on which Wellington College was situated. It gave rise to little confusions.' (The Earl of Derby once gave the outward half of his return ticket to a student.)

The fervidly High Church headmaster believed in three Chapel services a day to improve his boys, as well as a daily Bible-study class, and permitted only devotional books to be borrowed from the library on Sundays, prompting the Prince to ask Benson 'whether there may not be excessive employment in Religious Exercise in the present system of the College'. Benson replied that he thought not.

Libraries, although not of the Bensonian variety, meant much to Albert, who had just built out of his personal funds a library at Aldershot for the use of young officers, with its emphasis upon military history and technology. Readiness had become an obsession. He worried that Prussia, and possibly Coburg and Gotha, would be drawn in. 'The Emperor Napoleon', Albert wrote to his brother the next day, 'appears bent on producing the storm, and much blood will flow, amongst which a great deal of noble German blood. When, and how, we here are to be drawn into the vortex, I am unable to calculate. But, that we shall not be able to escape it in the long run, this I consider certain.'

The German states, Albert advised Ernest early in March, when Austria was proposing some withdrawals from Italy in the interest of peace, should do nothing warlike unless the Emperor attacked the Rhine. In the end it was not Napoleon, despite his seeking war, who was the aggressor, nor even ambitious Sardinia. Determined to rescue its position through a pre-emptive strike, Austria made the first move. Predicting it in his weekly letter to King Leopold on 19 April, Albert wrote, 'The Austrians seem bent on beginning the war, no doubt hoping to strike a decisive blow before the French can appear upon the field – a very hazardous venture, and one the issue of which is scarcely to be brought within the rules of probability. Here it will turn public opinion at a stroke against Austria and in favour of Sardinia.'

A foreshadowing of the imperial tragedy of 1914, Austria issued an ultimatum to King Victor Emmanuel at Turin demanding the disarmament of his troops. An impossible condition, and intended to be so, it was rejected, and the Piedmont was invaded. As expected, France mobilized against Austria, and Prussia mobilized against France, but only France entered the war. Prince William of Prussia, as Regent, used the emergency as an excuse to extend conscription; to increase the regular army, reducing the influence of the *Landwehr* (citizen army – an equivalent to the British Territorials); and to militarize every possible aspect of government. Albert's dreams of a constitutional Prussia were ending hardly a year after Vicky's marriage.

Although the Prince's first thoughts were of his daughter, he was overwhelmed by other concerns. 'My greatest of all anxieties', the Queen wrote to Vicky, 'is that dearest Papa works too hard, wears himself out by all he does. It makes me often miserable. If it were not for Osborne and Balmoral and then again at Windsor at Easter – I don't know what we would do . . .' She had become more activist as a result of the Crimea and the Mutiny, and – internally – the Cabinet instability that seemed now chronic. Yet regardless of where the Court relocated, Albert brought worries with him that went beyond the red dispatch boxes. Not only overwork was taxing his health.

There was a single bright day that spring in which the ego he was forced by his role to submerge was permitted a brief and rewarding exposure. Having opened in the Queen's name hundreds of events and edifices, on 2 May, at the broad estuary of the Tamar which separates Devon from Cornwall, the Prince formally opened the Royal Albert Bridge, a long arc that was centrepiece of the new Cornwall Railway, which required in its sixty-mile stretch seven tunnels and forty-three viaducts. Suspension cables from a mid-river pier supported on either side spans of 455 feet that represented nearly half of the bridge's 2240-foot length. Fifteen minutes after noon, booming cannon announced

Albert being greeted as he opens the Cornwall Railway's Albert Viaduct, 2 May, 1859.
(Illustrated London News)

the arrival of the royal train on the Plymouth side of the approaches. A battery on the Saltash shore fired a second salute as the train proceeded westward into Cornwall. There his Royal Highness alighted and, as was his practice, minutely inspected the bridge while crowds on both sides cheered.

The builder, Isambard Kingdom Brunel, his friend of Crystal Palace days, only fifty-three, was dying of kidney failure, and unable to share the acclaim. A few days later, lying in a couch placed on a carriage truck, he crossed his last bridge. He died of a stroke on 15 September 1859, ten days after he staggered away from a final look at his *Great Eastern* – the renamed *Leviathan* – which was about to sail on its maiden voyage, to Holyhead on the Welsh shore of the Irish Sea. No one had better epitomized Victorian-era engineering genius.

There would be other Albert Bridges, the one most associated with the Prince's name the neo-Gothic span of 1874 opened by the Queen. Inspired, perhaps, by ships' masts in the Thames, it would link Chelsea and Battersea in the western reaches of London.

Victoria would write to the Princess Royal that 'poor dear Papa' was 'very much fagged' yet would have to make the early morning journey and return 'the same night at one'. She did not accompany him. On 2 May as Albert clattered westward to Cornwall, the Queen wrote a long response to the eighty-fourth letter written to her by the unhappy and lonely Vicky. It did not help that Victoria assured her daughter that Papa could not 'enter into Fritz's ecstasy' about the infant Willy. Albert only felt warmly toward infants, she claimed, 'after a certain age if they are nice'. The Queen's own distaste (she considered babies little more than frogs and 'frightful when undressed') seemed deflected on to the warmer parent.

The reported death of the universal German genius Alexander von Humboldt, Victoria added, 'has deeply, deeply grieved us' – but very soon after, Humboldt's letters to writer and diplomat Karl Varnhagen von Ense (who had died the year before) were published, including one of 27 February 1847 in which he quoted Albert as telling him, on their meeting at Stolzenfels, 'I know you feel great compassion for the Poles under the Russian sceptre; but I am sorry to say, the Poles are as little deserving of our sympathy as the Irish.' He was, Humboldt explained to Varnhagen, 'severe only to the mighty ones of the earth, and this man impressed me very uncomfortably . . .' Among other lapses, Albert had read, in Humboldt's *Kosmos*, the metaphorical 'star-carpet' as 'star-terraces'. With Prussian snobbery, Varnhagen was told that it was 'a Coburg variation from my text, and *quite English* from Windsor, where there are nothing but Terraces'. To Humboldt, whose scientific writings the Prince (a former provincial) had praised, perhaps overly much, he was only 'the handsome husband of the Queen'. When the letters appeared in an English translation in 1860, Albert was briefly embarrassed. Offhand confidences had returned to haunt him before. Still, he dismissed the matter to Vicky as of no consequence, 'for what does one not write or say to his intimate friends under the impulse of the moment?'

In subsequent letters to her daughter, Victoria distracted the Princess Royal from self-pity by employing her to shop among eligible Protestant princesses for a bride for Bertie, as the Queen herself was exploring possible husbands for Alice, for a betrothal following her confirmation. Unable to bring the infant Prince Willy to visit – Prussian doctors ruled against it – Vicky, as soon as permitted, paid an emotional visit to Osborne late in May. Because of the troubled European situation, Victoria and Albert had to put off a return visit to see their first grandchild until the next year. The day before Vicky's arrival, 20 May 1859, the Austrians began paying for their arrogance with a defeat at Montebello. Further disasters followed at Magenta on 4 June and Solferino on 24 June. A revolt in Florence created what would become a predictable Italian solution – its puppet duke changed sides. 'All Italy is now up', Lord Malmesbury wrote from the Foreign Office. Seeing that, the unpredictable Napoleon III concluded a separate peace with Austria at Villafranca on July 8, having extracted what he wanted from the war.

Albert's cousin Alexander Mensdorff-Pouilly, an Austrian cavalry general on the scorching plains of Solferino, wrote to Ernest bitterly of the administrative incompetence of his side, which had snatched defeat from the jaws of victory. 'May the manes of the many fallen', he fulminated, 'sometimes appear in the dreams, and disturb the night's rest, of those who are meanwhile sitting comfortably at their writing desks, and laying political addle[d] eggs'.

In both peace and war the Emperor had deceived Albert, who broke off all attempts at friendly relations. Early that summer, however, the minority Derby ministry collapsed and the francophile Palmerston was back, his dream of a unified Italy apparently realized. Yet to the Prime Minister's disappointment, the Villafranca terms excluded Venetia and reinstalled Austrian puppet regimes in Modena and Tuscany. Despite the expanse of Austria's sprawling and multilingual European domains, the internally weak empire, like Ottoman Turkey, had to be propped up as a bulwark to Russian expansion, Prussian ambitions, and French designs. 'Germany ought to be heartily glad of it', Albert wrote acidly to his brother, 'and would be so, if she herself had contributed something toward this result'. What was saved for Austria, the Prince implied, was some role in the balance of Continental power. England's interest, at least, was to prevent any nation from dominating Europe. 'Prussia's situation', he continued, 'is excessively disagreeable and dishonourable. Palmerston is furious that his victim has escaped him, and his bosom friend has led him by the nose.'

To Palmerston, Albert drafted an ironic note for Victoria to copy in her own hand – that 'She is glad to be relieved by the happy news of the concluded Peace'. Feeling deceived by Napoleon, Palmerston protested to the French, sending a copy to the Queen, and again Albert drafted a tart message to the Prime Minister for Victoria's signature:

The Queen returns to Lord Palmerston the copy of his letter ... The effect of placing Austria in an Italian confederation will certainly be to legalise that influence for the future, the supposed illegal exercise of which was put forward as one of the conditions of peace bought by much blood and the loss of a rich province by Austria. We did not protest against the war and Lord Palmerston personally wished France success in it; we can hardly now protest against the peace, and Lord Palmerston will, the Queen is sure, see the disadvantage which would accrue to this country should he make it appear as if to persecute Austria was a personal object with the first minister of the Crown.

The Queen is less disappointed with the peace than Lord Palmerston appears to be, as she never could share his sanguine hopes that the '*coup d'état*' and the 'Empire' could be made subservient to the establishment of independent nationalities and the diffusion of liberty and constitutional government on the Continent. The Emperor follows the dictates of his personal interests and is ready to play the highest stakes for them, himself entirely uncontrolled in his actions; we are cautious, bound by considerations of constitutional responsibility, morality, legality, etc. – our attempts therefore to use him for our views must prove a failure (as the Russian peace has shown before) and exposes us rather to be made his dupes ...

Although royal impatience with Palmerston had returned, both Prince and Prime Minister would again mellow – but not before the affair of the new Foreign Office building. During the Derby interregnum, Sir Gilbert Scott, Albert's choice as architect, had been commissioned to design the edifice, and did so in the neo-Gothic style admired by the Prince. Despite Albert's patronage, and the advanced state of the plans, Palmerston vetoed them in favour of Regency neo-classicism, the style fashionable when he first came into the government. In the Commons, without mentioning Albert, he railed against the 'hideous Gothic structure' likely to be confused with a European cathedral. Forced to give way, but not give up on his concept, Scott took his design to the directors of the Midland Railway, friends of Albert's since Crystal Palace days, who adapted it for the St Pancras Railway Station, now considered a jewel of mid-Victorian architecture.

Despite the Queen's many messages to Palmerston and to ministers, all in what was clearly her own voice as they had heard it in many audiences, they knew that Albert was a superb mimic and her signature was often a convenient fiction. In return they often wrote directly to Albert, implying that their confidential letters to him were in effect to her informal private secretary. Reports of Cabinet meetings usually went directly to Albert rather than to the Queen. The increase in military readiness was also seen as accomplished under pressure from Albert. Although Panmure was supportive as Minister for War, Gladstone as Chancellor of the Exchequer was reluctant to part with an extra penny. Under Albert's pressure, a Volunteer Defence Force, first proposed by the Prince during the Crimean crisis, was funded by Parliament, and Victoria, now wary of her former friend across the Channel, was delighted. 'Fritz would have been surprised', she wrote to Vicky, 'to see 18,000 volunteers marching at Aldershot like the finest troops, many of the best-educated people, peers, gentry, [and] artists in the ranks.'

For Albert there was, now, almost always a physical price. After the heat of manœuvres, the Queen wrote to Vicky from Osborne, on 24 August 1859, 'Monday and yesterday at Aldershot and here were really fearful. Poor dear Papa had one of his stomach attacks on Monday, which made him look fearfully ill, but he remained in the field in that broiling sun the whole time and said he was all the better for it. He is however not quite right yet. He is so fagged and worked...' She blamed, without identification, since Vicky would understand the sly references to Palmerston and Russell, 'our 2 Italian Masters'. But Albert's recurrent 'stomach attacks' had nothing to do with European politics. For several days at Osborne he could keep down only milk and water, and fainted while attempting to dress. Rudolph Löhlein was alarmed; Albert attributed his weakness and subsequent 'malaise' – his description to Vicky – to 'worry about political affairs'.

On the evening of 29 August, three days after Albert's fortieth birthday, the Court left for Balmoral. From there he was to go on the fourteenth to the annual meeting of the British Association for the Advancement of Science at Aberdeen. A day and night *en route* were to be spent in Edinburgh, largely to consult with the Prince of Wales's frustrated tutors. (They spoke highly of him, of course.) Albert had been preparing his address to the Association for weeks, intending to make a major statement. At the close of the conference on 22 September many delegates were to be the Queen's guests at a Highland fête.

The royal railway journey to Edinburgh was his first by sleeping-car, an advance in travel technology. Albert had a specially designed carriage built at his and Victoria's expense. By 1859 their journey to Scotland was a precise operation. The line and stations were kept clear of other trains half an hour before the royal special was due, and all traffic in its vicinity stopped until the pilot locomotive following the train had passed. At stations where it was scheduled to stop, the public – according to a regulation meant largely for daylight hours – had to remain behind barriers, to prevent crowds from thronging near the halted carriages. At Edinburgh the train was shunted to a secondary line that would take the party to Braemar, where coaches waited to transport the royal family and suite to Balmoral. For the others the trip remained as exhausting as ever. There was only one sleeping car.

'I read thick volumes, write, perspire and tear what I have written into shreds', Albert claimed to Vicky before leaving for Scotland. *Punch* had already published a facetious 'Sights worth seeing in the metropolis' column which included 'Albert's night light. It could be seen without charge, when his Royal Highness is going to bed, by looking at Buckingham Palace . . . any night between the hours of eleven and six the next morning'. Looking from St James's Park it was 'on the third story, in the thirteenth and fourteenth windows, counting from the tail of the Duke of Wellington's statue'. The Prince's light, however, was often a reading lamp, which he used late at night and in the early post-dawn bleakness. He was making up for the hours snatched by ceremony.

Albert would be away from the Queen in Edinburgh only two days, which Victoria occupied in his absence, in crisp, sunny weather, with ghillies and her ladies in ascending Morven, and then Lochnagar, but to her uncle Leopold she bemoaned, in a letter, feeling 'so lost without him'.

As the Association's president for the year, Albert spoke to an audience of 2,500 for nearly an hour, accepting the honour because 'I felt that I could, from the peculiar position in which Providence has placed me in this country, appear as the representative of that large public, which profits by and admires your exertions, but is unable actively to join them.' Whatever the meanness of spirit he had encountered so recently and posthumously from Alexander von Humboldt, he introduced his name as the example of the need for science and government to work together, and for governments to heed the counsel of scientists. Humboldt's 'personal influence with the Courts and Government of most countries in Europe', Albert observed, 'enabled him to plead the cause of Science in a manner which made it more difficult for them to refuse than grant what he requested'.

The Prince sought more statesmen of Science, and also praised the Association for its encouragement of scientific interdisciplinarity by making it possible for investigators in any area to take part in discussions, learn of relevant ideas and problems, and meet their 'brethren'. Science, he hoped, would be less a province of pedants 'jealously guarding the mysteries of their profession'.

Albert was not only addressing a cause, and an audience, in which he had a genuine interest: he was shaping the modern monarchy. In letters to Ernest, who was more a sounding board than a sincere listener, and believed that people needed, for their own good, a proper dose of authoritarianism, Albert prophesied that European monarchies would either mesh into democratic systems, or disappear. As he watched the political and constitutional powers of the monarchy irreversibly wane, he redesigned its role on the traditional concern of the Crown for the well-being of the people. Without that commitment, the monarchy's relevance as national symbol would vanish. It was not enough, he saw, to cut ribbons and lay foundation stones and be titular patron of charities. Relevance meant responsibility, and he was wearing himself out at making the democratic monarchy meaningful.

On the twenty-second, two hundred scientists came to Balmoral for the afternoon to watch Highland games, unfortunately amid showers alternating with sunshine. After their departure the family had two more weeks in Scotland, disturbed by news of colonial setbacks in China that sent the Minister in Residence, Lord Elgin, twice back to London for Cabinet meetings. The third of the 'opium wars', it was ostensibly to defend the opening of trade, and there were neither scientists nor philosophers to excoriate opium's immoralities. To Britain, which had to fight off the angry Chinese with heavy French assistance, Victoria expressed the prevailing mood when she worried that 'in Eastern Asia[, France] will be looked on as the stronger Power'.

By mid-October the royal family was back at Windsor, where Albert, unable to conceal what he described as a severe chill (and there had been early frost), took to his bed. 'I hope by tomorrow or the next day', the Queen wrote to Vicky, 'he will be nearly his dear self again. Though of no real consequence whatever, it was the severest and most obstinate attack I ever saw him have, the more annoying as it was accompanied by violent spasms of pain; which he had both on Saturday and yesterday for two hours; he had to go to bed at three on Saturday, remained in bed all day yesterday till ten o'clock when he got up for an hour and a half and thank God today (*unberufen, unberufen**) – there has been no return of pain . . . But it has been such an unusual thing to see him in bed (never except for the measles) and naturally cast such a gloom over us all, but it seems as if everything were turned upside down when dear Papa is not able to go about.'

Stockmar knew of Albert's stomach pains; on a visit to Coburg the year before, the Prince had what he described in a letter to Victoria as 'headache and general *malaise*', and his usual cramps. 'I have eaten nothing all the day', he added, attempting to make light of the problem, 'to rob my stomach of the shadow of a pretext for behaving ill'. To the Baron he wrote, on 3 November 1859, claiming as his reason the need to damp down any exaggerated reports, that he was 'rallying from a gastric attack, under which I have been suffering for the last fourteen days, and which kept me two days in bed . . . The only new symptom I had was a violent cramp at the pit of the stomach, which lasted very sharply for two hours at noon, several days running . . . I am able today to move about the house.'

The Queen had characterized the return of Albert's ailment to Vicky as 'his old enemy'. An erstwhile physician himself, Stockmar did not dismiss the 'old enemy' that easily – and Victoria may have revealed less than she feared so as not to alarm the Princess Royal. Shaking off the apathy about responding to letters that had been exasperating Victoria for years, the elderly, rheumatic Stockmar wrote to Albert that the description of his illness 'has disquieted me, and made me very sad'. Among its causes, he suggested, apparently hoping that nothing worse than an ulcer was involved, were the physical and mental pressures upon the Prince, but he saw little way that Albert could avoid 'all disturbing agencies, and in everything he does be governed by prophylactic rules: for under certain circumstances it is possible for the physician to *prevent*, but under all it is difficult to *cure*'.

* Touch wood! Touch wood!

On 8 December, answering Stockmar, Albert wrote from Osborne of the irony of English suspicions of France. 'Throughout the country people think of nothing but measures of protection against our Ally; Volunteer Corps are being formed in all the towns. The lawyers of the Temple go through regular drill. Lords Spencer, Abercorn, Elcho, &c., are put through their paces in Westminster Hall by gaslight in the same rank and file with shopkeepers.' He also added that his stomach was 'decidedly *not* better'.

Osborne was choked with snow in December, but it was there that the family – without Prince Alfred, whose ship was at Corfu – celebrated Christmas. On the last day of the old year Albert penned another memorandum to himself for the record, venting more anger at Palmerston for failing to keep English interests at the top of his priorities. 'All his old tricks of 1848 and the previous period are revived again', he wrote. Having Lord John Russell in the Foreign Office only made matters worse, as his 'inefficiency...love for Italy and fear of Lord Palmerston makes him a ready tool and convenient ally; he tries to carry on a policy of revenge against Austria and to bind us to the Emperor Napoleon more than ever, regardless of all the interests of England or Europe, and if impeded by the Cabinet or Queen he is violent and overbearing, and if this be of no avail, [Palmerston] cheats and tricks'. He had even returned to having 'pamphlets written against me and the 'Coburg Influence' in order to bear down all opposition...'

It would be Louis Napoleon himself who would bring the Crown and the Cabinet together by coercing King Victor Emmanuel to cede to France, in return for past and future military assistance against Austria and the Papal States, the provinces of Nice and Savoy. The Emperor's appetite clearly remained unsatisfied, and ministerial passivity would not sit well with Parliament or the public.

Among Albert's New Year letters was one to Stockmar, reporting on the completion of a rail link from Cologne to Mayence (now Mainz), which would make it possible to travel from London to Coburg in thirty-one hours. The Prince hoped that meant he could see Stockmar again. 'We are all quite well,' he added, 'all except my stomach, which is in a state truly pitiable, and is responsible for my waking early in the morning, and being unable to sleep again – "a shocking bore", as the popular phrase here says.' But to Victoria he would minimize his sleeplessness and pain; and he would drive himself harder.

XVII

The Treadmill Donkey

1860–1861

T WO WEEKS INTO the new year, craving someone to talk to about European politics, and more at ease in German, Albert invited Baron Vitzthum to Windsor. On departing, the Baron penned a long entry in his diary for 14 January 1860. The Prince, he summed up, 'is still living in the Liberal circle of ideas which prevailed in our learned world between 1830 and 1840'. His 'high view of things' had not been crushed by the experience of 1848 and the relapse from it in Europe. He saw 'insoluble contradictions' besetting all the major powers, among which would soon be Italy. Napoleon III would need 'the halo of a campaign on the Rhine', but it would do him in. Prussia would soon dominate Germany, but the maintenance of 'Particularism' – the independence of the minor states but for foreign and military affairs – was essential as a balance to the 'overbearing temper' of Berlin. The Prince predicted that Napoleon would seize Belgium once the ageing King Leopold was gone. Albert worried, too, that the Emperor would ally himself to Denmark so that Prussia would find itself preoccupied with Holstein just long enough for France to attack the Rhineland. And he expected an Italian attempt to take Venetia from Austria, reopening that war. On he went with his concerns, many of which would become realities, although not as quickly as Albert anticipated in the anxieties of early 1860. 'Of politics I don't speak', the Queen wrote cautiously to her daughter four days later, 'as I hear only far too much of them as it is, and Papa is quite *absorbé* by them'.

With eight children still to marry off over the years, Victoria was absorbed in that process. No longer eager for dynastic coups, but keen to marry off her elder children early, she accepted a visit from a Dutch prince whom Lord Clarendon called 'the Orange Boy' and who lacked what seemed then the essential qualification of being German. Albert had little to do with it, and soon found the bland heir presumptive to the Grand Duchy of Hesse, Prince Ludwig, also paying a call. Victoria's political and diplomatic correspondence remained voluminous, however, with Albert drafting most of the missives and the Queen occasionally crossing out a paragraph that seemed not resounding enough. There were also other than marital plans for the children, more in the Albertine vein of establishing meaningful roles for the monarchy. The Prince of Wales was to go to Canada (soon the United States would be added) and Prince Alfred to South Africa. Bertie's progress was planned to take place before his next Oxford term, and Affie's between naval assignments. The Prince of Wales, Albert explained to his brother, 'is to represent England[,] and the Canadians wish to show the Americans how happy, free and yet monarchical it is possible to be'.

To Stockmar he elaborated upon his concept on 27 April, describing initiatives that went well beyond opening charity bazaars and gracing theatrical benefits. 'Almost in the same week in which the elder brother is to open the great bridge across the St Lawrence in Canada,* the younger will lay the foundation stone for the breakwater for the harbour of Cape Town, at the other end of the world.' The events would demonstrate not only British progress, but 'the useful co-operation of the Royal Family in the civilisation which England has developed and advanced'. And he expected that in 'both young colonies' the royal children would be accepted with 'conscious national pride'. Elaborating on his motives at a Trinity House dinner in May, Albert described the 'present greatness', 'past history' and 'future hopes' that his sons embodied, and 'how important and beneficent is the part given to the Royal Family of England to act in the development of these distant and rising countries, who recognise in the British Crown, and their allegiance to it, their supreme bond of union with the mother country and with each other'.

---

* The Victoria railway bridge at Montreal, on 25 September 1860.

Albert's responsibilities, all of them self-made over twenty years, ranged from urging his views about European affairs on the Foreign Office to pressing the Prime Minister to fill a vacant professorship at Cambridge. 'The Consort paid me an immense long visit', Lord Clarendon wrote to his most intimate correspondent, the Duchess of Manchester, on 2 May, '... & was by no means as violent about men & things foreign & domestic as I had heard – on the contrary he discussed them all in a very practical spirit but he totally forgot the sacred hour of 2 & Eliza' – Clarendon's code for the Queen; the Prince was often *Joseph* – 'will have waited or not waited ¾ of an hour for him.' (The royal couple usually lunched at two.)

After a hard winter and late-arriving spring, the royal family escaped to Osborne, where they attempted each year to mark Victoria's birthday on 24 May. For Albert, who was preparing for the speechmaking season in June and July, it was a welcome respite from conferences and audiences, and an opportunity to pore over books that were not essential to business. A new one (published in 1859) was Tennyson's *Idylls of the King*. The Prince wanted the poet's autograph. 'You would thus add', he wrote, sending his copy to his Isle of Wight neighbour, 'a peculiar value to the book, containing those beautiful songs, from the perusal of which I derived the greatest enjoyment. They quite rekindle the feelings with which the legends of King Arthur must have inspired the chivalry of old, whilst the graceful form in which they are presented blends those feelings with the softer tone of our present age.' Tennyson signed Albert's book, which contained the first four idylls. A later and fuller edition would bear a dedication beginning,

> These to His Memory –
> Since he held them dear,
> Perchance as finding there unconsciously
> Some image of himself.

'We spent the 24th in more than usual gaiety and good spirits', Victoria wrote to Fritz's mother, Augusta, on 26 May. 'Where could I point to another woman who after 20 years of such marital felicity still possesses it? My dearly beloved Albert shows me not only as much affection and kindness as ever, but as much love and tenderness as on the first day of marriage. How can I ever repay him for it? How can I be sufficiently thankful for his goodness?' They had music on the terrace; the weather was kind, and they danced.

Returning to take in the London social season, which went on luxuriously despite unabated war anxieties, the Queen and Prince went to an evening concert at the second Duke of Wellington's Apsley House, visited other great London mansions, and held their own State Ball at Buckingham Palace on 23 June. As guests filed into the dining-room, the American envoy, George Mifflin Dallas, noted in his diary, 'a tremendous crash, sounding like the fall of a chandelier, alarmed us all'. It proved only to be 'one of the golden ornaments, a superb vase, placed against a wall behind the fountain ... '

Although the leisured élite who had nothing else to do but dress for the next evening's ball could ignore the alarms from across the Channel, Victoria and Albert could not. Shortly after their ball, they left for the encampment at Aldershot, where eighteen thousand volunteers took to the field. King Leopold and Duke Ernest arrived in time to watch manœuvres executed, Ernest wrote, 'by 23,000 men with 56 cannons'. Since most of the troops were civilian reservists, newspaper coverage stressed the faultlessness of the review. Observing their movements as an officer trained in Prussia and Saxony, Ernest carped that their 'dispositions ... were of so extremely innocent a nature, that I thought I ought not to conceal from the English statesmen, how very little was to be expected from these performances, in the event of an actual war'. If the French emperor 'had not abstained from the much-apprehended invasion from other reasons', he claimed, 'the volunteer battalions assuredly would not have prevented him'. The importance of their being at Aldershot, however, was their very existence. They had made a difference in English attitudes toward France, and acted as a brake upon Palmerston.

Readiness, from Albert's standpoint, was a public relations matter as well as a military one. As a result there were 21,000 volunteers who, for two hours, paraded before the Queen in Hyde Park, six thousand of them paying their own way from places like Manchester, Leeds and Nottingham to demonstrate what they were able to do with only limited leisure for practice. The Prince rode at the side of the Queen's carriage.

It was already early Saturday evening when the militia dispersed. Albert rushed back to Buckingham Palace, dressed anew for the annual

Prince Albert watching as the Queen fires the first shot from a fixed rifle at the
National Rifle Association meeting on Wimbledon Common, 2 July, 1860.
(Illustrated London News)

Trinity House dinner, at which he presided, and in proposing a toast to
the Army and Navy, made the point that unlike other European
powers, the British armed services in times of danger were drawn largely
from non-professional volunteers. He hoped that the 'noble and
patriotic spirit' which actuated such sacrifices would remain 'ever
unimpaired'.

A week later came the much-publicized rifle-shooting competition
on Wimbledon Common. First prize went to a candidate using Joseph
Whitworth's new steel rifle with a spiral polygonal bore. A machine-
tool manufacturer from Manchester who had exhibited at the Crystal
Palace, Whitworth had been encouraged to upgrade weapons engineering by Albert. To make his point, it was arranged that the Queen open
the National Rifle Association event on 2 July, a Monday, by firing
a shot from a Whitworth weapon fixed in a stationary rest at four
hundred yards. She hit the bull's-eye at one-and-a-half inches above the

centre. Nevertheless the hidebound War Office rejected Whitworth's rifle as having too small a bore for military effectiveness. (Later rifles adopted would have even smaller bores.) Stealing a march on Whitehall and the Horse Guards, the French adopted the weapon – a paradox not lost on Albert.

In London in early July, the Prince Consort worked to secure funding for the South Kensington Museum, accompanied Bertie as far as Plymouth, where he was to sail for Canada, and returned to prepare the opening address for the fourth International Statistical Congress, the first to be held in England. It was an event that Albert was delighted to chair, for its founder had been Professor Lambert Adolphe Jacques Quételet, now sixty-four, the Brussels mathematician and probability theorist who had been one of his tutors when he had prepared for the university at Bonn. Only Russia among reasonably civilized nations failed to send delegates.

While the social season seemed fixed for the best spring weather, Albert's ceremonial obligations made him a man for all seasons. On 27 March he had opened the new hall of the Clothworkers' Company, described in his graceful address as one of 'these little independent republics of the City of London' which linked the generations, and to which he was admitted as a 'Liveryman'. The 'four-hours' dinner, toasts, and songs, [just] under 90° of heat', his having 'to take an oath, and make two speeches after dinner', and to drink to the Princess Royal's health, 'upstanding, three times three', he wrote to Vicky, was not 'the best specific' for his stubborn late-winter cough.

In May the demands were still accumulating. He recalled to Vicky, as always in German, his image of himself and his 'never-ending business' as the treadmill donkey on the Isle of Wight, 'my true counterpart. He too, would rather munch thistles in the Castle Moat, than turn round in the wheel at the Castle Well; and small thanks he gets for his labour.' Two public dinners were imminent, in which again he would be in the chair. 'The one gives me seven, the other ten toasts and speeches, appropriate to the occasion, and distracting to myself. Then I have to resign at Oxford the [year's] Presidency of the British Association [for the Advancement of Science], and later in the season to open the Statistical Congress... Between these come the laying of the foundation stone of the Dramatic College, the distribution of Prizes at Wellington College, &c. &c.; and this, with the sittings of my different Commissions, and Ascot races ... and the Balls and Concerts crowded into the month of June, over and above the customary business, which a distracted state of affairs in Europe, and a stormy Parliament ... make still more burdensome and dis-agreeable than usual.' However allegedly distasteful, he loved his work, and he realized that the Queen, as a woman barred from much of it, could not do what only he could.

To assist him with the Statistical Congress address, Albert called in William Farr, a pioneer in the application of 'vital statistics', and declared, 'now, Dr Farr, I wish to suck your brains!' Farr looked up a paper that he thought would update the Prince, and forwarded it, observing later that Albert had studied far more than the single govern-ment report he was sent, and that his address was 'entirely his own'. 'Statistical science', as Albert described it, had been condemned by clergymen as a pernicious scholarly conspiracy aimed at the destruction of religion by making the Almighty's world 'a mere machine working according to a general prearranged scheme, the parts of which are capable of mathematical measurement'. Statistics, the ultra-pious charged, 'deprives man of his dignity'.

'Is the power of God', the Prince asked, opening the sessions on 16 July, 'destroyed or diminished by ... the fact that the earth required three hundred and sixty-five revolutions upon its own axis to every revolution round the sun, giving us so many days to our year, and that the moon changes thirteen times during that period; that the tide changes every six hours; that water boils at a temperature of 212° according to Fahrenheit ...?' On the other hand, he observed, prob-ability theory had established 'that in the natural world there exist no certainties at all, but only probabilities', based upon calculations valid 'as long as the same causes are operating'. It was the essence of statistical science 'that it makes only apparent general laws, but that these laws are inapplicable to any special case; that, therefore, what is proved to be law in general is uncertain in particular ... Thus is the power, wisdom, and goodness of the Creator manifested, showing how the Almighty has established the physical and moral world on unchangeable laws, con-formable to His eternal nature, while He has allowed to the individual the freest and fullest use of his faculties, vindicating at the same time the majesty of His laws by their remaining unaffected by individual self-determination.'

The address was a graceful upholding of science in an era dominated by religious dogma, and was intended to be heard well beyond the Congress. In opening, the Prince apologized to his immediate audience of experts for being so 'inadequate an exponent', however much he owed to the 'privilege' of early instruction by Quételet. He hoped that their 'common method' would lead to the 'common end' of utilizing mathematical tools to improve the human condition.

As the applause swelled, then faded, crotchety old Lord Brougham, ever the troublemaker, saw George Mifflin Dallas in the *corps diplomatique* section, and shouted at him, aware that the slavery issue in the United States had reached a high tide of dissension, that there was 'a negro in the assemblage'. It was, the American Minister realized, an attempt to provoke him into some unseemly response, and he remained 'silent and composed'. However, Dallas noted in his diary, 'The gentleman of colour . . . rose, and requested permission of the Prince Consort, as chairman, to thank Lord Brougham for his notice, with an emphatic conclusion, "I am a man!" '

For Albert it had to be a relief that the dignity of the speaker defused the excitement in the hall, and he brought the meeting back to order. Two days later, when a delegate from Massachusetts called upon Dallas on Brougham's behalf to say that the abolitionist-minded peer had meant no personal disrespect, the Minister insisted that if he had an apology to make for the insult to the United States, 'he must do this in the very body where he had made the attack'. On the twentieth, Brougham called upon Dallas but found only his secretary, as the Minister was at the South Kensington Museum. 'You know,' Brougham claimed, 'you don't treat your negroes as well as they are treated in the Brazils!'* Slavery would not come up again in the Congress, but as a foreign policy matter it would continue to beset the Prince.

The Queen and Prince remained at Buckingham Palace through much of the parliamentary sitting, watchful over defence expenditures. Gladstone, the Chancellor of the Exchequer, guarded the national purse as if his own. 'Our Fortifications Bill is at last in the House of Commons', Albert reported to Stockmar from Osborne late in July. 'Gladstone continues in the Ministry but on the condition that he be

---

* Slavery was not abolished in Brazil until 1888.

free next year to attack and denounce the fortifications, to the construction of which he this year gives his assent, and the money. Palmerston laughingly yielded this condition to him.' The Prince would follow up his victory of readiness over penuriousness by urging Palmerston to raise a Naval Reserve, pointing out that such trainees would be doubly valuable through applying their skills in the merchant fleet.

It was at Osborne that Victoria and Albert learned of the birth of Vicky's second child, a girl, on 24 July. She would be named Victoria, although called by the last of her four names, Charlotte. For Albert it furnished the occasion to explain the facts of conception and birth to Alice, who was already on the verge of betrothal. 'Papa told her all', the Queen wrote to her eldest daughter the next day, having been reluctant to explain such intimate matters herself.

On 5 August, the day before the Court moved to Balmoral, an overnight expedition of a trainload of people and baggage, Albert wrote to the Prince Regent of Prussia to congratulate him on the birth of their granddaughter. It was an opportunity to raise such European matters as the likely unification of Italy (the Neapolitan regime was despised, and tottering), and his expectations for political reforms in Austria – a veiled encouragement for liberalization in Prussia. 'May the Emperor Francis Joseph go on with his reforms', Albert hoped, 'and cause justice to be done to Protestants, Hungarians, and Jews ... It is high time. It seems to me that one of his chief difficulties consists in fundamental differences between his and his people's way of looking at things. He proposes to make concessions as acts of grace; they, on the other hand, ask to have a legal status, and institutions not dependent on the good or ill will of the Sovereign.'

The terminus of the royal train at Edinburgh offered the occasion to schedule yet another three hours' review of volunteers, again with the Queen in an open carriage and Albert on horseback. As political a gesture as it was an act of preparedness, the gathering emphasized unity of will across Britain. Twenty-two thousand troops paraded, and 200,000 spectators cheered them on, Albert reported to Stockmar. 'The French are as much out of humour at this demonstration', he wrote on 21 August, 'as Messrs Cobden and Bright'. The Radical leaders were long-time pacifists, William Cobden remarking to an American – while both were then in Paris – that 'Prince Albert's rifle mania' was 'mere Germanism in the disguise of British patriotism'. 'The American despatched the whole conversation forthwith to the *New York Herald*', the Prince explained, 'from which it was come back to our papers!'

The Scots stay was to be abbreviated because of a planned trip to Germany, and Albert's rifle mania, at least when it came to hunting, was no longer what it had been, although he did bring down one stag. While in the Highlands early that September the Queen and Prince went off on a lengthy incognito journey, meant as psychological therapy for Victoria, whose recurrent depressive moods remained a quandary for Albert. In deliberately unsplendid carriages the small royal party travelled along the river Geldie to Loch Inch, crossed the Spey in a ferry, and bounced in 'very rough vehicles' to Grantown, over sixty miles from Balmoral. '*No* one knew us', she bubbled to Leopold – 'anywhere or at the little inn. We went under the names of Lord and Lady Churchill, and Lady Churchill and General Grey who went with us, under the names of Miss Spencer and Dr Grey! Two maids *only* went with us (whom we had sent round with our things), and *no* servants but our two excellent Highlanders, viz. Albert's first stalker or head keeper, and *my own Highland servant* and factotum – *both* excellent, intelligent, devoted people. *Only* when we had *left* was it found out.' Her Highland servant was John Brown, then thirty-four. On the journey he nearly gave the game away be calling Victoria 'Your Majesty' as she was getting into a carriage, and John Grant, head keeper at Balmoral, who was acting as Albert's servant, once called him 'Your Royal Highness'. The slips set the others tittering, and increased the deliciousness of the masquerade.

The secret had been imperfectly kept, as the dogcart in which they had begun the journey carried the Balmoral crest, and someone in the street recognized Albert. 'The lady must be terrible rich', one woman observed. Victoria's fingers were covered with rings. The Queen retorted that the other lady wore even more rings. The sense of freedom in Scotland to play at not being Queen enraptured Victoria. At the inn, Grant and Brown were to have waited on them, not an unusual procedure when a wealthy couple travelled with their own servants, but as Victoria and Albert tidied up in their room, the Highlanders made themselves 'wishful' (the Queen's word in her journal – Scots for *drunk*). A ringletted local woman waited on the royal couple and served them their bottle of wine, brought from Balmoral. The next day, permissive as usual about the tippling of her Highlanders, the Queen was up and ready early to complete the expedition without a word of reproof. 'To my dear Albert', she noted, they owed the lark, 'for he always thought it would be delightful'.

The much talked-of yet much delayed visit to Germany began from Buckingham Palace after their early return from Balmoral, but was in jeopardy almost until the day they departed because of Albert's recurrent stomach cramps. Sir James Clark, called in to review the symptoms, which included chills and aches, diagnosed exhaustion and recommended rest. Albert insisted that they meet their schedule.

To avoid any semblance of a state visit, Prussia was excluded from the itinerary. Instead, Vicky and her family would travel from Berlin to Coburg, which the wizened Stockmar, now seventy and more shrunken than ever, seldom left, and where Albert's stepmother, Dowager Duchess Marie, was in failing health. Lord John Russell accompanied the party to represent the government, as any political matters that were likely to come up were expected to be in his province as Foreign Secretary.

Late in the afternoon of 22 September 1860, they embarked at Gravesend on the *Victoria and Albert*. Princess Alice and a suite of attendants, including William Baly, the young physician who had just joined the Court medical staff, accompanied them. At Antwerp, they were met by King Leopold and his sons, who joined them by rail as far as the station at Verviers. With the Belgians was a telegram from Ernest in Coburg: 'Mama' Marie was dying. The journey should be put off for a day. Albert telegraphed back that it was impossible, and that he hoped for the best. At Frankfurt a further telegram awaited them. Duchess Marie had died.

'To our regret', Victoria wrote in her journal, 'we were received by a guard of honour and a band.' Only just in possession of the sad news, they were already in technical mourning. The next day, after staying overnight at the Hotel d'Angleterre, as they had done fifteen years earlier, they continued along the valley of the Main to Lichtenfels, where they transferred to the Thüringian railway to Coburg, arriving at five in the evening. The quiet welcome, as befitted bereavement, left Albert and Victoria even more agitated than any traditional greeting, in the brightest gala style, would have done. With Alexandrine, the Duchess of Coburg, at the Palace, was Vicky, 'in the deepest German mourning, long black veils . . .', the Queen wrote. 'A tender embrace, and then we walked up the staircase...Could hardly speak, I felt so moved, and quite trembled.'

Stockmar, whom they had not seen since his farewell visit to England in 1856, was there, looking 'a little weak', and also little Willy, 'a fine fat child' with 'very fair curly hair'.

Two days later was the Duchess's funeral, which left Albert shaken, but not nearly as much as he would be four days later, following quiet, nostalgic visits to familiar places. The Queen's journal for 1 October opens, 'Before proceeding, I must thank God for having preserved my adored one! I tremble now on thinking of it...The escape is very wonderful, *most merciful*!' Albert had been riding alone in a carriage drawn by four horses, which suddenly took flight. Two miles ahead lay a railway crossing with a bar across the road, and as Albert attempted to control his team he saw a wagon waiting. With a collision inevitable, he jumped for his life. Cut and bruised, but conscious, he rushed to the aid of the coachman into whose wagon his carriage had crashed. Of Albert's four horses, one was dead; the others raced on the remaining mile to Coburg.

In the town the runaway horses were recognized, and Colonel Ponsonby, the Prince's equerry, rushed to the scene of the accident with the party's young doctor, William Baly, and Carl Florschütz, the Duke's physician. Ponsonby then went on to summon the Queen, who found Albert lying on the bed of his valet, Löhlein, with lint compresses on his nose, mouth and chin. Victoria veered between horror and gratitude. 'I sent off many telegrams to England, &c., fearing wrong messages.' She would not know of Albert's curious confession to Vicky that when he realized his team had bolted, he sensed that his time had come ('*mein letzes Stündlein gekommen wäre*'*), and that he found himself welcoming oblivion.

At dinner that evening he chattered away in the nervous manner of someone pretending to be other than he was. The next day the Prince kept to his room, but claimed he was feeling better. 'Good Stockmar [was] there', Victoria wrote. 'He had been half distracted all night, thinking of what might have happened...Many dispatches and letters; Emperor and Empress of the French inquiring after dear Albert...My heart very full, but would not give way.'

---

* 'My last hour had come.'

Dispatches to England about Albert's brush with death offered an enterprising *Punch* editor the opportunity to pun, 'It is an extraordinary thing that any sort of vehicular indiscretion should have been manifested in the case of a Prince who has always been so remarkably Prudent in his Carriage.'

Among the letters forwarded from London, unrelated to the accident, was one from the Prince of Wales. On a tour of Canada and the United States – a highly successful venture that proved that whatever his failings with books, he had the social graces – Bertie had reached Niagara Falls.

On 4 October, the Queen drove with Princess Alice to Baron Stockmar's house in the Weber-Gasse, and met his '*zuvorkommende Frau*' (affable wife) for the first time. In none of his stays in England, the months adding up to many years, had she ever travelled with him.

Although Victoria and Albert would not leave until the tenth, every day for the Prince became a farewell, as he absorbed sights and sounds and smells he sensed he might never experience again. The weather, which had been gloriously autumnal, turned cold and wet, and made the process of drawing away somewhat easier. 'Had a last visit', Victoria wrote, 'from dear Stockmar, and talked over many things with him. Towards the end of his stay, dear little William came in and played about the room, and we got over the leave-taking without its upsetting Stockmar too much.'

In the last days, happily for Albert's peace of mind, came foreign affairs distractions from London – 'constant dispatches from Italy and about Italy', Victoria's journal notes. 'Matters become more and more complicated. The Emperor [of France] declares he shall protect the Pope in Rome... Albert too busy to go out.' The next morning he was also busy with diplomatic papers, but on Albert's last afternoon in Coburg, Ernest took his brother for a walk. Afterwards he remembered Stockmar's words. Having perceived Albert's despondency and melancholy – unrelated to the accident, Stockmar knew, as he had been in constant correspondence with Albert – he confided to Ernest, 'God have mercy on us! If anything serious should ever happen to him, he will die.'

Very likely something serious had already happened, and both Stockmar and Albert knew it. The Prince, at least, thought that he was slowly but surely dying. 'At one of the most beautiful spots', Ernest recalled, 'Albert stood still, and suddenly felt for his pocket handkerchief.' The

Duke assumed that Albert's facial abrasions had begun to bleed afresh, and went to help, but discovered instead 'that tears were trickling down his cheeks ... [and] he persisted in declaring that he was well aware that he had been here for the last time in his life'. The brothers turned back to the Rosenau in silence.

The slow return journey to London, in persistent cold rain, was a prolonged misery alleviated only by the continued presence of Vicky, who – though married to a German prince – had never travelled the Rhine. Victoria had a heavy cold, with a sore throat and fever. Albert, more ill than she knew, attempted to conceal his continuing headaches and stomach discomfort, his cramps and chills, until he was on home soil again, and in royal privacy.

At the railway station in Koblenz, Vicky's mother-in-law and Prince Frederick of Baden joined the party, planning to have the Queen and Prince sightsee along the Rhine and Moselle. In rain and hail, wobbly on their feet, they did what was expected of them, and remained overnight. On 13 October, after two days in Koblenz, they left for Cologne, where the Prussian party was joined by the Prince Regent, Vicky's father-in-law, who talked in the train with Victoria and Albert until Aix-la-Chapelle (Aachen), where the Prussians, 'little William' included, took their final leaves.

Leopold met the train at Verviers, shocked at the appearance of the royal couple. 'I could hardly walk when we got out', Victoria confessed in her journal, 'and with difficulty got up stairs ... Dr Baly found my throat very bad, that I had much fever; so I was ordered to remain lying down in my room and to see no one.' The dinner in Brussels that Leopold had scheduled in her honour was held without the Queen.

Even the final farewells in Belgium were delayed by weather. Before the yacht proceeded very far from Antwerp, the sky turned black and a deluge of rain forced the ship to drop anchor. Finally, at six in the evening on 17 October, a week after leaving Coburg, they reached Gravesend.

Shaken by her illness, and grateful for what she considered Albert's deliverance at Coburg, Victoria wrote to Sir Charles Phipps, the administrator of Her Majesty's Privy Purse, to explore the possibility of endowing a permanent charity at Coburg, to be distributed every 1 October – the anniversary of Albert's escape. A modest trust, the *Victoria-Stift* (Victoria Foundation) was established for little over

£1,000. The interest was to enable men and women 'of exemplary character belonging to the humbler ranks of life' to receive small sums for apprenticeships, for purchasing tools and equipment needed for work, or, in the case of women, to secure a small marriage dowry. It would become, in effect, the first Albert Memorial.

The Queen recovered more quickly than Albert. 'My attack', he claimed to Vicky on 11 December, once he was able to work again 'was the real English cholera'. 'English cholera', also called 'summer cholera', is a diarrhoeal disease usually lasting two to seven days, and accompanied by severe stomach cramps. Albert had such symptoms, but had been ill for two months. Now he had to act as if he were fit, for Empress Eugénie, staying in London at Claridge's without her philandering husband, was expected on a private visit ('there was not the slightest allusion to politics'); and in residence at Windsor was Alice's future husband, the amiable but empty Prince Ludwig of Hesse, soon to be 'Louis', for whose bad teeth the Queen found a dentist. Albert gave him some informal lessons on his own German history.

Christmas 1860 was celebrated at Windsor, with both the Prince of Wales and Prince Alfred at home. George Byng, seventh Viscount Torrington, 'in waiting' at the time, sent J.T. Delane of *The Times* an intimate account of what was to be the last family Christmas with the Prince Consort. Something of a sceptic and a wit, Torrington (signing his letter 'Your Windsor Special') was 'agreeably surprised and pleased' by the royal Christmas Eve:

> The Queen's private sitting-rooms, three in number, were lighted up with Christmas trees hung from the ceiling, the chandeliers being taken down. These trees, of immense size, besides others on the tables, were covered with bonbons and coloured wax lights. Some of the trees were made to appear as if partially covered with snow. These rooms contained all the presents for the royal family the one to the other. Each member gave a present to one another, so that, including the Prince of Hesse and the Duchess of Kent, every person had to receive or give thirteen presents...
>
> I have never seen a much more agreeable sight. It was royalty putting aside its state and becoming in words, acts, and deeds one of ourselves – no forms and not a vestige of ceremony. Even as in a public

bazaar, where people jostle one another, so lords, grooms, Queen, and princes laughed and talked, forgot to bow, and freely turned their backs on one another. Little princesses, who on ordinary occasions dare hardly to look at a gentleman-in-waiting, in the happiest manner showed each person they could lay hands on the treasures they had received . . . Prince Arthur (the flower of the flock) speedily got into a volunteer uniform, which, with endless other things, including a little rifle, fell to his lot, took a pot-shot at his papa, and then presented arms.

Some of the presents were beautiful in taste and suited to the receiver, and even the presents of children to their parents were selected so that even the Queen might find use for them . . . I received a supply of studs, sleeve buttons, and waistcoat ditto – handsome, plain gold; a pocket-book, and every one of us a large cake of Nuremberg gingerbread. Whether the Prince Consort had a quiet joke in his mind when he selected certain presents for Phipps, Biddulph, Grey, and Bruce,* I don't know, but Phipps had salt cellars resting on little fish with the *mouths open*, Biddulph a *bread* basket, Grey a sugar basket, and Bruce a claret jug . . .

I never saw more real happiness than the scene of the mother and all her children; the Prince Consort lost his stiffness, and your *Windsor Special* had much cheerful and friendly conversation with them both. Altogether, it was a sight I should have liked you to have seen . . .

On Christmas Day the windows at Windsor were clouded by frost, although a cold sun shone. The Duchess of Kent came to luncheon, and Leopold and Beatrice ('Baby') were permitted to join the family for dessert. Albert swung Baby in a large dinner napkin.

Christmas dinner was for adults only. Lord Torrington went to the kitchen to watch the roasting of turkeys, geese, and beef – 'a mighty sight: at least fifty turkeys before one fire'. By custom, he reported, the Lord Lieutenant of Ireland sent the sovereign at Christmas a large woodcock pie. Victoria's had one hundred birds in it – 'a worthy dish to set before a Queen'.

* Sir Charles Phipps, Private Secretary to the Prince Consort and Keeper of Her Majesty's Privy Purse; Colonel Thomas Biddulph, Master of the Queen's Household; General Charles Grey, Private Secretary to the Prince Consort and later to the Queen; General Robert Bruce, Governor to the Prince of Wales.

The dinner 'was really wonderful. How I live to tell the tale I don't know. I took some of the baron of beef, the boar's head, and the Lord Lieutenant's pie. Fortunately, I did not go to bed till near three o'clock, as we finished the evening with some pool and billiards, and Captain Du Plat and self cleared the remainder out of every silver coin they possessed. Altogether a jolly Christmas Day...'

As the Queen, with Albert, watched the final minutes of 1860 tick away, she worried aloud about war on the Continent and was anxious for England. 'My precious husband', she wrote in her journal, 'cheered me & held me in his dear arms saying "We must have trust, & we have trust that God will protect us." ' 10 February, however, was the real beginning of the year for her – that date in 1861 was the twenty-first anniversary of her wedding to 'that most perfect of human beings my adored Husband!' It was also her opportunity to record her guilt about her 'foolish sensitivity & irritability', which continued to mar relations with Albert. A woman whose instincts were so queenly that she never looked behind her when she sat down could not separate her husband from her other subjects when the royal temper was aroused. She resolved again to be calmer.

The new year was a difficult one in which to remain calm, punctuated as it was from the beginning by serious anxieties. Albert expected little good from it. Napoleon, Albert wrote to his brother, would brew trouble with both Austria and Prussia; Cavour's nucleus of a new Italy was already arming rebels in the sub-alpine Austrian principalities; and Prussia would be taking 'steps' against Denmark in Holstein.

On 2 January, just as the Court was about to leave Windsor for a brief stay at Osborne House, a telegram arrived reporting the death of Frederick William IV. His mind had failed years earlier. To Victoria and Albert the accession of Fritz's father, long the actual ruler of Prussia, seemed an event to celebrate quietly despite the official mourning. Vicky's husband was now the Crown Prince, and the new King, they hoped, would be liberal in outlook – although he would quickly succumb to his bellicose 'Iron Chancellor' Otto von Bismarck, whom he named Prime Minister the next year. In the first dawn of the elderly King William's regime, the dream of Victoria and Albert that their daughter might soon be queen of a progressive, unified Germany seemed to be approaching fulfilment.

Despite such prospects, letters from Vicky were filled with deathbeds and mourning, and the mail she received from England was in a similar vein. At just the time when enlightened medical help was needed in Victoria's household, William Baly, the Queen's new Physician-in-Ordinary, was the victim of a gruesome railway accident. He had arrived at Wimbledon Station, *en route* to Osborne, only to see the train steaming away. When he explained to the station-master that he was the Queen's doctor, the train was stopped and Baly climbed aboard. Soon afterward, the floor of his carriage collapsed, and he fell to his death on the tracks. He was the only passenger killed. '*Sehr traurig*'– very sad – Albert wrote in his diary.

For the Prince, Baly's death was especially sad, as the doctor had been treating him for continuing woes, including gum inflammations that had persisted for two years, and had become worse. 'Papa never allows he is any better or will try to get over it', the Queen wrote lightly to Vicky, 'but makes such a miserable face that people always think he's very ill. It is quite the contrary with me always; I ... never show it, so people never believe I am ill or ever suffer. His nervous system is easily excited and irritated, and he's so completely over-powered by everything.' Albert indeed felt wretched, although he persisted in his schedule, which expanded with the new parliamentary session.

With the less-than-competent Sir James Clark now semi-retired, a new physician was appointed, William Jenner – 'a great friend of our poor Dr Baly', the Queen wrote to Vicky. 'He is extremely clever, and has a pleasing clever manner.'

As the King of Prussia lay in state earlier in January, Victoria had confided to her daughter, about to confront a grim new experience, 'I have never even yet witnessed a death bed'. That would soon change. Dr Jenner had hardly assumed his duties when the Duchess of Kent began to fail. The Queen's priorities altered. She had been concerned with Albert's health, but not so much as to divert her from a continuing preoccupation with matchmaking, this time with the intention of settling the future of the Prince of Wales, whose shallowness had not been reversed by the social success of his trip to North America. Since Victoria was distracted by her mother's decline, the assignment to find Bertie a bride – almost certainly the future Queen – remained that of Vicky. Although she was situated where likely candidates existed, there were also Danish and Dutch possibilities; however, the Danish princess, though beautiful, seemed politically unacceptable as long as the dispute with Prussia over Schleswig and Holstein simmered.

Vicky had sent the Queen photographs, and Victoria responded about the Danish candidate, 'Princess Alexandra is indeed lovely!... What a pity she is who she is!' Albert's response to Victoria was more enthusiastic, although he might have been expected to be pro-German. 'From that photograph', he said, 'I would marry her at once.'

Bertie had been uncaged by the voyage to North America, but on 18 January 1861 he had been transferred from Christ Church, Oxford, to

LATEST FROM AMERICA.

Punch *satirizing Bertie's social growth as a result of his American travels. His father is not amused.*

Trinity College, Cambridge, both arrangements again implying matriculation rather than residence. Reports had come to Victoria and Albert
that the Prince of Wales had often been seen with a cigar in his mouth,
aping the more vulgar undergraduates, and remained gauche. At Cambridge he was housed with a staff appointed by his father at Madingley
Hall, four miles from college, and cantered to campus on his horse or
was driven in a phaeton. To bring him into closer contact with college
life, Dr Whewell allotted to the young prince rooms at the Master's
Lodge, where, Natty Rothschild discovered, 'the different Regius professors come and lecture to him'. Bertie was 'not allowed to take any
notes but has to write out the lectures when he gets back to Madingley'.
The eldest son of Lionel and Charlotte de Rothschild fancied that 'the
little spirit [which the Prince of Wales] ever had is quite broken' from
the strict regimen, yet Bertie played tennis – badly – every day, and was
'excessively fond of the chase' and of 'riddles and strong cigars'. His
'redeeming quality' was his excessive courtesy to every student without
exception, but, Natty predicted, if the Prince could follow his own
inclinations 'he would take to gambling and certainly keep away from
the law lectures he is obliged to go to now'.

An early marriage, Albert hoped, would draw Bertie from bad
company and bad habits, to both of which he was prone. The only
university education which seemed to stick to him was extra-curricular
and unhelpful. Any risk to foreign policy of a Danish bride seemed
worth chancing.

Foreign affairs remained Albert's overwhelming concern. Regardless
of the troubled area, he warned Palmerston, there were influential
'peace-at-any-price mongers'. To Disraeli, who had been at a Windsor
dinner on 21 January, the Prince warned that Napoleon hoped for a
'Gladstone–Cobden' government to disarm the country, and 'Dizzy'
promised the support of the Conservatives. 'What is the use of that?'
said Albert candidly; 'the country is governed by newspapers, and you
have not got a newspaper'. He copied down the gist of his conversation
with Disraeli and sent it to Palmerston the next morning.

Though rushing from meeting to meeting, and overseeing the
Queen's correspondence, the Prince was working at less than his usual
efficiency. Well into February he was still suffering through nights
made sleepless by a variety of aches and pains, and was seldom able to
eat his dinner. Then he found himself forced to handle even more

responsibilities. On 28 February, Sir George Couper, long the comptroller of the Duchess of Kent's household, died suddenly. Albert had to take those affairs in hand, a matter made more difficult by the weakened condition of the Duchess. At seventy-five, she was painfully crippled by erysipelas. An operation on her swollen right arm did nothing but hasten the end.

As 15 March waned into the next morning, Victoria went to the Duchess's room for the last time, to witness her first deathbed. 'I sat on a foot stool, holding her dear hand . . . I felt the end was fast approaching, as Clark went out to call Albert . . . Fainter and fainter grew the breathing. At last it ceased . . . The clock struck half-past nine at the very moment.'

Victoria was seized by paroxysms of grief that were in large measure feelings of guilt and remorse. When she began sorting her mother's papers after the funeral, her emotions gave way entirely. Her mother had saved every scrap of childhood memorabilia. She had really loved Victoria. All her villainy was long past and forgotten.

The Queen's mourning became so excessive that her family and the Court recognized that the hysterical indulgence in sorrow was a sign of a serious nervous collapse. She was now a 'poor orphan child', she wrote to Vicky. The Queen, Clarendon reported, 'was determined to cherish her grief & not be consoled'. For three weeks she took all her meals alone (the children were 'a disturbance'), and left Albert (in his words) 'well nigh overcome' with the Queen's business, the late Duchess's affairs, and those always left to his province. 'I hope this state of things won't last', Clarendon gossiped to the Duchess of Manchester, 'or she may fall into the morbid melancholy to wh[ich] her mind has always tended & wh[ich] is a constant cause of anxiety to P[rince] A[lbert].' In mid-April, Albert was still (to Clarendon) 'in a very melancholy tone', and when he confirmed to Palmerston that the Queen had approved of appointments or wished to comment about something, or was returning Dr Livingstone's 'interesting letter' from Africa, it seemed clear that her involvement in affairs remained minimal.

Recovery began with her agreeing, once more, to copy out in her hand such messages to the Prime Minister as suggested that she was overcoming her lassitude, but at the Royal Horticultural Show in South Kensington on 5 June, a pale, exhausted Prince Consort presided over the opening. The Queen was still unequal to public appearances, and

Albert brought his young family as if to compensate for her absence. Again his schedule was crowded. He had to hurry his return, in the rain, to Buckingham Palace in order to rush through dinner in time to go off again, eastward to John Adam Street, below the Strand, for a report to the Society of Arts on preparations for the 1862 reprise of the Great Exhibition. Next time, he had already cautioned the exhibition planners, he could not carry his former burdens. 'Am ill, feverish, with pains in my limbs, and feel very miserable', was a typical entry in his diary at the time.

Later in the month, King Leopold, now a gaunt seventy, made the Channel crossing to learn for himself about Victoria's breakdown, and found her not nearly as low as rumour had it; but he was disturbed by Albert's appearance, and wrote urgently to Stockmar. Returning a message via the King's agent, the Baron urged that Leopold use his good offices to end the morbid official Court mourning, which he suggested was a factor in undermining Albert's health. To Leopold's surprise, Albert declared that wearing black matched his mood, and that even half-mourning would be resisted by Victoria before the late Duchess's birthday in mid-August. The obsessive mourning – Victoria described herself as 'much shattered' – and the burden it had thrown upon a clearly ill Albert, had created, Leopold realized, serious strains between the Queen and Prince. He had little time to spare from the Queen's business to bring her out of her withdrawal from it.

To help, Princess Vicky was sent for, and her family visited for several weeks, much of which the Queen spent on marital plans for Bertie, almost her only therapy. Fortunately for Albert, the mausoleum on the Windsor grounds at Frogmore, where the Duchess had lived, was ready by her birthday for a visit by Victoria. Its 'repose and calmness', the Queen wrote to her daughter on August 17 – she had returned to Berlin – 'were most soothing. Beloved Papa is the cause of all this – he planned and designed it all!'

Externally, the anxieties for the Prince had also increased. The American Civil War had erupted that April. Eleven southern states had seceded and formed a Confederacy which the North was determined to undo, although the initial successes were all those of the slaveholding South. Palmerston's government had cautiously recognized the South not as a nation, but as a belligerent, a status reflecting the sea blockade of the Confederate States by the North. Concern rose about being drawn into the conflict, as Lancashire textile mills depended upon the

South's cotton. At the same time, the Queen and Prince were resisting efforts by Lord John Russell to furnish guarantees to Denmark, which denied Prussian claims to Holstein – 'a part of Germany' (the moribund Confederation), as a letter bearing Victoria's signature reminded her Foreign Minister.

Most sharply worded missives reflected Victorian emendations to Albert's more conciliatory language, and it may have been as true of her observations about the situation in North America as it was about Denmark and Prussia. Expectations in England were that the disunited States were likely to remain sundered, and that the North might attempt to repair its territorial losses at the expense of Canada. Rewriting Albert's draft, the Queen urged that Palmerston send additional artillery units to Canada rather than mere infantry, as 'the Colony' had no munitions industry. But, with no idea of Palmerston's Machiavellian designs to aid the South little short of war, Albert added, in Victoria's somewhat more caustic terms, 'The naval forces would, however, require strengthening even more. It is less likely that the remnant of the United States could send expeditions by land to the north while quarrelling with the South, than that they should commit acts of violence at sea.'

Near physical breakdown, Albert found himself nevertheless planning to go through with a trip to Ireland with the Queen, arranged to coincide with the Prince of Wales's ten weeks of army service there. An ambitious programme had been worked out to slide Bertie through the competency requirements of every officer grade – promoting him one rank every fortnight – until he could command a full battalion in view of the Queen and Prince when they visited the Curragh military grounds near Dublin in August. The reports from General Bruce, the Prince's governor, were discouraging. Meanwhile, Albert had to pull Victoria further out of her malaise so that royal guests could be met and entertained – the King of Sweden, the King of Belgium, her own son-in-law the Crown Prince of Prussia (and Vicky). These became more than mere protocol matters; European capitals were echoing with rumours that Victoria had suffered a breakdown so violent that she had to be restrained in a padded cell. Even Vicky had reported it – to her father – from Berlin. It was vital that Victoria be seen behaving like a queen.

That Bertie was unfit to command a company, let alone a battalion, was insufficient reason to call off the Irish visit. The Queen had not been there since 1849. Cancellation would give credence to the rumours of madness. The Queen and Prince came, visited the encampment at the Curragh on 24 August, and watched Bertie march past with a mere company of Grenadier Guards, his command a public airing of his non-progress. But Victoria's mind still dwelled self-indulgently only on her sorrows. In Ireland she was 'weak and very nervous', she wrote to Leopold; with her mother gone she felt (at forty-two!) 'as if we were no longer cared for'.

One member of the family thoroughly cared for was the Prince of Wales, who was overseen to absurdity. The other young officers, with whom he was ordered to have little to do, felt challenged to extract him from the royal cocoon. At a party before he left the Curragh, Bertie's brother subalterns conveyed into his bed Nellie Clifden, a young woman with a talent to amuse. The Prince of Wales saw to it that Nellie continued to amuse him. But no news of Nellie reached Victoria and Albert.

Only Scotland was perceived to have the healing qualities that the Queen felt she still needed. Albert carefully planned therapeutic expeditions away from Balmoral, including an incognito stay at the Ramsay Arms in Fettercairn, where the landlord and his wife – but no one else – were told in advance who their guests would be. Another outing took them to the inn at Dalwhinnie – where a maid recognized them. They went on daily walking tours. On their final expedition, they lunched on the Cairngorm heights, 'on a precipitous place, which made one dread anyone's moving backwards'. As they packed to leave, 'Albert wrote on a bit of paper that we had lunched there, put it into a Seltzer-water bottle, and buried it there, or rather stuck it in the ground'. Their Highland servant John Brown wished them well as they left, and added the hope that 'above all, you may have no deaths in the family'. The Queen took the bluff farewell as a reference to the Duchess of Kent. Later she wondered about second sight. She had forgotten her own remark to Vicky, on 7 October, after she and Albert had heard an Edinburgh minister preach a sermon that 'touched and enchanted us all', on a text from the Book of Amos, 'Prepare to meet thy God, O Israel'. The subject now affected her greatly, she wrote Vicky. 'I feel now to be so acquainted with death – and to be so much nearer that unseen world.'

Duty Done

1861

ALBERT'S SENSE OF fatality had intensified, and his nights, as he lay beside the sleeping Victoria, were troubled and waking. Confiding in the father-figure of his youth had often been his way of confronting adversity, even when he realized that his appeals would be unanswered prayers. The Prince's last letter to Baron Stockmar was dated 14 November 1861. 'I am fearfully in want of a true friend and counsellor', he wrote, 'and that *you* are the friend and counsellor I want, you will readily understand.' He knew that he was unlikely to receive any practical advice from Stockmar, and perhaps no response whatever. Infirm and reclusive, Stockmar would not leave Coburg.

On their return from Scotland, Windsor Castle had filled with invitees, and a band had played – the first time the Queen had permitted one since her mother's death – for Bertie's twentieth birthday on 9 November. The next day the Prince of Wales returned to his sham residency at Cambridge and Albert went off to London for a round of meetings, returning that night to pitch into his postponed paperwork. All of his schedule, including the birthday festivities, had been carried out in the gloom of his having discovered on the 6th that his cousin, Prince Ferdinand of Portugal, had died of typhoid fever, and that the ineffectual King Pedro, Ferdinand's elder brother, was dangerously ill. Soon he was dead, too, at twenty-five. The Saxe-Coburg-Kohary clan was ravaged. Albert was devastated. 'My Albert was very fond of him', Victoria wrote extravagantly of Pedro in her diary, 'and loved him like a son (as I did too), while he had unbounded confidence in Albert, and was worthy of him.'

The day before his plea to Stockmar, Albert had penned a lugubriously unconsoling letter to Vicky, who was also ill, closing with, 'Spare yourself, nurse yourself, and get completely well. The disaster in Portugal is another proof that we are never safe to refuse Nature her rights.' It was a startling reflection, indicative of the Prince's state of mind.

A calamity closer to home followed quickly. He should have realized months earlier that a young officer in the company of other moneyed young gentlemen in uniform would not acquire the facts of life from discreet fatherly confidences such as he had imparted to Princess Alice. A marriage was being arranged for her; Bertie, although older, had never been privy to such arcana. Now it was no longer necessary. On 16 November, two days after Albert's entreaty to Stockmar, he wrote to his son 'with a heavy heart upon a subject which has caused me the greatest pain I have yet felt in this life'. Lord Torrington, always attuned to gossip, had informed Albert of 'a story current in the Clubs' about Bertie's continuing involvement with Nellie Clifden, which explained his reluctance to consider the Danish betrothal scheme. A letter from Stockmar confirmed that allegations about an Irish 'actress' had already surfaced in Continental papers.

Too heartbroken to confront his son in person, Albert claimed, he had to protect Bertie, nevertheless, from the consequences of his misconduct, and urged him to tell all to General Bruce, who was, rather unsuccessfully, overseeing the Prince in Cambridge. In a second letter a few days later Albert forecast a melodramatic scenario of a future king compromised by blackmail and scandal. If the young woman were to become pregnant, Albert warned, there would be a press circus when the Prince of Wales was dragged into court to own up to his paternity. No particular of his 'profligacy' would escape 'the greedy Multitude' if Nellie Clifden herself were in the witness box to offer her own testimony. 'Oh horrible prospect, which this person has in her power, any day to realise! and to break your poor parents' hearts!' To channel such wanton impulses, he warned, Bertie would have to be hurried into an early marriage.

Victoria had already been told some of the circumstances, but not – she wrote later – 'the disgusting details'. Despite Bertie's contrite response, confessing that he had indeed yielded to temptation, but insisting that the affair was ended, she confided to her journal that she would never be able to look on her son again 'without a shudder'. Although Albert conceded to Bertie that further inquiries were useless, and that 'The past is past. You have to deal now with the future', he might not have informed the Queen in the first place had his head not reeled with illness, exhaustion, and agony over his proliferating problems. Given his caution, and his feelings about sheltering the monarchy from dishonour, he would have railed at his son in any case, although perhaps with less self-pity. He was at a low ebb physically, made worse by sleeplessness, and confessed to Victoria, '*Ich hange gar nicht am Leben; du hangst sehr daran*... [I do not cling to life; you do; but I set no store by it.]. 'I am sure that if I had a severe illness I should give up at once; I should not struggle for life. I have no tenacity of life.'

In retrospect, his fatalism appears more like self-diagnosis than prophecy. He was in no condition, mentally or physically, to fulfill a commitment to inspect the new buildings for the Staff College and Royal Military Academy at Sandhurst, long one of his goals, but he went anyway, on 22 November, despite a drenching rain – '*entsetzlicher Regen*' in his diary. He returned to Windsor wet and exhausted.

Still, Albert pushed himself further. When he returned from Sandhurst he was feeling too ill for the usual round of domestic activities that comprised much of the 'Court Circular' in the daily press, even failing to accompany the Queen on an afternoon walk. '*Bin recht elend*' – 'am very wretched' – he confessed in his diary on the 24th, but he had determined to have it out with his son, and ordered a special train to Cambridge for the next morning.

Rather than remain indoors for a heart-to-heart talk, he went out with Bertie despite a cold, intermittent rain and, although in no condition for an extended stroll, Albert had to go on longer than he anticipated because in the apparently emotional exchange they missed a turning. But Albert extracted assurances of appropriately princely conduct henceforth, and forgave his son, promising that there would be no investigation of the friends who had led him into wrongdoing. Remaining overnight at Madingley Hall, Albert returned on the 26th more exhausted than ever, admitting to pain in his back and legs, and to having slept little in two weeks of stress. The rheumatic symptoms, the

Queen suggested in her diary, were due to 'Bertie's mistaking the road during their walk'. Only on the 28th was Albert able to get about somewhat, although still suffering from pain and insomnia. That morning he learned of the *Trent* affair.

The first and worst diplomatic crisis of the American Civil War had begun on 8 November 1861 when the Confederate envoys (technically, 'Commissioners', as they had no diplomatic status) James Murray Mason of Virginia and John Slidell of Louisiana, were removed by force from the British West Indian mail packet *Trent* in the Caribbean. With their two aides, they had been taken aboard the American steam frigate *San Jacinto* commanded by Captain Charles Wilkes.

Secessionist president Jefferson Davis, frustrated by the failures of his agents in England and France to secure recognition of the Confederacy and eager to purchase ships and arms, had ordered Mason and Slidell to run the Union blockade to Cuba and find their way to Europe. Enemy communications were contraband of war. If the envoys carried nothing but oral instructions they could have been, legally, 'the embodiment of dispatches'.

The Confederate commissioners removed from the British mail packet Trent *(left) to the USS* San Jacinto. *(Engraving in the US Naval Historical Center, Washington, DC)*

Chasing the *Trent* down in the Old Bahama Channel, Wilkes ordered two warning shots to be fired across the ship's bow. The packet hove to, and Navy Lieutenant Donald M. Fairfax and a small detachment of marines boarded.

While Fairfax insisted upon custody of the Confederates, Mrs Slidell lectured him that Northerners were 'doing the very thing the South was hoping for – something to arouse England ... Really, Captain Wilkes is playing into our hands!'

When the Americans returned to their frigate, Wilkes watched the *Trent* steam away rather than head to a Federal harbour with a prize crew. He may have wondered why his deputy, against orders, had let the packet go, but Wilkes did nothing about it. He had his prisoners, who would, he expected, serve out the war in a Northern cell.

The news reached England on 27 November. London newspapers the next morning seethed with indignation and demands for revenge. Historian Henry Adams, then unpaid additional secretary to his father, Charles Francis Adams, the courtly new American Minister, wrote later that if the Atlantic cable had been in operation, Britain would have gone to war with the North. The undersea link from Ireland to Newfoundland had operated briefly in 1858 before breaking apart. Only in 1868 was it finally in service again. In a climate of immediate communications, the hotheads might have prevailed.

Palmerston and Russell appear to have looked forward to a confrontation with the Union – possibly short of war – as a pretext to support the cotton-rich South. 'It is in the highest degree likely', the Prime Minister minuted Russell, 'that the North will not be able to subdue the South, and ... if the Southern Union is established as an independent state, it would afford a valuable and extensive market for British manufactures. But the operations of the war have as yet been too inconclusive to warrant a [formal] acknowledgment of the Southern Union.' Palmerston was aware that a Union paddle-wheeler, the *James Adger*, had put into Southampton. He already knew that Mason and Slidell were planning to cross the Atlantic on a British steamer from St Thomas in the Virgin Islands, the *Trent*'s next destination. In the North it was thought that the emissaries had escaped the blockade of Charleston on the Confederate cruiser *Nashville* on a direct run to England, and Commander John Bonnett Marchand of the *James Adger* had left New York on 16 October in pursuit. The Prime Minister assumed that the *Adger*, coaling in Southampton harbour, was waiting for a packet flying the British White Ensign.

Although Palmerston had employed gunboat diplomacy against a weaker nation in the Don Pacifico affair, the pinnacle of his reputation for international truculence, on 11 November he called in his principal legal advisers for counsel. The United States was not puny Greece. What courses of action could England follow under international law, Palmerston asked, if a British vessel were accosted and the Southern envoys seized?

The question recalled the War of 1812, fought in part because the British claimed the right to board ships of other nations to remove Royal Navy deserters and to impress seamen claimed to be of British origin. That issue had been left unresolved by the Treaty of Ghent ending the war. A written opinion produced for Palmerston a day later concluded that the Americans had been right in 1812 and thus had no more lawful authority in 1861 to search a neutral vessel and remove passengers than the British did earlier. The document prompted the Prime Minister, who was anticipating (and possibly even welcoming) trouble, to summon Minister Adams. As the military fortunes of the Union had declined, and with them respect for him and his mission, Adams had endured a difficult year. American envoys were long considered to have substituted pallbearer's garb for Court dress because of State Department instructions that they be suited without aristocratic pretensions. When Adams had presented his credentials to the Queen and Prince on 19 May 1861, wearing traditional diplomatic costume, Victoria is said to have remarked tartly, 'I am thankful we shall have no more American funerals'.

With hardly more courtesy, Palmerston confronted Adams with the seaport rumour that the *James Adger* was awaiting an opportunity to intercept the Southern emissaries, warning, according to the Minister's report to Secretary of State William H. Seward, 'It would be regarded here very unpleasantly if the captain, after enjoying the hospitality of this country, [and] filling his ship with coals and other supplies, and filling his own stomach with brandy' – and here he laughed in his characteristic way – 'should, within sight of the shore, commit an act which would be felt as offensive to the national flag.'

Palmerston already knew that there would be no immediate difficulty from the American warship, as he had in his pocket a report from one of his operatives that the captain, 'having got very drunk this morning at Southampton with some excellent brandy, and find it blow heavily at sea', had decided not to weigh anchor. Not having the benefit of such up-to-date intelligence, Adams assured the Prime Minister that his apprehensions were groundless.

Adams's message to Seward about Palmerston's warning was still *en route* by sea to Washington when the *San Jacinto* docked in Norfolk on the evening of 15 November. (The Union controlled the chief ports of secessionist Virginia.) From there Secretary of the Navy Gideon Welles ordered Wilkes to take his prisoners to Fort Warren in Boston harbour. The news raced north quickly – that at noon on 8 November, a week earlier, the Southerners, then four thousand miles from the English Channel, had been encountered in waters north of Cuba, and taken captive.

The Queen and Prince learned of the anxieties in Whitehall on 13 November from Palmerston, who reviewed for them his conference at the Treasury. International law as accepted during the Napoleonic wars condoned a search, and the removal of the vessel to a harbour of the belligerent. Proceedings there for its seizure were justified 'if enemy dispatches were found on board, or any other contraband'. Palmerston had seen Adams, and assured him that the arrival of Slidell and Mason in England 'would have no more effect on the policy of her Majesty with regard to America than the presence of the three other Southern Deputies who have been here for many months'. Yet the Southerners had an informal legation in Suffolk Street, not far from the Houses of Parliament and Downing Street, had established contacts with MPs and sympathizers in the aristocracy, and were zealous in bargaining cotton for weapons.

In his distinctive third-person manner, Henry Adams recalled that on the afternoon of 27 November, while he languished in the American Legation in Mansfield Street, quiet during the absence of the Minister and Mrs Adams on a visit to Yorkshire, a Reuters telegram reporting the seizure of Mason and Slidell had come. The agency had facilities at Cork in Ireland, enabling Reuters to beat transatlantic news from ships arriving in Liverpool by several hours. 'All three secretaries, public and private, were there – nervous as wild beasts under the long strain on their endurance – and all three, though they knew it to be not merely their order of departure – not merely a diplomatic rupture – but a

declaration of war – broke into shouts of delight. They were glad to face
the end. They saw it and cheered it! Since England was waiting only for
its own moment to strike, they were eager to strike first.'

Second Secretary Benjamin Moran, less elated than Adams, wrote
anxiously in his diary, 'I am satisfied that the act will do more for the
Southerners than ten victories, for it touches John Bull's honor, and the
honor of his flag. I telegraphed the news at once to Mr Adams, and fear
it has not added to his enjoyment of rural retirement.'

The Adamses were at Fryston Hall as guests of Richard Monckton
Milnes, MP, soon to be Baron Houghton, who had arranged for the
literary company of Froudes, Gaskells and Forsters to show England at
its sophisticated best for the son and grandson of two American
presidents. 'Telegram delivered to Mr Adams while he was inspecting
Pomfret Castle announcing *the North* had captured Southerners off
Eng. ship', Annabel Monckton Milnes jotted down in her pocket diary
for 27 November 1861. To her sister she wrote, after the Americans had
rushed back to London by train, 'This terrible threat of War in the far
West is hanging over England! May God in his mercy avert such a
calamity!... *Richee* and *all England* are feeling anxious about this American dispute...'

Adams expected to have his passport returned as soon as Whitehall
learned the news, and was worried, as his hosts in Yorkshire had been,
that war was inevitable. Even before he had arrived back in London, the
Confederate commissioners there had rushed a memorandum to Russell and Palmerston contending that while envoys proceeding from an
enemy port to a neutral one were subject to seizure, whatever the flag, if
they were travelling from one neutral port to another, they were, under
international law, to be conveyed unmolested, as were their dispatches.
Only an admiralty tribunal, W.L. Yancey, P.A. Rost, and A. Dudley
Mann wrote, could decide otherwise, and no such hearing had been
held for the *Trent*. And they claimed for their imprisoned countrymen
'the full benefit of that protection to which every private person who
seeks shelter under the British flag and demeans himself according to
British law has heretofore ever before to be entitled'. A second letter
from the trio would emphasize 'the great outrage upon the British flag'.

In Richmond, President Davis had already addressed the Confederate Congress on the *Trent* affair, declaring on 18 November, 'These
gentlemen' – to the North they were rebel escapees – 'were as much

under the jurisdiction of the British Government upon that ship and beneath its flag as if they had been on its soil, and a claim on the part of the United States to seize them in the streets of London would have been as well founded as to apprehend them where they were taken'.

The London press occupied itself with American belligerent rights at sea. Palmerston's own law officers advised that Captain Wilkes had illegally taken international law into his own hands – or had been instructed to do so by Washington. As Adams phrased it, ruefully, 'Great Britain would have been less offended if the United States had insulted her a good deal more'. By then Palmerston and everyone else had forgotten about the *James Adger*, which had slipped out of Southampton and into the Atlantic. But the irrelevant *Nashville* was never sighted, and Marchand would arrive in Hampton Roads, Virginia on 2 December, while the *Trent* imbroglio was still unsettled.

In Anthony Trollope's *Phineas Finn* (1867–69), the fictional Prime Minister asks the young MP, 'Have you seen the news from America?' 'Yes', says Finn, 'I have seen it but do not believe it.' Provoking the Empire seemed beyond comprehension.

Among the Queen's guests on 28 November, a Thursday, was the ambitious Chancellor of the Exchequer, W.E. Gladstone, whom Albert had wooed long and hard for military funding, and who was envisioned as a future Prime Minister. Earlier in the year the Prince had sent him a draft 'Law for Ministerial Responsibility' for Prussia, which Vicky had drawn up for her husband, 'intended to be called for by the opposition in that country and dreaded by many advisers of the King'. It appeared 'so well argued, that I made the Prince of Wales translate it from the German'. Clearly, Albert had a preliminary hand in it. In liberal but ill-conceived good will, he had been interfering in the internal affairs of another sovereign nation, and then displayed the evidence as a gesture of confidence in Gladstone. Only two weeks before the dinner, the Prince, whose activities had inevitably fallen off with his illness, had, as Master of Trinity House, honoured Gladstone with an appointment as an Elder Brother. Gladstone had already received from Albert a printed copy of his British Association address at Aberdeen, and an article from the *Revue des deux Mondes*, which Albert read regularly, on the financing of imperial France.

Returning to London from Windsor, Gladstone noted laconically in his diary, 'The Queen and Prince spoke much of the American news, &

in the anti-Northern sense.' The evening saw Albert's first attempt at
dinner in many days: news of the outrage had animated him. The next
day, 29 November, because of the crisis, the Queen went into London
without him to learn what she could of a Cabinet debate on the affair,
but had to return before it was ended. Although Albert had reported
himself as '*noch immer recht miserable*' – 'still extremely miserable' – he
was determined to show himself and avoid gossip about his health, and
had stood that morning for twenty minutes to watch two hundred Eton
College Volunteers pass in review. The weather was unseasonably mild,
but the Prince wore a coat with a fur lining and walked very slowly. '*Ich
muss leider dabei erscheinen*', he confided weakly in his diary – 'Unhappily I must put in an appearance'.

That Friday evening Gladstone was deputed back to Windsor, '&
reported to Q. & Prince'. Before dinner he sent a note to the Queen
'that the Cabinet is of opinion that reparation for the seizure of Messrs
Mason and Slidell ought to be asked from the Government of the
United States and that Lord Russell is to prepare a dispatch on which
the Cabinet will deliberate tomorrow, for submission to Your Majesty'.

Confined to his bedroom all afternoon, Albert left it to learn what
had happened. By then his initial wrath over the *Trent* affair had begun
to moderate. During the first years of his marriage he had been involved
in the movement to suppress the slave trade, and must have recalled that
the Royal Navy in the early 1840s had claimed the right to search
American vessels suspected to be slavers. It was known in England that
Slidell when a Senator in 1850 had helped to draft the notorious
Fugitive Slave Law. In *The Times* that morning had appeared letters,
signed 'Templar' and 'Senex', from readers conversant in international
law, warning of the tenuous grounds for demanding reparations from
Washington. 'There can be no reason of principle', 'Templar' argued,
'why persons other than military may not be contraband if they be in
fact engaged in furthering the military operations of the enemy.' 'Senex'
raised the point that 'You may stop the Ambassador of your enemy on
his passage, but when he has arrived and taken up himself the functions
of his office and has been admitted in his representative character, he
becomes . . . entitled to peculiar [diplomatic] privileges, as set apart for
the relations of amity and peace.' Further, 'Senex' recalled, a declaration
by the Queen on 15 April 1854, early in the Crimean War, contained the
passage (very likely Palmerstonian), 'It is impossible for Her Majesty to

forgo the exercise of her right of seizing articles [that are] contraband of war, and of preventing neutrals from carrying [the] enemy's despatches.' And newspapers had published reports of interviews with Mrs Slidell, who had now arrived with her daughter, seventeen-year-old Rosina, on the *Trent*, revealing that she had concealed her husband's contraband papers under her capacious crinoline.

Although Victoria had admired Harriet Beecher Stowe, read her *Uncle Tom's Cabin*, and even arranged to meet the lady who was the best-known foe of the Fugitive Slave Law, her emotions were now confused. To Vicky in Berlin, she wrote, 'The great and all absorbing event of the day is the American outrage. The Government have decided (and they could not do anything else – as the act is quite illegal) to ask reparation and if this is not given – we know what must follow. They are such ruffians!' Ill as he was, Albert had a conversion to attempt once the Queen's guests took their leave.

The next day, Foreign Minister Earl Russell (as Lord John had become) would draw up a Cabinet-approved memorandum to Lord Lyons, Minister to the United States, directing 'that the Washington Government' – the very term was truculent, implicitly recognizing a rival capital in Richmond, Virginia – 'should be told that what has been done is a violation of international law, and of the rights of Great Britain, and that Her Majesty's Government trust that the act will be disavowed and that the prisoners set free and restored to British protection; and that . . . if this demand is refused, he' – Lyons – 'should retire from the United States'.

Reports from Unionists in London were much like that of George Francis Train in the *Boston Journal* – that 'the Army, the Navy, the Church, the Parliament, the Aristocracy, the Banker[s]', were supporting secession although ordinary people ('the pit and the gallery') were fearful of war and sympathetic with the Federal government. English vessels were shipping 'every sort of contraband to aid the rebellion', he claimed, and when Adams had protested to Palmerston, the Prime Minister had allegedly (so Train wrote) retorted, 'We know it; catch them if you can.'

Expecting that the *Trent* case would be a pretext for war, the *Boston Post* vowed 'Such a war will bring starvation to [British] doors. We have been their best customers; we have furnished them with bread, and we have bought their goods. The first hostile gun fired, and the doors of

Commerce will be slammed in the face of insolent Britannia. Not a bushel of grain – not a yard of cloth – shall cross the ocean.'

The enthusiasm of the Unionist press over the coup of the *San Jacinto* was interpreted in England to mean that Captain Wilkes had acted on the orders of Secretary of State Seward, to whom President Abraham Lincoln usually deferred in foreign relations matters. Seward and Lincoln now seemed captives of public opinion in the North. The shots across the bow of the *Trent* were not intended to provoke war with Britain – which should have been clear from a report in London that Fairfax had confided on boarding the *Trent* that his captain had acted on his own initiative. Yet the boarding of a ship flying the British flag seemed an insult to the empire. 'Bear this, bear all!' was the rallying cry in the London press. Eight thousand troops were ordered to Canada; warships were transferred to waters off the American coast; the sale of munitions to the North (but not to the South) was halted; arsenals in Britain were put on day-and-night shifts; and the Cunard steamer *Europa* sailed to New York with preliminary instructions to Lyons that could lead to a break in relations and possibly much more. On his own, he wrote on 19 November to Russell, 'I don't think it likely that they' – the North – 'will give in, but I do not think it impossible that they may do so, particularly if the next news from England brings a note of warlike preparation, and determination on the part of [our] Government and people.'

Having listened for two evenings to the Prince's moderating views on the *Trent* crisis, Gladstone wrote to Palmerston on Saturday morning, 30 November, after returning from Windsor on the 11.25 to Paddington. Later the same day, he noted in his diary 'Ld Russell's draft softened & abridged'. Revised Foreign Office drafts of instructions to Lyons arrived late on Saturday at Windsor while the Queen presided over yet another dinner for visiting dignitaries. The Prince, too ill to sit at the table, was absent. Yet he may not have been too ill to have seen that morning's *Times*, which would have been brought to him as usual. Prominent in it was another letter from a lawyer with an Inns of Court address, signed 'Justitia', which downgraded the seizure of the Confederate party to 'an irregularity...admitted even by those who are disposed to take the least inflammatory view of the subject'.

A Prize Court, the writer proposed, 'might have fairly taken the confession of Mr Slidell and his friends, that they were Southern

Commissioners, coupled with the occupation in which it is notorious that other Southern Commissioners are now engaged, as a sufficient proof of their mission. If the Court had come to such a decision, could the English Government have disputed their judgement as one in gross violation of law and justice? If not, it would have been binding on us, and the *Trent* would have been condemned as lawful prize.' Because the United States had not taken the *Trent* into port, the writer claimed that the act was illegal only in 'form', not in 'substance'.

The solution, 'Justitia' proposed, 'is this – what we are entitled beyond all question to demand is an apology for the illegal and irregular proceeding...and an undertaking that the offence shall not be re-peated...I cannot think that we are entitled to push our demand to the extreme point of requiring the restitution of the Commissioners. Such a demand would almost certainly be repelled. And England, before she can appeal to the arbitrament of arms, must have a quarrel good not only in *form*, but in substance.'

Whatever the legalities, another certainty was that a Palmerston government would not settle for less than the release of the Southerners. Albert had experienced enough confrontations with 'Pam' to realize that. The Prince had to reconcile, in any approach of his own, domestic needs with foreign policy pragmatism, and *The Times* had also held out the editorial hope that the seizure, as reported, was 'the act of the American commander, and was not expressly directed by his govern-ment'.*

Both Palmerston and Russell had prepared the Queen on Friday, 29 November, the day before, to receive a strong Cabinet draft, 'which will go to your Majesty about four o'clock tomorrow', and required '[no] loss of time', Russell urged, as the documents, in that pre-mechanical age, had to be recopied in time to make the Sunday evening mail packet

---

* Unknown yet in London was the congratulatory message from Secretary of the Navy Welles to Captain Wilkes – now promoted to Commodore – for his 'great public service' – but which also admonished him for failing to bring the *Trent* into port for adjudication. Not until 2 December would Congress pass an ill-considered joint resolution thanking Wilkes, and requesting President Lincoln to award Wilkes a special gold medal. 'I paid my respects to the President', Wilkes wrote in a memoir, '& had some conversation with him. He remarked that I had kicked up a breeze, but he intended to stand by me and rejoiced over the boldness, as he said, of my act.' But there was no gold medal, and despite his elevation in rank, no 'hearty welcome' from Welles when he visited the Navy Department in person.

to New York. Palmerston had been more inflammatory in his own preparatory letter, employing unsubstantiated allegations which suggested a reluctance to offer Washington anything it could honourably accept. The affair had been 'a gross outrage and [a] violation of international law has been committed'. The American response necessitated 'reparation and redress'.

Although Mrs Slidell had reported the boarding officer's admission of unilateral action, 'it was known', Palmerston claimed to the Queen, that the warship had put into St Thomas several weeks before 'and had there received communications from New York; and it is also said that General [Winfield] Scott, who has recently arrived in France, has said to Americans in Paris that he has not come on an excursion of pleasure, but on diplomatic business; that the seizure of these envoys was discussed in Cabinet at Washington, he being present, and was deliberately determined upon and ordered; that the Washington Cabinet fully foresaw that it might lead to war with England'. Further, Palmerston alleged, the elderly leader of the American war with Mexico (a doddering seventy-five) had been 'commissioned to propose to France in that case to join the northern States in war against England, and to offer France in that case restoration of [Quebec,] the French province of Canada'. Scott, he sneered, would 'find himself much mistaken', for the French government 'is probably thinking more about Cotton than about Canada'.

Palmerston seemed eager to raise the warlike hackles of a queen who had called herself 'a soldier's daughter'. England had been insulted, and America had been conspiring to draw her into war. In the Commons, Richard Cobden warned, 'Palmerston likes to drive the wheel close to the edge, and show how dexterously he can avoid falling over the precipice.'

Victoria brought the documents to Albert as he lay on a sofa awaiting the departure of her guests. He had already seen the Prime Minister's anticipatory invective, and now his ultimatum to the United States – it had that strident Palmerstonian tone – further agitated the Prince. 'This means war!' he warned.

As Albert lay, sleepless, into Sunday morning (1 December) – he had moved to a separate room days earlier to avoid disturbing Victoria – he pondered alternative approaches that could satisfy national pride and meet the government's minimum political requirements, yet might enable Washington to accede gracefully. Finally, in the lingering darkness that followed a December dawn he arose and struggled to draw up a response to the Cabinet for the Queen to re-draft and sign.

Palmerston and Russell, it was clear, had little expectation that Washington could afford, in the face of American public opinion, to submit to the British terms, even if Seward and Lincoln saw them as tolerable. While Adams waited for instructions from Washington, Seward was writing, too late to be of use, 'We have done nothing to anticipate the discussion [in Downing Street], and we have not furnished you with any explanations... because we feel it is more prudent that the ground to be taken by the British government should first be made known to us here...' Meanwhile, the Prime Minister expected – he wrote to Russell – that they would not get what they demanded from the United States 'without fighting for it', while *The Times* suggested that Seward wanted war in order to seize Canada as a replacement for the lost South. In Paris, the American consul, John Bigelow, saw British exploitation of the Mason–Slidell incident as an opportunity to split the Union. As Albert had told Disraeli, English newspapers orchestrated public opinion; indignation, with the lure of cotton in the background, and the salvage of industrial jobs, intensified daily, despite moral support in the Midlands for the anti-slavery North. 'That pink of modesty and refinement, *The Times*', Benjamin Moran seethed in his diary, 'is filled with such slatternly abuse of us and ours, that it is fair to conclude that all the Fishwives of Billingsgate have been transferred to Printing House Square to fill the ears of the writers there with their choicest phraseology'.

It was nearly eight o'clock when Albert shuffled to the Queen with his pages, confessing, as he handed them to her, '*Ich bin so schwach, ich habe kaum die Feder halten können*' – 'I am so weak, I have hardly been able to hold the pen'. In the margin of the manuscript Victoria would later note, 'This draft was the last the beloved Prince ever wrote...' He could eat no breakfast, and returned to bed.

Setting her agitation about Albert aside, Victoria examined his response, making few alterations. 'The Queen returns these important Drafts', she wrote to Palmerston,

which upon the whole she approves; but she cannot help feeling that the main Draft – that for communication to the American government – is somewhat meagre. She should have liked to have seen the

Albert confessed that he was so weak that he could hardly hold his pen when he drafted his response to the Cabinet's Trent *ultimatum on the morning of 1 December 1861.*

expression of a hope, that the American captain did not act under instructions, or, if he did, that he misapprehended them, – that the United States Government must be fully aware that the British Government could not allow its flag to be insulted, and the security of her mail communications to be placed in jeopardy; and Her Majesty's Government are unwilling to believe that the United States Government intended wantonly to put an insult upon this country, and to add to their many distressing complications by forcing a question of dispute upon us, and that we are therefore glad to believe that, upon a full consideration of the undoubted breach of International Law committed, they would spontaneously offer such redress as alone could satisfy this country, *viz*, the restoration of the unfortunate passengers and a suitable apology.

Palmerston read the Queen's message as he received further reports from New York – mail took ten to twelve days by sea to London – about the jubilation following Wilkes's exploit. The *New York Times* on 19 November had predicted, since it was 'such an exact imitation' of past English policy, that its government 'will [not] even remonstrate.' The *New York Tribune* suggested that English military assistance to the South was aimed at eliminating the United States as a commercial rival. Poet James Russell Lowell, later a much-admired American Minister to London, would capture public resentment of what seemed bullying from Britain in verses deploring,

> It don't seem hardly right, John,
> When both my hands was full,
> To stump me to a fight, John –
> Your cousin, *tu*, John Bull...

While Albert insisted on walking on the Castle terrace for half an hour, and, although looking pale and ill, to make a show – it was a Sunday – of attending Chapel with the Queen before returning to bed, Victoria's response on the *Trent* crisis was rushed by messenger to Whitehall. Refusing luncheon, Albert confessed to recurrent stomach pain and chills. Both Sir James Clark and Dr William Jenner came to see him but offered no new medication. The Prince also refused dinner and, shifting back and forth from sofa to bed, retired early but again could not sleep.

In London, Albert's expedient in the Queen's memorandum was immediately apparent to Palmerston and Russell. In a letter to Windsor on 29 November, which the Prince had read, Palmerston had acknowledged that the *San Jacinto* boarding-party had admitted to acting independently of Washington. The Prince preferred that explanation to the conspiratorial one attributed to ancient General Scott. Albert wanted Seward and Lincoln to have the opportunity, even if untrue, of denying responsibility for Captain Wilkes's breach of international law, and thereby to be able, without loss of dignity, to relinquish the Southerners. Despite the belligerence of the British press, Albert also saw no risk in removing from Palmerston's stipulations offensive expressions which might block a politic Federal retreat. *Punch*'s John Bull could warn Brother Jonathan – Uncle Sam's precursor – 'You do what's right, my son, or I'll blow you out of the water', but American honour precluded submitting to threats.

'Your Majesty's position is anyhow a good one', Palmerston (while still unaware how ill Albert was) conceded to the Queen. The conciliatory approach was not the one which the Prime Minister preferred, but Russell's instructions to Lord Lyons in Washington and the message he was to deliver to Seward reflected the temper of the Prince's draft, concluding,

> Her Majesty's Government, bearing in mind the friendly relations which have long subsisted between Great Britain and the United States, are willing to believe that the United States naval officer who committed this aggression was not acting in compliance with any authority from his Government, or that, if he conceived himself to be so authorised, he greatly misunderstood the instructions which he had received. For the Government of the United States must be fully aware that the British Government could not allow such an affront to the national honour to pass without full reparation; and Her Majesty's Government are unwilling to believe that it could be the deliberate intention of the Government of the United States unnecessarily to force into discussion between the two Governments a question of so grave a character, and with regard to which the whole British Nation would be sure to entertain such unanimity of feeling.

Her Majesty's Government therefore trust that, when this matter shall have been brought under the consideration of the United States, that Government will of its own accord offer to the British Government such redress as alone could satisfy the British nation, namely, the liberation of the four gentlemen, and their delivery to your Lordship, in order that they may again be placed under British protection, and a suitable apology for the aggression which has been committed.

Beneath the wooden diplomatic prose, the message was more tactful than Palmerston had intended. Frustrated in his pro-South subterfuges, he wrote hopefully to Russell on 6 December 1861 as their moderated provisos made their way on a mail packet to New York, 'It is difficult not to come to the conclusion that the rabid hatred of England which animates the exiled Irishmen who direct almost all the Northern newspapers, will so excite the masses as to make it impossible for Lincoln and Seward to grant our demands; and we must therefore look forward to war as the probable result . . . Republican nations or nations in which the masses influence or direct the destinies of the country are swayed much more by passion than by interest.'

When, on 19 December, the Foreign Minister received a surprisingly pacific reply from Seward, indicating that Mason and Slidell and their two aides would be released and put aboard a British steamer to Southampton, a decision confirmed by a Christmas Day Cabinet meeting, Palmerston suppressed the news until the press learned that the Southerners had actually sailed. Northerners were disgusted and unrepentant, but resigned. 'I had no right to object to the manner in which the Govt thought proper to act', Commodore Wilkes wrote, 'but when Mr Seward read me his dispatch to Lord Russell and asked my opinion of it, I frankly told him it was an act which I had not expected . . . I felt a glow of shame for my country . . . ' In 'Donelson', Herman Melville compared 'The bitter cup / Of that hard Countermand / Which gave the Envoys up' to 'wormwood in the mouth'. To London publisher Frederic Chapman, Anthony Trollope wrote, 'So we are to have no war; I for one am very glad.'

It remains one of the intriguing *ifs* of the age that without Albert's intervention, the last political act of his life, in defusing the belligerent Palmerston–Russell ultimatum, there might have been an

Anglo-American war which could have drawn in France,* and irrevocably divided both Canada and the United States.

In the early days of December, Albert continued to deteriorate. His sleeplessness aggravated his fatigue. Food nauseated him; even soup with a bit of brown bread caused vomiting. Dr Jenner examined him and saw no cause for concern, although he thought that 'a long feverish indisposition' would be dangerous. Still, Albert's malaise and general discomfort had not been followed by fever, which encouraged Victoria to downplay the illness when Palmerston, sincerely anxious, asked to have another physician called in. In a few days it will 'pass off', she assured him. 'In addition to Sir James Clark, the Queen has the advantage of the constant advice of Dr Jenner, a most skillful Physician, and Her Majesty would be very unwilling to cause unnecessary alarm, where no cause exists for it, by calling in a Medical Man who does not upon ordinary occasions attend.'

The lack of alarm showed in the casualness of Albert's treatment – or lack of it. When he could, he paced about his dressing-room, and sometimes changed bedrooms. He could keep little food down, even tea, and alternated between wild incoherence and being a competent host to his children, who came to talk or to read to him. In an age when nurses functioned only in hospitals, the Prince was tended by such personal servants as Rudolf Löhlein, Court retainers, and Princess Alice. Eighteen, with no previous responsibility of any sort, she filled the vacuum as head nurse with instinctive authority, following her father when he padded restlessly about.

On 8 December, a Sunday, the doctors around Albert even told the Queen, because he seemed to be no worse, that he appeared somewhat better, a verdict made plausible when he asked to hear some music. Alice played, as he requested, the Lutheran chorale 'A Mighty Fortress Is Our God', but he soon murmured, '*Das reicht hin*' – 'That's enough'. Later, Alice was permitted to play several German songs that she knew were his favourites, and he asked to have his sofa moved closer to the window so that he could watch the clouds drift across the sky. When

---

* The French Minister in Washington, and, after the fact, the Foreign Minister, sided with the British, but words and war are very different matters, and the opportunistic Napoleon III may well have attempted to regain Quebec much as he tried, vainly, in 1863 to seat a puppet emperor on a throne he created for Prince Maximilian in Mexico.

Alice thought he had dozed off, she covered him with a blanket. He opened his eyes. 'Were you asleep?' she asked.

'No,' he said, with a wan smile, 'but my thoughts were so happy that I did not want to drive them away by moving.'

In the evening, Victoria read to him from Walter Scott's *Peveril of the Peak*, but he had her stop when he decided to change bedrooms again, and walked from her own to the 'King's Room' – the Blue Room, in which both George IV and William IV had died. He was apparently preparing for his own death, yet everything that his attending physicians could possibly conceive as a sign of improvement was so interpreted, and his renewed activity appeared to them positive and welcome.

The next day, the two envoys who had been on a condolence visit to Lisbon, Lord Methuen and General Seymour (Albert's companion in Italy in 1839), arrived, and Albert insisted upon seeing them. If they were carrying typhoid from Portugal, he may have thought the disease could hardly hurt him now. Also at Windsor was gouty Lord Palmerston, leaning on canes, to urge again that other medical opinions be sought. Again the Queen refused, although she was increasingly worried because Albert's mind was wandering and he insisted on calling her '*gutes Weibchen*' – 'good little wife' – and holding her hand.

Since a low fever had been confirmed, doctors now remained in attendance day and night. Jenner possessed considerable clinical experience of typhoid fever – often euphemistically referred to as 'gastric fever' – and finally thought he saw evidence of the characteristic pink rash of the disease. That it should have taken Jenner so long to identify Albert's ailment, if indeed he had, remains a mystery, for when he was a young physician in 1845 (he was now forty-six) he had published a paper establishing the clinico-pathologic distinction between typhus and typhoid fever. In any case, whatever he identified as typhoid, given his special reputation, was almost certain to be accepted as such by most other physicians – and by the Queen, who later knighted him. To her, he explained the implications of the disease in a dismissive manner. It would run its course in a month if there were no 'bad symptoms', as Victoria put it in her journal. The Prince was not to know any more than that he had a 'feverish cold'.

Nor was the public. The previous Sunday, two days earlier, a bulletin had been issued by his doctors declaring exactly that, adding that there were 'no unfavourable symptoms'. No new bulletin would be issued to the press identifying typhoid, and fresh releases on 11 December and 12 December would be equally uninformative except for the ominous implication of the signatures of additional physicians. No cases of typhoid appeared otherwise in the vicinity of Windsor, nor had any emerged at Sandhurst, where, in any event, Albert had arrived too ill to have luncheon, and had drunk nothing.

Tuesday, 10 December, found Albert too weak and listless to make any attempt to dress. To the Prince's aides, his condition seemed grave. They remembered Palmerston's repeated appeals for better medical advice. The Prince and the Prime Minister had often been at odds, but the elderly politician had come to respect Albert's abilities, and was concerned about losing him. Recalling the Flora Hastings embarrassment twenty-two years earlier, before the advent of the Prince, and the persistence at Court of the medical authority of that era, Sir James Clark, now seventy-three, Palmerston had earlier urged on Sir Charles Phipps the necessity of forestalling an even more tragic misdiagnosis. 'If it is unavoidable that the highest interests of the nation be sacrificed to personal and professional jealousy,' he warned, 'there is no help for it and so it must be. I could say much about the past, but my thoughts are wholly engrossed with the future.' There was still the risk of war with the United States. If that occurred, he wanted Albert available. The monarchy without him was almost inconceivable, and the instructions to Lord Lyons were on a mail packet due to arrive in New York the next day.

Beyond the Prince's family, the most distraught observer of the inevitable, his feelings complicated by unhappy medical insight and the helplessness of distance, was Baron Stockmar in Coburg. By early December he was disregarding information from the Court on Albert's condition as unreliable, and queried Squires, the royal chemists, to find out what medication had been prescribed. Peter Squire handed the letter to his head apothecary, David Williamson, telling him, he later recalled to his son, 'that if he liked he could reply to it, but that he must be on the side of extreme caution'. Very likely the actual preparations would have evidenced that the Prince was not being treated with anything intended to be curative.

On the morning of the eleventh, Albert sat up in bed to drink beef tea. When his aide, General Grey, also brought him some unwelcome and useless medicine, he managed a wry joke, raising the glass weakly and saying, 'Your very good health, Grey'. The gesture did not deceive the Queen, who was more frank than usual with Vicky, perhaps preparing herself as well as her daughter for the worst. The Court physicians remained satisfied with Albert's condition, she wrote – 'though he gets sadly thin. It is a dreadful trial to witness this, and requires all my strength of mind and courage not to be overcome – when I look at him . . .' They were so 'fortunate in the doctors', she insisted, but it was necessary 'to satisfy the public to have another eminent doctor to come and see him, which I own distressed me much . . . however I submitted'.

Despite some resentment from Clark and Jenner, Thomas Watson, one of the Physicians Extraordinary to the Queen, and the equally veteran Sir Henry Holland were called in, and the Queen clasped Holland's hands in hers and cried, 'Oh, you will save him for me, Dr Holland! You will save him for me, will you not?'

Both physicians accepted the minimal therapy in progress, but Sir Henry, recognizing that the public had to be prepared for what was beyond medicine, drew up a bulletin for the press, beginning, 'Hitherto there has been no anticipation of danger . . .' When his text was submitted to the Queen she was unable to face the implication, and struck out 'Hitherto'.

Neither Clark nor the septuagenarian Holland, Lord Clarendon deplored, 'were fit to attend a sick cat', but Sir Henry, at the least, was a realist. Once physician to George IV's estranged Queen Caroline, he dismissed the Prince's wandering mind as 'of no consequence, though very distressing'.

As Victoria suggested to her daughter in Berlin, the eminent Dr Watson, author of a textbook on medicine and later Sir Thomas Watson, was superfluous, but only because the Prince could not benefit from his pharmacopoeia. Had the Queen recalled Lord Melbourne's remark that 'English physicians kill you; the French let you die', she might have understood that Albert's doctors were applying, despite their Anglo-Saxon training, the humane French method. Sedated with brandy and given little else, Albert was failing rapidly.

On the twelfth, when another innocuous bulletin was issued by the four physicians in attendance, the Prince coughed up a large quantity of mucus. He shuddered with chills and with quickened breathing, although he was able, briefly, to lay his head affectionately on Victoria's shoulder as she knelt at his bedside. His temperature had risen, and he was often delirious. He imagined that he heard the birds singing at the Rosenau, and was consumed by absurd worries, even about cousins he had not seen for years. More lucidly, he asked Alice, now almost constantly present, whether Vicky knew about his illness. 'Yes,' said Alice truthfully. 'I told her you were very ill.'

'You did wrong. You should have told her that I am dying. Yes, I am dying.'

Alice had seen her father try to confide much the same recognition to the Queen, who resisted by breaking into sobs and forcing him into silence. Now he appeared to want to confide something further to his daughter, and she pulled a chair close to the bed. He struggled to say something, but she could not understand the words.

One wonders whether Albert, having accepted his imminent death, might have recalled songs he had composed in the inexperience of youth, when their melancholy was only appropriated from *Lieder* tradition. In '*Trauenlied*' ('Lament') the singer recalled pursuing

> a gleam of happiness
> which always seemed to lead me on,

and that when he followed its 'glimmering light' it 'did ever flee ahead', uncaptured.

> All of a sudden, I don't know how,
> I found I had to turn back to see it.
> It shone behind me like the twilight.
> How did I pass it without noticing?
> It must have happened in a dream.

There had also been his 'Last Words of a Bard', whose creative fires are 'extinguished', and whose 'torrent of songs' has ended. The wind stirs in him 'sounds from forgotten times', and from the window he sees the sinking sun throwing 'a last gleam of light for me'.

> The gentle lyre no longer sings
> At many a festival's high ceremony.
> Soon I will lie silent in my grave…

The 13th was a Friday. Jenner told the Queen that the Prince's condition was stable, and that she could take a morning walk, but by late afternoon it seemed urgent for the family to gather – a step that Alice had anticipated by summoning Bertie. 'The breathing was the alarming thing', Victoria recorded, 'it was so rapid. There was what they call a dusky hue about the face and hands, which I knew was not good.' She told Jenner, who appeared alarmed. Then she saw Albert begin to arrange his hair and fold his arms, 'just as he used to do when well and dressing... Strange! as though he were preparing for another and greater journey.'

The public knew almost nothing, other than that the Prince Consort was ill with a fever, although members of the Household from the Master of the Horse on down had begun to break through the wall of discretion. Mail from Windsor Castle to London and the Home Counties was often delivered the same day. Finally, at five o'clock the first bulletin suggesting a grave outcome was issued, recording that the patient had passed a restless night and confessing that 'the symptoms have assumed an unfavourable character during the day'. No specific malady was identified. The Queen was told that Albert was sinking fast.

When alone with Lady Augusta Bruce that evening, Victoria collapsed into hysterical tears and prayer. Recovering, she called for Sir Charles Phipps and collapsed again into uncontrollable grief. Then, bracing herself, she went to sit calmly by Albert's bed. He seemed now warm and comfortable, and managed to recognize her, kiss her, press her hand, and weakly call her '*gutes Fräuchen*'. Waiting for the inevitable, Albert's doctors continued drugging him with brandy every half-hour. He had taken no solid food for many days.

Phipps was instructed to send a messenger to Palmerston with the warning, 'I deeply grieve to say that the Prince's disease has taken a very unfavourable turn, and that the Doctors are in the *greatest anxiety* – they have even fears for the night.' When the Prince of Wales arrived late Friday evening, summoned, Natty Rothschild wrote to his parents from Cambridge, from a 'gay party', there was concern that his presence might upset his father, but Albert's eyes, when open, now stared fixedly. All that Bertie had known from Windsor before Alice's message had been the untruth that there was a gastric fever 'epidemic' at the Castle, and that the Prince Consort had fallen victim to it.

Once the Queen and the younger children had left the sickroom for the night, Colonel Biddulph, Master of the Household, with Generals Grey and Bruce, shifted Albert's bed from the window prospect that had given him pleasure to the centre of the room, in preparation for the end. To their surprise, the Prince was able to arise while the move was in progress, but he had to be helped back into bed.

On the bright early morning of 14 December, the growing group of doctors permitted themselves some renewed optimism. In the first sunlight of Saturday, Albert's gaunt face looked younger, and even radiant. Dr Henry Brown, who had been the Duchess of Kent's physician, even suggested to the Queen that 'there was ground to hope the crisis was over', prompting her to telegraph as much to the frantic and hopelessly remote Vicky. If the illness were typhoid, that was at least possible. If Albert's affliction, however, was a long, slow, debilitating one – probably stomach cancer, which fits many of his self-confessed symptoms over at least four years – he had no resources left. Had his physicians – even the obtuse Dr Clark – fathomed this earlier, they also knew that their skills offered no remedies. Victoria, too, seemed to have sensed something potentially catastrophic and to have pushed it away, uncertain as to whether her fragile equilibrium could absorb that much reality.

As the morning wore on, the doctors retreated from their fantasy that the Prince was rallying. 'Alas!' Phipps messaged to Palmerston, 'the hopes of the morning are fading away . . .' At midday, Albert was given a spoonful of brandy, but no attempt was made to raise his head. 'He is not worse', Dr Watson told Victoria without conviction; 'the pulse keeps up'. Then he confessed to being 'very much frightened, but [I] don't and won't give up hope'.

A bulletin at nine had indicated no change, but at 4.30 p.m. the patient was declared to be in a 'most critical state'.

In the darkened room, members of the Household gathered, stood uneasily, then slipped out. After her own exit, Lady Biddulph rushed to her husband's office in the castle to write to Earl Spencer, Groom of the Stole to Albert and thus titular head of his Establishment, 'VERY VERY bad news. All the Household have just been up to the Prince's room to see for the last time him who is *fast sinking*. The doctors say there is no hope not the slightest of His Royal Highness's life being spared, but none may say how long it may go on . . .'

Now and then one of the physicians checked the Prince's weakening pulse, but did little else. Alice remained at one side of the bed, where she had posted herself, when awake, for days. At the foot of the bed were Bertie and Helena, and, as the day wore on, Louise and Arthur.

Alfred was at sea; the haemophiliac Leopold was in France for his health and Beatrice, at four, was too young for such scenes. The Prince's rapid breathing had become alarming. Victoria hastened to the side of the bed across from Alice and whispered to Albert, '*es ist Fraüchen*'. Then she bent toward him and asked for '*einem Kuss*', and he kissed her. Then he dozed again. Victoria, with a terrible calm, held his thin, cold hand until her misery became overwhelming. She burst from the room and broke down.

The Queen's notes, written later when she could bear the recollection, suggest a somewhat quieter scene than that described immediately afterwards by Lady Augusta Bruce. At a quarter to eleven, when the Prince's breathing began to change, Alice whispered to Lady Augusta, 'That is the death rattle.' Calmly, she went for her mother.

'Oh, yes, this is death!' Victoria cried on seeing Albert. 'I know it. I have seen it before.' She fell upon the still, cold body, and called him by every endearing name she could recall from their life together. Then she allowed herself to be led away.

How should a Prince die? The once-irreverent and even uncharitable *Punch* would shortly, in chivalric terms, ask that. In battle, 'with red spur deep in [a] maddening charger's flank'? Ending a day of pleasure with 'painted goblet fully drained'? Albert, the lament acknowledged, had been 'graced with gentler powers' for a later day, and although he died 'too soon', one might measure his years by the 'wise, and bold, and Christian duties done'. And, *Punch* concluded,

> Him whom she loved we loved. We shared her joy,
> And will not be denied to share her grief.

Afterword:
Legacy

'WHY HAS THE earth not swallowed me up?' Vicky mourned when the dreaded news came.

'Oh, my poor child', the Queen returned, 'Why may the earth not swallow *us* up?...How am I alive after witnessing what I have done? Oh! I who prayed daily that we might die together and I never survive Him! I who felt, when in those blessed Arms clasped and held tight in the sacred Hours of the night, when the world seemed only to be ourselves, that nothing could part us. I felt so v[er]y secure.' She would, she insisted, live to do her duty and to follow Albert's wishes. 'But how I, who leant on him for all and everything – without whom I did nothing, moved not a finger, arranged not a print or photograph, didn't move to put on a gown or bonnet if he didn't approve it[,] shall go on, to live, to move, to help myself in difficult moments?'

The children, Albert's staff, Victoria's ministers, her Household officials, had all come forward in the Red Room once the Prince had breathed his last, to offer not only sympathy but pledges of support in the transition from dependence upon Albert to a reign without him. 'You will not leave or desert me now?' she had asked pathetically. Turning to Sir Charles Phipps, she said, 'There is no one to call me Victoria now.' Albert had been confidant, adviser, collaborator, spouse, even surrogate sovereign. A queen could have no close friends. She was now alone.

Exhausted by lack of sleep and numb with grief, she permitted herself to be led away, first to Beatrice, who was asleep, then to her own room and to bed. In shock, but unable to sleep and given no sedative, she dozed off only in the early hours of the morning.

With Victoria out of the room and unlikely to return for some hours, a death mask of the Prince was made, for the record and to facilitate the work of later sculptors. Albert had been staunchly against the practice, but the handling of a body in the absence of any legal injunctions to the contrary is always the option of the survivors. Told about the mask later, Victoria refused to look at it and would not 'allow that sacred cast . . . to go out of the house'.

As midnight approached, the dull boom of the great bell atop St Paul's announced that the royal family had been struck by death, and throughout Sunday the bells of London tolled. At Buckingham Palace, people queued quietly to sign a condolence book. Next to it, on a table in the reception room, was a statement that although she was in great tribulation, her Majesty bore her affliction with as much calmness and fortitude as could be supposed.

On Monday morning the war-scare newspaper placards about the *Trent* affair disappeared, replaced by particulars of the Prince Consort's death. While the bells still tolled, newspaper hawkers did a record business, and readers discovered posthumous and sweeping concessions in the press to Albert's value to the kingdom. Less than a decade after rumours had put him in the Tower for treason, the turnabout would have pleased the Prince's shade. 'Placed in a difficult position', said the *Observer*, 'Prince Albert knew how to deport himself so discreetly and so well, that he has died without leaving a single enemy, while his friends were a host . . . He was a man of elegant mind, of cultivated tastes, of a clear understanding, and of high and lofty aspirations for the public good . . . Peace to his ashes! A good husband, a good father, a wise prince, and a safe counsellor, England will not soon "look upon his like again".'

Similar feelings were common among ordinary Londoners. Novelist Mary Elizabeth Braddon wrote of 'the dull light of the December day . . . when rough omnibus drivers forgot to blaspheme at each other, and tied decent scraps of crape upon their whips'. Fellow novelist Elizabeth Gaskell recalled that her friend Mary Ewart had passed through London on the Monday after the Prince's death – the sixteenth – and found that 'all the little shops in Shoreditch were shut up – all blinds were down – up to Buckingham Palace'. With crowds of others she went to Buckingham Palace to put her name down in the mourning book, and found 'a room hung with black, & lighted with wax'. The fashionable shops, unlike those in the East End, were open, but 'people could not give their orders at Lewis' & Allonbys for crying'.

These were insignificant consolations for the Queen – if she knew about them – for beneath her initial surface equilibrium, after the first convulsive grief, was a dazed shock not uncommon to sorrowing spouses. Only on the Monday evening after – an interval of two days – could she begin her first post-Albert letter to Vicky. And not until the twentieth could she write to her uncle, addressing him as 'Dearest, kindest Father', and describing herself as the 'poor fatherless baby of eight months' (as she had been), now 'the utterly broken and crushed widow of forty-two' – as she indeed was:

> My *life* as a *happy* one is *ended*! the world is gone for *me*! If I *must* live on (and I will do nothing to make me worse than I am), it is henceforth for our poor fatherless children – for my unhappy country, which has lost *all* in losing him – and in *only* doing what I know and *feel* he would wish, for he *is* near me – his spirit will guide and inspire me! But oh! To be cut off in the prime of life . . . is too awful, too cruel! And yet it *must* be for *his* good, his happiness! His purity was too great, his aspiration too *high* for this poor, miserable world! His great soul is now only enjoying *that* for which it *was* worthy!

Without instructions, the Lord Chamberlain's Department nevertheless began the necessary preparations, moving the Prince's body to the extra bedstead in the room where he had died. Löhlein and Albert's dresser, Macdonald, assisted. The Prince of Wales, next in authority to the Queen but only twenty and never called on before for advice, had to fix the date for the funeral. Consulting the Duke of Cambridge, he chose Monday, 23 December, nine days away. It was a brief interlude in which to organize a state ceremony, but it was crucial to keep the obsequies from colliding with Christmas – even with Christmas Eve, more important to many than the day itself.

The Lord Chamberlain's staff began with the assumption that the funeral of the Duchess of Kent, only months before, represented the wishes of the Queen as well as those of the Prince, and used that precedent for the arrangements. Although no equivalent panoply was called for, because Messrs Banting had been the undertakers at the

Duke of Wellington's funeral, they were called in as appropriate for Albert.

Dr Jenner filed a death certificate on 21 December, fixing the cause as 'typhoid fever; duration 21 days', the first time that the label was publicly applied; and although questions were raised in the *Lancet* and in the *British Medical Journal* about the discrepancies between the medical bulletins and the belated diagnosis, there was no autopsy. Instead, Jenner suggested to the Queen that death was 'due to the heart being over-strained by the Prince's heavy frame', and Clark added that three things had proved fatal – overwork, worry about the Prince of Wales's love affair, and 'exposure to chill when already sick'. In 1877 Jenner added further that '*no one* can diagnose typhoid at first'. Victoria underlined 'no one' in her memo of the conversation. Clark's 'when already sick' spoke further volumes.

Although Albert's own confidences about his failing health in his last years suggest stomach cancer – his mother had died of cancer at thirty, pointing to genetic predisposition – other possibilities unknown then to his doctors only emphasize their helplessness. In later decades, when physicians incorrectly attributed peptic ulcers to personality factors, Albert's stress-prone profile seemed ripe for chronic, wasting, ulcer disease. *Helicobacter pylori*, now known to cause peptic ulcers which can progress to stomach cancer, could have been involved. The bacterium was then unknown, as were curative antibiotics, and surgery was impossible – hopeless.

Calling the handling of Albert's illness, and his death, 'a national calamity of far greater importance than the public dream of', Lord Clarendon maintained to the Duchess of Manchester that the doctors had been contributing factors. 'Holland and Clark are not even average old women, and nobody who is really ill would think of sending for either of them. Jenner has had little [experience of] practice . . . Watson (who is no specialist in fever cases) at once saw that he had come too late to do any good.'

Early on Sunday morning, having rested for only a few hours, the Queen took the Duchess of Sutherland, Mistress of the Robes, into the Blue Room. Her doctors cautioned Victoria, citing the risk of infection, not to touch the body – a bit of nonsense, since she had embraced the dying Prince over and over again during his illness. She obeyed meekly, and instead embraced the clothes in which he was to be dressed. For years she would sleep with his nightshirt in her arms. Every night thereafter, she knelt at Albert's side of their bed before she put her head on her own pillow. In part, she would confide to Vicky, who had experienced the pleasures of the marital bed, the deprivations were profoundly sexual. 'My warm passionate loving nature', she confessed, '[remains] so full of that passionate adoration for that Angel whom I dared call mine. And at 42, all, all those earthly feelings must be crushed & smothered & the never quenched flame . . . *burns* within me & wears me out! . . . I am alas! not old – and my feelings are strong and warm; my love is ardent.'

To keep the sombre ambiance of the Blue Room from affecting her further, the Queen ordered that the room be cleaned and restored to usefulness, but not until the 'sad but lovely image' was photographed. She did not want it to remain as a *Sterbezimmer* – a death chamber – but intended to turn it into a room for her use that would nevertheless be a memorial. The 'sacred room', she wrote to Vicky, would have pictures and busts and china. Her precious cast of Albert's hand, made in happier days, would be kept in their bedroom, near her. In each of their homes, his dressing-room or study would be kept as it had been, even to the changing of linens, the daily replacement of towels and nightclothes, and – in the dressing-rooms – the bringing of hot water for shaving each morning, and a scouring of the unused chamber pot. Yet each room would continue to be used in some way by Victoria. At first her audiences in Albert's silent study or dressing-room were disconcerting in the extreme to her ministers.

In his diary on the sixteenth, Disraeli, having learned of the Curragh incident and its aftermath, wondered how the Prince of Wales would now fare. The matter was 'not seriously discreditable', Disraeli thought, 'but undignified'. The question about Bertie was 'into whose hands he may fall'. More crucial, with Albert gone, were the future influences upon the Queen, for she had 'long shown indications of a nervous or excitable disposition'. He recalled of Albert that 'nothing small or great was done but by his advice . . . I have myself . . . heard him at dinner, suggest to her in German to enquire about this, that, and the other: and the questions never failed to follow . . . The worst consequence possible is one, unluckily, not unlikely: that without being absolutely incapacitated for affairs, she may fall into a state of mind in which it will be difficult to do business with her, and impossible to anticipate what she will approve or disapprove.' The 'trying' situation he prophesied would quickly materialize. Victoria's sole immediate interest would be to embrace her grief.

Although the Queen, wearing her widow's cap, was hastened off to Osborne on the nineteenth, to be as far away from the funeral as was practical, her instructions for mourning fittings everywhere quickly exhausted supplies of black drapery throughout the kingdom. Dyeing establishments rushed to meet fresh orders. Christmas, following so soon after the funeral in Wolsey's Chapel, was darkened everywhere by official mourning. A grim extravaganza to parallel the Duke of Wellington's farewell, however, did not materialize. The Queen did not want it, and time was too short for ambitious preparations to proceed, or for many sovereigns or other state visitors to attend. From Osborne, Victoria sent word afterwards through Sir Charles Phipps that from reports she had received about the obsequies, everything had been conducted 'as she could have wished, with due solemnity and every mark of profound respect, and yet without any unnecessary form or state'.

Despite the insouciance he usually affected, Lord Torrington agreed with the assessment, writing to Delane, whose *Times* had set circulation records (an unprecedented 89,000 copies) on the Monday after the Prince's death, that the obsequies had been 'in every respect singularly well conducted – no confusion and no hurry. The music as fine as could be . . . I am inclined to think that more real sorrow was evinced at this funeral than at any that has taken place *there* [at Windsor] for a vast number of years.' Reverting to form, he added that 'the champagne went briskly; but then the company had suffered extreme cold for at least an hour and a half . . . Phipps looked his position, and ate a most excellent luncheon.' Disraeli's own private comment seemed not unreasonable in the circumstances: 'With Prince Albert we have buried our Sovereign. This German Prince has governed England for twenty-one years with a wisdom and energy such as none of our Kings have ever shown.'

On the dreariest Christmas Eve of her life, Victoria wrote again to her uncle from Osborne. She had been considering her future conduct as Queen.

I am . . . anxious to repeat *one* thing, and *that one* is *my firm* resolve, my *irrevocable decision* . . . that *his* wishes – *his* plans – about everything, *his* views about *every* thing are to be *my law*! And *no human power* will make me swerve from *what he* decided and wished . . . I am *also determined* that *no one* person, may *he* be ever so good, ever so devoted among my servants – is to lead or guide or dictate *to me*. I know *how he* would disapprove of it. And I live *on* with him, for him; in fact I am only *outwardly* separated from him, and only for a *time*.

The Prince of Wales had also been pondering appropriate responses. Albert had rejected the idea of a statue of himself in South Kensington to mark the Great Exhibition, and plans had been changed to make the principal figure that of the Queen. It had always been her wish, announced Albert Edward, that a likeness of the Prince Consort top the monument, and he would bear the cost. Executed by Joseph Durham and unveiled with great ceremony in June 1863, it faces, appropriately, the later Albert Hall.

Victoria would henceforth see everything through the lens of her bereavement. In that, she contributed nothing new to the vocabulary or symbolism of mourning. Oxford Street shops already existed for sable women's hats, sashed crêpe 'weepers' for men's tall hats, black armbands, deep purple clothes, black plumes for horses, and funeral accoutrements of every description. In Prussia or in Russia, the attention paid to the body of the deceased was greater; in France or Italy peasant women who became widowed, at whatever age, would wear black the rest of their lives; in England and Scotland, setting aside a room associated with the dead child or spouse, to keep it undisturbed as a document of the beloved's life, was commonplace. Few looked on such demonstrations as morbid. One indulged in what grief one could afford. Even Victoria's allegedly vicious uncle Ernest – King of Hanover after her accession – left the rooms of his queen, when she died in 1841, exactly as they had been. Night candles were lit, pages and dressers remained in attendance, and the King, who venerated her 'sweet and amiable character', went regularly to pray at the side of what had been her bed. In Prussia it was a royal custom to assemble on the anniversary of the death of an important member of the family for a religious ceremony in a room associated with the deceased.

The English poor could not afford the luxuries of such grief, and after the obsequies had to substitute the stiff upper lip. Still, in *David Copperfield*, Charles Dickens inveighed against the grotesque mummeries and extravagant expense of nineteenth-century lower-class funerals, and in 1903, Bernard Shaw wrote in the Devil's great speech in *Don Juan in Hell*, 'I saw a man die: he was a London bricklayer's labourer with seven children. He left seventeen pounds club money; and his wife spent it all on his funeral and went into the workhouse with the children the next day...On death she spent all she had.' In the wide black edges on her handkerchiefs and writing paper, and in her widow's weeds, in the planned memorials to Albert and in his portrait in a locket around her neck or in the bracelet around her plump wrist, the Queen was not turning her back on life any more than did other widows of her time.

The 'easing of that violent grief', Victoria wrote in 1867, 'those paroxysms of despair and yearning and longing and of daily, nightly longing to die...for the first three years never left me...' When Lord Canning, her Viceroy in India, died only six months after his wife (he was suddenly inconsolable, and had a nervous breakdown), Victoria wrote to his sister as if Canning had not been a flagrantly erring husband throughout the marriage, 'How enviable to follow so soon the partner of your life! How I pray that it be God's will to let me follow mine soon.' But she was Queen: there was civil war in America, into which her country might be drawn; there were conflicts brewing on the Continent nearby; there was social and political and religious agitation in England, and there were Fenian outbreaks in Ireland. Nothing of such external events emerges in Victoria's journal in early January, as she begins again to record her 'sad and solitary life'.

When Palmerston wrote to her on 9 January that the *Trent* affair had been concluded with the release of the Southerners to a British vessel, the Queen responded from Osborne the next day that 'the things of this world' were of no interest to her 'beyond the satisfaction she must experience if Peace is maintained and the country is in prosperity: for *her* thoughts are *fixed above*. She thinks with satisfaction, that the slight alterations in the draft to Lord Lyons, which the Queen suggested, and which was her precious husband's *last* work (which rendered it more easy for the American Government to comply with our request) have helped in bringing about this peaceful result, which she knows her dear Angel much wished for.'

To the Earl of Derby she wrote poignantly of herself (17 February 1862), 'She sees the trees budding, the days lengthening, the primroses

coming out, but she *thinks* herself still in the month of December.'
Victoria's desolation may have included a dimension of culpability – a
result of a long and unconfessed realization of the presence of mortal
illness, an unspoken secret she may have shared with her husband.
Certainly Albert knew, and had attempted to make it known, although
to deliberately deaf ears, and he had at times acted openly with a
fatalistic acceptance. A denial of that reality during Albert's decline
could only have added afterwards to Victoria's sense of complicity, a
shameful thing sometimes put aside by blaming the deceased for the
desolation in the survivor. She remained in seclusion, and the sovereign
as symbol disappeared except from currency, coinage, postage stamps,
and the *Court Circular* by which newspapers strained to see some
meaningful activity by the Queen.

Mirroring her mourning, the Household, at the Queen's instruction,
went about in black crêpe, broadcloth, and bombazine, underscoring
the gloom. For a year after Albert's death, no member of her Household
could appear in public except in mourning garb, a practice that might
have continued indefinitely had her ladies not sunk so much in morale
that Victoria relented sufficiently to permit 'semi-mourning' colours of
white, mauve, and grey. Even royal servants were obliged to wear a
black crêpe band on the left arm until 1869. At Windsor, Disraeli noted,
the two guest books that existed, for the Queen and the Prince, were
not discontinued – 'visitors write their names ... as before – calling on a
dead man'. Her efforts to recall him and memorialize him would be
constant, although the cult of the Prince Consort was imposed rather
than real. For many Englishmen he had been too German in his ways –
too interested in science and education, in good works, in efficiency and
energy.

Those who knew more than they read in the newspapers since 1840
had always had a different view. 'His character always comes out
honest', novelist Emily Eden, daughter of the first Lord Auckland, had
written to Mrs Drummond. 'I take it that he governs us really, in
everything.' To John Scott Russell, who had worked with the Prince
on the Great Exhibition and many later projects, Sir Charles Phipps
shared thoughts on their loss, writing, 'I feel that I can never look on his
like again. There was something in his character, an honesty, a straight-
forwardness, a purity of motive, and an ameliorating consistency of
action, which were quite unlike what I ever met in any other man ...

This country does not know, as you know, deeply as they mourn, one-tenth of what he did for them.'

Having worked so intimately on the highest level with Albert over many years, Phipps realized that whatever influence the Crown exercised in England, and whatever regard it had acquired after the Hanoverian era, and especially its culmination with Victoria's sleazy uncles, George IV and William IV, was to the Prince's credit. He had salvaged the Crown as a pillar of the emerging constitutional state.

The modern constitutional and 'corporate' monarchy, worldwide, owes much to Albert's example. Yet his early death, and Victoria's prolonged retreat into mourning and seclusion, eroded his efforts to mould the monarchy into a conspicuous pulpit as well as a national symbol. Disraeli had seen past eulogy when he declared that England had lost a sovereign rather than a consort. Nevertheless it was unlikely that anything but Albert's death would have brought him England's love. For his being perceived as an unwelcome outsider, one must look rather to those emotional and intellectual qualities that separated him from his adopted countrymen. He was hardly more German in lineage than the five kings who had preceded him, or than Victoria herself.

Albert had a Germanic sentimentality that caused him to wear his emotions on his sleeve at a time when a chilly heartlessness was more the aristocratic mode. He was an internationalist when his countrymen were still insular. He valued art and science and technology – indeed, the entire world of the intellect – when men of power in England preferred traditional, if obsolescent, learning. He had a passion for reform when his peers, whatever the inexorability of change, distrusted anything but the *status quo*. He valued work with a more-than-Puritan propensity for it when the aristocratic establishment which had no personal need for productive labour lavished empty hours on unproductive pleasure. He promoted the importance of earnestness over its mere show, and hardly veiled his contempt for the religiosity that seemed to be replacing religion – which in any case he emptied of theology and like Victoria, emphasized good works. He realized that although he could never become what was, in the perception of his peers, an Englishman, his eldest son and heir would epitomize, to Albert, potentially the most appalling sort of Englishman.

The Prince had apparently intuited, as had Baron Stockmar, that he was suffering from an inoperable and incurable malignancy. That melancholy understanding had contributed to the despondent and workaholic states of his last years. Unwritten powers accrue to those who use them effectively. What he had accomplished for the monarchy, he realized, would inevitably be buried with him.

Gifted beyond most men, he was limited by his curious position which denied him opportunities his driven conscience sought. As a recent historian has summed him up, Albert did more than create Osborne and Balmoral and make Windsor Castle and Buckingham Palace operate more efficiently. 'He composed songs and sacred music, and was a competent sketcher and etcher; he patronized Winterhalter and Landseer and collected early German and Italian paintings. He ran model farms at Windsor and Balmoral, and exhibited his livestock at shows throughout the country. He rode to hounds with skill and verve, and was a competent shot. He believed in better housing for the workers, better education at Cambridge University (of which he was chancellor), and better weapons for the army. He was president or chairman of innumerable societies; he chaired one Royal Commission charged with the decoration of the Houses of Parliament; and he chaired another that planned the Great Exhibition of 1851. And all this was only in his spare time, in those odd moments of respite from the treadmill of public engagements and official correspondence.'*

Burdened by what he had to do, Albert nevertheless was one of his era's unsung great men because of what he managed to do beyond his duty. He helped thrust England's institutions and power structure into the dynamic century which, decades into it, the Establishment still distrusted. And his and Victoria's example of a domesticated, democratizing monarchy (despite Albert's attempt to retain some executive power for the Crown) seemed to temper the revolutionary ardour that elsewhere in Europe overturned thrones and generated continuing instability. He was not only seen – sometimes derisively in the press – as 'Albert the Good', he contributed concretely to the nation's good.

Albert remains, too, a hero figure who shared a romantic, troubled, moving love story and marriage that possessed the stuff of high drama,

---

* David Cannadine also observes that Prince Albert was no Thomas Jefferson, an Enlightenment figure who had independence of action as well as real genius (*The Pleasures of the Past*, 1989). Jefferson, however, was not handicapped by cultural transplantation, beginning life anew in a new language.

even classic tragedy. From student prince to uncrowned king, his life was without parallel. None of his descendants on the throne of his adopted country have taken the name of 'Albert', although many were christened with it. They recognized the risks.

The Prince's vision for the modern monarchy died with him. It could not have been sustained without his intellectual qualities and his intensity of purpose, and he left no such potential in his spouse or progeny. Although he would have deplored the glamorous, ornamental, impotent Crown that emerged in the next century, his life was a prototype invalidated by time. Windsor Castle as co-ordinate executive branch with Downing Street was an impossible dream. Driven by his sense of mission, he wanted to sustain more than a symbolic and ceremonial monarchy, but faced the tide of history. Had he lived a less abbreviated life, might something of his vision have been realized? On a rare occasion a single life makes a difference.

Sources

The first reference to a source will be its fullest citation; further allusions will abbreviate the source. The published literature on Victoria and Albert is immense. Where facts are in common currency and found in a multiplicity of locations, no citation may be given below. Although many sources are cited in the notes, it can be assumed that the following books have been consulted at almost every stage: Charles Grey, *The Early Years of the Prince Consort*. Compiled for and annotated by Queen Victoria (1867); Theodore Martin, *Life of the Prince Consort*, 5 volumes (1875–1880), which include extracts from the diaries of both Queen and Prince; A.C. Benson and Viscount Esher, eds, *The Letters of Queen Victoria*, First Series, 3 volumes (1908); Kurt Jagow, ed., *Letters of the Prince Consort* (1938); Hector Bolitho, ed., *[Letters of] The Prince Consort and His Brother* (1933); Roger Fulford, *The Prince Consort* (1949); Elizabeth Longford, *Victoria R.I.* (1964); Cecil Woodham-Smith, *Queen Victoria, her life and times* (1972); Daphne Bennett, *King without a Crown* (1977); Hermione Hobhouse, *Prince Albert, His Life and Work* (1983); Robert Rhodes James, *Prince Albert* (1984); Stanley Weintraub, *Victoria* (1987; rev. 1996); Monica Charlot, *The Young Queen* (1991); and Hans-Joachim Neutzer, *Ein deutschen Prinz in England* (1992). In subsequent notes these may be referred to briefly by author/editor surname. Albert's post-marriage letters unless otherwise cited are from Jagow, Bolitho, Martin, the *Memoirs* of Ernest II, and Benson and Esher. Many sources not cited below may be inferred from the text itself.

Preface

For details of the *Omphale and Hercules* painting at Osborne House, see chapter VIII. Tennyson's lines are from the Dedication to his *Idylls of the King* (1862). Since the outlines of the narrative are drawn from Malory's *Morte d'Arthur*,

Swinburne – whose politics were to the left of republicanism – thereafter referred to the *Idylls* as the *Morte d'Albert.*

I Leaving for Good 1839–1840

Lady Wharncliffe's letter to Caroline Talbot is from *The First Lady Wharncliffe and Her Family,* ed. Caroline Grosvenor and Lord Stuart of Wortley (1927). Dickens's letters throughout are from the Pilgrim Edition (1959–). Extracts from Lord Clarendon's diaries are from George Villiers, *A Vanished Victorian. Being the Life of George Villiers Fourth Earl of Clarendon (1800–1870)* (1938). Grey furnishes the most details, as a participant and observer, on the partings at Gotha. Charles Greville's diaries and letters throughout are from Henry Reeve, ed., *The Greville Memoirs. A Journal of the Reigns of King George IV, King William IV, and Queen Victoria,* 8 vols (1896). John Wilson Croker's papers are from Louis Jennings, ed., *The Croker Papers. The Correspondence and Diaries of the Late Right Honourable John Wilson Croker,* 3 vols (1885). Stockmar's perspectives are from Ernst Stockmar, ed., *Memoirs of Baron Stockmar,* 2 vols (1872). Some of his correspondence with Albert is also in Jagow and Martin. Letters to and from Peel, other than from the Queen, are from Norman Gash, *Sir Robert Peel. The Life of Sir Robert Peel after 1830* (1972). Albert's bored doodling on his Windsor musical programme, saved by the Queen, is from RC/WPR, k-19 (f. 25). Disraeli's letters to his sister, Sarah, are from M.G. Wiebe *et al.,* eds., *Benjamin Disraeli. Letters: 1838–41* (1987), hereafter Wiebe.

II Silver Spoon 1819–1831

Biographies (including letters) of Duchess Louise, Albert's mother, include D.A. Ponsonby, *The Lost Duchess. The Story of the Prince Consort's Mother* (1958); Paul von Ebart, *Luise. Herzogin von Sachsen-Coburg-Saalfeld. Ein Lebensbild nach Briefen derselben* (1903); and G. Holler, *Louise von Sachsen-Coburg – Ihr Kampf um Liebe und Glück* (1991). Details of the Rosenau and the Ehrenburg in Coburg are from visits by the author and from descriptive brochures at each location. The diaries of Henry Richard Vassall Fox, third Lord Holland, are in A.D. Kriegel, ed., *The Holland House Diaries 1831–1840* (1977). Disraeli papers are from Wiebe. Hector Bolitho writes about the Duchess from her original letters in a chapter of his *A Biographer's Notebook* (1950). He also explodes the canard of Albert's alleged Jewish extraction, first proposed in Max W.L. Voss's *England als Erzieher,* from which Lytton Strachey eagerly and erroneously picked it up for his *Queen Victoria* (1921). For an account of the Duke of Kent's illegitimate Adelaide Victoire see Mollie Gillen, *The Prince and His Lady* (1970), and S. Weintraub's *Victoria.*

III The Student Prince 1832–1838

Anecdotes of Albert at Bonn University are from an unsigned biography in
the London *Pictorial Times*, 1845 volume, p. 370. Albert's matriculation
records at Bonn were furnished to me by Prof. Dr Rolf Lessenich, Universität
Bonn. Reminiscences of Bonn by Prince Ernest are from his *Memoirs of the
Duke of Saxe-Coburg-Gotha*, 4 vols (1888). Additional details about Albert at
Bonn are in A. Rimmer, *Early Homes of Prince Albert* (1883). Thomas Raikes's
diary is from *Portion of the Journal Kept by Thomas Raikes, Esq. from 1831 to
1847*, 2 vols (1858). Albert's education in Brussels is in part from Louis de
Lichtervelde, *Léopold First* (1930), and also from Hans-Joachim Neutzer, *Ein
deutschen Prinz* (1992), and from Stockmar. A biography of Pierre Bergeron is
in C. van der Kindere, *L'Université Libre de Bruxelles 1834–1884* (1884). Count
Mensdorff's reminiscences are in Ernest's *Memoirs* and in Bolitho's *Albert
Prince Consort* (1932). Wordsworth quotes W. Schlegel on Albert's prospects
in a letter of 28 November 1840 in Alan G. Hill, ed., *The Letters of William
and Dorothy Wordsworth*, vol. 7 (1967). Victoria's letters to Albert, 30 June
1837 and 3 December 1837, are in the Royal Archives; her letter to Duke
Ernest, that her marital intentions 'are still the same', is in Hector Bolitho,
The Reign of Queen Victoria (London, 1949). The references to President Van
Buren's marital interest in Victoria from Boston and Salem newspapers are
from a report in the Plymouth, New Hampshire *Journal of Literature and
Politics*, 5 August 1837.

IV Courting a Husband 1838–1839

The future General Sir Francis Seymour's letters are quoted in Sir James
Denham's *Memoirs of the Memorable* (1922). Identification of Ernst Platner was
made by Professor Gerhard F. Strasser at the Herzog August Bibliothek,
Wolfenbuettel. Albert's letters are from Martin, Jagow, and Duke Ernest II's
Memoirs, as well as Benson and Esher. Metternich's snide dismissal of Albert as
un-royal was delivered to the Earl of Aberdeen when he was Prime Minister,
according to a letter of 3 April 1861 from Lord Clarendon to the Duchess of
Manchester. His gossipy correspondence to her is in *My Dear Duchess*, ed. A.L.
Kennedy (1956). Melbourne's warning to Victoria about creating Albert 'King
Consort' is quoted by Lord George Russell in his anonymously published
Collections and Recollections (1898).

V Serene Highness to Royal Highness 1840–1841

For the Earl of Cardigan's 11th Dragoons see Richard Brett-Smith, *The 11th Hussars (Prince Albert's Own)* (1969), Cecil Woodham-Smith's *The Reason Why* (1954), and Piers Compton, *Cardigan of Balaclava* (1972). The quip from *John Bull* is quoted from his diary by Lord Malmesbury in his *Memoirs of an Ex-Minister*, 2 vols (1884). Princess Lieven to Lord Aberdeen is quoted from her *Correspondence* (1939). Her letters to Lady Palmerston are from the *Lieven–Palmerston Correspondence* (1943). Lady Palmerston's other letters are from *The Letters of Lady Palmerston*, ed. Tresham Lever (1957). Guizot's description of a boring evening at Windsor is from the London volume of his *Memoirs* (1862), *An Embassy to the Court of St James in 1840*. Victoria's reminiscences of her early years with Albert appear throughout her long correspondence with Princess Vicky, beginning in 1858 (6 vols, 1964–1990), the first five edited by Roger Fulford, the final one by Agatha Ramm. Thomas Carlyle's letters are from *The Collected Letters*, ed. Richard Charles Sanders (1970). Disraeli's letters are from Wiebe. Lady Charlotte Guest is quoted from the Earl of Bessborough, ed., *Lady Charlotte Guest. Extracts from Her Journal* (1950). Albert's letters to Lord Palmerston throughout are from the original correspondence at the University of Southampton.

Miss Barrett's letters are in Meredith B. Raymond and Mary Rose Sullivan, ed., *The Letters of Elizabeth Barrett Browning to Mary Russell Mitford 1836–1854*, 3 vols (1983). Monckton Milnes received the 'Prince Hallbert' song from Dickens; the letter to him from Robert Monteith is also quoted in James Pope-Hennessy, *Monckton Milnes. The Years of Promise 1809–1851* (1949). Albert's investiture as Fishmonger is recorded in the Bible awarded to him on the occasion, described in the Alan Rankin *Miscellany No. 45* catalogue, December 1995, Edinburgh, as item 19. The vicissitudes of the Gozlan farce about Victoria and Albert are described in the daily press and in Martha Katherine Loder, *The Life and Novels of Léon Gozlan* (1943). Sallie Stevenson's letters are in Edward Botkin, *Victoria, Albert, and Mrs Stevenson* (1957).

VI Taking Hold 1841–1843

Carlyle's letter to Monckton Milnes is from vol. 13 of the *Collected Letters*. The letters of Dickens, Disraeli, Lieven, Melbourne, Palmerston and others are also from previously credited sources, as are the references to Greville, Peel, Aberdeen, Victoria, and Albert. Mendelssohn's visits to Windsor are described from his letters to his mother and to Ignaz Moscheles. Sallie Stevenson is again quoted from Boykin. The E.M. Ward episode is recorded in S.M. Ellis, ed., *A Mid-Victorian Pepys. The Letters and Memoirs of Sir William Hardman* (1923). Albert's marital difficulties with Victoria are easily inferred from her own diaries, and are described as well by Robert Rhodes James in *Prince Albert* (1984) from Anson's notes and Albert's memoranda in the Royal Archives. *Bell's Life* was a contemporary gossip sheet claiming to be a sporting newspaper. Baroness Bunsen's *Life and Letters*, ed. Augustus J.C. Hare (1880), reports of an intimate Victoria and Albert in the first decade of their marriage, will be quoted further in later chapters. Tom Moore is quoted from Wilfred S. Dowden, ed., *The Journal of Thomas Moore, vol. 5, 1836–1842* (1983).

VII The Goldfish-bowl 1843–1844

G.P.A. Healy's memoirs are *Reminiscences of a Portrait Painter* (1894). For the couple's private life in general see S. Weintraub, *Victoria* (1987, 1996), and Clare Jerrold, *The Early Court of Queen Victoria* (1912). For Albert and Cambridge see especially John Willis Clark and Thomas McKenny Hughes, *The Life and Letters of the Reverend Adam Sedgwick* (1890). D.G.C. Allan's 'From Nobility to Royalty: The Background to Prince Albert's Election as President of the Society [of Arts]', in the *Journal* of the Royal Society for the Encouragement of Arts and Manufactures and Commerce, January 1986, is self-explanatory. A letter to the author from Dr David Painting, Law Librarian, University College of Swansea, 8 May 1994, explains the origin of 'the Prince Consort's Act' of 1843, Act 6 & 7 Vict. c. 36, known as the Scientific Societies Act. A letter from Bernard Shaw to Gilbert Murray, 3 December 1920, continued to refer to it under its Albertine connection. Albert's euphemistic allusion to the imminent birth of Princess Alice as 'an interesting event' occurs in a letter to Count Alphonse de Mensdorff-Pouilly, a Coburg cousin, quoted in the catalogue of the Sotheby (London) sale of 24 July 1995. The 'night-cap' verses appear as 'The Royal Riddles' in *The Satirist*, 15 January 1843. *Letters of the King of Hanover to Viscount Strangford* (1925) include some of the most hostile correspondence relating to Victoria and Albert, the King's niece and nephew, in print. The feeling was mutual.

VIII The Queen's Business 1845–1848

For Albert's tastes and art purchases, as well as inadvertent purchases, reproductions and documentation see Christopher Lloyd, *The Queen's Pictures* (1991), David Robertson, *Sir Charles Eastlake and the Victorian Art World* (1978), Winslow Ames, *Prince Albert and Victorian Taste* (1968), Benedict Read, *Victorian Sculpture* (1982), and the many pictures owed to the Victoria-and-Albert years still hanging on royal walls, including the Anton von Gegenbaur *Omphale and Hercules*, a fresco in an iron chassis, 6 ft. 3½ in. high, signed and dated Rome 1830, bought by the Prince in 1844 and hanging since at Osborne House. Many pictures acquired from Prince von Oettingen-Wallerstein are now hanging in the National Gallery, where Christopher Brown, Chief Curator, kindly showed them to the author. The note co-signed by Albert (dated 1 June 1847) on behalf of the Bavarian prince as security for his Rothschilds loan is in the Rothschild Archive, as is the message from Albert's German secretary, Dr Mayer, dated 12 May 1847, inviting Lionel de Rothschild to Buckingham Palace the next morning to arrange with the Prince for his signature and to explain the nature of the obligation.

Albert's unwillingness to have the family embarrassed by public sales of his chronically debt-ridden brother's art is revealed by letters to Ernest in Bolitho.

The National Gallery Archive history files indicate that Henry Mogford, acting as agent for the Prince, once he was left with the pictures, offered them for sale to the Gallery on 8 August 1851 and again on 31 March 1852. The Trustees declined purchase on 5 April 1852. On 7 September 1862 Charles Eastlake reported to the Trustees that the Queen intended to present the pictures in which the Gallery had expressed an interest, still then at Kensington Palace, to the Gallery. The pictures now identified as Nos. 701–722 were accepted on 1 October 1862 and removed to the Gallery in February 1863 along with the addition of No. 622, an anonymous Netherlandish painting, and No. 1864, a Netherlandish Virgin and Child.

For the Royal couple at Stowe, see the Disraeli *Letters* and editorial notes in Wiebe, vol. IV. Albert's campaign for Chancellor at Cambridge is thoroughly detailed in the *Life and Letters*, largely a memoir, of Professor Adam Sedgwick (1890), also covered very fully, if satirically, in the pages of *Punch*, and fully and admiringly in Martin. Carlyle's acerbic comment of 26 February 1847 to Erskine is in the Carlyle *Letters* ; Wordsworth's ode, 15 March 1847, is in the *Letters of William and Dorothy Wordsworth*. Albert's dozens of letters to Palmerston in this period, briefly extracted in Brian Connell's *Regina vs. Palmerston* (1961), are at Southampton. Lord Frederic Hamilton's account of the Earl of Abercorn's children being presented to the Queen and Prince at Ardverikie is in his *The Days before Yesterday* (1920). A contemporary source for the Scottish visits is *The Illustrated London News*, which looks externally at what the Queen notes privately in her journals; her entries themselves are extracted at length in David Duff, ed., *Victoria in the Highlands* (1968). Albert's letter to his Aunt Julie about 'cold' Windsor is extracted from the Sophie Dupré (Calne, Wilts) catalogue 34 as item 33.

A useful and comprehensive source for the relations between Napoleon III and the Royal couple is Jasper Ridley, *Napoléon III and Eugénie* (1969); a more romantic perspective appears in Theo Aronson, *Queen Victoria and the Bonapartes* (1992).

IX The Violent Year 1848

Letters and diary entries relating to the Queen, Albert, Ernest II, Palmerston, Peel, and Greville are from sources previously cited. Van der Weyer's story of his bringing the telegraphed news of the revolution in Paris to Albert is in Brison D. Gooch, *Belgium and the February Revolution* (1963). That Victoria and Albert discussed the revolutions spreading across Europe 'day by day and hour by hour' is recalled by the Queen in a letter of 11 August 1866 to Vicky. Albert's long memorandum on the future political composition of Germany and Europe is in the Palmerston Papers, Southampton. The letter from Julian Harney to Friedrich Engels alleging that Albert had 'bolted' from London is in *The Harney Papers*, ed. F.G. Black and R.M. Black (1969). The link of the proposed loan to Albert and the 'Jew Bill' is made by Richard Davis in *The English Rothschilds* (1983), quoting a letter of 10 May 1848 from Nathaniel de Rothschild to his brothers in London (RAL 109/73) in the Rothschild Archive, in which the idea is scoffed at as unrealistic. (Albert did keep an account with the Rothschilds, which his uncle, King Leopold, would supplement.)

Albert's letter to young Alice is reproduced in the Sophie Dupré catalogue 35 (1995), Calne, Wilts, as item 7. Victoria's handwritten prayer for the children, by which they were to recall their parents, is also from a manuscript catalogue. The Judge–Strange lawsuit by which Albert protected his and Victoria's rights to reproduce their own drawings was a long-running affair that dragged into 1849, and was covered in detail in the newspaper press, although afterwards long forgotten.

X Master Mason 1849–1851

Aside from full reports in the newspaper press, Albert's activities furthering manufacturing and technology come from the minutes and associated documents preserved in the [Royal] Society of Arts in John Adam Street, which include the John Scott Russell papers. The minutes and account sheets of the Exhibition Commission are also at the Royal Society of Arts. Additional documents are printed in Cole. A lengthy document setting out the legal basis for the Exhibition, beginning in 1845, is the *Statement of Proceedings Preliminary to the Exhibition of Industry of All Nations, 1851*, prepared by John Scott Russell, and printed by the Society in January 1850. The report of the Queen's Commission for the Exhibition of 1851, *Great Exhibition of the Industry of All Nations, 1851*, dated 3 January 1850, is in the archives of the Royal Society of Arts. See also E.F. Armstrong, 'The Influence of the Prince Consort on Science', *Journal of the Royal Society of Arts*, 23 November 1945, pp. 4–14, and Henry Cole, *Fifty Years of Public Work*, 2 vols (1884), a rich source for Crystal Palace documentation through 1851, as is Violet Markham, *Paxton and the Bachelor Duke* (1935).

The texts of Albert's major speeches are from *Addresses delivered on Different Public Occasions by His Royal Highness the Prince Albert.* Published by the Society of Arts in 1857, when he was its President, it was augmented posthumously in 1862. Also published in 1862 was a small volume of extracts, also used here, *Prince Albert's Golden Precepts; or, The Opinions and Maxims of His Late Royal Highness The Prince Consort.*

The Palmerston Papers contain a long English translation of a memorandum on the Schleswig-Holstein question by Ernest, responding to Albert's own views. The Prince passed the document on to Palmerston, as he did most of his personal foreign policy correspondence. For documentation of Faraday's relations with Albert beyond press accounts, see Geoffrey Cantor, *Michael Faraday: Sandemanian and Scientist* (1991), and Frank A.J.L. James, ed., *The Correspondence of Michael Faraday* (in progress).

The Prince's conversation with Edward Stanley, later Lord Stanley and afterwards the fifteenth Earl of Derby, is part of the entry of 20 July 1850 in John Vincent, ed., *Disraeli, Derby and the Conservative Party. Journals and Memoirs of Edward Henry, Lord Stanley* 1849–1869 (1978). Thackeray's musings connecting *Hamlet* and the imagined death of Albert are part of a letter to Mrs Edward John Sartoris, completed 3 November 1850, in Edgar F. Harden, ed., *The Letters and Private Papers of William Makepeace Thackeray* (a supplement to the Gordon Ray edition), vol. I (1994). For Peabody's benefactions at the time of the Exhibition see Franklin Parker, *George Peabody. A Biography* (1971). Albert's difficulties with Birch, Bertie's High Church tutor, are described amusingly by Disraeli in a letter of 22 April 1850, in Wiebe, vol. 5. The Athanasian Creed attack on Albert, refuted by Dean Wellesley, appears in Peter Levi, *Edward Lear* (1995), as Gibbs had refuted the charge to Lear, quoting Wellesley. The scotched knighthood to Darwin is reported in Adrian Desmond and James More, *Darwin* (1991), based upon James Bunting, *Charles Darwin* (1974).

XI The Palace of Glass 1850–1851

Facsimile reproductions of many items associated with the Crystal Palace, from a season ticket with Albert's signature to reproductions of pictures of the exhibits and souvenir-type ephemera, were published in 1971 as *Jackdaw No. 43, The Great Exhibition 1851* by Jackdaw Publications Ltd in London. Most were derived from the Victoria and Albert Museum. Albert commissioned two volumes of coloured lithographs of the exhibition areas, published as *Comprehensive Pictures of the Great Exhibition of 1851 from the originals painted...for H.R.H. Prince Albert* (1854). Minutes of the Crystal Palace Commissioners are in the Royal Society of Arts, as is a report of the success of the 'Public Waiting Rooms', this attached to the minutes of 23 June 1852.

Dickens's letters of the Crystal Palace period are in the *Letters 1850–1852* (Pilgrim edition), ed. Graham Storey, Kathleen Tillotson and Nina Burgis (1988). The comments by John Bright on the Exhibition are from his *Diaries*, ed. R.A.J. Walling (1931). For Lady Charlotte Guest's diaries, see V. Countess Granville's letter on the Exhibition, to Lady Rivers, was actually finished by a Mr Stuart, an old friend who had accompanied her, and appears in Susan H. Oldfield, *Some Records of the Later Life of Harriet, Countess Granville* (1901) as if by an amanuensis. Carlyle was quoted by George Eliot in a letter to Sara Sophia Hennell, 13 October 1851, in Gordon S. Haight, ed., *The George Eliot Letters* (1954). The children's illustrated book was *Aunt Busy-Bee's The Fine Crystal Palace the Prince Built*, published at sixpence (1851). The song 'How's Your Poor Feet?' was published at a penny by W.S. Fortey at Seven Dials, London (1851).

Albert's letter to the Prime Minister, Lord John Russell, 9 July 1851, recommending Exhibition Secretary Digby Wyatt for a new post was quoted in the Julian Browning (London) sale catalogue 14, 'The Nineteenth Century', as item 4.

XII From Glory to Grief 1852–1853

Captain Inglefield's Arctic naming adventures are described by Francis Spufford in 'Traces in the Snow. Victorian relics of human purpose at the poles', *TLS*, 28 July 1995. Albert Smith's vicarious adventures in the lecture hall are described in Simon Schama, *Landscape and Memory* (1995). Lord Malmesbury's reminiscences and diaries are in his *Memoirs of an Ex-Minister* (1884). Proposed expenditures from Great Exhibition surpluses are reported in John Scott Russell's itemizing of Exhibition Committee correspondence with Albert and his secretaries in a fifteen-page handwritten descriptive index to the forty-seven letters from Albert, or for him, in the Society of Art archives. That the Queen and Prince used the private courier service of the Rothschild firm to carry confidential messages to Germany is validated by a thank-you note from Albert's private secretary, Anson, as early as 4 July 1845, in the Rothschild Archive. This arrangement continued into 1861.

Thomas Mulock's Irish backgrounds were researched for me in the National Library of Ireland by Sean Ronan, who also found other letters, such as one from D.W. Cahill, DD, in *The Freeman's Journal* of 30 December 1853, the original having been sent to Albert as the one who presumably ran the affairs of government. The Revd Dr Cahill wrote on 'the disastrous condition of Ireland', which he hoped the Prince could rectify. It was an indication of public perception – or misperception – of Albert's actual powers. According to the Royal Librarian, Thomas Mulock remained a staunch defender of the Queen even after the Prince's death, and Mulock's move to England in the 1860s, as he is recorded as a correspondent as late as April 1863.

XIII Impeaching the Prince 1853–1855

Daphne Bennett's *King without a Crown* (1977) credits the letter under the initials 'M.P.' as having been written by Lord Maidstone, but Edward Stanley owns up to it in his diary entry for 3 January 1854. For Thomas Mulock, see XII. For broadsides of the time on the Prince, including 'Lovely Albert', published by E. Brown, Lower Street, London, see the bound volume of contemporary broadsides by contemporary printers in the British Library. Julian Osgood Field in his anonymously published *Uncensored Recollections* (1901) quotes the *Martin Chuzzlewit* perception about the Queen and the Tower as foreshadowing public ignorance in 1854. G.W. Dasent's *John Delane* (1908) quotes fully many letters of *The Times*'s editor, and Greville's diary furnishes Delane's conversations. Baroness Bunsen's are reported in the *Life and Letters of Baroness Bunsen*. Baron Charles Frederick Vitzthum von Eckstaedt's reminiscences, based upon his diaries, are published as *St Petersburg and London in the Years 1852–1864*, ed. Henry Reeve (1887). Many memoirs and histories already cited deal with the Crimean War, however the narrative more often referred to here aside from personal recollections is Cecil Woodham-Smith, *The Reason Why* (1954), from which comes Disraeli's ironic quip on war aims. Colonel Gordon's letters are quoted in the biography of his father, the Earl of Aberdeen.

XIV Albert's War 1855–1856

Exhibition Commission papers are in the Royal Society of Arts archives, as is Scott Russell's correspondence with Albert. Robert Mallet's siege gun counterpart to Albert's weapon is described by Thomas F. Arnold in 'The Venerable Mortar', *Military History Quarterly*, 8 (Winter, 1996). Palmerston's relations with Albert are derived primarily from the Southampton archive and from *Regina vs. Palmerston*. The arranged marriage for Vicky is best described in Hanna Pakula, *An Uncommon Woman. The Empress Frederick* (1995), Daphne Bennett, *Vicky* (1983), and Richard Berkeley, *The Empress Frederick* (1956). Albert's appearance at the pre-Exposition private view is described in Robertson, *Sir Charles Eastlake*. Albert's reorganization of the army is outlined in his letters to Palmerston, who acquiesced. His letters to his future son-in-law, Prince Frederick, are quoted by Pakula. Albert's gift of a charger to Col. Alexander Gordon for use in the Crimea is recorded in *Lord Aberdeen*, the life of his father. The background of the purchase of Paton's *Home: The Return from the Crimea* is described in Lloyd, *The Queen's Pictures*. The song overheard by Theodor

Fontane ('Bad luck they say/to...the Cobugs...') is quoted by him in his diaries, trans. Dorothy Harrison, *Journeys to England in Victoria's Early Days 1844–1859* (1939).

XV Managing Destiny 1856–1858

Tennyson's letter to Elizabeth Russell, 19 May 1856, on Albert's surprise visit to Freshwater, is in Cecil Y. Lang and Edgar F. Shannon, Jr, eds, *The Letters of Alfred Lord Tennyson, II, 1851–1870* (1987). George M. Dallas's letter to Lewis Cass, 24 April 1857, is in his *Diary*, ed. Susan Dallas (1892), as is his later letter on Napoleon III's visit to Osborne. Albert's letters to his daughter Vicky detail much of his activities. Albert's extensive memorandum of his long conversation on foreign policy with Napoleon III is reproduced in Martin, IV, and reported from his own conversation with Albert by Vitzthum. The Prince's address at the opening of the Art Treasures Exhibition at Manchester is published in the posthumous *Principal Speeches and Addresses*. Other sources were cited earlier or may be inferred from the text.

XVI Corporate Personality 1858–1860

Bertie's Albertine education is laid out in letters from his father and in both George Dangerfield, *Victoria's Heir. The Education of a Prince* (1941) and Philip Magnus, *King Edward the Seventh* (1964). Vitzthum's diary records the affair of Prince George of Saxony's visit. E.F. Benson writes of Albert's relationship to Wellington College in *As We Were* (1930). The Humboldt letter that embarrassed Albert had been published in the *Letters of Alexander von Humboldt to Varnhagen von Ense from 1827 to 1858* (1859, trans. by Friedrich Kapp, 1860). The royal routine at this time, and precision of the railway arrangements for the Balmoral journeys, are described in detail in Benita Stoney and Heinrich C. Weltzien, eds., Sheila de Bellaigue, trans., *My Mistress the Queen. The Letters of Frieda Arnold, Dresser to Queen Victoria* (1994). The letters begin in 1855. Fräulein Arnold left the Queen's services in 1859. Both Albert's letters and recorded conversations, and Victoria's more guarded comments in her letters and journals, attempting to conceal from herself her fears about Albert's health, record his progressive deterioration. So do Stockmar's responses to Albert. Clarendon's letters here and later are from *My Dear Duchess*, including the 'Eliza and Joseph' code for Victoria and Albert.

XVII The Treadmill Donkey 1860–1861

For Albert's letter to Tennyson on *Idylls of the King*, see XV. Ernest II commented upon the Aldershot encampment in his memoirs. Albert's Statistical Congress speech was covered very fully in the press and published in his posthumous *Addresses*. The Queen's Scottish adventures are recounted as always in her journals and in shorter form in her *Leaves from the Journal of Our Life in the Highlands* (1868), ghost-edited by Arthur Helps. Details of how Bertie was managed at Cambridge, and how he evaded discipline, are described in a letter from Nathaniel de Rothschild to his mother, Charlotte, in an undated letter, but early 1860, in the Rothschild Archive. Albert's remarks to Disraeli about the political power of newspapers are in Lord Stanley's diaries. Clarendon's gossip, here as earlier, is in Kennedy. Albert's letters to Stockmar and to Ernest on his visions for Royal princes as ambassadors to the Empire are in Martin and in Ernest's memoirs. Albert's accident with the runaway four-in-hand is described, along with its aftermath, in Ernest's memoir. Lord Torrington's description of the family Christmas at Windsor is quoted from Dasent's *Delane*. Dr William Baly's death in a grotesque railway accident is recalled in the *British Medical Journal*, 26 January 1901.

XVIII Duty Done 1861

Albert's distraught letters to Bertie are quoted in Magnus. Sources for the *Trent* affair include George E. Baker, ed., *The Works of William H. Seward*, vol. V (1884); Norman B. Ferris, *The Trent Affair* (1977); Gordon H. Warren, *Fountain of Discontent: The Trent Affair and Freedom of the Seas* (1981); 'God's Hand against the Rebellion', *Living Age*, May 1862; 'The Exact Law of the Trent Case', *The Economist*, 21 December 1861; Richard E. Winslow III, *Constructing Munitions of War: The Portsmouth Navy Yard Confronts the Confederacy, 1861–1865* (1995); David F. Long, *Gold Braid and Foreign Relations. Diplomatic Activities of U.S. Naval Officers, 1798–1883* (1988); Richard Rush and Robert H. Woods, eds., *Official Records of the Union and Confederate Navies in the War of the Rebellion*, Series 1, vol. 1, 19 January 1861 to 31 December 1862 (1894); W.J. Morgan et al., eds, *Autobiography of Rear Admiral Charles Wilkes, U.S. Navy 1798–1877* (1978); Martin Duberman, *Charles Francis Adams 1807–1886* (1960); Lord Redesdale, *Memories*, vol. 1 (1915); Ridley, *Lord Palmerston*; Connell, *Regina vs. Palmerston*; Ephraim Douglas Adams, *Great Britain and the American Civil War*, vol. 1 (1925); Edward Chalfant, *Better in Darkness. A Biography of Henry Adams. His Second Life* (1994); Henry Adams, *The Education of Henry Adams* (1918); James Pope-Hennessy, *Monckton Milnes. The Flight of Youth 1851–1885* (1951); S.A. Wallace and F. E. Gillespie, eds, *The Journal of Benjamin Moran*, vol. 1 (1948);

Philip Guedalla, *The Queen and Mr Gladstone* (1933); N. John Hall, ed., *The Letters of Anthony Trollope, 1833–1870*, (1983); H.C.G. Matthew, ed., *The Gladstone Diaries*, vol. VI (1978); and the American and British periodical press. John Wheeler-Bennett's 'The Trent Affair: How the Prince Consort Saved the United States', *History Today*, December 1961, is in a class by itself in asserting, by ignoring Palmerston's own writings, reproduced here, that the Prime Minister, 'contrary to general belief, was not spoiling for a fight'. The title suggests on the basis of no evidence whatever that the Union would have lost any conflict with Britain.

Albert's terminal illness, albeit misdiagnosed, is detailed at length in the many biographies of the Queen and Prince, especially in Martin, and in the recollections of courtiers; but only Daphne Bennett speculates in a one-page appendix to her *King Without a Crown* that typhoid fails to account for Albert's symptoms, and suggests a 'wasting disease'. My survey of the clinical particulars as described by Albert himself over the years 1858–1861, when offered to medical specialists, has elicited considerable scepticism over the typhoid diagnosis, as indeed existed among contemporaries cited. G.C. Williamson, *Memoirs in Miniature* (1933) quotes his father on Stockmar and the Royal chemists. The anonymous *Notebooks of a Spinster Lady 1878–1903* (1919) quotes Sir Henry Holland on the Queen's plea to him. Lady Mary Biddulph's urgent note from Windsor to John Poyntz, 5th Earl Spencer, is in P. Gordon, ed., *The Red Earl. Papers of the Fifth Earl Spencer 1835–1885* (1982). Nathaniel de Rothschild's letter to his parents from Cambridge, 16–17 December 1861, is in the Rothschild Archive.

Afterword: Legacy

Charles Phipps's letter to John Scott Russell, 11 January 1962 is in the archives of the Royal Society of Arts. Elizabeth Gaskell's description of London in mourning appeared in her letter to Marianne Gaskell, 26 December 1861, in J.A.V. Chapple and Arthur Pollard, eds, *Letters of Mrs Gaskell* (1967). Mary Elizabeth Braddon's observation appeared in the January 1862 instalment of her novel *Aurora Floyd*, in *Temple Bar* – obviously a timely addition to the text. Emily Eden's correspondence, ed. Eleanor Eden, was published as *Letters from India* (1972).

Acknowledgements

Writing *Victoria* made writing this parallel biography almost inevitable – to examine one of the most famous marriages in history from the perspective of the other spouse. Thus my acknowledgement to persons and to archives in that book can be assumed to carry over to this one. Some names are repeated, however, when I convey my appreciation here to Lucy Addington, Richard Altick, Herbert Appeltshauser, Melanie Askey, Richard Atkins, Stephen Belcher, Christopher Brown, Harry P. Clark, Sarah Curtis, Alison Derrett, Frances Diamond, Robert C. Doyle, Vivian Elliot, Ken and Jenny Emrys-Roberts, Oliver Everett, Bonny Farmer, Roland Fleischer, Peter Funnell, Peter Gadsden, Victor Gray, John Halperin, Alan and Eileen Hanley-Browne, Bridget and Heinz Henisch, Jürgen Kamm, Marlene Eilers Koenig, Heinz Kosok, Rolf Lessenich, Elizabeth Longford, Bonnie McEwan, Tom McGarrity, M.D., Grant McIntyre, Charles W. Mann, George Mauner, Anne Michel, Patrick Middleton, David Painting, Michel Pharand, Franz-Josef Post, Shirley Rader, Sue Reighard, Sean Ronan, Barbara Ryan, Mina Schwalb, Sandra Stelts, Gerhard Strasser, Wendy Trewin, Elliot S. Vesell, M.D., Rodelle Weintraub, James L.W. West III, M.G. Wiebe, Richard Winslow III, Muriel Winterscheid.

I owe a special indebtedness to my research 'home' since 1970, the Institute for the Arts and Humanistic Studies at the Pennsylvania State University.

Stanley Weintraub

The House of Coburg

Duke August of Saxe-Altenburg
1773 – 1822
m.
Duchess Louise Charlotte of Mecklenburg
1779 – 1801

Duke Francis of Saxe-Coburg-Saalfeld
1750 – 1806
m.
Augusta of Reuss zu Ebersdorf
1757 – 1831

Louise of Saxe-Gotha-Altenburg ——— m (1) ——— Duke Ernest I of Saxe-Coburg-Gotha
1800 – 31   1784 – 1844

m (2)   Marie of
         Wurttemberg
         1799 – 1860

Duke Ernest II of Saxe-Coburg-Gotha   Prince Albert of Saxe-Coburg-Gotha
1818 – 93   Prince Consort
m.   1819 – 61
Princess Alexandrine of Baden   m.
1820 – 1904   Victoria, Queen of England
                                              1819 – 1901

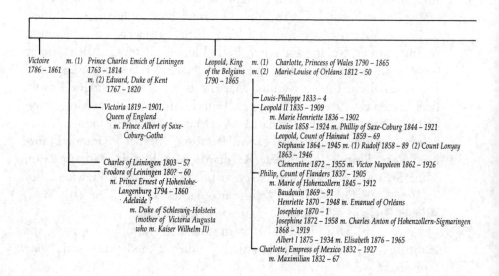

Victoire   m. (1) Prince Charles Emich of Leiningen   Leopold, King   m. (1)   Charlotte, Princess of Wales 1790 – 1865
1786 – 1861   1763 – 1814   of the Belgians m. (2)   Marie-Louise of Orléans 1812 – 50
                      m. (2) Edward, Duke of Kent   1790 – 1865
                      1767 – 1820
                                                                          ┌─ Louis-Philippe 1833 – 4
                          └─ Victoria 1819 – 1901,   ├─ Leopold II 1835 – 1909
                             Queen of England   m. Marie Henriette 1836 – 1902
                             m. Prince Albert of Saxe-   Louise 1858 – 1924 m. Phillip of Saxe-Coburg 1844 – 1921
                             Coburg-Gotha   Leopold, Count of Hainaut 1859 – 69
                                                                                Stephanie 1864 – 1945 m. (1) Rudolf 1858 – 89 (2) Count Lonyay
                                                                                1863 – 1946
                          ┌─ Charles of Leiningen 1803 – 57   Clementine 1872 – 1955 m. Victor Napoleon 1862 – 1926
                          └─ Feodora of Leiningen 180? – 60   ├─ Philip, Count of Flanders 1837 – 1905
                             m. Prince Ernest of Hohenlohe-   m. Marie of Hohenzollern 1845 – 1912
                             Langenburg 1794 – 1860   Baudouin 1869 – 91
                              Adelaide ?   Henriette 1870 – 1948 m. Emanuel of Orléans
                                m. Duke of Schleswig-Holstein   Josephine 1870 – 1
                                (mother of Victoria Augusta   Josephine 1872 – 1958 m. Charles Anton of Hohenzollern-Sigmaringen
                                who m. Kaiser Wilhelm II)   1868 – 1919
                                                                               Albert I 1875 – 1934 m. Elisabeth 1876 – 1965
                                                                          └─ Charlotte, Empress of Mexico 1832 – 1927
                                                                             m. Maximilian 1832 – 67

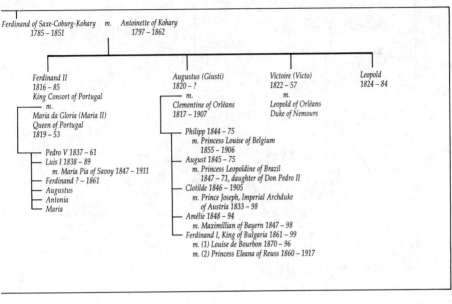

Ferdinand of Saxe-Coburg-Kohary   m.   Antoinette of Kohary
1785 – 1851   1797 – 1862

Ferdinand II
1816 – 85
King Consort of Portugal
— m.
Maria da Gloria (Maria II)
Queen of Portugal
1819 – 53
— Pedro V 1837 – 61
— Luis I 1838 – 89
     m. Maria Pia of Savoy 1847 – 1911
— Ferdinand ? – 1861
— Augustus
— Antonia
— Maria

Augustus (Giusti)
1820 – ?
— m.
Clementine of Orléans
1817 – 1907
— Philipp 1844 – 75
     m. Princess Louise of Belgium
     1855 – 1906
— August 1845 – 75
     m. Princess Leopoldine of Brazil
     1847 – 71, daughter of Don Pedro II
— Clotilde 1846 – 1905
     m. Prince Joseph, Imperial Archduke
     of Austria 1833 – 98
— Amélie 1848 – 94
     m. Maximillian of Bayern 1847 – 98
— Ferdinand I, King of Bulgaria 1861 – 99
     m. (1) Louise de Bourbon 1870 – 96
     m. (2) Princess Eleana of Reuss 1860 – 1917

Victoire (Victo)
1822 – 57
m.
Leopold of Orléans
Duke of Nemours

Leopold
1824 – 84

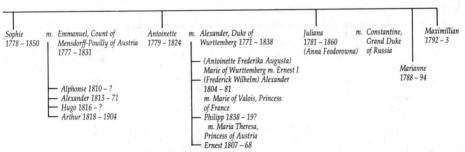

Sophie
1778 – 1850

m.   Emmanuel, Count of
     Mensdorff-Pouilly of Austria
     1777 – 1831
— Alphonse 1810 – ?
— Alexander 1813 – 71
— Hugo 1816 – ?
— Arthur 1818 – 1904

Antoinette
1779 – 1824

m.   Alexander, Duke of
     Wurttemberg 1771 – 1838
— (Antoinette Frederika Augusta)
     Marie of Wurttemberg m. Ernest I
— (Frederick Wilhelm) Alexander
     1804 – 81
     m. Marie of Valois, Princess
     of France
— Philipp 1838 – 19?
     m. Maria Theresa,
     Princess of Austria
— Ernest 1807 – 68

Juliana
1781 – 1860
(Anna Feodorowna)

m.   Constantine,
     Grand Duke
     of Russia

Maximillian
1792 – 3

Marianne
1788 – 94

The Descendants of Victoria and Albert

Victoria   m.   Albert, Prince Consort
1819 – 1901   1819 – 61

Albert Edward,   m.   Alexandra
Edward VII   of Denmark
1841 – 1910   1844 – 1925

Alice   m.   Louis IV,
1843 – 78   Grand Duke of
          Hesse-Darmstadt
          1837 – 92

George,
George V
1865 – 1936
m.
Victoria Mary
(May) of Teck
1867 – 1953

Victoria
1868 – 1935

Victoria
1863 – 1950
m.
Prince Louis
of Battenberg
(Mountbatten)
1854 – 1921

Irene
1866 – 1953
m.
Henry of
Prussia
1862 – 1929

Frederick
William
1870 – 3

Mary Victoria
1874 – 8

Albert Victor,
Duke of Clarence
1864 – 92

Louise,
Princess Royal
1867 – 1931
m.
Alexander Duff,
Duke of Fife
1849 – 1912

Maud
1869 – 1938
m.
Haakon VII,
► King of
Norway
1872 – 1957

Elizabeth
1864 – 1918
m.
Serge,
Grand Duke
of Russia
1857 – 1905

Ernest,
Grand Duke
of Hesse
1868 – 1937
m.
Victoria
Melita
1876 – 1936
(div. 1901)

Alix
1872 – 1918
m.
Nicholas II,
► Tsar of Russia
1868 – 1918

Victoria,
Princess Royal
1840 – 1901

m. Frederick III,
Emperor of Germany
1831 – 88

William II,
► Emperor of
Germany
1859 – 1941
m.
Augusta
of Schleswig-
Holstein-
Sonderburg-
Augustenburg
1858 – 1921

Henry
1862 – 1929
m.
Irene of
Hesse
1866 – 1953

Victoria
1866 – 1929
m. (1)
Adolphus of
Schaumburg-
Lippe
1859 – 1916
m. (2)
Alexander
Zubkov
1900 – 29

Sophie
1870 – 1932
m.
Constantine,
► King of Greece
1868 – 1923

Charlotte
1860 – 1919
m.
Bernard of
Saxe-Meiningen
1851 – 1928

Sigismund
1864 – 6

Waldemar
1868 – 79

Margaret
1872 – 1954
m.
Frederick
Charles of
Hesse
1868 – 1940

* *Gustav's second wife was Princess Louise
of Battenberg (1889 – 1965), one of the three
children of Victoria's granddaughter (Alice's
daughter) Victoria & Prince Louis of Battenberg*
► *Monarchs of other European counties*

and their marriages into the Royal Houses of Europe

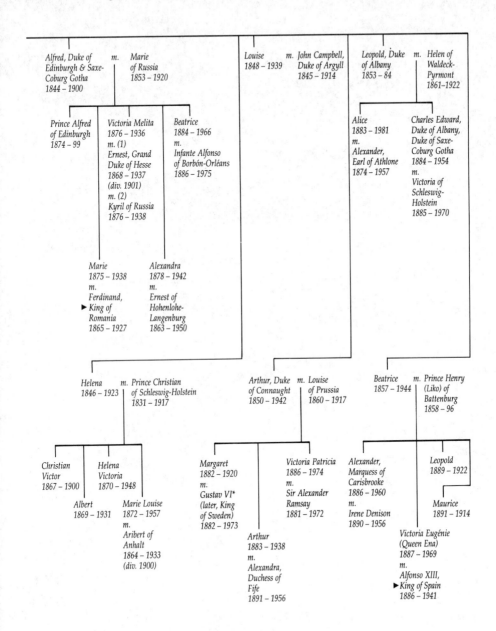

Alfred, Duke of
Edinburgh & Saxe-
Coburg Gotha
1844 – 1900

m.

Marie
of Russia
1853 – 1920

Louise
1848 – 1939

m.

John Campbell,
Duke of Argyll
1845 – 1914

Leopold, Duke
of Albany
1853 – 84

m.

Helen of
Waldeck-
Pyrmont
1861–1922

Prince Alfred
of Edinburgh
1874 – 99

Victoria Melita
1876 – 1936
m. (1)
Ernest, Grand
Duke of Hesse
1868 – 1937
(div. 1901)
m. (2)
Kyril of Russia
1876 – 1938

Beatrice
1884 – 1966
m.
Infante Alfonso
of Borbón-Orléans
1886 – 1975

Alice
1883 – 1981
m.
Alexander,
Earl of Athlone
1874 – 1957

Charles Edward,
Duke of Albany,
Duke of Saxe-
Coburg Gotha
1884 – 1954
m.
Victoria of
Schleswig-
Holstein
1885 – 1970

Marie
1875 – 1938
m.
Ferdinand,
► King of
Romania
1865 – 1927

Alexandra
1878 – 1942
m.
Ernest of
Hohenlohe-
Langenburg
1863 – 1950

Helena
1846 – 1923

m. Prince Christian
of Schleswig-Holstein
1831 – 1917

Arthur, Duke
of Connaught
1850 – 1942

m. Louise
of Prussia
1860 – 1917

Beatrice
1857 – 1944

m. Prince Henry
(Liko) of
Battenburg
1858 – 96

Christian
Victor
1867 – 1900

Helena
Victoria
1870 – 1948

Margaret
1882 – 1920
m.
Gustav VI*
(later, King
of Sweden)
1882 – 1973

Victoria Patricia
1886 – 1974
m.
Sir Alexander
Ramsay
1881 – 1972

Alexander,
Marquess of
Carisbrooke
1886 – 1960
m.
Irene Denison
1890 – 1956

Leopold
1889 – 1922

Albert
1869 – 1931

Marie Louise
1872 – 1957
m.
Aribert of
Anhalt
1864 – 1933
(div. 1900)

Arthur
1883 – 1938
m.
Alexandra,
Duchess of
Fife
1891 – 1956

Maurice
1891 – 1914

Victoria Eugénie
(Queen Ena)
1887 – 1969
m.
Alfonso XIII,
► King of Spain
1886 – 1941

Index

Index

TO THE LIBRARY OF
FROM YOUR ARMENIAN
FRIENDS AT ST. NERSESS
ARMENIAN SEMINARY,
ON THE OCCASION OF
DR. J. KOENIG'S AND FR. WRIGHT'S
VISIT TO OUR SEMINARY.

NEW ROCHELLE, NY

DN. HRATCH
TCHILINGIRIAN
RECTOR

11.11.92

Armenian-Americans

Armenian-Americans

From Being to Feeling Armenian

Anny Bakalian

Transaction Publishers
New Brunswick (U.S.A.) and London (U.K.)

E
184
.A7
B35
1992

Library of Congress Catalog Number: 91-32396
ISBN: 1-56000-025-2
Printed in the United States of America

Library of Congress Cataloging-in-Publication Data
Bakalian, Anny P.
    Armenian-Americans : from being to feeling Armenian / Anny
Bakalian.
    p. cm.
    ISBN 1-56000-025-2
    1. Armenian Americans—Cultural assimilations. 2. Armenian
Americans—Ethnic identity. I. Title.
    E184.A7B35 1992
    305.891'992073—dc20   91-32396
                                                                CIP

To the memory of Haigouhie and to her American
great-granddaughter Anoush
and
to all Armenian grandparents
who provide that chain of memory and love linking the ancestral past
to future generations

Contents

Acknowledgments

This book was written with two audiences in mind; social scientists concerned with race and ethnic relations and people of Armenian descent. Given my Armenian background and my sociological training, the motivation for researching and writing this volume might seem obvious. Yet, a number of fortuitous experiences led me to begin this investigation of Armenian-Americans. When I first came to New York City to pursue graduate work at Columbia University, I had not given ethnic studies much thought. Then, as I started attending functions hosted by the formally organized Armenian community and meeting people, I realized that ethnic identity and Armenianness in the United States were very different from what I was familiar with in the Middle East.

In May 1984, having finished my course work and comprehensives, I was searching for a dissertation topic when Loretta Nassar suggested I attend a conference on Armenian assimilation organized by NAASR (National Association of Armenian Studies and Research) in Cambridge, MA. In retrospect, that meeting was the catalyst that prompted this study. I found out that little had been written in the social sciences on contemporary Armenian-Americans, to the point where they had been labeled a "hidden minority." An empirical analysis was well overdue. It was an opportunity I could not miss. Not only would a survey of people of Armenian descent in the United States satisfy my personal curiosity, it could provide much-needed scientific evidence to pull this largely overlooked ethnic group out of the academic closet. I also believed the results of the study would eventually benefit the Armenian-American community. The journey since has spanned several years and stages in my professional career. My debts are many and long-standing.

First, I would like to thank the members of my dissertation committee. It was my great fortune to meet Professor Viviana Zelizer during my first semester at Columbia. She has been a teacher, a role model, a mentor, and, to my delight, a friend. She was there for me when I needed advice, and when I decided to switch my research topic to ethnicity; she continued her advisory role even though it was not in her area of expertise. Her comments on earlier drafts were incisive; they helped shape the parameters of the argument and enhanced its creativity. Viviana has also been instrumental in getting my manuscript published. Somehow words do not seem adequate to express my affection and infinite gratitude.

I am much obliged to Professor Bernard Barber for having sponsored the dissertation. I could not have had a more supportive sponsor. He gave me the freedom to learn to become an independent thinker and writer. Professor Allen Barton suggested the use of a snowball sample, and was particularly helpful in the quantitative component of this study. He read through several drafts, and discussed with me the topic in question among others of more general interest. Those conversations were highly enjoyable.

I was honored that Professor Nina Garsoian agreed to participate in my doctoral defense. Her historical precision with dates and sources improved the quality of the final document. My intellectual debt to Professor Herbert Gans is clearly visible throughout my work, even in the title of this book. While taking one of his courses, I finally admitted to myself my interest in ethnicity and proceeded to read the literature for the first time. As a student, I found Professor Gans's criticisms of my academic performance well-deserved, though painful. He must have known what he was doing because it made me strive harder to meet his approval. I am deeply touched by his opinion of the end product. His compliment stands in a class by itself.

For this publication, the original manuscript was completely revised to account for the rapid changes taking place in the Republic of Armenia and to include a discussion of all Armenian-Americans, not just those in metropolitan New York and New Jersey. In addition to interviews with California informants and visits to other communities, I have had to rely heavily on the previous works of my colleagues in this particular field. I have acknowledged each author in the text as I borrowed from his or her work, but I would like to single out Rouben Adalian, Claudia Der Martirosian, Vigen Guroian, Robert Mirak, Anahid Ordjanian, Susan Pattie, Harold Takooshian, and Khachig Tölölyan whose contributions were substantial.

Gerard Libaridian deserves special recognition. He read my work during different stages of its development. His criticisms were always incisive and constructive. Moreover, as director of the Zoryan Institute for Contemporary Armenian Documentation and Research, Inc., Gerard established the Open University Seminars and other colloquia that provided a forum for the exchange of ideas and observations on Armenianness in America and the diaspora. My participation in such meetings shaped many of my thoughts and arguments. In fact, it would be hard to delineate which particular insights are mine and which ones were generated from Zoryan-sponsored gatherings.

The late Archbishop Tiran Nersoyan also took an interest in my study. It was a humbling and encouraging experience to find such a remarkable individual who was still eager to learn something new. I will cherish his memory dearly. Louise Simone was generous in granting interviews and supplying mailing lists. Professor Irving Louis Horowitz reputed in the Armenian-American community as a friend of the Armenians, once again came through. I thank him for his courage in publishing this book. Esther Luckett at Transaction and Janet Schamehorn provided me with invaluable editorial assistance. At the College of Notre Dame of Maryland I found support for my scholarly endeavors especially from Sister Mary Ellen Dougherty and Sally Wall.

I owe much to my extended family. Without their help, in every sense of the word, I would have accomplished little. More specifically, I thank my Uncle Puzant and Aunt Shake for providing a home for me when I first came to New York; my Uncle Vasken for backing my goals without questioning them; my brother-in-law Hrant for keeping me up-to-date with the latest gossip on Armenia and the Armenians;

and my mother and sister for their love, understanding, and care, which typically for women, means feeding. I was particularly lucky, I ate haute cuisine.

Several institutions in metropolitan New York entrusted their mailing lists to me. Many people assisted with referrals, the pretests, and discussions. About thirty individuals on the East and West coasts became my informants for their local communities, sharing with me their expertise on things Armenian. I thank them all. Last but by no means least, my respondents, the 584 men and women who participated in the survey, deserve my deepest appreciation. They took time from no doubt busy schedules and demanding responsibilities to answer my long and detailed questionnaire. Their cooperation and enthusiasm for this study made the research personally and professionally rewarding. Without them all, I would have had no data and no book. *Shnorhagal yem!*

1

Introduction: Assimilation and Identity

My parents met through the Armenian Presbyterian Church, which both their parents helped found, in West New York, NJ. They were very active in the church and Armenian activities while they were growing up. [Father was U.S.-born and mother was born in Turkey but immigrated when she was four years old.]

After they married, and my sister and I were born, they moved to Fair Lawn, NJ, and bought a home. We were the only Armenians in town, except for an elderly minister who would visit us occasionally. I was two years old and my sister was five. That is when our separation from the Armenian community began. We grew up as Americans with American friends. Our parents didn't speak Armenian at home, and we never learned the language. As our older relatives became lost to us, our ties to our Armenian roots became obscure. As a teenager, I went through a time of intense pride and interest in my Armenian heritage, but with the turmoil of the 1960's, that was replaced by other concerns. My sister and I have married non-Armenians, and our children are another generation removed from our roots. We teach them, with pride, the history of the Armenians while we encourage their progress in America. (Forty-two-year-old male respondent)

I am a third-generation American-Armenian, regrettably I know little about the Armenian background of my grandparents. My grandmother came to this country when she was only sixteen, so she was more American than Armenian.

> I enjoy my Armenian roots, go to Armenian events whenever I can and always feel
> a common bond with other Armenians. (Fifty-one-year-old female respondent)

This book describes Armenian-Americans, individually and collectively. The above comments from two survey respondents illustrate the main themes that dominate the discussion: the assimilation of people of Armenian descent in the United States of America and their continued pride and identity in their ethnic heritage.

Assimilation has been a contentious subject for Armenian-Americans. With promises of wealth, power and prestige, the host society is assumed to lure immigrants and their descendants away from their ancestral roots. While few immigrants have actively embraced cultural change, welcoming a fresh start in life, most have tried to maintain their heritage and recreate new communities in the New World. The success of such efforts remains under dispute. The issue has consumed Armenian-Americans ever since they first landed in America over one hundred years ago. Assimilation has been widely debated by scholars and the lay public to the point where it has been likened to an obsession.[1] It has also been called the "white massacre," a poignant analogy to a people who have historically suffered numerous massacres and a genocide.[2]

Armenian-Americans see themselves as descendants of a very ancient people who emerged in the mountainous region of northeastern Asia Minor some twenty-five hundred years ago and have survived, against all odds, a long and turbulent history. At the threshold of the twenty-first century however, the Armenian people and their unique material and nonmaterial culture are perceived to be in jeopardy for lack of an autonomous homeland, their dispersion in a diaspora, and their small size (approximately 6 million worldwide). Moreover, to many, it seems that their very physical survival is repeatedly threatened by massacres, earthquakes, and political turmoil around the world. To mention but a few examples from the most recent past; one is reminded of the well-established Armenian communities in Lebanon and Iran that have been destroyed or uprooted, and the Armenians in Sumgait and Baku who have been killed or expelled from their homes. The precarious existence of the Armenian people and culture fuels this debate with urgency and timeliness. Armenian-Americans are burdened with the insecurity of a collective future, locally and globally. Not surprisingly, for Armenian-Americans, assimilation is a very sensitive topic that hovers, like a specter, in the forefront of their being.

On the one hand, there are some who have accepted assimilation as a foregone conclusion perceiving ethnic maintenance efforts as temporary palliatives. They have been too keen to notice the galloping erosion of the immigrant language and culture. This position is not new; even the earliest settlers were cognizant of the forces of assimilation. This is illustrated by an editorial that appeared in the Fresno (CA) Armenian paper, *Asbarez*, on July 7, 1911:

> The most important question confronting the Armenians of California, and in the United States in general, is that of remaining Armenian.

> The Americanization of Armenians is certain to come, all we can do is to delay the day. (Quoted in LaPiere 1930, 316-17)

On the other hand, there are those who have argued that Armenians are distinguished by unique historical and cultural features that make them resilient to the forces of assimilation.[3] Armenians take pride in their history, their persistence as a people for thousands of years, their unique language and alphabet, their national church, which has since its inception in the fourth century A.D. fused together the sacred and secular destinies of its people. The Genocide and its subsequent denial by Turkish governments remain at the forefront of Armenian collective consciousness, serving as a common denominator and strengthening the boundaries that carve up a separate sense of peoplehood.

Most recently, the survival efforts of the victims of the December 1988 earthquake in Soviet Armenia, and the resistance of the residents of mountainous Karabagh against the Azeries are taken as illustrations of the indomitable will of the Armenian people to endure and perpetuate their culture, much like the heroic courage of David in his stand against the giant Goliath. These sentiments are best portrayed by fellow Armenian-American author, William Saroyan (1984):

> I should like to see any power of the world destroy this race, this small tribe of unimportant people, whose wars have all been fought and lost, whose structures have crumbled, literature is unread, music is unheard, and prayers are no more answered. Go ahead, destroy Armenia. See if you can do it. Send them into the

desert without bread or water. Burn their homes and churches. Then see if they will
not laugh, sing and pray again. For when two of them meet anywhere in the world,
see if they will not create a New Armenia.

Indeed, the proponents of this viewpoint observe that, contrary to
predictions, the Armenian-American community has grown and
prospered over the years and many Armenian-Americans have
achieved prominence without denying their ancestral origins.

All this preoccupation with assimilation remains mostly rhetorical
and speculative. Armenians in the United States are a little-studied
group that have hitherto been called a "hidden minority" (Rollins
1981). Studies in the social sciences on Armenian-Americans have
been few and far between; mostly descriptive accounts of traditional
Armenian institutions.[4] This book aims to fill that gap. It provides a
sociological analysis of Armenianness as it unfolds with the passage
of time and generations in the United States. This entails an
examination of the processes of assimilation and ethnic maintenance
in personal expressions and an ethnographic description of Armenian-
American communal structures.

The empirical data used in this volume is based primarily on the
results of a large questionnaire survey that was mailed to men and
women of Armenian descent in metropolitan New York and New
Jersey in 1986. The main sample was chosen randomly from mailing
lists of all Armenian churches and voluntary associations in the study
area. It was supplemented with a snowball sample of individuals who
were not organizationally affiliated. The survey yielded 584
respondents; hereafter referred to as sample, survey, or New York
study. The qualitative data was derived from in-depth interviews with
informants actively involved in Armenian-American communities,
both on the East and West coasts; participant observation of the New
York/New Jersey community; and published material. Vignettes and
anecdotal evidence gathered from these sources are used to buttress
and humanize the quantitative evidence. Methods of data collection
and a description of the sample are explained in greater detail at the
end of this chapter.

Milton Gordon's (1964) conceptual framework on assimilation was
used to collect and analyze the data on Armenian-Americans. He
postulated that there are seven subprocesses of assimilation (explained
fully below), and that immigrant groups proceed at a variable pace

along each of these continua. The underlying assumption of this study is the "straight-line" model (Sandberg 1974), which predicts a decrease in adherence to ethnic culture and behavioral forms with length of history in the United States. Nonetheless, assimilation is understood as a dynamic process that may be reversed, at least in theory. The aim here is not to measure how Armenian-Americans have become similar to other ethnic groups or mainstream Americans, but to measure their departures from traditional Armenian value systems, behavioral forms, and life-styles.

The results of this survey establish that generational presence in the United States is the most powerful variable in explaining assimilation. The immigrant generation's cultural and behavioral patterns are taken as the statistical baseline, and all departures from that imply a movement along the continuum toward more assimilation. Therefore, change is measured in the degree difference between the first and subsequent generations. The foreign-born or immigrant generation is defined as the first generation. The second generation consists of the U.S.-born children of the immigrants. The third generation are men and women who with one or both parents are U.S.-born. And the fourth generation are those who with their parents and at least one grandparent are also U.S.-born.

The observations presented here are believed to be representative of Armenian-Americans. This term encompasses a wide spectrum of people. The universe of Armenian-Americans consists of men and women who reside in the United States and trace descent from the ancient land and culture of Armenia. This is a subjective definition based on identity; it inevitably produces wide within-group variations by generational presence in America, recency of immigration, legal status, country of birth, religious affiliation, mixed parentage, socioeconomic status, knowledge of Armenian language and culture, political/ideological beliefs, degree of involvement in ethnic communal activities, and so on.

This study demonstrates that American-born descendants of Armenian immigrants have undergone significant assimilation in the United States. For example, the Armenian language is no longer used as a means of everyday communication. The secular culture, even cuisine, is relegated to special occasions and acquires symbolic connotations. Frequency of attendance at Armenian religious services is gradually reduced, as is participation in communal life and activities sponsored by Armenian voluntary associations. Social ties, even intimate relations and conjugal bonds, with non-Armenians become increasingly the norm. But this is only part of the story. The majority of Armenian-Americans, even the great-grandchildren of the immigrant generation, continue to maintain high levels of Armenian identity, fierce pride in their ancestral heritage, and a strong sense of we-ness or peoplehood.

What might seem as two contradictory processes, a zero-sum pie, do indeed coexist. I propose here that processes of assimilation and maintenance of ethnic identity go hand in hand. This is possible because Armenianness changes in its form and function. Later-generation Armenian-Americans are best described by the concept of "symbolic ethnicity" (Gans 1979). Symbolic Armenianness is voluntary, rational, and situational, in contrast to the traditional Armenianness of the immigrant generation, which is ascribed, unconscious, and compulsive. Symbolic Armenians acknowledge and are proud of their ethnic origin. Symbolic Armenianness pertains to the realm of emotions but makes few behavioral demands. The generational change is from "being" Armenian to "feeling" Armenian.

Human action is assumed to be purposeful, creative. People use the little margins of freedom and limited choices they have to play an active part in structuring their social world. Assimilation and ethnic maintenance do not just "happen" to immigrant groups. Immigrants are not passive victims in the drama that forces them to make choices between their cultural survival and their mundane, existential survival. Armenians, like most immigrant groups in America, have established churches, schools, mass media, and myriad other organizations to enact their cultural heritage in a new land, under new conditions, as they have tried to pass their ancestral legacy onto subsequent generations. It should be noted, however, that the emergent structures are rarely exact replicas of the ones left behind in the "old country" or countries, as the case may be. The Armenian-American subculture is a creative adaptation to a new and different life. Likewise, assimilation and the changing nature of Armenianness are not acts of callous betrayal, but innovative responses to changing structural conditions and personal needs.

The ethnicity of later-generation Armenian-Americans is different in nature and degree from that of the immigrant generation. Ethnic identity for American-born generations is not at the core of their role expectations and self-image. American-born upper-middle-class symbolic Armenians have more freedom in deciding their personal identities. They may choose to be Armenian, Armenian-American, American-Armenian, American, or whatever else they want. Moreover, symbolic Armenians may change their identity as often as they want. Identities may fluctuate over the course of one's life, when facing specific audiences, and in response to changes in the larger environment or the diaspora.

For Armenian-Americans, the boundaries separating Armenians from non-Armenians, "us" from "them," are generally self-imposed, shallow, and mutable. By contrast, the identity of Armenians who lived in the Ottoman Empire, as those of the Middle East today, was ascribed by the social and political system they were born into. That is, the markers that separated Armenians from non-Armenians were imposed by forces outside the Armenian collectivity. It should be noted that an ascribed identity is far more likely to determine the life-styles and life chances of a group member than a voluntary identity. In sum, the varying versions of Armenianness should be recognized as the outcomes of complex historical and dialectical processes. Country of birth and childhood socialization, generation, and even cohort effect are important variables in understanding the behavior and attitudes of people of Armenian descent.

The study emphasizes the sentimental component of symbolic Armenianness, making a case for increased situational, individualistic forms of expression and the importance of convenience in its application. Most frequently, Armenianness is manifested during one's leisure time. Armenian identity for later generations is no longer exclusive, all-engulfing, but tangential to people's lives and daily preoccupations. Consequently, its liability is also limited, making it easier to be a symbolic Armenian.

It is generally hypothesized that the higher the social class, the less the ethnic identity and commitment. I find that Armenian-Americans with higher educational attainment in the sample are more likely to be structurally assimilated; that is, they are more likely to have non-Armenian friends and spouses. However, structural assimilation does not significantly alter their levels of Armenian identity. With continued assimilation and upward mobility, if Armenianness is to survive in the United States among large proportions of men and women of Armenian descent, it can only do so in its symbolic form.

It should not be forgotten that the popularity and renewed interest in ethnicity in recent decades coincides with its increased societal legitimation and the improved socioeconomic status of most white ethnic groups including the Armenians. With higher levels of education, occupational prestige, and income, later-generation Armenian-Americans are less ashamed to be vocal about their immigrant roots. Ethnicity is less embarrassing today than it was during the first half of the twentieth century precisely because it is only sentimental, romanticized ethnicity. The results of this study clearly show that there is no "return" or "revival" to behavioral forms of Armenianness.

The argument that ethnic resilience is caused by instrumental motives or material "interests" is somewhat limited in its application here. Overall, Armenian-Americans are characterized by middle-class to upper-middle-class status, and their social mobility as a group has been remarkably rapid. They have few social and economic reasons to mobilize as a group in the urban political arena. This is not to say that Armenian-Americans have not jumped on the bandwagon alongside other ethnic and racial groups competing for their share of the American pie. In Los Angeles, for example, Armenian brokers compete for public monies targeted to finance social services for Armenian refugees. Elsewhere Armenians contribute dollars, and votes whenever possible, to elect people of Armenian descent to public office. More recently, Armenian organizations have received federal funds for earthquake relief. There is somewhat more support for the ideological component of ethnic resilience because Armenianness is sustained by a myth of a common ancestor, a shared history, and a sense of peoplehood with Armenians around the world. This ideology stirs the hearts and minds of Armenian-Americans to express their roots, make token contributions to Armenian philanthropies, write letters to newspapers or politicians regarding the denial of the Genocide, and so on. The most active forms of mobilization, such as rallies, public demonstrations, whatever the motivation, are confined primarily to the first and second generations.

A small core of highly active men and women, overwhelmingly from the first and second generations, make up the "Armenian-

American Community" and constitute the audience for the numerous events and activities hosted by the voluntary associations. The large influx of new Armenian immigrants in recent decades has revitalized the communal structures and provided a cadre to man the churches, the schools, the old people's homes, the media, and the various organizations. This community is unable to attract the attention, let alone retain the participation, of the vast majority of people of Armenian descent.

It is impossible for American-born Armenians to find Armenianness meaningful or functional if they are not taught how to appreciate it. The dilemma in ethnic continuity has always been the conciliation of the American Dream with ethnic ideology. Only the most convenient modes of socialization and manifestations of ethnicity are acceptable and feasible. They are the most symbolic: those that do not hinder personal achievements and do not get into conflict with mainstream American society. The concern here is not whether Armenian institutional structures and a community of sorts will survive. There is no doubt that there will be in the foreseeable future some men and women of Armenian stock who will find it expedient to maintain some form of Armenianness, and as long as the larger American society tolerates it, they will individually and communally try to do so. The real issue is what proportion of the universe of men and women of Armenian descent will do so.

Immigration and Settlement

Mirak (1980; 1983), who has written the most comprehensive social history of early Armenian-Americans to date, observes that very few pioneering Armenians came to America before 1890. The earliest recorded immigrant is one "Malcolm the Armenian" who came to Jamestown in 1618 or 1619. Before 1870, perhaps 60 adventurous businessmen who had been schooled by New England Protestant missionaries arrived from Asia Minor. By the late 1880s the number of Armenians is estimated to have risen to 1,500. These were mainly artisans and laborers seeking economic opportunities. Then, in the last decade of the nineteenth century, over 12,000 frightened Armenians, fleeing the massacres and political unrest of the decaying Ottoman

Empire, took refuge on American soil. The annual immigration figures peaked to 2,500 by the mid-1890s.

The pace of immigration accelerated dramatically between 1900 and 1914. By World War I, there were some 60,000 Armenians in the United States. For example, in 1910 more than 5,500 Armenians entered the United States, and in 1913, the records indicate that another 9,355 arrived. Both push and pull factors contributed to this increase. On the one hand, political and economic conditions were rapidly deteriorating in Ottoman Turkey. The most significant incident during this period was the Adana massacres in 1909 that killed between 15,000 and 20,000 souls. On the other hand, the presence of relatives and friends in the New World triggered the migration chain and eased the process.

The prewar immigrants were predominantly from Asia Minor. They arrived in New York and settled in eastern cities. A much smaller number of Russian-Armenians, about 2,500, came between 1898 and 1914. They initially settled in Canada and then moved to southern California after 1908. Mirak (1980) suggests that economic and political conditions in Russian Armenia, while serious, were not as oppressive as those in the Ottoman Empire, nor did they have the benefit of Protestant missionaries to lure them to emigrate.

After World War I, emigration resumed. Survivors from the Armenian Genocide (1915) and the deportations perpetrated by the Young Turk Government continued to come to America in comparatively large numbers until the quota system went into effect in 1924. For example in 1920 alone, 10,212 Armenians, a record number, entered the United States. Again, between 1920 and 1924 an additional 20,559 came. Unlike prewar Armenian immigrants, over half of these were women and a fifth were children; many were widows and orphans who had been maimed and psychologically scarred by the atrocities they had experienced. A few had been rescued from Turkish homes, many came from orphanages and refugee camps run by Armenian charitable associations or European and American missionaries in Syria, Greece, and Egypt.

The quota system, which admitted immigration from various nations by the proportion of their countrymen in the 1870 U.S. census, obviously did not favor Armenians and brought their immigration to a halt. Nonetheless, during the period when the quota law was in effect,

1924-1965, some Armenians were able to bypass the restrictive barriers to immigration. Initially, several Armenians entered with so-called Nansen passports; refugee documents supplied by the League of Nations. Then, ANCHA (American National Committee for Homeless Armenians), established in 1947, was instrumental in relocating about 4,500 Armenians, mainly from the Soviet Union, who had been stranded in settlement camps in Germany and Italy after World War II. These were exempted from the nationality quota by the Displaced Persons Act. ANCHA later helped Armenians from Palestine after the creation of the State of Israel, those fleeing communist regimes in Romania and Bulgaria and those escaping the socialist Arab governments of Egypt, Syria, and Iraq. In all, about 25,000 Armenians immigrated to America as refugees under the auspices of ANCHA (Takooshian 1986-87).

The influx of Armenian immigration to the United States picked up once again, after the liberalization of the quota law in 1965. This time the Armenians were escaping the political turmoil of the Middle East. The rate peaked as never before with the start of the Civil War in Lebanon (1975) and the Islamic Revolution in Iran (1978) (see Takooshian 1986-87). According to the 1980 U.S. census, only 8 percent of Iranian-Armenians immigrated to the United States before 1959, about 25 percent between 1960 and 1974, and 65 percent between 1975 and 1980. Nearly three-quarters of Armenian immigrants from Iran settled in Los Angeles. In an extensive survey of 195 Iranian-Armenian heads of households in Los Angeles, Der-Martirosian (1989) found additional evidence; 35 percent of her sample had arrived between 1952 and 1978, 24 percent in 1979 alone, the year following the revolution, and 41 percent since then.

The Armenian population of Lebanon is estimated to have decreased from well over 250,000 in the early 1970s to less than 100,000 in the late 1980s. Of course, not all those who left Lebanon came to the United States, though a large proportion did. Takooshian's (1986-87, 138) guesstimates range from 60,000 to 160,000 Lebanese Armenians immigrating to the United States. Unfortunately, there are no reliable statistics to indicate how many Armenians from the Middle East, or elsewhere for that matter, have settled in the United States in recent decades. I should add that most of the numerical data on the Armenian population is based on conjecture. Armenian immigration to the United States has been "lost" in official counts for over a century. Early immigrants traveled with Ottoman papers and were often mislabeled as "Turk" or "Arab" while more recent ones obtained visas on Lebanese, Iranian, or other passports.

A group that has received little scholarly attention are Armenians who had remained or returned to their homes in Turkey after the Genocide and deportations. Most of the Armenian population of Turkey after the establishment of the Republic in 1923 lived in Istanbul. In spite of severe restrictions on their personal and collective freedom,[5] Istanbul Armenians (or *Bolcetzi*) sustained a communal life as best they could. They maintained an Armenian press, operated Armenian schools, and continued to worship in Armenian churches. Discrimination has barred Armenians in Turkey from a wide range of occupations. At present, except for a few professionals, the majority of the population tends to earn its livelihood through business enterprises.

The situation of Armenians who remained in the hinterland was deplorable. While scattered in small towns and villages, deprived of economic and educational opportunities, lacking access to Armenian religious and communal structures, most were able to hold onto their Armenian identity in private. Over the decades, the vast majority of these by then Turkish-speaking, semiskilled, or unskilled Armenians gravitated toward Istanbul. The late Patriarch Shnork Kaloustian, who traveled repeatedly to the interior of Turkey, was instrumental in helping them relocate and be integrated in the Armenian community of Istanbul. In the pursuit of freedom, Armenians with Turkish passports have emigrated in unprecedented numbers. In the early 1960s, it is estimated that more than 120,000 Armenians lived in Istanbul. At present, only about 30,000 remain. Armenians from Istanbul have come to the United States; Los Angeles alone is reputed to have received some 10,000 Istanbul Armenians in the last twenty years. There is also a sizable *Bolcetzi* population in the New York metropolitan area. Others though have settled in Canada, Australia, France, Germany, and Argentina.[6]

Starting in the 1970s and most recently in late 1980s, large numbers of Armenians were allowed to leave Soviet Armenia.[7] These were mostly those Armenians and their descendants who had repatriated to Soviet Armenia between 1946 and 1960 (an estimated 250,000) and had not been able to assimilate with the native population. Given a chance to leave, they did. Heitman (1988)[8] puts the total number of Armenians who emigrated from Soviet Armenia to the United States between 1971 and 1988 at 47,700 (71.3 percent came between 1971 and 1980, 13.4 percent between 1981 and 1986 and 15.3 percent came in 1987-88 alone). More are coming. Their favorite destination remains Los Angeles. Estimates suggest that between September 1988 and September 1989, another 13,500 Armenian refugees came from Soviet Armenia and Iran.[9]

With the exception of Fresno (CA), the earliest Armenian immigrants settled predominantly in urban industrial centers of the Northeast such as New York City, Providence (RI), Worcester (MA), and Boston (MA). Some moved soon to midwestern cities such as Chicago, Detroit (MI), Racine (WI), and Waukegan (IL) where jobs were more plentiful. The social and demographic characteristics of the migrant population determined their early settlement patterns. Typically at the beginning, when the immigrants consisted of single young men or married men who had journeyed without their families, Armenians shared living quarters in cheap, overcrowded boardinghouses or tenements. These residences tended to be in densely populated areas of the state with easy public access to factory jobs. The immigrants' aim was to save as much money as possible to send back home or to finance the travel of other family members. For many of this first wave of immigrants, their stay in the United States was perceived as temporary. However, the situation in Ottoman Turkey soon terminated such aspirations. In time, they were joined by women and children. As families regrouped, and others were formed, their living conditions improved and communal life flourished.

Compared to other immigrants of that period, the majority of the Armenians were literate, over a third were skilled artisans, and a few were businessmen and professionals. In spite of their skills and business acumen, most had no choice but to become laborers in manufacturing industries because they did not have proficiency in English and their capital resources were almost nonexistent. For many though, that was just a stepping-stone for private ownership in a small retail store. Fresno again was the exception. There, Armenians were engaged in agricultural production and packaging. Hard work (and the expansion of the U.S. economy) eventually paid off, especially after

World War II. Large proportions of the immigrants' children went to college, and entered white collar or professional occupations. The road to success was also the move to suburbia in the 1950s and 1960s.

Recent Armenian immigrants, like other post-1965 (legal) immigrants to the United States, do not conform to the stereotype of the poor, often illiterate peasant of earlier generations. For the most part, the newest arrivals come with greater resources than in the past. They are more likely to be proficient in English, have higher levels of educational attainment and occupational skills, and a few seeking political asylum from the turmoils of the Middle East have brought with them their fortunes. At the very least, the vast majority of these newest immigrants have experienced modern urban environments. Thus, it is possible to concur with Mirak's (1980, 142) suggestion that socioeconomic success for these newcomers was achieved at a faster pace than for those who came at the turn of the century. He explains that the majority of refugees who received loans from ANCHA were able to repay their debts within a few years.[10] Small business ownership was and continues to be the typical route to the American Dream for many Armenian immigrants. However, increasingly, one also tends to find among the immigrants sizable proportions of professionals, such as physicians, dentists, pharmacists, engineers, architects, scientists, and academics who manage to establish themselves relatively quickly in the United States.[11]

Estimates of Size and Location

Often-quoted estimates of the number of people of Armenian descent in the United States at the present time range from 600,000 to 800,000.[12] In the mid-1970s, the estimates stood between 350,000 and 450,000, with about 45 percent living in New England and the mid-Atlantic states, another 15 percent in Michigan, Illinois, Ohio and Wisconsin, and the remaining 25 percent in California (Mirak 1980; Avakian 1977b). In recent years, as the demographic characteristics of the Armenian-American population have changed so has their geographical distribution. Sizable communities have sprung up in Florida and Texas warranting the establishment of churches. Others, such as those in Seattle (WA) are in the process of organizing a congregation. Elsewhere, such as in Tucson (AZ), Atlanta (GA),

Baton Rouge (LA), Minneapolis (MN), Las Vegas (NV), voluntary associations were created. On the other hand, once well-established Armenian churches and communities have lost their vigor or ceased to exist. For example, the Protestant Armenian church of Haverhill (MA), emptied of parishioners, was dismantled in 1977 (Mirak 1980, 141). Similarly, the St John the Baptist Armenian Apostolic Church in Syracuse (NY) is apprehensive about its future. Its congregation has aged or died and few newcomers seem to be drawn to Syracuse (*Armenian American Almanac* 1990).

A rough measure of the dispersion of the Armenian-American population in various regions of the United States at the present time would be to count the number of Armenian churches that hold regular services in any given area. Typically, Armenians have established a church in a new location as soon as an optimum number of congregants were able to sustain one. I have tallied the total number of Armenian Apostolic, Protestant, and Catholic churches in the country and calculated their geographic distribution (see table 1.1). Fifty percent of all Armenian churches are located in the mid-Atlantic states and New England, 33 percent in California alone, 14 percent in the Midwest (WI, IL, MI), and the rest are in Texas and Florida. The fastest-growing Armenian-American population is undeniably the greater Los Angeles area.

The Armenian settlement in Los Angeles had a slow start. According to Aram Yeretzian, the very first Armenian in Los Angeles was a student who came from the East Coast for health reasons around 1900. Then an Oriental rug merchant arrived; and soon they were writing letters to their friends and relatives and asking them to join them. Yeretzian was a Protestant minister and social worker who had the opportunity to gather firsthand information on the Armenians in Los Angles which he presented as a thesis at the University of Southern California in 1923. He writes that there were between 2,500 to 3,000 Armenians at the time of his study. The majority had come from Turkey, but there were a few from Russian Armenia. There were three Armenian women who had married American men, and twelve men who had married American, Spanish, and other women. Armenians had established a number of voluntary associations and two churches; one Apostolic and one Protestant, the Armenian Gethsemane Congregational Church, which had more than seventy members. Yeretzian notes that 2.3 percent of the Armenian population in Los Angeles in the early 1920s were professionals, 39.5 percent were skilled laborers, 23.5 percent were farm laborers and the rest laborers in other occupations. In general, Yeretzian found Los Angeles Armenians to be hardworking, thrifty, enterprising, resourceful, and highly individualistic; most of all they were loyal and obedient citizens.

Since 1965, Los Angeles has attracted a large proportion of immigrants from Lebanon, Iran, Turkey, and the bulk of refugees from Soviet Armenia.[13] Metropolitan Los Angeles boasts twenty-two churches, more than three-quarters established after World War II. It also claims the lion's share of Armenian all-day schools (twelve schools, including five high schools). Indeed, all available data indicate that the Armenian immigration boom in Los Angeles is about twenty years old. According to the U.S. census, 52,400 Armenians lived in Los Angeles in 1980 (reported in Der-Martirosian, Sabagh and Bozorgmehr 1990).[14] Of these, only 28.1 percent were born in the U.S. (including 19.5 percent born in California), while the overwhelming majority (71.9 percent) were foreign-born.[15] The foreign-born consisted of those born in Iran (14.7 percent), the USSR (14.3 percent), Lebanon (11.5 percent); Turkey (9.7 percent), and other Middle Eastern nations (11.8 percent). The remaining 9.9 percent came from Eastern Europe or elsewhere. Furthermore, only 17.1 percent of those born in Turkey and 15.1 percent of those born in the USSR immigrated before 1950. The biggest influx of immigrants arrived after 1975: 74.8 percent of Iranian-born Armenians, 71.4 percent of Lebanese-born Armenians, 66.9 percent of those born in USSR, and 53.1 percent of those born in Turkey.

It should be noted that scholars find that these statistics from the 1980 census underestimate the actual number of Armenians in Los Angeles,[16] and elsewhere in the U.S. for that matter (see Lieberson and Waters 1988). Moreover, the massive influx of Armenians to Los Angeles did not stop in the 1980s; on the contrary, it seems to have accelerated (Der-Martirosian, Sabagh, and Bozorgmehr 1990). Elsewhere in the United States, foreign-born Armenians are estimated to constitute about 40 percent of the Armenian-American population. More specifically, the foreign-born make up 43.2 percent of Armenian-American population in San Francisco, 26.5 percent of those in Fresno, 30.7 percent of those in Boston, 32.3 percent of those in Worcester, and 33.3 percent of those in Chicago (Sabagh, Bozorgmehr, and Der-Martirosian 1988). These figures are comparable to the proportion of foreign-born found in the New York sample (38.8 percent).

In metropolitan New York and New Jersey where the survey was conducted, the Armenian-American community is relatively large.

TABLE 1.1
Distribution of Armenian Churches by Geographical Location

	Diocese	Prelacy	Protestant	Catholic	Subtotal	Total
California						38
Los Angeles	6	5	10	1	22	
Fresno	3	1	4	-	8	
San Francisco	2	1	3	-	6	
Sacramento	1	-	-	-	1	
San Diego	1	-	-	-	1	
Mid Atlantic						57
Metro NY & NJ	10	3	3	2	18	
NY State	4	3	-	-	7	
Watertown	2	1	2	1	6	
Worcester	1	1	1	-	3	
Massachusetts	4	3	-	-	7	
Providence	1	1	1	-	3	
New Hampshire	-	-	1	-	1	
Connecticut	3	1	-	-	4	
Philadelphia	2	1	1	1	5	
Washington, DC	1	1	-	-	2	
Richmond	1	-	-	-	1	
Midwest						16
Detroit	1	1	1	1	4	
Chicago	4		3	1	8	
Wisconsin	3	1	-	-	4	
South						4
Florida	2	1	-	-	3	
Houston	1	-	-	-	1	
	53	28	28	6		115

Unfortunately, the exact number of people claiming Armenian descent who live in this area is not known. Avakian (1977b) has estimated that 175,000 Armenians live in the Middle Atlantic States (NYC, Northern and Eastern NY State, NJ, Eastern Pennsylvania, metropolitan Washington, DC, and Richmond, VA). More specifically, he has estimated 35,000 people for the state of New Jersey and 132,000 for the state of New York. If I were to calculate my own estimates from the number of addresses on the mailing lists I was able to generate, the total number of households in the study area would number approximately 13,000. This figure translates roughly to 65,000 people (averaging five persons to a household), an estimate far below the figure provided by Avakian some ten years earlier. Probably, the universe of Armenian-Americans who are highly active in communal life and those in the periphery who identify as Armenian-American but attend communal events only sporadically, if at all, is nearer to 100,000 persons in the survey area.

Armenians have lived in New York and New Jersey since the beginning of their immigration to the United States in the last decades of the nineteenth century. Unlike other ethnic groups, Armenians were too few in number to take over entire city blocks to recreate a "little Armenia" in the New World. Nonetheless, there were some areas where their residential concentration warranted the building of a church and eventually a community hall for social activities. In Manhattan, on East Twenty-seventh Street[17] an Apostolic church was organized in 1903. Nearby on East Thirty-fourth Street, Protestant Armenians purchased a building in 1921, though prayer meetings had been held in the vicinity as early as 1881. In 1925, when the Armenian population increased in the Washington Heights area on One Hundred and Eightieth Street, the Holy Cross Church of Armenia was established (Mirak 1983, 125, 147-48, 198; Megerdichian 1983). In New Jersey, there were large groups of Armenians in Union City and Paterson (Kulhanjian 1986-87).

As the second-generation moved to the suburbs in the 1950s and 1960s, new churches, each with its own community center were established in Queens, Westchester, and New Jersey. At present, Armenian-Americans are residentially spread throughout the metropolitan area. Many of the more affluent families live in Bergen County (NJ), Westchester, and Long Island, while Sunnyside (borough of Queens) has a concentration of less-prosperous, relatively recent immigrants.

Armenian immigration to the United States is a continuing process.[18] As long as the U.S. government welcomes new immigrants, there will be some Armenians among the hordes of newcomers who will seek refuge on its soil.[19] Even when gatekeepers deny official access, men and women who want to emigrate, like those in the decades before them, will try to circumvent the law. In the past, many Armenians entered the United States on student or tourist visas, then decided to stay; a few may have even jumped ship or entered illegally. As Nathan Glazer has accurately remarked, "the United States, it seems, remains the permanently unfinished country" (1985, 3). So too it seems, Armenianness in the United States continues to be shaped and reshaped with the influx of new immigrants.

Local Reception to Armenian Immigration

What kind of a reception did Armenian immigrants face in the United States of America? Borrowing Talai's characterization of London Armenians, in general, Armenian presence in American towns and cities has been described by "relative anonymity"; that is, they "encountered blankness or at the very least decided vagueness as to their origins or ethnic identity" (Talai 1984, 203). Their small numbers and dispersion throughout the United States, with one notable exception, prevented outright discrimination or prejudice against Armenians.[20] Yet, they have not been spared stereotypes.[21] Because it would have been too much of a distortion if they were called lazy, stupid, or irresponsible, Armenians together with Jews, Greeks, Syrians, and American-Japanese are in a category that brands them as "too ambitious and with a crafty kind of self-interested intelligence" (Simpson and Yinger 1985, 101). The archetypical Armenian rug merchant is portrayed as a cunning trader, a wheeler-dealer, a person with haggling in his blood.[22] The rug merchant stereotype[23] may linger on but Armenian-Americans have come a long way and have achieved too many significant socioeconomic gains to allow such disparaging images to bother them or hinder their further progress into the American mainstream.

Fresno, California, from the turn of the century until World War II was the exception to the generally indifferent reception Armenian immigrants encountered in America. Mirak (1983, 144-47), in his historical survey of early Armenian settlements in the United States, found overt discrimination only in Fresno. In 1909, the state of California attempted to prohibit Armenians from purchasing land because of their alien, "Asiatic" status, until the U.S. Circuit Court of Appeals in the case of *re-Halladjian* ruled that they were indeed "Caucasian" upon the expert testimony of anthropologist Franz Boas (Ordjanian 1991, 60-61).

Still, Armenians in Fresno were prevented from owning property in the "better neighborhoods"; they were excluded from social clubs and professional associations, even from local Protestant churches; they were ill-treated by clerks, salesmen, and other townspeople in their daily transactions. Armenians were called "Turks," a label they resented bitterly, and other equally demeaning slurs. Schoolchildren were open to abuse from teachers and classmates alike, which often ended up in fights. Sociologist LaPiere (1930, 390-415; 1936), who studied the Fresno Armenians in the 1920s, discovered that they were stereotyped as dishonest, lying, deceitful, parasitic, relying heavily on community welfare, responsible for most crimes in the county, and of inferior morality; all claims that LaPiere was unable to validate. The more educated among the first generation, and the second generation were most conscious of the prejudice that existed in Fresno against Armenians.

Mirak (1983, 146) postulates that the hostility against Armenian immigrants in Fresno was caused by a combination of economic and social factors. A critical mass of Armenians settling and buying land in one county induced the fears of the natives; besides, these new immigrants appeared to be stubborn, proud, and independent in spirit, contrary to the servile attitudes the Fresnans expected from aliens. Furthermore, like many other immigrants, the Armenians dressed differently, had a darker complexion, and talked in a foreign language. Fortunately, Armenians avoided direct confrontation with the natives, a trait they had mastered under Ottoman rule, thus preventing the bloodshed that was the fate of other ethnic groups elsewhere in America. Moreover, because the Armenians were relatively anonymous in the rest of California, native Fresnans were unable to mobilize opposition against Armenians in their state to pass discriminatory legislation similar to the exclusionary laws against the Chinese. Rapid Americanization soon reduced the most visible distinctions between the Armenian immigrants and the host society.

Mirak observes that throughout the United States, "children of the pre-World War I years grew up amidst a virulent nationalist atmosphere characterized by 100 percent Americanism, which held in contempt most foreign habits and foreign-born peoples" (1983, 161). Second-generation Armenian-Americans, like most of the offspring of the immigrants arriving at the turn of the century, grew up in discriminating schools and with prejudiced teachers who called them names such as "immigrant" and "foreigner." Even later, children of ethnic descent were not spared discriminatory treatment. In the 1970s, after the civil rights movement, ethnicity become popular, something one could be proud of, though by that time, Armenian-Americans, like many other white ethnic groups had shed most of the visible peculiarities of their heritage and their ethnicity had become symbolic. Discrimination however, has not been wiped out.

The heavy concentration of Armenian immigrants in metropolitan Los Angeles in recent decades and their attempts to get organized has no doubt increased their visibility and alerted other ethnic groups competing for scarce resources in the public arena that they are a group to be reckoned with. Sociologists contend that such forces of boundary formation in the urban opportunity structure give rise to misunderstandings and stereotypes. Little is known of what non-Armenians think of Los Angeles Armenians; however, within the Armenian-American community, Soviet Armenian immigrants have become the butt of jokes and stereotypes. A well-circulated rumor suggests that supermarkets in Hollywood post signs saying; "No Dogs, No Armenians," presumably because Soviet Armenians are skilled shoplifters. These newcomers are also accused of cheating the welfare system,[24] of engaging in gang-related crime, for crowding the county jail, and for giving Armenians a negative press.[25] I should add that many individuals in leadership positions in the Armenian community in the United States have opposed Soviet Armenian emigration, interpreting the new immigrants' desire for a better life as a desertion, a betrayal of the nation.[26]

In a report to the County of Los Angeles Commission on Human Relations, Bobbi Kimble concurs with the above that, psychologically, many Soviet Armenian immigrants to Los Angeles "are unprepared for their experience in America."[27] They have problems in understanding the concept of private property, their expectations of the standard of living in the United States are highly exaggerated; furthermore, they assume that all Armenian-Americans are extremely affluent, possessing a wealth that they expect to share. They are disappointed when they realize that the privately owned, high per capita income of Armenian-Americans does not translate into a higher income for themselves. Soviet Armenian emigres are angry and frustrated at the amount of paperwork and long waiting lists they have to endure in order to be eligible for services. There are growing backlogs of applicants for English-language classes, for affordable housing, to health care, etc. In general, the immigrants behave in ways that are consistent with the norms of the USSR; for instance, they believe that public employees (including policemen who stop them for speeding on the freeway) expect to be bribed. Obviously, they end up in deeper trouble! On the other hand, service providers complain that Soviet Armenian clients are "demanding" and "pushy."

Soviet Armenians are, of course, not the only Armenians allegedly engaged in fraudulent or criminal activities. For example, a small number of "well-established" jewelers in downtown Los Angeles, immigrants from Syria and Lebanon, were charged by the FBI for money laundering for Latin American drug dealers in 1989.[28] The Soviet Armenian tendency for "playing the system," as one informant put it, appears to be a habit acquired in the Soviet Union; a useful skill that ensured their basic survival in that society. Moreover, crime and delinquency are by-products of the low socioeconomic status of many immigrant groups in the early stages of their settlement in the United States. For example, the Irish, the Greeks, the Jews, and Italians also had their deviant thugs and gangs in ethnic ghettos in the early part of the twentieth century. Eventually, with increasing assimilation and social mobility, Soviet Armenians, like others before them, will leave behind deviant goals and careers for more legitimate life-styles.

Distinguishing Features of Two Waves of Immigration

Armenian immigration to the United States can be roughly divided into two periods because of the demographic features of the population, the cultural baggage they brought with them, and the economic and political conditions in the host country. The first wave would consist of those who came before the quota law of 1924 and those who entered on Nansen passports or other methods until the end of World War II. The second wave would be those who entered the United States after World War II, starting roughly in the early 1950s and accelerating after 1965.

The following characteristics distinguish the two waves of Armenian immigration to the Unites States: First, most of this first wave of Armenian immigrants to the United States were from Asia Minor; directly or indirectly, they were survivors of the Genocide and deportations. They had been uprooted, orphaned, widowed, left with no kin; they were generally an oppressed, traumatized people. In contrast, the post-World War II Armenian immigrants to the United States were more likely to be members of younger cohorts; to many of them, the Genocide was not a personal experience.

Second, the earlier immigrants had firsthand experience of living on ancestral soil with deep roots to the land. In contrast, with the exception of Soviet Armenians, most postwar Armenian immigrants came from the diaspora. At the close of World War I, after being forced out of their ancestral lands, Armenians established new communities in Syria, Lebanon, Iraq, Egypt, Cyprus, Greece, Romania, Bulgaria, France, Argentina, Venezuela, and so on. This changed dramatically the provenance and social characteristics of Armenian immigrants to the United States after the 1950s.

Third, when the early twentieth century Armenian immigrants arrived in the United States, they were more likely to be shocked and overwhelmed by the complexity of modern technology and social relations they encountered. Industrialization had not penetrated as many aspects of life in Ottoman Turkey as it had in the United States. Again, in sharp contrast, an urban experience and a cosmopolitan outlook tend to be the norm for the post-World War II immigrants. Fourth, Armenians who entered the United States at the beginning of the twentieth century were only a fraction of one of the largest immigration movements in human history. They found a host society that was not welcoming of foreigners. The xenophobic mood that had created the "100 percent American Movement" was virulently hostile to ethnic cultures and life-styles. Attempts were made to "Americanize" the hordes of newcomers as quickly as possible because they were believed to be ignorant, uncouth, dirty, immoral, genetically inferior. On the other hand, the social climate in the United States, especially in the 1970s and 1980s was somewhat more tolerant of ethnic differences.

Fifth, in the second wave, Armenian immigrants were more likely to have high school, even college, education, occupational skills adaptable to an industrial economy, and some financial resources. In addition, they were more likely to be proficient in English. As mentioned above, the newcomers had an easier process of adaptation and integration into American society, a point that has become the cause of much animosity and conflict between the two groups. Sixth, the two Armenian immigration waves to the United States also differed in their psychological makeup and worldview. Those who came in the earlier wave were made to feel inferior to their hosts, the WASP elite, the "Old Americans" (Warner and Srole 1945). They had few resources at the time to bridge the social distance imposed upon them. Until the resurgence of ethnicity in the 1970s, calling someone an "ethnic" had a pejorative connotation. In comparison, the post-World War II immigrants were more likely to be self-confidant about their ethnic identity and place in the world, particularly those born in the Middle East who had developed a sense of Armenian superiority over their Arab neighbors.

Having been rejected by the local population as a burden, Armenian refugees survived initially on help by Western relief organizations and eventually developed a strong institutional system. Self-reliance for their material and emotional needs became their trademark. Moreover, Middle Eastern societies were just beginning to industrialize and modernize when the Armenians settled there in the early twentieth century in large numbers. Competing with relatively less modernized sectarian and ethnic groups who shared their environment, a sizable proportion of the Armenian population appropriated lucrative niches in many domains and achieved social mobility in a very short while. Consequently, their reputation as "smart" people[29] and their nouveaux riches status boosted their self-assurance, even arrogance, and translated into a generalized sense of well-being, a sense of Armenian prestige and power. Whether this was an empirically valid self-concept is beside the point. Though the post-1950s realities in the United States were different from the Middle East for many an immigrant, such feelings nurtured in childhood remain hard to crush.

Finally, the first wave did not have the advantage of a well-established Armenian-American community like the second wave did. This communal structure cushioned the shock of immigration and helped the integration process. In the 1970s, several Armenian-American organizations founded centers to provide social services to newcomers.[30] Established mostly with state and federal funds, these centers offered a wide range of services such as locating housing, finding jobs, placing students in schools, as well as providing referrals to technical training and certification centers, legal counseling, especially immigration matters, psychological and personal counseling, translation services, and classes in English and office skills. One such program in Los Angeles, the Armenian Relief Society, employs twenty-six staff members in four offices and operates on a budget of $900,000 a year.[31] Another program is the Armenian Evangelical Social Service Center of Hollywood. Established in 1977, it claims to have serviced 12,000 people in 1989-90 alone and is "one of the most successful of its kind in America."[32]

It should be noted that the vast majority (90-95 percent) of men and women of Armenian descent in the United States trace their roots to Western Armenia, that is present-day Turkey, rather than Eastern Armenia.[33] This background accounts for the cultural legacy Armenian-Americans inherited from their ancestors. Three significant characteristics distinguished the two groups at the turn of the twentieth century.[34] First, the Eastern Armenians had no experience of the *millet* (community) system nor of living among Muslims, while the Western Armenians were unfamiliar with Russian governments and people. Second, Western Armenians were direct targets of the Genocide and deportations. Third, the class structure and occupational traditions of Eastern and Western Armenians were different.

Eastern Armenians were more likely to be urbanized, educated, and a sizable proportion had traditionally been employed in the administrative and intellectual arenas of the Russian Empire.

Furthermore, a small number had been able to achieve significant mobility as industrial entrepreneurs, such as those in the oil business in Baku. In Western Armenia, on the other hand, the elite, consisting of the *amiras* (the aristocracy), the intelligentsia, and the professional and bourgeois classes resided in Constantinople. The rest of the population remained physically and socially alienated on the Anatolian Plateau. They were composed of a petty bourgeois minority (merchants, shopkeepers and artisans) who lived in the towns and cities; and a peasant majority (small land-holding subsistence farmers) who were scattered in the rural heartland. It was these common people who were uprooted and nearly annihilated. Given this information, one can explain the Armenian-American proclivity to self-employment; the inordinate imprint of the Genocide on the lives of the survivors and their offspring; their hatred of the Turks; the predominance of Western Armenian dialect; the popularity of "oriental" music using Near Eastern drums and fiddle (*davoul, zurna*); the frequency in which shish kebab, *beurek* (cheese puffs) and *dolma* (stuffed vegetables) is consumed, and so on.

Armenian-Americans are a very heterogeneous group. There are those who immigrated at the turn of the century, the "old-timers" who have lived in the United States most of their lives, by now in their late seventies and eighties. Then there are the post-1950s immigrants, a category spanning some forty years of immigration that is composed of a diverse group of people differing on their length of residence in the United States, characteristics they acquired in their country of birth, etc. And then of course, there are the American-born: the children, grandchildren, and great-grandchildren of the immigrants. All these collectivities are further divided by religious affiliation, ethnic background of parents, age, gender, and socioeconomic status. Nonetheless, the central thesis of this book is that generational presence in the United States of America is the most important variable in explaining an individual's expression of Armenianness.

At the collective level, the dynamics of Armenianness in various localities are shaped by the following variables: the proportions of foreign-born to U.S.-born, the country of birth and the length of residence in the United States of the foreign-born, and the socioeconomic composition of the group. As illustrated above, the Armenian-American community of Los Angeles is quite different from, let us say, the Boston community. Yet, there is an overarching pattern; these manifestations of Armenianness are not totally random.

A caveat is in order here. As historian Thomas Sowell has written: "No ethnic group has been wholly unique, and yet no two are completely alike" (1981, 4). The assimilative profile of Armenian-Americans is somewhat different from any other ethnic group's because of their particular socioeconomic characteristics, their cultural patrimony, their time of first settlement, the subsequent influx of newcomers, their size and dispersion, and the structural conditions of twentieth-century United States. However, these assimilative pathways are not unique. They are similar to those experienced by many white ethnic groups of the "new" immigration, that is those who arrived between 1890 and 1920, such as the Jews, Greeks, and Italians. Indeed, this study may primarily interest Armenian-Americans; however, it is of relevance to a wider audience because it documents an important process in American social life and history and contributes to the sociological literature on race and ethnic relations.

Overall, Armenian-Americans have made significant inroads into mainstream American society, in politics, industry, finance, medicine, the arts, and every other aspect of public and private life (see Armenian Assembly of America 1987). Many have gained fame and fortune, in little or big ways, while acknowledging their Armenian roots and feeling very proud of their ancestry. Armenian churches and communal structures have also multiplied and spread throughout the United States more than ever before. It is time for this small but vibrant ethnic group to come out of the intellectual closet. Armenian-Americans should no longer be considered a "hidden minority" in sociological discourse. In a way, this book celebrates their coming of age in America.[35]

Plan of this Book

In the chapters that follow, I will examine major components of Armenian-American culture and social relations. In chapter 2, I describe the religious and political culture of the early generations and how it has shaped and pitted Armenian-Americans into two rival camps characterized by bitter animosity and at times even bloodshed. I will begin with a description of the historical antecedents of the dispute, then look at the role of the Armenian church in maintaining communal life and identity. I will subsequently examine the traditional Armenian political parties and the challenging institutions that have emerged. Inevitably, this chapter also discusses the new realities in diaspora relations, especially the rapid changes that are taking place in the new Republic of Armenia.

In chapter 3, I describe the Armenian-American community and the subgroups that constitute this community. The typical features of collective life, the voluntary associations, the activities they sponsor, and their popularity with different generations are then examined. Instrumental motives for personal gain or profit are also discussed, though they only affect a small fraction of the population. In chapter 4, I look at the debate on language. Foreign-born Armenians, especially those from the Middle East, and the American-born dispute the need to establish and finance institutions that serve to perpetuate the Armenian language. These differences stem from the varying definitions of Armenianness that they possess. The debate is central at this juncture in Armenian-American history and has been magnified by the influx of large numbers of immigrants in recent decades.

After an analysis of the processes that transform immigrants into hyphenated Americans, chapter 5 explores sources of Armenian identity. The Genocide remains a core element in defining Armenian-Americans, but it is in the family that Armenian identity is ultimately nourished and sustained. Other factors are Armenian cuisine, travel to historic Armenia, and celebrities and media representations of Armenia and Armenians. In the last chapter, I examine variables that influence rates of Armenian intermarriage. Intermarriage is often blamed as the "cause" of assimilation. However, throughout this study the data demonstrates that the passing of generations is more significant in changing Armenianness. This final chapter also provides an ideal typical representation of symbolic Armenianness in the United States. It describes the most common personal expressions of such an identity and the institutional structures that are most congruent with symbolic Armenianness. But first, in the remainder of this chapter, I explain assimilation and ethnic identity in American society and define concepts used in this study. Last but not least, I describe the sources of the empirical data used here and provide a profile of Armenian-Americans from the study sample.

Assimilation and Ethnic Identity in America

The question of "who shall be allowed to become an American" (Glazer 1985, 3) has dominated the public agenda of the United States for about two centuries and continues to do so today. Armenians who immigrated to America at various points in the twentieth century faced policies that were a mixture of assimilation and cultural pluralism. As Simpson and Yinger have observed, the policies of the United States of America vis-à-vis its immigrants and the ideological atmosphere of the nation have been contradictory during the course of its history.

> [The United States is] basically assimilationist, not only permitting, but demanding conformity to a rather narrow range of options.... On the other hand, religious pluralism is now nearly fully the fact as well as the ideal; the country has followed a "hands-off" policy toward the private associations and foreign-language newspapers of many immigrant groups; there is some support for language diversity.... Blacks, Chicanos, Indians, Asians and others assert their separate identities with some approval and even support from the majority; and pluralism is widely accepted as a value. If America has never been so evenhanded in her treatment of different groups as her ideology would imply, neither has she been so utterly indifferent to the range of cultures and peoples as her most severe critics have declared. (Simpson and Yinger 1985, 18)

The ideological origins of American identity or national character were influenced by the English tradition of separation of church from state and the value of liberty, as well as the thinkers of the Enlightenment with their emphasis on universalistic principles (Gleason 1980, 31-32). The early settlers thought of themselves as "new men" produced from many different peoples, and throughout the nineteenth century, the open-door immigration policies were justified by the belief that newcomers could adjust and be absorbed into the American nation (Handlin 1959, 146). The significant characteristics of American identity were its openness to anyone who wanted to become an American, its newness, which unlike the European example was not only a model for tomorrow but would be realizable in the future (Gleason 1980, 32-33; see also Erikson 1963; 1974, 75-77). These abstract, ideological underpinnings of American national identity explain only partly the initial ambiguity toward the issue of immigration. Most significantly, the predominant Anglo-Saxon origins of the founding families and the relatively small numbers of immigrants who came to the United States before the 1830s[36] had much to do with the magnanimous attitude of the early Americans.

Following the potato famine, unprecedented numbers of Irish (and German) immigrants arrived in America. Their large numbers, their immigrant status, their poverty, and most of all their Catholicism triggered one of the earliest conflicts between the newcomers and the so-called Native Americans (Ravitch 1988, 56). By midcentury, the battles were being fought over the public schools, which were intended by the "native" Protestant majority to Americanize the Catholic foreigners with their potentially disintegrative influence. These confrontations were eventually settled with an accommodation: the Catholics could become Americanized (in common schools) without giving up their religion (Gleason 1980, 36; Ravitch 1988, 27-76).

The debates over the ethnic component of the American character started after the Civil War, but were most poignant with the advent of the "new immigrants" from about the 1890s to the passage of the restrictionist laws in 1924. Anglo-conformity, the melting pot, and cultural pluralism were the three perspectives that in response to specific historical circumstances offered models of assimilation in America. Rather than being realistic descriptions of behavior and explanatory hypotheses, these were ideologies about the desired outcome of the massive immigration movements. They were broad interpretations of the unity and multiplicity of the American national identity, each stressing one tendency over the other (Gleason 1980, 46; see also Gordon 1964; Handlin 1959, 146-66).

Anglo-Conformity

The basic assumption of the Anglo-conformity model was the superiority and desirability of the English language, institutions, and culture. It called for the total renunciation of the immigrants' imported language, value system, and traditions in exchange for active conformity to the influential Anglo-Saxon core group's culture. Its origins stemmed from the early English settlers who dominated the fledgling American nation (Gleason 1980, 41). In its mildest form, it remained their implicit assumption regarding immigration throughout American history (Gordon 1964, 80). However, this social doctrine became strongest and most popular at the turn of the twentieth century. It was a defense against the "new" immigration tides whose increasing numbers, foreign ways and developing political power were making the established elite "feel like aliens in their own homeland" (Gleason 1980, 42).

There was a widespread belief, imbued with elements of social Darwinism, that these new immigrants had "inferior genetic traits [that] would dilute the strong, industrious, pioneering spirit of the older racial strains and that this infusion posed a threat to the future of the nation.... Not only were the new immigrants charged with being ignorant, poor, dirty, immoral, and overly fecund, but their eagerness to work at any wage caused American workingmen to accuse them of stealing jobs, undercutting unionization, and depressing the American standard of living" (Ravitch 1988, 174). Therefore, there was a feverish urgency to Americanize the uncouth hordes by every means available. The society elite, like the Daughters of the American Revolution, and the Boston-based North American Civic League for Immigrants, volunteered their time, organizational skills, finances, and underlying value system to a multitude of social programs.

The settlement houses and adult education classes provided instruction in English, American history, and government, hygiene, domestic science, etc. Upper-class women were particularly active during this period in organizing classes, and lectures, publishing books and pamphlets,[37] supplying health care and child care services and so on (see Rothman 1978, 101-126). Most of all, the general opinion was that the public school system ought to take charge of the children of the immigrants, instead of their incompetent families and disintegrated communities (Ravitch 1988, 171), and turn them into stalwart American citizens, indoctrinated with patriotism, love of freedom, and democratic principles. The pressures to Americanize intensified during World War I when the political loyalty of the large German-American community and other hyphenated Americans was in question. The "100 percent American Movement" created a national hysteria that was instrumental in enacting the racist law of 1924. Overall, the push to Americanize was successful.

One cannot deny that immigrant groups made substantial contributions to American society by supplying the labor that furthered its development, as one cannot ignore the ethnic provenance of many American cultural elements such as pizza, frankfurters, chow mein, St Patrick's Day parades, blues, and jazz. Yet immigrant groups had little influence on the core or mainstream cultural patterns themselves, which remained predominantly Anglo-Saxon (Gordon 1978, 171; Steinberg 1981). As the case of Armenian-Americans will illustrate, Anglo-Conformity "substantially triumphed in the behavioral area ... acculturation without massive structural intermingling at primary group levels has been the dominant motif in the American experience of creating and developing a nation out of diverse peoples" (Gordon 1964, 114).

The Melting Pot

The "melting pot," an expression borrowed from Israel Zangwill's play, labeled an implicit ideology that existed long before the phrase was coined in 1908.[38] The open-door immigration policy was a reflection of America's belief in its ability to mold a national character from a large collection of nationalities, religions, races, and cultures (Handlin 1959, 146). It "assumed that the conditions of American life, particularly egalitarianism and the opportunity for material improvement, would automatically transform foreigners into Americans—with some help from the common schools" (Gleason 1980, 38). Unlike the earlier model, the melting pot ideology gave credit to the immigrants' heritage and assumed that each would contribute in a small way to the emergent American character, which was to remain basically Anglo-Saxon.

The single melting pot ideal was later refined to the "triple melting pot" hypothesis—incorporating Protestant, Catholic, Jew—because it was found that there was little assimilation across religious lines (Kennedy 1944, 1952; Herberg 1960). Will Herberg observed that there was a paradox in contemporary America of "pervasive secularism amid mounting religiosity" (1960, 2). The most Americanized descendants of the immigrant generation were increasing their church attendance and their identification with religious denominations (see Lenski 1963). Herberg argued that religious institutions had survived Americanization most successfully, and traditional forms of worship had changed to adapt to the new environment. Religious affiliation offered the ideal link to one's immigrant ancestors, yet remained an acceptable way to manifest one's commitment to the spiritual ideals of American ideology of freedom and democracy (see Gleason 1980, 50-51).

Borrowing Marcus Lee Hansen's (1938) "third-generation return hypothesis," Herberg explained that the immigrant generation had established churches and synagogues as the center of their communal life and the repository of their sacred symbols. Their children's generation had revolted against their immigrant parents and cast off all their ties to the past, including their religious affiliation. The grandson had no reason to feel inferior, but his problem was the need to belong. What kind of an American was he? Herberg's answer was that the third generation's affiliation to one of the three major religious communities satisfied that urge to belong, because nationality backgrounds had already been eroded by assimilation.

Cultural Pluralism

Unlike the first two models of assimilation, which assumed the disappearance of the immigrant's original culture and communal life, the cultural pluralism model advocated the preservation of the immigrant's heritage as a democratic principle. Its chief advocate was Horace Kallen, a German Jew who grew up in America and became a professor of philosophy and psychology. He believed that each immigrant culture had something unique to contribute to the larger society. Cultural pluralism was a counterattack against the excessive assaults of the Americanization movement on the human dignity and self-worth of the bewildered immigrants. It advocated a nonlinear perspective of assimilation whereby each ethnic group preserved its communal life and its culture but was integrated legally, economically, and politically into the American society. Thus, America was seen as a "mosaic," a "federation of nationalities," not a melting pot (Handlin 1959; Sowell 1981).

Kallen was not a pragmatist but a romantic and an idealist. The cultural pluralism model was the liberal, tolerant antidote for forced assimilation. Kallen never refined his concepts or formulated in detail how cultural pluralism would work. As a model it remained an underdeveloped vision that would be borrowed and reinterpreted during the ethnic "revival" period. With the participation of the United States in World War II, ethnicity faded once again as a dimension in American identity because the unity of the nation was at stake.

Park's Race-Relations Cycle

A pioneering attempt at constructing a theory of assimilation was Robert Park's four-stage race-relations cycle (see Coser 1977, 357-84). Park hypothesized that there were four progressive and irreversible processes: contact, competition, accommodation and assimilation. As a result of immigration, groups come into contact, and this results in competition between them, which is accompanied by conflict. Eventually there is some degree of accommodation between them, and finally assimilation results (Park and Burgess 1969). Park defined *assimilation* as "a process of interpenetration and fusion in which persons and groups acquire the memories, sentiments, and attitudes of other persons and groups, and, by sharing their experience and history, are incorporated with them in a common cultural life" (Park and Burgess 1969, 735). He argued that the most rapid assimilation would take place in intimate, intense relationships such as the ones with family members and friends; that is, through primary group ties. Secondary associations, such as the ones at the workplace, were more likely to facilitate accommodation. Yet for Park, assimilation does not totally eradicate individual differences nor stop competition and conflict (Park and Burgess 1969, 737).

Park's race-relations cycle was criticized because it was not readily applicable to many groups; the cycle was rarely complete; and its irreversibility was not substantiated. Overall, the traditional models of assimilation outlined above were vague and often overlapped. Precise formulations could not be derived from them to test their empirical validity. They did not take into account group distinctions, cohort effects, and historical circumstances.

W. Lloyd Warner and Associates

In recent reviews, W. Lloyd Warner's contribution to assimilation theory has not received the recognition it merits. Even though his value judgments on the hierarchical positioning of immigrant cultures and his deterministic approach regarding the certainty of assimilation are no longer acceptable, many of the underlying assumptions on assimilation held today are derived from his empirical observations. In

The Social Systems of American Ethnic Groups, part of the Yankee City series, Warner and Srole found that in spite of the variations in the cultural heritage of the eight ethnic groups they examined (which included the Armenians) and the differences in their emergent communities, there were nonetheless remarkable similarities among them. They postulated that an immigrant group's adjustment to American life is dependent on individual and group processes of social mobility. In other words, "each group enters the city at the bottom of the social heap (lower lower class) and through the several generations makes its desperate climb upward. The early arrivals, having had more time, have climbed farther up the ladder than the ethnic groups that followed them" (Warner and Srole 1945, 2). Thus, as groups assimilate, ethnic characteristics for determining status are substituted for social class criteria.

Warner and Srole argued that assimilation and social mobility are the products of the power of the host society to dictate its wishes on immigrant groups (by either subjugating them or by facilitating their absorption) and that of the immigrant group to resist such pressures. The degree of subordination of an immigrant group is calculated by the following criteria: "(1) freedom of residential choice, (2) freedom to marry out of one's own group, (3) amount of occupational restriction, (4) strength of attitudes in the host society which prevent social participation in such institutions as associations and cliques, and (5) the amount of vertical mobility permitted in the host society for members of the ethnic or racial group" (Warner and Srole 1945, 289). On the other hand, the strength of the immigrant group depends on the influence of its religious institution over its members; the competence of ethnic schools in socializing new ethnics; the effectiveness of its voluntary associations; and the political and economic coherence of the group.

It is hypothesized that the greater the cultural and racial differences of an immigrant group from white "old American" Protestant stock, the greater the social distance imposed between them, and the longer it will take to bridge that distance. Assimilation is measured in terms of proportions of individuals exiting the ethnic collectivity, the probability of the entire group being absorbed into the mainstream, and the openness of the host society to accept these changes. Thus,

Warner and Srole would predict that Protestant Armenians are more likely to be assimilated at a faster pace than Apostolic Armenians, a hypothesis that is validated by the results of the New York survey.

Gordon's Theory of Assimilation

Milton Gordon's theory of assimilation is one of the most comprehensive treatments of the subject. Gordon (1964) constructed a typology of seven subprocesses of assimilation, an ideal type construct in which assimilation in general and each type in particular can occur at varying degrees. Gordon postulated that cultural differences between immigrant groups would disappear gradually under the influence of public education and the mass media. The ossification of the immigrant's cultural heritage is called *cultural assimilation* or *acculturation*.

Culture is understood to be a people's material and nonmaterial way of life. It is language, art, architecture, literature, music, religious traditions, political institutions, as well as aesthetic preferences, recreational patterns, cuisine, dietary styles, and so on. It is also a group's norms, values, and belief systems. Gordon argued that acculturation to the values and life-style of the host society is more readily accepted than structural assimilation. He postulated that cultural assimilation is likely to take place first, and for some groups may stop there, either because the host society is unwilling to accept them as peers or because the group espouses a very strong ideology that discourages social relationships with out-groups.[39]

Structural assimilation is defined as the incorporation of an ethnic group on a large scale into the host society's institutional organizations on a primary group level; that is, through intimate face-to-face relationships.[40] The opposite of structural assimilation occurs when members of an ethnic group confine their intimate, diffuse relationships, or their leisure-time contacts to their own ethnic group. Mingling extensively with the host society on an open, personal basis leads to friendships with nonethnics and eventually to Gordon's third type of assimilation: *marital assimilation* or *amalgamation*.

The fourth subprocess of assimilation is *identificational assimilation*. Particularistic allegiances to the ethnic group are superseded by a shared feeling of peoplehood with the core or host society. Instead of ethnic or hyphenated identifications, people come to see themselves as "Americans." The fifth and sixth types measure the absence of prejudice and discrimination. The last type, *civic assimilation,* implies the absence of major value and power conflicts between the ethnic group and the host culture. These conflicts may be over political issues or civic ones such as abortion, school busing for minority children, capital punishment, and the like.

Gordon developed two other concepts that help explain behavioral outcomes. *Ethclass* is "the intersection of the vertical stratifications of ethnicity with the horizontal stratifications of social class" (1964, 51). People's social participation is generally confined to one's ethclass, that is, one's social class segment within one's ethnic group. Next, Gordon distinguished between historical identification and participational identification. *Historical identification* is a sense of peoplehood, or "interdependence of fate" provided by the ethnic group. *Participational identification,* on the other hand, is a feeling that one is most congenial with one's subsociety or ethclass.[41]

People tend to behave according to the subsociety they find themselves in. Acculturation is easier to accomplish than changing one's subsociety or reference group. Nonetheless, structural assimilation is crucial in the overall process, because according to Gordon, once it takes place, other types of assimilation are likely to follow.[42] The underlying assumption rests on the notion that intimate relationships are likely to reduce prejudice and hostility between groups while the opposite process of structural separation or compartmentalization is likely to promote ethnic stereotypes, negative attitudes, and overall conflict. What is a positive outcome for the whole society may not be so for the ethnic groups. As Gordon (1964, 81) notes, "the price of assimilation, however, is the disappearance of the ethnic group as a separate entity and the evaporation of its distinctive values." Following Warner's lead, it is assumed that the ethnic group will gradually lose its holding power over the individual. Ethnicity will be replaced by social class as a determinant of values, attitudes, and life-styles (Alba 1976, 1978, 1981; Crispino 1980; Gans 1979; Gordon 1964; Steinberg 1981).

Gordon's theory of assimilation has been criticized as static and biased in its implication that immigrant groups are "passive" and have a strong desire to assimilate (see Henry 1973, 6). It has also overlooked the distinction between immigrants who settle permanently in the host society and those who come as sojourners (see Portes and Bach 1985). The most constructive criticism has come from Alba who finds Gordon's approach

> ahistorical, individualistic and incrementalist—which, in other words, does not connect assimilatory processes to macrostructural dynamics, but instead conceives of them as individual decisions played out against a static background. Such a conception naturally places the emphasis on social psychological constructs, including the acceptability of a group's members to the majority or core and, perhaps more importantly, their motivation to merge with the majority. At the same time, it is implicitly one-directional: assimilating individuals are affiliating with a new group, thereby dropping the cultural and other garb of their original one. (1985b, 134-35)

Yet, Alba does not discard the whole theory, nor is he blind to the overwhelming statistical evidence that points to the assimilation of white ethnic groups. He suggests that a distinction must be made between two types of assimilation, individual and group forms. Though analytically these two are separate, empirically it is hard to distinguish between them. In the first one, people cross ethnic boundaries changing their reference groups while the boundaries themselves are not transformed. In the second type, the change occurs to the ethnic boundaries; they become porous and social markers become obsolete (see Alba 1985b, 135-36).

A theory of assimilation that includes structural processes of group formation and dissolution in its framework is believed to be more comprehensive. One such attempt has used the words *assimilation* and *dissimilation*[43] to describe a variable that can range in degrees of more or less "boundary reduction" between two or more societies or cultural groups that come into contact (Yinger 1981). *Assimilation* is used when distance between groups is reduced to a minimum; *dissimilation* when differences between groups are at a maximum. Pluralistic movements, separatist movements are examples of dissimilation. It should be noted that dissimilation may take place alongside assimilation. As the Armenian case demonstrates, "at this period in human history at any rate, it is not a matter of assimilation versus ethnicity, but of assimilation and ethnicity" (Yinger 1981, 261).

The underlying assumption of most of these theories of assimilation has been called the "straight-line" model (Sandberg 1974). This model describes a process along a continuum with complete segregation at one end and complete assimilation at the other; however, unlike the melting pot ideology, it does not make value judgments about the inferiority of immigrant cultures (Gans 1979, 194). The straight-line model assumes that the first generation, that is, foreign-born, is the most "ethnic" or culturally distinct. It is hypothesized that the longer the generational presence of ethnic groups in America, the less will be their adherence to a separate ethnic culture and behavioral forms. In conclusion, with one correction, Gordon's theory of assimilation, with its underlying straight-line assumption, remains the most powerful explanation to date. Assimilation *and* ethnic identity make up the pattern of Armenian-Americans and other white ethnic groups (see also Alba 1990; Waters 1990).

Defining Ethnicity

Ethnicity derives from the Greek *ethniko,* an adjective of *ethnos,* referring to people or nations (Cashmore 1984, 85-90; see also Petersen 1980). The term has gained currency, academically and popularly, in recent years.[44] Early emphasis on the ascriptive components of ethnicity are now perceived to be "static and descriptive" and the tendency is toward more "dynamic and analytic" conceptualizations (Patterson 1975, 305). Fredrik Barth's (1969) definition of ethnic groups in terms of boundary maintenance is widely accepted. Barth focuses on boundaries rather than cultural and social contents of a group. In this view, boundaries, or discrete categories persist, despite "osmosis" or movement of individuals entering and exiting the group. Moreover, cultural features and characteristics of individuals may change, even organizational forms may change, but the distinction between insiders and outsiders, "us" versus "them," remains the essence. It is the boundary that defines the group, determines members from nonmembers, organizes behavior and social relations, recognizes limits and shared worldviews, and reinforces differences.

Boundaries remain meaningful and ethnic groups survive if cultural differences persist between interacting groups. On the other hand, frequent communication with outsiders reduces cultural distinctiveness as each borrows from the other, resulting in congruence of cultural codes and values (Barth 1969, 15-16). Cultural matter may vary, be learned, change, but boundaries, or the criteria for membership, determine the continuity of a group. Elements of today's culture are not necessarily the result of the culture that was in the past. Barth recognizes that ethnic identity is a status that, like sex and rank, exerts role constraints on the individual. Individuals are permitted to choose from a limited number of other groups for their transactions in social situations. Furthermore, in social systems where there are power differences between groups, the culture of the more powerful group is perceived as superior, that is, worth emulating (Barth 1969, 21).

Ethnic boundaries have two sides, "us" and "them." The differences are both subjective and objective, real or perceived cultural markers. Boundaries are either self-imposed or imposed by others. For example, what constitutes Armenian identity in Boston is very different from that in Cairo. American ethnic identity is defined by insiders and is a voluntary, subjective boundary,[45] while that of minority groups in the Middle East is imposed by outsiders, their boundaries are far less permeable. An Armenian, a Jew, a Greek with an Egyptian passport is not an Arab and cannot be one. Similarly, Armenians in Lebanon have dual identities. As Lebanese citizens, Armenians have a set of privileges and responsibilities; for instance, they are allowed to work, vote, travel with Lebanese passports, but they have to pay taxes and are precluded from a number of government positions and political appointments. Births, marriages, divorces, deaths in Lebanon are registered with the religious sect that one's father belongs to. There are no separate personal status laws in Lebanon; marriages between Christians and Muslims cannot be registered unless the bride or the groom converts, homogenizing the religion of the couple. Middle Eastern Armenians have been called "traditional ethnics" (McKay 1982) in contrast to Armenian-Americans who are described here as symbolic ethnics.

Increasingly, scholars have come to recognize ethnicity as a variable that may be an essential resource, irrelevant or a crippling liability, depending on the context. For example, an Armenian-American salesman may choose to activate his or her Armenian identity to establish rapport and make a sale by saying: "I'm Armenian too." On the other hand, a Lebanese-Armenian may choose to "pass" as an Arab if the situation warrants it. "People often have a repertoire of ethnic attributes from which they can select the ones most suitable to a given situation" (see Hicks 1977, 17). However, one should not forget that not all ethnic labels are readily manipulated. Highly assimilated German Jews were as likely as their Orthodox brethren to find themselves in a concentration camp during World War II.

For immigrant groups in America, or their descendants, identity beyond the stage of cultural assimilation is based on double boundaries; from within, through socialization, from without through intergroup relations (Isajiw 1974). Complete assimilation takes place when insiders cease to socialize their young in the ethnic subculture and its identity, and when outsiders do not perceive any salient markers that distinguish them from others. However, once a collective consciousness is established and distinctive characteristics of an ethnic group recognized, the group "takes on a self-perpetuating quality and is passed from one generation to the next" (Cashmore 1984, 87). Inertia may sustain communal structures and institutional forms of ethnicity for a long time; moreover, it does not need large numbers to do so. "Polarization" of ethnic groups into a small but highly active core contrasted with a large, assimilated aggregate of symbolic ethnics is increasingly the pattern the Armenians and other white ethnic groups of the "new" immigration are adopting (see Cohen 1983, 51).

Ethnic Revival Hypothesis

In the 1970s, academic and popular interest in ethnicity increased (see Polenberg 1980). The assimilation of the "new" immigrants, those who had come to the United States at the beginning of the twentieth century, was challenged. This was possible because of the relative absence of empirical evidence (Crispino 1980; See and Wilson 1988; Simpson 1968). The proponents of the ethnic "revival" or "return" proposition charged that the melting pot perspective was a myth; assimilation had not been completed as assumed. Behavioral differences in family life, educational and occupational achievement, political participation, and religiosity between ethnic groups remained significant (e.g., Abramson 1973, 1975; Greeley 1974; Greeley and McCready 1975; Kobrin and Goldscheider 1978; Novak 1973). The literature was inundated with examples of how ethnicity was alive and strong. This "new ethnicity" became fashionable yet controversial in academia, the mass media, and popular culture.

The ethnic revival hypothesis had a number of prominent critics. Myrdal (1974, 19) dismissed the "return" as "upper-class intellectual romanticism." Thernstrom (1982, 19) declared it "the last gasp of groups nearing extinction." Alba (1985a, 159, 170) called it an "illusion" that "existed more in the eyes of its beholders." Others charged the new ethnicity to be a paranoid position in "defense and adaptation to conditions of shame, disillusionment, exposure, and despair" of white working-class Americans who did not fulfill the American dream (Stein and Hill 1973, 96). Indeed, the political and economic grievances of white working class people were seen by many to be the real issue in disguise (see Patterson 1979; Steinberg 1981; Stein and Hill 1977).

The ethnic resurgence hypothesis stems from Marcus Lee Hansen's "law of the third generation return." Hansen, in a speech delivered to the Augustana Historical Society (a Swedish group), in 1937, had predicted that "whenever any immigrant group reaches the third generation stage in its development a spontaneous and almost irresistible impulse arises which forces the thoughts of many people of different professions, different positions in life and different points of view to interest themselves in that one factor which they have in common: heritage—the heritage of blood" (1938, 12). The third generation of the "new" immigrants had matured by the 1960s and 1970s and were vociferously claiming back their ethnic roots and culture, or so it seemed to many observers. They were taking trips to the old country, showing an interest in the culture and arts of the ethnic group, and exhibiting a general nostalgia and compassion for their grandparents' life-style and values. To many, this was indeed the "revival" that Hansen (1938, 9) had foreseen: "what the son wishes to forget the grandson wishes to remember."

Several studies demonstrated that for descendants of immigrant stock beyond the third generation, ethnic membership and traditions fulfill their primal need to belong. Ethnicity offers them self-identity, self-worth, pride, and intimate, trusting relationships in a highly mechanized, impersonal social environment (Greeley 1974; see also Keller 1988). Recent surveys have also found that in spite of widespread mixed ancestry among whites, there is increased tendency among third-generation, college-educated men and women to identify with one single ethnic group. The data corroborate the resurgence thesis, though younger cohorts are consistently more assimilated on cultural indicators (Alba and Chamlin 1983).

The key to understanding the continued ethnic identity alongside assimilation is the distinction Glazer (1954) makes between "ideological" and "cultural" returns. Mere identification does not imply that there is a return to old-style ethnicity of the grandparents' generation. The fact remains that empirical studies have not been able to prove a cultural "revival" for white ethnic groups of the "new" immigration (Alba 1976, 1978, 1985a; Cohen 1983; Crispino 1980; Moskos 1989; Sandberg 1974).

Joshua Fishman (1985) corroborates that the "revival" was more attitudinal than behavioral. The 1960s and 1970s were not unique to a resurgence of ethnicity; they were also characterized by the Vietnam War, the civil rights movement, the feminist movement, the gay rights movement, etc. Fishman stresses not the end of ethnicity, but the broadening of the permissible limits of what it means to be an "American." The "revival" brought "sidestream ethnicity out of the family and neighborhood closet ... and made it salon-worthy" (Fishman 1985, 510; see also Alba 1985a, 172). He goes on to explain:

> Thanks to the revival, sidestream ethnicity has come to play a public role very similar to that of religion in American life.... A sidestream ethnicity is recognized as being not only "natural" but as being humanizing and strengthening in some very general sense, and those who implement or display it situationally are not outsiders in urban America.... It controls no domain of behavior completely but it is "a good influence" and makes for a more interesting, colorful, rooted life. It is family-stability-related, neighborhood-stability-related, personal-stability-related. Americans now expect each other to have some sidestream ethnicity; any sidestream ethnicity will do and all ethnicities are equally good ... because their role is no longer to help or hinder "being a success in America" ... but to provide "roots": meaningful cultural depth to individual and family life. Thus a sidestream ethnicity as part of one's background ... has become part of an enriched and overarching *American* experience.... There is no need to hide it.... What is worse, it would be denying an aspect of American identity. (Fishman 1985, 511, italic in original)

Predicting the doom of ethnicity in the 1960s and 1970s may have been premature; on the other hand, its continued vitality remains somewhat exaggerated (Alba 1976, 1045). There is little evidence of any cultural or behavioral "return" or "revival" to the foreign-born grandparents' life-style. Indeed, as Alba explains:

this ethnic resurgence was more in the eyes of the beholders than it was in the events among the Catholic [and other] ethnics and, moreover, that the increased visibility of ethnicity was paradoxically a product of the same forces sapping ethnicity's vitality. During the 1970s, ethnicity could be celebrated precisely because assimilation had proceeded far enough that ethnicity no longer seemed so threatening and divisive. Ethnicity was made more visible by the penetration of prominence in American life. (1981, 98)

Ethnic groups and communities of the "new" immigration are, to use Alba's fitting analogy, in their "twilight" phase. Yet, "it is a twilight which may never turn into night" (Alba 1981, 97).

Symbolic Ethnicity

Since there is little doubt that the process of cultural assimilation has been almost accomplished for most white ethnic groups, the task at hand is to explain the residuals. Ethnicity in contemporary America does not disappear altogether in later generations, instead, as Herbert Gans (1979) says, it becomes "symbolic." Later-generation ethnics do not need ethnic cultures and institutions in order to conduct their daily lives, be it in the workplace or at home. Instead, the use of visible symbols satisfies their need for belonging, furnishes a differentiating factor in a culturally homogeneous society, and for highly (geographically) mobile individuals, it offers a sense of commonality and continuity. Thus, ethnicity becomes expressive, a voluntary affiliation that can be pursued in one's leisure time. It loses its hold over the individual; it becomes an artificial commitment that can be easily reversed when the surrounding environment becomes less tolerant of ethnic differences.

Instead of "being ethnic," later-generation descendants manifest their ethnicity through personalized interpretations and "varying mental constructions of ethnic behavior" (di Leonardo 1984, 228). The American value of individualism, the vocabulary of freedom and human rights dominates the scene. The different components of identity: the sacred, the secular, the political, the structural, are more likely to be separated and adapted to individual ends. For example, Zenner (1985, 120) notes that before the eighteenth century there was no such thing as a Jewish atheist or a non-Jewish Jew. Similarly, being an Armenian some two hundred years ago meant being a member of the Armenian Apostolic church (e.g., see Sarkisian 1984, 41). "What has happened is that many former life-long commitments, including those relating to kinship and ethnicity, have become commodities" (Zenner 1985,130).

How is symbolic ethnicity manifested? Gans (1979) outlines the many ways in which ethnicity is expressed. Most of all, it is an awareness of one's immigrant origins, a nostalgia for the past, and an immense pride in the group, its culture, its traditions, its history, and its people, past and present. Gans goes on to add: "All of the cultural patterns that are transformed into symbols are themselves guided by a common pragmatic imperative: they must be visible and clear in meaning to large numbers of third-generation ethnics, and they must be easily expressed and felt, without requiring undue interference in other aspects of life" (1979, 205).

Symbolic ethnics follow Porter's admonition that "the obligation to conserve culture is different from the obligation to live it" (1975, 300). They consciously seek to preserve heritage cultures by sponsoring lectures, funding chairs or departments in major universities, by establishing scholarships in ethnic studies, by collecting arts and artifacts and setting small sections in existing museums or starting new ones, and so on. I call these depositories for heritage conservation "knowledge banks." Symbolic ethnics have an interest in the events of the homeland and its history, which they turn into another symbol, disregarding its domestic and foreign policy problems.

Visibility is an important characteristic of symbolic ethnicity. Cultural paraphernalia such as bumper stickers, T-shirts with ethnic symbols and slogans, photographs, or other representations of ethnic monuments and artifacts are displayed prominently on one's person, car, home. Famous ethnic personalities such as actors, artists, politicians, business tycoons, become a source of pride. Appropriating illustrious figures as one's own, by name-dropping or similar associations increases one's feelings of pride and we-ness. Symbolic ethnicity is also expressed through institutions that do not require active participation and combine ethnicity with other interests, such as dance, music, athletic clubs, travel clubs, festivals, parades.

Rites of passage (such as births, deaths, marriages), religious or civic holidays (such as Christmas, saints days, Thanksgiving) are occasions for enacting ethnicity with one's family and kin, often in the privacy of one's home. Ethnic food forms a central element in such rituals, and it is not surprising that it is often imbued with positive connotations of warmth and sharing. The continued success of these ceremonies is their sporadic nature and the fact that they are convenient and do not upset everyday life and its preoccupations. Family, food, and rituals are cornerstones upon which symbolic ethnicity is built, whether or not the food, the rituals, or even the family members are ethnic in actual content or composition; the important thing is that they are perceived as such.

Michael Schudson (1984, 179) makes an interesting case for the "emergence of 'convenience' as a desirable product characteristic" in the United States, in the 1920s. He uses the almost sudden adoption of the cigarette and its widespread popularity as a case in point. He argues that by the early twentieth century, the "tempo" of life in America had quickened; time was becoming scarce. People were realizing that they had new social worlds and possibilities to choose from. Moreover, goods were becoming democratized, standardized, and available at any time and in any place. Products/goods were getting milder, less offensive, and easier to use by all social groups. Schudson explains further: "Convenience becomes especially desirable only when 'time' becomes an objectified and precious commodity itself. Only when people come to conceive of their lives as involving the 'spending' of time do they come to care about the 'saving' of time by the use of convenience goods" (1984, 199).

Convenience became a desirable quality in the United States in the twentieth century, because the country by then had become affluent and the clock or watch omnipresent. America had become a "time famine" culture. Convenience, it should be noted, is not a "labor-saving" but rather a "suitability" factor. Schudson goes on to say that another desirable social goal in modern, urban societies is "connection" or "circulation." "People not only want to be valued in their own circles but want to be available to enter new social groups. People seek ways to increase their mobility or social circulation" (1984, 202). Thus another attribute of convenience is being socially "nonrepellent."

Schudson's analysis of convenience as an important attribute of consumerism can be expanded to include most aspects of modern life. The concept of convenience is applicable to ethnic commitment and participation in America (see also Kramer and Leventman 1961). Whether cooking an ethnic dish, learning a new language, listening to ethnic radio, attending ethnic rallies or church services, suitability or convenience guide conduct, because time, energy, and income limitations are serious preoccupations of ethnic Americans. An ethnic culture must be "easy," and within the reach of all; the less the prerequisites, the wider the appeal. That is why, eating ethnic food is the most democratic form of ethnic maintenance; it is even more convenient than cooking it. Furthermore, symbolic ethnics have moved out of the ghetto for good; ethnic practices that risk isolating people and reghettoizing them will be most unpopular.

What are the functions of symbolic ethnicity in later generations? Ethnicity, in America, in the latter part of the twentieth century, continues to fulfill social and psychological functions for individuals who crave rituals (Steinberg 1981, 262), roots, or a sense of belonging (Driedger 1976; Lambert and Taylor 1988), and community. In spite of homogenizing tendencies in the modern world today, there are diametrically opposite movements toward "traditional harbors—religion, family, ethnic groups, and neighborhoods" (Keller 1988, 176; see also Gordon 1978, 121).

Recently, Richard Alba (1990) has argued that ethnicity, in lieu of social class, continues to be an important marker of social boundaries in the United States. Moreover, for all those Americans who are the descendants of the big immigration waves of the nineteenth and early twentieth centuries, the very journey of their grandfathers and grandmothers from the Old Country, their early settlement patterns in the New World, their initial struggles and hard work toward social mobility have come to define an essential part of American experience and identity. The immigrants' stories are almost as significant as the *Mayflower* in describing what it means to be an American today. Alba proposes the emergence of a new ethnic group; the European-Americans. It is a group characterized by subjective consciousness of a kind; not by demographic or other objective indicators. Much of my own conclusions about Armenian-Americans fit into this thesis, with one caveat. Armenian-Americans are unlikely to blend into this nondescript European-American group in the near future, at least not yet, because their immigration experience is a recent and still unfolding process. Another obstacle may be their membership in the Apostolic church. Like the Jews and Greeks, this religious affiliation tends to reinforce ethnicity (see chap. 2).

Finally, there is a need to ask: Is symbolic ethnicity any less real for later-generation ethnics? Compared to traditional ethnics, it is acknowledged that there is little discrimination or prejudice against symbolic ethnics. Symbolic ethnicity has few costs for the individual. It is ideally suited for white-middle-class Americans who have contradictory goals. On the one hand, they seek a sense of community, the American need to know "where one comes from," and on the other hand, they desire individuality, freedom to choose, be it a product in a store or an ethnic heritage (Waters 1990). The boundaries separating symbolic ethnics from nonethnics are self-imposed and thus can be easily obliterated. Nonetheless, the varied ways in which symbolic ethnics desperately wish to "feel" ethnic must be subjectively real. W. I. Thomas's theorem comes to mind: "If men define situations as real, they are real in their consequences" (Coser 1977, 521). If Armenian-Americans and other white ethnics define their identity as real, then it should be real in its consequences, whether or not its content is substantiated by objective definitions of culture (see di Leonardo 1984, 228).[46]

Ethnicization or Ethnogenesis

Ethnicization or ethnogenesis is the process whereby an aggregate of immigrants from the same national or regional origin acquire self-consciousness as a collectivity and create an ethnic group out of their shared American experience (Greeley 1974, 291-317; Greeley and McCready 1975, 211; Sarna 1978; Stein and Hill 1973, 99). There is considerable consensus among scholars that ancestral cultures are not recreated in totality in the new environment. Rather, a "hybrid culture" (Shibutani and Kwan 1965, 526) or synthesis, a "product of interaction" containing elements from the ancestral heritage and others from the core or mainstream culture in the new environment emerge (Charsley 1974, 357; see also Kayal 1973, 419).

Each immigrant group, anxious to preserve its traditional ways, at first endeavored
to create a sub-culture of its own. In order to do so it was obliged to develop
separate religious, educational and benevolent institutions. But this step alone
showed how strong was the pressure toward conformity with the existing
American pattern, for these voluntary organizations, none of which had existed in
Europe, adopted a common American form. (Jones 1960, 317)

The ethnic subculture and subsociety is created in response to the
immigrant experience and the exigencies of the new environment. It
provides comforting commonality and familiarity to the immigrants
and mediates between the old world and the new (Gordon 1964, 242).
Ethnicization may be activated successfully by immigrant leaders and
brokers by manipulating symbols and emphasizing a bond to a
national origin. Such was the case of the Polish-American community.
Lopata (1964, 206) writes: "The consciousness of a bond between all
persons of Polish birth or descent living in America grew up gradually
as a result of the efforts of a number of different leaders." Similarly
Schiller (1977) describes how the Haitian ethnic group in New York
was created by one leader who exploited the American political
system and the Democratic party machinery to ethnicize an immigrant
collectivity for economic and political benefits.

The creation of an ethnic communal structure is essential to
socialize the American-born generations to carry on the ethnic
subculture and identity. Yet, there are fundamental differences
between the generations: "Fathers, sons and grandsons may differ
among themselves not only in the *degree* but also in the *nature* of their
identification with ethnicity" (Nahirny and Fishman 1965, 312, italics
in original). For the foreign-born, the ethnic background is a taken for
granted as a way of life. Not the American-born; estranged from the
tangible traits of the ancestral heritage, they have no memory or
loyalty to the old country. Yet, they become more "conscious" of their
identity; their tie is social not cultural (Nahirny and Fishman 1965,
322; see also Sengstock 1975, 151; Warner and Srole 1945, 124-27).
American-born ethnics need to study ethnic cultures to "know" and
"appreciate" their heritage, but their socialization is "usually kept
within reasonable bounds and need have little or no relevance to daily
life" (Nahirny and Fishman 1965, 323; see also Kramer and
Leventman 1961).

Instrumental or Ideological Mobilization

The primordialist and instrumentalist debate in explaining ethnic mobilization and boundary maintenance occupies a central place in ethnic studies. This debate stems from such early masters of sociological thought as Tönnies, Durkheim, Cooley, Thomas, Park, and Wirth, who had conceptualized human relations, affiliation, and allegiance in dichotomous terms; from Gemeinschaft to Gesellschaft, from mechanical solidarity to organic solidarity, from primary to secondary relations, from communal to individualistic emphasis, and so on. In this scheme, ethnic relations were irrational ties, assumed to disappear with increasing modernization and industrialization. Ethnic ties were characterized as ascribed, particularistic, diffuse, kinlike bonds. Shils (1957) was one of their first critics. He proclaimed that ascriptive networks or "primordialism" continued to be a significant element in the social, economic, and political life in the second half of the twentieth century (see also Bendix 1967; Gusfield 1967; Litwak 1985, 16-30; Mayhew 1968). A heated academic discussion developed around the nature of ethnic resilience and its continued vitality in modern societies.

To some, the salience of ethnicity in America was attributable to the distinctive features of the cultural heritage of the immigrant groups (e.g., Abramson 1973; Greeley and McCready 1975; Mindel and Habenstein 1981; Schooler 1976; Slater 1969). Others criticized the primordialism argument by saying that if ethnic allegiance is natural, then it needs no explanation. Rather, they conjectured, the tenacity of ethnicity in contemporary life was situational; it was sustained by structural (economic and political) conditions (e.g., Barth 1969; Portes 1984; Olzak and Nagel 1986; Yancey, Ericksen and Juliani 1976; Yancey, Ericksen and Leon 1985).

Ethnic allegiance was a tool used in boundary formation of goal-oriented groups competing for scarce resources (political, economic, and social) in the public arena (Bell 1975; Glazer and Moynihan 1970, 1975; Hannerz 1974). White working-class ethnics in urban centers in the United States were mobilized because of their fear of the expanding power of blacks and the threat they perceived to their homes, their jobs, and their general well-being. Ethnicity was just the idiom for promoting group solidarity. The situation was not unique to people of immigrant descent. For example, native Pan-Indianism (American "Indian" identity) is perceived as a sociopolitical entity, a unifying construct that cannot rely on cultural homogeneity or inherited traits. Not only were ancestral cultures widely divergent, but few "Indians" today share the culture of their forefathers (Wax 1973; Jarvenpa 1985).

Indeed, no one can deny that ethnicity, as much as social class, remains an important variable of identity and differentiation in the world today. As Keyes so succinctly says: "Primordial identities continue to serve as gyroscopes for those buffeted by uncertainties as to the best way to pursue their interests or for those alienated by the dehumanized agencies designed to organize the ordering of social ends in a rational way" (1981, 28).

McKay (1982) has tried to resolve the dichotomy between the purely ideal, affectional and the purely material, instrumental components of ethnicity by arguing that it is false and both viewpoints are interrelated (see also Burgess 1978; Johnston and Yoels 1977; Lal 1983; Williams 1977, 53-54, 68). He suggests that the linkages between the two need to be specified empirically. The primordialism thesis or compulsory ethnicity is essential for understanding the emotional basis and tenacity of ethnic ties, but it is a type of psychological reductionism that fails to offer comprehensive theoretical explanations. On the other hand, the mobilizationist perspective is guilty of materialism. Moreover, it overlooks socioeconomic, gender, and other differences within the ethnic group and does not ask whose interests are being pursued. Therefore, simplistic theories of economic and cultural determinism are unable to explain complex phenomena like ethnicity.

McKay proposes a typology of five kinds of ethnic behavior and identity (ethnic traditionalists, ethnic militants, ethnic manipulators, pseudo-ethnics, and symbolic ethnics) and locates them along a two-dimensional matrix. The horizontal axis measures degrees (from low to high) of ethnic manifestation that tend to be based on instrumental interests; the vertical axis measures degrees (from low to high) of ethnic manifestations that tend to be based on primordial interests. First, *ethnic traditionalists* describes "people who are culturally and socially 'rooted' in the symbols and primary relationships of their ethnic groups" (McKay 1982, 403). To such people, their socialization

processes and their history are more significant than political and
material interests in influencing behavior and identity. Their conflicts
are more likely to be based on normative differences. Examples of
ethnic traditionalists are the Hutterites and Amish in North America;
Armenians, Copts, Kurds, Maronites in the Middle East. They are high
on primordialism, low on materialism.

Second, *ethnic militants* interfuse interest and affect. These are
groups "culturally and structurally 'rooted' as traditionalists, but are
also intensely involved in conflicts over political and economic
resources" (McKay 1982, 405). The Basque ETA, the Quebec
separatists, and the Armenian Secret Army for the Liberation of
Armenia (ASALA) are examples. Ethnic militants testify that
modernization is not necessarily incompatible with primordialism. On
the contrary, it can change, modernize. In the last decade or so, there
has been a trend toward more militancy among ethnic traditionalists.
Of course, not all traditionalists advocate or espouse violence. Why
some do and others do not requires further investigation. Ethnic
militants are high on both measures of interest and affect.

Third, *ethnic manipulators* are sheer opportunists. Their goals are
primarily economic and political. Their cultural, linguistic, and other
primordial attributes are latent. Ethnic entrepreneurs or brokers are
examples of people who negotiate ethnic boundaries and mobilize
support for their cause. This category has medium amounts of each
measure of interest and affect. Fourth, *pseudo-ethnics* "try to make
their pursuit of political and economic goals more legitimate by
finding an ethnic foundation on which they can be based" (McKay
1982, 407). They transform dormant ethnic categories into a group but
they continue to resemble interest groups and social movements rather
than ethnic groups per se. This type is low on primordialism and
medium on material interest. Finally, *symbolic ethnics* have low levels
of interest and low levels of ideology. Most white ethnic groups in
America can be classified under this category.

McKay's matrix is useful for a number of reasons. It shows that
there is a spectrum of activities in ethnic behavior and identity that
ranges from simply feeling ethnic to cultural/folkloric participation, to
membership in militant organizations. It describes the various
combinations of interest and membership criteria different
collectivities exhibit. It allows longitudinal analysis of groups as they

change in form, function, and membership. And in this case, it explains the meaning of Armenianness in the various diaspora communities.

Middlemen Minorities and Enclave Economy

Historically Armenians have often been called middlemen minorities. The term *middlemen minorities* characterizes the orientation of the immigrants to their place of residence. First, they come as sojourners, "birds of a passage," mainly for economic profit but stay on for generations because the political climate in the homeland is unfavorable and because sojourning increases business success. Their ideology remains that of a sojourner because some day they intend to return to their ancestral lands. This ideology prevents them from establishing lasting social relationships with their host society; instead they turn inward to the ethnic group for trust, mutual assistance, social relationships, and marriage partners. They conduct and control community affairs and do not rely on public charity. They form highly organized communities with their churches, schools, press, cultural and recreational organizations. They are accused of being clannish, foreign, and unassimilable. These are mostly justifiable accusations because they are ethnocentric, their reference group being insiders. It is not surprising that they "often emphasize the importance of maintaining a good name or preserving the family honor within the community" (Bonacich and Modell 1980, 16).

High communal solidarity regulates the distribution of resources and keeps control over internal competition. The economic activity of the middlemen minorities is the key variable in their existence. They are mostly traders, independent professionals, skilled craftsmen, often economically successful. Their occupations can be characterized by liquidity and transportability. Middlemen minorities are criticized for their disloyalty, for draining the resources of the host society, but this hostility and conflict is functional because it isolates them and increases group solidarity. What starts off as a voluntary segregation for the sojourners may eventually become forced segregation. Relinquishing the ideology of an eventual return to the homeland implies assimilation. Economic and social integration is the doom of the middleman form (Bonacich 1973).

Recently, the concept of *enclave economy*, allegedly broader and less rigid than the middlemen minority form, has been used to explain the Latin (mostly Cuban) entrepreneurial success in Miami (Portes and Bach 1985). An enclave economy is established when political and economic structures of the host society prevent the structural assimilation of ethnic minorities. That rejection and "prior experience in buying and selling" forces new immigrants to look to their co-ethnics for capital, labor, and economic opportunities. Enclave economies may deal with trade or any type of small-scale production or manufacturing.

Enclaves offer more favorable economic conditions to workers by modifying the character of the class relationship between capital and labor. Employers exploit ethnic bonds to maintain a cheap and acquiescent labor force. In return, they are obligated to reserve supervisory positions for their fellow immigrants, promote their occupational skills, and help them establish self-employment when they eventually make the move (Portes and Bach 1985, 343). Armenian immigrants in Los Angeles and New York appear to have established an enclave economy in the jewelry business.

Recent evidence (Sanders and Nee 1987) demonstrates that the enclave economy is more profitable for ethnic entrepreneurs and business owners than to their employees; the latter do better economically when they assimilate into the larger society. This is because, first, the success of the enclave economy depends on the maintenance of a large pool of low-wage laborers. Second, the paternalistic assistance that ethnic entrepreneurs give to immigrant workers upon their arrival may not be so helpful in the long run because in the process immigrant workers accumulate a web of obligations and favors they might not be able to repay.

The middlemen minority form and the enclave economy are brought about by a combination of cultural variables pertaining to the immigrant group (as in Light 1972), contextual variables that are the properties of the recipient population (as in Blalock 1967), and situational variables such as that of being a sojourner (as in Bonacich 1973; see Turner and Bonacich 1980). The question that is of interest here, however, is how long can ethnic enclaves or middlemen minorities be sustained? Is it possible to retain these forms into the second and subsequent generations? From a case study of small businesses among Japanese-Americans, Bonacich and Modell (1980) suggest that leaving small businesses means decreasing ethnic solidarity. Those who moved to jobs in the corporate economy were less likely to retain close ethnic bonds and contacts. Later-generation upwardly mobile Americans of ethnic descent who do not depend for their livelihood on ethnic enterprises are most likely to become symbolic ethnics. The significance of instrumental motives for ethnic solidarity is indeed undeniable. Ideologies (of eventual return or otherwise) are also important but harder to sustain over time without an economic base.

Methods of Data Collection and Description of the Sample

The core of this study rests on Milton Gordon's theoretical framework on assimilation. As shown above, Gordon postulated that there were seven analytically separate processes or dimensions of assimilation. Each group that immigrates to America forges its unique trajectory because of variations in the time of arrival, socioeconomic conditions in the host society, the cultural baggage they bring with them, and so forth. All these variables affect the pace and outcome of each subprocess of assimilation and the overall process. Implicitly, Gordon's theoretical framework assumes that assimilation in the United States follows a straight-line model; that is, the longer the generational presence of an immigrant group, the greater the probability of assimilation.

In empirical terms, the degree of assimilation is measured as a percentage difference between the immigrant generation and each subsequent American-born generation. The first generation's cultural and behavioral patterns are used as the statistical baseline, and all departures from it imply a movement along the continuum toward "more" assimilation. It should be noted that the cultural heritage of the first generation is far from being homogeneous, and, of course, not all immigrants of Armenian descent are well versed in the Armenian language and cultural heritage. Thus, the distinctions between the various generations should be understood in relative not absolute terms.

In this study, an Armenian-American is defined as a person who resides in the United States of America (whether or not he or she is legally a citizen), whose ancestors originated in historic Armenia, and who implicitly claims Armenian descent by participating in the survey.[47] No behavioral preconditions are included in this definition. In addition, foreign-born Armenian-Americans may use other hyphenated labels to characterize themselves. The prefix Lebanese, French, Romanian, Middle Eastern, Soviet, Istanbul, Aleppo, and so on before the word *Armenian* designates the city, country, or region of birth or residence in the diaspora that a respondent identifies with.[48] These labels are not mutually exclusive; rather depending on the context, individuals use them discriminately to reduce (or increase) social distance.

Assimilation is the dependent variable in this study, that is, the phenomenon under investigation. The seven subprocesses of assimilation have been operationalized with a battery of questions and Likert-type attitude statements to measure empirically the assimilative profile of American-Armenians in metropolitan New York and New Jersey. The independent variables, that is those that influence the outcome of assimilation, used in this study were: generation,[49] respondent's place of birth (variable Origin),[50] religious affiliation (variable Religion),[51] ethnic origins of respondent's parents (variable Ancestry),[52] ideological beliefs or sympathy to Armenian political parties (variable Symparty),[53] age, gender, marital status. Finally, social class was measured by respondent's education, occupation, and income.

Sampling Procedures

Master mailing lists of the Apostolic (Sees of Echmiadzin and Cilicia),[54] Protestant, and Catholic Armenian churches were obtained.[55] These lists represent people of Armenian descent who have at some point in their lives participated in, or attended activities sponsored by ethnic voluntary associations, or contributed financially to Armenian churches or other institutions. The totality of these lists, it is assumed, make up the universe of Armenian-Americans who are either actively or very loosely connected to the formally organized Armenian-American community of metropolitan New York and New Jersey.

The Main Sample of the survey was selected randomly from the above mailing lists. Every twelfth address was chosen from the two Apostolic mailing lists and every sixth household from the two

Apostolic mailing lists and every sixth household from the two
Protestant and one Catholic church lists. If an address had already
been selected, the one directly below was picked. In spite of the care
taken not to duplicate addresses, two such mistakes were made. There
was some duplication in the two Apostolic lists, but less in the others.
Households whose names appeared on more than one mailing list had
a higher probability of being selected into the sample. It also implies
that they were more active ethnically. The Main Sample consisted of a
total of 1,145 households. The Apostolic addresses numbered 950 (83
percent). The Main Sample also included 87 addresses from the
Catholic list (7.6 percent) and another 108 from the New York and
New Jersey Protestant church lists (9.4 percent).

To redress the organizational bias in the sampling procedure, a
second group of names was generated through the snowball technique.
Respondents in both samples were asked to supply the names and
addresses of persons of Armenian descent who were believed not to be
affiliated with Armenian organizations. Some names were obtained
through my own network of friends and acquaintances who knew of
the study and through an advertisement that appeared in the *Armenian
Reporter*, the local English-language weekly. The Snowball Sample
yielded 144 addresses. All the names and addresses in the study area
that were sent to me were subsequently mailed a questionnaire.

The instructions for generating the Snowball Sample might have
been misunderstood because the names and addresses of some people
who were active in Armenian voluntary associations or churches were
also sent to me. Nonetheless, those who responded were included in
the Snowball Sample. This balances out those respondents whose
names appeared on the initial mailing lists but were not
organizationally active. Several of them wrote or called requesting to
be included in the Snowball Sample because they felt they did not
belong with the ethnically active group. They did not realize that there
was only one questionnaire for both samples. Their names had been
included on Armenian mailing lists because they had at some time in
the past made financial contributions to Armenian churches or
organizations in memory of a dead relative or had a similar incidental
involvement. The total number of questionnaires that were mailed was
1,289. The geographical parameters consisted of the state of New
Jersey, the five boroughs of New York City, as well as Long Island,

Westchester, and Suffern counties. Addresses outside this area that were sent in by the snowball technique were not included.

Attitude statements used in the survey were pretested on twenty college students of Armenian descent gathered for a panel discussion at Columbia University. An earlier version of the questionnaire was administered to twelve people of Armenian descent who were believed to represent a cross-section of the population in terms of age, generation, ancestry and socioeconomic factors. The Main Sample was mailed in April 1986; the Snowball Sample in the weeks that followed. The last completed questionnaire was received in December 1986. The survey was designed and conducted using Dillman's (1978) Total Design Methods (see copy of package in Appendix). That is, each envelope was individually typed; first-class stamps were used to ensure quick delivery and return in the case of wrong addresses; the cover letter explained the academic and educational purpose of the project and promised confidentiality of responses. An identification number was written on every questionnaire; it facilitated the telephone follow-up, but hindered some people from participating in the survey. It is impossible to estimate the number of potential respondents that were lost because of the lack of complete anonymity in the study. Two weeks after the first mailing, a postcard was sent to all potential respondents. Two weeks after that, I started telephoning households that had not responded. My personal appeals were able to persuade some people to reply.

Response Rate

From the Main Sample, 472 people responded to the survey, that is a 41 percent response rate. The response rate was much higher for the Snowball Sample, 78 percent or 112 replies. The combined sample, therefore, consists of 584 completed questionnaires by adult men or women of Armenian descent living in metropolitan New York and New Jersey (45 percent response rate for total sample). The response rate reaches a respectable 48 percent if I exclude the non-Armenian names, wrong addresses, and duplicates in the initial mailing.[56] Babbie (1979, 335) observes that a 50 percent response rate is adequate for analysis and reporting. He argues that a demonstrated lack of response bias and statistical biases are more important.

I was able to talk to and/or received letters from 102 men and women of Armenian descent who did not participate in the survey. I even visited with two potential respondents at their invitation. Of these almost 37 percent were too old or too ill. About 19 percent refused to participate because they said the survey was not anonymous, questions were too personal or political in nature, or because they would not participate in surveys on principle. Five percent said the questionnaire was too long or too difficult and demanding. Twelve percent said they were not interested, and 10 percent were too busy. An additional 77 potential respondents who were contacted by phone said they were too busy, promised to send in their responses, but did not. Six people said they had already sent in their completed questionnaires which I never received.

If I calculate the total number of completed responses, and the number of potential respondents I communicated with, there still remain 454 (35 percent) questionnaires that were sent out but for which I had no response. It is assumed that the reasons for their nonresponse is similar to the ones already accounted for. People are too busy, too old, too tired to devote time and energy to fill out a sixteen-page questionnaire. Old age, illness, death in the family, vacation, or moving house were reasons preventing potential respondents from participating in the survey. Older respondents, whose numbers were significant in the study, found some of the questions difficult to answer, even a 47-year-old second-generation woman observed: "I am exhausted thinking about all this—a good Armenian exercise."

Some people alluded to "Big Brother" in the use of survey information. One woman wrote, "It is not my policy to answer questionnaires of any kind." Still another woman sent me a letter from which I quote:

Before I received your questionnaire, as an American-born of Armenian parents, I, like many other Americans, was concerned about the intrusion of "Big Brother" into our lives. I was dismayed to find that there is, also an Armenian "Big Brother."

The intrusion into one's private and political affairs is often started with a comprehensive inquiry, the inquirer having the intention to keep this information confidential. However, control of the original inquirer and a second or third party makes this public, always professing well-intentioned reasons for releasing this information.

In trying to explain nonresponse on sample surveys, Goyder (1987) argues that it is fallacious to label all nonrespondents as deviant cases to be explained by social and demographic characteristics such as age, marital status, socioeconomic level, and so on. He advocates an exchange theory perspective in which the voluntaristic elements in human behavior enter into the picture. People balance costs and benefits for completing a particular survey. Some nonresponse arguments are situational, others are attitudes like sensitivity to privacy and confidentiality, or dislike of a particular form of survey or all forms. These are consistent across replications. Though an exchange "rate" for completing surveys is not clear, Goyder suggests that because of the multidimensionality of survey nonresponse, possibly one component helps nullify another, thus reducing biases.

The men and women who responded to the survey are a self-selected group who implicitly claim Armenian descent by participating in the study. Thus, the results are biased toward a more *ethnic* [57] representation of people of Armenian descent living in metropolitan New York and New Jersey. There were several differences between the Main Sample and the Snowball Sample. The reader is reminded that the Snowball Sample was in principle designed to tap men and women of Armenian descent who continue to identify with their ethnic roots but were not members of Armenian voluntary associations.

In general, the Snowball Sample tended to be younger in age (mean age was forty-three vs. fifty-seven years), predominantly U.S.-born (80 percent vs. 60 percent), more likely to have mixed parentage (23 percent vs. 8.5 percent), and twice as likely to be married to spouses who were not of Armenian descent. They were also more likely to have gone to college and beyond (65 percent v. 41 percent). On assimilation indices, respondents in the Snowball Sample were twice as likely not to speak or read Armenian (46 percent vs. 21 percent), had fewer Armenian friends, and attended activities hosted by Armenian organizations less often. They were also more likely to identify as American (12.5 percent vs. 7.4 percent).

This suggests that the Main Sample is skewed toward the immigrants and their children's generation while the Snowball Sample is skewed toward the more assimilated later generations. In spite of these differences, the two samples overlap. It was therefore decided to analyze the results of the two samples together, for both substantive and practical reasons. The data presented henceforth are the results of the combined samples numbering 584 completed questionnaires.

Generalization of the Study

The main bias in this study is inherent in the method of data collection. The mail questionnaire assumes respondents are literate and proficient in English. This makes the sample biased toward the more educated segment of the population. The follow-up telephone calls were meant to correct this bias, but failed to eliminate error. In addition, sampling from organizational mailing lists increases the chances of more ethnically involved individuals to participate in the study. The Snowball Sample was meant to redress this problem, and it is hoped it did. Also, this sample tends to miss the very recent immigrants, less-educated blue-collar workers of ethnic origin, but, more seriously, it misses the younger, later-generation descendants.

The results of the survey are believed to be representative of people of Armenian descent who acknowledge their ethnic ancestry and live in metropolitan New York and New Jersey. As an aggregate, these people tend to be predominantly in the second generation, occupying middle- to upper-middle status positions. With two caveats I can confidently declare that the results of this study are generalizable to all people of Armenian descent in the United States of America. The first cautionary note argues that people of Armenian descent living in areas where there are no Armenian institutions have an increased probability to rank higher on assimilation indices (Breton 1964).[58] Last but not least, because of sample bias, these findings tend to underestimate the actual amount of assimilation of men and women of Armenian descent in the United States of America.

Qualitative Data

In the early stages of this study, in-depth interviews were conducted with a number of individuals highly active in and knowledgeable about the Armenian-American community in New York and New Jersey. More recently, I have conducted additional interviews in Los Angeles and Washington, DC and reinterviewed a few individuals in

New York to get an update on the latest changes in the Armenian-American community, the Republic of Armenia, and elsewhere in the diaspora. In all, there were thirty such interviews, varying in length from less than one hour to three hours. In the last several years, I had the opportunity to visit the Armenian communities of Los Angeles, San Francisco, Boston, Philadelphia, Washington, DC, and Baltimore. My impressions confirmed the general trends I had found in New York.

I identify myself as an Armenian, but was unfamiliar with the Armenian-American scene until my arrival in New York City over a decade ago; that put me in the unique position of being an insider at one level, yet an outsider at another.[59] My outsider status and my sociological training sharpened my observational tools and made me seek and question behavior that might have been taken for granted by an American-born Armenian. My insider status gave me access to Armenian-American networks; those formally organized as voluntary associations, congregations, clubs, etc., and those private ties that eventually became my friends and acquaintances. Living in New York City, I was able to participate in as many types of ethnic events and programs sponsored by Armenian-American voluntary associations as possible. I attended concerts, church services, ethnic festivals, dinner dances, ethnic theater, a convention, lectures, seminars, etc.[60] I even attended bridal and baby showers, weddings, funerals, Thanksgiving dinners, and private gatherings to learn more about Armenian-Americans. In retrospect, my participant observation, the in-depth interviews, and the unsolicited comments of the respondents validated and confirmed the statistical evidence gathered by the survey. My personal observations and the survey data complimented each other and completed the picture. In other words, the qualitative component was as valuable as the quantitative part in reaching the conclusions of this study.

Description of the Sample: An Armenian-American Profile

Other than distribution frequencies, data presented in this book is in the form of simple cross-tabulations and all associations are statistically significant,[61] unless otherwise stated. It is important to note that measures of association do not determine causation. Also, the

between the variables. For example, it is often not quite clear which
independent variable has more power in accounting for a given
behavior.[62] More complex statistical methods and interval-level data
are needed to determine the relative significance of one variable over
the other in explaining assimilation and ethnic maintenance. The
prime purpose of this survey is descriptive; it is hoped more
explanatory studies will follow.

The demographic profile of men and women of Armenian descent
in metropolitan New York and New Jersey who responded to the
survey is shown below (see table 1.2). The data shows that this sample
is predominantly middle-aged (the mean age being 54.3 years). It is
characterized by a recent immigration history (84 percent of the
sample are from the first and second generations). Respondents in the
third and fourth generations tended to be younger (84 percent of them
below age 50) and single (about half were not married). Also, only 11
percent of the sample had a non-Armenian parent.

TABLE 1.2
Frequency Distribution of Demographic Variables of New York Sample

	Percentage of Total		Percentage of Total
Sex (N = 584)		Origin of Foreign-Born (N = 232)	
Male	54.5	Turkey	38.8
Female	45.5	Middle East	47.4
		Soviet Bloc	9.5
Marital Status (N = 584)		Other	4.3
Never married	14.7		
Married	69.0	Ancestry (N = 584)	
Widowed	10.1	Both parents Armenian	88.7
Separated/divorced	5.1	One parent Armenian	11.3
Remarried	1.0		
		Generation (N = 584)	
Age (N = 578)		Respondent foreign-born	37.5
20—29	5.5	Respondent U.S.-born of	
30—39	11.7	foreign-born parents	46.6
40—49	17.1	Respondent and one	
50—59	28.2	parent U.S.-born	6.2
60—69	21.1	Respondent and two	
70 +	17.3	parents U.S.-born	7.0
		Respondent parents &	
		grandparent(s) U.S.-born	2.7

With one exception (a man who arrived in 1902 at the age of one year, born in Alexandria, Egypt), almost 17 percent of the respondents arrived in the United States between 1914 and 1924. There is a noticeable decrease in the proportion of immigrants in the 1930s and 1940s, when the quota system was in effect, when about 5 percent of the respondents arrived in each decade. Then, after World War II, there is a gradual increase which reaches its peak immediately after 1965. Almost 9 percent of respondents arrived in the 1940s, 13 percent in the 1950s, 31 percent in the 1960s, and another 18 percent in the 1970s. As noted above, this sample misses some of the most recent newcomers, only 3 percent are included here; however, the bulk of the 1980s immigrants settled in Los Angeles, not New York. In all, 37.5

TABLE 1.2 Continued

Percentage of Total		Percentage of Total	
Occupation (N = 528)		**Year of Arrival in U.S. (N = 232)**	
Traditional professional	22.2	To 1924	16.8
Semi-professional	16.9	1925-1929	4.7
Business owner	24.6	1930-1939	4.7
Manager	11.2	1940-1949	8.6
White collar	14.6	1950-1959	12.9
Skilled blue collar	9.5	1960-1964	11.2
Semiskilled blue collar	1.1	1965-1969	19.8
		1970-1979	18.1
Education (N = 562)		1980-1986	3.0
Grade school or less	5.9		
Not finish high school	2.7	**Religion (N = 576)**	
High school	24.4	Apostolic Armenians	64.2
Some college/business school	19.4	Protestant Armenians	9.7
College	23.0	Catholic Armenians	3.8
Graduate or professional school	24.7	"Other" denominations	16.0
		No religion	6.3
Income (N = 471)			
0-19,999	15.0	**Symparty (N = 584)**	
20,000-29,999	10.4	Hunchag sympathizers	1.0
30,000-39,999	12.7	Ramgavar sympathizers	4.8
40,000-49,999	15.3	Tashnag sympathizers	18.7
50,000-59,999	10.2	*Chezok* (neutral/nonpartisan)	24.5
60,000-69,999	7.4	Indifferent to ethnic politics	30.3
70,000-79,999	5.3	Reject ethnic political parties	12.2
80,000-89,999	4.0	No answer	8.6
90,000-99,999	1.0		
100,000 +	17.6		

percent were foreign-born. This figure corresponds with the estimate of the 1980 census for foreign-born Armenians in the United Sates reported above (40 percent).

While most of the early immigrants were born in Ottoman Turkey, the largest proportion of those who came in recent decades were from the Middle East (38.8 percent of foreign-born). More specifically, 13.8 percent of the foreign-born came from Lebanon, 12.5 percent from Iran, 8.6 percent from Syria, 6.9 percent from Egypt and the rest from Iraq and Palestine/Israel. Another 10 percent of the foreign-born in the sample came from Eastern European countries, mainly Bulgaria and Romania, and the rest from such diverse places as Greece, France, Germany, Cuba, and Argentina. There were twenty-three respondents in the study (3.9 percent of the total sample) who were sponsored by ANCHA. It is interesting to note that as many foreign-born Armenians settled in the United States in the two decades since the liberation of the quota system (41 percent of the foreign-born sample) as they did in the four decades (1925-1964) when the quota system was in effect (42 percent). The impact of the post-World War II Armenian immigration (65.1 percent of the foreign-born sample, and 25.9 percent of the total sample) on Armenian-American communal structures is demonstrated throughout this study.

The majority of the respondents in this study (65 percent) were affiliated with the Armenian Apostolic church. The next biggest group (16 percent) were those people of ethnic descent who have left ethnic churches to become members of other nonethnic mainstream denominations; of these, close to 11 percent belonged to varied Protestant denominations, mostly Presbyterian (3.5 percent) and Episcopalian congregations (2.3 percent); the remaining 3 percent belonged to the Roman Catholic church. Armenian Protestants made up almost 10 percent of the sample,[63] while the Armenian Catholics about 4 percent.[64] Finally, about 7 percent of respondents said they had "no religion."

The socioeconomic attributes of this sample are surprisingly high. Twenty-three percent of the respondents graduated from college and almost 25 percent went to graduate or professional school. These figures are more than twice the U.S. average. According to the 1980 census, 21 percent of white males and 14 percent of white females completed college or more (Population Reference Bureau 1982, 34).

On the other hand, this sample is closer to the national average of American Jews; 59 percent of Jewish men and 47 percent of Jewish women have at least a college degree (quoted in Friedman 1989). Almost 60 percent of the sample occupy the three highest occupational categories—traditional professional, semiprofessional, and business owner. Nearly 80 percent of respondents declared their family income;[65] of these about 60 percent earn $40,000 or more per year, with almost 18 percent in the $100,000 or more income bracket.[66]

It is possible that these income levels have been inflated in reporting. As financial success is greatly valued in American society, those respondents earning higher incomes were proud to show off their achievements. Thus, it might be postulated that those respondents who did not declare their incomes in the survey (19.3 percent) are more likely to fall into the less prosperous income brackets. These results lend support to Ronald Stockton's hypothesis that the increasingly affluent upper-middle-class status of American-Armenians risks alienating working-class people of Armenian descent. He explains; "Armenian is what individual Armenians are. Even more, it is what those most influential Armenians are, for it is they who define Armenianness by controlling the organized structures through which Armenian individuals manifest their collective identity" (1983, 12).

The basic assumption behind this hypothesis is that upper-middle-class American-Armenians will want to control ethnic voluntary associations, churches and the like. This is the opposite of classical ethnicity theory that assumes that with increased socioeconomic status, people of immigrant descent assimilate into mainstream America, leaving such communal structures behind to the working-class ethnics. I suggest that Stockton's argument applies to the first and second generations, while the classical interpretation is true of later generations.

Seventy percent of the sample were married or remarried, 10 percent widowed and 5 percent divorced. It is interesting to note that 35.9 percent of the married, 15.2 percent of the widowed, and 55.6 percent of the separated/divorced had been married to non-Armenians. On the other hand, 4.3 percent of foreign-born, 5.4 percent of second-generation, and 9.5 percent of later generations over forty years of age were divorced and separated. Given these two pieces of data it is not possible to conclude that intermarriage increases the chances of separation and divorce, though the relationship certainly warrants further investigation. There is conflicting evidence in literature on the issue (see Cretser and Leon 1982, 10).

In spite of the efforts made to draw equal numbers of men and women of Armenian descent into the sample, slightly more men than women answered the questionnaire (45.5 percent versus 54.5 percent respectively), especially those comprising the Snowball Sample (59 percent were men). Women who marry out of their ethnic group and adopt their husband's family name are more likely to "disappear" from ethnic mailing lists, unless they remain active in ethnic associations. In addition, men who retain the "ian" ending in their family names are more readily traceable whether they marry Armenians or non-Armenians, and whether or not they participate in community activities. I cannot draw any conclusions from the available evidence on whether ethnic identity is transmitted patrilineally or matrilineally. In the United States (and traditional Armenian culture), children tend to take the family name of their fathers, but that does not mean that fathers are more successful in propagating their ethnic heritage.

It is interesting to note that gender differences were insignificant in this sample in almost every correlational matrix.[67] A survey on the assimilation of Italian-Americans in Bridgeport (CT) made a similar discovery (Crispino 1980). However, in 1958, Spindler and Spindler had found that immigrant women do not encounter the sharply disjunctive role expectations that men do. They argue that women continue to play feminine expressive roles and their position is more flexible. Similarly in a study of the integration of Armenians in Lebanon, Sona Jerejian (1976) in the 1970s found that women were more family bound and less integrated in the larger society.

It may be that surveys are inappropriate for teasing out subtle meanings in men's and women's ethnicity. Contradictory evidence comes from Micaela di Leonardo (1984) who used participant observation to study Italian-Americans in San Francisco. She suggests that men's ethnicity is manifested primarily through the nurturance and symbolically laden environment that women create. Through the celebration of holidays among kin and friends, women recreate materially and symbolically, time and time again what is perceived to be the perpetuation of ethnicity.

Di Leonardo argues that in negotiating their ethnic identities, ethnic women (compared to nonethnic American women) "must face ... an idealized patriarchal past in which women stayed at home and served men and children" (di Leonardo 1984, 228). She goes on to say that ethnic men lay claim to their own ethnicity through the "work of kinship" that mothers, sisters, wives, and daughters perform. Work of kinship implies telephoning family members, keeping the network informed of each others' activities, writing letters, sending birthday cards, buying Christmas presents, planning and cooking holiday meals for the whole family, and taking care of elderly parents and in-laws. Women cannot escape the work of kinship without feeling guilty or having a sense of failure. Therefore, ethnic women more than ethnic men have the added burden to live up to the idealized standards of their family and ethnicity.

Tables 1.3 to 1.10 show the distribution of selected background variables by generations in America. Together, these tables indicate that later-generation respondents in the sample tend to be young, still single, the offspring of intermarried couples, affiliated with non-Armenian churches or declare "no religion," and indifferent to Armenian political ideologies. They are also more likely to have gone to college, even graduate school, be employed in professional occupations, and earn above average incomes.

TABLE 1.3
Frequency Distribution of Age by Generation

	Foreign-Born	U.S.-Born of F.B. Parents	1 Parent U.S.-Born	2 Parents U.S.-Born	Grandparent U.S.-Born
N = 584	(219)	(272)	(36)	(41)	(16)
20-29	4.1	2.2	5.6	24.4	31.1
30-39	11.4	3.3	27.8	41.5	43.8
40-49	18.7	11.4	44.4	17.1	25.0
50-59	21.5	37.9	19.4	14.6	0.0
60-69	18.3	30.1	0.0	0.0	0.0
70 +	26.0	15.1	2.8	2.4	0.0
Total	100.0	100.0	100.0	100.0	100.0

TABLE 1.4
Frequency Distribution of Religion by Generation

	Foreign-Born	U.S.-Born of F.B. Parents	1 Parent U.S.-Born	2 Parents U.S.-Born	Grandparent U.S.-Born
N = 576	(215)	(270)	(35)	(41)	(15)
Arm. Apostolic	76.3	60.4	68.6	39.0	20.0
Arm. Protestant	12.6	8.9	2.9	9.8	0.0
Arm. Catholic	5.1	3.0	0.0	7.3	0.0
Other	5.1	21.5	14.3	19.5	66.7
No religion	0.9	6.3	14.3	24.4	13.3
	100.0	100.0	100.0	100.0	100.0

TABLE 1.5
Frequency Distribution of Ancestry by Generation

	Foreign-Born	U.S.-Born of F.B. Parents	1 Parent U.S.-Born	2 Parents U.S.-Born	Grandparent U.S.-Born
N = 584	(219)	(272)	(36)	(41)	(16)
2 Parents Arm.	90.9	93.9	86.1	75.6	12.5
1 Parent Arm.	9.1	6.3	13.9	24.4	87.5
	100.0	100.0	100.0	100.0	100.0

TABLE 1.6
Frequency Distribution of Sympathy to Armenian Political Parties and Ideologies
by Generation

	Foreign-Born	U.S.-Born of F.B. Parents	1 Parent U.S.-Born	2 Parents U.S.-Born	Grandparent U.S.-Born
N = 584	(219)	(272)	(36)	(41)	(16)
Hunchag	1.4	1.1	0.0	0.0	0.0
Ramgavar	5.5	5.5	0.0	0.0	6.3
Tashnag	27.9	15.1	13.9	4.9	0.0
Neutral (Chezok)	33.3	22.8	11.1	7.3	6.3
Indifferent	12.8	36.0	44.4	65.9	50.0
Rejects all parties	10.5	11.0	22.2	14.6	25.0
(No answer)	8.7	8.5	8.3	7.3	12.5
	100.0	100.0	100.0	100.0	100.0

Interestingly, occupation and income are not statistically related to generation. These figures question the general assumption in assimilation theory about the correlation of social class variables and generational presence in the United States. The hypothesis that ethnicity varies inversely with socioeconomic status is only valid for educational attainment, not occupation and income (see tables 1.9 and 1.10). That is, the later the generational standing, the higher the educational level completed, but there is no commensurate increase in occupational prestige and income levels. Foreign-born respondents

TABLE 1.7
Frequency Distribution of Education by Generation

	Foreign-Born	U.S.-Born of F.B. Parents	1 Parent U.S.-Born	2 Parents U.S.-Born	Grandparent U.S.-Born
N = 563	(204)	(266)	(36)	(41)	(15)
Grade school or less	13.7	1.9	0.0	0.0	0.0
Some high school	2.9	3.0	0.0	2.4	0.0
High school	26.5	28.2	11.1	12.2	0.0
Some college	15.7	24.1	19.4	7.3	18.8
College	21.1	19.2	41.7	36.6	31.3
More than college	20.1	23.7	27.8	41.5	50.0
	100.0	100.0	100.0	100.0	100.0

TABLE 1.8
Frequency Distribution of Marital Status by Generation

	Foreign-Born	U.S.-Born of F.B. Parents	1 Parent U.S.-Born	2 Parents U.S.-Born	Grandparent U.S.-Born
N = 584	(219)	(272)	(36)	(41)	(16)
Not married	9.1	13.6	16.7	34.1	56.3
Married	73.1	70.2	75.0	58.5	43.8
Widowed	14.2	10.3	0.0	0.0	0.0
Divorced/ separated	3.7	5.9	8.3	7.3	0.0
	100.0	100.0	100.0	100.0	100.0

were as likely as third- and fourth-generation respondents to earn high incomes and hold upper-echelon jobs, even when their age was held constant.

Religion is also an important variable in explaining assimilation. Respondents categorized as "other" (i.e., they were affiliated with non-Armenian churches) or "no religion" in the survey were, on average, the most assimilated. First, non-Armenian religious affiliations tended to increase with generational presence (.18*; see table 1.4). Second, the higher the likelihood of a respondent to declare "other" or "no religion," the higher his or her chances to be indifferent to Armenian political ideologies (.21*; see table 1.11). Third, non-Armenian church affiliations considerably increased the chances of mixed ancestry (.18*; see table 1.12). This leads me to infer that mixed ancestry affects assimilation through religion. That is, children of mixed marriages are more likely to be lost to Armenian churches because they follow the faith of their non-Armenian parent or no

TABLE 1.9
Frequency Distribution of Occupation by Generation

	Foreign-Born	U.S.-Born of F.B. Parents	1 Parent U.S.-Born	2 Parents U.S.-Born	Grandparent U.S.-Born
N = 570	(210)	(267)	(36)	(41)	(16)
Traditional prof.	18.6	19.1	25.0	34.1	25.0
Semiprofessional	11.4	15.4	25.0	26.8	25.0
Business owner	29.0	21.0	25.0	4.9	12.5
Manager	9.0	10.5	13.9	12.2	12.5
White collar	7.1	20.2	5.6	12.2	6.3
Skilled blue-collar	14.3	6.7	0.0	2.4	6.3
Semiskilled blue-coll.	1.4	1.1	0.0	0.0	0.0
(Homemaker)	8.1	5.2	5.6	4.9	0.0
(Student)	1.0	0.7	0.0	2.4	12.5
	100.0	100.0	100.0	100.0	100.0

religion than simply because they had a nonethnic parent. This is a hypothesis that needs to be tested in the future.

In addition to generational effects, there are cohort effects that seem to influence behavior. Younger respondents, irrespective of generation, were more likely to have higher levels of educational attainment, earn higher incomes, have a non-Armenian parent, and to hold prestigious occupational positions. These cohort effects are also observed between generation and education when age is controlled. Irrespective of generational differences, none of the twenty to twenty-nine year olds in the sample stopped with a high school diploma. For the thirties cohort, fully 50 percent of the foreign-born had a college degree or more. This figure increases to 78 percent for the second generation and 85 percent for later generations. There is also a

TABLE 1.10
Frequency Distribution of Income (in U.S. $) by Generation

	Foreign-Born	U.S.-Born of F.B. Parents	1 Parent U.S.-Born	2 Parents U.S.-Born	Grandparent U.S.-Born
N = 471	(176)	(209)	(35)	(35)	(16)
0-19,999	18.8	14.4	0.0	14.3	18.8
20,000-29,999	9.7	11.5	11.4	8.6	6.3
30,000-39,999	13.6	12.9	0.0	20.0	12.5
40,000-49,999	12.5	15.3	31.4	17.1	6.3
50,000-59,999	12.5	10.5	2.9	8.6	0.0
60,000-69,999	4.5	10.5	5.7	5.7	6.3
70,000-79,999	6.8	2.4	14.3	5.7	6.3
80,000-89,999	1.7	4.8	11.4	2.9	6.3
90,000-99,999	3.4	1.0	0.0	0.0	6.3
100,000 +	16.5	16.7	22.9	17.1	31.3
	100.0	100.0	100.0	100.0	100.0

generational increase in those who obtained a college degree or more for forty to forty-nine year olds (41 percent of first generation, 58 of second, 74 percent of third and 100 percent for fourth generation).

The differences are less marked for those in their fifties, but there is still a small generational increase in higher education from 44 percent in first generation, to 51 percent in second, to 54 percent in the third generation. The situation changes for the sixties and seventies cohorts. Here, the foreign-born have more college education than the second generation. For those between age sixty and sixty-nine, while 53 percent of the immigrant generation had a college degree or more, 32 percent of the second generation did. Again for those above age seventy, 22 percent of the foreign-born had higher education in contrast to 17 percent of second generation.

In sum, only respondents in their thirties and forties, the (American) baby boom cohort do better educationally than the foreign-born. For those born sixty or seventy years ago, there is even a reversal. This reflects the cohort effects in the history of American-Armenians. Respondents who grew up in the 1920s and the Great Depression were severely handicapped in terms of educational attainment. Starting with the outbreak of World War II and afterward, Armenian parents in the United States pushed their children to go to college and professional

TABLE 1.11
Frequency Distribution of Sympathy to Armenian Political Parties and Ideologies by Religious Affiliation

	Apostolic Armenian	Protestant Armenian	Catholic Armenian	Other (Non-Arm.)	No Religion
N = 584	(370)	(56)	(22)	(92)	(36)
Hunchag	1.1	0.0	4.5	1.1	0.0
Ramgavar	6.2	5.4	0.0	1.1	0.0
Tashnag	25.4	7.1	0.0	7.6	2.8
Neutral	29.7	23.3	27.3	9.8	11.1
Indifferent	19.5	37.5	45.5	54.3	63.9
Rejects all parties	9.7	12.5	18.2	17.4	16.7
(No answer)	8.4	14.3	4.5	8.7	5.6
	100.0	100.0	100.0	100.0	100.0

74   Armenian-Americans

schools. By then, it was easier to do so, besides they were not unique. Jews, Italians, and others of the "new" immigration did likewise (e.g., Alba 1985a, Cohen 1983).

When the educational attainment of the respondents is examined by their place of birth, holding constant their age, an interesting phenomenon is found. All younger cohorts show larger proportions of college and graduate school education, but the proportional increase is the least for those born in Turkey. For example, about 54 percent of respondents over sixty years of age who were born in Turkey have a high school diploma or less, dropping to 33 percent for thirty year olds. By contrast, the decrease for Armenians born in the Middle East is from about 80 percent for those over sixty to 30 percent for those in their thirties. The biggest drop is for U.S.-born respondents, from 54 percent to 12 percent for the same cohorts. This implies that the United States has been most conducive to educational attainment for Armenians in the last fifty-year-period. Those born in Turkey after the Genocide have had less of an opportunity to go to college. In between are those born in Middle Eastern countries.

Business ownership is the avenue for upward mobility and integration into the American economy for most Armenian immigrants. Nearly 30 percent of the entire sample said they were self-employed. Interestingly, there were no differences in self-employment between the Main Sample and the Snowball Sample in spite of the younger more assimilated profile of the latter. Several occupations have been popular with Armenians especially among the first and second generations. These are the (Oriental) rug business and

TABLE 1.12
Frequency Distribution of Religion by Ancestry

	Both Parents Armenian	One Parent Armenian
N = 576	(513)	(63)
Armenian Apostolic	69.0	25.4
Armenian Protestant	9.6	11.1
Armenian Catholic	2.9	11.1
Other denominations	13.5	36.5
No religion	5.1	15.9
	100.0	100.0

repairs, laundry and dry cleaning business, tailoring and dressmaking, and photoengraving. Mirak (1983) corroborates that Armenians in New York City became tailors, rug merchants, grocers, and dry cleaners. At the present time, Armenian immigrants, especially those from Turkey, tend to enter the jewelry business and a small enclave economy has developed in the Diamond District on Forty-seventh Street in Manhattan.

The U.S. census (1980) indicates that Armenians are overrepresented along with other historic middlemen minorities (i.e., Jews, Lebanese, Greeks) in small-business ownership (Waldinger and Aldrich 1990, 54-55). The business participation rates[68] of the fifty

TABLE 1.13
Frequency Distribution of Age by Place of Birth of Foreign-Born Respondents

	Turkey	Middle East	Soviet Bloc	Other
N = 233	(90)	(110)	(22)	(11)
20-29	3.3	6.4	4.5	0.0
30-39	6.7	17.3	4.5	0.0
40-49	5.6	27.3	22.7	9.1
50-59	6.7	25.5	40.9	45.5
60-69	28.9	13.6	13.6	18.2
70 +	48.9	10.0	13.6	27.3
	100.0	100.0	100.0	100.0

TABLE 1.14
Frequency Distribution of Education by Place of Birth

	U.S.A.	Turkey	Middle East	Soviet Bloc	Other
N = 563	(346)	(86)	(100)	(20)	(11)
Some high school	3.8	29.1	8.0	10.0	0.0
High school	22.8	23.3	30.0	25.0	36.4
Some college	22.5	11.6	15.0	15.0	27.3
College	23.4	17.4	27.0	20.0	18.2
More than college	27.5	18.6	20.0	30.0	18.2
	100.0	100.0	100.0	100.0	100.0

largest U.S. ancestry groups rank Armenians sixth at 94.5 (after Russian Jews at 117.4; Lebanese 106.6; Romanians at 104.3; Swiss at 104.2; and Greeks at 94.9). They are almost double the national average (48.9). In addition, self-employed Armenians rank thirteenth on mean income at $21,430 (average being $18,630).

In this sample, 1.4 percent of the respondents were in the rug business, 7.4 percent of their fathers and 2.7 percent of their spouse's fathers were in that business. Another 2.6 percent of the respondents were tailors, as were 6.7 percent of their mothers and fathers. A little over 1 percent of the respondents were in the jewelry business, together with 2.7 percent of their fathers, and 1.2 percent of their spouse's fathers. Three percent of our respondents were in the photoengraving business,[69] as were 7.5 percent of their fathers, 2.7 percent of their spouses, and 3.9 percent of their spouse's fathers.

Several respondents commented on being apprenticed with other Armenian photoengravers and being active in the union. A 63-year-old second-generation man describes:

> [My father] came to the City [New York] and obtained a job in a photo-engraving shop owned by Armenians. He became a member of the Photo-engraving Union. This was an important event for him. For the rest of his life he earned good union wages. He was a skilled etcher and was able to hold his job through the Great Depression. Those Armenians who now disparage unions should know that it was Photo-engravers Union wages that helped support the churches and other organizations in those years. Many Armenians obtained their college education

TABLE 1.15
Frequency Distribution of Occupation by Place of Birth

	Turkey	Middle East	Soviet Bloc	Other
N = 223	(89)	(102)	(21)	(11)
Traditional Prof.	21.3	15.7	23.8	9.1
Semiprofessional	9.0	13.7	4.8	18.2
Business owner	33.7	28.4	23.8	9.1
Manager	3.4	13.7	4.8	9.1
White collar	5.6	8.8	4.8	9.1
Skilled blue-collar	15.7	8.8	19.0	36.4
Semiskilled blue-coll.	2.2	1.0	0.0	0.0
Homemaker	9.0	7.8	14.3	9.1
Student	0.0	2.0	4.8	0.0
	100.0	100.0	100.0	100.0

because of their fathers' union wages. That was the case for my brother ... and I ...
I attended ... [technical school] then entered photo-engraving (stripper). My other
brother ... also became a photo-engraver (finisher). [Brother] and I were able to
enter the Union apprenticeship because our father was a member.

All this leads me to postulate that self-employment is an "ethnic" trait.
The experience of Armenian immigrants in New York and New
Jersey, whether in the past or at present, fits to some extent the
"middlemen minority form" discussed above. I will argue this point
further in chapter 3.

The survey supports the claim that Armenian immigrants to the
United States who arrived after World War II had more resources than
the earlier immigration wave. Tables 1.13 to 1.15 show the
distribution of foreign-born respondents' place of birth with age,
education, and occupation. The oldest immigrants came from Turkey
after the Genocide, 77.8 percent are over age sixty. They also tend to
be the least educated, 29 percent have not finished high school,
compared to 8 percent for immigrants from the Middle East. Turkish-
born respondents also tend to occupy blue-collar jobs more often, 17.9
percent compared to 9.8 percent for Middle Eastern-born respondents.
This can be explained by the deportations, massacres, and general
instability of Armenian lives in Turkey at the beginning of this
century. Although respondents born in Soviet Bloc countries tend to
have higher educational attainment than those born in Turkey, the
former tend to predominate in blue-collar jobs.

A caveat is in order here. The *embourgeoisement* of Armenian-
Americans should not be overrated, or too rosy a picture be painted of
their success story. Surveys often miss those who did not "make it" in
the system. The American Dream has eluded many who continue to
live modestly, not for lack of trying. Often physical and mental illness,
absence of or inappropriate skills and resources, even bad luck prevent
families from attaining their goals. The meteoric ascent of a few
Armenian-Americans and their national prominence in business,
professions, politics, and so on overshadows the painful and hard-
earned achievement, in small increments, of the majority.

The evidence provided by the sample of 584 men and women of
Armenian descent living in metropolitan New York and New Jersey
confirms the general events in Armenian history and the major trends

in U.S. immigration. It also supports the discussion on settlement of immigrant groups and their struggle for the American Dream. The assumptions of this study on assimilation and ethnic maintenance are borne out. The demographic profile of Armenian-Americans reveals that they are mostly middle-aged, predominantly from the first and second generation, about two-thirds have more than a high school diploma, and earn over $40,000 annually and are employed in professional occupations or are business owners. About two-thirds are affiliated with the Armenian Apostolic church, but about one fifth have left ethnic churches to join other nonethnic denominations or are not interested in organized religion. In the chapters that follow, I will describe "typical" patterns of behavior of Armenian-Americans and their ways of experiencing their Armenianness. I will also explain how they have, individually and collectively, created and perpetuated an Armenian subculture in the United States of America. I begin with the cornerstones of this subculture; the church and politics.

Notes

1. For example, Ferro and Mouradian (1982, 560) talk about "hantise de l'assimilation."
2. Several respondents in the study were reminded of the parallels, such as a young foreign-born professional woman who wrote: "Turks massacred us physically . . . [assimilation] is massacre emotionally, 'white' vs. 'red.'" Contemporary analysis of diasporan communities almost invariably allude to "jermag chart" (white massacre). See Pattie (1990, 26), Ordjanian (1991, 233) among others.
3. American Jews are often cited as a model of ethnic resilience because of their unique cultural and religious heritage. Armenians compare themselves to Jews because of several parallels in their history and culture, and hope to match their alleged ethnic cohesion and steadfastness. It is interesting, however, that the unassimilability of American Jews has been demonstrated to be more of a myth than an empirical fact (see e.g., Cohen 1983; Gans 1979; Steinberg 1981; Thernstrom 1982, 19). The results of a mid-1990 telephone survey of 2,441 households in which at least one person was Jewish or of Jewish heritage sponsored by the Council of Jewish Federation are similar to the findings of this study on Armenian-Americans. The survey indicated that in 43 percent of marriages after 1985 Jews married Jews, this is compared to 89 percent before 1965. Also, 31 percent of children under eighteen in mixed households grow up with no religion, 41 percent in other religions and only 28 percent are raised Jewish. See Ari L. Goldman, "Poll Shows Jews Both Assimilate and Keep Tradition," New York Times, 7 June 1991, p. A 14.
4. Even the ethnic press has reiterated the need for research, e.g. see Vartan Oskanian, "Research is Needed to Enhance our Knowledge about Ourselves,"

Armenian Mirror-Spectator, 15 February 1986, p. 2. Some of the most significant empirical studies in the social sciences on Armenian-Americans in chronological order are: LaPiere 1930; Warner and Srole 1945; Treudley 1946; Nelson 1953; Atamian 1955; Kernaklian 1967; Henry 1973; Phillips 1978; O'Grady 1979; Rustigian 1979; Der-Karabetian 1980; Davidian 1986; Takooshian 1986-87; Bakalian 1989; Der-Martirosian 1989; Ordjanian 1991; see Bakalian 1985 for other references.

5.   Armenians in Turkey were systematically discriminated against by the Turkish government. For example, the Armenian National Council (*azkayin joghov*) was outlawed in 1939, the Capital Tax of 1942 makes commercial and industrial ventures almost impossible, other laws required official permission to whitewash Armenian schools; Armenian history, including the Genocide, could not be taught in Armenian classrooms, and most forms of intimidation and harassment possible in civilian life were practiced against them. Most significantly, the violent demonstrations and looting of non-Muslim stores on 6 September 1955 stands out in the memory of the *Bolcetzi* as a frightening experience that could be repeated in the future (see Walker 1980, 372). It should be noted that up until the early 1960s, Istanbul had a viable Armenian community, a sizable professional and business class, an intelligentsia publishing literature and poetry and active in the local press. However, most of the college-educated *Bolcetzi* started emigrating as early as the 1950s. They were later followed by the rest of the population and those born in mainland Turkey.

6.   Kevork Imirzian, "Armenians of Istanbul: As the Once-vibrant Community Turns Increasingly Pale, the Struggle for Survival Continues in the face of Adversity, Attrition and Assimilation," *Armenian International Magazine*, November 1990, pp. 18-21.

7.   Both the national press and the ethnic press have repeatedly reported on Soviet immigration to the United States, for example, see *New York Times*, 6 December 1987, p. 1; *Armenian Reporter*, 26 November 1987.

8.   See also Sidney Heitman, "Parallels and Differences between Jewish, German, and Armenian Emigration from the Soviet Union," *Armenian Reporter*, 15 May 1986, p. 3; and "German and Armenian Emigration from the USSR," *Armenian Reporter*, 14 August 1986, p. 2.

9.   This information was supplied to me during my visit to Los Angeles in April 1990 by knowledgeable informants active in refugee rehabilitation services.

10.   This information was corroborated by Mr. Suren Saroyan, president of ANCHA, during my interview with him in New York City in 1984, and the late Mrs. Arpi Papazian, an active committee member in the New York area.

11.   The evidence is sketchy but the trend is clear. According to the 1980 U.S. census, 10 percent of foreign-born Armenian males have a four-year college degree and an additional 16.3 percent have completed graduate studies (of those born in Iran, 17.4 percent have a college education, and 24.6 percent professional education; of those born in Lebanon the figures are 9.6 percent and 15 percent respectively). For foreign-born females the proportions are lower, 7.9 percent have college and 7.4 percent more than college. The 1980 U.S. census also indicates that 26.6 percent of foreign-born males and 20.6 percent of foreign-born females have executive and professional occupations [comparable rates for American-born Armenians are 36.7 percent for males and 30.3 percent for females]. In a survey of 195 Iranian Armenian heads of households in Los Angeles (71 percent male),

16.9 percent had a college degree and 16.4 percent had professional or graduate training. Of these, 29.4 percent were employed in managerial and executive positions and 18.2 percent had a professional specialty (Sabagh, Bozorgmehr, Light, and Der-Martirosian 1989). In a 1989 survey of Armenian-American population of Pasadena (Los Angeles) found that 83 percent of residents were foreign-born, 11 percent had a college degree, 3.9 percent a masters degree and 2 percent a doctorate. The annual average income was $39,000 and 52.9 percent of sample owned their homes (S.C. Communications Group. *The Armenian-American Population in Pasadena: A 1989 Survey* [Whittier, CA, photocopied]; see also Vicki Torres, "Armenian Population Smaller than Pasadena Survey Expected," *Los Angeles Times*, 5 April 1990.

12. It should be noted; however, that in 1980, the U.S. census reported only 212,621 Americans of Armenian origin; a count based upon self-described cultural ancestry (Takooshian 1986-87).

13. According to one unpublished report (Los Angeles County Commission on Human Relations, "Impact of Soviet Armenian Immigration on Los Angeles County," report by Bobbi Kimble, 1989), 90-95 percent of Soviet Armenian refugees settle in Los Angeles. An estimated 200,000 residents of Los Angeles are of Armenian origin. Heavy influx of recent immigrants from Soviet Armenia and the Middle East (see Takooshian 1986-87) in the last decade or so have changed the character of the Los Angeles Armenian community. The incoming Soviet Armenian refugees and other Armenian immigrants have received widespread ethnic, local, and national coverage. For example see Pierre Papazian "From Bourj-Hammoud to Hollywood or 'To Live & Die in Los Angeles,'" *Armenian Reporter*, 19 February 1987, pp. 2, 4; *Daily News - L.A. Life,* 19 April 1987; reprinted in *Armenian Reporter*, 14 May and 28 May 1987; *New York Times,* 19 May 1988.

14. This figure is from the Public Use Microdata Sample File (5 percent) of the U.S. census.

15. The 1989 Pasadena Armenian-American population survey corroborates that only 17 percent of residents were American-born, 33 percent were born in Lebanon, 15.6 percent born in Armenia, 12 percent born in Syria, 8 percent born in Turkey, 3.5 percent born in Egypt, etc. The average number of years in the United States was 12.3. Armenians in Pasadena make up 5.16 percent of the city's estimated 13,250 residents.

16. Indeed, the census figures undercount the estimates of Armenian-Americans. For example, according to one authority on the matter, in 1970 there were about 65,000 Armenians in Southern California, especially the greater Los Angeles area (Avakian 1977a, 49). Surely by 1980, the number must have increased with all the immigration from the Middle East and Soviet Union.

17. Several respondents in the survey described their experiences of New York City, such as the seventy-six-year-old second-generation man who wrote: "Born and lived on the East side of Manhattan. In the apt we lived 22 out of 24 were Armenian."

18. Middle Eastern Armenians trying to obtain visas for the United States appear to wait out their hopes in Europe, in spite of major hardships. See article by Florence Avakian "New Breed of Armenian Refugees Flock into European Countries," *Armenian Reporter,* 8 October 1987, p. 21. A recent study has revealed that about 15,000 Armenian refugees awaiting permanent settlement are

stranded in various European capitals and in India and Pakistan. Plans are under way to help them immigrate to the United States because it is believed to be their only solution for a decent future for themselves and for their children (Armenian Assembly of America, *Armenian Refugees in Western Europe: A Profile, A Challenge,* Washington, DC, March 1988).

19. It is interesting to note that public opinion and the mass media in the United States, over the last century have been consistently restrictionist on the issue of immigration. In a content analysis of the American print media between 1880 and 1980, Simon (1985) found that the press continuously communicated a desire to reduce the number of immigrants coming to the United States and advocated the exclusion of different nationalities and people at all times; the list of undesirables changing with changes in peak tides of immigration and the provenance of the immigrants. In the last couple of decades, public opinion has remained exclusionist; Simon hypothesizes that if the general public dictated immigration policies, it is unlikely that the quota laws of the 1920s and restrictive statutes of the 1950s would have changed at all. Moreover, opinion polls find poorer Americans to be most hostile toward immigration. Lower-class Americans fear the competition of new immigrants in the job market, in housing, in social services, in education and in opportunities for social mobility. Immigrants represent a threat to their livelihoods and that of their children (Simon 1985, 222). Yet, it is remarkable that against this background of hostility and opposition, over 30 million immigrants arrived in the United States during this period, among them a few hundred thousand Armenians.

20. Similarly, Zenner (1982, 458) finds that the Syrians and the Lebanese, unlike other ethnic groups such as the blacks, Japanese and Jews have not been the object of major hostility because of their relatively small numbers.

21. It should be noted that there are no specifically negative stereotypes against Armenian-Americans like those of other ethnic groups. For example, blacks are said to be lazy or drug peddlers; Jews are said to control Wall Street and the Media; the Irish are stereotyped with drunkenness; Polack jokes assume Poles are dumb, uneducated; Italians are believed to be in the Mafia, and so on (e.g., see Helmreich 1982).

22. In popular fiction, Armenians are generally stereotyped as astute, crafty merchants. For example, in James Clavell's *Noble House* (Dell, 1981, pp. 144-45) the heroine, Miss K. C. Tcholok (for Kamalian Ciranoush Tcholokian) is of Armenian descent (third-generation). She is portrayed as a skilled negotiator with an inherited sense of business acumen.

23. Presently, it is more likely that poorer Armenians, those who did not achieve upward mobility, will suffer from the stereotyping of American-Armenians. As is the case with the Jews, "today's stereotype is the well-educated Jewish [or Armenian] professional" or prosperous businessman (Rosentraub and Taebel 1980, 212; see also Stockton 1983).

24. Armenians make up only a fraction of Los Angeles County's welfare recipients. In April 1988, 4,357 Armenian families with dependent children (Soviet and others) received welfare payments; they constituted 2.2 percent of the total. In April 1990, the figure went up to 7,132 families, that is, 3.3 percent of the total (see Viken Berberian, "Coming to America," *Armenian International Magazine,* June 1991, pp. 14-21).

25. One of my informants in Los Angeles told me that some sixty Armenian-

Americans work for the welfare department servicing the thousands of Armenian refugees, and the Los Angeles county court system employs several Armenian interpreters. In Pasadena, on the other hand, only fifteen Armenians are employed by the city, they make up less than 1 percent of the 1,600-member work force (See Vicki Torres. *Los Angeles Times*, 5 April 1990).

26. Of course, most of the Soviet Armenian refugees who have settled in the United States have become hardworking, honest citizens. Some have been exceptionally lucky, achieving fame and fortune in the short time they have settled here. A magazine article that portrayed five of these success stories reveals that these people have "made it" in a variety of fields with varying educational backgrounds. One was a fifty-six-year-old engineer and computer scientist who arrived in 1966; another is the owner of eight supermarkets who came in 1969. A young thirty-six-year-old man who arrived in 1977 is a jewelry designer and wholesaler whose estimated annual sales range between $10-15 million. Another man started off driving a cab in 1980 and now owns a garment sewing business with seventy full-time employees. The only woman in the article is a scholar who arrived in 1977 and is presently writing textbooks for Armenian-American schools. See Serge Samoniantz, "Soviet Armenian Immigrants Carve Path to Success," *Armenian International Magazine*, September 1990, pp. 18-20.

27. Los Angeles County Commission on Human Relations, "Impact of Soviet Armenian Immigration on Los Angeles County," (report by Bobbi Kimble, photocopied, 1989).

28. See *Armenian Reporter*, 2 March 1989.

29. In Lebanon, Armenians were stereotyped as smart, clever (in Arabic: *el Arman shatreen*).

30. For example, AGBU established a social service program in New York City in 1976 to help newcomers find jobs, housing, legal advice, and other basic needs. With additional federal funding, a program for teaching English as a second language and a six-month secretarial skills training course were also offered to all Armenians. The program was able to come to the assistance of hundreds of immigrants fleeing the political turmoil of the Middle East and the communist countries of Romania, Bulgaria and Soviet Armenia. It managed to survive initially in spite of severe opposition because of the sheer demand for help. In recent years, the program has succumbed to financial hardships caused by the belief that people should be self-sufficient and should not rely on welfare, whether it is federal, local or ethnic (see Bakalian, *Community Needs Assessment Report* [August 1988] — AGBU Social Services Program). It is noteworthy that the community press has reiterated similar views regarding the large influx of Soviet Armenian immigrants into California in 1987-89. It has been suggested that the Armenian social services programs that come to the assistance of incoming immigrants should be shut down in order to discourage further emigration from the "motherland."

31. Information supplied by Sarkis Ghazarian, director of the program in April 1990.

32. See ad in *Armenian International Magazine*, January 1991, p. 6

33. The vast majority of Eastern Armenians are presently scattered in the Soviet Diaspora, though a small number of their descendants are found in France.

34. I am indebted to Professor Nina Garsoian for pointing out these distinctions to me.

35. Even though Armenians trace their origin in the United States to the late

nineteenth century, the fourth generation of Armenian-Americans, that is the great-grandchildren of the earliest immigrant generation, is still predominantly young in age and proportionately small in size, while the foreign-born generation is relatively large because of continuing immigration. As an ethnic group, Armenian-Americans are considered relative newcomers to the United States of America when compared to the descendants of the early settlers who can enumerate at least eight generations of ancestors since independence (Gleason 1980, 56).

36. Bouvier and Gardner (1986, 9) report that before 1819, only about 250,000 immigrants settled in the United States. This is to be compared to the well over 52 million who came between 1820 and 1985.

37. It is interesting to note that an Armenian translation of Elizabeth C. Barney Buel's "American Citizenship" pamphlet was published by the Daughters of the American Revolution in Washington D.C., in 1926. An earlier version had been published in 1912.

38. For example, the idea of a melting pot was evident in the writings of J. Hector St John de Crevecoeur, *Letters from an American Farmer,* published in London in 1782 (for extracts see Gordon 1964, 116; Handlin 1959, 148-49; Scott 1968, 16-19).

39. This is a rare occurrence in American society. The exceptions are: the Hutterites (see John A. Hostetler and Gertrude Enders Huntington, *The Hutterites of North America,* [New York: Holt, Rinehart & Winston, 1967]); the Amish (see John A. Hostetler, *Amish Society,* 3d ed., [Baltimore: The Johns Hopkins University Press, 1980]); and the Hasidim (see Solomon Poll, *The Hassidic Community of Williamsburg,* [New York: Free Press of Glencoe, 1962]).

40. Other scholars have used the term integration for structural assimilation (e.g. Yinger 1981).

41. Kourvetaris and Dobratz (1976) tested empirically Gordon's ethclass hypothesis among three ethnoreligious groups — Greek Orthodox, Italian Catholic, and Swedish Lutherans. They corroborate Gordon's notion that people confine primary group relations to ethclass more than would be expected by chance alone.

42. Empirical evidence in the 1960s suggested that while ethnic groups of the "new" immigration had been acculturated, the process had stopped there. There was little evidence of structural assimilation at the time (for Jews see Kramer and Leventman 1961; Rosenthal 1960; for Italians see Gans 1962). In recent studies, indicators of structural assimilation such as nonethnic friendships and marriages and participation in ethnic communal activities and events show a totally different picture. Structural assimilation is well under way (for Jews see Cohen 1983; for Italians see Alba 1985a).

43. Abner Cohen (1974) uses *de-tribalization* and *re-tribalization* to explain the same type of process in African societies.

44. Glazer and Moynihan (1975, 1) reveal that the word *ethnic* did not make its appearance in English dictionaries until the 1960s.

45. Lynn Rapaport (1989) has found that children of the Holocaust survivors who were born and continue to live in Germany today use such subjective boundary markers to identify themselves. They deny "German" identity even though they may carry German passports, speak German, and be culturally assimilated. The Holocaust overshadows their lives and mobilizes them ethnically/culturally

(rather than religiously). This is not the case of Armenians and their descendants who survived the Genocide and have remained in Turkey. Their minority status is imposed upon them by their inability to become a Turk (a Muslim).

46. Arlene Avakian argues the same point in an editorial of a "feminist issue" of the literary magazine *Ararat*. She writes: "If people who do live outside the community identify as Armenians, does anyone have the right to question that self-identification? As a person who is the child and grandchild of survivors of the genocide, whose first language was Armenian and who was raised within the Armenian community, who has never chosen to be part of that community as an adult, but who presently identifies her Armenianness as central to her identity, I must argue that I am as 'real' an Armenian woman as anyone else" (1988, 4).

47. It should be noted that this definition does not include spouses of non-Armenian descent. In this survey, one completed questionnaire filled-out by a non-Armenian spouse was excluded from analysis.

48. In Armenian, the suffix *tzi* at the end of place names implies provenance, such as *Hayastantzi* (Soviet Armenian), *Bolcetzi* (Istanbul Armenian), *Haleptzi* (Aleppo Armenian).

49. Generation has been categorized in this study as follows: first, foreign-born respondent (except those who arrived at or below the age of six) also first generation or immigrant generation; second, U.S.-born respondent of foreign-born parents (includes those who arrived at or before age six) or second generation; third, respondent and one parent U.S.-born; fourth, respondent and both parents U.S.-born, or third generation; fifth, respondent, both parents and at least one grandparent U.S.-born, or fourth generation. Finally, the term *later-generation* is used to denote respondents with one or more U.S.-born parent(s) and grandparent(s). The rationale for including children under six years of age not born in the United States with the second generation is attributed to the power of the (public) school system and mass media in acculturation.

50. The country of birth of the foreign-born were grouped into: Turkey, Middle East, Soviet Bloc, and Other.

51. Religion has been classified into: Armenian Apostolic church, Armenian Protestant church, Armenian Catholic church, "other," and "no religion."

52. Ancestry is a dichotomous variable that measures the ethnic origins of the respondent's parents: both Armenian or mixed ancestry.

53. Variable Symparty was classified as follows: Hunchag, Tashnag, Neutral, Indifferent, and Rejects Parties. The differences between these nominal values are explained in the next chapter.

54. As I will describe in the next chapter, the Armenian Apostolic church in the United States and the diaspora is administered by two separate Sees or jurisdictions because of historical and political circumstances. Bitter conflict and animosity characterizes the relationship between the two. Since most Apostolics in North America choose to become members in churches affiliated with either the See of Echmiadzin or the See of Cilicia, it was essential to obtain both mailing lists from both sides.

55. Several organizations' mailing lists were also obtained, but these were not used (with one exception) because they were not comprehensive enough. The (Apostolic) master lists already included most of their addresses. One voluntary association's president had read about my research in the ethnic press and volunteered to send me their mailing list. Twenty names were sampled from it

and were included in the Main Sample. These tended to be more recent immigrants from the Middle East whose names were less likely to appear on the master lists.

56. Nineteen households in the Main Sample were not of Armenian descent. They had been put on the lists because their name ended with "ian" or they had attended a concert in an Armenian church or hall or some similar reason. Thirty-nine envelopes were returned by the post office, the time limitation for forwarding mail having expired, or the addressee having passed away. Six questionnaires were excluded from analysis because they were incomplete and the identification number had been torn off, making it impossible to call the respondent and complete the questionnaire.

57. According to Warner and Srole the "term *ethnic* refers to any individual who considers himself, or is considered to be, a member of a group with a foreign culture and who participates in the activities of the group" (1945, 28). In popular speech the word *ethnic* sometimes tends to have pejorative connotations. Here, I use the word *ethnic* more liberally, meaning simply people of ethnic descent who acknowledge their immigrant roots, irrespective of community participation.

58. For example, Chichekian (1987) finds that linguistic assimilation of Armenians in Canada depends first, on size of the ethnic community, second, on institutional completeness. Thus, Montreal and Toronto have the highest linguistic retention rates in Canada.

59. Robert Merton's (1972) analysis of insiders and outsiders in conducting research is relevant to my role in this study. I was born and raised as an Armenian in Beirut, Lebanon. Both my parents and grandparents were of Armenian stock from ancient Caesarea (Kayseri) in Turkey. My upbringing in Lebanon was atypical of most Lebanese-born Armenians. My Armenian identity was ascribed by the sociopolitical conditions of Lebanese society. As I was not sent to an Armenian day school, and as we did not live in an Armenian neighborhood, I was structurally removed from a more traditionally ethnic socialization. Consequently, even though my parents' primary relations were mostly with fellow Armenians, my own friends (personal network) were predominantly non-Armenian. Jerejian (1976), who studied differences between Lebanese-Armenian students attending Armenian schools and those attending non-Armenian schools, found that the latter were more integrated into the larger Lebanese society. This implies that I would have been categorized among the "more assimilated" Armenians in Lebanon.

60. In sampling the community activities, I tried to attend at least one event of each type that is routinely held in any given year, and is open to the public. This bars committee meetings of voluntary associations and private parties. My participation may be somewhat biased because it reflects my own interests. This means I oversampled lectures and concerts and only attended a token number of dinner dances and ladies guild luncheons. Nonetheless, from the list of activities used in this study (see chap. 3), I only missed sports matches.

61. Kendall's Tau c was used to test the strength of association of any two pairs of variables. It ranges in value from -1.0 to +1.0 and equals zero if the two variables analyzed are not related. The statistical package used in the analysis (SPSSX) reports the probability of association; thus if a relationship between two variables is significant at the .00001 level, it means that there is one chance in 100,000 that the observed association would have occurred by pure chance. It

should be noted that tau c measures are more conservative than Pearson's R measures of correlation, about two to one. This implies that the results of this study, whenever significant, are far from being fortuitous. An asterisk (*) is used above tau c measures of association to imply the relationship is significant at the .00001 level.

62. This issue is called multiple colinearity. For instance, variables Origin, Generation, Ancestry and Age tend to correlate with each other; thus, the later the generational presence, the higher the probability of respondents to be younger and have mixed ancestry. Similarly, variables Religion and Symparty are used as independent variables throughout the analysis, yet sacred culture and ethnic political culture are also used as assimilation (dependent) variables.

63. Armenian Protestants are estimated to make up 15 percent of the Armenian-American population while the Armenian Catholics 5 percent (see *Zoryan Notes* 3, n. 1, supplement [April 1988]).

64. According to one of the Armenian Catholic clergy I interviewed, their congregation consists of approximately 750 households in the study area. It is estimated that there are some 90,000 Armenian Catholics around the world.

65. It should be noted that the highest percentage of missing answers in the whole survey is in the Income category. This is not unique to Armenians. Income remains one of the most sensitive questions in survey research, even more sensitive than intimate sexual queries!

66. The median income of all white families in the United States for 1980 was $21,904 (Population Reference Bureau 1982, 35).

67. Gender was strongly correlated with Income (.23*) and knowledge of cooking Armenian food (.17*); otherwise there were only four less statistically significant associations in the study. Men were more likely than women never to attend Armenian church services (tau c .12 significant at .005), and more likely to report discrimination. On the other hand, women contacted their siblings more frequently than men (.18 significant at .0003), and more women disagreed that family needs are more important than the individual's (.12 significant at .0001). All the associations except the last one are in the predicted direction, and are corroborated by other studies (Crispino 1980). Faint echoes have started to surface among Armenian feminists questioning the patriarchal attitudes and behavioral forms expressed and sustained by Armenian communal structures (see Avakian 1988). I suspect these results hint at that direction. In any case, more systematic research needs to be done on the role of Armenian women in the maintenance of Armenianness. In a conference entitled: "Mother of God and Daughters of Hayk: Women and Gender in Armenian Culture" sponsored by the Armenian Center, Columbia University on 4 November 1989, I argued that communal forms in the expression of Armenianness lag far behind changes in individual lives; therefore, the question: "To be or not to be an Armenian Woman," is not such a formidable problem at the personal level because identities can be highly flexible and situational. However, at the collective level, Armenian-American women have to live up to idealized role models from the patriarchal past and beyond. Mother of God and Daughters of Hayk are incongruent images that mesh poorly with their daily needs and preoccupations.

68. The business participation rate = (# of self-employed)/(total # of persons in ethnic group) x 1000.

69. It is interesting to note that photography as a profession was not new to

Armenians immigrants. Miller (1981) has shown that photography was pioneered by Armenians in the Near East in the late nineteenth early twentieth century; because of the iconoclastic teachings of the Koran, Muslims were initially reluctant to adopt the use of this new invention.

2

Church and Politics

Two very important institutions Armenian immigrants carried with them to America as part of their cultural baggage were their religious and political institutions; more specifically, the three Armenian churches—Apostolic, Catholic and Protestant—and the three Armenian political parties—Tashnag, Ramgavar, and Hunchag. These historically intertwined institutions have had a significant effect on the lives of the Armenian-American population and subculture.

Communal life in the United States came to be organized around the churches. Immigrants would congregate initially in rented meeting halls or church buildings, but as soon as they had sufficient funds, they would buy or build their own edifices. These houses of worship doubled as locales for social gatherings; almost invariably, they were comprised of a sanctuary and a large hall (and kitchen) that became the hub of a burgeoning collective existence. Where there was a church, there was also politics. Armenian political parties from the start were an integral part of this emergent culture in the New World.

The church and political parties were essential organs for propagating divergent ideologies[1] about Armenians as a people; their ancestral origins, their raison d'être, and their future aspirations. The conflicting worldviews and the vested interests of clergymen, party politicians, and other players culminated in the schism within the Armenian Apostolic church[2] and the community at large. Consequently, internal competition, hostility, and animosity have characterized Armenian life in the diaspora throughout the twentieth century.

As supralocal formal organizations, the religious and political institutions provided links, both metaphorically and pragmatically, between men and women of Armenian descent in the United States and other Armenians around the world, weaving them into the diaspora. As a people, Armenians had traditionally been middlemen minorities (see chap. 1) who espoused a strong ideology of an eventual return to an autonomous homeland. Likewise, the early immigrants who settled in the New World at the turn of the twentieth century thought of themselves as sojourners (Mirak 1983). Though hopes for an immediate return were soon shattered with the Genocide and deportations in Western Armenia and the Sovietization of Eastern Armenia, as a collectivity, Armenian-Americans continued to see themselves as a diaspora, a stateless people scattered around the world.[3] In other words, the churches and the political parties have pushed and pulled the Armenians in diametrically opposite directions. They fostered unity between the diasporan communities, but within each community, they created dissonance and strife.

Armenian-Americans are at a critical juncture in their history. Throughout the twentieth century, while they were undergoing cultural and structural assimilation in their host society, they continued to sustain the ideology of an eventual return to an autonomous homeland. Now, the promise of that "free" Armenia is a definite possibility as a result of recent changes in the Soviet Union and the establishment of the Republic of Armenia. Will Armenian-Americans repatriate? What effect, if any, will the existence of the Republic of Armenia have on Armenian-Americans, individually and collectively? Will it increase or decrease the maintenance of their ethnic identities and subculture? What will future relations between Armenian-Americans and the spiritual homeland be like? Unfortunately, sociologists are not fortune-tellers, if they were, they might have become more popular. I cannot predict what the future will be like; however, a close examination of the Armenian sacred and political culture in the United States will provide the necessary premise for establishing new courses of action, new policies, and making projections. Here, I question the ideology of an eventual return, the significance of a diaspora, and the role and function of Armenian churches and political parties.

The New York survey confirms that Armenian-Americans are here, in the Unites States, to stay. They are ambivalent about the Armenian Apostolic church. On the one hand, they appreciate its style of worship, rituals, chants, but on the other hand, they find it alienating, unable to fulfill their contemporary needs. Moreover, they do not understand, nor care to know the differences between the various political parties because Armenian politics are irrelevant to their lives. Indeed, the analysis concurs with the critics[4] that both the churches and the political parties are divorced from present-day realities and their ideologies are vacuous.

Historical Background

In most ancient cultures, the sacred and secular components are often coterminous; for the Armenians this is even more so. The history of the Armenian Apostolic church[5] and that of the Armenian people have been fused together since the fourth century A.D. when the Armenians became the first Christian nation.[6] Moreover, in the fifth century, the Armenian church became autocephalous following a disagreement with its Greek and Roman brethren over the doctrine of the divinity and humanity of Jesus Christ.[7] Isolated from other Christian communions, a unique cultural heritage both sacred and secular evolved, and the fate of the Armenian people and that of the Armenian church became inseparable (see Dedeyan 1982; Mirak 1983, 180).

The union between church and state was reinforced after the middle of the fifteenth century, when the Armenian people became subjects of the Ottoman sultans. As a Christian minority in the Ottoman Empire, the Armenians came to be organized into the *Ermeni Millet* (in Turkish meaning "the Armenian race/community"). The *millet* has been defined as "a church organized into a nationality as a nationality organized into a church"[8] (Cahnman 1944, 527). The religious, political, economic, and social administration of the Armenian people eventuated under the leadership of the Armenian Patriarch in Constantinople. Though the manifest function of the millet was advantageous to the Armenians, granting them a measure of cultural and religious autonomy, its latent function was the creation of political inequality by increasing the social distance between the Armenians and their neighbors, thus encouraging all forms of oppression, institutional discrimination, and prejudice (Atamian 1955, 22 -27; Libaridian 1987).[9] The millet system affected the destiny of the Armenians until the beginning of the twentieth century and culminated in the Genocide (see Sanjian 1965).

In the eighteenth and early nineteenth centuries, the Armenians experienced a literary, artistic, and scientific renaissance. This new awakening did not spare the Armenian church from criticism. Some of the archaic and by then corrupt practices of the church were questioned, and new alternatives were sought. Given the inherent conservatism of the Apostolic church, and the proselytizing prowess of Roman Catholic and New England Protestant missionaries, a small proportion of the Armenian population in Asia Minor left the "mother church" to become Catholics and Protestants. The new converts, nonetheless, remained ethnically Armenian. The Ottoman authorities, recognizing these developments established the Armenian Catholic millet in 1831. This was followed in 1850 by the creation of the Armenian Protestant millet (see Dedeyan 1982; Tootikian 1981).[10] The Armenian Apostolic church retained the majority of its adherents, but the Patriarch was no longer the only spokesman for the Armenian people. For the first time in their history, Armenians came to belong to one of three separate religious denominations: Apostolic, Catholic, Protestant.

Armenians from all three religious persuasions immigrated to the United States, and like all immigrant groups their first effort at preserving their cultural heritage and identity was the transplanting of their churches (see Herberg 1960, 11; Lopata 1964, 210). Worcester, Massachusetts became the cradle of Armenian communal life in the United States. The very first Armenian church (the Armenian Congregational Church of the Martyrs) was founded there in 1881; the first Apostolic church was erected there in 1891; and the first political battles were also witnessed in Worcester (Mirak 1983, 183;

Megerdichian 1983,1).[11] Similarly, Armenian Protestants established
their own churches after discovering that they were unwelcome in
local Protestant congregations (Mirak 1983, 196; Tootikian 1981, 65-
67). In New York City, the first Armenian Protestant church began to
meet on a regular basis in 1897, and by 1923 they had their own
church building (Mirak 1983,198).[12] Armenian Catholics were
organized as a separate community in America relatively late. Small
parishes existed for some time in Detroit, Pennsylvania, and Paterson
(NJ). The Armenian Catholic Exarchate was established in New York
City, as recently as 1983.

At the present time, there are a total of 115 Armenian churches in
the United States (see table 1.1 in chap. 1). Of these, 53 are affiliated
with the Eastern and Western Diocese of the Armenian Church of
North America, that is, they are under the jurisdiction of the Holy See
of Echmiadzin (in the Republic of Armenia). Another 28 are affiliated
with the Eastern and Western Prelacy of the Armenian Apostolic
Church of America, that is, they follow the Holy See of Cilicia (in
Antelias, Lebanon). There are a total of 28 Armenian Protestant
churches, the majority (10) of these being in Los Angeles.[13] These
Protestant churches comprise a number of denominations; many are
Congregational, others are Presbyterian, Pentecostal, Church of the
Nazarene; still others call themselves Evangelicals or Brethrens. They
also vary in their emphasis on proselytism or evangelistic fervor, some
come close to resembling the southern right-wing Fundamentalists.
The Armenian Catholic (Eastern Rite) church is the smallest; it has
only six parishes (see *Armenian American Almanac* 1990).[14]

There has been a boom in church construction in the last few
decades reflecting the demand created by the influx of new
immigrants, the rising affluence of the parishioners, and their move to
suburbia. Constructing church edifices has been easier than preparing
officials to serve in them. A vast majority of the clergymen are
foreign-born and most have received their training in seminaries
overseas. Undoubtedly, this mirrors their worldviews and their
approach to their ministry; of course, there are some who have been
more responsive to American circumstances than others. Furthermore,
the congregations they serve increasingly consist of college-educated
men and women who demand sophisticated sermons and theological
arguments from their clergymen. There is only one Apostolic

seminary in the New World, Saint Nerses Armenian Seminary, in New Rochelle, on the outskirts of New York City.[15] On the other hand, according to the *Armenian American Almanac* (1990), there are two Protestant seminaries; Fuller Theological Seminary and Armenian Bible College, both in Pasadena (CA). Indeed, it seems appropriate to call the shortage of highly educated, well-trained clergymen in the Armenian church a serious crisis.

Modern Armenian political consciousness and political parties trace their origins to the late nineteenth century. During the final years of the Ottoman Empire, social, political and economic conditions in Anatolia had seriously deteriorated. Armenians, especially the peasantry, suffered from widespread corruption and oppression. Revolutionary political parties emerged when the reforms advocated by the traditional Armenian bourgeoisie and the Armenian Apostolic church proved to be ineffective. The most important party was the Tashnagtsutiun (Armenian Revolutionary Federation—ARF)[16] founded in 1890, whose goals were political emancipation and administrative autonomy for the Armenian people, as well as social-structural and economic reforms. The Tashnag party's agenda advocated the use of violence, and supplied *fedayees* [17] or freedom fighters to help Armenian peasantry defend themselves in Turkey at the turn of the century.

The nationalistic, socialistic platform of the Tashnag party appealed to the peasants, artisans, and the radicalized elements of the intelligentsia. In contrast, the commercial and industrial bourgeois classes were hostile to revolutionary movements. They did not want to antagonize government authorities and jeopardize their relatively advantaged position. They found expression to their interests in the Armenian Democratic Liberal party (ADL) commonly known as the Ramgavar party, established in 1921.[18] A third party, the Social Democratic Hunchagian party was established slightly earlier[19] than the Tashnag party. It advocated a more orthodox Marxist ideology, and was never able to attract a large following (Atamian 1955; Dedeyan 1982; Libaridian 1979; Ter Minassian 1984; Walker 1980).

Over the years, the political and ideological arena of the Armenian people has crystallized into two factions; the Tashnag and anti-Tashnag. As a political party, the Tashnagtsutiun commands the largest number of official members and can mobilize a wider following due to its revolutionary ideology, modes of recruitment, and operational tactics. The anti-Tashnag "side" consists of members and sympathizers of the Ramgavar and Hunchagian parties and a silent majority that call themselves *chezok* (literally "neutral," nonpartisan). The *chezok* do not necessarily endorse the Ramgavar or Hunchagian parties' platforms and agenda or identify with them, but are opposed to the militant ideology of the Tashnags (see Phillips 1978; O'Grady 1979).[20]

The main difference between the Armenian political parties at the time of their creation was the varying class interests each served. This is no longer the case for contemporary Armenian-Americans as the survey will indicate, though more economically and politically disadvantaged Armenians in the Middle East have found expression of their needs in the Armenian Revolutionary Federation. The short-lived Republic of Armenia (1918-1920) and the consequent Sovietization of the land is one of the major issues of conflict between the two factions (see Hovannisian 1971, 1982). The Tashnags made up the majority of the governing body of the independent republic. At its inception, the republic faced insurmountable problems. Besides the logistics of establishing a new state, the population, much of it refugees from the western provinces, was plagued by the ravages of war, famine, and disease. Moreover, the fledgling republic's powerful neighbors had a different agenda for its future. Besides, Western economic and military aid, which had been promised, failed to materialize. In 1922, Eastern Armenia formally became part of the Soviet Union.

Feelings of rejection and betrayal by fellow Christian nations in Europe, self-resentment on having relied on the West, disappointment at having lost an independent homeland, and frustration over their inability to change the situation, according to Atamian,[21] have resulted in the present Armenian worldview. "It is that *weltanschauung* which explains the non-rationality of the contemporary Armenian ideological conflict and the bitter, internalized self-aggression and self-hatred of the Armenian groups" (Atamian 1955, 251).

The Tashnags see themselves as the defenders of Armenian nationalism and identity, having fought against the Turkish tyrants and sacrificed many patriots to martyrdom. This gives them the vicarious sense of moral victory and courage that prevents them from feelings of inferiority and helplessness. A free, independent Armenia remains their political goal and raison d'être. It justifies the revolutionary doctrines, the strong esprit de corps among the rank and file, and aggressive relations with other Armenian groups. They perceive the "others" as cowards who did not fight the Turks. The emphasis is on values of self-respect, pride, patriotism, virility: all of them reminiscent of the nineteenth-century Armenian intellectual renaissance. Association with the Tashnagtsutiun is supposed to be more than a political party affiliation. It is identifying with the consciousness of a people, a people with a separate history, culture, and language (Atamian 1955). The Armenians who do not endorse the revolutionary values, militant tactics, and "terrorism" have come to form a collective ideology in opposition to the Tashnag party line. The adversary elements have been polarized in an anti-Tashnag stance, though they remain far from being an organized group or having a coherent political platform.

Having lost their independence and power base in an independent Armenia, the Tashnags were opposed to the Sovietization of their homeland. The weaker position of the Ramgavars led them to interpret the Soviet takeover more positively as the lesser of two evils. The Ramgavars rationalized that, as a small nation surrounded by powerful neighbors, Armenia was vulnerable. Thus, Soviet Russia was perceived as a protector of the Armenian people, their culture, language, and land, as well as a potential ally capable of punishing Turkey and taking revenge. The pro-Soviet policy of the Ramgavar party and the anti-Soviet policy of the Tashnag party is somewhat of a paradox. While a conservative, antirevolutionary organization (i.e., Ramgavars) with bourgeois interests supported the Soviet regime in Armenia, the socialistic, revolutionary Tashnags condemned it on the issue of nationalism. The two sides with their opposing political orientations and ideologies are split on the issue of Armenian national interests, each vying for the leadership of the Armenian people and claiming to speak for it. They have come through the years to dissipate their frustrations and hostilities at each other rather than at a remote, less accessible enemy.

After the Genocide, the dispersed Armenian refugees and immigrants abandoned hope of an immediate return to their homes and lands. The two political and ideological factions had to develop auxiliary organizations to fulfill the various functions required in a refugee/immigrant community. Besides the physical survival of the "starving Armenians"[22] the second most pressing task for the leadership became the maintenance of Armenian language and culture in host societies. Given the antagonistic orientations to Armenian national interests, the two factions duplicated their supporting organizations, a wasteful procedure considering the limited human and material resources. As a result, there are two churches, two women's auxiliaries, two youth/sports organizations, two charitable associations,[23] and so on, each affiliated with a political faction in nearly every Armenian-American and diasporan community. The adherents of each philosophy support their own activities and programs, almost totally avoiding the other "side." [24]

In the United States, the official schism of the Armenian community took place with the murder of Archbishop Tourian by Tashnag party members in New York City while he was celebrating Divine Liturgy on December 24, 1933. The archbishop was designated by the See of Echmiadzin (in Soviet Armenia) to assume the spiritual leadership of all the Armenians in America. The Catholicos, ecclesiastical head of the Armenian Apostolic church, was perceived by the Tashnag party to be under the control of the Soviets, therefore unable to assume the spiritual leadership of all the Armenian people.

The Armenian Apostolic church became the arena for the expression of conflict at the local level in various diasporan communities.[25] The church was said to be an instrument in the hands of Soviet authorities, dictating their political aims.[26] This incident split the Armenian-American community into two hostile warring factions. Members of the Tashnag party were expelled from the existing Armenian churches, forcing them to eventually build their own churches. The Tashnag congregation remained ecclesiastically independent until 1957 when it came under the jurisdiction of the See of Cilicia. Thus, the Armenian Apostolic church is united on religious doctrine, but it is administered by two separate bodies.[27] The murder of the archbishop is often given as a reason to justify the schism, but in fact it was the effect of a complex situation in which political, ideological, and social psychological elements were involved.

In 1956, there was further dissension in the Armenian diaspora. The newly elected Catholicos to the See of Echmiadzin came into conflict with the See of Cilicia as the two centers tried to increase their jurisdiction over the Armenian communities in the diaspora. The Cilician See came to be dominated by the Tashnag party while the opposing parties took up the defense of the See of Echmiadzin. Cold War politics were influential in the events; there were even allegations of CIA involvement which the Tashnag party has denied (see Phillips 1978, 142-55). An impassioned strife culminated in bloody battles between the two factions during the Lebanese civil strife in 1958.

With the end of the Cold War and other changes in the political climate between East and West, the political and ideological distinctions within the Armenian diaspora became blurred, and the rhetoric of strife and hostility mellowed. The Tashnag party came to accept Soviet Armenia as a homeland in the absence of the possibility of retribution for Armenian lands by the Turkish government in the foreseeable future and the ever-increasing threat of assimilation in the diasporan communities. The Soviet Armenian Republic, though not an ideal arrangement for the Armenian people, was perceived to be be an adequate solution, for the short term. There existed the possibility of salvaging the threatened Armenian language and culture and possibly of becoming a territorial base for an independent Armenia in the future. The Ramgavar and Hunchagian parties, on the other hand, recognized that Soviet Armenia was incapable of assuming the political and territorial aspirations of the Armenian people. Meanwhile, in the interest of better relations with the diaspora communities, the Soviet authorities made a number of compromises to Armenian cultural nationalism (Mouradian 1990; Libaridian 1979).[28]

The situation also changed in Lebanon, one of the bastions of Armenian political life in the diaspora (see Adalian 1989, 105). With the beginning of the Civil War in 1975, the three political parties, the Tashnags, Hunchags, and Ramgavars, were formally united and agreed on a policy of "positive neutrality" regarding the Lebanese crisis. This helped minimize the unavoidable loss of human lives and Armenian property, both private and public (see Libaridian 1979, 50). The resolution of the conflict within the Armenian-American community was not as successful. In the absence of any urgent reason to join forces, attempts at unity were plagued by lack of trust and the resurgence of old issues.[29] The reason behind the successful rapprochement of the Armenian political parties in Lebanon and the failed attempts in the United States can be understood by Georg

Simmel's proposition that conflict with an outside enemy increases cohesion within the group by providing a stimulus for change. I will elaborate on this point later in this chapter (Simmel 1955, 87-93; Coser 1956, 87-95).

The role of Armenian "terrorist" movements in the late 1970s and early 1980s,[30] in particular the ARA (Armenian Revolutionary Army, formerly Justice Commandos of the Armenian Genocide) and ASALA (Armenian Secret Army for the Liberation of Armenia),[31] have been analyzed as contenders for the political leadership of the Armenian diaspora. According to Tölölyan,[32] their attacks on Turkish targets were more a means for legitimating themselves in the eyes of the Armenian people than taking on their prospective, but as yet remote, enemy. The question is: Have these organizations been successful in awakening bourgeois Armenians of the diaspora to the plight of their less advantaged compatriots? Some analysts suggest so. Kurz and Merari (1985, 70) write: "The emergence of ASALA caused an urgent need for the more conservative streams in the diaspora to fight for recognition in world opinion" (see also Gunter 1986). What about the elusive Armenian Question: were the aims of the "terrorist" movements achieved? The answer is no. The government of Turkey has not as yet recognized the Armenian Genocide, nor, of course, moved toward retribution of land or property owned by Armenians.

In a content analysis of the evening news on American Network television, (ABC, CBS, and NBC) between 1968 and 1983, Ayanian and Ayanian (1987) counted forty-four stories mentioning Armenians or Armenia. They found that "if not for political violence, Armenians would have received essentially no coverage on the evening news during this period" (Ayanian and Ayanian 1987, 17). Coverage of the "terrorist" acts was able to increase "name-recognition," yet "the networks tended to reduce Armenians to terrorists (not freedom fighters).... [They] evaded the burden of investigation and education" (Ayanian and Ayanian 1987, 29). The question as to why these acts of violence were instigated was rarely asked, nor was there much discussion of the historical context (see also Saba 1989).

As a result of Mikhail Gorbachev's reform policies of glasnost and perestroika, the stage for the Armenian political theater has shifted to Soviet Armenia and the USSR since February 1988, where the scenes have been changing with dramatic speed. Soviet Armenians were the first to test the limits of Gorbachev's reforms. The rallies that started in the fall of 1987 over environmental issues eventually gathered momentum. Crowds of over one hundred thousand people—at their highest point even a million—were protesting daily in the streets of Yerevan. The rallies and strikes gave birth to the Karabagh movement and in February 1988 a group of intellectual activists formed the Karabagh Committee. It was also in the same month that the Sumgait pogroms in Azerbaijan took place, adding fuel to already raging fires.

The Karabagh movement was a struggle to reattach to Soviet Armenia a small (4,500 sq. km), mountainous piece of land, populated mostly by Armenians, and historically belonging to the Armenians until it was annexed to the Republic of Azerbaijan in 1923 by Soviet authorities (see Libaridian 1988; Mouradian 1990). However, the Karabagh movement became much more than that. It was a grass roots movement for radical change in Soviet Armenia. It was a protest against the inherent bribery and widespread corruption of the system and the local elites supporting the status quo. It rejuvenated nationalistic feelings, sparked interest in Armenian culture and history, and mobilized a whole nation, as well as other Armenians within the Soviet Union, to stand up for their rights as a people and as a nation (see Hovannisian 1988; *Armenian Reporter,* 23 February 1989, p. 18; Libaridian 1991).

In the midst of this social and political turmoil, an earthquake struck Soviet Armenia on December 7, 1988, adding tremendous physical damage. The earthquake focused world attention on Soviet Armenians as aid and money for reconstruction projects poured in. The political and socioeconomic demands of the people had to take a backseat, but only for a short while. In the meanwhile border clashes did not stop,[33] and in January 1990 Armenians were massacred again, this time in Baku. Finally, the people of Armenia triumphed when on May 20, 1990 they held their first free elections in seventy years, throwing the Communists out of power.

On August 4, 1990, the new government elected Levon Ter-Petrosyan president. And on August 23, 1990, the parliament declared its intention to secede from the Soviet Union. Landlocked, surrounded by unfriendly neighbors, and threatened by the military might of the Soviet Union, a formidable task faces the new leadership.[34] The stated goal of the Republic of Armenia is the well-being and survival of its people, something that it is believed can be attained through democracy and independence.[35]

It is too early to tell what the future holds for the Republic of Armenia. As the Soviet Union crumbles with bewildering speed, new opportunities, and of course pitfalls, open up for the Armenians. For the first time in almost a century, there is heightened optimism, hope that the dream of an autonomous homeland may be achieved soon. The Armenian people have turned a new page in their history. The Republic of Armenia is emerging as the legitimate "center" of Armenian life and culture. These changes have shaken the very foundations of collective structures and institutions in the diaspora. They question the sojourner's ideology of an eventual return; the rationale for Armenian political parties; and the role of the Apostolic church as the defender of the faithful. More specifically, they call for the reevaluation of the Armenian-American community's linkages with the new republic, and the schism within its midst.

Armenian Sacred Culture in the United States

It is the thesis of this book that assimilation and identity in the United States go hand in hand. Later-generation Armenian-Americans are less and less likely to know and practice the subculture of their immigrant parents and grandparents. Yet they continue to feel very strongly about their Armenian roots. Their expression of Armenianness is tailor-made to suit their individual personalities, their life-styles and the urban, postindustrial society they live in. I have also shown in the previous chapter that the historical conditions and ideological foundations of the United States made socioreligious subcommunities more likely to survive than purely ethnic communities. Therefore, it is hypothesized that the sacred culture is somewhat more resistant to forces of assimilation. Here, I measure the sacred culture with respondent's religious affiliation, frequency of participation in Armenian and non-Armenian worship services, attitudes toward the Armenian church, and maintenance of sacred traditions.

Sociologists postulate that in premodern societies, sacred beliefs and practices pervaded almost all aspects of one's daily life. I have shown that historically, being an Armenian meant membership in an

Armenian church: Apostolic, Protestant, Catholic.[36] An Armenian could not be a Jew[37] or a Muslim (Phillips 1978, 102). In the New York study, 64 percent of respondents were affiliated with the Armenian Apostolic Church, 9.7 percent with the Armenian Protestant church and 3.8 percent with the Armenian Catholic church. These figures are believed to be representative of Armenian-Americans in general. In spite of their continued identifications with Armenianness, the remaining 22.3 percent of respondents in the sample, who did not belong to any Armenian church, have gone a step further from historical tradition by separating their ethnic identity from their religious affiliation. Of these, 6.3 percent declared "no religion" and the rest were members of mainstream Protestant denominations (almost 11 percent) or the Roman Catholic church (3 percent).

In order to understand these changes in the sacred culture of Armenian Apostolics, I refer to Susan Pattie's distinction between religion and church. She defines religion as belief systems in spiritual life and the nature of ties between human beings and God or the supernatural; while church is the institution mediating and facilitating religion; it "includes the physical building, ecclesiastical hierarchy, doctrine, and services" (1990, 293). With increasing modernization, the yearly cycle of church traditions and celebrations take less and less time and are less likely to invade one's daily existence. Religious activities and the use of religious vocabulary become more and more specialized, distinct, "isolated and definable as a category of experience" (p. 294). Indeed, later in this chapter, I will show that two of the sacred traditions of the Armenian people are being forgotten. However, the church as an institution has remained durable. As mentioned already, it embodies both sacred and secular ideologies of the Armenian people. The lines between church and peoplehood/nationalism are blurred. This explains why "atheists, agnostics, and anti-clericals" attend Divine Liturgy, often several times a year; not only for weddings, baptisms, funerals, requiems *(hokehankist),* but also for April 24, and possibly *Vartanantz.*

I find Pattie's concepts most applicable to the immigrant generation, because for them their institutional affiliation is taken for granted. But they are less applicable for American-born generations, in whom religion, like ethnic identity, becomes voluntary, a choice individuals consciously make. In later generations, men and women of

Armenian descent are more likely to "shop around" for a congregation that will fulfill their needs in terms of style of worship, demographic composition of congregation, spiritual dogma, and so on. Therefore, as I will show, the Armenian churches, especially the Apostolics, need to become "competitive" in order to attract and retain adherents. From immigrant churches they need to adapt and become Americanized churches. The number of respondents who declared "no religion" or those who were affiliated with non-Armenian denominations provide evidence to the claim that Armenianness in America is becoming more and more individualized. People of Armenian origin want to choose their preferred mode of identity and their own particular way of expressing it. For some, religion may not even be a consideration; such is the case of a young professional whose Armenian paternal grandfather immigrated from Turkey. He would like to be ethnically connected to the Armenian secular community, but not to the church. Here are his comments:

> I would like to rediscover my Armenian heritage. As an Agnostic, joining a church is out, though I wouldn't mind attending functions at a church.

Pattie's London Armenian informants, predominantly from the immigrant generation, expressed the opposite of these sentiments. I quote from her work:

> We accept our church as it is. We don't go around shopping for the best church in the neighborhood, the one with the priest who gives the best sermon or whatever. Because it's not the particular priest who is important, it's the church and we have to support it no matter what the priest does or doesn't do. (Pattie 1990, 309)

Still, Pattie concedes that the future portends individualistic forms of religious affiliation and practice. Therefore, the Apostolic church in the Western diaspora, be it in England or the United States, is likely to receive increasing criticism from its members. She writes:

> Whereas some are satisfied and inspired by a church of atmosphere and ritual, others ask why they are not provided with intellectual food as well. The emphasis of some priests on nationalism (sermons on historical heroes, exhortations to be [metaphorically] soldiers for the Armenian nation) is welcomed by many while a vocal minority prefer more of Christian doctrine and spirituality. (Pattie 1990, 320)

I suggest that Gerhart Lenski's (1963, 23) distinction between *associational* and *communal* involvement is more useful in understanding the religious behavior of later-generation Armenian-Americans. The associational form of religious life denotes frequency of church attendance, while the communal form implies the confinement of one's primary group ties to one's socioreligious group.[38] Lenski has argued that with increasing Americanization of the immigrant communities (also increasing urbanization of the population, rising educational levels, and the spread of middle-class values), the associational aspect of religion increases. People in the third generation are more likely to attend church regularly than those in the first and second generation, even when class is held constant (Lenski 1963, 47, 55). At the same time, with increasing Americanization, the probability of friendships and marriage outside one's socioreligious subcommunity increases, therefore decreasing the communal influence. In other words, as the New York data demonstrates, the involvement of first- and second-generation Armenian-Americans can be characterized as communal; while in later generations, for those who consciously choose to invest their time and energy in what Pattie calls "religion," their involvement is more likely to be associational. That is, they are more likely to attend worship services regularly and to take that participation seriously.

Armenian Church Attendance

How often do Armenian-Americans attend an Armenian church? Simply put, not very often. There is almost a ninefold increase between the foreign-born generation (6.5 percent) and the fourth generation (56 percent) in the proportion of respondents who never attended an Armenian church during the year prior to the study (table 2.1). The increase in those who do not attend an Armenian church is steady and significant with each passing generation in America. It should be noted that foreign-born respondents are not frequent attenders either; most (40 percent) attend only "several times a year." Nonetheless, 33 percent of the first generation attend an ethnic church at least once a month compared to 23 percent of the second generation, 25 percent of respondents with one parent who is U.S.-born, 12 percent of respondents with two parents who are U.S.-born and 6.3 percent of respondents with two parents and at least one grandparent who are U.S.-born.

It is interesting to note that there are differences within the three Armenian denominations in mean frequencies of attendance. Apostolics are not frequent attenders. Any casual visitor to an Armenian Apostolic church would readily observe that it is rarely full on an ordinary Sunday, unless a requiem service *(hokehankist)*[39] is

TABLE 2.1
Frequency Distribution of Armenian Church Attendance by Generation

	Foreign-Born	U.S.-Born of F.B. Parents	1 Parent U.S.-Born	2 Parents U.S.-Born	Grandparent U.S.-Born
N = 580	(216)	(271)	(36)	(41)	(16)
Never	6.5	24.7	33.3	36.6	56.3
Once or twice a year	21.3	22.1	25.0	34.1	25.0
Several times a year	39.4	30.3	16.7	17.1	12.5
Once a month	13.9	12.5	11.1	2.4	6.3
Once a week	19.0	10.3	13.9	9.8	0.0
	100.0	100.0	100.0	100.0	100.0

TABLE 2.2
Frequency Distribution of Armenian Church Attendance by Respondents' Religious Affiliation

	Apostolic Armenian	Protestant Armenian	Catholic Armenian	Other (Non-Arm.)	Non Religion
N = 572	(366)	(56)	(22)	(92)	(36)
Never	7.4	12.5	22.7	57.6	58.3
Once or twice a year	21.0	21.4	22.7	28.3	30.6
Several times a year	41.3	16.1	27.3	12.0	11.1
Once a month	16.1	12.5	4.5	2.2	0.0
Once a week	14.2	37.5	22.7	0.0	0.0
	100.0	100.0	100.0	100.0	100.0

scheduled after the Divine Liturgy. Christmas and Easter are a different matter. Armenians may drive sometimes for an hour or two to partake in the ceremonial ritual, but also to see and to be seen. Only 14 percent of Apostolics attend about once a week compared to 38 percent of the Armenian Protestants (table 2.2). The Armenian Catholics are somewhere in between. A nonrandom survey conducted in metropolitan New York and New Jersey among Armenian Apostolics found similar frequencies of attendance. Of the 486 households that responded to that study, 22 percent said they attend "regularly," 13 percent once a month, 19 percent on religious holidays, and 20 percent for weddings and funerals *(Armenian Reporter,* 16 and 23 April 1987).

Respondents affiliated with other churches and those with no religion were more likely to attend an Armenian church because they were pressured by their families. It appears that they comply most often during high holidays and, of course, when there is a wedding or a funeral (see table 2.3). Even though third-generation Armenian-Americans may identify with their roots, they are reluctant to participate as often as their parents' generation in the Armenian world, sacred or secular. This is the case of a middle-aged second-generation mother who believes that her "[two] grown daughters are quite ambivalent regarding church attendance, but they love the Armenian Church and their Armenian heritage."

I attribute the differences in frequencies of attendance in the three Armenian denominations to varying church traditions. A favorite excuse among the Apostolic congregation for not attending Divine Liturgy is the length of the service. On a regular Sunday, Divine Liturgy is about two hours long, longer (three hours) on major holidays. Several respondents commented on the length of the services. For example, a fifty-year-old second-generation woman said: "Service should be shorter length of time!" Another reason for lack of frequent attendance in the Armenian Apostolic church is said to be the liberal attitude of the church in dogma and enforcement of strict observance rules. For example, one often finds a crowd of young men standing and chatting outside the church while the service is in progress inside. Others may go into the church, stay for half an hour or so, then leave. It has been suggested that this liberal attitude stems from the structure and organization of the Apostolic church. The extensive involvement of the laity in church administration, even to the election of the Catholicos, the head of the church, has decreased the social distance between the clergy and the faithful (see O'Grady 1979, 67-73).

The Armenian Apostolic church has been described as tolerant (Ormanian 1955, 100). In a study of the Armenian community in

TABLE 2.3
Frequency Distribution of Reasons for Attending Armenian Church by Religious
Affiliation
(multiple response)

	Apostolic Armenian	Protestant Armenian	Catholic Armenian	Other (Non-Arm.)	No Religion	Total
N = 473 (cases)	(344)	(48)	(19)	(43)	(19)	
Have always gone (190 responses)	85.3	10.5	1.1	1.1	2.1	100.0
Meet friends (81 responses)	76.5	14.8	1.2	6.2	1.2	100.0
Family expects it (36 responses)	63.7	8.3	5.6	8.3	13.9	100.0
Worship and pray (249 responses)	77.1	10.8	5.2	6.8	0.0	100.0
Enjoy singing (137 responses)	86.1	8.0	0.0	4.4	1.5	100.0
Make me feel better (137 responses)	87.6	5.8	2.2	2.2	2.2	100.0
Keep in touch with Armenians (261 responses)	77.0	11.1	3.4	6.9	1.5	100.0
Teach my children about Armenians (145 responses)	85.5	10.3	0.0	3.4	0.7	100.0
Attended wedding or funeral (34 responses)	26.5	5.9	5.9	38.2	23.5	100.0
Gone for holidays (14 responses)	42.9	0.0	0.0	35.7	21.4	100.0

Washington, DC, O'Grady found that the members of the Apostolic church held a wide range of beliefs and opinions on church doctrine and Christianity. As one of her informants told her, the Apostolics do not try to "intellectualize religion as the Protestant churches do. They emotionalize it" (1979, 60).[40] Likewise, one of Susan Pattie's informants in London, a woman in her early forties, an artist, made similar remarks:

> You see, I like the ritual. I don't want everything spelled out. I can't bear it.... I think it is the atmosphere which is created by [the *sharagans* (hymns)] ... the music, the liturgy is very beautiful and I like that—the fact that it leaves you free to think of yourself and just meditate, float about in your own mind. (Pattie 1990, 306-7)

Pattie explicitly specifies that Armenians are "born into" the Apostolic church; they "absorb" its tenets and doctrine, they do not "learn" them. With increasing intermarriage and assimilation, the church can no longer afford to be "absorbed" by osmosis. Presently, the Armenian Apostolic church is trying to institutionalize formal religious education for the youth; however, in the past many Armenians received their religious training in Protestant and Catholic Sunday schools (see O'Grady 1979, 60), remaining ignorant of the teachings of the Apostolic church, a fact supported in this survey. Typically, a middle-aged immigrant from the Middle East commented: "I don't understand *Badarak* [Divine Liturgy]." This respondent now attends a Seventh Day Adventist church in her local community. Though doctrinal beliefs in the Apostolic church are flexible, O'Grady found that by contrast, "beliefs in moral values are more conservative and well-defined, since moral values are taught not only by the church but also within the family" (1979, 62). This combination of factors produces an associationally liberal/tolerant but communally conservative mixture of religious influence for Armenian Apostolics.

It might not be far from reality to suggest that more people come to Armenian churches to attend secular activities than they do to worship and pray. A large proportion of Armenian-American collective events are held in the church compound (see O'Grady 1979, 34). The church actively encourages the development of "communal" ties among its members by scheduling a social hour or luncheon following Divine Liturgy. These face-to-face relationships and companionship fulfill significant functions for the immigrant and second generations.

Respondents' comments reveal the importance of this communal aspect of religion. For example, a fifty-eight-year-old, second-generation man points out:

> I grew up in the outskirts of Brooklyn where there was no Armenian church and very few Armenian families so I was raised with little outside influence. My wife on the other hand was raised in Washington Heights[41] where there was a very strong Armenian influence. Her friends were much more Armenian than mine. Because of this I feel the church was and is the only thing that can really bind and keep the Armenian community together.

Thus, if the manifest function of church attendance is to worship and pray, then its latent function is to create a sense of community, enhancing feelings of belonging and cohesion. This latter function seems to take precedence in the immigrant church. Not surprisingly, keeping in touch with the Armenian community received the highest number of responses (55 percent of cases, see table 2.3).[42] One can worship and pray in any nearby church, but Armenian immigrants and their children sometimes travel long distances to share the communal experience of an Armenian church. Outside the family, the Armenian church remains the repository of ethnic identity, affiliation, and the hub of social life (see Warner and Srole 1945, 218).

The findings of this study are corroborated by a survey conducted by AREC—Armenian Religious Educational Council of the Prelacy of the Armenian Apostolic Church of America—in 1985. In spite of the methodological limitations of the AREC study, it is useful to compare some of its results with mine.[43] A total of 344 questionnaires were answered by seventeen parishes belonging to the Prelacy. Because over half of the respondents were over fifty years of age,[44] additional questionnaires were completed by forty-eight young people under age thirty. Forty percent of the general sample attended Armenian church regularly, compared to 29 percent of the under-thirty sample. These percentages are much higher than those reported in this sample but can be attributed to the sampling bias.

Similar to my findings, the AREC study revealed that the Armenian church stands for more than just a place of worship. About one-fourth to one-third of the sample attended the Armenian church to socialize with other Armenians and perpetuate the Armenian culture and heritage. The report concludes: "This would seem to indicate that our churches fulfill a broad spectrum of needs other than religious." The

AREC survey further revealed the ignorance and confusion of the respondents about church beliefs such as life after death, the Nicene Creed, and the Holy Trinity. Nearly 50 percent did not know that the Armenian Apostolic church considers Jesus Christ to be truly God and truly Man. Though some of AREC's respondents were satisfied with church traditions, saying: "I'm devoted 100 percent to my church and fully *appreciate* it's lack of dogma," younger cohorts tended to be more frequently dissatisfied (italics in original). Forty-eight percent of the youth sample did not understand the *Badarak* [Divine Liturgy], the overwhelming majority (92 percent) of young people (i.e., the more Americanized) were more interested in religion per se and wanted to learn more about the Armenian liturgy. Considering the self-selection of these respondents into the AREC survey, these facts reveal only the tip of the iceberg.

With increasing Americanization, people are more likely to demand a basic understanding of the church liturgy, rituals, and doctrines, in contrast to the immigrant generation whose devotion to the Armenian church is taken for granted, as long as it serves its communal functions. A thirty-year-old woman, whose father is U.S.-born and whose mother immigrated from Syria, parted ways with the Apostolic church after a disagreement concerning her wedding ceremony. Her husband, being a non-Armenian and a nonbeliever in any organized religion, must have objected to some of the demands of the church.[45] Here are her comments, which illustrate the issues inherent in Armenian church affiliation that American-born Armenians face:

> We were not allowed to marry in my "supposed" church, unless he and his brother (best man) took communion, were baptized, and my husband promised to be a parishioner. We had numerous "talks" with my priest. It was hypocritical for us to marry there because it held no meaning to us. All the Armenian church cares about is procreating other "people" into their church, their way.

> I never cared about our church services growing up, I only went through the motions.... In College I attended services—basically Catholic geared—and I never enjoyed anything so much. There was real communication, discussion, and singing. All in understandable English, needless to say.

> I am so turned off by the Armenian church, as are a lot of people my age. Perhaps if I'd married an Armenian, we would be into the "church thing" now.

There is mounting evidence that the Armenian church needs to accommodate the growing numbers of Armenian-Americans who may continue to enjoy the communal involvement, like their parents, but over and above that, want to emphasize the devotional/associational component of the church.

Style of worship depends on individual needs and preferences. Generally, people of Armenian descent dissatisfied with the Armenian Apostolic church have searched elsewhere for their spiritual needs. A forty-year-old second-generation man wrote, "I attend non-Armenian church regularly. I go to Armenian church only on special occasions for family sake. I attend Baptist church. It is a Bible-preaching church. Armenian [Apostolic] churches are too liberal."

Several respondents deplored the lack of evangelistic fervor in the Armenian Apostolic church. Many of those were born-again Christians, but not exclusively so. A fifty-five-year-old third-generation woman wrote that her family supported the Armenian National church for thirty-two years but has decided to join the Reformed Church of America because "the people are sincere, not status conscious and love each other. The minister is truly a 'ministering minister.'" Another woman, thirty-nine years of age, who like her mother is U.S.-born attends an Episcopal church, replied, "Initially, because my husband is of the Episcopal faith. Now, because I find the sermons more relevant to my needs than the sermons in the Armenian church." Indeed, one should ask, where are the Bible study sessions, the explanations of the liturgy, the history of the Armenian church, discussions on the essence of Christianity? These events are so rare in the Apostolic church that they often go unnoticed and unattended.

The Armenian intelligentsia too has been increasingly critical of the Apostolic church. For example, Anahid Ter Minassian has observed that the Armenian church is facing a severe crisis in authority, vocation, discipline, and intellectual arena.[46] Similarly, Khachig Tölölyan (1988) has argued that the Armenian Apostolic church has neglected a metaphysical dialogue with its sacred traditions.[47] It has failed to produce a theology of exile, to reinterpret dogma. Islam has been the "other" of Armenian Christianity since the fourteenth century, a kind of a buffer state that has sheltered the Armenian church from outside influences, including positive ones. The fusion between church and state, indistinguishable for Ottoman and later Middle Eastern Armenians, has produced a politicized identity that is alien to symbolic Armenian-Americans. Furthermore, the Armenian church has not taken a position vis-à-vis divorce, homosexuality, gambling, abortion, nuclear war, or any of the contemporary issues that puzzle and concern modern men and women.[48] There is a growing concern among American-born Armenians that the Apostolic church needs to become more relevant to individuals living in postindustrial societies. It needs to update its sacred traditions and reinterpret them instead of being a blind conformist to tradition.

The most comprehensive critique comes from theologian Vigen Guroian, a third-generation Armenian-American. Guroian argues that the Armenian Christian world died in 1915 along with 1.5 million Armenians and the millet system. Yet, the Apostolic church claims it is the "soul of the nation" and projects the illusion that church and nation still function in unison.[49] It has become an instrument for national aspirations. In other words, in preserving Armenianness, the church is converted to a custodian for folk dance, food, artifacts, rituals, etc. Guroian characterizes the present status of the church as "secular religion of ethnicity." Then he asks: how does such a church "differ from the Girl Scouts, the local garden club, Republican club, or health spa?" His answer is that the church must be something more, something greater than just a vehicle for perpetuating Armenianness. It must have a biblical mission, a spiritual essence. Guroian[50] (1990, 26) advocates a diaspora theology that would acknowledge, on the one hand, that it is permanent because most Armenian-Americans will never return to a homeland, and on the other hand, that the diaspora is transitional because it is a phase in the process of acculturation into American life.

I find Guroian's observations on "unity" within the Apostolic church highly pertinent to my thesis (see discussion below and table 2.10). His reflections were spurred by a debate he witnessed at a national meeting of parish representatives. I quote, in full, a passage from his book, *Incarnate Love*:

The Armenian Church's reason for being has been misunderstood by its own people. Never once in all the debate was it argued: "Unity must be achieved because the people of God, who are called to holiness, must never do such violence to the body of their Lord." Nor did even one member say in so many words: "We cannot go on dividing our Lord's garments and crucifying him on a cross of ungodly political controversies." Instead, one heard: "We must have unity in order to save ourselves." By this was meant "save our ethnic identity." The Church, however, does not exist in order to save anyone's ethnicity. If Armenians continue to view their church as the means to such an end, they will not only fail to achieve unity in America; they also will fail to retain the great numbers of American-born Armenians now and in the future. (Guroian 1987, 170)

Indeed, the statistical evidence provided by the New York survey confirms Guroian's predictions.

Alternate Church Attendance

Are Armenian-Americans more likely to attend a non-Armenian church? Only 3 percent of respondents affiliated with the Apostolic church attend a non-Armenian church almost always, 16 percent of the Armenian Protestants, 46 percent of the Armenian Catholics, 63 percent of those who are affiliated with "other" denominations. Only 8 percent of those who profess no religious persuasions attend an alternate church some of the time, none of them frequently. Apostolics have no set preferences in attending an alternate church, some attend Roman Catholic churches (16 percent), some Protestant churches (15 percent). On the other hand, 39 percent of Armenian Protestants attend "American" Protestant churches, and 59 percent of Armenian Catholics attend Roman Catholic churches. The "other" category consisted mostly of members of mainstream Protestant denominations (71 percent).

At the turn of the century, Mirak estimated that approximately 80 percent of the Armenian immigrants in the United States belonged to the Apostolic church, while the Protestants made up the remaining 15 to 20 percent. The Armenian Catholics who came to America at that early date were too few to make up a separate community (see Mirak 1983, 195).[51] Given the estimates for the early twentieth century provided by Mirak and those of the New York study in religious affiliation, the attrition rate of the Armenian Protestant church can be calculated to be, in the least, double that of the Armenian Apostolic church.[52] Conversions to mainstream Protestant denominations were easier for the Armenian Protestants.[53] For example, a fifty-six-year-old woman said: "My father's family were devout Evangelicals,

making it easier to assimilate with the local Congregational church."
Another forty-seven-year-old second-generation woman wrote: "I am
a Presbyterian by birth—as were my parents (both Armenian). My
grandparents adopted this religion." Mirak's historical evidence
corroborates these conclusions:

> [The] Apostolic Church stressed the preservation of the old culture in the New
> World. Repeatedly, the Apostolic priests emphasized fidelity to Armenian
> traditions, the language, the family, and marriage within the group. By contrast, the
> Protestants acted as a willing acculturating mechanism in the New World. The
> Protestants did not emphasize the need to keep the old language and culture.
> Rather, while seeking to bring the Armenians to Christ, they promoted the adoption
> of New World and American ways. (1983,198-99)

Since Armenian Catholics attend Roman Catholic churches and
Armenian Protestants attend Presbyterian, Episcopalian,[54] and other
Protestant denominations (see chap. 1 for percentages), these results
confirm Will Herberg's (1960) thesis. Herberg argued that individuals
have a need to belong in some type of a community. At the turn of the
century, this need had been fulfilled by affiliation with an immigrant
group. However, with increasing assimilation by midcentury, religious
congregations were replacing immigrant communities as social
anchors. Herberg explains:

> To find a place in American society increasingly means to place oneself in one or
> another of these religious communities. And although this process of self-
> identification and social location is not in itself intrinsically religious, the mere fact
> that in order to be "something" one must be either a Protestant, a Catholic, or a Jew
> means that one begins to think of oneself as religiously identified and affiliated.
> (1960, 56)

The tripartite melting pot, however, excludes adherents of Orthodox
churches. Though a minority in the United States, an Orthodox
community free of ethnic colorings has been suggested as a fourth
division in Herberg's model because of doctrinaire and stylistic
differences with the Protestants and Catholics (see Kayal 1970, 459-
60; Guroian 1987, 166-78).

There is no evidence of Pan-Orthodoxy in America in the near
future. None of the respondents said they belonged to an Orthodox
church other than the Armenian Apostolic church, and only 2.4
percent said they occasionally attended Greek, Russian, or Bulgarian
Orthodox church services because it was their spouse's religion or

they lived close to such a church. The Armenian Apostolic clergy I interviewed were opposed to the idea of American Orthodoxy. As one clergyman told me: "We fear cutting the tie to the Middle East. We have to keep the Armenian church tied to its patrimony." Moreover, the other ethnic Orthodox churches are equally reluctant to advocate Pan-Orthodoxy (see Kayal 1970; Scourby 1980; Moskos 1989, 34-35). Herberg's tripartite model remains viable (see also Kayal 1983, 49).

What is the rationale for attending a non-Armenian church? Respondents affiliated with Armenian denominations cite "convenience" as the prime cause for attending a non-Armenian church (23 percent for Apostolics and Protestants, 30 percent for Catholics) while those with "other" affiliations cite membership (45 percent). Other reasons such as "spouse's church" are less significant for those belonging to ethnic churches, except for those with "no religion" (14 percent).[55] Doctrinaire reasons such as appreciating the teachings of a church or enjoying the service are least important for Apostolics. Less than 3 percent of Apostolics are members of non-Armenian churches; this figure increases to almost 8 percent for Armenian Protestants, and 30 percent for Armenian Catholics (see table 2.4).

Mixed ancestry and generational presence in the United States do not necessarily increase a person's attendance in an alternative church, but do open the door to those leaving organized religion. Interestingly,

TABLE 2.4
Frequency Distribution of Rationale for Attending Alternate Church by
Religious Affiliation

	Apostolic Armenian	Protestant Armenian	Catholic Armenian	Other (Non-Arm.)	No Religion
N = 559	(364)	(52)	(20)	(87)	(36)
Convenience	23.1	23.1	30.0	14.9	5.6
For Teachings	6.3	15.4	15.0	19.5	2.8
Member	2.7	7.7	30.0	44.8	2.8
Spouse's church	5.2	1.9	5.0	10.3	13.9
Special event	7.7	11.5	0.0	3.4	8.3
Not applicable	54.9	40.4	20.0	6.9	66.7
	100.0	100.0	100.0	100.0	100.0

those in later generations were not more likely to attend an alternate church, the correlation was not statistically significant. Yet, 16 percent of respondents who had an Armenian mother and father "never" attended an Armenian church compared to 53 percent of those with mixed ancestry. Also, while 27 percent of the former attended an Armenian church at least once a month, only 15 percent of the latter did so. Moreover, 68 percent of those with two Armenian parents "hardly ever" attend an alternate church compared to 53 percent of those with one Armenian parent. Generally, those who attend "most frequently" are most likely to be children of mixed ancestry (14 percent vs. 26 percent). This suggests that a generational decrease in Armenian church attendance does not necessarily mean a generational increase in alternate church attendance. The relationship between an individual's ancestry and church affiliation is not a simple one; an increase in intermarriage does not increase affiliation in non-Armenian denominational congregations. Rather, I hypothesize that the "no religion" category is more likely to increase in the future.

While almost none of the respondents gave any reasons to justify their attending an Armenian church, many did write to explain how they started attending a non-Armenian church. Few wished they could attend Armenian church more frequently; such was the case of a eighty-five-years-old foreign-born woman who said, "I depend on my family to take me, otherwise I'd go more often." The most frequent reason given for attending non-Armenian church was distance from home,[56] especially if the family has young children and is desirous of giving them a Christian education.[57] For example, a seventy-three-year-old woman, who immigrated as a child, attends a Baptist church at present. She wrote: "I started Sunday School in a Baptist church near our home at the age of 13. My friends had tried for quite a while to get me to go, my mother finally decided to let me rather than no religion training at all."

Another sixty-four-year-old second-generation woman who also goes to a Baptist church explained that she grew up in Maine where there were no Armenian churches.[58] Such is the case of a forty-seven-year-old second-generation woman who wrote: "I believe in a local church. If there was an Armenian Presbyterian-Protestant church in our community, I would go there.... Nearest [Armenian] church is 73 miles one way. A thirty-year-old third-generation woman similarly said: "When we were young we moved to a new town and began to attend the Trinity Reformed Church. My parents said it was due to convenience. The Armenian church was approximately 35 minutes away by car. Nevertheless, we visited St ... Armenian Church in ... , NJ 2-3 times per year and we were able to make a few friends through the years."

Like ethnic identity, attending an ethnic church is situational. Most of all, it must be physically feasible. A sixty-three-year-old second-generation woman who lived in Ohio for thirty years before retiring in New York City where she grew up, said she used to attend the local Presbyterian church in Ohio because "it was close to our home and the closest Armenian church was 2 hrs away." She now attends an Armenian church. A forty-five-year-old man who with his mother are U.S.-born, wrote: "Was brought up in the Episcopalian church. Have regularly attended the Armenian church only in the last 10 years and since our children started Sunday School." It might be relevant to mention that this man's wife is also of Armenian descent. He and his family might have behaved differently if she was not.

Attitudes Toward Armenian Church

In response to attitude statements on the Armenian church (table 2.5), about 55 percent of the New York sample agreed with the first statement: "If the Armenian Church does not use English in its services, the American-born youth will stop coming to church." This is to be expected because 25 percent of respondents do not speak and 60 percent do not read and write Armenian, and the percentages are much higher with later generations and younger cohorts. Only about 30 percent of respondents (mostly foreign-born) do not want to change the church language. Another 15 percent have no opinion, most of them in the third and fourth generation. I suspect that these are people who are so alienated from the church that such issues do not even command their attention or concern. The generational status, the age cohort, the ancestry, the socioeconomic background were not significantly correlated with the first statement.

Several respondents would have agreed with the thirty-five-year-old second-generation man who said: "the language used in church is, I think, irrelevant to the youth." It should be noted that the language of the Divine Liturgy in the Apostolic church is in classical Armenian; it is not even fully understood by those who speak conversational Armenian. However, there is a reluctance to use English exclusively. At present, in most churches the gospel readings and the sermon are often bilingual. There are some who believe that maintaining the use of the Armenian language is essential for identity.[59]

Similarly, about 51 percent of the sample agreed with the second statement that said, "Armenian priests should preach only the Holy Scriptures in their sermons and not concern themselves with Armenian issues." Respondent's education (.19*), occupation (.16*), age (.15*) and not generational presence in the United States were most significantly associated with this statement. It is very interesting that the higher the educational level, the less the respondent advocated a separation of church and state. This is contrary to assumptions in the ethnicity literature that the higher the socioeconomic background the less the ethnic commitment. Thirty-one percent of those who did not finish high school wanted to keep the ethnic component in the church,

TABLE 2.5

Frequencies of Respondents Scoring "High" (Ethnic Position) on Four Attitude Measures of Sacred Culture by Generation

(in percent)

	Foreign-Born	U.S.-Born of F.B. Parents	1 Parent U.S.-Born	2 Parents U.S.-Born	Grandparent U.S.-Born
N = 579-582	(216)	(272)	(36)	(41)	(16)
Statement 1	36.6	27.6	30.5	17.1	31.3
Statement 2	51.8	47.6	58.3	58.4	53.3
Statement 3	81.6	62.1	44.4	48.8	37.5
Statement 4	76.6	43.3	38.9	29.3	18.8

Statement 1: "If the Armenian Church does not use English in it services, the American-born youth will stop coming to church."

Statement 2: "Armenian priests should preach only the Holy Scriptures in their sermons and not concern themselves with Armenian issues."

Statement 3: "It is every Armenian's duty to support the Armenian national church morally and financially."

Statement 4: "Our people should get their families to the Armenian church on Sundays, even if it is far from one's home."

as did 42 percent of those with high school, 46 percent of respondents with some college, 55 percent of those who completed college, and 65 percent of those with more than college education. Similarly, traditional professionals were most likely to endorse Armenian nationalism in the church. Younger age cohorts were more likely to hold an ethnic position. About 59 percent of those below age forty disagreed to separation of sacred from secular, compared to 33 percent of those above seventy years of age. These results are hard to interpret, except to suggest that there is attitudinal, if not behavioral, support for the continuation of Armenian churches.

Overall, 67 percent of the sample concurred that "it is every Armenian's duty to support the Armenian National church morally and financially." Least likely to agree were those who were affiliated with non-Armenian churches (.41*), those in later generations (.27*), and those indifferent to Armenian political ideologies (.24*). Almost 54 percent of the sample agreed that "our people should get their families to the Armenian church on Sundays even if it is far from one's home." Again, those least likely to agree were those in nonethnic religious categories (.39*), those in later generations (.38*), those with higher education (.24*), and those indifferent to ethnic politics (.20*). There is about a 50 percent drop between the foreign-born generation and the fourth generation in willingness to support the

TABLE 2.6
Frequencies of Respondents Scoring "High" (Ethnic Position) on Four Attitude Measures of Sacred Culture by Religious Affiliation
(in percent)

	Apostolic Armenian	Protestant Armenian	Catholic Armenian	Other (Non-Arm.)	No Religion
N = 572-574	(370)	(56)	(21)	(92)	(35)
Statement 1	81.9	46.4	85.7	27.2	34.3
Statement 1	67.1	58.9	54.5	12.2	17.1

Statement 1: "It is every Armenian's duty to support the Armenian national church morally and financially."
Statement 2: "Our people should get their families to the Armenian church on Sundays even if it is far from one's home."

church. The drop is even greater for attending an Armenian church in spite of distance; from 77 percent for foreign-born to 19 percent for fourth generation.

Overall, respondents were more likely to strongly agree that it is every Armenian's duty to support the Armenian church than they were to support the attitude that families should attend Armenian church irrespective of the distance because the latter is more demanding. One can support the church by occasional attendance and sending in contributions, but going every Sunday to church is a different matter (see tables 2.5 and 2.6). As mentioned above, several respondents became members of non-Armenian churches primarily because they lived far away from an Armenian church. These responses are in the predicted direction. It should be noted that in the study area there are a total of nineteen Armenian parishes which makes it geographically feasible for most (especially the Apostolics) to attend regularly, unlike Armenians living in Knoxville (TN) or Charleston (SC) who, of course, have a valid excuse not to.

Though not without criticism on the efficiency of the Armenian church in America, respondents in the survey were aware of the dual role of the church as a preserver of sacred and secular culture. However, it should be noted that this support comes overwhelmingly from the first and second-generations. A fifty-four-year-old second-generation man wrote:

> The church is the instrument that has kept the people together all these years. (Even though I am an atheist I make donations to the church because it is the center of our people).... To keep the sheep in the church, the church will have to lighten up, English sermons, priest that can relate to young people, you have to sell the church as a product to keep the people coming.

Another second-generation respondent wrote:

> I also firmly believe that the Armenian church is the most important part of our Ethnicity.... The Armenian church is unique. It will keep Armenians Armenian.

And again, a forty-year-old man who with his mother are U.S.-born wrote:

> I wanted to point out that, although we are relatively inactive in Armenian circles, we do feel very close to the church (which is a considerable distance from our home). We feel that the church serves both spiritual and cultural functions. The

church is the glue that preserves the Armenians' ethnic identity in this country. The church and family are very much intertwined and lets hope it stays that way.

The Armenian Apostolic church in the United States, more than the Armenian Catholic and Protestant churches, has taken on the responsibility[60] of preserving the Armenian culture, but it is also better equipped to do so beyond the immigrant generation. The Apostolic church has its unique sacred traditions. The Armenian Protestant and Catholic churches, on the other hand, risk losing their distinctiveness once their ethnic component is removed. The Armenian Protestant church, for instance, contends that the role of the church is not to be a guardian of the secular culture: the history, the language, the arts, etc. An Armenian Protestant pastor pointed out to me during an interview that the main function of his church is "the provision of spiritual needs of the Armenian people." He went on to add: "The 'mother [Apostolic] church' perceives the church as a cultural enhancer in a foreign land.... It is not the church's responsibility to strengthen the culture. Schools and clubs should not be run in conjunction to the church. They should be separate."

Nonetheless, an ethnic church operating under the principle of religious distinctiveness is a more acceptable form of diversity than ethnic separateness (see Kayal 1973, 417); that is, American society encourages ethnic communities to become church communities. The case of the Melkite Church in America is illuminating. Though the Melkite Church is in communion with the Vatican, it is not a Latin but an Eastern Rite church, historically the church of the "Catholics" of the Near East. In the United States, the Melkites, like most immigrants wanting to be socially acceptable and upwardly mobile, latinized their religious traditions to become doctrinally and stylistically similar to any Catholic church in America. Instead of a religiously separate church, they became an ethnic church like the Italian Catholics or Polish Catholics. They substituted a new ethnic/national identity for the religious one. However, becoming Syrian Catholics was in the long run more vulnerable to assimilation (see Kayal 1970, 1983).

The Armenian Apostolic church in the United States has been the primary instrument by which structurally and culturally ethnicity is translated into behavioral expressions (Kernaklian 1967, 91). It has been more successful in retaining its adherents than the Armenian

Protestants and Catholics and continues to claim the biggest proportion of those who identify as Armenians in the diaspora (see Phillips 1978, 278). However, it cannot afford to rest on its laurels. The New York data suggests that later-generation descendants are less likely than their parents and grandparents to take their religious affiliations for granted. Mirak explains the inherent conflict in the Apostolic church: "[The Apostolic church] stood staunchly and resolutely for the preservation in toto of the Old; this was its historic justification, its rationale, and a source of its weakness" (1983, 201).

The influx of new immigrants has only postponed the crisis within the Apostolic church. These Armenian-speaking (and -reading) immigrants have supplied members to church councils and choirs; served as acolytes, deacons, and priests; and filled the pews on Sundays. But they have introduced a conservative influence that has alienated the American-born in later generations even more. Instead of forming a partnership between the different segments of the population, in some parishes the American-born have typically abdicated their role, leaving the institutions in the care of a handful of relatively recent newcomers. As a third-generation informant who is highly active in the community told me: "We let them, it shouldn't have been so easy." However, in other parishes, the second-generation have maintained hegemony over church councils, keeping both the post-1965 immigrants and their own children's generation out.

The church cannot rely on a constant stream of immigrants to fill its ranks. The time has come for the Apostolic church to modernize its sacred traditions. From an archaic institution, it needs to become a living institution, responsive to the spiritual needs of the men and women of Armenian descent, their increasingly *odar* (non-Armenian) spouses, and their mixed-bred children living in contemporary United States. In doing so, the church may in the short term lose some of its adherents who are nominally Christian, but in the long term, it will be serving the real religious needs of those who flock to it, by choice, for solace, inspiration and communion.

Sacred Traditions

The Armenian church as a formally organized religion has played a major role in maintaining the language and culture of the Armenian people throughout their history. But equally important have been what Susan Pattie calls "religious" beliefs and practices, the little traditions, such as the celebration of saint's names and the use of religious vocabulary in everyday conversation, keeping Lent, and fasting before communion. These sacred traditions were part of the seasonal life cycle of preimmigration Armenian culture in Asia Minor at the turn of the twentieth century and were kept alive afterwards in the Middle Eastern diaspora to a great extent. For example, a man named Vartan or Sarkis would be congratulated *(anoonoved abrees)* and a festive meal for kin and friends would be held for him on *Vartanantz* or *Sourp Sarkis* (St Vartan, St Sarkis); the actual saint's day, being in relation to Easter, is not fixed. A Mariam's name day celebration would be on the Sunday nearest August 15, *Asdvadzadzin* (the Feast of Assumption).

In the contemporary United States, this tradition is dying out for a number of pragmatic reasons. These days, parents are less likely to name their baby boys Vartan or Sarkis, but more significantly, since few Armenian-American households in later generations are likely to have access to an Armenian church calendar, they (let alone their *odar* [non-American] friends) may not even know the exact date of these saints' days. Similarly, ordinary speech is no longer peppered with religious vocabulary. Since few American-born Armenians speak the language, words like *Asvadz bahe* ("God keep him/her"), *Asdoudzme pareen* ("God send you good things"), *Asvadz hokeen lousavoree* ("God rest his soul"), and *Asvadz ouzene* ("God willing") are automatically lost (see also Pattie 1990, 311). Such ancient idioms sound strange in a secularized society like that of the United States. Besides, they lose much of their charm in translation.

To measure the maintenance of sacred traditions, New York respondents were asked how frequently they abstained from food the day they planned to take communion. A more demanding behavioral tradition in the Armenian church/culture is the custom of keeping the forty days of Lent, that is, refraining from eating meat (including fish) and all meat products. Respondents were asked how often they fasted or abstained from animal products or other items[61] during Lent or Holy Week before Easter. Evidently, it is easier to fast for a few hours before taking communion than to keep Lent. Therefore, the question was asked in a liberal way; keeping Holy Week before Easter was considered sufficient.

As expected, more people answered affirmatively to the question about abstaining before communion than to keeping Lent. Nonetheless, the percentages of those who almost always fast before communion are remarkably small. Overall, 34 percent of the sample abstain, almost always, before taking communion, compared to 16 percent who fast or keep Lent, frequently. There are few generational and age differences between respondents who said they abstain before communion, except for the very youngest cohort, who are least likely to do so. About 20 percent of the foreign-born generation keep Lent, 14 percent of the second generation, 11 percent of those with one U.S.-born parent, 19 percent of those with two U.S.-born parents, and 6 percent of those with U.S.-born grandparents. The proscription of each denomination is the most important factor in whether one keeps sacred traditions or not. While nearly 45 percent of Armenian Apostolics and Catholics abstain from food before communion, only 5.5 percent of the Armenian Protestants do so, because their church does not require it. In keeping Lent, the Catholic injunction is a stronger norm than the Apostolic one. Therefore, only 17.5 percent of Apostolics keep Lent compared to nearly 55 percent of Armenian Catholics. The Protestants trail further behind.

In conclusion, the Armenian Apostolic church continues to be the bulwark of Armenianness in America at the present time, though the passing of generations is a threat that cannot be ignored. As predicted, later generations had the lowest rates of church attendance. Armenian Protestant and Catholic churches are less resistant to assimilation; their attrition rates were estimated to be at least twice those of the Apostolics. About two-thirds of the respondents consider it their duty to support the church, but slightly more than half (mostly the foreign-born and their children's generation) would be willing to travel long distances to attend regularly (probably fewer proportions would actually do so). Most agree that more English should be used in the service; evidently, a two- to three-hour service in a language one does not understand is not a very meaningful or pleasant experience. Certainly, it is not to be repeated often. The Armenian church has been a "communal" church, and most want it to continue as such; however, younger cohorts would like to understand the doctrines of the church rather than blindly follow their ancestral faith. Finally, few people maintain sacred traditions because they are demanding and inconvenient. Most significantly, individual forms of expressing one's Armenianness are increasing; acknowledging Armenian descent does not automatically make a person a member of an Armenian church. Overall, there was little verbal renunciation of the sacred culture, but behavioral indicators tell a different story.

Maintenance of Armenian Political Culture

In summing up the experience of the early Armenian immigrants to the United States, Mirak wrote: "[Their] distinguishing characteristic was the intensity of their inner political life.... [They] inherited a bitter, cataclysmic irredentist struggle which generated passionate battles in the community. The conflicts ... left deep cleavages in their lives, and these cleavages would continue to disrupt community life for decades" (1983, 286). I have already described above that this violent, vicious strife was so pervasive that it divided the Armenian communal structures in the diaspora roughly into two factions: Tashnags and anti-Tashnags. Therefore, the questions that need to be addressed are: To what extent are these traditional political and ideological orientations being maintained at present? How has this political and ideological culture affected the manifestation of Armenianness?

It is generally postulated that an immersion in the ethnic milieu precludes participation in the larger society. Not true! The New York survey reveals that Armenian political parties and traditional ideological orientations have not been resistant to the forces of assimilation. Armenian-Americans are citizens of the United States of America; as such they exercise and are conscious of their political rights and responsibilities. In fact, the vast majority realize that their membership in the larger society has more serious repercussions on their daily lives and livelihoods than their membership in the Armenian world.

For the first and second generations, Armenian-Americans are equally at home in Armenian and American politics. However, in later generations, ethnic political parties cease to be functional or meaningful to them. Therefore, they are no longer active participants. Yet, many maintain emotional ties to their ancestral background and may, whenever convenient, become symbolically involved, through monetary contributions, writing letters to Congress, or providing technological expertise to earthquake victims. Additionally, with the creation of the Republic of Armenia, there are prospects of mobilizing Armenian-Americans into an "interest" group.

Retention of Traditional Political Orientations

Less than 3 percent of respondents were official members of Armenian political parties.[62] However, almost half (49 percent) of them sympathized with either one of the three parties or took a *chezok* (nonpartisan or neutral) position in the conflict, which was demonstrated to be a euphemism for the anti-Tashnag side. Specifically, 1 percent sympathized with the Hunchags, 4.8 percent with the Ramgavars, 18.7 percent with the Tashnags, 24.5 percent said they were *chezok*. By contrast, 30.3 percent were indifferent to Armenian politics, 12.2 percent rejected all parties, and the remaining 9.6 percent did not know or gave no answer (see totals column table 2.7).

Sympathy to Armenian political parties and ideologies was significantly correlated with generational presence in the United States (.19*; table 1.6 in chap. 1). Sympathy to the Hunchag and Ramgavar parties is predominantly a foreign-born phenomenon. The Tashnag party also gets most of its supporters from the foreign-born; however, their

TABLE 2.7
Frequency Distribution of Sympathy to Armenian Political Parties and Ideologies by Ancestry

	Both Parents Armenian	One Parent Armenian	Total
N =	(518)	(66)	(584)
Hunchag	1.0	1.5	1.0
Ramgavar	5.2	1.5	4.8
Tashnag	20.8	1.5	18.7
Neutral *(Chezok)*	25.7	15.2	24.5
Indifferent	28.0	48.5	30.3
Rejects all parties	11.0	21.2	12.2
(No answer)	8.3	10.6	8.6
	100.0	100.0	100.0

socialization techniques must be more effective than the others or their ideology more meaningful, because they are able to sustain partisans until the third generation. Yet, there is a remarkable monotonic decrease with each passing generation. Accelerating with the second generation, the proportion of respondents who are indifferent to Armenian politics increases dramatically. Likewise, those who reject parties and those in the "no response" category are mostly later-generation descendants who have little knowledge of the issues.

Sympathy to Armenian politics is also significantly related to religious affiliation (.21*). The majority of the non-Apostolic respondents in this survey (75.5 percent) did not favor any of the ideological positions. Respondents with non-Armenian church affiliations and "no religion" were even less (82 percent) sympathetic to Armenian politics (see table 1.11 in chap. 1). This is not surprising, because as mentioned above, the conflict was fought out within the Armenian Apostolic church. Those who are affiliated to the National church are more prone to be aware of the consequences of the schism. In choosing to attend one Apostolic church over another, willingly or unwillingly, one makes a political decision. Similarly, having a non-Armenian parent drastically decreases the chances of a respondent's partisanship (.13*; see table 2.7). Only 4.5 percent of respondents with mixed ancestry favored one or the other of the parties, nearly 50 percent said they were indifferent.

TABLE 2.8

Frequency Distribution of Sympathy to Armenian Political Parties and Ideologies by Place of Birth

	United States	Turkey	Middle East	Soviet Bloc	Other
N = 584	(351)	(90)	(110)	(22)	(11)
Hunchag	0.9	2.2	0.9	0.0	0.0
Ramgavar	4.0	7.8	5.5	0.0	9.1
Tashnag	12.3	18.9	31.8	40.9	45.5
Chezok	19.7	41.1	27.3	31.8	0.0
Indifferent	41.6	8.9	16.4	13.6	18.2
Rejects all parties	13.4	13.3	8.2	4.5	18.2
(No answer)	8.3	7.8	10.0	9.1	9.1
	100.0	100.0	100.0	100.0	100.0

Table 2.8 shows the frequency distribution of sympathy to Armenian politics by country of birth of respondents. It confirms that the majority of the followers of Armenian political parties and ideologies are foreign-born. Respondents born in Soviet Bloc countries are most likely to be pro-Tashnags. The one-time staunch anti-Soviet policies of the Tashnag party seem to have found ready allies in those who have experienced firsthand the Soviet system. Also, Armenians from the Middle East, especially from Lebanon and Syria, are more likely to be politicized. Ascribed ethnicity in those countries, the influential presence of Armenian political parties, and the historical incidences such as the bloody battles in Lebanon in 1958 have sensitized Middle Eastern Armenians.

Immigrants from Turkey, especially recent ones, are less political. As previously mentioned, for the few Armenians who remained in Turkey after the Genocide, community life was predominantly centered around the family (and the church for those in Istanbul), it precluded any form of political consciousness. By contrast, Turkish-born old-timers who immigrated to the United States before the 1920s are more likely to be politicized. They are also more likely to have witnessed the fights that split the Armenian-American community in 1933.

Occupation, education, and income are not significantly related to sympathy to Armenian political ideologies. The socioeconomic background of the members and advocates of the Hunchags, Ramgavars, and Tashnags appear to be similar: middle to upper middle class. This is a tremendous change from their class origins in the early twentieth century. As explained before, while the Ramgavar party spoke for the bourgeoisie, the Tashnags were spokesmen for the less privileged classes: the peasants, the artisans, and the intellectuals. I suspect that the situation in Greater Los Angeles is somewhat different. There are higher proportions of working-class and lower-middle-class Armenians because of the influx of new immigrants from the Middle East and Soviet Armenia. Undoubtedly, many of the former have carried with them their political affiliations and ideologies, reinstating their membership in Los Angeles branches.

There were three attitude statements that measured the political and ideological traditionalism of the men and women of Armenian descent who participated in this study. The first statement was: "The division of the Armenian community into various political groups, such as Hunchags, Ramgavars, Tashnags is irrelevant in this day and age." The second statement said: "I attend the Armenian church closest to my home, whether or not I sympathize with Echmiadzin or Antelias." The last statement read: "I attend the activities that interest me in the Armenian community no matter what the political affiliation of the organization sponsoring the activity." Irrespective of generational presence, ancestry, age, and socioeconomic background, on average, 65 percent of the sample found the split within the Armenian community to be irrelevant to this day and age (22 percent disagreed).

It is noteworthy that on all these statements, high proportions of respondents had no opinion (or did not answer). Later-generation respondents and those with mixed ancestry were most likely to say they do not know (see table 2.9). For example, 53 percent of respondents with two U.S.-born parents and 88 percent with U.S.-born grandparents preferred to have "no opinion" on the second statement, that is, attending the closest Armenian church irrespective of political sympathies. Similarly, third- and fourth-generation respondents averaged 32 percent of "no opinion" category on the third statement, that is, attending any activity no matter the political affiliation of the association sponsoring it. All three attitude statements on the schism within the Armenian community were most meaningful to first- and second-generation respondents.

Several respondents, in later generations and children of mixed marriages, wrote to say that they were not familiar with any of the political parties mentioned in the questionnaire. For example, a young woman whose father is a U.S.-born Armenian and whose mother is Italian wrote: "I do not understand any." A middle-aged woman whose mother, like her, is U.S.-born said: "I cannot sympathize with any political divisions primarily because I have no pertinent knowledge of any of them." Other respondents wrote, "I am *totally* unknowledgeable on all these groups," or "Not familiar with these organizations," or statements to that effect (emphasis in original). A forty-one-year-old man whose father is English and mother American-born Armenian wrote, "Have a lack of sympathy for the divisions. For one thing I can never get them all straight in my mind. For a race with a small population, Armenians seem to have more division per capita than any other race!"

Respondents found the effect of the political divisions within the Armenian community to be destructive[63] and a thing of the past. A forty-five-year-old woman who came from Turkey at age twelve wrote, "We have no room nor reason to pursue these political prejudices. They may have had a purpose in the past. At present, they will only weaken us even more as it's done so in the past." A fifty-five-year-old, third-generation woman observed that the division "has made them [the Armenians] so hateful—I detest this nonsense." A second-generation man wrote: "It's a thing of the past and should be forgotten." Yet another second-generation, middle-aged woman said that ethnic "political parties are obsolete in U.S.A. today." A community leader I interviewed also expressed the view that there is no future for Armenian political parties in the United States. He compared the situation in Lebanon with that of the United States. In Lebanon, political parties had to replace inefficient governmental agencies in dealing with the Armenian population, from marital disputes to obtaining a passport. In contrast, in the United States,

TABLE 2.9

Frequencies of Respondents Rejecting Armenian Communal Schism (and Those with No Opinion) Measured Through Three Attitude Statements by Generation (in percent)

	Foreign-Born	U.S.-Born of F.B. Parents	1 Parent U.S.-Born	2 Parents U.S.-Born	Grandparent U.S.-Born
N = 561-577	(215)	(269)	(36)	(41)	(16)
Statement 1	62.3	67.3	69.4	63.4	43.8
(No opinion)	(13.0)	(13.0)	(8.3)	(24.4)	(25.0)
Statement 2	55.9	31.4	42.4	30.0	0.0
(No opinion)	(17.1)	(33.3)	(30.3)	(52.5)	(87.5)
Statement 3	75.0	59.5	47.2	51.2	40.0
(No opinion)	(7.9)	(22.1)	(38.8)	(34.1)	(33.3)

Statement 1: "The division of the Armenian community into various political groups, such as Hunchags, Ramgavars, and Tashnags is irrelevant in this day and age."
Statement 2: "I attend the Armenian church closest to my home, whether or not I sympathize with Echmiadzin or Antelias."
Statement 3: "I attend the activities that interest me in the Armenian community no matter what the political affiliation of the organization sponsoring the activity."

ethnic political parties do not fulfill any functions necessary for the survival of their people.

Interestingly, the immigrant generation, no matter where respondents were born, were more likely than the U.S.-born to say that they would attend the Armenian church nearest their home whatever its political colorings.[64] I find that second-generation respondents are most likely to uphold the schism. This can be interpreted by the historical circumstances that many of the second-generation respondents witnessed while growing up: the 1933 murder of Archbishop Tourian that officially split the Apostolic church in America and the subsequent Cold War era. The reader is reminded that 83 percent of second-generation respondents were over fifty years of age. This behavior is a cohort effect.

As a result of childhood socialization, network connections, and habit, many Armenian-Americans inadvertently perpetuate the political and ideological schisms within the community by being members of one church rather than another; by supporting the social, cultural, educational activities, and fund-raising events of one association rather than the opposing one, and contributing financially or otherwise to projects and organizations of one faction instead of the rival ones. Preferences to Tashnag and anti-Tashnag orientations are mostly inherited, as several respondents in this survey remarked. For example, a middle-aged, second-generation woman wrote that she sympathized with the Ramgavar party "only because of my late father." Another woman declared a preference to the Tashnag Party, but she went on to say: "[It is] because of my parents. I feel somehow indifferent now." Again, a middle-aged, second-generation woman wrote that her father was a Tashnag. She added, "I still feel some sympathy but not for what they are today." Often the sympathy of American-born generations to Armenian political parties is not so much to the present performance of the parties, but in memory of their parents and the ideals they held.

Many Armenian-Americans unintentionally contain their social relations with other Armenians to the confines of one faction, as the present data illustrates. The Armenians they know and meet in their leisure time, such as family, relatives, friends, or acquaintances, happen to belong, in general, to the same churches and auxiliary associations as themselves (see also O'Grady 1979, 51). Attending a church service, a lecture, a concert, or a fund-raiser has a latent function of establishing and maintaining kinship and friendship ties. Considering the finite amount of time and energy (and finances) one has, one goes to the events where one is more likely to meet familiar faces and feel welcomed.

Some men and women, because of their close relationships and their ability to move freely in either "side," become brokers between the two factions. O'Grady (1979, 51-54) found that there are different categories of brokers. There are those who by virtue of being married into the opposing faction become brokers. People associated with the arts are coveted by all organizations; they too become intermediaries. There are also organizations, such as professional and student groups, that attract people from both factions. Ties between the two factions are not completely severed; however, conversions from one "side" to the other are rare. It is hard to find a person who was raised as a

TABLE 2.10
Reasons Favoring Church Unity

	percent
Eliminate image of division, more power	45
Reduce waste and duplication of resources	38
Strengthen identity, one nation, one church	28
Reduce assimilation, and keep youth in fold	23
Promote larger church attendance	11
Eliminate political domination	10
Improve cultural efforts, schools, etc	10
Strengthen Christianity and religion	7

Reasons Opposing Church Unity

	percent
Armenians are too split to unite	12
Power struggle will always continue	4
Competition is good	3
Political parties will dominate	3
Fear of Soviet influence	1

Source: *Armenian Reporter,* 23 April 1987, p. 1.

Tashnag and became a Ramgavar and vice versa (see also Phillips 1978, 268).

The Issue of Unity

In recent decades, with the end of the Cold War and changing diasporan relations with Soviet Armenia, "Unity Talks" have been held intermittently between the two Apostolic church factions. A recent poll found that 93 percent of respondents favored the unification of Armenian churches under one jurisdiction; only 6 percent of respondents were unfavorable, the remaining one percent had no opinion *(Armenian Reporter,* 16 and 23 April 1987).[65] The breakdown by church affiliation is interesting: 4 percent of those affiliated with the Diocese of the Armenian Church of America and 12 percent of those affiliated with the Prelacy of the Armenian Apostolic Church of America were opposed to unity. Furthermore, 61 percent of those who responded to the above survey were affiliated to the Diocese churches, 25 percent were affiliated to the Prelacy churches, 6 percent of respondents said they attended both churches, and the remaining 8 percent said they had no Armenian church affiliation.[66]

The most frequently stated reasons in favor of church unity are concerns for Armenian ethnicity, identity and fear of assimilation (see table 2.10). Unity is perceived to be more effective in projecting ethnic power and more efficient in terms of human and material resources. The poll does not specify the generational status of those who offered their views on unity, but I suspect a significant proportion to be from the first and second generations. In that respect, their answers are more comprehensible. As symbolic Armenians, they require that the administration of their institutions, whether or not religious, be unambiguous in their goals, rational in their procedures, and efficient in the allocation of human and material resources.

In the New York study, I did not ask any direct questions on unity within the Armenian Apostolic church; nonetheless, numerous respondents made comments on the issue, providing similar reasons to the ones mentioned in the above poll. A seventy-four-year-old immigrant woman who had come to the United States at age twelve, out of apprehension for the future of the Armenians, wrote:

My only concern now is Armenian unity. I was very disappointed when they didn't unite on the 70th anniversary of the Genocide—in Washington. It's something I will always remember.... [I] am thankful there are intelligent young Armenians concerned about the past, present and future of the Armenians.

A seventy-eight-year-old U.S.-born man whose ancestors came from Bulgaria sent in a typed "open letter" that advocated unity in order to fight back against the Turks and prevent assimilation. Here are some excerpts from his letter:

Dear Brother,

Divided we have failed for 70 years, United we have a chance.

The Turks are laughing at us, because we are struggling within ourselves. How can we fight the Turks? UNITY.

This letter further suggested that young Armenians should join ethnic organizations "otherwise *Odar* [foreign] country and none of our own, We are Lost."

On the other hand, a fifty-eight-year-old, second-generation man lamented the duplication of Armenian churches, implying the waste in resources. He wrote:

The greatest harm done to the Armenian people is the stubbornness of the two factions (priests) of the Armenian church in not uniting. As an adolescent in Syracuse, NY, many years ago, there was no Armenian church. Post World War II, a church supporting Echmiadzin was established—within a year another church was established (Antelias). From zero to two in 1 1/2 years.

A forty-nine-year-old Lebanese-born woman would agree with the above quotation. Her fear though is assimilation. Here are her remarks:

It is a shame that the Armenians are not forgetting their differences and working hand in hand to salvage Armenian ethnicity in America. I find it hard to believe that even in small towns where there are few Armenians (like Niagara Falls, NY) you find opposing Armenian churches next to each other and not working together.

Another middle-aged, second-generation man was concerned about unity because it could mean increased ethnic power for political action. Here are his comments:

I am not a party (political) person and therefore not a real believer in the Armenian churches. Unfortunately, they are one and the same. The *old* guard Armenians are keeping the Armenians divided and forcing the churches to do the same. Fear of losing their power base, and *not* the love of Armenia or Armenians is the only reason they can have for these policies. Unfortunately the only thing they agree on is that the Turks massacred the Armenians. Even on this occasion they *cannot* forget their differences and have a united rally, a united religious service or a united effort to pressure legislation. (Emphasis in original)

Similarly, a second-generation man regrets the political impasse caused by the schism. He believes that "the murder of Archbishop Tourian ... has separated Armenians *forever*—politically we have not advanced 1 inch in 50 years. All groups stand firm on quicksand" (emphasis in original).

The concern for unity is an example of the changing conditions within the Armenian community in the United States. This does not mean that unity will be easy to achieve. As a matter of fact, several attempts have so far ended in failure. The Unity Poll presented above indicates that a maturing generation of American-born Armenians who continue to identify with their ancestral church and culture have come to perceive the schism within their community with more objectivity. They have come to realize the futility of animosity within their ranks and between the churches. To many Armenian-Americans the jurisdictional dispute within the church and the traditional political and ideological orientations must appear like the skeletal remains of a dinosaur, the vestiges of a bygone era.

Effect of Political Ideologies on Armenianness

Having seen the frequencies of support for Armenian politics in the sample, both attitudinally and behaviorally, the question is: how have these sympathies to Armenian political ideologies affected the course of assimilation. In competing for the leadership of the Armenian community in the United States, the different political/ideological orientations vie for the ultimate task of ethnic maintenance. The loftier goals of an independent homeland, and the retribution for the loss of ancestral lands from the Turkish government remain latent; they do not exact the immediate energies and resources of the leadership and the community. It is a matter of emphasis as to which is the best way to maintain Armenianness in the United States; the idiom of organization is different for each faction. The Tashnags place more emphasis on culture, language and politics. Generally, the Tashnags tend to be irreligious; given their socioeconomic and revolutionary roots, this is not surprising. On the other hand, the anti-Tashnags stress the importance of church affiliation. In accordance with their predominantly middle-class interests, the anti-Tashnags have opted for a "safer" form of ethnicity that does not disturb their hard-won status (see O'Grady 1979, 149-51).

Table 2.11 shows the relationship between sympathy to Armenian parties and selected measures of assimilation. It should be noted that the Hunchag and Ramgavar categories have been recoded into the "other parties." The assimilation variables selected here are: speaking and reading Armenian adequately to very well, attending Armenian church once a month or more, sending one's child(ren) to Armenian day schools instead of public (American) schools, attending requiem services on April 24, commemorating the Genocide, and attending public gatherings for the same occasion.

The evidence suggests that the ideologies have been able to influence ethnic maintenance until the second generation. By stressing different aspects of Armenian culture, the idiom of organization or locus of control of each party/ideology has created variations in the responses, though the differences are by small margins of less than 10

TABLE 2.11
Frequency Distribution of Respondents with "High" Scores on Selected Measures of Assimilation (Ethnic Position) by Revised Classification of Sympathy to Armenian Political Parties
(in Percent)

	Tashnag	Other Parties	Neutral	Indifferent
N = 463	(109)	(34)	(143)	(177)
Speak Armenian well	93.6	85.3	90.2	54.8
Read Armenian well	65.1	55.8	48.9	18.1
Attend Armenian church often	28.0	33.3	29.4	19.2
Favor Armenian education for children	47.7	40.6	44.0	20.7
Attend Requiem on April 24	64.2	61.7	49.0	19.2
Attend public rally on April 24	47.7	38.2	31.5	13.6

percent. The Tashnag sympathizers have the highest rates of language maintenance and support for Armenian day-school education. They have the highest rates for attending public rallies and requiem services for April 24. However, they lag behind the anti-Tashnags and *chezoks* (neutrals) in regular church attendance. On average, being a partisan of any Armenian party or ideology increases one's involvement in "political" activities. Genocide commemoration rallies, even requiem services, can be designated as political behavior because they maintain the historical conflict with the Turkish government.

The Tashnags, anti-Tashnags, and *chezoks* (neutrals) stand in sharp contrast to the "indifferents." Less than one-fifth of the indifferents read Armenian, participate in Genocide commemoration services or attend public demonstrations, or attend church regularly. It is interesting, however, that over half of them speak Armenian adequately to very well. They are the most assimilated. In sum, political ideologies have been functional in the past for the immigrant generation and second generation if they are able to provide a focus for collective identity and a framework for organizing communal structures. But these political parties and ideologies have not been responsive to contemporary realities. Large proportions of Armenian-Americans in later generations no longer feel the holding power of traditions and nostalgia.

Armenian Case as Application of Simmel's Theory of Conflict

The schism within the Armenian diasporan community is an excellent application of Georg Simmel's conceptualizations on the sociological nature of conflict. The schism has been long lasting and intense for a number of reasons. First, conflict within the Armenian community has established boundaries between Tashnags and anti-Tashnags by strengthening the consciousness, sense of separateness, and identity of each "side" (Coser 1956, 34). Second, feelings and the expression of hostility have prevented these boundaries from disappearing. Moreover, as Simmel notes, "hostilities are often consciously cultivated to guarantee existing conditions" (1955, 18).

Third, the conflict within the Armenian community can be described as nonrealistic conflict because it is "not directly related to a contentious issue and is not oriented toward the attainment of specific results" (Coser 1956, 49). Nonrealistic conflicts often stem from originally realistic antagonisms that were denied expression and are perpetuated through socialization (Coser 1956, 54). Realistic conflicts are directed at objects that are the source of unmet demands or expectations of benefits. Functional alternatives, such as bargaining and compromise, can replace realistic conflict in achieving one's demands. However, in nonrealistic conflicts, the only functional alternative is in the choice of an adversary. Fourth, conflict has maintained the relationship within the social system by allowing members of each group to vent their frustrations at one another; otherwise, they might have despaired and withdrawn (Coser 1956, 47). As Simmel has written, "opposition gives us inner satisfaction, distraction, relief.... Our opposition makes us feel that we are not completely victims of circumstances" (1955, 19).

Simmel observed that in close social relationships there exists both converging and diverging tendencies, such as the feelings of love and hate in intimate relationships where the total personality is involved. This intensity produces greater violence in cases of disagreement and disloyalty. Similarly, in groups in which members are deeply committed to the group, conflict may become very violent. Furthermore, in such close relationships, because of frequent interaction, there are more occasions for feelings of hostility to explode (Simmel 1955, 23; Coser 1956, 60-65). In host societies, the closest social relations of Armenian immigrants were other Armenians; besides, their numerically small size contributed to their intensity of involvement and friction (see Coser 1956, 97).

Simmel found that "people who have many common features often do one another worse or 'wronger' wrong than complete strangers do" (1955, 44). For the Tashnags and anti-Tashnags, hostility was as rooted in their social ties to each other, their sense of belonging and unity as Armenians (Simmel 1955, 48), as it was in their survival as a people and as a culture. Finally, Simmel observed that when ideological considerations become important in a conflict, as in this case, when members of a group feel that they are not fighting for personal reasons but an ideal, the conflict becomes more radical and merciless (Coser 1956,118). In ideological conflicts, dissenters in each camp are not easily tolerated and are forced to withdraw (Coser 1956, 103). The descendants of Armenian immigrants to the United States who do not endorse the traditional political and ideological orientations become alienated and eventually drop out of the ethnic community as the data clearly shows. The most assimilated respondents, by most of the indices used in this study, are those who were "indifferent" to Armenian political parties and ideologies.

To summarize then, according to Simmel, the conflict within the Armenian community is partly a direct result of the structural and ideological properties of the case. The small, close-knit structure of Armenian communities, the total involvement of immigrants in their ethnic group, their constant interaction, their vested interests in the future of the Armenian people and the Armenian culture, their sense of belongingness and identity, the objectification of conflict, among other causes, resulted in the strengthening of the boundaries that separated the Tashnags from the anti-Tashnags and dissipated their frustrations by displacing their goals from the less attainable enemy to each other. It became a nonrealistic conflict that functioned more as a tension release mechanism than as an attempt to achieve any specific results. For a short while, this conflict was able to maintain the system; however, in the long run, such a conflict-ridden system is more likely to lose momentum, rigidify, and be unable to change (or change as quickly and as effectively) in response to changes outside the Armenian community.

Some Armenians have tried to justify the continuous conflict in their community as functional. It is believed that the opposition of the political orientations and the competition in supporting two sets of churches and auxiliary organizations have kept the Armenian identity alive in the diaspora (O'Grady 1979, 153). This may have been true for the immigrant generation, but it has alienated their American-born descendants as this study testifies. Simmel would agree that such a conflict can be costly. If conflict rigidifies a system, thus preventing it from modifying its structure, values, and rules in order to adapt to changing conditions, then it becomes dysfunctional (see Coser 1956, 48).

Indeed, Tashnag and anti-Tashnag political orientations and ideologies do not reflect present sociopolitical realities and do not address the issues that the diaspora-born generations face. Phillips corroborates this by adding that "there is among the youth a disenchantment with the Armenian [political] institutions and a demand for new institutions which will include all Armenian-Americans" (1978, 265). Two organizations, the Armenian Assembly of America and the Zoryan Institute for Contemporary Armenian Research and Documentation, may function as alternatives to the traditional political parties because they provide "American/symbolic" avenues of political and ideological expression for Armenian-Americans.

American Alternatives to Traditional Political Culture

The Armenian Assembly of America is an organization that is the product of a maturing generation of Armenian-Americans—a generation of educated, professional, affluent Americans who are conscious of their Armenian heritage. The Armenian Assembly was founded in 1972 in Washington, DC by a small group of professional Armenians to represent and promote the interests of Armenians. In their own terms, it is "an information and resource center and liaison between the Armenian community and the American government."[67] The rationale behind the creation of the Armenian Assembly is best explained in the words of historian Richard Hovannisian, one of the founders of the Assembly.

> Successful through the sweat of their brows in creating many new opportunities for their children, the Armenian immigrant generation nonetheless failed to pass on the secrets contained within the Armenian alphabet, that is the key to Armenian history, Armenian literature, and Armenian existence. And even recent immigrants, who had attended Armenian schools in the Middle East and for whom the Armenian characters were not simply unintelligible hieroglyphics, found in a very short time that they had to face the same problems as American-born Armenians. The challenge of finding the means to preserve the existence of a people in the dispersion and to achieve their aspirations demanded attention.

> It was out of concern for themselves and their children and out of a growing awareness of the enormous potential existing within the Armenian-American community, with successful and talented people in the arts, media, medicine, science, public service, business and many other fields, that a few individuals sought the means to tap that potential and provide it a channel for productive expression. It was a regrettable reality that most Armenian-Americans would not or could not replace their parents in Armenian political and compatriotic societies. In fact, most Armenian-Americans are involved in no Armenian organization, not even in the Church. Hence, the community has been deprived of the talents and ability of thousands of individuals who may identify personally with their Armenian heritage, but have not found or been offered a satisfactory avenue of

participation. Unwilling to commit themselves on the basis of their parents' faith alone, they demand businesslike operations, logical and tangible results. (*Armenians in America* 1987, 89)

Some of the projects supported by the Armenian Assembly at present are: the recognition of the Armenian Genocide by the government of the United States of America and research and educational programs making the discussion of the Genocide part of the school curriculum[68] and a subject of interest to the academic community. A popular project is the Summer Internship Program that allows college-aged students to work in Washington, DC to learn about the U.S. government and establish professional and fellowship networks. The Armenian Assembly also claims to have a "special responsibility toward the plight of Armenians who are in countries where the integrity of the Armenian community has been threatened and who have fled by the thousands to Europe and elsewhere ˜s refugees" (*Armenians in America* 1987, 91). To this end, it tries to maintain ties with Armenians in the diaspora.

Since the physical and "political" earthquakes in Armenia, the Armenian Assembly has established a bureau in Yerevan, like several other Armenian-American organizations. The Assembly had to respond to the immediate need for relief, and then to redefine its mission. In the words of the chairman of the Board of Trustees:

Armenia's Declaration of Independence last August marked the beginning of a new chapter in Armenia's history, and gave the people hope for the future. They are now looking to Armenians in the Diaspora to be a source of strength and to provide expertise, technically, economically, and in other ways. In 1990, the Assembly can be proud of its efforts that provided Armenia with new links in the U.S. government leaders, to international humanitarian organizations, and to the media.[69]

More specifically, the Armenian Assembly has hosted the first U.S. trip of President Levon Ter-Petrosyan, was awarded a grant from U.S. AID to support earthquake relief, and presented written testimonies to the Senate Foreign Relations Committee on mistreatment of Armenians in Azerbaijan. As an advocacy agency, the Armenian Assembly has found a new and deserving "client" that is in dire need of its services. Its "new" mission, which is still within the mandate of its original goals, is to help connect the West with Armenia and Armenia with the West.

The Armenian Assembly is *not* a political party, but it fulfills many of the functions of political groups. It represents the case of the Armenians in the nation's capital; it selects the collective goals and priorities of Armenian-Americans;[70] and like any political group, it reflects the socioeconomic interests and political aspirations of its leaders and members.[71] Even though the Armenian Assembly claims to hold at heart the interests of Armenians elsewhere in the world, its focus is predominantly American and its perspective mainstream (i.e., not radical). The recognition of the Genocide by the U.S. government (not Turkey!) is a moral issue that extends a visceral tie to all Armenian-Americans. Furthermore, it does not jeopardize the status quo or antagonize the general American public like the issue of "terrorism" and the reclamation of lands from Turkey. The internship program promotes the individual achievements of young Armenian-Americans in their fields of endeavor, and if by the same token it helps heighten feelings of ethnic pride and identity, few would dispute the need for such a program. Their projects, mostly educational and informational, are prudent and highly commendable.

In keeping with general trends in American society and emulating other ethnic groups, Armenian-Americans have created their own "interest group" in the Armenian Assembly of America—a goal-oriented group capable of demanding political, economic, and social benefits for the Armenians whenever or wherever necessary. The Armenian Assembly indirectly challenges the traditional political leadership[72] of the Armenian-American community by offering programs that are of particular relevance to American-born generations, feasible programs that are unlikely to offend many people. As a bureaucracy, it is managed in the best American tradition, with a well-trained, energetic staff, receiving commensurate salaries to their colleagues in the nonethnic world, accountable for their actions, judged on their efficiency; the office is equipped with modern technological innovations, and so on. By transcending the confines of the political culture of the immigrant generation, it offers an acceptable avenue for Armenian-American political action, vicariously.

The Zoryan Institute for Contemporary Armenian Research and Documentation, Inc. was established in Cambridge (MA) in 1982. As its name indicates it is not a political organization. Yet, like the

Armenian Assembly, it is an inadvertent contender for the traditional Armenian leadership in the diaspora, because it challenges the status quo, intellectually. The institute's body of associate scholars, its research interests, its publications, the open university seminars and other conferences it sponsors, all together address the collective consciousness of Armenians in the United States and in the diaspora. In their own words: "The Zoryan Institute takes a unique view of Armenian society.... This means examining the Armenian experience in relation to forces beyond the Armenian world and assessing the impact of historical events on our lives today.... The intent is to establish a new, self-critical standard in the Armenian community ..." (Zoryan Institute brochure 1988).

Among its accomplishments, the Zoryan Institute lists the following: publishing *The Karabagh File,* a compendium of historical documents and analysis of the movement less than one month after the issue gained international attention (see Libaridian 1988); the videotaping of oral histories of Genocide survivors; providing critical evidence for Permanent People's Tribunal session on the Armenian Genocide in 1984; establishing a computerized data bank for documents related to the Genocide; and providing research assistance to scholars, writers, journalists, and filmmakers. Representatives of the Zoryan Institute and the Armenian Assembly have appeared on national television and in the press as spokespersons for Armenian-Americans and Armenians around the world.

The Zoryan Institute exemplifies a new trend in the intellectual leadership of the Armenian-American community. With increasing acculturation and changes in the educational and occupational composition of the ethnic population, highly trained and accomplished academics and researchers who can function successfully in the larger American intellectual arena are favored. The majority (80 percent) of the institute's supporters, that is, dues-paying "friends" and "patrons," are in the words of their brochure, "well-educated professionals," the rest being business owners.[73] The institute is also a product of a new emerging partnership between second-generation Armenian-Americans and highly educated foreign-born Armenians (often U.S. trained) that reflects recent changes within the Armenian-American community, namely, the maturing of the U.S.-born symbolic Armenians and the influx of new immigrants from the Middle East and the Soviet bloc. Not surprisingly, the institute's supporters can be divided equally between the American-born and the foreign-born.[74]

In exchange for annual dues, supporters of the Zoryan Institute receive scholarly publications and the opportunity to participate in public forums or attend lectures or similar activities if one so desires. Essentially the commitment is financial, and no other involvement is required. Unlike traditional political organizations, both the Armenian Assembly and the Zoryan Institute are not greedy institutions. They do not demand the full energies, body or soul, of their supporters. Financial demands are relatively easy and convenient for symbolic Armenians. In form and function, these organizations correspond to the symbolic type of Armenianness. It is the only way any ethnic organization can succeed in America past the second generation.

In sum, Armenian-Americans are becoming increasingly indifferent to the traditional political parties because they are unable to represent their concerns, let alone alter their material circumstances. The majority of respondents regard the schism as obsolete. Changing traditional ideologies and political structures are, of course, more difficult to achieve than creating new institutions. The concern for church unity illustrates the type of changes that are necessary in the traditional Armenian institutions to correspond (and catch up with, if possible) with the changes that have taken place, for most people, in individual forms of Armenianness. Armenian institutions in the United States are being challenged to change. Their survival depends on their ability to adapt and serve the needs of symbolic Armenians. Emerging organizations like The Armenian Assembly of America are viable alternatives to the traditional political leadership. Their goals and their modes of operation are more congruent with the aspirations and the sympathies of symbolic Armenian-Americans. Though they are *not* political organizations per se, they are the only politicized alternative that can function successfully in the United States.

Political Participation in American Society

The first Armenians who came to America wanted to make money and then return to their birthplace, where most of their families had stayed. Some hoped that conditions would improve at home in the interim; nonetheless, the intention to return was sustained (Mirak

1983). Kaprielian, speaking of Armenian sojourners in Canada emphasizes: "Length of residence in the new location was largely irrelevant. As long as a man's heart, mind, and money were directed to the family back home, he could remain physically removed from his village for many years" (1986-87, 47). However, the Genocide and forced deportations from Western Armenia and the Sovietization of Eastern Armenia forced many Armenian sojourners to give up their dream of living again in their ancestral homeland.[75]

The post-Genocide diaspora, which included the booming settlements in the New World, was neither the first nor was it going to be the last exile community of the Armenian people. Sojourning had become an Armenian tradition. Armenians readily observe that before the modern era, they had established viable, often prosperous, communities in Lvov (Poland),[76] Calcutta, Madras, Singapore, Isfahan, Baku, Tiflis, Constantinople, Aleppo, Jerusalem, Venice, Vienna, Paris (see Adalian 1989; Dedeyan 1982; Sanjian 1965). Adalian, analyzing the historical evolution of Armenian diasporas, traces the earliest dispersion "to the time when the ancient world was being reshaped into medieval civilizations" (1989, 81). After existing for over a thousand years under the aegis of their chieftains and monarchs, anchored in statehood, the geographic location of the Armenian people became subject to constant change. It meant that henceforth a segment of the population would settle beyond the confines of the "homeland."

It is interesting to note that when the Armenians first established a diaspora, they had to coin a new word to describe their situation. Ironically, the word *gaghut* meaning community of exile, came from "the condition of *ghaributiun*, that of being among strangers *(gharib* in Arabic and Turkish meaning stranger)" (Adalian 1989, 88). Armenians also used the the word *spurk* (diaspora) after the 1920s, while Soviet authorities popularized the word *ardasahman* literally meaning "extramural" or "beyond the borders"; implying the "real" patrimony was Soviet Armenia (Mouradian 1990, 306).

At present, Tölölyan writes that an estimated 1,400,000 Armenians in thirty-four nations make up the diaspora.[77] On the other hand, a Soviet Armenian scholar has placed the diaspora Armenian population at 2,225,000 (see the *Armenian Reporter,* 20 February 1986, p 4). Ordjanian (1991, 47), who has combined and compared several sources, estimates that the Armenian diaspora (outside Soviet Armenia) between 1975 and 1989 stood at 3,084,000. Mouradian (1990, 142,169) puts the total number of Armenians in the world in 1988 between 6 and 6.7 million, of these 3,283,000 lived in Armenia. In any case, these figures suggest that approximately half of the Armenian population of the world lives on historical lands, the other half does not. Moreover, while less than 1 percent of the Armenian population lived in the West (Western Europe, America, Australia) in 1914, that proportion had increased to 20 percent by 1988 (Mouradian 1990, 170).

Sociologists postulate that the sojourner's ideology or the middleman minority form, which characterized early Armenian immigration to the United States, is antithetical to participation in mainstream American politics. However, once the dream is relinquished, the avenue to social and economic integration and hence to assimilation is open. Here, I need to make a distinction between individual and collective ideologies and strategies of social and political adaptation. In America, at the individual level, Armenians found a tolerant society; or more accurately, a background of affective neutrality, which increases the tendency toward rapid assimilation. Armenians were also charmed by America's modernism, its technological development; they were beguiled by its system of values, opportunities, and promise of achievement. Having lost hope of return, many aspired to become successful Americans.

Advancement for the early Armenian immigrants meant education, if not for themselves, then certainly for their children. Mirak (1983, 272) quotes the injunction many an immigrant father and mother repeated time and time again to their children: *Tbrots Kna vor mart ellas* (go to school to be a man). The public schools opened the doors to acculturation. In due course, higher education and corporate employment widened the structural pathways into mainstream America. The involvement of Armenians in American politics follows the same course. Again, I quote from Mirak: "First-generation Armenians were too few in number, too poor, and too inexperienced in American politics to constitute a legitimate ethnic bloc on state or national levels. Moreover, many were preoccupied with Old World issues" (1983, 283). Yet, the Armenian-American press and community spokesmen tried to educate the immigrant generation with American political issues. Gradually, Armenians took on dual identities and commitments, establishing new roots, getting involved in American politics alongside their Armenian loyalties, allegiances, and interests.

At the collective level, the dilemma of being in diaspora was enigmatic intellectually,[78] psychologically, and practically in terms of the day-to-day functioning of Armenian institutions. Once Armenians realized that their condition was permanent for all intents and purposes, the political parties and other organizations had to formulate a new raison d'être to legitimate their claim to the leadership of the diaspora. As described at the beginning of this chapter, the Tashnags, as a revolutionary party, reaffirmed the goal of a free, autonomous Armenia. Others were less articulate, but they continued to function as if they were still middlemen minorities. The dream survived, more or less. Maintenance of Armenianness, as it was practiced under the millet system, and self-preservation, at any cost, became the order of the day. Politics of exclusion, including the phobia of the *odar* (non-Armenian) spouse,[79] old-fashioned survival formulas, resistance to innovation were ultimately self-defeating. The traditional diasporan institutions culminated in the present stagnation and sorry state of affairs that I have described throughout this book. In sum, while on the collective front the Tashnags and anti-Tashnags continue to play out their antiquated battles, the majority of Armenian-Americans, in later generations and younger cohorts, are growing further and further away from most communal behavior. The exceptions are emergent organizations and structures, those made in the United States, that closely correspond to individual forms of voluntary, symbolic Armenianness.

Respondents in the New York sample were asked to specify their political affiliation. Overall, 26.8 percent of the sample said they were Democrats, 36.2 percent said they were Republican and the rest (37 percent) said they were independent (see table 2.12). The overwhelming majority of the sample said they voted in presidential elections in 1984 (83 percent); only 12.6 percent did not vote and another 4.3 percent said they could not vote because they did not have their American citizenship papers. Neither voting behavior nor party affiliation were statistically related to any of the other independent variables. However, slightly more foreign-born than later-generation ethnics did not cast their vote (see table 2.13).

TABLE 2.12

Frequency Distribution of Political Affiliation by Generation

	Foreign-Born	U.S.-Born of F.B. Parents	1 Parent U.S.-Born	2 Parents U.S.-Born	Grandparent U.S.-Born
N = 560	(204)	(267)	(36)	(38)	(15)
Democrat	22.1	29.2	16.7	36.8	46.7
Republican	38.7	38.6	30.6	15.8	26.7
Indifferent	39.2	32.2	52.8	47.4	26.7
	100.0	100.0	100.0	100.0	100.0

TABLE 2.13

Frequency Distribution of Voting During Presidential Elections by Generation

	Foreign-Born	U.S.-Born of F.B. Parents	1 Parent U.S.-Born	2 Parents U.S.-Born	Grandparent U.S.-Born
N = 578	(215)	(270)	(36)	(41)	(16)
Yes	68.8	92.6	86.1	85.4	100.0
No	19.5	7.4	13.9	14.6	0.0
Cannot vote	11.6	0.0	0.0	0.0	0.0
	100.0	100.0	100.0	100.0	100.0

Only 15.8 percent of the sample said they were politically active in backing local and national issues and candidates (see table 2.14). Of these, 8.1 percent had helped local candidates for office, 4.7 percent had helped national candidates, and 2.4 percent both. Another three respondents (.5 percent) said they had run for office themselves. Most people (14.2 percent) had helped campaigns in minor ways; canvassing, distributing pamphlets, calling prospective voters, and the like (excluding dollar contributions), while 1.6 percent of the sample had provided major help in election campaigns. Political activity was somewhat more significant with education (tau c .12 significant at .0003 level) and religious affiliation (tau c .08 significant at .002 level) than generational status. The higher the educational achievements, the more the political participation; respondents with more than college education helped in elections 23 percent of the time compared to 10 percent for those who had high school diplomas. Also respondents

professing "other" religions (21 percent) and "no religion" (36 percent), who were the most assimilated in the sample, were more likely to be politically involved than those with Armenian denominations (e.g., 14 percent for Apostolics).

TABLE 2.14
Frequency Distribution of Respondents Politically Active by Generation

	Foreign-Born	U.S.-Born of F.B. Parents	1 Parent U.S.-Born	2 Parents U.S.-Born	Grandparent U.S.-Born
N = 583	(218)	(272)	(36)	(41)	(16)
No	90.4	80.5	86.1	80.5	68.8
Yes	9.6	19.5	13.9	19.5	31.1
	100.0	100.0	100.0	100.0	100.0

New York respondents were asked to agree or disagree with the following statement: "I would vote for an Armenian political candidate at local or national elections regardless of party affiliation." The results were statistically significant by generational status (.17*). Foreign-born respondents were most likely to vote for an Armenian candidate irrespective of political affiliation (71 percent), followed by the second generation (56.6 percent). Nonetheless, even in the third generation, the proportion of respondents who agreed with the statement was considerable (46.8 percent).[80]

Most of the comments on voting behavior were conditional on the qualifications and platform of the candidate. The statement hints of nepotism; it contradicts American traditions of freedom, democracy, and fair play. The following comments were made by young and old alike, but predominantly by American-born respondents: "provided he was a good candidate," or "assuming I agreed with his/her views," or "I vote on qualifications," and again, "only if candidate is qualified and agrees with my principles." A more articulate young second-generation lawyer wrote: "If the candidate were in the mainstream, party affiliation is secondary. If the candidate is extreme, I wouldn't vote for him or her regardless of the particular political party."

There was only one comment that advocated an ethnic stand. This was a middle-aged immigrant woman from the Middle East who said:

"I vote for the person who endorses the Armenian issues." In spite of the above reservations for voting for Armenian candidates, when all other considerations are equal, Armenian-Americans would cast their vote for a fellow Armenian. I was told by one of the community spokespersons I interviewed that a 1984 Armenian-American candidate for Congress received generous campaign funds from fellow ethnics. They could not help with actual votes because not many Armenians live in the district the candidate was representing (Manhattan). Fund-raising banquets or other events for Armenian candidates in local or national elections have received strong support from the Armenian-American community.[81]

Armenians have come of age in the United States. Consequently, more and more Armenian-Americans are acquiring political savvy and some are running for public office.[82] George Deukmejian, former governor of California, as the highest ranking Armenian-American in public office to date, serves as a role model for future generations. Increasingly, Armenian-Americans are also supporting electoral candidates of Armenian descent with financial contributions and votes whenever possible.[83] It is of little significance whether a candidate has previously been involved in Armenian communal activities; most aspirants for public service have not. Yet the community rallies to the support of candidates who claim Armenian descent, and wisely most do so. This symbiotic association between politicians of Armenian descent and Armenian-Americans testifies to their growing maturity in the United States and the flexibility with which they maneuver their symbolic Armenianness.

Armenian-Americans do not only support the candidature of fellow ethnics but are discerning of other politicians who promise to represent their interests in local, state, or national arenas.[84] The comments of the survey respondents indicate the increasing awareness among Armenian-Americans of the need to get involved in the political process. For example, a forty-five-year-old woman who immigrated from Turkey at age twelve wrote:

In America, we Armenians should run for public office and be effective legislators to be visible locally, nationally, even internationally and so maybe through these types of channels people will recognize us more easily and want to know about our heritage. What I am saying is that credibility will be established and will be visible no matter how the Turks want to eradicate our history from the books.

America is no longer recognized as a melting pot but ethnicity is quite stylish now, and we should take advantage of it.

The community leaders I interviewed were more explicit in declaring that the token numbers of American politicians of Armenian descent, in spite of their lack of involvement in the formally organized Armenian-American community, have done more to enhance Armenian interests in the United States than all the Armenian political parties put together.[85] For instance one informant said: "With the example of Deukmejian, now others are saying let's also do the same. People like Chip Pashayan [congressman from California] have done more for Armenians than official [Armenian] party members. This is something new for Armenians. They realize they need representation."

What exactly are Armenian interests, one should ask? Besides the acknowledgment of the Genocide, I suggest it is cognizance and respect as a people, and as "good" citizens of the United States. It is also making sure that as many Armenian-Americans as possible attain positions of power and prominence in public and private life. That is, they want to receive what they consider to be their share of the American pie, even if for the majority it is only by proxy.[86]

In sum, Armenian-Americans are dutiful citizens, voting at presidential elections, and participating in the electoral process—a few as candidates and most as supporters and voters. Armenians are also very proud of their record as exemplary citizens of the United States of America.[87] Armenians see themselves as law-abiding, peace-loving, hard-working, self-reliant people. They are quick to note that few of their ranks are on welfare and fewer are criminals. The following quote from a respondent (professional male sixty-two, born in Turkey, immigrated at age twenty-five) is typical of this belief:

Armenians have displayed an exemplary behavior in any country and society they have gone to live outside their land. They are law-abiding, contributing, loyal and supportive. It seems to me that in their quest to make life for themselves, they feel, too, a human obligation to their host country—for admitting them—to be good citizens. It is their way of paying the host country back. Except for the struggle against the Turks, the crime rate of the Armenians in any country including the U.S. is zero or negligible. We are simply a grateful people by good behavior to any host country outside Armenia.

Observers (e.g., Antreassian 1981, 253; Phillips 1978, 113-14; Mirak 1983, 175; Yeretzian 1923, 70-71) have suggested that

Armenians are generally reluctant to go on welfare because they feel
they should not expose their weaknesses and deficiencies to outsiders.
This may reflect the traditional value of saving "face" and avoiding
shame *(amot)* and other social blemishes. Armenian immigrants are
not unique in being good citizens; studies have found that immigrants
are less likely than the population at large to be apprehended for
violations of the law (Tilly and Brown 1974, 110). This is not to say
there are no Armenian criminals (see chap. 1).

Numerous respondents wanted to share with me how they, their
parents, or grandparents had been good citizens of the United States of
America, giving back to their adopted country what they had received
in hospitality and opportunity. For example a middle-aged, second-
generation woman wrote: "I believe my parents were happy to come to
the U.S.... They are good citizens and are content in the U.S."
Another second-generation woman said: "They are good citizens of
the United States—my parents. Never taking, always giving. Neither
they nor any of the Armenians who came to this country at that time
were on welfare, which bothers me now when the newcomers go on
welfare first; they do not even try to work. The early Armenian
immigrants contributed much toward the development of America."

An eighty-five-year-old woman who immigrated from Turkey at
age seventeen wrote: "I am forever grateful to the United States for the
safe haven it has provided my family, and truly it has been a land of
opportunity. I believe your survey would be more complete if you had
provided a section to allow me to tell you of the accomplishments of
my children and grandchildren." A sixty-three-year-old, second-
generation woman wrote: "Armenians in America appreciate this
country and the freedom we have."

A fifty-seven-year-old man, who like his mother was U.S.-born,
told me the story of his immigrant father and father-in-law, self-made
men who worked hard to become successful in America. He
concluded with the following comments:

> I could go on and on, but the point I am trying to bring out is that Armenians as a
> minority like so many in their times did not throw their hands and demand their
> new founded government do everything for them; but rather, [they] proved
> themselves by helping not only themselves but their fellow man. I do hope your
> paper, while on Armenians, will reflect to other minorities and perhaps 3rd World
> people that you must take your own initiative and develop it and give it all you

have, and that when coupled with the right help and assistance, the path for better living opens. Then one realizes they did it mostly themselves.

Yet another middle-aged woman who like her mother was U.S.-born explained: "My grandparents (and father) were a total asset to America. My father came to this country as 'steerage' and ended his days (at age 85 yrs old) as a very well-respected member of his community and the State of N.J. He 'gave back' and was one of the proudest 'Americans' you could have hope to know."

Approximately 65 percent of the sample agreed (28 percent disagreed and 7 percent had no opinion) with the following statement: "Armenian 'terrorism' in the last few years has soiled the good name of Armenians in the U.S.A. as a law abiding and peace loving people." Moreover, several respondents (mostly in later generations) wrote to voice their disapproval of "terrorism." A fifty-five-year-old, third-generation woman wrote: "Damn right. It makes us look like a bunch of hoods." Similarly, a twenty-five-year-old, third-generation man said: "I think the use of terrorism to further nationalistic causes is abhorrent and antithetical to American and Western values. Political pressure should be resorted to." Yet another middle-aged, third-generation woman wrote: "I feel embarrassed when the Armenians and Turks kill each other today.... Most Armenians involved have such hatred, and I do not want to be part of hating any fellow man."

On the other hand, foreign-born respondents were more sympathetic to Armenian "terrorism," some correcting the language of the questionnaire, crossing out the word terrorism and replacing it with patriotism and freedom fighters. A sixty-five-year-old man, who was born in Iran and settled in the United States in his youth, wrote: "I sympathize with Armenian terrorists. We should help them more. They are keeping the Armenian Question open. Too bad if [the] American Government does not agree." Another foreign-born young woman who immigrated recently from the Middle East said: "I do support the Armenian terrorism, because they have helped Americans know Armenians. I hate Turks and wish them dead, all of them."

Most Armenian-Americans condone the U.S. government's policies and decisions, even when such policies are antagonistic to Armenian interests. U.S. aid (i.e., tax dollars) to the government of Turkey is the best example. About 68 percent of the sample disagreed (16.5 percent agreed and another 15.5 percent had no opinion) with the statement: "I would support Armenian 'terrorism' against Turkish military bases." Armenian-Americans continue to support their government even when their personal judgment is contrary to established policies. That is why only 33 percent of the sample disagreed with the statement (35 percent agreed and the rest had no opinion): "I believe that the interests of the U.S.A. are indeed furthered against the Communist Bloc by supporting Turkey." A twenty-eight-year-old, third-generation man wrote: "I am disgusted by America's idiotic support (and paranoid support) of Turkey, because of their obvious border with the 'dreaded enemy,' but so is America's stupidity throughout the world." Indeed, being openly critical of the U.S. government's policies is the best of American democratic traditions. The results clearly attest to the civic and political assimilation of Armenian-Americans in the use of the political machinery, voting behavior, running for public office, and supporting Armenian and non-Armenian candidates by financial contributions or otherwise.

Public Involvement for Armenian Issues

So far, this study has shown that Americans of Armenian descent are fairly well integrated as individuals into the American political process. However, as an interest group, they are unlikely to be mobilized to their optimum potential for a number of reasons. First, Armenian-Americans are too few in number and geographically scattered. With the exception of Los Angeles, they do not represent a significant voting bloc in the United States, thus are unable to sway public opinion through the ballot box alone. Second, Armenian-Americans are poorly organized and so far have not been able to articulate their objectives cohesively.[88] The schism has blinded them to such an extent that it has prevented collaboration for the common good. Third, the effect of assimilation is undeniable. Significant human and material resources are lost because the traditional institutions have not been able to engage the attention and interest of those in later generations.

One of the few objectives that most Armenian-Americans can agree upon is the official acknowledgment of the Genocide, "the *sine qua non* of the Armenian experience in the twentieth century" (Ayanian and Ayanian 1987, 25). Ideally, such ethnic goals should be translated into concrete action through political channels. Respondents were therefore asked whether they had used democratic processes to influence decision making in favor of the Armenians in their local governments and through their congressmen and senators in the nation's capital. There is evidence that such political processes are effective. For example, an analysis of statements related to Armenian issues from *The Congressional Record* between 1965 and 1983 suggests that both houses of Congress were clearly in favor of acknowledging the Armenian Genocide in spite of the pro-Turkish policies[89] of the administration (Yegparian 1987). There were no differences between Democrats and Republicans when representation and size were controlled. Most notably, it was found that more political statements were made in favor of the Armenians "when the money, votes, and political activity started flowing from the Armenian community" (Yegparian 1987, 62). Such statements help legitimize Armenian claims by sheer repetition and publication in official government records. The gain may seem small, but it fulfills the Armenian goal of respect and recognition.

First, survey respondents were asked whether they had ever written letters to their congressmen or visited Washington to help pass a bill that would make April 24 "A Day of Remembrance of Man's Inhumanity to Man."[90] Overall, 41.4 percent of the sample had written to Congress; by all counts a remarkably high level of participation! First and second-generation respondents were slightly more likely to have done so than later-generation respondents (see table 2.15) but the relationship was not very significant statistically (tau c .09 significant at .01 level). On the other hand, writing to Congress was strongly associated with religious affiliation (.25*) and with sympathy to Armenian political parties (.22*). As expected, respondents with non-Armenian or no religious affiliations were least likely to have written to Congress (see table 2.16). Likewise, respondents who were indifferent or rejected Armenian political ideologies were least likely to write to their congressmen to further the passage of a bill that would have the Armenian Genocide recognized officially by the U.S. government (see table 2.17).

Second, respondents were asked to indicate how many of the three types of public action listed, if any, they had been involved in: getting jobs for other Armenians, helping establish an Armenian school, and furthering Armenian interests in their community. Public action was not defined in the questionnaire, but it is suspected that many misunderstood the question to mean individual action. Overall, 27.4 percent of the sample said they helped get jobs for other Armenians, almost 20 percent said they helped start an Armenian school, and the highest affirmative response (33 percent) was for the vaguest statement, namely to further Armenian interests, which could have meant almost anything. This finding adds weight to a loose definition of symbolic Armenianness and convenience in ethnic participation. The fewer the constraints, the more the variations, the wider the following.

With each passing generation there is a monotonic decline in the percentage of respondents who report having been involved in public action to help fellow Armenians (see table 2.18); from 66 percent of

TABLE 2.15
Frequency Distribution of Writing to Congress on the Genocide Issue by Generation

	Foreign-Born	U.S.-Born of F.B. Parents	1 Parent U.S.-Born	2 Parents U.S.-Born	Grandparent U.S.-Born
N = 582	(218)	(271)	(36)	(41)	(16)
No	55.5	56.5	63.9	78.0	75.0
Yes	44.5	43.5	36.1	22.0	25.0
	100.0	100.0	100.0	100.0	100.0

TABLE 2.16
Frequency Distribution of Writing to Congress on the Genocide Issue by Religious Affiliation

	Apostolic Armenian	Protestant Armenian	Catholic Armenian	Other (Non-Arm.)	No Religion
N = 574	(368)	(56)	(22)	(92)	(36)
No	49.5	64.3	81.8	73.9	88.9
Yes	50.5	35.7	18.2	26.1	11.1
	100.0	100.0	100.0	100.0	100.0

the first generation to 46 percent of the second generation, to 39 percent of those who have one U.S.-born parent, 27 percent of those with two U.S.-born parents and 12 percent of those with U.S.-born grandparents. The first generation were also most likely to advocate Armenian day school education and help start such institutions.

Contributing tax-deductible dollars to Armenian political parties or para-political organizations is the most popular form of involvement. The New York survey has also demonstrated that for emotionally charged issues, such as the Genocide, individuals are willing to write to their political representatives, or to editors of local and national newspapers. More active forms of political participation trail behind

TABLE 2.17

**Frequency Distribution of Writing to Congress on the Genocide Issue
by Sympathy to Ethnic Politics**

	Ramgavar	Tashnag	Neutral	Indifferent	Rejects Parties
N = 527	(28)	(109)	(143)	(177)	(70)
No	42.9	43.1	53.1	68.9	70.0
Yes	57.1	56.9	46.9	31.1	30.0
	100.0	100.0	100.0	100.0	100.0

TABLE 2.18

**Frequency Distribution of Engaging in Public Action in Support of Fellow
Armenians by Generation
(multiple response)**

	Foreign-Born	U.S.-Born of F.B. Parents	1 Parent U.S.-Born	2 Parents + U.S.-Born	Total
N = 299 (cases)	(146)	(126)	(14)	(13)	
Find jobs for Armenians (159 responses)	53.5	38.4	4.4	3.8	100.0
Help start school (114 responses)	60.5	35.1	2.6	1.8	100.0
Armenian interests (192 responses)	45.8	43.8	5.2	5.2	100.0

by a significant distance. Public demonstrations, rallies, and the like do not attract large crowds. For example, during the last few years, in solidarity with their compatriots in the homeland and in response to their demands for political support, Armenian-Americans in New York, predominantly from the first and second generation, staged vigils in front of the Soviet Mission to the UN, marched to the United Nations headquarters, held rallies in Times Square, sent telegrams to Moscow and Washington, and held press conferences. The number of individuals who participate in such public gatherings is very small, often a few hundred, on rare occasions it may reach five thousand or so. Likewise in Los Angeles, and other cities with sizable Armenian populations, the number of participants in such public events have consistently been negligible in proportion to the universe of people of Armenian descent in the United States.

Here, I need to point out that even though the ethnic press keeps abreast of the latest developments in the Armenian world, it is often the only source of such information. The large numbers of Armenian-Americans who are not exposed to the Armenian media tend to remain

TABLE 2.19
Frequency Responses to Attitude Statement on "Free Armenia"

Statement	One	Two	Three	Four	Five
Total N =	(560)	(573)	(559)	(569)	(567)
Strongly agree	6.6	13.6	15.4	17.6	26.3
Mildly agree	7.1	12.0	14.1	17.6	25.0
No opinion	31.6	20.1	23.8	26.0	17.3
Mildly disagree	12.1	8.0	8.9	16.0	13.8
Strongly disagree	42.5	46.1	37.7	22.8	17.6
	100.0	100.0	100.0	100.0	100.0

Statements:
1 "Armenians in the Diaspora should eventually settle in Soviet Armenia to avoid assimilation."
2 "I would be willing to live in a free Armenia."
3 "If necessary, I would fight to free Armenia."
4 "I believe that one day in the distant future we will be able to have a free Armenia."
5 "I consider Soviet Armenia as the spiritual homeland of Armenians."

ignorant of the issues and ideological interpretations, and thus are unlikely to become engaged in political action, symbolic or otherwise. People of Armenian descent alienated from the Armenian community are more likely to accept the social construction of reality put forward by the national press and news media.

A case in point is the language bias of prestigious national newspapers. Armenian-American scholars have noted that the Armenian/Azeri conflict was described as "ethnic unrest" while similar conflicts in the Baltic Republics was called 'nationalistic.'[91] Similarly, in a content analysis of five major national dailies *(New York Times, Washington Post, Boston Globe, Los Angeles Times, Christian Science Monitor)* from February to August 1988, Chorbajian (1989) found that the reporting of the Karabagh issue was grossly misinterpreted. Instead of reporting a grass-roots movement for democratization, human rights, and self-determination, the U.S. dailies took their cue from the State Department and denied fair and accurate coverage of the movement. Chorbajian suggests that the wrong timing of the Karabagh movement from the American perspective made it a kind of nuisance in their eyes. It risked disturbing the thaw in U.S.-Soviet relations, and embarrassing NATO's ally, Turkey, by revealing the historical roots of the conflict.

In sum, there is a straight-line generational decline in involvement in Armenian issues and interests. Because the Genocide is a topic dear to the hearts of many Armenian-Americans, more people wrote to Congress than participated in action to help fellow Armenians. A general pattern seems to emerge. It characterizes all aspects of public involvement. The integration of first- and second-generation Armenian-Americans in the larger "American" society parallels their participation in the Armenian world. However, starting with the third generation, most people of Armenian descent limit their collective manifestations of their Armenianness to a minimum. As shown in the section above, Armenian-Americans, irrespective of generational status (except for the very recent immigrants), have become skilled in the use of the political machinery. Here, one finds that with the third generation their participation in Armenian issues is curtailed, especially the more demanding forms of involvement.

Diasporan relations have changed with the ebb and flow of East-West relations since the 1920s (see Phillips 1978, 196). Periodically,

Armenian-Americans have had to reevaluate their status and their rapport with the "motherland." Five attitude statements were included in the questionnaire on the issue of "free Armenia" (see table 2.19). It is remarkable that between one-fifth and one-third of the sample had no opinion on the matter. About one-half regarded Soviet Armenia as a spiritual homeland of Armenians. It is the highest affirmative position Armenian-Americans were prepared to take. It should be noted that these statements are not value-free. Those who espouse a pro-Tashnag ideology believe strongly in "freeing" Armenia, one day. The anti-Tashnag ideology, on the other hand, advocates the protection of a superpower for the survival of an Armenian nation (see also Phillips 1978, 268).

These complex statements on "free Armenia" were included in the survey to measure support for traditional ideologies. Very few respondents would ever consider living anywhere except in the United States of America. They vehemently indicated:

I'll stay in U.S. of America—Thank you (female 68, second generation).

I thank the Turks for being so nasty and evil because if not I might have been born there too.

Thank God for America.

America is the *only* country I will fight for (female 55, third generation).

I would never leave America. I am *American*. Was born *here* (male 53, third generation, mother Italian; emphasis in original).

The views of the "silent majority" of American-born Armenians are best summarized in a speech delivered on the occasion of the visit of Catholicos Vasken I to New York City in October 1987. The committee chairperson, a man who came to the United States with his parents at a very young age, is representative of second-generation ethnics. He said:

I am an American.... I am not a product of a separate Armenian community that happened to be located in this land. I am part and parcel of the mainstream of America. I am not a stranger or a guest or here by anyone's sufferance. If Diaspora means a return someday to another land, then I am not of it. This is home. I am American.[92]

The survey respondents are citizens of the United States of America and happy to be so. Armenia, Soviet or free, lies in the realm of the spirit. It is an emotional link.

Yet, Americans of Armenian descent do not live in a vacuum. Diasporan Armenians and international events have the power to influence their self-image and status. It has been suggested that "group trauma" may happen at any time (Bender and Kagiwada 1968, 370). An ethnic group may periodically gain or lose status because of the differential impact of international events. Group trauma may heighten self-appraisal of the ethnic group by its members and by the society at large. For example, anti-Semitism and the media's exposure of the Holocaust is more likely to keep Jewish ethnicity in "continual revival," while the absence of these factors may induce Italian ethnicity to become latent (see McKay 1982, 411).

The earthquake is an excellent illustration of "group trauma." When the massive earthquake hit Soviet Armenia on December 7, 1988, killing over 25,000 people, injuring 19,000, destroying fifty-eight cities, towns,[93] and villages and leaving over 500,000 men, women, and children destitute, world attention focused on the Armenians for days and weeks. The news media reported on Secretary Gorbachev as he interrupted his visit to New York City and flew back to the disaster scene. It gave updates on rescue efforts and the international teams that converged on Leninakan and Spitak. It broadcast news on volunteers, donations, and fund-raising efforts by charitable and humanitarian organizations. In the United States, the spotlight was also on Armenian-Americans.

Armenian-Americans were deeply saddened and grieved by the death and devastation in their spiritual homeland. They saw the earthquake as the last episode in a chain of calamities befalling their people. It was interpreted as a direct threat to their survival as a people, as a nation. They felt frustrated and betrayed by their historical destiny. Vartan Gregorian, president of Brown University and prominent Armenian historian, is reported in *New York Times* to have said: "Armenians feel like Job's people.... God has tested us for more than 2,000 years."[94] Yet, there was solace in the world's recognition of their tragedy and the rescue efforts that ensued. There was also hope in their belief in their creativity and ingenuity as a people to start anew once again. They would rebuild new lives, new cities, new communities.

The Armenian community in the United States officially went into forty days of mourning, and requiem services were held in Armenian churches. Upcoming Christmas and New Year celebrations sponsored by Armenian voluntary associations were all cancelled; some people even refrained from decorating Christmas trees and exchanging gifts in the privacy of their homes. Armenian-Americans volunteered their time, effort, expertise, and contacts at centers where aid was being collected.

Many men and women of Armenian descent who had not been active in communal structures brought in their contributions, even by a token check. Nonetheless, their reaction to the earthquake was first and foremost a humanitarian concern. It touched them as it had touched many, many others around the world, regardless of their race, nationality, religion, or social status. Even people who had never heard of Armenians in their lives were moved to participate in the relief effort. With a massive problem at hand, and a concrete objective to fulfill, it was easy to solicit help and obtain it.

The earthquake heightened the general American public's awareness of the Armenians. Unlike the group traumas caused by "terrorism," this time, Armenian-Americans were not ashamed to be identified with their ancestral roots. The world's reaction was compassionate, supportive. Watching television, people were able to empathize with a father holding his dead son in his arms or a little girl bewildered by the enormity of the chaos around her.

At times of crises such as these, when the images of the devastation in human lives are still fresh in people's memory, and the goals of fund-raising are clear to all, symbolic Armenians, even ex-ethnics, are pressed to set aside their alienation from their ancestral roots. However, this involvement should not be construed as a "return" to communal life or behavioral Armenianness. Feelings of sorrow and monetary contributions, even volunteering one's time at Armenian centers, does not signify a desire to return to traditional forms of Armenianness or a need to participate in events and activities sponsored by Armenian churches and organizations.

The "political" earthquake in Armenia has terminated the ideological impasse of Armenian institutions in the diaspora. A free, autonomous homeland is in the making. Now, the political parties and other traditional institutions can officially relinquish the dream of repatriation. Instead, they need to formulate fresh ideologies that reflect the realities and needs of Armenian-Americans; they need to account for the fact that the overwhelming majority are here to stay and their Armenianness is voluntary, symbolic. The new Armenia is the legitimate "center." Of course, support is not unanimous; not everybody will agree with the policies of the government in Yerevan. Already, many Armenian-Americans are apprehensive about the Republic's decision to open trade and other cooperative relations with the government of Turkey, the archenemy of the Armenians. Many question that decision and reflect on the historical record of this treacherous neighbor. Nonetheless, some reason that the physical survival of the people of Armenia and their welfare has to take precedence over emotional hobbyhorses of diasporan Armenians.[95]

As the "center" of Armenian existence, the Republic's population can shoulder the major responsibility for creating culture and perpetrating history. This does not mean that there is no role for Armenian-Americans. On the contrary, the relationship between Armenian-Americans and the Republic of Armenia can become functional. Analogous to Israel's ties to diasporan Jews, center and periphery can draw from each other's strength and achieve a mutually supportive co-existence. For the time being, Armenia is rebuilding itself: physically, economically, socially, intellectually, culturally, and any which way there is. Its need for assistance is urgent and monumental. Already, many Armenian-American organizations have initiated a variety of projects to share in that rebuilding. For many of these organizations, the decision to invest in the future of Armenia was not hard to reach. In their by-laws and constitutions, they had provisions for serving other Armenians in need. Is there a more compelling reason than coming to the rescue of a homeland, believed to be almost lost? Many Armenian-American organizations leaped to their new mission, like a child rushes to a mother who has suffered a traumatic accident and needs to be taken care of.

Paradoxically, setting up concrete, clearly defined goals and specific, tangible projects, such as building a cold-storage unit or a plant to construct prefabricated housing, training neurosurgeons or correspondents for Cable News Network with the latest technological innovations, are more likely to excite and engage symbolic Armenian-Americans in later generations. Indeed, Armenian identity in the United States may be easier to sustain when the goals for Armenian-American institutions become instrumental, than when self-preservation was an end in itself. But why would later-generation men and women of Armenian descent want to get involved in Armenian projects, albeit, in a limited, professional capacity? By lending their expertise and knowhow to someone in need, they may derive ego gratification, enhance their self-worth, and feel empowered by their group affiliation. These are exactly the same functions that symbolic Armenianness fulfills. Isn't the grass next door greener? Traveling to Yerevan, on occasion, adds significantly to the list of perks.

In this chapter, I have shown that two of the traditional Armenian institutions, the church and political parties, are suffering from their inability to adapt to the needs of their "clients." Most significantly, they have not been able to find the language to communicate with Armenian-Americans in later generations and younger cohorts. The Armenian Apostolic church has the advantage of offering a unique, "exotic" Christian tradition for those who seek diversification from the homogenizing tendencies of American society. Furthermore, it is easier to be a "church community" in America than an "ethnic community." The double boundaries of ethnicity and religion reinforce one another for the Apostolics, adding a buffer against forces of assimilation. Yet, Armenianness in later generations is not an ascribed status. The church cannot expect men and women who by an accident of birth have Armenian roots to automatically becoming parishioners and absorb its tenets by osmosis. The church needs to change in order to accommodate the symbolic Armenians; it needs to introduce more English and shorten the services, emphasize the devotional aspect of religion, and socialize future generations to appreciate its uniqueness. Like any other commodity in a competitive market, the church needs to become attractive to its potential "customers."

Armenian political parties are becoming more and more insignificant in the lives of later-generation descendants. The post-World War II immigration wave is the only reason why they are still in existence today. Young recruits are hard to come by. As Simmel predicted, the jurisdictional dispute is alienating more and more

Armenian-Americans and forcing them to drop out of most communal forms of participation. A handful of organizations, that have sprung up in the last few decades, are challenging the political hegemony of the traditional parties. These are attractive to symbolic Armenians because they demand only token participation and embody their goals and interests as Americans first and Armenians second.

The New York data shows that Armenian-Americans, irrespective of generation (except for newest arrivals), have become sophisticated in their knowledge and use of the American political system. About a third are Republicans, another third Democrats. The majority cast their votes in presidential elections. Some have been active in local and national politics and most realize the importance of political participation. They support their government even if they personally do not agree with its policies. Above all, Armenian-Americans see themselves as good citizens of the United States of America. Many feel that their image was tarnished by the Armenian "terrorism" of the 1970s, but they take heart that when the earthquake struck Armenia, the world came to its rescue.

Armenian-Americans have not been mobilized effectively to defend their interests, at home and in the diaspora. The recognition of the Armenian Genocide by the U.S. government is one of the few ideological motives that incites the participation of Armenian-Americans; about two-fifths of the respondents in the survey had written letters to Congress on the matter. Armenian-Americans do not sustain traditional ideologies on the eventual return to a free, autonomous homeland; though about half of the sample maintained that [Soviet] Armenia was a spiritual homeland. Adamantly, many wrote to say they were Americans and they were here to stay. Group trauma such as the physical and political earthquakes in Armenia have focused world attention on the Armenians in recent years, keeping their ethnicity in continual revival. But this does not change the fact that Armenianness in the United States is voluntary, symbolic. Armenian-Americans will not go back to the life-style of their grandparents. They will not start attending Divine Liturgy every Sunday nor become Hunchags, Ramgavars, or Tashnags.

Notes

1. *Ideology* is defined "as a pattern of ideas which simultaneously provides for its adherents: (1) a self-definition, (2) a description of the current situation, its background, and what is likely to follow, and (3) various imperatives which are 'deduced' from the foregoing. In ideology there is a strong tendency to merge fact and value, to superimpose upon 'things as they are' the things that are desired" (Matossian 1958, 218).
2. The Armenian Protestant and Catholic churches are not officially involved with the schism, though some of their adherents are members or sympathizers of Armenian political parties.
3. Ordjanian, using a political economy perspective, calls the Armenians "one of the world's 'non-state nations'; peoples who consider themselves temporarily disinherited, while worthy of attaining nation-statehood" (1991, 41).
4. Such ideas were brought forward at several Open University Seminars sponsored by the Zoryan Institute for Contemporary Armenian Research and Documentation, Inc. that I attended in the 1980s. For example, in a seminar on "Legitimacy and Democracy in Armenian Life" by Jivan Tabibian (3 December 1988, at Columbia University, New York City) the ideology of an eventual return was criticized as a myth that is hindering Armenian-Americans from becoming integrated as a more powerful 'interest' group in American mainstream politics, hence the world.
5. The Armenian Apostolic church is also known as the Armenian National church, Armenian Orthodox church, or the Gregorian church (after the evangelist Gregory the Illuminator). The church is called Apostolic after the apostles Thaddeus and Bartholomew, believed to have first preached the message of Jesus Christ to the Armenians.
6. Armenians believe that their national conversion came in the year 301 A.D. Some scholars have; however, postulated that 314 A.D. is more accurate since it comes after the Edict of Milan in 313 when Christians in the Roman Empire became officially tolerated.
7. Note that the Armenian Apostolic church shares theological agreement with the Coptic Church of Egypt, the Abyssinian Church of Ethiopia, the Syrian Church, and Malabar Church of India. The split came about when the Armenians failed to attend the Council of Chalcedon in A. D. 451 because of theological (over the monophysite formula) and political disagreements (asserting their independence from Byzantines and Nestorians in Iran). Armenians believe that in 451 their ancestors were fighting for the very existence of their faith. The legendary nobleman Vartan Mamigonian, at the head of a small army, was at Avarayr battling the formidable forces of the pagan Persians (Zoroastrians). Though defeated, the Armenians were allowed to practice Christianity (it seems the Persians conceded because they were facing political problems elsewhere). The moral victory at Avarayr has since become for the Armenians a symbol of self-determination, of surmounting all odds, and a reminder of the fusion of the church's interests with those of the state. Now, *Vartanank* is one of the "holy" days in the Armenian calendar. See Ordjanian (1991, 228-32) on how it is celebrated in an Armenian elementary school in contemporary U.S.A.
8. According to Cahnman, the origin of the millet system is an "Eastern" practice dating back to the Sassanid rulers of Persia who were then Zoroastrians. They

had found it advantageous to tolerate Christians and Jews. Islam carried the system further. Non-Muslim subjects were organized into homogeneous communities, and political power was delegated to their own ecclesiastical leaders. The millet lacked territorial cohesion and military power, but was an autonomous unit within the state. The laws of personal statute were based upon religious sanctions. In a similar vein to Emile Durkheim's description of the *Elementary Forms of Religious Life* (New York: Free Press, 1954) Eastern Christianity, traditional Judaism, and Islam "do not dissociate religion from social life, from community ties, from civic status, and from law" (Cahnman 1944, 256). Society is thus conceived as an enlarged family and perpetuated through religious worship. By contrast, modern nationalism is based on territorial boundaries and political contract. For example, the Armenian delegation at the Congress of Berlin in 1878 was a representative of the Catholicos of Armenians. Millets were initially quasi-religious, endogamous, living in close proximity, but became a "people" late in their history. It is the "time aspect of society rather than the space aspect" that is significant in the consciousness of such 'people' (Cahnman 1944, 256). Similar to the Armenians, the Greeks, who were organized under the same principle, continue today to regard the church and nationalism as inseparable (Scourby 1980, 70). It should be noted that remnants of the millet system persist in many Middle Eastern nations today, notably in Lebanon where the sociopolitical structure of the nation is based on proportional representation of religious communities in government and politics. At the beginning of the Civil War, the Armenian community in Lebanon was one of the seven most important religious groupings in Lebanese politics (see Bedoyan 1979).

9.   Libaridian, in tracing the development of Armenian political thought until the 1850s, observes that Mehmet II intentionally created the office of Patriarch in the fifteenth century to regulate the affairs of the millet and assist in collecting taxes. The Patriarch came even to dominate the catholicoci of Sis and Akhtamar who were above him in the ecclesiastical hierarchy. Moreover, the Patriarch was not elected nor accountable to the Armenians in the empire; ultimately his power within the millet was circumscribed by that of the Sublime Porte. Libaridian concludes: "Behind the facade of religious autonomy and cultural self-management, the millet system excluded the masses from any real participation in Ottoman political life while sustaining the impression of Armenian access to power" (1987, 94).

10. It should be noted that there were Armenian Catholics in Asia Minor well before the nineteenth century. One of the most famous converts was Abbot Mekhitar, a scholar and clergyman, who embraced Catholicism in 1695. In 1701, he founded the Mekhitarist Order whose primary aims included the promotion of literacy and education among the Armenian people through the training of teachers and translation and printing of classical western thought. On the other hand, the Armenian Evangelical Church was established on 1 July 1846 when thirty-seven men and three women met in Constantinople (Tootikian 1981, 11).

11. The Armenian Apostolic Diocese marks its 100th anniversary in 1991 with celebrations in Worchester (see *Armenian Reporter,* 20 June 1991, p 10). After being the hub of Armenian life in America, at present the city struggles to maintain a viable Armenian-American community. Estimates suggest that it lost more than half of its population since its heyday just before the Great Depression. About 4,500 Armenian-Americans are said to live in Greater Worcester today

(see Kevork Imirzian, "Trading Places: As the First Bastion of Armenian Immigration, Worcester Struggles to Keep the Memory Alive," *Armenian International Magazine,* May 1991, pp. 22-24).

12. See also "Brief History of the Armenian Evangelical Church of NY as 90th Anniversary Approaches," *Armenian Reporter,* 24 October 1985, p. 17. See Megerdichian (1983) for a brief history of Armenian churches in America and lists of parishes in North America.

13. Megerdichian (1983) estimates 25,000 Protestant Armenians live in the United States. I suspect this has increased in the last couple of decades. Tootikian (1981) numbers 24 Evangelical churches [19 of these being members of the Armenian Evangelical Union of North America (see list pp. 289-90)]. Los Angeles seems to witness the multiplication and revival of its Protestant congregations. Old church edifices are being renovated for more spacious surroundings or sold for more desirable locations. For example, the Armenian Cilicia Congregational Church in Pasadena first founded around 1922-27 has recently held dedication ceremonies for its refurbished new sanctuary (see *Armenian Reporter,* 20 June 1991, p. 14).

14. Megerdichian's (1983) list of Armenian parishes in the United States totals 123: 49 in Eastern Diocese, 17 in Western Diocese (total 66); 22 in Eastern Prelacy, 7 in Western Prelacy (total 29); 22 Protestant and 6 Catholic churches. Megerdichian includes in his list congregations that do not necessarily hold regular services every Sunday.

15. Saint Nerses Armenian Seminary, established in 1967 in conjunction with St. Vladimir's Orthodox Seminary in Crestwood (NY), offers a Master's degree in Divinity. Students (mostly men) take courses in Armenian language, history, liturgy, music, church doctrines, canon law, etc. The seminary is governed by a board of directors and is under the jurisdiction of the Eastern and Western Diocese. In May 1990, a young American-born woman became the ninth graduate of the school in the previous five years (see *News from St Nerses,* A publication of St. Nerses Armenian Seminary, Fall 1990, p.1). Still the church seems to suffer severe shortages. According to one account, in 1990, of a total of forty active parishes in the Eastern and Western Diocese, seven had no full-time priests (almost 20 percent). This figure ignores the twelve "missions" where young congregations will be needing priests in the years to come. Moreover, it is estimated that in the next ten years, 40 percent of the clergymen will be retiring (Michael Findikyan, "Priests Do Not Fall From Heaven," *Window* 4, n. 4 [Fall 1990]: 20-22). For a critical view of this (e.g., special issue: "Is the Collar Choking the Armenian Priest?" Fall 1990) and other matters related to the Apostolic church see *Window: View of the Armenian Church,* a quarterly published by The Armenian Church Research and Analysis Group, Reseda, California.

16. *Hai Heghapokhakan Tashnagtsutiune* or Tashnag for short, it is spelled Dashnak in Eastern Armenian dialect.

17. Ter Minassian (1984, 19) explains that the word *fedayee* comes from Persian and means "he who is committed" or "he who is sacrificed."

18. *Ramgavar Azadagan Gusagtsutiun,* or Ramkavar in Eastern Armenian dialect. This was a merger of three earlier groups including the original party, *Sahmanadir Ramgavar* party, which was founded in 1908 in Cairo (Walker 1980, 354).

19. The Hunchag party was established in 1887, *Hunchag* (meaning "bell") was the

name of the party organ. See also Aram Arkun. "Hunchakians." *Armenian International Magazine,* March 1991, pp. 25-28.

20. Opposition to Tashnag militant ideology does not prevent the *chezok* (nonpartisans) from attending cultural and educational programs of general interest to the Armenian people sponsored by organizations affiliated with the Tashnag party.

21. Atamian (1955) has produced an interesting sociological analysis of the Tashnag/anti-Tashnag ideologies and worldviews. However, his account is heavily biased toward the Tashnag position. It should be noted that the book was written during the Cold War period when superpowers had strongly penetrated Armenian thought and action, aggravating the internal schism and propelling it toward bloodshed (in Lebanon).

22. The term "starving Armenians" was used in the United States between the 1890s and 1920s when the plight of the Armenian people was a *cause célèbre.* Numerous fund-raising campaigns publicized the massacres and deportations and asked donations to help orphaned Armenians. By the beginning of World War I, there were more American missionaries in Turkey than anywhere else in the world, serving mainly the Armenians. The term "starving Armenians" became a household term as children were scolded into cleaning up their plates, and Protestant relief associations collected pennies from Sunday schools (see Dobkin 1977, 8; Papazian 1986, 48).

23. Organizations that were in existence prior to the schism took "sides" unofficially because of the political affiliations of their membership, such as the Armenian General Benevolent Union (AGBU). AGBU is a well-endowed charitable organization established by Boghos Nubar Pasha in Cairo, Egypt, in 1906. Though nominally the AGBU is not aligned politically, its members have been predominantly Ramgavar party members, partisans, or *chezok* (nonpartisans).

24. In her study of the Armenian community in Washington, DC, O'Grady corroborates that the pro- and anti-Tashnag churches were only five miles away from each other, "yet many active community members had never been in the opposing church either for church services or community activities" (O'Grady 1979, 33).

25. The post-Genocide Armenian community of Turkey (mainly Istanbul) is an interesting exception and remains to this day apolitical due to social pressures, intimidation, and suppression by the Turkish authorities (see Libaridian 1979, 43-46).

26. Claire Mouradian corroborates that Armenia SSR was *"nationale par la forme, socialiste par le contenu"* (1990, 307, italics in original). The Soviets tried to dictate diasporan life any which way they could, including the infiltration of the church by their agents (p. 318). The goal was to legitimate Soviet Armenia as the only national homeland in the eyes of the diasporan population. For example, the word *ardashman* (literally "extramural, beyond the borders") was the favorite Soviet term for diaspora, because Soviet Armenia was the "real" patrimony of the Armenians (p. 396). For example, Mouradian explains that Archbishop Tourian wanted to celebrate November 29, the date of the Sovietization of Armenia in the church, while he had refused to commemorate April 24 (the date for the commemoration of the Genocide). He was instrumental in enticing the "progressive" elements of the community to oppose the display of the tricolor flag in public events (see below), a conflict which eventually led to his murder (p.

318).

27. The Armenians are by no means unique in being internally divided. For example, Padgett (1980) writes that the Serbian Orthodox Diocese was split into two violently opposed groups in 1963, not because of religious differences, but because of accusations that the mother church in Yugoslavia had come under the influence of the Communist government. The opposing faction argued that it could fight communism more effectively if it supported the church in Belgrade. The Armenian experience is closely applicable to that of the Serbs. Padgett observes: "Despite virtually identical religions, cultural, and social practices, the two parishes have remained committed to their 'cause' with equal fervor" (1980, 60).

28. Mouradian makes a convincing argument that the Soviets had their own agenda in making these concessions. However, she writes, after the death of Stalin: "Les techniques de séduction de la diaspora se sont progressivement affinées" (1990, 335); from crass manipulation of patriotic themes, they adopted new campaigns aimed to "charm" and "seduce" the diaspora. After 1964, the Armenian Communist party created the Committee for Cultural Relations with the Diaspora, *(Spiurkahay-Komité),* equipped with with a staff of seventy, it aimed to promote the Armenian language and culture — *hayabahbanoum* ("conserve Armenianness"). For example, after the 1960s, about fifty teachers were trained each year in Armenia SSR; schoolbooks and other publications were diffused, often free of charge (300,000 between 1962-1980); several magazines and journals were distributed; Armenpress, a permanent information agency, started to transmit news directly from Yerevan (via Moscow) to Beirut in 1967, to New York in 1970, to Paris in 1972; the Mesrop Machtoz prize in education, the Komitas prize in music and the Sarian prize in fine arts were established for diasporan Armenians who deserved recognition; tourism flourished and artists and intelligentsia exchanged visits between the "berceau de la nation" (cradle of the nation) and diaspora. The Soviets also erected a memorial for the victims of the Genocide (though April 24 was not officially recognized as a holiday until 1988!). Mouradian goes on to observe: "La diffusion de la culture et de la langue arméniennes n'est pourtant pas tout à fait neutre" (1990, 337). The communist ideology remained omnipresent (for example in the text or photos of their publications), but more seriously, the word "liberty" was totally absent in all Soviet Armenian communications; instead they talked about "peace" and "security." The impression projected from all this was that Sovietization and Russification of Armenia had been in the best interests of the Armenian people; it had left a very positive impact. What the Soviets never mentioned was the question of human dignity and freedom. Mouradian concludes: "les Arméniens ont tirés de leur histoire une obsession de la durée et de la survie, à n'importe quel prix, fût-ce celui de vivre à genoux en attendant des jours meilleurs. 'Plutôt rouges que morts,' en somme" (1990, 345).

29. Often petty issues became the cause of violent disagreements. For example, the conflict over the tricolor flag goes back to the murder of the archbishop in 1933. The red, blue, and orange flag was the official flag of the short-lived independent republic and since then that of the Tashnag party. The fight over the display of the tricolor is merely symbolic of the greater conflict of what is best for the Armenian people, and what are the best means of achieving these goals. The issue of the flag has now been resolved. The Republic of Armenia has officially

adopted the tricolor as the emblem of its people and nation.

30. It should be noted that the very first "terrorist" act was the killing of two Turkish consular officials in Santa Barbara (CA) on January 28, 1973 by seventy-eight-year-old Gourgen M. Yanikian, a "survivor" who had lost most of his family to the Genocide (Gunter 1986, 32).

31. About 20 "terrorist" attempts are attributed to the ARA and about 150 to the ASALA (Mouradian 1990, 291).

32. See Khachig Tölölyan. Review of *ASALA - Irrational Terror or Political Tool,* by Anat Kurz and Ariel Merari, and *"Pursuing the Just Cause of Their People"* - A Study of Contemporary Armenian Terrorism, by Michael M. Gunter. In *Armenian Reporter,* 24 November 1988, p. 4.

33. For an example see Robert Cullen. "A Reporter at Large: Roots." *New Yorker,* 15 April 1991, pp. 55-76.

34. Among the new leadership are several members of the Karabagh Committee (transformed into the Armenian Pan-National Movement [*Hay Hamaskaine Charjoum*] in November 1989).

35. Armenian-American historian Gerard Libaridian (who was the first non-Soviet person to assume a government position in the Soviet Union as director of the Department of Research and Analysis, Presidium of the Parliament of Armenia [see *Armenian International Magazine,* May 1991, pp. 19-20]) argued, in a lecture delivered in New Jersey, 6 June 1991, that democracy and independence are inseparable goals. It is not possible to further democracy in Armenia without independence. He also noted that the Soviet constitution has provisions for the secession of its republics. The law requires that certain procedures be followed, including a referendum by the people. The process, until the severance of final ties, is scheduled to take five years. See also Libaridian's views in a speech he delivered at the Second Congress of the Armenian National Movement in Yerevan, 25 May 1990, reproduced in his edited volume *Armenia at the Crossroads* (1991).

36. Church and peoplehood were highly intertwined for women survivors of the Genocide. A recent study concurred that to be an Armenian was to be a Christian and vice versa (see Sarkisian 1984, 41).

37. There was one respondent in the study whose religious affiliation was Jewish. The number of Jewish Armenians is likely to increase in the future with increasing intermarriage. It would be interesting to see which one of their inherited identities, if any, they will adopt.

38. Two aspects of religion are are most likely to be sharply differentiated in large metropolitan communities. It has been observed that urban areas encourage less associational, devotional involvement, but more communal ties. However, in small towns, attendance in a local church is necessary to establish social ties, thus making the associational and communal aspects of religion more inseparable than in larger communities. In large places, especially if one felt strongly about organized religion, people do not have to attend services to have contact with members of their socioreligious subcommunity (Fischer 1982, 211-15).

39. Apostolics traditionally have special prayers said for their loved ones for the forty-day and first anniversary of their deaths. Often, other departed relatives are also mentioned in such services.

40. This is similar to the Greek Orthodox faith due to historical circumstances and the legacy of the Ottoman rule. "Religion is not a personal matter, nor is it a

guide to conduct" (Dorothy Lee, quoted in Scourby 1980, 70).

41. Holy Cross Armenian Church in Washington Heights in upper Manhattan is one of the oldest churches in this area and historically has played a pivotal role in Armenian-American history (see Atamian 1955). At present, only old-timers continue to live in the church neighborhood, most of their children and grandchildren having moved to the suburbs or other states. The congregation and administration of the parish is now in the hands of recent immigrants from Istanbul who commute to the church from surrounding suburbs. See also Avakian (1985, 81 et seq.) for a personal description of the Washington Heights Armenian community in the 1940s.

42. See Appendix for questionnaire. Weddings, funerals and holidays were volunteered responses. Had they been printed in the questionnaire, they would have received more responses.

43. The report does not describe the sampling procedure or methods of data collection used in the AREC survey, but it appears that it was a nonrandom sample. Using only Prelacy parishes is another source of bias, but in religious matters, it is assumed that the answers would have been similar if the Diocesan parishes were included. Further, it should be noted that the sample consists only of respondents affiliated with the Armenian church, thus their results are expected to be more conservative than the New York survey.

44. This reflects the average age of the communally involved member (both in sacred and secular spheres); it matches the mean age of participants in the New York sample.

45. The clergy I interviewed said that a non-Christian spouse marrying an Armenian in the Armenian church is asked to convert first. This is not the case for non-Armenian but Christian spouses, even those who are nominally Christian.

46. Quoted in Keoseyan (1981, 72) from *Nation et Religion,* 1980, Milano: ICOM.

47. See also Vigen Guroian. "The Armenian Church in the American Diaspora: Survival or Mission." *Armenian Reporter,* 20 August 1987, p. 2.

48. In sharp contrast, the clergymen I interviewed believed that such issues would not interest their congregations. A foreign-born informant also told me that the church does not have a position on such issues; it is so liberal that it allows every individual to decide on his or her own. What this informant missed is that individuals may want guidance in thinking through some of these issues. "Religion" in the sense used by Pattie above, is supposed to provide formulas for life and death, for suffering and misery, for ties with the supernatural, and so on.

49. See Vigen Guroian. "Armenian Nationalism and the Ferment of Faith." *Christian Century,* 27 February 1991, pp. 233-36.

50. See also "Toward a Diaspora Theology." 1990. *Window: A View of the Armenian Church* 1, n. 2 (Spring): 22-26.

51. Interestingly, these are the reverse proportions to those found in Lebanon (before the Civil War). Bedoyan (1979, 121) estimated that the Armenian Catholics constituted about 15 percent of the Armenians in Lebanon, while the Armenian Protestants were approximately 5 percent, the remaining 80 percent belonged to the Apostolic church. The United States was more attractive to Protestant Armenians than to Catholic Armenians because of their familiarity with the English language and the American culture that they had learned in Protestant missionary institutions. Similarly, Kayal (1970, 276) has noted that Protestant Syrians (and Lebanese) because of their affiliation with the American

Presbyterian church were "better prepared for their encounter with America" and their experience of social mobility was faster. See also Adamic (1940, 132-46) who gives similar reasons for the rapid adaptation of an Armenian Protestant family in America at the turn of the century. The Armenian Catholics were more likely to be francophone. It is only in the last couple of decades that relatively larger numbers of Armenian Catholics have immigrated to the United States. They fled the Arab nationalistic movements in Syria and Egypt and the Civil War in Lebanon.

52. There are approximately 15 percentage points difference in the Apostolic estimate between the New York survey's 65 percent and Mirak's 80 percent. This means 18.75 percent decrease in the number of Apostolics since the early twentieth century. In the Protestant case, the decrease is between 33.3 percent and 50 percent, depending on which of Mirak's estimates is considered, 15 or 20 percent (in the New York sample 10 percent were Protestant).

53. It should be noted that Protestant Armenians are perceived as heretics by the Apostolic majority. This gives the Apostolics a sense of superiority, and a feeling that they are the bona fide representatives of Armenianness.

54. Kayal (1970, 277) has observed that Episcopalians are conceived of as Western equivalents of Eastern Orthodoxy. Warner and Srole (1945, 100) make similar associations in their study of Yankee City and conclude that the "religious affinity between the Armenian Apostolic Church and the Episcopal Church, . . . led to affiliation between the two and more rapid acculturation [and social mobility] of the Armenian group." It is not surprising that a significant number of the respondents in this study (2.3 percent) were members of that congregation.

55. Lenski (1963, 55) has observed that conversion of spouses in mixed marriages to one or the other religion reduces conflict within the nuclear family. Data on such conversions for the New York study are not available. Those who profess no religion are unlikely to convert, yet they might occasionally accompany spouse and children to spouse's church.

56. A recent study suggests that contrary to popular assumptions, cities do not decrease religious attendance. Cities provide more access to churches, and to a variety of churches, all competing for adherents. This competition facilitates mobilization (see Finke and Stark 1988). This implies that where there are no Armenian churches in one's vicinity, one is likely to attend any local church. The case of the Protestant Armenians in Long Island is a case in point; most have become members of local Protestant denominations.

57. Evidence indicates that when a couple have children, there is "often a quickening of religious interest on the part of the new parents. This frequently develops when the problem of transmitting the cultural heritage to the children is faced" (Lenski 1953, 636; see also Mueller and Johnson 1975). The New York data supports these claims. Respondents who attended an Armenian church most frequently (about once a week) were parents of school-age children.

58. Kayal (1970, 276, n. 4) has found that the Syrian Orthodox in America were more likely to send their children to the nearest Protestant Sunday school rather than a Catholic school because of their traditional dislike of Catholics. It might be postulated that this is similar to Apostolic Armenians.

59. Likewise, in a study of young people's attitudes about the Greek Orthodox Church, Scourby (1980, 57) found a similar ambivalence about the use of English in the services. Her informants felt that some Greek should be kept in the service,

otherwise the Greek church would lose its essence. Nonetheless, Greek Orthodox parishes with predominantly later-generation congregations use mostly English and stress the religious over ethnic commitment (Saloutos 1973).

60. Most Saturday schools (for teaching the Armenian language and culture) are run in conjunction with the local church and on church premises (for more details on schools see chap. 4). Also the Armenian Diocese and the Armenian Prelacy each have their separate departments for language instruction. They have even initiated the writing and publication of series of books for teaching Armenian at Saturday schools. It is interesting to note that the Armenian Diocese in New York City offered a one-day crash course in Armenian language for a number of years on the anniversary of the Genocide for beginners, intermediate, and advanced levels. Undoubtedly, such a course serves a purely symbolic function. It is ideally suited for symbolic ethnics.

61. These days, some health-conscious individuals stop eating candy, chocolate cakes, and other sweets during Lent.

62. Phillips (1978) has found that there are approximately 2,000 Ramgavar party members and 3,000 Tashnag party members in the United States. Membership consists of people who have sworn allegiance to the party, pay dues, and attend meetings. According to a community leader I interviewed, there are a maximum of 150 official members of the Tashnag party in the New York and New Jersey area, the overwhelming majority (95 percent) being foreign-born. My informant said that he knew of only three U.S.-born official Tashnag party members. The Ramgavar party consists of 25 or 30 members in the New York area, all of them foreign-born. And there are no more than 5 foreign-born members of the Hunchagian party. The community leader added that to these members the party was a social reality; they had all grown up with it. According to this source, 20 to 25 percent of the Armenian population in New York/New Jersey is pro-Tashnag, an estimate that corresponds to the survey data above. According to a recent article on the Hunchags in *Armenian International Magazine,* on the East Coast the party supports an athletic club, a cultural union, and a monthly paper, *Yeridasrt Hayasdan;* while on the West Coast (i.e., Los Angeles) the party has an athletic club, a cultural union, a Sunday school, and a weekly newspaper, *Masis* . See Aram Arkun, "Hunchakians: Founded More Than a Century Ago to Liberate Armenians from Ottoman Rule, the Social Democratic Hunchakian Party is Now Involved in Strengthening the New Republic of Armenia," *Armenian International Magazine,* March 1991, pp. 26-28.

63. Phillips (1978) provides several incidences on the local scene that demonstrate how the political dichotomy is alienating the young (pp. 244, 259); how one woman was so disgusted with the strife that she became a Jehovah's Witness (p. 240), how a wedding never took place because the bride and groom came from opposite sides of the ideological conflict (pp. 223-30), and how an Italian Catholic daughter-in-law was preferred to one from "the other side" (p. 224).

64. Fifty-six percent of those born in Turkey (26 percent would not); 57 percent of those born in the Middle East (26 percent would not); and 64 percent of those born in Soviet Bloc countries (32 percent would not) said they would attend any Armenian church. By contrast, 29 percent of those born in the United States said they would attend any Armenian church (32 percent would not).

65. The poll was a nonrandom questionnaire distributed to the regular subscribers of the *Armenian Reporter* (mainly in New York and New Jersey) plus an additional

sample of households in Philadelphia and the Boston area). Four hundred and eighty six (486) households responded to this poll. The self-selection of the respondents into the study is biased toward Armenian-Americans who are active and concerned members of their churches and communities. A surprising 75 percent of the sample were dues-paying members of Armenian churches. The Coalition of Church Unity, the group that conducted this survey, has not published the response rate to the questionnaire. The response rate is not likely to be high considering that the *Armenian Reporter* has about 5000 subscribers according to its owner/publisher. Assuming they all received a questionnaire, about 10 percent appear to have responded to the poll.

66. The percentage of the nonaffiliated in the Church Unity Poll is far below the figures reported in the New York study. This confirms that my study included a larger number of American Armenians who were not active in the Armenian community.

67. According to a telephone conversation with an executive officer of the Armenian Assembly, 22 February 1988.

68. For example see special issue, "Teaching about Genocide," *Social Education* (Official Journal of National Council for the Social Studies) 55, 2 (February 1991). It includes an article by Rouben Adalian, academic affairs director of the Armenian Assembly, entitled; "The Armenian Genocide: Context and Legacy." The Armenian Assembly has also published a booklet to help educators entitled: *Armenian Genocide Resource Guide*, 1988.

69. Armenian Assembly of America, *Annual Report*, 1990, p. 1.

70. For example, the Armenian Assembly perceives its task to be the increased involvement of Armenians in the American democratic process, stressing the importance of human rights, promoting public understanding and awareness of Armenian issues (see pamphlet issued by Armenian Assembly of America, *Aims and Accomplishments*, Bulletin 05, no date).

71. The Armenian Assembly does not have grass-roots support, but has trustees who pay at least $1,000 annually. In 1990, there were approximately 350 trustees.

72. Officially, the Armenian Assembly is adamant in declaring that it "competes with no other organization, rivals no group, and is friend and supporter to all. It is non-sectarian and non-partisan in both the Armenian and American contexts. . . . [It] claims no exclusivity in dealing with issues, persons, or institutions" (see pamphlet published by Armenian Assembly, *Aims and Accomplishments*, Bulletin 05, no date).

73. *Zoryan Notes* 3, n. 1, supplement (April 1988).

74. Thirty-five percent of the latter have lived in the United States for over fifteen years and the remaining 15 percent are more recent arrivals (*Zoryan Notes* 3, n. 1 [April 1988]). With the resignation of Gerard Libaridian as director in early 1991 in order to assume a position in the government of Armenia, the Zoryan Institute was left with no one at its helm. Its future remains to be seen.

75. It should be noted that repatriation drives of diaspora Armenians to Armenia SSR were encouraged several times during the seventy-odd years of Soviet domination. On the numbers of *nerkaght* (repatriates), the precise dates, their reception upon arrival, their problems of adaptation, and integration see Mouradian (1990).

76. See special issue: "Armenians in Poland," *Ararat* 31, 124 (Autumn 1990).

77. See Khachig Tölölyan. Review of *ASALA - Irrational Terror or Political Tool*,

by Anat Kurz and Ariel Merari, and *"Pursuing the Just Cause of Their People"* - A Study of Contemporary Armenian Terrorism, by Michael M. Gunter. In *Armenian Reporter*, 24 November 1988, p. 4.

78. Diasporas have concerned Armenian intellectuals for a long time. It is no wonder that a scholarly journal on the subject was the brainchild of an Armenian (see *Armenian International Magazine*, April 1991, 28-31). As executive editor, in his preface to the first issue of *Diaspora: A Journal of Transnational Studies*, Khachig Tölölyan argues that diaspora is the "other" of nation-states. In the modern world, diasporas have proliferated, challenging the legitimacy and effectiveness of nation-states. The main problem of a diaspora is that of borders; the new manifesto calls for a fresh "vision of the world as a 'space' continually reshaped by forces — cultural, political, technological, demographic, and above all economic — whose varying intersections in real estate constitute every 'place' as a heterogeneous and disequilibriated site of production, appropriation, and consumption, of negotiated identity and affect" (Tölölyan 1991, 6). For example in North America, Jews, Armenians, and Greeks, to a lesser extent, have used the vocabulary of a diaspora.

79. A case in point is the election of Richard McOmber, an *odar pesa* (his wife is of Armenian descent), to the presidency of AGBU in 1988. This action was vehemently criticized in the Armenian community, and numerous letters were sent to the editors of the Armenian press (e.g., *Armenian Reporter*, 17 March 1988, p. 3 - letter to the editor).

80. Likewise it was found that Greeks in Norfolk (VA) voted predominantly for the Nixon-Agnew ticket in the 1968 presidential election. Agnew's Greek ancestry swayed the votes of most independents and some Democrats in spite of assimilation (Humphrey and Louis 1973).

81. A major fund-raising black tie banquet was held in Boston's Copley Plaza for about 1,000 guests on Saturday 10 October 1987, for California Governor George Deukmejian. Among the guests were Vice-President George Bush, and Senators Dole, Kennedy, and Pressler. See "Coming of Age of Armenians in Politics," *Armenian Reporter*, 15 October 1987.

82. The Armenian Assembly's special publication *Armenians in America* (1987) is a tribute to those who have succeeded in their respective fields of endeavor as Americans of Armenian descent. This publication enumerates the following Armenian-Americans in public service: George Deukmejian, governor of California; Congressman Charles Pashayan, Jr, representing the 17th district of California (Fresno); Chuck Haytaian, majority leader of New Jersey General Assembly; George Keverian, Speaker of the House of Massachusetts; Julia Tashjian, Connecticut's secretary of state. In addition to these prominent five, there are at least eight more men of Armenian descent who have served in local and national governments intermittently and several aspirants to public office.

83. For contributions to Governor Deukmejian, see e.g., *The Economist*, 21 September 1985.

84. The Armenian Assembly of America issued a report just before the 1988 presidential elections entitled: "Congressional Report Card, 100th Congress (1987-1988), and Presidential Candidate Questionnaire." Its aim was to supply Armenian-Americans with relevant information on the past record of their elected officials. It is pertinent to repeat here the avowed function of the Armenian Assembly. In their own words, it "seeks to promote the welfare and interests of

Armenian-Americans and to encourage greater community participation in government at the local, state and national levels." All this adds further evidence to the claim of the increasing sophistication of the population under study in the political affairs of the nation.

85. For example, the *New York Times* (22 May 1988) wrote that presidential candidate George Bush was accused by Democrats of pandering to the Armenian-American vote and hoping to elicit the endorsement of California Governor George Deukmejian. Bush used the term Genocide, contrary to Reagan administration policy, in campaign speeches in Fresno, California, where a sizable Armenian-American community resides and where Charles Pashayan, the only congressman of Armenian descent, has his constituency. This is the type of coverage and attention Armenian-Americans would like to receive a little more often.

86. Achieving positions of influence and decision making power is assumed to have a trickle-down effect in terms of rewards, kickbacks, etc. For example, George Deukmejian was asked by *Armenian International Magazine* journalists how many Armenian-Americans he had appointed or nominated for office during his tenure as governor of California. He replied: "You know, people have asked me, 'Why aren't you running again?' and in jest, I've replied: 'Well, I've run out of Armenians to appoint.' Seriously, though, I don't know the exact number, but it's in the hundreds." Then the journalists asked him: "Would it be between 200 and 300?" To this Deukmejian responded: "Yes, so I get kidded a lot by non-Armenians about that, but all of my appointees are extremely qualified individuals and are doing a superb job" (*Armenian International Magazine*, September 1990, p. 12).

87. It is interesting to note that the Armenian Student Association, an educational, social organization for young and not so young people, offers a "Good Citizen Award" (see *Armenian Reporter*, 3 September 1987).

88. On the Armenian lobby in Washington, DC see Tony Halpin and Vartan Oskanian, "Voices on the Hill," *Armenian International Magazine*, April 1991, pp. 10-22. According to the article, the basic tools of a lobbyist are "votes, money, friendship and accurate information." But above all, the issue in question must be in America's national interest. The reader is reminded that the first two prerequisites are in limited supply for Armenian-Americans.

89. The Turkish government is reported to have paid at least $2 million to its American lobbyists in 1989 (see Kevork Imirzian, "Turkish Lobby in America," *Armenian International Magazine*, July 1990, pp. 30-32).

90. To facilitate the task of the ordinary citizen of Armenian descent, ethnic organizations have prepared documents and facsimile letters and lists of officials with their addresses. This package is sent to all those on organizational mailing lists whenever there is a pending bill in Congress or similar need.

91. Zoryan Institute Open University Seminar, 22 October 1988 at Columbia University, New York City.

92. *Armenian Reporter*, 5 November 1987, p. 5.

93. See *Armenian Reporter*, 23 February 1989, p. 1.

94. Ari I. Goldman, "The Armenians, Still 'Like Job's People,'" *New York Times*, 18 December 1988, sec. 4, p. 2.

95. For a critique of diasporan fears of Pan-Turkism, the paralysis in the Armenian collective psyche that has produced a "nation of victims," and the negative

politics of distrust that rationalizes the need for a "third force" to defend the homeland, etc., see "Introduction" in Libaridian 1991.

3

The Armenian-American Community

In the previous chapter, two interdependent institutions, church and politics, cornerstones of the Armenian-American subculture and collective life were examined. The pattern that emerged indicates that these traditional institutions lose their holding power over those in later generations and younger cohorts. Yet, Armenian identity survives, and in a few cases, people seek alternative institutions that are more congruent with their voluntary brand of Armenianness. In this chapter, I look at the remaining aspects of communal life, concentrating on the structural relations of Armenian-Americans as they come together to form a "community" in the United States and on how that community evolves and changes with the passing of generations. Community comprises both the formally organized structure of voluntary associations and the activities they produce and the informal networks of friends and acquaintances—in other words, the Armenian-American subculture. This subculture emerged and developed in response to the specific economic, social, and political conditions consecutive waves of Armenian immigrants and their offspring encountered in the one hundred years they have lived in the United States of America, as a people.

The focus here is on group boundaries and social relations within and between groups. This is measured by computing the amount of traffic or social contacts across different types of boundaries. It should be noted that there are various levels of inclusion/exclusion and various definitions of insiders/outsiders. For instance, at one level, this study calculates the relative proportion of ties American-born Armenians have with Armenians born in the Middle East and those from Soviet Bloc countries; at another level, it counts the proportion of ties Armenian-Americans as a group have with members of non-Armenian groups. It is hypothesized that the greater the exodus from the Armenian fold, the weaker the boundaries that contain Armenianness and the greater the chances of dispersion into the mainstream.

In the early 1960s, analysts observed that white immigrant groups like the Armenians had adapted remarkably well to American life by altering certain aspects of their imported culture and borrowing other traits from their surrounding environment. Yet, it seemed that immigrant groups continued to retain relatively rigid boundaries. That is, while most Armenian-Americans interacted extensively with members of other ethnic and racial groups in the workplace and neighborhood, they confined their intimate, face-to-face contacts and leisure-time pursuits to fellow Armenians. In sociological terms, this means that structural assimilation had not been achieved because primary group ties were still limited to insiders. There was much speculation at the time whether there would ever be structural assimilation; that is, the dissolution of ethnic boundaries. Since then, one study after the other has conclusively shown that for white ethnic groups, the process has been accomplished. Even the advocates of the revival hypothesis in the 1970s have conceded that there is no return to behavioral forms of ethnicity.

What about the Armenians, the reader should naturally ask. Armenians are no exception. Data prove that a greater and greater proportion of social ties of Armenian-Americans are with non-Armenians. That does not mean that the decline of the Armenian-American community is imminent. Quite the contrary, ethnic communities, especially of numerical minorities like the Armenians, tend to persist in urban settings such as metropolitan New York and

Los Angeles. It is true that the group may be diluted and weakened by those who perforate ethnic boundaries and assimilate into other social worlds. However, as Claude Fischer observes, these "defectors" leave "behind a more purified core of committed ethnic-group members—'a saving remnant'" (1984, 153). In addition, as mentioned in chapter 1, the tendencies of the modern world toward globalization and homogenization make individuals seek different types of small-scale, face-to-face structures to satisfy some of their unmet needs. This desire for community is a nostalgic wish for what they imagine "the good old days" were. Men and women in postindustrial societies such as the United States cannot and do not want to go back to the communities of the past that were characterized by constraints of proximity, social class, caste, race, etc. Commitment to community, today, is a voluntary attachment on the basis of similarity and compatibility. Time and space are no longer fixed, but for short periods, communities of like minds, feelings, and purpose come together to fulfill a number of manifest and latent functions. Thus, ethnic communities among others, though small and volatile in spatial and temporal terms, may continue to thrive in modern contexts.

The Armenian Community in the USA

Even though Armenians are very small in size relative to other ethnic groups in the United States, in a few metropolitan areas their numbers have become sufficient to warrant the formation of a large array of communal structures. The largest Armenian communities in the United States are to be found in the vicinity of the following cities (in alphabetical order): Boston, Chicago, Detroit, Fresno, Los Angeles, New York, Philadelphia, Providence, San Francisco, and Washington, DC. Some of the smaller communities, often organized around a church and/or charitable organization, are to be found in Phoenix, Tucson (AZ), San Diego (CA), Hartford and other coastal cities (CT), Miami, Fort Lauderdale, Boca Raton (FL), Worcester, Springfield and other towns (MA), Asbury Park and other townships in South Jersey (NJ), Niagara Falls, Syracuse, Rochester (NY), Houston, San Antonio (TX), Racine and nearby cities (WI), and Richmond (VA).

With modern systems of transportation and communication, total isolation from the Armenian world is a matter of individual choice.

Nonetheless, there is evidence that those who have ready access to communal structures are more likely to maintain identity than those who do not. Even if those with easy access do not participate frequently in Armenian organizations and the events they sponsor, their ethnicity is kept in continual revival by chance contacts with Armenian persons, places, topics, and role relationships. Households of Armenian descent in districts with few or no co-ethnics can maintain ties with the Armenian-American community by subscribing to the Armenian press, by receiving the newsletters of various organizations, by telephoning and occasionally visiting relatives and friends (often for weddings and funerals) in places like New York, Los Angeles, and Boston. They can also have Armenian food, books, music, videotapes, and an assortment of souvenirs with Armenian lettering or symbols mailed to them, if they so wish.

In localities with a handful of Armenian families, people sometimes establish their own "mini" community by meeting informally a few times a year for a Labor Day picnic or Thanksgiving dinner, sharing Armenian food, music, gossip, and a game of *tavloo* (backgammon). In geographically isolated households, the options for involvement in the Armenian-American community are somewhat limited to informal ties with family and friends and vicarious participation through the mail and dollar contributions. It should be noted that in most immigrant groups, formal associations have been created as a result of ethnic size and success, rather than as a reaction to social isolation (Fischer 1984, 120).

Thus, a critical mass of Armenian-Americans in a given region is a necessary precondition for a community to exist and flourish. On the one hand, by sheer economies of scale, the larger the group, the greater the complexity of institutions it can carry and the more specialized audiences and clienteles it is able to satisfy. For example, in Los Angeles and New York, organizers of Armenian events can afford to cater to the needs, life-styles, budgets, and fantasies of a diverse group of people. They may offer a concert of chamber music performed by Armenian musicians, scholarly lectures and debates on Armenian history and literature, a dramatic production in Eastern Armenian dialect, a debutante ball for the sons and daughters of affluent families, an exhibition of the works of Archille Gorky, and so on. They are also in a position to nurture their own esoteric medley of voluntary associations; some of these might be Armenian only in composition, such as soccer teams and professional associations.

On the other hand, the supply side of Armenianness in areas with a heavy concentration of Armenians can stimulate sporadic participation and provide the illusion of vitality. By supply side I mean the availability (and abundance) of Armenian bookstores, grocery stores, restaurants, radio and TV programs, churches, voluntary associations, and so on. Therefore, the larger the size, the greater the complexity of the community, the easier it is to please a significant proportion of the Armenian-American population. Given that symbolic Armenianness rests on an individual's interpretation of ethnicity, one's residential location is an influential, but not a decisive factor in identity maintenance. There will always be men and women of Armenian descent in downtown Los Angles who will choose not to identify with their ancestry; while there might be others in Alabama, Hawaii, or Vermont who might actively try to maintain ties with the Armenian world.

The Armenian-American community, as it exists in centers enumerated above, is not a geographically bound structure. Armenians have not had their own ghettos in the United States, though they have had and still have neighborhoods and towns with high Armenian density, such as Fresno, Hollywood, and Watertown. Residentially, Armenian households are spread throughout a given metropolis and its surrounding suburbs; however, the churches, the church halls, and the premises of Armenian clubs and organizations constitute the ecological locale of the Armenian-American community (see also Phillips 1978, 262). In these locales, the bulk of Armenian communal life takes place: the religious services, the weddings, the funerals, the lectures, the concerts, the dinner dances, the bazaars, the committee meetings, and so on. Zenner's (1985, 124) very eloquent comments about the Jewish community are equally applicable to the Armenians.

> The synagogue, home observances of festivals, Jewish community centers and the like help demarcate a Jewish symbolic arena in both time and space. While many, if not most, Jews only move in and out of the arena a few times a year, others remain in the arena for a wide range of activities. While there is no corporate Jewish body, the activities within the arena and the movements through it indicate that American Jewry retains its vitality.

I define the Armenian-American community as a social construct, a mental image to both insiders and outsiders. The community consists of social networks of families, friends, acquaintances, as well as institutions and organizations. It comprises formal and informal relations among people of Armenian descent sharing a collective consciousness and concern for people and things Armenian. Instrumental ties often coincide with intimate association as when friends and relatives join the same compatriotic societies to organize fund-raisers or when family groups meet in the Armenian arena at dinner dances or summer picnics. Participation in programs sponsored by Armenian organizations, such as lectures and concerts, has the latent purpose of establishing and sustaining intimate, face-to-face associations with fellow Armenians. Involvement in such associations is likely to emanate we-feelings and be a source of social and emotional fulfillment.

Like the Calabrians, Palermans, and Venetians who were most trusting and loyal of their fellow *campanelismo,* the earliest Armenian immigrants who came to the United States before the Genocide or shortly thereafter, identified each other by the village, town, or district they came from in the "Old Country." Thus, some were *Aintabtzies,* others *Bitlistzies,* or *Vanetzies,* still others *Marashtzies* or *Gesaratzies* (i.e., those from Aintab, Bitlis, Van, Marash, and Caesara, towns in Turkey), and so on. These regional ties and loyalties led to the founding of compatriotic societies: charitable organizations whose aims were to promote educational endeavors in their hometown or province and care for refugees and orphans. According to Mirak (1983), these compatriotic societies started as local efforts in various Armenian communities throughout the United States, but soon developed regional and national unions. There were some twenty-seven Armenian compatriotic societies active in the United States by 1906.

If the manifest function of these compatriotic societies was educational and charitable, their latent function was to reconvene immigrants from the same region, at least occasionally, to exchange news and information and reminisce about old times in the ancestral village or town (Mirak 1983, 174). It is interesting to note that in contrast to compatriotic organizations of other ethnic groups in the United States, Armenian ones did not give "sickness or death benefits for their members. This peculiarity stemmed from the Armenian precept that such contingencies were the responsibility of the immediate family only and not of the community" (Mirak 1983, 175). Such sentiments continue to prevail today. There is a general reluctance to finance social service agencies (see chap. 1).

Many of these compatriotic societies continue to exist today, though much of their vigor has been sapped. The *Armenian American Almanac* (1990) lists some twenty of these organizations. For example, the Compatriotic Union of Koghi Khoops village (based in Dearborn Heights, MI) was founded in 1900. Its purpose is "to preserve the identity of Armenian men and women of Khoops descent through a group perpetuating fraternity and friendship, and to observe August 1, annually, as Khoops Memorial Day, to pay homage to all deceased Khoopsetzees" (p. 20). Similarly, the General Society of Vasbouragan, established in 1931 with eight chapters and headquarters in Detroit, aims "to keep alive in the hearts of the new generation of Vasbouragan descendants the love of their ancestral lands and strengthen their faith and confidence in the future; to preserve the historic and cultural heritage of the Armenian people; to extend financial aid to "Vanetzie" students to further their education" (p. 20). In other words, such compatriotic societies are limited in scope and their membership consists predominantly of "old-timers." They have little to offer to later-generation Armenian-Americans, except for the proceeds of small scholarship funds established in the past.[1]

Distinctions by towns and regions in Turkey are at present meaningless to most Armenian-Americans, except as historical references to the birthplace of their ancestors. In the place of such regional ties and identifications, Armenian immigrants who came to the United States after World War II distinguish themselves by the host countries they (and their parents) lived in. They are referred to as Iranian-Armenians, Lebanese-Armenians, Romanian-Armenians, Soviet-Armenians and so on. The sociopolitical conditions in these host societies created differences in the way Armenianness was experienced. First, it is worth repeating that Armenian identity in the United States is a matter of voluntary choice, while in most Middle Eastern countries it is ascribed by birth. Second, there are differences in the emphases or focal points various nationality subcommunities place on Armenian maintenance because of their prior experiences.

For instance, in Lebanon, powerful political parties influenced Armenian community life and politicized ethnicity; while in Istanbul, the church and schools were the only suprafamilial institutions allowed to function by the Turkish government; thus communal life came to be centered around them. Once in America, Lebanese-Armenians are more likely to join political and charitable organizations, such as the Homenetmen Armenian General Athletic Union, Hamazkayin Armenian Cultural Association, and others under the umbrella of the Tashnag party, or AGBU and Tekeyan Cultural Association, under the auspices of the Ramgavar party. Turkish-Armenian immigrants are more likely to support the Apostolic church by joining church choirs,[2] serving on parish councils, and becoming members of the Knights of Vartan—a fraternal organization whose purpose is to preserve Armenian culture (including the church) in the United States.[3]

The formal and informal groupings of the Armenian community in metropolitan areas crisscross each other. Some formal organizations have a broader set of aims and are open to and welcoming of both American-born and foreign-born members, while other organizations have more specific aims and generally cater to particular groups or subcommunities. Likewise, certain immigrants are more familiar with Armenian-American voluntary associations and readily join the local chapters once they settle in the United States, while others keep more to themselves and have established their own associations because of language, dialect, socioeconomic and other distinctions.[4]

AGBU (Armenian General Benevolent Union) is an example of an organization that covers a broad range of educational, cultural, and charitable projects in the United States and diaspora aimed at preserving and promoting Armenian language, identity, and heritage. It also plans and finances an extensive program of activities annually in many communities; occasionally, it has even hired professionals to take care of specific projects.[5] Its members are both American-born and foreign-born,[6] they are more likely to come from affluent socioeconomic backgrounds, and have Ramgavar and *chezok* (nonpartisan) political orientations.

On the other hand, alumni associations of Armenian high schools in Aleppo, Beirut, Cairo, Istanbul, and Nicosia are a common form of particularistic organization. Their membership is restricted to alumni, their families and friends; they sponsor several fund-raising activities per year, and at least part of their proceeds are earmarked for the schools in the "Old Country." For example, Essayan-Getronagan Alumni, Inc. represents a girls' and a boys' high school in Istanbul and has been active in New York City for the last couple of decades. Similarly, the Armenian Evangelical College Students' Association is for graduates of a coeducational high school in Beirut.[7] Other examples of particularistic organizations for recent immigrants are: The Armenian Society of New York, for predominantly affluent Iranian-Armenians whose communal life evolves mostly in their center in Little Neck, Long Island; and the Armenian-American Support and Educational Center in Palisades Park, New Jersey, which caters to Turkish-speaking, skilled and semi-skilled artisans, and small businessmen with relatively low educational skills.

Most of these particularistic voluntary associations, like the compatriotic societies before them, have charitable and educational objectives; however, their underlying purpose is to meet the social-psychological needs of the immigrant generation. These organizations cushion the assimilative process; while maintaining ties to their countries of origin, providing companionship and community, they promote acculturation. That is, they turn immigrants into American citizens who are proud of their ethnic identity. In the final analysis, by encouraging education, providing grants, loans, and scholarships, Armenian voluntary associations seek status and recognition for their people in the larger American society.

When Armenian-Americans talk about "the community," what do they mean? The Armenian-American community has an amorphous structure depending upon one's definition. At its core is a group of ethnics, predominantly from the first and second generations, who are highly active in the churches and formal organizations, both as audience and participants, and as leaders and organizers. Their primary group ties, that is their intimate relations and leisure-time pursuits, are likewise mostly with fellow Armenians. In terms of size, this group is the smallest in relative and absolute numbers. This core group is to be contrasted to those people of Armenian descent who continue to identify with and take pride in their Armenian heritage but are almost totally absent from organized communal life. Their family networks and friends are likewise predominantly inactive in the Armenian world. These are the most assimilated, the most symbolic of ethnics. In between those with maximum communal participation and those with almost none, there are those who sporadically attend Armenian religious services, cultural performances, or social events. Their primary associations are with both Armenians and non-Armenians. Even though all three groups described above are identified as Armenian-American, in this study, *the Armenian-American community* is understood to consist only of the core group of maximally involved Armenians in primary and secondary relationships and those in the periphery with intermediate degrees of participation.[8]

A caveat is in order here. I have described and referred to the Armenian-American community, but it would be more appropriate to discuss *communities or subcommunities*. The Armenian-American community is not a monolithic structure. To outsiders it gives the impression of a cohesive entity; however, internally the community is fragmented[9] into various subcommunities: politically/ideologically, generationally, by country of origin, by denomination, by social class, by cohort. Often the linkages between these groupings are not powerful enough or loyalties are too differentiated to mobilize very large numbers of people of Armenian descent. Moreover, I repeat my earlier contention that the Armenian-American community or subcommunities have almost no influence in drawing the support and participation of the organizationally unaffiliated people of Armenian descent.

I would like to argue further that there are few structural links between the various subcommunities. For example, in selling tickets for social benefits such as concerts, in spite of extensive advertising in community papers and mailings, the organization sponsoring the event is generally unable to induce the support and participation of people outside its own network. This should not be surprising because according to Katz and Lazarsfeld's (1955), research in diffusion and mass communication, people do not act on information supplied by the mass media unless it is transmitted by somebody they know. That is, word of mouth is more effective than media advertisement. Because of breaks in structural linkages between the various subcommunities, the spread of information and more active forms of mobilization on a massive scale is often handicapped. The commemoration of the Armenian Genocide is another example. As one of the most powerful symbols for rallying people of Armenian descent, public ceremonies so far have not been able to enlist the participation of large crowds, even for the seventieth and seventy-fifth anniversary. Overall, the total number of persons physically present at such rallies remains only a fraction of the estimated number of people of Armenian descent who live in the area where such events are organized.[10]

Structurally then, it might be argued that the Armenian-American community appears to be made up of semi-insulated subcommunities. Network theory provides a conceptual framework that may help explain the lack of social cohesion among Armenian-Americans. It has been suggested that if a community is partitioned into small networks and cliques, community-level organization and mobilization will be inhibited because paths or bridges from any given leader to community-wide rank-and-file followers will be reduced by lack of trust (Granovetter 1973). Indeed, there are few leaders that are known and respected by the entire Armenian-American community.[11]

Instead of a structural explanation, Talai (1984), after studying the Armenian community of Greater London, suggested that the absence of centralization and coordination among the voluntary associations is related to the lack of particularistic, instrumental, rational goals. She described these associations as diffuse; that is, they are to be contrasted to Max Weber's classic depiction of formal organizations—they do not have specific aims and do not follow rational bureaucratic procedures. Such associations maintain their viability if they can recruit a cadre of volunteer staff and members. Recruitment efforts have to rely on persuasion and subtle obligations to people's ascriptive identities. Members must want to join these associations, since most of Armenian communal life takes place in one's leisure time. Such associations are secondary or have little relevance to one's occupational and domestic life.

The more diffuse the organizational framework and the more ambiguous the aims of the association, the greater its capability of appealing to larger sections of a very heterogeneous Armenian population. About twenty-two autonomous, often competitive voluntary associations have emerged to serve the varying interests, attitudes, and experiences of the Armenian population in London. If, on the one hand, the diffuse and loosely articulated structures of these associations are functional for mobilizing a wider cross-section of Armenians, on the other hand, they have prevented the development of permanent overarching communal facilities and effective lobbying groups that could coordinate general interests of the community. Thus, the lack of community-wide cooperation, according to Talai, is due to the nature of the organizational structure of the Armenian community.[12] Talai adds:

> The objective of mobilizing an ethnic group en masse and the objective of promoting explicit and specific political, economic and social aims on its behalf are not easily reconcilable. For these objectives call forth organizational tendencies pulling in opposite directions. It is not surprising therefore that we often find that it takes rare moments of acute crisis for these objectives to truly merge. (1984, 201)

The Armenian community of London differs from that of New York or Los Angeles mainly in its smaller size[13] and the fact that the majority of its adult population are first-generation immigrants. However, the same rationale could be applied to the community in the United States. The various particularistic Armenian-American organizations described above could enlist the support and participation of most of the first generation and second generation; however, not a single organization is able on its own to speak for the entire community in the United States or mobilize it.

Organizational Participation of the New York Sample

The Armenian-American community in metropolitan New York and New Jersey boasts a rich array of voluntary associations to suit almost every life-style, and interest. Organizational participation is measured by questions on membership, positions of responsibility, and frequency of attendance in Armenian and non-Armenian voluntary associations; as well as by attendance at events and activities sponsored by ethnic organizations. The sample was provided with a list of eleven types of voluntary associations; respondents were asked to check the number of Armenian and non-Armenian organizations they belonged to in each category.

Membership in Voluntary Associations

About half of the respondents do not belong to any voluntary associations: Armenian (53.9 percent) or non-Armenian (48.9 percent). Professional associations (27 percent), charities (19 percent) and American political parties (16 percent) are the most cited organizational affiliations in the non-Armenian world. Within the Armenian community, charities (24 percent), church committees (23 percent), cultural organizations (12 percent) and compatriotic societies (11 percent) are the most popular. Armenian political parties (1.7 percent) have the lowest rate of appeal.

Generational presence in the United States is an important explanatory variable in organizational membership; as membership in

TABLE 3.1
Frequency Distribution of Membership in Armenian Voluntary Associations by Generation
(in rank order of multiple response)

	Foreign-Born	U.S.-Born of F.B. Parents	Later Generation	Total
N = 269 (cases)	(126)	(117)	(26)	
Charitable organization (138 responses)	50.0	43.5	6.5	100.0
Church group (134 responses)	42.5	48.5	9.0	100.0
Cultural organization (71 responses)	52.1	35.2	12.6	100.0
Compatriotic society (65 responses)	52.3	44.6	3.0	100.0
Choir (46 responses)	58.7	34.8	6.5	100.0
Scholarly association (39 responses)	43.6	41.0	15.4	100.0
Student association (32 responses)	46.9	40.6	12.6	100.0
Sports organization (25 responses)	48.0	40.0	12.0	100.0
Dance group (12 responses)	41.7	33.3	25.0	100.0
Professional association (11 responses)	63.6	27.3	9.1	100.0
Political party (10 responses)	90.0	10.0	0.0	100.0

Armenian voluntary associations decreases generationally, membership in non-Armenian ones increases (though the proportion of foreign-born respondents in nonethnic organizations is not negligible). Of all the foreign-born respondents in this sample, 57.5 percent belong to Armenian organizations; of those in the second generation, 43 percent belong to ethnic organizations; and of all the later-generation ethnics, 27.9 percent do so. In comparison, 35.6 percent of the first generation, 57.7 percent of the second-generation,

TABLE 3.2
Frequency Distribution of Membership in non-Armenian Voluntary Associations
by Generation
(in rank order of multiple response)

	Foreign-Born	U.S.-Born of F.B. Parents	Later Generation	Total
N = 298 (cases)	(78)	(157)	(63)	
Professional association (154 responses)	27.6	50.6	22.0	100.0
Charitable organization (110 responses)	24.5	57.3	18.2	100.0
Political party (93 responses)	22.6	54.8	22.6	100.0
Cultural organization (81 responses)	25.9	54.3	19.8	100.0
Scholarly association (73 responses)	17.8	58.9	23.3	100.0
Church group (58 responses)	22.4	63.8	13.7	100.0
Sports organization (53 responses)	17.0	54.7	28.3	100.0
Student association (29 responses)	27.6	55.2	17.1	100.0
Civic organization (21 responses)	28.0	68.0	4.0	100.0
Choir (18 responses)	22.2	61.1	16.7	100.0
Dance group (7 responses)	14.3	71.4	14.3	100.0

and 67.7 percent of the third or fourth generations belong to non-Armenian organizations (see tables 3.1 and 3.2).

For later-generation respondents, folk dance groups are the most popular type of ethnic organizational membership. Otherwise, they constitute less than a tenth of the membership of all organizations, and they are totally absent from Armenian politics. In sharp contrast, the foreign-born compose 90 percent of American political parties and they are the majority in every other type of organization with the exception of church committees where the second generation predominate. Foreign-born respondents constitute 50 percent of all members of Armenian voluntary associations, while they form less than 40 percent of the sample. Respondents born in the Middle East are most likely among the foreign-born to be "joiners" of voluntary organizations. Sixty percent of them join Armenian organizations and 39 percent of them non-Armenian ones.

There is a direct, monotonic relationship between education and membership in non-Armenian associations. The higher the educational level, the higher the probability that a person of Armenian descent will join nonethnic voluntary associations. That is, 3.4 percent of respondents with less than high school education 15.3 percent of those who have finished high school, 21.1 percent of respondents with some college education, 24.5 percent of college graduates, and 35.7 percent of those with more than a college degree join non-Armenian organizations. It is intriguing that education had little effect on joining Armenian voluntary associations. About 26 percent of respondents who have a high school diploma were members of Armenian organizations, as did 22 percent of those who completed college and 24 percent of those with graduate or professional education. It appears that for first and second generations, irrespective of educational attainment, the needs Armenian associations fulfill are not matched by American organizations in terms of providing prestige, status, and companionship. The observation that "I'd rather be a big fish here than nobody out there" (Lopata 1964, 216) is true of many people's fears and apprehensions in choosing to remain within the ethnic fold.

In examining organizational leadership, respondents were asked if they held a position of responsibility such as officer, secretary, treasurer, or chairperson in Armenian and non-Armenian voluntary organizations. Overall, slightly more respondents were active in

Armenian than in non-Armenian organizations (17.6 percent vs. 12.9 percent). This is to be expected given the general ethnic bias of this sample and the higher proportion of respondents who came from Armenian church mailing lists. Generation does not affect the leadership composition of Armenian voluntary associations, but religious affiliation does (see tables 3.3, 3.4). Typically, those affiliated with the Apostolic church are leaders in Armenian associations, and those with "other" denominations are leaders in non-Armenian associations. Protestant Armenians are almost equally divided in both worlds. Furthermore, 8.6 percent of later-generation respondents held positions of responsibility when later generations constituted 9.7 percent of all memberships in Armenian organizations. This means that past the second generation, when men and women of Armenian descent enter the Armenian world, they are highly motivated and committed to it and become very active in leadership roles. By then, participation in the Armenian-American community becomes a true choice, since one becomes comfortably American with enough distance from immigrant origins and parental pressure. Therefore, lukewarm ties are either strengthened or severed.

In examining the frequency of attendance at meetings of voluntary associations, it was found that nearly half (44 percent) of the sample remain almost totally absent from all types of organizational meetings, Armenian and non-Armenian. Fifteen percent attended Armenian meetings and only 9 percent attended non-Armenian meetings, almost always (see tables 3.5 and 3.6). Attending meetings of Armenian voluntary associations decreases with later generations (.18*), nonethnic denominations, or no religion (.21*). On the other hand, attending the meetings of a non-Armenian voluntary association was not statistically correlated with any of the independent variables.

Participation in Communally Hosted Events

To measure the frequency of participation in activities sponsored by Armenian voluntary associations, respondents were provided with a list of thirteen different types of events commonly held in the community, and were asked how often they attended each in the year prior to the survey. Frequency of attending activities sponsored by Armenian organizations is influenced by the number of times such

activities are held in any given year. For such an estimate, I have
tallied the total number of events in each category that were held by
the Armenian community of metropolitan New York and New Jersey
in 1986 by following the announcements published in the Calendar of
Coming Events section of the local English-language weekly, the
Armenian Reporter. These are the events that were open to the general
public, there were others that were not advertised in this particular
paper.[14] The figures presented below are for 1986; however, it is
believed that more or less an equal number of events were sponsored
by Armenian organizations in 1985, the year respondents were asked
to report about.

In 1986, there were approximately 74 dinner dances (including
banquets, cotillons, debutante balls, dances, etc), 10 *kef* nights,[15] 35
luncheons (such as Lenten luncheon, women saint's day lunch,
mother's day luncheon, Ladies' Guild brunch and fashion show; as
well as testimonials, ground-breaking and dedication ceremonies that
included lunch), and an additional 9 receptions/banquets for membership meetings, reunions, and the like. In the summer months, there
were 15 picnics and garden parties. These make up a total of 143
events that consisted of a meal, lunch, or dinner, plus other entertainment or program. On average, there were 3 such socials per week.

In contrast to mostly social gatherings, there were a total of 79
events that could be classified as cultural. There were 25 musical

TABLE 3.3
Frequency Distribution of Respondents Holding Positions of Responsibility in
Armenian and Non-Armenian Voluntary Associations by Generation
(in percent)

	Foreign-Born	U.S.-Born of F.B. Parents	1 Parent U.S.-Born	2 Parents U.S.-Born	Grandparent U.S.-Born
N = 582	(218)	(271)	(36)	(41)	(16)
Respondents in Armenian associations	18.9	19.2	11.1	10.0	0.0
Respondents in non-Armenian Associations	8.7	15.1	16.6	19.5	6.2

concerts including 1 at Avery Fisher Hall, Lincoln Center. Three folk
dance shows[16] were performed including 1 in Carnegie Hall. Only 5
art exhibitions were advertised, there could have been others because
of the high percentages of respondents who visited art shows. Thirty
lectures were given on Armenian history and culture, and 6 others on
non-Armenian subjects.[17] Lectures in the Armenian community,
whatever the subject matter, are generally delivered in English. There
were 10 theatrical events[18] comprising 3 plays, 2 talent shows, and 5
poetry readings and dramatizations.

The third type of activity was food sales, rug sales, bazaars, book
fairs, and the like. There were a total of 17 such bazaars and 1 major

TABLE 3.4

Frequency Distribution of Respondents Holding Positions of Responsibility in
Armenian and Non-Armenian Voluntary Associations by Religious Affiliation
(in percent)

	Apostolic Armenian	Protestant Armenian	Catholic Armenian	Other (Non-Arm.)	No Religion
N = 573	(268)	(56)	(22)	(91)	(36)
Respondents in Armenian associations	22.3	23.2	9.1	3.3	5.6
Respondents in non-Armenian associations	7.6	19.6	9.1	30.4	16.6

TABLE 3.5

Frequency Distribution of Respondents Attending Meetings of Armenian
Voluntary Associations by Generation

	Foreign-Born	U.S.-Born of F.B. Parents	1 Parent U.S.-Born	2 Parents U.S.-Born	Grandparent U.S.-Born
N = 580	(218)	(269)	(36)	(41)	(16)
Hardly ever	56.4	72.5	72.2	87.8	87.5
Some of the time	22.9	14.1	19.4	2.4	6.3
Almost always	20.6	13.4	8.3	9.8	6.3
	100.0	100.0	100.0	100.0	100.0

street festival, the One World Festival.[19] The sports events advertised in the weekly newspaper tally to only 2 regional championships, no doubt regular matches were not mentioned.[20] There were 11 conventions or weekends for a variety of age groups and organizations. Probably one of the most popular weekends with American-born Armenians is the long established Armenian Student Association's[21] annual convention held along the Northeastern seaboard in the summer. I counted 8 events for the commemoration of the Armenian Genocide on and around April 24. These consisted of 3 requiems[22] in the city, a rally at Times Square, a concert at Avery Fisher Hall, a march for the survivors, a tree planting ceremony, and a one-day crash course to teach the Armenian language for beginners and advanced students.

For comparative purposes I have also tallied the total number of activities listed in the Calendar of Events section of the three major English-language newspapers on the East Coast for 1990. The *Armenian Weekly* is published in Watertown by the Hairenik Association, for the Armenian Revolution Federation (Tashnag party), the *Armenian Mirror-Spectator* is also published in Watertown and is the organ of the Ramgavar party. The *Armenian Reporter*, as mentioned above, is nonpartisan and published in New York. Together these three weeklies provide a fairly accurate picture of Armenian communal life on the Eastern seaboard. I have tried not to duplicate the listings, because even though each paper specializes in a particular audience, set of sponsoring organizations, and region, all three tend to print ads that are sent to them.

TABLE 3.6
Frequency Distribution of Respondents Attending Meetings of Non-Armenian Voluntary Associations by Generation

	Foreign-Born	U.S.-Born of F.B. Parents	1 Parent U.S.-Born	2 Parents U.S.-Born	Grandparent U.S.-Born
N = 580	(217)	(270)	(36)	(41)	(16)
Hardly ever	82.0	65.9	75.0	73.2	81.3
Some of the time	9.2	24.1	16.7	22.0	12.5
Almost always	8.8	10.0	8.3	4.9	6.3
	100.0	100.0	100.0	100.0	100.0

TABLE 3.7
Ratio of Favorite Activity: Proportion of Sample Attended Activity by Number of
Times Activity Held per Year
(by rank order)

	Proportion of Sample	Number of Activities	Ratio
Festival	44.4	2	22.2
Folk dance show	27.6	3	9.2
Art exhibition	34.5	5	6.9
Sports matches	11.0	2	5.5
April 24 events	39.3	8	4.9
Picnic	51.8	15	3.4
Bazaar	54.9	17	3.2
Kef night	25.0	10	2.5
Theater	24.9	10	2.4
Concert	45.8	25	1.8
Lecture	30.7	36	0.85
Dinner dance	42.3	74	0.57

TABLE 3.8
Number of Activities Hosted by the Major Armenian-American Communities of
the East Coast in 1990 as Listed in the Calendar of Events of the *Armenian
Weekly,* the *Armenian Mirror-Spectator,* and the *Armenian Reporter*

	NY/NJ	Boston	Other MA	Philadelphia	Providence	Hartford
Folk dance show	3	2	-	1	-	-
Art exhibition	4	6	1	-	-	-
Sports matches	7	4	5	2	1	-
April 24 events	7	5	3	-	-	-
Picnic	16	9	2	-	1	1
Bazaar	11	8	2	-	2	-
Kef night	12	5	1	-	-	-
Theater	5	3	-	-	-	-
Musical concert	15	8	2	2	1	-
Lecture	26	24	4	1	2	-
Banquet/dance	74	61	7	9	9	3
Weekend	7	6	3	1	-	1
Total	187	141	30	16	16	5

The activities are categorized as above. The geographical areas are divided into New York/New Jersey; Greater Boston (which includes Belmont, Brookline, Cambridge, Lexington, and Watertown); other cities in Massachusetts (such as Lowell, Springfield, and Worcester); Philadelphia; and Providence and Hartford (includes New Britain). Table 3.8 shows the distribution of activities by region. In addition, the *Armenian Weekly* provided listings for the Midwest (i.e., Chicago, Detroit, Racine; a total of 17 events, mostly sports tournaments and April 24 commemorations); and Richmond (one picnic and two banquets/dances); and the *Mirror-Spectator* listed a total of three dinner dances for Chelmsford (NH). Comparing the 1990 with 1986 listings for New York and New Jersey suggests that there have been few changes during this short period of time. Interestingly, the minor decreases in number of events hosted are in theater productions, concerts, and lectures—all three categories with specialized audiences.

This tally proves the point I made at the beginning of this chapter. Metropolitan New York and Boston have, by far, the largest Armenian institutional structures on the East Coast. Even though I am unable to

TABLE 3.9
**Number of Times Respondents Participated in Activities Sponsored
by Armenian Voluntary Associations
(by rank order)**

	Never	1 to 2	3 to 5	6 & More	Total
N = 583					
Bazaar/ rug sale	45.1	41.3	12.7	0.8	100.0
Picnic	48.2	41.0	9.3	1.6	100.0
Concert	54.2	31.4	12.2	2.1	100.0
Armenian festival	55.6	42.5	1.4	0.5	100.0
Dinner dance	57.7	25.2	12.2	4.8	100.0
April 24 events	60.7	34.5	4.1	0.7	100.0
Art exhibition	65.5	29.0	4.8	0.7	100.0
Lecture	69.3	21.6	6.3	2.8	100.0
Folk dance show	72.4	23.4	2.9	1.0	100.0
Kef night	75.0	17.7	6.2	1.1	100.0
Armenian theater	75.1	18.4	6.0	0.5	100.0
Armenian convention	82.7	16.0	1.2	0.2	100.0
Sports matches	89.0	6.2	2.6	2.3	100.0

provide the same information for the West Coast, there is little doubt about the prominence of Los Angeles. It is easy to imagine that people of Armenian descent who live in Boston, Los Angeles, or New York have more choice in community participation than someone living in Richmond or Hartford. Economies of scale increase the supply side of Armenianness and allegedly help keep identity in continual revival.

TABLE 3.10
Frequency Distribution of Respondents Participating in Activities Sponsored by
Armenian Voluntary Associations by Generation
(in rank order of multiple response)

	Foreign-Born	U.S.-Born of F.B. Parents	Later Generation	Total
N = 484 (cases)	(197)	(221)	(66)	
Bazaar (320 responses)	40.9	49.4	9.7	100.0
Picnic (302 responses)	44.0	48.7	7.3	100.0
Concert (267 responses)	47.9	41.9	10.1	100.0
Festival (259 responses)	41.7	46.3	12.0	100.0
Dinner dance (246 responses)	46.7	43.1	10.2	100.0
April 24 events (229 responses)	53.7	37.6	8.7	100.0
Art exhibition (201 responses)	40.8	45.8	13.5	100.0
Lecture (180 responses)	47.8	40.6	11.6	100.0
Folk dance show (161 responses)	51.6	41.6	6.9	100.0
Theater (145 responses)	58.6	37.2	4.2	100.0
Kef night (144 responses)	41.7	44.4	13.9	100.0
Armenian convention (101 responses)	47.5	41.6	10.9	100.0
Sports matches (64 responses)	54.7	34.4	11.0	100.0

To have a rough estimate of the popularity of these communally held activities, I have tabulated a ratio of "favorite activity" from the percentage of the sample attending any given type of activity by the approximate number of times such an event was held in one year. Table 3.7 shows the results by rank order. Festivals are the most popular event. Even though these are held once or twice a year, record numbers of people attend such events. Ethnic festivals are *par excellence* the form of organizational participation ideally suited for symbolic ethnics. Concerts and lectures on the other hand, have very specialized audiences. Similarly, dinner dances are a particular form of entertainment with a small group of aficionados who repeatedly attend this type of event. Dinner dances, lectures, and concerts receive the highest frequency of repeat attendance (see table 3.9).

Generation remains the most significant factor in community participation. Table 3.10 further supports the claim that the Armenian-American community of metropolitan New York and New Jersey is predominantly a first- and second-generation phenomenon. Only 13.6 percent of the total participants in communal activities are from the third or later generations. There is almost a straight line increase in complete absence from communal activities by generation. In 1985, 10 percent of foreign-born, 19 percent of the U.S.-born with foreign-born parents, 31 percent of those with one U.S.-born parent, 22 percent of those with two U.S.-born parents and 44 percent of those with at least one U.S.-born grandparent did not take part in activities hosted by Armenian voluntary associations. Generally, American-born generations are proportionally more likely to participate in activities that are not too demanding and do not require knowledge of culture and language, such as bazaars, picnics, and festivals. Noteworthy is the popularity of Armenian theater with the foreign-born. Even lectures, concerts, and folk dance performances have proportionally more foreign-born audiences.

Foreign-born senior citizens who personally experienced the massacres and deportations are most prominently present at commemorative events for the Armenian Genocide (April 24).[23] With increasing generational presence in America, even the Genocide loses its impact and urgency on people of Armenian descent. This does not mean that they become insensitive to what happened to their forefathers at the turn of the century. As will be clarified in chapter 5, few respondents are indifferent; however, these sentiments do not easily translate into action. Fewer and fewer later-generation Armenian-Americans attend rallies, public marches, even requiems.

Rationale for Community Participation

Several respondents felt the need to justify their lack of involvement in the Armenian community. I have counted approximately eight different reasons for being alienated temporarily or permanently from Armenian communal life. One excuse is lack of time. A thirty-nine-year-old, third-generation woman wrote: "My own lack of involvement with participation in Armenian organizations has more to do with lack of time than lack of interest. More often than not, I am out of town when some meeting or function that would have interested me is taking place."

Other reasons are ill health, old age, death and sickness in the family, or a combination of these. A sixty-five-year-old woman, born in Turkey, who immigrated at age six, noted that she did not participate in any activities, adding, "I have in the past, due to ill health this year." Another middle-aged, second-generation woman said, "Low key last year because of death in the family." A foreign-born woman who grew up in the United States wrote, "When I was young I belonged to many Armenian functions. When you are seventy-eight years old???" Yet another foreign-born woman repeated, "I used to belong to these when I was younger." A ninety-two-year-old man who did not participate in any communal activities remarked, "Ill all of 1985—still too ill." A sixty-seven-year-old woman who grew up in America since she was three, observed: "We do not attend or participate in any [of] above [activities] now due to age and ill health. But in our earlier years as family with two children we attended to all of above and exposed our growing children to Armenian oriented environment." A foreign-born father was inactive because his twelve-year-old child was autistic and hyperactive and needed his parents' constant attention; he added, "No time or energy left to involve in the community activities as an active member. That is the reason for my passive life."

In the previous chapter, I quoted from several respondents who did not attend Armenian church regularly because of geographic distance.

For the same reason, people are not able to attend Armenian communal events. For example, a senior citizen wrote: "Not active in the community as don't drive and limited mostly to walking." Another retired man who was born in the United States of an Armenian father and an English mother wrote: "When we lived in North Jersey we did go to Armenian dinners, picnics etc., but since moving down to Cape May, NJ, we do not come in contact with many Armenians." A college student whose mother's parents were born in Turkey said: "Since I left for school my Armenian activities have decreased greatly because there are no organized groups here. I used to be more involved in NYC & Columbia groups & activities—attending lectures, parties, performances."

The passing away of the immigrant generation may sever the last ties a person of Armenian descent may have to the ethnic community. A fifty-three-year-old U.S.-born man with an Armenian father and an Italian mother wrote: "Have lost touch with Armenian activities since my father's death in 1969. He was active in his ethnic background." Disillusionment with Armenian factionalism is yet another reason for being alienated from communal life, especially when other alternatives are readily available. For example, a fifty-two-year-old, second-generation man wrote: "I was for many years very active in Armenian affairs. I became disillusioned with all of the fruitless factionalism and fighting. Upon marrying a non-Armenian, I found other organizations to work in, although I still have strong feelings and support for the Armenian people and its nationhood."

Some years are different from others. A middle-aged, second-generation woman who did not participate in any Armenian communal activities wrote: "1985 was an atypical year. We would sometimes attend festival, picnics etc." Indeed, communal involvement is not constant over time, nor is ethnic identity for that matter. Since ethnicity is contextual, one's absorption in ethnic circles may fluctuate during different stages of one's life course.

Several respondents observed that their interest and involvement in the Armenian community had changed over the years. For example, a thirty-three-year-old man who like his mother and father is U.S.-born wrote:

> My involvement with the Armenian community seems to be typical of many of my friends: no interest through high school and college because I had many American

friends to socialize with, despite the constant prodding of my mother to join the Armenian community. After college, when I entered new social environs, I took a chance with Armenian groups. My involvement over the last 10 years has steadily grown in various organizations, to a level today which is probably much heavier than the average person.

Similarly, another forty-five-year-old man who like his mother is U.S.-born said: "We were an Americanized family; as children, my sibling and I were reluctant participants in the Armenian community, although always cognizant of being Armenian. Interestingly though, as each of us reached our late teens we became more involved in our ethnicity and expanded our friendships in the Armenian community."

The last two quotes point to an identity search in early adulthood. This stage in the life course is also a time for establishing friendships, and for mating. Some young people of Armenian descent may find a ready-made community to fulfill their needs. Those who find spouses within the community are more likely to stay, others will search elsewhere, decreasing the probability of their staying in the ethnic fold subsequently. Several community leaders I interviewed believed that the lack of interest of the young people in church and Armenian community is temporary. A parish priest told me: "This is kind of natural, but they will come back to the Armenian community as soon as they get married and have their own children. They want to baptize their children in the Armenian church, send them to Sunday and Saturday school." The quantitative data does not support the life course hypothesis in community involvement. Even though empty nest couples were the most frequent attenders in Armenian communal life (92 percent), followed by singles of all ages (88 percent), and the least active were senior citizens (76 percent), the variations between the different stages of the life cycle were not statistically significant.

The Odar Spouse

Second only to generation, ancestry decreases participation in the organized Armenian community. While 14 percent of those who have two Armenian parents did not participate in any activity, 39 percent of those with mixed parentage did not. Knowledge of the way the Armenian-American community sanctions intermarried couples is impressionistic, to say the least. As a rule of thumb, however, the institutionalized community is not very welcoming of *odar* [non-

Armenian] spouses. The anger of a thirty-year-old intermarried respondent (father U.S.-born, mother born in Syria) portrays one outcome: "I've ... resented the fact that people who are married to other Armenians frown upon my marrying an 'odar.' There isn't one week that goes by without some alluding to this fact."

Some social critics find the laissez-faire policy of Armenian churches and organizations detrimental to the very survival of the community. Thus, according to Aharonian, who examined the extent of intermarriage in the parishes of the Eastern Diocese over several decades, "the problem is not intermarriage itself but our rejection of it and our general alienation of most of these mixed married couples thus losing to the community not only the non-Armenian spouses but also our many Armenian sons and daughters married to them" (1983, 116).

The testimonies of respondents in this study suggest that at the private, informal level, the Armenian-American reaction ɔ intermarriage is similar to the Greek-American pattern of the second generation. That is, parents and kin praise defensively the nonethnic in-law, suggesting there are good and bad people in all nationalities, but go on believing that common ethnic background makes a good marriage (Moskos 1989, 94). For example, a fifty-nine-year-old, second-generation woman who is married to a non-Armenian wrote: "My Mom loves my husband very much and tells her friends that if he was Armenian he couldn't treat her any nice [*sic*]; in other words, they have a good mother-in-law-son-in-law relationship."

Another middle-aged, second-generation woman explained that her son's and daughter's spouses were non-Armenian, adding: "[They] love our culture and customs and my grandchildren have been baptized in our Armenian Apostolic Church." Second-generation parents find consolation that their children "are happily married," or that their non-Armenian in-laws are "from fine upper-class families." Yet another third-generation woman has this to say about her Irish/German/French fiancé: "His family regards Armenian people very highly and is very receptive to my ethnicity. Hopefully, our children will learn to be proud of *both* their backgrounds" (emphasis in original).

As for the children of intermarried couples, one of four choices in their socialization is possible. Parents can either follow the ethnic background of the mother, or that of the father; or a little of both, producing pan-ethnics; or they may choose to follow neither backgrounds bringing forth nonethnic "Americans." I am unable to discern which is the most common pattern for the acculturation of the children of mixed parentage from the remarks of the New York respondents. The analysis suggests that mixed ancestry is generally less statistically significant than generation and religious affiliation in determining the degree of alienation from the Armenian world. Mixed marriages increase the likelihood of assimilation, but do not necessarily produce it. Here are some examples:

> I don't know if there is any value in mentioning that although my mother is Anglo-Saxon I was raised in an Armenian household (male 55, third-generation).

> Living in a mixed ethnic family, ethnic bonds were not developed in either nationality. However, I am proud to be both Polish and Armenian (male 50, second-generation, mother Polish).

> I married a non-Armenian who is very supportive of my heritage and we were married and baptized our children in the Armenian church and they go to Armenian church with me (female 40, respondent and mother U.S.-born).

> I am married to a non-Armenian but my children would be raised as Armenians (female 24, born in Iran came to the United States at age 16, husband Jewish).

Intermarriage is a fact of life in later generations.[24] The story of a fifty-eight-year-old, second-generation woman personifies some of these issues.

> As an American-Armenian who married an *Odar,* 36 years ago, I am aware that many social/religious/political Armenian-related activities tapered off considerably after my marriage. Though married to an empathetic [sic] 'Pesa' [groom], the situation precludes a totally committed involvement in more Armenian activity. I have two daughters in their early thirties, one married to an Armenian. Their daughter is being raised with a pride in her heritage.

> My second daughter is not married, successful in her career but sad at the odds in finding an Armenian mate to perpetuate her heritage.

> [I regret] ... the discouraging situation for young Armenian singles in this country vis-à-vis their meeting suitable marriage partners for the future.

The degree of accommodation the *odar* spouse needs to make depends on the generational status of the family he/she is marrying into. Those who marry foreign-born Armenians generally have more hurdles to overcome. Often, the most significant is the language gap.

The inability to speak or understand Armenian creates communication barriers that may make the *odar* spouse feel isolated and rejected. The spouse does not have to be a complete *odar;* American-born Armenians who marry foreign-born men and women have similar problems. A case in point is an interview writer Mary Ann Aposhian conducted with Christine, a third-gèneration wife, and Vahe, a foreign-born husband. Here are Christine's comments:

> I love being with Armenians, but sometimes I feel so lonely. We go to a lot of Armenian events ... the first-generation men want to bond with each other all the time at these events.... They sit in the living room; the women sit in the kitchen. I can't speak Armenian, so Vahe has to sit with me all the time because nobody will want to talk to me in English and because, well—truthfully—I'm snubbed to a certain extent.[25]

The New York survey reveals that there is very little linguistic acculturation. Less than 7 percent (N = 11) of *odar* spouses spoke Armenian, and a mere 1.8 percent read/wrote Armenian (see table 3.11).[26] Most of these spouses in question were also born and married in the Middle East. In general, *odar* spouses do their part to find acceptance and accommodation. They readily enjoy Armenian food, some daughters-in-law even learn to cook their husband's favorite dishes. They may be curious to learn about Armenian culture and history in general, and their spouse's ancestors in particular. However, participation in communally hosted events is an onerous obligation. They might sporadically agree to attend a picnic or concert to please their spouses and have peace with their in-laws. I should add that the less one attends community events, the more one is likely to feel isolated and surrounded by unfamiliar faces. This has nothing to do with Armenians. Acquaintances and friendships take time and effort to forge.

Of course, there are exceptional *odar* spouses, mostly of foreign-born Armenians, who have invested great amounts of time and energy in the formally organized community. They have had to be more royalist than the king to gain recognition. Yet, even then, they remain outsiders, literally *odars*. It is therefore not surprising that intermarried couples and their children prefer to shield themselves from feelings of rejection, and thus remain aloof from Armenian-American institutional circles.

Community Involvement for Symbolic Armenians

Oscar Handlin speaking at a conference on Armenian assimilation in 1984 observed that in spite of the homogenizing influences of the mass media, there are very few typically American rituals that deal with birth, marriage, and death. Thus, he argued, "ethnicity fills the vacuum," because people want traditions that are unique and more meaningful to them. Handlin explains: "People becoming Americanized are not just moving away from their pasts; they wish to move toward something that will apply to education and the rearing of children, to family life, and even to a search for rituals or ceremonies for their own sake" (1986-87, iv). Similarly, Joshua Fishman (1985, 503 italics in original) recognizes that there are certain *acts* and certain *events*, such as transitions of birth, death, coming of age that are more imbued with ethnic behavior and meaningfulness than others in modern urban life. There are also certain *persons* such as the grandmother, the parish priest who are interacted with in terms of shared ethnic world. As there are *places, topics* and *role relationships*

TABLE 3.11
Frequency Distribution of Ability of Spouse to Speak Armenian by Generation Controlled for Spouse's Ethnicity (married sample only)

	Foreign-Born	U.S.-Born of F.B. Parents	1 Parent + U.S.-Born
Spouse's ethnicity			
2 Parents Armenian			
N = (313)	(163)	(131)	(19)
Doesn't speak Armenian	3.7	9.2	21.1
Spouse speaks Armenian	96.3	90.8	78.9
	100.0	100.0	100.0
1 Parent Armenian			
N = (10)	(3)	(6)	(1)
Doesn't speak Armenian	33.3	33.3	0.0
Spouse speaks Armenian	66.7	66.7	100.0
	100.0	100.0	100.0
Non-Armenian Background			
N = (170)	(30)	(96)	(44)
Doesn't speak Armenian	83.3	96.9	93.2
Spouse speaks Armenian	16.7	3.1	6.8
	100.0	100.0	100.0

that are more likely to be marked off and colored by ethnic rituals, symbolism and connotations.

Armenian identity could indeed be functional in modern American society. Nonetheless, the question one needs to ask is: How prevalent is the desire to be married in an Armenian church or to baptize and raise one's children in the Armenian community? The results of the New York survey do not support the belief that any substantial proportion of people of Armenian descent beyond the second generation aspire to "return" to the Armenian community. On the contrary, the evidence speaks for itself; as shown above, most of the behavioral indicators drop sharply after the second generation. What this study proves, however, is that 'feelings' for one's Armenian background remain strong, and may occasionally be manifested by token behavioral gestures such as getting married in an Armenian church or making donations to Armenian charities or visiting one's Armenian grandmother. Even though I do not want to belittle the significance of such actions to the man or woman of Armenian descent, these are not behavioral patterns rooted in the daily routine and material circumstances of people's lives.

With increasing generations, alienation from the organized Armenian community is common. The remarks of a twenty-eight-year-old man whose paternal grandfather immigrated from Turkey are a case in point: "I have no desire to cling to other Armenians—or to go to every barbecue sponsored by Armenians. I only feel proud by other people's awareness of Armenians and their heritage." Similarly, the experiences of a fifty-nine-year-old, second-generation man are typical of many others.

> I attended Sunday school every Sunday, from my earliest youth through my senior year of high school. This experience was my closest contact with Armenians during my formative years, and except for family visits with Armenian friends and relatives, my only real contact. My day-to-day experiences were in a pleasant, small town environment, with "Americans," where I became totally assimilated into the [local] community.

To justify involvement in Armenian communal life some respondents provided specific instrumental reasons. A twenty-five-year-old man, both of whose parents were U.S.-born, said he had attended one or two Armenian conventions "for previously received scholarships." He went on to explain:

Although my family and I are not "active" in the so-called Armenian community, I do identify as an Armenian and am quite grateful to the various scholarships I have received over the years to defray the cost of attending the best schools in the nation. Such is a very important role that is played by the AGBU & ASA. In this way an Armenian-American is able to promote the reputation of Armenians while making a positive contribution to this United States.

Once scholarship funds are established, it might not be too difficult to find recipients of Armenian descent.[27] In much the same way, when asked about the future of Armenian organizations, one of my informants replied: "They'll survive, some are well funded organizations. Money means a lot. If there is a yearly income, they'll exist. If there is a staff, there will be projects and programs."

A fifty-nine-year-old, second-generation woman said she attended one dinner dance, adding: "Cotillon—my daughter was an Armenian debutante." Judging by the coverage they receive in the ethnic press, debutante balls have become increasingly popular among the American-born suburbanites in recent years. Cotillons emulate the behavior of the national elite listed in the *Social Register* and photographed in *Town and Country* that they are unlikely to belong to. It is an event that befits the social standing of many *nouveaux riches* Armenian-Americans. It provides a unique occasion for mothers and daughters for ostentatious display and at the same time an opportunity for mate selection among acceptable peers. Most important, these peers are from the same socioeconomic status; being of Armenian descent adds the icing on the cake. Debutante balls have high potential for attracting affluent symbolic Armenians into the community, at least temporarily.[28]

Economic Participation

Several respondents in the New York study remarked that they had not attended requiem services for the Genocide (or some other event) but had sent in a donation, implicitly suggesting that such monetary contributions were proof of their commitment to Armenianness. Given the above-average incomes of this sample, and possibly of many Armenian-Americans, monetary contributions, however large, may not be such a big sacrifice. Armenian leaders I interviewed agreed that "raising money has not been difficult in the Armenian community." One of them mentioned that according to Internal Revenue Service sources, the Armenian community raised approximately 20 million tax-deductible dollars for charities in 1984. Considering there are about 500,000 people of Armenian descent in the USA,[29] this amounts to an average of $400 per person. The published budget of the Armenian General Benevolent Union for 1988 was $9 million.[30] Vis-à-vis the small size of its population, the Armenian Protestant community in the United States has an impressive budget. For 1985-86, the Armenian Missionary Association of America, had a budget of over one-and-a-half million U.S. dollars.[31]

Philanthropic contributions are an important form of involvement in one's ethnic heritage and community. It makes one feel good about oneself, it is easy to accomplish, and it exemplifies yet another characteristic of symbolic ethnicity. I have called this "in absentia participation" in the Armenian world. It is the most convenient behavioral form of ethnic expression. If the case of Jewish Americans is an indication of what will be happening to the Armenians (Cohen 1983), it is probable that those in later generations and younger cohorts will be less likely to contribute their tax-deductible dollars as generously or as frequently. Besides, Armenian philanthropic associations are less likely to have their names on their mailing lists.

In conclusion, the Armenian-American community and the myriad voluntary associations that constitute it, consist of and cater to first- and second-generation ethnics. Only a small (mean 10 percent) proportion of people of Armenian descent beyond the second generation participate actively in organized communal life. Their participation is most likely to be in activities that are undemanding; that is, they do not require knowledge of the Armenian language or culture. That is why ethnic festivals are the favorite form of communal activity. It is remarkable though that Armenian organizations continue to sponsor a large number of banquets and dinner dances year after year when this type of event has the least base of support in the Armenian-American population.

Armenian organizations primarily serve a very small number of devoted followers whose lives outside the domestic and occupational spheres center around the ethnic community. As a community leader observed: "Every single function that is done, it's probably the same 2000 or so people who attend everything." This informant blamed the Armenian organizations for alienating younger cohorts.

We need new projects, the ones we have aren't any good. We need things that are interesting to the new generation. The new generation is not interested in stuffing envelopes and selling dinner tickets. We need projects within the professions of those people.

All Armenian projects so far have been sports oriented or dance or music, but not everyone is interested in such things. Our heritage is a little more than dance and music. We lose a lot of young people (ages 20 to 35). Young people are most interested in their jobs.

[The organizations are] catering for the people who have nothing better to do than go to dinners and sit though long speeches, I don't resent people who are not involved. It's our fault if that person is not interested enough. We all have different priorities in life.

Indeed, later-generation Armenian-Americans are not interested in attending dinner dances. More creative programming might induce some symbolic Armenians to participate in communal activities; however, since most of the leaders of Armenian organizations are from the first and second generation, I find it unlikely that they will be able to transcend their own needs and preoccupations to cater to a wider public of ethnic descent they have little knowledge of and hardly any contact with. The tendency to continue the present structure and programming is stronger. Once a community is established, it runs "by the principle of psychological inertia, comfortable social immersion, and vested interests" (Gordon 1964, 247).

Instrumental Motives for Community Participation

It is assumed that conscious, rational processes guide later-generation descendants of Armenian descent in choosing a dentist, a doctor, a lawyer, an accountant, or any other professional. These people are more likely to be referred to a professional on the basis of his or her competence and expertise in a given field of endeavor than particularistic characteristics such as ethnicity, religion, race, gender, or age. By contrast, immigrant generations are believed to seek (competent) ethnic professionals because they are more likely to have trust and confidence in them, and also for easier rapport and communication. To illustrate, here are the comments of a young third-generation respondent.

As a practicing dentist I find a third of my practice to be Armenian-American. I find my rapport with them to be often easier than with other patients. I find them easier to trust and I have seen proof that they trust me *beyond the normal expectations of a doctor-patient relationship.* This has been a major joy in my professional career. My Armenian patients are particularly kind to me and I love it!

Relative to the newcomers (e.g. Lebanese-Armenians, Iranian-Armenian etc) they come to me for dentistry as I am Armenian. [Emphasis in original]

Professional Services

Three questions measured use of Armenian professional services and businesses. First, respondents were given a list of four professionals they normally consult (doctor, lawyer, accountant, dentist) and asked to check which ones were of Armenian descent. The second question asked respondents whether they would be willing to employ Armenians in their business, if they had one. Finally, respondents were asked if they would patronize small businesses, such as gas stations, mechanics, grocery stores, dry cleaners, jewelers, watch repairers, among others, solely because they were owned and operated by Armenians.

All three measures were statistically significant by generation. The hypothesis holds that with increasing generational presence in the United States, people of Armenian descent are less likely to consult Armenian professionals (.16*), patronize Armenian small businesses (.18*), and employ fellow Armenians (.15*). Overall, only 11 percent of the sample utilize the services of three or more Armenian professionals, about 26 percent say they would, almost always, patronize Armenian businesses, and about 30 percent would employ Armenians, most of the time. Conversely, the proportions of those who hardly ever support Armenian businesses increase in the opposite direction. The discrepancy in these results can be attributed to the nature of the questions. Often, people say they would or would not do something, but their actual behavior does not necessarily concur with stated attitudes. The hypothetical question on willingness to employ fellow ethnics received the smallest proportion of negative responses. Patronizing Armenian shopkeepers and small enterprises occasionally is not as serious or costly to the individual as finding four competent and conveniently located Armenians for one's professional services.

Foreign-born Armenians are most likely to consult with the maximum number of Armenian professionals; however, there are few generational differences among respondents who utilize the services of one or two ethnic professionals (on average 40 percent; see table 3.12). This is attributed to the fact that many of these professionals are relatives or close friends, as several respondents penciled in. This is not surprising given the large proportions of professionals in the Armenian population. First-generation respondents are also most likely to patronize Armenian small businesses frequently. The percentages drop by half with each succeeding generation. Only about a quarter of the sample would not patronize an Armenian store just because it was Armenian (see table 3.13). Again, almost 50 percent of foreign-born respondents would be willing to employ, almost always, fellow Armenians in their business, while most of the American-born generations would be willing to do so, sometimes (approximately 5 percent of the sample added that they would employ an Armenian only

TABLE 3.12

Frequency Distribution of Respondents Consulting Armenian Professionals by Generation

	Foreign-Born	U.S.-Born of F.B. Parents	1 Parent U.S.Born	2 Parents U.S.-Born	Grandparent U.S.-Born
N = 584	(219)	(272)	(36)	(41)	(16)
None	38.4	49.6	75.0	53.7	62.5
One or two	43.8	42.3	22.2	41.5	37.5
More than three	17.8	8.1	2.8	4.9	0.0
	100.0	100.0	100.0	100.0	100.0

TABLE 3.13

Frequency Distribution of Respondents Patronizing Armenian Small Businesses by Generation

	Foreign-Born	U.S.-Born of F.B. Parents	1 Parent U.S.-Born	2 Parents U.S.-Born	Grandparent U.S.-Born
N = 584	(219)	(272)	(36)	(41)	(16)
Hardly ever	22.4	26.5	36.1	39.0	56.3
Some of the time	37.0	54.4	55.6	51.2	25.0
Almost always	40.6	19.1	8.3	9.8	18.8
	100.0	100.0	100.0	100.0	100.0

if he or she were qualified; see table 3.14). As expected, Apostolics, followed closely by Protestant Armenians, were somewhat more likely to support ethnic businesses (table 3.15).

Indeed, employing other Armenians hints of nepotism, and many respondents would have agreed with a twenty-nine-year-old, second-generation man who wrote: "I would not discriminate." Another young man reiterated the question as follows: "Just because they are Armenian? No! Because they're qualified? Yes!" Others observed: "If they were qualified, but wouldn't favor Armenians," or "depends on the business and ability of the person for the job (he or she could be Armenian)." Armenianness for later-generation ethnics is selective, as the remarks of a middle-aged, second-generation man demonstrate: "I look for Armenian names as a source of pride in achievement of our

TABLE 3.14
Frequency Distribution of Willingness to Employ Armenians in One's Business by Generation

	Foreign-Born	U.S.-Born of F.B. Parents	1 Parent U.S.-Born	2 Parents U.S.-Born	Grandparent U.S.-Born
N = 584	(219)	(272)	(36)	(41)	(16)
Hardly ever	9.1	13.6	11.1	7.3	18.8
Some of the time	40.6	58.5	77.8	80.5	56.3
Almost always	47.5	21.3	11.1	12.2	12.5
If qualified	2.7	6.7	0.0	0.0	12.5
	100.0	100.0	100.0	100.0	100.0

TABLE 3.15
Frequency Distribution of Respondents Supporting Armenian Professionals, Willingness to Employ Fellow Ethnics, and Patronizing Armenian Small Businesses "Almost Always" by Religious Affiliation

	Apostolic Armenian	Protestant Armenian	Catholic Armenian	Other (Non-Arm.)	No Religion
N = 576	(370)	(56)	(22)	(92)	(36)
Support Arm. Prof.	14.6	8.9	4.5	3.3	2.8
Employ Armenians	33.5	32.1	31.8	16.3	16.7
Patronize Arm. store	30.8	26.8	13.6	15.2	5.6

people. On the other hand I don't care to do business or make friends just because we are of the same nationality. Some of the Armenians in photo engraving business were as bad as you could find anywhere. Good and bad in all I guess."

Few respondents were candid and did agree that they would favor a fellow Armenian, given all other requirements were met. Such is the case of a twenty-five-year-old, third-generation man who wrote: "Would be hired on an ethnicity/nationality neutral basis—all other things being equal, probably lean toward Armenian."

Another middle-aged, third-generation respondent said: "Yes, given the same skills the preference would always go to the Armenian." "Why not?" was the comment of yet another respondent.

Overall, there is a willingness to help fellow Armenians in business endeavors as a respondent said: "To give them a chance." This is anecdotally called the "Double-Duty Dollar" (Hannerz 1974, 55). However, good will is conditional on qualifications and competence. The products or services must be competitive with the market, the rapport must be positive, and most of all, the business or office must be conveniently located. A foreign-born senior citizen who has lived in the United States most of his life, wrote: "Gladly, [would patronize a store] if their work or service is comparable in quality and price to non-Hyes [non-Armenians]. I prefer to go to Hyes [Armenians] and work with them but it must be on a competitive basis, not because they are Armenian per se." Convenience is an important consideration in identity maintenance; patronizing Armenian small businesses is no exception. The availability of such stores in one's geographic area is a prerequisite. For example, a forty-five-year-old, third-generation man said he did not go to any Armenian professionals "because none are located in our geographical area." Nonetheless, the first generation remains more vocal in supporting fellow Armenians in professions and businesses, and they are more likely to go out of their way to do so.

The ethnic enclave hypothesis postulates that the salience of ethnic solidarity in segmented labor markets helps immigrant minorities achieve socioeconomic success despite their initial disadvantages (see chap. 1). In the past, Armenians clustered in the oriental rug business, the photoengraving business, and the dry cleaning business. They hired fellow Armenians as apprentices if they owned their own business or promoted their recruitment by putting in a good word with the boss. However, Armenians were unable to control an entrepreneurial niche because of their size and dispersion. The nearest Armenians come to approximate an enclave economy in metropolitan New York and Los Angeles, at the present time, is in the jewelry business. According to one of my informants, Armenians, mostly born in Turkey and the Middle East, make up almost 10 percent of all businesses in the Diamond District on Forty-seventh Street (Manhattan) and control the market in downtown Los Angeles. These Armenian entrepreneurs employ Armenian immigrants in both skilled and semiskilled positions, teach them skills, and provide them with contacts. It is true that the entrepreneurs may reap more benefits from the enclave economy than their employees. Yet, many an immigrant, "off the boat" or plane without work papers has been saved by the opportunity to find potentially skillful employment immediately upon arrival and be sponsored for a "green card." A few have used it as a stepping stone on the path of the American dream.

It is has been suggested that the nature of the work environment is an important consideration in ethnic support and maintenance. According to di Leonardo (1984, 140), the exigencies of various work processes may be so organized that they may enhance ethnicity in some cases, such as that of speciality food stores, but stressing ethnicity in other cases, such as that of bureaucratic firms, may bring no material reward and may even be harmful. Work processes are defined as "social relations engendered and maintained in the course of doing one's job." These can be divided into three categories; "small businesspeople, workers in large firms, and independent professionals" (di Leonardo 1984, 136). The first and last of these categories may have large ethnic clienteles, making them most likely to have broad work-based ethnic networks. Thus, small business owners and independent professionals are more likely to claim membership in the ethnic community. Their work environment enables them to express their ethnic identity at work because they rely on ethnic patronage for their economic prosperity. Shopkeepers, doctors, lawyers, and the like often assume leadership in ethnic voluntary organizations, act as information brokers, displaying posters, selling tickets for community events, and volunteering information to insiders and outsiders about the community, and providing much of the necessary revenues for community activities by advertising or other contributions. Di Leonardo (1984,

156) further argues that the type of ethnic solidarity that is invoked by business owners and independent professionals is in the Durkheimian sense, organic.[32] Publicly, these people appeal to the mechanical solidarity of a broad spectrum of people of ethnic descent, but only privately reveal that ethnicity is good for business.[33]

While I was in Los Angeles recently, a Lebanese-born elderly gentleman told me an anecdote to demonstrate his disdain of some, in his opinion, opportunist Armenians. I find this story a fitting example of what I have attempted to explain above. My host was at a fundraiser for a local Armenian school and he happened to be sitting next to a medical doctor who had donated $3,000 on that particular occasion. When the elderly gentleman enquired as to why the doctor was giving so much money to such an endeavor when none of his three children attended Armenian schools, the doctor replied: "It's good business!" Apparently, the doctor has a large Armenian clientele. These insights help explain at least partially the proportionately higher percentages of business owners and traditional professionals in the sample[34] who are willing, almost always, to employ other Armenians (40.8 percent and 24.8 percent respectively) and patronize other businesses (37.7 percent). Business owners and professionals were also more likely to be active in Armenian voluntary associations.

A cursory look at the advertisements of any Armenian newspaper also suggests that business owners and self-employed professionals such as doctors, dentists, and lawyers are most likely to place ads in the ethnic press. For example, I have analyzed the ads that were placed in the *Armenian International Magazine*. I have chosen this monthly publication because of its novel approach to the Armenian community, its investigative style, its national readership, and the high-quality image (colorful, glossy paper) it projects. It is likely to appeal to symbolic Armenians.

Irrespective of the size of the ad, whether it was in black-and-white or in color, I have counted a total of 173 entries in the first eight issues of *Armenian International Magazine* (vol 1, nos. 1-3; vol 2, nos. 1-5). Naturally, there were few ads in the first three issues (an average of thirteen per month), but they have more than doubled since. I divided the ads into three categories: first, there were people of Armenian descent who were advertising their professional services and business products (which had nothing to do with Armenianness). These included lawyers, financial consultants, computer specialists, political candidates, architects, jewelers, painters/artists, model builders, travel agents, and owners of hotels in London and Paris. This category made up 48 percent of the total number of ads. Second, there were ads specifically targeted to the Armenian market. These included books, records, video cassettes, prints, and memorabilia (rugs or T-shirt with Armenian alphabet). This category made up 34 percent of the ads. The third category consisted of big companies such as Exxon, Bank Audi, Mercedes Benz, California Raisins. These ads might have been placed by Armenian executives, but such companies do not rely on the Armenian population to show them a profit. In sum, those with instrumental motives, the self-employed professionals and business owners, are most likely to reap economic or political benefits by claiming Armenian identity and increasing their exposure in the community.

Armenian Professional Associations

Several Armenian professional associations were established in the United States in the last decade or so. This type of ethnic association appears to be the formula for the future because it is adaptable to symbolic Armenianness. Such self-help networks allow their members to utilize ethnic ties to further individual achievements. Thus, like business owners and self-employed professionals, here too, the basis of solidarity is organic. Being of the same ethnic background is no longer a sufficient motivation to form an association either for American-born or for foreign-born professionals of Armenian descent. Unlike their grandparents' generation, these people are not interested in compatriotic societies.[35]

A popular association among young professionals of Armenian descent is the Armenian Network of America, Inc., established in 1983 with branches in New York, Boston, and Washington, DC. "The Network emphasizes career pursuits and Armenian identity, by creating a network of college youth, young professionals and established career people to promote community leadership and enhance participation of Armenians in the American society" (*Armenian American Almanac* 1990, 27). Computerized information on Armenians in professions and businesses helps the Network in this task. Meetings for different professions are held separately, but lectures and other events are open to the public. The popularity of the Armenian Network derives from its ability to combine professional interests with Armenianness among young, mostly single, adults. Though at present the Armenian Network numbers 150 members in the study area,[36] their fund-raising events and social gatherings draw very large crowds where young, later-generation ethnics socialize among peers furthering professional and personal interests.[37]

According to the *Armenian American Almanac* (1990), there are about 24 Armenian professional associations in the United States. For example, the Armenian-American Medical Association, founded in 1971 and based in Belmont, Massachusetts, aims "to develop bonds of friendship among physicians of Armenian parentage by meeting at least twice a year; to assist young Armenian-Americans desiring medical education; to assist newly arriving physicians or those starting practice" *(Armenian American Almanac* 1990, 42).[38] Similarly, the Armenian Engineers and Scientists of America, Inc.[39] founded in 1985 in Glendale (CA) aims "to bring together Armenian engineers and scientists to help Armenians and Armenian organizations by technical means" *(Armenian American Almanac* 1990, 43). The Armenian Artists Association of America, established in 1983 in Watertown (MA) aims to promote artists of Armenian descent. The Armenian-American Medical and Dental Association of Greater Philadelphia was also founded in 1983. Some associations are not specific to one profession; an example is the Armenian Professional Society of Bay Area founded in 1982. Unfortunately, the Almanac does not provide any information on the number of members and the type of programs these associations have.[40] Nonetheless, almost every liberal profession appears to be represented. So far there are associations for lawyers, dentists, medical doctors, nurses, pharmacists, engineers, scientists, behavioral scientists, artists, computer specialists, and broadcasters.

In conclusion, the absolute and relative numbers of people of ethnic descent who are members of Armenian professional associations remain very small. The data indicates that 64 percent of the membership of such associations is foreign-born, and only 10 percent come from later generations (see table 3.1). I suspect that more professionals of Armenian descent might join, if they are approached, because such associations are symbolic in nature; that is, not because such associations are symbolic in nature; that is, not demanding, and basically utilitarian. The results also confirm the hypothesis that later-generation Armenians and those with nonethnic religious affiliations are less willing to go to a doctor, a lawyer, or a dentist just because he or she is of Armenian descent; they are less likely to buy from a store because the owner is Armenian, and they are less willing to employ an Armenian in their business, especially if he or she is not qualified. Yet, this does not mean a total rejection of Armenianness. Here again, there is additional proof of the study's contention that increasing assimilation in behavioral patterns proceeds hand in hand with changes in the form of ethnicity. Outside the family circle, which will be analyzed in chapter 5, it is in such professional and business contexts that middle-class symbolic Armenian-Americans will be most comfortable in meeting fellow Armenians. Ethnic allegiances are attributes among many others that individuals can use to further their personal, business, and professional goals. Symbolic Armenianness manifests itself selectively when actors perceive a material or nonmaterial gain in their ethnic connections. This means that the organic aspect of ethnic solidarity is replacing the mechanical aspect. Kobrin and Goldscheider concur: "When ethnic membership is described as providing a 'sense of community' it may be that 'community' means not only comradeship, but the greater ability to command resources—clients, jobs, promotions, nominations—a useful property which might very well explain the continued salience of ethnicity" (1978, 242).

Social Networks of Armenian-Americans

When levels of prejudice and discrimination against a given group are high, social ties are likely to be confined to one's group, increasing the social distance between groups. In other words, the boundary that distinguishes "us" from "them" is likely to be clearly marked, allowing few to cross the line. So far the discussion centered on the formally organized sectors of the Armenian-American community. In this section, the ethnic composition of the personal networks of Armenian-Americans is examined, including prejudice and discrimination; social distance between various subcommunities within the Armenian-American population; social distance with other ethnic, racial and national groups; the conflict within the community, between Americanized Armenians and newcomers; and friendship ties. It is hypothesized that the longer the generational presence, the less likely will the personal network of an individual of Armenian descent be exclusively Armenian.

Experience of Prejudice and Discrimination

Self-reporting of discrimination and prejudice is not the best method for analyzing the level of such practices in a given society. Individuals may underestimate or overly exaggerate actual occurrence. In any case, the level of perceived discrimination and prejudice, or lack or it, influences the degree of assimilation of a group. New York respondents were asked whether they had been discriminated against because they were Armenian. They were given a list of five possible types of discrimination: in getting a job, in being promoted, in joining a club, in admission to a school or college, and in buying or renting an apartment or house. Respondents were also asked: "Do you think there is a great deal of prejudice against Armenian-Americans in this country?" Overall, only 5.3 percent of the sample felt there was prejudice against Armenians, most adding that it was in the past, in the 1930s and 1950s. Between 95 and 98 percent of the sample said there was no discrimination against Armenians in America. The highest discrimination reported was in getting a job (4.5 percent), followed by getting a promotion (3.4 percent), then joining a club (2.2 percent); the least discrimination found was in school admittance and renting or buying a home (1.7 percent).

Second-generation respondents reported the most counts of discrimination, followed by the immigrant generation (see table 3.16). Also, older respondents tended to report discrimination and prejudice more often than younger respondents. These results reflect a cohort effect; older respondents remember specific discriminatory periods in U.S. history. Moreover, because of their marginal situation, living between two social worlds, the immigrant generation and their children's generation are most susceptible to be conscious of discriminatory behavior toward them. Men reported somewhat more discrimination than women (50 to 85 percent compared to 15 to 50 percent for women); this is due to the traditional role of women. In the past, women were more likely to be sheltered at home, having fewer opportunities to compete in the open market and encounter discriminatory practices.

Generation was not very statistically significant with prejudice (tau c .04 significant at .006 level), though the foreign-born tended to find prejudice twice as often as the American-born (table 3.17). Those born in Turkey, Soviet Bloc countries and the Middle East reported three times as much prejudice as the U.S.-born (10 percent, 9 percent and 8 percent vs. 3 percent respectively). These results are in the expected

TABLE 3.16
Frequency Distribution of Reported Discrimination by Generation
(multiple response)

	Foreign-Born	U.S.-Born of F.B. Parents	Later Generation	Total
N = 57 (cases)	(20)	(33)	(4)	
Getting a job (26 responses)	23.1	76.9	0.0	100.0
Getting a promotion (20 responses)	55.0	40.0	5.0	100.0
Joining a club (13 responses)	15.4	69.2	15.4	100.0
Getting admitted to school (10 responses)	10.0	80.0	10.0	100.0
Renting an apartment (10 responses)	60.0	30.0	10.0	100.0

TABLE 3.17
Frequency Distribution of Perceived Prejudice by Generation

	Foreign-Born	U.S.-Born of F.B. Parents	1 Parent U.S.-Born	2 Parents U.S.-Born	Grandparent U.S.-Born
N = 583	(218)	(272)	(36)	(41)	(16)
No	90.4	95.2	95.1	95.1	100.0
Yes	8.3	4.0	2.8	2.4	0.0
Don't know	1.4	0.7	0.0	2.4	0.0
	100.0	100.0	100.0	100.0	100.0

direction. Foreign accents, mannerisms, names, and customs tend to attract attention even if socioeconomic variables are held constant.

Generally, older respondents tended to find the present situation more tolerant of ethnic differences. Several had experienced discrimination in finding jobs, joining social clubs, and the like, prior to the 1960s. For example, an eighty-one-year-old foreign-born woman wrote: "Came to U.S.A. in 1923 when Turkey was changing from an absolute monarchy into a republic. It was not easy for Armenians to be accepted by U.S.A. as an ethnic group as it is today. I would say they were considered as—white niggers—your generation is lucky, that being or belonging to an ethnic group is something to be proud of." A middle-aged, second-generation woman also observed: "I grew up in a non-Armenian community and felt prejudiced against. I feel the Armenians arriving in this country over the last 25 years have had it much better because it is much more acceptable to be of ethnic origin today and many have come with money and education."

A seventy-one-year-old, U.S.-born man said: "In applying for my first teaching job, 50+ years ago, some districts showed discrimination. After being hired for my first job, there were no further problems for new jobs, promotion, etc." A second-generation woman wrote: "I am 47. In my teens there was some social discrimination. Those years are gone—at least from what I observe. Ethnic is in." Another second-generation respondent (male, fifty-eight-years-old) believed he was discriminated against in joining a club adding, "in early 50's." Another respondent (female, fifty-three-years-old, second-generation) thought there was prejudice, though "not today. Yes in the 1930's in small towns." She went on to explain that they had lived in upstate New York, "a WASP community where all three children experienced discrimination in the schools. Most friends were Armenian, Greek, or Jewish. Some discrimination for parents."

Respondents suggested that the discrimination they experienced was not directed at them just because they were Armenian, rather it was a generalized attitude against all foreigners. For example, a retired writer, who immigrated from Turkey at age twelve explained: "Not because I was an Armenian-American, but because I was not a WASP, and visibly somebody of foreign extraction. Nonetheless, I was hired by Fortune Magazine for certain work for which I was qualified." Another foreign-born respondent also observed: "There is prejudice against *most* ethnics probably not clear against Armenians" (male fifty-five-years-old, born in Iraq came at age twenty-two; emphasis in original).

Many respondents seemed to agree that there was little discrimination because few non-Armenians seemed to know what an Armenian was. Here are their comments:

I am surrounded by people who do not know who and what an Armenian is. I spend most of my time trying to explain that to them (female 51, born in Lebanon came age 26).

They don't know what an Armenian is (female 57, second generation).

To qualify—Since Armenians don't blow their own horns, we have not been well known for 100 years (male 75, second generation).

They think we are Arabs, they don't know the difference (male 77, second generation).

Being of ethnic stock does not necessarily mean one will experience discriminatory behavior and prejudice. On the contrary, there were a few respondents who seemed to believe that their Armenian heritage had been an advantage to them. A fifty-eight-year-old, second-generation woman explained: "Quite the contrary, it seems to be an asset. Everyone seems to have 'a friend' who is Armenian and likes our food. If anything, it helped me and my children into prestigious places." A third-generation young respondent (female, age twenty) said: "Actually, I think being Armenian helped me with getting a job and admission to college." Another young third-generation woman wrote: "Absolutely the contrary—Armenians are highly regarded." In sum, there is no specific anti-Armenian sentiment in this country at the present time. On the other hand, it can be argued that comparatively few people in mainstream America know much about who and what Armenians are, even after all the media coverage of the earthquake and political turmoil in Armenia.

Social Distance

I have measured social relationships within the various Armenian subcommunities and with other non-Armenian ethnic and religious groups living in the study area. The famous Bogardus scale was used to measure social distance, that is, respondents were asked to indicate whether the closest relation they have had in each group was a relative (by blood or marriage), a friend, a neighbor, a co-worker, an acquaintance, or whether they had no acquaintance from that group. Six Armenian subcommunities and twelve (non-Armenian) ethnic and religious groups were listed in the questionnaire. Even though this is a crude measure[41] for network connectedness among different ethnic and religious groups living in metropolitan New York and New Jersey, it provides valuable information on social networks of Armenian-Americans.

These measures provide evidence to support the claim that the Armenian-Americans in the metropolitan area are fragmented into subcommunities by place of birth. The later the generational presence, the higher the proportions of respondents who have no acquaintances among any of the Armenian immigrant groups (table 3.18). Overall, within the Armenian subcommunities, most of the respondents had Armenian-American relatives (72 percent) or friends (19 percent). A

TABLE 3.18
Frequency Distribution of Respondents Having "No Acquaintance" among
Armenian Subcommunities on Social Distance Scale by Generation
(in percent)

	Foreign-Born	US.-Born of F.B. Parents	1 Parent U.S.-Born	2 Parents U.S.-Born	Grandparent U.S.-Born
N = 426-534	(151-254)	(198-254)	(28-36)	(36-39)	(13-16)
American-Armenians	2.1	1.2	0.0	0.0	6.3
Turkish-Armenians	15.2	34.0	30.0	51.4	53.8
Middle Eastern-Armenians	6.5	24.8	17.9	32.4	23.1
Iranian-Armenians	27.2	45.7	36.4	63.2	31.3
East European-Armenians	29.8	47.5	46.4	55.6	61.5
Soviet-Armenians	39.3	60.0	60.6	61.5	31.5

distant second were Middle Eastern-born Armenians (28 percent had relatives and 36 percent friends among them). Turkish-Armenians came third (28 percent relatives and 27 percent friends). By contrast, Iranian-Armenians, Eastern-European-Armenians, and Soviet-Armenians are least known. There are reasons for these factors.

Iranian-Armenians speak an Eastern Armenian dialect unlike the majority of other immigrants. Those who have come to the United States in recent years, especially after the Islamic Revolution, have created their own voluntary associations and tend not to mix freely with other ethnics. Iranian-Armenians who came earlier, like Bulgarian and Romanian-Armenians, are well-integrated into the Armenian community and would probably be considered Armenian-Americans by the New York respondents. Recent arrivals from Soviet Armenia are too few in number in the study area and the respondents' lack of acquaintances among them may be well-justified. Note that Los Angeles is the exception among Armenian communities in the United States because of its higher proportion of immigrants and large number of Soviet Armenians and Iranian-Armenians. The comments of a young, third-generation dentist illustrate some of the stereotypes about the immigrant subcommunities.

> I find that the newcomer Armenians [from Lebanon and Iran] in their dealings with me are more like Middle Easterners than the Armenian-Americans. They can at times be very trying. Very interestingly, the Turkish Armenians seem the most like Armenian-Americans! They are *very easy* people to deal with.

> I believe that the Armenian-Americans and the Middle East Armenians have become two subcultures and strangely enough, the Turkish Armenian immigrants are more akin the Armenian-Americans, perhaps more "European?" Also, the Egyptian-Armenians are very easy to work with, much like the Turkish Armenians. They are very classy people. (Emphasis in original)

Outside the Armenian-American community, respondents in the survey were closest to the following in descending order: Italian-Americans (11 percent have relatives, 53.5 percent friends), American-Jews (9.7 percent have relatives, 52 percent friends), Irish-Americans (11 percent have relatives, 48.6 percent friends), Anglo-Saxons (14.3 percent have relatives, 44.6 percent friends), and Greek-Americans (6 percent relatives, 47 percent friends). They are most likely to meet blacks and Hispanics in the workplace. Friendship choices with Italians and Jews are not surprising because large proportions of American-Jews and Italian-Americans live in metropolitan New York and New Jersey. Moreover, in terms of their immigration history and socioeconomic characteristics, they are not dissimilar to Armenians. It is noteworthy that Anglo-Saxon spouses are chosen most frequently over other groups, presumably the quick step to social mobility and assimilation in America.

Turks stand out as the least known people (see table 3.19). It is remarkable that over 70 percent of the sample have no Turkish acquaintances. This lack of contact is attributed to Armenian prejudice against Turks. The relatively small number of Turks who live in the study area, and their predominantly immigrant status may be another reason.[42] Foreign-born respondents have more Turkish acquaintances than all the U.S.-born together. This is understandable because a certain proportion of foreign-born respondents are recent immigrants from Turkey. Nonetheless, with increasing generational presence in

TABLE 3.19

Frequency Distribution of Respondents Having "No Acquaintance" among Ethnic and Religious Groups in Metropolitan New York and New Jersey on Social Distance Scale (in descending order from closest to least known) by Generation (in percent)

	Foreign-Born	U.S.-Born of F.B. Parents	1 Parent U.S.-Born	2 Parents U.S.-Born	Grandparent U.S.-Born
N = 352-526	(163-185)	(102-250)	(34-36)	(37-39)	(16)
Italians	17.4	2.0	5.7	5.1	0.0
Jews	10.3	5.0	2.9	2.6	6.3
Irish	22.6	6.7	8.6	0.0	0.0
Anglo-Saxon	26.9	11.1	8.3	7.9	6.3
Greeks	16.1	11.4	16.7	8.1	18.8
Poles	59.1	21.7	22.9	18.9	12.5
French	34.1	40.0	37.1	27.0	12.5
Blacks	37.1	25.1	17.6	7.7	12.5
Hispanics	41.7	27.3	23.5	7.9	25.0
Arabs	48.8	55.2	55.9	40.5	37.5
Asians	61.1	44.2	26.5	35.1	25.0
Turks	66.3	79.9	73.5	59.5	37.5

the United States, even Armenian animosity toward Turks tends to decrease. Later-generation Armenian-Americans are more likely to have Turkish acquaintances.[43]

Except for the foreign-born generation (notably those from Middle Eastern countries), Arabs are the second least-known ethnic group. This may be explained by American prejudice against Arab and Islamic peoples. Generally, later-generation Armenians tend to be more tolerant of almost all ethnic and religious groups and have at least an acquaintance in most groups. By contrast, the foreign-born generation does not have many acquaintances among minority groups such as Asians, Hispanics, and blacks. It is interesting to note that stereotypes about ethnic groups of non-European origin remain strong among the general U.S. population (college samples). On Bogardus's Ethnic Distance Scale, Armenians ranked twenty-first in 1977 in a list of thirty groups and received a mean score of 2.2. (U.S. whites scored 1.25 at the top of the list and Koreans 2.63 at the bottom). Surprisingly, Armenians have dropped in ranking in the last fifty years. In 1926, they ranked sixteenth and their mean score was 2.06 (at the top were the English with 1.06 and at the bottom the Indians (from India) with 3.91 [see Smith and Dempsey 1983]).

Conflict between Newcomers and American-born

The two attitude statements measuring social distance in the study were: "I feel more comfortable with Armenians who were born and raised in the same city/country as me," and "Unlike American-born Armenians, some recent Armenian immigrants are crude and clannish." Almost half of the respondents felt that they would be more comfortable with people who were born and raised in the same place as themselves. About a fourth of the sample also believed that new immigrants are crude and clannish, though a third had no opinion on the matter, mostly those in later generations. It is interesting that 37 percent of the foreign-born agreed that new immigrants were crude and clannish (see tables 3.20, 3.21). This may be because most of the foreign-born respondents have been living in the United States for over fifteen years (see chap. 1) and consider themselves American-Armenians, and thus are disdainful of newcomers. Surely, who is or is not a "newcomer" is an arbitrary label. This sentiment is not unique to

Armenians, most ethnic groups have similarly disowned their "off the boat" compatriots.

German Jews who had arrived in the United States before the Eastern European Jews felt that the latter would imperil their status and be a threat to American Jewish life. German Jews established clubs and erected social barriers to exclude the new immigrants (Kramer and Leventman 1961, 45-49). They even attempted to stop the flow of immigration (Sklare 1975, 264). Failing that, they tried to "Americanize" the newcomers (Rosentraub and Taebel 1980). The social chasm ended when the children of the East European Jews achieved social and economic parity with the earlier settlers (Gordon 1964, 185; see also Moskos 1989 for the Greek-American case). Similarly, when displaced persons from Poland arrived after World

TABLE 3.20
Frequency Distribution of Statement: "I Feel More Comfortable with Armenians Who were Born and Raised in the same City/Country as Me" by Generation

	Foreign-Born	U.S.-Born of F.B. Parents	1 Parent U.S.-Born	2 Parents U.S.-Born	Grandparent U.S.-Born
N = 584	(219)	(272)	(36)	(41)	(16)
Agree	58.4	41.2	44.4	36.6	18.8
No opinion	7.8	20.6	27.8	29.3	43.8
Disagree	33.8	38.2	27.8	34.1	37.5
	100.0	100.0	100.0	100.0	100.0

TABLE 3.21
Frequency Distribution of Statement: "Unlike American-Born Armenians, Some Recent Armenian Immigrants Are Crude and Clannish" by Generation

	Foreign-Born	U.S.-Born of F.B. Parents	1 Parent U.S.-Born	2 Parents U.S.-Born	Grandparent U.S.-Born
N = 584	(219)	(272)	(36)	(41)	(16)
Agree	37.4	47.8	50.0	39.0	12.5
No opinion	22.8	31.2	30.5	31.7	50.0
Disagree	39.7	21.0	19.4	29.3	37.5
	100.0	100.0	100.0	100.0	100.0

War II, hostility erupted. Lopata explains the Polish case, which is not dissimilar to the present situation among American-Armenians:

> The presence of the fresh arrivals seemed to have increased the Americanization of the original Polish residents, showing them how non-Polish they had become ... the new emigration Poles tend to be more conscious of Polish culture and more "proud" of its various aspects. Coming into contact with descendants of Polish peasant immigrants who are frequently ashamed of this background, the new immigrants have tended to increase the interest of Polonia in Polish literary culture. (Lopata 1964, 213)

This conflict between different waves of immigration is attributed to ethnogenesis. "The old immigrants tend to regard the more recent arrivals as foreigners and the more recent immigrants tend to dismiss their predecessors as peasants" (Greeley 1974, 312). It was stated in chapter 1 that the culture of the immigrant or ethnic community in America is a new synthesis between the imported culture and the conditions of life in the host country. The clashes between the newest immigrants and those who arrived before World War II are due to their respective definitions of Armenianness. It has been my contention in this study that the culture of the Armenian diaspora is not a uniform culture. Differences between the various subcommunities are the result of separate ethnogenesis for the Armenian people in various host societies. The social, political, economic conditions of life for Armenians in Beirut were different from those in Istanbul, in Marseille, in Fresno, and Buenos Aires.

The attitude statement on new immigrants being crude and clannish received a large number of comments from the respondents. Some of these were specific criticisms related to the wording of the statement, but others were general observations about "newcomers." The tension between new immigrants and the established ethnics is undeniable. Most of the community leaders I interviewed were concerned about it; and in recent years, several panel discussions have been organized on the subject.

Evidently, foreign-born respondents were more critical of the statement that recent immigrants are crude and clannish. For example, a fifty-four-year-old woman who had come from Iran six years previously, wrote: "The American-born don't want newcomers. They are clannish." Another Iranian-born lady who has been in the United States for fifteen years disagreed with the statement, she added: "Au contraire, [they] have larger cultural and political horizons." A forty-year-old man who came from Istanbul at age twenty-three said: "So are American-born Armenians." Another middle-aged woman who was born in Aleppo but lived most of her life in America wrote: "Some American-born are crude and clannish." On the other hand, several American-born respondents agreed with the statement. For example, a forty-five-year-old man who like his mother was U.S.-born strongly agreed, adding: "Rude, immoral and dishonest." Another second-generation man penciled in: "and very poor church supporters." A thirty-six-year-old woman whose parents were U.S.-born was equally harsh in her criticism of foreign-born Armenians. She wrote: "When I was younger I used to feel great pride saying I was Armenian because that is how I was brought up. However, the influx of Armenians particularly from Beirut (whom we call 'boatjobs') with their dishonest crude way, arrogant attitudes, and back-stabbing women has left me cold, to say the least."

A middle-aged second-generation man wrote the following comments about the Armenian community in general: "They are too cliquish. I went to the Armenian Festival at the Garden State Arts Center and really did not feel as though I belonged especially as we do not belong to any club or organization. My son is married to an *odar*. When I go to their church I am greeted and welcomed. At an Armenian affair if you are not known you might as well have leprosy." There were several American-born respondents who tried to qualify the statement on immigrants. A third-generation, middle-aged woman said that *crude* "seems rather a harsh word, 'ignorant' might be a better choice." Another second-generation man wrote: "Clannish but not crude—odd combination you chose." An elderly second-generation man noted: "New immigrants are like my parents' kind of people."

One reason for the tension between Americanized Armenians and more recent immigrants is the issue of supporting the Armenian church. Newcomers are blamed for not paying membership dues and not coming to church on a weekly basis. The newcomers find the practice of membership dues strange. They argue that every Armenian should be a church member as his or her birthright, whether or not he or she pays the fixed fees. Donations should be left to personal decisions. The American-born defend their position by saying that it contributes to administrative efficiency.[44] A fifty-two-year-old second-

generation woman wrote: "The American-Armenians place more emphasis on the church whereas the Armenians who come from abroad
stress the language more. We must make Armenians realize that—yes,
the schools are important but being a good Christian is also vital in a
child's life."

As mentioned in the previous chapter, generally, Middle Eastern-
born Armenians tend to define their Armenianness in terms of
language and culture maintenance, while the American-born find the
Apostolic church to be the catalyst of their ethnicity. The competition
often includes the issue of who is "more" Armenian. This is often
heard among community members, both old and new. For example, a
sixty-three-year-old second-generation man said: "we Armenians who
are born in the USA are mostly more Armenian than these
newcomers."

The priest of a suburban parish church I interviewed was critical of
the newcomers, though he himself is foreign-born. He said:

There is tension between the American-born and the newcomers. The native-born
are blamed for not speaking Armenian but they are the pillars of the community.
They resent the accusation and find the newcomers take a lot of things for granted.

Few of the new immigrants are interested in the church as such. They come on
special occasions such as Christmas, Easter, etc. The American-born attend Divine
Liturgy more regularly on Sundays. If it wasn't for them the church doors would
remain closed.

Newcomers bring their children to Saturday school but have little concern for the
church and its activities. Because of them, we are forced to have two types of
classes, their children speak Armenian at home. [The children of the foreign-born
are taught reading and writing only, while the children of the native-born are taught
reading, writing and conversation.]

Another suburban parish priest observed that due to the influx of
foreign-born Armenians, the composition of his congregation had
changed: "Originally, this parish was mainly English-speaking. In the
last 10-12 years, it has become Armenian-speaking. About 12 years
ago the sermons were in English, now in both English and Armenian."
The available evidence indicates that the invasion of foreign-born
Armenian-speaking parishioners has alienated the charter members. In
this particular case, over 60 percent of the dues-paying members were
American-born, while most of those who attended church were
foreign-born.

A second reason for conflict between the Americanized Armenians and recent immigrants is jealousy over the alleged easy and rapid upward mobility of the latter group. As mentioned in chapter 1, many newcomers defy the old stereotypes of what immigrants should be like in their socioeconomic characteristics. Here are the comments of a sixty-three-year-old man who emigrated from Lebanon with a professional education and capital. In the United States, he invested in real estate in the last twenty years and was successful.

> Financially we are very secure, emotionally we miss our friends and lifestyle. We compensate with new cultural activities [opera, concerts, etc.].
>
> Our non-Armenian friends like us and look for our company.
>
> Our *new* Armenian friends are a puzzle for us. We do not understand them. We feel they resent us, we feel; we came and are enjoying *their* America, they complain without hardship. Because we brought vast capital, European education, European manners, in a few years [we] live in nicest neighborhoods, and they complain we are snobs. To understand this feeling in our new Armenian friends is very hard for us. (Emphasis in original)

An Apostolic priest admitted to me that the tension between the American-born and the foreign-born Armenians was one of the "biggest problems" his church is facing. He went on to explain: "They have different cultural backgrounds, different languages. Economic differences are not important. In fact, most of the newcomers come with money, they establish new businesses, they have personal initiative. In fact, they may be better off than American-born Armenians."

I would like to note that such comparisons are made between foreign-born Armenians and the American-born who remain within the ethnic fold. However, the most successful (financially, professionally, socially, etc.) people of Armenian descent tend to be outside the ethnic community. The observations of a fifty-four-year-old, second-generation man summarize the discussion. "There appears to be a subtle resentment by the American Armenians toward the Middle Eastern Armenians—my guess as to why, is: * clannish * come to U.S. with money * get prosperous with relative ease * chauvinistic with females."

Friends

Friendships are judged according to criteria internal to the relationship. They have been defined as sociable relationships "that an individual enters into purposefully and voluntarily for primarily non-instrumental reasons" (Allan 1979, 2; see also Allan 1989). Friendships are not constructed and maintained haphazardly, but are patterned according to rules of relevance. They are achieved relationships between equals. Enjoyment is the essence of sociable relationships which involve spending time and sharing activities together. Friendships vary by social class, by geographical mobility, by position in the family cycle, and by gender.

Immigrant groups tend to restrict their rules of relevance to people of the same ethnic background because of value and status similarity. In later-generations, with increasing assimilation, sociable relationships are decontextualized; that is, the appropriateness of interaction in multiple settings and contexts is recognized. For example, friends met at work are not confined to the workplace. Furthermore, in later generations, people are less likely to be involved in the community, thus less likely to meet fellow ethnics. It is therefore hypothesized that the foreign-born generation chooses its best friends and acquaintances from within its ethnic circle. With increasing generational status, there is a fanning out of sociable relationships; social class replaces ethnicity as a basis for friendship.

In measuring friendship, the amount of interaction and frequency of contact are imprecise tools because "friend" is a subjective label applied to a relationship that is qualitatively special. For example, one of the respondents (male, age thirty-three, respondent and both parents U.S.-born) criticized the friendship questions with the following comment:

Relative to Armenian friends I feel the questionnaire does not ask the question properly. I have as many close Armenian friends as non-Armenian friends but the question as asked does not allow a proper explanation of this. My Armenian friends are not seen as frequently now as in the past but they are still close friends whom I have contact with on a monthly rather than weekly basis due to geography or difference in marital status. If the question were rephrased to close friends you see at least monthly or yearly, half of my friends are Armenian. I have a close Armenian friend (one of my best friends) with whom I go to professional events but with whom I never go to any Armenian events (we did once during a particular period of our lives but no longer) because of changes in our mutual lifestyles.

In recent years, Network Theory has developed sophisticated concepts and techniques of data analysis pertinent to this issue. Regretfully, they are beyond the scope of this study. Nonetheless, the simple frequencies of ethnic and nonethnic friends that are available here make it possible to estimate the magnitude and direction of the trend. In fact, in whichever way one tries to measure the relative proportion of Armenian versus non-Armenian friends, the pattern is clear; the further one gets from one's immigrant roots, the less likely it is that one has Armenian friends.

First, respondents were asked to provide background information on their "three best friends." About 52 percent of first friends and 44 percent of second and third friends were of Armenian descent.[45] There is a straight-line decrease with each succeeding generation; the longer the generational presence in the United States, the lower the probability of having a person of Armenian descent as a best friend and the lower the probability of having all three best friends of Armenian background (.24*; see table 3.22). Religious affiliation is as significant as generation in predicting whether one's three best friends are Armenian or not (.24*). Apostolics are most likely to have at least one close Armenian friend, and they are most likely to have all three best friends of Armenian descent (28.4 percent). In sharp contrast, those who have no religion are most likely to have no Armenian friends (72 percent vs 32 percent for Apostolics) closely followed by those with non-Armenian denominations (67 percent). The latter were also least likely to have all three best friends of Armenian descent (1.1

TABLE 3.22
Frequency Distribution of Respondents' Three Best Friends by Generation

	Foreign-Born	U.S.-Born of F.B. Parents	1 Parent U.S.-Born	2 Parents U.S.-Born	Grandparent U.S.-Born
N = 584	(219)	(272)	(36)	(41)	(16)
None Armenian	28.3	45.6	63.9	65.9	68.8
One Armenian	15.5	21.0	13.9	14.6	31.3
Two Armenian	20.5	17.6	16.7	9.8	0.0
All three Armenian	35.6	15.8	5.6	9.8	0.0
	100.0	100.0	100.0	100.0	100.0

percent). Mixed parentage reduces by more than half the percentages of those who have three Armenian best friends (.15*; 23 percent vs 9 percent for all three best friends and 38 percent vs 73 percent for none at all). Similarly, younger respondents were also more likely to have no Armenian friends (63 percent for twenty year olds vs 34 percent for sixty year olds) and least likely to have three best friends (9 percent for 20 year olds vs 28 percent for 60 year olds).

Best friends come from all ethnic and national backgrounds; about thirty-five different groups were mentioned by the respondents. Most

TABLE 3.23
Frequency Distribution of Respondents' Three Best Friends by Religious Affiliation Controlled for Generation

	Armenian Church	Roman Catholic	Protestant Denomination	Jewish	Other	Total
First generation						
Friend one N = 175	76.6	8.6	7.4	2.9	4.6	100.0
Friend two N = 168	72.6	10.1	7.1	5.4	4.8	100.0
Friend three N = 158	76.9	10.3	5.1	5.8	1.9	100.0
Second generation						
Friend one N = 229	45.0	23.6	17.9	7.4	6.1	100.0
Friend two N = 227	39.6	26.4	21.6	8.4	4.0	100.0
Friend three N = 222	34.7	31.5	20.3	9.5	4.0	100.0
Third generation						
Friend one N = 81	23.5	30.9	21.0	17.3	7.4	100.0
Friend two N = 84	23.8	36.9	17.9	14.3	7.1	100.0
Friend three N = 80	11.2	42.5	18.7	21.2	6.8	100.0

prominently, Italians average 9.1 percent of "three best friends," Jews average 8.3 percent, "Americans" average 5.9 percent, the Irish 5 percent, Germans 4.1 percent, and the English 2.7 percent. These choices in ethnic background are not surprising because Italians made up 18 percent of the population of metropolitan New York in 1980, the Irish made up 15 percent, the Germans 12 percent, the English 7 percent, and the Jewish population of New York was estimated at 13 percent (Lieberson and Waters 1987). To facilitate the analysis, I categorized friendship choices into Armenian churches (that is, Armenian Protestants, Armenian Catholics and Apostolics), the Roman Catholic church, Protestant denominations, Jewish congregations, and all others, including those who do not profess any religious persuasion.[46]

With each succeeding generation, the percentage of best friends belonging to Armenian churches decreases (table 3.23). While on average 75.3 percent of best friends in the first generation belong to Armenian churches, 39.8 percent of second-generation respondents and 22.8 percent of third- or later-generation respondents do so. The next highest percentage of best friends belonged to the Roman Catholic church. This is due to the high percentages of Italian, Irish, and Polish friends in the survey area. On average, in the first generation, 9.7 percent of best friends were Roman Catholic, 6.5 percent were Protestant and 4.7 percent were Jewish. By the second generation, the number of Roman Catholics and Protestants almost triples (27.2 percent and 19.9 percent respectively) and that of the Jews doubles (8.4 percent). In later generations, the number of Jewish friends doubles, that of the Roman Catholics also increases, but that of Protestants does not change. In other words, with increasing generational presence, ascribed characteristics such as religion and ethnicity become less meaningful than the intrinsic qualities of the relationship in establishing friendships. These results demonstrate that Armenian-Americans are well-integrated in the larger American society and social distance between them and other groups sharing their environment is narrowing considerably; the boundaries are being obliterated.

Second, respondents were asked to indicate the proportion of Armenian friends they had at the time of the survey other than their three best friends. For the foreign-born, not only are their "three best friends" highly likely to be of Armenian descent, but more than half of their other friends were also likely to be Armenian. This probability diminishes by half with each generation (see table 3.24;.36*). Respondents who profess no religious affiliation and those who have other than Armenian denominations are least likely to have a majority of Armenian friends (8.3 percent, 17.6 percent respectively, compared to 66 percent for Apostolics, 55 percent for Armenian Protestants and 27 percent for Armenian Catholics).

Socioeconomic variables were not significantly related to friendship choices with the exception of education (.16*). The higher the educational attainment, the less the circle of Armenian friends (40 percent for less than high school, 64 percent for high school, 47 percent for less than college, 45 percent for college and 40 percent for more than college). These findings corroborate the conclusions of previous studies; that is, immigrants associate with fellow ethnics, but

TABLE 3.24

Frequency Distribution of Proportion of Armenian Friends Now by Generation

	Foreign-Born	U.S.-Born of F.B. Parents	1 Parent U.S.-Born	2 Parents U.S.-Born	Grandparent U.S.-Born
N = 574	(214)	(267)	(36)	(41)	(16)
None	6.5	18.4	30.6	39.0	31.3
Less than half	15.4	39.3	44.4	43.9	62.5
More than half	78.0	42.3	25.0	17.1	6.3
	100.0	100.0	100.0	100.0	100.0

TABLE 3.25

Frequency Distribution of Armenian Friends When Respondent Was Eighteen Years of Age by Generation

	Foreign-Born	U.S.-Born of F.B. Parents	1 Parent U.S.-Born	2 Parents U.S.-Born	Grandparent U.S.-Born
N = 584	(219)	(272)	(36)	(41)	(16)
None	4.1	18.4	22.2	39.0	31.3
Less than half	12.8	34.2	38.9	34.1	62.5
More than half	83.1	47.4	38.9	26.8	6.3
	100.0	100.0	100.0	100.0	100.0

education and length of residence expands their networks (Breton and Pinard 1960).

Third, generation was also significantly related to the proportion of Armenian friends when respondent was seventeen or eighteen years of age (.35*; table 3.25). The sharpest drop is between the foreign-born generation and the second generation. Later-generation Armenians are more likely to grow up in communities where there are no or few Armenians. For example, a fifty-six-year-old, second-generation woman wrote: "Grew up in Newburgh, NY, not too many Armenians." A young man whose father is Jewish and whose mother's parents were Armenian immigrants from Turkey, remarked: "We lived in a section of New York in which no other Armenians resided—*None at all*" (emphasis in original). Some foreign-born respondents also grew up in environments with relatively few Armenians. Such is the case of a ninety-two-year-old man who was born in Berlin of a German mother and an Armenian father. He came to America when he was forty-five-years-old. When the proportion of Armenian friends at eighteen is compared to Armenian friends now, the former receives slightly higher frequencies in each generation. This suggests that in addition to generation, there is a decline over the life course in having Armenian friends. When households of Armenian descent are geographically isolated from metropolitan centers with heavy concentrations of Armenians, they are more likely to join other religious denominations. It is therefore not surprising that affiliation with non-Armenian denominations reduced significantly the chances of having numerous Armenian friends when young (21 percent vs 70 percent for Apostolics).

TABLE 3.26
Frequency Distribution of Armenian Friends When Respondent Was Eighteen
Years of Age by Education

	Some High School	Completed High School	Some College	Completed College	More than College
N = 563	(47)	(138)	(109)	(129)	(138)
None	6.2	13.0	14.7	16.3	20.9
Less than half	14.6	18.8	29.4	32.6	35.3
More than half	79.2	68.1	56.0	51.2	43.9
	100.0	100.0	100.0	100.0	100.0

It is noteworthy that in addition, higher educational attainment was significant with friendship with non-Armenians (table 3.26). People tend to meet and make friends in school or college. Therefore, the longer a person stays in an educational setting the more the chances that he or she will meet and befriend non-Armenians. Given the small proportion of Armenians in the United States, parents and community leaders go to great lengths to bring young Armenian-Americans into contact with each other. Summer camps, sports associations, youth organizations, debutante balls, and Armenian student clubs in major universities are examples of communally designed programs to fight against the odds.

Nelson's observations of third-generation Armenians in Fresno, California, after World War II illustrate the efforts parents make not to decontextualize friendships. They are applicable to many Armenian-American parents today.

> Armenian parents, incidentally, seldom made an issue of preventing their children from associating with *odars* while in school. After graduation from high school, they exerted some pressure for their children to join Armenian organizations, probably to encourage friendships with other Armenians and so prevent the possibility of mixed marriage. (Nelson 1953, 115)

The remarks of a respondent (female, thirty-years-old, respondent and father U.S.-born) suggest that the urging of parents, especially if they are foreign-born, to befriend fellow Armenians is overpowered by structural conditions and the ideology of romantic love. She wrote:

> Since my mother was from the other side—Syria ... [she] ... encouraged us (5 kids) at every opportunity to go to Armenian church dances for the youth and join ACYOA [Armenian Christian Youth Organization of America], etc, of which I attended plenty.

> With all this, I made many Armenian friends; I had gone through my share of dating Armenian guys, as did all my sisters.

> I never stopped having relationships with my *odar* friends. It made no difference to me whom I would someday fall in love with, whom I would marry. Well, it happened to be a guy who not only is not Armenian, but he has no religious convictions at all.

In conclusion, whichever way friendship choices are measured, whether best friends or acquaintances or youth friends, the proportion of Armenian to non-Armenian friends, decreases with each succeeding generation, non-Armenian denominational preference, mixed ancestry, youth, and higher educational attainment. Typically, foreign-born respondents are most likely to have an Armenian social network. Such as the ninety-three-year-old female respondent who wrote: "All my friends and relatives are Armenian and close to my age, born in Turkey." There is overwhelming evidence that the personal networks of the respondents, the people they choose to label as "friend," those they feel are their equals tend to be increasingly non-Armenian. Most later-generation Armenian-Americans would agree with the young woman who told me that she had more in common with her Irish-American friends than she did with Armenians coming from Lebanon or elsewhere in the Middle East, even when their socioeconomic backgrounds were comparable.

Conclusions

In this chapter, the structural relations of Armenian-Americans were demonstrated to increasingly fan outside the confines of the formal and informal community. The pattern established so far in this study also applies here. That is, with the passing of generations in the United States, with nonethnic denominational affiliation or no religious persuasion, with mixed ancestry among younger cohorts, and for those with higher levels of educational attainment, a distancing from Armenian social structures proceeds, slowly for the first and second generations, but at a very fast pace consequently.

The data shows that the Armenian-American community of metropolitan New York and New Jersey is a first- and second-generation phenomenon. The members of voluntary associations and the audience for activities and events hosted by such associations drops off sharply after the second generation. At the core of most collective happenings is a small group of frequent attenders or devotees who are to be contrasted with people who acknowledge their Armenian descent but hardly ever take part in collective manifestations of Armenianness. In between these two extremes are those with varying degrees of participation. Moreover, the Armenian-American community is not a monolithic structure; it is divided into subcommunities by country of origin, by generation, by political ideologies, by religious denominations, by socioeconomic status, by life-style and interest, and so on.

Over two hundred events and activities are sponsored year after year by the numerous voluntary associations that make up the formally organized structure of the Armenian-American community of metropolitan New York and New Jersey. This vitality is due to the large proportion of first- and second-generation Armenian-Americans in the population. Being an immigrant and the child of immigrants, irrespective of social class, heightens one's participation in the ethnic community. It also increases the probability of being a dues-paying member, and somewhat less the chance of attending meetings frequently. Involvement in the ethnic world does not preclude integration into the larger American society. Significant proportions of respondents, including the foreign-born, join non-Armenian voluntary associations, notably professional associations and political parties.

The survey results establish that the integration of Armenian-Americans into the larger "American" society parallels their immersion in the ethnic community for the first and second generation; one is not exclusive of the other. Significant proportions of foreign-born respondents were members of professional associations, charitable organizations, and mainstream political parties. Indicators of social distance and friendship choices used in the study also revealed that with the exception of Turks, respondents felt close to Italians, Jews, the Irish, "Americans," and other ethnic or religious groups who live in the study area. However, with the third and subsequent generations, about nine out of ten persons of Armenian descent confine most of their leisure-time activities to the nonethnic world.

Those who choose to remain within the ethnic fold past the third generation are a numerical minority, but strongly committed to their Armenianness. They are highly likely to assume positions of responsibility in voluntary associations. Thus the real loss across the generations is not so much in the leadership, but in the audience to collective events. Some types of voluntary associations and events are more appropriate for later-generation symbolic ethnics. Ethnic professional associations or business-related networks are examples of structures that further organic solidarity, combining instrumental gains with fellowship with co-ethnics. Festivals, street fairs, and folk dance shows are prototypes of events that are most likely to be popular by symbolic ethnics. It should be noted that the present results do not support Hansen's third-generation return hypothesis. There is no behavioral "return" to the ethnic world in the third or any other generation. Nor is there any measurable "return" by different stages in the life cycle. The high level of activity and visibility of communally structured programs testifies to the increasing acceptability of "sidestream" ethnicity and the influx of large numbers of new immigrants in the last couple of decades or so.

Notes

1.   The Union of Marash Armenians is a case in point. According to the report of their Student Fund Committee read at the 61st annual convention held in Los Angeles on 31 August 1985, a total of $3,400 was distributed that year. Nine college students, whose ancestors were born in Marash (Turkey), were awarded sums ranging between $300 and $500. The report further emphasized that "the real meaning of UMA scholarships is not their dollar value but in passing to our children two important traditions of Marash, namely, our concern for each other and our love for learning" (John Halajian, "Annual Report of the Student Fund Committee to the 61st UMA Convention," *Kermanig* [Boston] 55, no. 219-20 [January-June 1986]: 27). It should be noted that in this particular issue, four out of the thirty-four pages were in English, the rest in Armenian. This further adds to the evidence that compatriotic societies are characteristic of the immigrant generation.

2.   For example, the overwhelming majority of the Gomidas Choir of the Armenian Diocese in New York were born in Turkey and emigrated after World War II. The Gomidas Choir, like other Armenian organizations, is facing the challenge of replacing deceased and older, retiring members.

3.   The Knights of Vartan is a national organization established in 1919 with twenty-seven lodges in eighteen states. According to my informant, it is nonpartisan and nondenominational. That is, in recent years, it has encouraged the participation of Armenians from all political parties and religious affiliations. It is a semimilitary organization in its hierarchical structure and emphasis on discipline. In 1991, there were 2,500 male members and 2,000 female members, each paying approximately $50-$60 in dues annually. Of these, 75-80 percent were American-born. The average age of the members was fifty years. Most of its leaders and many of its followers have been individuals highly active in establishing churches in the United States and serving on parish councils. In the past decade, the Knights of Vartan contributed $500,000 toward the Center for Armenian Research and Publication, at the University of Michigan, Dearborn. In 1990, they gave $55,000 in scholarships; and like many other organizations, since the earthquake this fraternity has diverted some of its resources to Armenia. They donated a food-processing machine worth $115,000 to Leninagan. In the New York area, the Knights of Vartan have for the past several years organized (at times in collaboration with other organizations) the Times Square Genocide Commemorative Rally.

4. Asked about the conflict between the American-born and newcomers, one of the community leaders I interviewed had the following comments: "It's difficult but their children will no longer be foreign-born. It's a matter of time. It won't split the community further. There are differences in the foreign-born from different countries. Most organizations absorbed the Lebanese-Armenians because they were used to working in such contexts. The Iranian-Armenians formed their separate organizations. The Soviet-Armenians are not organizationally inclined."

5. For example, in the 1980s, AGBU Central Committee of America hired English-trained actor Krikor Satamian to direct the Ardashad Theatre Group. He produced and acted in a number of Armenian-language plays that toured several communities in the United States and Canada.

6. In the study area, AGBU had 1,488 official members in 1984 (AGBU Central Committee of America, *Annual Report 1984* presented 21 June 1985 at 71st National Convention, Los Angeles, California, p. 36). According to an AGBU director I interviewed, 65 to 70 percent of the New York and New Jersey chapter members are American-born, the rest foreign-born. In 1990, AGBU had 22,000 members worldwide.

7. According to a committee member, the group was organized in 1976; there are about one hundred alumni living in metropolitan New York and New Jersey. Their main activity is an annual dinner dance as a fund-raiser. Recently, they have taken charge of an Armenian Saturday school program in the Armenian Protestant Church of New Jersey (called the Sipan School). This alumni association has a branch in Los Angeles, and their annual dinner dance attracts larger crowds than on the East Coast. Haigazian College Alumni Association, established in 1977 in Glendale, has similar aims and activities and partly shares the same membership.

8. It is interesting to note that Boudjikanian-Keuroghlian (1978) has constructed a similar typology of Armenians in the Lyons district of France. First, there are the old-timers *(le retraité)*, those who came from the old country and have grown old in France. At the other extreme are the assimilated, those of Armenian descent who are lost to the community; I call them the "ex-ethnics" (see chap. 5). Then there is *l'Armenien moyen* (the "average" French-Armenian). They are the majority and would correspond to second-generation American-Armenians. Finally, the author finds a very small number of *militant engagé* (militant ethnics). It should be noted that the study was conducted in the 1970s at the height of Armenian "terrorism." With the French emphasis on political activism among other reasons, many young Armenian activists supported the movement openly. There are many similarities between French patterns of assimilation and American ones; however, there are also important differences. Until recently, France has been a closed, relatively homogeneous society, less welcoming of foreigners; Armenian immigrants faced severe prejudice and discrimination (for a personal account see Verneuil 1985).

9. Again, the Armenians are not unique in their experience. According to Zenner (1985, 121), "efforts at forming an umbrella communal structure" for Jewish groups failed initially at national and regional levels until ideological distinctions became less important.

10. According to one of the organizers of the annual Times Square Genocide Commemoration Rally around April 24, estimates of participants have rarely exceeded 2,000 individuals. In recent history, record crowds gathered for a

solidarity rally for Armenians in the Soviet Union. An estimated 5,000 people of Armenian descent assembled in New York City, on Sunday, 12 March 1988 to march from the United Nations to the Soviet Mission to the UN in support of Armenians in Karabagh who were demanding the reunification of the autonomous region with Armenia SSR (see *Armenian Reporter,* 17 March 1988). The record was broken in 1990. Close to 7,500 people were estimated to have attended the seventy-fifth anniversary of the Genocide at Times Square. I should add that this particular gathering was a joint effort between the two factions of the community; the Prelacy and Diocese groups (see the *Armenian Reporter,* 26 April 1990, p. 24).

11. A small nonprobability study asking people of Armenian descent who they thought were Armenian leaders in the diaspora today found that there were no viable political leaders who could be readily named. Respondents named clerics, a philanthropist, history professors. They also mentioned writers, freedom fighters, and men of arms who have long been dead (Khachig Tölölyan, "Who leads the Armenians of the Diaspora?" *Armenian Reporter,* 31 July 1986, p. 3). Similarly, one of my informants lamented that the Armenian community spends enormous fortunes on communal projects but there is no master plan, no list of priorities, because there is no community-wide leadership.

12. Lopata (1964, 216) makes a similar case for Polish-Americans. She argues that there are no unifying goals sufficiently broad to attract large numbers of Polish-Americans. Poles, like Armenians, blame their inner conflicts on their "Polishness" and individualism. She suggests that the greater the differentiation within the ethnic group, the more their assimilation, the less likely their ability to organize as an interest group.

13. The Armenian population of Greater London is estimated to range between 8,000 and 10,000 persons. Only about 1,500 of them are active members in voluntary associations, participating regularly in communal life (Talai 1984).

14. I was notified by an informant that activities sponsored by the Armenian Revolutionary Federation (Tashnags) and its allied associations are rarely advertised in the *Armenian Reporter.* The figures presented above are therefore lower than the actual number of events that take place in any given year.

15. *Kef* is a Turkish word meaning "merriment." A *kef* night is an informal gathering for dancing, eating, and drinking.

16. According to one observer there are approximately seventeen amateur Armenian folk dance ensembles in the United States that are somewhat active. See Gary Lind-Sinanian "Armenian Dance in the Diaspora - An Inquiry," *Armenian Reporter,* 19 December 1985, p. 2. From the *Armenian American Almanac* (1990), I was able to count six folk dance ensembles or troupes; three dance studios (in California); and one folk dance society whose purpose is "to preserve and perpetuate Armenian traditional folk dancing and music unchoreographed."

17. These were lectures of general interest, for example, lectures on wills and estates, taxes, computers, business ethics, and interpretation of dreams. Their sponsoring organizations cater mostly to the "Armenian yuppie" generation, American-born young professional symbolic Armenians. Later-generation ethnic organizations such as the Armenian Network, Inc. can draw the biggest crowds for such topics rather than traditional cultural and historical subjects ("Arm. Network Offers Varied Programs to Young Professionals," *Armenian Reporter,* 26 March 1987, p. 4.

18. See Parlakian (1983) for an account of "Armenian-American theatre" in the United States. Parlakian observes that initially, original Armenian plays and world drama in translation were produced for Armenian immigrant audiences. However, by the 1940s and 1950s, a new generation of American-born Armenians, thoroughly familiar with the English language did not need to see Shakespeare and others in translation. Thus, the repertoire of amateur theatrical groups was increasingly restricted to Armenian works. In the 1970s, there was a new surge of theatrical performances in the Armenian community of New York. Parlakian attributes this "cultural renaissance" to the renewed interest in ethnicity nationally, but mostly to the large numbers of immigrants from the Middle East. Nonetheless, audiences for ethnic theater remain limited. Parlakian mentions that at a hit show in 1979, 600 people packed the auditorium (p. 33). Similar figures were quoted to me by community leaders I interviewed. In 1985, about 700 people, mostly foreign-born, attended two performances of an Armenian play in New Jersey. The prevalence of foreign-born audiences in ethnic theater is understandable, when the small proportion of American-born ethnics who speak the Armenian language is taken into consideration.

19. In 1985, there were two major ethnic festivals, the One World Festival in New York City and another one in New Jersey. The One World Festival was a product of the 1970s "ethnic revival" movement; it was co-sponsored by the Diocese of the Armenian Church of America and the Mayor's Office of Special Projects and Events. It brought together, for sixteen consecutive years, a large number of folk dance groups, musicians, and entertainers from around the world, as well as vendors of souvenirs and food. Armenian parishes and organizations were prominent at the festival, but the *piece de resistance* was usually on Sunday afternoons when the Antranig Dance Ensemble performed for the large crowds. The festival was held on the weekend following Labor Day, at St. Vartan's Cathedral on 33 Street and its adjacent St. Vartan Park. The last festival was to be on September 10-11, 1988; and as in previous years, New York's popular mayor, Ed Koch, and numerous other politicians made an appearance (see *Armenian Reporter,* 29 September 1988, p. 8). The community's preoccupation with the earthquake in Armenia and New York City's fiscal crisis finally put an end to the One World Festival. In any case, it was ready to fold. It had served its purpose well while it lasted. After repeating the same program for sixteen years, the audience was ready for something new, and few people were willing to invest time and energy to organize such an undertaking.

20. Golf is becoming increasingly a favorite sport with American-born upper-middle-class suburbanites of Armenian descent. Golf tournaments were not advertised in the ethnic press during 1986; however, they have been mentioned occasionally since.

21. In spite of its name, the Armenian Student Association (ASA) does not depend on students for its membership. The ages of its members range from early adulthood to senior citizens. I attended the June 1985 convention in the suburbs of Boston. There was a *kef* night on the Friday evening, business meetings for the chapters the next day, and various sports tournaments; it culminated in a formal banquet on Saturday evening with dancing. A live band played Armenian tunes; during their long breaks a tape deck blasted American hits. A number of scholarships and awards offered by ASA were announced and presented at the banquet.

22. Undoubtedly, there were requiems in almost all parish churches that were not mentioned in the ethnic press.

23. It should be noted that organizers of April 24 events such as the annual Times Square rally (New York City) make a special effort to provide transportation and other amenities to the "survivors."

24. Armenian communities in America have created several youth associations and programs to encourage young people to build social relationships with Armenian peers. Community leaders hope that such groups will have the latent function of a matrimonial agency. What the Armenian communities have not realized is that too much familiarity with one's peers can be dysfunctional for romantic involvement. They have demystified love. Similar to peer groups that grow up in Israeli Kibbutzim (see Talmon 1964), Armenian youth active in community circles consider their local peers like siblings (O'Grady 1979, 91).

25. See Mary Ann Aposhian. "Clinging to Ethnic Heritage in America: Study Compares Extent of Assimilation between Earlier Generation, New Arrivals." *Armenian International Magazine*, February 1991, pp. 33-36.

26. For comparison, 70 percent of spouses who had one Armenian parent and 93 percent of those who had two parents spoke Armenian.

27. For an estimate of the amount of scholarships offered to people of Armenian descent in America, here are the figures of two major funding organizations. In 1985, AGBU received 180 applications for scholarships. It made 171 loans and 77 grants for a total of $138,325 (personal communication with director, 12 November 1985). According to the *Annual Report of the Armenian Missionary Association of America, Inc.* (AMAA) read at the Sixty-Sixth Annual Meeting, 20 October 1985, in Downey, California, in 1984 "$183,500 was granted and/or loaned to 198 students, of which 21 were theologically oriented. This year [1985] the total amount awarded was $137,500 of which $84,050 were outright grants and $53,450 were interest-free loans" (p. 89). Furthermore, for the 1990-91 academic year, AMAA granted a total of $139,250 to 120 students in outright scholarships and interest-free loans ranging from $500 to $3,500 (*Armenian Reporter*, 9 August 1990, p. 8). It is curious that most scholarships offered by Armenian philanthropies are paid in small increments of $500-$1,000. For example, according to one "Financial Aid Directory for Students of Armenian Descent," out of 46 awards or grants, only three pay up to $3,000; and the AGBU "Excellence" grant pays $5,000 annually (*Armenian Mirror-Spectator*, 6 January 1990, pp. 8-9). All this creates busy work for both the applicants and the granting organizations. With college fees averaging nowadays about $15,000 per annum, it would be more efficient to consolidate these monies into two or three substantial scholarships than keep the present system.

28. Golf tournaments are in the same league as debutante balls. They serve the needs of affluent American-born ethnics. Ethnic organizations that cater to symbolic ethnics are only structurally ethnic. Debutante balls, golf tournaments, bazaars, etc. have little culturally ethnic content.

29. As mentioned in chapter 1, estimates of the Armenian population in the United States fluctuate between 500,000 and 800,000.

30. *Armenian Reporter*, 11 February 1988, p 8.

31. See *Annual Report of AMAA, Inc*, read at 66th Annual Meeting, 20 October 1985, in Downey (CA). It should be noted that large sums of AGBU's and AMAA's budgets are targeted to Armenian schools, scholarships, and other social projects

in the Diaspora (e.g., Cyprus, Lebanon, Syria, etc.).

32. Organic solidarity is the social glue that ties a community through rational interdependence; it is contrasted to mechanical solidarity which nurtures social cohesion on the basis of similarity.

33. McKay and Lewins (1978, 420) similarly propose that ethnic "manipulators," "entrepreneurs," and "brokers" interact frequently in ethnic contexts for economic and political rewards without strong commitments. Examples of ethnic brokers are musicians who play in Armenian bands, academics who specialize in Armenian subjects, Armenian priests, politicians, and executives who work for Armenian organizations.

34. The reader is also reminded that almost 30 percent of this sample is self-employed.

35. In order to attract young, later-generation ethnics into the communal structures, several organizations have started internship programs for college students. The Armenian Assembly and AGBU are two such organizations where college students are placed during the summer months in fields of government, business, and industry of their choice for training and experience. The rationale behind these programs is similar to the professional associations: they further ethnic solidarity among people of Armenian descent by helping each other out and taking care of their own.

36. See *Armenian Reporter*, 17 March 1988, p. 6.

37. The Armenian Network has been very popular in New York/New Jersey (e.g., over 1,000 participants for their Christmas dance). This is due to the vacuum it fills in the institutional structure and most important its latent function. The Network caters to young upwardly mobile professionals of ethnic descent who shrug away from the forms of Armenianness of their parents' generation. One of their leaders boasted to me that they have been able to remove their gatherings from church basements and host their functions in hotels, restaurants, and university clubs. It is an organization by the young for the young, ideally suited for later-generation symbolic Armenians. Though structurally Armenian, much in its content (e.g., lectures) is not. In my opinion their popularity is due to their latent function. Informal meetings, cruises, dances serve as a marriage market for these Armenian "yuppies."

38. See also "Armenian Medical World Conference in LA Brings Together Over 400 Doctors," *Armenian Reporter*, 2 June 1988, p. 14.

39. For example, see advertisement for AESA's symposium in *Armenian International Magazine*, January 1991, pp. 32-33.

40. My knowledge about numbers of members and rate of convention participation is sketchy. For example, according to a recent newspaper report, the Armenian Bar Association has 220 members. It had its first annual meeting in California in January 1990, and about half of the members attended (*Armenian Mirror-Spectator*, 10 February 1990, p. 9). Also, about 30 academics and independent professionals of Armenian descent in social and behavioral sciences, out of a total of approximately 240 (12.5 percent), responded to an invitation and attended the first meeting of the Armenian Behavioral Science Association in New York City in 1987 (See Anny Bakalian, "Association for Behavioral & Social Scientists founded here," *Armenian Reporter*, 10 September 1987, p. 12). The goals of this association are professional networking, social science research on Armenian subjects, training and referrals to students of Armenian descent in the

field, and providing professional services to the Armenian community. ABSA publishes a newsletter and a directory (its 1989 edition lists 304 anthropologists, psychologists, political scientists, sociologists, and social statisticians). It meets regionally, several times a year, in conjunction with the annual meetings of national social science associations. For example, sociologists have met during the annual convention of the American Sociological Association in San Francisco in 1989 and Washington, DC in 1990. At any given time the number of sociologists did not exceed eight. I should add that there are less than a dozen sociologists of Armenian descent in the United States.

41. It does not control for group size, homogeneity of socioeconomic status, time of immigration or ethnic queue (see chap. 1), and respondent's generational and ancestral background. The labels used for the Armenian subcommunities were not readily familiar to the respondents. For example, Eastern-European Armenian was used to economize space, it stood for Bulgarian and Romanian-Armenians. Generally the question was considered difficult and "fussy" by respondents. Consequently, its response rate was far below optimum (missing up to 26 percent).

42. There are an estimated 125,000 Turks living in the United States, few of them in Brooklyn and Queens, New York City (Ghayur 1981).

43. This characteristic is not peculiar to Armenian-Americans. Younger Lebanese-Armenians responding to the "Ethnic Orientation Questionnaire" were more likely than the older generation to disagree with a statement that Armenians and Turks can never be friends (Der-Karabetian and Oshagan 1977).

44. Again, this issue of dues-paying church membership is not unique to Armenians; long ago, Treudley observed the same thing among the Greeks in Boston. She wrote: "local churches early face the problems occasioned by the voluntary financing of religion and learn in time to adopt American methods of raising money" (1949, 48).

45. Overall, 18.3 percent of the sample had one Armenian best friend, 17.6 percent had two, and 21.7 percent had three Armenian best friends. It should be noted that the category "none" which makes up the remaining 42.3 percent of the sample includes those who have no Armenian best friends, those who have no best friends, and those whose best friends have passed away, which is the case with some of the older respondents.

46. The reader is reminded that, 77.7 percent of respondents were affiliated with Armenian churches, 3 percent with the Roman Catholic church, 15.3 with Protestant churches .2 percent were Jewish, and the remaining 6.4 percent either had other or no religion.

4

The Debate over Language

"How can you be an Armenian if you do not speak Armenian? What kind of an Armenian are you?" With such callous remarks, foreign-born Armenians often reproach American-born Armenians. Indeed, these provocative accusations sum up the conflict between two definitions of Armenianness: the traditional and the symbolic. Traditional Armenianness was defined in this study as a status ascribed by accident of birth. It fosters a compulsive type of identity and unconscious behavioral responses. "Being" Armenian can only be sustained in an environment where there are linguistic, religious and other cultural markers that delineate the boundaries between Armenians and *odars*. Symbolic Armenianness was defined as voluntary, rational choice in identity maintenance. It tends to elicit a situational, emotional, personalized response toward one's ancestral heritage. It is not dependent on knowledge or practice of language or culture to survive. Rather, it is contingent on its effectiveness in fulfilling social-psychological functions for the individual and on the larger society's tolerance of ethnic differences.

Because of the recent influx of immigrants, significant proportions of Armenians born and raised in the Middle East and Soviet Union who conceive of their Armenian identity in traditional terms have come face-to-face with American-born Armenians whose Armenianness has evolved over the decades to become symbolic in form and substance. The two groups realize that even though they both claim the same cultural heritage, the way each interprets and enacts that culture at the present time is very different. As I briefly illustrated in the previous chapter, on the one hand, the American-born have been embarrassed to see, once again, people who espouse the Armenianness of their parents' and grandparents' generations. On the other hand, the foreign-born have been appalled by the prospect that their own children may grow up to become estranged from their roots, just as they assume the Americanized Armenians to be.

These clashes over language are symptomatic of a broader struggle for social and political dominance of the Armenian-American community. They are over whose definition of Armenianness should prevail, and who shall be allowed to decide the future course of Armenianness in the United States. After all, the foreign-born assert, language is the depository of culture. Without language, how is it possible to maintain a separate culture? Assimilation, the much dreaded enemy, will be sure to win. These views are effusively portrayed in Alice Baghdasarian's poem: "Mother's Last Word."[1]

> Take my message to the world, my child.
> To my people, my blood and my bones.
> Tell my people how hard it was to save our Language.
> Tell my people that our Language has to be alive, as long as we breathe.
> Tell them it has to be the language of our heart and mind.
> Tell them it has to be not replaced.
> Tell them it has to be passed to our next generations.
> . . . .
> Our language has to be alive
> Or else, we'll die.

But why do Armenians cherish their language so much? Traditionalists believe the language has played a vital role in shaping the historical destiny of their people. In this regard, the fifth-century monk who fashioned the original thirty-six letters[2] of the alphabet was instrumental in carving a separate existence for the Armenians. His translation of the Bible opened the way to other translations and new literary works, giving rise to a golden age of knowledge. It established Armenians as part of the civilized world and consolidated their Christian identity. In the words of one observer, there is little wonder that many present-day descendants "respect their unique alphabet almost to the point of reverence: pilgrims worship at the tomb of Mesrob Mashtots, its inventor; women wear it cast in gold as jewelry; privileged tourists view it sculpted in gold, marble and precious stones in the palace of the Armenian Catholicos in Echmiadzin" (Davidian 1986, 54).

The American-born do not deny the historical significance of the language, but accuse the defenders of "language at all costs" of operating in a vacuum; of being dream merchants who are oblivious of reality. They retort that they are proud to have surmounted tremendous constraints during their history in the United States and still have produced an impressive communal presence and a long list of sons and daughters who have achieved recognition in their fields of endeavor without denying their ancestral identity. They cite the numerous churches they have built; the multitude of organizations and activities they have sustained; the vast donations they have made to Armenian causes in this country and the diaspora; and the generations of Armenian-Americans they have nurtured with love of nation and church.

In other words, the proponents of traditional Armenianness argue that fluency in Armenian qualifies a person to be a legitimate member of the Armenian community. That is, Armenian identity is contingent on knowledge of language, hence culture. They advocate restrictionist and isolationist policies for the survival of Armenianness in the United States. The symbolic Armenians contend that under ideal conditions it is of course desirable to retain language use, but not if it is at the cost of their ability to make a comfortable living and achieve mobility in the dominant society. They live to prove that knowledge of language is not a necessary precondition to claiming Armenian identity or commitment to Armenianness. They measure membership in the community by concrete action, voluntary service, that is, donations of one's time, energy, skills, talents, resources, and of course, money. They further suggest that the well-being of the Armenian people and heritage are better served by their business or professional success and prominence in American society. They emphasize integration and the ability to function effectively in the world they live in.

The discourse over language is lively and emotionally charged for a number of reasons. First, it divides the Armenian-American community into opposing factions, each with its own social construction of reality. Second, it negates the contributions of the founding members. Third, it calls into question the principal means of communication of this emergent subculture. It should be noted that by the 1960s, before the arrival of the newcomers in massive numbers, English had become the official language of the community. Organizations communicated with their followers in English, the press published in English, literature was produced in English, even the Apostolic church was almost ready to start conducting its services in English.

Since the 1970s, however, the controversy over language and varying definitions of Armenianness have been played out in meeting after meeting, in the myriad secular and sacred institutions and the voluntary associations. With every decision over which type of project should be sponsored, and where the scarce resources should be allocated, the battle lines are drawn. The question as to whether monies should be used to subsidize Armenian day schools or to erect a monument for the Genocide, concretizes the issue. I should add that the ideological orientations of the foreign-born are not clear-cut. Not all of the foreign-born advocate traditional Armenianness. Moreover, as I mentioned in chapter 2, Apostolics and adherents of Tashnag ideology tend to overemphasize the significance of language.

More than any other subject, the language debate has centered on the role of all-day Armenian schools. As agents of socialization such schools are believed to be the best means of ensuring that the next generation will speak, read, and write Armenian. Maintaining high academic standards seems somewhat of an afterthought. Since 1964, the year the first all-day school was established in Encino (CA), Armenian-Americans have funded twenty-two such institutions. To keep the doors of these schools open requires not only constant financial investment, but also well-trained teachers, textbooks, other educational resources, and of course, pupils. The debate goes on.

Not a year goes by without a panel discussion or a symposium being held on the subject of Armenian day schools in Boston, Los Angeles, New York, or San Francisco.[3] The Armenian press is also replete with articles and letters to the editor expounding the pros and

cons of Armenian education and all-day schools.⁴ Paradoxically, most
of these exchanges are speculative, ideological diatribes. With a few
exceptions, systematic studies on the performance of these schools,
first as agents of socialization into the Armenian world, and secondly
in preparing their students to function effectively in the postindustrial
economy they live in, have yet to be undertaken.

The dilemma is not only at the collective level. Most parents of
Armenian descent, at some point or another, need to decide what kind
of a person they want their child to grow up to be. Their decisions take
into account the material circumstances of their lives, their ideological
orientations regarding their Armenian background, and last but not
least, their status as American citizens. For the intermarried in later
generations, the question of language is often moot, since the majority
are unlikely to speak it. In rare cases, such couples may decide to send
their child to an all-day Armenian school. For couples and/or
individuals who speak Armenian, the following questions are more
relevant and pressing: Should they speak Armenian at home? How can
they insist that their children speak Armenian? Should they send them
to Armenian Saturday school, or Sunday school; and what about
camp? What kind of compromises will they be able to live with? For
parents who live within commuting distance of an Armenian school
additional questions are in store. Should they send their child to an all-
day Armenian school? What kind of sacrifices will they have to make:
academic, social, financial? Of course, the financial assets of each
family may sway the vote one way or the other, but the real issue in
attending or not attending an all-day Armenian school remains
ideological.

Language Retention of the New York Sample

In the lore of immigrants who came to its shores, the United States
of America symbolizes opportunity. Yet, the American Dream, and
the value system that encourages individual success and achievement,
were overpowering for many immigrants. It lured them into
assimilation; not that they were unwilling partners. The process of
integration into American society was rewarded by the promise of a
higher standard of living. English proficiency became a prerequisite
for success, if not for the immigrant generation, then certainly for their

children. Thus, it is not surprising that ethnic languages, including
Armenian, could not compete successfully with the American Dream.
This is illustrated by a middle-aged, second-generation respondent
who explains his Americanization as follows: "We were raised as
Americans. In order to learn English herself, my mother had us speak
to her in English once we were in school. We gradually used less and
less of Armenian in home."

In the New York study, five measures of language maintenance
were used: three behavioral and two attitudinal. Table 4.1 shows the
breakdown by generation of the percentage of respondents scoring
"high" (ethnic position) on the five language measures: ability to
speak, read/write Armenian adequately to very well; frequency
Armenian spoken at home almost always; and agreeing (mildly or
strongly) with the following statements: "It is not possible to stay
Armenian without speaking Armenian" and "Our children should
learn to speak Armenian."

Overall, 73.7 percent of the New York respondents speak Armenian
adequately to very well, while only 40 percent read or write Armenian.
Nearly 30 percent of the sample speak Armenian at home almost
always, 23 percent some of the time, and 47.5 percent hardly ever or

TABLE 4.1
**Frequencies of Respondents Scoring "High" on Five Language Variables
by Generation
(in percent)**

	Foreign-Born	U.S.-Born of F.B. Parents	1 Parent U.S.-Born	2 Parents U.S.-Born	Grandparent U.S.-Born
N = 580-584	(219)	(272)	(36)	(41)	(16)
Speak Armenian	97.6	73.9	36.1	14.6	12.5
Read Armenian	78.1	19.1	13.8	4.9	12.5
Armenian at home	62.5	11.8	2.7	0.0	0.0
Statement 1	58.0	37.1	13.8	21.9	25.0
Statement 2	93.6	76.1	63.8	68.3	56.2

Statement 1: "It is not possible to stay Armenian without speaking Armenian."
Statement 2: "Our children should learn to speak Armenian."

never. These results are corroborated by a small nonprobability poll of Armenian-Americans in metropolitan New York and New Jersey (N = 486). They found that 33 percent of their sample spoke Armenian predominantly at home, while 65 percent did not (see the *Armenian Reporter* 16 and 23 April 1987).

The majority of those in the sample who speak Armenian were foreign-born. Only 3.2 percent of first-generation respondents did not speak Armenian.[5] The most striking change (a drop of 59 percentage points) is between the immigrant generation and their U.S.-born children in their ability to read and write Armenian. Seventy-eight percent of foreign-born men and women who answered the questionnaire said they read and wrote Armenian adequately to very well,[6] while only 19.1 percent of the second generation said so. It is easier to learn to speak a language as a child than to learn to read and write it. As a fifty-six-year-old second-generation woman wrote: "Both my parents read Armenian. Mother tried to teach me, but as a teenager, I refused to learn. They spoke 'clean' Armenian, as did my sister and I."

The decrease in ability to read/write the ancestral language is followed by an equally precipitous drop (50 percentage points) in its usage at home. While 62.5 percent of the immigrant generation speak Armenian at home most of the time, 12 percent of the second generation do so. Even though some 12 to 14 percent of the third and fourth generation can speak Armenian, hardly any of them use it predominantly at home (only 2.7 percent of respondents with one U.S.-born parent do, none beyond that). This indicates that the Armenian language ceases to be the "mother tongue" for American-born generations. That is, Armenian no longer serves as a means of communication; it is no longer an automatic, subconscious response. Words and phrases have to be thought of and formulated carefully.

Generation is the most significant variable with all five measures of language retention; the longer the generational presence, the lower the proportion of people of Armenian descent who can speak Armenian (.52*), read or write Armenian (.49*), and consequently the lower the frequency they speak Armenian at home (.50*). The later the generation, the less respondents believed that one must speak Armenian to be an Armenian (.22*), and the lower the proportions who wished that their children would speak Armenian (.15*). The relatively high proportions of Armenian-Americans in the sample who speak Armenian, at least adequately, is caused by the recency of Armenian settlements in the United States and the massive influx of newcomers. The reader is reminded that about 40 percent of this sample were foreign-born and almost two-thirds of them arrived after World War II. In other words, about 90 percent of respondents born in Turkey, the Middle East, and Soviet Bloc countries speak Armenian very well, compared to 34 percent of the American-born. In sum, living in America is clearly not conducive to Armenian proficiency.

For the second generation, as several participants in the survey said, Armenian was learned by rote from their foreign-born parents. In some cases, the children of the immigrants did not speak English until they went to school.[7] A second-generation male respondent wrote: "I was born in 1933, my parents only spoke Armenian. I was 5 years old before I learned to speak English." Likewise, a forty-year-old third-generation man remarked that his American-born mother "did not speak English until she entered public school." For those in later generations, the role of Armenian teacher is relegated to the grandparents. A second-generation, sixty-five-year-old female respondent said: "When I married, my parents lived with me and this encouraged my children to learn and speak Armenian fluently." Now that this respondent's son and daughter have grown up and married (non-Armenians), and have children of their own, she added: "At every opportunity, we try to teach our grandchildren the Armenian language. Hopefully, they will always remember their Armenian heritage."

The variance in responses to the two attitude statements is small by all independent variables. Most people disagreed that one must speak Armenian in order to be an Armenian (54.5 percent disagreed, 42 percent agreed, and 3.3 percent had no opinion), but they agreed that children should learn to speak Armenian (81 percent agreed, 10.2 percent disagreed, and 8.6 percent had no opinion). Agreeing on both statements was the ethnic position. The differences in the responses are related to the issues each item raises. Armenians born in countries where ethnicity is an ascribed status were most likely to advocate that language was a fundamental component of culture. Of those who agreed, 56 percent were born in Turkey, 60 percent in other Middle Eastern countries and 54 percent in the Soviet Bloc. Moreover,

American-born survey respondents would have created cognitive dissonance had they agreed with the first statement since most did not speak Armenian. The second statement, on a child having to speak Armenian is less threatening, an idealized state of affairs that would be hard to disagree with.

Several respondents commented to this effect. An elderly second-generation man said it was not necessary to speak Armenian to be Armenian because "it's in the blood," but that it would be nice to teach children because "it enriches them, and [gives them] sense of roots." Others said: "It would be nice but not necessary to be an Armenian," or "It would be nice if possible." A caveat should be added here. There is a wide gap in what people say they will do and what they actually do. Actual behavior invariably falls short of good intentions. This gap is clear in the responses. Nonetheless, these results bear out my earlier contention on significance of language for ethnic maintenance.

Empirical evidence shows that children with two foreign-born parents are most likely to learn their parents' non-English language; those with one foreign-born parent are less likely, and those with two native-born parents are least likely. "The disappearance versus persistence of non-English languages in the United States is largely an outcome of two processes: the passing of generations, and patterns of

TABLE 4.2
Frequencies of Respondents Scoring "High" on Five Language Variables by Ancestry
(in percent)

	Both Parents Armenian	One Parent Armenian
N = 580-584	(518)	(66)
Speak Armenian	79.7	31.8
Read Armenian	42.3	19.7
Armenian at home	31.8	9.1
Statement 1	43.7	30.7
Statement 2	83.4	63.6

Statement 1: "It is not possible to stay Armenian without speaking Armenian."
Statement 2: "Our children should learn to speak Armenian."

intra- and intergroup relations" (Stevens 1985, 82). These findings are also applicable to the Armenian case.

Mixed parentage decreases the odds of a child's likelihood of speaking Armenian. While 97.7 percent of the sample with Armenian mothers and fathers spoke Armenian adequately to very well, 31.8 percent of those who had a non-Armenian parent did so (see table 4.2). Understandably, the most noticeable difference is the decrease in the frequency that Armenian is spoken in the home for respondents with mixed parentage. Several respondents made comments to this effect. For example, a fifty-three-year-old U.S.-born respondent whose mother is Italian wrote: "I do not speak it. We live in this country. I also did not let my children learn German, my wife's origin. I want them to learn English." A thirty-year-old respondent (who like her father is U.S.-born) noted: "My home now is with [my] husband. He is not Armenian. When at Mom's home [we speak Armenian some of the time]."

Does socioeconomic achievement decrease language retention among Armenian-Americans? Overall, there is a steady decline in measures of language maintenance with increasing education, but the differences are not very sharp, nor uniform (see table 4.3). This could be explained by the large number of bilingual, college-educated,

TABLE 4.3
Frequencies of Respondents Scoring "High" on Five Language Variables by Ancestry
(in percent)

	Some High School	Completed High School	Some College	Completed College	More than College
N = 560-563	(48)	(138)	(109)	(129)	(139)
Speak Armenian	87.7	82.6	72.5	66.6	66.9
Read Armenian	62.5	44.2	29.3	39.5	30.2
Armenian at home	55.3	33.6	22.2	27.1	18.7
Statement 1	55.3	50.7	40.4	38.3	33.8
Statement 2	91.5	86.2	83.3	77.5	72.5

Statement 1: "It is not possible to stay Armenian without speaking Armenian."
Statement 2: "Our children should learn to speak Armenian."

recent immigrants. Occupation is not correlated with language maintenance, but interestingly, income levels were statistically significant with the frequency of Armenian spoken at home (.18*). Though the negative association was not monotonic; 16 percent of those earning $100,000 or more per annum spoke Armenian at home most of the time compared to 42 percent of those making less than $20,000 a year. Nonetheless, generation is a better predictor of language assimilation than socioeconomic variables.

Participants in the New York survey were invited to share their experiences of growing up Armenian in the United States. Their comments exemplify the pressures immigrants have had to face. A fifty-five-year-old, second-generation man wrote:

> Here in America, my other brother, born here, spoke with an accent in kindergarten owing to the Armenian spoken at home. A teacher warned my mother that Armenian must not be spoken at home (this was in the 1930's). As a result, my parents decided to speak only English in front of us. We did not learn Armenian.

Respondents in this study suggest that the 1930s and 1940s were harsh times for immigrants because the Depression curtailed economic opportunities, and immigrants had to comply to the dictates of the dominant group. The present-day immigrants are luckier. Their arrival coincided with the so-called ethnic revival movement, which induced a more tolerant atmosphere in the society at large; in addition, the economic conditions were generally more favorable.

The following quotation from a thirty-year-old woman exemplifies some of the factors that influence language retention.

> Since my mother was from the other side—Syria—we were raised speaking Armenian in the house, as well as English. She sent us to Saturday school— religion and also to school to learn about Armenian history and culture. Of course, I learned the language at Sat. School although I already knew the practical speaking of it. Also I attended Camp Nubar—Armenian Camp—for *nine* consecutive years. We participated in language, dance and culture classes. (Emphasis in original)

In other words, the larger American society does not discourage bilingualism, but it does not make it easy for the children and grandchildren of immigrants to learn their ancestral language. Bilingualism is costly. The maintenance of the Armenian language, like that of other ethnic languages, is dependent on the financial and other material and nonmaterial resources of the community, and most important, the willingness of parents to send their children to special Armenian schools and extracurricular activities.

The development of an Armenian ghetto in Los Angeles may be the exception to a well-established historical pattern. Bilingualism can also be a dangerous thing. Confining one's entire social world to the boundaries of this ghetto may turn the newest immigrants into marginal citizens and prevent them from achieving the American Dream. Observers of the Armenian-American community are worried. For example, in a recent editorial, Vasken Oskanian of *Armenian International Magazine* made the following remarks:

> Today, in Los Angeles—the city with the largest concentration of Armenians in the Diaspora—we have created an Armenian microcosm, where the community is self-sufficient in every conceivable aspect of everyday life. Linguistically, one can live here for a hundred years and not need to spell a word in English. Indeed, we have created a bilingual America for ourselves, where even some government transactions could be conducted in Armenian. Isn't that fantastic? No....
>
> There is nothing better than to speak both Armenian and English. But also, there is nothing more dangerous than to feel secure and fulfilled by speaking only Armenian, with total disregard and ignorance of the language to which is bound the promise of making it in America....
>
> For us, in order to operate in the mainstream of American society, we must extend ourselves beyond the confines of our narrow environment. We must achieve proficiency in linguistic skills, and adapt ourselves to the behavioral values of American life. (July 1991, p. 5)

The fact remains that English proficiency is a necessary condition if one is to function fully in American society. This does not mean that a person cannot be equally proficient in two or more languages, but the chances of this occurrence in the general population are small because the cultural policies of the United States have not supported bilingualism or multilingualism. In a comparative study of the latest cohort of foreign-born Armenians with third-generation Armenian-Americans, that is, the grandchildren of the first cohort of Armenian immigrants to the United States, Aposhian found that the former tended to be multilingual, while the latter tended to be monolingual.[8]

Aposhian's nonrandom sample consisted of sixty-eight informants; seventeen men and seventeen women in each generation, their ages ranging from thirty to fifty-one. When asked: "What language do you speak?" Sixty-one percent of the foreign-born said they spoke English, Armenian, and another language equally well; 13 percent were proficient in English and Armenian, only 3 percent spoke only English and 23 percent spoke mostly Armenian and some English. These figures are in contrast to the third generation, half of whom spoke only English, and the other half mostly English. When asked: "What language do you prefer?" Again, 64 percent of the third generation said English only, 32 percent mostly English, and only 3 percent were bilingual. Of the foreign-born, 13 percent preferred only Armenian, 32 percent mostly Armenian, 10 percent mostly English, and 45 percent were bilingual.

What prevents, then, the development of bilingualism in the United States? Should English proficiency have to be the demise of the ethnic language? Though bilingualism is part of the process of assimilation, it is only a transitory stage. Except for the very old, the vast majority of Armenian immigrants learn to speak English within a few years of their arrival.[9] Many may not be able to get rid of their accents, but this does not prevent them from functioning effectively in the larger society. Most of the second generation learn to speak Armenian in early childhood at home, but are not likely to master it. At school, however, they learn to possess English as a "mother tongue."

The chances for the third generation to speak, let alone to read and write, Armenian are slim. Other studies on Armenians in the United States corroborate these conclusions (LaPiere 1930; Nelson 1953; Kernaklian 1967; O'Grady 1979, 109). Writing about Fresno, LaPiere found that in the 1920s, "most of the second-generation cannot speak the Armenian language well and almost none of them can read it" (1930, 304). In the United States, the historical decision to use English as the official language and the success of the public school system in teaching immigrant children to adopt English as their only language was instrumental in nation formation. In the opinion of one expert in bilingual education, "the concept of bilingual education is contrary to the American experience of 200 years" (Cafferty 1982, 117).

In her comparative study of Armenians in Cyprus and London, Susan Pattie (1990) concurs that it is not unusual for Middle Eastern Armenians to be multilingual. However, "it does not seem natural in London to be multilingual" (Pattie 1990, 279). Learning several languages comes naturally to Armenians who grow up in the Middle

East. They manage to compartmentalize the various languages they can communicate with. For example, Armenian is private, it is the speech of intimacy, of informal social ties with family and close friends. For older cohorts, especially men, Turkish is used for joking, story telling, proverbs and curses (Pattie 1990, 256). Greek (in Cyprus) or Arabic (in Lebanon/Syria) is the language of the marketplace, of buying and selling, of haggling over prices. English and/or French are the languages of elite status, of higher education, of one's professional training.

It should be noted, however, that this compartmentalization is not strict. If one were to follow every word and every nuance in the informal conversations of multilingual Armenians, one would need a good knowledge of all the languages used. As Pattie so accurately observes, "when you hear pure Armenian speech, you can be sure that the person has made a mental note at some time, if not just then, to purify his or her speech and discover the Armenian equivalents of the more commonly used foreign phrases" (1990, 277-78). She further argues that multilingualism, not the Armenian language per se, is the key in understanding the thinking of Middle Eastern Armenians. Any single language does not frame one's worldview, but the multiple code-switching and language styles have a significant influence over the perceptions and thought formation processes of multilingual users.

I must add here that the Armenian language itself is divided into *krapar* (classical Armenian, literally meaning "written"), which remains the language of the Divine Liturgy in the Apostolic church, and the *ashkharapar* (the vernacular). Furthermore, eastern and western dialects subdivide the latter. According to linguist Davidian, "dialectical differences include phonological, grammatical (including conjugation and declension) and idiomatic variances" (1986, 57). All this makes it difficult for eastern and western Armenians to understand each other readily or follow the church services. It also compounds the problems of educators when deciding which dialect should be used in instructing the next generation. Several Los Angeles schools have to cater to Iranian and Soviet Armenian parents who insist on teaching their children the western dialect and to others who insist on the eastern dialect.

The United States of America, like England, is a monolingual society; that is, the media, the educational system, the government use the English language. In these societies, Pattie goes on to say, "speaking languages other than English, even on the simplest level, requires effort, determination, and a different attitude towards language than that of the host culture. This is not easy to instill in the younger generation" (1990, 280). For example, children of Armenian descent growing up in England or the United States, "want to blend in, to be the same as their friends (or would be friends).... Looking different is bad enough, but it is crucial to sound like the others in the neighborhood, in accent, vocabulary, and style" (Pattie 1990, 280). Why do people learn so many languages? For the same functional reasons that people learn only one language, that is for pragmatic and sociopolitical factors dictated by the host society. Indeed, learning English, French, Greek, or Arabic is a necessity for Armenians in the Middle East today. In this regard, Armenian is more of a luxury because it fulfils a sentimental need.

For the American-born, after the second-generation, learning Armenian is like learning a foreign language, but certainly a less popular choice for pragmatic reasons. A twenty-five-year-old, third-generation man wrote: "I'm not so much concerned with assimilation (and actually encourage it) but do *regret* not having been trained to speak/read/write Armenian fluently. Oddly enough I studied Spanish for 16 years and am fluent" (Emphasis in original). In general, prestige more than power determines the direction of acculturation and the language of communication when two linguistic groups come into contact as a result of conquest or immigration. For example, when the Roman Empire was invaded by 'barbaric' tribes, Roman ways and Latin continued. Immigrants to the United States have had to learn English, the language of the ruling elite, though interestingly without the imposition of the federal government. According to Zenner, English proficiency was accomplished successfully with "the zeal of English-speaking Americans at every level of society" (1985, 122). In the American case, power coincided with prestige, reinforcing the dominance of English over native Indian and other European languages.

By contrast, Armenians who settled in Lebanon after the Genocide opted for Western languages, especially French and English, before they spoke Arabic. The prestige of Arabic and the power of the Lebanese government was more disputable. As a multilingual culture,

Lebanon allowed Armenians to use their ancestral language in the privacy of their homes and communities. However, those who wanted to achieve parity with the local elite sent their children to non-Armenian schools. The diaspora Armenians did not have the power or the prestige to impose their language on others.[10] Few odars bothered to learn it.[11] Similarly in Soviet Armenia, the language of the powerful dominated in the public sphere; proficiency in Russian was a vehicle for upward mobility in the Communist system. But Armenian continued to be spoken in the privacy of the home and in the streets. This gave the *Hayastantzi* (Soviet Armenians) a measure of independence and autonomy (Samuelian 1986). The situation has changed since the declaration of independence. Now Armenian is the state language, and all schools are mandated to teach it.

In the second generation and beyond, for the relatively few who can speak Armenian, it is relegated to sporadic episodes such as its use in church, with grandparents, or exchanging "secrets" in public as a code system. Even those who do not speak the ancestral language tend to learn a dozen or so key words and idioms which they use to punctuate their English speech. A young Armenian-American who has explored Americanized Armenian speech, explains;

> if an Armenian is referring to someone who is of black or Jewish heritage, respectively, during an English conversation he would replace these words with *sev* or *her/yah*. Although discretion may dictate this in a public setting, these words have become automatic referents even in private settings, essentially erasing the need for English equivalents. This standard becomes even more absolute when referring to any non-Armenian, or *odar*. Indeed, *odar* is probably the one word of reference from which Armenians hardly ever stray.[12]

Other Armenian words that replace English equivalents have to do with family [*hireeg* (father), *medzmama* (grandmother)]; the nation [*hay em* (I'm Armenian)]; salutations [*parev* (hello), *eench bess es?* (how are you)]; swear words [*esh* (donkey), *khent* [crazy]]; and of course food. Words like pilav, lavash, baklava, shish kebab have entered the culinary dictionaries of America and do not need any translation.

Likewise, the Armenian alphabet takes on a symbolic value. A suburban parish priest I interviewed told me that less than 10 percent of the contents of the monthly parish bulletin (circulation 950) were in the Armenian language, adding: "The Armenian is mainly for emotional reasons. Few read Armenian." Key rings with letters of the Armenian alphabet, T-shirts with Coca Cola written in Armenian, gold chokers with one's name in Armenian letters, cross-stitch samplers with the thirty-eight letters of the alphabet, wall rugs depicting a *Khatchkar* (cross)[13] are other examples of the popular, albeit secondary, uses of the Armenian language. Indeed, the examples abound; one has only to visit an Armenian bookstore in a church basement or open the pages of Armenian newspapers and magazines[14] to get a deluge of such symbolic uses of language.

For Armenians who live in the diaspora, language is more than a means of communication. It is a link to the larger Armenian family, a cohesive symbol of identity. Even though fewer and fewer American-born Armenians speak Armenian,[15] language remains strong in the definition of their identity. In her study of the Washington, DC community, O'Grady writes that Armenians traveling overseas or in the United States communicate easily because of the shared language. "American Armenians often introduce themselves saying, 'Hay es? Yes Hay yem,' (Are you Armenian? I'm Armenian), speaking Armenian for a brief period and then lapsing into English" (1979, 108). Similarly, a sixty-six-year-old, second-generation respondent said: "Today, I regret not sending my children to a school at least to learn Armenian. It's great to have this learning when you travel. The more the languages the better." Relatively few Armenian-Americans come into contact with other Armenians of the diaspora when they travel. Men and women active in major Armenian organizations are more likely to do so. It was the case of a community leader I interviewed, who felt the need to learn Armenian as an adult, and was taking lessons (interviewee is U.S.-born of foreign-born parents). I quote: "In this country it [the language] is of no use. You don't have to speak Armenian to maintain a culture. But on the other hand, we've been very backward. We should develop better tools for those who want to learn the language—use modern audio techniques, cassettes, etc."

In sum, maintaining full use of the Armenian language serves three functions for ethnicity: first, it is a unifying force, fostering a sense of we-ness; second, it is a boundary marker distinguishing insiders from outsiders; third, it delays assimilation. I would argue further than even in its limited symbolic capacity, a few words of Armenian, here and there, displays of Armenian alphabet on one's person, living room wall, or office desk testify that language is an identity marker, it sends out signals that only insiders can readily decipher. Like the sharing of secrets, language bonds its users.

The dilemma between the American Dream, on the one hand, and Armenian preservation, on the other, is real but rigged against the latter. Many immigrants and their children find that American society does not encourage bilingualism. Even with an ideology of Armenian maintenance and competent institutional alternatives it becomes practically impossible to retain Armenian language for the majority of the population beyond the second generation, especially for those who live outside the major metropolitan centers with high Armenian density. The comments of a seventy-one-year-old second-generation woman illustrate this, though she speaks with the wisdom of hindsight.

> In my early childhood, I felt like a misfit growing up in mid-Manhattan in a predominantly Anglo-Saxon area—no one knew what an Armenian was. My grandmother ruled as the grand matriarch in the household and would not allow us to speak English at home. Her favorite words, "You were born Armenian, live as an Armenian and die as an Armenian." Consequently, I speak the language fluently, but deficient in English (at that time).

> I did not want my sons to grow up feeling as I did but of course today with all the explosions everyone has heard of Armenians—I should have taught them the language and regret I did not. I realize too late that they would not feel as I did in childhood as I could have helped them in English as well since I am not foreign-born as my parents were. Now at this late date I am trying to give them some conversational lessons in Armenian.

Only in exceptional cases do third- and fourth-generation descendants speak, read, and write Armenian. The data clearly indicate that the Armenian language is least likely to survive with the passing of generations in the United States. Yet, in the opinion of the majority of the New York respondents, this does not make them less Armenian.

Armenian Educational Institutions in the United States

Armenian parents, in particular those beyond the second generation, are unable to transmit the Armenian culture to the next generation on their own. This task requires "specialists." The perpetuation of a cultural heritage necessitates a conscious ideological socialization, such as full-time and part-time schools. Here New York respondents' attitudes toward Armenian educational institutions are examined. Specifically, the focus is on at day schools, Saturday schools, or supplemental types of schooling and summer camps. Parental attitudes are interpreted as outcomes of assimilation and varying expressions of Armenianness. It was not the goal of the New York survey to evaluate the performance of Armenian institutions or their effectiveness in transmitting identity and culture to the next generation; however, I will report the findings of two case studies on the subject. I will conclude this section with a brief discussion of the functions of Armenian higher education and research centers.

The New York Sample's Attitudes toward Armenian Schooling

It is hypothesized that recent immigrants and the more ethnically oriented will value Armenian education and send their children to all-day schools in the hope of perpetuating their cultural heritage and rooting their social structure in Armenian circles. On the other hand, later-generation respondents will more likely value "American" public (or mainstream private) schooling for their children. When convenient, that is, if time and energy restraints are easily surmountable, and if there are no conflicting personal goals, some may opt for supplementary Armenian socialization such as Saturday or Sunday schools and summer camps.

At present there are a total of twenty-two all-day Armenian schools in the United States (see table 4.4). The majority of these are in the Greater Los Angeles area, including the five high schools. Their total enrollment does not exceed 5,500 students. Armenian day schools are regular schools that in addition to a basic curriculum of general studies teach Armenian language, history, literature, religion, and culture. They are not bilingual institutions because students are taught all subject matter in English except for Armenian classes. For example, in the 1980s, in the Ferrahian High School in Los Angeles, Armenian classes totalled ten periods per week (Davidian 1986, 67, 182); and in the Armenian Sisters' Academy in Philadelphia, they constituted five out of a total of thirty-eight periods of weekly instruction (Ordjanian 1991, 126). Paradoxically, many public schools in Los Angles offer bilingual education at present because of the influx of newcomers from Soviet Armenia and elsewhere with limited English proficiency.[16]

Part-time or supplemental Armenian schooling is offered by most Armenian-American communities, large or small. The *Armenian American Almanac* (1990) lists 62 such schools. They are usually sponsored by church committees, voluntary associations, or political parties and held in church basements or meeting rooms. Generally, these classes are scheduled to meet for two or more hours on Saturday mornings, or any afternoon of the week after regular school. Their enrollment ranges from as few as 6 or 8 pupils to more than 100, ages

TABLE 4.4
List of Armenian All-Day Schools in the United States
(location, year established, enrollment in 1990, and highest grade level)

Name		Year Established	Enrollment	Grade Level
Southern CA				
AGBU Marie Manoogian	Canoga Park	1976	320 G & 280 B	12th
Armenian Mesrobian	Pico Rivera	1965	179 G & 175 B	12th
Holy Martyrs' Ferrahian	Encino	1964	329 G & 316 B	12th
Rose & Alex Pilibos Arm.	Los Angeles	1969	420 G & 382 B	12th
TCA Arshag Dickranian Arm.	Los Angeles	1981	130 G & 146 B	12th
Merdinian Arm. Evangelical	Sherman Oaks	1982	272	9th
Vahan & Anoush Chamlian	Glendale	1976	363	9th
Arm. Mekhitarist Fathers	La Crescenta	1979	350	8th
Ari Guiragos Minassian	Santa Ana	1986	44 G & 56 B	6th
Armenian Sisters' Academy	Glendale	1984	250	6th
Sahag-Mesrob Arm. Christian	Altadena	1980	195	6th
Alfred & Marguerite Hovsepian	Pasadena	1984	130	6th
Northern CA				
Arm. Community School	Fresno	1977	30 G & 56 B	6th
Krouzian-Zekarian Vasbouragan	San Francisco	1978	180	8th

six to fourteen. In Saturday schools, children of Armenian descent learn the rudiments of the Armenian alphabet, history, and culture.

There are six Armenian summer camps run by various political, philanthropic, or religious organizations. They recruit campers from all over the United States and even abroad. The more established ones, such as AGBU Camp Nubar in the Catskills (NY) and Camp Haiastan of the Armenian Youth Federation in Massachusetts offer several sessions over an eight-week period during July and August. Essentially, they focus on fun activities that eight to fifteen year olds can enjoy, such as swimming, sailing, canoeing, tennis, volley ball, hikes, crafts. In addition to Armenian songs and folk dance, each day simple, short lessons in history and language are taught. Being in an Armenian atmosphere and having the opportunity to establish friendships with fellow Armenians are the primary goals. Having the opportunity to pick up some of the Armenian language and culture is perceived as an additional benefit. Still, it is not to be taken too seriously.

TABLE 4.4 Continued

Name	Location	Year Established	Enrollment	Grade Level
Massachusetts				
Armenian Sisters' Academy	Lexington	1982	130	8th
St. Stephen's Arm. Day	Watertown	1984	70	8th
AGBU Arm. Elementary	Watertown	1970	117	6th
Michigan				
AGBU Alex Manoogian	Southfield	1969	184	12th
New Jersey				
Hovnanian Armenian	New Milford	1976	78 G & 77 B	6th
New York				
Holy Martyrs Arm. Day	Bayside	1967	95	6th
St. Illuminator Day	Woodside	1977	60	6th
Pennsylvania				
Armenian Sisters' Academy	Radnor	1967	82 G & 98 B	8th

Studies investigating ethnic schooling indicate that the same principles that apply to the cognitive aspect of education also apply to religious or ethnic education. Coleman and his associates in the classic *Equality of Educational Opportunity* (1966) found that community inputs such as the amount of money spent on school facilities, books, library, classroom size, teacher characteristics, morale, and so on had little effect on students' cognitive achievement and performance on tests. The variations in test scores were strongly associated to differences in the socioeconomic background of the students. Similarly, for Catholics and Jews, family values, attitudes, and religious maintenance at home were found to be pivotal in children's religious identity and observance (Greeley and Rossi 1966; S. Cohen 1974).

Parochial schools and *yeshivot* were not able to ingrain religious or ethnic identity in their pupils when little sympathy was found for it at home. Such schools can only buttress parental socialization; they cannot change it. Full-time religious schools were found to have the most powerful effect on identity maintenance, while supplementary forms of schooling had no or negligible effect (S. Cohen 1974, 325-26). In sum, the family unit is the most effective breeder of ethnic identification. Bock (1976), analyzing data from a national survey of American Jews, found that after a critical threshold of approximately 1,000 classroom hours of Jewish instruction, there was an increase in most conceptualizations of identification. Supplementary types of schooling were effective, but not efficient. Feelings about being Jewish (related to self-esteem) were mainly associated to family atmosphere and generational presence in the United States. On the other hand, behavioral indicators of identification increased with Jewish school experience.

In a survey of the alumni of the Ramaz High School, a progressive Jewish co-ed all-day school in New York City, on the occasion of its silver jubilee, Friedman (1989) found that it is possible to combine high academic standards with Orthodox Jewish instruction. A random sampling of the graduates of Ramaz demonstrated that overwhelming proportions had graduated from Ivy League colleges and universities. Subsequently, they were employed in professional occupations or in the business world and were earning incomes well above the national and Jewish community average. Most Ramaz alumni had realized the

American Dream, achieving intergenerational mobility. All the while, they had continued to measure strongly on Jewish identification, practiced ritual observance, and many were highly active members of their communities. Friedman concluded that the goals of the Ramaz founder have been fulfilled; it is possible to be American *and* Jewish, the two identities being fully compatible.

Encouraging as these results may be for ethnic maintenance and identity, parents as agents of socialization retain the power, at least while their children are still young, to determine if they will send them to ethnic schools. Whether their opinions on the academic standards or social milieu within such schools are validated or not, their attitudes are crucial. The results of the New York survey indicate that only a small proportion of Armenian-Americans advocate full-time schooling. Even if select, progressive, quality schools like Ramaz were available for Armenians, it is unlikely that they would serve more than a token number of future generations.

In response to a question: "Would you (do you) send your child(ren) to an Armenian day school?" almost 59 percent of the New York sample answered no, 35 percent said yes and the rest (6.4 percent) had no children, were not married, did not know, or did not answer (see table 4.5). Attitudes toward Armenian full-time education were most significant with generational status (.19*); half as many second-generation respondents (25.9 percent) were willing to send a child to such schools as foreign-born respondents (55.3 percent).

TABLE 4.5
Frequency Distribution of Respondents Willing to Send Their Children to
Armenian All-Day Schools
by Generation

	Foreign-Born	U.S.-Born of F.B. Parents	1 Parent U.S.-Born	2 Parents U.S.-Born	Grandparent U.S.-Born
N = 578	(215)	(270)	(36)	(40)	(16)
No	40.0	68.5	80.6	75.6	75.0
Yes	55.3	25.9	11.1	19.5	18.8
Not applicable	4.7	5.6	8.3	4.9	6.2
	100.0	100.0	100.0	100.0	100.0

Later-generation descendants were even less likely to advocate Armenian all-day schools. Respondents who did not, or would not send a child to an Armenian day school were asked to justify their answer (see table 4.6). About 28 percent of responses suggested that day schools were too far away (included are older respondents who added that there were no such schools when their children were young). Only 7.4 percent said such schools were expensive, almost 17 percent believed that their academic standards were too low, and about 9 percent regarded the social milieu to be inferior. A small number of respondents said they would not consider Armenian day schools because their spouse was not of Armenian descent.

The single highest response was the "other" category (34.5 percent of responses and 43 percent of cases). The volunteered answers were "too insulated," "too ethnic," or "too parochial." It should be emphasized that if this response category had been offered, a larger number of respondents would have chosen it as their rationale for not wanting to send a child to an Armenian full-time school. Foreign-born respondents were most likely to offer the expense and the low academic standard excuses. Twice as many later-generation respondents offered the "too ethnic or too insulated" argument as the first generation. There is a straight-line increase by generation in the belief that Armenian full-time schooling is insulating. Attitudes of

TABLE 4.6
Frequency Distribution of Reasons for Not Supporting Armenian All-Day Schools by Generation
(from negatives in table 4.5, multiple response)

	Foreign-Born	US.-Born of F.B. Parents	1 Parent + U.S.-Born
N = 282 cases	(72)	(145)	(65)
Multiple response N=(351)	(88)	(181)	(82)
Too far or no school available	29.5	29.8	21.9
Expensive	14.8	6.6	1.2
Low academic standards	26.1	16.0	8.5
Low social milieu	4.5	9.4	13.4
Too ethnic or insulated	22.7	33.2	50.0
Spouse non-Armenian	2.3	5.0	4.9
	100.0	100.0	100.0

second-generation parents were in between the foreign-born and those from later generations.

A fifty-eight-year-old man, born in Iran, immigrated at age nineteen, said: Children "should grow in a cross-section of U.S. population." A twenty-five-year-old, fourth-generation man wrote: "Integrated, diverse environment would be lacking." Another fourth-generation, thirty-six-year-old woman indicated: "I want my child to have a more secular, non-ethnic education." "When in America do like the Americans," retorted a twenty-two-year-old woman who immigrated from Beirut at age six. "Hints of segregation," observed a middle-aged, second-generation woman. "Don't believe in parochial schools," noted a young, third-generation male. "I feel if one lives in the U.S., the children should go to an American school," said a forty-year-old woman who immigrated as a child from Iran. Others wrote: "Strong advocate of public schools," and "I want them to be able 'ɔ relate, learn and socialize with people from all ethnic backgrounds"; yet again, "in some ways it can be delimiting in terms of living within the larger society." Last but not least, a fifty-four-year-old woman, born in Aleppo but raised in the United States, said: "Don't believe in segregation even for a good purpose, i.e., learning Armenian."

Because Saturday schools and summer camps do not replace basic education and are not a real threat to belief systems on educational attainment, more respondents, especially from later generations, agreed to the supplementary programs (see tables 4.7, 4.8). Overall, 67 percent of the sample would be willing to send a child to a part-time Armenian school (Saturday school) and 70 percent to summer camp; that is, twice as many as those who advocate full-time Armenian schools (35 percent). While 55.3 percent of the immigrant generation, 26 percent of the second generation, and only 16 percent of later-generation respondents do or would be willing to send a child to an Armenian day school (see table 4.6), the frequencies increase dramatically when it comes to supplementary forms of education. The percentages more than double for the second generation (65 percent) and increase by three and a half times for later generations (56 percent). Later-generation respondents were most likely to approve of summer camps, the least ethnic of institutions.

Irrespective of generational presence, the prime reason for sending a child to Saturday school is to learn the Armenian language, while the prime reason for going to summer camp is to make good friends. Otherwise, all reasons are equally valid for both types of institutions. The least given reason is to learn new sports at summer camps. It is interesting that parents did not consider the duty of Armenian organizations to teach sports. Ethnicity plays a specialized role in people's lives; one gets the impression that Armenian institutions should not be wasted on services that could be bought elsewhere. Later-generation respondents are less concerned about the primacy of Armenianness in everyday life. Yet, they believe that their spirit is Armenian. This has been the message that has been clearly repeated throughout this study.

If Armenian educational institutions have a good reputation, symbolic Armenians might consider enrolling their son or daughter in such a camp or school. With the increasing emphasis on global and multicultural education in the United States in recent years, I hypothesize that if an Armenian all-day school develops a prestigious academic reputation and is able to attract children from upper-middle-class families, then nonethnics, and later-generation ethnics, might consider sending their children to such a school. The school run by the Armenian Sisters of Immaculate Conception in Radnor (PA) approximates such a reputation, and boasts that approximately 15 percent of its student body comes from non-Armenian background.[17] Ordjanian (1991, 110-13) found that American-born parents support and encourage the enrollment of non-Armenian students, and would even favor increasing their proportion. They feel it is an important

TABLE 4.7
Frequency Distribution of Respondents Advocating Saturday Schools
by Generation

	Foreign-Born	U.S.-Born of F. B. Parents	1 Parent + U.S.-Born
N = 392 cases	(165)	(175)	(52)
Multiple response N = (843)	(364)	(364)	(115)
Learn the Armenian language	39.3	40.9	38.2
Learn Armenian history and culture	32.1	34.1	36.5
Make Armenian friends	28.6	25.0	25.1
	100.0	100.0	100.0

preparation for the pluralistic society their child lives in. The Ramaz High School in Manhattan is another example, where superior academic standards are maintained with Orthodox Jewish teachings. Over the years, as the school grew and established its select, progressive, and high academic reputation, more and more parents who were less religiously observant started sending their children to Ramaz (Friedman 1989).

Armenian schools also need to develop a reputation for first-quality teaching staff, textbooks, computers, science laboratories, sports fields, and other facilities. Symbolic Armenian-Americans expect teachers to be competent college graduates, specialized in their field of knowledge. Moreover, they assume that teachers be well-versed with the latest (American) pedagogical concepts and techniques in child development. They also know that well-paid teachers are happy teachers who want to keep their jobs, thus go out of their way to cater to their students. In recent years, educational councils such as ALLRC (Armenian Language Lab and Resource Center affiliated with the Diocese) and AREC (Armenian Religious Educational Council affiliated with the Prelacy) have organized conferences, developed curriculum, and sponsored the publication of textbooks and instruction material geared for American-born children. These efforts are a start but by no means sufficient to meet the overwhelming problems of Armenian all-day schools.

TABLE 4.8
Frequency Distribution of Respondents Advocating Summer Camp
by Generation

	Foreign-Born	U.S.-Born of F.B. Parents	1 Parent + U.S.-Born
N = 409 cases	(167)	(183)	(59)
Multiple response N = (1092)	(440)	(456)	(196)
Learn the Armenian language	21.6	20.4	18.4
Learn Armenian history and culture	25.9	26.8	23.0
Make Armenian friends	29.3	30.9	24.5
Have a good time	15.9	16.7	22.4
Learn new sports	7.2	5.3	11.7
	100.0	100.0	100.0

There seems to be a consensus among educators of children of Armenian descent in the United States that the available textbooks in Armenian are for the most part unsatisfactory. The majority of textbooks are either published in Beirut or Yerevan (a few others are published in Syria, the Mekhitarist Press in Venice and the United States). According to Ordjanian (1991, 142-143; 236-238), Armenian-American children find the material culture and social habits portrayed in the illustrations and text puzzling; they are also not familiar with the vocabulary and idioms used. The children reject the history books as myths, typically interpreting events as a battle between good and evil. They expect instead scientific data. Most significantly, foreign publishers do not seem to incorporate childhood developmental and learning theory in their products. Aesthetically, the books are not as appealing as the American ones the children are used to; they lack pictorial illustrations, the quality of the paper is poor, the illustrations are crude, photos are mostly in black and white, etc. Consequently, it is not surprising that these books do not provide a pleasurable learning experience for children growing up in America; they are not able to command their attention. Children often get bored and frustrated with the books.

Yeranouhi Garabedian, Armenian Studies Program Director at Krouzian-Zekarian School in San Francisco, concurs with the above remarks. She further adds that role models provided in the stories are highly inadequate for the American environment. Talking at a symposium on Armenian day schools she said: "I teach Armenian to 5th graders from 'Mayreni Lezou Book 4.' Every time we start reading a new short story, they ask the same question: Does this have a sad ending, too?" Garabedian observed that in the three stories her students had read during one month, one of the main characters had died tragically. Moreover, characters were orphans or poor or otherwise deprived, and the setting was a small village.[18]

Respondents' objections to Saturday school or summer camp are less intense, precisely because these are supplementary in nature and do not conflict with the values or structural requirements of American middle-class life. Armenian-Americans would like their children to speak Armenian, (only 10 percent disagreed that children should speak Armenian); however, implementing that decision is inconvenient. Several respondents found even Saturday schools to be taxing for the busy schedules of their children. A second-generation woman wrote: "They went to school enough during the week. They need time for themselves." A third-generation man said: "Five days of school is enough." Another third-generation respondent indicated: "They are involved with sports activities in the community." A second-generation man commented: "No problem here [on principle] ... but we have not [sent our children to Saturday school]. They are too busy." Again a Middle Eastern-born woman who has lived in this country for about thirty-five years wrote: "I would, but didn't. It conflicted with sports and other interests."

For many foreign-born respondents, the Armenian language is an essential component of Armenianness. In one of the earliest studies of the Armenian day-school movement in the United States, Rustigian reported that the underlying philosophy of most school officials is that "the Armenian identity can only be preserved by the continued use of the language" (1979, 82). Therefore, it is not surprising that the communities with the largest number of recent immigrants were the first to open Armenian day schools after the mid-1960s (Rustigian 1979, 10, 147).[19]

For example, 50 percent of parents who sent their children to the Armenian Sisters' Academy in Philadelphia were born in the Middle East and North Africa (28 percent of these in Lebanon and Syria alone). Thirty-five percent were born in the United States, this included those who were not of Armenian descent, and 5 percent were born in Europe and Latin America (Ordjanian 1991, 114). Similarly, at Ferrahian High School in California, even though 33 percent of students were born in the United States, the vast majority of their parents were first generation. The rest of the students were foreign-born, these included 24 percent from Lebanon, 10 percent from Iran, and 5 percent from Turkey (Davidian 1986, 124).

For American-born ethnics, loyalty to the ancestral language conflicts with symbolic ethnicity. Learning a language is a demanding task. As seen above, some believe that sending a child to an Armenian full-time school may hinder his or her social mobility. The distinction between the immigrant generation and the U.S.-born is reflected in Saturday and Sunday schools that each group patronizes, respectively. The emphasis in Sunday schools is on teaching Christian principles, church doctrine, and religious history. Armenian words and phrases are taught, but that is not the primary object of the Sunday schools, unlike the Saturday schools. From my interviews with community spokespersons, it became clear that the parents of children attending Saturday schools are more likely to be foreign-born, while the American-born are more likely to send their children to Sunday schools. As a second-generation, middle-aged woman aptly notes: "The Armenian-Americans place more emphasis on the church whereas the Armenians who come from abroad stress the language more. We must make Armenians realize that yes, the schools are important but being a good Christian is also vital in a child's life."

In constructing an ideal-typical model of attitudes toward Armenian educational institutions, I postulate that at one extreme, the most ethnically immersed immigrants would send their children to Armenian all-day schools; at the other end, the most Americanized, who continue to identify with their ancestral background, would send their children to Sunday schools in Armenian churches. In between, the least ethnic foreign-born and the most ethnic second generation and beyond would send their children to Saturday schools. Excluded from this typology are people of Armenian descent who are too alienated from the Armenian community to even consider any form of involvement or socialization for their children.

When all is said and done, Armenian all-day schools only cater to a very small proportion of the Armenian-American population; a little over five thousand students nationwide. The vast majority of children of Armenian descent in the United States attend public schools and a select group of affluent sons and daughters attend private elite schools. Even in the immigrant generation, most parents send their children to public schools. According to one estimate, the probability of attending Armenian schools in Los Angeles is between 15 and 20 percent (Davidian 1986, 66, 305).

Even though tuition in most Armenian all-day schools is subsidized by the community at large, costing parents about half of what it costs to run the schools (also a third to a fourth of what nonethnic private schools charge), still there are many new immigrant families in Los Angeles and elsewhere who cannot afford these rates. Ordjanian notes that school fees at the Armenian Sisters' Academy in Philadelphia are kept purposefully low. The rates are determined according to the median U.S. family income, yet for many it is a sacrifice. She goes on to say that the annual school budget averages $400,000, but only half of it is derived from tuition (Ordjanian 1991, 111-12).

Recently, *Armenian International Magazine* reported that school fees had been raised several times in the last five years. Many parents voiced their concerns about the economic strain of Armenian education. AGBU, for instance, gave $140,000 to the Armenian Elementary School in Watertown in 1990 to cover its costs, and the Marie Manoogian School in Canoga Park had a deficit of $160,000. What are the solutions? The article quotes educator Gabriel Injejikian, the founder of the first Armenian school in the United States, as suggesting that "Armenian parents should make an added sacrifice, even at the cost of not buying a house for the sake of their children's national education." He also suggested that a national tribute *(azkayin doork)* could be levied by the church to finance communal services and schools. Such a system prevails in Lebanon, where Armenian families pay an annual duty depending on their income.[20] Both solutions to the tuition crisis, and in fact to the problem of operating Armenian all-day schools, are clear examples of the traditional form of ethnicity I described earlier. Suggesting that parents forgo the American Dream of owning their own house, imposing an income tax based on one's ascribed status are unlikely to be endorsed. They are downright un-American!

It is noteworthy that the influx of massive numbers of newcomers from Soviet Armenia and elsewhere has created serious problems for the public school boards in the Greater Los Angeles area. For example, the Glendale Unified School District recently reported that Armenians now make up the single largest, and growing, contingent of students with limited English proficiency. In 1990, there were 4,859 students making up 42.6 percent of all the students with limited English proficiency in the district. Of these, 61 percent were in the nineteen elementary schools, 21 percent were in the four junior high schools, and the rest were in the four high schools of Glendale. The rate of Armenian students with limited English proficiency has been increasing almost exponentially in the last decade; that is, there were 1,000 students in 1983, 2,309 in 1988, 3,654 in 1989, and 4,859 in 1990. In addition, there were 889 Armenian students, or 22.3 percent of those with fluent English proficiency in Glendale schools in 1990.[21] Other school districts suffer similar problems. For instance, in 1990, Le Conte Junior High School in Hollywood had 750 Armenian students, mostly from Soviet Armenia. The ten or so other schools in the Hollywood district had equivalent numbers of Armenian students. The school boards have had to hire bilingual teachers to bridge the linguistic and cultural gaps of their students and set them on the road to acculturation.

Armenian All-Day Schools: Two Case Studies

How effective are Armenian all-day schools in socializing the next generation? So far, only two comprehensive case studies have been carried out on the subject: Richard Davidian (1986) examined the Ferrahian Armenian High School in Encino (CA), and Anahid Ordjanian (1991) analyzed the Armenian Sisters' Academy, which uses the Montessori system and teaches preschoolers to eighth graders, in the suburbs of Philadelphia. Each of these studies has its particular methodological and theoretical perspective. Davidian's goal as a linguist was to test the proficiency of students in English and Armenian. He surveyed 102 students in the eleventh and twelfth grades on a number of items and interviewed eleven additional students for ethnographic data. All but one of his informants were foreign-born, they had lived in the United States for an average of 7.5 years. Ordjanian, as a cultural anthropologist, used participant observation during her seventeen months of fieldwork and in-depth interviews with parents, teachers, and school board members. Using a political economy perspective, her goal was to answer questions as to why parents send their children to an Armenian school, what ideologies does the school, in general, and the Armenian studies curriculum, in particular, impart to its students.

Davidian found that, on average, English proficiency overtakes and surpasses the Armenian. "Pressure for Armenian young people to learn English is everywhere, even among Armenian peers. In Ferrahian school, those who don't speak it are teased by those who do" (Davidian 1986, 260). Students tend to compartmentalize the languages they speak, depending on their interlocutors and the topic. For example, 85 percent spoke Armenian with their grandparents, 75 percent with their parents, 60 percent with their siblings, and 46 percent with their friends (Davidian 1986, 268). There was a steady decline with each generation in the use of the Armenian language and a reciprocal increase in English usage. Interestingly, on average, 51 percent of students thought and reflected with themselves in Armenian. Moreover, the longer students had lived in the United States, the more likely they were to use English.

Yet, Davidian also found that the longer the student stayed in an Armenian school the higher were his or her chances of becoming fluent in two languages. Over 80 percent of students said they spoke, read, and wrote English and Armenian very well, and over 90 percent said they spoke both languages very well. Additionally, the longer they were in an Armenian school, the more likely they were to choose to speak Armenian with their friends. That is, those who spent one to six years in Armenian schools had a 30 percent probability of speaking Armenian with friends, those who spent seven to twelve years had a 45 percent probability, and those who spent thirteen to eighteen years had a 58 percent probability (Davidian 1986, 275). The study found that the school is successful in teaching Armenian, but only if the student's family environment actively reinforces identity maintenance and encourages participation in the organized Armenian-American community. These results are consistent with those of other ethnic groups that I have mentioned above.

Thus the empirical evidence confirms the fears of those who perceive assimilation as a plague. "The young people are adopting much of the American culture which surrounds them in spite of the sheltered Armenian environment found in the Armenian school" (Davidian 1986, 287). Consistent with the results of the New York survey, that is only part of the story. In Davidian's opinion, Ferrahian High School is trying to walk a fine line, advocating two, almost contradictory, goals. On the one hand, it promotes economic and political integration in the dominant society; on the other hand, it tries to avoid cultural and structural assimilation. In other words, the school instills in students the idea "that group worth is enhanced by individual achievement outside of the Armenian community" (Davidian 1986, 296); at the same time, it provides formal instruction in Armenian culture and language and indoctrinates them with the ideology of cultural preservation.

Ordjanian is more candid in her conclusions that the Armenian school she observed in Philadelphia does not fulfill its stated goals of preserving the Armenian culture, "in the sense of preserving the ways of life of past generations" (Ordjanian 1991, 256). Rather, the school teaches a reinvented Armenian culture, a symbolic or polyglot version. This is done explicitly through the Armenian studies curriculum; and implicitly through the annual reenactment of ceremonial rituals such Vartanantz and Genocide commemoration day; the folk dance styles children are taught to perform in public and private; and the culinary and dietary habits, labeled Armenian, that students practice in the Cooking Club. All these are symbolic markers that define and distinguish what is Armenian from what is not Armenian *(hai* versus *odar)*.

The new culture borrows something old from the past and something new from neighboring cultures. It homogenizes the varying definitions of Armenianness by finding a common denominator acceptable to a broad spectrum of people. It is a culture that adapts effectively to the needs of collective life in the United States at the threshold of the twenty-first century. The emergent traditions and symbols consciously minimize the diversity within the group. By emphasizing interdependence and responsibility toward one's family, church and ethnic group, and fostering communal ties, the school teaches that on the one hand, students are members of an ethnic group "who can cooperate politically as an 'interest' group" in the American arena; on the other hand, they are members of a diasporan people.

Most significantly, the school provides "quality" education. It fulfills the real and immediate educational requirement of preparing students to compete successfully in the American system (Ordjanian 1991, 257). Students learn the necessary skills, habits, and values that are essential to achieve social mobility and assume rewarding roles in the postindustrial economy they live in. For example, they learn self-reliance, self-discipline, critical thinking, creativity, emotional self-control, reliability, and the ability to work for long periods. Parents and friends of the school measure success by the number of "acceptances" the alumni receive from prestigious schools and colleges and the high-status jobs they eventually hold.

What about Armenian proficiency? Ordjanian writes, "immediate economic and practical needs take precedence over those of ethnic affiliation" (1991, 157). Even though students progressively learn more and more of the Armenian language as they move from one grade to the next, the five periods of Armenian instruction per week

(13.2 percent of total) indicate that the subject does not have high priority. Ordjanian's analysis supports my contention in this chapter. She found that there is little consensus among the parents as to what Armenian proficiency means. Lebanese and other Middle Eastern-born parents are more likely to demand that their child be highly literate in Armenian, even insisting that the the number of instruction periods be increased.

The advocates of language note that learning Armenian provides students with a mastery of a rare language, a sort of elite knowledge that solidifies their membership not only in the Armenian community in the United States but also in the diaspora. Moreover, they note that such knowledge increases the cognitive skills of students, making it easier for them to learn other languages. Some even find that knowledge of the Armenian language is useful in admitting a child into an elite high school or an Ivy League college because of the new popularity of multicultural education and the conscious policy of admissions officers to create a diverse student body.

In contrast, American-born parents who do not speak Armenian themselves find the expectations of some teachers unrealistic, especially those not trained in the United States. To them conversational knowledge of Armenian is sufficient. They think too much stress on learning Armenian is a waste of time, and unfair. More specifically, they are angered that a low grade in Armenian will lower the grade-point average of their child and disadvantage him/her when competing for reputable high schools. Ordjanian further remarks that

> while pleased if their child is bilingual, [American-born parents] recognize the difficulties of transmitting the language in the United States, where a speech community does not, for all intents and purposes, exist. Therefore, their concern is towards the level of their child's achievement in mastering English, which represents, for them, a skill unequivocally necessary not only for survival in the U.S. but for social mobility (a goal which they aspire to and which the U.S. system makes it possible for them to achieve). (1991, 214-15)

Last but not least, Ordjanian found that contrary to assumptions, the Armenian studies program is not able to teach pride in the ancestral heritage because "Armenians still seem convinced of the inferiority of Armenian society vis-à-vis Western society" (1991, 222). Like a child who will not love his/her mother less because she is not very pretty, students are taught that their culture and history may not have been brilliant or prestigious, but it is still their own. Ordjanian advocates the creation of a new, revised history which I will describe below. Albeit, the school heightens the students' awareness of the injustices suffered by the Armenians throughout their history and teaches them to challenge American and generally Western cultural superiority.

In conclusion, the all-day Armenian schools do not reproduce traditional Armenians as many of their advocates believe. A review of the two case studies indicates that these schools socialize young men and women to function in the mainstream, without relinquishing their ancestral identity. These schools produce second- and third-generation Armenian-Americans somewhat more steeped in their ancestral language and heritage than previous cohorts. However, the culture they impart to their charges is a symbolic one, constructed to match the requirements of ethnic life in the United States. Furthermore, the community in which the parents hope their children will participate as adults is unlikely to be a speech community. Finally, I need to ask, how representative are these case studies of all-day Armenian schools in the United States? They are probably two of the more successful institutions because of their longevity and the reputations they have gained; yet the issues and problems they face are fundamentally similar to all the others.

Armenian Higher Education and Research Centers

The development of higher education and research in Armenian studies in the United States had to await the coming of age of the second generation. Growing up in the first half of the twentieth century was difficult for children of all the "new" immigrant groups, including the Armenians. Public school teachers, who were in charge of the Americanization process, rarely missed a chance to belittle their charges' "foreign" behavior or their "less enlightened" parents. Peers were no less tolerant (e.g., Dobkin 1977). What the American-born children learned in public about their ancestral heritage, or, more accurately, its distinctive absence from all subject matter, contradicted what their families told them in private. It was hard to convince oneself that one's ethnic background had any value. Upon maturity and familiarity with the American system, a whole generation wanted to prove to themselves and to the world that Armenian history and culture was indeed worthwhile. It certainly deserved mention in mainstream texts and reference books. To gain acceptance and legitimacy as a people, on a par with the "advanced" nations of the world, Armenian-American specialists had to use the methodological techniques and theoretical perspectives of Western scholarship.

In 1955, the National Association of Armenian Studies and Research (NAASR) was founded "to foster the study of Armenian history, culture, and language on an active, scholarly, and continuous basis in America" *(Armenian American Almanac* 1990, 16). More specifically, one of its main aims was "to work for the establishment of endowed professorships, fellowships, scholarships, departments, and courses of instruction in Armenian studies at American colleges, universities, and other institutions of higher learning."[22] As a result, in 1961, Professor Avedis K. Sanjian became assistant professor of Armenian studies at Harvard University. "This marked the first instance of the appointment of a scholar to a full-time professorship in Armenian Studies anywhere in the United States" (Adalian 1990-91, 80).

The timing was fortuitous for two reasons: first, America was soon to experience the so-called ethnic revival movement. Ethnic heritage studies were fashionable, even the government was providing funding. Second, the massive immigration from the Middle East and Soviet Bloc brought in new energy, enthusiasm, and candidates and staff for Armenian studies. Consequently, a whole gamut of research institutes,[23] endowed chairs,[24] departments, and programs for Armenian studies, associations for Armenology scholars[25] mushroomed, just like the other types of schooling I have discussed above.

At present, Harvard, Columbia (established 1979), and the University of California, Los Angeles (established 1969) have endowed chairs in Armenian history and culture and grant MA and PhD degrees in Armenian studies (see Adalian 1990-91). There are also many universities and colleges that offer undergraduate courses in Armenian language and literature, ancient and modern history, history of art and architecture, and so on. Among those that do so on a regular basis are: the American Armenian International College, La Verne (CA); Boston University; California State University, Fresno; Cleveland State University; Tufts University; University of Connecticut, Storrs; University of Michigan, Ann Arbor; University of

Michigan, Dearborn; and the University of Pennsylvania.

Undergraduate courses in Armenian history and language serve a number of functions. They satisfy the curiosity of young men and women about their ancestral background during a period in their life course when they are most likely to be in search of an ethnic or religious identity. Course content is assumed to instill pride in their roots by explaining scientifically the role of Armenian history and culture in world events. Such courses can be attractive to college students because of their utilitarian value. As I have stated before, convenience is the key to practice. Furthering one's knowledge about one's ethnic background while earning elective credits is well suited to symbolic Armenian-Americans. Undergraduate courses in Armenian studies also serve latent functions. If a young person's interest in Armenianness is sustained, the community gains an active participant. These courses also provide essential preparatory training for future cadre for the ethnic church and organizations.

In addition to regular semester-long or quarter-long courses, students interested in Armenian studies have increasingly more options to choose from. Among these are a couple of study-abroad programs in Venice[26] and Yerevan[27] during the summer months. Through intensive instruction in language and culture, students earn college credits, and on top of that have the opportunity to travel and have fun. Among other programs available,[28] the Siamanto Academy is noteworthy. It provides college credits by offering Saturday classes during a three-year period.[29] This variety is attractive to young Armenian-Americans. Brought up in a consumer-oriented society, they have developed a wide range of individualized needs that they expect to be fulfilled. Moreover, Armenian studies, in general, and the summer or travel abroad programs, in particular, increase structural ties among young people of Armenian descent and enhance feelings of belonging.

With the declaration of independence in the Republic of Armenia and the removal of ideological controversies, homeland-diaspora relationships can in the future be strengthened or reestablished in earnest. Like American Jewish youngsters who spend a few months to a year on a kibbutz in Israel, it may become easier for American-born Armenians to study in Yerevan during the summer months, even spend their "junior year abroad." College programs are only one option in such an exchange. Work camps may be another. They too are learning experiences that serve similar functions to those mentioned above. For example, the Land and Culture Organization, Inc. organizes groups of young people to restore historic Armenian buildings and monuments on ancestral lands.[30]

Taking a course or two in Armenian history, traveling throughout Armenia during the summer months, and restoring ancient monuments are congruent with symbolic ethnicity. Making a career out of one's ethnicity is an option that only a select few have taken or are likely to take. In the last couple of decades, a number of men and women have earned MA and PhD degrees in Armenian studies. Not many others are encouraged to follow their example because upon graduation, these "specialists" face limited opportunities for full-time employment. Only the lucky few continue to earn a living in their field of specialization.

Since the majority of symbolic Armenian-Americans do not use the ancestral culture, they have an urgent need to preserve it for posterity. They need what I call "knowledge banks" such as Armenian studies programs and research institutes to meet their goals, in addition to preparing specialists to do so. The task at hand is to translate Armenian classics into English, transcribe the music, document and codify other art forms, catalogue and reference sources, and so on. In other words, the objective is to make Armenian culture and history readily accessible to nonnatives. Ultimately, centers for Armenian research and scholars working in Armenian studies need to validate the prestige and standing of this culture in the eyes of the Western world. Through this process they vicariously boost the self-esteem of symbolic Armenian-Americans.

Ordjanian (1991) concurs that scholars working on Armenian studies serve an important function for Armenian-Americans. By fostering positive views, they help them achieve upward mobility. Still, she criticizes these specialists for not challenging the basic Western premise that Armenian culture is less valuable. So far, studies produced by American-trained scholars have argued that Armenian history and culture is similar, even "equal" to, or "as good as" Western societies. She goes on to say, "comparisons of societies, as if they represent the sum of similar historical experiences, has robbed a subjugated people like Armenians of a dignified view of their past, as well as present, circumstances" (Ordjanian 1991, 258).

Ordjanian proposes that a political economy perspective be adopted for studies of Armenian history. She argues that such an approach would "reveal the differing interests of social groups" (Ordjanian 1991, 261), even those of certain Armenian classes, groups, and political parties that have dominated other Armenians during various historical periods. By explaining the consequences of political and economic action by foreign and domestic forces and the vested interests of various players, a clearer image of the past can be achieved. Ordjanian suspects, however, that her suggestion may be resisted by the elite. This is true because the moneyed elite in the Armenian-American community, as elsewhere in the diaspora, provide the major donations that keep "knowledge banks" in business.

What has been the role of Armenian educational institutions in the United States, then? Writing for the special issue of *Ararat* magazine on Armenian-Americans, Nishan Parlakian (1977, 74) concludes his article, "ABC to PhD: Armenian Studies in America" as follows:

> The reason for this expansion [in Armenian educational institutions] is clear enough. It has to do with the continued growth of ethnic identity and pride as well as the deep need for understanding of a unique language, history and people and with a shared holocaustic agony. It is part of a continual effort to keep the Armenian spirit alive.

> Detractors may say that the growth is a kind of unnecessary chauvinism in a country so democratic as the United States. But it is necessary just as the same sort of thing is necessary to other ethnics—more so perhaps because Armenians number so few in the world. Nor is it relevant to say the lower schools are havens for segregationists who want clean private schools for their children. Without the Saturday and Day Schools, there would be fewer qualified Armenians from whose ranks must come the Armenian leaders and clergy of the future and there would be fewer scholars to carry on research, scholarship, and teaching of Armenology on the highest levels.... If the Bicentennial has made anything obvious, it is that the wonder of America is in the richness and strength of its diversity. We now recognize that the rich second heritage of each individual people and culture is important and needs to be preserved.

Indeed, much of Parlakian's remarks sum up this section as well. Yet, I need to add a caveat. Lest the reader forgets, the rich second heritage that is mentioned above is to be enjoyed in the sidestream. All the rush to preserve heritage and prepare leadership is precisely because language and the ancient culture is no longer taken for granted, it is no longer part of a living tradition.

The Emergent Armenian-American Subculture

According to one of the community leaders I interviewed, there is much confusion among Armenian-Americans as to what constitutes their patrimony. My informant said:

> In 1915 we lost our intelligentsia. The Armenians who came to America after the massacres were peasants. They didn't know much about their history, background, etc. They didn't have the intellectual class to interpret culture for them. They were unable to pass on the ideals of a high culture to the second-generation. The second and third generation born in America are ashamed of their background. They equate Armenian culture with a peasant culture.

Moreover, because of the tragic events at the turn of the twentieth century, the exodus from historic lands, the near annihilation of the intellectual class, the forces of industrialization, modernization, and assimilation, much of the ancient culture of the Armenian people has been lost.

What constitutes the cultural heritage of an immigrant group in America? I define *culture* as an idea system that creates and sustains material and nonmaterial products compatible with its goals and requirements. It is the way of life of a people that includes their values, goals, norms, belief systems, ideologies, body of knowledge, rituals, and as well as architecture, painting, sculpture, music, literature, crafts, dance, and so on. The heritage of a people consists of the high culture and the popular culture (Gans 1974); the great traditions and the little traditions (Redfield 1955; Singer 1972), both sacred and secular. The material and nonmaterial products of the ruling classes make up the high culture. They are more likely to have survived the turbulent forces of history than the popular culture of the ordinary people. The ancient cultural remains that make contemporary Armenians proud, such as the illuminated manuscripts and the architectural monuments, were once the possessions of a small privileged elite.

The great traditions of a people are generalized belief systems and rituals that permeate all levels of society. For example, Armenians as a Christian nation believed in the crucifixion and resurrection of Jesus Christ, which they reenacted annually during Holy Week. The little traditions are more likely to be localized; they vary by region, by social status, and by urban-rural residence. They are beliefs, customs, and practices the family and local community observe during rites of passage and daily living, such as those surrounding betrothal, marriage, childbearing and rearing, health and disease, life and death. The little traditions also include customs related to the celebration of seasonal changes and events in the sacred calendar, such as the blessing of the grape harvest on *Asdvadzadzin* (Feast of Assumption), and the fast of young virgin women before the Saint Sarkis name day, in the hope of finding a suitable match. Additionally, they include the oral traditions: the legends, proverbs, the songs, the dances, the cuisine, and so on.

The cultural baggage Armenian immigrants brought with them to the United States at the turn of the twentieth century consisted of the great and little traditions, the popular culture of the peasant and petit bourgeois (artisan and merchant) classes. Out of their original context, many of these imported traditions proved to be cumbersome, even meaningless. Besides, immigrants were too busy trying to survive in a hostile environment they were ill-prepared for. They did not see the need to sustain practices and beliefs that were no longer functional. Instead, Armenian immigrants adapted what they could of their cultural legacy to the requirements of American society. A new culture emerged; albeit a symbolic one.

The ancient high culture had to await the second generation to be rehabilitated and owned by Armenian-Americans. It was the task of the knowledge banks I have described above to appropriate the elite culture and reclaim the historical episodes that would make present-day descendants proud. These were more likely to be periods of territorial expansion and military triumphs, and eras of stability and prosperity that gave rise to golden ages of literary and artistic innovations. For instance, illuminated manuscripts are a testimony to a heroic and glorious past. When visiting the Freer Gallery of Art in Washington, DC or the Walters Art Gallery in Baltimore where several of these manuscripts are found, Armenian-Americans ask to see them and demand they be displayed more prominently.

Contemporary Armenian-Americans also preserve and cherish whatever heirlooms their ancestors may have left them. Grandmother's embroidered wedding dress or ceramic dishes from Kutahia, great-uncle's watch or Armenian Bible, great-aunt's needle lace doilies or old photographs[31] are displayed prominently in the homes of Armenian-Americans. A few items become museum pieces. At present, the American Museum of Natural History in New York, the Immigration Museum at Ellis Island, and the Armenian Library and Museum of America, Inc. in Watertown have small collections of Armenian artifacts, needlework, rugs, textiles, coins, metalwork, etc. These too are knowledge banks, for the popular culture

With the fading of Armenian language proficiency with each passing generation in the United States, the oral traditions—the legends, fairy tales, songs, proverbs, among others—pass away unnoticed. Similarly, the family customs and practices of over a hundred years ago are not as easily retrievable either. Sociologists trying to measure change are at a loss because there are few sources that describe the little traditions of the Armenian past. The exceptions are few and far between. Noteworthy is the study of the changing pattens of family life of Armenian immigrants and their descendants in Fresno by Nelson (1953). A more recent study relied on the recollections of elderly Armenian immigrants to document village life before 1914 (Villa and Matossian 1982).

Armenians in America today, even recent immigrant cohorts, follow predominantly American customs at weddings and funerals, as they have adopted the practice of bridal and baby showers[32] and the celebration of birthdays, anniversaries, and Thanksgiving. Said a community spokesman describing wedding ceremonies among Armenian-Americans: "These are presents of Hollywood. All religions, all groups have adopted it. The source is the same. People feel this is great source of satisfaction. It is part of the local culture."

Likewise, after documenting the traditional Armenian custom of ceremonial or mock abduction at weddings among Fresno immigrants after World War II, Nelson (1953) noted that it is being practiced less often because fewer and fewer young people know about it.[33] He found that the peripheral elements of the wedding ceremony, such as clothes, number and composition of attendants, and music follow American custom. Interestingly, he goes on to say,

> While peripheral elements have generally been accepted without much difficulty, certain changes considered more significant apparently met with obstacles overcome only by societal insistence. Armenian society succeeded by boycotting, or threatening to boycott, the church that would not "modernize" its ceremonies, and consequently, the church was compelled to accept changes thus forced upon it. (Nelson 1953, 217)

I asked several of the community leaders I interviewed to suggest what they believed to be "typical" Armenian values. The following is a list they provided: generosity and hospitality;[34] hard work and industriousness; resourcefulness and ingenuity *(jarbeeg);* filial respect and loyalty; parental sacrifice and keeping the good name, honor and reputation of the family *(badeev)* by avoiding shame *(amot).* Similarly, some of the respondents in the New York study associated these values with Armenian culture, such as the seventy-six-year-old, second-generation, Protestant Armenian lady who wrote somewhat chauvinistically, "Armenians are a fine race of people, I am proud to be one. All are intelligent, hardworking, respectable people, kind, generous, sympathetic. Any Armenian home you visit, there is always a generous amount of food and love shown to the family, friends, neighbors, etc."

Many of the values suggested above as typically Armenian are rather inherent characteristics of all small, face-to-face, close-knit communities with agrarian economic means of production. Moreover, for several centuries, the Armenian family was organized patrilineally; that is, descent was traced through the male line. The patriarch, the eldest male member of the household, controlled the communal assets, including the labor of all the members. Women and younger men were not favored by such a system. Upon marriage, a woman joined the household of her husband, and often, until she gave birth to a male heir, her position there was virtually powerless. In other words, filial duty, family honor, and shame are common in many agrarian, patriarchal, folklike societies.

Other values might have been borrowed from neighboring societies. For example, the Armenian traditional concepts of family honor[35] and shame are very similar to to the Arab concepts of *ird* and *Sharaf* (e.g., see Antoun 1968), or the Greek *philotimo* (Kourvetaris 1981, 176; Moskos 1989, 93, 104, 110), the Italian *onore della famiglia* (Johnson 1985, 108). The issue of punctuality is anecdotal. Armenians are reputed to be late. Many social functions sponsored by Armenian associations start late, consequently called "Armenian time" *(Haygagan Jumm).* But this is not unique to Armenians; Greeks have "Greek time" (Moskos 1989, 96), Italians have "Italian time," Jews have "Jewish time," and so on.

Given the ambiguity about the great and little traditions, also given the unanimous agreement among my informants that old customs and practices have changed, I am unable to analyze the prevalence of the popular cultural heritage of the Armenians. The study of changing values, norms, and traditions merits a separate investigation. Instead, I examine the extent of utilization of the emergent secular culture of Armenian-Americans among the New York respondents. Whatever its exact provenance, this emergent culture is produced and enacted in the United States by men and women of Armenian descent. It includes the language, literature, music, song, dance, architecture, paintings, sculpture, crafts, cuisine, as well as the values, norms, rituals, etc.

The New York Sample's Maintenance of Secular Culture

New York respondents were asked whether they read Armenian literature, either in Armenian or in translation, and whether they ever bought any works of art, such as paintings, sculpture, embroidery, or antiques especially because they were made by Armenians. Use of the Armenian media was measured by two questions: one, the approximate number of Armenian newspapers and/or magazines (in English or Armenian) the respondent usually received; second, the frequency of listening to Armenian radio programs.

Overall, only 13.6 percent of respondents said they almost always read Armenian literature, 32.1 percent said they read sometimes, and the remaining 54.4 percent said they hardly ever read Armenian literature. Table 4.9 shows the distribution of generational status by respondents scoring "high" (ethnic position) on reading Armenian literature, buying Armenian art (sometimes to almost always), and receiving two or more Armenian newspapers and magazines. Foreign-born respondents read Armenian literature about twice as often as American-born generations (.27*). The latter are most familiar with the English-language works of fellow Armenian-Americans. A thirty-five-year-old third-generation man exemplifies this. He remarked that he had not read Armenian literature "except for Michael Arlen and William Saroyan." Saroyan needs no introduction to the American public. Arlen, on the other hand, achieved some recognition in the mid-1970s with his work "Passage to Ararat," first published in *The New Yorker*.

There is support of Armenian literature and art, but it is weak, in each case less than 7 percent of the answers were in the "always" category on a five-point scale of never to always. Only 8.2 percent bought art made by Armenians almost always, 28 percent sometimes, and about 64 percent hardly ever. First-generation respondents were also most likely to collect art, though the differences between the generations were less sharp (.12*). Responses for receiving publications were higher. Only 26.8 percent of all respondents do not receive any Armenian newspapers or magazines, about 60 percent receive between one and three, and the remaining 13.6 percent receive more than four. Again, more foreign-born respondents scored high (60 percent) on receiving Armenian publications than the American-born (.19*); however, about 40 percent of the second generation continued

TABLE 4.9
Frequencies of Respondents Scoring "High" on Three Variables of Secular Culture by Generation
(in percent)

	Foreign- Born	U.S.-Born of F.B. Parents	1 Parent U.S.-Born	2 Parents U.S.-Born	Grandparent U.S.-Born
N = 581-583	(218)	(271)	(36)	(41)	(15)
Read Arm. literature	63.8	34.4	36.1	22.0	37.5
Buy Arm. art	44.5	33.9	25.0	21.9	26.7
Get Arm. newspapers	60.5	41.0	40.0	24.4	25.0

TABLE 4.10
Frequencies of Respondents Scoring "High" on Three Variables of Secular Culture by Religious Affiliation
(in percent)

	Apostolic Armenian	Protestant Armenian	Catholic Armenian	Other (Non-Arm.)	No Religion
N = 581-583	(369)	(56)	(22)	(92)	(36)
Read Arm. literature	52.6	48.2	36.4	23.9	33.3
Buy Arm. art	41.7	44.6	13.6	23.6	13.9
Get Arm. newspaper	54.9	50.0	36.4	25.0	22.2

to do so. Receiving a newspaper, magazine, or newsletter is not a demanding task. Moreover, receiving does not mean reading. Often Armenian organizations send their in-house magazines or newsletters free of charge to households on their mailing lists, as a respondent noted: "It is sent to me."

The proportions of respondents affiliated with non-Armenian denominations and those with no religion were about half of the proportions of the Apostolics on all three variables measuring secular culture (see table 4.10). Similarly, about 58 percent of respondents who were partial to Armenian political ideologies (Hunchag, Ramgavar, Tashnag, *Chezok* [nonpartisan]) read Armenian literature most frequently, compared to 30 percent of those who were indifferent, and 35 percent of those who rejected ethnic politics. Again, about 50 percent of the partisans bought art frequently, versus 20 percent of the indifferents. Mixed parentage reduces the proportion of people receiving Armenian newspapers by more than half, from 50 percent for respondents with two Armenian parents to 23 percent for those with one Armenian parent. There are equal declines in reading Armenian literature (48 percent to 30 percent) and buying art (32 percent to 22 percent).

Interestingly, socioeconomic variables were not statistically significant with all three variables used to measure maintenance of secular heritage. Like a young graduate student who found the question on buying art "a rather class-biased question," I had assumed that with more income, a person could afford to buy more artwork and subscribe to more publications. Contrary to these assumptions, people who make less than $20,000 bought more Armenian art than those who make double or triple that amount. How is this possible? Art comprises a wide range of collectibles. It could be high art, such as an oil painting by Gorky or a sculpture by Nakian, or it could be popular crafts or artifacts such as a lace doily made by grandmother, a souvenir *khatchkar* (cross) from Yerevan, or a record of Khachaturian's *Sabre Dance*. The comments respondents made reflect this. A fifty-two-year-old, second-generation man said: "I do enjoy my collection of Armenian music." Another elderly man who immigrated as a child wrote: "Oh Yes, I have two Tolegians, a Yaghjian (prof at a Southern Univ.); Art books, collectibles, embroidery. I also have a Khachaturian, records, etc."

Armenian-Americans feel positive about their cultural heritage. They are very proud of both their ancient and modern high culture. They admire the illuminated manuscripts of Toros Roslin, the architecture of the cathedral at Akhtamar, the music of Gomidas Vartabed, and the paintings of Aivazovsky. They particularly enjoy showing off to their non-Armenian friends and acquaintances that Arshile Gorky, William Saroyan, and Alan Hovaness among many others were (or are) their compatriots. Additionally, Armenian-Americans cherish their family heirlooms and old photographs, as they find many of the popular Armenian music and the folk dances delightful. In general, Armenian-Americans would like to pass this pride and heritage to their progeny.

For example the statement: "Our children should learn Armenian dance and music" received unanimous approval in the pretests. Even when respondents disagreed mildly with such statements, the objection was not against Armenian culture per se. A twenty-eight-year-old woman whose father is an Armenian immigrant and mother a Midwesterner reacted to the statement "Public schools should teach something about the history and culture of the Armenian people" by saying: "There are *many, many,* races in the world. The public schools already have a heavy burden" (emphasis in original). In sum, these sentiments and displays of one's ancestral legacy are typical of symbolic ethnics, especially where no prior knowledge of the language or history is required. Practicing the culture is another matter. As a rule, they would encourage the perpetuation of Armenian culture as long as it is in the sidestream, and as long as it does not become a burden.

Armenian Press and Radio

The *Armenian American Almanac* (1990) lists a total of sixteen Armenian newspapers published in the United States. These papers and other magazines, journals, and newsletters are distributed by mail. Though a West Coast paper might take up to ten days to reach New York City or New Jersey, it is not unusual for area residents to receive West Coast publications and vice versa. Four newspapers are published in Watertown (MA), one in Queens (NY), and one in Paramus (NJ). All the others are published in the Los Angeles area. Of the sixteen, two are daily newspapers,[36] two biweekly, ten are weeklies, and the rest monthlies or periodicals. Besides newspapers, there are less than half a dozen literary and scholastic journals that are published in the United States and a large number of in-house magazines and newsletters of organizations, churches, and research libraries and centers.

Five of the six papers that are published only in the Armenian language are organs of the three Armenian political parties.[37] Their circulation is relatively small, ranging from 1,000 to 2,500 copies. The one exception targets an immigrant clientele, and is written in Eastern Armenian. Three other newspapers are bilingual, and in one case trilingual (Armenian, English, French). These bilingual papers also cater to the new immigrant population. All three are published in Los Angles, and their circulation is impressive—6,000 for the *Asbarez* daily (10,000 for its Saturday edition), and 16,500 for *Hai Gyank* and the trilingual *Nor Gyank*.

One can easily deduce from this information that the readers of the Armenian language press are almost exclusively from the first generation. Armenian-Americans do not need to know how to read and write Armenian to sporadically participate in communal activities, to take pride in their cultural heritage, or to feel Armenian. The Armenian-American subculture can be maintained while the vast majority of Armenian-Americans are not proficient in the ancestral language. In fact, I was clearly told by the owner/publisher of the *Armenian Reporter* that there is no market for Armenian language publications in the United States. He explained to me that in 1967 when his paper started, it had an Armenian language supplement. After a couple of years, the supplement had to be discontinued. It had lost money due to lack of readers. While political parties may be able to afford to publish Armenian-language newspapers that are economically not profitable, independent entrepreneurs cannot.

The *Armenian Reporter* is the only English-language newspaper in the research area with a circulation of about 4,800. It is an independent weekly (nonpartisan in terms of ethnic politics), individually owned and operated by a Middle Eastern-born Armenian. The yearly subscription cost $35 at the time of the survey. It has since gone up to $55. Other than regional news and ideological/political proclivities, Armenian-American newspapers cover roughly the same type of stories, features articles and classified ads. To illustrate the focus of these papers and the interests of their readers, I collected a sample of the headlines that appeared in ten issues of the *Armenian Reporter* between April 3 and June 5, 1986, approximately corresponding to the period the New York survey was being conducted. Below is a selection of the headlines. I have classified these by the following categories: lead stories, feature stories, letters to the editor, calendar of events, and classified ads.

Sample Headlines from the Armenian Press

Lead Stories

Edouard Balladur, No. 2 Man in French Cabinet, Said To Be of Armenian Origin

Turks May Allow Repairs of Armenian Church in Iskenderun

Turks Said to Soon Release Very Rev. Manuel Yergatian Congressional Delegation Reports after Visit to Turkey

Massachusetts Gov. Dukakis to Participate in Armenian Martyrs' Day Memorial Services

Armenians in Holland Want to Buy Back Europe's 1st Armenian Church

"American-Turkish Day" Planned by Turkish groups in New York City for April 19

Soviet Armenians Said to Fear Nuclear Disaster Similar to Chernobyl Accident

4 Armenians Murdered in W. Beirut in 2 Days

Unidentified Underground Group Claim International Magazines Assassinations Will Continue until Armenian Presence Is "Terminated"

Feature Stories

Proxmire and Aspin to receive "Friends of Armenia" Award

Dr Grigorian's Lectures at Columbia University Are Well Attended; Many Young People Are Present

Senators Link Armenians and Jews at Celebration of Genocide Convention Passage

Armenian Catholics Celebrate Annual Mid-Lenten Dinner-Dance

Genocide Class Featured at Cal State

Competition Very Keen between Armenian Independent & Partisan Publications in Los Angeles as They Strive to Corner the Armenian Reading Market

British Library Oriental Dept. Reports on Recent Acquisitions

Thirteen Lovely Young Debutantes Take Part in St Thomas 29th Annual Cotillon & Ball, Proud Fathers Present Their Daughters to the Community Saturday April 5, 1986

Sale of Two William Saroyan Houses Upsets Many Fresnans

Keeping Their Roots Strong: Armenians Take Crash Course to Keep Language Alive

German TV Features Documentary on Turkish Massacres

Armenian Terrorists Written about in Reader's Digest: "Bomb on the loose!" Armenians Urged to Participate in Kodak's "America's Family Album"

Armenian Doctor Elected to Britain's College of Surgeons

Prelacy Ladies Gather for Elegant Mother's Day Lunch and Fashion Show at St Regis in New York City

Armenian Research Center at U. M. receives $1,000 Contribution from U.S. Senator Donald Riegle

Letters to the Editor
Joseph Vosbikian, a Man of Courage and Dedication
Bravo to Ara Baliozian for His Excellent Essays
Protests AGBU Fashion Show Held Near Martyr's Day
Everyone Should Pitch and Help the Mekhitarists
The People Shall Judge the Leaders

Calendar of Events
Violinist Gerard Kantarjian Will Perform April 27
Diocese to Mark Birth Anniversary of F. Nansen, a Friend of the Armenians
NY AGBU Golf Season to Open April 23 at Plandome Country Club
Rep. Bill Green Will Be Honored at Reception Hosted by Armenian-Americans
Fundraiser for Armenian Nursing Home Will be Held at the Copley in Boston

Classified Ads
Oriental Rugs
Mortgage Money Available
Funeral Directors Service—any Distance—any Hour
Chiropractor, MD, Eye Physicians, etc. Open New Offices
Armenian Restaurant
Florist
Jewel Consultant—Appraisals
Armenian Furrier
Brokerage—Apartments, Homes, Commercial
Musical Ensemble of Armenian, Arabic, Greek Music for Parties
Travel Service Offers Special Summer Tour to Armenia, Moscow, Leningrad
Piano Tuning
Books for Sale

Samples of headlines from an Armenian newspaper published in the United States suggest that the cultural and communal life of Armenian-Americans is supported by the press. There is a symbiotic relationship between the press and the organized community. Each derives benefit from the existence of the other. The voluntary associations rely upon the press to advertise the programs and events they sponsor, while the newspapers fill up their pages with reports and photographs of those activities, and sell subscriptions. The press also announces personal news of weddings, funerals, high school and college graduations, as it publicizes the successes of men and women of Armenian descent in their fields of endeavor. Most important, the Armenian press contributes to the development of Armenian pride and sense of community by highlighting the accomplishments of Armenian individuals around the world and the longevity and greatness of Armenian culture.

Noteworthy is the fact that the Armenian-American community derives glory and sense of achievement by association with prominent national or mainstream personalities. When senators, governors, or other illustrious (non-Armenian) individuals pay attention to Armenian-Americans or Armenian issues, this is perceived by the community as a sign of validation of their culture and existence. Headlines of the Armenian press reveal that the reference group of Armenian-Americans is the larger American society. I have also observed this repeatedly among the community leaders I interviewed. The younger leaders, in particular, consider it their duty to introduce the general American public to Armenian culture and history. As one of them, criticizing the established Armenian organizations, said to me, "We must look at the non-Armenian view. How can we publish and produce films to acquaint the rest of the world about our culture? So far all we've done is entertain the Armenians themselves." Another community leader, when asked whether Armenian-Americans promote their young ethnic artists, replied, "They do not know much about art. They think it's worthless unless it is accepted by the American community. The reference group is still the American society. For example, Gorky is now considered to be great."[38]

It has been established that the function of the ethnic press is to develop an ethnic ideology through the positive portrayal of the ethnic culture (Sandberg 1974, 28). For example, readers of the *Armenian Reporter* in the 1980s were encouraged to identify Armenia as a "spiritual homeland." This was done by printing news of Soviet Armenia in almost every issue, most of it being positive. Since the physical and political earthquakes in Armenia, the headlines have become bigger and bigger, and more and more pages are devoted to cover the events there. Another ideology is reinforcing a sense of diaspora. News of Armenian communities around the world appears regularly in the weekly press, stressing the cultural commonalities between the reader and his or her distant compatriot.

The newly created news magazine *Armenian International Magazine* explicitly advocates a diasporan ideology. Its timing is not only indicative of the collapse of ideological barriers between the homeland and the diaspora, but also the prominence of the Armenian-American community. Outside Armenia, this community remains the largest and most influential. Through the magazine, Armenian-

Americans have claimed a voice in the future of the Armenian people and the leadership of the expatriate communities. As an opinion maker, the magazine is most likely to propagate the views of symbolic Armenian-Americans and promote the class and political interests of its sponsors. It is therefore not surprising that the *Armenian International Magazine* is published in English, not Armenian. Indeed, English has become the *lingua franca* of the Armenian diaspora.

As with other aspects of Armenian-American communal life, several newspapers compete with each other over the ideological orientations of their sponsors and readers.[39] The focus of the Armenian press in English is very narrow. Essentially it is self-expository,[40] concentrating on Armenian news locally, nationally, and internationally. Non-Armenian news is totally excluded. The American-born generations have to rely on the American news media for national and international news and information. By contrast, the Armenian-language dailies in the past covered a broader spectrum of news and events, both Armenian and non-Armenian, because these papers were the principal source of information for the immigrant generation.[41] The new cohort of foreign-born immigrants, as reported above, are more likely to be bilingual.

How often do Armenian-Americans listen to ethnic radio? Nearly 58 percent of the New York respondents had never listened to an Armenian radio program, and another 23.4 percent have done so only rarely. Only about 6.3 percent listen to Armenian radio almost always, and 12 percent sometimes. These figures are not surprising because many respondents were ignorant of the existence of such radio programs, or did not know at what time or to which station to tune to. They wrote, "Didn't know there was one," or "Haven't known about it," or "Do not know when it's on." Alternatively, several respondents believed they were unable to receive the station. They noted, "No radio programs in our geographic area," or "Don't get any here," and again "Only because it's not available."

There were three radio programs in the New York and New Jersey metropolitan area at the time the survey was being conducted. They continue to operate today, though their schedules may have changed somewhat. These are the "Armenian Radio Hour of New Jersey" broadcasting for three hours on Sunday afternoons and another hour on Tuesday evenings; "Sound of Armenia" broadcasting Wednesday evenings for half an hour; and "Armenian Outreach Radio Program" broadcasting on Tuesday mornings for half an hour. Each of these programs serves a specific purpose. The oldest program, "Sound of Armenia," was established in 1978 to promote the sales of an Armenian record store. It is an individualistic effort, financed by advertisements and promotional concerts by Armenian popular (semiprofessional) singers and orchestras. By contrast, the "Outreach" program broadcasts Armenian historical and cultural information and is funded by the Prelacy of the Armenian Church of America.

The most impressive program, the "Armenian Radio Hour of New Jersey," established in 1979, broadcasts news in English and Armenian. It focuses on news about Armenian individuals, communities, and issues in the United States, the diaspora, and, of course, Armenia. The station, affiliated with a local university, is federally funded, though additional support for the program comes from Armenian individuals and organizations. According to its producer, the goals of the program are to provide cultural nourishment, information, and community services to its listeners, "old-timers who are hungry for that type of programming."

In many respects, the news and information content of the Armenian radio programs has the same function as the ethnic press. The following list consists of programs of the "Armenian Radio Hour of New Jersey" as advertised in the *Armenian Reporter* in the "Calendar of Events" section during 1986. There was a program dedicated to William Saroyan, another to French (Armenian) singer Charles Aznavour, one to composer Aram Khachaturian, a program about the Armenian community in Lebanon, yet another about the One World Festival in New York City. Additionally, the program hosts, about once a month, a bilingual immigration lawyer who answers call-in queries on legal matters, and occasional guests who discuss current issues in Armenia.

Given the enormous odds against even the existence of such radio programs, the fact that they have survived for some years must be a measure of success for the producers and staff who volunteer their services. Nonetheless, such programs remain limited in achieving their goals and reaching out to any significant number of people of Armenian descent. As a sixty-three-year-old second-generation man wrote: "The Armenian Radio Hour is *not as regular* as the other foreign radio broadcasts" (emphasis in original). Indeed, a total of five broadcasting hours per week for the Armenian community in the New York area is inconvenient, one can easily forget to tune in. A major problem is the difficulty of producing quality programming for any significant amount of time on a voluntary basis. As an elderly respondent said, he does not listen to Armenian radio, but "I would if time and place were known and convenient. Those I listened to in the past were very unprofessional, boring." It should be noted that all three producers are foreign-born, and the majority of listeners are also foreign-born.

The radio programs are a typical first-generation phenomenon common to many ethnic groups (Fishman 1985). Since the Armenian language is decreasingly used for communication, the few hours of broadcasting per week can only play a vestigial role in maintaining functional fluency of Armenian. As Armenian music and songs are less demanding, they are more likely to take over larger and larger segments of programming time in the future.

The *Armenian American Almanac* (1990) lists twenty radio programs in the United States (including the three already mentioned). Most of the major centers of Armenian communal life have a radio program. For example, there is at least one program in each of the following cities: Chicago, Cleveland, Fresno, Detroit, Houston, Philadelphia, Providence, New York, San Francisco, Watertown, Worcester,[42] and of course, Los Angeles. Most stations broadcast in Armenian and English, and feature news items and music. Typically, they go on the air for an hour or two on weekends or on weekday evenings. The one exception is the "Voice of All Armenians, Inc." Established in 1982 in Los Angeles, it is a private subscription frequency via satellite which is on the air for twenty-four hours, seven days a week.

California also boasts four Armenian television programs. Since 1979, "Armenian Teletime" can be seen on Saturday and Sunday mornings. "Horizon" was established in 1989 and provides programming for an hour on Saturday evenings. Also since 1989, "*Hye*-Air" telecasts on Mondays and Thursdays at 6:00 P.M. All three stations use KSCI-TV, channel 18, and are available to viewers in Los Angeles and occasionally in San Francisco. "The *Hye* Light" is a cable channel and is on the air on Tuesdays, Wednesdays, and Thursdays at

8:00 P.M. All this adds up to a token twelve or so hours of Armenian television per week. The Armenian television shows I watched while in Los Angeles consisted of news reports read by an announcer, sometimes accompanied by film clips. They covered events in the U.S. communities, the diaspora, and Armenia. Otherwise, there was much singing and musical interludes. Programing was frequently interrupted for lengthy commercials. I was told that occasionally dramatic productions or comic sketches are produced. In sum, the press, radio, and television have more or less the same content and serve the same functions.

Conclusion: What is Armenian-American Culture?

Can Armenian traditional culture survive in America? That is, can the imported culture of the immigrant generation, or more accurately of succeeding immigrant cohorts, be preserved in its totality? The literature on ethnicity indicates that immigrant cultures become ossified with the passage of time unless, like the Amish and the Hasidim, the group voluntarily segregates itself from the rest of society. However, through a process of "ethnogenesis" or "ethnicization" (see chap. 1), a hyphenated culture emerges in the United States.

Richard Alba, after careful analysis of Italian Americans, concluded:

> culture is malleable, and signs of change were already visible with the emergence of the second generation. The culture of the group continued to change as its position did. The story of the Italian Americans thus testifies to endless creativity of human beings, who fashion culture in order to help make sense of the world they know and are capable of reworking it in response to changes in their surroundings. (1985a, 170-71)

Likewise, men and women of Armenian descent, in response to particular social, economic and political experiences in the United States have created the Armenian-American subculture. It is a dynamic product that adjusts to the demands of the larger society and incorporates the goals and preferences of new waves of immigrants who join the fold.

Throughout this chapter, I have argued that the debate over language hides a conflict between two definitions of Armenianness:

the traditional and the symbolic. Traditional Armenianness espouses an ascribed, compulsive type of identity and insists that the Armenian language is central to its survival. The symbolic, on the other hand, conceives of Armenianness including language proficiency as voluntary, to be enjoyed in the sidestream as along as it does not become a burden and hinder the pursuit of the American Dream. Foreign-born Armenians, especially from the Middle East, tend to defend the retention of language at all costs, while the American-born advocate individual choice in identity and community participation.

Ethnic languages fare poorly in the United States; the Armenian language is no exception. The language is the component of culture that is the least likely to be retained after the second generation. For American-born children, Armenian is not a "mother tongue." Even when 74 percent of the second generation learn to speak Armenian at home, by rote, less than 20 percent can read and write it, and, most significantly, less than 12 percent are likely to use Armenian as a means of communication at home. By the fourth generation, only a select few choose to learn to speak, read, and write Armenian. The United States is a monolingual society, and throughout its history English has been a prerequisite for economic and political integration and a chance to achieve the American Dream.

The debate over language focuses on the educational institutions as socializers of future generations. The New York data has shown that support for Armenian all-day schools comes predominantly from the post-1965 immigrant cohorts. Overall enrollment in Armenian educational institutions is very small, about 5,000 nationally. Such students represent a fraction of the universe of Armenian-American children. Even though some schools and communities have managed to prove that it is compatible to be Armenian *and* American, most of the New York sample believed that it is inconvenient and un-American to send one's child to an all-day Armenian school.

Review of two case studies of Armenian all-day schools suggests that the longer the students remain in school, the more proficient they become both in English and in Armenian. However, contrary to commonly held assumptions, these schools do not reproduce traditional Armenianness. With Armenian classes comprising less than 15 percent of instruction periods per week, American-born children get the message that their primary goal is to be successful in the larger society.

Moreover, the all-day schools propagate a symbolic Armenian culture. It is the only version that is feasible in the American environment. Yet, the all-day schools remain controversial. Middle Eastern-born parents fight for additional Armenian classes and the exclusion of non-Armenian students, while the more Americanized parents threaten to pull their children away if low grades in the Armenian language get in the way of a high grade-point average and advocate a multicultural student body that reflects American pluralism.

The Armenian radio and television programs are in the same category as the all-day schools. They cater to the Armenian-speaking immigrants who conceive of their Armenianness in traditional terms. Keeping in mind that the majority of the radio and television producers are foreign-born, as "taste-makers" they have promoted over the airwaves a type of Armenian music known as "boulevardier" or "estrada," in the style of Charles Aznavour and Julio Iglesias. It is a genre that was popularized by composers and singers in Beirut and Yerevan in the last few decades. The "estrada" style is to be contrasted to the *à la turqua* variety that Armenian communities in the United States were accustomed to. The earliest immigrants had brought to the New World their "Oriental" drums and fiddles *(davoul* and *zurna)* and the tunes and lyrics they had played and sung in their native towns and villages on the Anatolian Plateau. Paradoxically, what the recent cohort of foreign-born Armenians condemn as "Turkified" music,[43] the American-born define as "traditional" Armenian music. This has became another battleground between the two definitions of Armenianness; even though it is recognized that musical tastes are not as consequential to the well-being of individuals as all-day schools.

Since the start of the Lebanese Civil War, Los Angeles has replaced Beirut as the Mecca for Armenian popular music. There are about a dozen Middle Eastern-born "stars" who live and record in Los Angeles, but frequently tour the Armenian communities in North America to perform at concerts or dinner dances hosted by various voluntary associations. Additionally, a few of them can be seen more regularly at Middle Eastern restaurants and night clubs in Los Angeles. These "stars" sing almost exclusively in Armenian, though a couple of them have ventured into Persian, Greek, Arabic, French, Italian, and English. Their repertoire consists of old revolutionary and nationalistic songs and romantic ballads. Most borrow, even translate songs, but some have created their own scores and lyrics. However, outside a very small circle of fans, overwhelmingly from the first generation, the names of Adis Harmandian, Pamboukian, Manuel, Vatché, Yorgantz remain unrecognizable by most Armenian-Americans.

Many second-generation Armenians active in communal life are unhappy with the new genre. One of them lamented in an Armenian newspaper: "Our dance and music, in our attempt not to be of 'Turkish' flavor, has degenerated to a point that I can no longer understand or enjoy."[44] Linguistic barriers and lack of stylistic familiarity prevent symbolic Armenian-Americans from appreciating the contemporary music produced in Yerevan or Los Angles. They are more likely to enjoy some of the bands that play live Armenian music at weddings, dinner dances, picnics, and other community gatherings. Many of these bands specialize in the "Turkified" style that is more conducive to folk dancing. Dancing is indeed more fun than listening to a song in a language one does not comprehend. One can learn the few basic steps fairly quickly; besides, one does not need a partner from the opposite sex to participate. Young and old, male and female link their hands, side by side, in a human chain and move sideways around the dance floor. There are about a dozen bands on each coast whose efforts at creating new music are insignificant. Overall, there is a limited market for these ethnic musicians; almost none of them can survive on the sale of their cassettes and live performances alone.

Nonetheless, the numbers of Armenian educational institutions, newspapers, and radio and television programs in the United States are not negligible. In a study of the community resources of ethnic languages, Fishman and his colleagues (1985, 204) found that Armenian press, radio, television, schools, and churches are proportionately overrepresented compared to other ethnic or religious groups, given the demographics of people of Armenian descent living in the United States. Fishman explains this institutional overrepresentation (in contrast to populational representation) by the ethno-religious nature of Armenian ethnicity in America as follows: "Obviously, their language institutions are maintained by multiple boundaries. But it is the *strength* of boundaries vis-à-vis mainstream society rather than their *number* that is crucial" (Fishman 1985, 269; emphasis in original). Fishman further argues that the need to teach the liturgical/ecclesiastic language to the next generation leads organizations (including churches) to sponsor supplementary schools.

Supplementary forms of ethnic socialization such as Saturday schools, Sunday schools, summer camps, and college courses both in the United States and abroad are more acceptable. The undergraduate courses also serve as a recruiting and training ground for future leaders of the community. The chairs for Armenian studies and research centers serve somewhat different functions. As "knowledge banks" their role is to document, codify, and translate Armenian culture and history and enhance its status in the eyes of symbolic Armenian-Americans and more importantly, the Western world. Remnants of both the high culture and popular culture of the past are salvaged and lodged in museums. Family heirlooms are similarly displayed prominently in one's home. An illuminated manuscript, an ancient coin, a rug with Armenian lettering, grandmother's lace doilies, or some old photographs provide Armenian-Americans with pride and roots. Even the Armenian alphabet becomes a symbolic marker that delineates insiders from outsiders. Its original function displaced, the alphabet is more likely to be worn or hung on a wall.

Social critics have argued that in an effort to preserve the past, the Armenian cultural heritage in America is being "fixed" to traditional forms and symbols, thus excluding the possibility of change and development and failing to recognize the overwhelming majority of talented and creative Armenian-Americans. Alice Scourby, in her analysis of the Greek community in America, provides clues as to why first-generation ethnics tend to be fixated with the past. She writes: "In order to relieve the pressure of rejection and the subsequent feelings of inferiority, the immigrant overidentified with the Old World customs and traditions. The Old World's style of life became the only stabilizing pattern. Any deviations, by either himself or his children became a threat to his identity" (1980,14-15).

Ancient forms in architecture, visual arts, even crafts are repeatedly copied instead of being inspirational elements of cultural continuity in new creations. It is surmised that the Armenian-American culture, instead of being alive and vibrant, is believed to be a "dead" culture. Furthermore, it has been suggested that the Armenian-American communal structures work on the centrifugal principle, throwing out all talented, creative individuals from their core.[45] In other words, the community holds narrow parameters of what Armenian culture entails. Artists too have said that they feel suffocated; intellectually, if they become too immersed in the community and financially, if they rely upon it for patronage. Yet, these critics are partly correct.

The devotion of the second-generation Armenian-Americans to the "Turkified" style of music is similar to their effort at preserving other aspects of their ancestral heritage in "knowledge banks." They cherish the music because they have inherited it from their parents and grandparents and because they associate it with childhood memories and warm family atmospheres. Likewise, when building an Armenian church in the United States, Armenian-Americans insist on the conical dome, the architectural trademark. In a similar vein, those who insist on traditional definitions of Armenianness tend to exclude the works of American-born authors like William Saroyan, Peter Najarian, Diana Der Hovanessian, Nancy Kricorian because they were not originally published in Armenian. They refuse to see that their spirit and the essence of their writings is Armenian.

The critics, however, seem to miss the broader picture. They tend to disregard the attractiveness of the dominant American society and its overpowering capacity to absorb talented individuals, artists, architects, musicians, among many others. Those who venture beyond the confines of the Armenian-American community have the opportunity to reap significantly greater rewards. In many respects, symbolic Armenianness encourages, even expects that leap because it is believed that the individual's success can be shared by the ethnic group, however vicariously. The Armenian-American community reclaims its sons and daughters who have "made it" in the mainstream. When Eric Boghosian's talent as a comedian became known, several voluntary associations in New York invited him to appear as a guest speaker on their programs. Similarly, when Ruth Zakarian (alias actress Devon Pierce on the soap opera "The Young and the Restless") became Miss Teen U.S.A. in 1983, she was courted by numerous Armenian organizations to appear at their banquets or dinner dances.[46]

The quantitative and qualitative data presented here demonstrate that there is a generational decrease in maintenance of traditional Armenian culture; less people read Armenian literature; buy art objects made by Armenians; and receive Armenian newspapers, magazines, and newsletters; and it is assumed that even fewer people read such publications. They are also less likely to listen to Armenian radio, let alone attend concerts by popular Armenian singers or buy their cassettes. The art forms that use the ancestral language—poetry, fiction, nonfiction, lyrics, etc.—are most likely to become the first victims. In the final analysis, the Armenian-American community is not a speech community; if it is to survive it cannot afford to alienate those who do not speak Armenian.

Notes

1. The poem is quoted by Nicole E. Vartanian in her article "Language as a Gift of Life," in *Armenian Reporter*, 29 November 1990, p. 4 and 6 December 1990, p. 5.
2. It should be noted that two additional letters have been added to the alphabet, totalling thirty-eight at the present time.
3. To mention but a few examples: a symposium was organized by the Bay Area Professional Society in November 1988, on "Armenian Day Schools: Prospects and Challenges" (transcripts of proceedings c/o Suzy Antounian, 2400 Broadway, San Francisco, CA 94115). A round-table was hosted by the Hairenik Association on 4 August 1990 in Watertown (proceedings published in "Armenian Day Schools: Where do We Go from Here?" *Armenian Weekly*, 18 August 1990, pp. 10-11, 14). Yet another panel discussion in Watertown was sponsored by the Tekeyan Cultural Association (in Armenian) on 26 October 1990, entitled: "The Role of Armenian Day Schools and Saturday Schools in the Preservation of Ethnicity." The Tekeyan Cultural Association also sponsored a panel discussion in New York City on 3 May 1991, entitled: "New York and New Jersey Armenian Schools: Problems and Prospects." See write up in *Armenian Reporter,* 23 May 1991, p. 7.
4. For example see "Are Armenian Schools Better?" *Armenian International Magazine* September 1990, p. 52. See also Pergrouhi Svajian, "Observations on Armenian Education — Parents and the Armenian School," *Armenian Reporter,* 6 September 1990, p. 1.
5. Being a foreign-born Armenian does not imply that one speaks, reads, and writes Armenian. There were several respondents whose ancestry was mixed. It should be noted that in certain regions of Turkey in the nineteenth century, Turkish was spoken at home. With the cultural renaissance in the latter part of the century, Armenian schools were established for boys and girls in most of the regions where Armenians lived. Thus, among the very old, it is possible to find Turkish-speaking people (sometimes exclusively so). Also the few Armenians who stayed in mainland Turkey after the Genocide had to speak Turkish to keep a low profile, and with the closing of Armenian schools their children never had a chance to learn the language of their ancestors. Many of those who had stayed behind on their ancestral lands eventually moved toward Istanbul in the 1960s and 1970s, and some of them subsequently immigrated to the United States.
6. There is a wide gap between spoken and nonspoken language retention, even among the foreign-born. Many Armenians born in Iran, Lebanon, Bulgaria,

Romania, and so on had their formal schooling in non-Armenian institutions, though at home they spoke Armenian. For example, Claudia Der-Martirosian (1989) found that among the 195 Iranian Armenian households she surveyed in Los Angeles in the late 1980s, 97 percent spoke Armenian while growing up between the ages of seven and eighteen. However, only 37 percent said they wrote Armenian most comfortably, and 21 percent said they read Armenian most often.

7. Nelson (1953), in a study of the Armenian family in Fresno (CA), found that most children raised before the 1930s spoke only Armenian before going to school.

8. See Mary Ann Aposhian. "Clinging to Ethnic Heritage in America: Study Compares Extent of Assimilation between Earlier Generation, New Arrivals." *Armenian International Magazine,* February 1991, pp. 33-36.

9. All questionnaires in the New York study were answered in English, except for four completed over the phone in Armenian.

10. Margaret Mead suggested once that Armenian be used as an international language at the United Nations (see Pattie 1990, 269 n. 9).

11. The few exceptions, whether in Cyprus, Beirut, Aleppo, or Cairo were maids or apprentices who worked for Armenians. In Fresno too, several Chinese immigrants learned Armenian when they worked for Armenian bosses in the early part of the century.

12. Nicole E. Vartanian, "Language as the Gift of Life: Keeping the Armenian Language Alive in America," *Armenian Reporter,* 29 November 1990, p. 4.

13. Such a Khatchkar rug commemorating the seventy-fifth anniversary of the Genocide is being marketed for $630. It is handmade of wool, measuring 2' 6" x 4', has Armenian inscriptions (see ad in *Armenian International Magazine,* November 1990, p. 15).

14. To illustrate, *Armenian International Magazine's* November 1990 issue (p. 43) carried such ads entitled: "Armenian International Magazine Christmas Mart." Included are magic Armenian letters, [historical] map puzzle for children, durable two-sided wooden lettering blocks, and Mashtots Armenian lettering stencil. On the same page are other typically symbolic items: an Armenian cookbook, and prints of landscapes and still-life paintings of Armenian-American artist Manual Tolegian.

15. It is worth noting that it is hard to maintain a distinctive language in any diaspora. Samuelian (1986, 87) writes: "it appears that it is not much easier to maintain Armenian as a second language in the Armenian Diaspora of the Soviet Union than in the Diaspora outside of the Soviet Union."

16. During my visit to Los Angeles in April 1990, I sat in at a bilingual class at Le Conte Junior High School in Hollywood. For students with limited English proficiency even American history is taught in Armenian!

17. In the 1980s, during Ordjanian's field work (1991, 111), parents of the non-Armenian students described themselves as: English, German, Greek, (East) Indian, Italian, Irish, Native American Indian, Dutch, Polish, Scottish, Slav, or a combination of these.

18. See *Armenian Day Schools: Prospects and Challenges,* a symposium sponsored by the Bay Area Armenian Professional Society (c/o Suzy Antounian, 2400 Broadway, San Francisco, CA 94115), November 1988, p.17.

19. Arkun (1987) found that eleven full-time Armenian schools mushroomed in the

Los Angeles area in the last twenty-five years. To repeat, very little is known about the academic quality of these schools and their effectiveness in ethnicity maintenance.

20. Raffi Shoubookian, "Back to School: Caught between Rising Tuition Costs and Armenianism, Parents Face a Difficult Choice," *Armenian International Magazine,* September 1990, pp. 44-45.

21. Unpublished paper by Glendale Unified School District, Language Census Report, Spring 1990.

22. See *Journal of Armenian Studies* 2 (Spring/Summer 1985).

23. The list includes among others: NAASR (which organizes conferences, sponsors exhibits, maintains a reference and research library, offers the Armenian book clearing house, publishes popular and scholarly works, etc.); the Zoryan Institute (see chap. 2); the Center for Armenian Research and Publication at the University of Michigan, Dearborn; the Krikor and Clara Zohrab Information Center of the Diocese of the Armenian Church (New York).

24. There are at present eight occupied chairs for Armenian studies in the United States; one each at Harvard and Columbia, two at University of California, Los Angeles, two at University of Michigan at Ann Arbor, one at California State University, Fresno, and the most recent one at Tufts University.

25. For example, the Society for Armenian Studies is an institutional member of the Middle East Studies Association (MESA). It sponsors several panels at MESA annual conferences. It publishes a newsletter (semi-annually) and the award-winning *Journal of the Society of Armenian Studies* (annually) with a circulation of 500 each. Its 1991 "Roster of Members" lists 191 entries, though according to Richard G. Havannisian, in his Chairman's Midyear Report (30 July 1991) only 125 have paid dues ($25 per year) and are in good standing.

26. Intensive summer courses (five levels of competency) are offered at the University of Venice and taught by Mekhitarist fathers from their nearby monastery at St. Lazaro. See *NAASR Newsletter* 7, 1-2 (Winter/Spring 1991): 6.

27. Yerevan Summer Institute is administered by the University of Michigan Armenian Studies Program and sponsored by AGBU. Students meet four hours a day, five days a week to earn eight credits. They also get the chance to discover Armenia. As one student who participated in the program in 1990 said: "The Institute provides an opportunity to become skilled in speaking, reading, and writing Armenian in a relatively short time, and to sample the richness of all aspects of Armenian culture — its art, religion, history, music, dance and more" ("Yerevan Institute Offers Language Study and More to 17 Students," *News from AGBU, Armenia-Aid,* February 1991, p.8; see also "AGBU Language Instruction Program in Yerevan," *Armenian Reporter,* 8 September 1988).

28. For example see "ACYOA Armenian Summer Studies Program," *Armenian Church* 2, 7 (August 1988). Another program was sponsored by AREC and held at the campus of the University of Hartford (CT), see "Armenian Summer Language Intensive For Teens Concludes," *Armenian Reporter,* 20 September 1990, p. 7. The Mekhitarist fathers have initiated a month-long summer Armenology course in Los Angeles. Classes include "language instruction in Classical Armenian as well as Modern, History of the Armenian People, History of Armenian Art, Communities, Commerce, Philosophy, Theater, Medicine, Monarchism, Spirituality, Church Liturgy, Canon Law, etc." (*Armenian Reporter,* 16 May 1991, p. 13).

29. The Siamanto Academy established in 1980, sponsored by the Armenian Religious Educational Council of the Prelacy of the Armenian Apostolic Church (AREC) and the Armenian Relief Society is designed to prepare future leaders for the community. Highly motivated and academically successful high school students take courses in Armenian language, history, literature, etc. The program is accredited as a college-level course in a number of universities and colleges in the United States. Upon graduation, students are eligible for six credits in history and three in literature. In 1990 the program had twenty-six students. Moreover, a preparatory division was instituted recently for junior high school students (see the *Armenian Reporter,* 13 September 1990, p. 5).

30. This organization has been in existence in the United States since 1986. It started as a modest grass-roots experiment in France in 1978. Young Armenian-American men and women have already completed the restoration of an old church in Kessab, Syria. Since the earthquake, they have been working on projects in Armenia. See full-page advertisement in *Armenian International Magazine,* February 1991, p. 23.

31. Project SAVE is yet another example of a knowledge bank. It is a photographic archive on Armenian life. It was started in the mid-1970s by Ruth Thomasian in Watertown (MA). Its mission is "to collect and document photographs of people and places in Historic Armenia and the diaspora. . . . Project SAVE has become a facilitator in connecting generations. Older Armenian-Americans have the chance to verbalize their past as well as preserve it visually with their photographs, and younger generations now have access to this source of information about their background. In a society with such ethnic and cultural diversity, it is extremely important for people to understand their own heritage" (from Project SAVE 1991 Calendar).

32. It is noteworthy that after 1928 all Armenian weddings in Fresno were preceded by a shower (Nelson 1953, 201).

33. Reading about traditional wedding ceremonies seems foreign and strange to most Armenians today. For example, see Fr. Arten Ashjian, "Armenian Weddings of Bygone Days," *Armenian Reporter,* 31 October 1985, p. 3.

34. See Lemyel Amirian, "Notes in Transit: Armenian Hospitality," *Armenian Reporter,* 7 August 1986, p. 2. The writer notes that traditionally, for Armenians, hospitality was paramount. The term "a guest is a king in my house" was used to describe this value. By contrast, he continues; "the Americanized or Europeanized Armenians won't ask you to their home . . . for fear they'll have to offer you a glass of water."

35. One of my interviewees suggested the word *namous* for family honor. The term was coined for a novel by A. Shirvanzade (1858-1935), a Caucasian-Armenian literary figure, which he himself borrowed from Arabic and Turkish. In 1925, the popular novel was adapted by Bek-Nazarian to the cinema. The movie was entitled: *Namous.* Mouradian (1990, 45, 57) argues that the Soviet system used cinema to preach modernism and denounce the excesses of the patriarchal family. It is the story of a young potter who is promised to the daughter of the tailor. Discovering that the young lovers are impatient, the tailor gives his daughter to the merchant Rostom. The latter, upon finding out the real story, kills the young woman; and the potter commits suicide. Interestingly, the audiences did not react to the film in the way that the Soviet authorities had expected. Instead of denigrating the cruel customs of the past, they felt very proud. The film

represented their own lives. The issue here is, to what extent does the concept of family honor prevail in the Armenian community of the United States at present? Murder and suicide are highly unlikely to ensue from premarital relations these days. However, the double standard of morality that condones sexual permissiveness in males, and condemns it in females still lingers on.

36. One of the dailies is *Hairenik,* the longest running Armenian language paper in the United States. The other is *Asbarez,* a bilingual paper established in Fresno in 1908, but now operating out of Los Angeles.

37. These are (in alphabetical order): (1) *Baikar* - weekly (Ramgavar party) published in Watertown since 1922; (2) *Eritassard Hayastan* - monthly (Hunchag party) published in Paramus (NJ) since 1903 with a circulation of 1,000; (3) *Hairenik* - daily (Tashnag party) published since 1899 in Watertown with a circulation of 2,000; (4) *Massis* - weekly (Hunchag party) published in Pasadena with a circulation of 1,000; (5) *Nor Or* - biweekly (Ramgavar party) published since 1922 in Altadena with a circulation of 2,500. The only nonpartisan Armenian language paper is *Paros,* a biweekly established in 1984 in North Hollywood. The political parties also have their English-language weekly newspapers: The *Armenian Mirror Spectator* (Ramgavar) published since 1932 in Watertown; and the *Armenian Weekly* (Tashnag) published since 1933 also in Watertown.

38. Anecdotally, I was told that Arshile Gorky once gave one of his paintings to an Armenian charity in Massachusetts. It was auctioned at $7.50, much to Gorky's outrage.

39. For example see the *Armenian Reporter,* 10 April 1986, pp. 18-19; and article by Larry Gordon of the *Los Angeles Times* reprinted in the *Armenian Reporter,* 28 August 1986, "Legal Dispute and Competition between Two Armenian Language Weeklies Draws Attention of Local American Press." For parallels with the Polish community in America see Sandberg (1974, 28).

40. The Armenian press is also self-serving and not a "free press." The political and ideological leanings of a given paper seem to make it color-blind to the weaknesses and faults of its leadership, organizations, and membership. One critic has likened this to the *Washington Post* reporting information by publishing the press releases of the White House or other federal agencies. This lack of reliability and intellectual integrity of the Armenian press is a consequence of the chauvinism and parochialism of communal life. See Jack Antreassian, "The Community and You," *Armenian Church,* 4, 5 (May 1990) and 4, 6 (June 1990); and "Armenian Print Media: A Blessing and an Embarrassment," *Armenian International Magazine,* November 1990, p. 52.

41. Personal communication with Gerard Libaridian, director of The Zoryan Institute for Contemporary Armenian Research and Documentation, Inc., Cambridge (MA). See also Moskos (1989, 80) for similarities with Greek press.

42. The May 1991 issue of *Armenian International Magazine* reports (p. 23) that since July 1986, Worcester has an "Armenian Heritage Program." It airs on Sundays between nine and eleven in the evening. Its producer is also foreign-born.

43. Indeed, it is hard to define what "pure" Armenian music is, or should be, when Armenian culture was influenced by 400 years of Ottoman subjugation. Politically conscious and nationalist elements in Soviet Armenia and the diaspora have tried to "clean" Armenian music of Turkish influence, the same way the

nineteenth-century Armenian literary and cultural renaissance established schools, published books, etc., teaching to a new generation their "mother tongue" as their parents spoke predominantly Turkish. As the Republic of Armenia becomes the center for diasporan life and culture, it is expected that it will have a stronger voice in deciding what type of music will be produced. However, in the United States, Armenian-Americans will reserve the right to choose what is best suited for them.

44. See "An Ongoing Debate: What is the Authentic Music, Dancing?" *Armenian Reporter,* 15 January 1987, p. 3.
45. The analogy of the centrifugal system was discussed by Gerard Libaridian at a seminar sponsored by The Zoryan Institute in their Open University Seminar series, on 21 March 1987 at Columbia University, New York.
46. See *Armenian International Magazine,* June 1991, pp. 30-31.

5

Sources of Identity

It is the contention of this study that the assimilation of Armenian immigrants in the United States proceeds hand in hand with changes in the nature of Armenianness. Behavioral and attitudinal changes characterize the transition from traditional to symbolic Armenianness. The evidence presented in the previous chapters demonstrates that with later generational status, with mixed ancestry, with non-Armenian religious affiliation men and women of Armenian descent in the United States are less and less likely to speak the ancestral language, attend services in their grandparents' church, participate in communally hosted programs and activities, become members of voluntary associations, and find ethnic politics very meaningful. Yet repeatedly, the data also showed that identification, sense of peoplehood, and pride in one's ancestral roots do not wane with the passage of generations, intermarriage, and religious conversion as quickly as other aspects of traditional Armenianness. What explains these differences? I argue that while the behavioral components of Armenianness are typical of the traditional form, the emotional components exemplify, *par excel-*

lence, the symbolic. Here, I explore sources that nourish, replenish, and energize Armenian identity in the United States.

The Making of Hyphenated Americans

When immigrant groups settle in America, the world they had taken for granted is shattered. Their new neighbors and hosts question their identity. "Who are you?" they ask. The self-identification labels they had used prior to immigration are often irrelevant in their new environment. They have to redefine themselves by new self-placement tags. For this, they need to use categories that are readily understood in their host society over and above those that reflect their place of origin and historical roots. Through this process of self-identification, immigrant groups become "ethnics" or hyphenated Americans (Greeley 1974, 301-2). In the United States, this dual identity is not denied, but encouraged (De Vos and Romanucci-Ross 1982, 378). Initially, processes of ethnicization take place alongside processes of acculturation. For example, post-1965 Armenian immigrants from Romania had to get accustomed to the already existing Armenian community that welcomed them upon their arrival and identify themselves as Armenian-Americans. All along, they had to adjust to the larger American society and learn to function effectively in its economic, political, and social systems.

In the long run, the straight-line assimilation theory posits that following cultural, structural, and marital assimilation, the ethnic component of self-identity will be relinquished. That is achieved when an individual develops a "sense of peoplehood based exclusively on host society" (Gordon 1964, 71; see also Shibutani and Kwan 1965, 479, 505). It is important to distinguish between individual and group changes in ethnic identity. Some individuals may identify themselves as "American" as early as the first generation. However, it takes a group several generations for the majority of its members to identity themselves as American. Estimating the number of generations necessary for a group to be fully assimilated is a tricky issue. As discussed in chapter 1, several variables related to the internal dynamics of the group and the external environment influence the outcome. Some groups may be arrested or almost arrested at the symbolic phase forever. A few groups, like the Hasidim, remain traditional by choice.

Ethnic identity is an extension of Cooley's concept of "looking glass self." The self is a social product. It is a subjective consciousness developed during early socialization as the child realizes a sense of "I /Me" in contrast to others. Initially, the child acquires this sense of self through imitation and role-playing. Positive evaluation and feedback of his/her behavior by significant others are reflected back through verbal and nonverbal cues. These result in a strong sense of self and feelings of pride. Neglect or negative sanctions, on the other hand, produce feelings of self-mortification. Next, the child takes the roles of generalized others; the notion of self is expanded to include a collectivity. We-feelings are likewise nurtured by comparison to an out-group. The "I/We" is rooted in the past, connected to the individual's and group's history (Cooley 1983).

The social self is a dynamic and flexible mechanism. It is transformed or transmuted contingent on its real or fantasized reference groups. Moreover, the image of self that is projected to others is negotiated and achieved by impression management. Individuals inhabit a multiplicity of social worlds separated by cognitive boundaries, each world having its own rules and communication channels. An ethnic environment is one of several past-oriented[1] social worlds that people may occupy. Citizenship in a political state, membership in a religious congregation, affiliations to professional or occupational groups and class loyalties are some of the other social worlds people have access to.

Ethnic identity is buttressed by two principles that legitimize a sense of belonging to a social entity (De Vos and Romanucci-Ross 1982, 364-71). First, are myths of origin, traditions that provide a scripted continuity between the past and the future. Through one's parents, individuals trace their genealogy and bind the generations to a common ancestor. Shared origins of a collectivity establish an individual's rights and responsibilities toward the group, direct one's loyalties and affections to the in-group, and vent one's aggression to the out-group. In essence, ethnic identity is a kind of moral commitment to "personal survival in the historical continuity of the group" (De Vos and Romanucci-Ross 1982, 17). Second, ethnic identity specifies rules of comportment. It highlights the behavior of insiders in contrast to that of outsiders. Group expectations reinforce "correct" behavior by social sanctions that reward those who comply and punish, even ostracize, those who deviate from the norms. Ideally, recruitment to an ethnic group is by birth *and* socialization; however, one aspect may be emphasized more than the other at different times and in different places in a group's history. Criteria that determine exclusion or inclusion in an ethnic group are altered by expanding or restricting ethnic boundaries. For example, ethnic identity may be inherited bilineally or unilineally.[2] Code of conduct may be demanding and strictly sanctioned or it may be fluid and enforcement lax, allowing for greater compliance or variation in behavior.

In the United States, immigrants, their children, and grandchildren have a choice in their presentation of self from a range of identities; at one end is traditional identity, at the other "American" identity, and in between are hyphenated combinations. Traditional ethnic identity is qualitatively different from that of later-generation hyphenated identities. I hypothesize that traditional ethnic identity tends to be more salient or central to one's concept of self. It permeates most of the roles one routinely engages in during the course of one's daily life. Furthermore, one's role attachment to being ethnic or one's emotional involvement in ethnicity tends to be stronger. Because the "stakes" are higher, the individual is more likely to be more committed to his/her ethnic background. In other words, traditional ethnic identity is a master status; it is at the core of one's economic, social, and even physical survival as an individual.

In the United States of America, membership in ethnic groups is optional, and group boundaries are permeable (mostly outwards). Ethnic identity is achieved in competition (or through lack of it) with other interests and allegiances in people's lives. In contrast to traditional ethnic identity, symbolic identity tends to be less central to one's conception of self. Symbolic or emblematic identity is described with malleable "ego boundaries" adaptable to almost any situation or context (Barth 1969). It is activated or muted, expanded or contracted, both collectively and individually, whenever the situation or interpersonal encounter warrants one or the other reaction. "Passing" behavior, identity switching, alter-casting,[3] maintaining a facade, name changes are part of the vocabulary of adaptive, contextual ethnicity.

Opportunities for manipulating ethnic identities are not infinite. According to Lyman and Douglas (1973, 351-54) there are five kinds of structural and personal constraints on ethnic impression management. First, inasmuch as skin color cannot be changed and accents are hard to lose, there are limits on "passing" behavior. Second, ethnicity is not the only aspect of self. In certain situations ethnicity is irrelevant, or subordinate to other attributes of self. At times, one's gender identity or socioeconomic status may be more significant. Third, because of differentiation, compartmentalization, and specificity in modern life, individuals do not have to project a coherent image of themselves at all times. Inconsistencies in identity and behavior allow actors to portray one aspect of self to one audience without jeopardizing another. Fourth, in plural societies ignorance, stereotyping, and restrictive repertoires about other ethnic groups and the host society are common. Ethnic (minority) groups are at a disadvantage because their early socialization does not equip them with a thorough knowledge of the dominant culture, or other ethnic groups for that matter. Thus, they are unable to manipulate identities to maximize their gains. Finally, individual actors may lack the skills or mental requisites to enact a presentation of self different from the one they were socialized into.

The development of Armenian-American identity follows the same processes. First, one can be an Armenian by nature, substance, genealogy, or blood; that is, one is born *Hye* (term used by insiders for Armenian) in opposition to *odar* (foreigner, outsider); *Hye* and *odar* being two mutually exclusive terms. Second, one can be an Armenian by following a code of behavior; by learning and using the Armenian language; attending Armenian church; caring for family members; or sharing common sentiments such as the importance of the family, homeland, and hatred of the Turks. In her analysis of Armenian-Americans in Washington, DC, O'Grady argues that the community perceives intermarriage as inevitable and the Armenian "substance" endangered by dilution. Therefore, she says, the community is trying to expand and alter the rules of relevance of who is entitled to be an Armenian (O'Grady 1979, 119-123).

The emphasis is shifting from concepts of origin to a code of conduct. That is, non-Armenian spouses are being increasingly welcomed into the community. Moreover, tracing descent bilineally is becoming more and more acceptable. For example, children of mixed ancestry are awarded scholarships and other grants irrespective of whether the father or mother is of Armenian descent. Traditionally, Armenians traced descent patrilineally, and the few non-Armenian wives who married into the Armenian community remained *odars* even though they had to be resocialized into the husband's culture. They had to learn the language, the norms and values, and the small and great traditions alike. On the other hand, if on rare occasions an Armenian woman married outside her congenital community, she was considered lost.

Demographically, the proportion of people who are one-half, one-fourth, one-eighth, or one-sixteenth Armenian will increase exponentially to become eventually a majority of the universe of people of Armenian descent in America. Definitions of Armenianness cannot but be set in very flexible terms; descent will have to be bilineal and code of conduct very fluid. At the collective level, whoever defines Armenianness will have to accept an emblematic identity with a multitude of individualistic interpretations and expressions. Empirical evidence suggests that white ethnic communities in the United States such as the Jews, Greeks, and Italians more and more are accepting intermarried people in their midst. Despite O'Grady's observations above, I find Armenian-Americans have been slower to follow suit. Because of the large influx of new immigrants in recent decades, Armenian institutional structures have, as yet, not felt the void left by the alienation of the intermarried and the assimilated from the community.

Individuals who are not Armenian by blood or marriage are not considered for recruitment into the Armenian Apostolic church or the institutionalized community. One hears occasionally of complete outsiders who became members of the Armenian Apostolic church. Aharonian (1983) mentions such an example and suggests that church doors be opened to all people who want to join, irrespective of descent or marital ties. Recently, another example appeared in the ethnic press. David Luhrssen, a non-Armenian by blood or marriage, had written a short essay explaining why he became a member of St John the Baptist Armenian Church of Greenfield (WI).[4] These are truly rare examples. My interviews with clerics and community leaders suggest that neither the church nor the community, at the present time, are considering the inclusion of *odars* as a technique for increasing the church's congregation. Public debates in Armenian newspapers over the controversial presidency of a non-Armenian spouse as head of the largest Armenian philanthropic organization in America illustrate that even the acceptance of *odar* spouses in influential leadership positions is still not totally acceptable.[5]

Self-identification of New York Respondents

New York respondents were asked: "How do you think of yourself?" Surprisingly only 8.4 percent of the sample said they were "American"[6] 18 percent said they were "Armenian" and the rest gave hyphenated labels to identify themselves. The majority of the sample (64.3 percent) were "American-Armenians" (N = 583). This figure includes 3.1 percent who said they were "Armenian-Americans" and a very small proportion of respondents (.9 percent) who said they were of Armenian descent. I have used the title "Diaspora-Armenians" to describe 9.3 percent of the sample who as foreign-born respondents continued to identify with their place of birth. Diaspora-Armenians include Istanbul/Turkish-Armenians (2.6 percent), Iranian-Armenians (2.1 percent), Lebanese-Armenians (2.1 percent), Syrian-Armenians (.5 percent), French-Armenians (.5 percent), Bulgarian-Armenians (.3 percent), Jerusalem-Armenians (.3 percent), Soviet-Armenians (.3 percent), Latin American-Armenians (.3 percent), and Egyptian-Armenians (.2 percent). It should be noted that even those who identified themselves as American did not deny their Armenian roots

TABLE 5.1
Frequency Distribution of Self-Described Identity by Generation

	Foreign-Born	U.S.-Born of F.B. Parents	1 Parent U.S.-Born	2 Parents U.S.-Born	Grandparent U.S.-Born
N = 583	(219)	(272)	(36)	(40)	(16)
Armenian	37.0	5.9	13.9	5.0	6.3
Armenian-American	38.4	82.7	72.2	72.5	68.8
Diasporan-Armenian	22.4	1.8	0.0	0.0	0.0
American	2.3	9.6	13.9	22.5	25.0
	100.0	100.0	100.0	100.0	100.0

because participation in this study automatically assumed that respondents recognized their Armenian descent.

Even though with each passing generation there is a straight-line increase in the proportion of people who identify as American, the association between generation and identity is not statistically very significant (see table 5.1). Approximately, 70 percent of third- and later-generation respondents continue to identify as Armenian-Americans. On the other hand, ancestry and religious affiliation were somewhat more significantly related to self-described identity (tau c .10* for both). Mixed ancestry increases seven times the number of those who identify as American (5 percent versus 35 percent for those with one Armenian parent; see table 5.2). Those with "other" and no religion were least likely to say they were Armenian, and most likely to say they were American (see table 5.3). Yet, about 65 percent of

TABLE 5.2
Frequency Distribution of Self-Described Identity by Ancestry

	Both Parents Armenian	One Parent Armenian
N = 583	(517)	(66)
Armenian	18.8	12.1
Armenian-American	66.7	45.5
Diasporan-Armenian	9.5	7.6
American	5.0	34.8
	100.0	100.0

TABLE 5.3
Frequency Distribution of Self-Described Identity by Religious Affiliation

	Apostolic Armenian	Protestant Armenian	Catholic Armenian	Other (Non-Arm.)	No Religion
N = 575	(370)	(56)	(22)	(92)	(35)
Armenian	21.4	19.6	13.6	7.6	5.7
Armenian-American	65.1	62.5	59.1	66.3	65.7
Diasporan-Armenian	10.3	8.9	22.7	3.3	5.7
American	3.2	8.9	4.5	22.8	22.9
	100.0	100.0	100.0	100.0	100.0

those with mixed ancestry and nonethnic religious persuasions continue to identify as Armenians or hyphenated Armenians.

Respondents were asked to agree or disagree with the statement: "You can be for your own people first and still be a good American." This view was most significantly associated with sympathy to ethnic politics, religious affiliation, and generational status (.11* for all three). Those who were indifferent to Armenian political parties and ideologies (see table 5.4), and those who had no religion and "other" religions (see table 5.5) were least likely to agree that people can have dual identities and allegiances. First- and second-generation respondents tended to agree somewhat more that a person could be a good Armenian and a good American (see table 5.6). Again, the overall differences were minor. The question is: Why does Armenian identity defy the theoretical assumptions of Milton Gordon and others? How can these results be interpreted?

Reasons for Persistence of Ethnic Identity

The results of the New York sample are corroborated with other studies.[7] In a study of ethnic identification using national samples of native-born whites, Alba and Chamlin (1983) found that contrary to common assumptions, ethnic identification remained relatively high with generation, age, higher educational status, and mixed ancestry. They further observed that people with mixed parentage have a tendency to identify with one group. Younger people, those with college education, and those living in large urban settings, show

TABLE 5.4

Frequency Distribution of Attitude Statement: "You Can Be for Your Own People First and Still Be a Good American" by Sympathy to Ethnic Politics

	Anti-Tashnag	Tashnag	Neutral	Indifferent	Rejects Parties
N = 523	(32)	(109)	(141)	(173)	(68)
Agree	96.9	82.6	85.8	61.8	66.2
No opinion	0.0	2.8	2.8	11.6	4.4
Disagree	3.1	14.7	11.3	26.6	29.4
	100.0	100.0	100.0	100.0	100.0

surprising rates of identification with one background in spite of their mixed or ambiguous ancestry. This phenomenon is likewise typified by the comments of one of the New York respondents; a thirty-four-year-old, fourth-generation woman whose father is Armenian-Assyrian and mother German-English, who wrote: "I am only 1/4 Armenian, however I do tend to identify myself as an Armenian-American." Alba and Chamlin explain, "ethnic identifications remain salient in an era when increasing numbers of Americans have mixed ancestry (and many others have intermarried). In part, ethnic identification may remain an issue, even for the socially assimilated, insofar as ethnic differentiation remains a prominent axis of social life" (1983, 246).

Another survey conducted in Boston and Kansas City found that most people could trace their ancestry back several generations; however, Catholics, those from lower classes, and those living in lower-status neighborhoods were most likely to identify as "all-around Americans" (Barthel 1978, 105). Many of those reluctant to specify an ethnic group, felt no pride in their background and uncomfortable with fellow ethnics. The dilemma in reconciling assimilation with ethnic identity and continuity is resolved with the allocating of the latter to the sidestream. Respondents in Boston and Kansas City overwhelmingly advocated the Melting Pot ideology, equating Americanism with melting to become better, stronger, united, less prejudiced. They felt that ethnic groups "should 'mix' yet retain a sense of their own background and a respect for that of others" (Barthel 1978, 101). The author goes on to say:

TABLE 5.5

Frequency Distribution of Attitude Statement: "You Can Be for Your Own People First and Still Be a Good American" by Religious Affiliation

	Anti-Tashnag	Tashnag	Neutral	Indifferent	Rejects Parties
N = 565	(364)	(55)	(22)	(89)	(35)
Agree	81.3	76.4	81.8	64.0	51.4
No opinion	4.1	5.5	9.1	9.0	11.4
Disagree	14.6	18.2	9.1	27.0	37.1
	100.0	100.0	100.0	100.0	100.0

Ethnic groups are taken as "good" for the individual, insofar as the identities they provide yield a certain sense of belonging and heritage. They are "good" for the country, insofar as they remain to remind us that we are a "nation of nations"—they are what has made America unique. Yet, they lead to prejudice and limit individual expression, and "bad" for the nation when they stress loyalty to the group and to what it can get from the system rather than stressing working together as Americans. In sum, we find a solid level of support for the melting pot ideology and a distrust for any social movement or philosophy that could lead to an intensification of ethnic group identification. (Barthel 1978, 108)

What explains the durability of identification with one ethnic group? The results of the New York study have repeatedly demonstrated that there is no real revival in behavioral forms, as they amply illustrate that symbolic Armenianness is most acceptable in the sidestream. Armenians, like the majority of the white immigrant groups that arrived to the United States at the turn of the century, are no longer poor, barely literate peasants. They no longer live in inner-city ghettos, occupy working-class positions, and feel politically insecure. Additionally, the post-World War II immigrants have not significantly set back the progress already achieved by their predecessors. It is too early to tell what the most recent refugees from Soviet Armenia will do. Therefore, men and women of Armenian descent are not likely to deny their identity nowadays. Armenianness is easier, safer, and more attractive than in the early part of this century. Empirical evidence from other studies concurs that ethnic identity is stronger among groups that are sufficiently secure in their socioeconomic position, with still relatively low proportions of intermarried (such as the Armenians). Economically comfortable

TABLE 5.6
Frequency Distribution of Attitude Statement: "You Can Be for Your Own People First and Still Be a Good American" by Generation

	Foreign-Born	U.S.-Born of F.B. Parents	1 Parent U.S.-Born	2 Parents U.S.-Born	Grandparent U.S.-Born
N = 572	(214)	(265)	(36)	(41)	(16)
Agree	84.1	74.0	50.0	70.7	68.8
No opinion	3.3	6.4	8.3	7.3	18.8
Disagree	12.6	19.6	41.7	22.0	12.5
	100.0	100.0	100.0	100.0	100.0

ethnic groups have the best of both worlds; they "enjoy the folkloric aspect of ethnicity while protecting against its more negative aspects" (Barthel 1978, 110).

What are the functions of ethnic identity for later generations? A study of seven groups in Winnipeg, Canada, suggests that people have a psychosocial need to identify with either their ethnic group or the host society, depending on whether they are from a minority or a majority group. Positive, sufficiently dynamic historical and cultural experiences will produce a well-rounded concept of self, while their absence (e.g., lack of institutional completeness for some ethnic groups) will lead to feelings of inferiority, of being restricted, of annoyance, discomfort, and a general sense of marginality (Driedger 1976). De Vos and Romanucci-Ross provide another explanation for identification with one ethnic background for individuals with mixed ancestry. They suggest that such people often choose the more exotic background in lieu of the host society's because

> this type of identity decision refers to the issues about a contemporary democratic sense of integrity reflected in a felt necessity to affirm rather than deny the less prestigious segment of one's ancestry. This sense of integrity runs counter to previous patterns which emphasized identification with one's more socially elevated ancestors—a common mode of tracing genealogies practiced in aristocratically oriented societies. (De Vos and Romanucci-Ross 1982, 378)

A recent study corroborates that individuals of mixed ancestries, sometimes having as many as eight ancestries, choose from their background the one ethnicity that is the most unusual or interesting. This gives them a chance to stand out in a crowd, to feel one in a thousand (Waters 1990, 154). Men and women with only one Armenian grandparent are in a similar position.

Armenian identity provides the descendants of the original immigrants the chance to feel affiliated with a smaller, often historically older, and culturally richer collectivity. In a way, it provides relief from the homogenizing forces of modern American society and the anonymity of the metropolis. Ethnicity adds "spice," "fun" and "color" to a "bland post-industrial existence" (Barthel 1978, 111). It also offers the opportunity for bonding with ready-made allies in instrumental and expressive encounters.[8] "It gives a sense of heritage and roots to a highly mobile population" (Barthel 1978, 111).

To illustrate how an individual's instrumental and expressive interpersonal relations with fellow ethnics is important in fostering confidence and goodwill or denial and marginality, here are the comments of two of the New York respondents. A thirty-year-old woman, who like her father is U.S.-born, in her anger and disappointment at the Armenian church and clergy regarding her marriage to a non-Armenian, said: "I am sick and tired of calling myself an Armenian, when in fact, I am but an *American* with Armenian roots." On the other hand, in spite of her identification as an American, another respondent, also female, similar in age and generational status wrote:

> I feel a strong connection to being Armenian, but it is not reflective of my responses on this survey. I feel it in my *spirit* and responses to the world around me. This is possibly because the richness culturally that I was exposed to as a child. I like being Armenian and have never received anything but positive reaction and reinforcement from people about it.
>
> I am not religious and do not seek out Armenians in the course of life, [but] I am interested in them and feel a trust and bond more easily. (Emphasis in original)

In addition to all the reasons already mentioned for identifying with an ethnic group in America, essentially beyond the third generation, insiders have suggested that unlike other white ethnic groups, people of Armenian descent have special reasons to hang onto their historical definition of self. Armenians as a nation managed to survive for thousands of years; they survived wars, famines, occupations, persecutions, deportations, a multitude of invaders. To culminate this turbulent history, they survived the Genocide at the hands of the Young Turk government at the turn of this century. It would therefore be a grave injustice to the past, if the continuity of this unique cultural heritage were terminated at this time of ease and opulence and in this country of opportunities. Furthermore, insiders argue that the precarious situation of the historical Armenian homeland, part of it in Turkish hands, and the other trying to achieve full independence from Soviet domination, places more responsibility on the Armenians of the diaspora to perpetuate the culture. I have heard several young, later-generation Armenian-Americans say that there is too much to give up: culture, history, the church. They would feel guilty in facing history if they severed the link with the past out of negligence. Rather, they feel it is their responsibility to impart this heritage to the next generation.[9]

How prevalent is this rationale among the Armenian-American population? It is hard to say; however, judging from the results of the New York study, this notion cannot be very popular or widespread.

In any case, there is a need for further research, especially among the intermarried and their children, for a better understanding of the intensity and forms of Armenian identity. Erikson, who was the first person to popularize the notion of identity, had similar thoughts several decades ago. He wrote: "[W]e begin to conceptualize matters of identity at the very time in history when they become a problem. For we do so as a country which attempts to make a super-identity out of all the identities imported by its constituent immigrants; and we do so at a time when rapidly increasing mechanization threatens these ... identities" (Erikson 1963, 285).

Qualitative Evidence

New York respondents wrote about the intensity of their Armenian identity and the forms it took. For example, three respondents (first and second generation) said they were "100 percent Armenian." While another wrote: "I am not an outwardly staunch Armenian, but I am Armenian—Westernized and well-educated" (professional male forty-seven, born in Iran, immigrated at age ten). Another forty-three-year-old woman (respondent and mother U.S.-born, married to a non-Armenian) said, "I've always been proud of my heritage and although I have not followed a strict Armenian upbringing in the rearing of my children, I have instilled in them, I believe, a sense of pride in the fact that they are *half* Armenian."

Two kinds of qualifiers were used by the respondents to describe their ties or connection to their ancestral culture and group. Some were mathematical concepts such as percentages or fractions, others were simple adjectives (staunch, strict). These subjective measures may or may not be matched by objective criteria. Similar to self-placements in social class terms, people's subjective perceptions about Armenianness are important inasmuch as they guide behavior.

Respondents wrote profusely about their identity. There were two common themes they reiterated, over and over again. First, they were immensely proud to be of Armenian descent. Second, they were overwhelmingly grateful to the United States of America. I begin with people's pride in their roots, in their ancestors. This was elicited directly from the love and respect they felt for their parents and grandparents. Here are some of their comments:

I'm proud of my parents and of being *Armenian!!* (female fifty-eight, second generation).

Our parents were proud of being Armenian and taught us to be proud of our heritage (female thirty, third generation).

As an American Armenian I have always felt very proud to repeat time and time again that I am an Armenian and in as much as I would have been very proud to marry one, being raised to believe that [as] Armenians, male or female, you also come first—type attitude prevailed through all our acquaintances of Armenian background. My grandparents, I am glad to say, left for me everything anyone could want, pride, joy and happiness. They all were victims in some form or fashion of the genocide.... May Armenians always be proud to say YES HYE EM! [I am Armenian] (female thirty-three, respondent and both parents U.S.-born).

I am proud to be an Armenian in America. I have raised my children in America and proud that I have raised them as Armenian speaking Armenians. And I have raised them with a religious background (male seventy-two, born Baghdad, came to the United States at age six).

We are Armenians and proud of our ethnicity (male eighty-three, born in Turkey, lived in Romania, came to America at age sixty-eight).

Even though the majority of the respondents claimed dual identity, the foreign-born were more likely to emphasize the Armenian part. On the other hand, the American-born stressed the American part. Irrespective of generation, respondents spared no words in praise of America. To illustrate, I quote:

I am an American—but also proud to be Armenian (female thirty-three, fourth generation).

I am very happy to have been born a United States citizen, but I am very proud of my Armenian heritage (female sixty-five, second generation).

We love Armenians, and we are very proud of our heritage, but we must never forget we are Americans (male forty-six, respondent and mother U.S.-born).

Armenian-American, since the Armenian part came first (1909) and the Americanization followed (1921). I have never liked the use of the hyphen. It fractures both identity and unity (male, born Greece).

I am proud to be an Armenian but I also love my adopted country, USA (male seventy-seven, born Soviet Armenia, came age forty-one).

We should remember and act Armenian but never forget that we are blessed by being Americans (male seventy-six, born Turkey, came age twenty-six).

I am very proud of being Armenian.... God Bless America. American first, Armenian second, but both are second to none (female forty-nine, second generation).

I am a first generation American Armenian [sic.]. All my early friends were sons of Irish, Italian, Jewish, German etc immigrants. Our household was Armenian in language and food but in every other way we were American and greatly proud of it. We were also fiercely proud of our Armenian blood. Best of both worlds. Always found nothing but high regard and respect for Armenians (male sixty, second generation).

Even though I have never hid my Armenian origins, I have been always proud to be one; I am an American by choice. I respect this country and feel it as my own. My loyalties are to the U.S.A. (male forty-one, born in Romania, came age twenty-one).

I am forever grateful to the U.S. for the safe haven it has provided my family and truly it has been a land of opportunity (female age eighty-five, born Turkey arrived at age seventeen).

The hypotheses of this study are supported by the comments above. First, Armenian identity is more central to the self-conception of traditional Armenians, most characteristic of the immigrant generation. Second, symbolic Armenians are not ashamed of their ancestral roots; on the contrary, they proudly declare their ancestral origins. Third, respondents affirm unconditionally their allegiance to the United States of America. As long as their Armenian loyalties do not come into conflict with their American status, they will be happy to carry on their Armenianness in the sidestream.

Ex-citizens and Ex-ethnics

Though reasons for the continued maintenance of Armenian identification of the New York respondents have been explored, there is still a need to explain the variability in their answers. This is best described by the concept of role exit proposed by Ebaugh (1988). It is the process of becoming an ex-citizen, an ex-ethnic. Ebaugh defines "the process of disengagement from a role that is central to one's self-identity and the reestablishment of an identity in a new role that takes into account one's ex-role constitutes the process ... [of] role exit"

(1988, 1). The ex-role is characterized by unique expectations and norms that relate to one's previous status. Being a non-member is different from being an ex-member of a group. A change in self-identity involves withdrawing physically and emotionally from rights and obligations of a given role but is also a process of incorporating past identifications into one's new identity. The experiences of immigrants fit the role-exit process.[10] The process of leaving one's country of birth, coming to America, learning a new language, acquiring a new reference group, shifting friendship networks, and, most important, presenting oneself with a new identity makes one an ex-citizen and opens the way to becoming a hyphenated American.

Ebaugh has found that there are four stages or "moments" in the process of role exit: first doubts, seeking alternatives, turning points (i.e., anticipatory socialization, role rehearsals, shifting reference groups) and creating ex-role identity. She finds that "the essential dilemma involved in the ex-role is the incongruity and tension that exists between self-definition and social expectations" (Ebaugh 1988, 150). However, the issue that is of concern in this process is that even when an ex-role is created, residuals, "remnants or leftovers" from the previous one remain and "cloud and impact on one's current one" (Ebaugh 1988, 174). Role residual is sometimes beneficial as in the case of immigrants adjusting to a new social world; an experience often perceived as humiliating. Holding onto their past identity provides immigrants with meaning, comfort, and strength. More specifically Ebaugh finds that role residual "helps in coping with the fears and uncertainties that the future holds while believing that one's present self is the same as it was in the past. Since that self dealt successfully with life's complexities, it can and will continue to do so" (1988, 174).

The role-exit process may take months or years, and for some people the cycle may never come to an end. I suggest that the empirical variability observed in ethnic identification is related to the successful resolution of the process of role exit, or lack of it, and the different degrees of role residuals one retains. The Armenian case somewhat complicates the issues because only a fraction of immigrants come from an Armenian state; the majority are citizens of other host nations. Becoming an ex-citizen of a previous host nation is easy, but embracing a new hyphenated identity is a different matter. To illustrate, here are the comments of a respondent (male professional sixty-two, born in Turkey, immigrated at age twenty-five):

> I do not think one has to be a hyphenated citizen of our country. In my view, being a U.S. citizen (which I am) does not diminish my feelings of being an Armenian. I was born as an Armenian and I will die as an Armenian. I chose to be an American citizen and I will exercise all my obligations—including love and respect—with great willingness and delight in my chosen country. Still, I do not wear two hats. I am and will ever be an Armenian of U.S. citizenship. I love each one equally well and hope never to be asked to choose between them.

Likewise, the nearly 10 percent of New York respondents who identified themselves as Lebanese-Armenian, Iranian-Armenian, etc., did not complete the role-exit process. They held onto their preemigration identities.

There is also another type of role exit one encounters in ethnic studies. When American-born men and women of ethnic descent, reared in the ethnic ghetto or community decide to exit from their ascribed status, they become ex-ethnics. Then, a more thorough identificational assimilation is completed. Ex-ethnics are most likely to identify themselves as American. These are in a minority in the New York sample basically because of the design of the study, though it is hypothesized that empirically ex-Armenians will become increasingly numerous. In sum, the process of role exit is equally applicable to the ethnicization process for early immigrants as it is for those who have completed their assimilation process.

In conclusion, the rate of people who claim Armenian descent in later generations and in spite of mixed ancestry is remarkably high compared to cultural, structural, and marital indicators of assimilation. Nonetheless, Armenian identity remains only an acceptance of Armenian heritage. It is doubtful that this emotional, expressive, verbal affiliation with a group will be translated into goal-oriented action. Moreover, the rates of those who claim American identity increase steadily, if slowly, with each succeeding generation.

Sense of Peoplehood

Closely following identity, sense of peoplehood or we-ness endures as the most popular expression of symbolic Armenian-Americans. What does sense of peoplehood imply? It involves a profusion of

feelings and sentiments toward others of Armenian descent: feelings
of affinity, of closeness, of belongingness, of group worth and esteem.
At home or abroad, when Armenian-Americans recognize an
Armenian name or person in movie credits, in the media, or on a
storefront, or hear the accomplishments of a man or woman of
Armenian descent who has gained prominence in the arts, in science,
in business, in politics, in sports, it touches their heart. In other words,
a sense of peoplehood entails positive feelings toward one's roots. It
should be noted, however, that we-feelings do not mean a desire to go
back to daily contact with fellow Armenians, or any behavioral
participation in the Armenian community. Sense of peoplehood is in
the spirit, and that is where Armenian-Americans want it to stay.
Peoplehood is commonly expressed when Armenian-Americans
recognize fellow Armenian celebrities and take pleasure in their
accomplishments. Travel to the ancestral homeland is also an
important source of we-ness ideally suited for symbolic Armenian-
Americans because of its sporadic, leisure-time nature.

Celebrities and Others

There was almost universal endorsement of a statement that read:
"When I notice an Armenian name on a shop or in the media (such as
movie credits, press) I feel happy, proud." Exactly 96.4 percent of the
New York sample agreed, mildly or strongly, with the statement, only
1.7 percent disagreed. By all counts, this is a remarkable phenomenon.
Even though there is a slight decrease of about 10 percentage points
between the first and fourth generations, this drop is not statistically
significant (see table 5.7). When an individual of Armenian descent
achieves prominence in the mainstream, it is indeed heartwarming and
a matter of pride. It is proof that one belongs to a group of talented and
successful people. Such was the joy of a forty-seven-year-old second-
generation woman who wanted to share her discovery with me. She
wrote, "Did you know that an Armenian boy's song was selected for
the honoring of Statue of Liberty this July 4th? His name is Turo
Pashayan and the song is 'America, I love you.' ... Armenians are so
colorful." This is a typical example of the sort of behavior that causes
Armenian pride. Expressing vocally positive sentiments about one's
Armenian background does not have costs or any disadvantages to

speak of. This is not unique to Armenians; most white ethnic groups in America share similar feelings toward their heritage (e. g., for Greeks see Moskos 1989, 146,148; also for Armenians, see O'Grady 1979, 111). Pride and affect are concordant with the definition of symbolic ethnicity.

A large number of respondents shared the feelings of a middle-aged, second-generation man who wrote on the questionnaire in capital letters: "I AM PROUD OF MY ARMENIAN HERITAGE." Yet, sense of peoplehood is not a constant quantity. It increases with positive reinforcement, both explicit instruction and implicit feedback, as it decreases and withers away when it is not continuously nourished and propped with affirmative evaluations. Some information about one's ancestral history and culture justifiably enhances one's stance, such as the young third-generation woman who wrote: "I have always been proud to be of Armenian descent because of my knowledge of my heritage." Similarly, a fifty-one-year-old man reminiscing about his immigrant parents and the sentiments they instilled in him said: "As I've grown older and wiser, I do see that there is a wealth of heritage

TABLE 5.7

Frequencies of Responses (Ethnic Position) on Two Measures of Peoplehood
by Generation
(in percent)

	Foreign-Born	U.S.-Born of F.B. Parents	1 Parent U.S.-Born	2 Parents U.S.-Born	Grandparent U.S.-Born
N = 580-583	(218)	(272)	(36)	(41)	(16)
Agreeing on statement 1	97.7	96.3	94.3	95.1	87.5
(no opinion)	(0.9)	(1.8)	(2.9)	(2.4)	(12.5)
Disagreeing on statement 2	87.2	82.5	83.3	78.0	75.0
(no opinion)	(5.0)	(11.2)	(13.9)	(12.2)	(25.0)

Statement 1: "When I notice an Armenian name on a shop or in the media (such as movie credits, press), I feel happy, proud."

Statement 2: "It is alright to change your name so that it will not be taken for an Armenian."

to be proud of. I also recognize the distinction of Armenians vs. Turkish historical achievement." On the other hand, the case of a young second-generation woman (mother Italian) exemplifies what one is more and more likely to find in the future: "Unfortunately, I was never educated on any of my ancestry. However, I would very much like to learn, but do not know where to begin."

Trying to nurture pride in the next generation and teach them something about Armenian history and culture seems to cause much concern among first- and second-generation parents and grandparents. A middle-aged U.S.-born mother wrote, "I love my rich, ancient, cultural heritage and have tried very hard to impart it to our sons who are now 2nd generation American/Armenians [*sic*]. I hope they have our feelings as well." When parents and grandparents find that their offspring share their feelings of pride, they are overjoyed. Such is the case of the second-generation grandmother who wrote, "As you c' ᄀ see I did not marry an Armenian, nor did my daughter. However, she is proud of her Armenian heritage. As a result of this both of her children attend the Hovnanian Armenian school in NJ."

Pride in the ancestral background is also expressed occasionally through colorful books Armenian-Americans give as Christmas or birthday presents to *odar* in-laws, friends, acquaintances, or business associates. Coffee-table books, beautifully illustrated and printed on fine paper, on Armenian art or architecture make ideal gifts. They are aesthetically elegant tokens of Armenian culture and history, easy to flip through and be enlightened without having to read much except the captions underneath the photographs, in case one's curiosity gets carried away. Cookbooks are likewise on the bestseller lists of Armenian bookstores. They are deemed appropriate gifts for *odar* girlfriends and daughters-in-law. The illustrated editions introduce Armenian culture, in a symbolic way, without being overbearing or embarrassing. Similar to grandmas who parade "brag albums" of their grandchildren's favorite photos, symbolic Armenian-Americans show off their ancestral heritage through stunning photographs and handsome volumes they give away as gifts, or leave on coffee tables in their living rooms. They want everyone to see that they are proud of their Armenianness.

Armenian Names

The majority of the New York respondents (81 percent) were reluctant to agree with the following statement: "It is alright to change your name so that it will not be taken for an Armenian." There was a generational increase in respondents advocating name change. The foreign-born were most likely to preserve the Armenian name (87 percent), and those in fourth generation least likely (75 percent). However, the differences were slight, not uniform nor statistically significant (see table 5.7). The same statement on name change was used in a study of Italian-Americans in Bridgeport (CT). Nearly 90 percent of the sample (N = 455) disagreed because it was believed that changing one's ethnic name is like "betraying one's family and people; it is a rejection of the group, a threat to its survival and, as such, is resisted vehemently" (Crispino 1980, 63). Indeed, an Armenian name is like a treasured heirloom, even though one need not know much about its provenance or significance.

Many participants in the survey commented on name change. The "ian" at the end of a surname is a sign of Armenian descent and identity. A middle-aged woman, in spite of being alienated from the Armenian community by marriage and divorce (to a non-Armenian), wrote: "Father used to say that if you meet any Armenians it's like meeting a member of your family, as very few of us are left. I always recognize the 'ian' at the end of names and go up to Armenians and kiss them."

Because of the xenophobic atmosphere in the United States in the 1920s and 1930s, many Armenians, like immigrants in other groups, felt the need to change their names. Several respondents described how their fathers or grandfathers had done so. A fifty-three-year-old man whose father was an Armenian immigrant (mother Italian) made the following comment to the statement on name change: "My father felt this way and did so. I wish he had not, but will not change it back." If some Armenian immigrants to the United States were motivated to change their names to avoid discrimination and prejudice, others had names that were difficult to pronounce and hindered business relations. An elderly respondent wrote: "My father changed our family name of [Barangozian] to [Baron] not to hide being an Armenian but because people could not pronounce our name and he had a lot of trouble in his business dealings" (I have used pseudonyms here to maintain the respondent's confidentiality).

A small proportion of New York respondents who approved of name change did so for pragmatic reasons. A middle-aged woman who was born in Aleppo (Syria) but raised in the United States wrote: "If the name is very difficult, it could be changed." Another Turkish-born woman justified name change by saying: "Most Armenian names are of Turkish origin."[11] Indeed, during four hundred years of Ottoman rule, many Armenian family names had acquired Turkish roots, though most had the "ian" ending.[12] More recently, during Ataturk's rule, those who had remained in Turkey were coerced into Turkifying their names even further, dropping the "ian" ending, or exchanging it to the Turkish suffix *oglu,* meaning "son of." An elderly gentleman, born in France, agreed to name change adding: "But it must be a real Armenian name!" It should be noted that one can change one's name to become more Armenian. I know of several recent immigrants from Turkey who reinstated the "ian" ending to their family names after becoming U.S. citizens.

At present, Armenians no longer have the same motives to avoid an ethnic-sounding name. A sixty-six-year-old second-generation man, recalling his childhood experiences with an Armenian name, wrote: "As an Armenian it was embarrassing to hear teachers stumble over the name. At times, I wished I was one of the more simple names like Jones, etc. Now I wouldn't change it for a million. Love those different sounding names. I look for Armenian names as a source of pride in achievement of our people." Similarly, a young lawyer, Armenian on his father's side, Greek on his mother's reflected, "I really have had little contact with my Armenian heritage. My grandfather dropped the 'ian' ending from his name when he arrived here. I suppose to avoid being known as an Armenian. I am seriously considering adding it back."

Indeed, the Armenian people in the United States have come a long way from their humble immigrant origins. As an elderly respondent said: "It was the style years ago [to change names], not any more." Armenian-Americans are at present predominantly a middle- to upper-middle-class community, with many of them having achieved fame and fortune in the larger American society. The "ian" is no longer embarrassing, even the most assimilated of Armenian descendants are reluctant to drop the "ian" deliberately. A middle-aged second-generation woman made the following observations about her family: "Many of my relatives are no longer Armenian with regard to religion, interest or association due to marriage with other ethnic spouses. My youngest relatives are fourth generation born in the U.S. However those with Armenian surnames have not changed their names or the spelling."

The emerging norm in the United States among career-oriented professionals who get married is to keep both their surnames; by creating a double-barrelled combination, husband, wife, and children assume the same family name. However, for the vast majority of the American population, the patrinomial system remains the norm; that is, a child takes the family name of his/her father. Armenians too have traditionally used the patrinomial system; with few exceptions they continue to do so today. Since Armenian names ending with "ian" function as a symbolic marker that delineates Armenians from non-Armenians, an unusual looking and sounding name entices non-Armenians to ask, what kind of a name is that? This simple question opens the door for disclosure of identity. It also sends messages to fellow Armenians that this person is "one of us." It helps establish rapport and affinity.

Consequently, in the case of mixed ancestry, if one's heritage is traced through the male line, and one's family name retains the "ian" ending, then that person will be reminded of his/her Armenian roots more often than an individual who traces descent through the matri-line. Of course, this is not to say that individuals who trace Armenian-ness through their mother cannot have a strong sense of peoplehood. On the contrary, mothers as principal caretakers and agents of social-ization may exert a stronger impact on their children's identity by overemphasizing their Armenian roots. Moreover, not everybody in the United States with an "ian" name ending will acknowledge his/her Armenian identity.[13] Middle Eastern-born Armenians cannot under-stand how somebody can say: "I'm American, but my parents are Armenian." As I have already explained, Armenian identity in the United States is a matter of choice. Children are likely to drop their Armenian identity if they are not socialized to evaluate it positively.

Currently, the mood in the general U.S. population indicates a tolerance of exotic sounding names. One can readily observe the profusion of unusual first names among African-Americans. I have observed that young parents, especially among the immigrant and second generation, are fond of giving their children Armenian first names. Granted, the names they choose are short and easily pronounced by Americans (see also O'Grady 1979, 11). Armenian-Americans parents can consult several sources before naming their child. On the market, there are a couple of small books that list Armenian boys' and girls' names and provide their English equivalent and/or significance. The pocket-size agenda published by the Prelacy of the Armenian Church, issued annually in the last several years, also carries such lists in the back. In sum, Armenian first names and family names are a sign of identity and peoplehood. A respondent in the New York survey appropriately said that I should have included the following item in the questionnaire: "Are the names of your children pure Armenian?"

Travel to Spiritual Homeland

Throughout the twentieth century, the spiritual homeland of the Armenian people has been divided between the Republic of Turkey and the Soviet Union. Though most Armenian-Americans trace their roots to towns and villages on the Anatolian Plateau in Turkey, few have been adventurous enough to venture beyond Istanbul and the major coastal cities on the Mediterranean. This is because traveling conditions in the hinterland are primitive in terms of transportation, accommodation, and availability of English-speaking guides. Most of all, Armenians fear an unfriendly reception. Those who attempt such a journey are such a rarity that upon their return to the United States, they show their slides to Armenian audiences and narrate their experiences.

For example in 1986, three men from the New York/New Jersey area climbed to the top of Mount Ararat. Paradoxically, Mount Ararat, one of the most cherished symbols of Armenian identity, is at present located within Turkish borders. For the three adventurous American-born Armenians, this was a second attempt. The previous year the Turkish authorities had forbidden the climb. The slide show I saw in Manhattan was very well attended and very emotional. Subsequently, several articles appeared in the Armenian press recounting this symbolic climb.[14] Another trip to historic lands has been recorded for posterity by Theodore Bogosian in his documentary, "An Armenian Journey."[15] Bogosian accompanied Mariam Davis, a survivor of the Genocide, and her daughter back to the towns in Eastern Turkey where she was born, deported, lost all her family, and lived for about five years as a homeless child (towns of Terjan, Egin, and Arabkir). The traveling party concealed their Armenian identities from the local people and left town as soon as their suspicions were aroused.

Travel to Soviet Armenia has been largely dependent on U.S. foreign policy toward the Communist Bloc. During the Cold War period, ties were understandably hostile. As soon as East-West relations began to thaw and Armenian political parties redefined their policies vis-à-vis Soviet Armenia, tourism became popular. Claire Mouradian writes that starting in 1967, there were direct bi-weekly flights from Beirut to Yerevan, altogether avoiding the stopover in Moscow. In 1978 alone, Armenia SSR welcomed 60,000 tourists, a big proportion of them being diaspora Armenians (1990, 334). Several travel agencies in New York, Boston, and Los Angeles specialized in organizing group tours and chartering planes to Yerevan. A major incentive was that these trips were affordable for most.

Typically, Armenian-American tourists visit museums, ancient monuments, churches and monasteries, and spend an evening or two at the ballet or opera in Yerevan. The more privileged among them participate in Divine Liturgy in Echmiadzin and get invited for an audience with the Catholicos in his private quarters. Overall, individuals who visit Armenia are pleasantly surprised to be in the midst of a society where everyone around them speaks Armenian, all the signs on the streets are in Armenian, the radio and television are in Armenian, and where most people have dark hair and a complexion similar to themselves. For a fleeting moment in their lives, they feel they belong, they are a member of the majority. The experience is generally overwhelming.

According to one of the community leaders I interviewed who owns a travel agency that charters trips to Armenia, for a while in the mid-1980s, business was slowing down with the passing away of the older generation. In his opinion, younger people, in later generations, were not as frequent visitors. However, since the earthquake and political changes within Armenia and in the Soviet Union, diaspora-homeland relations are at the threshold of a new era. Tourism is again gaining momentum. The Armenian church and voluntary associations are sponsoring pilgrimages, and the advertisements of travel agencies appear regularly in the Armenian press.[16] With increasing political stability, and improvement in hotel accommodations and other services in Yerevan, more Armenian-American tourists will be likely to visit the spiritual homeland during their vacation.

Because of space limitations, the final version of the New York questionnaire did not include items on travel to the ancestral homeland. Their absence was noted. For example, a thirty-five-year-old second-generation man who had visited Soviet Armenia and Turkey wrote: "In your next survey you might ask if the respondents have visited *Hayastan* [Armenia] and why." Several respondents were eager to share with me their connectedness to the Armenian spiritual homeland. A seventy-one-year-old, second-generation man said: "We plan to visit there this summer." A fifty-five-year-old woman whose mother is U.S.-born said: "I plan on going to Armenia in the fall." A middle-aged, third-generation woman wrote: "I visited Soviet Armenia a few years ago, and found that to be a wonderful experience." Another middle-aged, second-generation woman wrote: "My parents made two trips to Soviet Armenia which they enjoyed." A young second-generation man was even more adventurous. He visited Soviet Armenia as well as Armenian ancestral lands in present-day Turkey. Here are his comments: "I have visited Hayastan twice and Dikranagerd (Dyarbekir, Turkey) once, to become better acquainted with (and out of ethnic and family history see) [sic] my ancestral homeland." Like Israel for American Jews (see Cohen 1983, 168-69) and Greece for American Greeks (see Moskos 1989, 95), a trip to Armenia, the spiritual homeland, is a pilgrimage for Armenian-Americans. Unlike any other trip, this journey is imbued with meaning, symbolism, a unique experience in search of roots. It is the ultimate expression of one's Armenian identity.

Yet, for the Armenian-Americans, a sense of peoplehood is not confined to the geographical boundaries of the present-day Republics of Armenia or Turkey. Included on the itinerary of the Armenian tourist are historic sites and cultural centers of the diaspora. For example, when traveling in the vicinity of Venice, it is considered a must to visit the tiny island of San Lazaro where an Armenian

Catholic monastery, library, and printing press have existed since the eighteenth century. Motor boats, scheduled to stop at the island several times a day, are greeted by Mekhitarist monks who guide visitors through the museum and other areas open to the public. In the same way, it is a must to visit the Armenian Quarter when in Jerusalem, admire the ancient manuscripts, silver and gold relics, the Kutahia tiles, and other displays; maybe even kiss the ring of the Patriarch. When in Calcutta, Madras, or Singapore, one makes time to see the Armenian church and graveyard.

Armenians have "kin" wherever people of Armenian descent are to be found. Ethnic brokers and ideologues foster this diasporan sense of we-ness by emphasizing the commonality, interdependence, and shared past (and possibly future) of all who trace their roots, their bloodline, to historic Armenia. As demonstrated in previous chapters, the Armenian media is instrumental in promoting the ideology of an Armenian diaspora. News of other Armenian communities is featured regularly, thus indirectly propagating the message that Armenians around the world are one people.[17] The traditional Armenian organizations (religious, philanthropic, and political) that were established in the Old World have a diasporan character and interests. Through the years they have developed an infrastructure that necessitates communication between the leadership of the various communities, at least for administrative purposes. At the communal level, cultural exchanges are crucial in demonstrating commonality of culture and projecting a feeling of peoplehood. Folk dance ensembles, choirs, musicians, painters, sculptors, academic personalities are sporadically sponsored to perform, exhibit, or lecture in various Armenian communities. And lest one forgets, financial assistance to needy communities continues to be the backbone of diasporan relations.[18]

The universal sense of Armenian peoplehood often remains anecdotal. One hears stories of Armenian-Americans meeting other Armenians during their travels. They either overhear a conversation in Armenian or see the "ian" name ending on a shop or even look up common Armenian names in telephone directories and get in touch with them.[19] It is interesting to note that less than 4 percent of the New York sample have family living outside the United States. The unaffiliated, later-generation individual of Armenian descent is least likely to test his or her "closeness" to fellow diasporan Armenians.

The concept of an Armenian diaspora remains an ideal that does not touch the daily lives of most Armenian-Americans. For most of them, Armenians around the world are linked by make-believe emotional ties. That is why I have called the ancestral territory the *spiritual homeland*. Armenian-Americans consider the United States of America their real home. They have no intention of settling elsewhere. Yet, whenever travel is possible and is realized, it heightens feelings of peoplehood and creates strong memories that nourish the individual for a long time to come. The popularity of travel is ultimately its sporadic, leisure-time convenience.

Centrality of the Genocide in Armenianness

Even though mass killings and deliberate destruction of human societies have been common in history since early antiquity, the term genocide was not coined until the 1930s. Since then, however, it has entered everyday discourse, acquiring highly negative loading. The term has been popularized to such an extent that it has become difficult to examine the phenomenon scientifically. Moreover, because of the vested political interests of various governments, a consensus on a universal definition of genocide has not been achieved. As a result, systematic analyses of the anatomy and processes of genocide and theory building remain at an elementary stage (Chalk and Jonassohn 1990). Nonetheless, experts seem to concur that genocide is "a structural and systematic destruction of innocent people by a state bureaucratic apparatus" (Horowitz 1980, 17). It entails one-sided mass killings, aimed at exterminating an entire collectivity. More specifically, it is the "ruthless ... pursuit of human life-taking without regard to individual guilt or innocence. It is a punishment for identification with a particular group, not for personal demeanor or performance" (Horowitz 1984, 2).

There is no doubt that the Armenian case is a prototype of genocide. In 1915, the deliberate and systematic policy of the Young Turk government was to annihilate the Armenian people and eradicate their presence from their ancestral lands. Seventy-five years later, the trauma of the Genocide and deportations continues to hover in the forefront of Armenian collective consciousness. Adding insult to injury, Turkish governments have repeatedly denied any wrongdoing and, of late, they have pursued aggressive revisionist policies that have infuriated Armenians. The literature on the Armenian Genocide and the debate with the Turkish revisionists has increased considerably in recent years (e.g., see Dadrian 1975a, 1975b, 1986a, 1986b, 1988, 1990; Dedeyan 1982; Horowitz 1980, 1984, 1986; Hovannisian 1986; Kuper 1981; Libaridian 1984, 1986; Papazian 1986; Permanent Peoples' Tribunal 1985; Walker 1980). The major concern here, however, is the impact of the Genocide on Armenian-Americans and its role in manifestations of Armenianness.

The tragic events at the turn of the twentieth century radically transformed the demographic, social, and psychological makeup of the Armenian people. It is important to stress that the process of genocide was not confined to one segment or proportion of the population. It was truly widespread. The Genocide continues to have significant repercussions on Armenian-American lives today. Its memory remains not only vivid in the minds of the survivors, the generation that witnessed firsthand the atrocities, but also their offspring who have not been spared their share of grief and psychological problems. Even the survivors' grandchildren have been deeply touched by the the stories they have heard or read. Respondents in the New York study described the consequences the cataclysmic events have had on their lives and that of their parents. For many of them, the Genocide was a fact of daily life.

The massacres and deportations left deep psychological, social, and physical scars. The remarks of a second-generation respondent testify to this effect: "My father was born in October, 1895, a week before the first massacres came to Shebin-Karahissar. He showed signs of infant malnutrition all his life." Social consequences were no less devastating; the world Armenians had taken for granted collapsed. They were chased out of their homes, their homeland; their social networks were broken, their communal infrastructure was shattered. Furthermore, Armenian refugees immigrated to alien societies with strange customs and languages; adding physical and social distance between them and their past. Nothing was the same anymore.

Even though the perpetrators did not make any distinctions by gender, age, or social status, each age cohort was affected in a different way by the tragic events. Those who were still children when the events occurred became orphans; they suffered malnutrition as in the case quoted above. Their schooling was disrupted, influencing their ability to earn a living as adults. Young women in their teens and twenties, especially the pretty ones, had the highest probability of being raped. Older cohorts of women became widows. Many lost all their children and with that the possibility of ever becoming grandmothers. The loss of a husband also meant the loss of one's means of livelihood and future security. Irrespective of one's social status before the events, poverty was widespread in the post-Genocide era. Poverty was not only financial. Refugees lacked material assets and human resources. Becoming an orphan or a widow increased the chances of long-term poverty.

Psychologically, survivors suffered guilt, anxiety, and reactive depression. They were not alone; their children shared their pain and nightmares. For example, a seventy-three-year-old foreign-born woman who immigrated as a child, explains:

> My mother suffered psychologically from these terrible experiences (losing my father, her child, etc) and as a result before I graduated from high school she broke down completely and was institutionalized the rest of her life. The Turks scarred not just those who were directly under their control but many, many who went away and left them. Visiting her for all those years (39) as I grew up, married, etc. was a constant reminder of what the Turks stood for.

Likewise, a second-generation woman recalled that her grandmother who witnessed the fire of Smyrna "always wore black and seldom smiled." Another woman said her grandmother "could not talk about the old country as she was reduced to tears when we questioned her." Similarly, several respondents indicated their parents or grandparents did not talk about the massacres, such as the woman who wrote: "My father kept to himself all that happened during the Massacres [and] never really came out and told us; I guess it brought back too many sad memories." For some, assimilation into American society was a way of forgetting a painful past. Like many others, a little Armenian girl was orphaned, then saved by American missionaries who placed her in an orphanage in Beirut, Lebanon. Her fifty-four-year-old American-born son wrote: "I suspect my mother needed to put all those terrible memories of her girlhood behind her and Americanization was the quickest way to do it." Yet, as psychiatric evidence shows (see below), repression of traumatic experiences could not have been a cure.

There were survivors who clung to their church, to the remaining members of their families, to their Armenian identity, and testified to the horrors and painful events they witnessed. A young third-generation woman wrote: "As a child I listened to many stories from my grandparents of the massacres and struggles of Armenians then." A thirty-six-year-old woman who emigrated from Lebanon at age eighteen said that she had lost her grandparents and four uncles in 1915; then described her perception of the Genocide: "I still remember those cold winter nights when my father used to tell us the story of his family who were killed by the Turks with tears in his eyes.... How could I forget those stories, those tearful eyes which I can't see anymore?" Some parents and grandparents tempered the stories they told their offspring. A forty-one-year-old man who is of Armenian descent from his mother's side wrote: "My mother very deliberately (in my opinion) downplayed stories of Turkish massacres (always balancing stories of attacks with recitals of the fact that Turkish neighbors would hide my grandmother from harm)."

Surprisingly, there are few systematic studies of the psychological impact of the massacres and deportations on survivors and their offspring. One of the rare scientific investigations of the subject is Donald and Lorna Miller's (1986) analysis of the oral histories of ninety-two survivors in California. The Millers argue that reactions to the massacres and deportations must be understood within the framework of a typology of six responses: repression, rationalization, resignation, reconciliation, rage, and revenge. The first response, repression, involves unconscious or conscious denial or forgetting of events "too horrible to contemplate... [because they] are tinged with guilt and shame: memories of rape, forced nudity, humiliation of parents, the abandonment of siblings, coerced conversion to Islam" (Miller and Miller 1986, 192). The second, rationalization is finding political, pragmatic, and religious explanations in order to derive some positive benefit or meaning from the ordeal. The third is resignation; it is rooted in helplessness. The Millers elaborate as follows:

> The dehumanization, degradation, and humiliation that occurred during the deportations—expressed especially when deportees were forced to walk naked, when caravans were marched by water sources and not allowed to drink, when parents were forced to abandon children, to say nothing of acts of plunder, rape, torture, separation from parents—established the experiential basepoint from which some survivors have never recovered.

The fourth category in the typology of responses to genocide is reconciliation. Survivors interpret their experiences as part of life and point to the exceptions such as Turks who were helpful to them. However, the researchers retort, denial precludes complete reconciliation and healing because as the survivors suggested, it is as if the Turkish government was rubbing salt into their wounds. The fifth response is rage or extreme forms of anger and frustration. This is most vividly typified by hatred of the Turks. Miller and Miller write, "the very word Turk clearly elicits very visceral reactions from many Armenians" (1986, 199). Finally, the researchers suggest that the second and third generations are more revengeful than the survivors because militancy requires a position of strength. Retaliation for something unjust can take the form of "terrorism" or rely on divine retribution or other symbolic forms.

Further, Miller and Miller contend that feelings toward the traumatic experiences are not constant. They vary by different stages of the life course. More specifically, between the ages of six and fifteen, survivors were consumed with physical survival, there was no room for political consciousness. Only when they were established in their own families and occupations, during later stages of their life course, did survivors start to reflect upon their experiences and realize its enormity; thereupon "bitterness and anger began to fester" (Miller and Miller 1986, 188). For a few, advanced age meant reconciliation, but the majority became increasingly preoccupied with thoughts of the massacres.

Miller and Miller found also that seven intervening variables could have tempered the responses of survivors. These include the degree of suffering and deprivation one endured; whether one or both parents survived, losing both parents increased feelings of total abandonment. Many orphans underwent religious conversion during their tutelage under Protestant missionaries; such an experience changed their interpretation of what had happened to them. In some orphanages, survivors formed surrogate families and received formal education and occupational training; others were not as lucky. Women tended to be more reconciled than men. Those who later became members of Armenian political parties were more militant in spirit. Last but not least, those who lived with Turkish families projected their particular treatment (positive or negative) upon Turkish people in general. In conclusion, the Millers' study is significant for showing the variability and complexity of responses to genocide. But most of all, by delineating common patterns, they have moved the analysis a giant step forward toward theory building. Human behavior is after all not altogether random.

Psychiatrists Boyajian and Grigorian's article (1986) compliments the above findings. They describe the "survivor syndrome." Survivors feel that they have to apologize for living. They have a strong sense that the good family members died, leaving the unworthy ones like themselves behind. The dead are elevated to the status of martyrs: martyrs of the church, martyrs of the nation. It is little wonder that Genocide memorials have been built in almost every major diasporan center. Writing about the survivors who emigrated to the United States, Boyajian and Grigorian describe their inability to enjoy their good fortune, their freedom, and the fruits of their labor; adding, "as if enjoyment would bring punishment, misfortune, and disaster" (1986, 178).

Genocide survivors undergo identity crises. They feel robbed of their faith and their patrimony, besides they see no hope of ever returning "home." While witnessing the atrocities, survivors cultivate psychological skills that help them cope with their unbearable experiences. By developing a sense of detachment and lack of affect, survivors imagine they are observers to the events rather than subjects. However, the survivors cannot forget the memories, which keep haunting them as long as they live. Repeatedly, pictures from the past come to their minds in the form of nightmares.

Boyajian and Grigorian further note that Armenian-American survivors who had access to compatriotic societies, Armenian churches, and communal life were able to talk about their sufferings and collectively mourn their losses. In contrast, survivors who were geographically isolated from other Armenian families were reluctant to verbalize and share their feelings. Unable to unburden their guilt and anxieties, they tried to repress them—not very successfully. These observations are corroborated by the results of a study of twenty women survivors in Providence (RI) and Watertown (MA). Interestingly, Sarkisian found that there is no single word in Armenian for "coping." The Genocide was "not seen as coping; but rather as survival." Above all, it was an *ongoing* phenomenon that was never resolved (1988, 55). Nonetheless, these New England Armenian women had coped remarkably well because their "commitment to their religion and to family helped them adapt to the adversities of the event, and continues to help them cope with life in their old age" (Sarkisian 1984, 44). Evidently, those who coped with the trauma best lived long enough to tell their stories. In any case, the data proves that collective mourning is a mechanism that heals survivors and integrates generations and communities.

What about the children of the survivors of the Genocide? Boyajian and Grigorian argue that "a dominant theme that emerges is the feeling of being 'special'; special in the sense that there is an obligation that was placed upon them directly or indirectly, to be the bearers of the hopes and aspirations, not only of a given family but of a whole people" (1986, 181). Such children are overprotected, bear the names of dead relatives, carry some of the shame and guilt of their parents, but most of all, they see life as a "serious business; ... they [are] required to be serious and in some sense, almost sad" (1986, 181). It is as if they do not deserve happiness or joy. Boyajian and Grigorian support my contention (see above) that children and grandchildren of Genocide survivors carry the burden of ethnic continuity. That is, the second-generation Armenian-Americans are most likely to be susceptible to their parents' urges to marry within the group and perpetuate their Armenian identity. The third generation is not released of that obligation; though by then the elders lose their power to demand compliance. In sum, the Genocide is shared by *all* three generations; it is the quintessential Armenian experience of the twentieth century.

Finally, Boyajian and Grigorian ask: Why has the Genocide had such a strong influence on Armenian identity irrespective of generations? Here is their answer:

> it is not something that one can put aside and say that it has happened in the past and should be forgotten, because one cannot do that when it has never been accepted as a fact. One must clear one's name and set the record straight. It is not that Armenians wish to take on an identity of martyrs and victims; it is simply that those ghosts won't go away.
> ...
>
> The nonrecognition of the Armenian genocide generates an identity formation problem in the life cycle of Armenians. This identity devaluation may continue for

generations to come unless and until it is resolved by proper recognition of the genocide by the world at large. (1986, 183-84)

The Genocide is remembered every year on April 24. On that day in 1915 the Turkish government rounded up all the Armenian intellectuals in Istanbul. They were all subsequently murdered. April 24 stands for all the acts of violence committed against the Armenian people during that period. In the United States, the Genocide is commemorated by requiems in all Armenian churches as well as public gatherings, marches, rallies, speeches, and special events like tree-planting and wreath-laying ceremonies, concerts, plays, and so on. New York respondents were asked to describe their feelings about Turkey's denial of the Genocide. They could choose one or several of the following answer categories: indifference; Armenians need justice; anger; frustration; and other. Interestingly, respondents felt the need to add "forget past" to the list. Respondents were also asked whether they attended memorial services and public gatherings on or around April 24 during the year preceding the survey.

As with other variables examined throughout this study, behavior falls short of attitudinal intentions. The New York survey shows that about 95 percent of the sample have strong feelings toward the Genocide, but less than half participate in commemorative events. More specifically, 41 percent of the sample attended requiem services and 27.4 percent attended public gatherings for April 24 (see also chap. 3 for similar results). Feelings toward the Genocide received higher percentages: 61.3 percent said Armenians need justice, another 60.7 percent said they felt angry, 9.4 percent were humiliated by it. Only a very small proportion of the sample (about 5 percent of

TABLE 5.8
Frequencies of Respondents Attending Genocide Commemorative Activities (Requiem and Public Gatherings) by Generation (in percent)

	Foreign-Born	U.S.-Born of F.B. Parents	1 Parent U.S.-Born	2 Parents U.S.-Born	Grandparent U.S.-Born
N = 581-584	(219)	(272)	(36)	(41)	(16)
Requiem	57.5	33.5	30.6	17.1	18.8
Public gathering	40.6	19.9	25.0	14.6	12.5

responses) were not awed by the historic events; 4.5 percent felt indifferent, and 2.8 percent said that one should forget about the past and carry on with life.

There is a decrease with each passing generation in behavioral measure, but little attitudinal change (see tables 5.8, 5.9). The longer the generational presence, the less likely respondents were to attend memorial services (tau c .28*) as well as, rallies, meetings, marches, and other types of public events (tau c .20*). The biggest drop is between the immigrant generation and the second generation (24 percentage points for requiems and 21 points for public gathering). On the other hand, there were few generational differences in feelings of anger toward the Turkish denial of the Genocide or revindication of justice. The first generation is most likely to feel humiliated, but this is not a widespread feeling. There is a very small but steady increase in respondents who feel indifferent toward the Turkish revisionists. American-born generations are also most likely to suggest that Armenians should forget the past.

Respondents affiliated with Armenian denominations were most likely to attend requiem services commemorating the Armenian

TABLE 5.9
Frequency Distribution of Respondents' Feelings toward Turkey's Denial of the Genocide by Generation (multiple response)

	Foreign-Born	U.S.-Born of F.B. Parents	1 Parent U.S.-Born	2 Parents U.S.-Born	Grandparent U.S.-Born
N = 573 (cases)	(215)	(270)	(35)	(38)	(15)
Need justice	46.8	42.1	41.5	48.9	35.0
(351 responses)					
Anger	43.3	44.3	43.9	42.5	45.0
(348 responses)					
Humiliation	8.0	7.2	2.4	0.0	5.0
(54 responses)					
Indifference	1.9	3.7	2.4	6.4	10.0
(26 responses)					
Forget past	0.0	2.7	9.7	2.1	5.0
(16 responses)					
	100.0	100.0	100.0	100.0	100.0

Genocide (tau c .32*; see table 5.10). While half of the Apostolics attended requiem services, only one-tenth of those who had "other" religious affiliations did so (a drop of almost 41 percentage points). Those who profess no religious persuasion understandably were even less likely to attend church services; slightly more attended public gatherings. Respondents with "other" religious affiliations were also least likely to attend public gatherings (.24*). Here again, attitudes were in sharp contrast to actual behavior. Religious affiliations did not change one's feelings (see table 5.11).

Approximately 60 percent of respondents who sympathized with Armenian political parties (Tashnag, Ramgavar, and Hunchag) attended memorial services compared to 49 percent of *chezok* (nonpartisan), 19 percent of those who were indifferent to such ideologies, and 37 percent who rejected Armenian politics. The Tashnag party, as discussed in chapter 2, is the most militant of Armenian political parties. Consequently, Tashnag sympathizers were most likely to attend public gatherings (47.7 percent), followed by Ramgavars (39.3 percent), *chezoks* (31.5 percent), those who reject Armenian political parties (21.4 percent), and least of all, the indifferents (13.6 percent; tau c .22*).

The Genocide and its subsequent denial by Turkish governments is therefore a symbol of collective Armenian identity. It affected not only one segment of the population, but almost everyone. It serves as a common denominator, an equalizer of all differences between Armenians: national, regional, religious, ideological, political, socioeconomic, generational, and so on. Armenian community brokers and intellectuals have used the Genocide as a tool to mobilize men and

TABLE 5.10
Frequencies of Respondents Attending Genocide Commemorative Activities
(Requiem and Public Gatherings) by Religious Affiliation
(in percent)

	Apostolic Armenian	Protestant Armenian	Catholic Armenian	Other (Non-Arm.)	No Religion
N = 573—576	(370)	(56)	(22)	(92)	(36)
Requiem	51.6	39.3	40.9	10.9	5.6
Public gathering	36.0	21.4	18.2	5.4	8.3

women of Armenian descent, to foster a sense of we-ness, and to maintain their ethnic allegiance. The Genocide has become an ideology. By selecting such a symbolic framework, Armenian-Americans have been provided with a sense of peoplehood, cultural rebirth, and historical continuity. So far, it has been fairly successful.

Some Armenian scholars and activists feel the Genocide has not been politicized sufficiently.[20] On the other hand, there is a small but growing group of critics who argue that the idiom of the Genocide has been overworked. They contend that Armenianness cannot and should not be equated only with Genocide. They suggest Armenian-Americans have reached a saturation point; they can no longer rest their entire being on mourning the past. It is time to think about the future as well. Armenian culture is rich, surely more positive symbolic frameworks could be selected from the past that would offer a sense of continuity. Several of my interviewees suspected that the sadness that pervades the Armenian collective psyche is alienating younger cohorts, making them reluctant to get involved in Armenian communal life. One informant told me that she had often wondered about the meaning of "kef nights." In her mind it was as if Armenians

TABLE 5.11
Frequency Distribution of Respondents' Feelings toward Turkey's Denial of the Genocide by Religious Affiliation
(multiple response)

	Apostolic Armenian	Protestant Armenian	Catholic Armenian	Other (Non-Arm.)	No Religion
N = 565 (cases)	(366)	(54)	(22)	(89)	(34)
Need justice (346 responses)	45.1	49.3	51.8	40.3	31.7
Anger (341 responses)	44.3	38.0	37.0	42.1	53.7
Humiliation (53 responses)	7.6	5.6	7.4	5.3	2.4
Indifference (26 responses)	2.1	7.0	0.0	7.9	2.4
Forget past (15 responses)	0.9	0.0	3.7	4.4	9.8
	100.0	100.0	100.0	100.0	100.0

could not have fun any other time. In addition, Libaridian (1991, 1-2) has argued that the Genocide impedes rational political discourse because the specter of Pan-Turkism hovers around the collective consciousness of the Armenian people, turning them psychologically into victims, obsessed with an overburdened past, fearful of more massacres.

These sentiments are corroborated by a few respondents in the New York study, such as the seventy-year-old second-generation man who was more interested in living up to the standards of mainstream society than of making an issue of the denial. Here are his views:

> A waste of time and energy for no purpose.... Why do you and many Armenians re-live and dwell on the past. When will we stop pleading for sympathy—meaningless and worthless sympathy? Let's not grovel and squirm and try to impress the world by what Armenians suffered. On the contrary let's raise our heads up high and be proud of the accomplishments of present day Armenians in industry, science, government, sports, education, and art.

Likewise, the almost 3 percent of the sample who suggested that Armenians should forget the past testify to this increasing impatience with living in the past. Such was the answer of a forty-seven-year-old, second-generation woman: "I am more interested in looking forward than back. God and the Armenian people and any well educated person knows history. That is enough." Another thirty-year-old woman, who like her father was U.S.-born, commented that she felt "No indifference, but it is not so vital to me, that they admit to it. Everyone else knows they did it, so what's the big deal?"

It is not true that "everyone" knows that the Turkish government perpetrated the Armenian Genocide; human beings have short memories, and history is continuously rewritten. In a historical analysis of American public opinion concerning the "Armenian Question," Papazian (1986) describes how from a "cause celebre" in the early twentieth century the Genocide came to be "alleged" in the 1970s (see also Malkasian 1984). Similarly, a content analysis of Armenian issues in the *New York Times* from 1965 to 1983 found that "distortions of history progressively increased" (Sinanian 1987, 49).

While some want to forget the Genocide and the Turkish denial, others want to resolve the controversy so that they can go on with the business of living. Indeed, there is a growing awareness among Armenian-Americans that Turkey's denial of the Genocide is a serious issue that needs to be addressed professionally and politically. Here are some of the respondents' suggestions as to what should be done. A sixty-year-old second-generation respondent said: "When a Turk killed an Armenian he did not ask his political affiliation. Armenians should unite their efforts to right the Genocide of 1915. Church masses are not enough. United demonstrations must be organized and made effective. Advertisements in important newspapers and journals." Similarly, a forty-six-year-old third-generation man observed: "Both my wife and I lost grandfathers in the Turkish Massacres of 1921 but we feel education and prudent political activism is the best way of helping the 'Armenian Cause.'"

On the other hand, a seventy-one-year-old second-generation man well-aware of diasporan conditions wrote: "I ... feel what is to be gained by an admittance of guilt, would only make it a greater problem for the few of our people remaining in Turkey." Suggestions aside, there is little consensus as to what actions should be taken, what the goals of such action would be politically and ideologically, and who should speak for the Armenians. As the present study has shown over and over again, it is hard to mobilize symbolic ethnics for political or any other action, even when sentiments are not lacking.

In conclusion, the survey indicates that while feelings toward the Genocide are almost universal, Armenian-Americans are not likely to participate in commemorative events at the collective level. These results are not surprising for symbolic ethnics, as consistently observed, behavior lags behind feelings. Kramer and Leventman's (1961, 17) observations that "sentiment exceeds commitment" remain valid even for something as dear to Armenian-Americans as the Genocide. Obviously, some actions are easier and less conspicuous than others. Attending church services is not as demanding as participating in a rally in Times Square (NYC) or marching up a street with banners and signs. Only the most politicized of ethnics, mostly from the first generation and those sympathetic to Armenian political parties and ideologies are willing to attend public events.

Yet, affect vis-à-vis the Genocide and its denial are not lacking. Only one respondent in the entire sample (forty-five-year-old third-generation professional, affiliated with non-Armenian church) asked: "What is April 24?" The survey findings support the notion that the Genocide and its denial are central elements in Armenianness today. It is central to such an extent, and the burden of its proof weighs so heavily on the collective consciousness of the survivors and their descendants that the richness of the Armenian culture and experience have a tendency to be reduced to the Genocide, to martyrdom. One of my informants showed me a book on nationalities where the following entry occupied a full page in bold print: "ARMENIANS ARE ALWAYS MASSACRED." He believed that it was a fitting description. Not only do insiders see themselves as victimized people, but they are likely to be perceived in the same way by outsiders. For example, whenever news of Armenians appears in the mass media, it is often coupled with mention of the Genocide.

Armenian Cuisine

Food has been called "the last bastion" of ethnicity (Steinberg 1981, 63-65). Is it the case for Armenian-Americans? Two questions in the New York survey examined the maintenance of ethnic food: first, the frequency of eating Armenian food at home; second, ability of respondents to cook Armenian dishes. The change in behavior is in the predicted direction; the longer the generational presence, the less the frequency of eating Armenian food at home (.24*) and the fewer Armenian dishes one knows how to cook (.24*). While 75.5 percent of foreign-born respondents eat Armenian food at home at least once a week, this percentage decreases gradually to 18.8 percent for fourth-

TABLE 5.12
Frequency Distribution of Eating Armenian Food by Generation

	Foreign-Born	U.S.-Born of F.B. Parents	1 Parent U.S.-Born	2 Parents U.S.-Born	Grandparent U.S.-Born
N = 582	(218)	(270)	(36)	(41)	(16)
Few times per year	10.1	18.1	22.2	39.0	31.3
Few times per month	14.2	25.8	27.8	39.0	50.0
Once a week or more	75.7	56.1	50.0	22.0	18.8
	100.0	100.0	100.0	100.0	100.0

generation respondents (see table 5.12). Again, while about 63 percent
of the first generation were able to cook thirteen dishes or more, only
about 20 percent of the third generation were able to do so (see table
5.13). Obviously, it is easier to eat a dish than to prepare it.

This trend is corroborated by Aposhian's[21] comparative study of
foreign-born Armenians with third-generation Armenian-Americans.
When she asked her respondents what they considered their food
preference at home to be, 42 percent of the foreign-born replied
exclusively Armenian and Middle Eastern, while none of the
American-born had such a preference. Another 26 percent of the first
generation said it was mostly Armenian, compared to 3 percent of
third-generation. The majority of American-born (62 percent) enjoyed
both Armenian and American cuisine in contrast to 32 percent of the
first generation. Finally, none of the foreign-born said they preferred
mostly American food, while 35 percent of the third generation said
so.

Yet, it is remarkable that 68.8 percent of respondents with the
longest generational presence in the United States eat Armenian food
at least several times a month. Similar findings are reported for other
ethnic groups, a trait anecdotally called "the patriotism of the
stomach" (Moskos 1989, 96 n.12). For example, it was found that
most Italians "prefer pasta over potatoes and wine over beer or hard
liquor" (Johnson 1985, 39). Likewise, a survey found that more than
four out of five third-generation Greek-Americans regarded Greek
food to be very much part of their diet (Moskos 1989, 96). What do

TABLE 5.13
Frequency Distribution of Knowledge of Cooking Armenian Dishes
by Generation

	Foreign-Born	U.S.-Born of F.B. Parents	1 Parent U.S.-Born	2 Parents U.S.-Born	Grandparent U.S.-Born
N = 581	(217)	(270)	(36)	(41)	(16)
0-5 Dishes	8.8	20.3	25.0	48.8	50.0
6-12 Dishes	28.1	34.3	33.3	31.7	25.0
>13 Dishes	63.1	45.4	41.7	19.5	25.0
	100.0	100.0	100.0	100.0	100.0

these results mean? Armenian food continues to be favored intergenerationally, but is changing from being a routine, almost daily occurrence to an occasional, "special" event.

Had I asked respondents whether they enjoy eating Armenian food, I am almost certain the answer would have been unanimously affirmative. Armenian-Americans, like the rest of America, live increasingly in two-income households and are committed to their occupations plus a number of other interests. In short, they have very busy schedules in a time-hungry society. The life-style of the average family has changed yet again with the advent of the postindustrial economy. Now more than ever, individuals and families "eat out." Even when they are at home, they are likely to call in for a pizza or heat up a frozen entrée in the microwave. In any case, contemporary Americans, including those of Armenian descent, tend to simplify and shorten the process of meal preparation. On special occasions, however, they will indulge themselves with the time and energy required to fix more elaborate Armenian or other dishes.

A recent survey of Armenian restaurants on five continents supports my observations. *Armenian International Magazine* correspondents were not able to find any Armenian sit-down restaurants in Jerusalem, Cairo, Damascus, Amman, or Tehran in spite of their well-established Armenian communities. The editors attribute this discrepancy to "the eating habits and family traditions in these communities that make ethnic dining establishments superfluous" (June 1991, p. 34). Indeed, in these communities where Armenianness is taken for granted, where identity is ascribed, Armenian food is part of daily life, and women of the family are the most accomplished chefs. Why would anyone want to pay for something that is readily available, at its best, at home? Changes in eating habits of Armenian-Americans are attributed not only to processes of assimilation, but also to transformations in the nature of the economy and means of production.

Respondents who were affiliated with non-Armenian denominations or profess "no religion," and those with mixed parentage were similarly least likely to eat Armenian food often at home (.26* and .17* respectively). Armenian Apostolics tended to eat Armenian food at home most frequently (70 percent), next in descending order came Armenian Protestants (68 percent), Armenian Catholics (41 percent), those with non-Armenian denominations (33 percent) and finally those with "no religion" (19 percent). The threefold decrease in eating Armenian food between Apostolics and those with no religious persuasion may be attributed to the latter's less traditional views, and, it seems, less traditional behavior.

A non-Armenian parent more than halves the chances of eating Armenian food at home. About a quarter of those who had mixed parentage ate Armenian food at least once a week in contrast to about two-thirds of those with two Armenian parents. It is interesting to note that the integration of non-Greek wives was found to be smoother when she learned to cook Greek food (Moskos 1989, 96). I have observed the same phenomenon among Armenian-Americans. An *odar* wife is spoken of highly when she masters the art of making baklava, or stuffed vine leaves, or produces a lavish display of her culinary skills at a Thanksgiving or Christmas family gathering (see also O'Grady 1979). Similarly, a forty-three-year-old U.S.-born respondent whose husband was *odar* wrote with great delight: "My non-Armenian relatives have learned to make boreg, shish kebab, and pilaf, Armenian culture, no?"

I have argued in chapter 1 that women play a very significant role in ethnic maintenance because of their labor in food preparation and other contributions necessary for the sustenance of the family unit. The New York survey supports these claims. Several respondents wrote that they eat Armenian food when they visit their parents' home, or when their mother sends them care packages. Ethnic food is one of the few dependent variables that was statistically significant with gender (.17* for knowledge to cook and .14 significant at .003 level for frequency of eating Armenian food). Not surprisingly, women in the New York sample knew how to cook the maximum number of Armenian dishes (58 percent for women compared to 42 percent for men). After all, women's traditional domain has been the kitchen. Women were also more likely than men to eat Armenian food at home most frequently, presumably because they can cook the dishes they feel like eating (66 percent for women vs 54 percent for men). In this regard, men are dependent on women, especially those vested in the patriarchal system.

Eating ethnic food is an easy ethnic trait that does not come into conflict with modern middle-class American society. On the contrary, ethnic food has become popular in the United States in the last couple of decades. Americans have become adventurous with their taste buds. People are no longer exclusively loyal to the cuisine of their ancestors; rather, variability is the norm. Chinese, Japanese, Indian, Mexican, Thai, Ethiopian cuisines among many others have become very fashionable in gourmet dining. This craze has even trickled down to the general public. Street fairs, festivals, and bazaars in major American towns and cities are havens for all ethnic cuisines. For example, during its eighteen years of existence, the One World Festival in New York City featured vendors from different ethnic groups who peddled their specialities. In the midst of Thai, Vietnamese, and Mexican vendors, Armenian parish councils and voluntary associations sold shish kebab, stuffed vine leaves, *boreog* (cheese, meat or spinach in *filo* or streudel dough), *lahmejoun* (Armenian meat pizza), and of course, baklava.

What does America's craze with ethnic cuisines imply? According to Steinberg (1981, 64), it symbolizes the melting pot, not ethnic pluralism. Surely, one does not have to be Jewish to enjoy a pastrami sandwich, or Italian to like pizza, or Armenian to crave shish kebab and pilaf; these have become "American" dishes. It has also been argued that the persistent preference for Italian cuisine among later-generation Italian-Americans is due to its acceptance by the larger American public. Alba explains:

> Among the outward manifestations of culture, cuisine is probably unique in the sense that its weakening among Italians and its acceptability in the wider society bring about a convergence, in which acculturation occurs as a two-way process of interaction between ethnic group and host society, rather than as a one-way imposition of the host culture on the new group. (1985a, 133-34)

The same generalizations apply to Armenian cuisine or any ethnic cuisine for that matter.

In the last couple of decades, the average American palate has become more cosmopolitan. The abundance of ethnic restaurants in most U.S. towns and cities has certainly contributed to an increased experimentation with food tastes and styles. Additionally, purveyors of ethnic staples have become increasingly astute in marketing their goods. For instance, pita bread, lavash crackers, Armenian string cheese, and Colombo's yogurt[22] (and its competitors) are now sold in most supermarkets. I contend that if *lahmejoun* (Armenian meat pizza) were readily available in supermarkets, and if Armenian restaurants or eateries were as omnipresent as Chinese takeouts or pizzerias, not only would more Armenian-Americans be eating Armenian food, so would the general public.

Writing about Armenian food one is always confronted with the following question: What is authentic Armenian cuisine anyway? During their historic migrations, Armenians inevitably exchanged with their host societies a number of cultural items, including dietary habits. It is therefore natural that Armenians developed distinctive regional cuisines, as it is natural that they share many dishes, cooking styles, and tastes for certain staples and ingredients with neighboring Middle Eastern or Mediterranean peoples such as the Greeks, Turks, Lebanese, Sephardic Jews, Persians, and Yugoslavs. In the United States, this regional commonality of Middle Eastern cuisines has been advantageous. Through economies of scale, Armenian consumers have had increased access to speciality food stores. Today in many American cities, there are stores that cater to Middle Eastern ethnic groups.

According to some observers, ethnic food in the United States is becoming less and less authentic. In her study of later-generation Italian Americans, di Leonardo found that there was little regional loyalty (i.e., North Italians would bake Sicilian cookies) and no "typical Italian foods" that all her respondents included on their menus for special occasions. She argued that "aside from the proliferation of Italian-named food stuffs, these family holiday patterns seem typically American Christian" (1984, 218). New York respondents too were uncertain about what would be considered typical Armenian food. A fifty-five-year-old third-generation women said her family ate Armenian food at home almost every day, adding: "If you count pilaf." A forty-three-year-old male respondent whose mother is a U.S.-born Armenian and his father English reported that they eat Armenian food almost daily "at least one dish every meal" and cook thirteen to twenty-four dishes and "probably more but do not think of them as 'Armenian.'"

An emergent Armenian-American cuisine is accommodating "American," Middle Eastern, and other dishes and traditions. The more pungent spices and other objectionable ingredients have been tamed or eliminated to adapt to the American palate, which has been described as bland, even tasteless (Steinberg 1981, 64). California-made *pasterma* (dried beef with garlic, tumeric and other spices) no longer leaves undesirable odors.[23] Also, *hommos* (chick pea dip with sesame seed oil), *taboulé* (parsley and mint salad) and *baba ghanouj* (egg plant salad), which are Lebanese, not Armenian, specialities are becoming standard items on Armenian menus in private homes and public affairs. Even the most recent Armenian immigrants seem to borrow dietary customs rather quickly from their host environment. Typically, at Thanksgiving, which is celebrated almost universally, a roast turkey graces the table. However, instead of (or rather, in addition to) sweet potatoes with marshmallows and cranberry sauce, rice pilaf, *boreog,* and stuffed vine leaves accompany the bird.

The specialized skills of Armenian grandmothers in rolling dough for baklava or cheese *boreog* may be a thing of the past. Packaged substitutes (such as *filo* or streudel dough) are readily available, making the cook's task easier and faster. Also easily available are canned (e.g., stuffed vine leaves) and frozen foods (e.g., *lahmejoun*). In addition, no Armenian-American anywhere in the United States need crave Armenian food. Mail-order firms can ship most staples within a day or two, even ready-to-eat goods. As for the cooking enthusiasts, those who turn their love of Armenian food into a hobby, there are a large number of cookbooks, in English with simple instructions and standard measures.[24] As a fifty-eight-year-old, second-generation respondent commented, she could cook over twenty-five Armenian dishes "with a little help of my cookbook."

I was able to enumerate fifteen Armenian cookbooks in English currently on the market. The oldest was published in 1949 by the Detroit chapter of an Armenian philanthropic association. There were three books published in the 1960s, one in 1975, and the rest (ten) in the 1980s. Of the fifteen, twelve were single authored, all but one by women; three women having written more than one book. Three cookbooks were group projects by Armenian churches or voluntary associations. One book was published in England, one in Beirut (Lebanon), the remaining thirteen in the United States. The question is: Why this surge in cookbooks in the United States in the 1980s? The resurgence of ethnicity popularizing ethnic cuisine, the women's movement encouraging women to achieve something for themselves,[25] the immigration of large numbers of Armenians from the Middle East (several of the authors are from the Middle East) are some of the possible motivating factors.

I suggest though that the proliferation of Armenian cookbooks published in English in the last few years is a by-product of becoming symbolic ethnics. A need develops to "store," to codify the ethnic culture in some permanent form, because one feels that it is being "lost." The traditional techniques and know-how are no longer taken for granted or perpetuated automatically from mother to daughter because of lack of time, interest, or break in the human chain. Therefore, this body of knowledge has to be documented for posterity, so that future generations (and non-Armenian spouses) may have the possibility of learning from it, if they so wish. Cookbooks are not an isolated phenomena. Armenians have written books on traditional lace embroidery and rugs; they have recorded patterns in folk costumes, folk dancing, and so on. In the last chapter, I called these "knowledge banks." The only difference is that cookbooks have a higher utility value, more popular appeal, and may be more profitable for authors and publishers.

Cookbooks, and, to a lesser extent other manuals of traditional Armenian culture, have another function. They establish an emergent Armenian-American culture, a common ethnic culture among a variety of Armenians from different regions of ancient Armenia and the diaspora. As I have argued above, Armenian-American cuisine now includes Lebanese, American, and other dishes and traditions. Cookbooks not only explain the secrets of *taboulé, baba ghanouj,* and stuffed turkey with cranberry sauce, they popularize and legitimize their inclusion in the Armenian-American culinary repertoire.

Similarly, a standardized Armenian-American menu is emerging in most banquets and dinner dances hosted by Armenian associations. Typically, the appetizer consists of cheese *boreog* or *hommos* or stuffed vine leaves, or a combination of these. The main course is usually lamb or beef, though chicken is also common, accompanied by rice or *bulghour* [crushed wheat] pilaf and vegetables (peas or string beans) or a salad (lettuce, tomato, and cucumber). Occasionally, a yogurt and cucumber dish replaces the salad. Desert is baklava or one of its numerous varieties (see also Ordjanian 1991, 202-4). Such a menu would have been alien to pre-Genocide Armenians, as it is to others in the diaspora today. However, it fits all the necessary requirements of American society; it is different without being offensive.

In conclusion, the pattern is clear. In spite of a general acceptance and availability of Armenian and Middle Eastern food, the longer the generational presence in the United States, the less Armenian cuisine constitutes an integral part of a family's daily diet and the fewer dishes one is able to cook. The following quotation from a seventy-seven-year-old respondent (born in Greece, who immigrated at age twelve) illustrates the trend.

> Since my wife was born in the U.S.A. of Aintabtzi [from Aintab, Turkey] parents the "Armenian" part of our food consists of pilaf, dolma, lahmejoun, home-made yogurt. When my parents lived it was different. It was then *ALL* Armenian.

Nonetheless, Armenian cuisine continues to be popular when readily available. The preparation of such dishes at home is relegated to special occasions, family get-togethers or holidays such as Christmas and Easter, even American ones like Thanksgiving.

For symbolic Armenian-Americans eating Armenian food occasionally is the most convenient form of participation in their ancestral heritage. Armenian food can be eaten at a family celebration, in an Armenian restaurant, at a street fair; it can be bought at a local supermarket, or a Middle Eastern speciality store, or ordered through the mail. The choices abound. With minimal commitment, the experience is almost always immensely gratifying. Moreover, food conjures images of childhood memories, of festive occasions with tables piled up with colorful dishes and succulent tastes, pungent aromas emanating from the kitchen, grandmother's comforting voice mixed with sounds of laughter and music. Such mental images come to represent for symbolic Armenian-Americans what it feels like to be of Armenian descent. Food occupies center stage in these cognitive reconstructions. In the final analysis, the essence of Armenianness is felt with one's heart, and whenever possible one's palate.

The Family

So far in this chapter, I have analyzed the sources that breed and invigorate Armenian identity in the United States. The family unit is the repository of Armenian culture and the web of social relations. As an agent of socialization, the role of the family in passing Armenian identity and pride to the next generation is undeniable. Given the sidestream nature of ethnicity, it is my contention that at the individual level, the family will remain the most significant, and in some cases the only, tie of later-generation men and women of Armenian descent to their ancestral heritage. Even though the maintenance of a viable collective presence requires more than the contributions of the family, ultimately the future of Armenianness in the United States may well depend on its performance. Therefore, it is necessary to explore the characteristics of the Armenian-American family system and examine the nature of its social relations.

The Changing Patterns of the Traditional Armenian Family

It has been argued that second only to social class, ethnicity causes the major variations in the American kinship structure (Schneider 1980, 122). In the Armenian case, these differences are minor, and likely to diminish with time. The contemporary Armenian-American family is not different from the "American" family in its structure or functions. Its distinguishing features lie in emphases on certain values, norms, and behavioral patterns retained from the original immigrants and the emergent ethnic subculture in the United States.[26] What is the legacy of the present-day Armenian-American family? What were the characteristics of the early twentieth-century family? How have they changed?

The pre-Genocide family *(endanik)* in historic Armenia has been portrayed as patriarchal, patrilineal, patrilocal, and patrinomial (see Bamberger 1986-87; LaPiere 1930; Mazian 1983, 1984; Nelson 1953; Villa and Matossian 1982; and for a bibliography of the Armenian family see Bakalian 1985). Power and authority rested in the hands of the male elders of the family. A child's welfare was the responsibility of his/her father's family. An Armenian father passed on his identity to his children, irrespective of their mother's ethnic background. In addition, children inherited the material and nonmaterial assets that their families enjoyed. The clan *(Kertasdan)* was a larger kin group that like a corporate body regulated family life, especially at times when the central government was weak. It provided extrafamilial protection, assistance during calamities, and mediated disputes. As in most agrarian economies, the Armenian family functioned as a unit of production. In the villages and towns on the Anatolian Plateau, where the majority of the Armenian population lived until the deportations, family members labored jointly to produce the goods and services necessary for survival.

A strong sense of family honor, described as "Mediterranean" (Bamberger 1986-87, 81) focused on the purity of female members of the family. Fathers and brothers jealously guarded their honor by protecting female kin from illicit relationships with men. Marriages were arranged. Marriage between close kin was prohibited. Betrothal was at an early age for women. Age differences between the bride and groom were wide. Patrilocal residence patterns were the norm; after the wedding ceremony, the couple lived with the groom's family. In the extended household, the newlyweds were allocated a separate quarter, a room, or a corner of the domicile depending on their economic status. The bride *(hars)* served her in-laws in silence, and initially was not allowed to visit her family of origin for an extended period of time. She remained a junior member in her husband's household until the birth of a son. Given the high incidence of infant and childhood mortality, women gave birth to a large number of children to ensure that a few would survive into adulthood. With more children and increasing age, her position was elevated, and her authority increased over junior members in domestic matters. After menopause and the acquisition of the status of mother-in-law, some women attained significant respect and authority within the household and community.

The Genocide, migration, and forces of modernization changed the structure and functions of the Armenian family. Nelson's (1953) analysis of three generations of Armenian-American families in Fresno (CA) outlines the distinguishing themes of the early immigrant family. Child rearing was characterized by discipline, "strictness," and obedience to parental authority (Nelson 1953, 49, 157). Elders were highly respected and initially, there was a reluctance to place elderly parents in old people's homes because it was considered shameful[27] (Nelson 1953, 82). The family unit, often consisting of grandparents, parents, and children, was described as close-knit (Nelson 1953, 173); moreover, members were reported to "do things together" as a group (Nelson 1953, 41). An important leisure-time activity that was practiced over several generations was visiting. On Sundays or holidays, parents visited kin, compatriots, and friends, and they took their children with them. Nonetheless, Nelson observes that this was "a family unified by parental pressure." It was an adult-centered family and "children were fitted into [their parents'] program" (Nelson 1953, 44).

The family name and its reputation in the ethnic community were important values in Armenian lives (Nelson 1953, 125-26). Concern for the family name is typically the product of a folklike, face-to-face society where knowledge of other people's behavior is pervasive. In such societies, the collectivity sanctions normative behavior by gossip, ridicule, even ostracism. The immigrant Armenian family was responsible for the behavior of its members. Armenian children were taught at an early stage not to discredit the family, or cause disunity in its midst by any behavior that would bring shame *(amot)* to the family name. The concern for "what will people say?" was paramount in regulating social conduct and sanctioning deviant behavior (see also Boudjikanian-Keuroghlian 1978, 112). The "good" families were those whose reputations were untarnished. They were highly sought after for marriage alliances. When parents negotiated the marriages of their children, they made sure their son or daughter was not married into a family with a history of disease, illness, crime, laziness, avarice, scandal, divorce, desertion, and other such unsavory traits (Nelson 1953, 125).

Matchmaking continued to prevail as a mode of mate selection for the immigrant generation in the first half of the twentieth century (Nelson 1953, 150). "Picture brides" (Mirak 1983, 153) or "pen-pal couples" (Bamberger 1986-87, 84) were common. Immigrant men would send for wives they had seen only in a photograph; sometimes they would correspond, and sometimes they would travel back to Near Eastern orphanages or Marseille to choose a bride. Women continued to marry young and several years separated their ages from that of their husbands. Many of the New York respondents' parents and grandparents were married in this way. Here are some of their stories.

A second-generation respondent explained that her mother was placed in an orphanage after the massacres. Her father had escaped the Turkish army and settled in New York State. "Dad went to Corfu when given her picture by her cousin, who was father's brother-in-law. They liked each other and married." He was eighteen years older than his wife. Another second-generation man wrote: "Father went to

France—for a wife—mother and father married in an arranged marriage—father was thirty years old, mother was seventeen years old, when married." Yet another second-generation respondent wrote: "My mother and her mother were brought here by my father in 1923 and were married in 1924. She was introduced to my father by letter through my aunt (my mother's sister) who was already married and living in New York." And again, a second-generation mechanic said:

> My father arrived before the massacres and worked as a laborer. My mother went through the massacres and was saved by American missionaries and grew up in an American orphanage in Beirut. My father returned to Beirut with a friend. They both met and married Armenian girls there. My parents arrived in 1929 from Beirut and had three children, born here.

A young, third-generation man wrote:

> My grandfather on my mother's side saw a picture of my grandmother sometime after he came to this country. Back then all of the Armenians were particularly close and my grandfather knew her family and arranged for her to be sent here. My grandmother was sixteen and the oldest child in a family where the mother had died four years earlier. Therefore she felt a strong responsibility to stay but her father convinced her to go. After a journey lasting around one year, she arrived on Ellis Island in 1906. Although she had only just met my grandfather, she had to marry him there on the island in order to gain entry to the country. They had nine children and forty-three grandchildren.

The traditional Armenian value of female purity and virginity at marriage lingered in disguise in American society during the early period (Nelson 1953, 73). Arranged marriages after the first generation gave way to chaperoned dating and eventually—by the third generation—to more "casual" dating (Nelson 1953, 115). Young Armenian boys and girls were characterized by "shyness" because they did not mix easily (Nelson 1953, 113-14). Armenian men preferred marriage partners "who have not 'been around' very much" (Nelson 1953, 73). Armenian women could not date "indiscriminately"; an "easy date" was considered not marriageable (Nelson 1953, 79, 127). Intention of marriage was a prerequisite for dating in order to avoid community gossip. Even though by the third generation dating among ethnic peers was substituted for parental matchmaking, Nelson observed, it was "fashioned and shaped by Armenian values" (1953, 173). That is, young Armenian men and women, unlike their nonethnic peers did not "experiment" with several partners; instead, they carefully narrowed the field of eligible mates "to a minimum and then concentrate[d] on those few" (Nelson 1953, 174). Dating continued to be subject to parental approval in later generations.

Though Nelson found the power of the Armenian-American father in early generations to be absolute, the universality of this rule is disputable because with the death of a large proportion of the Armenian male population, in many families women must have filled the vacuum.[28] Armenian men and women growing up in the post-Genocide era remember matriarchal grandmothers dominating their images of their childhood. The Armenian grandmother continues to be a source of inspiration and prominent subject matter in the prose and poetry of Armenian-American authors.[29] For example, Dobkin writes: "My grandmother is a central figure in this world" (1977, 6) when she remembers the Armenian world of her youth. The grandparent is a symbol of the Genocide, of survival, of love. She is a link to the past, to one's roots, to one's identity. Some respondents also portrayed their Armenian mothers or grandmothers as powerful figures in their lives. The comments of a seventy-one-year-old, second-generation woman quoted in the previous chapter illustrate this: "My grandmother ruled as the grand matriarch in the household."

At present, the Armenian-American family is changing in the direction of equalitarian relationships between husbands and wives and between parents and children; neolocal residence (i.e., upon marriage spouses establish their own home); and descent is being traced bilineally through both parents. Parental influence remains strong, but the absolute authority of the historical Armenian patriarch has disappeared.[30] Young daughters-in-law no longer serve in silence, but cannot deny their in-laws from visiting their son and grandchildren without inviting their anger and gossip. Safeguarding the "good" name of the family and fear of being gossiped about is less meaningful in today's society where individuals inhabit a multitude of social worlds with insulated boundaries. In addition, the behavior of a daughter or a brother does not necessarily reflect upon the good standing of the family as it did in the past. Nonetheless, within communal circles, families still care about their reputation. They try to avoid losing face unnecessarily.

Relations between the sexes, mate selection, and courting are similar to conservative American norms. Those who are immersed in the Armenian-American community tend to uphold more traditional values and norms. Avakian supports this claim by saying that "antiquated attitudes" continue to be prevalent at the collective level. "Armenian women ... [are] held to sexual standards much more restrictive than those for non-Armenian women" (1988, 2).[31] Matchmaking has almost disappeared, though kin and friends occasionally introduce eligible Armenian men and women to each other. Also, among the newest immigrants from the Middle East, one occasionally hears of foreign-born men officially asking a woman's hand in marriage before dating her.

Yet, the contemporary Armenian-American family continues to be a close knit unit. As I will show below, frequent contact is maintained with immediate kin. Even when relatives live far away from each other, making contact more time and energy consuming, close ties endure through telephone calls, occasional visits. Mutual assistance is the backbone of family cohesiveness; it varies from baby sitting services to substantial financial transfers. I find Bamberger's characterization of the modern Armenian-American family quite apt; what makes it somewhat different than other ethnic or mainstream American families is its "strong sense of family duty [bardaganutiun] and a continuing concern for family solidarity" (1986-87, 78).

Household Composition

Nuclear families, with father, mother, and their children living under one roof, were most numerous in the New York sample (43.9 percent). The second largest category was couples living alone (22.5 percent); and third, respondents living alone (16.5 percent). The extended household or three-generational family consisted of less than 15 percent of the sample; it was highest among the immigrant generation. The remaining 2.3 percent, predominantly fourth generation, shared living arrangements with a nonrelative, often a friend or a lover (see table 5.14). It is interesting to note that the Armenian-American family has come a long way since its early immigrant origins when many households took on fee-paying boarders to supplement their income. This was a common occurrence among most immigrant groups during early twentieth-century America (for Armenians see Mirak 1983, 158; for other groups see Modell and

Hareven 1978). It is also worth noting that of the 5.3 percent of respondents who reported their exact relationship to their in-law in the extended household (2.1 percent did not), almost three times as many of the wife's father and/or mother lived with the nuclear family as did parents of the husband (3.9 percent vs 1.4 percent). As mentioned above, the opposite situation was the norm in the past.

The household composition of the respondents was statistically not significant with any of the assimilation variables, except for respondent's age (.17*) and stage in the household cycle (.38*; see

TABLE 5.14
Frequency Distribution of Household Type by Generation

	Foreign-Born	U.S.-Born of F.B. Parents	1 Parent U.S.-Born	2 Parents U.S.-Born	Grandparent U.S.-Born
N = 569	(214)	(264)	(35)	(41)	(15)
Nuclear family	42.1	42.0	65.7	46.3	40.0
Extended family	20.1	14.4	5.7	2.4	6.7
Couple only	19.6	26.9	11.4	24.4	6.7
Single household	16.8	15.5	14.3	19.5	26.7
Nonkin household	1.4	1.1	2.9	7.3	20.0
	100.0	100.0	100.0	100.0	100.0

TABLE 5.15
Frequency Distribution of Household Type by Household Cycle

	Single <40 yrs	Early Family	Child in School	Adult Child	Empty Nest	Single >41 yrs	Senior Citizen
N = 569	(33)	(34)	(160)	(101)	(105)	(60)	(76)
Nuclear family	21.2	97.1	76.3	89.1	87.6	3.3	40.8
Extended family	9.1	2.9	22.5	10.9	12.4	28.3	5.3
Single household	45.5	0.0	0.0	0.0	0.0	63.3	53.9
Nonkin household	24.2	0.0	1.3	0.0	0.0	5.0	0.0
	100.0	100.0	100.0	100.0	100.0	100.0	100.0

table 5.15). This means that the Armenian-American household structure varies with age and stages in the life cycle more than by generation. Young adults live alone or with a nonrelative; some continue to reside under the same roof as their family of origin. When young adults get married and start childbearing, the overwhelming majority establish neolocal residences. By the time a nuclear family has school-age or college-age children, older grandparents may move in. Other senior citizens maintain separate residences with a spouse or alone. There is nothing unusual about these arrangements. The Armenian-American family fits in with Winch and Kitson's conclusions that "there is and always has been a plurality of types of American families" (1977, 50).

Familism

Two statements were used from Bardis's (1959) "Familism Scale" which measures strong family feelings, goals, and mutual support. The first statement read: "A person should always consider the needs of his family as a whole more important than his own." The second statement said: "A person should always help his parents with the support of his younger brothers and sisters if necessary." These values are reminiscent of the early Armenian families in Fresno that Nelson described just after World War II.

> [M]arried children felt obliged to assist their parents and they rendered economic assistance if necessary and kept them in the household without grumbling if this was necessary. Children maintaining close ties with their parents, did not consider marriage a device enabling them to move to a remote community away from their parents. Parents liked to have their married children near them, and most children complied by settling in Fresno and its surrounding area with visiting back and forth at least several times a week. (Nelson 1953, 55)

New York respondents reiterated that the family was important and one should help one's siblings. For example a third-generation respondent noted that his wife was non-Armenian, then went on to say,

> She recognized the uniqueness of being an Armenian the first time she went out with me. Unlike many other minorities the Armenians in this country have never lost sight of the value of the FAMILY; we hope to pass on that tradition to our six-month-old daughter.

Another middle-aged, third-generation respondent explained that his father-in-law had arrived to the United States at the age of sixteen and worked as a photoengraver, "first to support his parents and siblings and then his own family and his parents."

Armenian-Americans, irrespective of generations in the United States, maintain a very high regard for the family and its needs (see tables 5.16, 5.17). Almost 80 percent of respondents in the sample agreed that family needs take precedence over individual needs, and 86 percent agreed that people should assist parents with the support of younger brothers and sisters, when need be. Yet, there is a slight decrease by generation in agreement on both statements. Third- and fourth-generation respondents were less apt to agree than first- and second-generation respondents, but compared to other assimilation variables, these differences were minor. Overall, the statement on supporting siblings received slightly higher agreement responses than the other.[32]

Throughout this survey, gender differences have generally not been significant with most assimilation variables. Here is an exception (tau c .12 significant at .0001); twice as many women disagreed that family needs were more important than individual needs (22.9 percent vs 10.4 percent). The never-married, the separated, and divorced in the sample were also twice as likely to disagree as the married that family needs were more important than individual needs (31.4 percent, 26.7 percent respectively vs 13.7 percent). There was a straight-line increase by age in agreement with the statement that family needs are more important

TABLE 5.16

Frequency Distribution of Attitude Statement: "A Person Should Always Consider the Needs of His Family as a whole More important than his own" by Generation

	Foreign-Born	U.S.-Born of F.B. Parents	1 Parent U.S.-Born	2 Parents U.S.-Born	Grandparent U.S.-Born
N = 584	(219)	(272)	(36)	(41)	(16)
Agree	84.0	78.7	80.6	70.7	56.3
No opinion	4.1	4.8	0.0	2.4	12.5
Disagree	11.9	16.5	19.4	26.8	31.1
	100.0	100.0	100.0	100.0	100.0

than one's own. The older the respondent, the more he or she was likely to agree that family needs should take precedence (31 percent of twenty year olds, 21 percent of forty year olds, 11 percent of sixty year olds and 7 percent of those over seventy disagreed with the statement). It can be concluded that, unlike the statement on supporting siblings, the statement on family needs is influenced by life status events not generational standing. A small group of independent women, singles and younger people—those who deviate from the marriage norm—are less likely to comply with family pressure, but such people are also least likely to reap the benefits of family life.

It is remarkable that supporting siblings and putting family needs before one's own continues to have high priority in the lives of men and women of Armenian descent. Nelson had found that one of the characteristics of the Armenian family unit was its closeness. He wrote: "Kinship is important, and informants speak of the warmth within Armenian families they don't believe exists in the families of their *odar* friends" (Nelson 1953,117-18). It is hypothesized in the ethnicity literature that with increasing generational presence in America, people feel closer to friends than to family; that is, ascriptive relations take second place to the more compatible relationships one establishes with nonkin. Is this true of Armenian-Americans?

Respondents were asked how many of the five people they felt closest to in their lives were family members; second, married respondents were asked how close they felt to their spouse's relatives. These correlations were statistically not significant with most of the

TABLE 5.17
Frequency Distribution of Attitude Statement: "A Person Should Always Help His Parents with the Support of His Younger Brothers and Sisters if Necessary" by Generation

	Foreign-Born	U.S.-Born of F.B. Parents	1 Parent U.S.-Born	2 Parents U.S.-Born	Grandparent U.S.-Born
N = 584	(219)	(272)	(36)	(41)	(16)
Agree	92.7	84.6	83.3	70.7	68.8
No opinion	3.6	7.7	8.3	7.3	12.5
Disagree	3.7	7.7	8.3	22.0	18.8
	100.0	100.0	100.0	100.0	100.0

independent variables of the study (see tables 5.18, 5.19). Overall, only 18 percent of the sample did not feel close to any of their kin, about 33 percent felt close to one or two relatives, and the remaining 50 percent or so felt close to more than three (including 25.5 percent who felt close to all five).[33] It is interesting that there was a slight increase of about ten percentage points in feeling close to more than three family members by generation. This is in the opposite direction than predicted. On the other hand, there was a decrease in the predicted direction in feeling close to one's spouse's relatives. About half of the married sample did not feel close to their in-laws. The hypothesis that generational presence decreases one's feeling of closeness to one's kin group is refuted. Armenian-Americans repeatedly say they feel close to their family and would put its interests first, if necessary. They interpret the traditions of their ancestors to mean a sense of duty and solidarity toward their families.

Family Contacts

To bridge the gap between attitudes and behavior, respondents were supplied with a list of the following relatives: father/mother, children, sister/brother, grandparents, in-laws, aunts/uncles, cousins, and nephews/nieces, and asked to indicate how many times in the two weeks prior to the survey they had seen or telephoned each set of kin (see table 5.20). To control for geographical distance, respondents were asked to name the city/state each set of relatives lived in.

TABLE 5.18
Frequency Distribution of Respondents Feeling Closest to Five Relatives by Generation

	Foreign-Born	U.S.-Born of F.B. Parents	1 Parent U.S.-Born	2 Parents U.S.-Born	Grandparent U.S.-Born
N = 541	(191)	(261)	(34)	(39)	(16)
None	22.0	16.1	11.8	20.5	12.5
One or two	30.4	33.7	44.1	29.2	31.3
More than three	47.6	50.2	44.1	50.3	56.3
	100.0	100.0	100.0	100.0	100.0

Distance was categorized into: same as respondent; adjacent (New England, Pennsylvania, Washington, DC); other states in the United States and Canada; and abroad (see table 5.21).

Out of the eight sets of kin provided by the questionnaire, Armenian-Americans are most likely to be in frequent contact with their children. All respondents who had children and did not live under one roof saw or phoned their children at least once in the two weeks prior to the study. Almost a third of them had contact with their children every day, and another quarter had contact at least every other day. Parents were next; a third of all respondents whose parents were still alive saw or phoned their parents every other day or more frequently. Of the six respondents (2.5 percent) who had no contact whatsoever with their parents, five were foreign-born and their parents lived abroad, and one was a third-generation respondent whose parents were in another state. Siblings were the third most frequent kin respondents maintained contact with. While only 11 percent saw or talked to a brother or sister every day, over 70 percent did so once to seven times in two weeks.

It is interesting that Armenian-American kin relations are in sharp contrast to those reported for the English. According to Allan, secondary kin such as aunts, uncles, nephews, nieces in England were considered of "little importance in people's patterns of sociability." They were seen "comparatively rarely, and when interaction [... occurred it was] often perceived as a consequence of fortuitous

TABLE 5.19
Frequency Distribution of Respondents Feeling Closest to Five In-Laws by Generation

	Foreign-Born	U.S.-Born of F.B. Parents	1 Parent U.S.-Born	2 Parents U.S.-Born	Grandparent U.S.-Born
N = 543	(191)	(262)	(34)	(39)	(16)
None	50.3	53.4	55.9	50.0	50.0
One or two	29.3	21.8	17.6	15.0	6.3
More than three	9.4	9.9	5.9	2.5	0
Not applicable	11.0	14.9	20.6	32.5	43.8
	100.0	100.0	100.0	100.0	100.0

circumstances rather than conscious design" (1979, 111-12). I have no information on whether contact with secondary kin is fortuitous for Armenian-Americans. However, over two-thirds of the sample had contacts with aunts, uncles, cousins, nephews, and nieces at least once or twice in the two weeks before the survey (see table 5.18). This indicates a fairly busy kin circle. The majority of the sample had relatives living in the same city and state. Only about 5 percent of respondents had kin living abroad. Children were the least likely to be abroad and grandparents the most. This reflects the continuous chain of migration of younger family members followed by older ones.

TABLE 5.20
Frequency Distribution of Times Family Members Contacted in Two Weeks
Prior to Survey by Kinship Categories

	Parent	Child	Sibling	Grand-parent	In-Laws	Nephew/Niece	Aunt/Uncle	Cousin
N.A.	(327)	(329)	(140)	(508)	(293)	(206)	(314)	(171)
N =	(240)	(243)	(414)	(50)	(265)	(342)	(235)	(375)
Zero	2.5	0.0	7.5	50.0	13.9	23.7	33.2	31.5
1-2	29.9	16.9	42.5	26.0	47.9	43.9	45.5	40.0
3-7	35.4	29.2	28.7	18.0	24.5	23.4	15.7	22.6
8-13	15.8	25.1	10.1	4.0	7.9	6.1	2.5	2.9
Daily	16.6	28.8	11.1	2.0	5.7	2.9	3.0	2.9
	100.0	100.0	100.0	100.0	100.0	100.0	100.0	100.0

TABLE 5.21
Frequency Distribution of Times Family Members Contacted in Two Weeks
Prior to Survey by Geographical Location

	Parent	Child	Sibling	Grand-parent	In-Laws	Nephew/Niece	Aunt/Uncle	Cousin
N. A.	(327)	(329)	(140)	(508)	(293)	(206)	(314)	(171)
N =	(236)	(247)	(392)	(43)	(246)	(284)	(193)	(314)
Same	77.1	75.1	70.9	65.1	74.4	72.9	67.9	71.3
Near	7.6	10.1	9.9	11.6	10.6	12.0	8.8	10.8
Far	9.7	13.7	15.1	11.6	11.8	12.0	17.6	12.8
Abroad	5.5	1.3	4.1	11.6	3.2	3.1	5.6	5.1
	100.0	100.0	100.0	100.0	100.0	100.0	100.0	100.0

When controlled for geographical distance, foreign-born respondents were most likely to see or talk to their children (see table 5.22). They were also more likely to contact their parents (see table 5.23) and siblings (see table 5.24) very often. Keeping in touch with family members diminishes with each succeeding generation for those living

TABLE 5.22
Frequency Distribution of Respondents Contacting Their Children by Generation, Controlled for Geographical Distance

	Foreign-Born	U.S.-Born of F.B. Parents	1 Parent + U.S.-Born
Same city			
N = 179	(67)	(101)	(11)
1 to 7 times	29.9	42.6	63.6
8 times to daily	70.1	57.4	36.3
	100.0	100.0	100.0
Other (excluding abroad)			
N = 58	(14)	(43)	(1)
1 to 7 times	71.4	81.4	100.0
8 times to daily	28.6	18.6	0.0
	100.0	100.0	100.0

TABLE 5.23
Frequency Distribution of Respondents Contacting Their Parents by Generation, Controlled for Geographical Distance

	Foreign-Born	U.S.-Born of F.B. Parents	1 Parent + U.S.-Born
Same city			
N = 180	(54)	(71)	(55)
1 to 7 times	57.4	66.2	65.5
8 times to daily	42.6	33.8	34.5
	100.0	100.0	100.0
Other (excluding abroad)			
N = 40	(9)	(14)	(17)
1 to 7 times	100.0	92.9	88.2
8 times to daily	0.0	7.1	11.8
	100.0	100.0	100.0

in the same geographical area. There are less discernable patterns for those who do not live in same place. It is interesting that women were in contact with kin more frequently than men. They were twice as likely as men to keep in touch with siblings every other day or more times in a fortnight; the relationship is slightly more significant when controlled for the same city or state (35 percent vs 18 percent for same place, 10 percent vs 4 percent for distant location; tau c .18 significant at .0003 level).

This is not surprising; keeping in touch with family members comprises what has been called "the work of kin" which women do for the family without being recognized for it. In the same category are sending birthday cards, buying Christmas presents, cooking holiday meals and taking care of elderly relatives. On the other hand, when siblings live in other states, younger people are more likely to have frequent contact with them than older people (33.3 percent of twenty year olds compared to 26.7 percent of thirty year olds, 5 percent of forty year olds and 3.2 percent of fifty year olds). Keeping in touch with one's children does not vary by socioeconomic status, but the higher the class the slightly less the contact with siblings, and parents.

TABLE 5.24
Frequency Distribution of Respondents Contacting Their Siblings by Generation, Controlled for Geographical Distance

	Foreign-Born	U.S.-Born of F.B. Parents	1 Parent + U.S.-Born
Same city N = 277	(80)	(142)	(55)
Zero	1.3	2.8	3.6
1 to 7 times	61.3	75.4	81.8
8 times or daily	37.5	21.8	14.5
	100.0	100.0	100.0
Other (excluding abroad) N = 98	(33)	(46)	(19)
Zero	9.1	10.9	26.3
1 to 7 times	81.8	87.0	57.9
8 times or daily	9.1	2.2	15.8
	100.0	100.0	100.0

In sum, the majority of Armenian-Americans say they feel close to their family members; their behavior affirms it, more or less. Parents and children are most often in contact with each other, siblings come next, especially for younger people. The comments of the respondents support these findings. A thirty-year-old third-generation woman wrote, "While growing up our family (parents, grandparents, aunts, uncles, cousins, sisters/brothers) was close. This closeness and love continues today." Another third-generation, middle-aged lady said: "I was raised very Armenian. All Armenian friends and our social life was with our family basically." Generation was not significant with feelings of closeness to family members; however, it was more significant with actual behavior. This confirms the hypothesis that later-generation Armenian-Americans maintain high levels of affect but are low on actual behavior. It appears that this is also true in family relations.

Family contacts change with stages in the life cycle. The birth of a baby increases communication, and the death of a parent reduces it. A young mother whose mother is U.S.-born, and husband and father non-Armenian wrote: "Always close to immediate family especially mine, but with newborn baby seeing them even more often." On the other hand, a middle-aged, second-generation woman wrote: "We had a great family life. Went to Hantese [festive parties] every Sunday as a family—family gatherings. After parents passed away, the closeness lessened. But still keep in touch with all my mother's relatives."

Geographical distance and economic conditions are also important in family contacts. A second-generation respondent explained that his mother was an orphan. "Her sister ended up in California. I saw her

TABLE 5.25
Frequency Distribution of Visiting Armenians When Growing Up by Generation

	Foreign-Born	U.S.-Born of F.B. Parents	1 Parent U.S.-Born	2 Parents U.S.-Born	Grandparent U.S.-Born
N = 582	(217)	(272)	(36)	(41)	(16)
Hardly ever	5.1	5.9	11.1	19.5	43.8
Some of the time	13.8	27.6	38.8	51.2	37.5
Almost always	81.1	66.5	50.0	29.3	18.8
	100.0	100.0	100.0	100.0	100.0

once when I was nine.... My father's brother also went to California and since we were definitely not affluent we were not able to see each other." On the other hand, a first-generation respondent was luckier because his parents were more affluent. Here is his story: "I had no [Armenian] friends as such as we lived in Mineola, LI, completely detached from Hyes [Armenians]. But our family always associated with Hyes all the time; we'd visit, they'd come to our home. I had one close friend.... We met at the Catskills (where our families vacationed)."

Visiting

The last question in this section analyzes the imbeddedness of the respondent's family in the informal Armenian network of friends, acquaintances, compatriots, and second cousins while he or she was growing up.[34] It is important to measure a family's bridges with the wider Armenian-American community because such contacts allow a child additional opportunities to reinforce his/her ethnic identity and provide the possibility of getting involved in the collective manifestation of Armenianness. For three generations of Armenian-Americans in Fresno some forty years ago, "visiting, with the children accompanying their parents, and being visited ... [was] one of the most frequent recreational pursuits of the family" (Nelson 1953, 51; and 84-117 for second- and third-generation visiting).

The findings of the New York study corroborate the importance of visiting. Overall, 67 percent of the sample did so most of the time, while only about 8 percent hardly ever visited Armenian families when they were growing up (see table 5.25). The informal ties of the Armenian-American family with fellow ethnics diminish with each succeeding generation (24*). Nonetheless, a significant proportion of third- and fourth-generation respondents were exposed to other Armenians during their formative years.

Visiting Armenians while growing up was also highly significant with religious affiliation, sympathy to Armenian political parties, and mixed ancestry. For example, 5 percent of those with two Armenian parents hardly ever visited Armenians versus 30 percent of those with mixed ancestry (.16*). Again, almost 4 percent of Armenian Apostolics and Protestants hardly ever visited other Armenians compared to

20 percent of those with non-Armenian religious affiliations and 11 percent of those with "no religion." This leads me to deduce that respondents with "no religion" were brought up within the ethnic community but have since moved away from collective manifestations of Armenianness; by contrast, those with non-Armenian denominational affiliations have had less of an ethnic socialization while growing up. In sum, the data reveals that the immigrant family and the second-generation family are almost totally immersed in the Armenian world of family, kin, friends, and acquaintances. Visiting each other is a central activity in this informal network; it decreases somewhat in intensity by the third and later generations.

In conclusion, the Armenian-American family remains the hub of social exchanges, mutual assistance, and affection. Such close ties cannot but engender positive associations in the minds of its members. Descendants of the immigrant generation have a high regard for their parents and grandparents and value the hard work and dedication that contributed to their present well-being and status. Maintaining Armenian identity is the debt they owe to their forebears. For their sake or for their memory, they feel strongly about Armenia and the Armenians. But this commitment to the past does not translate into action very easily, nor is it allowed to become an obsession. It should be noted that the New York study is a typical portrayal of the first three generations, it does not do justice to the subsequent generations, nor does it predict the future. I suspect, however, that with the passing away of the immigrant generation, those in fourth and fifth generations will have fewer opportunities to develop a sense of moral responsibility either toward their ancestors or their heritage.

The family unit with its social ties and its traditions embodies an important source of Armenian identity, which it tries to pass down to next generation. Without the support of educational, religious, and other formal institutions, parents and grandparents can teach their children to identify themselves as Armenian-Americans; to be proud of their cultural background and the achievements of their people, to feel a sense of kinship to fellow Armenians in the diaspora; to be outraged by the Genocide, even develop animosity toward the Turks for its denial; to have a weakness for Armenian cuisine; to sporadically participate in communal endeavors or at least to contribute financially to Armenian concerns. In sum, they can teach the next generation to *feel* Armenian rather than *be* Armenian. Given the parameters of American society, this is what most people can and will probably do.

Men and women of Armenian descent in the present-day United States are happy to identify with their ancestral background and perpetuate their heritage as long as it is in the sidestream. Insofar as Armenianness does not come into conflict with the serious business of earning a living, one's allegiance to the United States, and the American Dream, Armenian-Americans will continue to express their pride and sentiments in people and things Armenian. The results of the New York study corroborate Barthel's very poignant observations:

> In sum, respondents seem to feel that ethnicity should remain on the "team sports" level of identification—it should give you someone to root for when what is at stake seems little more than a game. It becomes a basis for choice on election day when a choice must be made among candidates for minor office and there is no information to go on beyond name. It becomes the basis for celebrations when an Italian boy "makes good" on the athletic field or a Greek girl becomes an award-winning actress; the feeling that he or she is "one of us" adds to the excitement.... When this choosing-up of sides deepens, then people feel that it is carrying a good thing too far; they believe ethnic identification should be left as a matter of games and sentiment, not elevated to a level where it affects important decisions. (Barthel 1978, 114)

In this chapter, I have shown that identification, pride and sense of peoplehood do not decrease significantly with the passing of generations, with non-Armenian denominational affiliation or "no religion," with indifference to Armenian politics, or mixed ancestry. The majority of the respondents in the New York study identified themselves as Armenian-Americans. They felt extremely proud to be of Armenian descent. They rejoiced when they heard or recognized the names of men and women of Armenian descent who were successful in the arts, media, science, business, sports, or politics. They cherished their Armenian family name like a heirloom and said they would not change it to sound less ethnic. When they encountered other Armenians on their travels or visited historic lands, they felt strong bonds of kinship.

What do these patterns mean? Why do men and women of Armenian descent continue to identify with their ancestral heritage and maintain a sense of peoplehood? Unlike language, communal involvement, ethnic politics, and so on, I suggest identity and sense of peoplehood in one's ethnic background are maintained for two reasons. One is changes in the nature of ethnicity paralleling the group's social mobility. From an ascribed, behavioral, traditional identity ethnicity becomes a voluntary, emotional, symbolic identity. Two, greater tolerance, even popularity of folkloric or sidestream ethnicity in America. Ethnicity provides much-needed excitement and rituals to an otherwise bland, homogenizing culture.

Sense of peoplehood, the Genocide, Armenian cuisine and the family are sources that nourish and energize Armenian identity in the contemporary United States. Pride in the accomplishments of fellow Armenians enhances the value of the collectivity, it proves that one descends from a group of talented, creative, smart, hardworking people. Traveling to the "spiritual homeland" is a leisure-time, sporadic occurrence that is likely to heighten one's sense of roots while it satisfies one's adventurous spirit and pursuit of pleasure. The Genocide and its denial by Turkish governments makes Armenian-Americans very angry and arouses their sense of justice and equity. It is one of the rare issues that touches the hearts of nearly all Armenian-Americans. Yet, participation in commemorative events is far below the level of affect. Symbolic Armenian-Americans have strong feelings, but are not likely to transform their sentiments into action

Armenian cuisine continues to be enjoyed by Armenian-Americans, though more people eat it than cook it, and instead of being the daily diet, it is relegated to special occasions and family reunions. Yet food is one of the most convenient methods of satisfying one's urge to belong in one's ancestral world with minimum probability of disappointment. Ultimately, the burden of the perpetuation of Armenianness in the United States rests on the family. The New York sample indicates that the contemporary Armenian-American family is a close-knit unit, characterized by frequent contact among immediate kin, and a strong sense of obligation and concern for the welfare of its members. Most significantly, the family breeds Armenian identity and we-ness through a personal sense of love and obligation toward one's parents and grandparents. Overall, the family remains an important component in the lives of the men and women who participated in this study and the root of Armenian feelings, pride, and identity.

Notes

1. According to De Vos and Romanucci-Ross (1982, 18-24), there are three types of group allegiance, those that are ideological or future-oriented such as revolutionary or religious movements; the functional or present-oriented loyalties to a state or occupation; and the past-oriented commitments to family and cultural heritage of which ethnicity is a prime example.

2. For instance, presently in the United States, most children acknowledge the ethnic background of both their parents, i.e., bilineally. Whereas in unilineal societies, descent can be traced only partilineally, i.e., through one's father (e.g., most Middle Eastern societies), or only matrilineally, i.e., through one's mother (e.g., some West African tribes).

3. Alter-casting is defined as way people cast others in roles that fit the scenario they want to enact (see Lyman and Douglas 1973, 358).

4. David Luhrssen, "A non-Armenian Comments — Why the Armenian Church?" *Armenian Reporter,* 9 May 1991, p. 3.

5. See the *Armenian Reporter,* 17 March 1988, p. 3 - letter to the editor.

6. Given the fact that the survey was specifically on Armenians, it probably induced more respondents to check the "American-Armenian" category. These same individuals may have used other identity tags under different circumstances.

7. Other ethnic groups portray similar tendencies to identify themselves as hyphenated Americans. For example, for Lebanese-Maronite communities in Detroit see Ahdab-Yahia (1980, 150); for Italians in Bridgeport, see Crispino (1980, 97); for Chaldeans in Detroit see Sengstock (1969).

8. This is similar to the distinction made in chapter 2 between mechanical and organic types of ethnic solidarity.

9. These views were aired at an Open University Seminar organized by The Zoryan Institute, held at Columbia University, 24 January 1987. The seminar was chaired by Prof. Khachig Tölölyan.

10. Other examples of ex-roles provided by Ebaugh are ex-nuns, ex-doctors, divorcées, widows, alumni, ex-alcoholics, transsexuals, etc.

11. See also Dr. Puzant Hadidian, "Turkish Invasion of Armenian Family Names," *Armenian Reporter,* 13 February 1986, pp. 3, 12.

12. For example, my own family name, Bakalian, is Turkish, meaning "grocer."

13. It should be noted that some Persian names also end with "ian." However, it is usually not too difficult to recognize the difference; Armenians would not call their child Ali or Mohammad.

14. See the *Armenian Reporter,* e.g., 12 September 1985; 4 September 1986; 4 December 1986; 19 and 26 March 1987; 2 and 9 April 1987; and "Another Armenian Successfully Climbs Mt. Ararat," 6 August 1987 . A video film of this historic climb, narrated by Mike Connors is now on sale for $49.00 (see ad in *Armenian International Magazine,* July 1990, p. 15).

15. The film was produced by WGBH, Boston in 1988 with funding from the Alex and Marie Manoogian Foundation, the Louise Simone Fund, and public television viewers.

16. For example, the Diocese is sponsoring a pilgrimage to the Cathedral of Echmiadzin to witness the making of *Holy Muron* (holy oil ceremoniously mixed once every seven years), and a audience with the Catholicos in October 1991.

Also see ad in *Armenian International Magazine,* June 1991, p. 55.

17. Like the Armenians, the Jews and Greeks have their own diasporas. Describing the Hellenic case, Moskos elaborates on the concept: "The paradigm of the diaspora is that one's cultural roots and political sensitivities must be nourished by a responsiveness to contemporary Greek realities — even at a distance. The underlying presumption is that, whether residing or even born in the United States, Greeks in America share a destiny somehow connected with other people who call themselves Hellenes" (1989, 145-46).

18. For example, major fund-raising campaigns were targeted to help the impoverished Lebanese Armenians. See "Lebanon in Financial Turmoil," *Armenian Reporter,* 19 November 1987; and *Outreach* 10, 7 (November 1987). The major thrust is now geared toward the Republic of Armenia.

19. See Kerop Bayman "Impressions of a Visit to Argentina & Brazil: From South America with Love," *Armenian Reporter,* 19 February 1987, pp. 4 and 13. The writer, upon arriving in Rio de Janeiro called up Armenian names from the telephone directory to find out that there were approximately 100 families of Armenian descent, most of whom did not speak Armenian. There was no Armenian church in Rio de Janeiro, nor an organized community.

20. For example, one of them has written that "it is pitiful to see the Genocide being the only common issue to all Armenians and probably the only one which could enhance some type of national consciousness among Armenians, [it] has not been exploited as a most important political issue" (Keoseyan 1981, 70).

21. See Mary Ann Aposhian. "Clinging to Ethnic Heritage in America: Study Compares Extent of Assimilation between Earlier Generation, New Arrivals." *Armenian International Magazine,* February 1991, pp. 33-36.

22. Colombo's yogurt company was established by an Armenian from Massachusetts who sold the company for a sizable profit in recent years.

23. Likewise, according to the survey of Armenian restaurants quoted above, the chef of Sayat Nova in Chicago told the reporter that she "strives 'to make Armenian food more palatable to the American public'" (*Armenian International Magazine,* June 1991, p. 34).

24. Traditionally, Armenian cooks rarely weighed or measured their ingredients. Long years of practice had taught them to cook by "instinct" — *atchkee chap* (eye measure).

25. Following the lead of American chefs who have gained celebrity and fortune by going on (public and cable) television, a few enterprising cooks have videotaped their Armenian culinary techniques. These cassettes are advertised in the ethnic press.

26. For parallels with Greek-Americans see Kourvetaris (1981, 185).

27. Elkholy (1981, 158) corroborates that Arab-Americans shun nursing homes for their aged parents. According to the *Armenian American Almanac* (1990) there are eight Armenian old people's homes in the United States that offer a variety of services, including one in New Jersey and one in Queens. I asked the director of the New Jersey facility whether the notion that it is a shame to place one's elderly parents in an institution still prevailed. I was told that it was true in the past, but not any more.

28. Writer and poet Lorne Shirinian (1990) who has analyzed Armenian-North American literature makes an interesting analogy. He found that the father figure seems to be absent in most writings and sons seem to be abandoned. He attributes

this to the state of being in a diaspora, loss of territory, and gradual disappearance of language.

29. At a conference entitled "Armenian-American Literature: Old and New Directions," organized by The Armenian Center and The Columbia University Program in Armenian Studies, at Columbia University, New York City, 9 April 1988, a group of six fiction writers and three poets (all U.S.-born, second and third generation) observed the major influence their Armenian grandmothers (and grandfathers) had had in their lives and in their writings. Women authors, slightly more than men, emphasized the role their grandmothers had played in their lives. For a sample of Armenian-American fiction, see special issue of *Ararat* 28, 2 (Spring 1987). The mother/grandmother figure is of course not unique to Armenians; Gans (1962, 33) suggests that her role in ethnic maintenance is related to the importance of food in the family and her responsibility in cooking it (see also Fishman 1985, 503; Schneider 1980, 5).

30. Education professor Pergrouhi Svajian observes that vestiges of the authoritarian system survive today. Instead of reprimanding children with *amot eh* (shame, shame) and *mekhk eh* (pity, pity), she suggests that parents and educators in Armenian schools should develop children's individualism, initiative, and independence. She argues that it might have been functional in an agrarian traditional society under Ottoman rule exert authoritarian control; however, this is not the case in modern society where roles are no longer fixed and stable over time. Rather she points out flexibility and adaptability are valued in today's economic and social system. Svajian also notes that family relations in present-day Armenia remain extremely traditional, patriarchal. For example, even among the highly educated professional families, sons do not help themselves to water when thirsty, even when a faucet is nearby. Instead they demand that the (equally well-educated) *hars* (daughter-in-law) serve them. Moreover, daughters-in-law are rarely called by their names, they are beckoned by the generic *hars*. See Pergrouhi Svajian, "Three Faces of Parent-Child Relationship," *Nor Gyank* 13, 1 (20 December 1990): 25.

31. Similar observations were made in a study of French-Armenians over a decade earlier. Boudjikanian-Keuroghlian argues that the double standard of morality in the Armenian community allows Armenian men to date French women freely, but more conservative standards are set for women who were taught to be "honorable et vertueuse." The author goes on to suggest that this has produced confusion and ambiguity between personal aspirations and traditional upbringing and has inflated the rates of mixed marriages. "Le dépassement de ces contradictions aboutit au mariage mixte pour les uns et pour les autres. Il s'est créé un déphasage entre les convictions traditionelles et les aspirations individuelles actuelles que ni les familles — qualifiées de "vieux jeu" par les jeunes — ni la nouvelle génération n'arrivent à atténuer" (1978, 112).

32. Kassees (1972) used Bardis's Familism Scale on two samples of Christian Arabs from Ramallah, Occupied West Bank (Israel); one group was living in the original hometown, the other in the United States. Most significantly, the study found that Ramallah emigrés scored higher on the familism scale than those who had remained in the native land. The author suggests: "Familistic attitudes, instead of disappearing, become more emphasized when an ethnic group moves from its familistic culture to an individualistic one" (Kassees 1972, 543). For extended familism among upper-middle-class suburban Jews, see Winch, Greer

and Blumberg (1967).
33. The comparative percentages for Italian-Americans in Crispino's (1980, 81) study show that 41 percent of his respondents felt close to three or more of their relatives and only 7 percent felt close to their spouse's relatives. The straight-line model fits the Italian-American case better than the Armenian-American one.
34. The question was: "While you were growing up, did you and your family visit other Armenians excluding relatives?"

6

Conclusions:
Intermarriage, Symbolic Armenianness

The marriage of men and women of Armenian descent with non-Armenians *(odars)* is assumed to be the key to assimilation that will obliterate Armenian presence in the United States—the final straw on the camel's back, so to speak. It is perceived as the culprit of all the woes of Armenian-Americans: the loss of the ancestral language; the alienation of younger cohorts from Armenian churches, political parties, voluntary associations, and communal activities; the atrophy of the cultural heritage; the abandonment of family traditions; in sum, the cause of all the changes in the life-style that the immigrant generation had taken for granted.

Interestingly, Armenian-Americans do not realize, as the evidence from the New York survey has shown that statistically intermarriage is of secondary significance to the passing of generations in the United States and religious affiliation. Children of mixed ancestry do not as a rule exhibit all those supposedly "undesirable" characteristics I have listed above. A non-Armenian parent decreases the likelihood of participation in the ethnic world; however, the organized community's reactions are as significant, if not more so. Their attitudes and behavior send the message that *odars* are not welcome in their midst.

The aim of this study was to analyze the pervasive question of assimilation that has perplexed Armenians ever since they settled in the United States of America over a century ago. While some lamented the ossification of the immigrant culture, skeptics surmised that the primordial forces of Armenianness would prevail; after all, they had managed to survive as a people for thousands of years. They survived numerous invading armies, centuries of foreign domination, several natural and man-made calamities, and as if all that was not enough, their long and turbulent history culminated in the first Genocide of the twentieth century. In spite of the obsession with the "white massacre," there was scant empirical proof of what was happening to Armenianness in America. Yet, there was no limit to myths and speculative theories. Therefore, the motivating factor behind this investigation on Armenian-Americans was to put to rest the contentious subject of assimilation.

The empirical evidence in this book came predominantly from a lengthy mail questionnaire survey that yielded 584 responses. The sample was randomly selected from the mailing lists of Armenian churches and organizations in metropolitan New York and New Jersey and supplemented with a snowball sample of respondents who were organizationally not affiliated. The results are believed to be generalizable to all men and women of Armenian descent in the United States of America. Moreover, the findings are applicable to other white ethnic groups of the "new" immigration (i.e., those who came to the New World at the turn of the twentieth century), and somewhat less to racial groups such as blacks, Hispanics, and Asian-Americans because of higher levels of discrimination and prejudice against them. In other words, the assimilative profile of Armenians presented here is by no means unique; the impact of social, economic, and political conditions in the host society are considerable. Yet, as I said in chapter 1, no two ethnic groups are exactly alike because of the specific circumstances of their arrival, the various waves of immigration, their timing, size, and dispersion; and, of course, the cultural baggage brought with them.

The assimilation that the earliest Armenian immigrants in Fresno as elsewhere had feared is indeed well under way. However, what the pioneers had not foreseen was the changing nature of Armenianness. Indeed, they would have been pleasantly surprised to learn that their grandchildren and great-grandchildren continue to hold onto their Armenian identity and are immensely proud of their heritage. The change is from traditional Armenianness, which is typical of the foreign-born generation, to symbolic Armenianness, which is characteristic of American-born generations, though the distinctions are not absolute. It is the thesis of this book that processes of assimilation and changes in the nature of Armenianness go hand in hand.

The differences in the two forms of Armenianness are best portrayed through the debate over language. The traditional Armenians who understand their ethnicity as an ascribed, behavioral, corporate entity insist that one cannot be an Armenian without speaking Armenian and being immersed in an Armenian subculture. They realize that parents in the United States are incapable of single-handedly imparting to their children a solid grounding in the basics of reading and writing Armenian, as well as knowledge of the history and culture of their ancestors. Thus, traditional Armenians are fervent advocates of all-day Armenian schools.

The symbolic Armenians, on the other hand, conceive of their ethnic identity as a choice, expressed in terms of pride in one's heritage and strong feelings toward people and things Armenian. They gauge an individual's commitment to his/her Armenian background in terms of voluntary actions. Contributions of one's time, energy, and money to Armenian concerns are valued. No less important are the personal accomplishments of men and women of Armenian descent in their fields of endeavor. Through their successes, those who achieve fame and fortune testify that Armenians come from a fine stock of talented, hardworking people—a group worthy of recognition by the rest of the world.

All this implies that manifestations of symbolic Armenianness are confined to the sidestream, to one's leisure time and private life. By no means should one's ethnic background interfere with one's economic, social, and political integration in the larger society. Therefore, symbolic Armenian-Americans perceive all-day schools as too parochial or too ethnic, essentially because such learning environments do not reflect the pluralism of American society. On the other hand, less demanding forms of secondary socialization into the Armenian world, such as Sunday schools, college courses, or travel abroad summer programs, are favored because they are more congruent with their definition of Armenianness. Ideally, one should compete effectively in the larger economic and political arena while recognizing one's roots and being proud of one's ancestral patrimony.

Assimilation is not a unitary process. I have used in this study Milton Gordon's theoretical perspective, which postulates seven analytically separate subprocesses of assimilation, each progressing at its own pace. So far I have analyzed all the dependent variables except marital assimilation. Intermarriage is not an isolated phenomenon; it is an integral part of the changes that take place in the nature of Armenianness. An understanding of the dynamics of mate selection is warranted here.

Armenian Intermarriage in the United States

Variables Affecting Rates of Intermarriage

It has been argued that marital assimilation is the "inevitable by-product of structural assimilation" (Gordon 1964, 80). Interethnic and interreligious marriages have been explained as the natural outcome of assimilation and the closing of social and cultural distance between immigrant groups in the United States. Other factors influencing such marriages are sex ratio, size of a group, propinquity, availability, incidence of chance meetings, and homogamy. Generally, interethnic and interreligious marriages increase between immigrant groups and with the host society when there is a decrease in residential segregation, when variation in socioeconomic status decreases; and when there are changes in attitudes.

More specifically, it has been argued by Peres and Schrift (1978, 429) that the rate of interethnic and interreligious marriages depends upon "(1) variation in the reservoirs (i.e., the number of individuals in the relevant population who satisfy certain requirements); or (2) changes in the prerequisites for becoming eligible (i.e., in the attitudes or preferences of individuals who are active in the marriage market)." When immigrant ethnic and religious groups (or minority groups in Peres and Schrift's designation) have comparable distribution of socioeconomic resources, the field of eligibles increases. However, the lowest stratum of the host society is generally very ethnocentric and fearful of losing its relative advantage. Therefore, it is unlikely to intermingle with outsiders or newcomers, let alone marry into such groups. Members of the minority consequently need to bypass this barrier group and achieve educational and occupational parity with a higher, more tolerant stratum of the society (Peres and Schrift 1978, 429-30). In other words, a prerequisite for marital assimilation for immigrant groups is a big leap up the socioeconomic ladder.

Mate selection systems, past and present, have been based on the rule of homogamy; that is, like marries like. People choose spouses who have traits similar to their own; such as manners, tastes, traditions, life-styles, language, subcultures, race, religion, caste, ethnicity, and social class. Rules of exogamy proscribe marital unions between members of the same group, while rules of endogarr y prescribe the groups one must marry into. For the early immigrant groups in America, communal segregation and cultural differences restricted marriages into out-groups; however, ethnic and religious exogamy proscriptions have since been replaced by milder ethnocentric preference rules.

Transformations in marriage preference patterns have been brought about by changes in the family system and in the immigrant cultures. First, in mate selection, the family system has put the decision-making process increasingly on the individuals entering the union. The "romantic love complex" has replaced the matchmaker. Romantic love is a bait that lures mates into matrimony; it transfers loyalties from one's family of origin into one's family of procreation and provides an emotional cushion during the transitional process into new role relationships. In industrial societies such as the United States, love has been institutionalized as a prerequisite for marriage. Second, acculturation processes have shed the conspicuous characteristics that distinguished immigrant subcultures, such as language, dress, and mannerisms, making ethnic groups more homogamous. Other factors contributing to increases in marital assimilation in the United States include

the philosophical concept of freedom, a relatively open arms immigration policy since the nation's birth, unplanned migration which limited the number of potential in-group marriage partners available to any cohort in the marriage market and a system of stratification which rewards merit rather than family background and places more importance on class status than ethnic, cultural, or racial background. The rates of intercultural and interracial marriage have been especially advancing with the ever changing communication and transportation technology closing space and providing time to test and experiment with one's interpersonal relationships. (Jeter 1982, 110-11)

Scholars have debated whether the opportunity structures that enhance interethnic and interreligious encounters are more powerful than value systems that encourage ethnocentrism in mate selection. This argument is illustrated by Wesley Fisher's (1980) analysis of the Soviet marriage market. Fisher found that sociodemographic factors, and not ideology or nationalistic feelings, were responsible for the low intermarriage rates in Soviet Armenia. Others have disagreed with these conclusions contending that religion, an indicator of national consciousness, is the single best predictor of ethnic endogamy in the Soviet Union (Silver 1978).

Peter Blau's work on heterogeneity and inequality has provided significant support to the structural hypothesis of intermarriage. He and his associates have postulated that "cultural values discouraging intermarriage are not sufficient to nullify structural influences encouraging it" (Blau, Blum, and Schwartz 1982, 48; see also Blau and Schwartz 1984). Heterogeneous environments increase chance encounters between people who come from diverse backgrounds. Without these fortuitous meetings congenial or intimate relationships would not be possible. Blau, Blum, and Schwartz have demonstrated that measures of ethnic heterogeneity (among other types of heterogeneity) in the American metropolis[1] were highly correlated with intermarriage rates (Weighted Least Squares for national origin was .94, for mother tongue .86, and for ethnic background .75). They conclude that "the structural constraints of heterogeneity foster intergroup relations initially in the face of ingroup values engendering opposite tendencies, and in the long run by weakening the ingroup values themselves" (Blau, Blum, and Schwartz 1982, 54).

Any subcommunity that has a distinctive identity, such as a linguistic environment,[2] encourages ethnic endogamy. Stevens and Swicegood (1987) have found that second- or later-generation ethnics who retain their mother tongue (i.e., have not switched to English at home) are more likely to marry within their ethnic group. The larger the size, the more the geographical segregation, the greater the ethnic language retention of U.S.-born subgroups, then the higher their rates of endogamy. However, Stevens and Swicegood add "the erosion of non-English languages over time has been accompanied by declining levels of ethnic endogamy. This implication is congruent with recent research, which also argues that levels of endogamy have been declining because of the growing number of persons for whom ethnicity is either a vague or a bilateral notion and thus a less important factor in marital preferences and choices" (1987, 81). It should be noted that ethnocentric preference rules in mate selection are not altogether salutary. Indeed, ethnic endogamy may be desirable to perpetuate cultural distinctions and retard the assimilation of immigrant groups, but it also sustains social inequality (Crispino 1980, 103).

In another study, Stevens and Schoen (1988) support the assimilationist perspective (rather than cultural pluralism) and confirm that there is an inverse relationship between linguistic homogamy and educational attainment; the higher the educational level, the less the linguistic homogamy. This is attributed not to the greater facility of using English but "to the higher degree of social interaction with majority group members that takes place within higher educational institutions and to the role education plays in promoting the importance of achieved versus ascribed criteria in American society" (Stevens and Schoen 1988, 277). Moreover, the study also found that there is an exchange relationship in the marriage choices of men and women. Women with English-language backgrounds and lower educational levels tend to marry men with higher educational attainment but non-English backgrounds. This is similar to the pattern of hypergamy described long ago by Davis (1941) and Merton (1941) for interracial marriages. They argued that upper-class black men exchange their advantageous socioeconomic position for the white lower-class female's higher caste position.

Ruby Jo Reeves Kennedy's (1944; 1952) examination of marriage records in New Haven (CT) from 1870 to 1950 demonstrated the national trend toward the "triple melting pot" of Protestant, Catholic, and Jewish assimilation. Kennedy found that there were few interreligious marriages but significant interethnic marriages. In later generations, the Irish, Italian, and Polish Catholics were intermarrying; so were British-Americans, Germans, and Scandinavian Protestants;

and the Jews married each other.[3] The empirical generalization of ethnic exogamy but religious (denominational) endogamy is applicable to most immigrant groups in the United States. For example, it has been observed that among Arabic-speaking groups, Syrian Jews tend to marry American Jews, Syrian Christians tend to marry other Christians, and Syrian Muslims tend to marry other Muslims (Zenner 1982, 474).

Given the above theoretical contributions, one can predict that the higher the generational status, the higher the rate of Armenian exogamy will be for the following reasons: First, the largest concentration of eligible mates for the endogamous marriage market are the institutionally affiliated Armenian-Americans. Yet as shown in chapter 3, for the overwhelming majority of third- and fourth-generation Armenian-Americans, the formally structured community is unable to attract or retain their interest. Second, even in large metropolitan areas like New York, Los Angeles, Boston, and San Francisco where the concentration of the Armenian-American population forms a "critical mass," their absolute numbers are too small to insure fortuitous encounters between people of Armenian descent. It goes without saying that in the rest of the country, men and women of Armenian descent have even lower probability of meeting fellow Armenians in the course of their daily lives. It is true that casual meetings do not necessarily end in marriage, but in the currently acceptable mate selection system, they are a prerequisite for the development of intimate ties that may develop into marital unions.

Third, the middle- to upper-middle-class status of most Armenian-Americans, their prestigious occupational standing, their college or higher educational attainment, and their predominantly above average incomes make them highly acceptable and desirable mates by other groups. Fourth, for those in later generations, the ethnic background of one's spouse is of secondary significance to interpersonal attributes and compatibility. On the one hand, they are less likely to have retained a distinctive Armenian culture; as seen in chapter 4, they are highly unlikely to speak, read, or write Armenian. On the other hand, they are more likely to have imbued the American ideals of merit and personal achievement over ascribed status; that is, they tend to judge a potential mate on his/her social and psychological qualities rather than an ethnic or religious background. Moreover, they are more likely to have intermingled extensively, privately and publicly, with people from a variety of ethnic, racial, and religious backgrounds.

In sum, culturally and structurally, Armenianness ceases to be a less pressing factor in the marriage market for those in later generations. Borrowing the words of Tinker in describing the high rates of Japanese-American intermarriage and assimilation, I conclude that likewise, Armenian-Americans "are not trying to deny their past, their intermarriage is just the natural expression of their dispersion into the larger society" (1982, 72). Indeed as several of the New York respondents remarked, intermarriage does not necessarily indicate a rejection of their Armenian identity.

Armenian Exogamy

Sixty-four percent of the married sample[4] have spouses with Armenian mothers and Armenian fathers, and only 2 percent (N = 10) have spouses with one Armenian parent, the rest (34 percent) were non-Armenian. Respondents in the New York study were married into the numerically largest ethnic and religious groups that live in metropolitan New York and New Jersey. They are the same groups that the respondents chose their best friends and acquaintances from (see chap. 3). Spouses of Italian descent make up 3.7 percent of the married sample, the "Americans" approximate 3.4 percent of spouses, the Irish 3.1 percent, the Jews 3.1 percent, the Germans 3 percent, the Polish 1.5 percent, and the English 1 percent. In addition, there were national/ethnic backgrounds that reflected the country of birth of the immigrant generation, for example Arab Christians, Assyrians, Greeks, and Bulgarians. These collectively represented about 3 percent of spouses. It should be noted that Armenians are less likely to marry blacks, Hispanics and Asian-Americans, especially in the early generations. Armenians are no less racist than the rest of white America. Members of such minorities are not considered desirable marriage partners. Unions with minorities would be tantamount to marrying down; status considerations remain a priority even as ethnicity and religion become less so.

If the rate of intermarriage is defined as the proportion of mixed couples in the population of all married couples (Peres and Schrift 1978; see Cretser and Leon 1982, 8-9 for other computations) then the rate of out-marriage of the New York sample is 34.5 percent. As far as this sample is representative of the Armenian-American population,[5] this rate then reflects the percentage of the ethnically intermarried in that population, irrespective of generation. The reader is reminded that this rate of intermarriage mirrors the past, it does not predict the future. A significant proportion of the early immigrant generation is still alive, and new waves of immigration have revitalized the pool in recent decades.

The ethnic background of respondent's spouse is highly significant with generational standing; the longer the generational presence in the United States, the higher the probability of Armenian exogamy (see table 6.1). About 85 percent of the foreign-born were married to Armenian spouses (one or two parents of Armenian descent). There is a drop of about 25 percentage points by each generation. Thus, the second generation were 59 percent endogamous, and later generations about 30 percent or less. It should be noted that fourth-generation respondents tended to be younger in age (75 percent below age thirty-nine) and over half (56 percent) of them were not married at the time of the survey. Later-generation respondents were also more likely to be the children of mixed marriages, as they were more likely to have at least a college degree. All these factors increase their probability of marrying non-Armenians.

There were no intermarriages between later-generation Armenian-Americans and foreign-born Armenians and only about 15 percent of

TABLE 6.1
Frequency Distribution of Spouse's Ethnicity by Respondent's Generation
(married sample only)

	Foreign-Born	U.S.-Born of F.B. Parents	1 Parent U.S.-Born	2 Parents U.S.-Born	Grandparen t U.S.-Born
N = 493	(196)	(233)	(30)	(27)	(7)
Armenian parents	84.7	58.8	33.3	37.0	0.0
Parents non-Armenian	15.3	41.2	66.6	62.9	100.0
	100.0	100.0	100.0	100.0	100.0

the second generation had foreign-born Armenian spouses. This adds further evidence to my earlier claim that later-generation descendants are alienated from the Armenian community and have few contacts among the immigrants.[6] It is surmised that foreign-born Armenians are not likely to be homogeneous mates to those in later generations; at the very least their worldview and understanding of Armenianness tend to be different even if their socioeconomic characteristics are compatible.

It is interesting to note that U.S.-born generations are almost twice as likely to remain single after age forty as the immigrant generation. The data presented here is corroborated by a study of French-Armenians that found a high rate of celibacy among older cohorts. The author attributes this to the contradictions of their "marginal" existence between the French and Armenian worlds.[7] In the New York survey, those over forty years of age who had never married comprised f 5 percent of the immigrant generation, 10.9 percent of the second generation, 11.9 percent of the third and fourth generations (7.7 percent in total sample). In recent years, several dating organizations have advertised their services in the Armenian press. For example, the "Armenian Connection, Inc." provides a toll-free telephone number, operative twenty-four hours a day, and invites members with the following message: "Join this exciting club and meet professional and social friends throughout the United States. We will search for an Armenian friend for you if you are in graduate school or already have a graduate degree and are between 21 and 51" *(Armenian International Magazine,* January 1991, p. 42). The *Armenian American Almanac* (1991) lists an additional four dating services.[8] No information is at hand on these organizations. Studies of dating agencies generally conclude that they supply numerous dates, but hardly any marriages. I suspect the same for these Armenian agencies.

The rate of Armenian exogamy is likely to be compounded over time because in addition to generational status, mixed ancestry of respondents more than doubles their chances of marrying non-Armenians (see table 6.2). Given the one-time, cross-sectional nature of the New York data, one needs to find methods of comparing rates of intermarriage over time (within the sample). One way of looking at change in interethnic marriages is to compare the respondents' ancestry with those of their spouses'. Mixed ancestry in the sample is

11.3 percent non-Armenian while respondents' spouses' ancestry is 36 percent non-Armenian. Another method is to compare the ancestry of younger respondents with older cohorts. There is a negative monotonic relationship in mixed marriages by each age category in the sample; the younger the age cohort, the higher the mixed ancestry. Respondents in their seventies had 5 percent intermarried parents, those in their sixties had 6.6 percent, those in their fifties 9.8 percent, forty year olds had 11.1 percent, thirty year olds had 20.6 percent, and those in their twenties had 37.5 percent. Age and spouse's ethnicity are also inversely related; the younger the respondent, the higher the probability of interethnic marriage, irrespective of generation.

No statistical data on the marital choices of respondents' children's generation is available. Nonetheless, respondents' comments indicate that a significant number of their children marry outside the Armenian-American community. All of the following remarks were made by middle-aged, second-generation mothers and fathers.

My son and daughter went away to college and married non-Armenians.

My three children have married non-Armenians, but I'm happy to say they are happily married.

I have three children who grew up in a non-Armenian community (not by choice). All three are married to non-Armenians who are from fine upper class families. I am disappointed that at least one did not marry an Armenian. (We came close).

All five children are married—very happily to non-Armenians.

TABLE 6.2
Frequency Distribution of Spouse's Ethnicity by Respondent's Ancestry
(married sample only)

Respondent's	Both Parents Armenian	One Parent Armenian
N = (493)	(447)	(46)
Spouse's		
1 Armenian parent	1.6	6.5
2 Armenian parents	67.6	23.9
Parents non-Armenian	30.9	69.6
	100.0	100.0

Although my sons are married to non-Armenians, they have much regard, great respect and a very positive attitude toward the Armenian nation.

All our four children married non-Armenians.

These quotations among many others, humanize the statistical evidence on the increasing marital assimilation of Armenian-Americans.

Those who have "other" religious denominations or "no religion" in the sample are least likely to marry ethnic Armenians or members of Armenian Apostolic, Protestant, or Catholic churches (see tables 6.3 and 6.4). Apostolic marriages comprised 80 percent of all endogamous marriages (N = 304). Furthermore, those who married into Armenian

TABLE 6.3
Frequency Distribution of Spouse's Ethnicity by Respondent's Religious Affiliation
(married sample only)

	Apostolic Armenian	Protestant Armenian	Catholic Armenian	Other (Non-Arm.)	No Religion
N = 487	(323)	(47)	(16)	(76)	(25)
2 Parents Armenian	76.2	78.7	56.3	17.1	16.0
1 Parent Armenian	2.5	0.0	6.2	1.3	0.0
Parents non-Arm.	21.4	21.3	37.5	81.6	84.0
	100.0	100.0	100.0	100.0	100.0

TABLE 6.4
Frequency Distribution of Spouse's Religion by Respondent's Generation
(married sample only)

	Foreign-Born	U.S.-Born of F.B. Parents	1 Parent U.S.-Born	2 Parents U.S.-Born	Grandparent U.S.-Born
N = 474	(204)	(230)	(27)	(26)	(7)
Apostolic	70.6	46.9	40.7	30.8	0.0
Arm. Protestant	11.9	6.1	0.0	3.8	0.0
Arm. Catholic	6.0	2.6	0.0	3.8	0.0
Other	11.4	44.4	59.3	61.5	100.0
	100.0	100.0	100.0	100.0	100.0

denominations other than their own were most likely to marry Apostolics. And, later-generation Armenians who married fellow ethnics were also most likely to marry a member of the Apostolic church (table 6.4). In marital assimilation, as in cultural and structural assimilation, the Armenian Apostolic church has provided an extra buffer to Armenian ethnicity in fighting forces of assimilation. However, one cannot infer from this data whether it is the effect of sheer size[9] or that of the intrinsic attributes of the Armenian Apostolic church. Indeed, one finds here the classic sociological question: Are structural aspects more significant than cultural ones? Research findings quoted above tend to suggest the power of structural ties over ideology.

There were too many denominational affiliations and too small a sample size to be able to cross-tabulate the spouse's "other" religious affiliations with those of the respondent's. Nonetheless, the rough estimates available (see table 6.5) suggest that with the exception of the very small proportion of Armenian-Americans who marry Jews (3 percent of sample), the "triple melting pot" rule of religious endogamy holds for the Armenian case as well. Protestant Armenians were most likely to find mates from mainstream Protestant denominations; the Armenian Catholics were most likely to marry members of the Roman Catholic church; and Armenian Apostolics tended to marry Presbyterians and Episcopalians (see also chap. 2).

Greeley (1970) corroborates these findings with evidence from national samples that at least three-quarters of the American

TABLE 6.5
Frequency Distribution of Spouse's Religious Affiliation by Respondent's Religious Affiliation (married sample only)

	Apostolic Armenian	Protestant Armenian	Catholic Armenian	Other (Non-Arm.)	No Religion
N = 470	(314)	(46)	(12)	(75)	(23)
Apostolic	76.7	15.2	25.0	4.0	4.3
Arm. Protestant	2.2	63.0	0.0	1.3	0.0
Arm. Catholic	2.2	2.2	75.0	1.3	0.0
Other	16.9	19.6	0.0	92.0	56.5
No religion	1.9	0.0	0.0	1.3	39.1
	100.0	100.0	100.0	100.0	100.0

population marry within their religious denomination. He speculates that

> the strain toward denominational homogeneity is rooted in the American belief that religious differences between husband and wife are not good either for the marriage relationship or for the children of the marriage. This belief is probably reinforced by the fact that it is simpler and more convenient that everyone in the family belong to the same denomination. (Greeley 1970, 951)

Spouses of Catholics are likely to convert to Catholicism, while Jews and Catholics tend to marry within their denomination. Protestants marry across denominational lines, but will shift affiliations to maintain religious homogeneity in the family. Further research is needed on denominational conversions within the three Armenian churches to find what percentage of non-Armenian spouses convert or become members of Armenian churches.

The data presented here attest that interreligious marriages are more likely to be caused by indifference to religion than by conversions. Cohen's remarks about the Jewish American population are also applicable to Armenian-Americans. He writes:

> In today's secularized society, Judaism may be more vulnerable to threats from forces promoting indifference to religion than to the allure of competing major religions. In other words, Christianity and Judaism in America paradoxically may be natural allies in a struggle against secularity which may hold greater peril for all major faiths than do the ostensibly competing religious systems for one another. (Cohen 1983, 124)

About 6 percent of the New York sample declared "no religion" and most of them were young and in later generations. It has been shown throughout this study that respondents professing "no religion" rate highest on assimilation variables. I predict their chances for marrying non-Armenians to be equally high (see table 6.5).

It is hypothesized that the higher the educational attainment of the respondent, the higher the frequency of ethnic exogamy (see table 6.6). Indeed, there is a straight-line increase in non-Armenian spouses with each level of education (.21*). The proportion of nonethnic spouses among the most educated in the sample is more than double those of the least educated. Occupation and income, on the other hand, were not significantly associated with ethnicity of spouse. These results are corroborated for other ethnic groups (e.g., Cohen 1977; Kobrin and Goldscheider 1978, 240). One can conjecture that higher education is more significant with marital assimilation because opportunities to meet non-Armenian friends and potential spouses increase the longer one stays in institutions of higher learning. Additionally, college and graduate education are believed to exert a liberating influence on people's value system. Furthermore, the rule of class homogamy measured by education holds true for the New York sample. Between 65 and 80 percent of respondents married people who had completed approximately similar levels of education as themselves. On the other hand, status homogamy, measured by father's occupation and respondent's occupation, was not significant.

One way of measuring rates of intermarriage is through cross-sectional surveys such as my own study. Another method is to examine vital statistics. Two studies have attempted to do that for the Armenian-American population. One used church records and the other public records. Each source has its advantages and disadvantages. For example, vital statistics do not show generational status and other characteristics of the spouses, while surveys do not reflect trends over time, unless they are periodically administered. Yet the two complement each other. Unfortunately, all three data sets reported here are regional. Nationwide samples or vital statistics of Armenian-Americans have yet to be gathered.

Aharonian's (1983) study of marriages conducted in the churches of the Diocese of the Armenian Apostolic Church in New England found a monumental increase in intermarriage rates. The percentage of mixed marriages for the period between 1950 and 1954 was 21

TABLE 6.6
Frequency Distribution of Spouse's Ethnicity by Respondent's Educational Attainment
(married sample only)

	Some High School	High School	Some College	College	More than College
N = 476	(44)	(126)	(98)	(102)	(106)
2 parents Armenian	77.3	76.2	59.2	54.9	52.8
1 parent Armenian	2.3	1.6	5.1	1.0	0.9
Parents non-Arm.	20.4	22.2	35.7	44.1	46.2
	100.0	100.0	100.0	100.0	100.0

percent, by 1975-76 the figure had gone up to 78 percent. It should be noted that these rates do not include marriages conducted in the churches of the Prelacy of the Armenian Apostolic Church, in the Armenian Protestant and Catholic churches, in other (non-Armenian) churches and synagogues, and those registered with justices of the peace. Nonetheless, it is assumed that current figures from these other sources should be approximately the same, or higher than the ones reported. Indeed, Aharonian estimates that the annual percentage of Armenian exogamy at present is closer to the 90 to 95 percentage range when all marriages of people of Armenian descent are taken into consideration (Aharonian 1983, 37; see also Aharonian 1986-87).

The second study, by Jendian,[10] investigated the marriage records in Fresno County in 1930, 1960, and 1990. In addition, the author had access to similar statistics for 1940 and 1980. From a total of 324 marriages for the five selected years, the rate of out-marriage for men and women of Armenian descent in Fresno was calculated as 50.9 percent. The study found that rates of intermarriage increased for the children of the foreign-born, but stayed around 90 percent for the children of the U.S.-born. More specifically, among those with foreign-born parents, 10.4 percent of the thirty-four marriages enacted in 1930 were out-marriages; the proportion went up to 16.9 percent in 1940 (out of sixty-five marriages); to 44.9 percent in 1960 (out of forty-nine marriages); to 72.7 percent in 1980 (out of twenty-two marriages); to 42.3 percent in 1990 (out of twenty-six marriages). For the offspring of American-born parents, all (100 percent) marriages celebrated in 1960 were to non-Armenians (out of thirteen marriages); 94.4 percent in 1980 (out of thirty-six marriages) and 90.6 percent in 1990 (out of thirty-two marriages). Furthermore, Jendian found that 32.1 percent of marriages celebrated in an Apostolic church; 31.4 percent of those officiated in an Armenian Protestant church; 92.5 percent of weddings conducted in a non-Armenian religious institution, and 66.7 percent of civil ceremonies were out-marriages.

Ethnocentric Preference Rules

There were two statements in the New York survey that measured the attitudes of the respondents toward Armenian endogamy. The first read: "A good Armenian should marry another Armenian." The second was: "It is important for me that my children marry someone of my own ethnic background." The first statement received high frequency of disagreement; 47.5 percent of the sample disagreed (47.5 percent agreed). The value-loaded wording compounded the negative responses. On the other hand, 35 percent of the sample disagreed with the second statement (50 percent agreed).[11] There were numerous comments on intermarriage. One respondent said it "would be nice," another said, "depends on circumstances but would make life easier." A third respondent asked: "What is a 'Good' Armenian? Personal choice by God's guidance." A foreign-born woman wrote: "I would like that [children marry Armenians], but this is only a dream. How can we do this when our children are exposed to other ethnic groups?" Another foreign-born elderly man wrote: "Same religion would help to deter them from calling each other degrading names."

Both attitude statements on Armenian endogamy were highly significant by generational status[12] (tau c .34* for both; see tables 6.7 and 6.8). Those who did not approve of ethnic endogamy tended to have later generational status, non-Armenian denominations, or "no religion," and mixed ancestry. They were also more likely to be younger in age and single. It is noteworthy that the small proportion of divorced and separated respondents in the sample were more likely to disagree with the statements that Armenians should marry Armenians, and women disagreed somewhat more often than men. The gap observed throughout this study between attitudes and behavior is applicable here as well. People of Armenian descent are more likely to uphold ethnocentric attitudes than they are willing to live by them. In

TABLE 6.7

Frequency Distribution of Attitude Statement: "A Good Armenian Should Marry Another Armenian" by Generation

	Foreign-Born	U.S.-Born of F.B. Parents	1 Parent U.S.-Born	2 Parents U.S.-Born	Grandparent U.S.-Born
N = 581	(218)	(270)	(36)	(41)	(16)
Agree	67.9	33.0	13.9	12.2	0.0
No opinion	5.0	13.7	11.1	12.2	6.3
Disagree	27.1	53.3	75.0	75.6	93.8
	100.0	100.0	100.0	100.0	100.0

any case, later-generation Armenian-Americans are least likely to endorse ethnic endogamy both in attitude and in behavior.

In today's American society, marriages are based on personal attraction, romantic love, and psychological compatibility. Armenians are no exception, they follow the same norms. Other than altruistic sentiments about the welfare of their children, parents do not have economic or political interests in their marriage partners. Consequently, the marriage market is not controlled by elders as in traditional agrarian societies. This also explains why divorce rates are high in postindustrial societies. Because of the increasing economic independence of women, among other reasons, when spouses are unhappy in a relationship there are few ulterior factors to keep them tied in matrimony.

Given the small size and geographical dispersion of Armenian-Americans, their relatively high socioeconomic status, the absence of prejudice and discrimination against them, the compatibility of the Armenian-American subculture with mainstream American societal requirements, it is almost inevitable that men and women of Armenian descent will meet, fall in love and marry outside their ethnic group. In other words, the rates of intermarriage are caused by two processes: one, the changes in the family system and social relations that are typical of a postindustrial economy; second, cultural changes in the traditional Armenianness of the immigrant generation.

High rates of Armenian exogamy are a fact of life for Armenian-Americans at the turn of the twenty-first century. While many community leaders denounce intermarriage for all their afflictions, I

TABLE 6.8
Frequency Distribution of Attitude Statement: "It Is Important That My Children Marry Someone of My Own Ethnic Background" by Generation

	Foreign-Born	U.S.-Born of F.B. Parents	1 Parent U.S.-Born	2 Parents U.S.-Born	Grandparent U.S.-Born
N = 577	(215)	(269)	(36)	(41)	(16)
Agree	74.9	38.7	36.1	17.1	18.8
No opinion	7.9	18.6	19.4	22.0	18.8
Disagree	17.2	42.8	44.4	61.0	62.5
	100.0	100.0	100.0	100.0	100.0

argue that the issue lies in the inability of institutional structures to accommodate the transformations in individual forms of Armenianness, from traditional to symbolic. The Armenian-American community continues to maintain narrow boundaries of inclusion and exclusion. Marrying a non-Armenian does not mean a negation of one's ancestral heritage. I have reported in chapter 3 that individuals who marry non-Armenians and still want to maintain active involvement within the communal structures are shunned because of their *odar* spouses. If the churches and voluntary associations were more receptive and welcoming of non-Armenian spouses and the children of mixed marriages, more of them would be willing to enjoy the benefits of ethnic affiliation.

Summary of Results from New York Survey

Tables 6.9 to 6.12 summarize the statistical data from the New York survey. Table 6.9 shows, in rank order, the assimilative variables that change the most from the first to the second generation, and table 6.10 shows indicators with the most changes from foreign-born respondents to fourth-generation respondents. In table 6.10 "later-generation" is calculated as an average of third- and fourth-generation respondents (N = 93). Estimates for later generations are higher than would be expected for the fourth and subsequent generations. Also, some of the indicators of assimilation summarized in table 6.10 are artificially inflated by averaging lower levels of ethnic maintenance than those used in the body of the text. For example, 71 percent of later-generation respondents attend an Armenian event or activity at least once a year. This does not mean they are frequent attenders; on the contrary, one activity a year is a very low participation rate.

Cultural Changes

Language suffers the most by the passing of generations. Ability to perpetuate the written word decreases by about 60 percentage points from immigrant parents to their U.S.-born children's generation (table 6.9). The oral traditions fare slightly better because they do not need specialists to perpetuate them. Children learn to speak Armenian at home, by rote. Nonetheless, it is no longer an unconscious process, a "mother tongue." By the second generation, Armenian ceases to be the language spoken most frequently in the home, dropping by 50 percentage points (table 6.9). In later generations, less than one in ten men and women who identify themselves as Armenian-American can speak, read, or write Armenian (table 6.11).

Attitudes about the place of language in the definition of Armenianness change by the second generation (table 6.9). In order to avoid cognitive dissonance, U.S.-born generations no longer include knowledge of the language as a necessary precondition for their Armenian identity. This becomes one of the salient points of conflict between the American-born and the foreign-born, especially those from the Middle East. An often heard criticism addressed to the former by the latter is: "What kind of an Armenian are you, if you don't speak Armenian?" It is therefore not surprising that institutions that require knowledge of the Armenian language are supported

TABLE 6.9
Greatest Percentage Decrease on Indicators of Assimilation from Foreign-Born
Generation to Second Generation

Measures of Assimilation	% Decrease
1. Read Armenian	- 59.0
2. Frequency Armenian spoken at home	- 50.0
3. Proportion of Armenian friends when young and now	- 35.7
4. Attitudes favoring ethnic endogamy	- 35.0
5. Willingness to travel far to an Armenian church	- 33.3
6. Spouse non-Armenian	- 33.0
7. Read Armenian literature (in original or translation)	- 29.4
8. Willingness to employ Armenians in business	- 26.2
9. Attend requiem services for April 24	- 24.0
10. Indifference to Armenian political parties	- 23.2
11. Speak Armenian adequately to very well	- 23.1
12. Willingness to patronize Armenian-owned businesses	- 21.5
13. Believe a good Armenian must speak Armenian	- 21.0
14. Attend public gatherings for April 24	- 21.0
15. Eat Armenian food once a week or more	- 19.6
16. Receive several Armenian publications	- 19.5
17. Believe one's duty is to support the Armenian church	- 19.5
18. Attend Armenian church several times a year	- 19.2

predominantly by the Armenian-speaking immigrant generation and somewhat less by their children's generation. These include the Armenian churches, all-day schools, traditional political parties, Armenian language newspapers and radio, contemporary Armenian singers, Armenian theater, and literature written in Armenian. Without the arrival of new immigrants, the use of the Armenian language would become vestigial in the population.

Other aspects of Armenian culture become less and less a part of the everyday life of Armenian-Americans (table 5.12 in chap. 5). Fewer people read Armenian literature in the original or in translation, including works written in English by fellow Armenian-Americans such as William Saroyan and Michael Arlen. Fewer households receive Armenian newspapers, magazines, or other publications (in English). Surely, even fewer people actually read them. Armenian food is enjoyed and remains popular with almost everybody, but it is no longer eaten frequently at home. Instead of being eaten as a routine occurrence, it is relegated to "special" ceremonial occasions to be cooked by older women of the family or bought from speciality stores ready-made.

TABLE 6.10
Greatest Percentage Decrease on Indicators of Assimilation from Foreign-Born
Generation to Fourth Generation

Measures of Assimilation	% Decrease
1. Spouse non-Armenian	- 88.6
2. Speak Armenian	- 84.5
3. Proportion of Armenian friends when young	- 76.8
4. Proportion of Armenian friends now	- 71.7
5. Read Armenian	- 65.5
6. Frequency Armenian spoken at home	- 62.5
7. Visit Armenians almost always	- 62.3
8. Willingness to travel far to an Armenian church	- 57.8
9. Eat Armenian food once a week or more	- 56.9
10. Wish children would marry Armenians	- 56.8
11. Indifference to Armenian political parties	- 55.5
12. Attend Armenian church several times a year	- 53.2
13. Willingness to vote for a political candidate of Armenian descent	- 52.2

Lack of exposure to the Armenian press and radio and other opinion-shaping institutions makes later-generation descendants accept the mainstream media's interpretations of national and international news concerning Armenians, rather than insider versions. There is empirical evidence that the national press gets its cues from the State Department or other official sources and interprets events in terms of the administration's policy on such matters. The notorious example is the Reagan administration's attribution of the label "alleged" to the Genocide. Another illustration concerns the labeling of Baltic peoples' struggles for independence from the Soviet Union as "nationalist aspirations" while belittling the same types of movements in Soviet Armenia as "ethnic unrest." On a different matter, New York respondents alienated from communal life tended to find that Armenian "terrorism" in the 1970s had soiled the good name and reputation of Armenian-Americans as law-abiding citizens. By contrast, foreign-born respondents were more likely to perceive the "terrorists" as freedom fighters. In general, later generations are less likely to be influenced by ideologies that reinforce the ethnic boundaries of "us" versus "them."

The greater acceptance of denominational differentiation and plurality and the greater legitimacy of religious freedom in the United States has had a tendency to turn ethnic communities into church communities. Because of its larger size, its unique religious tradition, and its fusion with the national interests of the Armenian people, the Armenian Apostolic church has to some degree been able to maintain firmer boundaries of inclusion and exclusion. Overall, adherents of the Armenian Apostolic church maintain higher levels of traditional ethnic behavior and attitudes than members of the Armenian Protestant church and the Armenian Catholic church. The attrition rate of the Armenian Protestant church is calculated to be at least double that of the Apostolics (19 percent for Apostolics versus about 40 percent for Protestants).

Yet with increasing generational presence there is a tendency to separate the ethnic and religious components of one's heritage. Acknowledging Armenian descent does not make one a member of an Armenian church. About 23 percent of the sample were in that category; 16 percent belonged to a number of mainstream Protestant denominations or the Roman Catholic church, and the rest declared "no religion." Religious conversions to non-Armenian denominations are less of a threat to the future of Armenian churches than those who profess "no religion." For example, mixed parentage reduced Armenian church attendance, but it did not increase attendance in an alternate church. The trend toward secularization in the larger society affects Armenians as well. While foreign-born agnostics and atheists may be willing to use the Apostolic church as an arena for social encounters and support it financially as a focal center for their national interests, the American-born are not.

TABLE 6.11
Percentage Change in Ethnic Behavior between Generations, Frequency of
Behavior in Later Generations, and Tau Measures of Association

Measures of Assimilation	% Change from F.B. to Later Generations	Frequency in Later Generations (in percent)	Tau C
1. Cultural Assimilation			
Armenian food eaten once a week or more	- 43.4	32.3	.26*
Speak Armenian	- 74.4	22.6	.52*
Write Armenian	- 68.4	9.7	.49*
Read Armenian literature (original or translation)	- 32.3	31.5	.27*
Receive Armenian newspapers	- 30.1	30.3	.19*
Attend Armenian church several times a year or more	- 39.0	33.3	.22*
Sympathize with Armenian political parties or ideologies (including neutrals)	- 50.9	17.2	.19*
2. Structural Assimilation			
Membership in Armenian voluntary associations	- 37.1	9.7	Sig ¥
Leadership in Armenian voluntary associations	- 10.3	8.6	Not sig
Attend meetings of Armenian voluntary associations some of the time or more	- 25.2	18.3	.18*
Attend at least one Armenian event hosted by voluntary associations per year	- 19.0	71.0	Sig ¥

At least one professional he or she deals with is of Armenian descent	- 25.0	36.6	.16*
Feels very close to family	+ 1.8	49.4	Not Sig
Family needs are more important than individual's	- 12.0	72.0	Not Sig
Willing to support parents with care of younger siblings	- 17.4	75.3	.08*
Visit with other Armenians frequently	- 45.6	35.5	.24*
At least one of three best friends is Armenian	- 37.3	34.4	.24*
More than half of friends (other than best friends) are Armenian	- 59.7	18.3	.36*
More than half of friends when 18 years of age were Armenian	- 55.1	28.0	.35*

3. Marital Assimilation

Spouse's parent(s) Armenian	- 53.4	31.3	Sig ¥

4. Identificational Assimilation

Identify as American-Armenian or Armenian	- 17.3		80.4
Feelings of pride	- 10.2	87.5	Not sig

5. Absence of Prejudice and Discrimination

Perceived prejudice	- 6.2	2.1	Not sig

6. Civic Assimilation

Voted in presidential election	+ 19.4	88.2	Not sig
Active in local and national politics	+ 9.7	19.3	Not sig
Wrote letters to Congress regarding Genocide issue	- 19.5	25.0	Not sig
Feel strongly about denial of Genocide	- 13.1	85.0	Not sig

* significant at .00001 level

¥ tau c not available because of multiple response category

Though there is little verbal renunciation of the sacred culture and traditions among respondents, it becomes less central in their lives. Hardly anyone practices the ancient tradition of fasting during the forty days of Lent; few people abstain from food and drink before taking communion; and church attendance is reduced to once or twice a year, mostly high holidays such as Christmas and Easter. In later generations, few believe that it is their duty to support an Armenian church, morally or financially, and fewer are willing to travel far or be inconvenienced in other ways to attend services.

Furthermore, it is unlikely that the majority of Armenian-Americans who do not speak Armenian will be willing to attend Divine Liturgy every Sunday and sit still for three hours when they do not understand the language or the significance of the rituals enacted in front of them. Attending a wedding, a christening, or a funeral, or a memorial service for the Genocide to please one's parents, spouse, or in-laws is a different matter. As I have explained, contemporary American society is a "time-famine" culture, and Armenian-Americans like the rest of their fellow citizens, are highly unlikely to sacrifice this precious asset to something they do not find meaningful or spiritually fulfilling.

About two-thirds of the immigrant generation sympathize with one of the three traditional Armenian political parties (Hunchag, Tashnag, and Ramgavar) or hold a neutral position *(chezok)*. Slightly less than half of the second generation do so. In later-generations, the frequency

TABLE 6.12
Highest Frequencies (or least change) on Indictors of Assimilation in Fourth Generation

Measures of Assimilation	Frequency (in percent)
1. Pride in heritage	87.5
2. Has strong feelings toward Turkey's denial of the Genocide	85.0
3. Armenian identity	75.0
4. Disagree to change Armenian family name	75.0
5. Attitude favoring dual identity: American and Armenian	68.8
6. Willingness to help parents with support of younger siblings	68.8
7. Considers family needs more important than one's own	56.3
8. All five persons one feels closest to are kin	56.3

drops to less than a fifth (8.6 percent for parties only; see table 6.11). Moreover, according to the comments of the respondents, many in the third and fourth generations did not know the differences in the political ideologies, and none of them officially joined these parties. One can confidently generalize that traditional Armenian politics becomes obsolete for the majority of American-born Armenians past the second generation because the parties are unable to represent their interests and concerns, let alone make a difference in their material circumstances.

The results of the New York survey suggest that traditional institutions have not caught up with changes in the personal forms of ethnicity. In other words, the churches, political parties, and other collective structures tend to advocate a traditional form of Armenianness. They assume that Armenian identity is an ascribed status: by virtue of having Armenian blood, a man or woman of Armenian descent is somehow obligated to become a member of the community. They do not realize that at the individual level, the vast majority of Armenian-Americans perceive their identity as a choice, and participation in collective life as voluntary action. The traditional institutions have not recognized that Armenianness in the United States is a commodity. Members will not flock to their doors unless they attract them by promising to fulfill some of their real or socially induced needs. Even then, members will not retain their membership if they are in any way dissatisfied. In order to survive, like any other commodity, Armenianness must remain competitive and serve specific functions.

Structural Changes

Churches, voluntary associations, political parties, and other communal organizations define the collective consciousness of Armenian-Americans and provide the structural parameters for the collective expression of Armenianness. The Armenian-American community is a first- and second-generation phenomenon. At the core of the community is a proportionally small group of first- and second-generation Armenian-Americans who are fully immersed in its formal (i.e., voluntary associations) and informal (i.e., networks of relatives, friends, and acquaintances) structures. Those who are least likely to take part in collective manifestations of Armenianness are in sharp contrast to the core group. They are most likely to have the following attributes: later generation, non-Armenian affiliation or "no religion," mixed ancestry, indifference to Armenian ideologies, higher education, and younger cohort. Yet, nonparticipation in communal life does not diminish their levels of Armenian identity. In between these two extremes are individuals of Armenian descent with varying degrees of communal participation; their personal attributes are somewhere in between as well.

Membership in Armenian voluntary organizations drops to less than 10 percent in later generations (table 6.11). Joiners are most likely to be attracted to folk dance groups and scholarly and cultural associations. Such organizations have specific goals and tend to be congruent with symbolic ethnicity. Old World organizations such as compatriotic societies and political parties cease to be meaningful to the American-born. Interestingly, the proportional decrease in those who attend meetings frequently and those who hold positions of responsibility in voluntary associations is much smaller (table 6.11). A very small ratio of later-generation Armenian-Americans who consciously choose to maintain active participation in communal life tend to be highly dedicated to their cause. Consequently, they assume positions of responsibility and leadership. The pool from which leaders are chosen does become smaller with the passage of generations (decreases 10 percentage points from the first generation), but the real loss is in the size of the audience to communal events (about 37 percentage point decrease from first generation).

Structural assimilation escalates in the third generation and beyond, both in formal and informal relations. First, there is a sharp drop after the second generation in participation in activities and events sponsored by Armenian voluntary associations (later generations make up only 10 percent of all participants in community events). Averaging the proportion of later-generation respondents who attended such events by the number of times these events are held annually demonstrates that ethnic festivals are the most popular; trailing far behind are sports matches, art exhibits, and folk dance shows. All these activities do not require knowledge of the Armenian language or culture. Later-generation Armenian-Americans are least likely to attend dinner dances. Paradoxically, the dinner dance is the single most hosted event in the Armenian social calendar (at least 74 out of a total of 207 "events"). For instance, in metropolitan New York, about two thousand or so aficionados seem to repeatedly go to dinner dances hosted by various Armenian associations. Second, there is a reduction in the fourth generation in the informal ties with fellow Armenians, measured by visiting patterns and friendship networks (table 6.11). However, the magnitude of this drop is not as significant as that in formal ties.

While the first and second generations have acculturated to the larger American society, they have remained somewhat more entrenched structurally in Armenian communal life, both in the private sphere of their families and friends and in the public arena of Armenian church and voluntary associations (the average decrease from the first to the second generation is about 27 percentage points). Gordon's concept of "ethclass" describes the communal participation of the first two generations. Their intimate networks consist of fellow Armenians, often from the same country of origin or region of emigration, and, most important, of similar educational, occupational, and income backgrounds.

The patterns of ethnic involvement suggest that first- and second-generation individuals participate in two worlds, the Armenian and non-Armenian. Being a member of Armenian voluntary associations and going to events and activities does not preclude membership in the nonethnic environment (most significantly professional associations and mainstream political parties). Respondents proved that they can be equally integrated in both worlds, the Armenian and the American. The change takes place in the third generation when involvement in the Armenian community is reduced to a trickle, if not a halt. Sociability is an important function of collective structures for the immigrant generation. In later generations, one is less likely to look for events sponsored by Armenian voluntary associations to fulfill one's companionship needs.

Reliance on fellow Armenians in business and professional relations decreases with the passing of generations. Later-generation Armenian-Americans are less willing than earlier generations to patronize small businesses or stores owned and operated by Armenians if it is not convenient or if their goods and services are not competitive. Respondents in third and subsequent generations with their own businesses hesitate to employ fellow ethnics because they are concerned about qualities, and credentials or do not want to be guilty of nepotism and favoritism. They are also less likely to intentionally seek the services of a doctor, a lawyer, a dentist, an accountant, or other professional because he/she is of Armenian descent. Nonetheless, about a third of later-generation respondents in the sample continued to deal with at least one Armenian-American professional, generally because that person was a relative or a friend (table 6.11).

Second-generation respondents compared to their parents' generation are more likely to have non-Armenian friends and marry non-Armenians (table 6.9). By the fourth generation, the proportion of Armenian friends decreases on all of the measures used in the survey (three best friends, proportion of Armenian friends now, friends when young). Beyond the second generation, Armenian exogamy becomes the norm. The small size of the community, the romantic love ideology, and the American value system that rewards merit and class over ascribed status overcome ethnocentric preference rules. There is an almost 90 percentage point decrease from the first to the fourth generation in respondents who marry Armenians (table 6.10). Other sources corroborate that in later generations the rate of Armenian intermarriage fluctuates around 90 percent.

Other Changes

Armenian-Americans find little discrimination and prejudice against them at the present time in the United States. "Affective neutrality" describes the reaction of the ordinary American citizen vis-à-vis Armenianness. Social distance indicators show that the sample is closest, by marriage or friendship, to white Americans of European ancestry, notably, Italians, Jews, the Irish, and WASPs. Italians, Jews, and Armenians feel particularly close. They have shared the trials and tribulations of the big immigration waves and the xenophobic atmosphere of the host society in the early decades of the twentieth century. Later-generation respondents are most likely to have at least an acquaintance in most groups with large population concentrations in metropolitan New York and New Jersey. It should be noted though that individuals of Armenian descent are no less racist than other whites.

Armenian-Americans no longer fit the sojourner or "middlemen minority form" that characterized the earliest immigrants. As individuals they have relinquished the dream of an eventual return to a real or mythical homeland. A few may visit the "spiritual homeland," historical territory presently spread between the Republics of Armenia and Turkey, or feel obligated to send monetary contributions to less fortunate Armenians in the diaspora, but home is in the United States. Armenian-Americans are here to stay. The traditional political parties, on the other hand, have found it more difficult to relinquish ideologies of an eventual return to an autonomous homeland because their rationale for being would have been at stake.

Recent developments in Armenia have changed the political and ideological impasse in diasporan relations. An independent and democratic Armenia is likely to become a center for Armenian life and culture. It would relieve the diasporan communities of the burden of cultural maintenance and at the same time become a source for revitalizing Armenian identity. Tired spirits who travel to the ancestral homeland would return energized and younger cohorts on study abroad programs would come back infused with pride in their roots and new language skills. In return, leaders in the Armenian-American community, as self-proclaimed representatives of the largest and most affluent diasporan collectivity, might play a more active role in supporting their fellow brethren with special technological assistance programs, foreign investments, and political advocacy. Many hope to build a symbiotic relationship between an autonomous Armenia and the diaspora similar to the one operant between Israel and American Jews.

Armenian-Americans are well-integrated into the larger American society; that is, in the use of the political machinery and the acceptance of the ideological precepts of the nation. They accept the ideals of democracy: equal opportunity, hard work, fair play, and the promise of the American Dream. There were no significant differences among the New York respondents in party affiliation; about a third were Democrats, another third Republicans, and the rest independents. The majority of respondents vote at presidential elections, and a few are volunteers during political campaigns. Several Armenian-Americans have run successfully for public office, locally and nationally. Younger cohorts are more likely to follow suit and surpass their predecessors.[13]

Is it possible to mobilize Armenian-Americans? Would instrumental goals be more powerful than ideological goals in mobilizing them? Armenian-Americans are too few in number and too spread out to become a powerful voting bloc; besides, there are no significant value differences that would cause serious conflict between them and other ethnic and nonethnic Americans in the urban opportunity structure. Even in Los Angeles where massive numbers of recent refugees from Soviet Armenia and elsewhere have strained the resources of the local government, serious class cleavages prevent Armenian-Americans from being mobilized as a cohesive group on one side of an issue against groups on the other side. Therefore, at the grass-roots level, it is highly improbable that domestic issues will cause hostility in Armenian-Americans' relations with their non-Armenian neighbors, co-workers, acquaintances, and friends.

Foreign policy issues are a different matter. Armenian-Americans do not endorse their government's protection of Turkey, nor the millions of aid dollars that are funneled to their historic enemy each year. Had the government of Turkey admitted and apologized for the Genocide this might not have been an issue. Imbued with American principles of justice and equity, they feel terribly wronged. Another potential source of contention might be the dismemberment of the Soviet Union. Even though the U.S. government has recently recognized the independence of the Republic of Armenia, the future policies of the United States remain unclear. Many Armenian-Americans sympathize with the goals of the Armenian population for self-determination and want to support them.

How do Armenian-Americans voice their political opinions? Those in the first and second generations are most likely to engage in the most active forms of political mobilization. They are likely to march up the streets of New York City to the headquarters of the United Nations with banners and signs; demonstrate in front of the Turkish Consulate in Los Angeles to protest Turkey's denial of the Genocide; visit politicians in Washington, DC to endorse a resolution that declares the Genocide a crime against humanity; hold candlelight vigils in front of the Soviet Mission to the United Nations in support of their brethren in Armenia; or send telegrams to Moscow and Washington to object to the pogroms and unfair treatment of Armenians in Azerbaijan.

Even among the first generation, those who resort to such conspicuous and strenuous forms of protest and advocacy are proportionally few. Nonetheless, the rate of mobilization of the Armenian-American population should not be underestimated. For example, 40 percent of the New York sample wrote letters to Congress regarding the Genocide. This is an impressive figure by any calculation. As expected, however, later generations are least likely to engage in grass-roots politics for Armenian causes. Most prefer to make financial contributions to professional lobbying agencies and let them pursue their political goals by proxy.[14]

In spite of a slow start, Armenian-Americans are maturing as an interest group in mainstream American politics. They are acquiring more political savvy in endorsing politicians that reflect their goals and aspirations, lobbying Congress for aid to the earthquake victims in Armenia, or granting visas to Armenian refugees from the Middle East stranded in European capitals. As an interest group, Armenian-Americans would like to receive recognition as a loyal constituency in the United States, as law-abiding, dutiful citizens. They also would like to see more of their people elevated to the coveted positions of this nation in politics, finance, military, and so on.

Thus their goals are both ideological and instrumental. Ordinary individuals of Armenian descent in the United States are unlikely to receive any concrete material benefits. However, by opening up opportunity structures, more of their ranks will achieve high status and thus indirectly enhance the well-being and prestige of Armenians in general. Also, when Armenian individuals or advocacy groups are able to broker financial, professional, or technical aid packages from the U.S. government, philanthropic foundations, or other agencies to help needy Armenians in the spiritual homeland or elsewhere in the diaspora, the psychological rewards are tremendous.

Exceptions to the Assimilation Model

The fact remains that the assimilative profile of Armenian-Americans does not fully fit into Gordon's theoretical framework. The indicators of assimilation that change the least through the generations are the following: self-described identity, pride in one's roots, memory of the Genocide and feelings of anger toward its denial, centrality of the family (see table 6.12). In other words, about 80 percent of later-generation respondents identified themselves as American-Armenian, Armenian-American, Armenian, or of Armenian descent. Over 90 percent felt very proud of their roots and its culture; they had a strong sense of peoplehood. The majority of respondents said that of the five closest people in their lives, two or more were family members. Familism statements, which measure strong feelings, goals, and mutual support of one's family, received high agreement scores (80 to 86 percent). Last but not least, 85 percent were angered by Turkey's denial of the Genocide and said justice needs to be done. Even in the fourth generation, Armenian-Americans were least likely to have Turkish acquaintances, let alone friends.

Nonetheless, this does not mean that these measures do not change over the generations, only the pace is much slower. For example, Armenian identity drops by 23 percentage points from the foreign-born generation to the fourth, and attitudes favoring change in Armenian names drop by 12 percentage points. Attitudes toward the importance of the family drop an average of 26 percentage points between the immigrant and later generations. Even though the Genocide is fervently felt by almost every Armenian-American, about 10 percent of the fourth generation were indifferent to its denial by Turkish governments, and 5 percent said that one should forget the past. Fewer proportions of the fourth-generation attend requiem services (19 percent, a 39 percentage point decrease from the first generation) and even fewer participate in commemorative rallies, marches and demonstrations (12.5 percent, a 28 percentage point decrease from the first generation).

Identity and familism do not measure actual behavior. Overall, American-born generations profess verbal allegiance to their ethnic heritage, but they are less likely to transform it into action. One may continue to feel very close to one's family, as all of the indicators showed, but spend most of one's leisure time with one's friends. Indeed, less than one-third of the parents in the sample contacted their children, by person or phone, daily. Frequency of contact among other family members was much lower. Affect exceeds action in family relations as in most things. Assimilation can continue its course, at least for some time, without substantially decreasing levels of Armenian identity, sense of peoplehood and familism. These findings confirm that assimilation and ethnicity, in its symbolic form, can coexist. It does not have to be a zero-sum equation.

Armenian identity does not wane with higher socioeconomic achievement; an attribute characteristic of symbolic Armenian-Americans. Upper-middle-class status screens off the unpleasant aspects of ethnicity, thus making it easier for people to acknowledge and identify with their ancestral origins. Middle- and upper-middle-class Armenian-Americans who identify with their immigrant roots feel very close to family members and maintain a large network of Armenian institutional and communal activities. Owing to their predominance in middle- to upper-middle social classes, symbolic Armenian-Americans in the early generations are increasingly likely to define Armenianness and set the boundaries of inclusion and exclusion in communal life. The events sponsored by Armenian-American voluntary associations are increasingly geared toward the life-style, interests, and budget of upper-middle-class status, such as golf tournaments, debutante balls, and black tie testimonials for mainstream politicians. Tickets and donations for participation in such events are exclusionary. They are well beyond the capacity of working-class incomes, thus leaving out Armenian-Americans who have not achieved upward mobility. This contradicts the hitherto expressed assumption that ethnic allegiance and maintenance is synonymous with working-class status. Rather, if corporate or traditional ethnicity is strongly correlated with working-class status, symbolic ethnicity is then an upper-middle-class phenomenon.

New Immigration and Rejuvenation of Communal Structures

The influx of large numbers of immigrants from the Middle East and Soviet Union in the last twenty-five years or so has had significant repercussions on Armenianness in the United States. This has changed the ratio of American-born to immigrant stock and the age distribution of the latter. Two-thirds of the immigrant generation in the survey came to the United States after World War II. These newest arrivals do not conform to the stereotype of the illiterate peasant. Like other post-1965 legal immigrants, they tend to be more educated, have a higher proportion of professionals among them, and come with greater financial resources than in the past. The overall impact of this wave of immigration was to slow down the rate of assimilation of Armenian-American communal structures.

Newcomers who predominantly speak Armenian have rejuvenated tired and depleted voluntary associations established by the first wave of Armenian immigrants. They have infused new blood into several church communities, fortifying Armenian choirs, adding to the number of officiating clergy, deacons, and acolytes. They have lent their expertise and knowledge of the language and culture to promote full-time and part-time schools, press and radio, theater, popular songs, and the traditional Armenian political parties. At the same time, they have been a ready-made audience for the events and activities sponsored by voluntary associations and other institutions. The more educated among the newest immigrants, especially those who received their university education in the United States, in partnership with the second generation have founded institutions that are more congruent with the reality of American life and symbolic ethnicity, such as university chairs for Armenian studies, research institutes, professional associations, and political action groups.

Where there was no infrastructure, or it was already appropriated by the American-born, the newest immigrants proceeded to create their own organizations according to their understanding of Armenianness and the way they had been habituated in the Middle East, Eastern Europe, Soviet Armenia, or wherever they came from. The purpose of these compatriotic or other associations remains twofold: First, they provide familiarity and companionship to recent immigrants experiencing cultural shock. Psychologically, socially, they cushion their transition into the new environment. Second, they promote the goals and norms of the emergent Armenian-American subculture and turn their members into dutiful citizens of the United States. That is, they speed both their acculturation process into the ethnic world and their economic and political integration into mainstream society.

As with other ethnic groups, the newest arrivals and the American-born have not coexisted in total harmony. Conflict and animosity over their understanding and expression of their Armenianness is common. This will probably continue to be the status quo until the newcomers acculturate further and their American-born children mature. Indeed, the Armenian-American community is not a monolithic structure; it is more appropriate to speak of communities. These subcommunities are crisscrossed by allegiances to place of birth; by recency of immigration; by religious affiliation; by political and ideological sympathies; by age; by life-style and interest; and by education, occupation, and income levels. Except for those in leadership positions and those in intellectual circles, there is very little contact between the rank and file of these subcommunities.

The Armenians of Los Angeles deserve special mention. A large proportion of the post-1965 immigrants, especially the overwhelming majority of the Soviet Armenian refugees have made Los Angeles their destination. Los Angeles has become a sort of Mecca for traditional Armenianness. It has the highest per capita concentration of Armenian schools, churches, voluntary associations, newspapers, radio and television programs, nursing homes, and clubs. It also has significant proportions of independent professional firms and other businesses, not to mention the speciality food stores and restaurants. Since 1980, Greater Los Angeles has even had an Armenian telephone directory—a bilingual edition with business and residential listings.[15]

In Los Angeles, the supply side of Armenianness increases the likelihood of chance encounters between people of Armenian descent in their daily lives and business dealings. It keeps Armenian identity alive, but the cost may be too high. Armenianness in Los Angeles is highly visible and conspicuous, especially among the less affluent who cannot afford the more exclusive neighborhoods in the suburbs, the elite private schools, or the luxurious shopping malls, restaurants, and recreational facilities. Indeed, many have no option but to settle in places like Hollywood, which has become an Armenian ghetto. When ethnicity is no longer a choice, it risks increasing prejudice and discrimination against group members. Since many of the refugees who arrived in the 1980s from Soviet Armenia and the Middle East are poor, not well-educated, and unfamiliar with the American way of life; and since they have already developed a reputation for breaking local laws and going on welfare, stereotypes have inevitably surfaced. For many of the less advantaged, Armenianness is likely to remain an ascribed status.[16] That runs contrary to a century of Armenian experience in America and a solid record of personal and group achievements. In conclusion, lest the reader forget, Los Angeles is not representative of Armenian-Americans or of the Armenian-American community.

Resumé: Assimilation Rates for Sample

The rate of cultural assimilation for the sample is estimated at 48 percent, structural assimilation at 30 percent, and overall assimilation at 23 percent. These rates confirm Gordon's predictions for initial acculturation followed by structural assimilation. These rates are also indicative of the large proportion of foreign-born Armenians in the study (37.5 percent; 25 percent of sample came after WW II). Overall, behavioral measures show the greatest degree of change as American-born descendants of Armenian immigrants become more and more distanced from their roots, its culture, and communal life. The data prove that later-generation Armenian-Americans have successfully achieved assimilation. The average decrease in indicators of assimilation from the first to the fourth generation is 60 percentage points.

What then is the probability of the continuity of Armenian-American collective structures? Even though reliable demographic statistics are not available, I have used whatever estimates there are to project the size and growth rate of the Armenian-American community of metropolitan New York and New Jersey in one generation's time (thirty years). I have used the rates generated in this study and other published estimates. For the birth and death rates, I used U.S. population figures. These calculations show that if the rate of assimilation of the fourth generation is used, the number of those who identify as Armenian-American will remain more or less the same (1.8 percent increase) in the next generation in spite of births and immigration.[17]

The reader is reminded that these are very gross estimates, and more seriously, they reflect the xenophobic past of American society in the first half of the twentieth century and the cultural baggage of the earliest Armenian immigrants. Besides, human ingenuity has often proved statistical predictions wrong. This should be taken merely as an exercise for those trying to plan the future of Armenian collective structures and to set policies for religious, educational, and other institutions—a sort of "worst case scenario" if no changes alter the given structural and cultural variables.

Two important criteria make these projections implausible. First, the larger American society has been more tolerant of sidestream ethnicity in the last couple of decades. Ethnicity remains an important social boundary in modern American society, and the emergence of ethnic-based interest groups is generally welcomed, if not encouraged. Second, post-1965 Armenian immigrants are not peasants nor are they overwhelmed by the technological superiority of their host society as was the case in the late nineteenth century. Social forces that shape Armenianness in the contemporary United States are very different from those that were operant during the last hundred years. History does not repeat itself in exactly the same fashion.

The viability of the collective forms of Armenianness in the United States in the future will in the final analysis depend heavily on the success of a variety of recruiting and socializing agencies and the ability of traditional institutions to adapt to the changes warranted by symbolic Armenianness. If future cohorts of American-born Armenians are not taught how to appreciate their ancestral heritage, how can they be blamed for forsaking it? For individual forms, on the other hand, the family remains the most effective cradle of identity, pride, and affection.

Components of Symbolic Armenianness

For the grandchildren and great-grandchildren of the immigrant generation, Armenianness is no longer the taken for granted way of life, nor an immersion in an ethnic culture and communal relations. For American-born generations, Armenian identity is a "preference" (Zenner 1985, 118) and Armenianness is a "state of mind" (Crispino 1980, 160). The behavior of later-generation descendants is not Armenian in form or content. Yet, they feel Armenian, they identify themselves as American-Armenian, and they are fiercely proud of most things and people Armenian. Armenianness becomes voluntary, conscious, rationalistic, segmental, transitory, sporadic, that is, symbolic. Sentiment and convenience become the *modus vivendi* for maintenance of almost all aspects of Armenianness. Feelings run high, but when it comes to behavioral participation, convenience is the key.

With increasing generational presence, in the United States, with non-Armenian denominational affiliation or no religious preference, with indifference to Armenian politics, with mixed parentage, and with higher education, Armenianness loses it traditional attributes. One can say one is an Armenian without speaking Armenian, marrying an Armenian, doing business with Armenians, belonging to an Armenian church, joining Armenian voluntary associations, or participating in the events and activities sponsored by such organizations. Armenianness becomes more individualistic; that is, it is tailored to suit the personal needs and interests of symbolic Armenians. Diversity in forms of expression is another characteristic. Being Armenian means different things to different people. It can be any one or a combination of the following: church affiliation, network of relatives and friends, bonding with fellow Armenians, positive feelings of belongingness, a taste for Armenian cuisine, and so on. Armenianness changes from an emphasis on behavioral patterns to mental reconstructions of what individual Armenian-Americans think Armenianness is.

American-born men and women of Armenian descent do not callously discard or consciously plot to sabotage the cultural heritage of their ancestors. Rather, the cultural baggage brought over to America with the immigrant generation ceases to be functional. Two intertwined dynamics propel the emergence of a symbolic Armenian subculture in the United States: First, there are the requirements of the subsistence technologies and modes of production. More specifically, the Armenian immigrants who came to the United States in the early 1900s moved in a short while from a predominantly agricultural to a predominantly industrial society. Ottoman Turkey, especially the hinterland where most of the Armenian population had lived for centuries, consisted of agrarian, homogeneous, folklike communities where social relations were mostly face-to-face, diffuse, personal, enduring. It was a world where work and leisure were not separated in time and space and the absence of modern means of transportation and communication isolated small collectivities physically and socially from each other. The United States, on the other hand, was an industrial, urbanized, highly heterogeneous society where social relations were specific, purposeful, and impersonal, except for one's intimate ties, which were confined to one's private world of family, friends, and ethnic group or religious congregation. Inevitably, some of the great and little traditions of the Armenian people that reflected the agrarian environment they came from soon became obsolete in the densely populated American cities they now called home.

Second, the constraints imposed by the specific blend of American political, ideological, and social conditions also influenced the emergent Armenian subculture. In other words, the post-Genocide Armenian immigrants to France and the United States entered similar types of societies based on industrial modes of production; however, the specific cultural and structural conditions in each nation were different. In the United States, Armenians found an opportunity structure that was more open, relatively lower levels of prejudice and discrimination, a host society tolerant of ethnic subcommunities and religious pluralism, a pervasive ideology that encouraged hard work and individual accomplishment, and a public education system that made such achievement possible.

Therefore, many of the behavioral and attitudinal patterns that characterize symbolic Armenianness in the United States are by necessity by-products of the particular postindustrial economic system they live in today. For example, as inhabitants of a "time famine" culture, Americans value convenience. This also explains its importance in behavioral manifestations of Armenianness. Similarly, the current mate selection process dictates that future cohorts of Armenians will get married to those they fall in love with, irrespective of ethnic and religious background. Since Armenian-Americans not active in communal circles have little probability of fortuitous encounters with fellow Armenians, their chances of intermarriage are very high.

Likewise, the sentimentalization of symbolic Armenianness follows a general trend toward steeping one's intimate social relations with affect. The evidence for this trend comes from various studies that have observed historical changes in the last century or so in the United States in husband-wife relations, parent-child relations, grandparent-grandchild relations, and friendship ties. I explain: One, the romantic love complex has been institutionalized as a prerequisite for marriage in industrial societies since the late nineteenth century (Goode 1970; Shorter 1977). Love is also the glue that keeps spouses tied to their matrimonial vows. The long-range pattern of climbing divorce rates throughout this century (with the exception of those who produced the baby boomers) indicate that marriages are increasingly built on volatile sentiments rather than economic and social calculations.

Two, Viviana Zelizer (1985) has demonstrated that in the United States between the 1870s and the 1930s, there was a radical transformation in the cultural meaning of a child fourteen years of age or younger. The definition of a child changed from a commodity-like entity with instrumental motives to an exaltation of its sentimental, intrinsic worth. Instead of contributing to the welfare of the family unit through his/her labor in the fields or as hired hand, a child became a consumer, a source of expenditure because it had become the object of his/her parents' love and affection. Any harm that befell a child such as a serious illness, kidnapping, or death was now interpreted as an emotionally insurmountable experience for the parents. Instead of investing in quantity, parents started to value quality; they sacrificed themselves for the welfare of their child. Every child became unique, precious, irreplaceable. The family system changed from an adult-centered to a child-centered unit. In sum, the transition was from economically "useful" to "useless" but emotionally "priceless" child.

Three, relationships between grandparents and grandchildren became likewise sentimental. Grandparents were no longer the stern, remote, authoritarian figures of the agrarian system. Instead of obligation, the bond between generations came to be based on sentiment. A new style of grandparenting developed, one based on egalitarian or joking relationships that has been called a "companionate style" (Cherlin and Furstenberg 1986). Four, even friendship ties came to be infused with sentiments. By the late nineteenth century, friendships between women were seen as special, heartfelt (Cott 1977). Friends were no longer chosen for proximity, but for their intrinsic worth and compatibility.

Since symbolic Armenianness functions in the sidestream; that is, it is expressed during one's leisure time, in one's private life, with one's intimates, it has, like the other interpersonal ties, become imbued with sentiment. Symbolic Armenian-Americans feel very close to fellow Armenian-Americans, even Armenians in the diaspora. After all, one's ethnic group is an extension of one's self. Co-ethnics share the same ancestors, myths of origin, the same bloodline, and the same history; they are in a sense bonded like one gigantic kin grouping. The ties of Armenian-Americans with fellow Armenians are more expressive than instrumental. For instance, when the earthquake hit Soviet Armenia in 1988, symbolic Armenian-Americans felt very keenly the agony and misery of their compatriots thousands of miles away. However, this did not make them desire to become structurally embedded in Armenian networks. They did not join Armenian voluntary associations nor attend dinner dances.

In sum, the Armenian subculture emerging in the United States is more congruent with changes in the political economy and the American historical experience than the traditional culture of the immigrant generation. I have constructed an ideal typology of the collective and individual forms of symbolic Armenianness. It consists of six components which I will analyze next.

Sidestream Ethnicity

Symbolic Armenian-Americans display signs of their Armenianness on their person, possessions, home. Hanging a photograph of Mount Ararat, wearing a T-shirt with Armenian lettering, even using the Armenian credit card[18] satisfies their urge to express their heritage. They flaunt such tokens of their ancestral roots for everyone to see because they believe Armenianness is something one should be proud of. Similarly, they are unlikely to change their Armenian name or drop the "ian" ending. Armenian-Americans are not ashamed of their status and who they are. The higher socioeconomic standing of most Armenian-Americans at the present time decreases the stigma of ethnic affiliation, and their social mobility in the United States makes them proud of their group's achievements. Moreover, the increasing legitimacy of sidestream ethnicity makes it possible, even fashionable or quaint, to be of ethnic descent at the present time in large urban centers. To be a symbolic Armenian today in metropolitan New York, Boston, Chicago, or San Francisco is far less costly than it might have been in the past or in other places.

It is worth repeating that there is no "return" in the third generation toward behavioral forms of ethnicity. Furthermore, the so-called "revival" or "resurgence" of ethnicity in the post-civil rights era has not meant a resumption of traditional or behavioral forms of ethnicity. The change has been in the greater tolerance of symbolic ethnicity in the larger society. Armenian-Americans are first and foremost citizens of the United States of America. They are proud, grateful, and in their opinion exemplary citizens and as such their primary allegiance is to this nation and to the American Dream. Ethnic expression remains most acceptable in the sidestream; on the "teamsports level" to be enjoyed during one's leisure time and not to interfere with the serious business of earning a living or the democratic principles of this United States.

Affect Replaces Action

Symbolic Armenians are highly unlikely to be mobilized at the grass-roots level in the urban opportunity structure as an "ethclass" group in competition with other groups for coveted resources. First- and second-generation Armenian-Americans might be mobilized (though weakly) for ideological reasons. A small fraction of the Armenian population might be summoned to hold candlelight vigils, march up the streets of New York, Los Angeles, or Washington, DC with banners and signs as they did in solidarity with the Karabagh movement in Soviet Armenia and in protest against the pogroms in Soviet Azerbaijan. The vast majority of men and women of Armenian descent will at the utmost be moved to contribute financially for a worthy cause.

The Genocide remains at the forefront of Armenian collective consciousness. The overwhelming majority of Armenian-Americans feel angry and outraged about its denial, the revisionist historical interpretations, and the concerted media campaigns aimed at whitewashing Turkey's reputation. However, commemorative events and requiem services held annually around April 24 attract only a fraction of the Armenian-American public. Somewhat more people might be induced to write letters to Congress to help pass a resolution making April 24 "A Day of Remembrance of Man's Inhumanity to Man," because it is easier to draft a letter from a facsimile provided by lobbying institutions in the comfort of one's home than to attend a public rally in Times Square.

International events of a traumatic nature can periodically refocus the attention of Armenian-Americans on their Armenianness, stirring them ideologically into heightened levels of self-awareness. Following the earthquake in Soviet Armenia in December 1988, unprecedented numbers of men and women of Armenian descent who had never been involved in communal life flocked to contribution centers to volunteer their time, energy, and know-how. Even more people were moved to send in their checks. Nonetheless, the impact of such incidences is unlikely to be of long duration, or to mobilize them back into a corporate group. Dinner dances and other activities hosted by Armenian voluntary associations are highly unlikely to appeal to symbolic Armenians. To derive pleasure from such collective entertainment, one's structural ties must be densely populated with Armenian acquaintances, friends, and relatives, which is not the case for those in later generations. In addition, diasporan relations for symbolic Armenian-Americans are elusive. Travel to "spiritual homelands" is infrequent. Financial commitment remains the backbone of their sense of diasporan peoplehood. At best, traumatic events rekindle identity questioning and the reassessing of peoplehood boundaries, keeping them from a premature death.

The elements of the Armenian culture that are learned easily without resorting to specialized agencies have a higher probability of being practiced. Retention of Armenian cuisine requires cookbooks, in English, of which several are readily available, and ingredients that are increasingly sold in local supermarkets. By contrast, reading and writing Armenian requires schools, teachers, textbooks, and the concerted efforts of parents and students to attend classes and do homework, not to mention financial expenditure, and the valuable time and energy spent in learning Armenian rather than doing something else. Therefore, cooking and eating Armenian food once in a while is the most widespread mode of Armenian manifestation.

With the greater acceptance of ethnicity in the United States, festivals, food fairs, street bazaars, parades, and the like have become more popular and visible. All these are events and activities that do not need knowledge of the language, the culture, or history. They are generally considered to be 'fun' for the whole family. Non-Armenian spouses and children of mixed parentage can participate in such events without having the feeling of being an outsider. They have few restrictions; one can spend as little or as much of one's time and money as one wants. Since such events make few demands on participants, it is no wonder that they are popular with symbolic Armenians. Moreover, festivals celebrate ethnicity per se. They exemplify the pluralism and diversity of the American population without being too serious or offensive.

Symbolic Armenianness pertains to the realm of emotions. As such, it fulfills significant psychological functions in modern highly mechanized environments. It provides comfort, warmth, belongingness, roots. It offers relief from the bland homogeneity of mainstream culture by enriching one's life with colorful epics, myths, great and little traditions, and a horde of social bonds. Given the small size and dispersal of Armenians in the United States, it is a particularly fortuitous occasion to encounter another Armenian in the course of one's business or professional dealings. It makes one feel unique, precious, one in a million.

Armenianness is a form of cultural capital. Especially for geographically and socially mobile Armenian-Americans, it provides ready access to a whole network of social relations and a wealth of information. Hyphenated Armenians are willing to say they are of Armenian descent when they are asked, and when the situation is to their advantage. In business transactions with fellow ethnics, one may say "I am Armenian too," to enhance rapport and make a sale. Political candidates claim Armenian descent to solicit campaign contributions and votes. Business owners, self-employed professionals, and ethnic brokers (e.g., clergymen, academics, singers, editors of ethnic press) are more likely to activate their Armenian ties and networks than those employed in bureaucratic jobs because of possible gains in ethnic clientele. Their solidarity is mostly organic, in the Durkheimian sense. On the other hand, symbolic Armenians will only consent to buy products in an Armenian store, or consult an Armenian professional, or vote for an Armenian candidate, if and only if, all other things are equal.

Armenian-Americans are proud of the accomplishments of their fellow ethnics. They do not miss an occasion to remind their non-Armenian friends, co-workers, and acquaintances which celebrities are of Armenian descent. However, few have read the works of William Saroyan, or visited a museum to view a retrospective of Arshile Gorky's paintings, or attended a concert to listen to Alan Hovhaness conduct his music, or gone to a theater or a movie house to see Eric Bogosian perform, live or on film, or bought tickets for a tennis match to see Andre Agassi play. Strong sentiments toward people and things Armenian do not easily translate into behavior. In the concretization of ethnic action, convenience is generally the rule.

Knowledge Banks and Voluntary Associations

The institutional forms that have the greatest probability for longevity are those that are, like the personal forms of ethnicity, symbolic. There are those institutions that I call "knowledge banks" that are analogous to a dying sage in his urgency to codify his wealth of knowledge before his demise. University chairs for ethnic studies; research centers; display cases or wings in museums; publications of cookbooks or traditional handicrafts; collections of artifacts, old photographs, folk costumes, and the codification and documentation of musical forms, folk dances, folk tales, and customs all exemplify the passing of the mundane, but living tradition into the realm of the emblematic. Symbolic Armenian-Americans consciously seek to conserve their cultural heritage. Their higher educational attainment equips them with the know-how to do so.

Knowledge banks function as vehicles for enhancing status and increasing self-esteem. They are a way for Armenian-Americans to carve a niche for their cultural heritage in the pantheon of mainstream knowledge. By presenting it in language and formats that are readily acceptable to the American intellectual elite, the Armenian culture becomes more acceptable in their own eyes. Their reference group is the larger American public. They turn to it for legitimacy, for acknowledgment of their value as a people and the worthiness of their cultural heritage. Similarly, an artist, a writer, a performer of Armenian descent is claimed back into the fold of the Armenian world only when he or she has been successful in the mainstream.

For symbolic Armenian-Americans, voluntary associations need to combine an instrumental motive in conjunction with ethnicity in order to attract members. Associations that combine professional interests, scholarly or academic interests, (mainstream) politics, dance, sports, or other recreational interests with ethnic allegiance are more likely to be successful. Symbolic Armenian-Americans insist that the voluntary associations and institutions they want to support be run professionally. They have little patience for amateurs, inefficient bureaucracies, and mediocre results. Moreover, such organizations should not be greedy institutions; they must not be too demanding of one's time, energy, or financial resources.

Quest for Armenianness

The inherent tensions in modern American society of increasing secularization on the one hand and increasing quest for community and meaningfulness on the other will induce some Armenian-Americans to look to the Armenian Apostolic church for a rich spiritual experience. They do so consciously, rationally. It is no longer the blind faith, or indifference, and taken-for-granted affiliation of traditional Armenians. Consequently, they want to understand and study the doctrines of the church and the significance of the rituals. In order to meet the sacred needs of those in later generations, the Apostolic church must concentrate more on its unique Christian tradition and less on the perpetuation of Armenianness. It also has to use more English in the services and instruction manuals, since the vast majority of symbolic Armenian-Americans do not read and write Armenian.

Similarly, there are small numbers of Armenian-Americans who are interested in the secular heritage of their ancestors: the language, the history, the arts, the music, the crafts, and so on. Some, such as the academics, the clergy, the writers, the musicians, and so on, will make a career of their Armenianness. However, most will turn this quest for Armenianness into a hobby. Lectures and seminars attract large crowds because they are the least demanding form of instruction, and on top of that they are a form of entertainment. University courses, whether in the United States or abroad (e.g., Venice, Yerevan), mostly serve students who take them for credit, or the aficionados. Symbolic Armenian-American parents do not advocate all-day Armenian schooling because they believe it is un-American. Supplementary forms of ideological socialization of future generations, such as summer camps and professional internship programs, are more acceptable and popular because the Armenianness they propagate is in essence symbolic.

Economic Solvency

Making financial contributions to Armenian nonprofit organizations is undeniably the most prevalent method of token participation in the Armenian world. It is convenient and makes one feel good about oneself. While it sustains the appropriate social distance from the old-world milieu, it keeps the symbolic Armenian-Americans safe from contamination and discomfort. Nonetheless, it is predicted that contributions will dwindle with the passage of generations as ties and interest decrease. Symbolic Armenian-Americans need more aggressive, professional fund-raising techniques to move them to contribute. Because of the widespread individual variations in conceptualizations of Armenianness, men and women of Armenian descent in the United States will only make their deductible donations to the specific projects that appeal to their professional, religious, or artistic interests or those they associate with memories of their grandparents or other childhood episodes.

In many respects, the economic solvency of Armenian institutions and voluntary associations will determine the survival of Armenian-Americans as a collectivity. As such, financial contributions are highly significant for ethnic maintenance and should not be dismissed as tokens. As long as contributions keep pouring in, it will be possible to sustain communal forms of Armenianness. When Armenianness becomes symbolic, there is a shift from reliance on voluntarism and amateurish projects to an increasing demand for professionalism and efficiency in the administration of the ethnic organizations and the events they host. With the appropriate financial resources, it is possible to organize, commission, and host any number of activities. With professional management, advertising, and artists or performers of Armenian descent it is possible to draw larger audiences (not necessarily of Armenian origin) to concerts, art shows, and the like. Opening up Armenian art and culture to wider audiences has a higher probability of ensuring its survival.

The Family

Ultimately, it is within the family that Armenianness is nourished and sustained, and it is within the family that it finds its most frequent expression. Armenian traditions and rituals, or what are believed to be so, provide meaning, color, and drama and spice up people's routine existence. Most prominently, Armenianness is expressed during rites of passage and holidays. Typical examples are weddings, funerals, and christenings in an Armenian church. Christmas, Easter, anniversaries, and birthdays are also flavored with connotations of Armenianness, even though there is often nothing Armenian about them except maybe a dish or two on the menu. Family gatherings for whatever occasion inevitably mean food, hospitality, and generosity. The most recurrent and salient mental reconstructions of what Armenianness is for most symbolic Armenian-Americans are such warm family atmospheres.

Armenian grandmothers and grandfathers also have a special place in this symbolic firmament. They are remembered with reverence and nostalgia for bygone days and the stories they used to tell of even older times, before one's existence, and of places one has rarely known. Grandparents are the most tangible link of that human chain that extends to the spiritual homeland, to ancient Armenian forebears, and to fellow Armenians, past and present. Symbolic Armenianness, when all is said and done, is firmly logged in people's feelings and sentiments.

Notes

1. The units of analyses were taken from a national sample of SMSAs - standard metropolitan statistical area.
2. Linguistic diversity in the United States is attributed to immigration for the first generation; additionally, linguistic homogamy or ethnic endogamy perpetuates this diversity for American-born generations (Stevens and Schoen 1988, 277).
3. Noteworthy are psychosocial characteristics associated with interreligious marriages. Heiss (1960, 53) has found that the religiously intermarried tend to have nonreligious parents, have greater dissatisfaction with parents when young, greater family strife, less early family integration, and greater emancipation from parents at time of marriage.
4. In this section I have analyzed the married respondents in the New York sample only (N = 493). The married make up 70 percent, the widowed 10 percent, and the divorced or separated 5 percent of the total sample. The married sample includes all these categories. The never married, 86 respondents or 14.9 percent of the total sample, are excluded from analysis.
5. As mentioned in chapter 1, these results underestimate the proportion of the assimilated who have completely lost touch with people and things Armenian; thus, they also underestimate the proportion of the intermarried.
6. The exceptions are few. Foreign-born Armenians who date or marry third-generation Armenians soon realize that their ethnic homogamy is often deceptive. Significant cultural differences drive a wedge between their worldviews. For a case study see Mary Ann Aposhian, "Clinging to Ethnic Heritage in America: Study Compares Extent of Assimilation between Earlier Generation, New Arrivals," *Armenian International Magazine*, February 1991, pp. 33-36.
7. Boudjikanian-Keuroghlian writes: "Les célibataires agés(es) sont nombreux dans la communauté. Conditionés par les contradictions que vit la collectivité, leur

existences se déroulent à la lisiére des deux mondes français et arméniens. . . . Désorientées dans leur vie affective, solicitées par des aspirations contradictoires, elle souhaitent en vain un compagnon arménien" (1978, 112-3).

8. These services are Armenian Dating Service in Stow (MA); Armenian Singles Group in Downey (CA); Armenian Singles Unlimited in Houston (TX); Hye Mates, Inc. in Clawson (MI). When I called the 800 number of Armenian Connection, a recorded message reiterated the same contents as the ad. For an annual fee, photos and specifics are provided on Armenian professionals nationwide. I surmise that more later-generation Armenian-Americans might try the services of these organizations than those in earlier generations and more women than men.

9. Apostolics comprised 64.2 percent of the sample, Protestant Armenians were 9.7 percent, Catholic Armenians were 3.8 percent, "other" denominations were 16 percent, and those with "no religion" made up 6.3 percent of the sample (N = 576).

10. See Matthew Jendian 1991, "Intermarriage among Armenian-Americans in Fresno County: A Sociological Perspective," *Hye Sharzhoom,* supplement to *Daily Collegian - The Newspaper of the California State University* 12 (4): 3.

11. The comparative figures for Italian-Americans in Crispino's (1980, 113) study show that 3 percent agree that children should marry co-ethnics while 34 percent agree that children should marry of the same religion. It appears that Armenian preference norms are somewhat more salient than those of Italian-Americans. This may be a result of the large numbers of recent immigrants in the sample.

12. It is interesting to compare the opinions of other recent immigrant groups to the United States with this sample. Simon (1983) reports on Soviet Jewish and Vietnamese immigrants, the majority of whom have lived in America for an average of two years. She interviewed fifty pairs of mothers and adolescent daughters (ages fifteen to twenty), and fifty pairs of fathers and sons in each refugee group. All Soviet Jewish fathers wanted their sons to marry a Jew, 40 percent of them preferred a Soviet Jew. The majority of the sons expected to match their father's hopes in marrying Jews, only a third of them said ethnic and religious differences were not important. All Soviet Jewish mothers expected their daughters to marry Jews and Soviet Jews were preferred over American Jews. On the other hand, 24 percent of the daughters thought ethnicity was not important. All but 10 percent of daughters expected to marry Jews. Likewise, Vietnamese parents wanted their children to marry within the ethnic fold or with other Asian-Americans. Overall, Jewish identity was more salient than Soviet identity. It is also the case with the immigrant Armenian groups, their Armenian (ethnic) identity is more salient than their identity to their country of origin or religious denominations.

13. See Yvette Harpootian and Margaret Simonian, "The Pursuit of Power: Young Armenians Learn the Governing Game," *Armenian International Magazine,* July 1991, pp. 16-19.

14. Professional lobbyists seem to think that Armenian-Americans do not engage in grass-roots politics. According to one of them, "letter-writing is one of the most important elements that affect the legislation. Armenians are behind any other group in that respect." Maybe the Genocide is an exception to the general pattern because it is so close to people's hearts. In general the Armenian lobby in Washington, DC seems to be in its infancy; insiders concur that they lack

coordination and focus. See Tony Halpin and Vartan Oskanian, "Voices on the Hill: The Armenian Lobby, How Effective is it?" *Armenian International Magazine,* April 1991, pp. 10-20.

15. *Armenian Directory* is published by Bernard Berberian, Uniarts Advertising, Glendale, CA.

16. For example see Viken Berberian, "Coming to America . . . Without Rubles, Riches or Refugee Status," *Armenian International Magazine,* June 1991, pp. 14-23.

17. Size of Armenian-American population in metropolitan New York and New Jersey = 100,000 (chap. 1). Birth rate = 1.8 births per woman + 15 percent infertility (*Population Bulletin* 1982). Sex ratio = 45.5 percent (chap. 1). Death rate = 6 per 1,000 population (*Population Bulletin* 1982). Immigration = 340 per year (estimated from 2,000 per year, of which 17 percent settle in NY and NJ; Takooshian 1986-87, 142). Assimilation = 60 percent for fourth generation (this chap.). Generation = 30 years.

    Population - assimilation + immigration - deaths + births = population projections
    (100,000) - (60,000) + (10,200) - (18,000) + (69,615) = 101,815

18. A couple of Armenian entrepreneurs have initiated and marketed in the last several years the Armenian Exchange U.S.A. MasterCard credit card. Mount Ararat features prominently on the card. In their advertisements, the sponsors state: "Every time you use your card you'll be identifying your affiliation with a great people, and you'll be showing your pride and loyalty to them." Furthermore, the sponsors pledge to donate 25 percent of their net profits to religious, cultural, educational, and charitable Armenian organizations. For an assessment of the card and its sponsors see Viken Berberian, "Plastic Patriots? Charges and Countercharges: The Facts on an Armenian Credit Card's Worthiness," *Armenian International Magazine,* July 1991, pp. 27-30.

References

Books, Journals, and Reports

Abramson, Harold J. 1973. *Ethnic Diversity in Catholic America.* New York: Wiley.

———. 1975. "The Religioethnic Factor and the American Experience: Another Look at the Three-Generation Hypothesis." *Ethnicity* 2, n. 2 (June): 163-77.

Adalian, Rouben Paul. 1989. "The Historical Evolution of the Armenian Diasporas." *Journal of Modern Hellenism* 6: 81-114.

———. 1990-91. "Avedis K. Sanjian: Thirty Years of Armenian Studies in the United States." *Journal of Armenian Studies* 5 (Winter/Spring): 79-93.

———. 1991. "The Armenian Genocide: Context and Legacy." *Social Education* 55, n. 2 (Spring): 99-105.

Adamic, Louis. 1940. "The Tashjians: A Family from Armenia." In *From Many Lands.* New York: Harper & Brothers.

Aharonian, Aharon G. 1983. *Intermarriage and the Armenian-American Community.* Shrewsbury, MA: By the author, P. O. Box 67.

———. 1986-87. "Armenian Intermarriage in the United States, 1950-1976," *Journal of Armenian Studies* 3 (1-2): 103-10.

Ahdab-Yehia, May. 1980. "The Detroit Maronite Community." In *Arabic Speaking Communities in American Cities,* edited by

Barbara C. Aswad, 137-53. New York: Center for Migration Studies and Association of Arab-American University Graduates.

Alba, Richard D. 1976. "Social Assimilation among American Catholic National-Origin Groups." *American Sociological Review* 41, n. 6 (December): 1030-46.

———. 1978. "Ethnic Networks and Tolerant Attitudes." *Public Opinion Quarterly* 42, n. 1 (Spring):1-16.

———. 1981. "The Twilight of Ethnicity among American Catholics of European Ancestry." *Annals of American Academy of Political and Social Science* 454 (March): 86-97.

———. 1985a. *Italian Americans: Into the Twilight of Ethnicity.* Englewood Cliffs, NJ: Prentice-Hall.

———. 1985b. "The Twilight of Ethnicity among Americans of European Ancestry: The Case of Italians." In *Ethnicity and Race in the U.S.A.—Toward the Twenty-First Century,* edited by Richard D. Alba, 134-58. London: Routledge & Kegan Paul.

———. 1990. *Ethnic Identity: The Transformation of White America.* New Haven: Yale University Press.

Alba, Richard D., and M. B. Chamlin. 1983. "Ethnic Identification among Whites." *American Sociological Review* 48, n. 2 (April): 240-8.

Allan, Graham A. 1979. *A Sociology of Friendship and Kinship.* London: George Allen & Unwin.

———. 1989. *Friendship: Developing a Sociological Perspective.* Boulder, CO: Westview Press.

Antoun, Richard. 1968. "On the Modesty of Women in Arab Muslim Villages." *American Anthropologist* 70, n. 4 (August): 671-97.

Antreassian, Jack. 1981. "The Armenian in America: A Personal Viewpoint." In *The Armenian Image in History and Literature,* edited by Richard G. Hovannisian, 251-6. Malibu, CA: Undena.

Arkun, Aram. 1987. "A Study of Armenian Language and History Instruction in Los Angeles Primary and Secondary Schools." Los Angeles: Armenian Alumni Association. Photocopied.

Armenian American Almanac. 1990. Edited by Hamo B. Vassilian, 2d ed. Glendale, CA: Armenian Reference Books Co.

Armenian Assembly of America. 1987. *Armenians in America— Celebrating the First Century On the Occasion of the National*

Tribute for Governor George Deukmejian, October 10, 1887. Washington, DC: Armenian Assembly of America.

———. 1988. *Armenian Genocide: Resource Guide.* Washington, DC: Armenian Assembly of America.

Armenian Religious Education Council (AREC). 1985. "Armenian Church—Questionnaire Report." New York: The Armenian Prelacy of America. Photocopied.

Atamian, Sarkis. 1955. *The Armenian Community—The Historical Development of Social and Ideological Conflict.* New York: Philosophical Library.

Avakian, Arlene Voski. 1985. "Culture and Feminist Theory: An Armenian-American Woman's Perspective." Ed.D. diss., University of Massachusetts.

———. 1988. "Introduction: Tradition and Resistance to Tradition." *Ararat* 29, n. 4 Special Feminist Issue (Fall): 2-6.

Avakian, Arra S. 1977a. *The Armenians in America.* Minneapolis: Lerner Publications.

———. 1977b. "Armenians in America: How Many and Where." *Ararat* 18, Special Issue: Armenians in America, n. 1 (Winter): 125-35.

Ayanian, Mark Armen, and John Z. Ayanian. 1987. "Armenian Political Violence on American Network News: An Analysis of Content." *Armenian Review* 40, n. 1 (Spring): 13-29.

Babbie, Earl R. 1979. *The Practice of Social Research.* 2d ed. Belmont, CA: Wadsworth.

Bakalian, Anny P. 1985. "The Armenian Family and Related Topics: A Bibliography." *Armenian Review* 38, n. 4 (Winter): 23-40.

———. 1987. "Attitudes Towards Armenian Educational Institutions in New York and New Jersey." *Locus -UCLA Armenian Student Association Journal* (Spring): 25-39.

———. 1988. "Community Needs Assessment Report." New York: Armenian General Benevolent Union, Social Services Program. Photocopied.

———. 1989. "From Being to Feeling Armenian: Assimilation and Identity among American-Armenians in Metropolitan New York and New Jersey." Ph.D. diss., Columbia University.

Bamberger, Joan. 1986-87. "Family and Kinship in an Armenian-American Community." *Journal of Armenian Studies* 3 (1-2): 77-86.

Bardis, Panos. 1959. "A Familism Scale." *Journal of Marriage and Family Living* 21, n. 4 (November): 340-1.

Barth, Fredrik. 1969. Introduction to *Ethnic Groups and Boundaries,* edited by Fredrik Barth. Boston: Little, Brown.

Barthel, Diane. 1978. "The Role of Ethnicity." In *Social Standing in America—New Dimensions of Class,* edited by Richard Patrick Coleman and Lee Rainwater, 92-116. New York: Basic Books.

Bedoyan, Hratch. 1979. "The Social Political and Religious Structure of the Armenian Community in Lebanon." *Armenian Review* 32 (2): 119-30.

Bell, Daniel. 1975. "Ethnicity and Social Change." In *Ethnicity: Theory and Experience,* edited by Nathan Glazer and Daniel P. Moynihan, 141-74. Cambridge, MA: Harvard University Press.

Bender, Eugene I., and George Kagiwada. 1968. "Hansen's Law of 'Third-Generation Return' and the Study of American Religio-Ethnic Groups." *Phylon* 29, n. 4 (Winter): 360-70.

Bendix, Reinhard. 1967. "Tradition and Modernity Reconsidered." *Comparative Studies in History and Society* 9 (3): 292-346.

Blalock, Hubert M., Jr. 1967. *Toward a Theory of Minority-Group Relations.* New York: John Wiley & Sons, Capricorn Books.

Blau, Peter M., Terry C. Blum, and Joseph E. Schwartz. 1982. "Heterogeneity and Intermarriage." *American Sociological Review* 47, n. 1 (February): 45-62.

Blau, Peter M., and Joseph E. Schwartz. 1984. *Crosscutting Social Circles: Testing a Macrostructural Theory of Intergroup Relations.* Orlando, FL: Academic Press.

Bock, Geoffrey Ephraim. 1976. "The Jewish Schooling of American Jews: A Study of Non-Cognitive Educational Effects." Ed.D. diss., Harvard University.

Bonacich, Edna. 1973. "A Theory of Middleman Minorities."*American Sociological Review* 38, n. 5 (October): 583-94.

Bonacich, Edna, and John Modell. 1980. *The Economic Basis of Ethnic Solidarity—Small Business in the Japanese American Community.* Berkeley, CA: University of California Press.

Boudjikanian-Keuroghlian, Aida. 1978. *Les Arméniens dans la Région Rhone-Alpes—essai géographique sur les rapports d'une minorité ethnique avec son milieu d'accueil.* Audin-Lyon: Association des Amis de la Revue de Géographie de Lyon.

———. 1982. "Un Peuple en Exil: La Nouvelle Diaspora (XIXe-XXe Siecles)." In *Histoire des Arméniens,* edited by Gerard Dedeyan, 601-70. Toulouse: Privat.

Bouvier, Leon F., and Robert W. Gardner. 1986. "Immigration to the U.S.: The Unfinished Story." *Population Bulletin* (Population Reference Bureau, Inc., Washington, DC) 41, n. 4 (November).

Boyajian, Levon, and Haigaz Grigorian. 1986. "Psychological Sequelae of the Armenian Genocide." In *The Armenian Genocide in Perspective,* edited by Richard G. Hovannisian, 177-85. New Brunswick, NJ: Transaction Publishers.

Breton, Raymond. 1964. "Institutional Completeness of Ethnic Communities and the Personal Relations of Immigrants." *American Journal of Sociology* 70, n. 2 (September): 193-205.

Breton, Raymond, and Maurice Pinard. 1960. "Group Formation among Immigrants: Criteria and Processes." *The Canadian Journal of Economics and Political Science* 26, n. 3 (August): 465-77.

Burgess, M. Elaine. 1978. "The Resurgence of Ethnicity: Myth or Reality?" *Ethnic and Racial Studies* 1, n. 3 (July): 265-85.

Cafferty, Pastora San Juan. 1982. "The Language Question: The Dilemma of Bilingual Education for Hispanics in America." In *Ethnic Relations in America,* edited by Lance Liebman, 101-27. Englewood Cliffs, NJ: Prentice-Hall.

Cahnman, Werner. 1944. "Religion and Nationality." *American Journal of Sociology* 49, n. 6 (May): 524-9.

Cashmore, E. Ellis. 1984. *Dictionary of Race and Ethnic Relations.* London: Routledge & Kegan Paul.

Chalk, Frank, and Kurt Jonassohn, eds. 1990. *The History and Sociology of Genocide: Analyses and Case Studies.* New Haven: Yale University Press.

Charsley, Simon Robert. 1974. "The Formation of Ethnic Groups." In *Urban Ethnicity,* edited by Abner Cohen, 337-68. London: Tavistock.

Cherlin, Andrew J., and Frank F. Furstenberg, Jr. 1986. *The New American Grandparent—A Place in the Family, a Life Apart.* New York: Basic Books.

Chichekian, Garo. 1987. "Linguistic Assimilation and Cultural Completeness of Armenian Communities in Canada." *Armenian Review* 40, n. 3 (Fall): 1-15.

Chorbajian, Levon. 1989. "Karabakh and the U.S. Press: A Study in Mythmaking." Paper presented at the annual meeting of the American Sociological Association, San Francisco, 9-13 August.

Cohen, Abner. 1974. "Introduction: The Lessons of Ethnicity." In *Urban Ethnicity,* edited by Abner Cohen, ix-xxiv. London: Tavistock.

Cohen, Steven Martin. 1974. "The Impact of Jewish Education on Religious Identification and Practice." *Jewish Social Studies* 36, n. 3-4 (July-October): 316-26.

———. 1977. "Socioeconomic Determinants of Interethnic Marriage and Friendship." *Social Forces* 55, n. 4 (June): 997-1011.

———. 1983. *American Modernity and Jewish Identity.* New York: Tavistock.

Coleman, James et al. 1966. *Equality of Educational Opportunity.* Washington, DC: U.S. Government Printing Office.

Cooley, Charles Horton. 1983. *Human Nature and the Social Order.* New Brunswick, NJ: Transaction Publishers.

Coser, Lewis A. 1956. *The Function of Social Conflict.* New York: Free Press.

———. 1977. *Masters of Sociological Thought—Ideas in Historical and Social Context,* 2d ed. New York: Harcourt Brace Jovanovich.

Cott, Nancy F. 1977. *The Bond of Womanhood: "Woman's Sphere" in New England, 1789-1835.* New Haven: Yale University Press.

Cretser, Gary A., and Joseph L. Leon, eds. 1982. *Marriage and Family Review* 5, Special Issue: Intermarriage in the United States, n. 1 (Spring).

Crispino, James A. 1980. *The Assimilation of Ethnic Groups: The Italian Case.* Staten Island, NY: Center for Migration Studies.

Dadrian, Vahakin N. 1975a "The Common Features of the Armenian and Jewish Cases of Genocide: A Comparative Victimological Perspective." In *Victimology: A New Focus,* edited by Israel

Drapkin and Emilio Viano, 99-120. Lexington: Lexington Books/DC Heath.

———. 1975b. "A Typology of Genocide," *International Review of Modern Sociology* 2 (Autumn): 201-12.

———. 1986a. "The Naim-Andonian Documents on the World War I Destruction of Ottoman Armenians: The Anatomy of a Genocide." *International Journal of Middle East Studies* 18, n. 3 (August): 311-60.

———. 1986b. "The Role of Turkish Physicians in the World War I Genocide of Ottoman Armenians." *Holocaust and Genocide Studies* 1 (2): 169-92.

———. 1988. "The Anticipation and Prevention of Genocide in International Conflicts: Some Lessons from History." *International Journal of Group Tensions* 18 (3): 205-14.

———. 1990. "Towards a Theory of Genocide Incorporating the Instance of Holocaust: Comments, Criticisms and Suggestions." *Holocaust and Genocide Studies* 5 (2): 129-43.

Davidian, Richard Dale. 1986. "The Maintenance of the Armenian Language and Culture in the United States among Immigrant Armenian High School Students." Ph.D. diss., Northwestern University.

Davis, Kingsley. 1941. "Intermarriage in Caste Societies." *American Anthropologist* 43 (3): 376-95.

Dedeyan, Gerard, ed. 1982. *Histoire des Arméniens*. Toulouse: Privat.

Der-Karabetian, Aghop. 1980. "Relation of Two Cultural Identities of Armenian-Americans." *Psychological Reports* 47, n. 1 (August): 123-8.

Der-Karabetian, Aghop, and Levon Melikian. 1974. "Assimilation of Armenians in Lebanon." *Armenian Review* 27, n. 1 (Spring): 65-74.

Der-Karabetian, Aghop, and Emma Oshagan. 1977. "Ethnic Orientation of Armenians in Lebanon." *Armenian Review* 30, n. 2 (Summer): 164-75.

Der-Martirosian, Claudia. 1989. "Ethnicity and Ethnic Economy: Armenian Iranians in Los Angeles." M.A. thesis, University of California, Los Angeles.

Der-Martirosian, Claudia, George Sabagh, and Mehdi Bozorgmehr. 1990. "Subethnicity: Armenians in Los Angeles." Paper presented at California Immigrants in World Perspective Conference, University of California, Los Angeles, 26-27 April.

De Vos, George, and Lola Romanucci-Ross. eds. 1982. *Ethnic Identity—Cultural Continuities and Change*. Chicago: University of Chicago Press.

di Leonardo, Micaela. 1984. *The Varieties of Ethnic Experience— Kinship, Class, and Gender among California Italian-Americans*. Ithaca: Cornell University Press.

Dillman, Don A. 1978. *Mail and Telephone Surveys—The Total Design Method*. New York: John Wiley & Sons.

Dobkin, Marjorie Housepian. 1977. "The Melting Pot Myth," *Ararat* 18, n. 1 (Winter): 5-8.

Driedger, Leo. 1976. "Ethnic Self-Identity: A Comparison of In-Group Evaluations." *Sociometry* 39, n. 2 (June): 131-41.

Ebaugh, Helen Rose Fuchs. 1988. *Becoming an Ex: The Process of Role Exit*. Chicago: University of Chicago Press.

Elkholy, Abdo A. 1981. "The Arab American Family." In *Ethnic Families in America—Patterns and Variations*, edited by Charles H. Mindel and Robert W. Habenstein, 2d ed., 145-62. New York: Elsevier.

Erikson, Erik H. 1963. *Childhood and Society*. New York: W. W. Norton.

———. 1974. *Dimensions of a New Identity*. New York: W. W. Norton.

Ferro, Marc, and Claire Mouradian. 1982. "L'Arménie Soviétique (1921-1980)." In *Histoire des Arméniens*, edited by Gerard Dedeyan, 525-66. Toulouse: Privat.

Finke, Roger, and Rodney Stark. 1988. "Religious Economies and Sacred Canopies: Religious Mobilization in American Cities." *American Sociological Review* 53, n. 1 (February): 41-9.

Fischer, Claude S. 1982. *To Dwell Among Friends—Personal Networks in Town and City*. Chicago: University of Chicago Press.

———. 1984. *The Urban Experience*. 2d ed. San Diego: Harcourt Brace Jovanovich.

Fisher, Wesley Andrew. 1980. *The Soviet Marriage Market—Mate-Selection in Russia and the USSR*. New York: Praeger.

References   453

Fishman, Joshua A. et al. 1985. *The Rise and Fall of the Ethnic Revival: Perspectives on Language and Ethnicity*. Berlin: Mouton.

Friedman, Nathalie. 1989. "The Graduates of Ramaz: Fifty Years of Jewish Day School Education." In *Fifty Years of Orthodox Judaism in America, 1937-1987—Essays in Honor of the Jubilee of Ramaz School*, edited by Jeffrey S. Gurock. New York: Ktav Publishing.

Gans, Herbert J. 1962. *The Urban Villagers—Group and Class in the Life of Italian-Americans*. New York: Free Press.

———. 1979. "Symbolic Ethnicity: The Future of Ethnic Groups and Cultures in America." In *On the Making of Americans: Essays in Honor of David Riesman*, edited by Herbert J. Gans, 193-220. Philadelphia: University of Pennsylvania Press.

Ghayur, M. Arif. 1981. "Muslims in the United States: Settlers and Visitors." *Annals of the American Academy of Political and Social Science* 454 (March): 150-63.

Glazer, Nathan, ed. 1985. *Clamor at the Gates—The New American Immigration*. San Francisco: Institute for Contemporary Studies.

Glazer, Nathan, and Daniel Patrick Moynihan. (1963) 1970. *Beyond the Melting Point—The Negroes, Puerto Ricans, Jews, Italians, and Irish of New York City*. 2d ed. Cambridge, MA: Massachusetts Institute of Technology Press.

Glazer, Nathan, and Daniel Patrick Moynihan, eds. 1975. *Ethnicity: Theory and Experience*. Cambridge, MA: Harvard University Press.

Gleason, Philip. 1980. s.v. "American Identity and Americanization." In *Harvard Encyclopedia of American Ethnic Groups*, edited by Stephan Thernstrom, Ann Orlov, and Oscar Handlin. Cambridge, MA: Harvard University Press.

Goode, William. 1970. *World Revolution and Family Patterns*. New York: Free Press.

Gordon, Milton M. 1964. *Assimilation in American Life*. New York: Oxford University Press.

———. 1978. *Human Nature, Class and Ethnicity*. New York: Oxford University Press.

———. 1981. "Models of Pluralism: The New American Dream." *Annals of the American Academy of Political and Social Science* 454 (March): 178-88.

Goyder, John. 1987. *The Silent Minority—Nonrespondents on Sample Surveys*. Boulder, CO: Westview Press.

Granovetter, Mark S. 1973. "The Strength of Weak Ties." *American Journal of Sociology* 78, n. 6 (May): 1360-80.

Greeley, Andrew M. 1970. "Religious Intermarriage in a Denominational Society." *American Journal of Sociology* 75, n. 6 (May): 949-51.

———. 1974. *Ethnicity in the United States: A Preliminary Reconnaissance*. New York: John Wiley & Sons.

Greeley, Andrew M., and William C. McCready. 1975. "The Transmission of Cultural Heritages: The Case of Irish and Italians." In *Ethnicity: Theory and Experience*, edited by Nathan Glazer and Daniel Patrick Moynihan, 209-35. Cambridge, MA: Harvard University Press.

Greeley, Andrew M., and Peter H. Rossi. 1966. *The Education of Catholic Americans*. Chicago: Adline.

Gunter, Michael M. 1986. *"Pursuing the Just Cause of Their People"—A Study of Contemporary Armenian Terrorism*. New York: Greenwood Press.

Guroian, Vigen. 1987. *Incarnate Love: Essays in Orthodox Ethics*. Notre Dame, IN: University of Notre Dame Press.

Gusfield, Joseph R. 1967. "Tradition and Modernity: Misplaced Polarities in the Study of Social Change." *American Journal of Sociology* 72, n. 4 (January): 351-62.

Hamalian, Arpi. 1973. "Lebanese-Armenians: A Study of Generational Differences in Assimilation." M.A. thesis, American University of Beirut.

Handlin, Oscar. 1973. *The Uprooted*, 2d enlarged ed. Boston: Little, Brown.

———, ed. 1959. *Immigration—A Factor in American History*. Englewood Cliffs, NJ: Prentice-Hall.

———. 1986-87. Introduction. *Journal of Armenian Studies* 3 (1-2).

Hannerz, Ulf. 1974. "Ethnicity and Opportunity in Urban America." In *Urban Ethnicity*, edited by Abner Cohen, 37-76. London: Tavistock.

Hansen, Marcus Lee. 1938. *The Problems of the Third Generation Immigrant*. Rock Island, IL: Augustana Historical Society.

Heiss, Jerold S. 1960. "Premarital Characteristics of the Religiously Intermarried in an Urban Area." *American Sociological Review* 25, n. 1 (February): 47-55.

Heitman, Sidney. 1988. "The Third Soviet Emigration." *Soviet Jewish Affairs* 18, n. 2 (Summer-Autumn): 17-42.

Helmreich, William B. 1982. *The Things They Say Behind Your Back: Stereotypes and the Myths Behind Them.* New Brunswick, NJ: Transaction Publishers.

Henry, Sheila Eileen. 1973. "Occupational Mobility and the Ethnic Community: A Comparative Study of Armenians and Japanese Americans in Los Angeles." Ph.D. diss., University of California, Los Angeles.

Herberg, Will. 1960. *Protestant, Catholic, Jew.* New York: Doubleday.

Hicks, George L. 1977. "Introduction: Problems in the Study of Ethnicity." In *Ethnic Encounters: Identities and Contexts,* edited by George L. Hicks and Philip L. Leis, 1-20. North Scituate, MA: Duxbury Press.

Horowitz, Irving Louis. 1980. *Taking Lives—Genocide and State Power.* New Brunswick, NJ: Transaction Publishers.

———. 1984. "Genocide and the Reconstruction of Social Theory: Observations on the Exclusivity of Collective Death." *Armenian Review* 37, n. 1 (Spring): 1-21.

———. 1986. "Government Responsibilities to Jews and Armenians: Nazi Holocaust and Turkish Genocide Reconsidered." *Armenian Review* 39, n. 1 (Spring): 1-9.

Hovannisian, Richard G. 1971. *The Republic of Armenia.* Vol. 1, *The First Year, 1918-1919.* Berkeley, CA: University of California Press.

———. 1982. *The Republic of Armenia.* Vol. 2, *From Versailles to London, 1919-1920.* Berkeley, CA: University of California Press.

———. 1988. "National Ferment in Armenia." *Freedom at Issue* 105 (November/December): 29-35.

Hovannisian, Richard G., ed. 1986. *The Armenian Genocide in Perspective.* New Brunswick, NJ: Transaction Publishers.

Humphrey, Craig Rand, and Helen Brock Louis. 1973. "Assimilation and Voting Behavior: A Study of Greek-Americans." *International Migration Review* 7, n. 1 (Spring): 34-45.

Isajiw, Wsevolod W. 1974. "Definitions of Ethnicity." *Ethnicity* 1, n. 2 (July): 111-24.

Jarvenpa, Robert. 1985. "The Political Economy and Political Ethnicity of American Indian Adaptations and Identities." In *Ethnicity and Race in the U.S.A.—Toward the Twenty-First Century,* edited by Richard D. Alba, 29-48. London: Routledge & Kegan Paul.

Jerejian, Sona Movses. 1976. "The Social and Cultural Integration of Lebanese-Armenian Youth: A Sample Survey Conducted in Beirut, 1970." Ph.D. diss., University of California, Los Angeles.

Jeter, Kris. 1982. "Analytical Analysis: Intercultural and Interracial Marriage." *Marriage and Family Review* 5, Special Issue: Intermarriage in the United States, edited by Gary A. Cretser and Joseph J. Leon, n. 1 (Spring): 105-11.

Johnson, Colleen Leahy. 1985.*Growing Up and Growing Old in Italian-American Families.* New Brunswick, NJ: Rutgers University Press.

Johnston, Barry V., and William C. Yoels. 1977. "On Linking Cultural and Structural Models of Ethnicity: A Synthesis of Schooler and Yancey, Ericksen and Juliani," *American Journal of Sociology* 83, n. 3 (November): 729-41.

Jones, M. A. 1960. *American Immigration.* Chicago: University of Chicago Press, 317 (quoted in Charsley, 1974, 355).

Kaprielian, Isabel. 1986-87. "Early Armenian Settlement in Canada: An Overview," *Journal of Armenian Studies* 3 (1-2): 47-59.

Kassees, Assad S. 1972. "Cross-Cultural Comparative Familism of a Christian Arab People." *Journal of Marriage and the Family* 34, n. 3 (August): 539-44.

Katz, Elihu, and Paul F. Lazarsfeld. 1955. *Personal Influence: The Part Played by People in the Flow of Mass Communications.* New York: Free Press.

Kayal, Philip Mitchell. 1970. "The Churches of the Catholic Syrians and Their Role in the Assimilation Process." Ph.D. diss., Fordham University.

————. 1973. "Religion and Assimilation: Catholic 'Syrians' in America." *International Migration Review* 7, n. 4 (Winter): 409-26.

————. 1983. "Arab Christians in the United States." In *Arabs in the New World—Studies on Arab-American Communities,* edited by Sameer Y. Abraham and Nabeel Abraham, 45-63. Detroit: Wayne State University.

Keller, Suzanne. 1988. "The American Dream Community: An Unfinished Agenda." *Sociological Forum* 3, n. 2 (Spring): 167-83.

Kennedy, Ruby Jo Reeves. 1944. "Single or Triple Melting-Pot? Intermarriage Trends in New Haven, 1870-1940." *American Journal of Sociology* 49, n. 4 (January): 331-39.

————. 1952. "Single or Triple Melting Pot? Intermarriage in New Haven, 1879-1950." *American Journal of Sociology* 58, n. 1 (July): 56-9.

Keoseyan, Susy N. 1981. "The Question of the Armenian State: Building a National Consciousness." In "Armenians in the Eighties—Prospects and Challenges: Proceedings of Conference in Berkeley, California (September 11-13)" by California Council of the Armenian Assembly and Armenian Student Association at University of California, Berkeley, 65-75. photocopied.

Kernaklian, Paul. 1967. "The Armenian-American Personality Structure and its Relationship to Various States of Ethnicity." D.S.S. diss., Syracuse University.

Keyes, Charles F. 1981. "The Dialectics of Ethnic Change." In *Ethnic Change,* edited by Charles F. Keyes, 4-30. Seattle: University of Washington Press.

Kobrin, Frances E., and Calvin Goldscheider. 1978. *The Ethnic Factor in Family Structure and Mobility.* Cambridge, MA: Ballinger.

Kourvetaris, George A. 1981. "The Greek American Family." In *Ethnic Families in America: Patterns and Variations,* edited by Charles H. Mindel and Robert W. Habenstein, 2d ed., 163-88. New York: Elsevier.

Kourvetaris, George A., and Betty A. Dobratz. 1976. "An Empirical Test of Gordon's Ethclass Hypothesis among Three Ethnoreligious Groups." *Sociology and Social Research* 61 (October): 39-51.

Kramer, Judith R., and Seymour Leventman. 1961. *Children of the Gilded Ghetto—Conflict Resolution of Three Generations of American Jews.* New Haven: Yale University Press.

Kulhanjian, Gary A. 1986-87. "From Ararat to America: The Armenian Settlements of New Jersey." *Journal of Armenian Studies* 3 (1-2): 35-46.

Kuper, Leo. 1981.*Genocide—Its Political Use in the Twentieth Century.* New Haven: Yale University Press.

Kurz, Anat, and Ariel Merari. 1985. *ASALA—Irrational Terror or Political Tool.* Boulder, CO: Westview Press and Tel Aviv University, Jaffee Center for Strategic Studies.

Lal, Barbara Ballis. 1983. "Perspectives on Ethnicity: Old Wine in New Bottles." *Ethnic and Racial Studies* 6, n. 2 (April): 154-73.

Lambert, Wallace E., and Donald M. Taylor. 1988. "Assimilation versus Multiculturalism: The Views of Urban Americans." *Sociological Forum* 3, n. 1 (Winter): 72-88.

LaPiere, Richard Tracy. 1930. "The Armenian Colony in Fresno County, California: A Study in Social Psychology." Ph.D. diss., Stanford University.

———. 1936. "Type-Rationalizations of Group Antipathy." *Social Forces* 15, n. 2 (December): 232-37.

Lenski, Gerhard E. 1953. "Social Correlates of Religious Interest." *American Sociological Review* 18, n. 5 (October): 533-44.

———. 1963. *The Religious Factor.* New York: Anchor Books.

Libaridian, Gerard J. 1979. "Armenia and Armenians: A Divided Homeland and a Dispersed Nation." In *Soviet Asian Ethnic Frontiers,* edited by William O. McCagg, Jr. and Brian D. Silver, 27-60. New York: Pergamon Press.

———. 1987. "The Ideology of Armenian Liberation. The Development of Armenian Political Thought before the Revolutionary Movement (1639-1885)." Ph.D. diss., University of California, Los Angeles.

Libaridian, Gerard J., ed. 1984. *Armenian Review* 37, n. 1 (Spring). Special Issue: The Genocide of the Armenian People.

———. 1986. *Armenian Review* 40, n. 1 (Spring). Special Issue: Beyond Scholarship—The Genocide and its Discontents.

————. 1988. *The Karabagh File—Documents and Facts on the Question of Mountainous Karabagh 1918-1988.* 1st ed. Cambridge, MA: Zoryan Institute.

————. 1991. *Armenia at the Crossroads: Democracy and Nationhood in the Post-Soviet Era, Interviews and Speeches by the Leaders of the National Democratic Movement in Armenia.* Watertown, MA: Blue Crane Books.

Lieberson, Stanley, and Mary C. Waters. 1988. *From Many Strands: Ethnic and Racial Groups in Contemporary America.* New York: Russel Sage Foundation.

Light, Ivan H. 1972. *Ethnic Enterprise in America: Business and Welfare Among Chinese, Japanese and Blacks.* Berkeley, CA: University of California Press.

Litwak, Eugene. 1985. *Helping the Elderly.* New York: Guilford.

Lopata, Helena Znaniecka. 1964. "The function of Voluntary Associations in an Ethnic Community: 'Polonia.'" In *Contributions to Urban Sociology,* edited by Ernest W. Burgess and Donald J. Bogue, 203-23. Chicago: University of Chicago Press.

Lyman, Stanford M., and William A. Douglas. 1973. "Ethnicity: Strategies of Collective and Individual Impression Management." *Social Research* 40, n. 2 (Summer): 344-56.

Malkasian, Mark. 1984. "The Disintegration of the Armenian Cause in the United States, 1918-1927." *International Journal of Middle East Studies* 16, n. 3 (August): 349-65.

Matossian, Mary Kilbourne. 1958. "Ideologies of Delayed Industrialization: Some Tensions and Ambiguities." *Economic Development and Cultural Change* 6, n. 3 (April): 217-28.

Mayhew, Leon. 1968. "Ascription in Modern Societies." *Sociological Inquiry* 38, n. 2 (Spring): 105-20.

Mazian, Florence. 1983. "The Patriarchal Armenian Family System: 1914." *Armenian Review* 36, n. 4 (Winter): 14-26.

————. 1984. "Armenian Wedding Customs 1914: From Sacred to Profane." *Armenian Review* 37, n. 4 (Winter): 1-13.

McKay, James. 1982. "An Exploratory Synthesis of Primordial and Mobilizationist Approaches to Ethnic Phenomena." *Ethnic and Racial Studies* 5, n. 4 (October): 395-420.

McKay, James, and F. Lewins. 1978. "Ethnicity and Ethnic Groups: A Conceptual Analysis and Reformulation." *Ethnic and Racial Studies* 1, n. 4 (October): 412-27.

Megerdichian, Robert. 1983. *The Armenian Churches in North America: Apostolic, Protestant and Catholic—A Geographical and Historical Survey*. Cambridge, MA: Society for Armenian Studies.

Merton, Robert K. 1941. "Intermarriage and Social Structure: Fact and Theory." *Psychiatry* 4: 361-74.

———. 1972. "Insiders and Outsiders: A Chapter in the Sociology of Knowledge." *American Journal of Sociology* 78 (July): 9-47.

Miller, Dickinson Jenkins. 1981. "The Craftsman's Art: Armenians and the Growth of Photography in the Near East." M.A. thesis, American University of Beirut.

Miller, Donald E., and Lorna Touryan Miller. 1986. "An Oral History Perspective on Responses to the Armenian Genocide." In *The Armenian Genocide in Perspective*, edited by Richard G. Hovannisian, 187-203. New Brunswick, NJ: Transaction Publishers.

Mindel, Charles H., and Robert W. Habenstein, eds. 1981. *Ethnic Families in America—Patterns and Variations*, 2d ed. New York: Elsevier.

Mirak, Robert. 1980. s.v. "Armenians." In *Harvard Encyclopedia of American Ethnic Groups,* edited by Stephan Thernstrom, Ann Orlov, and Oscar Handlin. Cambridge, MA: Harvard University Press.

———. 1983. *Torn Between Two Lands: Armenians in America, 1890 to World War I*. Cambridge: Harvard University Press.

Modell, John, and Tamara K. Hareven. 1978. "Urbanization and the Malleable Household: An Examination of Boarding and Lodging in American Families." In *The American Family in Social-Historical Perspective*, edited by Michael Gordon, 2d ed., 51-68. New York: St Martin's Press.

Moskos, Charles C., Jr. 1989. *Greek Americans—Struggle and Success*, 2d ed. New Brunswick, NJ: Transaction Publishers.

Mouradian, Claire. 1990. *L'Arménie: De Staline à Gorbatchev, Histoire d'une République Soviétique*. Paris: Editions Ramsay.

Mueller, C. W., and W. T. Johnson. 1975. "Socioeconomic Status and Religious Participation." *American Sociological Review* 40, n. 6 (December): 785-800.

Myrdal, Gunnar. 1974. "The Case Against Romantic Ethnicity." *Center Magazine* 7, n. 4 (July-August): 26-30.

Nahirny, Vladimir C., and Joshua A. Fishman. 1965. "American Immigrant Groups: Ethnic Identification and the Problem of Generations." *Sociological Review* 13, n. 3 (November): 311-326.

Nelson, Harold. 1953. "The Armenian Family: Changing Patterns of Family Life in a California Community." Ph.D. diss., University of California, Berkeley.

Novak, Michael. 1973. *The Rise of the Unmeltable Ethnics—Politics and Culture in the Seventies*. New York: Macmillan.

O'Grady, Ingrid Poschmann. 1979. "Ararat, Etchmiadzin and Haig (Nation, Church, Kin): A Study of the Symbol System of American Armenians." Ph.D. diss., Catholic University of America.

Olzak, Susan, and Joane Nagel, eds. 1986. *Comparative Ethnic Relations*. New York: Academic Press.

Ordjanian, Anahid Victoria. 1991. "Children of Ararat: Political Economy and Ideology at an Armenian Ethnic School in the United States." Ph.D. diss., Temple University.

Ormanian, Patriarch Malachia. 1955. *The Church of Armenia*. London: A. R. Mowbray.

Padgett, Deborah. 1980. "Symbolic Ethnicity and Patterns of Ethnic Identity Assertion in American-born Serbs." *Ethnic Groups* 3 (December): 55-77.

Papazian, Dennis R. 1986. "The Changing American View of the Armenian Question: An Interpretation." *Armenian Review* 39, n. 4 (Winter): 47-72.

Park, Robert E., and Ernest W. Burgess. 1969. *Introduction to the Science of Sociology*, 3d rev. ed. Chicago: University of Chicago Press.

Parlakian, Nishan. 1977. "ABC to PhD: Armenian Studies in America." *Ararat* 18, Special Issue: Armenians in America, n. 1 (Winter): 68-74.

———. 1983. "Armenian-American Theatre." In *Ethnic Theatre in the United States,* edited by Maxine Schwartz Seller, 19-35. Westport, CT: Greenwood Press.

Patterson, G. James. 1979. "A Critique of 'The New Ethnicity.'" *American Anthropologist* 81, n. 1 (March): 103-5.

Patterson, Orlando. 1975. "Context and Choice in Ethnic Allegiance: A Theoretical Framework and Caribbean Case Study." In *Ethnicity: Theory and Experience,* edited by Nathan Glazer and Daniel Patrick Moynihan, 305-49. Cambridge, MA: Harvard University Press.

Pattie, Susan Paul. 1990. "Faith in History: Armenians Rebuilding Community in Cyprus and London." Ph.D. diss., University of Michigan.

Peres, Yochanan, and Ruth Schrift. 1978. "Intermarriage and Interethnic Relations: A Comparative Study." *Ethnic and Racial Studies* 1, n. 4 (October): 428-51.

Permanent Peoples' Tribunal. 1985. *A Crime of Silence—The Armenian Genocide,* edited by Gerard J. Libaridian. London: Zed Books Ltd and Zoryan Institute.

Peterson, William. 1980. s.v. "Concepts of Ethnicity." In *Harvard Encyclopedia of American Ethnic Groups,* edited by Stephan Thernstrom, Ann Orlov, and Oscar Handlin. Cambridge, MA: Harvard University Press.

Phillips, Jenny King. 1978. "Symbol, Myth and Rhetoric: The Politics of Culture in an Armenian-American Population." Ph.D. diss., Boston University.

Polenberg, Richard. 1980. *One Nation Divisible: Class, Race, and Ethnicity in the United States Since 1938.* Harmondsworth: Penguin Books.

Population Reference Bureau staff and guest experts. 1982. "U.S. Population: Where We Are; Where We're Going." *Population Bulletin* (Population Reference Bureau, Inc., Washington, DC) 37, n. 2 (June).

Porter, John. 1975. "Ethnic Pluralism in Canadian Perspective." In *Ethnicity: Theory and Experience,* edited by Nathan Glazer and Daniel Patrick Moynihan, 266-304. Cambridge, MA: Harvard University Press.

Portes, Alejandro. 1984. "The Rise of Ethnicity: Determinants of Ethnic Perceptions among Cuban Exiles in Miami." *American Sociological Review* 49, n. 3 (June): 383-97.

Portes, Alejandro, and Robert L. Bach. 1985. *Latin Journey*. Berkeley: University of California Press.

Rapaport, Lynn. 1989. "Life After Death: A Study of Second-Generation Jews in Frankfurt Am Main." Ph.D. diss., Columbia University.

Ravitch, Diane. (1974) 1988. *The Great School Wars—A History of the New York City Public Schools*. New York: Basic Books.

Redfield, Robert. 1955. "The Social Organization of Tradition." *Far Eastern Quarterly* 15, n. 1 (November): 12-21.

Rollins, Joan H., ed. 1981. *Hidden Minorities*. Lanham, MD: University Press of America.

Rosenthal, Erich. 1960. "Acculturation without Assimilation? The Jewish Community of Chicago, Illinois." *American Journal of Sociology* 66, n. 3 (November): 275-88.

Rosentraub, Mark, and Delbert Taebel. 1980. "Jewish Enterprise in Transition: From Collective Self-Help to Orthodox Capitalism." In *Self-Help in Urban America: Patterns of Minority Business Enterprise,* edited by Scott Cummings, 191-214. Port Washington, NY: Kennikat.

Rothman, Sheila M. 1978. *Woman's Proper Place—A History of Changing Ideals and Practices, 1870 to the Present*. New York: Basic Books.

Rustigian, Stella Sachaklian. 1979. "The Armenian Day School Movement in the United States." M.A. thesis, University of Connecticut.

Saba, Paul. 1989. "The Armenian National Question." In *Power and Stability in the Middle East,* edited by Berch Berberoglu., 173-201. London: Zed Books.

Sabagh, George, and Mehdi Bozorgmehr. 1987. "Are the Characteristics of Exiles Different from Immigrants? The Case of Iranians in Los Angeles." *Sociology and Social Research* 71, n. 2 (January): 77-83.

Sabagh, George, Mehdi Bozorgmehr, and Claudia Der-Martirosian. 1988. "Socioeconomic and Demographic Characteristics of Armenians in the United States in 1980." Paper presented at conference on the International Migration of Middle Easterners and North Africans: Comparative Perspectives, University of California, Los Angeles, 19-21 May.

Sabagh, George, Mehdi Bozorgmehr, Ivan Light, and Claudia Der-Martirosian. 1989. "Internal Ethno-Religious Differentiation of Immigrant Groups: Iranians in Los Angeles." Paper presented at annual meeting of Population Association of America, Baltimore, 30 March -1 April.

Saloutos, Theodore. 1973. "The Greek Orthodox Church in the United States and Assimilation." *International Migration Review* 7, n. 4 (Winter): 395-407.

Samuelian, Thomas J. 1986. Review of *Linguistic Composition of the United Nations of the World. vol. 5, Europe and the USSR,* by H. Kloss and G. D. McConnell. In *Armenian Review* 39, n. 3 (Autumn): 81-99.

Sandberg, Neil C. 1974. *Ethnic Identity and Assimilation: The Polish-American Community.* New York: Praeger.

Sanders, Jimmy N., and Victor Nee. 1987. "Limits of Ethnic Solidarity." *American Sociological Review* 52, n. 6 (December): 745-73.

Sanjian, Avedis K. 1965. *The Armenian Communities in Syria under Ottoman Dominion.* Cambridge, MA: Harvard University Press.

Sarkisian, Zarouhi. 1984. "Coping with Massive Stressful Life Event: The Impact of the Armenian Genocide of 1915 on the Present-Day Health and Morale of a Group of Women Survivors." *Armenian Review* 37, n. 3 (Autumn): 33-44.

———. 1988. "Armenian Women: Strength and Survival." *Ararat* 29, Special Feminist Issue n. 4 (Fall): 53-5.

Sarna, Jonathan D. 1978. "From Immigrants to Ethnics: Toward a New Theory of Ethnicization." *Ethnicity* 5, n. 4 (December): 370-78.

Saroyan, William. 1984. "The Armenian and the Armenian." *Ararat* 25, 2 (Spring): 7. [First published in 1936, as *Inhale an Exhale.* New York: Random House.]

Schiller, Nina Glick. 1977. "Ethnic Groups are Made, Not Born: The Haitian Immigrant and American Politics." In *Ethnic Encounters: Identities and Contexts,* edited by George L. Hicks and Philip L. Leis, 23-35. North Scituate, MA: Duxbury Press.

Schneider, David M. 1980. *American Kinship: A Cultural Account,* 2d ed. Chicago: University of Chicago Press.

Schooler, Carmi. 1976. "Serfdom's Legacy: An Ethnic Continuum." *American Journal of Sociology* 81, n. 6 (May): 1265-86.

Schudson, Michael. 1984. *Advertising: The Uneasy Persuasion.* New York: Basic Books.

Scott, Franklin D., ed. 1968. *World Migration in Modern Times.* Englewood Cliffs, NJ: Prentice-Hall.

Scourby, Alice. 1980. *Third Generation Greek Americans: A Study of Religious Attitudes.* New York: Arno Press.

See, Katherine O'Sullivan and William J. Wilson. 1988. "Race and Ethnicity." In *Handbook of Sociology,* edited by Neil J. Smelser, 223-42. Newbury Park, CA: Sage.

Sengstock, Mary C. 1969. "Differential Rates of Assimilation in an Ethnic Group: In Ritual, Social Interaction, and Normative Culture." *International Migration Review* 3, n. 2 (Spring): 18-32.

———. 1975. "Kinship in a Roman Catholic Ethnic Group." *Ethnicity* 2, n. 2 (June): 134-52.

Shibutani, Tamotsu, and Kian M. Kwan. 1965. *Ethnic Stratification.* New York: Macmillan.

Shils, Edward. 1957."Primordial, Personal, Sacred, and Civic Ties." *British Journal of Sociology* 8 (June): 130-45.

Shirinian, Lorne. 1990. "Lost Fathers and Abandoned Sons: The Silence of Generations in Armenian Diaspora Literature." *Armenian Review* 43, n. 1 (Spring): 1-17.

Shorter, Edward. 1977. *The Making of the Modern Family.* New York: Basic Books.

Silver, Brian D. 1978. "Ethnic Intermarriage and Ethnic Consciousness among Soviet Nationalities." *Soviet Studies* 30, n. 1 (January): 107-16.

Simmel, Georg. 1955. *Conflict and the Web of Group-Affiliations.* New York: Free Press.

Simon, Rita J. 1983. "Refugee Families' Adjustment and Aspirations: A Comparison of Soviet Jewish and Vietnamese Immigrants." *Ethnic and Racial Studies* 6, n. 4 (October): 492-504.

———. 1985. *Public Opinion and the Immigrant—Print Media Coverage, 1880-1980.* Lexington, MA: Lexington Books/ D. C. Heath.

Simpson, George Eaton. 1968. s.v. "Assimilation." In *International Encyclopedia of the Social Sciences,* edited by David L. Shils. New York: Macmillan/Free Press.

Simpson, George Eaton, and J. Milton Yinger. 1985. *Racial and Cultural Minorities—An Analysis of Prejudice and Discrimination,* 5th ed. New York: Plenum Press.

Sinanian, Zaven V. 1987. "Coverage of Armenian Issues in *The New York Times,* 1965-1983." *Armenian Review* 40, n. 1 (Spring): 31-49.

Singer, Milton. 1972. *When a Great Tradition Modernizes: An Anthropological Approach to Indian Civilization.* Chicago: University of Chicago Press.

Sklare, Marshall. 1975. "American Jewry: Social History and Group Identity." In *Majority and Minority,* edited by Norman R. Yetman and C. Hoy Steele, 2d ed., 261-73. Boston: Allyn & Bacon.

Slater, Miriam. 1969. "My Son the Doctor: Aspects of Mobility among American Jews." *American Sociological Review* 34, n. 4 (June): 359-73.

Smith, Tom W., and Glenn R. Dempsey. 1983. "The Polls: Ethnic Social Distance and Prejudice." *Public Opinion Quarterly* 47, n. 4 (Winter): 584-600.

Sowell, Thomas. 1981. *Ethnic America: A History.* New York: Basic Books.

Spindler, L., and G. Spindler. 1958. "Male and Female Adaptations in Cultural Change." *American Anthropologist* 60, n. 2 (April): 217-33.

Stein, Howard F., and Robert F. Hill. 1973. " The New Ethnicity, and the White Ethnic in the United States: An Exploration in the Psycho-Cultural Genesis of Ethnic Irredentism." *Canadian Review of Studies on Nationalism* 1, n. 1 (Fall): 81-105.

———. 1977. "The Limits of Ethnicity." *American Scholar* 46 (Spring): 181-89.

Steinberg, Stephen. 1981. *The Ethnic Myth—Race, Ethnicity, and Class in America.* Boston: Beacon Press.

Stevens, Gillian. 1985. "Nativity, Intermarriage, and Mother-Tongue Shift." *American Sociological Review* 50, n. 1 (February): 74-83.

Stevens, Gillian, and Robert Schoen. 1988. "Linguistic Intermarriage in the United States." *Journal of Marriage and the Family* 50, n. 1 (February): 267-79.

Stevens, Gillian, and Gray Swicegood. 1987. "The Linguistic Context of Ethnic Endogamy." *American Sociological Review* 52, n. 1 (February): 73-82.

Stockton, Ronald R. 1983."Who defines the Armenians?" *Armenian Review* 36, n. 4 (Winter): 6-13.

Stone, Frank Andrews. 1981. "The Armenians in North America." In *Hidden Minorities—The Persistence of Ethnicity in American Life,* edited by Joan H. Rollins, 101-39. Lanham, MD: University Press of America.

Szaz, Z. Michael. 1983. "Armenian Terrorists and the East-West Conflict." *Journal of Social, Political, and Economic Studies* 8: 387-94.

Takooshian, Harold. 1986-87. "Armenian Immigration to the United States from the Middle East." *Journal of Armenian Studies* 3 (1-2): 133-55.

Talai, Vered. 1984. "Mobilization and Diffuse Ethnic Organization: The London Armenian Community." *Urban Anthropology* 13 (Summer & Fall): 197-218.

Talmon, Yonina. 1964. " Mate Selection in Collective Settlements." *American Sociological Review* 29, n. 4 (August): 491-508.

Tavakoliyazdi, Mohammad. 1981. "Assimilation and Status Attainment of Middle Eastern Immigrants in the United States." Ph.D. diss., University of Minnesota.

Ter Minassian, Anaide. 1984. *Nationalism and Socialism in the Armenian Revolutionary Movement (1887-1912),* translated by A. M. Berrett. Cambridge, MA: Zoryan Institute.

Thernstrom, Stephan. 1982. "Ethnic Groups in American History." In *Ethnic Relations in America,* edited by Lance Liebman, 3-27. Englewood Cliffs, NJ: Prentice-Hall.

Thomas, William I., and Florian Znaniecki. 1984. *The Polish Peasant in Europe and America,* edited and abridged by Eli Zaretsky. Urbana, IL: University of Illinois Press.

Tilly, Charles, and Harold Brown. 1974. "On Uprooting Kinship and the Auspices of Migration." In *An Urban World,* edited by Charles Tilly, 108-133. Boston: Little, Brown.

Tinker, John N. 1982. "Intermarriage and Assimilation in a Plural Society: Japanese-Americans in the United States." *Marriage and Family Review* 5, Special Issue: Intermarriage in the United States, edited by Gary A. Cretser and Joseph J. Leon, n. 1 (Spring): 61-74.

Tölölyan, Khachig. 1988. "The Role of the Armenian Apostolic Church in the Diaspora." *Armenian Review* 41, n. 1 (Spring): 55-68.

———. 1991."The Nation-State and Its Others: In Lieu of a Preface." *Diaspora: Journal of Transnational Studies* 1, n. 1 (Spring): 3-7.

Tootikian, Vahan H. 1981. *The Armenian Evangelical Church.* Southfield, MI: Armenian Heritage Committee, P. O. Box 531.

Treudley, Mary Bosworth. 1946. "An Ethnic Group's View of the American Middle Class." *American Sociological Review* 11 (February): 715-24.

———. 1949. "Formal Organization and the Americanization Process, with Special Reference to the Greeks of Boston." *American Sociological Review* 14, n. 1 (February): 44-53.

———. 1953. "The Ethnic Group as a Collectivity." *Social Forces* 31, n. 3 (March): 261-65.

Turner, Johnathan H., and Edna Bonacich. 1980. "Toward a Composite Theory of Middlemen Minorities." *Ethnicity* 7, n. 2 (June): 144-58.

Verneuil, Henri. 1985. *Mayrig.* Paris: Robert Laffont.

Villa, Susie Hoogasian, and Mary Kilbourne Matossian. 1982. *Armenian Village Life Before 1914.* Detroit: Wayne State University Press.

Waldinger, Roger and Howard Aldrich. 1990. "Trends in Ethnic Business in the United States." In *Ethnic Entrepreneurs: Immigrant Business in Industrial Societies*, edited by Roger Waldinger, Howard Aldrich, Robin Ward and associates, 49-78. Newbury Park, CA: Sage Publications.

Walker, Christopher J. 1980. *Armenia—The Survival of a Nation.* New York: St Martin's Press.

Waters, Mary C. 1990. *Ethnic Options: Choosing Identities in America.* Berkeley, CA: University of California Press.

Warner, W. Lloyd and Leo Srole. 1945. *The Social Systems of American Ethnic Groups.* New Haven: Yale University Press.

Wax, Murray. 1973. "Cultural Pluralism, Political Power and Ethnic Studies." In *Learning and Culture: Proceedings of the 1972 Annual Spring Meeting of the American Ethnological Society,* edited by Solon T. Kimball and Jacquetta H. Burnett, 163-74. Seattle: University of Washington Press.

Waxman, Chaim I. 1981. "The Fourth Generation Grows Up: The Contemporary American Jewish Community." *Annals of American Academy of Political and Social Science* 454 (March): 70-85.

Williams, Robin M. Jr. 1977. *Mutual Accommodation: Ethic Conflict and Cooperation.* Minneapolis: University of Minnesota Press.

Winch, Robert F., Scott Greer, and Rae Lesser Blumberg. 1967. "Ethnicity and Extended Familism in Upper-Middle Class Suburb." *American Sociological Review* 32, n. 2 (April): 265-72.

Winch, Robert F., and Gay C. Kitson. 1977. "Types of American Families: An Unsatisfactory Classification." In *Familial Organization—A Quest for Determinants,* edited by Robert F. Winch, 11-52. New York: Free Press.

Yancey, William L., Eugene P. Ericksen, and Richard N. Juliani. 1976. "Emergent Ethnicity: A Review and Reformulation." *American Sociological Review* 41, n. 3 (June): 391-403.

Yancey, William L., Eugene P. Ericksen, and George H. Leon. 1985. "The Structure of Pluralism: 'We're All Italian Around Here, Aren't We, Mrs. O'Brien?'" In *Ethnicity and Race in the U.S.A.—Toward the Twenty-First Century,* edited by Richard D. Alba, 94-116. London: Routledge & Kegan Paul.

Yegparian, Garen. 1987. "Armenian Issues in *The Congressional Record,* 1965-1983." *Armenian Review* 40, n. 1 (Spring): 51-68.

Yeretzian, Aram S. (1923) 1974. *A History of Armenian Immigration to America with Special Reference to Los Angeles.* San Francisco: R. & E. Research Associates.

Yinger, J. Milton. 1981. "Toward a Theory of Assimilation and Dissimilation." *Ethnic and Racial Studies* 4, n. 3 (July): 249-64.

Zelizer, Viviana A. 1985. *Pricing the Priceless Child: The Changing Social Value of Children.* New York: Basic Books.

Zenner, Walter P. 1982. "Arabic-Speaking Immigrants in North America as Middleman Minorities." *Ethnic and Racial Studies* 5, n. 4 (October): 457-77.

————. 1985. "Jewishness in America: Ascription and Choice." In *Ethnicity and Race in the U.S.A.—Toward the Twenty-First Century*, edited by Richard D. Alba, 117-33. London: Routledge & Kegan Paul.

Newspapers, Magazines Cited

AGBU News (Saddle Brook, NJ)
Ararat Quarterly (AGBU, Saddle Brook, NJ)
Armenian Church (Armenian Diocese of North America, New York)
Armenian International Magazine (Glendale, CA)
Armenian Mirror-Spectator (Watertown, MA)
Armenian Reporter (Flushing, NY)
Armenian Weekly (Watertown, MA)
Christian Century (Chicago, IL)
Economist (London)
Hye Sharzhoom (University of California, Fresno and Armenian Studies Program)
Los Angeles Times
NAASR Newsletter (Belmont, MA)
Nor Gyank (Glendale, CA)
Outreach (Armenian Apostolic Church—Eastern Prelacy, New York)
The New York Times
The New Yorker
Window: A View of the Armenian Church (Reseda, CA)
Zoryan Notes (Cambridge, MA)

Appendix

The Questionnaire Package

This appendix provides the reader with a complete package of the questionnaire used in data collection. First, there is a letter from the sponsor of the project and its Armenian translation; a second letter from the researcher. This is followed by an exact replica of the questionnaire. Next, there is a request for the snowball sample that was enclosed with the questionnaire and the follow-up postcard. The last entry is a notice that appeared in the ethnic press and was sent to all the community leaders interviewed.

Columbia University in the City of New York | *New York. N. Y. 10027*

DEPARTMENT OF SOCIOLOGY   Fayerweather Hall

April 15, 1986

It gives me great pleasure to introduce to you Anny Bakalian. She is a doctoral student in Sociology here at Columbia University. She is writing her dissertation on <u>Armenians</u> <u>and</u> <u>their</u> <u>Descendants</u> <u>in</u> America: <u>A</u> <u>Study</u> <u>of</u> <u>the</u> <u>Patterns</u> <u>of</u> <u>Ethnic</u> <u>Manifestation</u> <u>in</u> New <u>York/</u> New <u>Jersey</u>. No comprehensive survey of Armenians in the USA has ever been done.

The results of this study will increase our understanding of persisting ethnicity and assimilation in America. Such information should also be invaluable to Armenian organizations, community leaders and citizens in planning policies and programs.

The research findings will appear initially in the form of a doctoral dissertation at Columbia University. And it is hoped it will be published shortly thereafter.

We urge you to complete your questionnaire and return it now. What we sociologists call a probability sample is essential to ensure good results. As your name has been drawn in such a random sample, your answers are very important. Let us assure you that your answers will remain anonymous and confidential.

Anny Bakalian and I appreciate your assistance in helping her carry forward this important and noteworthy project.

Yours sincerely

Bernard Barber

BERNARD BARBER
Professor
Project Sponsor

Columbia University in the City of New York | *New York, N.Y. 10027*

DEPARTMENT OF SOCIOLOGY   Fayerweather Hall

Ապրիլ 15, 1986

Սիրելի Բարեկամներ,

Հաճույքով կը ներկայացնեմ ձեզի իմ աշակերտներէս Անի Պազալեանը, թեկ-
նածու ``Ֆի-էյ ճ-Տի`` տիտղոսին Գոլումբիա Համալսարանի Ընկերաբանութեան ամ-
պիոնին: Անոր աւարտաճառին նիւթն է ``ԸՆԿԵՐԱԲԱՆԱԿԱՆ ՈՒՍՈՒՄՆԱՍԻՐՈՒԹԻՒՆ ՄԸ`
ՀԱՅՑՐԸ ՆԻՒ ԵՈՐՔԻ ԵՆ ՆԻՒ ՃՐՉԻԻ ՄԷՋ``: Տակաւին այսպիսի ամբողջական աշխա-
տասիրութիւն մը չէ կատարուած Ամերիկայի Միացեալ Նահանգաց մէջ:

Այս ուսումնասիրութիւնը ի յայտ պիտի բերէ Հայ ազգին ցեղային դարաւոր
յատկանիշներն ու ժուլման պատճառները: Այս արժէքաւոր տեղեկութիւնները օգ-
տակար պիտի հանդիսանան Հայ կազմակերպութիւններուն, համայնքի ղեկավարներուն,
ինչպէս նաեւ իրաքանչիւր Հայ անհատի:

Այս ուսումնասիրութեան արդիւնքները մաս պիտի կազմեն Անիի ``Տոքթո-
րայի`` աւարտաճառին, որ յոյսով եմ թէ ներկայացուելէն ետք պիտի հրատարակուի:

Կը խնդրուի ձեզմէ որ պատասխանէք բոլոր հարցումներուն եւ հարցարանը
վերադարձնէք ներփակեալ պահարանով: Կը փափաքիմ ձեզի տեղեկացնել թէ ձեր ա-
նունը պատատական կերպով ընտրուած է` որպէս զի կարելի չափով այլազան պա-
տասխաններ մէկտեղուին: Կը վստահեցնենք ձեզի որ այս հարցումներուն տրուած
պատասխանները գաղտնի պիտի պահուին:

Անի Պազալեանը եւ ես կը գնահատենք ձեր օժանդակութիւնը ի նպաստ այս
կարեւոր ուսումնասիրութեան:

Շերդ

Bernard Barber

Փրոֆ. Պէրնարտ Պարպըր

Յ.Գ. Եթէ կը նախընտրէք Հայերէն լեզուով
պատասխանել հարցումներուն, եւ կամ
որեւէ հարցում ունիք` կրնաք հեռա-
ձայնել Անիին (212 246-6215):

Columbia University in the City of New York | *New York, N.Y. 10027*

DEPARTMENT OF SOCIOLOGY   Fayerweather Hall

April 15, 1986

Dear Fellow Armenian,

This survey aims to fill a gap in our knowledge and understanding of men and women of Armenian descent in America today. Please help me by completing the enclosed questionnaire.

Your household is one of a number in which people are being asked to give their opinions and family histories. It was drawn in a random sample from the mailing lists of Armenian churches and organizations in the New York and New Jersey Metro area. In order that the results will truly represent the thinking of people of Armenian descent, it is important that we have about the same number of men and women participating in the study. Thus, we would like the questionnaire for your household to be completed by an adult female of Armenian descent. If none is present, then it should be completed by an adult male of Armenian descent. (In other households, adult males will be filling out the questionnaire).

The results of this study need to be compared with a sample of men and women of Armenian descent who are not involved with Armenian organizations and community affairs. Please send the name(s), address and telephone number of a relative or friend who fits this description so a copy of this questionnaire be sent to him/her. A postcard is provided for this purpose.

You may be assured of complete confidentiality. The questionnaire has an identification number for mailing purposes only. This is so that your name may be checked off the mailing list when your questionnaire is returned. Your name will never be placed on the questionnaire.

I would be happy to answer any questions you might have. Please write or call. The telephone number is (212)246-6215.

Thank you for your assistance.

Yours sincerely,

A. Bakalian

ANNY BAKALIAN

ARMENIANS AND THEIR DESCENDANTS IN AMERICA:

A STUDY OF THE PATTERNS OF ETHNIC MANIFESTATION IN
NEW YORK/NEW JERSEY

Ethnic parades, festivals, and food fairs in American cities
increased in popularity in the last couple of decades, suggesting
a revival of ethnic identification and pride. Hardly anything
has been written about the achievements (or failures) of
Armenians in America.

By answering the questions in this survey you will help us
understand ethnicity in America in general, and people of
Armenian descent in particular.

Please answer all of the questions. If you wish to comment on
any questions or qualify your answers, please use the margins or
a separate sheet of paper. Your comments will be read and taken
into account.

Thank you for your help.

Please return this questionnaire in enclosed envelope to:
        ANNY BAKALIAN
        BOX 60 FAYERWEATHER HALL
        COLUMBIA UNIVERSITY
        NEW YORK   NY 10027

PLEASE CIRCLE NUMBER OF YOUR ANSWER

Q-1   How do you think of yourself, as an: (Circle one answer)
1   ARMENIAN
2   AMERICAN-ARMENIAN
3   AMERICAN
4   ISTANBUL-ARMENIAN
5   IRANIAN-ARMENIAN
6   SOVIET-ARMENIAN
7   LEBANESE-ARMENIAN
8   OTHER (SPECIFY)_____

Q-2   How often do you eat Armenian food at home?
1   NEVER
2   A FEW TIMES A YEAR
3   A FEW TIMES A MONTH
4   ABOUT ONCE A WEEK
5   ALMOST EVERY DAY

Q-3   How many Armenian dishes can you (or your spouse) cook?
1   NONE
2   LESS THAN 5
3   BETWEEN 6 AND 12
4   BETWEEN 13 AND 24
5   MORE THAN 25

Q-4   Do you speak Armenian?
1   NOT AT ALL
2   VERY LITTLE
3   ADEQUATELY
4   WELL
5   VERY WELL

Q-5   Do you read/write Armenian?
    1   NOT AT ALL
    2   VERY LITTLE
    3   ADEQUATELY
    4   WELL
    5   VERY WELL

Q-6   How often do you speak each of these languages at home?
(Circle one number in each column)

ENGLISH	ARMENIAN	OTHER (SPECIFY)	
1	1	1	NEVER
2	2	2	SELDOM
3	3	3	SOME OF THE TIME
4	4	4	MOST OF THE TIME
5	5	5	ALWAYS

Q-7   Do you listen to the Armenian Radio Hour?
    1   NEVER
    2   RARELY
    3   SOME OF THE TIME
    4   MOST OF THE TIME
    5   ALWAYS

Q-8   Do you read Armenian literature (either in Armenian or in translation)?
    1   NEVER
    2   RARELY
    3   SOME OF THE TIME
    4   MOST OF THE TIME
    5   ALWAYS

Q-9   Have you ever bought any works of art (painting, sculpture, embroidery, antiques) especially because they were made by Armenians?
1   NEVER
2   RARELY
3   SOME OF THE TIME
4   MOST OF THE TIME
5   ALWAYS

Q-10   Do you receive Armenian newspapers or magazines either English or Armenian?
1   NONE
2   ONE
3   TWO TO THREE
4   FOUR TO SIX
5   MORE THAN SEVEN

Q-11   Which of the following professionals you deal with are Armenian? (Circle your answers)
1   DOCTOR
2   LAWYER
3   ACCOUNTANT
4   DENTIST
5   NONE OF THE ABOVE

Q-12   Suppose you own your own business, would you employ other Armenians?
1   NEVER
2   RARELY
3   SOME OF THE TIME
4   MOST OF THE TIME
5   ALWAYS

Q-13   Have you patronized a gas station, mechanic, grocery store, dry cleaner, jeweler, watch repair, etc. solely because they were Armenian?
1   NEVER
2   RARELY
3   SOME OF THE TIME
4   MOST OF THE TIME
5   ALWAYS

Q-14   Have you in the last year attended requiem services for April 24?
1   NO
2   YES

Q-15   Have you in the last year participated in marches, demonstrations, public ceremonies for April 24? (exclude requiems)
1   NO
2   YES

Q-16   How do you describe your feelings towards Turkey's denial of the Armenian Massacres? (You may circle more than one answer)
1   INDIFFERENCE
2   HUMILIATION
3   ARMENIANS DESERVE JUSTICE
4   ANGER, FRUSTRATION
5   OTHER (SPECIFY) _____

Q-17   Have you ever written letters to your Congressman or visited Washington to help pass a bill that will make April 24 "A Day of Remembrance of Man's Inhumanity to Man?"
1   NO
2   YES

Q-18   Which of the following public actions have you been involved in? (You may circle more than one answer)
1   GET JOBS FOR OTHER ARMENIANS
2   HELP ESTABLISH AN ARMENIAN SCHOOL
3   FURTHER ARMENIAN INTERESTS IN YOUR COMMUNITY
4   NONE OF THE ABOVE

Q-19   Do you think there is a great deal of prejudice against Armenian Americans in this country?
1   NO
2   YES

Q-20   Have you ever been discriminated against because you were an Armenian in America? Circle 1 for NO, 2 for YES for each of the following questions:

NO	YES	
1	2	GETTING A JOB
1	2	GETTING A PROMOTION
1	2	JOINING A CLUB
1	2	ADMISSION TO SCHOOL OR COLLEGE
1	2	BUYING/RENTING AN APARTMENT OR HOUSE

Q-21   While you were growing up, did you and your family visit with other Armenians excluding relatives?
1   NEVER
2   RARELY
3   SOME OF THE TIME
4   MOST OF THE TIME
5   ALWAYS

Q-22   Next, think of the friends you had when you were 17 or 18. How many were Armenian?
1   NONE
2   LESS THAN HALF
3   ABOUT HALF
4   MORE THAN HALF

Q-23   Think of your three closest friends today. Please, provide the following information for each: sex, age, place of birth, religion, ethnic background, occupation, education, and social class (i.e., upper class, upper middle class, middle class, working class). How long have you known each (in years)?

	SEX	AGE	PLACE OF BIRTH	RELIGION	ETHNICITY
FRIEND 1	___	___	_____	_____	_____
FRIEND 2	___	___	_____	_____	_____
FRIEND 3	___	___	_____	_____	_____

	OCCUPATION	EDUCATION	SOCIAL CLASS	TIME KNOWN
FRIEND 1	_____	_____	_____	_____
FRIEND 2	_____	_____	_____	_____
FRIEND 3	_____	_____	_____	_____

Q-24   Bedsides your three closest friends, think of the other friends you have today. How many of them are Armenian?
1   NONE
2   LESS THAN HALF
3   ABOUT HALF
4   MORE THAN HALF

Q-25   How many of them belong to the same social class as you?
1   NONE
2   LESS THAN HALF
3   ABOUT HALF
4   MORE THAN HALF

Q-26   Now, think of the five persons you feel closest to. How many of the five are relatives of yours?

If married, how many of the five are relatives of your spouse?

Q-27   Would you (do you) send your child(ren) to an Armenian day school?
1   NO
2   YES (go to Q-29)

Q-28   If not, why? (You may circle more than one answer)
1   TOO FAR AWAY
2   EXPENSIVE
3   LOW ACADEMIC STANDARDS
4   INFERIOR SOCIAL MILIEU
5   OTHER (SPECIFY)_____

Q-29   Do you, would you send your child to an Armenian Summer camp? Why? (You may circle more than one answer)
1   NO
2   YES, TO LEARN ARMENIAN
3   TO LEARN ARMENIAN HISTORY AND CULTURE
4   TO MAKE ARMENIAN FRIENDS HIS/HER OWN AGE
5   TO HAVE A GOOD TIME
6   TO LEARN NEW SPORTS
7   OTHER (SPECIFY)_____

Q-31   Do you, would you, send your child to an Armenian Saturday school? Why? (You may circle more than one answer)
1   NO
2   YES, TO LEARN ARMENIAN LANGUAGE
3   TO LEARN ARMENIAN HISTORY AND CULTURE
5   TO MAKE ARMENIAN FRIENDS HIS/HER OWN AGE
6   OTHER (SPECIFY)_____

Q-32   What is the main reason you attend an Armenian church?
        (You may circle more than one answer)
        1   BECAUSE I'VE ALWAYS GONE TO AN ARMENIAN CHURCH
        2   TO MEET MY FRIENDS
        3   FAMILY AND FRIENDS EXPECT IT
        4   TO WORSHIP GOD AND PRAY
        5   I ENJOY THE SINGING
        6   TO MAKE ME FEEL BETTER
        7   KEEPS ME IN TOUCH WITH ARMENIAN COMMUNITY
        8   TEACH MY CHILDREN ABOUT ARMENIAN
             CHURCH AND CULTURE
        9   OTHER (SPECIFY)_____

Q-33   Do you attend non-Armenian church?
        1   NEVER (Go to Q-36)
        2   RARELY
        3   SOME OF THE TIME
        4   MOST OF THE TIME
        5   ALWAYS

Q-34   Please specify which non-Armenian church you go to.

Q-35   Why do you attend this non-Armenian church?

Q-36   Do you abstain from food the day you plan to take
        communion?
        0   DO NOT TAKE COMMUNION
        1   NEVER
        2   RARELY
        3   SOME OF THE TIME
        4   MOST OF THE TIME
        5   ALWAYS

Q-37   Do you fast or abstain from animal products, or other items, during Lent or Holy Week before Easter?
1   NEVER
2   RARELY
3   SOME OF THE TIME
4   MOST OF THE TIME
5   ALWAYS

Q-38   In the last year, how many (if any) activities did you attend that were sponsored by Armenian organizations? Some activities are held only once a year, others more often. Please circle number(s) for each type of activity listed below.

	TIMES ATTENDED (IN 1985)				
ARMENIAN FESTIVAL/ONE WORLD FEST.	0	1-2	3-5	6-10	11+
DINNER DANCE (BARAHANTES)	0	1-2	3-5	6-10	11+
"KEF NIGHT"	0	1-2	3-5	6-10	11+
MUSICAL CONCERT	0	1-2	3-5	6-10	11+
FOLK DANCE	0	1-2	3-5	6-10	11+
ART EXHIBIT	0	1-2	3-5	6-10	11+
BAZAAR/BAKE SALE/RUG SALE	0	1-2	3-5	6-10	11+
APRIL 24 COMMEMORATIONS	0	1-2	3-5	6-10	11+
LECTURE/PANEL DISCUSSION	0	1-2	3-5	6-10	11+
PICNIC	0	1-2	3-5	6-10	11+
THEATRICAL EVENT	0	1-2	3-5	6-10	11+
SPORTS MATCHES	0	1-2	3-5	6-10	11+
ARMENIAN CONVENTION/WEEKEND	0	1-2	3-5	6-10	11+

Q-39　How many voluntary organizations do you presently belong to? How many of these are Armenian? A list is provided below to help you remember. Please list ALL organizations you belong to of each type listed, then write the number of Armenian organizations in the second column. Write Zero (0) if you do not belong to an organization of the type listed.

	TOTAL # OF ORGANIZATIONS	# ARMENIAN
COMPATRIOTIC SOCIETIES:		
POLITICAL PARTIES:		
CHARITABLE ORGANIZATIONS:		
CULTURAL/ARTISTIC ASSOC.:		
SPORTS ORGANIZATIONS:		
FOLK DANCE ENSEMBLE:		
CHOIRS:		
SCHOLARLY ASSOCIATIONS:		
PROFESSIONAL ASSOC.:		
STUDENT ASSOCIATIONS:		
CHURCH COMMITTEES:		
OTHER (SPECIFY):		

Q-40　Have you in the last year assumed any position of responsibility in any of these organizations? Specify.

Q-41　How often do you attend activities/meetings of Armenian voluntary organizations in general?
1　NEVER
2　RARELY
3　SOME OF THE TIME
4　MOST OF THE TIME
5　ALWAYS

Q-42   How often do you attend non-Armenian voluntary
organizations?
1   NEVER
2   RARELY
3   SOME OF THE TIME
4   MOST OF THE TIME
5   ALWAYS

Q-43   Please respond to the questions below by putting a number
from 1 to 5 in the slot next to each statement. The numbers
range from 1 (strongly agree) to 5 (strongly disagree), as
indicated in the following scale:

1	2	3	4	5
STRONGLY AGREE	MILDLY AGREE	NO OPINION	MILDLY DISAGREE	STRONGLY DISAGREE

_____   It is not possible to stay Armenian without speaking
Armenian.

_____   Armenian "terrorism" in the last few years has soiled the
good name of Armenians in the USA as a law-abiding,
peace-loving people

_____   When I notice an Armenian name on a shop or in the media
(such as movie credits, press) I feel happy, proud.

_____   Unlike American-born Armenians, some recent Armenian
immigrants to America are crude, clannish.

_____   I believe that sending a child to an Armenian day school will
hinder his/her chances of getting into a good college and
improving himself/herself in life.

_____   I feel more comfortable with Armenians who are born and
raised in the same city/country as me.

_____   If the Armenian church does not use English in its services,
the American-born youth will stop coming to church.

_____   Armenian priests should preach only the Holy Scriptures in
their sermons and not concern themselves with Armenian
issues.

_____   It is every Armenian's duty to support the Armenian
national church morally and financially.

1	2	3	4	5
STRONGLY AGREE	MILDLY AGREE	NO OPINION	MILDLY DISAGREE	STRONGLY DISAGREE

_____ The division of the Armenian community into various political groups, such as Hunchags, Ramgavars, Tashnags, is irrelevant in this day and age.

_____ Women who join the Women's Movement are typically frustrated and unattractive people who feel they lose out by the current rules of society.

_____ I attend the Armenian church closest to my home, whether or not I sympathize with Etchmiadzin or Antelias.

_____ It is alright for women to work, but men will always be the basic breadwinners.

_____ I would vote for an Armenian political candidate at local or national elections regardless of party affiliation.

_____ You can be for your own people first and still be a good American.

_____ A woman should be expected to change her name when she marries.

_____ Our children should learn to speak Armenian.

_____ I would support Armenian "terrorism" against Turkish military bases.

_____ A woman should not expect to go to the same places or have the same freedom of action as a man.

_____ A person should always consider the needs of his family as a whole more important than his own.

_____ A good Armenian should marry another Armenian.

_____ A person should always help his parents with the support of his younger brothers and sisters if necessary.

_____ Armenians in the diaspora should eventually settle in Soviet Armenia to avoid assimilation.

_____ I would be willing to live in a free Armenia.

_____ If necessary, I would fight to free Armenia.

_____ I believe that one day in the distant future we will be able to have a free Armenia.

1	2	3	4	5
STRONGLY AGREE	MILDLY AGREE	NO OPINION	MILDLY DISAGREE	STRONGLY DISAGREE

_____ Realistically speaking, most progress so far has been made by men and we expect it to continue that lay.

_____ I consider Soviet Armenia as the spiritual homeland of Armenians.

_____ It is alright to change your name so that I will not be taken for an Armenian.

_____ I believe that the interests of the U.S.A. are indeed furthered against the Communist block by supporting Turkey.

_____ It is important for me that my children marry someone of my own ethnic background.

_____ Our people should get their families to the Armenian church on Sundays, even if it is far from one's home.

_____ I would rather visit with my friends than with my relatives.

_____ I attend the activities that interest me in the Armenian community no matter what the political affiliation of the organization sponsoring the activity.

Q-44   Listed below are a number of ethnic/religious groups.
       Consider each group one at a time and indicate the <u>closest</u>
       relation you have had with each. In front of each entry please
       indicate your answer:
       1 relative (by blood or marriage)
       2 friend
       3 neighbor
       4 co-worker
       5 acquaintance
       6 no acquaintance

___	AMERICAN-ARMENIANS	___	ISTANBUL-ARMENIANS
___	SOVIET-ARMENIANS	___	MIDDLE EAST ARMENIANS
___	IRANIAN-ARMENIANS	___	EAST EUROPEAN ARMENIANS
___	POLISH	___	ANGLO-SAXON
___	ASIAN	___	TURK
___	ARAB	___	JEWISH
___	ITALIAN	___	BLACK
___	IRISH	___	HISPANIC
___	FRENCH	___	GREEK

Q-45   Finally, we would like to ask a few questions about yourself
       for statistical purposes. Are you presently:
       1 EMPLOYED
       2 UNEMPLOYED
       3 RETIRED
       4 FULL-TIME HOMEMAKER
       5 STUDENT

Q-46   What is your main occupation now? (If retired, unemployed,
       what was your occupation when you were working?)

Q-47   Are you self-employed?
       1 NO
       2 YES

Q-48   What is or was the main occupation of your father?

Q-49   What is or was the main occupation of your mother?

Q-50   What is the highest grade you completed in school? (If you have a technical or professional degree please indicate)

Q-51   What city/country were you born in?
1   USA (Go to Q-54)
2   OTHER (SPECIFY)_____

Q-52   If you were not born in the USA, at what age did you come here?

Q-53   Were you or your family sponsored by ANCHA?
1   NO
2   YES

Q-54   Please indicate for each of the following: place of birth, ethnic background, religious affiliation, and (approximate) year of arrival in the USA. (Write "NA" for Not Applicable.)

		CITY/ TOWN	ETHNICITY	RELIGION	YEAR
1	YOUR MOTHER	_____	_____	_____	_____
2	YOUR FATHER	_____	_____	_____	_____
3	YOUR MOTHER'S MOTHER	_____	_____	_____	_____
4	YOUR MOTHER'S FATHER	_____	_____	_____	_____
5	YOUR FATHER'S MOTHER	_____	_____	_____	_____
6	YOUR FATHER'S FATHER	_____	_____	_____	_____

Q-55   What is your religious affiliation?
     1   ARMENIAN APOSTOLIC CHURCH (LOUSAVORCHAGAN)
     2   ARMENIAN PROTESTANT CHURCH
     3   ARMENIAN CATHOLIC CHURCH
     4   OTHER (SPECIFY)_____

Q-56   What is your marital status?
     1   NEVER MARRIED (PLEASE GO TO Q-69)
     2   MARRIED
     3   WIDOWED
     4   SEPARATED
     5   DIVORCED

NOTE: In answering the following questions, please consider your current spouse if you are remarried. If widowed, separated, divorced, consider your previous spouse.

Q-57   How long have you been married?

Q-58   What is (or was) your spouse's main occupation?

Q-59   What is or was the main occupation of your spouse's father?

Q-60   What was the highest grade your spouse completed in school?

Q-61   Does (did) your spouse speak Armenian?
     1   NO
     2   YES

Q-62   Does (did) your spouse read/write Armenian?
     1   NO
     2   YES

Q-63   Where was your spouse born?
     1   USA (Go to Q-65)
     2   OTHER (SPECIFY)_____

Q-64   If he/she was not born in the USA, at what age did your spouse come here?

Q-65   What is your spouse's religious affiliation?
1   ARMENIAN APOSTOLIC CHURCH (LOUSAVORCHAGAN)
2   ARMENIAN PROTESTANT CHURCH
3   ARMENIAN CATHOLIC CHURCH
4   OTHER (SPECIFY)_____

Q-66   Was your spouse raised in this denomination?
1   NO, THEN WHAT DENOMINATION WAS YOUR
       SPOUSE RAISED IN? (SPECIFY)_____
2   YES

Q-67   What is the ethnic background of your spouse's father?
1   ARMENIAN
2   OTHER (SPECIFY)_____

Q-68   What is the ethnic background of your spouse's mother?
1   ARMENIAN
2   OTHER (SPECIFY)_____

Q-69   Do you consider yourself a:
1   DEMOCRAT
2   REPUBLICAN
3   INDEPENDENT
4   OTHER (SPECIFY)_____

Q-70   Did you vote in the 1984 Presidential elections?
1   NO
2   YES
3   CAN'T VOTE

Q-71   Have you ever done work for one of the major political parties or candidates?

For whom did you work?

What did you do?

Q-72   Please list all persons who presently live in your household (include unmarried children at school). Please indicate their relation to you, age, and marital status.

RELATION	AGE	MARITAL STATUS

Q-73   In the last two weeks, how many times did you telephone or see the following people? (Write 0, 1, 2, 3, etc., in the appropriate column and indicate where each person lives [city or state]. If dead or do not have any, write "NA"/Not applicable.)

	PHONED	SEEN	CITY/STATE
MOTHER/FATHER:			
SISTER/BROTHER:			
IN-LAWS:			
GRANDPARENTS:			
AUNT/UNCLE:			
COUSIN(S):			
NEPHEW/NIECE:			
CHILDREN:			

Q-74   Are you officially a member of an Armenian Political party?
   1   NO
   2   ARMENIAN ASSEMBLY
   3   HUNCHAGIAN
   4   RAMGAVAR
   5   TASHNGAGZOUTUN
   6   OTHER (SPECIFY)_____

Q-75   Do you sympathize with any of the following Armenian political divisions?
1   HUNCHAGIAN
2   RAMGAVAR
3   TASHNAGZOUTUN
4   NEUTRAL (CHEZOK)
5   INDIFFERENT
6   OTHER (SPECIFY)_____

Q-76   Which social class do you belong to?
1   WORKING CLASS
2   MIDDLE CLASS
3   UPPER MIDDLE CLASS
4   UPPER CLASS

Q-77   Into which of the following categories does your total annual family income from all sources (before taxes) fall? Include only yours and your spouse's; do not include earnings from any other person in your household.

1	0-14,999	9	55,000-59,999
2	15,000-19,999	10	60,000-64,999
3	20,000-24,999	11	65,000-69,999
4	25,000-29,999	12	70,000-79,999
5	30,000-34,999	13	80,000-89,999
6	40,000-44,999	14	90,000-99,999
7	45,000-49,999	15	100,000+
8	50,000-54,999		

Q-78   How old are you?

Q-79   Please indicate your sex:
1   MALE
2   FEMALE

Is there anything else you would like to share with me? In the space provided below, I invite you to write down briefly the story of your Armenian family's journey from the Old World to America. From where did you or your ancestors come? When and how? Who were they? What did they do for a living in the Old World and in America?

Also, any comments you wish to make that you think may help our understanding of Armenians in America will be appreciated, either here or in a separate letter.

Your contribution to this effort is very greatly appreciated. However, we hope that you can be of further assistance to us. We are trying to generate a sample of persons who have an Armenian parent or grandparent yet are not actively involved in the Armenian community of New York/New Jersey. If you have a close relative(s) or friend(s) who fits this description, please write his/her name, address and telephone number on the back of this card. You do not need to mention your name on this card. You may mail this card to our address separately or enclose it with your completed questionnaire. We assure you that we will be as confidential with these names as we will with yours.

Thank you for your help.

Sincerely,

ANNY BAKALIAN

April 29, 1986

Two weeks ago a questionnaire about Armenians in America was mailed to you. Your name was drawn in a random sample of Armenian households in the New York/New Jersey Metro Area.

If you have already completed and returned it to us, please accept our sincere thanks. If not, please do so today. Because it has been sent to only a small, but representative sample of NY/NJ Armenian residents, it is extremely important that yours also be included in the study if the results are to accurately represent people of Armenian descent in this area.

If by some chance you did not receive the questionnaire, or it got misplaced, please call me right now (212-246-6215) and I will get another one in the mail to you today.

Sincerely,

SURVEY OF ARMENIANS BEING CONDUCTED IN NY/NJ METRO AREA

Anny Bakalian, a Ph.D. candidate in sociology at Columbia University, is currently conducting a survey of men and women of Armenian descent in the New York/New Jersey Metropolitan area. This study aims to fill a very conspicuous gap in our knowledge and understanding of Armenians in the USA. While numerous books and articles have been written about other ethnic groups in America, Armenians have remained a "hidden minority."

A sample of over a thousand Armenian households was selected randomly from lists of ALL types of Armenian churches and organizations in the metro area. This scientific technique is essential for ensuring unbiased results. Similarly, in order for the findings to reflect reality, it is essential that all those people who were selected and receive the questionnaire in the mail complete it and return it to Anny Bakalian. These results will be compared with a sample of men and women of Armenian descent who are not actively involved in Armenian community life at present.

The results of this research project will appear initially as Anny Bakalian's doctoral dissertation entitled "Armenians and Their Descendants in America; A Study of the Patterns of Ethnic Manifestation in New York/New Jersey." And it is hoped it will be published shortly thereafter. Columbia professors Bernard Barber, Allen Barton, and Viviana Zelizer are sponsoring this project. The information gathered from this study should be useful specifically to Armenian organizations, community leaders, and citizens in planning policies and programs that will better serve the needs of the Armenian people in this area.

We urge the Armenian public to help Anny Bakalian carry forward this important and noteworthy project. For further information, please contact Anny Bakalian at Box 60, Fayerweather Hall, Columbia University, New York, NY 10027; tel: (212) 246-6215.

Index

510   Armenian-Americans

symbolic Armenian, 427
Sojourner, 144-145, 422-423
defined, 53
Soviet Armenia, 163. *See also* Republic
of Armenia
history, 98-100
Hunchag, 98
immigration, 12-13
new immigrant, 427, 429
Ramgavar, 98
succession, 100-101
Tashnag, 98
travel, 344-345
Soviet Armenian, 21
discrimination, 21
Los Angeles Armenian, 429
problems, 22
public school, 281-282
social distance, 227
Spurk, 145
Stereotype, 19, 229
Structural assimilation
defined, 36
generation, 420-421
rate, 430
Study bias
language, 61
snowball sample, 61
Study generalization, 61
Study representativeness, 61
Sumgait pogrom, 100
Summer camp, 310
generation, 277
objections, 278
Sunday school, 279-280, 310
Survivor syndrome, Genocide, 352
Symbolic Armenian, 6, 307, 395. *See
also* Symbolic ethnicity
affect instead of action, 436-438
Armenian-American community,
community involvement, 208-210
Armenian-American culture, 311
Armenian educational institution,
academic reputation, 276-277
components, 431-442, 435-436
economic participation, 210-212
financial contributions, 440-441
Genocide, 436

knowledge bank, 439
language, 253
manifestations, 395-396
nature, 6-7
postindustrial economic system, 433
psychological functions, 437-438
quest for Armenianness, 440
sense of peoplehood, 337-347
sentimentalization, 433-434
sidestream ethnicity, 435-436
socioeconomic status, 427
subculture dynamics, 432-433
voluntary association, 439
voluntary identity, 7
sentimental component, 7
Symbolic ethnicity, 53. *See also*
Symbolic Armenian
assimilation theory, 44-48
defined, 44
ethnic food, 45-46
functions, 47
later-generation, 48
manifestations, 45
rites of passage, 45
visibility, 45

Tashnag, 94-99
by ancestry, 126
anti-Soviet policy, 96
Apostolic, 97
conflict theory, 138-140
ethnic identity, 135-137
history, 94-99
language, 254
Lebanon, 98
membership, 174n
by place of birth, 127-128
political goal, 95-96
raison d'etre, 95-96
by religion, 127
Soviet Armenia, 98
See of Cilicia, 97
Third generation, defined, 5
Third generation return law, 42
cultural, 43
ideological, 43
religion, 33
Tradition, 291-292
Traditional Armenianness, 307, 395